GARDNER'S ART THROUGH THE AGES

EIGHTH EDITION

Horst de la Croix

Richard G. Tansey

HARCOURT BRACE JOVANOVICH, PUBLISHERS

San Diego New York Chicago Atlanta Washington, D.C.

London Sydney Toronto

ISBN: 0-15-503763-3 (hardbound)
            0-15-503764-1 (paperbound, Vol. I)
            0-15-503765-X (paperbound, Vol. II)
Library of Congress Catalog Card Number: 85-60874 (hardbound)
                                                              85-80092 (paperbound)

Printed in the United States of America

New illustrations by Felipe Fernandez.

Picture credits appear on page 992, which constitutes a continuation of the copyright page.

PREFACE

Since publication of the first edition in 1926, Helen Gardner's *Art through the Ages* has been a favorite with generations of students and general readers, who have found it an exciting and informative survey. Miss Gardner's enthusiasm, knowledge, and humanity have made it possible for the beginner to learn how to see and thereby to penetrate the seeming mysteries of even the most complex artistic achievements. Every effort has been made in this volume to preserve her freshness and simplicity of style and, above all, her sympathetic approach to individual works of art and to the styles of which they are a part.

Miss Gardner completed the third edition shortly before her death in 1946. The fourth edition was prepared in 1959 by Professor Sumner Crosby and his colleagues at Yale University. Our fifth edition was published in 1970, the sixth in 1975, and the seventh in 1980. We were led to prepare this edition by the popularity of those earlier editions and by suggestions we received for further improvement. The eighth edition of Gardner's *Art through the Ages*, we hope, will continue a tradition of 60 years as a standard and reliable survey of the history of world art.

In this edition, in addition to emendations made throughout the book, the text and the number of pictures have been expanded to include works of art recently discovered, restudied, or considered by the editors to be particularly characteristic of their periods and illustrative of developmental trends. Fuller treatment has been given to periods and monuments when warranted. Many new pictures are in color, and a large number of black-and-white pictures in previous editions have been converted to color in this edition. Every effort has been made to accommodate the results of recent research in as comprehensive and detailed a survey of the material as the physical limits of a textbook of this scope permit.

In making a balanced historical introduction to the art of the whole world, which *Art through the Ages* uniquely achieves, the hardest task is selection—in effect, limitation—of the monuments to be discussed and illustrated. Though a corpus of monuments essential to the art-history survey course has long been forming, and though there seems to be considerable agreement as to what constitutes it, there will naturally be differences of choice deriving from differences of emphasis. A radical departure from the corpus might well obliterate the outlines of the study. To avoid the random, systemless distribution of material that might result, we have generally adhered to the corpus and occasionally introduced monuments not well known, newly discovered, or not customarily treated in a survey. Our aim throughout has been to present and interpret works as reflections of an intelligible development rather than merely as items of a catalogue or miscellany. We have tried particularly to give coherence to the best assortment of materials by stressing—in the descriptions of sculpture and painting—the theme of representation as it passes through the many historical variations behind which operate the crucial transformations of humankind's view of itself and of the world.

Various teaching aids accompany the eighth edition of *Gardner's Art through the Ages*. A Study Guide by Kathleen Cohen and Horst de la Croix contains chapter-by-chapter drills on identification of geographical locations, time periods, styles, terms, iconography, major art movements, and specific philosophical, religious, and historical movements as they relate to particular works of art examined in the text. Self-quizzes and discussion questions enable students to evaluate their grasp of the material. A geographical index of locations of works of art illustrated in the eighth edition is also included.

A computer-generated, coded key is available to adopters for use in obtaining commercial slides of the works and monuments illustrated in the eighth edition. In addition, a computer disk will generate printed slide labels for all illustrations in the eighth edition, as well as printouts of lists of illustrations categorized by artist, title, date or period, medium, genre, and geographical location.

A note on style. Given a contemporary sensitivity, reported by some of our readers, to traditional English usage that would seem to disparage women, the editors disclaim at the outset any prejudice in the use of words like "man" or "mankind." These, through centuries of English speech and writing, have been generic terms for humanity and the human race and are inclusive of both sexes. Our disclaimer extends to such locutions as "the artist . . . he," which could not, we feel, be altered without clumsy misuse, neologism, or circumlocution destructive of English sense and style; nevertheless, we have made changes wherever they were appropriate and neither obtrusive on good form nor offensive to our readers' feelings. We would deeply appreciate the forbearance of concerned readers in this matter, especially since we do not believe ourselves to have the authority or the competence to introduce extraordinary changes in the language as it now stands.

A work as extensive as a history of world art could not be undertaken or completed without the counsel and active participation of experts in fields other than our own. In some cases, this took the form of preparation of chapters or portions of chapters; in others, of reviews of work in progress or already prepared. For such contributions to this edition and to previous ones, we offer our sincere thanks to Professor James Ackerman, Harvard University; Professor Marjorie P. Balge, University of Virginia; Professor Jacques Bordaz, University of Pennsylvania; Professor Louise Alpers Bordaz, Columbia University; Professor James Cahill, University of California, Berkeley; Professor Herbert M. Cole, University of California, Santa Barbara; Professor George Corbin, Lehman College, City University of New York; Professor Mary S. Ellett, Randolph-Macon Woman's College; Professor Roger K. Elliott, Central Virginia Community College; Professor Ian Fraser, Herron School of Art; Professor Oleg Grabar, Harvard University; Professor M.F. Hearn, University of Pittsburgh; Professor Howard Hibbard, late of Columbia University; Professor Joel Isaacson, University of Michigan; Professor M. Barry Katz, Virginia Commonwealth University; Professor Robert A. Koch, Princeton University; Professor William L. MacDonald, formerly of Smith College; Professor A. Dean McKenzie, University of Oregon; Professor Diane Degasis Moran, Sweet Briar College; Dr. Harry Murutes, University of Akron; Professor Edith Porada, Columbia University; Professor Bruce Radde, San José State University; Professor Raphael X. Reichert, California State University at Fresno; Professor Grace Seiberling, University of Rochester; Dr. Peter Selz, University of California, Berkeley; Professor David Simon, Colby College; Professor Pamela H. Simpson, Washington and Lee University; Professor Richard Vinograd, University of Southern California; Professor Joanna Williams, University of California, Berkeley; and the Art History Department, Herron School of Art, Indiana University–Purdue University at Indianapolis. We owe a special debt of gratitude to Luraine Collins Tansey, art librarian and slide consultant, who compiled the bibliography and made valuable suggestions on its content. In addition, she designed the geographical index for the Study Guide, prepared the computer-generated coded key, and completed and made available the personal computer diskette. Rod Scher, HBJ Electronic Publishing, and also Charles Edgin and Jo Ellen Hardester Herrick, CCOC Computer Center, San Jose, managed the technical problems in the diskette's production. Edith Crowe did indispensable bibliographical research.

Among those who have contributed their efforts, often in demanding and painstaking capacity, to the efficient management of an enormously detailed manuscript are our editors, Albert Richards, Mary George, and Andrea McCarrick; our art editor, Susan Holtz, and her assistants on this project, Avery Hallowell, Alice Harmon, and Rebecca Lytle; our designer, Jamie Fidler; and our production manager, Sharon Weldy.

We should like, as we thank all those who have helped immeasurably in the production of this book, to affirm that we alone are responsible for whatever may be its deficiencies.

Horst de la Croix
Richard G. Tansey

CONTENTS

THE MODERN WORLD 802

ART
THROUGH THE AGES
EIGHTH EDITION

INTRODUCTION

The goal of art history—the subject of this book—is the discerning appreciation and enjoyment of art, from whatever time and place it may have come, by whatever hands it may have been made. Outside the academic world, the terms *art* and *history* are not often juxtaposed. People tend to think of history as the record and interpretation of past (particularly political) human actions, and of art—quite correctly—as something *present* to the eye and touch, which, of course, the vanished human events that make up history are not. The fact is that a visible and tangible work of art is a kind of *persisting event.* It was made at a particular time and place by particular persons, even if we do not always know just when, where, and by whom. Although it is the creation of the past, art continues to exist in the present, long surviving its times; Charlemagne has been dead for a thousand years, but his chapel still stands at Aachen.

THE BASES OF ART HISTORY

Style

The time in which a work of art was made has everything to do with the way it looks—with, in one key term, its *style.* In other words, the style of a work of art is a function of its historical *period.* The historiography of art proceeds by sorting works of architecture, sculpture, and painting into stylistic classes on the bases of their likenesses and the times or periods in which they were

Dancers (detail of FIG. 3-35), wall painting from
the tomb of Nebamun (?), Thebes, *c.* 1450 B.C.

3

produced. It is a fundamental hypothesis of art history that works of art produced at the same time (and, of course, in the same place) will generally have common stylistic traits. Of course, all historiography assumes that events derive their character from the time in which they happen (and perhaps from their "great men," also products of their time); thus, we can speak of the Periclean Age, the Age of Reason, even—as with the title of a recent historical work—of the Age of Roosevelt. We also must know the time of a work if we are to know its meaning—to know it for what it is. Yet if the work of art still stands before us, persisting from the past, isn't this sufficient? By virtue of its survival, isn't the work in a sense *independent* of time? May not a work of art speak to people of all times as long as it survives? The key to this last question is the word "speak." Indeed, it may speak, but what is its language? What does it say to us? Art may be more than a form of communication, but it is certainly that; and it is the business of art history to learn the "languages" of the art of many different periods as they are embodied in the monuments from their respective times. We can assume that artists in every age express in their works some sort of meaning that is intelligible to themselves and others. We can get at that meaning only by setting a particular work in relation to other works like it that were made about the same time. By grouping works in this way, we can infer a community of meaning as well as of *form;* a style will then be outlined. In a chronological series of works having common stylistic features, we may find that the later and the earlier works show stylistic *differences* as well. The art historian tends to think of this phenomenon as reflecting an evolution, a *development*.

It is obvious that before stylistic development can be inferred it is necessary to be sure that the chronological sequence is correct (that each monument is correctly dated); without this certainty, art-historical order and intelligibility are impossible. Thus, an indispensable tool of the historian is *chronology*, the measuring scale of historical time; without it there could be no history of style—only a confusion of unclassifiable monuments, impossible to describe in any sequence of change.

The table of contents of this book reflects what is essentially a series of periods and subperiods arranged in chronological order—the historical sequence that embraces the sequence of art styles. Until the later eighteenth century, the history of art was really a disconnected account of the lives and the works of individual artists. We now regard art history as a record of the dynamic change of styles in time, and the art of individual masters as substyles of the overall period styles. Although one speaks of "change" in the history of art, the objects themselves obviously do not change; as we have said, they persist, although each naturally suffers some material wear and tear with time. But the fact that works of art from one period look different from those of other periods leads us to infer that *something* changes. This something can only be the points of view of the human makers of works of art with respect to the meaning of life and of art. Modern historiography is much influenced by modern philosophies of change and evolution, and, from the terms and data of biological science, our modern history of art was bound to borrow a sense of continuous process to help explain art-historical change.

In art history, as in the sciences and in other historical disciplines, we have gone far in knowing a thing once we have classified it. Art historians, having done this, resemble experienced travelers who learn to discriminate the different "styles" peculiar to different places. Such travelers know that one must not expect the same style of life in the Maine woods as on the Riviera, and when they have seen a great many places and peoples—like art historians who are familiar with a great many monuments—they are not only at ease with them, but can be said to know and appreciate them for what they are. As their experience broadens, so does their discrimination, or perception of distinctive differences. As world travelers come to see that the location contributes to the unique quality and charm of a town, so students of art, viewing it in the historical dimension, become convinced that a work's peculiar significance, quality, and charm are a function of the time of its making.

But isn't the historical "placing" of a work of art, so visibly and tangibly present, irrelevant to the *appreciation* of it? After all, isn't art-historical knowledge *about* a work of art different from the direct experience of it? The answers lie in the fact that uninstructed appreciators, no matter how sincere, still approach a work of art with the esthetic presuppositions of their own time, rather than of the time of the work itself. Their presuppositions can be tantamount to prejudices, so that their appreciation, even if genuine, may well be for the wrong reasons; it will, in fact, be undiscerning and indiscriminate, so that dozens of works of art may be viewed in the same way, without any savor of the individual significance and quality of each. Thus, as a work of art is intended for a particular audience at a particular time and place, so may its *purpose* be quite particular, and its purpose necessarily enters into its meaning. For example, the famous *Vladimir Madonna* (FIG. 7-62, p. 291) is a Byzantine–Russian icon, a species of art produced not as a work of "fine art" so much as a sacred object endowed with religio-magical power. It was considered, moreover, the especially holy picture of Russia that miraculously saved the city of Vladimir from the hosts of Tamerlane, the city of Kazan from the later Tartar invasions, and all of Russia from the Poles in the seventeenth century. We may admire it for its innate beauty of line, shape, and color, its expressiveness, and its craftsmanship, but unless we are aware of its special historical function as a wonder-working image, we miss the point. We can admire many works of art for their form, content, and quality, but we need a further characterizing experience; otherwise, we are admiring very different works without discriminating their decisive differences. We will be confused, and our judgment will be faulty.

Although our most fundamental way of classifying works of art is by the time of their making, classification by *place of origin* is also crucial. In many periods, a general style (Gothic, for example) will have a great many regional variations: French Gothic architecture is strikingly different from both English and Italian Gothic. Differences of climate helped to make French Gothic an architecture with no bearing walls (and with great spaces for stained-glass windows) and Italian Gothic an architecture with large expanses of wall wonderfully suited to mural painting. Art history, then, is also concerned with the spread of a style from its place of origin. Supplementing time of origin with place of origin therefore adds another dimension to the picture of art monuments in the process of stylistic development.

The *artist*, of course, provides a third dimension in the history of art. Early "histories" of art, written before the advent of modern concepts of style and stylistic development, were simply biographies of artists. Biography as one dimension is still important, for, through it, we can trace stylistic development within the career of the artist. We can learn much from contemporaneous historical accounts, from documents such as commission contracts, and from the artist's own theoretical writings and literary remains. All of this is useful in "explaining" an artist's works, although no complete "explanation" exhausts the meaning of them. Relationships to their predecessors, contemporaries, and followers can be described in terms of the concepts *influence* and *school*. It is likely that artists are influenced by their masters and then influence or are influenced by fellow artists working somewhat in the same style at the same time and place. We designate a group of such artists as a *school;* by this, we do not mean an academy, but a classification of time, place, and style. Thus, we may speak of the Dutch School of the seventeenth century and, within it, of subschools like those of Haarlem, Utrecht, and Leyden.

Iconography

The categories of time and place, the record of the artist, influences, and schools are all used in the composition of the picture of stylistic development. Another kind of classification, another key to works of art, is *iconography*—the study of the subject matter of and symbolism in works of art. By this approach, paintings and sculptures are grouped in terms of their themes rather than their styles, and the development of subject matter becomes a major focus of critical study. Iconographic studies have an ancillary function in stylistic analysis; they are often valuable in tracing influences and in assigning dates and places of origin.

Historical Context

Another very broad source of knowledge of a work of art lies outside the artistic region itself, yet encloses it and is in transaction with it. This is the *general historical context*—the political, social, economic, scientific, technological, and intellectual background that accompanies and influences specifically art-historical events. The fall of Rome, the coming of Christianity, and the barbarian invasions all had much to do with stylistic changes in architecture, sculpture, and painting in the early centuries of our era. The triumph of science and technology had everything to do with the great transformation of the Renaissance tradition that took place in what we call "modern art"—the art of our own time. The work of art, the persisting event, is, after all, a historical document.

THE WORK OF ART

The work of art is an object as well as a historical event. To describe and analyze it, we use categories and vocabularies that have become more-or-less standard and that are indispensable to an understanding of this book.

General Concepts

Form, for the purposes of art history, refers to the shape of the "object" of art; in the made object, it is the shape that the expression of content takes. To create forms, to make a work of art, artists must shape materials with tools. Each of the many materials, tools, and processes available has its own potentialities and limitations; it is part of the artists' creative activity to select the tools most suitable to their purpose. The technical processes that the artists employ, as well as the distinctive, personal way in which they handle them, we call their *technique.* If the material that artists use is the substance of their art, then their technique is their individual manner of giving that substance form. Form, technique, and material are interrelated, as we can readily see in a comparison of the marble statue of *Apollo* from Olympia (FIG. 5-40, p. 149) with the bronze *Charioteer of Delphi* (FIG. 5-37, p. 148). The Apollo is firmly modeled in broad, generalized planes, reflecting the ways of shaping stone that are more-or-less dictated by the character of that material and by the tool used—the chisel. On the other hand, the Charioteer's fineness of detail—the crisp, sharp folds of the drapery—reflects the qualities inherent in cast metal. However, a given medium (the material used) can lend itself to more than one kind of manipulation. The technique of Lehmbruck's bronze *Seated Youth* (FIG. 1), for example, contrasts strikingly with Rodin's *The Thinker* (FIG. 2), also in bronze. The surfaces of Lehmbruck's figure are smooth, flowing, quiet; those of Rodin's figure are rough, broken, and tortuous. Here, it is not so much the bronze that determines the form as it is the sculptor's difference of purpose and of personal technique.

Space, in our common-sense experience, is the bounded or boundless "container" of masses of objects. For the analysis of works of art, we regard space as bounded and susceptible of esthetic and expressive organization. Architecture provides us with our most common experience of the actual manipulation of space; the art of painting frequently projects an image (or illusion) of our three-dimensional spatial world onto a two-dimensional surface.

Area and *plane* describe a limited, two-dimensional space and generally refer to surface. A plane is flat and two-dimensional—like this page and like elements dealt with in plane geometry (a circle, square, or triangle). An area, which also can be described in terms of plane geometry, is often a plane or a flat surface that is enclosed or bounded. Bernini created an area when he defined the essentially plane surface in front of St. Peter's by means of his curving colonnades (FIG. 19-3, p. 714).

Mass and *volume*, in contradistinction to plane and area, describe three-dimensional space. In both architecture and sculpture, mass is the bulk, density, and weight of matter in space. Yet the mass need not be solid; it can be the exterior form of enclosed space. For example, "mass" can apply to a pyramid (FIG. 3-7, p. 78), which is essentially solid, or to the exterior of Hagia Sophia (FIG. 7-41, p. 278), which is essentially a shell enclosing vast spaces. Volume is the space that is organized, divided, or enclosed by mass. It may be the spaces of the interior of a building, the intervals between the masses of a building, or the amount of space occupied by three-dimensional objects like sculpture, ceramics, or furniture. Volume and mass describe the exterior as well as the interior forms of a work of art—the forms of the matter of which it

1 WILHELM LEHMBRUCK, *Seated Youth,* 1918. Bronze. Wilhelm-Lehmbruck-Museum, Duisburg.

2 AUGUSTE RODIN, *The Thinker,* 1880. Bronze. Metropolitan Museum of Art, New York (gift of Thomas F. Ryan, 1910).

is composed *and* the forms of the spaces that exist immediately around that matter and interact with it. For example, in the Lehmbruck statue (FIG. 1), the expressive volumes enclosed by the attenuated masses of the torso and legs play an important part in the open design of the piece. The absence of enclosed volumes in the Rodin figure (FIG. 2) is equally expressive, closing the design, making it compact, heavy, and locked in. (Yet both works convey the same mood—one of brooding introversion.) These closed and open forms, manifest throughout the history of art, demonstrate the intimate connection between mass and the space that surrounds and penetrates it.

In the definition of mass and volume, *line* is one of the most important, but most difficult, terms to comprehend fully. In both science and art, line can be understood as the path of a point moving in space, the track of a motion. Because the directions of motions can be almost infinite, the quality of line can be incredibly various and subtle. It is well known that psychological responses are attached to the direction of a line: a vertical line being positive; a horizontal line, passive; a diagonal line, suggestive of movement, energy, or unbalance; and so on. Hogarth regarded the serpentine or S-curve line as the "line of beauty." Our psychological response to line is also bound up with our esthetic sense of its quality. A line may be very thin, wire-like, and delicate, conveying a sense of fragility, as in Klee's *Twittering Machine* (FIG. 22-30, p. 914). Or it may alternate quickly from thick to thin, the strokes jagged, the outline broken, as in a 600-year-old Chinese painting (FIG. 12-20, p. 455); here, the effect is of vigorous action and angry agitation. A gentle, undulating, but firm line, like that in Picasso's *Bathers* (FIG. 3), defines a *contour* that is restful and quietly sensuous. A contour continuously and subtly contains and suggests mass and volume. In the Picasso drawing, the line is distinct, dark against the white of the paper. But line can be felt as a controlling presence in a hard edge, profile, or boundary created by a contrasting area, even when its tone differs only slightly from the tone of the area it bounds. A good example of this can be seen in the central figure of the goddess in Botticelli's *The Birth of Venus* (FIG. 16-60, p. 690).

When a line serves as an element along which forms are organized, it is known as an *axis*. The axis line itself may not be evident; there may be several axis lines (usually with one dominant), as in the layout of a city. Although we are most familiar with directional axes in urban complexes, they occur in all the arts. A fine example of the use of axis in large-scale architecture is the plan

3 PABLO PICASSO, detail of *Bathers*, 1918. Pencil drawing. Fogg Art Museum, Harvard University, Cambridge, Massachusetts (bequest of Paul J. Sachs).

of the Palace of Versailles and its magnificent gardens (FIG. 19-67, p. 761). Axis, whether vertical, horizontal, or diagonal, is also an important compositional element in painting.

Perspective, no less than axis, is a method of organizing forms in space, but perspective is used primarily to create an illusion of depth or space on a two-dimensional surface. Because we are conditioned by exposure to Western, single-point perspective, an invention of the Italian Renaissance (see pp. 600–630), we tend to see perspective as a systematic ordering of pictorial space in terms of a single point—a point at which lines converge to mark the diminishing size of forms as they recede into the distance (FIG. 17-17, p. 612). Renaissance and Baroque artists created masterpieces of perspective illusionism. In Leonardo's *The Last Supper* (FIG. 4), for example, the lines of perspective (dashed lines) converge on Christ and, in the foreground, project the picture space into the room on the wall of which the painting appears, creating the illusion that the space of the picture and the space of the room are continuous. Yet we must remember that Renaissance perspective is only one of several systems for depicting depth. Others were used in ancient Greece and Rome; still others, in the East. Some of these other systems, as well as the Italian Renaissance perspective, continue to be used. There is no final or absolutely correct projection of what we "in fact" see.

Proportion deals with the relationships (in terms of size) of the parts of a work. The experience of proportion is common to all of us. We seem to recognize at once when the features, say, of the human face or body are "out of proportion"—if the nose or ears are too large for the face or the legs are too short for the body. An instinctive or conventional sense of proportion leads us at once to regard the disproportionate as ludicrous or ugly. Formalized proportion is the mathematical relationship in size of one part of a work of art to the other parts within the work, as well as to the totality of the parts; it implies the use of a denominator that is common to the various parts. Recently, it has been shown that the major elements of Leonardo's *Last Supper* exhibit proportions found in harmonic ratios in music—12:6:4:3 (FIG. 4).

4 LEONARDO DA VINCI, *The Last Supper, c.* 1495–1498. Fresco. Santa Maria delle Grazie, Milan. (Perspective lines are dashed; lines indicating proportions are solid white or black.)

These figures (with the greatest width of a ceiling panel taken as one unit) are the horizontal widths, respectively, of the painting, the ceiling (at the front), the rear wall, and the three windows (taken together and including interstices); they apply to the vertical organization of the painting as well. Leonardo found proportion everywhere: "not only in numbers and measures, but also in sounds, weights, intervals of time, and in every active force in existence."* The ancient Greeks, who considered beauty to be "correct" proportion, sought a canon (rule) of proportion, not only in music, but also for the human figure. The famous Canon of Polykleitos (p. 161), expressed in his statue of the *Doryphoros* (FIG. 5-61, p. 160), long served as an exemplar of correct proportion. But it should be noted that canons of proportion differ from time to time and culture to culture and that, occasionally, artists have deliberately used disproportion. Part of the task of the students of art history is to perceive and adjust to these differences in an effort to understand the wide universe of art forms. Proportional relationships are often based on a *module,* a dimension of which the various parts of a building or other work are fractions or multiples. A module might be the diameter of a column, the height of the human body, or an abstract unit of measurement. For example, the famous "ideal" plan of the ninth-century monastery of St. Gall (FIG. 8-19, p. 331) has a modular base of 2½ feet, so that all parts of the structure are multiples or fractions of this dimension.

Scale (like proportion) refers to the dimensional relationships of the parts of a work to its totality (or of a work to its setting), usually in terms of appropriateness to use or function. We do not think that a private home should be as high as an office building or that an elephant's house at the zoo should be the size of a hencoop—or vice versa. This sense of scale is necessary to the construction of form in all the arts. Most often, but not necessarily, it is the human figure that gives the scale to form.

Form, with which we began this list of fundamental concepts, is mediated primarily by *light.* The function of light in the world of nature is so pervasive that we often take it for granted. Few of us realize the extraordinary variations wrought by light alone, whether natural or artificial, on our most familiar surroundings—as daylight, for example, changes with the hour or season. Few of us realize the full extent to which light affects and reveals form. One who did—the French artist Monet (pp. 855–57)—painted the reflections in a waterlily pond according to their seasonal variations and, in a series of more than 40 canvases of the façade of Rouen Cathedral, revealed its changing aspect from dawn until twilight in different seasons (FIG. 5 and FIG. 21-55, p. 856). Light is as important for the perception of form as is the matter of which form is made.

One function of light is *value.* In painting, and in the graphic arts generally, value refers to lightness, or the amount of light that is (or appears to be) reflected from a surface. Value is a subjective experience, as FIG. 6 shows. In absolute terms (if measured, say, by a photoelectric device), the center bar in this diagram is uniform in value. Yet where the bar is adjacent to a dark area, it *looks* lighter, and where the bar is adjacent to a lighter area, it looks darker. Value is the basis of the quality called, in Italian, *chiaroscuro* (*chiaro,* or light; *scuro,* or dark), which refers to the gradations between light and dark that produce the effect of *modeling,* or of light reflected from three-dimensional surfaces, as exemplified in Leonardo's superb rendering of *The Virgin and Child with St. Anne and the Infant St. John* (FIG. 17-2, p. 602).

In the analysis of light, an important distinction must be made for the realm

*Thomas Brachert, "A Musical Canon of Proportion in Leonardo da Vinci's *Last Supper,*" *Art Bulletin,* Vol. 53, No. 4 (December 1971), pp. 461–66.

of art. Natural light, or sunlight, is whole or additive light, whereas the painter's light in art—the light reflected from pigments and objects—is subtractive light. Natural light is the sum of all the wavelengths composing the visible spectrum, which may be disassembled or fragmented into the individual colors of the spectral band. (Recent experiments with lasers—*l*ight *a*mplification by *s*timulated *e*mission of *r*adiation—have produced color of incredible brilliance and intensity, opening possibilities of color composition that, until now, were unsuspected. The range and strength of color produced in this way approach, although at considerable distance, those of the sun.) Although the esthetics of color is largely the province of the artist and can usually be genuinely experienced and understood only through intense

5   CLAUDE MONET, façade of Rouen Cathedral, early 1890s. *Left:* Museum of Fine Arts, Boston (bequest of Hanna Marcy Edwards); *below:* National Gallery of Art, Washington, D.C. (Chester Dale Collection).

6   Effect of adjacent value on apparent value. Actual value of center bar is constant.

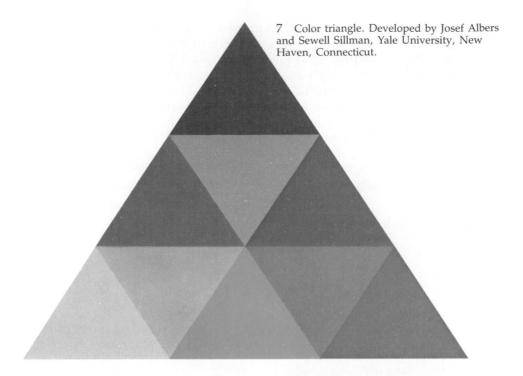

7 Color triangle. Developed by Josef Albers and Sewell Sillman, Yale University, New Haven, Connecticut.

practice and experimentation, some aspects can be analyzed and systematized. Paint pigments (as well as those of the human body) produce their individual colors by reflecting a segment of the spectrum while absorbing all the rest. "Green" pigment, for example, subtracts or absorbs all the light in the spectrum except that seen by us as green, which it reflects to the eye. (In the case of transmitted, rather than reflected, light, the coloring matter—as in stained glass—blocks or screens out all wavelengths of the spectrum except those of the color we see.) Thus, theoretically, a mixture of pigments that embraced all the colors of the spectrum would subtract all light—that is, it would be black; actually, such a mixture of pigments never produces more than a dark gray.

The name of a color is its *hue*—red, blue, yellow. Although the colors of the spectrum merge into each other, artists usually conceive of their hues as distinct from each other, giving rise to many different devices for representing color relationships. There are basically two variables in color—the apparent amount of light reflected and the apparent purity; a change in one must produce a change in the other. Some terms for these variables are (for lightness) *value* and *tonality* and (for purity) *chroma, saturation,* and *intensity.*

One of the more noteworthy diagrams of the relationships of colors is the triangle (FIG. 7), once attributed to Goethe, in which red, yellow, and blue (the *primary colors*) are the vertexes of the triangle and orange, green, and purple (the *secondary colors,* which result from mixing pairs of primaries) lie between them. Colors that lie opposite each other (such as red and green) are called *complementary* colors, because they complement, or complete, one another, each absorbing those colors that the other reflects and resulting in a neutral tone or gray (theoretically, black) when mixed in the right proportions. The inner triangles in FIG. 7 are the products of such mixing.

Color also has a psychological dimension—red and yellow, quite naturally, connoting warmth; blue and green, coolness. Generally, *warm* colors seem to *advance* and *cool* colors seem to *recede.*

The quality of a surface (rough, smooth, hard, soft, shiny, dull) as revealed by light is *texture.* The many painting media and techniques permit the creation of a variety of textures. The artist may simulate the texture of the materials represented, as in Kalf's *Still Life* (FIG. 19-56, p. 752), or create arbitrary surface differences, even using materials other than canvas, as in Picasso's *Still Life with Chair-Caning* (FIG. 22-14, p. 902).

Specialized Concepts

The terms we have been discussing have connotations for all the visual arts. Certain observations, however, are relevant to only one category of artistic endeavor—to architecture, or to sculpture, or to painting.

IN ARCHITECTURE

Works of architecture are so much a part of our environment that we accept them as given, and scarcely notice them until our attention is summoned. People have long known how to enclose space for the many purposes of life. Of all the arts, it is in architecture that the spatial aspect is most obvious. The architect makes groupings of enclosed spaces and enclosing masses, always keeping in mind the function of the structure, its construction and materials, and, of course, its design—the correlative of the other two. We experience architecture both visually and by moving through and around it, so that we perceive architectural space and mass together. The articulation of space and mass in building is expressed graphically in several ways; the principal ones follow.

A *plan* is essentially a map of a floor, showing the placement of the masses of a structure and, therefore, the spaces they bound and enclose (FIG. 7-44, p. 280). A *section*, like a vertical plan, shows placement of the masses as if the building were cut through along a plane—often one that is a major axis of the building (FIG. 3-8, p. 78). An *elevation* is a head-on view of an external or internal wall, showing its features and often other elements that would be visible beyond or before the wall (FIG. 5-56, p. 158).

Our response to a building can range from simple comfort to astonishment and awe. Such reactions are products of our experience of a building's function, construction, and design; we react differently to a church, a gymnasium, and an office building. For one thing, the very movements we must make to experience one building will differ widely and profoundly from the movements required to experience another. These movements will be controlled by the continuity (or discontinuity) of the plan or by the placement of its axes. For example, in a central plan—one that radiates from a central point, as in the Pantheon in Rome (FIG. 6-53, p. 223)—we perceive the whole spatial entity at once; but in the long axial plan of a Christian basilica (FIG. 7-27, p. 268) or a Gothic cathedral (FIG. 10-17, p. 383), our attention tends to focus on a given point—the altar at the eastern end of the nave. Mass and space can be interrelated to produce effects of great complexity, as, for example, in the Byzantine Church of the Katholikon (FIG. 7-48, p. 283) or in Le Corbusier's church at Ronchamp (FIG. 22-106, p. 964). Thus, our experience of architecture will be the consequence of a great number of material and formal factors, including training, knowledge, and our perceptual and psychological makeup, which function in our experience of any work of art.

The architect must have the sensibilities of a sculptor and of a painter and, in establishing the plan of a building, must be able to use the instruments of a mathematician. As architects resolve structural problems, they act as (or with) engineers who are cognizant of the structural principles underlying all architecture (FIG. 8). Their major responsibilities, however, lie in the manner in which they interpret the *program* of the building. We are not talking in architectural terms when we describe a structure simply as a church, a hospital, an airport concourse, a house. Any proposed building presents an architect with problems peculiar to it alone—problems related to the site and its surroundings, the requirements of the client, and the materials available, as well as the function of the building. A program, then, deals with more than function; it addresses itself to all the problems embodied in a specific building.

8   Basic structural devices: (a) post and lintel; (b) corbeled arch; (c) arch; (d) cantilever; (e) suspension.

IN SCULPTURE

Like architecture, sculpture exists in the three-dimensional space of our physical world. But sculpture as image is closer to painting than is architecture. Until recently, sculpture has been concerned primarily with the representation of human and natural forms in tangible materials, which exist in the same space as the forms they represent. However, sculpture also may embody visions and ideals and has consistently presented images of deities and people in their most heroic as well as their most human aspects (FIGS. 17-20, p. 616, and 5-77, p. 170). Today, sculpture often dispenses with the figure as image, and even with the image itself, producing new forms in new materials and with new techniques (FIGS. 22-79 through 22-86, 22-89, and 22-91, pp. 946–53).

Sculpture may be intimately associated with architecture, often to such a degree that it is impossible to disassociate the two (FIG. 10-14, p. 381). Sculpture is called *relief* sculpture when it is attached to a back slab or back plate (FIG. 3-42, p. 100); *high relief*, if the figures or design project boldly (FIG. 5-79, p. 171); and *low relief*, or *bas-relief*, if the figures or design project slightly (FIG. 3-42, p. 100).

Sculpture that exists in its own right, independent of any particular architectural frame or setting (FIG. 17-47, p. 636), is usually referred to as *freestanding* sculpture, or "sculpture in the round," although, in the art of Greece and of the Renaissance, freestanding sculpture has been closely allied to architecture on many occasions. Indeed, sculpture is such a powerful agent in creating a spatial as well as an intellectual environment that its presence in city squares or in parks and gardens is usually the controlling factor in creating their "atmosphere" or general effect (FIG. 19-74, p. 765).

Some statues are meant to be seen as a whole—to be walked around (FIG. 17-47, p. 636). Others have been created to be viewed only from a restricted angle. How a sculpture is meant to be seen must be taken into account by the sculptor, and by those who exhibit the work. The effect of ignoring this is illustrated in FIG. 9. The left photograph is taken directly from the front, as the piece is now seen in the museum; the right photograph is taken from below, at approximately the same angle from which the statue was originally meant to be seen in its niche on the facade of the cathedral of Florence.

In sculpture, perhaps more than in any other medium, textures, or tactile values, are important. One's first impulse is almost always to handle a piece of sculpture, to run one's finger over its surfaces. The sculptor plans for this, using a great variety of surfaces from rugged coarseness to polished smoothness (FIGS. 10-56, p. 407, and 16-50, p. 581). Textures, of course, are often intrinsic to a material, and this influences the type of stone, wood, plastic, clay, or metal that the sculptor selects. There are two basic categories of sculptural technique: *subtractive* and *additive*. Carving, for instance, is a subtractive technique; the final form is a reduction of the original mass (FIG. 10). Additive sculpture is built up, usually in clay around a framework, or armature; the piece is fired and used to make a mold in which the final work is cast in a material such as bronze (FIG. 16-52, p. 583). Casting is a popular technique today, as is the direct construction of forms by welding shaped metals (FIG. 22-80, p. 947), also an additive technique.

Within the sculptural family, we must include ceramics and metalwork, and numerous smaller, related arts, all of which employ highly specialized techniques described in distinct vocabularies. These will be considered as they arise in the text.

9 DONATELLO, *St. John the Evangelist*, 1412–1415. Marble. Museo del Duomo, Florence. *Left:* as seen in museum; *right:* as intended to be seen on façade of Florence Cathedral.

IN THE PICTORIAL ARTS

The forms of architecture and sculpture exist in actual, three-dimensional space. The forms of painting (and of its relatives, drawing, engraving, and the like) exist almost wholly on a two-dimensional surface, on which the artist creates an illusion—something that replicates what we see around us or something that is unique to the artist's imagination and corresponds only vaguely or slightly to anything we can see in the optical world. Human discovery of the power to project illusions of the three-dimensional world onto two-dimensional surfaces goes back thousands of years and marks an enormous step in the control and manipulation of the things we perceive. To

10 MICHELANGELO, *Unfinished Bound Slave,*
1519. Marble. Accademia, Florence.

achieve this illusion, the artist configures images or representations drawn from the world of common visual experience. Throughout the history of art, this has been interpreted in an almost infinite variety of ways. Undoubtedly, there is much that all people *see* in common and can agree on: the moon at night, a flying bird, an obstacle in one's path. They may differ, though, in their interpretation of the *seen,* for seeing and then representing what is seen are very different matters. The difference between *seeing* and *representing* determines the variability of artistic styles, both cultural and personal. For what we *actually* see (the optical "fact") is not necessarily reported in what we represent. In other words, in art, there is and need be little agreement between the *likeness* of a thing and the *representation* of it. This makes for a persisting problem in the history of art. How are we to interpret or "read" images or replicas of the seen? Is there a "correct" vision of the "real" world?

THE PROBLEM OF REPRESENTATION

The conundrum of seeing something and making a representation of it is artfully illustrated in FIG. 11, a cartoon of a life-drawing class in ancient Egypt that Gombrich uses to introduce his invaluable work *Art and Illusion.* The cartoon and the actual representation of an Egyptian queen (FIG. 12) raise many questions: Did Egyptian artists copy models exactly as they saw them? (Did Egyptians actually *see* each other in this way?) Or did they translate what they saw according to some formula dictated by conventions of representation peculiar to their culture? Would we have to say—if what was seen and what was recorded were optically the same—that this is the way Egyptians must have looked? Or wished to look? Beginning students usually have questions somewhat like these in mind when they perceive deviations in historical styles from the recent Western realism to which they are conditioned. They

11 ALAIN. Drawing. Copyright © 1955, 1983 The New Yorker Magazine, Inc.

12 *Queen Nofretari,* from her tomb at Thebes, *c.* 1250 B.C. Detail of a painted bas-relief.

will ask whether the Egyptians, or other artists, were simply unskilled at matching eye and hand, so to speak, and could not draw from what they saw. But such a question presupposes that the objective of the artist has always been to match appearances with camera-like exactitude. This is not the case, nor is it the case that artists of one period "see" more "correctly" and render more "skillfully" than those of another. Rather, it seems that artists represent what they *conceive* to be real, not what they *perceive.* They bring to the making of images conceptions that have been instilled in them by their cultures. They understand the visible world in certain unconscious, culturally agreed-on ways, and thus bring to the artistic process ideas and meanings out of a common stock. They record not so much what they *see* as what they *know* or *mean.* Even in the period of dominant realism in recent western European art, great deviations from camera realism have set in. Moreover, in our everyday life there are images familiar to all of us that distort optical "reality" quite radically; consider, for example, the images of the ubiquitous comic strip.

Solutions to the problem of representation compose the history of artistic style. It is useful to examine some specimens of sharp divergence in representational approach. Compare, for example, the lion drawn by the medieval artist Villard de Honnecourt (FIG. 13) and lions drawn by the Renaissance artist Albrecht Dürer (FIG. 14). In the de Honnecourt lion—which, it is important to notice, the artist asserts was drawn from life—the figure is entirely adequate for identification but preconceived and constructed according to the formulas of its time. Dürer's lions, drawn some three centuries later, obviously are a much different report of what the artist saw. So are the Assyrian lions of the hunting reliefs (FIG. 2-30, p. 61), the *Lion from the Processional Way* of the Ishtar Gate (FIG. 2-32, p. 62), the lion in Henri Rousseau's *The Sleeping Gypsy* (FIG. 21-77, p. 876), or (in slight shift of species) Barye's sculpture of a jaguar in his *Jaguar Devouring a Hare* (FIG. 21-8, p. 814). In each case, *personal vision* joins with the *artistic conventions* of time and place to decide the manner and effect of the representation. Yet, even at the same

13 VILLARD DE HONNECOURT, *Lion Portrayed from Life, c.* 1230–1235. Drawing. Cabinet des Manuscrits, Bibliothèque Nationale, Paris.

14 ALBRECHT DÜRER, *Two Lions, c.* 1521. Drawing. Staatliche Museen Preussischer Kulturbesitz, Kupferstichkabinett, Berlin.

time and place (for example, nineteenth-century Paris), we can find sharp differences in representation when the opposing personal styles of Ingres and Delacroix record the same subject (FIGS. 21-24 and 21-25, pp. 826–27).

A final example will underscore the relativity of vision and representation that differences in human cultures produce. We recognize, moreover, that close matching of appearances has mattered only in a few times and places. Although both portraits of a Maori chieftain from New Zealand (FIG. 15)—one by a European, the other by the chieftain himself—reproduce his facial tatooing, the first portrait is a simple, commonplace likeness that underplays the tatooing. The self-portrait is a statement by the chieftain of the supreme importance of the design that symbolizes his rank among his people. It is the splendidly composed insignia that is his image of himself, the European likeness being superficial and irrelevant to him.

Students of the history of art, then, learn to distinguish the works before them by scrutinizing them closely within the context of their time and place of origin. But this is only the beginning. The causes of stylistic change in time are mysterious and innumerable; and it is only through the continuing process of art-historical research that we can hope to make the picture even fragmentarily recognizable, never complete. Incomplete though the picture is, the panorama of art, changing in time, lies before the students; and, as their art-historical perspective gains depth and focus, they will come to perceive the continuity of the art of the past with that of the present. It will become clear that one cannot be understood without the other and that our understanding of the one will constantly change with changes in our understanding of the other. The great American poet and critic T.S. Eliot has cogently expressed this truth for all of art in a passage that suggests the philosophy and method of this book:

> . . . what happens when a new work of art is created is something that happens simul-taneously to all the works of art which preceded it. The existing monuments form an ideal order among themselves, which is modified by the introduction of the new (the really new) work of art among them. . . . Whoever has approved this idea of order . . . will not find it preposterous that the past should be altered by the present as much as the present is directed by the past.*

*T.S. Eliot, "Tradition and the Individual Talent," in *Selected Essays 1917–1932* (New York: Harcourt Brace Jovanovich, 1932), p. 5.

15   *The Maori Chief Tupai Kupa, c.* 1800. *Left:* after a drawing by John Sylvester;
right: a self-portrait. From *The Childhood of Man* by Leo Frobenius, 1909. Reproduced
by permission of J.B. Lippincott Company.

As new works of art continue to be created, old ones, buried by time, are recovered and others, known to have existed, disappear. Many come to light by chance, and many are destroyed by catastrophe or neglect. Restoration and reconstruction either damage or rescue them. The whole domain of art constantly shifts in outline and population, as does our knowledge of it. Identification of a work of art may be accepted at one time, rejected at another. Attribution of certain works to certain artists may be challenged. The chronology of stylistic change may be readjusted; the dating of particular works, debated and revised. Critics may disagree as to the number of works to be ascribed to a single artist. (Some allow Rembrandt as many as 600 paintings; some, as few as 350.) Reinterpretation of the meanings and functions of works of art is an ongoing process, as is the reassessment of their artistic value and stylistic importance. Our knowledge of art history is as much in flux as artistic creation itself; what seems to be certain at one time proves to be inconclusive or erroneous at another. Evidence for our conclusions is never all in; more of it is always turning up, and much of it cannot be found.

Students are therefore cautioned not to expect this book to contain an outlay of facts that are incontestable beyond all alteration. The facts are the works of art themselves, as made palpable to our senses; our descriptions of these works—our dating, attributions, classifications, interpretations—are forever provisional and open to doubt. What is not open to doubt is the presence in our world of a small universe of objects of art that expresses, in myriad, arresting forms, the highest values and ideals of the human race. It is essential to the quality of our own experience to encounter, comprehend, appreciate, and preserve these precious works of human hands.

I

THE ANCIENT WORLD

The Christian civilizations of the Western world early distinguished an ancient past from a new age—the times, respectively, before (B.C.) and after (A.D.) Christ. For them the ancient world—the world of the Old Testament—had the character of a preparation; it was related to the new era as promise is related to fulfillment. This slightly condescending view toward antiquity changed during the Renaissance, when scholars and artists deeply admired the Greek and Roman past and often debated the question of which was superior, the "ancient" or the "modern." Interest in Greco–Roman antiquity was later broadened to encompass the great civilizations that preceded it—the pre-Greek Mediterranean, the Egyptian, the Near Eastern, and the very remote, prehistoric cave cultures of western Europe.

From the end of the eighteenth century to the present, archeologists and art historians, utilizing ever-improving methods of investigation, have recovered great tracts of forgotten history to fill out with increasing accuracy, our picture

The Great Sphinx, Gizeh, Upper Egypt,
c. 2530 B.C. Sandstone, 65' high, 240' long.

of the distant past. Within the past three decades, evidence of the existence of civilizations that flourished as early as 7000 B.C. has been provided, and the sequence of development that viewed early Egypt and Mesopotamia as existing concurrently has been shown to be incorrect; Mesopotamia, in fact, preceded Egypt by many centuries.

Historical perspective is likely to produce a distortion of view similar to that of the early Christian depreciation of the pre-Christian world. Until we have become familiar with the ancient world, it seems to us to be simply *that* (ancient, exceedingly old), and we imagine it in terms and images of faded inscriptions, dusty ruins, fallen idols, and long-outdated institutions. More properly, we should see *ourselves* as ancient—as living in the later eras of a great epoch at the beginning of which, thousands of years ago, some of our most fundamental beliefs, institutions, folkways, and art and science had their inception.

The precarious, furtive life of the cave-dwelling hunter and the later nomadic herdsman was, given the development of agriculture and the widespread domestication of animals, succeeded by the more sedentary, predictable, and ordered life of the village farmer. Aside from the technological revolutions of our times, this leap from food-gathering to food production brought perhaps the most significant transformation of the human condition and made possible all that has followed. In Mesopotamia, Asia Minor, and Egypt, more complex forms of human community were created—cities, city-states, and kingdoms. Formal religion and codes of law were developed to regulate the relationships among men and between gods and men. Writing was invented, as well as numbers and the art of calculation. The courses of the stars were plotted in order to predict the seasons and the times for planting and harvesting. Architecture, sculpture, and painting flourished in the service of kingly magnificence. The sacred books of Judaism and Christianity were produced in the shadow of mighty and hostile empires, and the legacy of Israel, which has contributed so much to the formation of the Western spirit, was preserved through all the vicissitudes of a remarkable people.

With the Greeks, there emerged what might be called the specifically "Western intelligence," with its respect for reason, scientific inquiry, the physical concept of nature, and the humanistic view of man. The city-states of Greece were more than seats of commerce and government; the loyalties of the citizens of each city-state had social, educative, and local religious bases as well. It was in some of these city-states—Athens in particular—that democracy first evolved in a limited form. About 2,500 years ago, the government of Athens was largely in the hands of a council of citizens, who were chosen by lot, and a kind of legislative assembly composed of all citizens—although citizenship did not extend to women or to the slaves who made up nearly half the population.

With the repulsion of the Persian invaders in the fifth century B.C., the Greeks inaugurated the first authentic phase of European culture—the content and spirit of which, commingled with Hebraism, is still largely with us in our patterns of life and thought today.

Rome, although never matching the Greek achievement in intellectual and artistic culture, produced the greatest empire of the ancient world. During a period of approximately 800 years, Rome passed from its beginnings as a trading center under Etruscan kings to the zenith of its empire, which extended from what are now the borders of Scotland to Jordan and to the far shores of the Black Sea, asserting its dominance over a multitude of peoples and lands. The dynamic and aggressive Roman spirit was reflected in and supported by an astonishing military machine and technology, although

Roman control over diverse peoples was exercised as much by the encouragement of their participation in the empire as by the naked assertion of Roman power. The Romanization of western Europe—through the Roman genius for government and the "Roman Peace"—still has much to do with the character of Europe, and the Roman ideal of a single, peaceful community of all humankind is very much in our view today as at least an ideal and a hope.

PREHISTORIC EUROPE

PALEOLITHIC

Franco-Cantabrian region
● Cave art
▲ Mobiliary art

MESOLITHIC

East Spanish region

NEOLITHIC

■ Megaliths

Stonehenge

Carnac

Font-de-Gaume

Lascaux

Altamira

Niaux

La Madeleine

Willendorf

Castellón

| 0 | 100 | 200 | 300 | |
| | | | | MILES |

| 0 | 160 | 320 | 480 | |
| | | | | KILOMETERS |

1

THE BIRTH OF ART

NOTE: Most of the time spans shown on the chronology have been determined by the method of *radiocarbon dating* invented in 1955. This is such an effective dating method that archeologists have called it "the radiocarbon revolution." Radiocarbon dating is based on the fact that living organisms continually absorb carbon isotopes, including the radioactive carbon-14, which continually disintegrates into nonradioactive nitrogen-14. On the death of the organism, absorption ceases but disintegration continues. Because the rate of disintegration is known, the age of organic matter—such as charcoal or carbonized bone—can be calculated on the basis of the amount of carbon-14 remaining in it.

In recent years, however, the chemical "clock" provided by the disintegration of carbon-14 has sometimes been out of phase with known dates before about 1000 B.C., making them later than they should be; it may be that other energy phenomena interfere with the regularity of this chemical "clock." Radiocarbon dating has therefore been supplemented and corrected by another dating technique—called *dendrochronology*—which determines the age of timber. By counting the annual rings of trees, visible in the cross sections of their trunks (notably, the very ancient bristle-cone pines of California), accurate dates as far back as about 4000 B.C. can be obtained.

The result of using these two dating methods in correlation—now called *calibrated dating*—has been to update the end of the Paleolithic period to about 9000–8000 B.C., to push back the date of the Neolithic period, and to bring much more closely together in a continuity of development the Paleolithic, Mesolithic, and Neolithic epochs of human culture in relation to the historical periods, the Bronze and Iron ages, and our own times.

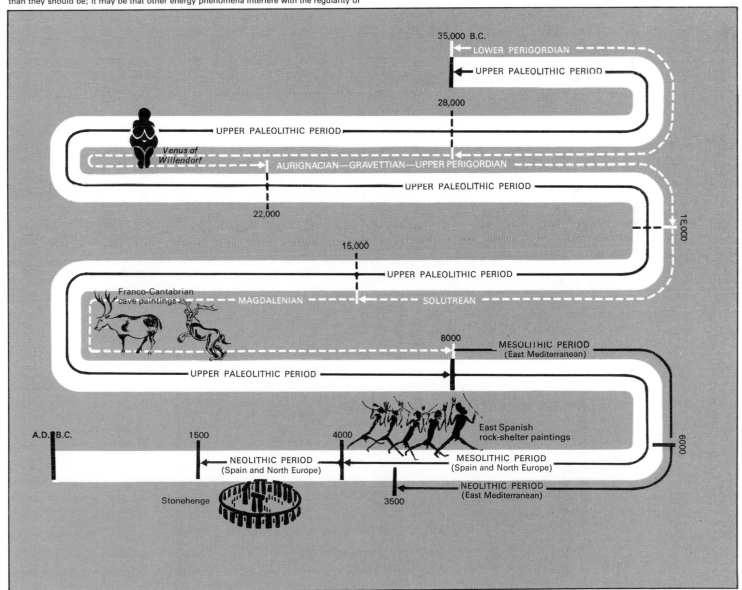

WHAT GENESIS is to the biblical account of the fall and redemption of man, early cave art is to the history of his intelligence, imagination, and creative power. In the caves of southern France and of northern Spain, which were discovered only about a century ago and are still being explored—as well as in central Europe, North Africa, and Asia—we may witness the birth of that characteristically human capability that has made man master of his environment—the making of images and symbols. By this original and tremendous feat of abstraction, upper Paleolithic men were able to fix the world of their experience, rendering the continuous processes of life in discrete and unmoving shapes that had the identity and meaning of the living animals that were their prey. Like Adam, Paleolithic man gathered and named the animals, and the faculty of imagination came into being along with the concepts of identity and meaning.

In that remote time during the last advance and retreat of the great glaciers, man made the critical breakthrough and became wholly human. Our intellectual and imaginative processes function through the recognition and construction of images and symbols. We see and understand the world pretty much as we are taught to, according to representations of the world that are familiar to our particular time and place. The immense achievement of Stone Age man, the invention of *representation*, cannot be exaggerated.

THE LATER OLD STONE AGE (UPPER PALEOLITHIC)*

The physical environment of the cave peoples over thousands of years would not appear to be favorable to the creation of an art of quality and sophistication; survival alone would seem to have required most of their energies. Although the Aurignacian period began between the early and main advances of the last glaciers and for a while was temperate, it grew cold toward its end. The great ice sheet advanced

*The prehistoric periods "Paleolithic," "Mesolithic," and "Neolithic" refer to the stone (Greek *lithos*) technology that prevailed through thousands of years of early human life; the prefixes "paleo," "meso," and "neo" mean "early," "middle," and "late," respectively. These terms were coined in the nineteenth century and no longer fit the facts precisely as modern archeology now classifies them, but they are used habitually and are difficult to replace. For convenience, we will use them here. Subdivisions within these three prehistoric periods are named for the sites (mostly in France) at which characteristic artifacts, like tools and weapons, have been found ("Perigoridan," "Aurignacian," "Solutrean," "Magdalenian"). The terms "lower" and "upper," placed before these names, signify the earlier and later phases of a period.

south from Scandinavia over the plains of north central Europe, and glaciers spread down from the Alps and other mountain ranges to produce a tundra and forest-tundra climate. With the end of the Magdalenian period about 8000 B.C., the final recession of the ice and the onset of temperate weather began. In the cold periods, man—the hunter and food-gatherer—took refuge in caves. It was here that Cro-Magnon man, who first appeared during the Aurignacian period, replacing Neanderthal man, took the remarkable turn that made him not simply a fabricator of stone tools, but an artist.

Cave Art

The first example of cave art was discovered—by amateurs and by accident—in 1879 near Santander in northern Spain. Marcelino de Sautuola, a local resident interested in the antiquity of man, was exploring the Altamira Caves on his estate, in which he had already found specimens of flint and carved bone. With him was his little daughter. Because the ceiling of the debris-filled cavern was only a few inches above the father's head, it was the child who was first able to discern, from her lower vantage point, the shadowy forms of painted beasts on the cave roof. De Sautuola was the first modern man to explore this cave, and he was certain that these paintings dated back to prehistoric times. Archeologists, however, were highly dubious of the authenticity of these works, and at the Lisbon Congress on Prehistoric Archeology in 1880, the Altamira paintings were officially dismissed as forgeries. But in 1896, at Pair-non-Pair in the Gironde district of France, paintings were discovered partially covered by calcareous deposits that would have taken thousands of years to accumulate. These paintings were the first to be recognized by experts as authentic. The conviction grew that these remarkable works were of an antiquity far greater than man had ever dreamed. In 1901, Abbé Breuil discovered and verified the cave art of Font-de-Gaume in Dordogne, France. The skeptics were finally convinced.

The caves at Lascaux, near Montignac, also in the Dordogne region of France, were discovered accidentally in 1940, and their paintings are now generally regarded as the most outstanding of all known prehistoric art (FIG. 1-1). Although they had survived more than 17,000 years in the sealed and dry subterranean chambers, many of these paintings have deteriorated rapidly since the caves were opened to the public in recent decades. At Lascaux, for example, it was found that moisture and carbon dioxide exhaled by hordes of visitors settled on the walls and encouraged the growth of fungi destructive to the paintings.

1-1 *Hall of Bulls* (left wall), Lascaux, *c.* 15,000–13,000 B.C. Dordogne, France.

For this reason, and to prevent further damage, the caves have been closed to the general public since 1963.

The Lascaux caverns (FIG. 1-2), like the others, had served as subterranean water channels, a few hundred to some 4,000 feet long. They are often choked, sometimes almost impassably, by faults or by deposits, such as stalactites and stalagmites. Far inside these caverns, well removed from the cave mouths that he chose for habitation, the hunter–artist engraved and painted on the walls pictures of animals— mammoth, bison, reindeer, horse, boar, wolf. For light, he used tiny stone lamps filled with marrow or fat, with a wick, perhaps, of moss. For drawing, he used chunks of red and yellow ocher; for painting, he ground these same ochers into powders that he blew onto the walls or mixed with some medium, like animal fat, before applying. A large flat bone served him as a palette; he could make brushes from reeds or bristles; he could use a blowpipe of reeds to trace outlines of figures and to put pigments on out-of-reach surfaces; and he had stone scrapers for smoothing the wall and sharp flint points for engraving. Along with the more famous paintings, more than 1,000 engravings have recently been found on the walls and ceilings of the Lascaux caverns, indicating that engraving was as much a practiced technique as painting—and quite as important for our appreciation of the art of the caves (FIG. 1-3).

During the years that the caves of Lascaux have been closed to tourism, archeologists, like the late Abbé André Glory, who made careful tracings of all the engravings, have worked indefatigably, recovering artifacts that provide firm evidence of the Magda-

1-2 Diagram of the caves of Lascaux. Dordogne, France. (After Arlette Leroi-Gourhan.)

1-3 Engraved reindeer, Lascaux, *c.* 15,000 B.C. Engraving on rock, 28" long. Dordogne, France. (Simplified copy of a tracing by Abbé André Glory.)

lenian artists' methods and materials. Some 130 stone lamps have been found, and from the remains of their burnt tallow and wicks, it has been shown that their light must have been as strong and steady as candlelight and must have lasted for an hour at a time. Numerous flat stones have been found that served as palettes for mixing colors. The colors themselves have been found, lumps of pigment have been chemically analyzed, and the different mineral powders that composed them have been ascertained. Recesses cut into the rock wall some seven feet or more above the floor must have held joists for a scaffolding that could support a platform made of saplings lashed together. This permitted the painters access to the upper surfaces of the caves, where they could occupy themselves for hours if need be; remains of meals indicate that they could take them without having to descend. Carbon-14 analysis of the charcoal in the lamps and of bone artifacts associated with the various strata of the paintings confirms a date for the art of Lascaux of around 15,000 B.C. It is thought likely that the period of artistic activity may have extended over a relatively short span of time, coinciding with only several centuries of human occupation of the caves. This would help to explain the stylistic unity of the paintings and engravings, which suggests a continuity of tradition and a common training.

The artist's approach to the figures, as seen at Lascaux and at other sites, is *naturalistic*; he attempts to represent as convincing a pose and action as possible. Each painting reflects the keen observation and extraordinary memory of the hunter–artist, whose accuracy in capturing fleeting poses is hardly surpassed by today's camera (FIGS. 1-1 and 1-6). Yet this observation was selective; the artist saw and recorded only those aspects that were essential to interpret the appearance and the character of the animal—its grace or awkwardness, its cunning, dignity, or ferocity. It is almost as if the artist were constructing a pictorial definition of the animal, capturing its very essence.

Any modern interpretation of this cave art must, of course, remain pure speculation. Properties common to all these paintings, however, provide some fairly definite clues as to what they meant to their creators. For instance, the fact that the paintings are never found in those parts of the caves that were inhabited or near daylight rules out any purely decorative purpose. The first paintings at Font-de-Gaume were encountered about 70 yards behind the cave mouth, and the painted animals in the "Salon Noir" in the cave at Niaux were found some 850 tortuous yards from the entrance. The remoteness and difficulty of access of many of these sites and the fact that they appear to have been used for centuries strongly suggest that the prehistoric hunter attributed magical properties to them. Therefore, the paintings themselves probably had magical meaning for their creators. As Abbé Breuil has suggested, "by confining the animal within the limits of a painting, one subjected it to one's power in the hunting grounds." Within this context, the artist's aim to be realistic may be explained by his probable conviction that the painting's magical power was directly related to its lifelike characteristics.

The naturalistic pictures of animals are often accompanied by geometric signs, some of which seem to represent man-made structures, or *tectiforms* (FIG. 1-4); others consist of checkers, dots, squares, or other arrangements of lines. Several observers have seen a primitive form of writing in these representations of nonliving things, but more likely they, too, had magical significance. The ones that look like traps or snares, for example, may have been drawn to ensure success in hunting with these devices. In many places, representations of human hands, most of them "negative," appear where the artist placed his hand against the wall and then painted or blew pigment around it (FIG. 1-5). Occasionally, he would dip his hand in paint and then press it against the wall, leaving a "positive" imprint. These handprints, too, may have had magical significance, or may simply have been the "signatures" left by whole generations of visitors to these sacred places, much as modern tourists leave some memento of their presence.

The figures are in themselves marvelous approximations of optical fact, but their arrangement on the cave walls shows little concern for any consistency of placement in relationship to each other or to the wall space, although this has been claimed. Certainly, we find no compositional adjustment to suggest the perspective effect and no notion of separation and enframement. Figures, far from being proportionally related, are often superimposed at random and are of quite different sizes (FIGS. 1-1 and 1-3). Generations of artists, working in the same sanctuaries, covered and recovered the crowded walls, although often pains seem to have been taken not to break through the outlines of an earlier figure. It seems that attention to a single figure, the rendering of a single image, in itself fulfilled the purpose of the artist.

The hunter–artist made frequent and skillful use of the naturally irregular surfaces of the walls—of their projections, recessions, fissures, and ridges—to help give the illusion of real presence to his forms. An outward swelling of the wall could be used within the outline of a charging bison to suggest the bulging vol-

1-4 *Three Cows and One Horse,* ceiling of the Axial Gallery, Lascaux, *c.* 15,000–13,000 B.C. Approx. life-size. Dordogne, France.

1-5 *Spotted Horses and Negative Hand Imprints,* Pech-Merle, *c.* 15,000–13,000 B.C. 11′ 2″ long. Lot, France.

ume of the beast's body. The spotted horse at Pech-Merle (FIG. 1-5) may have been inspired by a rock formation that resembles a horse's head and neck (on the right of the figure), although the artist's eventual version of the head is much smaller than the formation and is highly abstract. Natural forms, like those of foliage or clouds, the profile of a mountain, or the shapes of eroded earth and rock, can represent for any of us—sometimes quite startlingly—the features of men, animals, or objects. Thus, man's first representations may have followed some primal experience of resemblance between a chance configuration of a cave wall and the animal he had just been hunting. This might have had for him the effect of an awesome apparition of the very animal—a miraculous and magical reappearance of its vanished life. With the impulse to give the apparition even more presence, he could have "finished" the form by cutting an outline around the relief and continuing it until a silhouette, more or less complete and familiar, emerged. The addition of color would enhance the reality of the image.

THE MAGICAL FUNCTION

We have evidence that the hunters in the caves, perhaps in a frenzy stimulated by magical rites and dances, treated the painted animals as if they were alive. Not only was the quarry painted as pierced by arrows, as in the *Chinese Horse* at Lascaux (FIG. 1-6), but hunters may have thrown spears at the images—as sharp gouges in the side of the bison at Niaux (FIG. 1-7) suggest—predestinating and magically commanding the death of the animals. This practice would be analogous to the kind of magic, still cultivated in parts of the world today, that is based on the belief that harm can be done to an enemy by abusing an image of that person.

This art produced in dark caverns deep in the earth must have had, as most scholars are now convinced, some profound magical functions. Familiar in religious architecture, which had its beginning thousands of years after the era of the caves, are the cave-like spaces of the sanctuary where the most sacred and hidden mysteries are kept and where the god dwells in silence. The sacred has meant the mysterious; in many cases, this means a place of darkness, lit only by fitful light, where, at the culmination of rituals, absolute silence reigns. These features of the sacred environment were already present in the "architecture" of the caves, and the central theme has never been lost despite its myriad variations.*

It is significant that the miracle of abstraction—the creation of image and symbol—should take place in such secret and magical caverns. Abstraction is representation, a human device of fundamental power, by which not only art but ultimately science comes into existence. Both art and science are methods for the control of human experience and the mastery of the environment. And that, too, was the end purpose of the hunter–magician—to control the world of the beasts he hunted. The making of the image was, by

*About this time, magic may have been developing into religious ritual and communal belief. Recently, at the El Juyo cave site near Santander in northern Spain (the neighborhood of the Altamira caves), a sanctuary was uncovered containing an altar-like slab of stone that weighs nearly a ton and is supported by vertical slabs of stone. It appears to be the shrine of the sanctuary, the focus of a group religion. The shrine area, covering 118 square feet, contains clay-faced mounds that cover trenches in the floor. The trenches hold a variety of deliberately arranged objects that may have been used as sacred accessories in ceremonies of some sort. Structured cave, sanctuary, shrine, and repositories—the rudimentary elements of religious architecture—are already here in primitive form. The site dates from about 12,000 B.C.

1-6 *Chinese Horse* (detail of FIG. 1-4), Axial Gallery, Lascaux, c. 15,000–13,000 B.C. Approx. 56" long. Dordogne, France.

itself, a form of magic. By painting an animal, the hunter fixed and controlled its soul within the prison of an outline; from this initial magic, all the rest must follow. Rites before the paintings may have served to improve the hunter's luck. At the same time, prehistoric man must have been anxious to preserve his food supply, and the many representations of pregnant animals (FIG. 1-6) suggest that these cavalcades of painted beasts may also have served magically to assure the survival of the actual herds.

But magic must not be considered the sole function of cave art; other functions have been suggested. The processions and groupings of the animals are not entirely haphazard and seem to express an order in terms of the preferences and concerns of the hunter (cattle and horses, for example, regularly appear together). The *palimpsest effect*—images superimposed on one another—may be a spatial representation of time (one hunting season taking the place of another, a sort of mark-off calendar). The animals may be a kind of heraldic-totemistic image, representative of their blood relationship to different tribes. Or they may be objects of worship, as was the buffalo for the Indians of the North American plains. The fact is that we have not found a completely satisfactory answer to the enigma of the caves.

THE REPRESENTATION OF MAN

The figure of man is almost completely excluded from representation among the vivid troops of painted animals. There are at least two notable exceptions. A very puzzling picture at Lascaux (FIG. 1-8) shows a stick-figure man, falling or fallen, before a huge bison that has been disemboweled, probably by the rhinoc-

1-7 *Bison with Superposed Arrows*, Niaux, *c.* 15,000–13,000 B.C. 50″ long. Ariège, France.

eros at the left, which slouches away from the scene. The two animals are rendered with all the skilled attention to animal detail we are accustomed to in cave art: the rhinoceros heavy and lumbering; the buffalo tense and bristling with rage, its bowels hanging from it in a heavy coil. But the birdfaced (masked?) man is rendered with the crude and clumsy touch of the unskilled at any time or place. His position is ambiguous. Is he dead or in an ecstatic trance? The meaning of the bird on the staff and of the spear and

1-8 *Well Scene*, Lascaux, *c.* 15,000 B.C. Bison 55″ high. Dordogne, France.

throw stick is no more obvious. We will not add to the already abundant speculation on the meaning of this picture. A more important question is why are the man and the animal figures treated differently? Does man in this dawn of magic distinguish himself so much from the beast that he can find no image suitable to self-depiction? Or is he afraid to cast a spell on himself, as he casts it on the animals, by rendering his image visible?

At Trois Frères in the Pyrenees, there is a very strange humanoid creature, masked and wearing the antlers of a reindeer (FIG. 1-9)—the so-called *Sorcerer*. Is this the memory sketch of a shaman or witch doctor? If so, one can imagine how the fearsome composite apparition—the paws of a bear, tail of a wolf, beard of a man, corporal parts of a lion—could have struck terror into the heart of its audience. The chamber in which the figure appears is crowded with beasts, and Abbé Breuil has suggested that the figure may be their god, who has descended into the witch doctor and filled him with his bestial power. It has also been suggested that this is only a hunter camouflaged to stalk deer, but it would again appear that, for Paleolithic man, mankind simply is not to be counted among the animals; at least his figure must be so disguised—perhaps to avoid magical self-involvement—as to be unrecognizable as a man.

QUALITY

In explaining the great accomplishment of Stone Age man—who pictured the world in order to magically control it—we must not forget that his art is *art*. It is not simply that he made images, but that he made them skillfully and beautifully. Ancient and modern art have produced, along with masterpieces, images that are dull, prosaic, and of indifferent quality. The art of the caves is of an extraordinary level of quality. The splendid horse in the Axial Gallery at Lascaux (FIG. 1-6) has been called the *Chinese Horse* because its style strangely resembles Chinese painting of the best period. Not only do the outlines have the elastic strength and fluency that we find in Chinese calligraphy and brushwork, but the tone is so managed as to suggest both the turning under of the belly of the pregnant animal and the change of the color of the coat. At Font-de-Gaume, there is a painted reindeer (FIG. 1-10) executed with deft elegance in the contours and remarkable subtlety in the modeling tones. The grace of the antlers is effortlessly translated into an upward-sweeping line that renders the natural shapes with both strength and delicacy. Abbé Breuil, while copying the originals, discerned some highly sophisticated pictorial devices that one expects to find only in the art of far later times; for example, note the darkening of the forward contour of the left hind leg to bring it nearer to the observer than the right leg.

The pictures of cattle at Lascaux and elsewhere (FIG. 1-4) show a convention of representation of the horns that has been called *twisted perspective*, because we see the heads in profile but the horns from a different angle. Thus, the approach of the artist is not strictly or consistently *optical*—(organized from the perspective of a fixed viewpoint). Rather, the approach is *descriptive* of the fact that cattle have two horns. Two horns would be part of the concepts "cow" and "bull." In strict optical-perspective profile, only one horn would be visible, but to paint the animal in such a way would, as it were, amount to an incomplete definition of it. And for the cave artist, this would have been a defective image, without magic. When we discuss the art of the ancient Near East and Egypt, we will note this peculiarity and its significance.

Sculpture

The principal bequests of the hunter–artists are their paintings and engravings; we have seen that both abound at Lascaux. They have also left us sculpture—in stone, ivory, bone, and antler. In the *Bison with Turned Head* (FIG. 1-11), we are impressed by the striking vitality and the simplicity with which the formal beauty is expressed—a simplicity and economy of means that distinguishes the great paintings. The head is so turned that it is entirely framed by the massive bulk of the body, and there is a vivid play of curve and countercurve and a surface contrast obtained by the use of decorative hatching to indicate the mane. The artist would have been perfectly familiar with the method of incision of surfaces; incising the outlines of a figure before the tones were introduced was the usual procedure for painting. But the artists of the caves went farther than incision and produced sculpture in *deep relief* and in the *full round*. An example of the first is a horse in deep relief (FIG. 1-12) found in the rock shelter of Cap Blanc, not far from Lascaux. The figure is part of a frieze of sculptured horses and bison, some of the figures almost a

foot in depth and masterpieces of relief modeling. Although the figures have been eroded by weather, we can perceive their characteristics well enough. They are not simply "filled-out" natural rock contours; in parts, they are strongly modeled. The eyes are sharply incised, and, as in the case of the bison incised in reindeer horn (FIG. 1-11), the manes, forelocks, and portions of the head and muzzle have been carefully indicated by hatching.

It is important to note that engraving and sculpture preceded, by many thousands of years, the highly developed painting of the Magdalenian caves; at least no painting contemporary with existing engravings and sculptures has survived. Moreover, the Magdalenian culture and the cultures that went before were not uniquely French–Spanish. A distinct culture, *Gravettian–Pavlovian*, began in the Upper Paleolithic period, and its artifacts are found from the Rhine to Russia, especially in central Europe. Best known

1-11 *Bison with Turned Head*, La Madeleine, *c.* 11,000–9000 B.C. Reindeer horn, 4⅛" high. Dordogne, France. Musée des Antiquités Nationales, St. Germain-en-Laye.

1-12   Relief horse, Cap Blanc, *c.* 13,000–11,000 B.C. 7' long. Dordogne, France.

1-13   *Venus of Willendorf, c.* 25,000–20,000 B.C. Stone, actual size. Naturhistorisches Museum, Vienna. (Cast of original.)

among these are small sculptures in the full round representing the female figure (formerly called "Venus figures" by archeologists), an exception to the rule of exclusion of the human figure from the cave artist's vocabulary of forms. Perhaps the most famous of these is the *Venus of Willendorf* (FIG. 1-13), a figurine of a woman that is composed of a cluster of almost ball-like shapes. The anatomical exaggeration suggests that this and similar statuettes served as fertility fetishes; the needs for game and human offspring were one in the dangerous life of the hunter. But again the artist's approach to the human figure differs from his approach to animals. He obviously does not aim for that heightened realism so characteristic of his animal representations; facial features, for instance, are seldom indicated in these statuettes, and not even the heads are shown in some specimens. Evidently, the artist's aim was not to show the female of his kind, but rather the idea of female fecundity; he depicted not woman, but fertility.

THE MIDDLE STONE AGE (MESOLITHIC)

Rock-shelter Paintings

As the ice of the Paleolithic period melted in the increasing warmth, the reindeer migrated north, the wooly mammoth and rhinoceros disappeared, and the hunters left their caves. The Ice Age gave way to a transition period, the Mesolithic, during which Europe became climatically, geographically, and biologically much as it is today. In this period, a culture flourished and produced art that complements—and, indeed, may have partially originated from—cave art. Since 1903, diminutive, extraordinarily lively paintings of animals and men in scenes of the hunt, battle, ritual dance, and harvest have been discovered on the stone walls of shallow rock shelters among the barren hills of the eastern coast of Spain (the Spanish Levant). The artists show the same masterful skill in depicting the animal figure as did their predecessors of the caves, and it may be that we have here specimens of a lingering tradition or long-persisting habit of vision and representation of animals. But what is strikingly new is the appearance of the human figure—not only singly, but in large, coherent groups with wide variety of pose, subject, and setting. We have seen that the human figure almost never appears in cave art; the falling or fallen man of the *Well Scene* (FIG. 1-8) at Lascaux is quite exceptional. In the rock-shelter paintings, the new sentiment for human themes and concerns and the emphasis on action in which man dominates the animal are central. The new vocabulary of forms may have migrated across the Mediterranean from North Africa, where many paintings similar to those in the Spanish Levant have been found. There has been much learned debate about the dating of the whole development, and there is now some agreement that its beginnings were around 8000 B.C. and that the style may have lasted (with many variations) until about 3000 B.C.

Some characteristic features of the rock paintings appear in an energetic group of five warriers (FIG. 1-14) found in the Gasulla gorge. The group, only about nine inches in width, shows a customary tense exaggeration of movement, a rhythmic repetition of basic shape, and a general sacrifice of naturalistic appearance to narrative and to unity of action. Even so, we can distinguish details that are economically descriptive—bows, arrows, and the feathered headdress of the leader. The widely splayed legs communicate a leaping stride, perhaps a march to battle or a ritual dance.

Other such paintings show an even greater uniformity of basic shape and a nervous, sharp angularity, which suggest the *pictograph* or, as we have proposed, even the *phonetic hieroglyph*. And over the millennia, rock-painting styles did become more abstract and schematic, more symbol than picture; it is likely that they recorded a step in the evolution of the *symbolic* from the *pictorial*—an evolution that, in the Near East, culminated in the invention of writing. Later on, the liveliness and spontaneity of the rock paintings were lost in the rigid uniformities of almost letter-like shapes repeated as if from a limited stock of signs.

Like the cave paintings, the rock paintings are

1-14   *Marching Warriors* (ritual dance?), Gasulla gorge, *c.* 8000–3000 B.C. Approx. 9" wide. Castellón, Spain.

probably of magical–religious significance, although some observers believe them to be no more than pictorial records of memorable events. The rock paintings are concentrated at particular sites that were used for long periods; nearby places, better suited for painting, were not used. This suggests that the sites were held sacred, not only by the Mesolithic painters but also by those working well into the historical period. Iberian and Latin inscriptions indicate that supernatural powers were ascribed to some of these holy places as late as the Roman era.

THE NEW STONE AGE (NEOLITHIC)

In Paleolithic art, man, in a supreme feat of intellection, learned to abstract his world by making a picture of it. He sought to control the world by capturing and holding its image. In the Neolithic period, man made the giant stride toward the actual, concrete control of his environment by settling in fixed abodes and domesticating plants and animals. His food sup-

ply assured, he changed from hunter to herdsman, to farmer, and, perhaps as early as 7000 B.C. in the Near East, to townsman. The wandering hunter settled down to organized community living in villages surrounded by cultivated fields. Then began the long evolution toward the incredible technological command of the physical environment that exists today.

Recent research seems to indicate that local Neolithic populations in several areas of western Europe developed, as early as 4000 B.C., a monumental architecture consisting of graves and of rows of circles of massive, rough-hewn stones. The very dimensions of the stones, some as high as 17 feet and weighing tons, have prompted the historian to call them *megaliths* (great stones), and the culture that produced them *megalithic*.

There are several types of megalithic structures. The *dolmen* consists of several great stones set on end, with a large covering slab. Dolmens may be the remains of passage graves from which a covering earth mound has been washed away. The *passage grave*, the dominant megalithic tomb type (literally thousands exist in France and England) has a corridor lined with

1-15 Stonehenge, *c.* 2000 B.C. 97' in diameter. Salisbury Plain, Wiltshire, England.

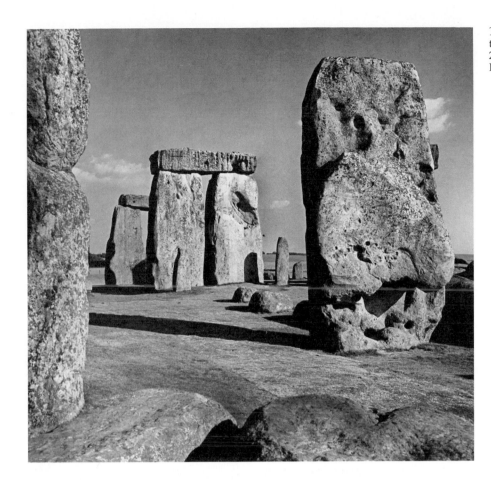

large stone slabs leading to a circular chamber often having a *corbeled* vault, in which each of numerous rings of stones projects inward beyond the underlying course, until the rings close at the top. These graves were frequently built into a hill slope or covered by mounds of earth. At Carnac in Brittany, great single stones, called *menhirs,* set on end, were arranged in parallel rows, some of which run for several miles and consist of thousands of stones. Their purpose was evidently religious and may have had to do with the cult of the dead or the worship of the sun. Sometimes these huge stones were arranged in a circle known as a *cromlech;* among the most imposing cromlechs are those at Avebury and at Stonehenge in England (FIGS. 1-15 and 1-16). The structure at Avebury is surrounded by a stone bank about four-fifths of a mile in diameter. The remains at Stonehenge are of a complex of rough-cut sarsen stones and smaller ''bluestones.'' Outermost was a ring of large monoliths of sarsen stones capped by lintels. Next was a ring of bluestones, which, in turn, encircled a horseshoe (open end facing east) of *trilithons*— five lintel-topped pairs of the largest sarsens, each weighing 45 to 50 tons. Standing apart and to the east is the ''heel-stone,'' which, for a person looking outward from the center of the complex, would have marked the point at which the sun rose at the midsummer solstice.

Stonehenge seems to have been built in several phases around 2000 B.C., according to recently corrected radiocarbon dates. Computer-based calculations have raised something of a controversy—not so much over the date as over the purpose of Stonehenge, which seems to have been a kind of astronomical observatory. The mysterious structure, believed in the Middle Ages to have been the work of the magician Merlin, who spirited it from Ireland, or the work of a race of giants, comes in our own time to be thought of as a remarkably accurate calendar—a testimony to the rapidly developing intellectual powers of man. Even in their ruined condition, the monoliths of Stonehenge possess a solemn majesty, created by heroic human effort, physical and intellectual. At Avebury, as at Stonehenge, there is, in the series of concentric circles with connecting curvilinear pathways or avenues, a feeling for order, symmetry, and rhythm that is evidence not only of well-developed and systematized ceremonial rituals, but perhaps also of a maturing geometrical sense born of observation of the apparent movement of the sun and moon.

2

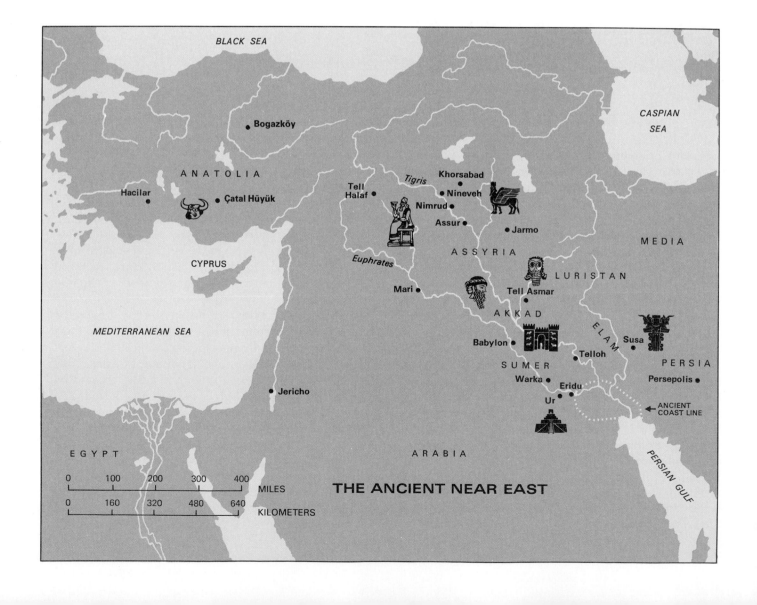

BLACK SEA

CASPIAN
SEA

Bogazköy

ANATOLIA

Khorsabad

Hacilar ● Çatal Hüyük

Tell
Halaf ●

Tigris

● Nineveh

● Nimrud

MEDIA

Jarmo ●

● Assur

ASSYRIA

Euphrates

LURISTAN

CYPRUS

Mari ●

Tell Asmar

AKKAD

ELAM

MEDITERRANEAN SEA

Babylon ●

Susa ●

PERSIA

Telloh ●

SUMER

Warka ● Eridu ●

Persepolis ●

Jericho ●

Ur ●

← ANCIENT
COAST LINE

EGYPT

ARABIA

0   100   200   300   400
MILES

THE ANCIENT NEAR EAST

0   160   320   480   640
KILOMETERS

PERSIAN GULF

THE ANCIENT NEAR EAST

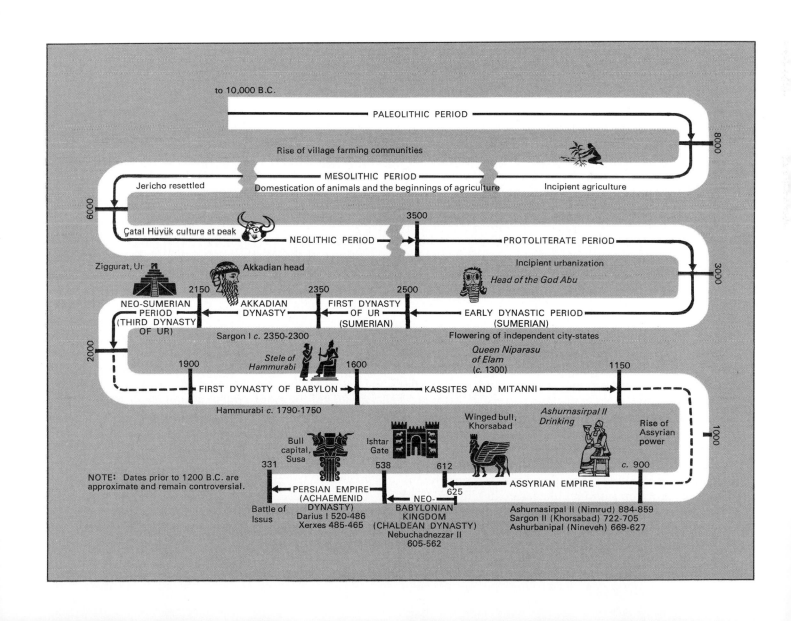

to 10,000 B.C.

PALEOLITHIC PERIOD

8000

Rise of village farming communities

MESOLITHIC PERIOD

Jericho resettled

Domestication of animals and the beginnings of agriculture

Incipient agriculture

6000

3500

Çatal Hüyük culture at peak

NEOLITHIC PERIOD

PROTOLITERATE PERIOD

3000

Ziggurat, Ur

Akkadian head

Incipient urbanization

Head of the God Abu

2150   2350   2500

NEO-SUMERIAN
PERIOD
(THIRD DYNASTY
OF UR)

AKKADIAN
DYNASTY

FIRST DYNASTY
OF UR
(SUMERIAN)

EARLY DYNASTIC PERIOD
(SUMERIAN)

2000

Sargon I c. 2350-2300

Flowering of independent city-states

*Queen Niparasu
of Elam
(c. 1300)*

1900   *Stele of
Hammurabi*   1600   1150

FIRST DYNASTY OF BABYLON

KASSITES AND MITANNI

1000

Hammurabi c. 1790-1750

Winged bull,
Khorsabad

*Ashurnasirpal II
Drinking*

Rise of
Assyrian
power

Bull
capital,
Susa

Ishtar
Gate

331   538   612   c. 900

NOTE: Dates prior to 1200 B.C. are
approximate and remain controversial.

PERSIAN EMPIRE
(ACHAEMENID
DYNASTY)

ASSYRIAN EMPIRE

Battle of
Issus

Darius I 520-486
Xerxes 485-465

NEO-
BABYLONIAN
KINGDOM
(CHALDEAN DYNASTY)
Nebuchadnezzar II
605-562

625

Ashurnasirpal II (Nimrud) 884-859
Sargon II (Khorsabad) 722-705
Ashurbanipal (Nineveh) 669-627

Just how and why the state of human society we call civilization began, we are not certain; we are more certain where and when it began. Since the Second World War, archeologists have been uncovering the sites in the Near East where the immense transformation began and have pushed back its date as far as 8000 B.C. The onset of civilized life is marked off from all that went before by the development of agriculture. The conventional three-part division of the time preceding recorded history into the Paleolithic, Mesolithic, and Neolithic periods, based on the development of stone implements, is not as basic and decisive as the simpler distinction between an age of food-gathering and an age of food production. In this scheme, the Paleolithic period corresponds roughly to the age of food-gathering, and the Mesolithic period, the last phase of that age, is marked by intensified food-gathering and the domestication of the dog. The proto-Neolithic period of incipient food production and greater domestication of animals precedes the Neolithic period, when agriculture and stock-raising became man's major food sources.

According to one view, the area we know today as the Near East (Egypt, Israel, Syria, Iraq, Iran, and Turkey) dried out into desert and semidesert after the last retreat of the glaciers, compelling the inhabitants to move to the fertile alluvial valleys of the Nile in Egypt and the Tigris and Euphrates in Mesopotamia (parts of modern Syria and Iraq). But this view is no longer tenable in light of recent archeological and paleo-environmental findings. The oldest settled communities are found not in the river valleys but in the grassy uplands bordering them. These regions provided the necessary preconditions for the development of agriculture. Species of native plants (like wild wheat and barley) were plentiful, as were herds of animals (like goats, sheep, and pigs) that could be domesticated; there was also sufficient rain for the raising of crops. It was only after village farming life was well developed that settlers, attracted by the greater fertility of the soil, moved into the river valleys and deltas. There, in addition to systematic agriculture, civilized societies originated government, law, and formal religion, and such instrumentalities and techniques as writing, measurement and calculation, weaving, metalcraft, and pottery.

For a long time, it was thought that these developments occurred concurrently in Egypt and Mesopotamia. But again, archeology is forcing a revision of our views. It is becoming clear that Mesopotamia and its neighbors were far ahead of Egypt temporally. Village farming communities like Jarmo in Iraq and Çatal Hüyük in southern Anatolia (Turkey) date back to the mid-seventh millennium B.C., and the remarkable fortified town of Jericho, before whose walls Joshua appeared thousands of years later, is even older. The oldest villages in Egypt, in the Faiyum district near the Delta, do not seem to have been founded before 4500 B.C.; moreover, an urban society like that of Mesopotamia seems never to have developed there. The invention of writing in Mesopotamia preceded writing in Egypt by several hundred years, and it may be that the whole development of Egyptian civilization was the result of Mesopotamian influence. Traditionally, the history of art in the ancient world begins with Egypt and then passes on to Mesopotamia. Archeological studies of Egypt are older, scientific archeology having been begun there at the end of the eighteenth century. In addition, the chronology of Egypt is more firmly established, and the general cultural picture is more complete. Nevertheless, in view of the array of new facts presented by the latest archeological investigations, the traditional sequence should be reversed: Mesopotamia and its neighbors should be placed at the beginning of the study of ancient art.

THE BEGINNINGS

Jericho

By 7000 B.C., agriculture was well established in at least three Near Eastern regions: Jordan, Iran, and Anatolia (Turkey). Although no remains of domestic cereal grains have been found that can be dated before 7000 B.C., the advanced state of agriculture at that time presupposes a long development; indeed, the very existence of a town like Jericho gives strong support to this assumption. The site of Jericho—a plateau in the Jordan river valley with an unfailing spring—was occupied by a small village as early as the ninth millennium B.C. This proto-Neolithic village underwent a spectacular development around 8000 B.C., when a new town was built with houses of mudbrick on round or oval stone foundations. As the town's wealth grew and powerful neighbors established themselves, the need for protection resulted in the first known permanent stone fortifications. By the middle of the eighth millennium B.C., the town, estimated to have had a population of over 2,000, was surrounded by a wide, rock-cut ditch and a five-foot-thick wall. Into this wall, which has been preserved to a height of 12 feet, was built a great circular stone tower, 30 feet in height and diameter (FIG. 2-1). Not enough of the site has been excavated to determine whether this tower was solitary, like the keeps in Medieval castles, or one of several similar towers that formed a complete defense system. In either case, a structure like this, built with the aid of only the most primitive kinds of stone tools, was certainly a tremendous technical achievement.

Around 7000 B.C., the Jericho site was abandoned by its original inhabitants, but new settlers arrived in the early seventh millennium. They built rectangular mudbrick houses on stone foundations and carefully plastered and painted their floors and walls. Several of the excavated buildings seem to have served as shrines—the plan of one of them being remarkably similar to that of the later Greek *megaron* (see FIG. 5-20). These settlers fashioned statuettes of a mother goddess and of animals associated with a fertility cult. Most striking is a group of human skulls on which the features have been "reconstructed" in plaster (FIG. 2-2). Subtly modeled, with inlaid seashells for eyes and the painted hair (a painted mustache has been preserved on one specimen), their appearance is strikingly lifelike. Because the skulls were detached from the bodies before burial and displayed above ground, they may have been regarded as "spirit traps," implying a well-developed belief in survival after the death of the body.

2-2 Human skull, Jericho, 7000–6000 B.C. Features molded in plaster.

2-1 Proto-Neolithic fortifications, Jericho, 8000–7000 B.C.

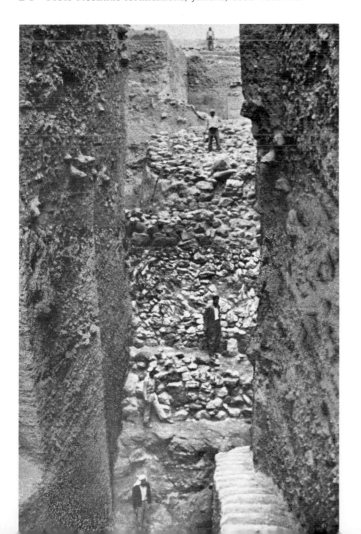

Çatal Hüyük

Perhaps even more remarkable than the Jericho finds are recent discoveries in Anatolia. Excavations at Hacilar and Çatal Hüyük have shown not only that the central Anatolian plateau was the site of a flourishing Neolithic culture between 7000 and 5000 B.C., but also that it may well have been culturally the most advanced region of its time. Twelve successive building levels excavated at Çatal Hüyük between 1961 and 1965 have been dated between 6500 and 5700 B.C. On a single site of 32 acres (of which only one acre has been explored), it has become possible to retrace, in an unbroken sequence, the evolution of a Neolithic culture over a period of 800 years.

Along with Jericho, Çatal Hüyük has been called "one of man's first essays in the development of town life." The regularity of the town plan suggests that it was built according to some *a priori* plan. A peculiarity of the town is its complete lack of streets; the houses adjoin each other, and access is provided over their roofs (FIG. 2-3). Impractical as such an arrangement may appear today—although it survives in parts of central Anatolia (Turkey) and western Iran—it did offer some advantages. The buildings, being attached, were more stable than freestanding struc-

2-3　Schematic reconstruction of a section of Level VI, Çatal Hüyük, *c.* 6000–5900 B.C. (After J. Mellaart.)

tures and, at the limits of the town site, formed a perimeter wall well suited to defense against human or natural forces. Thus, if an enemy managed to breach the exterior wall, he would find himself not inside the town, but inside a single room with the defenders waiting for him on the roof—a dismal prospect at best.

Here and there, the dense building mass at Çatal Hüyük is interrupted by an open court, which served as a garbage dump. Liberal amounts of ashes mixed in with the refuse acted as sterilizers, although probably not as deodorants. The houses, constructed of mudbrick walls strengthened by sturdy timber frames, varied in size but were of a standard plan. Walls and floors were plastered and painted, and platforms along walls served for sleep, work, and eating. A great number of shrines have been found intermingled with standard houses. Varying with the

different levels, the average ratio is about one shrine to every four houses. This may not hold true for the whole town, only about one-thirtieth of which has been excavated.

The shrines (FIG. 2-4) are distinguished from other houses by the greater richness of their interior decoration, which consisted of wall paintings, plaster reliefs, animal heads, bucrania (bovine skulls), and cult statuettes. Bulls' horns, which adorn most shrines, sometimes in considerable numbers, were set into stylized, remodeled heads of bulls or into benches and pillars and may have been thought to protect the inhabitants and ward off evil. Nothing, however, suggests that the bull, or any other animal, was re-

2-4　Reconstruction of a shrine, Level VI, Çatal Hüyük, *c.* 5900 B.C. (After J. Mellaart.)

2-5　*Seated Goddess*, Çatal Hüyük, *c.* 5900 B.C. Fired clay, approx. 2″ high.

garded as a deity. Cult statuettes found at Çatal Hüyük indicate that the people believed their gods to have human form, both male and female. When represented in association with animals (the female deity usually with leopards; the male, with a bull), the animals are always shown as subservient.

The statuettes are of stone or baked clay and are quite small; most are 2–8 inches high, and a few reach 12 inches. All the female figures, which predominate, seem to represent a mother goddess, but in a great variety of aspects: young, old, in ritual marriage, in pregnancy, giving birth, and as ruler of wild animals. These figures are described explicitly, and although the bulbous forms of the headless *Seated Goddess* (FIG. 2-5) may remind us of the *Venus of Willendorf* (FIG. 1-13), the artist's approach toward his subject is quite realistic. Unlike the Paleolithic artist, who tried to represent the abstract concept of fertility, the Neolithic sculptor converts an abstract being (a goddess) into a human figure. The breasts are sensitively modeled, the small hands carefully rendered, and, judging from other examples, it may be safely assumed that the lost head had fairly well described facial features. The figure is painted with cross-like floral patterns that are known also from wall paintings and may endow the goddess with the specific function of an agrarian deity.

Fertility and agricultural symbolism dominate the art of the upper (later) levels of Çatal Hüyük. But hunting also played an important part in the early Neolithic economy, and Paleolithic hunting rituals survived far into the Neolithic period. Numerous crude animal figurines, broken and damaged, have been found at Çatal Hüyük; they may have served as animal surrogates during hunting rites and then have been buried in pits. The importance of hunting as a food source (until about 5700 B.C.) is reflected also in wall paintings, in which, in the older shrines, hunting scenes predominate. In style and concept, the *Deer Hunt* (FIG. 2-6) recalls the rock-shelter paintings of the Spanish Levant (the east coast of Spain), but the figures at Çatal Hüyük are more full-bodied and rendered with greater realism. The artist used a full range of pigments, primarily derived from minerals, which he applied with a brush to the white background of dry plaster. A fragment from the *Deer Hunt* shows a dancing hunter (FIG. 2-7) dressed in a white loincloth and a leopard skin, holding a bow in one hand; the speed of his movement is effectively emphasized by the manner in which the leopard skin whirls around his waist. Once the apparently ritual function of these paintings had been fulfilled, they were covered with a layer of white plaster and later replaced with a new painting of a similar or a different subject.

In one of the older shrines at Çatal Hüyük, a painting was uncovered that has been interpreted as a pure landscape (FIG. 2-8). As such, it would be unique for thousands of years into the future. According to carbon-14 dating, it was painted soon after 6200 B.C. In the foreground is what may be a town, with rectangular houses neatly laid out side by side, perhaps representing Çatal Hüyük; behind the town, on a smaller scale, as though far away, appears a mountain with two peaks; dots and lines issuing from the higher of the two cones may represent a volcanic eruption. The mountain has been tentatively identified as the 10,600-foot Hasan Dag, which was located within view of Çatal Hüyük and was the only twin-peaked volcano (now extinct) in central Anatolia. Because the painting appears on the walls of a shrine, the conjectured volcanic eruption would have had some religious meaning. Although the artist may have linked the event with the underworld and witnessed it with fearful awe, his dread may have been mingled with gratitude to a bountiful Mother Earth, for it is believed that Çatal Hüyük derived much of its wealth from trade in obsidian—a vitreous volcanic stone easily chipped into fine cutting edges and highly valued by Neolithic tool- and weapon-makers.

The rich finds at Çatal Hüyük give the impression of a prosperous and well-ordered society that practiced a great variety of arts and crafts. In addition to painting and sculpture, weaving and pottery were well established, and even the art of smelting copper and lead in small quantities was known before 6000 B.C. The society seems to have been conservative in its long retention of Paleolithic traditions and practices, but it was also progressive in its slow but relentless achievement of a complex, fully food-producing economy. In the arts, this development is perhaps mirrored in a de-emphasis of realism in favor of a more abstract symbolism, in the disappearance of hunting scenes, and in a gradual decline in the production of statuettes representing male deities. At the same time, representations of the mother goddess increased in number, perhaps reflecting a corresponding change in the importance, if not the social position, of woman. As agriculture took precedence over hunting, female occupations, like the milling of grain, baking, weaving, and the care and feeding of domestic animals, became ever more important. At Çatal Hüyük, the conversion to a fully agrarian economy appears to have been completed by about 5700 B.C. Less than a century later, the site was abandoned. A probably related culture at Hacilar, some 200 miles to the west, provides an afterglow. But by about 5000 B.C. the limelight shifts eastward toward the Mesopotamian valley and Iran, and southward to Syria.

2-6 *Deer Hunt*, detail of a copy of a wall painting from Level III, Çatal Hüyük, *c.* 5750 B.C.

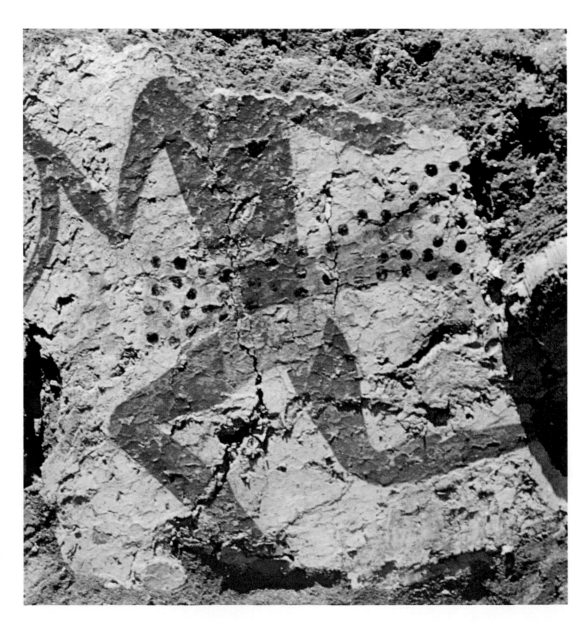

2-7 *Dancing Hunter*, fragment of a wall painting, a part of which is shown in copy in FIG. 2-6.

2-8 *Landscape with Volcanic Eruption* (?), detail of a copy of a wall painting from Level VII, Çatal Hüyük, *c.* 6150 B.C.

SUMER

Some time in the early fourth millennium B.C. in Mesopotamia, a critical event—the settlement of the great river valleys—took place. It was after this that writing, art, monumental architecture, and new political forms were introduced in Mesopotamia and Egypt, but with striking differences in function. As Henri Frankfort describes it:

> The earliest written documents of Mesopotamia . . . facilitated the administration of large economic units, the temple communities. The earliest Egyptian inscriptions were legends on royal monuments or seal engravings identifying the king's officials. The earliest representations in Mesopotamian art are preponderantly religious; in Egyptian art, they celebrate royal achievements and consist of historical subjects. Monumental architecture consists, in Mesopotamia, of temples; in Egypt, of royal tombs. The earliest civilized society of Mesopotamia crystallized, in separate nuclei, a number of distinct, autonomous cities—clear-cut, self-assertive polities—with the surrounding lands to sustain each one. Egyptian society assumed the form of the single, united, but rural domain of an absolute monarch.*

Thus, not one, but *two* civilizations emerged, each having its own special character. From this time forward, world history was to be the record of the birth, development, and disappearance of civilizations and the rise and decline within them of peoples, states, and nations. It is with these two mighty, contrasting civilizations bordering the eastern Mediterranean

*Henri Frankfort, *The Art and Architecture of the Ancient Orient* (Baltimore: Penguin, 1971).

region that the drama of Western mankind truly begins. It must not be thought, however, that these two distinct societies were geographically or culturally isolated from one another. Ancient Palestine (land of the Phoenicians) and Syria connected them on the west. On the east, Mesopotamia adjoined the vast territory of Iran and the North Indian civilization of the Indus river valley, with its important city of Mohenjo-Daro. Thus, a continuous range of more or less comtemporaneous city civilizations existed from Egypt to India, linked by trade, cultural diffusion, and conquest, and ringed about by nomadic peoples or sedentary farmer villages in Arabia, North Africa, and northern Eurasia.

In the fertile lower valley of the Tigris and Euphrates, man may have found the equivalent of the Garden of Eden celebrated in Genesis and long a part of Mesopotamian tradition. Once he had learned the art of irrigation and, to a degree, the control of floods, the possibility of creating a great oasis was before him, and he realized it. The turbulence of its history strongly suggests that this land, with its promise of a hitherto unknown life of abundance, was enormously attractive.

At the dawn of recorded history, the lower Mesopotamian valley was occupied by the Sumerians, whose origin is still one of the great puzzles of ancient history. It has been suggested that they came from the east in the Preliterate period, from the area bordering on the Persian gulf that is now western Iran. Their migration to southern Mesopotamia was preceded by that of a people whose culture is given the name (from its site in Iraq) *Jamdat Nasr*.

To the Jamdat Nasr period is assigned a handsome *minotaur* (man–bull) figure in soldered silver plates of exquisite craftsmanship (FIG. 2-9). Seated and making an offering of a vessel, which it holds between the hooves of its extended forelegs, the statuette is an early example of a universal theme of Ancient Near Eastern art: the man–animal monster (familiar as the Egyptian Sphinx). We shall see it often, in miniature and monumental form. Here, the sculptor shows his grasp of the essential form of the bodies of beast and man, the natural sweep of planes and contours. He gives us, with an astonishing sureness of touch, a gesture that is both solemn and graceful. This could only be the result of a long tradition of observation of natural form and of the craft of metalwork. The religious import of this figure (it is performing a ritual act of some sort) must also express a long tradition of religious art that goes back millennia—a tradition that, through its long development, came to align the figures of the great beasts with the figure of man. It is the tradition received and shared by the Sumerians and their successors in Mesopotamia.

The Sumerians were an agricultural people who learned to control floods and built strong-walled towns, such as Uruk, the biblical Erech and the modern Warka, and Lagash, the modern Al-Hiba. Sumerian influence, especially through language, extended widely from its base in southern Mesopotamia—eastward to Susa in Iran, northward to Assur, and westward to Syria, where recently discovered archives at Tell Mardikh (ancient Ebla), consisting of thousands of clay tablets in the Sumerian language, testify to the far-flung network of contacts Sumer made throughout the Ancient Near East as it engaged in a kind of cultural colonialism. After several centuries, Semitic nomad shepherds came from the western desert; they adopted agriculture, absorbed much from Sumerian culture, and built their own cities farther north—Kish, Akkad, Mari, Ebla, and Babylon. Over the centuries, dominion oscillated between the two peoples, but the Semites produced two of the mightiest kings, Sargon and Hammurabi.

From as early a time as the Paleolithic caves, we have evidence of man's effort to control his environment by picture magic. With the appearance of the Sumerians and the beginning of recorded history, the older magic was replaced by a religion of gods, benevolent or malevolent, who personified the forces of nature that often contended destructively with man's hopes and designs. In the fertile valley of the Tigris and Euphrates, the fiery heat of summer and the catastrophic floods, droughts, blights, and locusts easily persuaded man that there were powers above and beyond his control, powers that he must somehow placate and win over. Formal religion, a kind of system of transactions between gods and men, may have

2-9 *Kneeling Man-Bull,* Ancient Iran, *c.* 3,000 B.C. Silver, 6½" high. Metropolitan Museum of Art, New York (Joseph Pulitzer Bequest).

begun with the Sumerians; no matter how it has been systematized and diversified since then, religion has retained its original propitiatory devices of prayer, sacrifice, and ritual, as well as a view of man as imperfect by nature and dependent on and obligated to some higher being. The religion of the Sumerians and of those who followed them centered about nature gods: Anu, god of the sky; En-lil (Bel), a creator and ruler of earth and "lord of the storm"; Ea (or Enki), lord of the waters (a healing, benevolent god); Nannar (Sin), the moon god; Utu (Shamash), the sun god; and Inanna (associated with the planet Venus), goddess of love and fertility, who, as Ishtar, is later also endowed with the functions of battle goddess.*

The City-State and the Ziggurat

Religion, which dominated life and invested it with meaning, determined the form of society as well as its expression in architecture and art. The Mesopotamian city-state was under the protection of the god of the city; the king was his representative on earth and the steward of his earthly treasure. The relationship

*"Bel" and "Shamash" are Akkadian names; "Sin" is Babylonian.

of the king to the gods above and to his subjects below may be read in the prayer of an early Sumerian king to the god En-lil of the city of Nippur:

O En-lil, the king of the lands, may Anu to his beloved father speak my prayer; to my life may he add life, and cause the lands to dwell in security; may he give me warriors as many as the grass; the herds of heaven may he watch over; the land with prosperity endow; the good fortune which the gods have given me, may he not change; and may I ever remain the shepherd, who standeth at the head.

The plan of the city reflected this centrality of the god in its life, his temple being its monumental nucleus. The temple was the focus not only of the religion of the city but also of its administrative and economic process. It was indeed the domain of the god, who was regarded as a great and rich holder of lands and herds as well as the protector of the city. The whole function of the city was to serve the god as a master, as the function of all men in general was to serve the gods. The vast temple complex, a kind of city within a city, had a multitude of functions. A temple staff of priests and scribes carried on the business of the city, looking after the possessions of the god and of the king. It must have been in such a setting that writing developed into an instrument of precision; the very earliest examples of it have to do with the keeping of accounts and the description of simple transactions, stores, and supplies.

The most prominent part of a temple compound, and indeed the most characteristic structure of the Mesopotamian valley, was the *ziggurat*, or temple tower. Neither the origin nor the purpose of these huge, multi-storied brick structures is known. They have been interpreted as stairways by which the gods of the country mounted to heaven every night. An old Babylonian text (*c.* 1900–1600 B.C.) reads

The gods and goddesses of the country—
Shamash, Sin, Adad, and Ishtar—
have gone home to heaven to sleep.
They will not give decisions or verdicts [tonight].

It is generally thought that the roof of the shrine (at the top of the ziggurat) was the setting in which priests prayed to the "gods of the night" (the planets and constellations), or prepared a meal for them, or sacrificed a lamb for an omen.

Most of the ruined cities of Sumer—Ur, Warka, Nippur, Larsa, Eridu—are still dominated by their eroded ziggurats. A good example is the ziggurat at Ur, dating from the period called Neo-Sumerian (from the twenty-second to the twenty-first century B.C.) when builders were attempting to attain the greatest heights possible. In one view (FIG. 2-10), we see the huge mound of sun-dried brick, truncated and edge-worn by time, weather, and depredation; in the other (FIG. 2-11), we see a conjectural reconstruction. On a massive base, 50 feet high, stand two successively smaller stages, of which presumably the uppermost served as a pedestal for the shrine. Three ramp-like stairways of 100 steps each converge toward a tower-flanked gateway from which another flight of steps probably led to the shrine, access to which was forbidden to any but officiating priests. The structure is a solid mass of mudbrick, its lower two stages faced with baked brick laid in bitumen. This facing has withstood floods and weathering so

2-10 Ziggurat at Ur, *c.* 2100 B.C.

2-11 Reconstruction of the ziggurat at Ur. (Adapted from a drawing at the British Museum, London.)

well that the ziggurat at Ur is the best preserved temple tower in southern Mesopotamia. The loftiness of the great ziggurats—especially of the one at Babylon, which was about 270 feet high and intended by its pious builders to reach into heaven—made a profound impression on the ancient Hebrews, who memorialized the Babylon ziggurat as the tower of Babel, a monument to the insolent pride of man.

The three great inventions of the Sumerians—a system of gods and god–man relationships, the city-state itself, and the art of writing—provided the basis for a new order of human society. In the city-state, consecrated by the presence of the civic deity, men experienced new interrelationships with their god and with each other, and formalized and gave permanence to these interrelationships by recording them in writing. Life became regularized, and the community assumed functions, such as defense against man and the caprices of nature, that formerly had been left to the individual. This and the division of labor *(specialization)*, which is encouraged where large numbers of people are concentrated in a coherent community, emancipated the inhabitants from the consuming necessities of daily life, so that they could develop and apply skills and talents unthinkable in fluid and unintegrated societies. The relatively fixed character of the city-state also conferred on the community a permanent identity as a city ruled by king and god who were known and present. This sense of identity extended to the individual inhabitant as well, who received his identity from his membership in the community, discovering himself in his interrelationships with the city, god, king, and citizens. The new written language may also have contributed to this growing identification through which the individual perceived himself as a name among the names for other things and actions. Thus, from the Sumerian creation of stable patterns of life begins that sense of identity—that self-awareness of historical man—that will mature and reach its highest development in the civilization of Greece.

Sculpture

In the animal paintings of the caves, the figure of man almost never appears; he has not yet entered the area of self-awareness. Although the rock paintings of the Spanish Levant do indeed represent the human figure, they do so only schematically and almost in the form of picture-writing. Thus, we are not prepared for the beautiful female head from Warka (FIG. 2-12). Its ancestry is unknown. Dating from the so-called Protoliterate period, when writing first appeared, it is not a complete head but a marble face meant to be attached to a wood backing and wigged, perhaps, in gold. The deep recesses for the eyebrows were filled with colored shell or stone, as were the large eyes. The subject is unknown (goddess, priestess, queen?), but our ignorance of it and of the history of

2-12 *Female Head*, Warka, c. 3500–3000 B.C. Alabaster, approx. 8" high. The Iraq Museum, Baghdad.

2-13 Statuettes from the Abu Temple, Tell Asmar, *c.* 2700–2600 B.C. Marble, tallest figure approx. 30″ high. The Iraq Museum, Baghdad, and The Oriental Institute, University of Chicago.

the head does not diminish our appreciation of its exquisite refinement of feature and expression, despite the mutilations of time and accident. The soft modeling of the cheeks, the sensitivity of the mouth, the hesitancy of the expression between the sweet and the somber not only render for us a person in herself beguiling and mysterious but also suggest a sophistication in the artist beyond our expectation of his time.

One notices at once in the Warka head the disproportionately large eyes. This is a trait of a whole group of figures from Tell Asmar (FIGS. 2-13 and 2-14). The reason for this convention, which is not only Sumerian but appears throughout ancient art, can only be guessed. Long before Aristotle asserted that man is distinguished from the animals by being rational and that sight is the most "rational" of the organs of sense, men must have perceived and feared the power of the eye to hold, charm, and hypnotize for ends good or ill. The "evil eye" was feared in the ancient world, as it still is feared. It is a popular belief and a part of folklore that one can learn much about another's intentions and character by "looking him straight in the eye," and the modern affectation of dark glasses (curiously Sumerian when oversized!) may be both a defense and a badge of attractive mystery. To the ancient artist, the eyes, the "windows of

the soul," could have had several associations. Large eyes fixed in unflagging gaze see all, and frontal, binocular vision, distinguishing human from mere animal seeing, represents the all-seeing vigilance and omniscience of the gods and the guarantee of justice.

2-14 *Head of the God Abu* (detail of FIG. 2-13), Tell Asmar, *c.* 2700–2600 B.C. Marble. The Iraq Museum, Baghdad.

In the conventionalization of the human image, vision understandably becomes a peculiarly human trait—in its lesser physical sense as well as in its greater intellectual, spiritual, and theistic sense. God-like vision as the foundation of law and justice is evident in the stories of the great law-givers of the ancient world, including Hammurabi of Babylon, Moses, Lycurgus of Sparta, and Solon of Athens.

Although it may be that none of our speculations entered the mind of the artist of the Tell Asmar figures, some association of vision with supernatural powers seems to be indicated by the fact that the two largest figures, identified as deities by emblems on their bases, also have the largest eyes in relationship to their heads. The other statuettes represent worshipers (the larger ones, priests; the smaller ones, laymen). With their hands tightly clasped across their chests in the attitude of prayer, their large eyes seem to express reverent awe in the presence of their gods. The purpose of these votive figures was to offer constant prayers to the gods on behalf of their donors; thus, their open-eyed stares may symbolize the eternal wakefulness necessary to fulfill their duty.

CONVENTIONALIZATION

Just as the Sumerians, at the dawn of recorded history, created a new kind of human experience through formal religion and civic life they found a new way to represent that experience through writing and figurative art. Writing had been invented by simplifying pictures into signs, or wedge-shaped (cuneiform) strokes in numerous combinations, pressed by a stylus into wet clay tablets. In figurative art, by an analogous process of simplification, the multitude of appearances of things in the optical world was reduced to a few telling traits sufficient to present the human figure and human action. This process of simplification is variously named schematization, stylization, conventionalization, generalization, and formalization. *Conventional* simplifications of the human figure are universal and are not characteristic only of ancient art. Indeed, all artistic styles are conventional in that, in the societies in which they prevail, they are tacitly accepted as a comprehensible means of representation. The conventions may be broad or narrow, slow to change or under continual revision, as in our times. In any case, such criteria as fidelity to optical "fact" should not be used in evaluating a style. Although the main trends in modern art since the 1800s have been away from optical "fact" and today's artists often deliberately disregard photographic "truth," the images they make—such as those seen in comic strips and in commercial art and advertising—are perfectly recognizable to us.

The Sumerians, working out patterns and conventions that regulated the new life that they had in ef-

fect devised, also established conventions for the construction of the human image. The large eyes of the Warka and Tell Asmar figures are not the only conventionalized details. In the small figures of a shell-inlaid box, the so-called *Standard of Ur* (FIG. 2-15), we find several devices of representation that simplify the narrative, explain the action, and even convey the impression of motion. The panel shown depicts a Sumerian military victory—the advance of the foot soldiers, the charge of the chariots. A second panel (not shown) represents the aftermath of the victorious battle, with lines of prisoners and servants bringing in booty and the king relaxing, drinking with his nobles, listening to harp and song. The figures are carefully arranged in superimposed strips, each strikingly suggestive of a film or comic strip; doubtless, the purpose is the same—to achieve a continuous narrative effect. They are carefully spaced, with little overlapping. (Compare this regularized, formal presentation with the casual, haphazard placement of the figures in Paleolithic and Mesolithic art.) Poses are repeated, as in the line of foot soldiers, to suggest large numbers. The horses of the war chariots, the lines of the legs repeated to suggest the other horses of the team and their alignment in space, change from a walk to a gallop as they attack. The figures are essentially in profile, but it is a convention almost universal in the Ancient Near East that the eyes—again, very large—are in front view, as are the torsos. The artist indicates the parts of the human body that enter into our concept of what it looks like, and he avoids positions, attitudes, or views that would conceal or obscure the characterizing parts. For example, were the figures in strict profile, an arm and perhaps a leg would be concealed, the body would appear to have only half its breadth, and the eye would not "read" as an eye at all, because it would not have its distinctive flat oval shape and the pupil, so important in the Tell Asmar figures, would not appear. We could call this approach "conceptual" rather than "optical," because the artist records not the immediate, fleeting aspect of things but rather his concept of the distinguishing and abiding properties of the human body. It is the fundamental forms of things and his knowledge of them, not their accidental appearance, that direct his hand. But this is simply a reflection of the general *formalism* that was imposed at the beginning of the historical period in an effort to create an enduring order. This formalism continued to rule human conduct throughout history in thousands of customs, conventions, and ceremonies regarded as sacred and above change. In Greece, many centuries later, Plato conceived the famous philosophy of Forms, claiming that the world of pure form, in which the ultimate and unchanging truths of mathematical figures and relationships exist, is the

2-15 *Scenes of War*, panel from the *Standard of Ur, c.* 2700 B.C. Panel inlaid with shell, lapis lazuli, and red limestone, approx. 8″ × 19″. British Museum, London.

real world, whereas the world we see, the world of mere appearance, is the realm of the unreal, of illusion, of change, and of death.

THE UNION OF THE FORMAL AND THE NATURAL

On the inlaid soundbox of a harp from Ur (FIG. 2-16), there are figures representing, in the top register, a Sumerian hero wrestling with two man-headed bulls and, in the lower registers, real and fantastic animals preparing a banquet. The topmost register of the panel presents the figures in heraldic symmetry, and, except that the heads are in front view, they exhibit the conventional formalized pose of the *Standard of Ur*. On the other hand, the animal figures in the other registers exhibit a markedly relaxed formalism. The dog wearing a dagger and carrying a laden table, the lion bringing in the wine service, the ass playing the harp, the jackal playing the zither, the bear steadying the harp (or is he dancing?), and the gazelle offering goblets of wine to the scorpion–man—all are seen in more-or-less true profile. Torsos naturally cut off the view of the far arms, and the near legs obstruct the far legs. Shoulders are properly placed, and features are carefully noted and designated. The heroic human figures have the formality we find in the stylized animals on a coat of arms, but the banquet animals are at ease and seem almost to be burlesquing a stately pa-

rade of servants and musicians. Long before the figure of man appeared in art, naturalistic animal figures were painted in the Paleolithic caves. Then for a long time, as if by rule, man was represented with rigid formality, but the animal figure looked and moved much as it would appear to the eye. The soundbox panel shows a delightful Aesop-like scene (the comedy of which may not have been intended) in what is probably a representation of ancient myths. Surely it is a very early specimen of the theme in both literature and art in which animals act as people; thus, we pass from the artist of this panel to Aesop's fables, to the Medieval bestiaries, to the zoological creations of Walt Disney.

On the same harp is a splendid bull's head, finished in gold leaf with beard and details in lapis lazuli (FIG. 2-17). (Note where the head is attached to the harp, as it is shown on the third register from the top in FIG. 2-16). The bull, an exemplification of fertility and strength, naturally would have been worshiped by early herdsmen, who would have invoked its power against the natural enemies of cattle—drought and predatory beasts. The archaic artist shares with his prehistoric predecessor the genius for rendering with sharp perception the features, almost the personality, of animals. Throughout the Ancient Near East and the Mediterranean, the bull was revered. In

2-16 Soundbox of a harp, Ur, *c.* 2600 B.C. Shell inlay, approx. 12″ high. University Museum, Philadelphia.

2-17 Bull's head from the harp soundbox shown in FIG. 2-16. Gold leaf and lapis lazuli with inlaid eyes over a wooden core, approx. 18″ high. University Museum, Philadelphia.

this example, the beard may represent some supernatural amplification of the bull's power. The beard and such humanizing features as the man-heads added to the bulls in the top register of the soundbox panel foreshadow the man-headed bulls and lions that appeared much later in Assyria.

The contest between natural and supernatural forces in the Mesopotamian world is expressed as a struggle between animals and monsters. Such a struggle we find represented in miniature on a cylinder seal only 1½ inches high (FIG. 2-18), a design cut with exquisite refinement. A seal consisted of a cylindrical piece of stone, usually about an inch or so in height and pierced for the attachment of a cord. Made of various colored stones, both hard and soft, such as rock crystal, agate, carnelian and jasper, lapis lazuli, marble, and alabaster, the seal was decorated with a design in *intaglio* (incised), so that a raised pattern was left when it was rolled over soft clay. With this device, the Sumerian sealed, signed, and identified his letters and documents, which were written on clay tablets. Our illustration shows both a detail of the seal and the more complete relief design made from it. A hero fights a bull, and a being (half-man and half-bull) fights a lion. The heraldic attitudes and groupings reflect the formal method of representation, but even in the small area of the seal, the skillful artist shows such mastery of animal form that we can almost hear the roaring and bellowing of the struggle.

2-18 Cylinder seal (detail) and its impression, Ur.
c. 2700 B.C. Stone, approx. 1½″ high. The Oriental Institute,
University of Chicago.

AKKAD

At about 2300 B.C., the loose group of cities known as Sumer (where the tremendous change from prehistory to civilization had begun) came under the domination of a great ruler, Sargon of Akkad. The Akkadians, although Semitic in origin and speaking a language entirely different from that of Sumer, had assimilated Sumerian culture. Under Sargon and his followers, they introduced a new concept of royal power; its basis was unswerving loyalty to the king rather than to the city-state. During the rule of Sargon's grandson, Naram-Sin, governors of cities were called "slaves" of the king, who, in turn, called himself "King of the Four Quarters" (of the universe)—in effect, ruler of the earth. A magnificent bronze head of a king from Nineveh (a portrait of Naram-Sin?) embodies this new concept of absolute monarchy (FIG. 2-19). The elaborate coiffure, Sumerian in style, attests to the persistence of the tradition of Sumer and serves as crown to the unforgettable face with its expression of majestic serenity. The sensitive mouth, the large eyes, made even larger by the absence of the precious stones once embedded in the sockets, and the emphatic ridge like brows seem to echo a long tradition that extends back even to the Warka head (FIG. 2-12). Here, we see to particular advantage that union of the formal with the natural so common in Mesopotamian art. The symmetry of the head and the stylized motifs of the curly locks of hair manage to be consistent with the projection of personality—a strong-minded and commanding one, but in a pensive and composed mood, with perhaps just a trace of irony. The age of metals has come, and the piece demonstrates the craftsman's sophisticated skill in casting and in the engraving of details.

Roughly contemporary with the Akkadian portrait is the copper cast head of a ruler whose name we do not know (FIG. 2-20); nor do we know the provenance of it or its sure date. The head rivals that of the Akkadian king in its masterly blending of formal simplicity and firmness, with carefully observed particu-larity of detail. The features are those of a specific individual—large eyes, prominent nose, the compressed lips of a wide mouth, a beard that adds strength to the jaw—the speaking likeness of a man grave, thoughtful, and wise. The sculptor sets the features within spare, firm contours, composing a mask of dignity and authority. A sensitive reading of personality is thus disciplined by a convention that imposes a certain immobility of expression; this is characteristic of the formality of portraiture in the Ancient Near East, especially of persons of high rank.

2-19 *Head of an Akkadian Ruler*, Nineveh, c. 2300–2200 B.C.
Bronze, approx. 12″ high. The Iraq Museum, Baghdad.

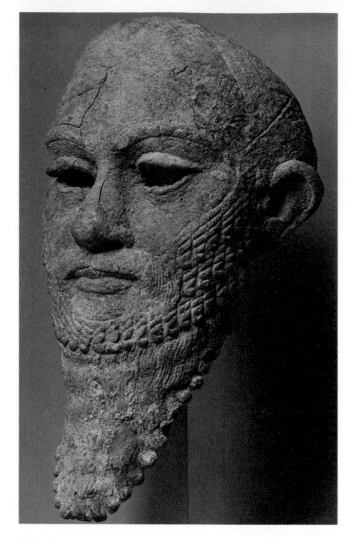

2-20 *Portrait Head of a Ruler*, Ancient Iran (Elam?), *c.* 2100–2000 B.C. Copper, 13½" high. Metropolitan Museum of Art, New York (Rogers Fund).

spears and flying banners as they encounter the shattered enemy (seven figures), one of whom falls headlong down the mountain side. In comparison with the stele figures, those of the *Standard of Ur* seem rather static and formal. The Naram-Sin artist is a daring inventor, and although he adheres to older conventions, especially in the figures of the king and his soldiers (in simultaneous profile and front view), he nevertheless relies on his own perception to create the first landscape in Near Eastern art since Çatal Hüyük (FIG. 2-8).

The achievements of Akkad were brought to an end by an incursion of barbarous mountaineers, the Guti, who dominated life in central and lower Meso-

2-21 *Victory Stele of Naram-Sin, c.* 2300–2200 B.C. Pink sandstone, approx. 6' 6" high. Louvre, Paris.

We will presently see it in the portraits of Egyptian pharaohs.

The god-like sovereignty claimed by the kings of Akkad may be seen proclaimed in another masterpiece of Akkadian art, the great *Victory Stele of Naram-Sin* (FIG. 2-21). On the stele, the war-like grandson of Sargon is represented leading his victorious armies up the slopes of a wooded mountain and through the routed enemy, who are crushed underfoot, fall, flee, die, or beg for mercy. The king stands alone, far taller than his men, treading on the bodies of two of the fallen enemy. He wears the horned helmet that signifies his deification, and two auspicious astral bodies, representing Shamash and Ishtar, shine on his triumph. The artist shows an almost startling originality, not only in his ingenious management of the theme but also in the variety of poses and in the setting. The king's troops, a whole army suggested by eight figures marching in two orderly files, carry

2-22 *Gudea Worshiping*, Telloh, c. 2100 B.C. Dolerite, approx. 42" high. Louvre, Paris.

lar size and shape were usually not large enough to permit the sculptor to execute the whole length of the standing figure without sacrificing its natural proportions; hence, its stumpiness. The sculptor emphasized the portrait head at the expense of the rest of the body, often preferring the seated to the standing figure. The capped figure of Gudea stands in the formal frontal pose that descends from the age of Tell Asmar; the great eyes and eyebrow ridges are in the Mesopotamian tradition. One shoulder and arm are bare; the drapery pulls about the torso and under the arm and falls almost vertically from the other arm. The overall contour is simple in the extreme, with no irregular or complex relief. There is a singular unity and compactness to the figure that arises from the artist's conception of it as a cylindrical or conical form that resides in the mass of the finely textured stone. The smooth sweep of its contours, the elegance of the profile, and the richness of the polished dolerite all complement each other.

BABYLONIA

Lagash, which had retained its independence during the Guti invasion, became a dependency of Ur during that city's brief resurgence in the late third millennium B.C. For a little over a century, the Third Dynasty of Ur ruled over a once-more united realm. Its last king fell before the attacks of foreign invaders, and the following two centuries saw the return of the traditional Mesopotamian political pattern in which several independent city-states existed side by side. One of these was Babylon, until its most powerful king, Hammurabi, was able to reestablish a centralized government that ruled the whole country. Perhaps the most renowned king in Mesopotamian history, Hammurabi was famous for his codification of the confused, conflicting, and often unwritten laws of the Mesopotamian towns. Although not the first to try to bring order out of the chaos, Hammurabi was the first to succeed; echoes of his code are found in the Law of Moses.

The code, beautifully inscribed on a tall, irregularly surfaced black basalt stele, is capped by a relief sculpture of Hammurabi receiving the inspiration for the laws from the flame-shouldered sun god, Shamash (FIG. 2-23). The god is seated on a mountain, indicated by a scale pattern beneath his feet. He holds the symbols of divine power, ring and staff, in a hand stretched toward Hammurabi, represented in a gesture of reverent attention, his hand raised in prayer. We find here again the Mesopotamian artist's instinct for cylindrical volume. Shamash is represented in the familiar convention of combined front and side

potamia for about 60 years, when the cities of Sumer, responding to the alien presence, reasserted themselves and established a Neo-Sumerian polity under the kings of Ur. During this age, the most conspicuous contribution came from the city of Lagash, under its ruler, Gudea. There are about 20 statues of Gudea, showing him seated or standing, hands tightly clasped, and sometimes wearing a woolen cap; the statue illustrated is characteristic (FIG. 2-22). Gudea, who attributed his good fortune and that of his city to the favor of the gods, was a zealous overseer of the performance of their rites; his statues were numerous so that he could take his (symbolic) place in the temples and there render perpetual service to the benevolent deities. The standing Gudea shown is, like the others, of dolerite, an extremely hard stone that the sculptor works with consummate skill, making an opportunity out of difficulty. That difficulty was made greater by the fact that stone, almost nonexistent in southern Mesopotamia, was rare and costly, having to be imported. Blocks and boulders of irregu-

2-23 *Stele of Hammurabi* (upper part), Susa, *c.* 1880 B.C. Basalt, entire stele approx. 7'4" high. Louvre, Paris.

the concept of guardian beasts—Mesopotamia, Syria, or Egypt—the Hittite realization of it is original, the figures being strongly bound to and dominated by the architecture, rather than freestanding and in the round.

ASSYRIA

While Sumer, Akkad, and Babylon flourished in southern Mesopotamia, what was happening in the northern sector of the great river valley? For a long time, archeologists thought of it as a kind of empty region—a staging area for nomadic migrations southward, an unstable territory without significant settlement. But we now know that many centuries before the later Assyrian empire extended its sway over all of the Ancient Near East, a king named Shamshi Adad, a contemporary of Hammurabi, had dominated the north, building his palaces at a site in northeastern Syria near the later Assur, which gives Assyria its name. Shamshi Adad called his city Shubat Enlil (Shagar Bazar) and built it on the ruins of a great city more ancient than his own by two millennia. The immense walls of the city—50 feet high and about 60 feet thick—have recently been uncovered beneath the two palaces of Shamshi Adad. The walls form a two-mile perimeter of what must have been the capital of a northern empire as powerful and perhaps older than Sumer. Its origins are still a mystery; its language was neither Semitic or Sumerian, and it has been suggested that its people may have been Indo-Aryans from the east. Below this level are still earlier remains of human habitation going back to the sixth millennium B.C.

The later Assyrians, familiar to us from the Old Testament and from their inscriptions and monuments, were frustrated in their impulse to power by the kingdoms of the south—Sumer, Akkad, and Babylon—and, on the northwest, by the Mitanni, to whom they were subject for a while. Their opportunity came when their Mitannian overlords were broken by the Hittites and when the weak Kassite kingdom that had succeeded the Babylonian dynasty proved incapable of effective resistance. By about 900 B.C., the Assyrian destiny was already becoming an actuality, and for the next three centuries, Assyria was the dominant power in the Near East. Assyrian kings became military commanders, and Assyria itself, with its center successively at Calah (the modern Nimrud), Dur Sharrukin (the modern Khorsabad), and Nineveh, became a garrison state with an imperial structure that extended from the Tigris to the Nile and from the Persian Gulf to Asia Minor. Centuries of unremitting warfare against their neighbors and often rebellious subjects hardened the Assyrians into a cruel and merciless people whose atrocities in war-

views, which gives his figure great breadth; Hammurabi, his servant, is shown in a position closer to profile, so that he occupies far less space. This confrontation between god and man expresses the increasing humanization of natural and supernatural forces, as man, increasingly self-aware, began (in Babylon) to attribute human form to the gods.

Hammurabi's Babylonian empire was brought down by the Hittites, who, after sacking Babylon around 1595 B.C., retired to Anatolia, the seat of Hittite power, leaving Babylonia in the hands of marauding mountaineers, the Kassites. The Hittites, who spoke an Indo-European tongue, developed an art of great power and originality. Their strongly fortified capital, near the modern Turkish village of Bogazköy, was fronted with massive stone gates set between towers (FIG. 2-24). Projecting from the Cyclopean stones (so different from the brick of Mesopotamian architecture!) are rugged figures of lions, blunt and brutal in aspect. Whatever the source for fare were bitterly decried throughout the ancient world. Although they held the restless Babylonian south in thrall, the Assyrians respected the religion and the culture of Sumer–Babylon and were, in fact, dependent on its advanced civilization—as the large library of Ashurbanipal attests. (Discovery of this library in the nineteenth century opened an immense field of knowledge about Assyria.)

Architecture

The unfinished royal citadel of Sargon II of Assyria, built at Khorsabad, reveals, in its ambitious plan, the confidence of the "great kings" in their all-conquering might (FIG. 2-25). The palace covered some 25 acres and had over 200 courtyards and rooms. The city, above which the citadel-palace stood on a mound 50 feet high, is itself about a square mile in area. The palace may have been elevated solely to raise it above flood level, but its elevation also served to put the king's residence above those of his subjects and midway between them and the gods. Although the builders probably aimed at symmetry, the plan is rambling, embracing an aggregation of rectangular rooms and halls grouped around square courts (FIG. 2-26). The shape of the long, narrow rooms and the massiveness of the side walls suggest that the rooms

were covered by brick *barrel vaults* (see FIG. 6-54), the most practical roofing method in a region that lacks both timber and good building stone. Behind the main courtyard, each side of which measures 300 feet, were the residential quarters of the king, who received foreign emissaries in state in the long, high, brilliantly painted throne room. Such visitors entered from another large courtyard, passing through the central entrance between huge guardian demons, some 13 feet in height, and into the presence of en throned power. Waiting in the court for the audience, visitors had time to meditate on their own insignificance in comparison with the awesome strength of the king, for the walls of the court were lined with giant figures of the king and his courtiers.

Sargon II regarded his city and palace as an expression of his grandeur, which he viewed as founded on the submission and enslavement of his enemies. He writes in an inscription: "I built a city with [the labors of] the peoples subdued by my hand, whom Assur, Nabu, and Marduk had caused to lay themselves at my feet and bear my yoke at the foot of Mount Musri, above Nineveh." And in another text, he proclaims: "Sargon, King of the World, has built a city. Dur Sharrukin he has named it. A peerless palace he has built within it."

In addition to the complex of courtyards, throne

2-25   Reconstruction drawing of the citadel of Sargon II, Khorsabad, c. 720 B.C.

2-26   Plan of the inner precincts of the citadel of Sargon II, Khorsabad.

room, state chambers, harem, service quarters, and guard rooms that made up the palace were the essential temple and ziggurat. The ziggurat at Khorsabad may have had as many as seven stages, of which four have been preserved, each 18 feet high and each painted a different color. The ascent was made by a continuous ramp that spiraled around the building from its base to its summit.

The palace façade consisted of a massive crenelated wall broken by huge rectangular towers flanking an arched doorway. Around the arch and on the towers were friezes of brilliantly colored glazed tiles, the whole effect being sumptuous and grand. Dazzling brilliance seems also to have been part of the royal Assyrian plan to overwhelm the visitor. The doorway was guarded by colossal winged bulls with human heads, called *lamassu* (FIG. 2-27). These man-headed bulls, derived from age-old composite creatures of Mesopotamian art, served to ward off enemies, visible and invisible, and to guard the kings whose traits their faces probably reflect. They are partly in the round and partly in high relief, and they combine the front view at rest with the side view in movement,

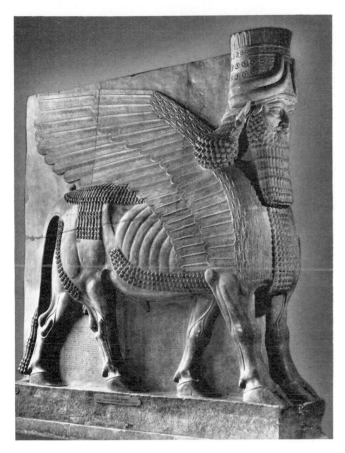

2-27 *Winged Human-Headed Bull (lamassu)*, Khorsabad, *c.* 720 B.C. Limestone, approx. 13′ 10″ high. Louvre, Paris.

contriving this combination by the addition of fifth legs. The gigantic size, the bold, vigorous carving, the fine sweep of wings, and the patterning of the surface by the conventional treatment of details together produce a splendor and a stupendous strength that are awesome even today. But we may think of them in all their majesty not so much as guardians of the king but as augmentations of his regality. They wear the horned crowns of the god–kings of Akkad and the large-eyed, bearded masks familiar ever since Sumer. The bull and lion bodies and eagle wings of the Khorsabad gate figures suggest the superhuman strength and fierceness of the king and his swiftness to bring justice or vengeance. The virtues of Assyrian kingship are written large in these hybrid beasts. Ancient art repeatedly testifies to man's persisting fear and admiration of the great beasts that serve as his metaphors for the powers of nature and for the gods themselves.

Relief Sculpture

Although the kings of Assyria had their power depicted in nonhuman forms, they considered themselves very much a part of the world and expected their greatness to be recorded in unmistakably exact and concrete terms. In conformity with his position between his subjects and his gods, every action of the king had importance. Thus, his conquests in battle had the significance of auspicious events, and the same appears to have been true of his successes in hunting. These two royal activities were recorded in the throne rooms of the earlier palaces; later, they were also carved on the walls of what may have been less official rooms. The style of the reliefs, different in the reign of each king who left them, reflects the Assyrian desire for factual reporting, which is also found in the accounts of the campaigns given in bands of inscription that accompany the reliefs.

The history of Assyrian art is mainly the history of relief carving; very little sculpture in the round survives. Even the great winged beasts are thought of as relief sculpture and are locked into their stone slabs, presenting three relief surfaces. To narrate the royal feats pictorially required flat, continuous surfaces on which could be repeated, almost without end, the campaigns, sieges, conquests, slaughters, hunts, and, even more important, especially in the earlier period, scenes of ritual significance. For the narrative scenes, the artists devised a vocabulary of forms that, although conventional, was sharply descriptive. At first, continuity was broken by the edges of the fitted block; in their most developed stage, the reliefs extended over the entire wall or walls of a room or corridor.

The astonishing multiplicity of a relief of Ashurnasirpal II at war (FIG. 2-28) compels careful study of the composition in order to discriminate its details. The king stands in his chariot drawing his bow. He is accompanied by officers, and, in the sky above him, the winged god of Assyria, Ashur, draws his bow and leads him on. The king's team, the reins tight, is passing an enemy chariot that is already breaking up; its driver has been thrown down and one horse has fallen. Assyrian foot soldiers cut the throats of the wounded enemies. At the upper center, an Assyrian soldier slays a foe while his comrade tries to save him. Behind them a soldier is lying dead; in the upper right, enemy bowmen desperately defend the towers of their city. What is remarkable is the ease with which we read the incidents, although they are not depicted in perspective or in logical sequence. The artist uses the space of his block as a field to be divided as narrative convenience and his own sense of both the factual and the dramatic dictate. The liveliness of individual poses and movements is exceptionally fine and convincing, and despite the formality that exists in Mesopotamian art side by side with naturalistic details, sophisticated spatial devices ap-

2-28 *Ashurnasirpal II at War*, Nimrud, *c.* 875 B.C. Limestone, approx. 39″ high. British Museum, London.

pear throughout. One is the overlapping of figures to suggest greater or lesser distance from the observer; the king overlapping his officers is a good example.

The formality of Assyrian art at its most rigid can be seen in another relief of Ashurnasirpal II (FIG. 2-29), in which the king, seated right of center, solemnly raises a ceremonial cup, while the presence of an august personage at the far left, a winged genius who sprinkles holy water, makes the king's act part of a sacred ritual. The slow gestures and stately mien are what we would expect of some grave liturgy; we recognize these characteristics in religious services today. The cuneiform inscriptions on the flat, thin slabs of relief continue across the shallow recesses between the slabs, accentuating the neutrality of the planes and suggesting that the carving is meant to be not so much a three-dimensional form (that casts shadows) as a report of an event in pictures as well as writing. An interesting Assyrian convention nevertheless makes itself felt—the representation of the human body as thickset and weighty and the limbs as bulging with muscle (witness the advanced left leg of the genius and the arms of the king). The calf and forearm muscles are exaggerated, and the veins are like cables—an example of realistic observation converted to a kind of symbol of brute human strength. Also noteworthy is the way in which the profile view of the arms comprises, with the front-view torso, a kind of three-quarter view. The artist, although subject to the conventions of his time, is experimenting with the problems of representing what his eye sees.

Two centuries later, in a relief from Nineveh showing Ashurbanipal hunting lions (FIG. 2-30), the conventions of the time of Ashurnasirpal II persist, al-

2-29 *Ashurnasirpal II Drinking*, Nimrud, *c.* 875 B.C. Limestone, approx. 7′ 8″ high. British Museum, London.

2-30　*Ashurbanipal Hunting Lions*, Nineveh, *c.* 650 B.C. Alabaster, approx. 60″ high. British Museum, London.

though more realistic elements are introduced. In this relief, lions released from cages in some large, enclosed arena charge the king, who, in his chariot and with his servants protecting his blind sides, shoots down the enraged animals. The king, menaced by the savage spring of a lion at his back, is saved by the quick action of two of his spearmen. Behind his chariot lies a pathetic trail of dead and dying animals pierced by what would appear to be far more arrows than are needed to kill them. A wounded lioness (FIG. 2-31) drags her hindquarters, paralyzed by arrows that pierce her spine. Blood streams from her wounds—a detail recurring in Assyrian art and revealing the savage character of its patrons. The artist gives a ruthless reading of the straining muscles, the swelling veins, the corrugations of the muzzle, the flattened ears—once more a hard realism under control of the formality of silhouette in low relief. Modern sympathies make of the scene of carnage a kind of heroic tragedy, with the lions as protagonists; but it is unlikely that the artists of the king had any intention other than to aggrandize his image by piling up his kills, by showing the king of men pitting himself against the king of beasts and conquering him.

2-31　*Dying Lioness*, Nineveh, *c.* 650 B.C. Limestone, figure approx. 23″ high. British Museum, London.

NEO-BABYLONIA

The Assyrian empire was never very secure, and most of its kings had to fight revolts in large sections of the Near East. The seventh century B.C. saw a steady rise of opposition to Assyrian rule, and, during the last years of Ashurbanipal's reign, the empire began to disintegrate. Under his son and successor, it collapsed before the simultaneous onslaught of the Medes from the east and the resurgent Babylonians from the south. Babylon rose once again, and, in a brief renewal (612–538 B.C.), the old southern Mesopotamian culture flourished, especially under the storied King Nebuchadnezzar, whose exploits we read of in the Book of Daniel. Nebuchadnezzar made Babylon a fabulous city once again, and its famous "hanging gardens" one of the seven wonders of the ancient world. Of its temple to Bel—the Hebrews' Tower of Babel—only a little of the great ziggurat remains. But Herodotus, the ancient Greek traveler and "father of history," has left us, in his brief account of his visit to the temple complex during the fifth century B.C., this description:

> In the one [division of the city] stood the palace of the kings, surrounded by a wall of great strength and size; in the other was the sacred precinct of Zeus-Bel, an enclosure a quarter of a mile square, with gates of solid brass, which was also remaining in my time. In the middle of the precinct, there was a tower of solid masonry, a furlong in length and breadth, on which was raised a second tower, and on that a third, and so on up to eight. The ascent to the top is on the outside, by a path which winds round all the towers. When one is about halfway up, one finds a resting place and seats, where persons are wont to sit some time on their way to the summit. On the top-most tower, there is a spacious temple, and inside the temple, stands a couch of unusual size, richly adorned, with a golden table by its side. . . . They also declare that the god comes down in person into this chamber, and sleeps on the couch, but I do not believe it.

A grand approach to the temple complex led down a walled processional way lined with 60 stately figures of lions done in brightly colored glazed bricks (FIG. 2-32). These remarkable beasts, sacred to the goddess Ishtar, are molded in relief and glazed in yellow-brown and red against a ground of turquoise or dark blue. The Babylonian glazes are opaque and hard; possibly, each brick was molded and enameled separately. Also, it may be that, as a result of this technique, these animals, whose vigor is suggested by snarling muzzles, long, nervous tails, and carefully depicted muscles, are more stylized than those of the Assyrian hunting reliefs.

The processional way passed through the monumental, brilliantly glazed Ishtar Gate (FIG. 2-33), the design of which, with its flanking crenelated towers,

2-32   *Lion from the Processional Way*, Ishtar Gate, Babylon, *c.* 575 B.C. Glazed brick, approx. 41" high. Louvre, Paris.

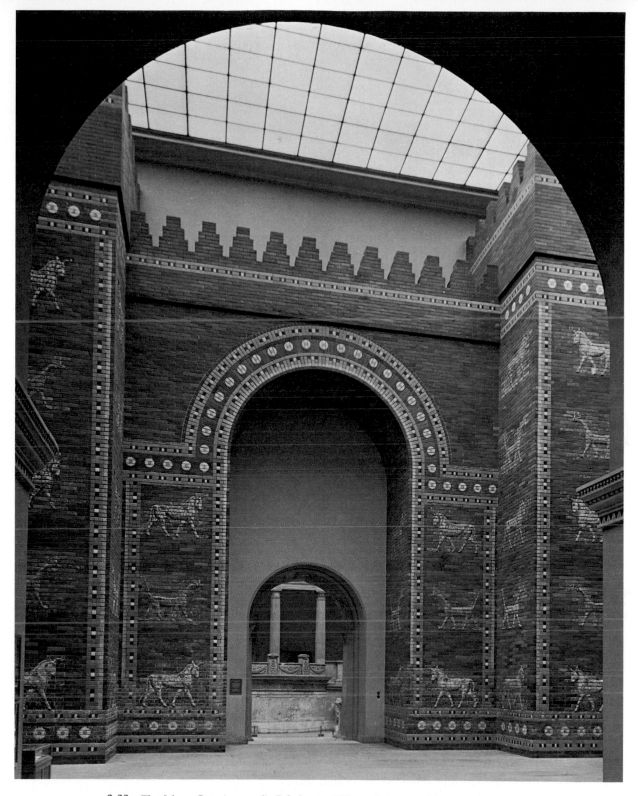

2-33   The Ishtar Gate (restored), Babylon, *c.* 575 B.C. Pergamon Museum, East Berlin.

conforms to the type of gate found in earlier Babylonian and Assyrian architecture. Glazed tiles had been used much earlier, but the surface of the bricks, even of those on which figures appeared, was flat. On the surfaces of the Ishtar Gate, laboriously reassembled, are superposed tiers of figures in profile, the dragon of Marduk and the bull of Adad alternating. Here is characteristic Mesopotamian formality at its best. The figures compose a stately heraldry proclaiming the gods of the temples toward which the Sacred Way leads. The lessons of architectural sculpture from Bogazköy and Khorsabad have been well learned, and the perfect adjustment of figure to wall found in the Ishtar animals rarely has been surpassed; certainly, in the history of architecture, few more colorful and durable surface ornaments are known.

ANCIENT IRAN: ELAM AND ACHAEMENID PERSIA

The later Persian empire that came into conflict with the Greeks was preceded at a considerable distance in time by a civilization contemporary with the civilizations of Akkad and Old Babylon and regularly in cultural and political transaction with them. Situated in western Iran, it was known by the biblical name, Elam.* The empire of Elam corresponded roughly to the Iranian province of Khuzistan. Although most often dominated by Mesopotamia, Elam was strong enough on one occasion to plunder Babylon and to carry off the stele of Naram-Sin and the stele of Hammurabi (FIGS. 2-21 and 2-23). The empire of Elam was destroyed by the Assyrian king, Ashurbanipal, who, in 641 B.C., sacked its capital Susa—a city that would rise again to great importance under the Achaemenid Persian empire.

During a relatively brief flowering of Elamite culture, around 1300 B.C., a sculptor cast in bronze a freestanding portrait statue of Niparasu, a queen of Elam (FIG. 2-34). Although sadly mutilated, enough remains of the work to show how obedient the sculptor was to the conventions of Mesopotamian art: the tight silhouette, strict frontality, firmly clasped hands held close to the body—what we have seen in the Tell Asmar and Gudea figures. Yet within these rigid conventions of form and pose, the artist manages to create refinements that could only be the result of close observation of appearance: the feminine softness of arm and bust, the grace and elegance of the long-fingered hands, the supple and quiet bend of the wrist, the ring and bracelets, the brocaded gown and the wave pattern of its hem. The figure presents the ideal in queenly deportment, with just a touch of demureness to mitigate the severity of the conventional pose. As we have seen in Assyrian sculpture, it is possible to wed convention with observed details, as the Elamite artist does so successfully here.

The Assyrians succumbed to the Babylonians, who were to fall, in their turn, once and for all. The later Babylonian King Nebuchadnezzar, Daniel's "King of Kings," boasted: "I caused a mighty wall to circumscribe Babylon . . . so that the enemy who would do evil would not threaten . . . [and] of the city of Babylon [I] made a fortress." Nevertheless, the handwriting on the wall appeared, and the city was taken by Cyrus of Persia (559–529 B.C.), founder of the Achaemenid dynasty, who traced his ancestry back to a mythical King Achaemenes and who may have

*It has been suggested that the fine portrait head of a ruler seen earlier in this chapter (FIG. 2-20) may have originated in Elam at the time when Sumer was at its peak of influence.

2-34　*Statue of Queen Niparasu,* Susa, Elam (Ancient Iran), *c.* 1300 B.C. Bronze, solid cast, 56″ high. Louvre, Paris.

been descended from an Elamite line. The impetus of the Persians' expansion carried them far beyond Babylon. Egypt fell to them in 525 B.C. By 480 B.C., the Persian empire extended from the Indus to the Danube, and only the successful resistance of the Greeks in the fifth century prevented it from embracing southeastern Europe as well. The Achaemenid line came to an end with the death of Darius III in 330 B.C., after his defeat in the Battle of Issus and the fall of his empire to Alexander the Great.

Architecture

The most important source of our knowledge of Persian building is the palace at Persepolis (FIG. 2-35), built between 520 and 460 B.C. by Darius I and Xerxes I, successors of Cyrus. Situated on the high plateau to the east of the Mesopotamian river valley, the heavily fortified palace stood on a wide platform overlooking the plain toward the sunset. Although destroyed by Alexander the Great in a gesture symbolizing the destruction of Persian imperial power, its still impressive ruins permit a fairly complete reconstruction of its original appearance.

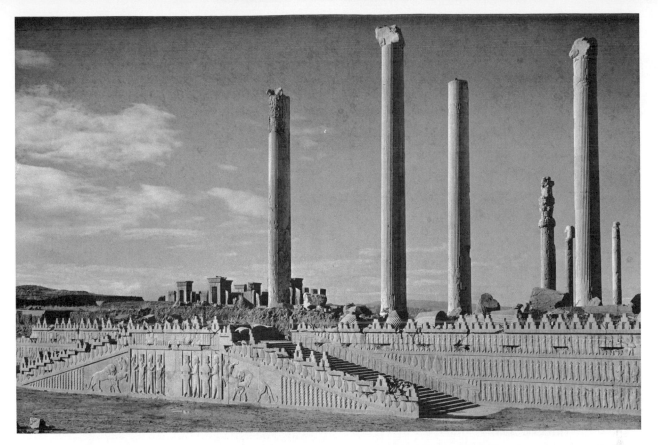

2-35 Royal audience hall and stairway, Persepolis, c. 500 B.C.

1. Treasury
2. Harem
3. Palace of Xerxes
4. Palace of Darius I
5. Audience hall of Darius I
6. Throne hall of Xerxes
----- Partially excavated

N

Unlike the Assyrian palace, which was tightly enfolded around courts (FIG. 2-26), the Persepolis buildings, although axially aligned, were loosely grouped and separated from each other by streets and irregular open spaces (FIG. 2-36). The dominant structure was a vast columned hall, 60 feet high and over 200 feet square. Standing on its own rock-cut podium, which is about 10 feet high, this huge royal audience hall (*apadana*) has been called "one of the noblest structures of the ancient world." It contained 36 columns (each 40 feet high) with slender, fluted shafts and capitals composed of the foreparts of bulls or lions, arranged to provide a firm cradle for the roof timbers. A well-preserved example from the somewhat later palace of Artaxerxes II at Susa is shown in FIG. 2-37. These unique capitals are an impressive and decorative Persian invention with no known antecedents or descendants. Unknown also remains the genesis of the square, many-columned hall so characteristic of the Persepolis palace. It has been suggested that it may have been derived from Median architecture, which has remained a blank page in archeologists' books. The Medes were the northern allies and later subjects of the Persians and are believed to have been the intermediaries through whom Persian art received a variety of Iranian stylistic elements.

2-36 Plan of the palace complex at Persepolis.

0   100   200
FEET
0   30   60
METERS

2-37 Bull capital from the royal audience hall of the palace of Artaxerxes II, Susa, *c.* 375 B.C. Gray marble, 7′ 7″ high, 12′ 3″ wide. Louvre, Paris.

Stone, easily available at the site, was used liberally at Persepolis for platforms, gateways, stairs, and columns; brick was used for the walls, however, and the smaller columns and the roofs were made of wood. The ruins of the palace at Persepolis (FIG. 2-38) show that stone also was used for door and window frames. The forms are derived from Egyptian architecture, which had impressed Darius, but here the frames are not composed structurally of posts, lintels, and sills but are cut in an arbitrary manner and used as sculptural ornaments. In fact, the entire complex of buildings, and particularly the apadana, seems to have been designed primarily for visual effect; it is a gigantic stage setting for magnificent ceremonials celebrating not only traditional festivals but also the greatness of the Persian empire and the power of its king.

Sculpture

The approach to the apadana leads through a monumental gateway flanked by colossal man-headed bulls and then at right angles toward the elevated great hall, ascent to which is by broad, ceremonial stairways, designed as though for a stage. The walls of the terrace and staircases are decorated with reliefs representing processions of royal guards, Persian and

2-38 Palace of Darius, Persepolis, *c.* 500 B.C.

Median nobles and dignitaries, and representatives from the subjected nations bringing tribute and gifts to the king (FIG. 2-39). These reliefs are thought to represent, in a shorthand version, the actual ceremonies that took place at Persepolis during the great New Year festivals. Traces of color found on similar monuments at other Persian sites suggest that, at least in part, these reliefs were colored. Their original effect must have been even greater than it is today, as the rows of figures sparkled in a blaze of colors rivaling that presented by the court during the festivals. On the other hand, the present denuded state of the reliefs makes it easier for us to appreciate their highly refined sculptural style. The cutting of the stone, both in the subtly modeled surfaces and the crisply chis-

eled details, is technically superb. Although they may have been inspired by Assyrian reliefs (FIGS. 2-28, 2-29, 2-30), these Persian reliefs are strikingly different in style. The forms are more rounded, and their projection from the background is greater; there is less emphasis on such details as straining sinews and bulging muscles; and, most important perhaps, the figures seem organically more unified, as the torsos are now shown in natural side view and are thus more convincingly related to heads and legs. The supposition that most of these modifications of traditional formal elements are the result of Greek (Ionian) influence becomes almost a certainty when we note how the garments worn by the figures have been stylized in accordance with Greek Archaic practice

2-39 *Subjects Bringing Gifts to the King* (detail), from the stairway to the royal audience hall, Persepolis, *c.* 500 B.C. Limestone.

(see FIGS. 5-14, 5-18, 5-27). Despite the modifications, the Persepolis reliefs represent a triumph of Near Eastern formality in art. Their purpose and function—to glorify the king in a manner both decorative and monumental—is fulfilled most successfully.

Craft Art

Love for well-ordered forms enabled Persian designers to create, on a vast scale, a rich and unified setting for official ceremonials. But the Persians could also work successfully on a much smaller scale. They were excellent goldsmiths and silversmiths; the example shown, a jar handle in the form of a winged ibex (FIG. 2-40), typifies their exquisite and enduring art. Made of silver inlaid with gold, the ibex rears up on a palmette growing from the head of a satyr. The leap of the lithe body rises into the higher leap of the horns,

2-40 Jar handle in the form of a winged ibex, Persia, 400–300 B.C. Silver inlaid with gold, approx. 10½″ high, Louvre, Paris.

2-41 Ceremonial cauldron, Luristan, eighth century B.C. Bronze, approx. 12″ high. Cincinnati Art Museum (The Mary Hanna Fund).

and the suave curves of the wings smooth the motion. All that is needed of truth to nature is here, and none of it intrudes on the effortless play of fancy.

As with most elements of Persian art, it is not difficult to trace the genesis of this winged ibex. Although the animal's body has regained its organic unity, probably through Mesopotamian influence, its original source of inspiration is to be found among the Luristan bronzes. Luristan, a mountainous region to the east of the Mesopotamian valley, inhabited at different times by Kassites, Medes, and other seminomadic tribes, was the home of a flourishing bronze industry that reached its peak during the eighth and seventh centuries B.C. It produced a variety of portable objects, such as cups, bowls, weapons, bridles, and articles of personal adornment that, collectively, are referred to as ''nomad's gear.'' Although we do not know by and for whom these objects were made, they form a homogeneous group that is rooted in an old and widespread tradition: its exponents delighted in working with animal forms. This so-called "animal style" may have originated in the Luristan region; at any rate, it spread over much of the ancient world, from the Asiatic steppes to central and western Europe. The Luristan bronzes are characterized by a high degree of abstraction that converts the representations of animals into purely decorative devices. In the handle of the ceremonial cauldron illustrated in FIG. 2-41, the two rearing ibexes make interlocking arcs that echo in linear form the three-dimensional shape of the vessel to which they are attached. Although wingless, their pose, attitude, and purpose leave little room for doubt that they are the forerunners of the Persian ibex. And, incidentally, the source of inspiration for the Persian animal's wings seems to appear in the embossed decoration of the bowl, where the Luristan artist has boldly copied Assyrian winged bulls and sacred emblems in Assyrian style and technique.

Eclecticism of Achaemenid Art

Thirty years ago, Achaemenid art was called eclectic— that is, derivative and lacking originality. Today, as more knowledge has been accumulated about the earlier periods of art in Iran, much art that seemed to have been brought in from the outside also can be shown to have had roots in earlier Iranian periods and to have been accepted in a new form from that source. Thus, the platforms of the palaces at Persepolis are similar to those found in Mesopotamia, but the fact that Persepolis was built on the terrace of a mountain spur may reflect ancient Persian custom. The inhabitants of southwest Iran carved rock reliefs with lines of marching figures, the monotony of which has been compared with some of the reliefs adorning the stairway façades at Persepolis. On the other hand, the guardian figures are of Assyrian origin, the machine-like precision in the carving of details is reminiscent of Assyrian relief sculpture, the columned halls may have been influenced by Egyptian or Median models, and the fluting of columns is derived from Greek (Ionian) practice. Yet the manner in which these various elements have been combined produces an ensemble that is quite new and different from the art of those nations from which they may derive. A Persian column cannot be mistaken for an Egyptian or a Greek one, and nothing like the Persian apadana has been found in earlier architecture. With all their derivative elements, the architecture and sculpture of Persepolis produce a coherent and majestic impression.

Prior to their conquest of the Near East, Persian art had consisted mainly of small-scale nomad's gear. Their monumental art was created "on the spur of the moment," one might say, when they found themselves masters of the Near East and heirs to its rich culture. To glorify and eternalize their military and political achievements, the Persians not only adopted those features of foreign and conquered cultures that seemed to serve this purpose but also brought into the country the artisans who could best realize their ambitious projects. A building inscription at Susa names Ionians, Sardians, Medes, Egyptians, and Babylonians among the workmen who built and decorated the palace. But under the single-minded direction of its Persian masters, this mixed crowd, with a widely varied cultural and artistic background, created a new and coherent style that was perfectly suited to the expression of Persian imperial ambitions. A court style, like that of Louis XIV over two millennia later, it compelled its contributors into an artistic synthesis that was to remain remarkably uniform during the 200-year reign of the Achaemenid dynasty.

3

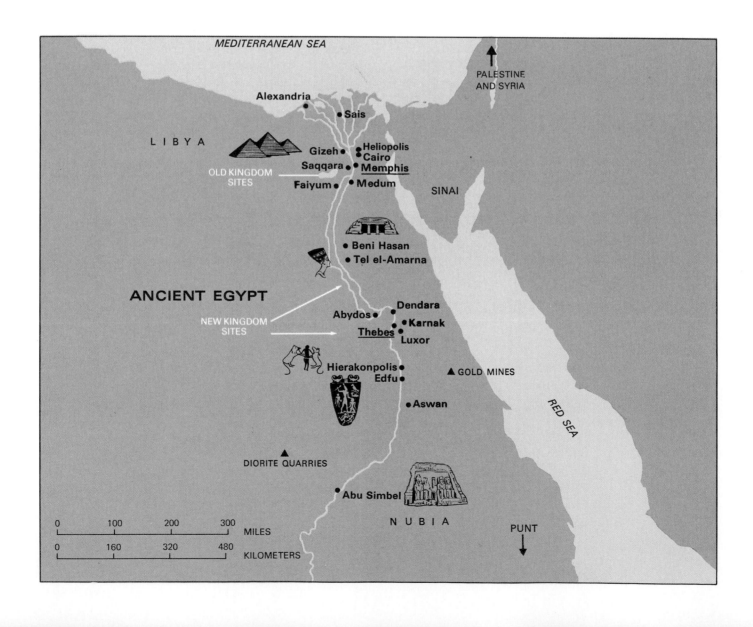

MEDITERRANEAN SEA

PALESTINE
AND SYRIA

Alexandria

Sais

LIBYA

Gizeh
Saqqara
OLD KINGDOM
SITES
Faiyum

Heliopolis
Cairo
Memphis
Medum

SINAI

Beni Hasan
Tel el-Amarna

ANCIENT EGYPT

NEW KINGDOM
SITES

Dendara
Abydos
Karnak
Thebes
Luxor

Hierakonpolis
Edfu

▲ GOLD MINES

Aswan

RED SEA

DIORITE QUARRIES

Abu Simbel

NUBIA

PUNT

| 0 | 100 | 200 | 300 | MILES |

| 0 | 160 | 320 | 480 | KILOMETERS |

THE ART OF EGYPT

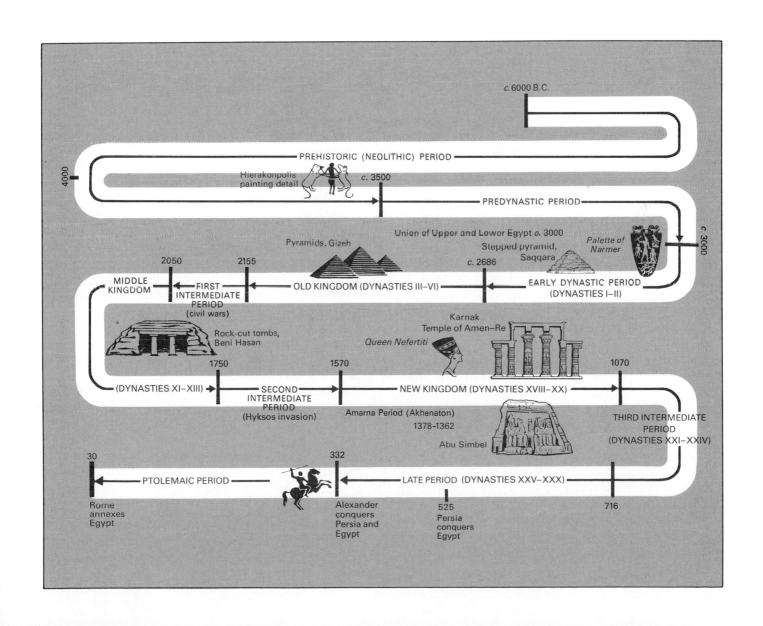

c. 6000 B.C.

4000

PREHISTORIC (NEOLITHIC) PERIOD

Hierakonpolis painting detail   c. 3500

PREDYNASTIC PERIOD

Union of Upper and Lower Egypt c. 3000

Pyramids, Gizeh

Stepped pyramid, Saqqara

Palette of Narmer

c. 3000

2050   2155   c. 2686

MIDDLE KINGDOM   FIRST INTERMEDIATE PERIOD (civil wars)   OLD KINGDOM (DYNASTIES III–VI)   EARLY DYNASTIC PERIOD (DYNASTIES I–II)

Karnak Temple of Amen–Re

Rock-cut tombs, Beni Hasan

Queen Nefertiti

1750   1570   1070

(DYNASTIES XI–XIII)   SECOND INTERMEDIATE PERIOD (Hyksos invasion)   NEW KINGDOM (DYNASTIES XVIII–XX)   THIRD INTERMEDIATE PERIOD (DYNASTIES XXI–XXIV)

Amarna Period (Akhenaton) 1378–1362

Abu Simbel

30   332   716

PTOLEMAIC PERIOD   LATE PERIOD (DYNASTIES XXV–XXX)

Rome annexes Egypt

Alexander conquers Persia and Egypt

525 Persia conquers Egypt

OVER 2,000 YEARS AGO, the admiring Herodotus wrote: "Concerning Egypt itself I shall extend my remarks to a great length, because there is no country that possesses so many wonders, nor any that has such a number of works which defy description." A little later, he added: "They [the Egyptians] are religious to excess, far beyond any other race of men." People of discernment, aware of the profusion of monuments left to the world by the ancient Egyptians, have long been in agreement with these observations. Although the Egyptians built their dwellings of impermanent materials, they made their tombs (which they believed would preserve their bodies forever), their temples to the immortal gods, and the statues of their equally immortal god–king of imperishable stone. The stone cliffs of the Libyan and Arabian deserts, from which that material was hewn, and the Nile flowing between them could represent, respectively, the timelessness of the Egyptian world and the endless cycles of natural process. Religion and permanence—these are the elements that characterize the solemn and ageless art of Egypt and express the unchanging order that, for the ancient Egyptians, was divinely ordained.

Even more than the Tigris and the Euphrates, the Nile, by virtue of its presence, defined the cultures that developed on its banks. Originating deep in Africa, the world's longest river descended through many cataracts to sea level in Egypt, where, in annual flood, it deposited rich soil brought thousands of miles from the African hills. Hemmed in by the narrow valley, which reaches a width of only about 12 miles, even in its widest parts, the Nile flows through regions that may not have a single drop of rainfall in a decade. Yet, crops grew luxuriantly from the fertilizing silt. Game also abounded then, and the great river that made life possible entered the consciousness of the Egyptians as a god and as a symbol of life.

In Predynastic, or prehistoric, and Pharaonic times, the river held wider sway than it does today. Egypt was a land of marshes dotted with island ridges, and what is now arid desert valley was grassy parkland well suited for hunting and grazing cattle. Amphibious animals swarmed in the marshes and were hunted through tall forests of papyrus and rushes. The fertility of Egypt was proverbial, and, at the end of its history, when Egypt had become a province of the Roman empire, it was the granary of the Mediterranean world.

Before settled communities could be built along the Nile's banks, however, it was necessary to control the annual floods. Instead of attempting to control the flow of the river, the Egyptians built dams to divert flood waters into fields; the communal effort put forth to construct these dams provided the basis for the growth of an Egyptian civilization, just as the irrigation projects in the Mesopotamian valley had furnished the civilizing impetus for that region a few centuries earlier.*

In the Middle Ages, when the history of Egypt was thought of as part of the history of Islam, Egypt's reputation as an ancient land of wonders and mystery lived on in more-or-less fabulous report. Until the later eighteenth century, its undeciphered writing and its exotic monuments were regarded as treasures of occult wisdom, locked away from any but those initiated in the mystic arts. Scholars knew something of the history of Egypt from references in the Old Testament, from the unreliable reports of ancient and modern travelers, and from a history of Egypt written in Greek by an Egyptian named Manetho in the second century B.C. Manetho described the succession of pharaohs, dividing them into the still useful groups we call *dynasties;* but his chronology is very inaccurate, and his account is untrustworthy.

Scientific history—or, at least, scientific archeology—had its start when, at the end of the eighteenth century, modern Europe rediscovered Egypt. Egypt became the first subject of archeological exploration, followed by the uncovering of the ancient civilizations of the Tigris and the Euphrates. In 1799, Napoleon Bonaparte, on a military expedition to Egypt, took with him a small troop of scholars, linguists, antiquarians, and artists. The chance discovery of the famed *Rosetta Stone,* now in the British Museum, gave the eager scholars what they wanted—a key to the until then undeciphered Egyptian hieroglyphic writing. The stone bears an inscription in three sections: one in Greek, which was easily read; one in *demotic* (Late Egyptian); and one in formal hieroglyphic. It was at once suspected that the inscription was the same in all three sections and that, using Greek as the key, the other two sections could be deciphered. More than 20 years later, after many false starts, a young linguist, Jean François Champollion, deduced that the hieroglyphs were not simply pictographs but the signs of a once-spoken language—vestiges of which survived in Coptic, the later language of Christian Egypt. Champollion's feat made him a kind of Columbus of the new science of *archeology,* as well as of that special branch within it, *Egyptology.* Those who followed Champollion, like Auguste Mariette and Gaston Maspero, sought to build classified collections and to protect Egyptian art from the unscrupulous. Men like Flinders Petrie introduced techniques of excavation, preparing the groundwork for

---

*The construction of the Aswan High Dam in recent times marks the ultimate human control of the great river.

the development of sound methods for validating knowledge of Egyptian civilization.

Ideally, the foundation of archeological knowledge is a reliable chronology. Yet, as the body of archeological evidence enlarges and new scientific methods of dating are developed, the chronology must change to accommodate them. Sometimes, what was thought to be close to certain becomes problematical; sometimes, what was guesswork or speculation suddenly becomes probable. Because this is more often the case the further back we travel in time, the Predynastic beginnings of Egyptian civilization are chronologically vague, as are those of Mesopotamia. Some time around 3500 B.C., a people of native African stock may have been exposed to influences from Mesopotamia, or it is possible that, as in Sumer, the sudden cultural development may have been due to an actual incursion of a new people. A wall painting from the Late Predynastic period, found in a shrine at Hierakonpolis in Upper Egypt (FIG. 3-1), represents, men, animals, and boats in a lively, helter-skelter fashion. The boats, symbolic of the journey down the river of life and death, are painted white and seem to carry a cargo of tombs mourned over by women. Also shown are a heraldic grouping of two animals (lions?) on either side of a human figure, many figures of gazelles, and, in the lower right corner, men fighting. The heraldic group, a compositional type usually associated with Mesopotamian art, suggests that, by this time, influences from Mesopotamia not only had reached Egypt but had already made the thousand-mile journey upstream. The stick figures and their apparently random arrangement remind us of the Mesolithic rock paintings from the Spanish Levant (the east coast of Spain) and North Africa, the style of which flourished also in the central Sahara and may have been another impetus to the development of Egyptian art.

The Hierakonpolis mural is the earliest known representative of that millennia-long tradition of painting that reveals to us the *funerary customs* of Egypt, so much at the center of Egyptian life. Most paintings are found in tombs and provide the principal archeological evidence for the historical reconstruction of Egyptian civilization. Religion pervaded that civilization. In Herodotus's words, the Egyptian was "religious to excess," and his concern for immortality amounted to near obsession; the overall preoccupation in this life was to ensure his safety and happiness in the next life. To this preoccupation was dedicated the major part of the monuments the Egyptians left behind them.

The sharp distinction between body and soul, long familiar to Christianity and other later religions, was not made in the religion of the Egyptians. Rather, they believed that, from birth, one was accompanied by a kind of other self, the *ka*, which, on the death of the fleshly body, could inhabit the corpse and live on. For the ka to live securely, however, the dead body had to remain as nearly intact as possible; to see that

3-1 *Men, Boats, and Animals,* wall painting from a shrine at Hierakonpolis, Upper Egypt, *c.* 3500 B.C. (After Quibell.)

it did, the Egyptians developed the technique of embalming to a high art; their success is evident in numerous well-preserved mummies of kings (like Ramses II), princes, and nobles, as well as of some common persons. The first requirement for immortality, *mummification,* was followed by others. Food and drink had to be provided, as well as clothing, utensils, and all the apparatus of life, so that nothing would be lacking that had been enjoyed on earth. Images of the deceased, sculptured in the round and placed in shallow recesses, guaranteed the permanence of his identity by providing substitute dwelling places for the ka in case the mummy disintegrated. Wall paintings (for the use and delectation of the ka) recorded, with great animation and detail, the recurring round of human activities—a cycle of "works and days" that changed with the calendar and the seasons. The Egyptians hoped and expected that the images and inventory of life—set up and collected within the protective massive stone walls of the tomb—would ensure immortality; but almost from the beginning of the elaborate interments, the thorough plundering of tombs became a profitable occupation. Only one royal burial place remained close to intact—that of King Tutankhamen of the Eighteenth Dynasty; its discovery, in 1924, revealed to a fascinated world the full splendor of a pharaoh's funerary assemblage.

THE EARLY DYNASTIC PERIOD AND THE OLD KINGDOM

Egypt has been known as the "Kingdom of the Two Lands," a reference to its very early physical and political division into Upper Egypt and Lower Egypt. The upper land was dry, rocky, and rustic in culture; the lower land was opulent, urban, and populous. Even in Predynastic times, there must have been conflict between the two, for the ancient Egyptians began the history of Egypt, as we do, with the forcible unification of the two lands by a certain Menes.

The *Palette of Narmer*

Menes is thought to be King Narmer, whose image we find on a slate slab from Hierakonpolis (FIG. 3-2). The slab, or *palette* as it is called, was originally used as a tablet on which eye makeup (to protect the eyes against sun-glare and irritation) was prepared. The *Palette of Narmer* is an elaborate, formalized version of a utilitarian object common in the Predynastic period. Its importance is great, not only as a historical document that records the unification of the two Egypts and the beginning of the Dynastic period, but also as a kind of early blueprint of the formula of figure representation that was to rule Egyptian art for some 3,000 years. On the palette's back, the king, wearing

3-2   *Palette of Narmer* (front and back), Hierakonpolis, Upper Egypt, *c.* 3000 B.C. Slate, 25" high. Egyptian Museum, Cairo.

the high, bowling-pin-shaped crown of Upper Egypt, is about to slay an enemy as a sacrifice. Before him a hawk—symbol of the sky god, Horus, protector of the king—takes into captivity a man-headed hieroglyph for land from which papyrus grows (a symbol for Lower Egypt). Below the king are two fallen enemies; above, two heads of Hathor, a goddess favorably disposed to Narmer. The other side of the palette shows Narmer wearing the cobra crown of Lower Egypt and reviewing a pile of the beheaded enemy. In both cases, it is significant that the king—towering over his own men and the enemy—by virtue of his superior rank performs his ritual task alone. The superhuman strength of the king is symbolized by a great bull knocking down a rebellious city, perhaps Hierakonpolis. Historical narrative, as we find it in Mesopotamian reliefs (see the *Victory Stele of Naram-Sin*, FIG. 2-21), is not of primary importance in this work. What is important is the concentration on the king as a deified figure, isolated from all ordinary men, far above them, and alone responsible for his triumph. As early as the Narmer palette (about 3000 B.C.), we see evidence of this Egyptian convention of thought, of art, and of state policy—namely, that the kingship is divine, that its prestige is one with the prestige of the gods.

If what belongs to the gods and to nature is unchanging and if the king is divine, then his attributes must be eternal. We have already seen that, in Mesopotamian art, the ever-changing natural shapes are formalized into simple poses, attitudes, and actions. The same thing happens in Egypt, even though the instinct for convention leads to a somewhat different style. In the figure of Narmer, we find the stereotype of kingly transcendence that, through several slight variations, will be repeated in subsequent representations of all Egyptian dynasts except Akhenaton (see FIG. 3-36) in the fourteenth century. The king is seen in a perspective that combines the profile views of head, legs, and arms with the front views of eye and shoulders. Although the proportions of the figure would change, the method of its representation would become a standard for all later Egyptian art. Like a set of primordial commandments, the *Palette of Narmer* sets forth the basic laws that would govern art along the Nile for thousands of years. In the Hierakonpolis painting (FIG. 3-1), figures had been scattered across the wall more-or-less haphazardly; here, a surface has been subdivided into a number of bands, and the pictorial elements have been inserted into their organized setting in a neat and orderly way. The horizontal lines that separate the bands also define the ground that supports the figures—a mode that would persist in hundreds of acres of Egyptian wall paintings and reliefs.

3-3 *Panel of Hesire,* Saqqara, *c.* 2750 B.C. Wood, 45″ high. Egyptian Museum, Cairo.

Three centuries later, we find the basic conventions of Egyptian figure representation that were fixed in the *Palette of Narmer* refined and systematized on a carved wooden panel representing Hesire, a high official from the court of King Zoser (FIG. 3-3). The figure's swelling forms have been modeled with greater subtlety, and its proportions have been changed to a broad-shouldered, narrow-hipped ideal. The artist uses the conceptual approach (see page 50), rather than the optical, representing what he knows to be true of the object, instead of some random view of it, and showing its most characteristic parts at right angles to the line of vision. This conceptual approach expresses a feeling for the constant and changeless aspect of things and lends itself to systematic meth-

3-4 The *Later Canon* ("rule of proportion") of Egyptian Art. (After Panofsky.)

ods of figure construction (FIG. 3-4). Although perhaps not quite as simple as his description of it, the system is explained by Erwin Panofsky as follows:

> With its more significant lines permanently fixed on specific points of the human body, the Egyptian network [of equal squares] immediately indicates to the painter or sculptor how to organize his figure: he will know from the outset that he must place the ankle on the first horizontal line, the knee on the sixth, . . . and so on. . . . It was, for instance, agreed that in a [lunging] figure, . . . the length of pace . . . should amount to $10\frac{1}{2}$ units, while this distance in a figure quietly standing was set at $4\frac{1}{2}$ or $5\frac{1}{2}$ units. Without too much exaggeration, one could maintain that, when an Egyptian artist familiar with this system of proportion was set the task of representing a standing, sitting, or striding figure, the result was a foregone conclusion once the figure's absolute size was determined.*

In addition to recording an important historical event and to laying down ground rules for the pictorial arts, the *Palette of Narmer* also illustrates several stages in the development of Egyptian writing. The story of Narmer's victories is represented in the different registers, with varying degrees of symbolism. Straight pictorial narrative is used to show the king following his standard-bearers in triumphal proces-

*Erwin Panofsky, *Meaning in the Visual Arts* (Garden City, NY: Doubleday, 1955), pp. 58–61.

sion and inspecting the bodies of his slain enemies. This simple picture-writing becomes symbolic when, in a bottom register, the king is shown as a bull breaking down the walls of an enemy fortress. The symbolism becomes more abstract in the pile of decapitated foes; here, each body, its severed head neatly placed between its legs, is probably a numerical symbol representing a specific number of fallen enemies. Finally, in the signs appearing near the heads of the more important figures, pictographs take on phonetic values, as the names of the respective individuals have been written in true hieroglyphs.

Architecture

Similar principles of permanence and regularity appear in the design of the Egyptian tomb—that symbol of the timeless, the silent house of the dead. We find its standard shape in the *mastaba* (FIG. 3-5), which is Arabic for "bench"—a rectangular brick or stone structure with battered (sloping) sides erected over a subterranean tomb chamber connected to the outside by a shaft. The form was probably developed from

3-5 Mastabas *(bottom)*, with plan *(middle)* and schematic section *(top)*.

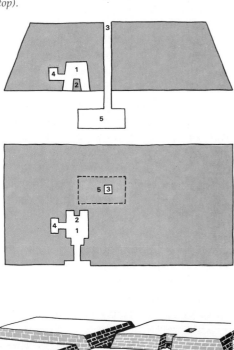

1. Chapel
2. False door
3. Shaft into burial chamber
4. Serdab (chamber for statue of deceased)
5. Burial chamber

3-6 Imhotep, Stepped Pyramid of King Zoser, Saqqara, *c.* 2610 B.C.

mounds of earth or stone that covered earlier tombs. It is significant that in Mesopotamia there was relative indifference to the cult of burial and to the permanence of the tomb, whereas in Egypt such matters were considered to be of the first importance.

About 2610 B.C., the Stepped Pyramid of King Zoser of the Third Dynasty (FIG. 3-6) was raised at Saqqara, the ancient *necropolis* (city of the dead) of Memphis. Possibly Egypt's oldest stone building, it was the first monumental royal tomb. In form a kind of compromise between the mastaba and the later "true" pyramids at Gizeh, it is in fact a piling of mastabas of diminishing size, one on the other, forming a structure resembling the great ziggurats of Mesopotamia. Unlike them, Zoser's pyramid is a tomb, not a temple, and is elevated above the funerary complex arranged around it.

A tomb such as Zoser's had a dual function: to protect the mummified king and his possessions, and to symbolize by its gigantic presence his absolute, godlike power. This structure, with its temples (now thought to be a medical shrine), complex of chambered terraces, and great courtyard, was the work of Imhotep, the first artist of recorded history. Grand vizier to King Zoser and a man of legendary powers,

he was celebrated in the ancient world not only as an architect but also as a wise man, wizard, physician ("the father of medicine"), priest, and scribe—a kind of universal genius who later came to be worshiped as a deity.

At Gizeh, near modern Cairo but across the Nile (the dead were always buried on the side where the sun sets), lie three pyramids of pharaohs of the Fourth Dynasty (FIG. 3-7)—Khufu (the Greek Cheops), Khafre (Chephren), and Menkure (Mykerinus). Built around 2500 B.C., these pyramids have been associated with mystery and with "hidden" knowledge and have served as symbols for several things— primeval wisdom, Egypt itself, eternal stability, and the arts of magic. The pyramids of Gizeh represent the culmination of an architectural evolution that began with the mastaba. They did not evolve out of necessity; kings could have gone on indefinitely piling mastabas, one on top of another, to make their weighty tombs. Rather, it has been suggested that when the kings of the Third Dynasty moved their permanent residence to Memphis, they came under the influence of nearby Heliopolis. This city was the seat of the powerful cult of Re, the sun god, whose fetish was a pyramidal stone, the *ben-ben*. By the

3-7   Great Pyramids of Gizeh. *From left:* Menkure, *c.* 2460 B.C.; Khafre, *c.* 2500 B.C.; Khufu, *c.* 2530 B.C.

Fourth Dynasty, the pharaohs considered themselves the sons of Re; hence, his incarnation on earth. For the pharaohs, then, it would have been only a step from the belief that the spirit and power of Re resided in the pyramidal *ben-ben* to the belief that their divine spirits and bodies would be similarly preserved within pyramidal tombs.

Is the pyramid form, then, an invention inspired by a religious demand, rather than the result of a formal evolution? We need not decide here. Our concern is with the remarkable features of the Fourth-Dynasty pyramid. Of the three pyramids at Gizeh, Khufu is the oldest and largest. Except for the galleries and burial chamber, it is an almost solid mass of limestone masonry—a stone mountain built on the same principle as the Stepped Pyramid of King Zoser, the interior spaces in plan and elevation being relatively tiny, as if crushed out of the scheme by the sheer weight of stone (FIG. 3-8). The limestone was quarried in the eastern Nile cliffs and floated across the river during the seasonal floods. After the masons finished cutting the stones, they marked them with red ink to indicate the place of each stone in the structure. Then great gangs of laborers dragged them (the wheel was not yet known) up temporary ramps and laid them

course on course. Finally the pyramid was surfaced with a casing of pearly white limestone, cut with such nicety that the eye could scarcely detect the joints. A few casing stones can still be seen in the cap that covers the Pyramid of Khafre, all that remain after many centuries during which the pyramids were

3-8   Section of the Pyramid of Khufu, Gizeh. (After Hoelscher.)

1. Silhouette with original facing stone
2. Thieves' tunnels
3. Entrance
4. Grand gallery
5. King's chamber
6. So-called "queen's chamber"
7. False tomb chamber
8. Relieving blocks
9. Airshafts?

stripped to supply limestone for the Islamic builders of Cairo. The immensity of the Pyramid of Khufu is indicated by some dimensions in round numbers: At the base, the length of one side is 775 feet and its area is some 13 acres; its present height is 450 feet (originally 480 feet). According to Flinders Petrie, the structure contains about 2,300,000 blocks of stone, each averaging $2\frac{1}{2}$ tons in weight. Napoleon's scholars calculated that the blocks in the three pyramids were sufficient to build a wall 1 foot wide and 10 feet high around France. The art of this structure is inherent not only in its huge size and successful engineering but also in its formal design. The proportions and immense dignity are so consistent with its funerary and religious function and so well adapted to its geographical setting; the four corners are oriented to the cardinal points of the compass, and the grave and simple mass dominates the flat landscape to the horizon. The ironic outcome of this stupendous effort may be read from the cross section shown in FIG. 3-8. The dotted lines at the base of the structure (2) indicate the path cut into the pyramid by ancient graverobbers. Unable to locate the carefully sealed and hidden entrance, they started some 40 feet above the base and tunneled into the structure until they intercepted the ascending corridor. Many royal tombs were plundered almost as soon as the funeral ceremonies had ended; the very conspicuousness of the pyramid was an invitation to despoilment. The hard

lesson was learned by the successors of the Old Kingdom pyramid-builders; they built few pyramids, which were relatively small and inconspicuous.

From the remains around the middle pyramid of Gizeh, Khafre, we can reconstruct an entire pyramid complex (FIG. 3-9): the pyramid itself, within or below which was the burial chamber; the chapel, adjoining the pyramid on the east side, where offerings were made, ceremonies were performed, and cloth, food, and ceremonial vessels were stored; the covered causeway leading down to the valley; and the valley temple, or vestibule, of the causeway. Beside the causeway and dominating the temple of Khafre rose the Great Sphinx (FIG. 3-10) carved from a spur of rock to commemorate the pharaoh. The rock was cut so that the immense figure, adjacent to the temple's west front, could give visitors coming from the eastern entrance the illusion that it was resting on a great pedestal. The lion figure with a human head, possibly a portrait of Khafre, again shows us the conjunction of a powerful beast with the attributes of absolute kingship, as we have seen in the hawk and the bull of the *Palette of Narmer* (FIG. 3-2). For centuries, the huge head of the Great Sphinx stood up above the drifting tides of desert sand that covered the body, providing generations of ancient and modern travelers with an awe-inspiring and unforgettable image of mysterious power. FIG. 3-11, showing a group of British soldiers of a century ago clustered about the head,

3-9   Reconstruction of the pyramids of Khufu and Khafre, Gizeh. (After Hoelscher.)

1. Pyramid of Khafre
2. Mortuary temple
3. Covered causeway
4. Valley temple
5. Great Sphinx
6. Pyramid of Khufu
7. Pyramids of the royal family and mastabas of nobles

3-10 The Great Sphinx (Pyramid of Khafre in right background), Gizeh, *c.* 2530 B.C. Sandstone, 65' high, 240' long.

before the rest of the figure had been excavated, helps to give scale to the colossus. Raising this overwhelming monument from the earth is in a way symbolic of the whole enterprise of modern archeology.

The valley temple of the Pyramid of Khafre (FIG. 3-12) was built on the post-and-lintel system—upright supports, or posts, with horizontal beams, or lintels, resting on them. Both posts and lintels were huge, rectangular, red-granite monoliths, finely pro-

portioned, skillfully cut and polished, and devoid of decoration. Alabaster slabs covered the floor, and seated statues—the only embellishment of the temple—were ranged along the wall. The interior was lighted by a few slanting rays filtering in from above. Although the Egyptians knew the arch and the vault and had used them occasionally in Predynastic tombs, they rarely used them again after about 3000 B.C., the beginning of the Dynastic period. Egyptian

3-11 The Great Sphinx in the nineteenth century, Gizeh.

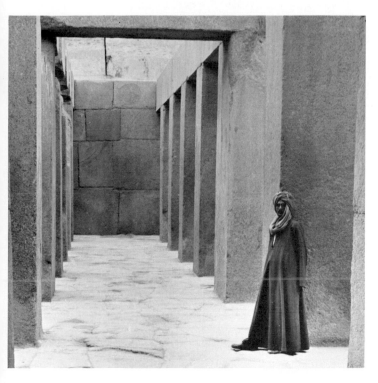

3-12 Middle aisle of the hall of pillars, valley temple of the Pyramid of Khafre, Gizeh, c. 2500 B.C.

architects preferred the static forms of the post-and-lintel system, which, if cast into the heavy, massive shapes of the Khafre temple, expressed, perhaps better than any other architectural style, the changeless and the eternal.

Sculpture

In Egyptian tombs, we have already noted that sculpture in the round served the important function of creating an image of the deceased that could serve as an abode for the ka (the other self) should the mummy be destroyed. For this reason, an interest in portrait likenesses developed early in Egypt. Hence, too, permanence of style and material were essential. Although wood, clay, and bronze were used, mostly for images of those not of the royal or noble classes, stone was the primary material: limestone and sandstone from the Nile cliffs, granite from the cataracts of the upper Nile, and diorite from the desert.

A seated statue of Khafre (FIG. 3-13), who ruled 2558–2533 B.C., was one of a series of similar statues carved for Khafre's valley temple near the Great Sphinx. These statues—the only organic forms in the geometric severity of the temple structure, with its flat-planed posts and lintels—must have created a striking atmosphere of solemn majesty. Khafre is seated on a throne on the base of which is carved the intertwined lotus and papyrus, symbol of united Egypt. Sheltering his head are the protecting wings of the hawk, symbol of the sun, indicating Khafre's divine status as son of Re. He wears the simple kilt of the Old Kingdom and a linen headdress that covers his forehead and falls in pleated folds over his shoulders. The representation of the king is strongly individualized yet permeated with an imperturbable calm, reflecting the enduring power of the pharaoh

3-13 *Khafre* (side and front), Gizeh, c. 2500 B.C. Diorite, 66" high. Egyptian Museum, Cairo.

and of kingship in general. This effect, common to royal statues of the ka, is achieved by devices of form and technique that we can still admire. The figure has great compactness and solidity, with few projecting, breakable parts; the form manifests the purpose—to last for eternity. The body is attached to a back slab, the arms are held close to the torso and thighs, the legs are close together and attached to the throne by stone webs. Like Mesopotamian statues, the pose is frontal, rigid, and bisymmetrical. This repeatable scheme arranges the parts of the body so that they are presented in a totally frontal projection or entirely in profile. As Erwin Panofsky observed:

> . . . we can recognize from many unfinished pieces that even in sculpture the final form is always determined by an underlying geometrical plan originally sketched on the surfaces of the block. It is evident that the artist drew four separate designs on the vertical surfaces of the block . . . that he then evolved the figure by working away the surplus mass of stone, so that the form was bounded by a system of planes meeting at right angles and connected by slopes. . . . there is a sculptor's working drawing . . . that illustrates the mason-like method of these sculptors even more clearly: as if he were constructing a house, the sculptor drew up plans for his sphinx in frontal elevation, ground plan, and profile elevation . . . so that even today the figure could be executed according to plan.*

This *subtractive* method of "working away the surplus . . . stone" accounts for the block-like look of the standard Egyptian statue, which strongly differs from the Mesopotamian cylindrical or conical shape seen, for example, in the Gudea statues (FIG. 2-22). The hardest stone was used to ensure the permanence of the image—and Egypt, again unlike Mesopotamia, was rich in stone. Even so, the difficulty of working granite and diorite with bronze tools (much of the finishing had to be done by abrasion) made production too expensive for all but the wealthiest.

As the figure was cut to plan, so were its proportions determined beforehand. A canon of ideal proportions, designated as appropriate for the representation of imposing majesty, was accepted and applied quite independently of optical fact. The generalized anatomy persisted in Egyptian statuary even into the Ptolemaic period, when Greek influence might have been expected to shift it toward realism. The Egyptian sculptor seems to have been indifferent to realistic representation of the body, preferring to strive for fidelity to nature in the art of portraiture, at which the Egyptians have not been surpassed.

*Erwin Panofsky, *Meaning in the Visual Arts* (Garden City, NY: Doubleday), pp. 58–59.

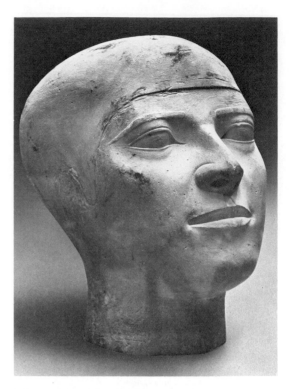

3-14 *"Reserve" Head of a Prince*, Gizeh, *c.* 2500 B.C. Limestone, life-size. Egyptian Museum, Cairo.

An example of their skill is a so-called "reserve" (duplicate, or spare) head of a prince of the family of Khufu (FIG. 3-14). Attention is given only to the execution of the face, which shows the union of the formal with the realistic that gives distinction to so many portrait busts of its type. "Reserve" heads were placed outside the burial chamber, and their purpose is not understood. This head displays the extraordinary sensitivity of Old Kingdom portraiture. The personality—sharply intelligent, vivacious, and alert—is read by the sculptor with a penetration and sympathy seldom achieved in the history of sculpture.

In the history of art, especially portraiture, it is almost a rule that formality is relaxed and realism is increased when the subject is a person of lesser importance. The famous wood statue of Ka-Aper (Sheikh el Beled) is a case in point (FIG. 3-15). The work is a lively representation of a man whose function was to serve the king in the spirit world as he had in life. The face is startlingly alive, an effect that is heightened by eyes of rock crystal. The sheikh stands erect in conventional frontal pose, left leg advanced. His paunchy physique lacks the idealized proportions found in representations of royalty and nobility; he was, after all, only a minor official. The wood medium permitted the artist to omit the back slab and try a freer pose. Actually, what we see is the wood core that was originally covered with painted

3-15 *Ka-Aper (Sheikh el Beled)*, from his tomb at Saqqara, *c.* 2400 B.C. Wood, approx. 43" high. Egyptian Museum, Cairo. (Partially restored.)

plaster, a common procedure when soft or unattractive woods were used.

Painting and Relief

The scenes in painted limestone relief that decorate the walls of the tomb of an Old Kingdom official, Ti, typify the subjects favored by the patrons. Most often they are of agriculture and hunting (FIG. 3-16), activities that represent the fundamental human concern with nature and that are associated with the provisioning of the ka in the hereafter. Ti, his men, and his boats move slowly through the marshes, hunting birds and hippopotamuses in a dense growth of towering papyrus. The slender, reedy stems of the plants are delineated with repeated fine grooves that fan out

3-16 *Hippopotamus Hunt*, tomb of Ti, Saqqara, *c.* 2400 B.C. Painted limestone relief, approx. 48" high.

gracefully at the top into a commotion of frightened birds and stalking beasts. Beneath the boats, the water, signified by a pattern of wavy lines, is crowded with hippopotamuses and other aquatic fauna. Ti's men seem frantically busy with their spears, while Ti himself, looming twice their size, stands impassive and aloof in the formal stance we have seen in the figure of Hesire (FIG. 3-3). The outsize and ideal proportions bespeak Ti's rank, as does the conventional pose, which contrasts with the realistically rendered activity of his diminutive servants and particularly with the precisely observed figures of the birds and animals among the papyrus buds.

A rare and fine example of Old Kingdom painting is the frieze called the *Geese of Medum* (FIG. 3-17). In the prehistoric art of the caves, the rock paintings, and the art of Mesopotamia, we have admired the peculiar sensitivity of early artists to the animal fig-

3-17   *Geese of Medum, c.* 2530 B.C. Tempera on plaster, approx. 18" × 68". Egyptian Museum, Cairo.

ure. They seem to have empathized with the non-human creature, to have possessed what Keats called "negative capability"—the power almost to share the being of the animal and to feel as it feels.

The *fresco secco* technique used, in which the artist lets the plaster dry before he paints on it, lends itself to slow and meticulous work, encouraging the trained professional to take pains in rendering the image and in expressing his exact knowledge of its subject. The delicate, prehensile necks of the geese, the beaks, the suppleness of the bodies, and the animals' characteristic step and carriage are rendered with an exactitude and discernment that would elicit the admiration of an Audubon. The firm, strong execution of the figures is the work of an expert, with superbly trained eye and hand, probably conscious of his power and proud of it. It is probable, too, that religious motives mingled here with esthetic ones, for, after all, once a tomb was sealed no mortal eyes were ever expected to see the paintings again. It must have been thought that, in the darkness and silence, the pictures worked their own spell, creating a force that would serve the ka eternally; some of the magic working of the cave paintings seems to persist here.

The art of the Old Kingdom is the classic art of Egypt in that its conventions, definitively established, remained the basis of subsequent styles of Egyptian art through three millennia.

THE MIDDLE KINGDOM

About 2150 B.C., the power of the pharaohs was challenged by ambitious feudal lords; for about a century, the land was in a state of civil unrest and near anarchy. Eventually, a Theban ruler, Mentuhotep II, managed to unite Egypt again under the rule of a single king. In the Eleventh, Twelfth, and Thirteenth Dynasties (the *Middle Kingdom*) that followed, art was revived and a rich and varied literature appeared.

Rock-cut Tombs

Among the most characteristic remains of the Middle Kingdom are the private rock-cut tombs at Beni Hasan (FIG. 3-18). One of the best preserved is the tomb of Khnumhotep, who boasted in an inscription of its elaborateness, saying that its doors were of cedar, seven cubits (about 20 feet) high. Expressing the characteristic Egyptian attitude toward the last resting place, he added:

> My chief nobility was: I executed a cliff-tomb, for a man should imitate that which his father does. My father made for himself a house of the *ka* in the town of Menofret, of good stone of Ayan, in order to perpetuate his name forever and establish it eternally.

The rock-cut tombs of the Middle Kingdom largely replaced the Old Kingdom mastabas. Hollowed out of the living rock at remote sites, these tombs, fronted by a shallow, columned portico, contained the fundamental units of Egyptian architecture—portico or vestibule, columned hall, and sacred chamber (FIG. 3-19). The interior of the rock-cut tomb of Amenem-

3-18   Rock-cut tombs, Beni Hasan, *c.* 1900 B.C.

3-19 Plan *(bottom)* and section *(top)* of a rock-cut tomb. (After Sir Banister Fletcher.)

0 10 20 30 FEET
0 3 6 9 METERS

3-20 Interior of the tomb of Amenemhet, Beni Hasan, *c.* 1930 B.C.

het (FIG. 3-20) shows the hall, the *reserve columns* of which serve no supporting function, being, like the portico columns, continuous parts of the rock fabric. (Note the broken column in the rear, suspended from the ceiling like a stalactite.) Tomb walls were decorated with paintings and painted reliefs, as in former times, and the subjects were much the same.

Painting and Sculpture

A painting from the tomb of Khnumhotep (FIG. 3-21) shows servants feeding oryxes (antelopes), the domesticated pets of the Egyptian gentry. Here the artist has made a daring attempt to present the shoulders and backs of both human figures by

3-21 *Feeding of Oryxes*, fresco from the tomb of Khnumhotep, Beni Hasan, *c.* 1900 B.C.

3-22 *Sesostris III* (ruled 1878–1843 B.C.), originally from the Temple of Medamud. Granite, 11" high. Egyptian Museum, Cairo.

foreshortening. However, working within the rigid framework of convention, he simply joined their front and side views in an unusual combination. As a result, the action reads convincingly enough, but the figures fall short of optical consistency.

In portrait sculpture of the Middle Kingdom, a somewhat deepened perception of personality and mood can be noted, as shown in a partially damaged head thought to be of Sesostris III (FIG. 3-22). The head, detail of a sphinx, has a pessimistic expression that, interestingly, reflects the dominant mood of the literature of the Middle Kingdom. The strong mouth, the drooping lines about the nose and eyes, and the shadowy brows show a determined ruler, who had also shared in the cares of the world, sunk in brooding meditation. The portrait is strangely different from the typical realistic and "public" Old Kingdom face, being personal, almost intimate, in its revelation of the mark of anxiety a troubled age might leave on the soul of a king.

THE HYKSOS AND THE NEW KINGDOM

This anxiety may have reflected premonitions of disaster. The Middle Kingdom, like the one that pre-

ceded it, disintegrated, and power passed to a line of migrant Semitic Asiatics from the Syrian and Mesopotamian uplands—the Hyksos, or Shepherd Kings, who brought with them a new and influential culture and that practical instrument, the horse. The invasion and domination of the Hyksos, traditionally thought to have been a disaster, was latterly reassessed as a seminal influence that kept Egypt in the mainstream of the Bronze Age culture in the eastern Mediterranean. In any event, the innovations introduced by the Hyksos, especially in weaponry and the techniques of war, contributed to their own overthrow by native Egyptian kings of the Seventeenth Dynasty. Ahmose I, final conqueror of the Hyksos and first king of the Eighteenth Dynasty, ushered in the New Kingdom (the Empire)—the most brilliant period of Egypt's long history. At this time, Egypt extended her borders by conquest from the Euphrates in the east deep into Nubia (the Sudan) to the south. Wider foreign contact was afforded by visiting embassies and by new and profitable trade with Asia and the Aegean islands. The booty taken in wars and the tribute exacted from subjected peoples made possible the development of a new capital, Thebes, which became a great and luxurious metropolis with magnificent palaces, tombs, and temples along both banks of the Nile. Thutmose III, who died in the fifty-first year of his reign in the second half of the fifteen century B.C., was the greatest pharaoh of the New Kingdom, if not of all Egyptian history, and his successors continued the grand traditions he established. The optimistic mood of the new era is recorded in an inscription above the heads of revelers in a painting now in the British Museum:

> The Earth-god has implanted his beauty in every
> body.
> The Creator has done this with his two hands as balm
> to his heart.
> The channels are filled with waters anew
> And the land is flooded with his love.

Architecture

If the most impressive monuments of the Old Kingdom are its pyramids, those of the New Kingdom are its grandiose temples. Burial still demanded the elaborate care shown earlier, and, partly following in the tradition of the Middle Kingdom, nobles and kings hollowed their burial chambers deep in the cliffs west of the Nile. In the Valley of the Kings, the rock-cut tombs are approached by long corridors, extending as deep as 500 feet into the hillside. The entrances to these burial chambers were carefully concealed, and the mortuary temples were built along the banks of the Nile at some distance from the tombs. The temple, which provided the king with a place for worshiping his patron god and then served as a mortuary chapel after his death, became elaborate and sumptuous, befitting both the king and the god.

The noblest of these royal mortuary temples, at Deir el-Bahri, was that of Queen Hatshepsut (FIG. 3-23), who preceded the conquering pharaoh Thutmose III. A princess who became queen when there were no legitimate male heirs, she boasted of having made the "Two Lands to labour with bowed back for her." Built about 1450 B.C. along the lines of the neighboring Middle Kingdom temple of Mentuhotep I, the structure rises from the valley floor in three colonnaded terraces connected by ramps. It is remarkable how visually well suited the structure is to its natural setting. The long horizontals and verticals of the colonnades and their rhythm of light and dark repeat, in man-made symmetry, the pattern of the

rocky cliffs above. The pillars of the colonnades, which are either simply rectangular or *chamfered* (beveled, or flattened at the edges) into 16 sides, are esthetically proportioned and spaced. Statues in the round, perhaps 200, were intimately associated with the temple architecture. So also was the brightly painted low relief that covered the walls and whose remnants may still be seen. The relief represented Hatshepsut's birth, coronation, and great deeds. In her day, the terraces were not the barren places they are now but gardens with frankincense trees and rare plants brought by the queen from an expedition to the faraway "land of Punt" on the Red Sea, an event that figures prominently in the temple's relief decorations.

The immense rock-cut temple of Ramses II, Egypt's last great warrior–pharaoh, who lived a little before the exodus from Egypt under Moses, was built far up the Nile at Abu Simbel. Ramses, proud of his many campaigns to restore the empire, augmented his

3-23 Mortuary Temple of Queen Hatshepsut, Deir el-Bahri, *c.* 1450 B.C.

3-24   Temple of Ramses II, Abu Simbel, 1257 B.C. Colossi approx. 60' high.

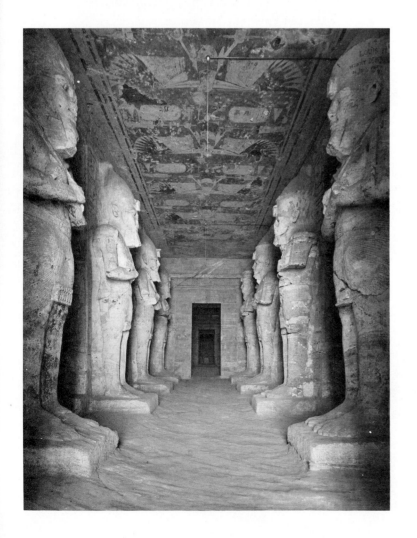

greatness by placing four colossal images of himself in the temple façade (FIG. 3-24). The whole monument was moved in 1968 to save it from submersion in the new Aswan High Dam reservoir. In later times, the glories of kings and emperors in periods of conquest and imperial grandeur were also celebrated in huge monuments; gigantism seems characteristic of much of the art of empires that have reached their peaks. Here, Ramses' artists use the principle of augmentation both by size and by repetition. The massive statues lack the refinement of earlier periods, because much is sacrificed to overwhelming size. The grand scale is carried out in the interior also (FIG. 3-25). The giant figures of the king, formed as columns, face each other across the narrow corridor; their exaggerated mass appears to appropriate the architectural space. The columns are *reserved* (hewn from the living rock) and have no bearing function; in this respect, they resemble the columns in the tombs at Beni Hasan. The figure-as-column, the *caryatid* form, will appear later in Greek architecture, and its presence at Abu Simbel may be its earliest use.

Distinct from the mortuary temples were the edifices built to honor one or more of the gods and often added to by successive kings until they reached gigantic size, as seen in the temples at Karnak and Luxor (FIGS. 3-30 and 3-31). These temples all had similar plans. A typical *pylon temple* plan (FIG. 3-26) is bilaterally symmetrical along a single axis that runs

3-25   Interior of the Temple of Ramses II, Abu Simbel.

3-26 Plan of a typical pylon temple.

1. Pylon
2. Court
3. Hypostyle hall
4. Sanctuary

5. Girdle wall
6. Colossal statues of the pharaoh
7. Obelisks
8. Avenue of recumbent animals

from an approaching avenue through a colonnaded court and hall into a dimly lighted sanctuary. The dominating feature of the statuary-lined approach is the façade of the pylon, simple and massive, with sloping walls. The pylon shown in FIG. 3-27 is from the Temple of Horus at Edfu, which was constructed during the Ptolemaic period and is a striking monument to the persistence of Egyptian artistic traditions. Its broad surface is broken by the doorway with its overshadowing cornice, by deep channels to hold

great flagstaffs, and by sunken reliefs. Moldings finish its top and sides. Within is an open court colonnaded on three sides, followed by a hall between court and sanctuary, its long axis placed at right angles to that of the entire building complex. This "broad" or *hypostyle* hall (that is, having a roof supported by columns) is crowded with massive columns and roofed by stone slabs carried on lintels that rest, in turn, on impost blocks supported by the great capitals. In the hypostyle hall of the Temple of Amen-Re

3-27 Pylon Temple of Horus, Edfu, *c.* 237–212 B.C.

3-28 Plan of the Temple of Amen-Re, Karnak. (After Sir Banister Fletcher.) Dates in parentheses indicate time of construction.

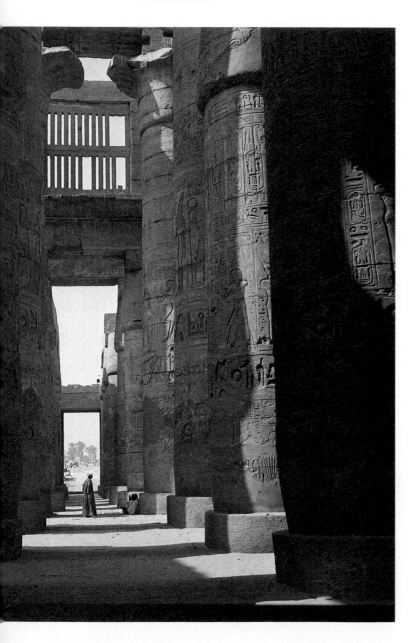

3-29 Hypostyle hall, Temple of Amen-Re, Karnak, *c.* 1280 B.C.

(a variant reading is Imen-Re) at Karnak (FIGS. 3-28, 3-29, 3-30), the columns are 66 feet high, and the capitals are 22 feet in diameter at the top, large enough to hold 100 men. The Egyptians, who did not use cement, depended on the weight of the huge stones to hold the columns in place. In many hypostyle halls, the central rows of columns were higher than those at the sides, raising the roof of the central section and creating a *clerestory.* Openings in the clerestory permitted light to filter into the interior. This method of construction appears in primitive form as early as the Old Kingdom in the valley temple of the Pyramid of Khafre. Evidently an Egyptian invention, it has remained an important architectural feature down to our times and was particularly important in the design of Medieval cathedrals.

The Egyptian temple plan evolved from ritualistic requirements. Only the pharaoh and the priest could enter the sanctuary; a chosen few were admitted to the hypostyle hall; the mass of the people was allowed only as far as the open court, and a high mudbrick wall shut off the site from the outside world. The conservative Egyptians did not deviate from this basic plan for hundreds of years. The *corridor axis*, which dominates the plan, makes the temple not so much a building as, in Oswald Spengler's phrase, "a path enclosed by mighty masonry." Like the Nile that it almost symbolizes, the corridor may have been an expression of the Egyptian concept of life. Spengler suggests that the Egyptian saw himself moving down a narrow, predestined life-path that ended before the judges of the dead. The whole of Egyptian culture can be regarded as illustrating this theme (FIG. 3-29).

A model of the hypostyle hall at Karnak (FIG. 3-30)

3-30 Model of hypostyle hall, Temple of Amen-Re, Karnak, c. 1280 B.C. Metropolitan Museum of Art, New York (bequest of Levi Hale Willard).

shows the smooth-shafted (as opposed to fluted) Egyptian columns with the two basic types of capitals: bud-shaped and bell-shaped, or campaniform. Although the columns are structural members—unlike the reserve "columns" of the Middle Kingdom tombs at Beni Hasan and the figure-columns at Abu Simbel (see FIGS. 3-20 and 3-25)—their function as carriers of vertical stress is almost hidden by horizontal bands of relief sculpture and painting, suggesting that the intention of the architects was not to emphasize the functional role of the columns so much as to utilize them as surface for decoration. This contrasts sharply with later Greek practice, which keeps the vertical lines of the column emphatic and its function clear by freeing the surfaces of the shaft from all ornament.

The courts and colonnades of the Temple of Amen-Mut-Khonsu at Luxor (FIG. 3-31) exhibit the columnar

3-31 *Left:* court and pylon of Ramses II, *c.* 1280 B.C.; *right:* court and colonnade of Amenhotep III, *c.* 1370 B.C. Temple of Amen-Mut-Khonsu, Luxor.

style especially well. The post-and-lintel structure of the temples appears to have had its origin in an early building technique that used firmly bound sheaves of reeds and swamp plants as roof supports in adobe structures. Evidence of this origin is seen in the columns themselves, which are carved to resemble lotus or papyrus, with bud-cluster or bell-shaped capitals. Painted decorations, traces of which still can be seen on the surfaces of the shafts and capitals, emphasized these natural details. In fact, the flora of the Nile valley supplied the basic decorative motifs in all Egyptian art. With respect to a possible Mesopotamian influence, it is important to note that, until the time of Persia, Mesopotamian architecture seldom employed the post-and-lintel system; the column was rarely seen. Moreover, the formalization of plant forms into the rigid profiles of architecture is precisely the same thing as the formalization of human bodies and action that the Egyptians achieved so skillfully in tomb painting and sculpture.

3-32 *Senmut with Princess Nefrua*, Thebes, *c.* 1450 B.C. Black stone, block statue approx. 40″ high. Staatliche Museen, Berlin.

3-33 *Fowling Scene*, wall painting from the tomb of Nebamun (?), Thebes, *c.* 1450 B.C. Painting on dry plaster. British Museum, London.

Sculpture and Painting

This radical simplification of form, which preserves in the ka figures the cubic essence of the block, can be seen to advantage in the statue showing Senmut (Queen Hatshepsut's chancellor and architect of her temple at Deir el-Bahri) with Princess Nefrua (FIG. 3-32). This curious design, evidently popular in the New Kingdom, concentrates attention on the portrait head and leaves the "body" a cubic block, given over to inscriptions. With surfaces turning subtly about smoothly rounded corners, it seems another expression of the Egyptian fondness for volume enclosed by flat, unambiguous planes. The polished stone shape has its own simple beauty.

The persistence of the formulas for projection of an image onto a flat surface can be seen in wall paintings in the tomb of Nebamun (?) at Thebes (FIG. 3-33), which dates from the Eighteenth Dynasty. The deceased nobleman is standing in his boat, driving the birds from a papyrus swamp with his throwstick. In his right hand, he holds three birds he has caught; a wild cat, on a papyrus stem just in front of him, has caught two more in her claws and is holding the wings of a third in her teeth. His two companions, perhaps his wife and daughter, their figures scaled down in proportion to their rank, are enjoying the lotuses they have gathered. Although the water and the figures are represented by the usual conventions, cat, fish, and birds show a naturalism based on visual perception similar to what we see in the *Geese of Medum* (FIG. 3-17).

The tomb chamber, as we see it in the well-preserved New Kingdom tomb of Nakht at Thebes (FIG. 3-34), is similar to the tomb chambers of the Old Kingdom. In the mural, the system of registers still preserves the rigid separation of the zones of action; but some innovations of detail appear: here and there, a new liveliness and a closer inspection of life. Another fresco fragment probably from the tomb of

3-34 Tomb of Nakht, Thebes, c. 1450 B.C. Fresco on rear wall 60″ × 55″.

Nebamun (FIG. 3-35) shows four ladies watching and apparently participating in a musicale and dance in which two nimble little nude dancing girls perform. The overlapping of the girls' figures, facing in opposite directions, and the rather complicated gyrations of the dance are carefully and accurately observed and executed. Of the four ladies of the audience, two at the left are represented conventionally, but the

3-35 *Musicians and Dancers*, detail of a wall painting from the tomb of Nebamun (?), Thebes, c. 1450 B.C. Fragment 11¾″ × 27¼″. British Museum, London.

other two face us in what is a most unusual and very rarely attempted frontal pose. They seem to beat time to the dance; one of them plays the reeds, and the artist takes careful note of the soles of their feet as they sit cross-legged. This informality constitutes a relaxation not only of the stiff rules of representation but also of the set themes once thought appropriate for tomb painting. We also may have here the reflection of a more luxurious mode of life in the New Kingdom; at this point, the ka may have required not only necessities and comforts in the hereafter but formal entertainment as well.

Akhenaton and the Amarna Period

These small variations of age-old formulas heralded a short but violent upheaval in Egyptian art—the only major break in the continuity of its long tradition. In the fourteenth century B.C., the emperor Amenophis IV (Amenhotep IV), later known as Akhenaton (or Ikhnaton), proclaimed the religion of Aton, the universal and only god of the sun. He thus contested and abolished the native cult of Amen, sacred to Thebes and professed by the mighty priests of such temples as Karnak and Luxor, as well as by the people of Egypt. He blotted out the name of Amen from all inscriptions, and even from his own name and that of his father, Amenophis III. He emptied the great temples, embittered the priests and people, and moved his capital downriver from Thebes to a site now called Tel el-Amarna, where he built his own city and shrines to the religion of Aton.

This action by Amenophis IV—now Akhenaton—although it might savor of the psychotic or of the fanaticism of sudden conversion, was portended by events in the formation and expansion of the power of the great Eighteenth Dynasty. Egyptian might had formed the first world empire. The conquering imperialist pharaohs—ruling over Syria and Nubia, bordered by the Hittites, and checking the penetration of the Mitanni—had gradually enlarged the powers of their old sun god, Amen, to make him not simply god of the Egyptians, but god of all men. Even before Egypt had become the main force in the Mediterranean world—before, as James Breasted describes it, "the Egyptian supremacy [was] undisputed from the Greek islands, the coasts of Asia Minor, and the highlands of the Upper Euphrates on the north to the Fourth Cataract of the Nile on the south"—Thutmose I, a founder of the fortunes of the dynasty, could say of the sun god that his kingdom extended as far as "the circuit of the sun." And the military pharaoh, Thutmose III, said of this aggrandized god: "He seeth the whole earth hourly." Thus, Akhenaton was exploiting already-gathering forces when he raised the imperialized god of the sun to be the only god of all the earth and proscribed any rival as blasphemous. He appropriated to himself the new and universal god, making himself both the son and prophet, even the sole experient, of Aton. To him alone could the god make revelation. Akhenaton's hymn to Aton survives:

> Thou art in my heart.
> There is no other that knoweth thee
> Save thy son Ikhnaton.
> Thou hast made him wise
> In thy designs and might.
> The world is in thy hand,
> Even as thou hast made them . . .
> Thou didst establish the world,
> And raise them up for thy son,
> Who came forth from thy limbs,
> The king of Upper and Lower Egypt,
> Living in Truth, Lord of Two Lands . . .

Egypt has left us the ingredients, as it were, of the later monotheisms so influential in the world. Akhenaton's brief theocracy seems to have embodied the seeds of later concepts of one god, of an eternal

3-36 *Akhenaton*, from a pillar statue in the Temple of Amen-Re, Karnak, *c.* 1375 B.C. Sandstone, approx. 13' high. Egyptian Museum, Cairo.

3-37 *Queen Nefertiti*, Tel el-Amarna, *c.* 1360 B.C. Limestone, approx. 20″ high. Ägyptisches Museum, Berlin.

son who is also a king, of a world created by that one god, and of the intimate revelation of that god's spirit to a chosen one.

One effect of the new religious philosophy seems to have been a temporary relaxation of the Egyptians' preoccupation with death and the hereafter and a correspondingly greater concern with life on this earth. In art, this change is reflected in a different attitude toward the representation of the human figure. Artists aimed for a new sense of life and movement, expressed in swelling, curvilinear forms; their long-fostered naturalistic tendencies, thus far confined largely to the representation of animals, were extended not only to the lowly human figure but, significantly, to royalty as well. A colossal statue of Akhenaton (FIG. 3-36) from Karnak retains the standard frontal pose; but the strange, epicene body, with its curving contours, and the long, full-lipped face, heavy-lidded eyes, and dreaming expression, show that the artist has studied his subject with care and rendered it with all the physiognomical and physical irregularities that were part of the king's actual appearance. The predilection for curved lines stresses the softness of the slack, big-hipped body that is a far cry indeed from the heroically proportioned figures of Akhenaton's predecessors. In a daring mixture of naturalism and stylization, the artist has given us an informal and uncompromising portrayal of the king that is charged with both vitality and a psychological complexity that has been called expressionistic.

The famous painted limestone bust of Akhenaton's queen, Nefertiti (FIG. 3-37), exhibits a similar expression of entranced musing and an almost mannered sensitivity and delicacy of curving contour. It may be that the sculptor was deliberately alluding to a heavy flower on its slender stalk when he exaggerated the weight of the crowned head and the length of the almost serpentine neck. One thinks of those modern descendants of Queen Nefertiti—the models in the fashion magazines, with their gaunt, swaying frames, mask-like, pallid faces, and enormous, shadowed eyes. As the modern mannerism shapes the living model to its dictates, so the sculptors of Tel el-Amarna may have had some standard of spiritual beauty to which they adjusted the actual likenesses of their subjects. Even so, one is made very much aware of the reality of the queen through her contrived mask of beauty, a masterpiece of cosmetic art. The Nefertiti bust is one more example of that elegant blending of the real and the formal that we have noticed so often in the art of the Ancient Near East.

During the last three years of his reign Akhenaton's co-regent was his half-brother, Smenkhkare. A relief from Tel el-Amarna may show Smenkhkare and his wife Meritaten (FIG. 3-38) in an informal, even intimate, pose that contrasts strongly with the traditional formality in the representation of exalted persons. Once-rigid lines have become undulating curves, and the pose of Smenkhkare has no known precedent. The prince leans casually on his staff, one leg at ease—an attitude that presumes knowledge on the sculptor's part of the flexible shift of body masses, a principle not really grasped until the Classical period in Greece. This quite realistic detail accompanies others that are the result of a freer expression of what is observed: details of costume and the departures from the traditional formality, such as the elongated and bulging head of Meritaten and the prominent bellies that characterize figures of the Amarna School. Proportions of figures no longer depend on rank; the princess is depicted in the same scale as her husband on the basis of their natural proportions.

We have seen some slight loosening of the conventions of sculpture and painting even before Akhenaton. But the Amarna style (and a subsequent re-

3-38 *King Smenkhkare and Meritaten* (?), Tel el-Amarna, *c.* 1360 B.C. Painted limestone relief, approx. 9½" high. Staatliche Museen, Berlin.

turn to the earlier tradition) marks a break too abrupt and emphatic to permit us to conclude that the style was simply a local, native flowering. It is at least possible that there was some influence from the Mediterranean world. We know that Egypt dealt commercially with Crete beginning in the Predynastic period, and the livelier, less convention-bound art of the Minoans could have proved suggestive and stimulating to the Amarna artists. Although the Cretan palace culture came to an end around 1400 B.C. (see Chapter 4), and Akhenaton did not ascend the Egyptian throne until 1378 (first as co-ruler with his father), the time lag does not seem too great to preclude such an influence. It may be that some Cretan artists, finding refuge in Egypt and a sympathetic artistic climate under Akhenaton's rule, fertilized the Amarna style.

The Tomb of Tutankhamen and the Late Period

The survival of the Amarna style is seen in the fabulously rich art and artifacts found in the uniquely unplundered tomb of the young pharoah Tutankhamen (1361–1352 B.C.), known in modern folklore as "King Tut." The treasures of the tomb—sculpture, furniture, jewelry, and accessories of all sorts—were uncovered in 1922; the adventure of their discovery gained world renown. Installed in the Egyptian Museum in Cairo, a selection of these treasures were made available to a larger public when, in the late 1970s, they were sent on a tour of museums throughout the world. It has been estimated that the collection attracted the greatest number of visitors recorded for any single tour of works of art. It reawakened public interest in the legend of "King Tut" and undoubtedly stimulated appreciation of ancient Egyptian art.

The principal monument in the collection is, of course, the tomb of the king himself (FIG. 3-39). The royal mummy reposed in the innermost of three coffins, nested one within the other and shaped in the form of Osiris, god of death. This was the most sumptuously wrought of the three. Made of beaten gold (about a quarter ton of it) and inlaid with such semiprecious stones as lapis lazuli, turquoise, and carnelian, it is a supreme monument to the sculptor's and goldsmith's craft. The portrait (death) mask, which covered the king's face, shows his features relaxed in a kind of musing serenity that betokens his confidence in eternal life (FIG. 3-40). Despite a lingering Amarnan sensitivity and softness of contour and

3-39   The second coffin of Tutankhamen (ruled 1361–1352 B.C.). Gilded wood inlaid with glass paste, 6' 7" long. Egyptian Museum, Cairo.

3-40 Death mask of Tutankhamen, innermost coffin. Gold with inlay of semiprecious stones. Egyptian Museum, Cairo.

subtlety in the reading of personality, there is a general effect of grandeur and richness expressive of Egyptian power, pride, and affluence at the time of the onset of empire.

That the king must have defined his mission as imperial conqueror, and would have himself so represented, is shown in the panels of a painted chest from the treasures of Tut's tomb (FIG. 3-41). The lid panel shows the king as a great hunter, pursuing droves of fleeing animals in the desert, and the side panel shows him as a great warrior—the double advertisement of royal power familiar in Assyrian art. From a war chariot drawn by spirited, plumed horses, Tutankhamen draws his bow against a cluster of bearded, Asian enemies, who fall in confusion before him. He slays the enemy, like game, in great numbers. Above him, the sun disc shines on his victory and the vulture goddess Nekh-bet, his special protectress, shelters him with her wings. Behind him are three tiers of war chariots in diminutive scale, which serve to magnify the figure of the king and to increase the count of his warriors. The themes are traditional, but the fluid, curvilinear forms, the dynamic compositions with their emphasis on movement and action, and the disposition of the hunted, overthrown animals and enemy—who, freed of conventional ground lines, race wildly across the panels— are features reminiscent not only of the Amarna style but, as we shall see, of the lively naturalism of Cretan art as well.

The pharaohs who followed Akhenaton reestab-lished the cult and priesthood of Amen, restored the temples and the inscriptions, and returned to the old manner in art. Akhenaton's monuments were wiped out, his heresy anathematized, and his city abandoned. The conservative reaction can be seen in a relief of the pharaoh Seti I (FIG. 3-42). The rigid, flattened shapes repeat the formula of the *Palette of Narmer* (FIG. 3-2) and the static formality of Old Kingdom art.

Seti I and his successor, Ramses II, were builders both of the Egyptian empire and the titanic colonnades of Karnak at Thebes, where their victories are celebrated in thousands of feet of relief sculpture and hieroglyphic inscription. Karnak was a monument to the Theban god Amen, restored to favor after the her-

3-41 Painted chest, tomb of Tutankhamen, Thebes, *c.* 1350 B.C. Approx. 20″ long. Egyptian Museum, Cairo.

3-42 *Seti I Offering*, Temple of Seti I, Abydos, *c.* 1300 B.C. Painted limestone. Louvre, Paris.

esy of Akhenaton. In addition to his building at Karnak, Seti I constructed, some 16 miles northwest of Karnak at Abydos, a great temple to the death god Osiris, whose religion he expanded from a local to a national one. The gods of Thebes were official, belonging to the state religion; their temples were in the care of an elite, privileged priesthood isolated from the people. But Osiris—god of the dead and king of the underworld, but also giver of eternal life—became the object of devotion for all Egyptians, the humblest among them. According to the myth of Osiris, he is slain and dismembered but rises again and, by his resurrection, conquers death; thus, he becomes the source of immortality for all humanity.

The ritual of the cult of Osiris is recorded in collections of spells, prayers, formulas, and counsels that compose the so-called "Book of the Dead." Illuminated papyrus scrolls, some as long as 70 feet, were the essential equipment of the tombs of well-to-do persons. The papyrus scroll of Hu-Nefer, found in his tomb in the Theban necropolis, represents the final judgment of the deceased (FIG. 3-43). At the left, he is led into the hall of judgment by Anubis, the jackal-headed god of embalming. Anubis then adjusts the scales to weigh the heart of the dead man against the feather of the goddess Maat, protectress of truth and right. A hybrid monster, half hippopotamus and half

3-43 *Psychostasis* ("soul-raising") *of Hu-Nefer*, Thebes. Papyrus scroll 2¾" high. British Museum, London.

lion, the devourer of souls awaits the decision of the scales; if it is unfavorable to the deceased, the monster will destroy his soul on the spot. The ibis-headed god Thoth records the proceedings. Above, the gods of the Egyptian pantheon are arranged as witnesses. Having been justified by the scales, Hu-Nefer is brought by Osiris' son, the falcon-headed Horus, into the presence of the green-faced Osiris, the goddess Isis (wife of Osiris and mother of Horus), and the goddess Nephtys (the sister of Isis and Osiris) to receive the award of eternal life.

The figures have all the formality of stance, shape, and attitude—all the flat linearity—that we find in the art of the Old Kingdom. Alike abstract figures and hieroglyphs are aligned rigidly along the same planar surface. There is nothing here of the flexible, curvilinear style suggestive of movement that is evident in the art of Amarna and Tutankhamen. The conservatism is complete, as it is in the Seti I relief.

And so, in essence, it remained through the last centuries of Egyptian figural art. During this time, Egypt lost the commanding role it once had played in the Near East. The empire dwindled away, and the land was invaded, occupied, and ruled by foreign powers, Assyria and Persia, and peoples from the west (Libya) and south (Nubia–Ethiopia). From the period of the last-mentioned reign in Egypt, a portrait statue, *Mentemhet the Governor* (FIG. 3-44), survives that easily could be mistaken for a Memphite work of the Old Kingdom (FIGS. 3-13 and 3-15)—yet it dates from the Twenty-fifth Dynasty in the seventh century B.C. The Old Kingdom formulas, conventions, and details of representation are all here in summary: the rigidity of stance, frontality, spareness of silhouette, arms at the side, one leg advanced, the kilt, the headdress—even the material (granite) and the carving technique recall the Old Kingdom. Only the realism of the head, with its rough, almost brutal, characterization, differentiates the work from that of the earlier age. The pharaohs of the late period deliberately referred back to the art of Egypt's classical phase to give authority to their royal image; religious and political motives only partly explain this deliberate archaism, however. As we noted at the beginning of this chapter, conservatism is a trait of the Egyptian character—perhaps the principal one. The Egyptians' resistance to significant change over a period of almost 3,000 years may stem from a profound religiosity inspired by the steady sun, the eternal desert, the slow pulse of the Nilotic seasons, and the enduring conviction that life is not really interrupted by death.

3-44 *Mentemhet the Governor, c.* 650 B.C. Granite, 53" high. Egyptian Museum, Cairo.

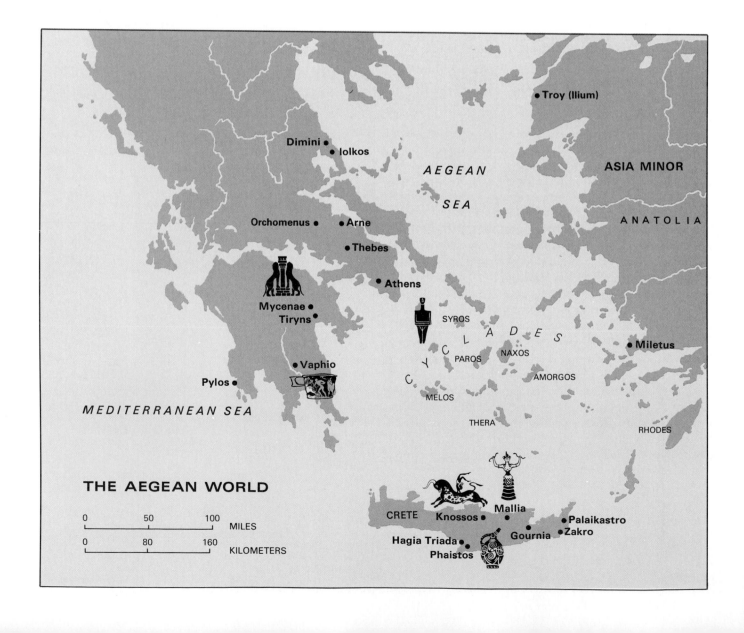

4

THE AEGEAN WORLD

Troy (Ilium)

ASIA MINOR

ANATOLIA

AEGEAN

SEA

Dimini
Iolkos

Orchomenus
Arne

Thebes

Athens

SYROS

C   L   A   D   E   S

Mycenae
Tiryns

Miletus

PAROS
NAXOS

Vaphio

AMORGOS

Pylos

MELOS

MEDITERRANEAN SEA

THERA

RHODES

Mallia

Palaikastro

CRETE   Knossos

Gournia
Zakro

Hagia Triada

Phaistos

0   50   100   MILES

0   80   160   KILOMETERS

THE ART OF THE AEGEAN

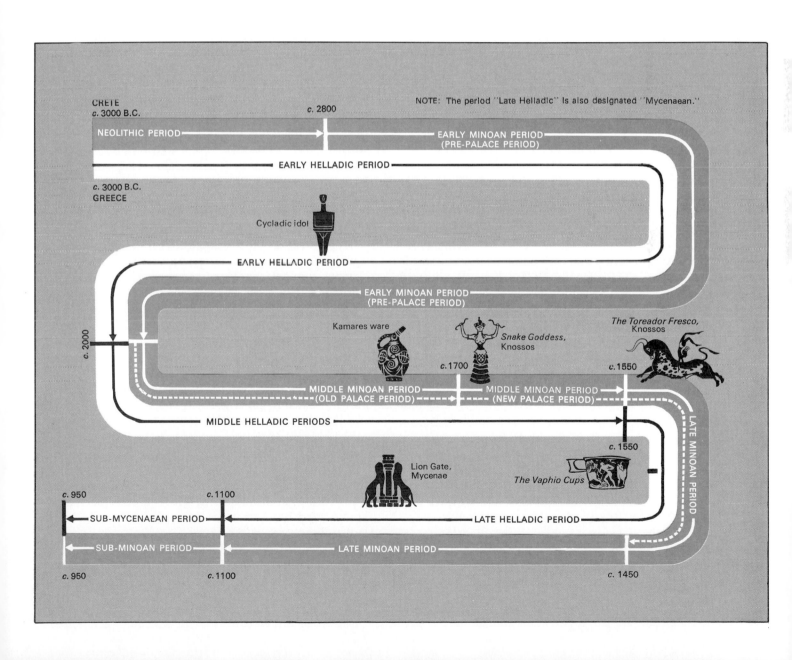

CRETE
c. 3000 B.C.   c. 2800   NOTE: The period ''Late Helladic'' Is also designated ''Mycenaean.''

NEOLITHIC PERIOD ——→   EARLY MINOAN PERIOD ——→
                                                            (PRE-PALACE PERIOD)

—————————— EARLY HELLADIC PERIOD ——————————

c. 3000 B.C.
GREECE

Cycladic idol

———— EARLY HELLADIC PERIOD ————

—————— EARLY MINOAN PERIOD ——————
           (PRE-PALACE PERIOD)

Kamares ware   Snake Goddess,   The Toreador Fresco,
                        Knossos   Knossos

c. 2000   c. 1700   c. 1550

←—— MIDDLE MINOAN PERIOD ——→ ←—— MIDDLE MINOAN PERIOD ——→
       (OLD PALACE PERIOD)   (NEW PALACE PERIOD)

←———— MIDDLE HELLADIC PERIODS ————→

                                              c. 1550

                        Lion Gate,
                        Mycenae   The Vaphio Cups

c. 950   c. 1100

←—— SUB-MYCENAEAN PERIOD ——→ ←————————— LATE HELLADIC PERIOD ——————————→

←—— SUB-MINOAN PERIOD ——→ ←————————— LATE MINOAN PERIOD ——————————→

c. 950   c. 1100   c. 1450

LATE MINOAN PERIOD

H OMER, IN THE *Iliad*, wrote of the might and splendor of the Achaean host deployed for war against Troy:

So clan after clan poured out from the ships and huts onto the plain of Scamander, and . . . found their places in the flowery meadows by the river, innumerable as the leaves and blossoms in their season . . . the Locrians . . . the Athenians . . . the citizens of Argos and Tiryns of the Great Walls . . . troops from the great stronghold of Mycenae, from wealthy Corinth . . . from Lacedaemon . . . from Pylos . . . Knossos in Crete, Phaistos . . . and the other troops that had their homes in Crete of the Hundred Towns. . . .

The list goes on and on, outlining the peoples and the geography of the Aegean world in intimate detail. Until about 1870, historians of ancient Greece, although they acknowledged Homer's superb art, discounted him as a historian, attributing the profusion of his names and places to the rich abundance of his imagination. The prehistory of Classical Greece remained shadowy and lost—as the historians believed—in an impenetrable world of myth. That they had done less than justice to the truth of Homer's account—or, for that matter, to ancient Greek literary sources in general—was proved by a German amateur archeologist, Heinrich Schliemann, who, between 1870 and his death 20 years later, uncovered some of the very cities of the Trojan and Achaean heroes Homer celebrates: Troy, Mycenae, Orchomenus, Tiryns. In 1870, at Hissarlik in the northwest corner of Asia Minor, which Schliemann's knowledge of the *Iliad* had led him to believe was the site of Homer's Troy, he dug into a vast *tell*, or mound, and found there a number of fortified cities built on the remains of another, together with the evidence of their destruction by fire. Schliemann continued his excavations at Mycenae on the Greek mainland, from which, he believed, Agamemnon and Achilles had sailed to avenge the capture of Helen, and here his finds were even more startling. Massive fortress-palaces, elaborate tombs, quantities of gold jewelry and ornaments, cups, and inlaid weapons revealed a magnificent pre-Classical civilization.

But further discoveries were to prove that Mycenae had not been its center. An important Greek legend told of Minos, king of Crete, who had exacted from Athens a tribute of youths and maidens to be fed to the Minotaur (half-bull, half-man), which was housed in a vast labyrinth. Might this legend too be based on historical fact? The lesson of Schliemann's success in pursuing hunches based on the careful reading of ancient legends was not lost on his successors. An Englishman, Arthur Evans, had long considered Crete a potentially fertile field for investigation, and Schliemann himself, shortly before his death, had wanted to explore the site of Knossos. In 1900, Evans began work on Crete and a short time later uncovered extensive unfortified palaces of the old sea-kings of Crete, which indeed did resemble labyrinths (FIG. 4-6). His findings, primarily at Knossos, were augmented by additional excavations there and at Phaistos, Hagia Triada, and other important sites along the southern coast of Crete. In 1962, excavation of another palace was begun on the eastern tip of Crete at Kato Zakro; more recently, in 1966, a queen's burial chamber judged to be about 3,400 years old was discovered near Knossos.

MINOAN AND CYCLADIC ART

The civilization of the coasts and islands of the Aegean emerged about the same time as the river-valley civilizations of Egypt and Mesopotamia. Although there was close contact at various times and active exchange of influences, each civilization manifested an originality of its own; the Aegean civilization, however, has a special significance as the forerunner of the first truly European civilization—that of Greece. The sea-dominated geography of the Aegean contrasts sharply with that of the Near East, as does its temperate climate. In the ancient world, this produced a busy, commercial, seafaring culture with decentralized authority and a vigorous, vivacious, and pleasure-loving way of life. This is especially true of Crete, the ancient center of Aegean civilization from which its creative forces radiated. As a commercial crossroads for the ancient world, Crete was strategically placed in the eastern Mediterranean, and her products, both of agriculture and manufacture, were exported widely. The sea provided a natural defense against the frequent and often disruptive invasions that checker the histories of land-bound civilizations like Mesopotamia, and the navies of the sea-kings maintained a prosperous maritime empire that served for the transmission of ideas and influences as well as goods. The controlled accessibility to Crete of impulses from abroad, especially from Egypt and Mesopotamia, may account for the emergence and influence of its culture, which was felt in all of the Aegean area. Modifications of it on the Greek mainland and in the islands of the Cyclades north of Crete have been identified. Thus, the art of Crete itself is called Minoan, after King Minos; that of the mainland, Helladic; and that of the islands, Cycladic. The culture associated with Mycenae on the mainland—the Mycenaean—is classed under Late Helladic (about 1550–1100 B.C.).

The archeological problems confronting investigators of Near Eastern civilizations were much less difficult than those that confronted archeologists working in the Aegean area. Here there survived very few documents like the chronicles and inscriptions of Egypt and Mesopotamia with which to correlate the archeological findings and no "absolute" dates that could be expressed numerically. Evans had to construct a "relative" dating in terms of different periods of ceramic and decorative style from various sites on Crete, in the Cyclades, and at Mycenae. Evans' tripartite division of Minoan art into Early, Middle, and Late Minoan and the further division of each large period into three subperiods are a classic example of a relative chronology, used by archeologist–historians who lack absolute dates. A greater firmness was given the Minoan chronology when points of contact with the chronology of Egyptian art were established. Imported objects of a certain style from the one country were uncovered in datable contexts in the other; in this way, for example, the Middle Minoan period was found to be roughly contemporary with the Middle Kingdom in Egypt.

The two earliest of several scripts found on Crete seem to have been inspired by Egyptian hieroglyphs. Of the later scripts, Linear A and Linear B, only the latter has been deciphered (as late as 1953); it is a pre-Homeric form of Greek, but the tablets inscribed with it almost exclusively represent inventories and tallies of objects and are of little aid in delineating the Minoan culture. For Minoan history, pottery remains have provided by far the greatest evidence, since figurative art is relatively scarce and often so fragmentary and diminutive as to preclude building a stylistic continuity on it. (*Potsherds* are one of the mainstays of archeology when documentary and monumental evidence is sparse or missing. Broken pots—kitchenware, for example—were often thrown on a garbage heap, where, over the years, the perishable materials decayed, leaving only the pottery sherds, which settled into firmly stratified mounds. Careful excavation of such mounds can produce relative chronologies.) Although the sequence of Cretan pottery styles was well established by Evans, some archeologists now feel that his method of dating is inadequate in view of increased knowledge of the Minoan civilization. A new chronology has been suggested that is based on the construction of the great Cretan palaces. Its relationship to the traditional chronology is shown on page 103.

Nevertheless, absolute dates are few, and our knowledge of Minoan history remains vague and provisional. Even the origin of the Cretans is problematical. Some believe that they may have come from Anatolia as early as 6000 B.C.—bringing with them a well-developed Neolithic culture, complete with pottery—and that the Bronze Age may have

been ushered in by a new wave of immigrants (also from Anatolia?) around the year 2800 B.C.

The Early Minoan Period

The Early Minoan (pre-Palace) period is known to us primarily through pottery and a few scattered pieces of minor sculpture. There is the Mochlos stoneware (named after the site at which it was found and apparently copied from Egyptian pieces of the First to Fourth Dynasties), and there are hand-made clay pots decorated with incised geometric patterns.

The most striking and perhaps the most appealing Aegean products of the Early Bronze Age are the numerous marble statuettes from the Cyclades. Most of them are representations of nude females with their arms folded across their abdomens. Varying greatly in size from a few inches in height to life-size, these flat "plank idols" are highly schematized descendants of the Neolithic mother goddess (see FIG. 2-5). Their styles are as varied as their sizes and range from figures of almost normal proportions to shapes that resemble violins rather than human figures. The example shown (FIG. 4-1) occupies a middle ground: the organic forms have been converted into geometric shapes (triangles, rectangles, ovals, and cylinders),

4-1   Cycladic idol, Syros, *c.* 2500–2000 B.C. Marble, 8½″ high.

but the reference to the female figure remains clear, and the manner in which the various stylized parts have been combined has considerable esthetic appeal. Traces of paint found on some specimens show that at least parts of these figures were colored. The eyes were usually painted, and additional color touches were provided by painted necklaces and bracelets.

Occasionally, male figures also occur in the Cycladic repertoire. They usually appear as musicians, like the *Lyre Player* (FIG. 4-2), who, wedged between the echoing shapes of chair and lyre, performs a task that seems to have been a part of funerary rituals. In the rendering of the figure, the disk-shaped head and the long, tubular neck are in the same style as the plank figures, but the body has gained mass and volume, and the composition has a three-dimensional quality lacking in the plank idols. Although it has not been possible to establish a chronological sequence for these Cycladic figurines, most seem to date from the second half of the third millennium B.C.; the *Lyre Player* is believed to belong to the end of the line and may have been contemporary with the Cretan palaces.

4-2 *Lyre Player*, Keros, *c.* 2000 B.C. Marble, 9" high.

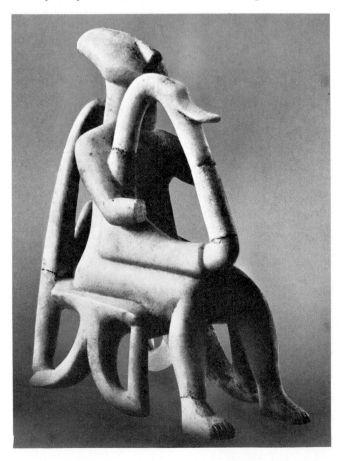

The Middle Minoan Period

The Middle Minoan period is marked by the founding of the old palaces around the year 2000 B.C. Building in Crete emphasized neither tombs, temples, nor fortresses, but instead palaces for the king and his retainers, around which grew up royal towns. The absence of fortification on Crete is conspicuous in the Aegean world (fortified sites appear everywhere in the Helladic and Cycladic areas), attesting either to the power of the Cretan navies, or to a long-enduring insular peace, or to both. But after only about three centuries, around 1700 B.C., these old palaces were destroyed, probably by one of the frequent earthquakes that ravage this part of the Mediterranean region.

An important technological advance of the beginning of the Old Palace period was the introduction of the potter's wheel, which permitted the throwing of vessels with thinner walls and subtler shapes and led to the development of a thriving industry. In this so-called "eggshell ware," the Minoan potter's art reached a degree of excellence that deserves our highest admiration, if for the delicacy of the ceramic technique alone. But the Cretan artist also developed a style of decoration that complemented the delicate fabric and sophisticated shapes of his pottery. Beginning with relatively simple, curvilinear patterns painted dark on light (FIG. 4-3), he moved toward a fully polychrome style of decoration that found its culmination in the splendid pottery (FIG. 4-4) discovered in the cave at Kamares on the slope of Mount Ida. On a surface swelling robustly with the peculi-

4-3 Small storage jar, Psyra, *c.* 2000–1850 B.C. 11" high.

4-4 Kamares pitcher, Phaistos, c. 1800–1700 B.C. Approx. 10″ high. Archeological Museum, Herakleion.

The Late Minoan Period

Somewhere between 1600 and 1500 B.C. began the New Palace period, when the destroyed palaces were rebuilt and the Golden Age of Crete produced the first great Western civilization. The bulk of the surviving archeological material—the evidence of an age of unsurpassed creative energy and precocious artistic achievement—dates from this era, which ended about 1400 B.C.

THE PALACES
The palaces rebuilt for the kings and their retainers were large, comfortable, and handsome, with ample staircases and courtyards for pageants, ceremonies, and games. Archeologists have recovered their ruins, along with rich treasures of art and artifacts that document the power and prosperity of Minoan civilization. Similarly laid out, the principal palace sites on Crete are at Knossos, Phaistos, Mallia, and, most recently excavated, Kato Zakro, situated at the eastern tip of the island. The largest of the palaces, that at Knossos (FIGS. 4-5 and 4-6), is a rambling structure built against the upper slopes and across the top of a low hill rising from a fertile plain. The great rectangular court, around which the units of the palace are grouped, had been leveled in the time of the old palace; the manner of the grouping of buildings suggests that it was not preplanned but that several building nuclei grew together, with the court as the major organizing element. A secondary organization of the palace plan is provided by two long corridors. On the west side of the court, a north–south corridor separates official and ceremonial rooms from the *magazines*, where wine, grain, oil, and honey were stored

arly Minoan feel for the vigor and buoyancy of active life, we find a lustrous black ground on which a quasigeometric pattern of creamy white is interspersed with yellow and red to form a colorful and harmonious decoration. As in Egypt, the motifs derive from natural forms; here, they are simplified into a play of spirals, beautifully adjusted to and integrated with the shape of the vessel.

4-5 Palace at Knossos, c. 1600–1400 B.C. (view from the east).

1. West porch
2. Corridor of the Procession
3. South propylon
4. Central court
5. "Theater area"
6. North-south corridor
7. Pillar hall
8. Magazines
9. Throne room
10. Palace shrine and lower verandas
11. Stepped porch
12. Grand staircase
13. Light well
14. East-west corridor
15. Hall of the Double Axes (principal reception room)
16. Queen's Megaron

Reconstruction

Earlier structures { Existing
Reconstruction

4-6 Plan of the palace at Knossos.

in large jars *(pithoi)*. On the east side of the court, an east–west corridor separates the king's and queen's quarters and reception rooms (south) from the workmen's and servant's quarters (north). At the northwest corner of the entire building complex is the "arena," a theater-like area with steps (seats?) on two sides—a possible forerunner of the later Greek theater. Its purpose is unknown, but it is a feature that, like the central court, appears in other Cretan pal-

aces. For the Greeks, the complexity of the palace's plan came to be associated with the cult of the double axe *(labrys)* celebrated there, perhaps giving rise to the Greek myth of the Cretan *labyrinth*. Certainly, it was the product of wealth and luxurious tastes and of a love for the convenient. Beneath the palace is a remarkably efficient drainage system of terra-cotta pipes that must have made Knossos one of the most sanitary cities existing before the twentieth century.

4-7   View of the magazine, west wing of the palace at Knossos, with large pithoi *in situ*.

The practical storage system is exhibited in the magazines of the west wing (FIG. 4-7), where some of the pithoi are still in place. Some of the rooms had flat floors; others, like those shown here, had stone-lined pits. The walls were quite thick, as must have been the roofing over these magazines; the masonry may have been covered with earth to keep the interior cool. In most parts of the palace, the masonry composing the walls was rough, consisting of unshaped field stones imbedded in mortar; ashlar masonry, made of shaped blocks of stone, was used at building corners and around door and window openings.

The palace had as many as three stories, with interior staircases built around light and air wells (FIG. 4-8), which provided necessary illumination and ventilation. Distinguishing features of the Minoan columns, which were originally fashioned of wood but were restored in stone (with, it is now thought, mistakenly bulky proportions), are their bulbous, cushion-like capitals and the manner in which the column shafts taper toward the base. Strong evidence that the column had religious significance for the Cretans is its central position in the Lion Gate at Mycenae (FIG. 4-25) and the fact that the base of a column in one of the lower stories of the palace at Knossos is surrounded by a trough that was used for libations.

4-8   Reconstruction of a stairwell, palace at Knossos.

PAINTING

A view into the Queen's Megaron, with its pillared hall and light well (FIG. 4-9), shows the typically elaborate wall decoration of the more important rooms at Knossos. Here, plastered walls were painted with frescoes, which, together with the red- or blue-shafted columns, must have provided an extraordinarily rich effect. The frescoes depicted many aspects of Cretan life (bullfights, processions, and ceremonies) and of nature (birds, animals, flowers and—as here—marine life, with dolphins frolicking among other fauna of the sea).

4-9 Reconstruction of the Queen's Megaron, palace at Knossos.

4-10 *Cupbearers in Procession*, reconstruction of fresco from Knossos, *c.* 1500 B.C. Approx. 60″ high. Archeological Museum, Herakleion.

4-11 *The Cupbearer*, Knossos, *c.* 1500 B.C. Fresco, approx. 60″ high. Archeological Museum, Herakleion.

One of the most memorable figures from the art of Crete is from the *Cupbearers in Procession* fresco of the south propylon at Knossos (FIG. 4-10).* *The Cupbearer* (FIG. 4-11) is the only one preserved from a sequence, shown in two registers, that may have contained over 500 figures—if those from the Corridor of the Procession (FIG. 4-6) are included. The ceremonial *rhyton* (vessel for pouring ritual libations) carried by the youth has a typically Minoan shape, found nowhere else except as a Minoan import. And the figure itself is unmistakably Minoan. The youth has long curly hair, wears an elaborately embroidered loincloth with a silver-mounted girdle, and has ornaments on his arms, neck, ankles, and wrist. Although the profile pose with the full-view eye was a familiar convention in Egypt and Mesopotamia, the elegance of the Cretan figure, with its pinched waist, proud, self-confident bearing, and free movement, distinguishes it from all other early figure styles. The angularity of the older styles is typically modified in the curving line that suggests the elasticity of the living and moving being.

*The scarred, patchy, and broken surface that makes the figure of *The Cupbearer* hard to discern is a good illustration of the fact that Minoan painting—unfortunately, like so much painting throughout the world—has survived only in fragments. To make sense of them, the archeologist has had to reconstruct or restore the ruined painting to some semblance of its original appearance. Using exact, painstaking methods, experts have replaced fallen fragments in agreement with those remaining on the wall, and—by careful deduction and often by conjecture and guesswork—they have achieved the complete picture. The task is like putting together an enormously complex jigsaw puzzle when many parts are missing and many completions are possible. A key to reading *The Cupbearer* and other fragmentary pictures will help: the smooth, lighter tonal areas show what is missing; the streaked and mottled, darker tonal areas are surviving fragments that have remained attached or that have been picked up and replaced. The cupbearing figures from Knossos are completely reconstructed from only traces of the original work (FIG. 4-10).

Vivacity and spontaneity characterize *The Toreador Fresco* (FIG. 4-12). Although only fragments of it have been recovered, they are extraordinary in their depiction of vigorous movements of the girls and the young man who is shown in the air, having, perhaps, grasped the bull's horns and somersaulted over its back. We have seen how important the bull is in the Near East, especially in Mesopotamian art. The difference in the Minoan paintings is in the relationship of the bull—it may be that here he is even a god—to human beings. In this fresco, man and beast contest with each other in a dangerous game that takes place in the here and now, the human beings as conspicuous in the action as the bull. In a powerful characterization of the natures of both man and beast, the poise and agility of the toreadors play off against the exploding energy of the bull. (We are reminded of the charging bulls of the Paleolithic caves; see FIG. 1-1). Everywhere within the frame are curving lines, the directional lines of action, and nowhere are they more conspicuous and vital than in the electric energy of the line that sweeps from the head of the bull to the whip of his tail.

Because of her cosmetic prettiness—like that of a sophisticated, modern woman—a girl represented in a fragment of another fresco has been labeled *La Parisienne* (FIG. 4-13). With her conventionally enlarged and front-view eye, her turned-up nose, full red lips, and elaborate coiffure, she is almost disturbingly of our own times, especially as we conventionalize her type in popular art. Surely, there is nothing quite like this sprightly charm, freshness, and *joie de vivre* in the art of the Ancient Near East. The painting method used is appropriate to the lively spirit of the Minoans. Unlike the Egyptians, who painted in the dry-fresco (*fresco secco*) technique, the Minoans used a *true*, or *wet*, fresco method, which required rapid execution

4-12   *The Toreador Fresco*, Knossos, *c.* 1500 B.C. Approx. 32" high, including border. Archeological Museum, Herakleion.

4-13 *La Parisienne*, Knossos, *c.* 1500 B.C. Fragment of a fresco, approx. 10" high. Archeological Museum, Herakleion.

and a skill in achieving quick, almost impressionistic effects. If one is to catch an interesting but fugitive aspect of an object or a scene, one must work quickly, even spontaneously, allowing for happy accidents. Thus, because the wet-fresco technique compelled the artist to work rapidly, the spirit of *La Parisienne* is also a product of the resultant verve of his hand, and the simple, light delicacy of the technique exactly matches the vivacity of the subject. It is the Minoan sense of immediate life and the skill in catching it that strike us as novel in the ancient world and prophetic of great changes in man's outlook on nature.

This sense and skill is vividly present in wall paintings recently found in ruins on the island of Thera (modern Santorini) some 60 miles north of Crete. Thera, a volcanic island, was the site of an enormous seismic explosion around 1500 B.C., perhaps the greatest of the post-glacial age, that left a huge crater in the center of the island. The effect of this mighty explosion on the palaces of Crete to the south is still a matter of debate, but it is generally felt that later invasions from the mainland of Greece, not the Thera ca-

tastrophe itself, brought the final destruction of the Minoan palaces and their culture.

In any event, Thera is regarded as a kind of early Pompeii, so well preserved are the remains of its streets, buildings, and especially its painted walls. We can feel the freshness and vitality of the Minoan vision of nature in the lovely mural *The Springtime Fresco* (FIG. 4-14). Here, the undulating earth, the graceful lillies, and the darting swallows express vernal qualities—the vigor of growth, the delicacy of flowering, and the lightness of birdsong and flight. In the lyrical language of curving line, there is a celebration of the breezy rhythms of spring. Landscape painting of this naturalistic sort is a Minoan innovation—the first of its kind, as far as we have yet discovered, in the art of the ancient world, and the forerunner of Greek and Roman landscape.

Another painting from Thera, in addition to its quality, gives us a detailed picture of scenes from Minoan life. Seascape and landscape combined, *The Flotilla Fresco* (FIG. 4-15) shows a fleet of ships plying between two ports. The details of ship design and of

4-14 *The Springtime Fresco*, from Room Delta 2, Akrotiri, Thera (Santorini), *c.* 1500 B.C. Approx. 7' 6" high. National Museum, Athens.

4-15 *The Flotilla Fresco,* from Room 5, West House, Akrotiri, Thera (Santorini), *c.* 1500 B.C. 17″ high. National Museum, Athens.

sailing are carefully observed, as if by one who knew ships well. Just as carefully observed are the placements and poses of steersmen, supercargoes, sailors, rowers, and passengers. There is little of the conventional stereotyping and repetition that we find, for example, in much of Ancient Near Eastern art (FIG. 2-15); instead, there is an almost casual arrangement of figures and variation of pose according to the roles they play—steering, tending to the sail, rowing, or simply sitting and conversing. Dolphins resembling those in the Queen's Megaron at Knossos (FIG. 4-9) frolic about the ships; and on the shore (at the upper left), a lion pursues fleeing deer. The ports—the one at the left encircled by a river represented as arching above it—show quays, houses, and streets occupied by a variety of people attentive to the coming of the ships, waiting to unload them, or simply going about their business. The whole composition has the openess and lightness of the seagirt lands of Crete and the Greek islands, suggesting the freedom of movement of a people for whom seafaring is second nature, and nature—with all its flora and fauna—is, in itself, delightful and worthy of representation.

A painting of a young fisherman holding his abundant catch in both hands is yet another indication of the keen attention the Minoan artist paid to natural appearances (FIG. 4-16). What at first appears to be the Egyptian convention of pose, frontal and profile views combined, can be read as an adjustment of the figure to allow both clusters of fish to be seen at the same time—much as a modern sport fisherman, proud of his catch, might turn slowly to display it as

his picture is being taken. The informality of the young fisherman might be compared with the strict formality of profile found in the cupbearers at Knossos (FIG. 4-10), the contrast reflecting differences of rank and occupation, the lesser rank and humble occupation of the fisherman calling for, or permitting, a more realistic representation. We have found elsewhere in ancient art that lesser persons, and scenes from common life, are treated with less formality and greater realism than are kings and nobles, or scenes of royal and religious ritual.

4-16 *Young Fisherman Fresco,* from Room 5, West House, Akrotiri, Thera (Santorini), *c.* 1500 B.C. 53″ high. National Museum, Athens.

4-17 *The Octopus Jar,* Gournia, *c.* 1600 B.C. Amphora approx. 8″ high. Archeological Museum, Herakleion.

POTTERY

The Minoan feeling for the dynamics of living nature, revealed in their figurative and landscape art, is no less visible in their pottery, which is among the finest in history. In the Kamares ware (FIG. 4-4), this interest in animate nature did not appear at once; the taste was for abstract spiral forms, scrolls, whorls, and the like. As time went on, the tendency toward naturalism in decoration increased. Motifs were derived from sea life, such as dolphins, seaweed, and octopuses. The tentacles reaching out over the curving surfaces of *The Octopus Jar* from Gournia (FIG. 4-17) embrace the piece and emphasize its elastic volume. This is a masterful realization of the relationship between the decoration of the vessel and its shape, always a problem for the ceramist. From the Kamares silhouetting of light, abstract forms on a dark ground, we progress, in *The Octopus Jar,* to a silhouetting of dark naturalistic forms on a light ground. This manner lasted from about 1600 to 1500 B.C., when the fluid, open, and lively naturalistic style became increasingly stiff and abstract. This late style can be seen in a three-handled jar of about 1425 B.C. from Knossos (FIG. 4-18). The stalks of its papyrus decoration grow symmetrically, and the flowers turn into stylized scrolls and fans, symmetrically balanced. Wavy bands, simple concentric circles with crosses,

and other rudimentary space-fillers occupy the surface rather than adjust to it and embrace it. Such devolution from naturalism to formalism and abstraction can be observed frequently in the history of world art.

An increasing self-awareness, which we have watched evolve slowly in ancient art, requires that man represent himself ever more as he is, in more conditions and situations, with fewer restrictions imposed by tradition. *The Harvester Vase* (FIGS. 4-19 and 4-20), made of steatite (soapstone), gives a sharp new glimpse of man as he is in his usual physical context. The egg-shaped rhyton, its lower half missing, shows a riotous crowd of olive harvesters, singing and shouting. Their forward movement and lusty exuberance are vividly expressed. The pattern of pitchforks fills the upper part of the band; the figures below, in higher relief, create a variation in surface. The entire design, like the octopus of the Gournia jar (FIG. 4-17), hugs the shape so tightly that it seems to be an integral part of the wall of the vase. But the figures themselves are depicted with a gusto that matches their mood. They are led by a man who carries a *sistrum,* or rattle, and beats time, while his lungs are so inflated with air that his ribs show. The harvesters' facial expressions are rendered with as-

4-18 Three-handled jar with papyrus decoration, Knossos, *c.* 1425 B.C. Approx. 53″ high. Archeological Museum, Herakleion.

4-19 Detail of *The Harvester Vase* (FIG. 4-20). Archeological Museum, Herakleion.

4-20 *The Harvester Vase*, Hagia Triada, *c.* 1500 B.C. Steatite, approx. 5″ wide. Archeological Museum, Herakleion. (Lower part is lost.)

tonishing exactitude; there are degrees of hilarity and degrees of vocal effort, all marked in the tension or relaxation of facial muscles. This reading of the human face as a vehicle of emotional states is without precedent in ancient art before the Minoans.

SCULPTURE

There is little sculpture in the round in Minoan art, and what there is generally is small; there is no monumental sculpture of gods, kings, and monsters, such as we find in Mesopotamia and Egypt—at least, none has been found. This absence of large-scale sculpture may reflect an absence of systematic and formal religion, although this is entirely speculation due to our ignorance of Minoan religion. The small figures of "snake goddesses" like the one shown from Knossos (FIG. 4-21) are hardly more than of talisman or fetish size. They exhibit most of the rigid conventions, including the frontal pose, found in Egypt and Mesopotamia, but the arms have been released from the core of the block and are held forward or aloft. Thus, they are shown to be active and, somehow, seem more alive than their Near Eastern or Egyptian cousins. The Cretans seem to have worshiped a mother goddess sacred to many places and manifest in many forms. Whether or not these miniature figures brandishing snakes are images of her is not certain, but they are clearly identified as Minoan by their costume—the open bodice and flounced skirt worn by Minoan women, as we find them depicted many times over. This touch of the real may be another example of man fashioning his gods in his own image.

The circumstances under which the Minoan civilization came to an end are still disputed, although it is now widely believed that Mycenaeans moved onto the island and established themselves at Knossos without meeting major resistance. From the repaired palace at Knossos, they appear to have ruled the island for at least half a century, perhaps much longer. Parts of the palace continued to be occupied until its final destruction around 1200 B.C., this time by the Dorians, but its importance as a cultural center faded soon after 1400 B.C., as the focus of Aegean civilization shifted to the Greek mainland.

4-21 *Snake Goddess*, Knossos, c. 1600 B.C. Faïence, approx. 13½″ high. Archeological Museum, Herakleion.

MYCENAEAN ART

Not only the end of the Minoan culture, but also the origins of the Mycenaean culture are still being debated. The primitive Greeks may have moved onto the mainland about the time that the old palaces were being built in Crete—that is, about the beginning of the second millennium B.C. Doubtless they were influenced by Crete even then, and some believe that the mainland was a Minoan colony for a long time, although the mainlanders developed and held to many cultural features of their own. At any rate, Mycenaean power rose on the mainland in the palmy days of the new palaces on Crete, and by 1500 B.C., a new and splendid culture was flourishing in Greece to which, 700 years later, Homer was to give the epithet "rich in gold." It is possible that the Mycenaeans made close contact in this new era not only with Crete but also with Egypt, with which they may have been allied against the Hittites during the early part of the New Kingdom; and the Mycenaeans' taste for gold, as well as their actual treasure, may have been acquired in the mercenary service of Egypt, which was known in the ancient world for its lavish use of the metal. Thus, the awakening of the Mycenaean world may have been the consequence of a kind of three-way route of influence connecting the mainland, Crete, and Egypt. The destruction of the Cretan palaces left the Mycenaean (mainland) culture supreme, but new waves of migrating proto-Greek peoples, the Dorians, finally submerged the Mycenaean civilization. The steady infiltration of these peoples had already led to the development of a fortress architecture (unnecessary in Crete), and by about 1200 B.C., the fortified citadels of the mainland were overwhelmed by the invaders. The heroes and battles of these last centuries of Aegean civilization must have provided the tradition that, hundreds of years later, Homer would immortalize in the first great European epics, the *Iliad* and the *Odyssey*.

Although Mycenae appears to have been the cultural center of the mainland development, the remains of other large citadels have been found at Vaphio, Pylos, Orchomenus, Arne, and (most recently) at Iolkos. The best preserved and most impressive Mycenaean remains are those of the fortified palaces at Tiryns and Mycenae, both built at the beginning of the Late Mycenaean period, about 1400 B.C., and razed (along with the others) between 1250 and 1200 B.C.

Architecture

The Citdel of Tiryns (FIG. 4-22)—located only 10 miles from Mycenae, so that at times they may have been

4-22 Plan of the Citadel of Tiryns, *c.* 1400–1200 B.C.

REFUGE (?)

APPROACH
RAMP

MAIN
GATE

MEGARON

OUTER
PROPYLON

N

0   25   50   75   100 FEET

0   10   20   30 METERS

4-23 Plan of the
megaron, Tiryns.

under the same lord—was known by Homer as Tiryns of the Great Walls and by the ancient world as the birthplace of Herakles (Hercules), the mythic hero of great strength. The ancient sightseer and guide-book writer, Pausanias, considered the walls of Tiryns to be as spectacular as the pyramids of Egypt.

The heavy walls contrast sharply with the open Cretan palaces and clearly reveal their defensive character. The buildings within the 20-foot-thick walls are aligned axially and seem to have been laid out according to a predetermined plan. Unlike the rambling and often confusing layout of the Cretan

4-24 Corbeled gallery, Tiryns.

capped with a huge lintel, above which the layers of stone form a corbeled arch, leaving a triangular opening that serves to lighten the weight to be carried by the lintel. The triangular space is filled with a slab on which two lions, carved in high relief, confront each other on either side of a column of the probably sacred Minoan type, resting their forepaws on its base. (This column of the Lion Gate supplies evidence of what the vanished wooden Minoan columns looked like.) Holes near the top of the animals indicate that the heads, now lost, were made of separate pieces of stone or metal. The lions are carved with breadth and vigor, and the whole design admirably fills its triangular space, harmonizing in dignity, strength, and scale with the massive stones that form the walls and gate. We find similar groups in miniature on Cretan seals, and one senses that these lions are not too distant from Mesopotamian heraldic composition.

palaces, the Mycenaean plan is an example of a clear and simple arrangement of the units. The *megaron* (FIG. 4-23)—the three-chambered structure at the heart of the design and the center of the life of the citadel—embodies the germ of the Classical temples of Greece. This fundamental building type does not appear in the palaces of Crete, but does appear, surprisingly, at Troy as early as 2000 B.C. A hall of state, the megaron was rectangular, with a central hearth and four columns supporting the roof.

The massive fortification walls at Tiryns and other Mycenaean sites, built of unhewn or roughly dressed stone, were called "Cyclopean" by later Greeks, who imagined them to have been built by that mythical race of giants, the Cyclopes. Through the walls at intervals run corbeled galleries (FIG. 4-24), which may have been part of the defensive structure or part of a complicated and dramatic ceremonial path leading, through a porch and vestibule, to the chief room of the palace—the megaron. The corbeled gallery pictured makes use, as its name indicates, of the primitive corbeled arch. The rough appearance of these Cyclopean structures is most impressive in its crude monumentality; it possesses an earthy dynamism not found in other, more sophisticated, ancient architectural styles.

The sternness of these fortress-palaces was relieved by frescoes, by carvings, and, at Mycenae at least, by monumental architectural sculpture—the Lion Gate (FIG. 4-25). This outer gateway of the stronghold, protected on the left by a wall and on the right by a projecting bastion, is formed of two great monoliths

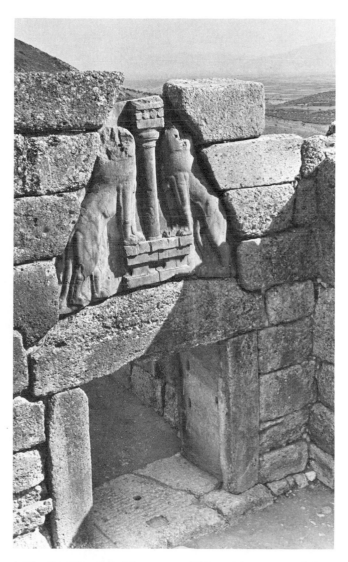

4-25 The Lion Gate, Mycenae, *c.* 1300 B.C. Limestone, relief panel approx. 9½' high.

4-26   Plan and sections of the "Treasury of Atreus," Mycenae, *c.* 1300 B.C.

Within the gate and to the right lies the *grave circle*, an enclosure containing a number of simple shaft graves, stone-lined pits serving as tombs for kings and their families, covered and marked by a stele. Another similar grave circle was recently discovered outside the walls of Mycenae. Both grave circles date from about 1600–1500 B.C. But, at this time, shaft graves were gradually being replaced by the so-called *beehive tombs*, of which the best preserved is the remarkable "Treasury of Atreus" (FIGS. 4-26 and 4-27), misnamed by Heinrich Schliemann, who thought it— the most imposing of a group—to be the storehouse for the treasure of Atreus, father of Agamemnon and Menelaus. Built into a hill and approached by a long passage, or *dromos*, the beehive shape of the round tomb chamber, or *tholos*, was achieved by use of corbeled courses of stone laid on a circular base, splendidly cut to the curve of the wall and ending in a lofty dome, which, in this fine example, is about 40 feet high. This vaulted structure without interior supports was the largest unified space in all antiquity until the Roman Pantheon was built 1,500 years later.

4-27   Interior of the tholos, "Treasury of Atreus," Mycenae. Vault approx. 40' high.

Pottery, Relief, and Craft Art

Most of the beehive tombs had been thoroughly looted long before their modern rediscovery. On the other hand, rich finds were made in shaft graves at Mycenae. Some bronze daggers, inlaid with gold and silver, found in these graves reveal the influence of the Minoan figure style (FIG. 4-28). On the longest of the three blades illustrated, three hunters with spears, bows, and shields attack a lion that has struck down a fourth hunter, while two other lions flee. The subject is of Mesopotamian derivation, but the costumes are Cretan and the vigorous, spirited movements of the hunters, the lithe strength and spring of the lions, are Minoan.

Beaten gold (repoussé) masks were found in the shaft graves, attached to the faces of the mummified Mycenaean princes (FIG. 4-29). Powerfully realistic in their record of the features of the deceased, they also testify to the influx of gold from Egypt. This and the

4-28 Inlaid dagger blades from the royal tombs at Mycenae, c. 1600–1500 B.C. Bronze, longest blade approx. 9″ long. National Museum, Athens.

4-29   Funeral mask from the royal tombs of Mycenae, *c.* 1500 B.C. Beaten gold, approx. 12" high. National Museum, Athens.

elaboration of funeral practices lend strong support to the supposition that the impulse that started this high phase of Mycenaean civilization originated partly in Egypt and partly in Crete.

The golden culture of Mycenae produced such masterpieces as the famous cups from Vaphio (FIG. 4-30). Found in a beehive tomb, these beautiful vessels are still the subject of warm debate among experts who see them as originating in Crete and those who insist that, despite their undoubted resemblance to Minoan figure style, they are Mycenaean. The cups are a pair, each made of two plates of gold—one worked in *repoussé* for the outside, the other left plain to make a smooth surface for the inside. The plates were fastened together, the handles riveted on, and some of the details then engraved. The subject seems to be Minoan (the men are costumed in the Minoan manner) and related to the bull-leaping ritual; bulls

are being trapped and snared, with a cow used as a lure in one case. One cup shows a bull caught in a net. A second bull, charging furiously, impales with its horns a man whose companion falls to one side; a third bull dashes madly from the fracas. The other cup presents a quieter scene. At the right, the bull moves toward the cow; in the center, he stands beside her; at the left, captured and hobbled, he is bellowing. The three scenes are integrated by the trees and the man, and the whole design is admirably composed to fit the space. In both cups, areas not filled by the animal and human figures contain landscape motifs of trees, rocks, and clouds similar to those in contemporary painting. The shallowness of the relief and the conventional treatment of the trees produce a rich play of light and shade and a variety of textures.

The Warrior Vase (FIG. 4-31) represents a file of Mycenaean soldiers strikingly different in costume,

4-30   *The Vaphio Cups, c.* 1500 B.C. Gold with *repoussé* decoration, approx. 3½" high. National Museum, Athens.

physiognomy, and beards from the Cretan figure types we have seen in Minoan art. This would seem to strengthen the argument that the Mycenaeans were of entirely different racial stock from the Minoans and the indigenous builders of their own civilization. It may be, too, that we are looking here at the last Myceanean warriors who marched forth to meet the Dorian invaders, under whose onslaught the Mycenaean civilization collapsed after 1200 B.C. The Dorians carried iron weapons, superior to the softer

bronze of the Mycenaeans, and their success illustrates the historical commonplace that a superior technology can overcome an otherwise more highly developed civilization. The centuries-long "dark age" that followed the obliteration of Aegean culture, although little survives from it, cannot be considered merely a historical void. New energies were gathering that would form one of the greatest civilizations the world has known—a civilization new, bold, self-confident, and modern.

4-31   *The Warrior Vase,* Mycenae, *c.* 1200 B.C. Approx. 14" high. National Museum, Athens.

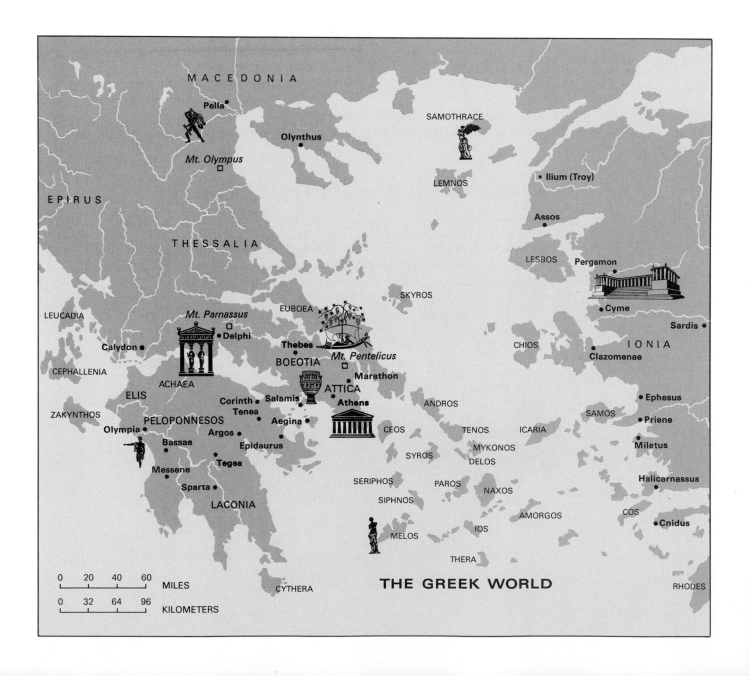

5

THE GREEK WORLD

MACEDONIA

Pella

Mt. Olympus

Olynthus

SAMOTHRACE

LEMNOS

Ilium (Troy)

Assos

EPIRUS

THESSALIA

LESBOS

Pergamon

LEUCADIA

Mt. Parnassus

Delphi

EUBOEA

SKYROS

Cyme

Sardis

Calydon

CEPHALLENIA

ACHAEA

Thebes

BOEOTIA

Mt. Pentelicus

CHIOS

IONIA

Clazomenae

ELIS

Corinth
Tenea

Salamis

Marathon

ATTICA

Athens

ANDROS

Ephesus

SAMOS

Priene

ZAKYNTHOS

PELOPONNESOS

Aegina

CEOS

TENOS

ICARIA

Miletus

Olympia

Argos

Bassae

Epidaurus

SYROS

MYKONOS
DELOS

Halicarnassus

Tegea

SERIPHOS

PAROS

NAXOS

Messene

SIPHNOS

AMORGOS

COS

Sparta

LACONIA

MELOS

IOS

Cnidus

THERA

0   20   40   60   MILES

0   32   64   96

KILOMETERS

CYTHERA

THE GREEK WORLD

RHODES

THE ART OF GREECE

1200 B.C.   *c.* 1100

DORIC INVASIONS — PROTO-GEOMETRIC PERIOD

c. 900

GEOMETRIC PERIOD

1000

Dipylon Vase   *c.* 700

Orientalizing Period

ARCHAIC PERIOD

800

First Olympiad

776   POLYKLEITOS   from *c.* 730 B.C.   EXEKIAS

Doryphoros   Foundation of Italian colonies   *Dionysos in*

Parthenon   *Apollo,* Olympia   Treasury of   *a Sailboat*

480   the Siphnians,

Delphi

CLASSICAL PERIOD

Early Classical — Transitional

Pericles 444–429   *c.* 450   Sack of Athenian   Persian Wars 497–479   Pythagoras

Acropolis

Peloponnesian

Wars 431–404

c. 400   PRAXITELES

Hermes and Dionysos   Pella pebble

mosaic, detail

323

Late Classical   Early Hellenistic

HELLENISTIC PERIOD

Alexander the

Great 336–323

Aphrodite   *Nike of*

of Melos   *Samothrace*

200

Late Hellenistic ("Greco-Roman")

30   146

Battle of Actium   Roman "liberation"

APOLLONIUS (?)   of Greece

Seated Boxer

Altar of Zeus and Athena,

Pergamon

FOR WE ARE LOVERS of the beautiful, yet with simplicity, and we cultivate the mind without loss of manliness. . . . We are the school of Greece." In the fifth century B.C., the Golden Age of Athens, Thucydides had Pericles make this assertion in praise of the Athenians, comparing their open, democratic society with the closed, barracks-state of their rivals, the Spartans. But Pericles might have been speaking in general of Greek culture, as we have received it, and of the ideal of humanistic education and life created by that culture. In the humanistic view, man is what matters, and he is, in the words of Protagoras, the "measure of all things."

For the Greeks, what set man apart was his intelligence, and human intelligence, trained in reasoning, was the highest function nature had created. Moreover, Aristotle assured us that "all men by nature desire to know." And what we know is the order of nature, which is one with the order of human reason.

The order of both nature and reason, said the Greeks, is beautiful and simple, and the beauty of things is one with our knowledge of them; thus, the good life, the achievement of the "beautiful soul," follows on compliance with that typically Greek command, "Know thyself!" One achieves the good life, then, through an intellectual process; one lives "according to nature," according to the natural laws of life discoverable by rational man. The self now becomes of first importance, and as man comes to full self-awareness, he necessarily becomes aware of nature as well.

Man is regarded as the highest creation of and value in nature, and it was the Greeks who created democracy as well as the natural image of man in art. A late, great scholar of Classical Greece, Werner Jaeger, wrote of their exaltation of man: "As against the Oriental exaltation of one God–king . . . and the . . . suppression of the great mass of the people . . . , the beginning of Greek history appears to be the beginning of a new conception of the individual. . . . the history of personality in Europe must start with them [the Greeks]."*

This honoring of the individual—and through the individual, the laws of human nature—is so completely part of our habit of mind that we are scarcely aware of it and of its origin in the minds of the Greeks.

From the Paleolithic period, we have been surveying man in a world dominated by the great beasts—threatened by them, fighting them, dependent on them (or their embodiment), worshiping them, conceding their might and man's own weakness. Now, in Greece, he asserts that his own peculiar power—

the power of intelligence—puts him far above the beasts. But the Greek mind was not dryly or pallidly rationalistic; it knew well the forces of the irrational against which reason must struggle constantly. In fact, Greek art constitutes with Greek culture a compact synthesis of opposites, a harmony between profound passion and rational order. Its clarity and symmetry are not cold but vital; its forms can be rigorous and mathematical, yet full of life.

In marked contrast to Egypt, with its long horizontals of alluvial plain between desert plateaus and seemingly invariable sunshine, Greece is a country of diversified geography and climate. The bays of its deeply indented, rugged coastline make the country half land and half sea; mountain ridges divide it into many small units. The climate is vigorous—cold in winter, dry and hot in summer. There is almost always a breeze from the sea. The unusually clear, almost crystalline atmosphere is often softened by a haze. Both sky and sea are brilliant in color. It is little wonder that the Greeks, attuned to nature, should people their mountains, woods, streams, sky, and sea with divinities—that they should picture Zeus, the king of this realm of gods, as reigning from their loftiest peak, Olympus; the Muses as dwelling in the deep, cool groves on the long slopes of Parnassus and Cithaeron; and Apollo as speaking from the awe-inspiring rocky clefts of Delphi.

Nature worship evolved into *personification*. The Greek gods assumed human forms whose grandeur and nobility were not free from human frailty; indeed, unlike the gods of Egypt and Mesopotamia, their only real difference from men was that they were immortal. It has been said that the Greeks made their gods into men and their men into gods. Man, becoming the measure of all things, in turn must represent, if all things in their perfection are beautiful, the unchanging standard of the best; to create the perfect individual became the Greek ideal.

The Greeks, or Hellenes, as they called themselves, appear to have been the product of an intermingling of Aegean peoples and of Indo-European invaders. This intermingling may have been a vitalizing factor that should be considered, together with the climate and the strongly diversified mountain–valley terrain of the Greek peninsula, in hypothesizing the causes of the peculiarly high competitive and creative energy of the Greek peoples.

The first of the invaders began to drift into the area about 2000 B.C., and after 1600 B.C., as we have seen, they formed the Mycenaean civilization on the Greek peninsula. After about 1200 B.C., the Mycenaeans were apparently overwhelmed in turn by new invaders from the north—the Dorians and perhaps the Ionians. The Dorians made the Peloponnesos the center of their power and may have forced the

*Werner Jaeger, *Paideia: The Ideals of Greek Culture* (New York: Oxford University Press, 1939), Vol. 1: p. xix.

Ionians eastward across the Aegean to the coast of Asia Minor. The origin of the Ionians is still a matter of dispute. Some scholars feel that proto-Ionians lived at Athens during Mycenaean times and that they were displaced during the Doric invasions. Others hold that they developed on the coast of Asia Minor between the eleventh and eighth centuries B.C. out of a mixed stock of settlers. In either case, the Ionians seem to have been more individualistic than the tribally ordered Dorians, whose most characteristic city became conservative Sparta.

In Ionia, on the east coast of Asia Minor, epics of individual greatness had come to be celebrated by the eighth century B.C., and by the seventh century, the rational philosophers of Miletus had begun to interpret the world in terms of reason rather than religion, beginning that immense transformation of the worship of nature into the science of nature, the science that is still expanding today. Between Ionia and the Peloponnesos lay Attica, and there, in Athens, a conservative tribal order and individualistic striving combined to produce the most fruitful of all the *poleis*, or city-states, of Greece—the one that Thucydides could boast was the "school of Greece."

By the eighth century B.C., the separate Greek-speaking states had held their first ceremonial games in common, the Olympiad of 776 B.C., from which time the historical Greeks calculated their chronology. From then on, despite their chronic rivalries and wars, they regarded themselves as Hellenes, distinct from the surrounding "barbarians" who did not speak Greek. The enterprising Hellenes, greatly aided by their indented coasts and island stepping-stones, became a trading and colonizing people who enlarged the geographic and cultural boundaries of Hellas. Tribal organizations had evolved into city-states, each an individual unit. Political development differed from state to state, but a kind of pattern emerged in which rule was first by kings, then by nobles, then by tyrants who seized personal power. At last, in Athens, appeared the dynamic balance that was called *democracy*.

Athens has in many ways become the symbol of Greek culture; many of the finest products of Greek civilization were created by Athenians or by others closely associated with Athens and its traditions. Athens, at the time of its brief flowering after the Persian Wars, was an active business city of about 100,000 people. Above its olive groves and rooftops towered the Acropolis, or higher city, formerly a Mycenaean fortress but, in this age, crowned with temples rising in bright colors against an intensely blue sky. Under the covered colonnades *(stoas)* that surrounded the city's central marketplace *(agora)*, the citizens congregated to discuss the latest political development or philosophical idea. Among the Athe-

nians, argument was both a public and a private exercise that went on wherever a few disputants could be assembled. This love of intellectual contest, the vigorous forerunner of science itself, was astonishingly popular; whether in the house of a rich man or in the marketplace, in the gymnasium, or on the street corner, such discussion was the key to the intense political and intellectual life that developed in the Greek city-state. Bodily exercise also played a large part in education and daily life, and the Athenian aim of a balance of intellectual and physical discipline, an ideal of humanistic education, is expressed in the Latin, *mens sana in corpore sano*, "a sound mind in a sound body."

The tragedies of Aeschylus and Sophocles, played before the eager citizens, presented the individual as having an obligation to the gods and the rise and fall of his fortunes as reflecting the contest between blind fate and the new-found power of reason.

The constants of Greek culture were man, nature, and reason, and the Greeks understood goodness to be the harmony of all three. On this elementary conviction, new to the world, they built their grand achievements in art, poetry, mathematics, philosophy, logic, history, and science—the heritage on which the modern Western world in turn was constructed. In discovering man, the Greeks discovered and confronted the problem of persistence and change; men pass away, but mankind remains. And although they aspired toward the timeless ideal, the Greeks realized the changes that produce growth and development.

To modern eyes, the realities of Greek life and society may seem to fall well short of what we would call "ideal," although the word has a different meaning in Greek philosophy than it does in modern usage. Slavery was regarded as natural, even beneficial, and was a universal institution among the Greeks. Aristotle declared at the beginning of his *Politics:* "It is clear that some are free by nature, and others are slaves." Women were secluded in their homes and played no part in public or political life. Aristotle may have been expressing the general view when he described woman as "more dispirited, more despondent, and more given to falsehood than the male. . . . she is more envious, more querulous, more slanderous, and more contentious." Womanly virtues were beauty, temperance, and industriousness. In the man's world of Greece, love between men was not considered illicit; in Plato's *Symposium*, Socrates is praised by the lascivious Alcibiades for his almost superhuman imperviousness to seduction. Although the Greeks invented and passed on to us the concept and practice of democracy, most Greek states, even when constituted as democracies, were ruled by the wellborn and affluent, in effect by aristocrats, and the virtue long most admired was not wisdom or justice, but statecraft and military valor. Greek men were educated in the values of the heroes of Homer and the athletic exercises of the *palestrae*. War among the city-states was chronic and often atrocious. Fighting among themselves and incapable of unifying, the Greeks eventually fell prey to the autocracy of Macedon and the imperialism of Rome.

In our own time, the uncritical admiration of Greek art and culture that characterized the eighteenth and nineteenth centuries has undergone sharp revision; Greek art is no longer regarded as perfect and without peer, worthy of imitation. What we call "modern art" turns its back on the ancient Greek example (Gauguin called Greek art "a lie!"), Greek language and literature is rarely studied in schools, and Greek ideals and values, even the best of them, are clearly not to the modern taste. Yet insofar as the Greeks sought for and revered ideal beauty, found it in the order of nature—above all, in the human body—and revealed it in art, we may still enjoy the art of Greece if we approach it with a sympathetic comprehension of its contexts, intentions, and archetypal forms.

The remains of Greek civilization enable us to reconstruct the development of the Greek style in art. That the Greek style should in fact have *developed* is in itself significant. Development in the art of Egypt, for example, was minimal; the pattern of ritual and of form was not to be broken. Change in Egypt occurred, when it did, *despite* the pattern of the culture as a whole. Of course, we must remember that an important factor in the sudden appearance of Greece on the summit of historical eminence was the base from which it rose—the civilizations of Egypt and the Near East, the quality and matter of which the Greeks quite honestly acknowledged borrowing. From these older civilizations, they acquired ideas, motifs, conventions, and skills. But from the beginning, the Greeks embraced experiment, even while adopting and holding to the older forms. Development and change were inherent in Greek culture (as conservatism was in Egyptian culture), and change has recognizable forms, as in the recurring stages of human life from infancy to old age. Greek art displays much more readily discernible stages than the relatively unchanging art of the Ancient Near East.

THE GEOMETRIC AND ARCHAIC PERIODS

Pottery serves, as no other artistic medium can, to link the very late Mycenaean (sub-Mycenaean) period with that of historical Greece. For one thing, it has survived. We can trace a continuity from the sub-Mycenaean period into the Classical fifth century B.C. entirely in terms of the figurative decoration of Greek ceramic ware, which shows the artist's confrontation with radically new ideas and problems and his equally radical interpretations and solutions. It is appropriate, then, given this continuity and the Greek concept of the development of forms, to begin the study of Greek art with vase paintings that illuminate changes that were profoundly influential in human history and that take place in a curiously logical order.

Already, we have seen numerous examples of how man represents himself, from the strange, falling stick figure in the *Well Scene* at Lascaux (FIG. 1-8) to the agile Minoans of *The Vaphio Cups* (FIG. 4-30). Now we can review changes in the representation of the human body that are the result not of accidental differences of convention but of carefully accumulated increments of knowledge. These were firmed into a tradition of technical procedure that did not backslide—as was the case in the Egyptian return to old forms after the death of the innovative Akhenaton (see Chapter 3). In the Archaic Greek vases, man became the subject of intense analytical study for the first time. As the Greek philosopher questioned man's nature and purpose, the Greek artist began to inquire how man looks to others of his kind in the world of optical experience. The conceptual way of placing him and enumerating his features, which we have seen in the art of older civilizations, gradually was given up and replaced by a method of painstaking observation of the pose and motion of the body in life. This did not happen all at once; centuries were involved in the great transformation, and the dated sequence of vases reveals the ordered phases of the change. It is useful to describe these changes at the outset, for, from its earliest appearances on vases, the human figure remained the principal motif of Greek art, as man was central to its thought and interest.

Vase Painting

A proto-Geometric *amphora* (FIG. 5-1), a two-handled jar for wine or oil, from the tenth century B.C. shows us the formative phase of what is called the *Geometric style*. Although it borrows the decorative devices of the earlier sub-Mycenaean style, its execution is neater and more painstaking. As the Geometric style developed, the Minoan stock of curvilinear forms was gradually replaced by rectilinear shapes arranged in tight bands covering more and more of the vessel.

The human figure reappeared in the decorative scheme during the period of the culminating Geometric style, specifically in the so-called *Dipylon Vase* (FIG. 5-2), from the eighth century B.C., named after the Dipylon cemetery in Athens, where it was found.

5-1 Proto-Geometric amphora, Dipylon cemetery, tenth century B.C. Approx. 16½″ high. Keramikos Museum, Athens.

5-2 *Dipylon Vase* (Geometric amphora), eighth century B.C. Approx. 59″ high. National Museum, Athens.

The figures are hardly more than symbols, fashioned of diamond and wedge shapes that fit the severe, regular, geometric characteristics of the banded shapes. These extremely abstract figures are arranged on the shoulders of the vessel, toward which the design builds up from below, the decorative bands generally becoming wider as their placement on the body of the vase becomes higher.

Another type of Greek vase, the *krater*, had a larger body and wider mouth than the amphora. A krater from the Dipylon cemetery (FIG. 5-3), possibly of the same date as the *Dipylon Vase* (FIG. 5-2) or somewhat later, shows a certain loss of refinement as the geometric ornament becomes secondary. The figures represent a funeral procession, with horse-drawn chariots occupied by warriors carrying shields; in the old conceptual manner, both wheels of each chariot are represented, the horses are carefully distinguished, and their legs are correct in number. The warriors are standing behind their shields, which are

shown in front view. The number of figures represented is markedly greater than the number shown in FIG. 5-2, suggesting that the artist was intrigued with the rediscovery of a subject—the human figure—that had been absent from mainland pottery decoration for over 400 years.

The Geometric period was succeeded by the Orientalizing phase of the Archaic period, a time of marked commercial and colonial expansion that brought the Greeks into closer contact with Ancient Near Eastern civilizations. A consequence of these new relationships was the frequent appearance of Oriental animals and composite monsters on Greek vases, motifs familiar to us from Mesopotamian and Egyptian art: lions, sphinxes, griffins, and centaurs. Stylistically, a vase from Eleusis (FIG. 5-4), typical of the Orientalizing period, represents a complete and radical break

5-3 Geometric krater, Dipylon cemetery, eighth century B.C. Approx. 40½″ high. Metropolitan Museum of Art, New York (Rogers Fund).

5-4 *The Blinding of Polyphemus* and *Gorgons* (proto-Attic amphora), Eleusis, c. 675–650 B.C. Approx. 56″ high. Museum, Eleusis.

with the orderly Geometric manner. The figurative decor occupies most of the vessel; the arrangement of the motifs is loose, almost casual, and the shapes are mostly curvilinear. It is almost as if the artist were intentionally throwing off the Geometric straitjacket as an awkward restraint on a new interest—the representation of narrative scenes, some from Homeric legend. On the amphora in FIG. 5-4 (where Polyphemus, the one-eyed giant, is being blinded by Odysseus), the human figure—resembling those of the Geometric period, but much more filled out, rounded, and active—now occupies the largest areas of the vessel, and the ornament retreats to the smaller areas in the neck, shoulder, and base. It was in the Geometric period that the Homeric themes were collected in the great epics; the Orientalizing period marks their diffusion and their achievement of universal popularity in Greece. The illustration of the epics was to occupy the surfaces of vases for centuries to come; it might almost seem that this first great reflection of man and his actions, in Greek epic, launched the enterprise of representing him in art.

During the Geometric and Archaic periods, numerous pottery centers developed throughout the Aegean world. They have been divided into two main groups—those of the mainland and those of eastern Greece (the regions east of the mainland). On the mainland, the most important centers were Athens in Attica and Corinth in the Peloponnesos; after 550 B.C., Athens became the principal ceramic center and the largest exporter of vases in the Mediterranean basin. In this brief survey, we shall confine ourselves to Athenian wares.

The number of basic Attic vase shapes was limited to six or seven, each subject to four or five variations. The shapes developed out of specific usages and were entirely functional (FIG. 5-5).

The François Vase (FIG. 5-6), which was named after its discoverer and is perhaps the finest extant example of an Early Archaic krater, with its volute handles and extraordinarily vigorous shape, was found in an Etruscan necropolis. (We are indebted to the Etruscans for their avid collecting of Greek vases; many of the best preserved have been found in Etruscan tombs.) It is especially important, not only for its high quality but also for the fact that it is signed by both ERGOTIMOS, the potter ("Ergotimos made it"), and KLEITIAS, the painter ("Kleitias drew it"). Signed vases appear for the first time in the early seventh century B.C. and suggest that their makers had pride in their profession and that their art had at least as much prestige as that of the sculptor or wall painter.

5-6 ERGOTIMOS and KLEITIAS, *The François Vase* (Attic black-figure krater), Chiusi, *c.* 575 B.C. Approx. 26" high. Museo Archeologico, Florence.

5-5 Greek vase shapes: (a) the *hydria* (from the Greek for "water"), a water jar with three handles, two for lifting and one for carrying; (b) the *lekythos,* an oil flask with a long, narrow neck adapted for pouring oil slowly, used chiefly in funeral rites; (c) the *krater* (from the Greek "to mix"), a bowl for mixing wine and water, the usual beverage of the Greeks; (d) the *amphora* (meaning "to carry on both sides," referring to the two handles), a vessel for storing provisions (wine, corn, oil, honey), with an opening large enough to admit a ladle and usually fitted with a cover; (e) the *kylix* (from the Greek "to roll," referring to the vase being turned on the potter's wheel), chief form of the drinking cup; (f) the *oenochoe* (from the Greek "to pour out wine"), a wine jug, the lip pinched into a trefoil shape to facilitate pouring.

The François Vase is ornamented with over 200 figures distributed in bands around the vessel. Representing almost the entire Greek pantheon, the figures provide us with one of our first pictorial glimpses of the forms and personages of Greek religion. The subject is the wedding of Peleus, with the gods in attendance; in addition to the scene of the gods and Peleus, father of Achilles, are depictions of the Calydonian boar hunt and the funeral games for Patroclus. On the foot of the vase is an account of an animated battle between cranes and pygmies, above which rays felicitously augment the swelling surface of the krater. The lively scenes are rigidly organized in six bands of varying widths, the widest placed on the vessel's shoulders, a return to the discipline and formality of the Geometric style after the casual and permissive Orientalizing style of the vase from Eleusis (FIG. 5-4).

The François Vase is decorated in an early form of the so-called *black-figure* technique, which is shown fully developed and at its best in a *kylix* (drinking cup) by the potter–painter EXEKIAS (FIG. 5-7). Dark figures are silhouetted against the light background of the natural reddish clay. Details are incised into the silhouettes with a sharp, pointed instrument to expose the red beneath; touches of white and purple, particularly on the earlier wares, add color to the dominantly monochrome decoration. Although the black areas are customarily referred to as "glazes," it should be pointed out that the black on these Greek pots is neither a pigment nor a glaze but *engobe,* a slip of finely sifted clay that originally is of the same color as the clay of the pot. In the three-phase firing process used by Greek potters, the first (oxidizing) phase turns both pot and slip red; during the second (reducing) phase, the oxygen supply into the kiln is shut off and both pot and slip turn black; in the final (reoxidizing) phase, the coarser material of the pot reabsorbs oxygen and becomes red again, while the smoother, silica-laden slip does not and remains black. After long experiment, Greek potters developed a velvety, jet-black "glaze" of this kind. The touches of white and purple were used more sparingly, with the result that

the figures stood in even stronger contrast against their reddish backgrounds. This superb formal control provides the framework for a wealth of naturalistic detail, some of it strikingly novel.

Exekias' kylix, with a representation of Dionysos sailing over the sea carrying his gifts to mankind and accompanied by sporting dolphins, his boat's mast entwined by a joyful grapevine, introduces a still more spectacular innovation—one that heralds the beginning of a revolution in world art. In his drawing of the boat's sail, Exekias does not show a traditional and conventional symbol that "reads" as a sail, but a sail as a sail would actually look, bellying out and filled with wind. It is an image of the action of wind itself, the wind made palpable as a force, and it must have come from a new awareness of the *physical* presence of nature. This awareness was abroad; it is in the Ionian speculations about the physical constitution of the world and in the reality-charged poetry of Homer: "But soon an off-shore breeze blew to our liking—a canvas-bellying breeze. . . . The bows went plunging . . . sails cracked and lashed out . . . ."

Although in Homer the gods are still the manipulators of the elements, it is men who feel their effects, who hear the howl of the great winds, smell the brine, and feel the harsh ropes and drenching rain. Man's experience of the world, as well as the world itself, begins to be understood by him in physical terms. Such a profound change in man's awareness of his relationship to nature and, in consequence, of his own nature is one that is bound to make itself felt in art. From Exekias' sail on, Greek art manifests an increasing comprehension of physical nature as it is apprehended by vision.

Exekias' skill and subtlety also solve to perfection a difficult compositional problem: how to fix the ship within its circular frame. Part of his solution lies in the down-branching weight of the loaded vines; part in the reverse hook-like dolphins, which seem to stitch the composition to its frame.

Around 530 B.C., a new painting technique was invented that reversed the black-figure style by making the background black and leaving the figures reserved in red. The figures of men and animals no longer were dark and earthy, massive against a light ground, but instead luminous, like light and air, shining forth from the black background. In this new *red-figure technique*, the major interior markings were rendered with relief lines applied with a syringe-like instrument that squeezed out the black "glaze" matter evenly and smoothly. Secondary markings, such as those representing hair, muscles, and sometimes

5-7 EXEKIAS, *Dionysos in a Sailboat* (interior of an Attic black-figure kylix), Vulci, *c.* 550–525 B.C. 12″ in diameter. Staatliche Antikensammlungen, Munich.

5-8 ANDOKIDES PAINTER, *Herakles and Apollo Struggling for the Tripod* (detail from amphora), *c.* 530 B.C. Outline drawing at right indicates relation to whole vessel. Portion shown approx. 11″ high; whole vessel approx. 23″ high. Staatliche Museen, Berlin.

5-9 EUPHRONIOS, *Herakles Strangling Antaios* (detail from krater), Cerveteri, *c.* 510–500 B.C. Outline drawing at right indicates relation to whole vessel. Portion shown approx. 12″ high; whole vessel approx. 19″ high. Louvre, Paris.

even shading, were painted in "dilute glaze" (engobe diluted with water), which could be applied with a fine brush. The style is freer and more facile than the earlier black-figure style, which it largely replaced within 20 years. The artist felt no need to enlarge his limited color scheme; the polished coppery red against a velvety black created an effect that was rich and elegant. The artist usually credited with the invention of the red-figure technique is the ANDOKIDES PAINTER, who is named for the potter Andokides, several of whose signed vases he decorated. Sometimes considered to be a student of Exekias, the Andokides Painter uses pictorial devices that are rooted in the style of the older master. On an amphora that shows *Herakles* (Hercules) *and Apollo Struggling for the Tripod* (FIG. 5-8), he shows an interest in rich drapery ornaments and textural effects such as are found in the work of his presumed master. His work lacks some of the warmth and sympathy of Exekias', because he is more concerned with exploiting the possibilities of his newly discovered technique. And there he breaks new ground, experimenting with novel and varied effects of color (he liked to use both purple and white) and, in a technique that dispenses with the laborious process of incision, creating new decorative schemes of great elegance.

A krater painted by EUPHRONIOS, one of the most forceful red-figure painters working near the end of the sixth century B.C., shows *Herakles Strangling Antaios* (FIG. 5-9). Euphronios was among the first to devote himself seriously to the study of anatomy and was famous for this in his time. Here, he shows two male figures in a complicated wrestling pose—one figure from the side, the other from the front. He at-

tempts such radical experiments as the doubled-under leg of Antaios and the rendering of Antaios' face in white to suggest the pallor of impending death. He makes an effort to describe Herakles' and Antaios' straining, powerful bodies with painstaking attention to the musculature, and although he does not entirely succeed in producing a correct representation, his attempt to apply knowledge gained through observation of bodily action is most significant.

EUTHYMIDES was a contemporary and competitor of Euphronios and, like him, an experimenter. As we can see from his picture of *Revelers* done on an amphora (FIG. 5-10), Euthymides is less concerned with anatomical description than with the problems of foreshortening in the figures and of showing them from different viewpoints. The fairly tipsy dancers, mightily enjoying themselves, are a rather popular subject on Late Archaic and Early Classical vases and celebrate the Hellenic sense of the comic that served as counterpoise to its genius for tragic art in the drama. In this case, it gave Euthymides an opportunity to present the figures in informal motion and in fairly successful three-quarter back and front views. The turning and twisting of the figures indicate that the artist is beginning to think of them as three-dimensional volumes that have free mobility in a space deeper than the flat, two-dimensional surface of the picture plane—a significant departure from pre-Greek tradition. The maturing self-consciousness of the Greeks is shown not only in their concern for the figures of man, but also, of course, in their consciousness of themselves as artists. They signed their names to their work and they were aware that they were doing new and revolutionary things as collaborators and rivals in a common professional enterprise. Euthymides, in an inscription on this amphora (FIG. 5-10), proclaimed with naïve pride: "Euphronios never did anything like it."

As revolutionary as Euphronios and Euthymides had been, the BRYGOS PAINTER (an anonymous artist who is named after the potter whose vases he decorated) took a significant step beyond them, around the year 490 B.C. Again the *Revelers* theme, with its gaily swinging movement, gave the experimenting artist his opportunity (FIG. 5-11). For some 2,500 years, since the *Palette of Narmer* (FIG. 3-2), painted figures and figures in relief had advanced the *far* leg to show a stride—which, after all, is the best way if the torso is to be shown in front view with minimum distortion of the figure. Euthymides had broken this rule, advancing the *near* leg of a figure to show it in a three-quarter rear view (FIG. 5-10). But the Brygos Painter, for the first time, presents a striding figure with the near leg advanced and its shoulder turned diagonally toward the observer (see the two central figures in FIG. 5-11). The result is the first true *contrapposto* stance that we have. The figure is now understood as an acting unit, not merely an assemblage of parts; the problem of its engineering has been solved to the extent that it can be represented in convincing

5-11 BRYGOS PAINTER, *Revelers* (detail from kylix), Vulci, *c.* 490 B.C. Outline drawing at right indicates relation to whole vessel. Portion shown approx. 10″ wide; whole vessel approx. 13″ wide. Martin V. Wagner Museen der Universität, Würzburg.

movement. At first, this may seem to be a small matter, but an apparently superficial detail may be the manifestation of an epoch-making change in the concept of what human beings perceive.

Sculpture

Trends in the development of sculpture in Greece are just as evident as those we have traced in vase painting, although much less sculpture survives. The earliest pieces go back to the beginning of the ninth century B.C. and consist of small-scale representations of animals (horses, oxen, deer, birds) and of human figures in various materials: copper, bronze, lead, ivory, and terra cotta. Some of these figures were ornaments on larger objects, like vases and bronze tripods; others, found near ancient sanctuaries, were separate votive offerings. At Olympia, these figures seem to have been manufactured on the spot for sale to visitors to the shrines.

A bronze warrior from the Acropolis of Athens, from the late eighth century B.C. (FIG. 5-12), shows all the clear simplifications of the Geometric period. The figure, a favorite type in Geometric art, is solid cast. (Given the figure's diminutive size, this would be the reasonable casting method; hollow casting, which was understood at this time, would not have saved much bronze.) The warrior originally held a spear in one raised arm and a shield in the other, although both shield and spear are missing in most surviving examples of such figures. The rather carefully rendered head and face, with the large eyes and broad grimace (later to become known as the standard "Archaic smile") attest to the fact that this figure is a late specimen of a type whose earlier examples had heads and faces that were little more than shapeless lumps. Moreover, the later body forms have become smoother, losing some of their former angularity, as if the artist were trying to rid himself of centuries-old conventions of Geometric figure representation before the new approach—the visual one—could be

5-10 EUTHYMIDES, *Revelers*, Vulci, *c.* 510–500 B.C. Approx. 24″ high. Staatliche Antikensammlungen, Munich.

5-12 Geometric bronze warrior (front and back views), Acropolis, Athens, late eighth century B.C. Bronze, approx. 8" high. National Museum, Athens.

5-13 *Mantiklos "Apollo"* (front and back views), Thebes, *c.* 680 B.C. Bronze, approx. 8" high. Museum of Fine Arts, Boston (Francis Bartlett Fund).

tried. It is believed that these warrior statuettes were Syrian in inspiration, but a difference important in the evolution of Greek sculpture should be noted: the Greek figures are represented nude, while the Syrian prototypes wear loincloths. As early as the eighth century B.C., the Greek instinct for the natural beauty of the human figure, which peculiarly and permanently distinguishes Greek art, is set in contrast with the Near Eastern traditional prejudice against the representation of the nude in sculpture in the round.

Kouros and Kore

A bronze figure of a youth from around 680 B.C. (FIG. 5-13) stands at the beginning of the Archaic period; it is a small forerunner of the later *kouros* figures (see FIGS. 5-15 and 5-16). The silhouette remains essentially geometric, with a triangular torso, a narrow waist, and bulging thighs; but the forms have gained volume, and the modeling of the pectoral muscles and the description of other anatomical details by means of incised lines show an incipient interest in the structure of the body.

Monumental, freestanding sculpture (life-size or larger) first appeared about 600 B.C., in the earlier stages of the Archaic period. Its rise is contemporary with the Orientalizing period in vase painting and was probably inspired by foreign sources, most likely Egypt and Mesopotamia—the only areas at that time that could show monumental sculpture in abun-

dance. An early example of this monumental, freestanding sculpture is the *Hera* from Samos (FIG. 5-14), which is over six feet tall and has a cylindrical shape that could have been derived only from Mesopotamia (compare FIGS. 2-22 and 2-23). The goddess stands in

5-14 *Hera* from Samos, *c.* 560 B.C. Marble, approx. 6' 4" high. Louvre, Paris.

a frontal pose, feet together, the right arm held tightly to the side, the left bent to the breast and probably originally holding some attribute, or symbol, of authority. The goddess is in the form of a sheathed column (in origin, a tree?), as were the deities of Crete and Mycenae, but here the Greek artist displays his extraordinary sensitivity for surface ornamentation. The stability of the lower portions—where the striations of the *chiton,* or tunic, are placed against the plain surface of the *himation,* a kind of cape—contrasts with the movement in the upper portions, where the himation is drawn in gracefully curving folds around the delicate modeling of the swelling bosom.

The early kouros figures (FIGS. 5-15 and 5-16) remind us of the Egyptian statues. Some of these figures are of youths who are dedicated to a god and are apparently advancing into his presence; others are memorial statues that stand over the graves of noblemen. Thus, they are of men, not gods (not, as once thought, "Apollos"), and this is significant—this glorification of men in monumental statues that commemorate their triumph and give them a god-like scale and presence. The kouroi recall Egyptian stat-

ues in the pose (the left foot advanced), in the broad, square shoulders, and in the rigidly frontal and symmetrical design. The Egyptian and Mesopotamian thought of the sculptured human body as a smooth envelope of stone, but the Greek was interested in the structural parts and how they fitted together. The kouros from Tenea (FIG. 5-15) shows us characteristic traits of the figure type, although the kouroi differ markedly from each other. Because the figures were freestanding, without the Egyptian stone slab for support, most kouroi have been found broken at the ankles. Obviously, the Greek sculptor was not aiming for Egyptian permanence as much as for fidelity to appearance, and one of his first steps toward that goal was the liberation of the figure from the original block of stone. On the broad planes of the figure, anatomical details are carefully modeled, as we see in the chest and the knee joints. The head is geometrically simplified into flat planes: the eyes are large and protruding, and the nose, mouth, ears, and headdress are all highly stylized attributes of the almost cubic mass of the head. Although still almost provincial Egyptian, the Tenea kouros is quite un-Egyptian in its nudity and in its more dynamic, half-striding

5-15 Kouros from Tenea, *c.* 570 B.C. Marble, approx. 60″ high. Staatliche Antikensammlungen, Munich.

5-16 *Kroisos* (kouros) from Anavysos, *c.* 540–515 B.C. Marble, approx. 6′ 4″ high. National Museum, Athens.

stance. Moreover, this figure is slender and elegant, with the alert, elastic physique of a sprinter. Description of the anatomy by incised line, typical of the earlier models, has been given up, and the torso, thighs, and calves are modeled in the full round with ever-closer approximation of anatomical truth.

With the *Kroisos* from Anavysos (FIG. 5-16), we come to the verge of a breakthrough similar to the one we have seen in vase painting. The statue is, according to an inscription on its base, a funerary monument of a youth, Kroisos, who died a hero's death in battle. Where the anatomy of the Tenea figure is still somewhat generalized, here it becomes specific and accurate. The artist not only understands the structural parts of the figure and their natural relationship and how to represent their surfaces by modeling the stone, but he is able to give us what amounts to a *portrait* of the body, a likeness of a particular physique—in this case, that of a muscular wrestler, heavier and more massive than the taut, spare Tenea figure. It is noteworthy that the Greeks began their monumental sculpture with portraits not of the head but of the body. This "bodiliness" of Greek sculpture persisted for centuries until it became lost in a realism that compelled the sculptor to use illusional devices more appropriate to painting.

What we might think of as companion figures to the *kouroi* (youths) are the draped *korai* (maidens), contemporaneous with the former and manifesting in their own style similar features of concept and design. The *Peplos Kore* (FIG. 5-17), contemporary with the *Kroisos*, is one of numerous figures found on the Acropolis of Athens, thrown down by the Persians during their sack of the city in 480 B.C. Their purpose is obscure, but they may have been votive figures attending the deities in a kind of permanent and perpetual ritual. In contrast with earlier types, the face of this kore is more expressively modeled; the chin, cheeks, and corners of the mouth are subtly planed. The great eyes, originally with painted lids, may have been intended to have hypnotic power: we think back to the ancient head from Warka (FIG. 2-12). The missing left arm was extended, a break from the frontal compression of the arms at the sides in Egyptian statues. The body itself is modeled with a soft smoothness that takes account of the figure beneath the drapery, much like the earlier *Hera* from Samos (FIG. 5-14), but is a great deal more anatomically real. Traces of paint may be seen on parts of the figure; all Greek stone statues were painted, the powder-white of Classical statues being an error of modern interpretation. But the Greeks did not smear their statues garishly with bright colors, indifferent to their place and effect; only the decisive parts, such as the eyes, lips, hair, and edges of drapery, were painted to provide accents and contrast with the color of the soft

5-17 *Peplos Kore*, Acropolis, Athens, *c.* 530 B.C. Marble, approx. 48″ high. Acropolis Museum, Athens.

marble itself, the latter being waxed and polished. The whole purpose of coloring was to make the statue more lifelike, more convincing as a kind of person confronting visitors to the shrines of the Acropolis. The remarkable permanence of the color partly

5-18 Kore from Chios (?), *c.* 510 B.C. Marble, approx. 21½″ high. Acropolis Museum, Athens.

can be ascribed to the technique of *encaustic,* in which pigment is mixed with wax and applied to the surface while hot. This method was widely used in ancient wall painting and on wooden panels, as well as in the embellishment of statues.

The preservation of the color of many of the kore statues is also a result of the Athenians' use of fragments of broken statues and temples as rubble fill in rebuilding the temples and retaining walls of the Acropolis after the Persian destruction. In this material, modern archeologists have found works such as the kore from Chios (?) (FIG. 5-18). The luxurious gowns of these figures may be evidence that they were made in Ionia, where the wealthy Greek states cultivated the Oriental taste for rich ornamentation in both life and art. Ionian influence was strong in Athens during the Archaic period, and Ionian fashions, featuring the intricately folded, chic chiton, interested not only women but sculptors, who found in the representation of delicate texture and fold a peculiarly difficult challenge. For some time, sculptors seemed to delight in working out the complexities of the pleats and folds made by the thin, soft material and were content to let the matter remain one of decoration rather than structure. At this point, much

must have been learned of the movement of a surface independent of the body beneath it, but the kore figures remained frontal and basically unchanged for a considerable period. Although there were slight changes, the scheme of this example was repeated over and over until the end of the Archaic period. The attractive problem of surface texture appears to have deflected the sculptors of the kore figures from larger issues.

The larger issues involve not the draped female figure but the nude kouros figure type we have been describing; at least, it is there that the break with age-old sculptural traditions takes place. The female nude does not appear in ancient sculpture, with some minor exceptions, until the fourth century B.C. We will see that its appearance in Greek art accompanies changes of a fundamental kind in Greek culture and morals. Why the Greek artist should have represented the male figure nude some 300 years before he represented the female nude is not known. He may have found, as any student of the living model in art has found, that the male figure is much more revealing of human structure. Male models would have been present for observation in exercises and at the games; we know that in the Dorian world, of which Sparta was the capital, the Greek artist would also have been able to observe female models, yet the male figure was given priority. By the time of Plato, nudity in the context of athletics was commonplace in the Greek world, and the prejudice against it could be regarded as barbarous—that is, merely a prejudice of the non-Hellenic Near East. In Plato's *Republic,* Socrates remarked:

> Not long ago . . . the Hellenes were of the opinion, which is still generally received among the barbarians, that the sight of a naked man was ridiculous and improper. . . . But experience showed that to let all things be uncovered was far better than to cover them up . . . .

Certainly by about 520 B.C., the male nude must have been familiar enough for the artist to construct a convincingly real image from the observation of it. The establishment of a new convention, the propriety of the nude, implied the setting aside of the 3,000-year-old convention of the pre-Greek world that inhibited—probably because nudity was the badge of slavery—the study of the structure of the human body as given to the eye.

In the *Kroisos* figure (FIG. 5-16), the independent elements of the body are sufficiently described. The question must now be: how do the elements work together? From the time of King Narmer, there had been more or less successful approximations of the human figure with enumerated parts, the attitudes universally stiff and immobile. What can put these parts into motion? The answer appears in a late kouros (if we can still call it that) found in the Acropolis rubble and dating from just before the Persian destruction. The statue, which must have been the consequence of a mind deliberating on what had already been done, is called the *Kritios Boy* (FIG. 5-19), from the name of its presumed sculptor. It is not in action, but stands at rest; that is to say, it *really* stands at rest, not merely in a stiff-legged pose or a pose bound to a block. The secret of this new and radical naturalness lies in the artist's knowledge of the principle of *weight shift,* the shifting of position of the main parts of the body around the vertical, but flexible, axis of the spine. The shifting of the human body in life never takes place in a rigid stiff-legged manner; indeed we laugh at, or are in terror of, the science-fiction monster that moves in this ponderous, mechanical way. Rather, when we change place and move, the elastic musculoskeletal structure of our bodies dictates a harmonious, smooth motion of all the elements of the body. Greek artists were the first to grasp this fact, and the artist of the *Kritios Boy* was the first to represent it. The youth turns his head only very slightly

away from the central axis. There is the slightest dip to the shoulders and to the hips, indicating the shift of weight onto the left leg; the right leg is at ease. (One can easily assume this pose and the contrasting flat-footed poses of the earlier kouros statues.) Once the principle of weight shift has been realized, all motion of the human figure is possible in the world of representation—not simply in terms of the signs of motion evident in simple gesture, but also in terms of motion of the whole body as we see *and* experience it. After the *Kritios Boy,* Greek sculpture rapidly passes through the possibilities of the figure understood as having its own physical principle of motion, a principle revealed to the eye in ordinary optical experience and confirmed by the observer's own physical sense of motion.

So far, we have been considering sculpture apart from architecture. But the decoration of buildings, especially temples, with sculpture, both in relief and in the round, offered the Greek sculptor a major opportunity. Because sculpture was applied only to very specific and limited areas of temples, it is necessary first to become acquainted with the basic structure of the various buildings that it adorned.

5-19 *Kritios Boy* (front and side views), Acropolis, Athens, *c.* 480 B.C. Marble, approx. 34″ high. Acropolis Museum, Athens.

Architecture

Greek architecture and its Roman and Renaissance descendants and hybrids are almost as familiar to us as modern architecture. The "revival" of it by European architects in the late eighteenth century brought about a wide diffusion of its style; official public buildings (court houses, banks, city halls, legislative chambers), designed for impressive formality, especially imitated the architecture of Classicism, which was fundamentally Greek in inspiration. Although their homes were unpretentious places, they had no monarchs to house royally until Hellenistic times, and they performed state religious rites in the open, the ancient Greeks were industrious builders. Their significant buildings began primarily as simple shrines to protect the statues to their gods. More and more attention was lavished on these structures, until possibly the belief arose that the qualities of the god were embodied in the buildings themselves. Figure sculpture played its part in this construction program, partly to embellish the protective building, partly to tell something of the deity symbolized within, and partly as a votive offering. But the building itself also was conceived as sculpture, abstract in form and possessing the power of sculpture to evoke human responses. The commanding importance of the sculptured temple, its inspiring function in public life, was emphasized in its elevated site, often on a hill above the city (the *acropolis*). As Aristotle stipulated: "the site should be a spot seen far and wide, which gives due elevation to virtue and towers over the neighborhood." And the reverent awe that must have been attached to the temple and to the genius of its founders was echoed by Plato: "Gods and temples are not easily instituted, and to establish them rightly is the work of a mighty intellect."

Although still a matter of ardent debate, one theory holds that the earliest temples were made of wood, and that these wooden forms were in time translated into the more permanent materials of limestone and sometimes marble. Marble was expensive, but mountains of it were available: from Hymettus, just east of Athens, with its bluish-white stone; from Pentelicus, northeast of the city, its glittering white stone particularly adapted for carving; and from the islands of the Aegean, Paros in particular, which supplied marble of varying quantities and qualities.

In its plan, the Greek temple discloses a close affinity with the Mycenaean megaron and, even in its most elaborate form, retains the latter structure's basic simplicity (FIG. 5-20): a single or double room (the *naos*) with no windows and one door (two for a double naos) and with (a) a portico with two columns between the extended walls (columns *in antis*), or (b) a colonnade across the front (*prostyle*), or (c) a colonnade across both front and back (*amphiprostyle*), or any of these plans surrounded by (d and e) a single (*peripteral*) or (f) a double (*dipteral*) colonnade. What strikes the eye first in the Greek scheme, after what

has been seen of the architecture of the Ancient Near East, is its remarkable order, compactness, and symmetry, in contrast, say, to the relative irregularity of the Egyptian temple. The difference lies in the Greeks' sense of *proportion* and in their effort to achieve ideal forms in terms of regular numerical relationships and the rules of *geometry*.

We can discern in the plans a kind of development from quite simple to more complex units, without, however, any fundamental change in the nature of the units or of their grouping. For Classical Greek architecture, like classical music, has a simple core theme from which a series of complex, but always quite intelligible, variations is developed. And, to change the analogy, the development of the temple scheme is like that other great invention of the Greeks, geometry, in which theorems, propositions, and their corollaries are deduced from a simple original set of axioms. The insistence of the Greeks on proportional order guided the experiments with the proportions of temple plans. The earlier, Archaic temples tended to be long and narrow (FIG. 5-20d), with the proportion of the ends to the sides roughly expressible as 1:3. Late Classical and Hellenistic plans approached but rarely had a proportion of exactly 1:2, with Classical temples tending to be a little longer than twice their width (FIG. 5-20e) and Hellenistic temples tending to be a little shorter (FIG. 5-20f). Proportion in architecture and sculpture, and harmony in music, were much the same to the Greek

5-20 Six representative plans of the Greek temple: (a) Treasury of the Athenians at Delphi, a temple *in antis*, in which the portico is formed by the projecting side walls with two columns set between their ends (*antae*); (b) Temple B at Selinus, Sicily, a *prostyle* temple, in which the columns stand in front of the naos and extend to its width; (c) Temple of Athena Nike on the Acropolis at Athens, an *amphiprostyle* temple, in which the prostyle plan has a porch added at the rear; (d) Temple of Hera at Olympia and (e) Temple of Aphaia at Aegina, *peripteral* temples, in which a single colonnade surrounds the naos; and (f) Temple of Apollo at Didyma, near Miletus, a *dipteral* temple, in which two colonnades surround the naos. (*Drawings are not to scale.*)

mind and indeed reflected and embodied the cosmic order, just as did the rationally pursued "good life."

The elevation of a Greek building is described in terms of the platform, column, and *entablature* (FIG. 5-21); this combination and relationship of three units is called an *order*. The three orders developed by Greek builders are differentiated partly by details but chiefly by the relative proportions of the parts. Each order served different purposes and embodied different meanings. The earliest of the Greek architectural orders to be formulated were the *Doric,* of mainland Greece, and the *Ionic,* of Asia Minor and the Aegeans (FIG. 5-21). The *Corinthian* order followed much later.

The columns, which rest on a platform (*stylobate),* have two or three parts, depending on the order: the *shaft,* which is marked with vertical channels (*fluting);* the *capital;* and (in the Ionic and Corinthian orders) the *base.* As the shaft rises, its diameter decreases gradually, giving the profile a subtle curve (*entasis);* the top (in the Doric) is marked with one or several horizontal lines (*necking)* that furnish the transition to the capital. The capital has two elements, the lower of which (the *echinus)* varies with the order: in the Doric, it is convex and cushion-like; in the Ionic, it is small and supports a bolster ending in scroll-like spirals (the *volutes);* and in the Corinthian, it is shaped like an inverted bell and is decorated with a design of stylized acanthus leaves. The upper element, present in all orders, is a flat, square block (the *abacus)* that provides the immediate support for the entablature. The entablature has three parts: the *architrave,* the main weight-bearing and weight-distributing element; the *frieze;* and the *cornice,* a molded horizontal projection. In some buildings, the third part, with two sloping (*raking)* cornices, forms a triangle that enframes the *pediment.* The architrave is usually subdivided into three horizontal bands (*fasciae)* in the Ionic and Corinthian orders. The frieze is subdivided

into *triglyphs* and *metopes* in the Doric order and is left open in the Ionic to provide a continuous field for reliefs.

The Doric order is massive in appearance, its sturdy columns firmly planted on the stylobate. Compared with the weighty and severe Doric, the Ionic order seems light, airy, and much more decorative. Its columns are slenderer and rise from molded bases. The Doric flutings meet in sharp ridges (*arrises),* but the Ionic ridges are flat (*fillets).* The most obvious differences among the three orders are, of course, in the capitals—the Doric, severely plain; the Ionic and Corinthian, highly ornamental.

In ancient times, the Doric and Ionic orders were contrasted as masculine and feminine. The Corinthian order was not developed until the fifth century B.C., when it appeared inside the temple, like a natural form growing in the darkness of the interior. On the exteriors of buildings, however, it was not widely used until Roman times. Since the Renaissance and until about two generations ago, much of the architecture in the Western world was considered to be in essence the display of the refined beauty of these architectural orders.

According to one theory, many of the parts of the Doric order seem to be translations into stone of an earlier timber architecture. Pausanias, writing in the second century A.D., noted that in the even-then ancient Temple of Hera at Olympia (FIG. 5-20d), a wooden column was still in place; the others had been replaced by stone columns. It has been inferred, from the varying proportions of these columns, that the wooden columns were replaced at different times, probably as the wood of the original columns rotted. One feature of the Doric order can best be explained as a translation from the wooden original into stone—the organization of the frieze into triglyphs and metopes. The triglyphs most likely de-

5-21 Doric and Ionic orders. (After Grinnell.)

rived from the ends of crossbeams that rested on the main horizontal support, the architrave. The metopes would then correspond to the voids between the beam ends in the original wooden structure.

Sculptural ornament, which played an important part in the design of the temple, was concentrated on the upper part of the building, in the frieze and pediments. The sculpture was gaily painted in red and blue, with touches of green, yellow, black, and perhaps a little gold, and was usually applied only to those parts of the building that had no structural function or that suggested a former structural function. This is true particularly of the Doric style, in which decorative sculpture was applied only to the "voids" of the metopes and of the pediment. Ionic builders, less severe in this respect, were willing to decorate the entire frieze and sometimes even the lower drums of columns. Occasionally, they replaced their columns with female figures (caryatids), something the Doric builder would probably not have done. Using color, the designer could bring out more clearly the relationships of the structural parts, soften the glitter of the stone at specific points, and provide a background to set off the figures. Although it is true that color was used for emphasis and to mitigate what might have seemed too bare a simplicity (in Doric as well as in Ionic buildings), the primary dependence in Greek architecture—as in Greek mathematics, science, and philosophy—was on the setting of clear limits. This thesis had to begin with the axiom that the limits themselves must never be encroached on, must always contain, and must never be vague. The three Greek architectural orders just described were embodiments of codified limits that appeared plainly to the eye as functioning realities. To the Greek, it was unthinkable to use surfaces in the way that the Egyptian used his gigantic columns—as fields for complicated ornamentation. The very building itself, the Greek temple as given to the eye, must have the clarity of a Euclidean demonstration. This is borne out not only by its plan, elevation, and function-enhancing ornamentation, but also by its "dry-jointed" construction (construction without mortar), which provides evidence that Greek architects looked on their temples not as "buildings" but as monumental pieces of sculpture.

The placement of the building strengthened its sculptural aspect. Unlike Egyptian temples, Greek temples faced outward. Rites were performed at altars in front of the temple, and the building itself served to house the cult statue and perhaps trophies and treasure. Private cults were frowned on, and public ritual prevailed. Thus, it was on the exterior of the building and its surfaces that the architect generally concentrated his efforts to make the temple a suitable monument to the deity. The studied visual relationships of solids and voids, of light and shade in the colonnades, and the lighter accents of the entablature made a sculptural form out of the rectangular mass of the temple. The history of Greek architecture is the history of the Greek artist's unflagging efforts to express the form of the temple in its most satisfactory (that is to say, what he believed to be perfect) proportions.

The experiment in proportions can be followed rather easily if we begin with the Archaic Doric architecture of the Greek colonies—especially in Sicily and southern Italy—for it is here that the best-preserved examples of Archaic temples are found. (In examining Greek architecture, it is useful to keep in mind the development of the human figure in Greek painting and in sculpture; the architectural events are not only contemporaneous, but reflect a similar concern with proportions.) The "Basilica" at Paestum, south of Naples, dates from about 550 B.C., and is a typical example of Archaic Doric style (FIG. 5-22). Called the

5-22 The "Basilica," Paestum, Italy, c. 550 B.C.

"Basilica" after a Roman building type that early investigators felt it resembled, it is a peripteral temple with heavy columns of pronounced entasis, closely spaced, with large, bulky, pillow-like capitals, supporting a high and massive entablature that makes the columns seem proportionately squat. These parts of the order will be gradually adjusted until a lighter and taller combination is achieved. There is a structural reason, perhaps, for the heaviness of the design and the narrowness of the spans between the columns. The Archaic builders, uncertain of the strength of their materials, may have been providing a broad margin of safety. A detail of the "Basilica" colonnade (FIG. 5-23) shows the extreme spread of the cushion capitals and exaggeration of the supporting surface in relationship to the spans bridged by the architrave. The columns are built up of separate, dry-jointed "drums," fitted with square metal plugs to prevent turning as well as shifting. The whole temple was of this typically Greek construction, the blocks of stone in a horizontal course being held together by metal cramps, while those of different courses, one above the other, were joined vertically by metal dowels. Through the "Basilica" colonnade can be seen the nearby Temple of Hera, which was built 80 to 90 years later with columns of strikingly different proportions from those of the "Basilica."

The diagram showing the evolution in the propor-

5-24 Evolution of Doric-order proportions, Archaic to Classical. (*Examples are not drawn to same scale.*)

tions of the Doric order from Archaic to Classical (FIG. 5-24) emphasizes the thesis that Greek art evolved in conjunction with a certain logic—whether in its figurative or its architectural forms—that moved toward a conclusion that was as satisfactory as it was true. Plato, in speaking of the imitative arts, declared the degree of their truth or rightness to be determined by the proportionality of their elements and that, if they were to be judged at all, they must be judged by the "standard of truth, and by no other whatever." In this diagram, we see the architects working toward proportions that could be thought of as "true" and final. Some of the earliest columns (not shown) were extremely slender, under massive capitals. The shafts soon thickened to the shape of the "Basilica" type, as the builders searched for a better relationship between the shaft and the capital. From then on, the forms were constantly refined, the shafts becoming more slender, the entasis subtler, the capitals smaller, and the entablature lighter. The final Classical proportions were considered to be ideal ones, beyond which further refinement was impossible.

The Temple of Hera at Paestum (FIG. 5-25) dates from about 460 B.C.; although the forms have been refined, the columns are still massive and closely spaced. This temple was erected at a time when, on the Greek mainland, the Doric order had already achieved its Classical proportions (as early as 490 B.C.) in the Temple of Aphaia at Aegina. There was a considerable time lag between developments on the mainland and their adoption by the colonies in Italy

5-23 "Basilica" colonnade, with view of the Temple of Hera beyond.

5-25   Temple of Hera at Paestum, Italy, *c.* 460 B.C.

and Sicily, so that the colonial architecture exhibits the usual provincial conservatism characteristic of styles distant from their source of inspiration in the cultural capital. The plan and section of the Temple of Hera (FIG. 5-26) show a noteworthy peculiarity in the support structure of the interior, the columns of which rise higher than the outer, peripteral columns. Each of the two rows of small Doric columns that support the roof is made up of two sets of columns, one resting on a stone course that rests on the set of columns below. This was a standard form where Doric columns were used to support the roof; the reason for this may have been that a single row of large columns, as in the ''Basilica,'' would produce a distortion of scale and look out of proportion and op-

pressive inside the relatively small naos. Later, the support problem was solved by using Ionic or Corinthian columns in the interior, because they were taller than the Doric ones in relation to their diameters.

One of the earliest Ionic buildings in Greece is the Treasury of the Siphnians at Delphi, constructed about 530 B.C. (FIG. 5-27). Although it has no Ionic columns (the supporting function is assumed by luxuriously carved caryatids), it has the identifying Ionic feature—the continuous frieze—that appears here as part of a heavy Archaic entablature. The caryatids, with their elaborate costume and very irregular silhouettes, would never have fitted into a context of Doric architecture, with its severity of line and disdain of ornament.

5-26   Plan *(left)* and section *(right)* of the Temple of Hera at Paestum. (After Sir Banister Fletcher.)

5-27 Treasury of the Siphnians from the Sanctuary of Apollo at Delphi, *c.* 530 B.C. Museum, Delphi. (Façade reconstructed.)

Architectural Sculpture

We have noted already that decorative sculpture was applied only to those parts of a temple that had no evident structural function—the frieze and the pediment. The caryatids are exceptional, but their use is fairly rare. Ordinarily, the weight-carrying columns and the weight-distributing architraves were not decorated, although it may be that war trophies were hung on the blank Doric architrave. In the Doric order, only the metopes bore relief sculpture. It might be argued that the fluting of columns is a form of decoration, but, in fact, the fluting simply explains and emphasizes the form and function of the column, stressing its verticality. It also exhibits the column's rotundity, for when the sunlight strikes sharply on the shaft (FIG. 5-23), the fluting throws numerous shadows of graduated width and darkness that lead the eye around the shaft in a series of graded steps, making the effect of roundness more evident than in the nonfluted column, in which the sunlight creates a single, indistinct line separating the light and dark sides.

The Greek architectural sculptor faced a problem similar to that of the Greek vase painter: how to adjust the image to the surface on which it is placed. This is not apparent in the frieze from the Treasury of the Siphnians (FIG. 5-28), for here the sculptor has a continuous blank zone to manage and can arrange his figures in a simple file, their heads on the same level,

5-28 *Battle of the Gods and Giants,* from the north frieze of the Treasury of the Siphnians. Marble, approx. 26" high. Museum, Delphi.

each filling a unit of space of approximately the same dimension. This is a good example of the formalizing effect of architectural line on figurative composition, as the surface of the ceramic vessel imposed its necessities on the vase painter, encouraging simplicity and elegance of style. In fact, there is a stylistic resemblance between the Siphnian figures and such contemporary painting as that of the Andokides Painter (FIG. 5-8). But an awkward space like that of the triangular pediment of the Archaic Temple of Artemis (early sixth century B.C.) on the island of Corfu (FIG. 5-29) is more troublesome to manage. Here, the figures are heraldically arranged and bring to mind compositions that go back beyond the Lion Gate at Mycenae (FIG. 4-25) to the symmetrical man–beast compositions of Mesopotamia (FIG. 2-9). On the thin panel of stone that fills the space between the cornices of the pediment, the sculptor presents a Gorgon flanked by spotted panthers. The Gorgon, a guardian monster, grimaces hideously, exposing her boar's teeth (her look could turn men to stone) and fulfilling her function as a winged demon to repulse all enemies from the sanctuary of the goddess. To the left and the right of the central Gorgon appear, on a smaller scale, the figures of Chrysoar and Pegasus, those mythological creatures that, according to legend, sprang from the Gorgon's head when she was struck by the sword of Perseus. Still smaller are two groups of figures beyond the panthers: Zeus slaying a giant (on the observer's right) and one of the climactic events of the Trojan War, Neoptolemus killing Priam. In the outer ends of the pediment, recumbent figures represent a fallen Trojan and a dead giant. As pieced together from the surviving fragments, the artist's narrative intention is clear enough, but the odd shape of the surface on which he worked compelled him to distribute his figures somewhat haphazardly around the central ones and to show them on different scales. As time progressed, the Greek artist attempted to fill the space more organically, with figures grouped so that they appeared to be of the same size and participating in a unified way in a single event.

5-29   Reconstruction drawing superimposed on a photograph of the remaining fragments of the pediment of the Temple of Artemis at Corfu, *c.* 600–580 B.C.

Toward the end of the Archaic period, Greek sculptors were arriving at a solution to the problem of pedimental composition. In the pedimental sculptures of the Temple of Aphaia at Aegina (FIGS. 5-30, 5-31, 5-32), we find that the figures, in different poses but of the same scale, have been fitted into the difficult triangular space. The exact original arrangement is still a matter of dispute, and various solutions have been suggested. The figures—heavily cleaned and over-restored in the nineteenth century, but recently re-restored to their original condition—probably represent some episode of the Trojan War. Athena, with aegis and spear, stands in the center, with fighting groups on either side. We notice most the freedom of movement and the variety of pose. The figures are modeled with great vigor and an understanding of the human physique that, as we have seen in the contemporary vase paintings, reflect a careful observation of nature. The figure of the *Fallen Warrior* from the left angle of the pediment (FIG. 5-31) exhibits the daring with which the sculptor tackles the challenging problem of a difficult twisted pose. The bold composition of the turning masses of the body manifests his new confidence in his mastery of the science of *representation*. The dynamics of muscular tension and relaxation are appreciated and are close to life in their rendering. Mistakes are still made, and the transition from chest to pelvis has not been fully solved in this complex pose (note the misplaced navel). However, these rather technical considerations should not blind us to the marvelously expressive power of this figure. The *Fallen Warrior* brings to mind the spare and monumental nobility of Homer's heroes—and particularly the Homeric simile, "darkness came down upon his eyes, and he crashed in the battle like a falling tower."

The figure of the archer *Herakles* (FIG. 5-32), from the same pediment, is another instance of the Greek sculptor's triumph over age-old taboos and difficulties of representation. It is thought that this nimble archer is executing a maneuver hard to perform without long practice but required in the Greek war games

5-30   Reconstruction drawing of the east pediment of the Temple of Aphaia at Aegina, *c.* 490 B.C.

5-31   *Fallen Warrior*, from the east pediment of the Temple of Aphaia at Aegina. Marble, 6' long. Staatliche Antikensammlungen, Munich.

5-32 *Herakles,* from the east pediment of the Temple of Aphaia at Aegina. Marble, approx. 31" high. Staatliche Antikensammlungen, Munich.

and in actual combat. Running forward, he has dropped suddenly almost to one knee, and, from this tense position, takes aim and fires a flight of arrows in a matter of seconds. Soon he will spring to his feet to run forward again. The practiced strength and poise demanded by such a feat are beautifully caught in the elastic, though momentarily rigid, pose. One might read here the expression of a new spirit in Greek life and art—a spirit buoyant and optimistic as it meets the great challenge of the Persians at Marathon and looks to a future that the Ancient Near Eastern world could never envision and never encompass.

THE FIFTH CENTURY

The Transitional Period

The 30 or so years of the Transitional period constitute the heroic age of the Athenians and of all the Hellenes who joined forces against the invasion of Greece by the Persians. Just as we look back to the age of the American Revolution and of the founding fathers of the republic for our models of heroism and civic wisdom and virtue, so the Greeks of the later fifth century revered the men of Marathon, Thermopylae, and Salamis—the battles that daunted and finally turned back the mighty hosts of Asia led by Xerxes. The new world of the Greeks, which they attributed to the Homeric feats of their heroes, turned away from Asia, barbarism, tyranny, and ignorance (it was all the same to the Greeks) to build a Hellenic civilization productive of a new species of mankind.

Typical of the time were the views of the great dramatist Aeschylus, who celebrated, in his *Oresteia,* the triumph of reason and law over barbarous crime, blood feud, and mad vengeance. Himself a veteran of Marathon, Aeschylus repudiated in majestic verse all the slavish and inhuman traits of nature that the Greeks at that time of crisis tended to associate with the Persians.

Shortly after Athens was occupied and sacked in 480 B.C., the Greeks won a great naval victory over the Persians at Salamis. This resilient toughness of the Athenians signified a new pride that was to mature into a sense of Hellenic identity so strong that thenceforth the history of European civilization would be distinct from—even though in interaction with—the civilization of Asia. The period of struggle with the Persians, calling repeatedly for courage and endurance, produced in the Hellenes a kind of austere grandeur that is manifested in the art of that period, usually referred to as the *severe style.* Stern simplification of outline and surface, fixed pose, firm stance, and immobility of expression characterize the severe style as we find it in two superb, life-size bronze statues of warriors, recently recovered from the sea (1972) and restored to their original appearance (FIGS. 5-33, 5-34, 5-35, 5-36). *The Riace Bronzes* take their name from Riace Marina, a shore resort in

5-33 *The Riace Bronzes, Warrior Figure,* 460–450 B.C. Bronze, silver teeth and eyelashes, copper lips and nipples; figure 6' 1" high. Archaeological Museum, Reggio Calabria.

5-34 Back of *Warrior with Headband* (before restoration).

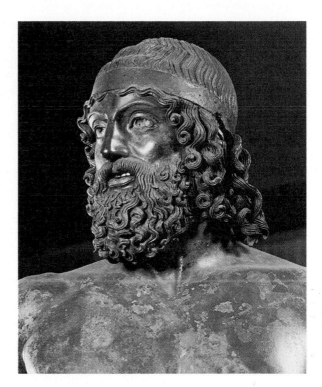

5-36 Detail of head of *Warrior with Headband*.

Reggio Calabria, the site of an ancient Greek colony at the toe of the Italian boot. They were found by an underwater swimmer just offshore, buried in the sand some 25 feet beneath the surface of the sea. Painstakingly restored (FIGS. 5-34 and 5-35)—the restoration itself a masterpiece of the modern restorer's art—these statues are now generally regarded as original Greek bronzes of the Transitional period of the so-called "severe style," which preceded the Classical period, and as priceless additions to the history of world art. Because these statues are life-size, weight, cost, and the tendency of large masses of bronze to distort when cooling would have made castings in solid bronze impractical, if not impossible. Larger sculptures in bronze were, and are, hollow-

5-35 *Warrior with Headband*, rear view (restored).

cast in the *cire perdue* (lost-wax) method (see Glossary). This art of bronze casting, used since Sumerian times and probably learned by the Greeks from the Egyptians in the sixth century B.C., is found here in all perfection, as is the craft of working the metal surfaces to produce the greatest subtlety of detail. The mastery of material and technique is matched by the sculptor's sure knowledge of the structure and dynamics of the human body. Although one leg of the *Warrior with Headband* is advanced (FIG. 5-33) in the tradition of the Archaic kouroi (FIGS. 5-15 and 5-16), the weight shift, which we noted in the *Kritios Boy* (FIG. 5-19), is more pronounced, and the articulation of the body masses is at once more defined and fluent (FIG. 5-35). The slight turning of the head and tilting of the shoulders, the unlocking of the arms from the body, and the lifting and crooking of the left arm (perhaps meant to be holding a shield)—all of these features break through the rigid "slab" of space that confines the Archaic kouros, suggesting the beginning of natural movement and the shift of viewpoint from the strictly frontal aspect. The massive physique and the alert, menacing stance express extraordinary strength and a brutal ferocity—a will to confront an enemy, whether Homeric or Persian. The face (FIG. 5-36), its silver teeth bared in a snarl, could be imagined as the very mask of merciless "War," defined by Homer as "the bane of men."

The high quality of *The Riace Bronzes* can be found again in another fine bronze, *The Charioteer of Delphi*

(FIG. 5-37). The statue belonged to a grouping that included chariot and horses, probably erected to commemorate the victory of King Polyzalos of Gela at the races in 478 B.C. *The Charioteer of Delphi* represents a youthful aristocrat, who stands firmly on both feet, holding the reins in his outstretched hand. He is dressed in the customary garment of a driver, girdled high and held in at the shoulders and the back to keep it from flapping. The hair is confined by a band tied behind the head. The eyes are made of glass paste and shaded by lashes of hair-like pieces of bronze. We feel the sharp clarity of Archaic work in the figure, especially in the lower part, where the folds of the dress have almost the quality of a fluted column, in the sharp lines of the brow, and in the conventional way in which the hair is worked. But we notice also the skillful modeling of the hand and the feet, and the slight twist of the torso, giving the feeling of an organic structure beneath the drapery. These subtleties are not seen at first, and we might mistake the statue for another example of the Archaic formula of rigid frontality. But it is only the formality of the pose, not ignorance of the principle of weight distribution, that determines the tight composure of the figure; it is as "alive" as the pose of a soldier at parade rest. The statue is probably a portrait, yet there are few individualized traits. This is typical of most works of the Greek Classical period and distin-

5-38 MYRON, *Discobolos*. Roman marble copy after a bronze original of *c.* 450 B.C., life-size. Museo Nazionale Romano, Rome.

5-37 *The Charioteer of Delphi,* from the Sanctuary of Apollo at Delphi, *c.* 470 B.C. Bronze, approx. 5' 11" high. Museum, Delphi.

guishes Greek from Egyptian portrait statues, which had a religious function (the preservation of the deceased's likeness to preserve the ka). Although, with the Greeks, man comes to complete self-consciousness ("Know thyself!") and although the *figure* of man is idealized, no individual is regarded as being true or perfect or, consequently, an appropriate subject for representation. In the words of Bruno Snell:

> If we want to describe the statues of the fifth century in the words of their age, we should say that they represent beautiful or perfect men, or, to use a phrase employed in the early lyrics for purposes of eulogy, "god-like" men. Even for Plato, the norm of judgment still rests with the gods, and not with men.*

Thus, our observations at the beginning of this chapter must be modified. Although, according to the philosopher Protagoras, "man is the measure of all things" for art, the gods are the measure of man, and to achieve the ideal is to achieve the "god-like."

The rapid process of liberation from Archaic limits continues in the renowned *Discobolos* of the sculptor MYRON (FIG. 5-38), from about 450 B.C. Like most freestanding statues by the "Great Masters" of Greek sculpture, the *Discobolos* has survived only in Roman

*Bruno Snell, *The Discovery of the Mind: The Greek Origins of European Thought* (New York: Harper & Row, 1960), p. 247.

5-39   Reconstruction of the west pediment of the Temple of Zeus at Olympia, 468–460 B.C. Approx. 91' wide.

marble copies after the bronze original (see pp. 160–61). Myron's representation of an athlete engaged in the discus throw, still an athletic event in the Olympic Games, was revolutionary as a result of its vigorous and convincing movement; it has been widely reproduced in both the ancient and modern worlds. However, the motion of the *Discobolos* has clearly been restricted to one plane, which means that only two distinct views are possible. The figure, represented at the point between the backward swing and the forward thrust of the arm, becomes, by means of certain formal devices, an expression of concentrated force. The composition is in terms of two intersecting arcs, creating the impression of a tightly stretched bow a moment before the string is released.

The "severe" early style of the Transitional period finds its clearest and most representative expression in the pedimental sculptures of the Temple of Zeus at Olympia (FIG. 5-39). On the west pediment, the combat of centaurs and Lapiths at the wedding feast of Peirithous is represented. The centaurs (half man, half beast) had been invited to the celebration, but they became drunk and attempted to abduct the bride and her maidens. They were prevented from doing so by Peirithous and Theseus, and Apollo, appearing above the combat, approves the heroes' chastisement of this breach of hospitality. The scene symbolizes three things: the Greek victories over the Persians; the sacred truce of Olympia (which outlawed strife within or on the approaches of the consecrated pre-

cincts of the temple); and the responsibility of men, who, unlike animals, acknowledge the rule of law.

The grouping of the figures in the Olympia pediments shows considerable improvement over the older Aegina grouping (FIG. 5-30) in the adjustment of the poses to fit the triangular pediment. In the center, Apollo thrusts out his arm amid the tumult (FIG. 5-40). The figure should be compared with the Archaic kouroi (FIGS. 5-15 and 5-16). From its formality and such lingering archaisms as the tight, decorative treatment of the hair, it seems the last of that great line, although the new understanding of bodily structure shows in the splendid and exact modeling of the athletic physique. The musculature is no longer schematic, but swelling with life and power. The transitions from one group of muscles to another are smoothly and subtly made, and this soft flow of planes and contours belies the formal rigidity of the pose.

The face of the *Apollo*, like those of *The Charioteer of Delphi* and the *Discobolos,* is composed in the expressionless mask of regular beauty deemed appropriate to gods and god-like men, despite their action or potential for action. This ideal mask, expressing the conviction of Greek philosophy that reason must be above and in control of the passions, precludes the distortion of the face by any strain of emotion, even in scenes of the most violent action. In the twisted complication of the group of *Hippodameia and the Centaur* (FIG. 5-41), where the bride of Peirithous tries to

5-40   *Apollo,* from the west pediment of the Temple of Zeus at Olympia. Marble, over life-size. Museum, Olympia.

5-41   *Hippodameia and the Centaur,* from the west pediment of the Temple of Zeus at Olympia. Marble, slightly over life-size. Museum, Olympia.

wrench from her breast the centaur's clutching hand, the girl's face remains serenely neutral. Her predicament is dire, as the artful sculptor dramatically describes it; yet, and significantly, it is only the centaur's face that is distorted, as befits the low creature that it is, surrendering to drunkenness and lust. This distinction between the calm of noble men and women and the frenzy of the creature abandoned to impulse prevailed for centuries in Greek art. The Greeks were convinced that overwhelming disaster awaited the man who yielded to the spell cast by the dark god of intoxication and madness, Dionysos; this conviction is reflected in their drama and in their persistent appeal to reason and order, both in art and life. Against Dionysos they attempted to raise the shining figure of Apollo, god of light, beauty, and wisdom. Thus, it was with the pediments of Olympia that the visual arts moved into the realm of philosophy and drama, and it was in the presence of these sculptures that the Greek athletes took their oath at the altar of Zeus before the Olympic Games.

The Early Classical Period

The prestige that the Athenians won by their leading role in the repulse of the Persians, and by virtue of the powerful fleet they built in the process, made them the dominant political force in the Greek world. They acquired a sea empire disguised as a religious and more-or-less democratic alliance of city- and island-states throughout the Aegean. Members of the alliance, which was called the Delian League, had cause enough to complain bitterly that they were more the subjects of Athens than her allies and that she siphoned off a large part of the common treasury (raised as a fund for defense against Persia) for her own uses. Despite chronic warfare within the alliance (and between it and the rival league led by Sparta), Athens, under the leadership of its adroit statesman, Pericles, became an immensely prosperous and

5-43   Plan of the Acropolis of Athens, restored as of 400 B.C.

proud community. The brief period of her glory under Pericles saw a concentration of human creative energy and a triumph of drama, philosophy, and art that has been known in no other place or time in all of the Western world.

Disdaining to reassemble the desecrated stones of the Athenian Acropolis after the sack of the city in 480 B.C., the Athenians, led by Pericles, signalized their new power and independence by completely rebuilding the Acropolis, undertaking one of the greatest building projects of antiquity before Roman times. Their success stands as a rare human achievement against the larger history of human failure. The beauty of the buildings, set on a towering platform of rock with difficult access (FIGS. 5-42, 5-43, 5-44), was recognized and celebrated in ancient times as it is today. Plutarch, writing some 500 years after the rebuilding of the Acropolis, commented:

5-42   The Acropolis today, Athens (view from the southwest).

Pericles' works are especially admired, as having been made quickly, to last long. For every particular piece of his work was immediately, even at that time when it was new, recognized as ancient, because of its beauty and elegance; and yet in its vigor and freshness it looks to this day as if it has just been done. There is a sort of bloom and newness upon those works of his, preserving them from the touch of time. . . .

Architect Eric Mendelssohn (1887–1953) made almost the same observation when he first visited Athens. Expecting to be depressed by the view of that original source of the academic Classicism from which his generation was fighting to free itself, he found himself exclaiming that the Parthenon is "modern," meaning that good architecture is always good, and so, always "modern."

Time, vandalism, accident, and neglect had, by the nineteenth century, reduced the buildings of the Acropolis to a clutter of ruins. Modern archeologists have cleared away centuries of encumbering, later structures and accumulated rubble that obscured and defaced the original design and have restored the Periclean works to some broken semblance of their former splendor. Today, the buildings are threatened by a uniquely modern blight, the corrosive emissions of automobile exhausts, which are decomposing the ancient marbles; the smog-laden air of the modern traffic-clogged city is the solvent of ancient stone. Steps are now being taken to encase the buildings in materials that will resist further damage from corro-

5-44 Restoration (model) of the Acropolis of Athens toward the end of the fifth century B.C.: the Parthenon *(upper center)*, the Erechtheum *(left center)*, and the Propylaea and the Temple of Athena Nike *(right foreground)*.

sion. The restoration and preservation of a priceless heritage become a modern obligation and task.

THE PARTHENON

Of the buildings on the Acropolis, the Parthenon (the temple sacred to Athena Parthenos) was the first and the largest to be constructed (FIG. 5-45). Its architects were IKTINOS and KALLIKRATES, and its sculptural ornamentation was produced under the direction of PHIDIAS, friend of Pericles and one of the great sculptors of all time. In plan (FIG. 5-43), the Parthenon is a peripteral temple, its short side slightly less than half the length of its long side. Its naos is subdivided into two parts: the larger contained the cult statue of Athena Parthenos in ivory and gold, some 40 feet in height, the work of Phidias; the smaller had been

5-45 IKTINOS and KALLIKRATES, the Parthenon, Acropolis, Athens, 448–432 B.C. (view from the northwest).

designed to serve as treasury of the Delian League, but most of the revenues contributed by the Aegean members were expended on Pericles' ambitious building projects. The interiors of the two rooms are organized differently. The naos proper had two double rows of small columns for roof support; although long disputed, the purpose of the rows was, according to some, to provide a second-story gallery from which visitors could view the statue, the foundation of which is still visible. The treasury had four single Ionic columns—one of several Ionic features in the otherwise Doric building, another being the continuous frieze of sculpture that runs around the top of the naos wall on the exterior. Except for these Ionic elements, the Parthenon is the epitome of the Classical Doric temple, exhibiting that order at the peak of its refinement.

Seen today, the building is a partial restoration. Through the centuries, the Parthenon has undergone many transformations, having been at one time a Greek temple, at another time a Christian church; then, after the Ottoman conquest of Greece, a Turkish mosque was built inside its naos. In 1687, the naos was being used as an ammunition dump by the Turks, who were then at war with the Venetians. A Venetian rocket scored a direct hit, and the resultant explosion blew out the center of the building. During the past century the colonnades have been reassembled, but the core of the structure remains a ruin.

Despite its dilapidated condition, the Parthenon is probably the most carefully surveyed and measured building in the world. The consequence of this searching study is the revelation that the builders aimed for unsurpassable excellence in every detail; the "refinements" of the structure have become almost a subtopic in the history of Greek architecture. If there is anything we are led to expect from the severe Doric order, it is that its lines must be rigidly and consistently straight and plumb; yet there are few straight structural lines in the Parthenon. The stylobate is convex, so subtly as to be almost imperceptible as a curve; only if one sights along it from one end does the curvature, which is repeated in the entablature, become visible. The columns tilt slightly inward and are not uniformly spaced, standing closer to each other at the corners of the buildings. Moreover, not all the columns are of the same diameter; those at the corners have a somewhat greater girth than the rest. The entasis, which gives a kind of muscle-tense elasticity and buoyancy to the profile of the column, has the same subtlety seen in the curvature of the stylobate and the entablature.

These deviations from the mechanical, plumb-line, straight-edged norm are plainly intentional; most have been found in other temples. But interpretations of these refinements do not agree; some feel that they are purely functional; the curvature of the stylobate, for example, may have been designed to facilitate drainage, or perhaps in anticipation of the settling of the central part of the building. Others believe that the deviations were intended to offset marginal distortions in the human visual field—optical illusions that might make columns with exactly vertical profiles look pinched and weak. Still other speculation is that the refinements were required by Greek instinct for completeness in the look of the building and for integrity with its surroundings; for example, the downward-tending curve of the stylobate would find its limit in the earth, making a visually stable and strong base for the building's aspect. A reasonable conjecture would be that the Parthenon was intended to be more than a product of engineering logic—that it was to be viewed and appreciated as a great work of sculpture, having the elasticity, resilience, and life of the human figure in statuary. Thus, the particulars would be designed to work in smooth relationship to each other and to the whole structure in an organic way in which, of course, the curved line predominates over the straight. The Parthenon columns especially display this in their entasis, appearing to respond to the burden they bear by the seeming swell of their compressed contours—expressing their function not mechanically, but organically.

Parts of the building were painted. This painting provided background against which sculpture could be seen clearly and, perhaps more important, delineated the upper parts of the building against the bright sky, so that the temple's basic proportions were crisply shown and could not be misread. Color also ensured that the visible parts of the building would be clearly defined and distinguished from one another.

The insistence on clarity in argument, which led to the invention of *logic* by the Greeks, operates just as strongly in the "arguments" of their architectural design. Unfortunately, that early triumph of Greek thought, the *syllogism*, with its three propositions ending in a logically correct conclusion, cannot quite be matched in the Doric order. As examination of a corner of the Parthenon (FIG. 5-46) will show, Greek architecture was not as "rational" as Greek logic. The Doric frieze was organized according to three inflexible rules: (1) a triglyph must be exactly over the center of each column; (2) a triglyph must be over the center of each intercolumniation; and (3) triglyphs at the corners of the frieze must meet, so that no space is left over. But the architectural "syllogism" is faulty, for the conclusion cannot be harmonized with proposition (1): if the corner triglyphs must meet, then they cannot be placed over the center of the corner col-

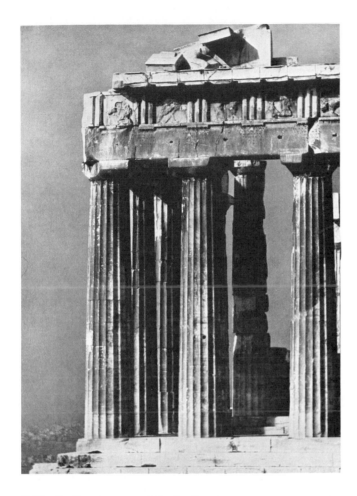

5-46 Southeast corner of the Parthenon.

The main purpose of the Parthenon, as already noted, was to house the cult statue of Athena Parthenos. Because the image of Athena—for whom the city of Athens was named—was made of ivory and gold, it did not survive centuries of depredation, although it seems to have been in existence as late as the second century A.D. We know the look of it only from accounts by Pausanias and others and from a few small replicas that differ in detail. Plutarch, in his *Life of Pericles*, tells us that its artist, Phidias, probably the scapegoat in an anti-Pericles plot, was convicted of stealing some of the gold intended for the statue and died in prison (although we know from other sources and recent excavations that Phidias was working on a statue of Zeus at Olympia after he left Athens and that he died in exile). Because work on the colossal cult statue for the naos of the Parthenon must have taken up most of Phidias' time, it is quite likely that he planned and designed the pedimental groups and friezes but left the carving of these architectural sculptures to his students and assistants. Nevertheless, they undoubtedly reflect his style, and they are among the most marvelous of all surviving Greek works of sculpture and among the supreme masterworks of all time. The sculptures of the pediments, the metopes, and the great frieze compose the most elaborate sculptural program in the history of Greek art. As in the cases of Aegina and Olympia, the arrangement of the pedimental statues is still debated by scholars, who differ in their interpretations and reconstructions. There seems to be agreement that the east pedimental group depicted the birth of Athena, the tutelary goddess of Athens; the west, her contest with Poseidon for possession of the city. The import is clear: the immortal glory of Athens is manifested in its divine genealogy and patronage.

Most of these sculptures are now in the British Museum in London, where they are popularly known as the "Elgin marbles." Between 1801 and 1803, while Greece was still under Turkish rule, Lord Elgin, the British ambassador to the Ottoman court at Constantinople, was permitted to dismantle some of the Parthenon sculptures and to ship the best-preserved ones to England. He eventually sold them to the British government at a great financial loss to himself. Although he was severely criticized for having "stolen" the treasures of Athens (the Greek government is attempting to retrieve them), Lord Elgin's quite civilized motives in saving the statues from almost certain ruin are no longer in doubt. During his time, there seemed to be no prospect that the statues, surrounded by rubble and neglected for centuries, might one day be salvaged and protected against further damage and decay.

The figure of *Dionysos* (identified by some as

umn. Although irremediable, this might seem to us a minor flaw, even in a building that aimed at perfection in all details. The Greeks wanted to be sure, and they worked out, in logic, a method for making series of statements conform to a rule for validity. But in Doric architecture, there was something left over, something that did not fit. To the Greeks, it must have appeared to be like one of the incommensurable "irrational" numbers (such as the square root of 2)—a disturbing thing with no limit or definition. (According to a singular and significant Greek legend, the man who first revealed the mystery of the irrationals perished by shipwreck, "for the unspeakable and the formless must be left hidden forever!".) In much the same manner as mathematicians and logicians faced with some disturbing contradiction in their results, the architects and artists who aimed at perfection must have found this problem of the corner triglyph a constant irritation and embarrassment. Indeed, it may have contributed to the eventual decline of the Doric order, which began in the fourth century B.C., and to the rise of the Ionic and Corinthian orders, the continuous friezes of which eliminate the problem.

5-47 *Dionysos (Herakles?)*, from the east pediment of the Parthenon. Marble, over life-size. British Museum, London.

Herakles) from the Parthenon (FIG. 5-47) shows the final relaxation of all the limitations of Archaic figurative art. Phidias and his assistants are in full possession of the knowledge of the organic, coordinated human body and render it effortlessly and with entirely convincing consistency in all its parts. This fidelity to nature was a revelation, even in an age (the nineteenth century) that was at the end of a long tradition of respect for nature in art. Artist Benjamin Robert Haydon, writing in that time, described his reaction to the reclining figure of *Dionysos (Herakles?)*, which he called Theseus:

> But when I turned to the Theseus, and saw that every form was altered by action or repose—when I saw that the two sides of his back varied, one side stretched from the shoulder blade being pulled forward, and the other being compressed from the shoulder blade being pushed close to the spine, as he rested on his elbow, with the belly flat because the bowels fell into the pelvis as he sat—when I saw in fact the most heroic style of art, combined with all the essential detail of actual life, the thing was done at once and forever. . . . Here were principles which the great Greeks in their finest time established . . . .*

*In F.H. Taylor, *The Taste of Angels* (Boston: Little, Brown, 1948), p. 502.

These principles seem indeed to be the monumental or heroic style "combined," as Haydon wrote, "with all the essential detail of actual life," the calm grandeur and simplicity of the one being in no way weakened by the precise, dynamic, anatomical logic of the other.

The *Three Goddesses* from the east pediment of the Parthenon (FIG. 5-48) shows even more than the *Dionysos (Herakles?)* the reinforcing and complementary actions of the principles of monumentality of scale and simplicity of pose with the "essential detail of actual life." The statues are typically Phidian in style, at once majestic and utterly "real" in the reading of the relaxed forms. In thin and heavy folds, the drapery alternately reveals and conceals the main and lesser masses of the bodies, at the same time swirling in a compositional tide that subtly unifies the group; the articulation and integration of the bodies produce a wonderful variation of surface and play of light and shade. Not only are the bodies fluidly related to each other, but they are related to the draperies as well, although the latter remain distinct from the bodies materially. The treatment of body and drapery as obviously different but in functional relationship to one another illustrates the thoroughly reasoned laws of appearance that Phidias and his generation had come to know and respect.

In addition to the statuary of the pediments, sculptured metopes were set between the triglyphs in the outer face of the Doric colonnade (FIG. 5-46). Within the colonnade, at the top of the external naos wall, a continuous Ionic frieze ran around the four sides of the building—an unbroken band of *bas-relief* sculpture some 524 feet long (FIG. 5-49). The metope sculptures provide an accent of movement, notably by the use of diagonal forms in successive compositions of pairs of struggling, interlocking figures in *high relief*—centaurs and Lapiths, gods and giants, Greeks and Amazons. The metope illustrated (FIG. 5-50) shows a battle between a Lapith and a centaur, the theme of

5-48 *Three Goddesses*, from the east pediment of the Parthenon. Marble, over life-size. British Museum, London.

5-49 Metopes and Panathenaic frieze from the Parthenon (west front).

the Apollo pediment at Olympia (FIG. 5-39). Although some of the metope designs are more successful than others, the figures generally are accommodated with great adroitness to the square spaces, and the whole series displays the ingenuity of the Phidian School in varying the poses and attitudes of the figures and avoiding the monotony that a regularly repeated space could impose. It is interesting also that the fortunes of the contestants are about equally balanced, the Greeks seeming to win or lose as often as their opponents.

The inner Ionic frieze of figures (FIGS. 5-51 and 5-52) was seen from below in reflected light against a colored ground. It enriched the plain wall and directed attention toward the entrance to the temple. It may represent the Panathenaic procession, which took place every four years, when the citizens of Athens gathered in the marketplace and carried to the Parthenon the *peplos*, or robe, for the statue of Athena—not Phidias' ivory and gold statue, but an older, Ar-

chaic one, kept, ultimately, in the Erechtheum of the Acropolis. This is the first known representation of a nonmythological subject in Greek temple reliefs.

The Panathenaic frieze is unique in the ancient world for its careful creation of the impression of the passage of time, albeit a brief fragment of it. The effect is achieved by use of a sequence of figures so posed as to present a gradation of motion—a rudimentary picture of time as an acceleration or deceleration. In order to experience the illusion, the observer must also be in motion, following the frieze around the colonnade of the temple. In the part of the frieze that decorated the western side of the naos the viewer can see the procession forming: youths are lacing their sandals and holding or mounting their horses; they are guided by marshals who stand at intervals, and particularly at the corners, to slow movement and guide the horsemen at the turn. In the friezes of the two long sides of the naos, the procession moves in parallel lines, a cavalcade of spirited youths, chariots, elders, jar-carriers, and animals for sacrifice. Seen throughout the procession is that balance of the monumental-simple and the actual, of the

5-50 *Lapith and Centaur,* metope from the Parthenon. Marble, 56" high. British Museum, London.

5-51 *Horsemen,* from the west frieze of the Parthenon. Marble, approx. 43" high. British Museum, London.

5-52 *Head of the Procession*, from the east frieze of the Parthenon. Marble, approx. 43" high. Louvre, Paris.

tactile and the optical, of the "ideal" and the "real," of the permanent and the momentary that, again, is characteristically Greek and the perfect exemplification of the "inner concord of opposites" that Heraclitus, the philosopher, wrote of in the sixth century B.C. The eye follows the movement of light and shade in the drapery, pausing at any point by shifting focus to the broad areas of planes, with their sharply linear outlines. The movement of the procession becomes slower and more solemn as it nears the eastern side of the naos, when, after turning the corner, it approaches the seated divinities, who appear to be guests of Athena at her great festival. Standing figures—to note one device of the artists—face against the general movement at ever-closer intervals, slowing the forward motion of the procession (FIG. 5-52).

OTHER BUILDINGS OF THE ACROPOLIS

To reach the Parthenon, the Panathenaic procession would have wound its way from the lower level of the city of Athens, up the steep slope of the Acropo-

lis, and through the gate called the Propylaea (FIGS. 5-43 and 5-53), another structure of the Periclean project. Built by MNESIKLES between 437 and 432 B.C., the Propylaea was begun immediately on the completion of the Parthenon but was never finished, partly because of the financial drain of the Peloponnesian War and partly, it is believed, because one of its wings would have trespassed on the sanctuary of Artemis Brauronia. The design is a monumental and subtle elaboration of a gate unit leading through a city wall, the gate hall itself being flanked by buildings containing a library and perhaps the first picture gallery (*pinakotheke*) in history. Here, members of the procession could rest in beautiful surroundings after the steep climb and before they passed on to the sacred buildings on the summit. The Propylaea shows modifications of Doric regularity in the broadening of the space between the central columns to make the passageway more commodious, and, like the Parthenon, the gateway includes Ionic elements, such as the columns lining the corridor for the purpose of giving

5-53 MNESIKLES, the Propylaea, Acropolis, Athens, *c.* 437–432 B.C. (view from the east).

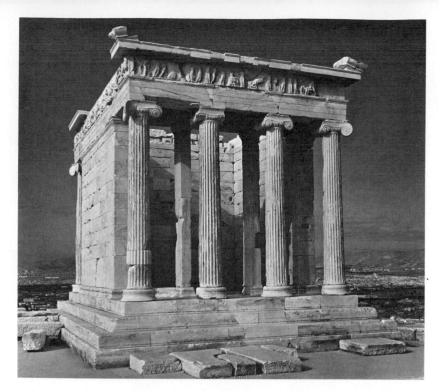

5-54 Temple of Athena Nike, Acropolis, Athens, 427–424 B.C.

greater height where necessary to support the central roof structure. Mnesikles innovated here in another respect. Greek buildings, whether religious or secular, ordinarily existed in isolation, self-sufficient and relatively independent of their surroundings. Here, for the first time, buildings of different types and functions (propylon and halls) were combined into an axially aligned grouping that looks ahead to later Hellenistic designs and the axial compositions of the Roman Imperial forums (FIG. 6-47).

The beautiful, little Ionic Temple of Athena Nike (Athena Victorious), built under the direction of Kallikrates between 427 and 424 B.C. (FIGS. 5-20c, 5-43, 5-54), is the earliest completely Ionic building extant on the Acropolis. Before this time, the Ionic order had been employed in the construction of a whole build-

ing only in the cases of a few treasuries at Olympia and Delphi on the Greek mainland (for example, the Treasury of the Siphnians, FIG. 5-27), and these buildings had been constructed by Aegean islanders, not by Greeks of the mainland. It was through Athens' rule of the islands that it became open to eastern Greek and Ionian influences. The little amphiprostyle Ionic temple stands on what used to be a Mycenaean bastion near the Propylaea, to the Doric severity of which this slender, exquisitely proportioned building offers a striking contrast, heightening the effects of both.

Another Ionic building situated on the Acropolis is the Erechtheum (FIGS. 5-43, 5-55, 5-56), the last of the Periclean program. Constructed between 421 and 405 B.C., the Erechtheum is most unusual in plan and

5-55 The Erechtheum, Acropolis, Athens, 421–405 B.C. (view from the south).

5-56 Reconstructed elevations of the east and west façades of the Erechtheum, Acropolis, Athens.

5-57 Porch of the Maidens, the Erechtheum.

quite unlike any other Greek temple. It was named after a mythical Athenian hero, Erechtheus, to whom it was in part dedicated. Its many unusual features are due partly to the irregularity of its site and partly to the number of shrines included within it. According to Pausanias, the Greek geographer and historian of the second century A.D., the Erechtheum stood on the traditional site of the contest between Poseidon and Athena for dominion over Athens—the theme of the sculpture group in the west pediment of the Parthenon. Also at the site were a rock supposed to be at the imprint of Poseidon's trident, the spring of salt-water that the stroke of the trident produced, Athena's olive tree, and the tomb of the legendary King Kekrops. The asymmetrical plan of the building resulted from the need to bring these traditionally revered sites together and from the fact that pious reluctance to disturb the sacred places precluded terracing of the uneven ground. Hence, this unique building stands on several levels, with different porches projecting from three sides and an unusual screen wall closing off the fourth. The irregularity of the structure, so uncommon in Greek architecture, was formerly explained as the result of a kind of hurried, *ad hoc* completion necessitated by political and financial problems brought on by the duress of the Peloponnesian War; now it is believed that the Erechtheum was finished according to plan and that the architect adjusted his design with great ingenuity to the difficult demands of ritual and site. In no way an esthetic failure, the asymmetrical form of the struc-

ture offers an effective counterpoint to the symmetrical unity of the nearby Parthenon; the graceful caryatids of the Porch of the Maidens (FIG. 5-57) strikingly complement the severity of the Parthenon's Doric columns, and the building's carved details are among the most refined and subtle in all of Greek art. The Erechtheum beautifully balances its larger neighbor, the Parthenon, setting Ionic complexity and elaboration against Doric simplicity and monumentality, repeating on a major scale the juxtaposition of the Propylaea and the Nike temple at the entrance of the *temenos* (sacred precinct).

SCULPTURE
The Porch of the Maidens, the south porch of the Erechtheum, is so called because its caryatids are its dominating feature (FIG. 5-57). It brings to mind that earlier Ionic caryatid design, the Treasury of the Siphnians (FIG. 5-27), and comparison of the two is useful. Unlike the Siphnian caryatids, those of the south porch of the Erechtheum do not carry a full entablature, but one that consists of architrave and cornice only, the topmost *fascia* (flat, horizontal bands) that make up the architrave being decorated with medallions to simulate the missing frieze. This seems to be a deliberate, proportional adjustment undertaken by the sculptors of the Erechtheum figures to avoid the effect seen in the Siphnian caryatids, which look

overloaded by the entablature; the sculptors must have been aware that figures graceful in attitude and dimension could scarcely harmonize with a massive architectural superstructure they would be presumed to be supporting. There are technical as well as esthetic reasons for the Erechtheum adjustment. Although the weight of a full entablature was borne by the Siphnian caryatids, in this case the load could have been too great for the necks of the figures, their weakest point; however, esthetic considerations were probably the more persuasive. Thus, again, we find the Classical architect–sculptor balancing in his wonderfully trained judgment the realities of structure with the necessities of ideal beauty. The figures have enough rigidity to suggest the structural column and just the degree of flexibility necessary to suggest the living body. The compromise is superbly executed. The corner figures determine the stance by representing the weight as falling on the outer leg. The inner figures repeat this pose, so that the legs not carrying the weight and, bent at the knee, do not determine the architectural verticals or disturb their natural plumb-line straightness. These figures have all the monumental majesty of the Phidian figures on the Parthenon pediments; the pleats and folds of their draperies reveal the quiet power of their bodies, and the very obligation imposed on them by the architecture serves only to strengthen their noble poise.

The Phidian style dominated Athenian sculpture until the end of the fifth century B.C. Due to the Peloponnesian War, fewer large-scale sculptural enterprises were launched, although the style lingered on in smaller works, such as the popular grave steles produced in considerable numbers for both local use and export. One of the most harmoniously designed of these is the *Grave Stele of Hegeso* (FIG. 5-58), which was found in the Dipylon cemetery. As is often the case in grave reliefs of the Classical period, the figures are placed in an architectural framework. The deceased is seated on a chair with sweepingly curved back and legs that provides an effective transition from the frozen forms of the architecture to the organic forms of the figures. Hegeso is contemplating a necklace (originally rendered in paint) that she has taken from the box held by her girl servant. The quiet glances of mistress and servant are directed at Hegeso's right hand, which, placed exactly in the center of the panel, is the compositional focal point. Although the stele was carved toward the end of the fifth century B.C., it is devoid of the sentimentality found in many other works of its day; the solemn pathos of the scene links the stele with the grandiose conception of the Parthenon sculptures.

The relief of *Nike Fastening Her Sandal* (FIG. 5-59), from a parapet constructed around the Temple of Athena Nike about 410 B.C., shows how sculptors,

5-58 *Grave Stele of Hegeso*, Dipylon cemetery, *c.* 410–400 B.C. Marble, 59" high. National Museum, Athens.

5-59 *Nike Fastening Her Sandal*, from the parapet of the Temple of Athena Nike, Acropolis, Athens, *c.* 410 B.C. Marble, approx. 42" high. Acropolis Museum, Athens.

having achieved the Classical perfection of the human form, now exhibited their virtuosity. The function of the concentrically arranged draperies, heavy and clinging to the form as if drenched with water, is to reveal the supple beauty of the young body. The interplay of the intricately moving drapery and the smooth volumes of the body seen in the *Three Goddesses* of the Parthenon (FIG. 5-48) is here refined to make a deliberately transparent veil for the female figure, which now fully emerges from the elaborate costume of the kore tradition.

A freestanding, bronze statuette of a nude girl (FIG. 5-60) displays the Classical artist's skill in representing the undraped body in natural pose and movement, its dynamics perfectly understood. The head, torso, and legs of the indolent figure are suavely and harmoniously related as they twist slowly in the contrary motion of *contrapposto*. The closed, quiet volumes, supple forms, undulant contours, and flowing surfaces of the dreaming girl's body are obviously presented for the sake of sheer beauty. No other meaning need be looked for; the esthetic effect is enough. This is the artist's translation of his vision of a living perfection of nature into the still medium of sculpture—the preservation of an image of the ideal

from the real flux of time and accidental appearance. The work beautifully expresses the Greek worship of the eternal order of nature imaged in an idealized human form.

In contrast with the Ionian sumptuousness of the Phidian style is a work of the Argive School of southern Greece, the *Doryphoros* (FIG. 5-61) of POLYKLEITOS, a sculptor whose fame rivaled that of Phidias in the ancient world. The work shown here, the original of which is dated 450–440 B.C., is a Roman copy made much later.

Almost all extant works of the so-called Great Masters of Greek sculpture are replicas, the originals having disappeared. Originals of Roman copies can be identified through descriptions by ancient authors, especially Pausanias and Pliny the Elder, and occasionally through representations on ancient coins. There are a number of reasons for the disappearance of the originals. In war, statues made of precious materials were often pillaged, and bronze statues were melted to make weapons or utensils; during the barbarian invasions, in the time of the fall of the Roman empire, marble statues were used to make lime for mortar. After the Romans conquered Greece in the second century B.C., they took Greek works of

5-60 Statuette of a young woman, *c.* 420 B.C. Bronze, 10″ high. Staatliche Antikensammlungen, Munich.

5-61 POLYKLEITOS, *Doryphoros.* Roman marble copy after a bronze original of *c.* 450–440 B.C., 6′ 6″ high. Museo Nazionale, Naples.

art to Rome to adorn the Imperial palaces and the villas of the rich. Numerous copies were made of some statues, reflecting their popularity and fame. Many of the copyists took liberties with the originals; changes were made to conform with popular taste, and very few of the copies even approach the quality and refinement that the originals must have had. When the Romans were copying bronze in marble, they used awkward devices to strengthen weak points—such as placing a tree trunk next to a statue's leg or adding braces and struts to prevent breakage of the arms, as can be seen in the *Doryphoros*. Nevertheless, the copy of the *Doryphoros* does provide evidence of the appearance of the original, and we can compare its blocky solidity and strength with the subtle grace of the Phidian style. Although the unity and equilibrium that pervade the works of Phidias are also in the Polykleitan statue, the origins differ; the artists at work on the Parthenon seem to have achieved their results with a deft, spontaneous translation of natural appearances, but Polykleitos worked according to a canon of proportions in which he formulated the principles that gave rise to unity. Although Polykleitos' own treatise enunciating his canon has been lost, Galen, the second century A.D. physician, interpreted it as follows in his *Placita Hippocratis et Platonis:*

> . . . [beauty consists] in the proportions, not of the elements, but of the parts, that is to say, of finger to finger, and of all the fingers to the palm and the wrist, and of these to the forearm, and of the forearm to the upper arm, and of all the other parts to each other, as they are set forth in the Canon of Polykleitos.

It has been said that in the *Doryphoros* Polykleitos had not simply made a statue but had manifested sculpture itself, and Aristotle used "sculptor" and "Polykleitos" interchangeably. As the Greeks saw proportion as the central problem in architecture, so they did in sculpture, and they viewed Polykleitos' canon as the embodiment of proportional rationality for sculpture.

In the *Doryphoros*, movement, which began to be expressed successfully in the early fifth century B.C., is disciplined through the use of an imposed system of proportions. The mighty body, with its broad shoulders, thick torso, and muscular limbs, strikes us as the embodiment of the Spartan ideal of the warrior physique, the human equivalent of the Doric order. And, like the Doric order, the figure appeals to the intellect and must be studied long and carefully before it fully reveals itself to the observer. The slow forward walk, the standard Polykleitan pose, stresses the principle of weight shift—the maneuver that must be made before we can move at all and with which the whole development of the representation of the moving human figure begins. What appears to be a casually natural pose is, in fact, the result of an extremely complex and subtle organization of the various parts of the figure. Note, for instance, how the function of the supporting leg is echoed by the straight-hanging arm to provide the right side of the figure with the columnar stability needed to anchor the dynamically flexed limbs of the left side. If read anatomically, on the other hand, the tensed and relaxed limbs may be seen to oppose each other diagonally (that is, the right arm and the left leg are relaxed, and the tensed supporting leg is opposed by the flexed left arm, which held a spear). Thus, all parts of the figure have been carefully composed to achieve the utmost variety within a compact and stable whole. A most circumspect and subtle artist has combined realism, monumentality, and diversity in a unified design that seems to be beyond the cavil of even the most discriminating critic.

PAINTING

Of Greek wall (mural) painting, little remains. Our knowledge of what it looked like must be drawn, for the most part, from vase painting and from the later Roman painting derived from it. From a tomb at Paestum, a painting, *The Diver* (FIG. 5-62), does survive that dates from the early fifth century B.C. A youth dives from a masonry platform, his figure a vivid silhouette against a flat, featureless background framed by stylized tree branches and ornamental palmette motifs of the kind found regularly on the rims, necks, and bases of Greek vases (FIGS. 5-8, 5-9, 5-10).

5-62 *The Diver*, fresco painting from a Greek tomb, Paestum, early fifth century B.C. Museo Archeologico Nazionale, Paestum.

The sharp outline, without shading, is the equivalent of sculpture in low relief, which emphasizes form rather than color and guides the method of Greek painting. The quick motion, arrested in space, reminds us, in its liveliness, of the naturalism of Minoan painting. Yet the diver may not be simply a subject represented for its human interest, but rather a kind of pictorial metaphor appropriate to a tomb; perhaps the plunge of the soul into the nether world—we are not sure of its meaning.

We know from ancient accounts that great painters lived and worked throughout the whole period of Greek art. The mural painter POLYGNOTUS enjoyed almost as much fame in antiquity as his contemporaries, Phidias and Polykleitos. Unfortunately, none of his works survive. On the basis of ancient literary sources, it is believed that his style is reflected in the vase decoration of the NIOBID PAINTER, whose *Argonaut Krater* (FIG. 5-63) illustrates a radical break with the traditional decorative style. For over two centuries, figures had been arranged *isocephalically* (with all the heads at one level) in horizontal bands, not only in Greek vase decoration but also in monumental painting. Evidence to support the latter seems to be provided by surviving Etruscan frescoes, which presumably reflect contemporary, or slightly earlier, Greek mural styles (see Chapter 6). On the *Argonaut Krater*, the figures have been placed on different lev-

5-63　NIOBID PAINTER, *Argonaut Krater*, Orvieto, *c.* 455–450 B.C. Outline drawing at right indicates relation to whole vessel. Portion shown approx. 15″ high; whole vessel approx. 21″ high. Louvre, Paris.

els, and the ground lines on which they stand or recline attempt to introduce into painting the illusion of depth—an effect that is thwarted, however, by the uniform size of the figures. It has also been reported that Polygnotus modeled his figures in dark and light, aiming for three-dimensional and sculptural effects. This last feature was not adopted by the

5-64　PHIALE PAINTER, *Hermes Bringing the Infant Dionysos to Papposilenos* (krater), Vulci, *c.* 440–435 B.C. Approx. 14″ high. Vatican Museums, Rome.

Niobid Painter, whose style remains linear and does not reveal what must have been an impressive statuesque quality of Polygnotan figures. Although important as reflecting—dimly, to be sure—the monumental manner of Polygnotus, the Niobid Painter's works also represent the decline of vase painting, as the figurative decoration loses contact with the body of the vessel, the earlier cohesion of figure and surface becoming mere adhesion.

Although the work of the Niobid Painter may provide us with some idea of the general compositional schemes of Polygnotus, it tells nothing of his use of color. A pale reflection of it may be found in the so-called *white-ground* vases of the fifth century B.C. Experiments with the white-ground technique date back to the Andokides Painter, but the method became popular only toward the middle of the fifth century B.C. The white-ground technique is essentially a variation of the red-figure technique; the pot was first covered with a slip of very fine white clay that, when burnished, provided a glossy or *matte white* surface on which to draw in black glaze or dilute brown wash. The range of colors remained severely limited (purple, brown, and several kinds of red); few colors known to the Greeks could survive the heat of the kiln. Also, the white slip, although highly effective as background for drawing and coloring, was not durable and tended to flake off. Crucial for wares that saw daily use, such as cups and kraters, this impermanence was less so in vessels that had a more limited use, such as funerary *lekythoi* (oil flasks), which were not handled after they had been deposited in the tomb. After mid-century, the white-ground technique was reserved almost exclusively for funerary vases of this type, some of which were even painted in full polychrome *after* the vase had been fired—naturally, at an even greater cost in durability.

The example by the PHIALE PAINTER shown in FIG. 5-64 uses the conservative colors that could withstand firing. It shows Hermes handing the infant Dionysos to Papposilenos ("granddad-satyr") and the nymphs in the shady glens of Nysa, where Zeus had sent Dionysos—one of his illegitimate sons—to be raised, safe from the possible wrath of his wife, Hera. The artist has used reds, brown, purple, and a special snowy white—the last for the flesh of the nymphs and for such details as the hair, beard, and shaggy body of Papposilenos. Despite this rather limited color scheme, the painting's effect is warm and rich; in combination with the compositional devices of the Niobid Painter, it may provide a shadowy idea of the appearance of the famed Polygnotan murals, which had so impressed ancient viewers.

The grandeur of the age of Phidias and Polykleitos, when their styles briefly dominated Greek art, passed with them. What followed, although exquisite and virtuoso, constituted a descent from their heights, becoming elegant, slight, more and more naturalistic, less concerned with lofty themes and majestic forms. The statues of "god-like" men became statues of men of this world.

THE FOURTH CENTURY AND THE HELLENISTIC PERIOD

The Late Classical Period

The disastrous Peloponnesian War, which ended in 404 B.C. with the complete defeat of Athens, left Greece drained of its strength. Sparta and then Thebes took the leadership of Greece, both unsuccessfully. In the latter half of the fourth century B.C., the Greek states lost their liberty to Philip of Macedon. Athens lost its precedence, and the whole structure of life changed; the traditional balance between the city-state and the individual was lost. The serene idealism of the fifth century, born of a simple, robust concept of mind and matter, of man and the state, gave way to chronic civil wars, social and political unrest, skepticism, and cynicism.

The Apollonian command "Know thyself," which Socrates had taught the people as he spoke with them in their daily gathering places, inevitably changed the Greek point of view to a more individualistic one. Euripides, too, seems to have regarded the individual as paramount, and his dramas depict a whole spectrum of human passions and crises. Aristophanes, however, ridiculed both Socrates and Euripides for their apparent departures from the good old Classical ways and customs, and especially for their emphasis on the role and value of the individual. During the fourth century B.C., man's intellectual independence was firmly established by Plato (however much he himself regretted the passing of the old ways), whose doctrine of such eternal forms as "virtue," "justice," and "courage" served as the rational model on which the individual could construct his life. Aristotle, perhaps the most versatile of all thinkers, formulated the operations of reason in the science we call "logic," converting reason into an instrument applicable to all human experience. Aristotle turned his attention systematically on just about everything that could be of interest to man, and among his fundamental contributions is the outline of the sciences of nature.

Thus, gradually separating himself from the old assurances—the gods, their oracles, and time-honored custom—as prime interpreters of the meaning of life, the Greek carried on his search to know himself and to achieve knowledge of the world and life through observant experience. His dependence on the city-state lessened, until he boasted with Diogenes: "I am a citizen of the world." Knowing the real, for whatever purpose, became the conspicuously Greek faculty and value. In the midst of political disaster, Greece, in the fourth century, enacted a daring drama of human discovery.

SCULPTURE

The humanizing tendency that had been gathering force throughout the fifth century B.C. achieved characteristic expression in the sculpture of the fourth century B.C.; themes lost something of the earlier, solemn grandeur and representations of the greater gods gave way to those of lesser gods, and the naturalistic view of the human figure became fully focused. *Hermes and Dionysos*, attributed to PRAXITELES (FIGS. 5-65 and 5-66), is a work of such high quality that some authorities insist it must be by Praxiteles himself and not a mere Roman copy. The god is represented standing, with a shift in weight from the left arm (supporting the upper body) to the right leg, so that there is a double distribution of the weight, giving the pose, with its fluid axis, the form of a sinuous, shallow S-curve that becomes a manner with Praxiteles. On his arm, Hermes holds the infant Dionysos, who reaches for something (probably a bunch of grapes) Hermes held in his right hand. Hermes is looking off into space with a dreamy expression, half smiling. The whole figure, particularly the

head, seems in deep reverie, the god withdrawn in self-admiration. The modeling is deliberately smooth and subtle, producing soft shadows that follow the planes as they flow almost imperceptibly one into another. The delicacy of the features is enhanced by the rough, impressionistic way in which the hair is indicated, and the deep folds of the realistic drapery are sharply contrasted with the flow and gloss of the languidly graceful figure. We need but a comparative glance at Polykleitos' *Doryphoros* (FIG. 5-61) to see how broad a change in artistic attitude and intent took place from the mid-fifth to the mid-fourth century. Majestic strength and rationalizing design are replaced by sensuous languor and an order of beauty that appeals more to the eye than to the mind. Praxiteles' esthetic of the human nude, slenderer in its proportions, with its emphasis on the exquisitely smooth modeling that reproduces the tones of resilient flesh, naturally led him to popularize the nude female statue. His *Aphrodite of Cnidos* was widely regarded in antiquity as the most beautiful of all statues and was the pride of Cnidos, the city that owned it. Its charm can best be understood, not from the inferior Roman copy of it, but from a much later, Hellenistic work, the *Aphrodite of Cyrene* (FIG. 5-67), which, two centuries removed, conveys a Praxitelean poetry of sensual beauty. For both the male and female

5-65   Attributed to PRAXITELES, *Hermes and Dionysos, c.* 340 B.C. Marble, approx. 7' high. Museum, Olympia.

5-66   *Head of Hermes* (detail of FIG. 5–65).

5-67 *Aphrodite of Cyrene,* North Africa, *c.* 100 B.C. Marble, approx. 56" high. Museo Nazionale Romano, Rome.

5-68 Attributed to SCOPAS, *Warrior's Head,* from the Temple of Athena Alea at Tegea, *c.* 350 B.C. Marble, approx. 11¾" high. National Museum, Athens.

was king of Caria, a non-Greek state in southwest Asia Minor, and was in the service of the king of Persia. The colossal portrait-statues of the king (FIG. 5-69) and queen date from about 355 B.C. Presumably, they

nude, Praxiteles set a new, more personal and naturalistic ideal of physical beauty.

Although his style was greatly admired and his theme of the bathing Aphrodite was represented again and again long after his time, Praxiteles was not the only influential sculptor of the Late Classical period. A fellow Athenian, Scopas, is known for a robust and vigorous style more suited to the representation of action and perhaps derived from Polykleitos. A fragmentary head from Tegea in Greece (FIG. 5-68) illustrates Scopas' style and shows a hitherto undepicted tension of facial expression, the features broad and strong, the eyes large, round, and set deeply under knitted brows. As a reflection of inner states through varied facial expressions, this work breaks with the Classical tradition of benign, serene features and prefigures later Hellenistic art, when the depiction of emotion became more important to sculpture.

The monumental Tomb of Mausolus, another of the seven wonders of the ancient world, was built for King Mausolus and his queen, Artemisia. Mausolus

5-69 *Mausolus,* from the mausoleum at Halicarnassus, *c.* 355 B.C. Marble, approx. 9' 10" high. British Museum, London.

are intended to be likenesses; the sculptor, who is unknown, is particular about the hair—curiously reminiscent of the Archaic—and the dynamics of the drapery. He continues that study of the drapery masses begun in the previous century and is at pains to read them so closely and realistically that he differentiates folds and pleats from the minute creases thin drapery would acquire in use. The colossal monument and the large figures reflect an Eastern influence, and already we sense that mingling of East and West that is to compose the Hellenistic styles of the last centuries before Christ.

The most renowned sculptor of the second half of the fourth century B.C. was LYSIPPOS, court sculptor to Alexander the Great. Although Lysippos was very prolific, his work is extant in copies only, including, notably, the *Apoxyomenos* (FIG. 5-70), which represents a young athlete scraping oil and mud from his body before taking his bath. The figure embodies two important innovations of the time, which may be creditable to Lysippos. One was a new canon of pro-

5-70 LYSIPPOS, *Apoxyomenos*. Roman marble copy after a bronze original of *c.* 330 B.C., approx. 6′ 9″ high. Vatican Museums, Rome.

portions, replacing the Polykleitan canon and reflecting a change in taste noticeable in all the arts. The new canon required a more slender, supple, and tall figure, a conception toward which we have already seen Praxiteles moving. This innovation may indeed have been influenced by the second (also foreshadowed in earlier works)—the full realization of the figure as if moving in space, not in the two dimensions of the figures hitherto examined (whether Phidian, Polykleitan, or Praxitelean), but in *three* dimensions. Thus, the figure now seems to move in a kind of free spiral through the space around it; it is made to be seen from a variety of angles, and it is related to things in its environment other than itself. The earliest Greek figures had been in a stiff frontal position, with the planes closely related to the stone block from which they had been carved; they were best seen from only one or two positions. Even when the figure was treated less rigidly, so that the torso as well as the arms and legs moved in a curve, it was still seen satisfactorily only from one or two points of view. In this respect, the Archaic kouros (FIG. 5-16) and the *Hermes and Dionysos* of Praxiteles (FIG. 5-65) are more nearly alike than are the *Hermes* and the *Apoxyomenos* of Lysippos. In the last, the arms curve forward, the figure enclosing space in its reach and twisting in it; the small head is thrown into stronger perspective by the large hand interposed between it and the viewer. Lysippos said that he wished to make men the way the eye sees them, allowing for accidents of perspective.

A bronze figure of a youth (FIG. 5-71), recently recovered from the Adriatic Sea near Fano, so expresses the Lysippic intention to show the human body in natural movement through space, that, given its recognizably Lysippic traits, some scholars believe it may be an original from that sculptor's own hand. The tall, slender, elegant young man, whose proportions are certainly Lysippic and whose individualized physique is more that of a runner than a wrestler, appears to be gliding past the observer. His gesture, it has been suggested, is that of an athlete at the games, placing on his head the wreath of victory. The facial features are like those we find in the Roman copies of the statues of Lysippos that record his style, and the naturalness of physique and pose in this masterful work clearly shows the artist's wish to render an image of nature given momentarily to the eye.

Although Lysippos' art tends toward the visually real, something of the older Polykleitan ideal persists in the sculpture of the fourth century, suppressing some features of the real in the interest of ideal form. Indeed, at this time, two stylistic tendencies, *idealizing* and *naturalizing*, prevailed—sometimes moving separately, sometimes merging. In the *Antikythera*

Youth (FIG. 5-72), we find them merging. The head is Polykleitan, as are the massive physique and the forward-walking stance; the unengaged left arm and hand resemble, in attitude and flexure, the right arm and hand of the *Doryphoros* (FIG. 5-61). But in the free sweep of the far-extended right arm and in the slenderer proportions and flowing outline, we sense the influence of Lysippic style. The gesture the youth makes suggests a subject; he is not simply an athlete throwing a ball, but perhaps a Perseus holding up the severed head of Medusa, or a Herakles reaching for the golden apple he has sought in the Garden of the Hesperides. The meaning of the statue is uncertain, but its exquisite refinement of form and its technical perfection make this one of the finest examples of the Greek art of the human figure in bronze.

As Praxiteles prepared the way for developing optical realism in his subtle surface effects, so Scopas and Lysippos foreshadowed Hellenistic themes, demanding force, action, and dramatic emotion. Before the new drama could develop in sculpture, however, space had to be understood in a new way—not as merely the limit of the body, but as an environment in which the body could act freely, as in nature.

5-71 LYSIPPOS (?), *Athlete (The Getty Bronze)*, late fourth century B.C. Bronze, 6' high. J. Paul Getty Museum, Malibu, California.

5-72 *Antikythera Youth*, late fourth century B.C. Bronze, 6' 4½" high. National Museum, Athens.

It is noteworthy that, in its full development of the Corinthian order, the architecture of the fourth century also produced a "body" that offered a complete aspect from any angle. The first Corinthian capital—the order differs from the Ionic only in its capital—appeared on the inside of the naos of the Temple of Apollo at Bassae, around 450 B.C. It crowned a column that, because it stood as a divider between two parts of the naos, could be seen from all sides. Presumably designed for this purpose, the Corinthian capital provided a much more satisfactory solution than the Ionic capital, which was designed to be seen effectively from two sides only. When Ionic colonnades were required to turn corners, as on peripteral structures, special "corner capitals" had to be designed that looked the same on the two sides that faced outward. The sharply projecting edge formed by the two meeting volutes never quite satisfied Classical architects, who may also have felt that this solution was achieved only at the expense of the structural logic of the Ionic capital and by a distortion of its functional parts. The problem was solved by the Corinthian capital, which can be seen to equal advantage from all sides. Its original design has been associated with the relief sculptor and metalworker Callimachos, who may have been at Bassae when the Temple of Apollo was built and of whom the sentimental story was told in antiquity that he was inspired to design the capital when he saw acanthus leaves—which decorate the Corinthian capital—growing up around a slab-weighted votive basket on the grave of a maiden. Be that as it may, although the Corinthian order appeared in the fifth century B.C., it was used only on the inside of the temple for almost a century. It is uncertain whether this is to be attributed to religious conservatism, which would tend to preserve a feature that had taken on a certain sanctity from its function at the temple's center, or whether Ionic experiments were continuing and a Doric tradition persisting. In any event, full emergence of the Corinthian order on a public exterior takes place about the same time as Lysippos' freeing of the sculptured figure from its two-aspect limits.

A capital from the tholos at Epidaurus (FIG. 5-73), where a ring of Corinthian columns stood inside the naos of a Doric structure, illustrates a step along the elaborative route of the Corinthian order, which culminates in the characteristic Hellenistic and Roman luxuriance. Here, the bell of the capital is clothed with carved acanthus leaves and manifests that same increasing attention to the deep and detailed sculpturing of stone surfaces noted in sculptured figures.

The monument of Lysicrates (FIG. 5-74), constructed in Athens in 334 B.C., shows the first known use of the Corinthian order on the outside of a build-

5-73   Corinthian capital from the tholos at Epidaurus, c. 350 B.C. Museum, Epidaurus.

ing. Significantly, the innovation appears not on a religious but on a commemorative monument. The graceful cylinder to which the Corinthian columns are engaged memorializes the victory of a choric group, patronized by Lysicrates, which had won the prized trophy of the tripod in the wild, dithyrambic contest of song in honor of Dionysos. The little tholos serves as a base for the monumentalized tripod.

5-74   The monument of Lysicrates, Athens, 334 B.C.

Henceforth, the Corinthian order was to be more and more in use on the exterior of public buildings, enjoying particular favor among Roman builders. In addition to having solved the vexing problems of both the Doric and Ionic orders—the corner-triglyph and the corner-volute dilemmas—the Corinthian order, with its ornateness, was bound to suit the developing taste for sumptuous elaboration of form and realistic representation that guided artistic effort in the Hellenistic world.

The Hellenistic Period

Philip of Macedon brought the once-free Greek city-states into subjection. His son, Alexander the Great, educated in Hellenism, the culture of Greece, by none other than Aristotle, returned the visit the Persians had made to Greece a century and a half before, overthrew their empire, and conquered all the Near East, including Egypt. Greek conquest of this vast area produced a culture and period called Hellenistic— a curious mingling of Western and Eastern ideas, religions, and arts—and a long period of Greek cultural and partly political dominance that made her the cosmopolitan heir of Sumer, Babylon, Egypt, Assyria, and Persia. Greedy for the lands their young leader had conquered, his generals asked Alexander on his death bed, "To which one of us do you leave your empire?" In the skeptical manner of the age, but also with more than a tinge of an older irony, he is supposed to have answered, "To the strongest." Although probably apocryphal, this exchange points up the near inevitability of what followed—the division of Alexander's far-flung empire among his Greek generals and their subsequent naturalization among the Orientals, whom they held subject.

In the late 1970s, excavations at Vergina in Northern Greece, within the territory of ancient Macedonia, turned up what is now widely regarded to be the grave of Alexander's father, King Philip of Macedon. Among the rich finds, which only a royal tomb might be thought to yield, were five tiny portrait heads in ivory, presumably representing Philip, Alexander, and other members of the family. The portrait thought to be that of King Philip (FIG. 5-75) shows in miniature those tendencies toward realism, already appearing in the earlier fourth century B.C., that ripened to maturity in the Hellenistic period. The king's features are highly personalized, vividly mobile, and expressive—broadly and surely modeled in the details. There is little doubt that the sculptor was closely familiar with his king and patron's face, so confident is he in the representation of it. In the Hellenistic world, the relationship of royal patron and artist was to draw ever closer.

The centers of culture in the Hellenistic period

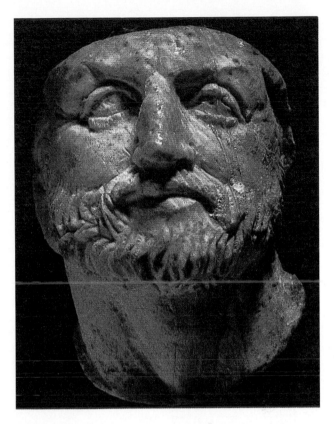

5-75   *Philip of Macedon* (?), Vergina, late fourth century B.C. Ivory, 1¼" high.

were the court cities of Greek kings—Antioch in Syria, Alexandria in Egypt, Pergamon in Asia Minor, and others. An international culture united the Hellenistic world, and its language was Greek. Hellenistic princes became enormously rich on the spoils of the East, priding themselves on their libraries, art collections, scientific enterprises, and skills as critics and connoisseurs, as well as on the learned men they could assemble at their courts. The world of the small, austere, and heroic city-state passed away, as had the power and prestige of its center, Athens, and a "world" civilization, much like today's, took its place.

SCULPTURE

The tendencies traced thus far all the way from the Archaic period were not interrupted by this change but simply proceeded to anticipated completions. In sculpture, the "environment" that opened up around the *Apoxyomenos* of Lysippos (FIG. 5-70) opened up still more around the *Nike of Samothrace* (FIG. 5-76). The goddess of victory is represented as alighting on the prow of a war galley, triumphant in some conflict among the successors of Alexander in the Greek world around 190 B.C. One of the masterpieces of the Hellenistic age, the *Nike of Samothrace*, windswept, her wings still beating, brings strength, weight, and airy grace into an equipoise one would not expect to be achieved in the hard mass of sculptured marble.

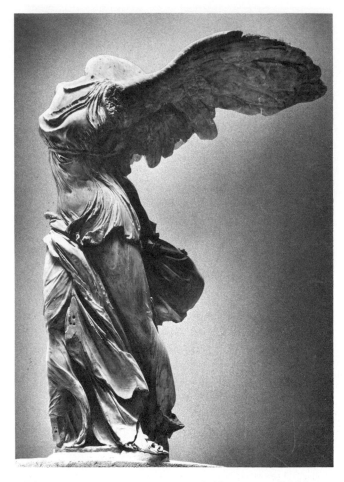

5-76 *Nike of Samothrace, c.* 190 B.C. Marble, approx. 8' high. Louvre, Paris.

Here, the sculptors have worked their stone with a freedom emulative of painters, achieving shadows and gradations of shadows by variations of surface carving, almost as if they were using heavy instead of light brush strokes. The gauze-like stretch of material across the stomach and the waves of drapery around the striding thighs and legs amount not only to an exercise in virtuosity of stonecraft but a successful ef-

fort to make stone do what poetry and painting do—render at the same time the visual nuances of the moment and the ongoing essence of action. In the end, the sculptor wants us to sense, from the figure itself, an atmosphere of wind and sea. We recall the billowing sail of Exekias' *Dionysos in a Sailboat* (FIG. 5-7), where it all seems to have begun.

The extension of the spatial environment of the figure, so as to suggest a stage on which it may and does act, appears in sculptures associated with the Hellenistic kingdom of Pergamon and the island republic of Rhodes, in the third, second, and first centuries B.C. From a group dedicated by Attalus I of Pergamon (241–197 B.C.), a figure, in Roman copy, survives of a *Dying Gaul* (FIG. 5-77). The figure is on stage, realistic, and also historical, representing a Gallic casualty in the wars Attalus had just fought with barbarian invaders. Comparison of the *Dying Gaul* and the *Fallen Warrior* from Aegina (FIG. 5-31) shows that, in a little more than two centuries, the principle of uniformity of movement had been well learned. The Gaul, dying from a chest wound that bleeds heavily, slowly loses strength, his weight falling rapidly on his last support, the trembling right arm; its collapse will be his own. This the observer reads at once from the lines and planes of the body—visually, with no need to interpret or expand the meaning. The statue is a triumph of realism. It may mark also the surrender of the interests of sculpture to the stage, where, we know, spectacles of human suffering painted with all realism of detail were sapping the great tradition of drama and diminishing human life in bloody scenes that could only present it as worthless. With the *Dying Gaul,* the sculpture of action degenerates into brutal stagecraft. Realism can go no further, even while it triumphs.

A later school of Pergamon exhibits a realism not quite so explicit, yet nonetheless belonging to the Hellenistic taste for tableaux of monumental suffering. A section of the great frieze of the *Battle of Gods*

5-77 *Dying Gaul.* Roman marble copy after a bronze original from Pergamon of *c.* 240 B.C., life-size. Museo Capitolino, Rome.

5-78 Altar of Zeus and Athena, Pergamon, *c.* 175 B.C. Staatliche Museen, Antiken-Sammlung, East Berlin. (West front restored.)

and Giants from the Pergamon Altar of Zeus and Athena (FIGS. 5-78 and 5-79) illustrates the highly dramatic kind of figurative sculpture that descended from Scopas and Lysippos. The altar was erected about 175 B.C. by the son and successor of Attalus I to glorify his father's victories. In a representation less factual than the group of dying Gauls, the artists here revert to the traditional Greek approach of presenting historical events in mythological disguise. The suffering and death, the writhing gesticulation, are somewhat formalized, and we do not feel so much that we are in the presence of pain that ordinary men might feel. In the figure of Alcyoneus, the young giant whom Athena takes by the hair (FIG. 5-79), one finds the anguish of the face to be based on Scopas and the twisting of the figure on the athleticism of both Scopas and Lysippos. The tragic content is read through the increasingly dramatic style of stonecraft. The

Greek revision of the climactic instant is still seen against a neutral background. Now, however, the background is almost obscured by shadows, from which the figures project like bursts of light. All these devices are "baroque" and closely related to those developed in seventeenth-century Europe. The unity of the design is achieved by a fluid, yet binding organization of parts—not unlike that of the figures of the *Three Goddesses* of the Parthenon (FIG. 5-48). Indeed, the two major figures of the frieze, Zeus and Athena, are directly inspired by the figures of Poseidon and Athena from the Parthenon pediments; yet this dynamic integration of the whole composition is unlike the carefully studied relationships of *separate* parts seen in the Early Classical period. In such pictorial unity, produced by the movement of light and the contrast of shade, we again recognize the strong influence of painting.

5-79 *Athena Taking Young Alcyoneus by the Hair*, from the frieze of the Altar of Zeus and Athena, Pergamon. Marble, 7' 6" high. Staatliche Museen, Antiken-Sammlung, East Berlin.

The theme of suffering is so pervasive in the Hellenistic world and its art that it could almost be understood as *the* interpretation of life by men who felt the hopelessness attendant on the decline of an older, more reasonable system. A late work of Hellenistic sculpture is the *Laocoön* group, a product of a still quite active school of Rhodes (FIG. 5-80). It shows the Trojan priest, Laocoön, and his sons being strangled by sea serpents—some say because of his defiance of Apollo; others, because he offended Poseidon (who sided with the Greeks) by warning his Trojan compatriots of the strategy of the Trojan Horse. Whatever his offense, Vergil described his plight with unsparing realism:

> Laocoön . . . they [the sea serpents] seize and bind in mighty folds; and now, twice encircling his waist, twice winding their scaly backs around his throat, they tower above with head and lofty necks. He the while strains his hands to burst the knots, his fillets steeped in blood and black venom; the while he lifts to heaven hideous cries, like the bellowings of a wounded bull that has fled from the altar and shaken from its neck the ill-aimed axe.

The spectacular torment of Laocoön and his sons is presented with all the devices of rhetorical realism available to artists as well as poets—the tortuous poses, straining muscles, and swelling veins—yet, curiously, there are lapses from consistent visual fact, as in the perhaps deliberate disproportion of the size of the sons in relationship to the size of the father, indicating them as *sons*, although they appear simply as small men.* The exceedingly popular group was reproduced frequently, sometimes on a colossal scale; in the eighteenth century, the analysis of it by Gotthold Lessing led to his designation of art and poetry as opposed in function and to the foundation of the branch of philosophy called *esthetics*.

Pliny named AGESANDER, ATHENODORUS, and POLYDORUS—three Rhodians—as the sculptors of the *Laocoön* group. The same three names are inscribed on the stern of a marble ship (FIG. 5-81) that formed part of one of several sculptured groups, fragments of

*It has been suggested that the second son—on the viewer's right—was added by the sculptors when working from an earlier group that had only two figures. The greater compositional integration of the two left figures is obvious.

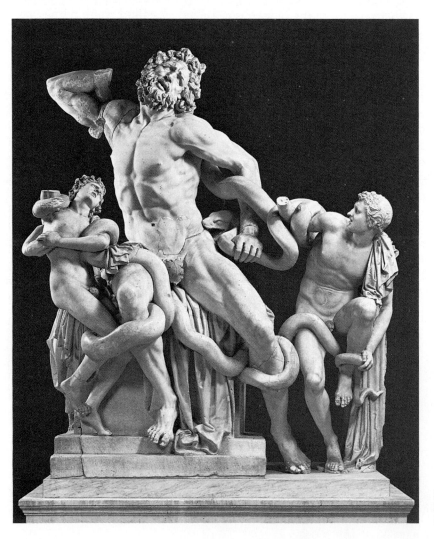

5-80 *Laocoön* group, early first century B.C. (?). Marble, 8' high. Vatican Museums, Rome. (Partially restored.)

which have been found in a large grotto near the sea at Sperlonga, some 80 miles south of Rome. The cave, adjacent to a large Imperial Roman villa built early in the first century A.D., had been used as a kind of dining room. Multifigured, sculptured groups appear to have been displayed in two niches and in a round central pool within the grotto. At least some of the sculptures must have been brought from Rhodes and were installed in the grotto around A.D. 29, when the cave was refashioned after a partial collapse.

A definitive interpretation of the scenes is most difficult, because the groups were found only in fragments, the figures evidently having been smashed to make lime or out of religious fanaticism. Three scenes from the *Odyssey* seem to have been represented: the blinding of Polyphemus (among the finds are the legs of a colossus that must have stood nearly 20 feet high), Scylla attacking Odysseus' ship, and a sinking ship. Shown is the terrified helmsman falling from the stern of the sinking vessel (FIG. 5-81). The dramatic group may have been placed—strikingly—against the dark, stalactite-covered walls of the cave. Probably the finest of the fragments is the *Head of Odysseus* (FIG. 5-82) from another group. Less convulsed and emotional than Laocoön's head, it nevertheless reflects strikingly the horrifying situation and the fear of impending death. The effect is produced—without the use of grimaces or the exaggerated eyes and anguished mouth of Laocoön—by the wind-tossed, whirling hair and beard that frame the face of the Homeric hero. While the dating of the Sperlonga sculptures remains a matter of ardent debate, it is felt

that they must be earlier than the *Laocoön* group, because they show the expressive power of the Rhodian sculptors at its height, before it succumbed to the theatrical exhibitionism that marks the latter group.

Side by side with the drama of suffering, Hellenistic sculpture continued the tradition of ideal, Praxitelean beauty seen in the *Aphrodite of Cyrene* (FIG. 5-67). Another Hellenistic descendant of this Praxitelean line is the *Aphrodite of Melos* (FIG. 5-83), the famed *Venus de Milo*. Here, as in the former *Aphrodite of Cyrene*, the ideal is taken out of the hypersensible world of reasoned proportions and made into an ap-

5-82 AGESANDER, ATHENODORUS, and POLYDORUS, *Head of Odysseus*, late second century B.C. to first century A.D. (?). Marble, life-size. Sperlonga Museum.

5-83   *Aphrodite of Melos, c.* 150–100 B.C. Marble, approx. 6′ 10″ high. Louvre, Paris.

5-84   *Old Market Woman,* second century B.C. Marble, 49½″ high. Metropolitan Museum of Art, New York (Rogers Fund).

adults at the height of their physical development, the Hellenistic artist expanded his subject matter to include not only the very old by also the very young. A group of two figures, *Eros and Psyche* (FIG. 5-85),

5-85   *Eros and Psyche, c.* 150 B.C. Marble, 49″ high. Museo Capitolino, Rome.

parition of living flesh—like the coming alive of Pygmalion's statue of Galatea. The feeling for stone as stone has quite surrendered to the ambition of making stone look as though it were the soft, warm substance of the human body. Such effects as these can be obtained only by an artist with brilliant technical facility working in the conviction that the business of the artist is to produce from stone a vision of beauty, faithful to optical reality but modified to make the keenest appeal to the senses as a flawless manifestation of the human form. Faithfulness to optical fact can also lead the sculptor to represent, with unflattering explicitness, the opposite of beauty, as seen in the *Old Market Woman* (FIG. 5-84). This bent, hobbling creature is offered to the viewer as an object of contempt, pity, or disgust, depending on one's temperament.

The disparity in subject of these two works reflects the wide scope of theme and the visual curiosity of Hellenistic sculptors. The sculptor aims to move the observer in terms of the theme of his work. He wishes, moreover, for recognition by the observer of those traits in the statue that the observer knows in life, so that a large part of the response to the statue comes from the observer's familiarity with its model or type in the context of one's own experience. Thus, while the Classical sculptor generally showed young who symbolize love and the human soul, represent adolescents in fond embrace, oblivious to all but themselves. The story of Eros and Psyche was popular in the Hellenistic and Roman worlds, and often retold; the reader can find a late and beautiful retelling of their story in Apuleius' *The Golden Ass.* The repertory of worldly and profane (that is, not religious in any formal sense) subjects was opened wide in Hellenistic art, and a principal theme, erotic art, was not overlooked. Plumply sensual, the nude and half-nude figures turn together in an artfully managed contrary motion, not unlike that of a slow, insinuating dance. The rhythmic flow of contour and plane enhances the softly amorous effect, although the artist's intent seems to be to convey prettiness and charm rather than blunt sexuality. In any event, he is now in complete possession of the formal and technical means to render whatever subjects he might choose—or might be chosen for him.

It seems unlikely that a fifth-century B.C. sculptor would have imagined that a *Boy Strangling a Goose* (FIG. 5-86) could be a subject worthy of representation. The sculpture may strike us as somewhat unpleasant, with its sadistic overtones, but doubtless it was intended to be "cute" and to elicit fond smiles as well as praise of the artist, BOETHUS, for his ingenuity in inventing a curious subject. And it must be admitted that Boethus has succeeded, from the formal point of view, in converting a trivial subject into a remarkably effective work of art. The swirling forms have been contained in a compact, pyramidal composition, at once complex and unified, in which the voids, like the solids, have been carefully studied and used as functioning parts of the whole.

5-86 BOETHUS, *Boy Strangling a Goose,* second century B.C. Marble, approx. 33" high. Staatliche Antikensammlungen, Munich.

The *Seated Boxer* (FIG. 5-87), attributed to APOLLONIUS, a very late Hellenistic work (perhaps more properly referred to as Greco–Roman, since it dates about a century after the absorption of Greece into the Roman empire), shows a heavily battered veteran of the arena resting, perhaps beaten and listening to the berating of his manager. The boxer is a man of huge physique, but his smashed face, broken nose, and deep scars tell the gist of his story. The sculptor appeals not to our intellect but to our emotions, as he strives to evoke compassion for the battered hulk of a once-mighty fighter. Story, realism, and human interest became the Hellenistic artist's interests at the end of the development of Greek sculpture, which ran, in a few centuries, a spectrum of possibilities and realizations from the *Apollo* of Olympia (FIG. 5-40) to a brutish boxer past his prime. This should in no sense be construed as a decline of artistic quality or a failure of spiritual force. Hellenistic art is to be appreciated within the whole history of art for its thematic variety, its virtuosity of technique, its power and passion in expressing the drama of human life. Its strength is felt throughout the development of Roman art, which, in many ways, is the extension of it.

5-87 Attributed to APOLLONIUS, *Seated Boxer* (found in Rome), *c.* 50 B.C. Bronze, approx. 50" high. Museo Nazionale Romano, Rome.

5-88 Interior of the Temple of Apollo at Didyma (the Didymaion), near Miletus, Anatolia (Turkey), begun 313 B.C.

ARCHITECTURE

The greater variety, complexity, and sophistication of Hellenistic culture called for an architecture on an imperial scale and of wide diversity—far beyond the requirements of the Classical city-state. Building activity shifted from the old centers on the Greek mainland to the opulent cities of the Hellenistic monarchs in Asia Minor—sites more central to the Hellenistic world. Great scale and ingenious development of interior space, the latter peculiarly a feature of Hellenistic architecture, are shown in the oracular Temple of Apollo at Didyma (the Didymaion) near Miletus, the old Ionian city on the west coast of Asia Minor (FIGS. 5-20f and 5-88). This dipteral Ionic temple, begun in 313 B.C., is raised on a seven-stepped base some 13 feet above the level of the large naos, which was intentionally left open to the sky (hypaethral). The temple is 167 feet by 358 feet, and the great columns are over 64 feet high. The deep and column-filled pronaos precedes an antechamber from which oracles may have been delivered. Entrance to the temple's interior was not through this room, which has a threshold some five feet high, but through two lateral, barrel-vaulted tunnels that sloped down toward the inner court, which was planted with bay trees in honor of Apollo. In the back of this court stood a small prostyle shrine that protected the cult statue, the foundations of which may be seen in the illustration. On the opposite end of the court a stairway some 50 feet wide rose majestically toward three portals leading into the oracular room, which, approachable from both front and back, was the focal point of the entire design. This complex spatial planning of large interiors leads directly into later Roman practice and marks a sharp departure from Classical Greek architecture, which stressed the exterior of the building almost as a work of sculpture and left the interior relatively undeveloped.

Another example of dexterous planning of uncovered space is the theater at Epidaurus, which Pausa-

5-89 View of the theater at Epidaurus, Greece, c. 350 B.C.

nias declared to be the best in Greece (FIGS. 5-89 and 5-90). Although the building (about 350 B.C.) is Late Classical rather than Hellenistic, it is already highly sophisticated and has all the functioning units and formal arrangement of later theaters. The slightly more than semicircular auditorium is built into the side of a hill; the diameter of its projected circle is 387 feet. Staircase aisles, laid out on radii projected from the center of the circular *orchestra*, where the plays were performed, separate blocks of stone benches, which themselves are separated into two tiers by a broad corridor. The orchestra, the *proscenium*, and the *skene* are arranged for maximum convenience of view of the performance and of the preparations of the actors. The *parodos* (passageway between stage and seats) on each side is wide enough to permit rapid exit. Such careful planning for the convenience of an audience marks, as do the New Comedy plays acted at this time, an increasing concern for individual views and responses.

The thoughtful adaptation of space to serve human uses, rather than, as in ancient times, to honor gods and to satisfy the whims of kings, is part of Greek humanism's contribution to history. The Hellenistic Greeks also broadened their conception of architectural design to take in whole cities. The regular street patterns of the gridiron type, which date from the Archaic period in Greece, were systematized during the fifth century B.C. by HIPPODAMUS, a Milesian architect, whose name has been linked with the rec-

tangular plans of urban Hellenistic foundations.* The *Hippodamian plan*, as illustrated by the city of Priene (FIG. 5-91), consists of a close-meshed network of streets that intersect at right angles, without any particular axial emphasis that might suggest dominant traffic patterns. Here, the plan has been superimposed on an irregular, sloping site, without regard to the nature of the terrain. Only the defensive walls on the city's perimeter closely follow the topographical contours, with the result that walls and street plan are unrelated. On the other hand, the system is neat and orderly and, by making few distinctions of either a social or economic nature, essentially democratic.

The major ordering principles of so-called Hippodamian plans were the rectangle and rectangular relationships. The *agora* was centrally located and easily accessible to all citizens. It was partially surrounded by long, roofed, colonnaded *stoas*, which housed markets and offices and were the architectural expression of the public life of the city. Here, its business and politics, its administration and its gossip went on, and it is from the fact that they taught their rational, moral discipline in a stoa that the philosophy of the Stoics takes its name.

*Knowledge of ancient urbanism is rather scanty, since archeologists generally prefer to investigate limited sites, and it is rarely economically feasible for them to uncover and trace miles of city streets. The fragmentary evidence shows, however, that cities with regular, usually rectangular street plans existed in both ancient Egypt and Mesopotamia.

5-90 Plan of the theater at Epidaurus.

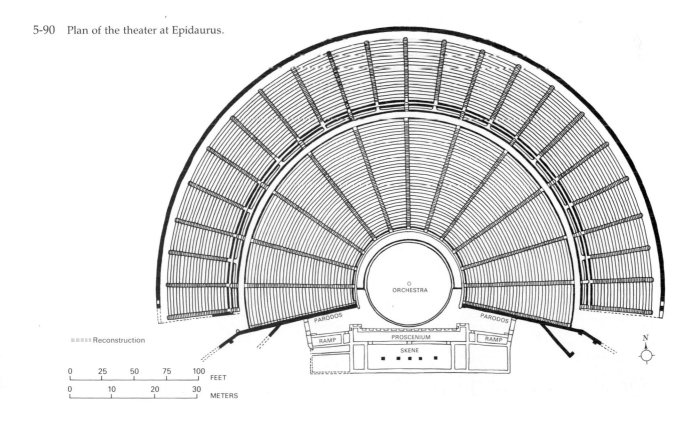

===== Reconstruction

0 25 50 75 100 FEET

0 10 20 30 METERS

ORCHESTRA

PARODOS   PARODOS

RAMP   PROSCENIUM   RAMP

SKENE

N

1. Temple ruins
2. Wells
3. Fish and meat market
4. Sanctuary of Olympian Zeus
5. Gymnasium
6. Bouleuterion
══─── Speculative

5-91 City of Priene, fourth century B.C. *Above:* Simplified ground plan. Shaded rectangle indicates area shown in detail at *left.*

As important as the stoa to the life of the civic organism (and forming part of the agora) was the *bouleuterion,* a meeting place of the city council, which required a large, roofed and enclosed space within which lines of sight were uninterrupted and acoustics were good. Efforts to fulfill these requirements came to fruition in the late third century B.C. in a new building type, an impressive example of which is the bouleuterion of Miletus (FIGS. 5-92 and 5-93). Here, the architectural problems were solved by incorporating a curved, theater-like auditorium of steeply rising tiers of seats into a rectilinear masonry shell with a timber roof supported by four columns, ingeniously placed so as not to obstruct the audience's view of the rostrum (FIG. 5-93).

It is at this point in the history of architecture that we can speak of domestic building as such and discover the look of a human dwelling capable of being

called a "house" (FIG. 5-94). Typically, the lot on which the Hellenistic house stood was enclosed by a wall to shut out the dirt and noise of the narrow street. A single door opened into an office, or service quarters, from which a covered passage led to the main unit through a courtyard, into which roofed chambers opened. Wealthier residents had, in addition to a forecourt (similar to the Roman *atrium*), a colonnaded garden, the *peristyle.*

The residential requirements of ordinary people without means were recognized and occasionally satisfied in Classical and Hellenistic Greece by planned housing projects. Such a development was built in a suburb of Olynthus in the late fifth century B.C. Here, groups of 10 houses were arranged in rectangular blocks of about 300 feet × 120 feet, neatly fitted together in a Hippodamian grid pattern (FIG. 5-95). The individual houses varied in plan, but one feature, a spacious central courtyard with verandahs, was common to all. Residential groupings of this sort predate

5-92 Bouleuterion at Miletus, late third century B.C.

5-93 Reconstruction of council chamber, bouleuterion at Miletus.

5-94 Plan of House XXXIII, Priene. (Partially restored.)

the Roman *insula,* an even more integrated housing plan not unlike that of a modern apartment house. On a small scale, the Priene and Olynthus houses reflect the general interest in designing convenient, interior spaces, as well as the growing concern for utility and convenience in the daily life of the ordinary individual.

Priene was a provincial town, and its houses were relatively unpretentious. It was in the capitals of the Hellenistic kingdoms—at Alexandria in Egypt, Pergamon in Asia Minor, and Pella in Macedonia—that life unfolded its richest and most sumptuous aspects. Here, the kings and their retainers surrounded themselves with luxury that became proverbial, and their way of life set a standard that was to be surpassed only by the Roman emperors in later antiquity.

The great, urbanized citadel of the Attalid kings at

5-95 Plan of residential blocks, Olynthus, late fifth century B.C.

Pergamon was a wonder of the ancient world and, even in its present, ruined state, still commands our admiration. Beautifully accommodated to its dramatic, mountainous site, the city proper was linked with the acropolis, some 800 feet above it, by an agora, a gymnasium, and the Sanctuary of Demeter, which were sited on intermediate levels. On the acropolis stood the fortress-palace of the rulers and, grouped around a theater, temples and sanctuaries like the Altar of Zeus and Athena (FIGS. 5-78 and 5-79). It was here that Pergamon achieved its greatest splendor in a sophisticated and dynamic grouping of architectural masses (FIGS. 5-96 and 5-97). The deployment of the structures along flexible axes for maximum visibility is a free departure from the symmetric regularity of the Hippodamian plan and must have produced, at a distance, the faceted effect of a great gem, reflecting in its brilliance the wealth and power of the Pergamene dynasty. We have already seen the sculptural celebration of Pergamon's victories over the Gauls, and it is noteworthy that the At-

5-96 Plan of the acropolis, Pergamon.

1. Upper agora
2. Altar of Zeus and Athena
3. Gateway to Acropolis
4. Sanctuary of Athena
5. Theater
6. Palaces
7. Barracks
8. Storehouses and arsenal
9. Temple of Trajan

5-97 Model of the acropolis, Pergamon. Staatliche Museen, Antiken-Sammlung, East Berlin.

talid kings were known in Hellenistic times as patrons of culture and art just as much as for their statecraft and their prowess in war.

MOSAICS

Among the most lasting symbols of Hellenistic luxury were the floor mosaics with which the wealthy residents of these court cities embellished their houses. As an art form, mosaic had a rather prosaic and utilitarian beginning. (The Sumerian custom of covering walls with baked-clay cones and the technique of shell inlay, as found in the *Standard of Ur*, FIG. 2-15, were not long-lived.) In the Mediterranean region, the mosaic technique seems to have been invented primarily for the purpose of developing a flooring that was both inexpensive and durable. Originally, small pebbles collected from beaches and riverbanks were set into a thick coat of cement. It was soon discovered, however, that the stones could be arranged in decorative patterns. At first, these were quite simple and confined to geometric shapes; examples of this type, dating back to the eighth century B.C., have been found at Gordium in Asia Minor. Eventually, the stones were arranged to form more complex pictorial designs, and, by the fourth century B.C., the technique had developed to the point that mythological subjects could be represented on a large scale and with a rich variety of colors.

The most famous of these fourth-century pebble mosaics were found at Olynthus, which was destroyed by Philip of Macedon in 348 B.C., and at Pella, the Macedonian capital under King Archelaus around 400 B.C. Although almost forgotten until the late 1950s (excavations there were begun in 1957), it was at Pella that Alexander was born, that Aristotle taught, and that Euripides died. Under Alexander, Pella virtually became the capital of the world, and he ruled his vast empire from there. Although little has been preserved of the buildings' superstructures, furniture, or other works of art, the uncovered floor mosaics provide ample evidence of the luxury and beauty of Pella's houses. A detail from one of several well-preserved pebble mosaics shows an almost life-sized figure from a scene representing a lion hunt (FIG. 5-98). The stones that have been arranged to form the picture are neither hewn nor shaped, but natural pebbles. A variety of colors has been used to produce a polychrome effect, but the chief pictorial impact is derived from a strong dark and light contrast. Some outlines and interior markings are defined with thin strips of terra cotta—a refinement that increases the clarity of the design but that was to enjoy no lasting favor.

Because they were cheap and durable, pebble mosaics remained popular through Roman times; in fact, they are still used for decorative pavements in Mediterranean countries. However, the desire for ever-greater pictorial realism led to the simple, but revolutionary, practice of cutting stones to desired shapes, so that they could be fitted together more closely. At first, these shaped stones, or *tesserae*, which permitted more precise description of detail, were used together with pebbles in limited areas that were felt to require greater definition. Perhaps originating in Hellenistic Sicily, "true" mosaics, composed entirely of cut stones, were designed at Pergamon and Delos by the second century B.C., at which time the technique had been perfected to include colored glass (*smalto*) for strong colors, such as pure blue, red, and green, rarely found in natural materials. One of the most durable of the artistic media, mosaic was highly refined and popular in Roman times and became one of the chief vehicles for the pictorial expression of early Christian and Byzantine artists.

While Alexander and his successors were Hellenizing the East, a power was rising in the western Mediterranean that, in its own way, would, like Greece, greatly determine the history of Europe and the Europeanized world. In one fateful year, 146 B.C., that power—Rome—sacked the Greek city of Corinth and destroyed an old enemy, Carthage, absorbing the small Greek states into the Roman province of Achaea and constructing around the ruins of Carthage the province of Africa. Thus, in a double stroke, Rome took under its aegis the culture of Greece and brought to an end in the Mediterranean West the Ancient Near Eastern civilization that had continued to flourish in the old Phoenician (eastern contemporary of the Minoan) sea-empire. Although this constituted another step in the Westernizing of the ancient world, it did not mean a blocking of the channels of commercial and intellectual intercourse with the East.

For what Rome adopted from Greece it passed on to the Medieval and modern worlds in a form much transformed by the Oriental message of Christianity. If Greece was peculiarly the inventor of the European spirit, Rome was its propagator and amplifier.

5-98 *Hunter,* detail of the *Lion Hunt* mosaic, Pella, *c.* 300 B.C. Pebble mosaic, approx. 66" high.

6

ROME ABOUT A.D. 350

1 Aurelian Wall		**7** Arch of Constantine
2 Forum Romanum		**8** Imperial Forums
3 Colosseum		**9** Baths of Caracalla
4 Trajan's Column and Basilica Ulpia		**10** Arch of Titus
5 Pantheon		**11** Circus Maximus
6 Temple of Fortuna Virilis		**12** Mausoleum of Hadrian
		13 Ara Pacis Augustae

ITALY ABOUT 500 B.C.

Area of Etruscan domination

Areas of Greek colonization

Areas of Carthaginian colonization

Area of Italic domination

0	50	100	MILES
0	80	160	KILOMETERS

VENETI

LIGURIANS

Mediolanum

Mantua

Adria

ILLYRIANS

Felsina

Faesulae

Volaterrae

CORSICA

Clusium · Perusia

ADRIATIC SEA

ETRUSCANS

Volsinii

Aleria

Vulci

Tarquinii

Veii

Caere · Fidenae

Roma · Praeneste

Tusculum

ITALIC

PEOPLES

Olbia

IAPYGIANS

Capua

Cumae · Neapolis

Tarentum

Paestum · Metapontum

Hydrus

SARDINIA

TYRRHENIAN SEA

Sybaris

Croton

Rhegium

Panormus

Messana

Selinus

SICILIA

GREEK COLONIES

Agrigentum

Syracusae

Carthago

AFRICA CARTHAGINIANS

ETRUSCAN
AND ROMAN ART

B.C.

8th CENTURY

ASSUMED ARRIVAL OF ETRUSCANS IN ITALY

- - - - - - GREEK COLONIZATION OF SOUTH ITALY - - - - - -

c. 700

c. 510   *She-Wolf of the Capitol*

753
Foundation of Rome (traditional)

ETRUSCAN DOMINATION

Tarquinians in Rome

509
Expulsion of kings

c. 400   c. 615
Siege of Veii
405–395

Peace between Rome
and Caere 353

Peace between
Rome and Tarquinii 351

DECLINE OF ETRUSCAN POWER

ROMAN REPUBLICAN PERIOD

Unification of Italy c. 350–275

300

ROMAN REPUBLICAN PERIOD

Conquest of Hellenistic Kingdoms

Punic Wars 264–201

200

280
Sack of Volsinii

Republican portrait

Augustus of Primaporta

30

B.C. A.D.

EARLY IMPERIAL PERIOD

44
Assassination of Caesar

27
Augustus proclaimed
emperor

79
Destruction
of Pompeii

98

Trajan

Marcus
Aurelius

Pantheon

117

284

EARLY IMPERIAL PERIOD

Barracks Emperors

Severans

Antonines

Hadrian

Diocletian

235

192

Ptolemy

136

Column of
Trajan

Arch of
Constantine

305

313

Constantine

LATE IMPERIAL PERIOD

c. 400

Sack of Rome by
Visigoths (Alaric) 410

c. 500

FALL OF WESTERN ROMAN EMPIRE

300

337
*Constantine
the Great*

Division of the empire c. 395

402
Honorius moves
capital to Ravenna

455
Sack of Rome
by Vandals

488
Occupation of
Italy by Ostrogoths

500

THE PEOPLE of Italy, while touched at an early date by the radiance of Greece, had deep and tenacious qualities of their own. Etruscan (or Etrurian) and Roman art, like any other, must be recognized as a synthesis of influences from outside sources and of elements indigenous to the country. Roman art, the immediate heir of all earlier Mediterranean cultures, was in many ways a synthesis of the arts of antiquity, in a manner quite distinct from that of Greek art. Rome was also deeply involved in bringing civilization to western Europe and to North Africa. The art of Rome was, therefore, in later times often regarded as the symbol of the art of antiquity.

In terms of political development, the early histories of Greece and Italy are roughly parallel, but the vigorous advance in Greece after the Persian Wars of the fifth century B.C., culminating in the Age of Pericles, found no counterpart in Italy, where culture was retarded by the bitter struggles among competing Italic peoples and between them and the Etruscans.

THE ETRUSCANS

The origin of the Etruscans, like that of the Mycenaeans, has long been one of the mysteries of the ancient world. Their language, although written in a Greek-derived script and extant in inscriptions that are still obscure, is unrelated to the Indo-European linguistic family. Ancient historians, as fascinated by the puzzle as modern scholars, generally felt that the Etruscans emigrated from Asia Minor; Herodotus, the "father of history," specifically declared that they came from Lydia. This tradition has persisted, and because the Etruscan culture emerges as distinct from those of other Italic peoples around 700 B.C., its arrival in Italy has long been put at the eighth century B.C. Such a view seems too simple, however, and does not explain adequately the evident connections between the Etruscan and earlier Italic cultures. Some modern scholars feel that the Etruscans are the direct descendants of very old pre-Indo-European people who had moved into Italy from the north. But this theory, in turn, cannot fully account for certain elements of the Etruscan culture, particularly the elaborate burial cult, which seems to be linked with Oriental customs.

A compromise theory points out that Herodotus gives no dates and that the migration to which he referred could well have occurred during the period of the great Mediterranean shifting of peoples, occurring around 1200 B.C., that caused the collapse of the Mycenaean civilization. At that time, immigrants from Asia Minor could have settled in Italy, mingled with the native population, and produced the culture of the so-called Villanovans, who, in turn, may have been the direct predecessors of the Etruscans. The changes that produced the Etruscan culture proper then would have to be explained in terms of increasing exposure to foreign influences—first Oriental, then Greek—brought about by expanding commerce and trade. In this connection, it is noteworthy that the Etruscans enjoyed high repute as skilled seafarers (or disrepute as pirates) in antiquity and that they emerged into the light of history during the so called Orientalizing period.

It is now generally conceded that Etruscan art developed largely as a consequence of the Greek colonization of southern Italy during the eighth and seventh centuries B.C. Although responsible for halting further Greek expansion northward along the Tyrrhenian coast, and despite deep-rooted distrust and antagonism toward their southern neighbors, the Etruscans—without relinquishing any of their native characteristics—eagerly absorbed Greek influences. Using the Greek colonial cities as a model, the Etruscans shifted from village life to an urban civilization and established themselves in strongly fortified hilltop cities. By the sixth century B.C., they controlled most of northern and central Italy from such strongholds as Tarquinii (modern Tarquinia), Caere (modern Cerveteri), Veii, Perusia (modern Perugia), and Volsinii (modern Orvieto). But these cities never united to form a state, and so it is improper to speak of an Etruscan "nation" or "kingdom." The cities coexisted, flourishing or fading independently and at different times, and any semblance of unity among them was based primarily on common linguistic ties and religious beliefs and practices. This lack of political cohesion eventually made the Etruscans relatively easy prey for the Roman aggressors. During the ten-year siege of Veii, for instance, no Etruscan city came to the aid of its beleaguered cousin.

ARCHITECTURE
Little is known of Etruscan architecture. The cities were either razed or rebuilt by the Romans, and those that survived were located on sites so well chosen that they continue to be inhabited to this day, making excavation impossible. Scattered remnants suggest that the Etruscans, at least during their later history, made considerable use of the masonry arch—a structural device not favored by the Greeks,* but one that was to become of profound importance in later Roman building.

The early Etruscan house is known to us chiefly from clay models that served as cinerary urns and from tomb chambers in which domestic interiors were re-created. To judge from the interior of the

---

*However, a masonry vaulted corridor from 320 B.C. was recently excavated at Nemea.

fifth-century B.C. Tomb of the Reliefs (FIG. 6-3), an originally simple, rectangular structure with a sloping roof grew progressively more elaborate, reaching its climactic development in the *atrium* houses of Pompeii and Herculaneum. Invention showed itself in the development of the atrium—a high, square or rectangular central hall that was lighted through a large opening in the roof and around which the other rooms were symmetrically arranged. This atrium was the focus of family life and the shrine for the *lares* and *penates*, the household gods. The ancient sacred hearth of Mediterranean family religion found an appropriate architectural expression in the noble atrium, which gave to Italic domestic architecture an importance and dignity beyond that developed by the Greeks.

Our knowledge of the Etruscan temple (FIG. 6-1) is based on a few preserved foundations and on a description given by the ancient Roman authority on architecture, VITRUVIUS. It may very possibly have had its origins in Greece. Its plan, for example, closely resembles the Greek prostyle plan (FIG. 5-20b). Yet the Etruscan adaptation, in typical fashion, developed its own characteristics. Resting on a high base (*podium*), with steps at one end only, it was constructed mostly of wood and sun-dried brick in a post-and-lintel system and had a heavy wooden superstructure richly decorated with brightly painted terra-cotta reliefs. The Etruscan emphasis on a highly ornate façade, with relatively spare treatment of the sides and rear, concentrated attention on the entrance porch. The axial organization was quite different from that of the Greek temple. Behind the sunlit pavilion of the porch, the shrine—divided into three *cellae* of equal size—formed dark cave-like spaces. The temple was not meant to be seen as a sculptural mass from the outside and from all directions, as the Greek temple, but instead was intended to function primarily as a confined interior space for the cult god. It was a place of shelter, protected by the wide overhang of its roof.

It is in the remains of their elaborate burial grounds, however, that the Etruscans have revealed themselves with the greatest clarity. In the rich array of wall paintings and painted reliefs with which they decorated the interiors of their tombs, they recount their zestful lives, their banquets, and their dances, which, in their suppleness and verve, seem partly Ionian (the Greek cities of the coast of Asia Minor) and partly barbarian. They tell us both of their athletic contests and of their wars. Their rise and fall from power is reflected in a gradual change from optimism to pessimism and in the choice of ever-more morbid and bloodthirsty subjects as their political fortunes declined. Although the Etruscans' reputation for cruel and unrestrained behavior is based largely on the testimony of the ancient Greeks and Romans, who were their enemies, elements in their tomb paintings indicate that many aspects of their society were in fact violent and extravagant. Indeed, these qualities may have played a decisive role in the formation of an energetic and creative culture that was to contribute to the rise to world rulership of their Roman successors.

6-1 Plan (*top*) and elevations (*bottom*) of an Etruscan temple. (After Vitruvius.)

The Etruscans built their cemeteries at some distance from their cities. Hundreds of tombs arranged in orderly manner along a network of streets produce the effect of veritable cities of the dead (*necropolises*). The tombs varied according to region and local custom. In the northern part of Etruria, they were usually constructed above ground; in the south, they were often excavated from the live rock, particularly in areas where tufa soil facilitated digging. Tufa, primarily strongly compressed volcanic ash, is easily excavated and hardens to a concrete-like consistency on exposure to the atmosphere; tufa can also be cut into durable building blocks that require no firing. It was used extensively by the Etruscans and Romans, and a minor tufa-brick industry flourishes in Italy today.

A characteristic Etruscan tomb type is the *tumulus*, a round structure that has been partially excavated and covered with earth (FIG. 6-2). This form was favored in Caere and, in view of its domical shape, seems to carry on an ancient Mediterranean tradition.

The majority of Etruscan tomb interiors, however, including those of the tumuli, are rectangular and reproduce the rooms of domestic architecture. A striking example is the Tomb of the Reliefs (FIG. 6-3), a large underground chamber in Caere (Cerveteri), in which massive piers with pseudo-Ionic (Aeolic) capitals support a slanting, beamed ceiling. The piers are *reserved*—that is, formed by cutting away the live tufa until the remaining rock assumes the shape of a pier or column, as in the Egyptian rock-cut tombs at Beni Hasan (FIG. 3-18). This, like most Etruscan tombs, was designed for multiple burials, the final resting place of an entire family and its servants. Sarcophagi, cinerary urns, and other tomb furnishings were placed in niches and on the bench-like projection at the base of the walls. Decoration in the Tomb of the Reliefs consists of painted plaster reliefs representing weapons, tools, and kitchen utensils, and displays a generous inventory of Etruscan objects of daily use. Occasionally, Caeran tombs were also decorated with mural paintings.

6-3 Tomb of the Reliefs, Caere (Cerveteri), fifth to fourth century B.C.

6-4 *Revelers*, detail of a wall painting from the Tomb of the Leopards, Tarquinii (Tarquinia), *c.* 470 B.C. Approx. 3' 6" × 6' 4".

PAINTING

Like the Caerans, the Tarquinians adorned the walls of their subterranean tomb chambers with colorful and lively murals. Although the subjects of tomb painting in Etruria are sometimes drawn from Greek legend, they are more often concerned with scenes of banquet and revel, as in the Tomb of the Leopards of Tarquinia. This small chamber tomb is decorated in the manner favored in Tarquinii during the fifth century B.C.: a banquet scene on the wall opposite the entrance, and groups of dancers and musicians on the side walls. These wonderfully vital pictures express especially well the peculiarly life-affirming exuberance that fills Etruscan art, as it must have filled Etruscan existence. Three young men (FIG. 6-4), one clad only in a light scarf, the other two in the elegant *chlamys* (cloak), seem to be hurrying through a grove of graceful little laurel trees, the leader carrying a cup of wine and beckoning the others, who play the double flute and the seven-stringed lyre. They already seem to be dancing, facing rhythmically in opposite directions, as if performing some circling step. The gestures have a kind of choreographic exaggeration, especially those of the enlarged hands and fingers of

the flutist, which hold and touch the instrument with such sureness and delicacy. It is rare in the painting of the ancient world that spirited movement is portrayed so convincingly, and it would be difficult to find from that time so fitting a monument to the beauty of youth, springtime, music, and the dance. The picture is a kind of fresco painting on a thin slip applied to the living rock wall or on a stucco paste made from the rock. The colors (blacks, blues, blue-greens, and ocher-reds) still retain much of their original freshness and harmonize easily and naturally with the creamy yellow ground.

But the later Etruscans seem to have surrendered their native, joyous vigor for a quiet, classicizing formalism like that in the *Woman of the Velcha Family* (FIG. 6-5), from a chamber in the Tomb of Orcus (Hades) in Tarquinia. The composed, even reflective, expression of this splendidly painted head suits the somber theme that is its context—the sufferings of the dead in Hades in the midst of the menacing demons of the underworld. The earlier Etruscan euphoria has disappeared, extinguished by the more cosmopolitan religions of the Hellenistic world, which stressed not the last happiness of the funeral revels, but the sadness of man's fate.

6-5 Detail of the *Woman of the Velcha Family*, wall painting from the Tomb of Orcus (Hades), Tarquinii (Tarquinia), fourth century B.C.

SCULPTURE

The Etruscan tombs yield a notable furniture of sculptured objects in both clay and bronze, materials that the Etruscans apparently preferred, although numerous stone sarcophagi survive. The forms are modeled rather than carved, modeling being a technique congenial to the impetuous temperament and fluid style characteristic of the Etruscans. Funerary urns and sarcophagi with recumbent portrait figures present some of the best examples of Etruscan sculpture. A canopic (cinerary) urn (FIG. 6-6) from Clusium (modern Chiusi) has a terra-cotta head for a lid, and the urn is set in a bronze model of a chair; the head is obviously intended to be a portrait likeness of the deceased whose ashes the urn contained. The strongly rounded form of the urn has a crude vitality that is carried into the head, with its blunt, aggressive

6-6 Canopic urn, Clusium (Chiusi), second half of the seventh century B.C. Hammered bronze with terra-cotta head, approx. 33" high. Museo Etrusco, Chiusi.

features and massive neck. In the reclining effigies of a man and his wife on the lid of a sarcophagus from Caere (FIG. 6-7), we read the traits of Archaism as we have found them in early Greek art. The work is a kind of three-dimensional formalization of the animated banquet scenes painted on Etruscan tomb walls to satisfy the demands of some cult ritual of the dead, the details of which are unknown. But there is nothing here of the solemn or the macabre, and the Etruscan instinct for the lifelike is preserved. The figures shown are relaxed and genial—much in contrast with the funerary formality of Egyptian statues—and the Archaic features of style, although present, produce no stiffness or awkwardness.

The *Apollo* from Veii (FIG. 6-8), an *acroterium* figure from the ridgepole of an Etruscan temple, is evidence that, like the Greeks, the Etruscans made use of architectural sculpture. But the Greek Archaic elements—the frontality, the grimacing mask, the closed contour—although immediately evident, are superficial; the awkward, lurching vigor of the powerful figure is a forceful example of Etruscan clay-modeling techniques and the use to which the confident, quick-conceiving, and quick-executing sculptor could put them. In contrast with, say, the serene majesty of the *Apollo* at Olympia (FIG. 5-40), this Apollo moves like a dangerous giant. His overpowering physical presence reflects small concern for the Greek preoccupation with harmonious proportions or idealized humanity. The Ionian elaboration of the drapery lines bespeaks the Eastern component in Etruscan art, but the animal force, the huge, swelling contours,

and the plunging motion are anything but Ionian and little of mainland Greek. The *Apollo* from Veii, given its architectural function, naturally differs from the painted Etruscan forms we have seen; yet it has in common with them the peculiarly Etruscan strength, energy, and excitement.

The absorption of Greek influences by the Etruscans continued during the height of their power—when the Etruscans were sending their own art commodities throughout the Mediterranean, including Greece—and through the centuries of their decline. The so-called *Mars from Todi* (ancient Tuder) (FIG. 6-9) exemplifies the Etruscan interpretation of the Greek Classical style in the beginning of the fourth century B.C. The figure, dressed in more-or-less contemporary military garb, executes a peculiar movement of the whole body, involving sideways and contrary directions of head, torso, arms, and legs, without seeming to move from his position. The sculptor may have been exaggerating the Polykleitan weight-shift stance, but there is a kind of agility to it, quite unlike the Polykleitan balance of weight and poise. We find again, as in the much earlier *Apollo* from Veii, that an Etruscan interpretation of prevailing Greek style

6-8 *Apollo*, Veii, *c.* 510 B.C. Terra cotta, approx. 70" high. Museo Nazionale di Villa Giulia, Rome.

6-7 Sarcophagus, Caere (Cerveteri), *c.* 520 B.C. Terra cotta, approx. 6' 7" long. Museo Nazionale di Villa Giulia, Rome.

6-9 *Mars from Todi,* early fourth century B.C. Bronze, approx. 56″ high. Vatican Museums, Rome.

her fame not simply to her antiquity and her magnificence as a work of art, but also to the fact that, for centuries, she has been the totem of the city of Rome. Ancient legend tells us that the founding heroes of Rome, Romulus and Remus, being abandoned as infants, were suckled by a she-wolf. The cult of Romulus and Remus was as old as the fourth century B.C., and we know that a statue of a she-wolf was dedicated on the Capitoline Hill in Rome in 296 B.C. We do *not* know whether the present statue of the she-wolf on the Capitoline Hill is the original (the suckling infants were cast during the Renaissance); its dating has been hotly debated, but its Etruscan origin is now widely accepted. Here, the vitality we have noted in the human figure of Etruscan art is concentrated in the tense, watchful animal body, with its spare flanks, gaunt ribs, and taut and powerful legs. The lowering of the neck and head, alert ears, glaring eyes, and ferocious muzzle render the psychic vibrations of the fierce and, at the same time, protective beast; the incised lines along the neck describe its rising hackles as it watches danger approach. Not even the great animal reliefs of Assyria can match, much less surpass, this profound reading of animal temper.

Somewhat later, we encounter the splendid *Chimera* (FIG. 6-11) from Arretium (modern Arezzo), a bronze monster with a rough-maned lion's head, a serpent's tail (restored in the Renaissance by Benvenuto Cellini), and a second head—that of a goat—whose right horn is seized by the serpent. Although the *Chimera* bears the wounds inflicted by the hero Bellerophon, who hunted and slew it, the figure is not merely illustrative of the event but almost cer-

brings out the native quality of energy, whether in the blunt drive of the *Apollo* or in the almost sprightly stance of the *Mars.*

One of the most famous animals in the history of world art, the *She-Wolf of the Capitol* (FIG. 6-10), owes

6-10 *She-Wolf of the Capitol,* c. 500 B.C. Bronze, approx. 33½″ high. Museo Capitolino, Rome.

tainly has some further demonic significance. The Etruscans, much of whose art is associated with mortuary ritual, had a well-developed *demonology*, an aggregation of demonic types that plague the dead in the underworld. Unlike the Greeks, who preferred to humanize their demons, the Etruscans, with their roots partly in Asia, employed their customary expressive force to represent them as dreadful animal hybrids. The precedents for the monster types go back to the sphinxes of Egypt and the winged, man-headed bulls of Mesopotamia, as well as to the ornamental animal bronzes of Luristan and the associated animal-heraldic style of much of the metalwork of central Asia. It may be that these traditions lingered in the Etruscan spirit, and the manifestation of them in such powerful form as the *Chimera*—so anti-Greek and so Asiatic—attests most firmly to the Eastern component in Etruscan culture. By the time of the Middle Ages, a whole population of monsters swarmed through the art of the West.

Also assimilated from the East and passed on by the Etruscans to the Romans was the practice of *divination*, whereby the future, as a product of arcane forces (personified as gods or demons), was thought to be predictable to some degree. On the assumption that all nature constituted a universe of affinities, prediction—the art of the priesthood—was based on the state of the viscera of sacrificed animals (especially the liver), the flights of flocks of birds, and unseasonable and unusual events. The engraved back of a bronze mirror (FIG. 6-12)—exquisitely wrought, with all the refinement for which the Etruscan craft arts were celebrated—represents a winged figure labeled Calchas, a priest in Homer's *Iliad*, divining from a liver that he holds in his hand and on which he

muses. The figure is a kind of miniature emblem for that world of benign and malign forces that surrounded ancient men and that they tried to approach or fend off by prophecy, sacrifice, oracle, omen, spell, incantation. Greek rationalism made little headway against the ancient world's overwhelming faith in the magical manipulation of nature.

Closely related to the delicately incised, Classical mirrors of the fourth century B.C., like the Calchas mirror, are the bronze cists of Praeneste (modern Palestrina), which undoubtedly echo the styles of the great Greek masters of mural painting—Polygnotus,

6-12 Engraved back of a mirror, *c.* 400 B.C. Bronze, approx. 6″ in diameter. Vatican Museums, Rome.

Euphranor, and others. Etruscan bronze vessels and mirrors with incised mythological scenes were famous and highly prized objects in Greece. Perhaps the outstanding member of this type is the *Ficoroni Cist* (FIG. 6-13). Most significantly, the artist, NOVIUS PLAUTIUS, is not Etruscan; he signed his work in Latin and made it in Rome. Here, Plautius has skillfully adapted a frieze of Greek figures, faithfully taking over the idealized naturalism of the Late Classical period. Naturalistic innovations appear: figures seen entirely from behind or in three-quarter rear view, complicated seated poses, figures on several levels rather than rigidly attached to a single groundline, details of landscape, and a kind of approximate perspective space. In his work, the artist represents the passing of the Etruscan genius and the acceptance of the irresistible influence of Greece. Yet something of the Etruscan sense for the real was to persist through the formal Classicism of Greece and, in turn, partly direct the course of the art of Rome; this earlier Etruscan sense would sharpen into the characteristic Roman taste for the factual in art, as in human affairs.

THE ROMANS

The Roman power that succeeded and replaced the Etruscan and Greek colonial powers on the Apennine peninsula compelled the contesting peoples of Italy into a Roman state and, eventually, the peoples of western Europe, the Mediterranean shores, North Africa, and the Near East into the Roman empire. The rise and triumph of Rome, and the awesome spectacles of its decline and fall, make, in the stately words of its great historian, Edward Gibbon, "a revolution which will ever be remembered, and is still felt, by the nations of the earth." From the Tigris and Euphrates to the borders of Scotland stretched a single government; under its energetic and efficient—if sometimes ruthless and brutal—rule lived people of innumerable races, creeds, tongues, traditions, and cultures: Britons, Gauls, Spaniards, Germans, Africans, Egyptians, Greeks, Syrians, and Arabs, to name only a very few. If the Greek genius, as we review it, shone most brightly in art, science, philosophy, history, and, in general, creations of the intellect and imagination, the Roman genius shone in the realm of worldly action—in law and in government. Roman monuments of art and architecture are distributed throughout the world that the Romans governed and are the most conspicuous and numerous of all the remains of the ancient civilizations we have studied thus far. But Roman monuments of a kind also survive in our concepts of law and government, in our calendar, in our festivals, rituals, languages, and religions, in the nomenclature of many of the sciences, and, for our special interest here, in the concept of art as worthy of historical study and criticism.

The main energies of Rome were devoted to conquest and administration, with conquest opening the way for the spread of Roman civilization. Roman cities sprang up not only all around the Mediterranean basin but also as far north as the Danube, the Rhine, and the Thames. Each city was a center for the propagation of Roman government, language, and customs and was closely connected with the city of Rome itself by a well-planned system of roads and harbors. By about A.D. 200, Rome was the capital of the greatest empire the world had ever known—an empire efficiently organized with 50,000 miles of sea routes and expertly engineered highways safe for travel and commerce. Rome itself was both cosmopolitan and splendid. The size, power, and complexity of the empire called for an impressive capital. The practical demands arising from the administration of a great empire required engineering skills for the construction of bridges, roads, sewers, and aqueducts, but the imperial ideal also called for public buildings that would express the dignity and diversity of the state.

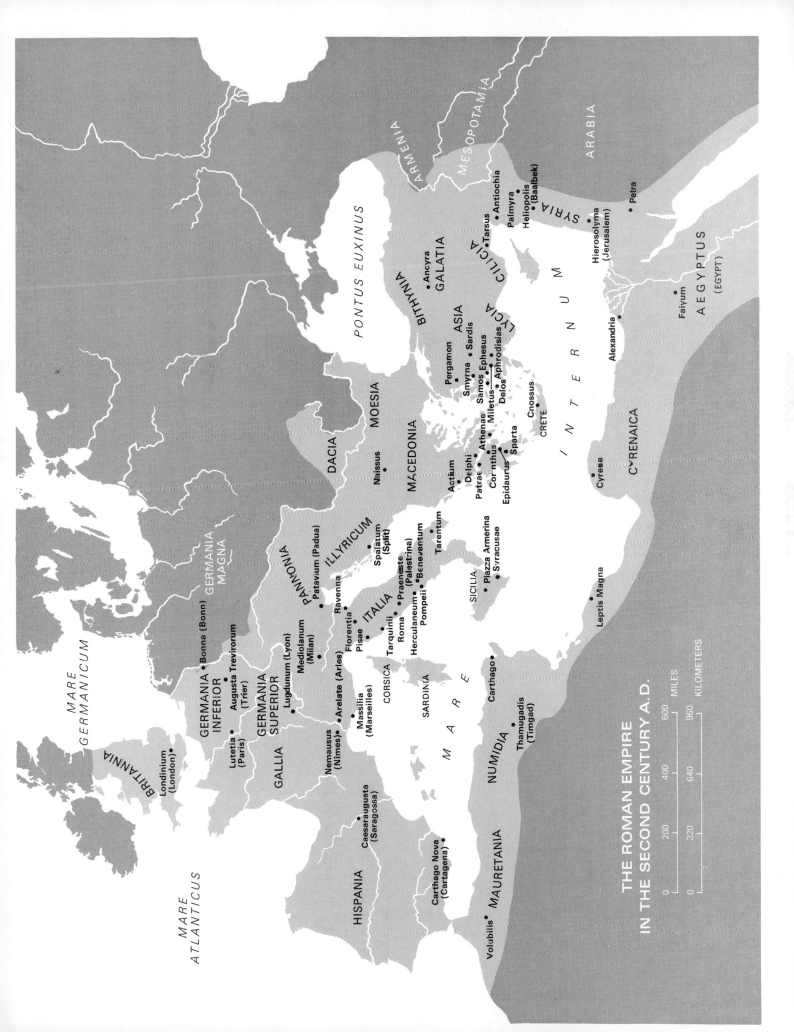

THE ROMAN EMPIRE
IN THE SECOND CENTURY A.D.

MARE
ATLANTICUS

MARE
GERMANICUM

BRITANNIA

Londinium
(London)

GERMANIA
MAGNA

Bonna (Bonn)
Augusta Trevirorum
(Trier)

GERMANIA
INFERIOR

Lutetia
(Paris)

GERMANIA
SUPERIOR

GALLIA

Lugdunum (Lyon)

Nemausus
(Nîmes)

Arelate (Arles)
Massilia
(Marseilles)

HISPANIA

Caesaraugusta
(Saragossa)

Carthago Nova
(Cartagena)

Volubilis

MAURETANIA

Thamugadis
(Timgad)

NUMIDIA

Carthago

SARDINIA

CORSICA

Mediolanum
(Milan)

Patavium (Padua)

PANNONIA

ILLYRICUM

Spalatum
(Split)

Ravenna

ITALIA

Florentia
Pisae
Tarquinii
Roma
Herculaneum
Pompeii

Praeneste
(Palestrina)
Beneventum

Tarentum

SICILIA

Piazza Armerina
Syracusae

MARE
INTERNUM

Leptis Magna

DACIA

Naissus

MOESIA

MACEDONIA

Actium
Delphi
Patrae
Corinthus
Epidaurus
Sparta

Athenae

PONTUS EUXINUS

BITHYNIA

Ancyra
GALATIA

ASIA

Pergamon
Smyrna
Sardis
Samos Ephesus
Miletus Aphrodisias
Delos

Cnossus

CRETE

CYRENAICA

Cyrene

ARMENIA

MESOPOTAMIA

CILICIA

Tarsus

LYCIA

Antiochia
Palmyra
Heliopolis
(Baalbek)

SYRIA

Hierosolyma
(Jerusalem)

ARABIA

Petra

AEGYPTUS
(EGYPT)

Faiyum

Alexandria

0   200   400   600   MILES
0   320   640   960   KILOMETERS

Roman art takes its character in large part from the imperial role the Roman state was required to play.

Although early under both Etruscan and Greek influence, Roman art came to have its own quite distinctive characteristics. The Romans, almost from the beginning of their rise to power, had been fully aware of Greek art, but it was only in the later Republican and Augustan ages that Hellenism became a conscious fashion. "Conquered Greece," wrote Horace, "led her proud conqueror captive." Shiploads of Greek marbles and bronzes were brought to Rome by generals and provincial governors to adorn their mansions, and, when the supply was exhausted, copies were made or Greek artists were employed to create new works. Fashionable art for a time became, to a large extent, the mere copying of Greek works. Finally, a deeper assimilation took place, and the art of Imperial Rome emerged, a product of its richly varied heritage and its unique genius.

This art-historical view of Roman art is comparatively new. Until about 1900, scholars saw Roman art merely as decadent Greek art, unoriginal and inferior. It is true that, drawing as it necessarily does on what went before, it does not have the degree of originality that distinguishes the great styles of Egypt, Mesopotamia, Greece, and even Etruria. Yet it is more than a mere "propagator and preserver of the classical heritage"; it is the "first comprehensive stage of western European art." Roman art makes use of Classical forms, but expresses non-Classical concepts. It combines an interest in individual personality with an interest in such abstract concepts as "law," "state," and "civilization." The vast body of the material of Roman art—found on three continents, with much of it still not evaluated and with much more still underground—almost suggests methods of mass production, in which the anonymous artist (almost no names survive, in contrast with Roman writers and poets) became the servant of his patron: private or public, wealthy connoisseur or the Roman state. Nevertheless, in the collective as well as in the individual case, Roman art has survived as an imposing style that took its own course in the days of the late republic.

The Republican Period

The Roman republic was founded after the last of the (possibly Etruscan) kings had been driven out. From the fifth century B.C. to the collapse of the republic and the assassination of Julius Caesar in 44 B.C., the external business of Rome was expansion abroad and the consolidation of imperial power in the Western world. In a succession of wars, the most harrowing and dangerous of which were the wars with Carth-

age, the Romans developed their peculiar qualities of character: disciplined valor, tenacity, practicality, obedience to authority, and a pitiless realism in recognizing the facts of power. Yet the constitutional structure of the republic, adequate to a limited city-state, could not begin to meet the requirements of an empire. Internal quarrels between classes—the *patricians* and the *plebeians*—were inflamed by disputes over disposition of the enormous wealth won abroad. When successful armies led by popular generals intervened in the politics of the republic, civil war began. Lasting almost a hundred years, during which dictators like Marius, Sulla, Caesar, and Pompey ruled, the war exhausted the state and destroyed its constitution. When the great-nephew of Julius Caesar, Octavian, finally found himself alone at the head of the Roman world (when he called himself Augustus), the republic was little more than a pious, ritualized memory.

It is in this period of the crisis of the republic, even while Greek influence became increasingly strong, that Roman art began to emerge as an entity distinguishable from the Late Hellenistic style. In 146 B.C., when Greece was absorbed into the Roman empire as the province of Achaea, a sculptural style came into being that we call *Greco–Roman*—the term, an admission that the two styles cannot be readily separated. Much of the original sculpture of the period was produced by Greek immigrant artists—for instance, the *Seated Boxer* (FIG. 5-87). But the growing Roman fascination with individual traits of personality is apparent in portrait sculpture, a field in which the Romans made one of their most original contributions (the others being architecture and landscape painting) and in which they achieved a quite typical, uncompromising, and often unflattering realism. However, the Hellenizing idealism that is found balancing this hard Roman realism in the last days of the republic bears witness to the peculiar dualism in the Roman attitude toward the defeated Greeks—admiration for their art and grace, and contempt for their "unmanly" cleverness and for their lack of skill in managing their own affairs as a people. Cicero described this Roman ambiguity of sentiment and scored the Greeks on their un-Roman insincerity in terms a little like those of nineteenth-century American travelers commenting on the French:

I grant them literature, I grant them a knowledge of many arts, I do not deny the charm of their speech, the keenness of their intellects, the richness of their diction; finally, if they make other claims, I do not deny them. But truth and honor in giving testimony that nation has never cherished. . . . Greeks never trouble to prove what they say, but only make a display of themselves by talking.

But it was the idealism of Greek art that again and again captivated the Romans. Greek statues in great profusion stood in the Roman forums and in both public and private buildings; villas and baths were museums of Greek sculpture—whether originals, copies, or adaptations to suit Roman taste. We read of 285 bronze and 30 marble statues brought from Corinth in 146 B.C., after the barbarous sack of that city, and of 500 bronzes brought from Delphi by Nero; when the stockpile of originals ran low, the demand for Greek sculpture was satisfied by copies made after Greek works.

PORTRAIT SCULPTURE

But even while under the spell of Hellenism, Roman portraitists produced works that have no parallel in Greek art. During the Hellenistic period, the quality of generalization that had distinguished earlier portraits had already given way to a style that was more particularizing and descriptive. The Roman's desire for literalness, together with his custom of keeping in his house, always before his eyes, the *imagines* (death masks, usually of wax) of his ancestors, influenced the sculptor to accentuate individual traits still further. Also operative was the Etruscan influence, which, with its expressionistic realism, persisted in Late Republican portraiture. The *Head of a Roman* (FIG. 6-14), for example, is striking by virtue of its "character," at once alive and mask-like. But the character may simply be accidental, the result of the artist's painstaking report of each rise and fall, each bulge and fold, of the facial surface, executed as if he were

proceeding like a mapmaker, concerned not to miss the slightest detail of surface change. The artist apparently tries neither to idealize the subject—that is, to improve him in conformity with an ideal, as in Greek practice—nor to interpret his personality. The blunt and bald record of his features, the kind given by a life mask or a death mask, is quite enough. Thus, this *verism*, a kind of superrealism, is the artist's objective, and it is determined not so much by esthetic motives as by religious convention. The habit of mind that demands faithful records of this kind is familiar to us in our curiosity about the fidelity of photographs of our forebears.

A quite different approach to the portrait subject can be seen in a bust of *Pompey the Great* (FIG. 6-15). A sculptor confronting a powerful and famous man may be conscious of the need for a method different from mere recording; he may want to idealize, but also to personalize—to interpret the subject's personality. We, coming 2,000 years after Pompey, bring to our scanning of him far more knowledge of the man than we could ever bring to the contemplation of a portrait of an unknown Roman. Pompey was first the partner and then the rival of Julius Caesar in the devastating civil war that wrecked the Roman republic in the first century B.C. We know of him as a great general, successful in war and the near proprietor of all the Eastern world held by Rome. We know of him also as a political incompetent and as an ambitious man of the middle class who allowed himself to be made the dupe of the extremists of the Senatorial party. We know of him as hopelessly irresolute, dis-

6-14 *Head of a Roman, c.* 80 B.C. Marble, life-size. Palazzo Torlonia, Rome.

6-15 *Pompey the Great, c.* 55 B.C. Marble, life-size. Frank E. Brown Collection, Rome.

appointing even his closest friends because he was unable to make up his mind. We know that he lost to Caesar in the bloody battle of Pharsalus, after which he was ignominiously assassinated by one of his own men. Yet he was a good man who refused to enrich himself by plunder of the provinces, a practice from which most of his contemporaries did not refrain. Cicero wrote of Pompey to a friend: "I knew him as a man honest, grave, and high-minded."

Thus, Pompey is a complex of traits played on by the accidents of history; yet what kind of man of only slightly more than good talent could have bested Caesar? Knowing what we do about Pompey's strengths and weaknesses, his triumphs and ultimate failure, we naturally approach his portrait bust as we might approach a bust of Washington or Lafayette—with curiosity about the individual man and his history. In the same way, it is likely that the artist of the bust, although different from us in his cultural responses, would still have cared to make a likeness that would be more than a mere facial record. This is evident in the work, which has none of the rigidity of the death mask and possesses a subtly modeled surface, over which the light plays softly. The modeling is obviously contrived to suggest rather than to describe. The strong lines of the broad head and the somewhat flat surfaces of the face are softened by a curiously ambiguous expression. Would we be wrong to read in it self-doubt mingled with affectation or bluster under an official mask of power? At any rate, the very fact that we are tempted to such interpretation testifies to the sophisticated artist's power to make us thoughtful before his image of a great and unfortunate man.

ARCHITECTURE

As striking as the manifestation of Roman originality is in its naturalistic portraiture, it is even more so in Roman architecture. During the Republican period, the Roman identity was first and most fully expressed in architecture and city planning. Unlike the religious architecture of the civilizations (including that of the Greeks) that preceded it, the Roman temple was not particularly inventive or conspicuous. Rather, it was on imposing and utilitarian civic structures and plans that the Roman builders concentrated, although they also built temples, modeled on plans that blended Greek and Etruscan elements in unique fashion. The Temple of "Fortuna Virilis" in Rome (FIG. 6-16), dating from the late second century B.C., looks at first glance like an Ionic, peripteral temple. The temple, now thought to have been dedicated to Portunus, god of the harbor, consists of a large cella located behind a deep porch (see FIG. 6-1). But the building stands on a high podium, which may be of Etruscan origin, and the cella occupies its entire width. This

6-16 Temple of "Fortuna Virilis," Rome, late second century B.C.

means that only the porch columns are freestanding and that the columns along the exterior walls of the cella are *engaged*, being purely decorative and having no supporting function. Seen from a distance, the engaged columns give the illusion of being freestanding—hence, the designation "pseudoperipteral" for this type of construction. A favorite with Roman builders, this temple type has survived in many examples, most of them larger than the one shown and employing the Corinthian order.

The same superficial resemblance to Greek architecture appears in the Temple of the "Sibyl" (or "Vesta"?, FIG. 6-17) at Tibur (modern Tivoli). Built in

6-17 Temple of the "Sibyl" ("Vesta"?), Tibur (Tivoli, Italy), early first century B.C.

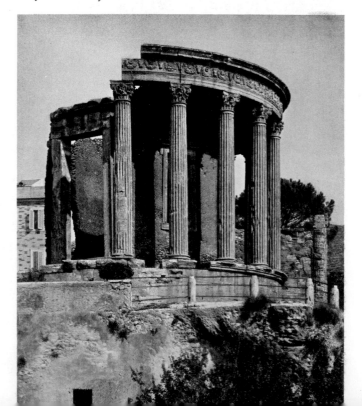

the early first century B.C., it looks at first like a Corinthian tholos. However, like the "Fortuna Virilis," the "Sibyl" stands on a podium, ascent to which is by means of a single flight of stairs that leads to the entrance of the cella. This arrangement introduces an axial alignment, not found in Greek tholoi, that serves to lessen the isolation of the building from its surroundings, diminishing somewhat the independent sculptural aspect so prized by the Greeks. A closer examination of the Temple of the "Sibyl" reveals other un-Greek features. The columns are *monolithic* (all of one piece) and not built up in the drum sections that were usual with the Greeks; the Romans preferred to use the monolithic column, often on great scale, wherever possible. The frieze is embellished not with figure sculpture, as would be the case in Greece, but with a favorite Roman decorative motif—garlands held up by the heads of oxen, a motif rhythmically repeated around the whole frieze.

(These are not the *bucrania,* or ox skulls, that became popular in later Imperial architecture.) Finally, and also in contrast with Greek practice, the cella wall is built, not of cut stone, but of concrete, into which blocks of tufa have been set in an ornamental pattern.

These significant departures from the Greek model are seen even more clearly in the sanctuary at Praeneste (FIGS. 6-18 and 6-19), which was dedicated to Fortuna (Fate) Primigenia and built under the first Roman dictator of the republic, Sulla, around 80 B.C. (or perhaps some 50 years before) at a site where oracular lots had long been cast. The great size of the sanctuary reflects the growing taste for colossal Hellenistic designs during the Late Republican period. Seven terraces rising against the hillside were placed with rigid, axial symmetry. The top terrace carried a semicircular, double colonnade that contained the sanctuary proper, probably in the form of a small, round temple. Although something of it had been

6-18 Sanctuary of Fortuna Primigenia, Praeneste (Palestrina, Italy), 120–80 B.C. (?)

6-19 Model of the reconstructed Sanctuary of Fortuna Primigenia. Museo Archeologico, Palestrina.

6-20   Detail of the Sanctuary of Fortuna Primigenia.

studied, we have full knowledge of the great temple only by an accident of war: Palestrina, modern successor of the Medieval town that had been built over Praeneste, was bombed during World War II, and clearing of the resultant ruins disclosed the impressive remains of the Roman buildings. The Roman builders had converted an entire hillside into a man-made design in a symbolic and ostentatious display of power and dominion. This assertive subjection of nature to man's will and rational order is the first full-blown manifestation of the Roman Imperial spirit and contrasts with the more restrained Greek bent—to crown a chosen hill with sacred buildings rather than to transform the hill itself into architecture.

The substructures for the terraces (FIG. 6-20) were built in concrete *(opus caementicium),* and it is here that we can find, in grand scale, the use of that favorite Roman building material, developed in the second century B.C. and applied for centuries wherever the necessary ingredients were available. Concrete (of generally inferior quality) had been used in the Near East, chiefly for the building of fortification walls, but its combination with the arch and the vault, as here at Praeneste, was revolutionary. As perfected during the Early Imperial period, concrete vaulting permitted Roman builders to cover, without interior supports, spaces of a scale never dreamt of before. Its use enabled the Roman architect to think of architecture in radically different terms from those of earlier build-

ers—as an architecture of space rather than of sheer mass, as was the case in the Egyptian pyramid, or the Mesopotamian ziggurat, or even the lighter, but still space-encumbering, post-and-lintel systems of the Greeks. (See discussion of the Roman Pantheon, pp. 221–23.) Roman concrete—a mixture of lime mortar, water, and volcanic dust found in limited areas, chiefly in central Italy—was poured over rubble that had been laid in courses between forms. Once solidified, this rubble concrete was cohesive and strong, although rough in appearance; but it was the custom to face the rough surfaces with marble slabs, plaster, or ornamental brick- or stonework. In Praeneste, the concrete is faced with small, flat, irregularly shaped stones that produce a figuration called *opus incertum.*

In the eighteenth century, the imagination of Europe was excited by the discovery of the buried cities of Pompeii and Herculaneum, which had been overwhelmed by an eruption of Mount Vesuvius in A.D. 79. Their discovery, prior to the first archeological expeditions to Egypt, fascinated Europe and provided the initial impetus for modern archeological curiosity. What made the discoveries—new ones are still being made in the excavations of both cities—of such poignant human interest, as well as so infinitely valuable for scientific history, was that they revealed to modern eyes, in almost perfect preservation and detail, the everyday communal life of these times and places past. Pompeii, a prosperous city of about

20,000, had been stopped dead in the very motion of everyday life and had been preserved intact in volcanic ashes, invisible and forgotten for some 1,600 years. The remains of the city permit us to reconstruct the Roman way of life during the Early Imperial period with a completeness far beyond that achieved at any other archeological site. The fullness of its record, its appeal to our sense of the dramatic and terrible accidents of life, and its usefulness for describing the architectural and artistic environment of quite ordinary people in an ancient city warrant considerable attention.

Although destroyed during the Early Imperial period, the city and many of its architectural monuments date from the Republican period. The plan of Pompeii, as seen in the parts excavated thus far (FIG. 6-21), is not that of the ideal *castrum* type, but rather the irregular plan of a *grown* city that was subjected to revisions and regularizing at various periods. The Roman castrum type of city plan, based on the layout of a military camp, was used in the outlying, frontier, colonial regions and had its major development during the Early Imperial period (see FIG. 6-44), although an early form of it was used at Ostia in the fourth century B.C. Pompeii, which started as a small, unplanned settlement in the vicinity of the Greek colony of Neapolis (modern Naples), was founded in the sixth century B.C. by the Oscans, early local rivals of the Romans. It was seized in 425 B.C. by the Samnites, also rivals of the Romans, who fortified and replanned it under the influence of expanding Greek concepts of rational, urban planning. But the Greek grid system could not be rigidly applied without tearing down most of the city; as a result, the main organizing features—the north–south and east–west thoroughfares—do not intersect at right angles, and the blocks between them are irregular. The city was conquered by Sulla in the 80s and refounded as a Roman colony in 80 B.C. In A.D. 62, it was partially destroyed by an earthquake; it had not yet been entirely rebuilt by the time of its final destruction 17 years later. Pompeii has been especially valuable to the historian of Roman architecture; many building types that later were to become standard are found there in their early, if not earliest, examples, including the oldest amphitheater extant and the earliest known public baths.

Next to the Roman Forum, from which it differs significantly in design, the forum of Pompeii (FIGS. 6-22 and 6-23) is the most important example of an early Roman civic center. The Pompeian forum is a rectangular court in the proportion of $3\frac{1}{2}$:1, unified by—and the boundaries of which are defined by—continuous colonnades around three sides. The other

6-21   Aerial view of the excavated portion of Pompeii, Italy. Area enclosed by rectangle near center of photograph is shown in FIG. 6-22.

6-22 Plan of the forum of Pompeii. Area diagrammed is indicated in FIG. 6-21 by rectangle inscribed near center of photograph.

1. Temple of Jupiter
2. Macellum (provisions market)
3. Sanctuary of the City Lares
4. Temple of Vespasian
5. Building of Eumachia (fullers hall)
6. Comitium (voting hall)
7. Duovirs' (chief magistrates') office
8. Council chamber
9. Aediles' (junior magistrates') office
10. Basilica
11. Temple of Apollo
12. Control of weights and measures
13. Cereals market
14. Commemorative arches

type of plan, represented by the Roman Forum, is bordered by more monumental, but individual and disconnected, structures. Like most Roman forums, the Pompeian forum was set apart from major traffic arteries and vehicles could not enter it. Its long, north–south axis is dominated by the Capitolium—a large temple set on a high podium and dedicated to the three gods who protected Rome and her colonies. Several smaller temples flank the long sides of the forum. At the south end stands the triple hall of the Curia (city council), representing civic authority, and the Basilica, the seat of law and business. (This basilica, dating back to about 100 B.C., is an early example of one of the most important and influential classes of Roman buildings—the one from which the basic form of the Christian church building will derive.) Thus, the forum combines the functions of a religious, commercial, and administrative civic center

and is the heart of the town. In the same way, it is a kind of imperial center in miniature, and this combination of functions, as architecturally expressed in the Roman Forum, would come to represent the central concerns and focus of the whole Roman empire.

One would not expect the formality of a civic center to be found in the streets that surround it. These would be less monumental and regular; their spaces, less ample—even narrow and cramped. The streets had heavy flagstone pavements with flanking sidewalks. Stepping stones for pedestrians crossing the street were spaced so that they could be straddled by the wheels of vehicles. Most intersections had continuously flowing public fountains. The problem of human convenience in an urban society—although not dealt with on the enormous scale that it is today, was worked out in Pompeii with an efficiency we can believe suited the needs of the people. The town had

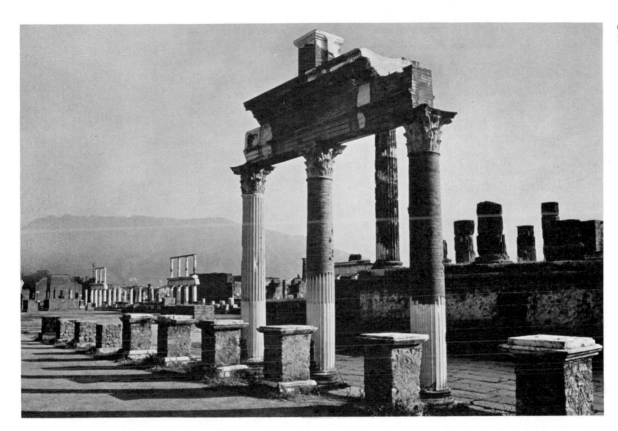

its commercial sections, like that of the Via dell' Ab-
bondanza, where the streets were flanked by rows of
small shops, offices, taverns, bakeries, and where we
can still see many painted advertisements on the
walls. Here and there, the rows of shops were interrupted by a gateway leading into a private residence,
which spread out in the back of the shops and was
entirely enclosed and isolated from them and from
the noise and dust of the street.

The private house is probably the most precious
and best-preserved record of urban life to come from
Pompeii. The town houses of the well-to-do—like the

House of Pansa (FIG. 6-24), an atrium type—
protected in Pompeii and Herculaneum by the volcanic ash and lava in which they were buried, are
extraordinarily well preserved, with their mural decorations still fresh and some equipment and household utensils intact. Such a house stood flush with
the sidewalk. Through a narrow door, one entered a
vestibule that led into the *atrium*. The latter had an
opening in the center of the roof (the *compluvium*) and
a depression in the floor below it (the *impluvium*) to
collect rainwater. Along the sides were small rooms;
at the end, where the atrium extended the full width

6-24 Plan of the House of
Pansa, Pompeii, second
century B.C. (After
Sir Banister Fletcher.)

1. Shops	6. Impluvium	11. Wagon shed
2. Main entrance	7. Separate house	12. Gardener's shed
3. Baker's shop	8. Atrium	13. Winter dining room
4. Bake house	9. Peristyle	14. Dining room (triclinium)
5. Oven	10. Portico	15. Reception room (oecus)

16. Office
17. Kitchen
18. Tablinum
19. Alae

of the building, were two wings, or *alae*. Behind the atrium was the *tablinum*, in which family archives and statues were kept. The tablinum could be shut off or could afford a passage to the *peristyle*, a large colonnaded court of Hellenistic origin. This court contained fountains and a garden, around which were arranged the family's private apartments. At the back, there was sometimes a vegetable garden or an orchard. Along the outer sides of the house and opening onto the street were the shops. Thus the house faced inward, depending on its courts for light and air. Whenever space allowed it, units were symmetrically arranged on a long axis that reached back from the street and, when opened through its entire length, afforded a charming vista of open court, gardens, fountains, statues, colored marbles, mosaics, and brightly painted walls. Some of the largest of these atrium houses in Pompeii rivaled, if they did not surpass, the palaces of Hellenistic kings; the House of the Faun, in which *The Battle of Issus* mosaic (FIG. 6-38) served as a floor ornament, covered almost 30,000 square feet. Of course, these houses, popular particularly in the region around Mount Vesuvius, were the homes of patricians and rich merchants; artisans, craftsmen, and shopkeepers lived in much more modest quarters, the last often in single rooms in back of or above their shops.

In their fullest development in the late Roman republic, the elaborate, skillfully planned houses of the great Romans combined an older Italic nucleus with features of the Hellenistic house and represented the highest achievements of domestic architecture in antiquity. That domestic architecture occupied a prominent place in Roman civilization was manifest in every part of the empire. The character of Roman domestic religion, which exhibited a traditional Italic feeling for the home, family, and hearth as sacred, helps to explain the careful elaboration of the domestic architecture.

PAINTING AND MOSAIC

The interiorizing design, with its open and independent arrangement of units, guaranteed complete privacy. Because of the small number of doors and windows, it also offered considerable stretches of wall space suitable for decoration, as the atrium of the House of the Silver Wedding in Pompeii (FIG. 6-25) clearly shows. The decorations commonly used varied between types that emphasized the wall as a barrier and others that visually opened the wall and enhanced the space of the room. The colors were sometimes delicate greens and tans, sometimes striking reds and black (to throw the panels or figures into relief), and there was rich creamy white in the borders. The Romans obtained a certain brilliance of surface by careful preparation of the wall. After the plas-

6-25 Atrium of the House of the Silver Wedding, Pompeii, second century B.C.

6-26 First-style (*incrustation*) wall painting from a Samnite house, Herculaneum, second century B.C.

ter, which was specially compounded with marble dust, was laid on in several layers, it was beaten with a smooth trowel until it became very dense and was then polished to a marble-like finish.

The progression from flat to spatial wall decoration in Pompeii and Herculaneum has been divided, somewhat arbitrarily, into four successive, but overlapping, styles. The first style (about 200–60 B.C.), called *incrustation*, divides the wall into bright, polychrome panels of solid colors with occasional, schematically rendered textural contrasts (FIG. 6-26). This style is a continuation of Hellenistic practice, and examples of it have been found in houses at Priene and on the island of Delos. A wall painting from the Villa Boscoreale, near Pompeii (FIG. 6-27), shows the second, or *architectural*, style (about 60–20 B.C.), in which decoration is no longer restricted to a single visual plane. The space of the room is made to look as if it extends beyond the room itself by the representation of architectural forms in a visually convincing,

but not really systematic, perspective. Columns, pilasters, and window frames painted on the wall serve to enframe distant views of cities and landscape. In the *herringbone perspective* used here, the *orthogonals*, or lines of perspective projection, do not converge on a single vanishing point on the horizon (as in Renaissance perspective); rather, *several* vanishing points (with associated orthogonals) tend to be distributed on an axis that runs vertically through the center of the panel. Although not consistently employed, this method does give a rather convincing illusion of objects receding in space.

A second-style mural in the Villa of the Mysteries near Pompeii (about 50 B.C.) displays painted figures that are among the finest to have come down to us from the ancient world (FIG. 6-28). Although other rooms in the villa are decorated in a style very similar to the pure architectural style of the Villa Boscoreale, the second-style illusionism here is confined to a painted ledge that looks like a shallow extension of

6-27 Second-style (*architectural*) wall painting from the cubiculum of the Villa Boscoreale, near Pompeii, first century B.C. Metropolitan Museum of Art, New York.

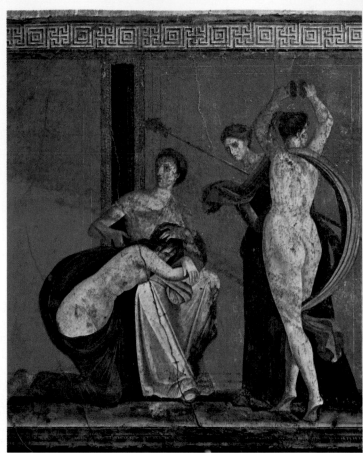

6-28　Second-style wall painting, details of a frieze from the Villa of the Mysteries, near Pompeii, *c.* 50 B.C. Figures approx. 60″ high.

the room proper and affords the figures a kind of narrow, supporting stage. The figures, set against a red-paneled background, in the style of a relief, are part of a large composition that circles the walls of the room, which may have doubled as a banqueting room and as a place for the celebration of the rites of some mystery cult, perhaps that of Dionysos. The meaning of these scenes is in dispute; we may, however, be fairly certain that this group represents the initiation of a young novice into the cult. Whipped by a winged genius or deity, she crouches for solace in the lap of a solicitous older woman, while a splen-

6-29　*Ulysses in the Land of the Lestrygonians* (scene from the *Odyssey Landscapes*), second-style wall painting from a house in Rome, late first century B.C. Approx. 60″ high. Vatican Library, Rome.

didly painted nude dances in Bacchic frenzy. The mystery cults, discussed later in connection with Christianity, made their way into the Roman empire in increasing numbers and variety from the Hellenized East. All included mysteries that were never to be divulged by the initiate, and that, when understood after painful introduction into the secret rites, would afford salvation through mystical union with a deity. The pictured ceremony from the Villa of the Mysteries is not only a work of art of high order, but a most important record of one aspect of the gradual religious transformation of the Roman world by the westward migration of Oriental spiritualism. As always with Roman paintings of quality, we question whether this is an original Roman work or a derivative from a Hellenistic Greek original in some temple that is now lost? No decisive answer can be given.

The question arises again, and more insistently, when we look at the second-style *Odyssey Landscapes* (FIG. 6-29) from a house on the Esquiline Hill in Rome. In these landscapes, dating from the late first century B.C. and now in the Vatican, painted piers divide the otherwise continuous stretch of landscape into eight compartments, in which scenes from the Homeric epic are represented. The shimmering landscapes extend the space of the room and their luminosity almost absorbs the subordinated, rapidly sketched figures. At the same time, the landscapes seem to be brought into the room almost magically—the flickering play of color and light, and especially the shaded edges of the solids, providing a stage-like presence, as of easily shifted props, that suggests distance and isolated action. The second style, although "architectural," here exhibits its versatility, for the sole purpose of the rigid frames is to create the illusion of open and unconstrained landscape. If it could be established that the conception of an "all-encompassing" space in works like the *Odyssey Landscapes* is original with Rome, then a solid Roman contribution to the history of art could be acknowledged.

The architectural quality of the second style faded toward the end, and the triumph of the *illusionism* evident in the *Odyssey Landscapes* may be seen in the detail of a wall painting from the House of Livia in Primaporta, near Rome, made toward the end of the first century B.C. (FIG. 6-30). The extension of the

6-30 *Garden Scene,* detail of a second-style wall painting from the House of Livia, Primaporta, late first century B.C. Portion shown approx. 9' wide. Museo Nazionale Romano, Rome.

6-31 Third-style (*ornate*) wall painting from a villa at Boscotrecase, near Pompeii, early first century A.D. Museo Nazionale, Naples.

space of the room and its complementary effect, the bringing of the landscape into the room, creates the image of a garden just outside the limit of the wall. (This is a curious anticipation of the widely popular "picture window" of recent modern architecture, in which one enjoys the "view" by fixing it within a frame, at the same time thinking of the landscape as continuous with the room.) Here, "deep" perspectives and distant views are not desired, but rather the intimacy and freshness of natural beauty easily within contact. In the second style, as it developed, the "view" comes ever closer, until one may think that it is one's own garden, free of any human intrusion, enclosed and isolated by the painted limits of the fence and by the back-stopping of the foliage itself, which occupies a plane close to the viewer and shuts out distance.

The passing of the wall from serving as a framed view into nature to serving as a mere support for smaller framed views occurred in the third, or *ornate*, style (about 20 B.C.–A.D. 60), during the time of the early Roman empire. Simulated architecture disappeared, as the wall was subdivided into a number of panels by means of vertical and horizontal bands filled with vine scrolls or other decorative designs (FIG. 6-31). The flat nature of the wall is here reaffirmed, and illusionism is confined to the pictures set into and emphasized by the decoratively patterned framework. At times whimsical and capricious, this style is characterized by delicate forms and colors, graceful elegance, and a deliberate rejection of the monumental constructions of the second style.

The fourth Pompeian wall style, the *intricate*, dates from around A.D. 60 to A.D. 79 and may be seen to good advantage in the Ixion Room from the House of the Vetii (FIG. 6-32). Here, the painters, under the influence of contemporary Roman theatrical design, returned to the use of architectural frames and open vistas. However, an aerial perspective, rather than a linear one, is created by areas of color flooded with light and atmosphere, which unite the wall in a complex way, incorporating all the lessons of previous experiments in optical illusion. In fact, the fourth style is a kind of résumé of its predecessors. The incrustation style appears along the lower walls, and architectural panels are set into the ornate, third-style wall articulation, which is also reflected in the individual picture panels. Although the aerial perspective produces a certain unifying effect, there is no single point of view from which the designs can be taken in or from which they can be related; obviously, it is intended that we pass the pictures as we do in a gallery, stopping at each one, aware that it need have no relationship in subject or style to its neighbor.

A masterpiece of the fourth style (FIG. 6-33), from the Domus Aurea of the emperor Nero (A.D. 54–68) in Rome, the architecture of which we will presently consider, shows a thinning out and simplification of

6-32 Fourth-style (*intricate*) wall painting from the Ixion Room, House of the Vetii, Pompeii, first century A.D.

the compositional intricacies of the Ixion Room paintings. Here, there is the greatest elegance and delicacy in the placing and rendering of details and in the proportions and spacing of the panels. The artist makes a virtue of vacant space and slender enframements, avoiding all crowding and busyness. The effect is one of precise symmetry, but with subtle variations of balancing. The color scheme is a harmony of white, gold, and accents of blue, deftly placed. The ornamental vocabulary is intentionally limited to a few motifs: in the transom panels, masks and sea-gods; below, birds, garlands, and architectural vistas. Centered in the main panels are framed landscapes, providing window-like extensions of the space of the

6-33 Fourth-style wall painting from the Domus Aurea of Nero, Rome, A.D. 60–67.

room. In the history of ancient painting and interior decoration, this work has scarcely an equal.

A still life with peaches and a carafe, from Herculaneum (FIG. 6-34), about A.D. 50, demonstrates that the Roman painter sought illusionistic effects in depicting small objects as much as he did in depicting architectural forms and landscape spaces. Here, his method involves light and shade, with scrupulous attention to contour shadows and to highlights; undoubtedly, he worked directly from an arrangement he made himself—the fruit, the stem and leaves, and the translucent jar being set out on shelves to give the illusion of the casual, almost accidental, relationship of objects in a cupboard. But the picture is exact in neither drawing nor perspective, and the light and shade are approximate. Still, the illusion the painter contrives here marks the point of furthest advancement made by the ancients in the technique of representation. He seems here to have an inkling that the look of things is a function of light, and he strives to paint *light* as he strives to paint the touchable *object* that reflects and absorbs it. It is interesting that painters like Paul Cézanne—often called the founder of modern art—in discarding the systematic, organizing devices of perspective and *chiaroscuro* (light and dark), produced distortions and irregularities in painted objects that resemble those of this ancient still life.

A painting from the House of the Dioscuri in Pompeii (FIG. 6-35) offers evidence of the high degree of

6-34 *Still Life with Peaches*, Herculaneum, *c*. A.D. 50. Wall painting transferred to wood, approx. 14″ × 13½″. Museo Nazionale, Naples.

6-35 Genre scene (?) from the House of the Dioscuri, Pompeii, first century A.D. Detail of a wall painting transferred to wood, entire painting approx. 15" × 17". Museo Nazionale, Naples.

skillful illusionism achieved by the painters of the fourth style. The subject may be a scene from mythology or a genre scene. A woman seated before a stone building and a small hut receives a cup from a bowing man—or does she extend the cup to him? It is difficult to decide. Whatever the interpretation, the brush technique is a deft *impressionism,* the strokes firm and practiced; and the painter is entirely sure of the poses and the relationship of the figures in space. The problems of figural attitude, anatomy, movement, and proportion, which we have seen confronting the ancient artist for millennia, seem now to have their familiar solutions, so that the artist of this work proceeds easily and confidently, his brush quickly expressive of his knowledge.

That the style of the Dioscuri painting was contemporaneous with other, quite different styles is apparent from a painting from Herculaneum representing Herakles finding the infant Telephos, being nursed by a doe, in Arcadia (FIG. 6-36). The subject indicates that the picture was copied from some Hellenistic original—or originals, for the artist proceeds as if he were lifting figures from different sources and arranging them with little relationship to one another. Thus, the personification of Arcadia, the large seated figure, is not in proportion to Herakles, nor is the treatment the same. The statuesque Arcadia exhibits the pale, hard modeling we associate with sculpture, while the play of light and highlight on the supple surfaces of the Herakles figure is closely related to the effects we expect in pictorial illusionism, although the technique is by no means the free, "painterly" one we see in the Dioscuri work. All the figures are precisely modeled, with firm outlines. The artist is concerned chiefly with the solid volumes of the bodies—not with light or with the space the whole group occupies; each figure is contained, as it were, by its own particular space, the space it "fits." The depiction of space as an enveloping and unifying factor in picto-

rial design may not be characteristic in Greek art, and this picture, as we have said, copies a Greek model. On the other hand, the special Roman contribution to painting may be precisely the representation of space as *surrounding* the whole group of objects and figures in any given composition, rather than merely coming between them.

It still seems to be a general tendency to deny any originality in Roman paintings and to insist that they are direct copies of, or closely inspired by, Hellenistic originals. Many Roman paintings do appear to be di-

6-36 *Herakles and Telephos,* Herculaneum, c. A.D. 70. Wall painting, approx. 7' 2" × 6' 2". Museo Nazionale, Naples.

6-37 *Idyllic Landscape* (detail of FIG. 6-31).

rect copies—among them the *Herakles and Telephos* just discussed and *The Battle of Issus* mosaic shown in FIG. 6-38. In fact, many paintings were probably done by transplanted Greek artists, and we might even grant that the Greek-derived style was the dominant one. But the Roman *landscape* seems to represent a radically different approach, particularly in its expression of a concept of space that is simply not evident in Greek art, and all attempts to derive Roman landscape painting from Hellenistic Greece lead us into extremely tenuous speculation based on unknown (or nonexistent) Greek prototypes. All extant Greek works show the Greek artist thinking in terms of solid volumes, like those of human figures (as in the *Herakles and Telephos* painting) and confining the role of space to a mere separating function, rather than an all-containing one. Thus, it might be much simpler to credit the Romans with the development of a new concept in painting: the projection of an enveloping, unifying volume of space on a flat surface. This refinement of abstraction—in which space, filled with air and light, is actually represented as being just as real as the objects it surrounds and contains—would complete the long development of rep-

resentation that began with the silhouettes of early Egypt and Mesopotamia, or even earlier. At any rate, many now accept the view that the architectural illusionism of the second style was a Roman development and that this illusionism was a step in the transition to the spaces depicted in the smaller landscape panels (FIG. 6-37). For an artist thinking of the wall surface as a kind of extension of the space of the room (as in architectural illusionism), the next step would be to take a segment of the wall and convert it, window-like, into a small block of framed space that extends "through" the wall and contains its little universe of depicted objects.

In any case, the artist of the fourth style, chiefly interested in representing space, made the objects as small as possible and unified the whole composition, as we have seen, with light and atmosphere. Of course, recession in depth is suggested, not accurately projected. The Romans had no system of mathematical perspective; instead, they employed (effectively, if unsystematically) the diminution of figures and objects and, particularly, atmospheric perspective, with its hazed and sketchy outlines, the shift from local color toward blue, and the blurring of distant contours (compare FIG. 6-29).

The love of country life and the idealizing of nature—what we may call the Arcadian spirit—prevails in these landscapes. Characteristically, they contain shepherds, goats, fauns, little temples, garlanded columns, copses of trees, and other accessories, which from their mood—part religious, part idyllic—have been called *sacral-idyllic* scenes (FIGS. 6-31 and 6-37). The Arcadian spirit of the time speaks in the formal, pastoral poetry of Vergil and, in one of his odes, Horace, proclaiming the satisfactions afforded the city man by his villa in the countryside, where life is beautiful, simple, and natural in contrast with the urban greed for gold and power, asks, "Why should I change my Sabine dale for splendor full of trouble?"

The attitude that celebrates the virtues of rustic life must be very closely associated with an original Roman development in architecture. Many Arcadian landscapes have been found in *villas*—country houses developed by the Romans when congestion in the cities became severe, as it did in Pompeii during the first century B.C. The villas were never located very far from town (one might call them "suburban"), so that their wealthy owners could enjoy the advantages of city life and the quiet of the countryside. The very spaciousness of the landscape around the villa came to be the subject matter of the wall paintings we have been examining. The modern desire to escape the tensions of the city and to return to nature is ancient in its architectural and pictorial expression, not to mention its appearance in literature. We will encounter this Arcadianism again and again in the history of the West, in the Renaissance and in

6-38 *The Battle of Issus*, from the House of the Faun, Pompeii, *c.* 80 B.C. Mosaic, approx. 8′ 10″ × 16′ 9″. Museo Nazionale, Naples.

the nineteenth and twentieth centuries, as urban pressures begin to strain human nerves.

The floors as well as the walls of Roman buildings were ornamented, usually in mosiacs.* *Mosaic* had its beginnings in the Ancient Near East (see pp. 180–81). It was used by the Greeks, often in geometric patterns, in place of carpets. The Romans continued the practice and, from the first century A.D. on, even applied mosaic to walls. A striking aspect of Roman mosaics is the frequent attempt to copy not only the subject matter of painting but also the painter's technique in modeling, shading, and the like. This was possible only if extremely small *tesserae* (the bits of glass or stone composing the mosaic) were used, as, for example, in the famous mosaic from the House of the Faun in Pompeii (FIG. 6-38), which is apt to be a copy of a Hellenistic original and perhaps should be thought of as more Hellenistic than Roman. The mosaic, which represents the rout of Darius and his army by Alexander the Great at the battle of Issus, has those qualities of Greek style we have noted: the essentially sculpturesque emphasis on the solid forms, space defined by the forms themselves, and no attempt to show an enveloping space. Nevertheless, a remarkable taste for fidelity to appearance is shown in the details of action. The horses plunge into and out of the picture at the most daring angles, and the human figures are posed in such a variety of descriptive attitudes as to convince us the artist was

pursuing an ultimate realism. In keeping with this is the high degree of tonal smoothness achieved by the setting-in of tesserae so small that some 50 separate bits were used to describe a single eye perhaps 1½ inches wide. The Romans appear to have developed a taste for this kind of minute workmanship, and the technical quality of mosaics must have been judged by the size of the tesserae used—the smaller, the better. Since, after all, the mosaics were seen at a distance of only five or six feet (one walked on them), such a criterion seems natural enough. The standard changed during the Early Christian period, when mosaics were placed high on church walls and apse vaults, making such minute differences scarcely noticeable and such a painstaking technique meaningless.

The vast range of subjects represented in mosaics is comparable to that of Roman painting. Themes from Classical mythology vied in popularity with historical subjects or with topical ones, such as genre aspects of rural existence and scenes from the popular theater, gladiatorial battles, chariot races, and hunting.

Stylistically, the development was toward simplification of the extremely complex and detailed work exemplified in *The Battle of Issus* mosaic (FIG. 6-38). Tesserae tended to become larger; the designs, flatter and less illusionistic. From the middle of the first century A.D. on, human figures and animal forms appeared in black silhouette on white ground, prefacing the black and white mosaics that were to become the favorite floor decorations in Italy during the second and third centuries A.D. They were especially popular

*The Romans used the words *tesselatum* (hence, "tesserae") for floor mosaics and *musivum* (source of "mosaic") for wall mosaics.

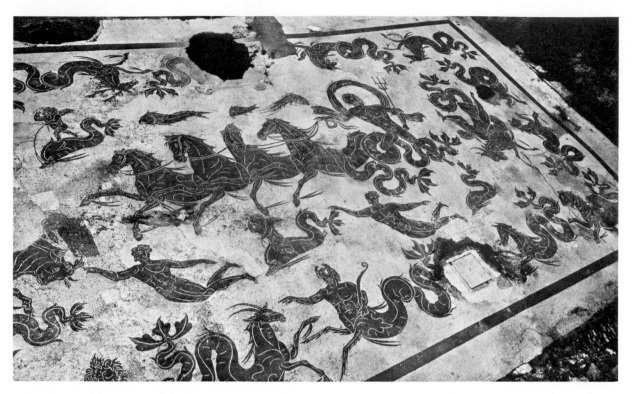

6-40 Wall mosaic from the House of Neptune and Amphitrite, Herculaneum, c. A.D. 70.

in bathing establishments, and a masterpiece of this type was found in the Baths of Neptune at Ostia (FIG. 6-39). Here, appropriately enough, marine divinities, accompanied by Nereids and Tritons, are carried across the waters by dolphins and horses with fishtail bodies. The fluid, dynamic design is based on a repetition of curvilinear forms that evokes the movement of the sea.

At the same time, polychrome mosaics moved up the walls—at first, to decorate grottoes and fountains, but eventually to cover entire walls (FIG. 6-40). Less exposed to wear from sandaled feet, wall mosaics permitted the use of relatively fragile materials, such as glass paste (smalto) and enamel, and the achievement of stronger coloristic effects than were possible with colored stone or marble tesserae. The brilliant blue of the wall mosaic in the House of Neptune and Amphitrite in Herculaneum (FIG. 6-40), due largely to the liberal use of smalto, also contributes to the rich tonality in the modeling of the figures, recalling the glassy surfaces in the Herakles figure from *Herakles and Telephos* (FIG. 6-36).

Painting, with all its advanced illusionistic devices, remains the standard for mosaic representation. What was achieved by way of subtle, pictorial effect can be seen equally in mural painting and, on a smaller scale, in the painted panel. We may judge the quality of panel painting by a portrait from Faiyum in Egypt, some 60 miles south of modern Cairo (FIG. 6-41). In Greek and Roman times, Faiyum was a busy, populous province, and its cemeteries have yielded some 600 portraits painted on wood and attached to the mummy cases of the deceased. The making of such portraits must have been a regional custom, as very few have been found elsewhere; they supply for us our largest gallery of ordinary people from the vast Roman Imperial world when it was at the height of its power. Some Pompeian wall frescoes hint at what Greek murals may have looked like, but the Faiyum portraits give us the best idea we have of Hellenistic Greek painting techniques. Most of the portraits are done in the *encaustic* technique (pigments in hot wax; see pp. 136–37), but *tempera* (pigments in egg yolk) was used occasionally. Easel painting, on small, portable panels, had been highly esteemed in Greece, where the encaustic technique had a long tradition. Polygnotus had worked in it in Classical times, and, as mentioned earlier, it had been used for the architectural decoration of buildings like the Parthenon. The example here (FIG. 6-41) shows the very highest level of craftsmanship—refined brushwork, soft and delicate modeling, and the subtlest possible reading of a sensitive subject. The Faiyum portraits were probably painted from living persons, and, in this instance, we have the meeting of an unusually perceptive artist with a subject whose

6-41 *Mummy Portrait of a Man,* Faiyum, *c.* A.D. 160–170. Encaustic painting on wood, approx. 13¾″ × 8″. Albright-Knox Art Gallery, Buffalo (Charles Clifton Fund, 1938).

personality would try his whole skill to render. The composure, the emphasized thoughtful eyes, and the Hellenizing hairstyle are familiar in portraits made during the time of the Stoic emperor Marcus Aurelius (about A.D. 160) and in the portraits of the emperor himself. The calm demeanor of the subject, the gaze that "sees the world steadily and sees it whole," evokes the philosophy of the emperor himself as set forth in his *Meditations*. As earlier we confronted the bust of Pompey, familiar with his history, so it is an aid to us in meeting this image from the age of the

Antonines to read the philosophic emperor as we read the painted features of our subject:

> Every moment think steadily as a Roman and a man to do what you have in hand with perfect and simple dignity. . . . do every act of your life as if it were the last, laying aside all carelessness and passionate aversion from the commands of reason, and all hypocrisy, and self-love, and discontent with the destiny which has been given to you.

Our history has taken us beyond the period of the republic into that of the empire to show how Rome carried the ancient world's representation of landscape and of human individuality—begun in Mesopotamia and Egypt—to its fullest expression.

The Early Empire

When Octavian Caesar, the nephew and heir of Julius Caesar, routed the forces of Antony and Cleopatra at Actium in 31 B.C., he brought to an end some 90 long years of destructive civil war that had shattered the Roman republic. Although Octavian believed and proclaimed himself to be the restorer of the republic and the protector of its constitution and traditions, he became, in fact, the first emperor of Rome and—to all intents and purposes—ruled as emperor, taking the venerable name "Augustus," which was bestowed on him by a grateful Senate. The peace that began with Augustus has been called the "Pax Romana," for, under the auspices of a long line of emperors, peace prevailed within the Roman world for 150 years—a record in world history.

Augustus (27 B.C.–A.D. 14), determined to establish his authority unshakably, kept command of the military and financial resources of the empire in his own hands and deliberately set out to build a new and magnificent Rome to give a splendid image to the Imperial reality. As they carried the boundaries of the empire further in all directions, the Julio–Claudian emperors, Augustus' successors in the first century A.D., continued his policy of glorifying the visible aspect of empire, sometimes to an extravagant degree, in architecture, art, and a vast variety of public works. In the second century, the empire—under Trajan, Hadrian, and the Antonines—reached its greatest geographical extent and the summit of its power (see map, p. 193). The might and influence of Rome was unchallenged in the Western world, although there was always the pressure of the new, Germanic peoples on its northern borders, of the Berbers in the south, and of the Parthians and resurgent Persians in the east. These pressures increased in the third century and—combined with the decline of Imperial authority within the empire, disintegration of the economic and administrative structure, and military anarchy—almost brought the empire to collapse. In A.D. 285, it was restored by the last pagan emperor, the capable Diocletian, who became the overseer of the savage persecution of a sect called the "Christians." Within a generation, the triumph of this sect would mark a major turning point in the history of the world.

ARCHITECTURE AND PUBLIC WORKS

The grandiose Imperial designs of the early Roman empire are reflected, perhaps most conspicuously, in its architecture. The relatively stable conditions produced by the Pax Romana facilitated the Romanization of the provinces, and *urbanism*—the planning and building of cities—played a principal role in this process. The rapid growth of population, especially city population, has already been cited as a reason for the escape to the "suburban" villa. The pressure of population in the city itself made the sprawling atrium house, which was wasteful of space, obsolete. In Rome, a population of close to one million had to be housed in multi-story apartment blocks (*insulae*). Some 45,000 of these—built to the maximum legal height of five stories (60–70 feet high)—accommodated almost 90 percent of Rome's population. Most of the almost 50,000 inhabitants of Ostia, the port city of Rome, were housed in such apartment houses, built primarily of brick-faced concrete, some of which have been preserved to the level of the third story. The ground floors were occupied by shops, above which were the apartments, accessible by individual staircases. Many of the apartments were substantially more spacious than are most of ours today, the suites sometimes containing as many as 12 rooms arranged on two levels. A reconstruction of an Ostian insula (FIG. 6-42) shows the apartment blocks built around a central court; some of the larger courts may have been landscaped to contain a small shrine. Apparently, many apartments had balconies, still a standard feature of modern Italian apartment houses. Only deluxe apartments had private toilets; others were served by community latrines, usually on the ground floor. The insulae had no private baths, but public baths were conveniently located throughout various quarters of the city and were equipped with highly developed heating systems, which private houses and apartments lacked. (This is still true of parts of modern Italy.) The crowded conditions encouraged rent-gouging and jerry-building. Deficiency in materials was often compounded by bad design, such as a foundation area too small in relationship to the height of a building—a means of maximal exploitation of the limited space available. The poet Juvenal wryly complained about the poorly constructed city buildings:

> . . . we inhabit a city propped up for the most part by slats: for that is how the landlord patches up the crack in the old wall, bidding the inmates sleep at ease under the ruin that hangs above their heads.

6-42 Reconstruction of an insula, Ostia, Italy.

To an extent greater than is commonly known, the convenience of the ancient Roman of ordinary and less-than-ordinary means depended on facilities provided by the state—by authority imperial, provincial, or municipal. Millions of individuals depended on the government for food distribution, water supply and sanitation, recreation and entertainment, and roads and bridges, not to mention the protection afforded by police and firefighters. The administration of these services in the great days of the empire was efficient even by our standards, given, of course, the limitations we would expect from a less highly developed technology and communications system. Second only to food distribution, an adequate water supply for the populations of the overcrowded cities was the most imperative need. The Romans methodically developed water-supply systems as part of urban planning. The city of Rome began to build *aqueducts*

for itself as early as the fourth century B.C., and Roman aqueducts or their ruins still stand in many former Roman cities, both in Italy and in the provinces. Water was carried from the source to the city by gravity flow, requiring the building of channels with a continuous gradual decline over distances often exceeding 50 miles; we can appreciate, even in modern terms, what an outstanding achievement of surveying and engineering this represents. The Pont du Gard (FIG. 6-43) near Nemausus (modern Nîmes) in southern France is one of the most impressive specimens of Roman engineering skill. Each large arch spans some 82 feet and is constructed of uncemented blocks weighing up to two tons each. The quickening rhythm of the small top arches (which carry the channel), placed in groups of threes over the larger arches, manifests the Roman engineer's sense for the esthetic as well as the practical. The finished aqueduct carried

6-43 Pont du Gard, near Nemausus (Nîmes, France), first century B.C.

water to Nemausus over a distance of some 30 miles and provided each inhabitant with about 100 gallons a day. Services like this, and the awesome structures through which they were provided, could not help but impress on the diverse peoples who had come under the rule of Rome the advantages of compliance with such practical power and the benefits that could come from Romanization.

If the construction of aqueducts showed the value of homage to Rome, how much more the erection of a whole city! At Thamugadis (modern Timgad) in North Africa (FIG. 6-44), the Romans built a city, around A.D. 100, that lasted until its destruction by the Arabs in the sixth century A.D. Built along a major military road 100 miles from the sea, Thamugadis was probably planned to house a military garrison to keep local tribes in check. But this primary function was soon expanded, and no costs were spared to make this little provincial town into an attractive focal point for the local inhabitants. Here, the empire was a physical presence to the Africans, the city representative of the authority of the emperor and the civilization of Rome. Like many other colonial settlements, Thamugadis served as a key to the process of Romanization. The town was planned with great precision, its design probably based on the layout of the Roman military encampment, the *castrum*. (The ques-

tion of precedence remains unresolved: the castrum may have been based on the layout of the Roman colonial city.) The typical provincial Roman city has the form of a square divided into equal quarters by two main arteries crossing at right angles—the *cardo* being the north–south axis; the *decumanus*, the east–west axis. The *forum* is located near this crossing. The quarters are subdivided into square blocks, and the forum and public buildings, like the theater, baths, and library, occupy areas that are multiples of these blocks. At Thamugadis, monumental gates led into the city, the streets of which were colonnaded. The city covered some 30 acres, and its original population of 2,000 soon grew to 15,000. The whole plan was essentially a modification of the Hippodamian plan (see FIG. 5-95), but more rigidly ordered and systematized, with the forum set off from the main traffic pattern. The fact that most of these colonial settlements were laid out in the same manner—whether in North Africa, the Near East, or England—expresses more concretely than any building type or other construction project the unity and centralized power of the Roman empire at its height.

The architectural images of Rome set up in the far reaches of the empire had their even more monumental equivalents in the capital itself. When all roads did indeed lead to Rome, they found their sym-

6-44   Plan of Thamugadis (Timgad, Algeria), founded *c.* A.D. 100.

1. Forum
2. Theater
3. Library
4. House of Januarius, baptistry
5. East bath
6. North bath
7. Small baths
8. Temple of Ceres

bolic terminus in such stupendous works as the Colosseum (FIGS. 6-45 and 6-46), which, for modern men, still represents Rome as does no other building. So closely was it identified in the past with the city and the empire that an aphorism out of the early Middle Ages stated: "While the Colosseum stands, Rome stands; when the Colosseum falls, Rome falls; and when Rome, the world!"

The Flavian Amphitheater—popularly renamed the Colosseum, after a now-lost colossal statue of Nero that stood nearby—was begun by Vespasian (A.D. 69–79), first in the Flavian line of emperors. It was dedicated in A.D. 80 by his successor, Titus (A.D. 79–81), who employed prisoners from the Jewish Wars as builders (see FIGS. 6-61 and 6-62). The building type is an invention of the Romans, who expanded the *theater* into an *amphitheater*, which is essentially two facing theaters enclosing an oval space, the *arena*. The Roman Colosseum is the largest of its type, but most major cities in the empire had an amphitheater. Some, like the one at Verona, are still being used today for theatrical performances or games. The Colosseum was originally designed for the staging of lavish spectacles—battles between animals and gladiators in various combinations. The mythical beast–men struggles represented in Mesopotamian art here came to bloody reality. The extravagantly inhuman shows cost thousands of lives, among them those of many Christians, and the Colosseum has never quite outlived its infamy. The emperors competed with each other concerning who could produce the most elaborate spectacles. For the opening performance in A.D. 80, the arena was flooded and a complete naval battle, with over 3,000 participants, was duplicated.

The oval arena of the Colosseum (FIG. 6-45) is surrounded by steeply rising rows of seats, which could accommodate over 50,000 spectators. Its substructure consists of a complex system of radial and concentric corridors, covered by concrete vaults that rise to support the upper rows of seats. Originally, tall poles around the top of the structure supported ropes on which awnings could be spread to provide shade for the spectators. The basements below the arena proper contained animal cages, barracks for gladiators, and machinery for raising and lowering stage settings as well as the animal and human combatants. A great deal of technical ingenuity involving lifting tackle was employed to suddenly hurl hungry beasts from their dark dens into the violent light of the arena.

Roman ingenuity in the management of architectural space to fit a complex function may be observed

6-45   Aerial view of the Colosseum, Rome, A.D. 70–82.

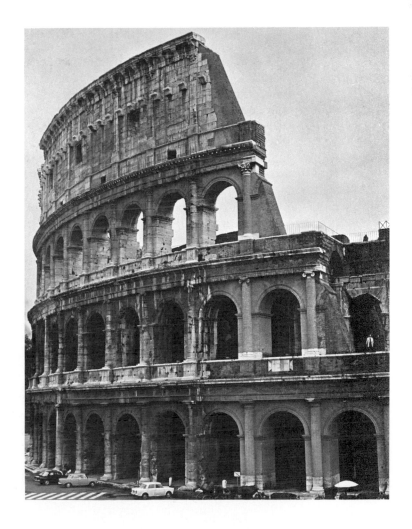

6-46   Outer wall of the Colosseum.

even in the exterior of the Colosseum—namely, the arcuated entrance–exit openings that must have permitted rapid filling and emptying of the vast interior space. (There were no less than 76 numbered entrances.) The relationship of these openings to the tiers of seats within was very carefully thought out and, in essence, may be observed in the modern football stadium. The Colosseum exemplifies the Roman talent for matching public and private convenience within large-scale service structures.

The exterior of the building (FIG. 6-46), with its numerous functional openings, consists of *ashlar masonry*, in which dry-jointed blocks are held together by metal cramps and dowels, as in Greek architecture. Its present pock-marked appearance (as if it had been blasted by large shrapnel) is due to the fact that the metal fittings were pried from the joints during the Middle Ages, when metal was very hard to come by. With these jointing units gone, vibrations from modern traffic have been shifting the stones, and the entire structure is in danger of collapse. The exterior walls are 161 feet high, and each of the three stories shows the characteristic combination of the Roman arch-and-vault construction with one of the ornamentally enclosing Greek orders. This setup, in which an arch is enframed by two engaged columns that carry a lintel, appears in triumphal arches and other Roman buildings, and, revived in the Italian Renaissance, has a long, illustrious history in Classical architecture. For the moment, it is necessary only to note that although this exterior feature serves no structural purpose, it does provide the esthetic function of integrating the units of the surface by rhythmic, horizontal and vertical repetition of the enframed arch. Although the arrangement of the orders finds no correspondence of a functional nature in the interior of the Colosseum, the rule of the arrangement is strict, following the standard, Roman, vertical sequence for multi-storied buildings: Doric–Ionic–Corinthian, from the ground floor up. This sequence, is based on the proportions of the orders, with the Doric, appearing to be the strongest, taken to be capable of supporting the greatest load.

The Imperial forums of the emperors rivaled the Colosseum as majestic expressions of the Imperial ideal. These forums were erected not as much as fundamental civic units of direct service to the people as ostentatious glorifications of Imperial power. They stood witness to the "piety, might, good fortune, magnanimity, and happiness"—as their triumphal inscriptions so often proclaimed—of the successive emperors who built them. They were not planned as a unit; each forum was added to another, their unity being achieved by strict, axial alignment (FIG. 6-47). Most of these forums consisted of large colonnaded courts; some were designed to set off a temple dedi-

6-47   Plan of the Imperial forums in Rome.

cated to the god who was the special protector of the emperor. The demands of impressive scale and great, sweeping vistas sometimes led to the massive transformation of whole neighborhoods. The building of the Forum of Trajan required the rebuilding of a market district and the modification of an entire hillside.

Dominating the Forum of Trajan was the huge Basilica Ulpia (Trajan's family name was Ulpius; he ruled from A.D. 98–117) of about A.D. 112 (FIG. 6-48). A larger version of the basilica in Pompeii, it was of a type that was perhaps the most characteristic of those developed by the Romans. The *basilica* was a public hall designed to accommodate large numbers of various kinds of business people. It was the locale of stock exchanges, law courts, business offices, and administrative bureaus and must have provided a

6-48 Reconstruction (*left*) and plan (*below*) of the Basilica Ulpia, Rome, *c.* A.D. 112. (After Sir Banister Fletcher.)

center for civic services analogous to those of multiple-building municipal centers today. Later, the Christians adapted the basilica (but more especially its subtype, the *palace audience hall*) to religious purposes, modifying it into the typical Christian church building. In plan, the basilica was rectangular, with two or more semicircular *apses*. In the Basilica Ulpia, one of the apses contained the Shrine of Liberty, where slaves were set free; the other may possibly have served in ceremonies of the emperor's cult. The entrance was on one of the long sides of the basilica—an orientation that was changed by the Christians. The building was vast—400 feet long (without the apses) and 200 feet wide; illumination for this great interior space was afforded by *clerestory windows*, provided by elevation of the timber-roofed nave above the colonnaded aisles. In the Basilica Ulpia, we once again encounter the Romans' instinctive feeling for broad, uninterrupted, architectural spaces, enclosed for the convenience of human transaction. Despite an imposing exterior, the interior space is what counts here, and although it is a colonnaded space, its effect is not like that of the externally perceived Greek temple, but rather like a dipteral Greek temple inverted: it is to be experienced from within, not from without.

The official style of public buildings during Trajan's administration was conservative and Hellenizing, and, like the deliberately classicizing style during the time of Augustus, expressed prosperous stability. At the same time, however, the native Roman School continued to work with and to exploit the properties of concrete—mainly in connection with private, commercial, and utilitarian structures. It is in this field that Rome made its great and original contribution to the history of architecture. Some of the most significant experiments occurred in the second half of the first century A.D., during the design and construction of the large, semiprivate, Imperial palaces of Nero and Domitian.

Augustus, who led an unobtrusively simple life, had been content to live in the house of a well-to-do citizen. His successors were neither as politically astute nor as frugal. Both Nero (ruling A.D. 54–68) and Domitian (ruling A.D. 81–96) built huge palaces for themselves. Nero's, never quite completed, was largely built over in later periods; Domitian's, which continued to be in use until the sixth century A.D., became the prototype for later Imperial and vice-Imperial residences throughout the Roman Empire.

The great fire of A.D. 64 destroyed large sections of

Rome, including Nero's old palace, the Domus Transitoria. The city was rebuilt in accordance with a new code that required greater fireproofing, resulting in the increased use of concrete, which was both cheap and fire-resistant. This gave rise to an entirely new attitude toward a still relatively new material—an attitude that found one of its first full expressions when Nero's architect, SEVERUS, was given the opportunity to use concrete inventively in the building of Nero's new palace, the Domus Aurea, or Golden House (FIGS. 6-49 and 6-50).

As described by the Roman historians Tacitus and Suetonius, Nero's new palace was a huge and luxurious country villa in the heart of Rome, extending from the Palatine to the Esquiline Hill. With a mile-long portico, it faced an artificial lake (later drained to become the site of the Colosseum) that was surrounded by a landscaped park in which tilled fields and vineyards alternated with pastures and woods filled with great numbers of wild and domestic animals. Probably, the palace was never completed. In the 70s, Vespasian, in a shrewd move to ingratiate himself with his subjects, turned most of the park over to the people. Domitian preferred the Palatine Hill and had a new palace built there. What stood of

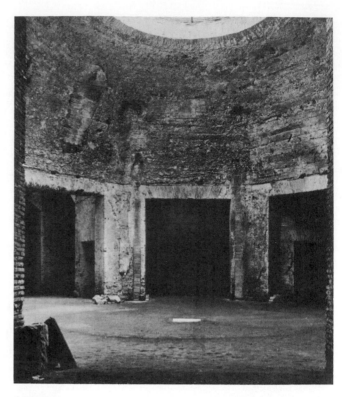

6-50 SEVERUS, the Octagonal Hall, the Domus Aurea of Nero, A.D. 60–67.

6-49 SEVERUS, plan (*above*) and section (*below*) of the Octagonal Hall, the Domus Aurea of Nero, Rome, A.D. 60–67.

the Domus Aurea was largely built over by later emperors, who, like Domitian, preferred to live on the Palatine.

The so-called "Esquiline Wing" of the Domus Aurea is the largest fragment of the Neronian palace known today; most of it was found imbedded in the basements of the Baths of Trajan. The excavated area measures about 660 feet long and 200 feet wide and contains a great number of rooms of uncertain purpose; their walls and piers are of brick-faced concrete, most of them covered by vaults. The more important rooms of the wing seem to have been located on its southern side, where they faced the artificial lake; traces of rich decorations, with marble paneling and painted and guilded stucco, have been found in them. The wing's general plan was fairly conventional, derived from the seaside villas, represented on Pompeian frescoes, that faced the ocean with porticoed façades. But, in what may have been the wing's central axis, a group of rooms expresses an entirely new approach to concrete architecture. An octagonal room is covered by a dome that modulates from an eight-sided to a hemispherical form as it rises toward a round central opening, the *oculus* ("eye"). Radiating outward from the pavilion's five inside sides (the other three, directly or indirectly, face the outside) are smaller, rectangular rooms, alternately covered by barrel and groin vaults (FIG. 6-49). These satellite rooms were enlivened by decorative recesses and, in the middle one, by a cascade. Their lighting was achieved in a most ingenious manner through what may be described as an inversion of a modified clerestory system. But most significant in the design of this group of rooms is that here, for the first time, we are confronted with an interior in which the architect appears to have been thinking of the architectural solids—the walls and vaults—not as space-limiting but as *space-molding* agents.

Today, deprived of its marble and stucco incrustation, the concrete shell stands without disguise and may appear crude to the casual observer (FIG. 6-50). Indeed, neither camera nor drawing board can capture the spatial complexity of the design that reveals itself only to the visitor who actually walks through the rooms. Then the central, domed octagon is found to be defined not by walls, but by eight angled piers—the wide, square openings between them so large that the rooms beyond appear to be mere extensions of the central pavilion. The grouping of spatial units of different sizes and proportions under a variety of vaults constitutes a dynamic, three-dimensional composition that is at once complex and unified. It reveals Severus as an original and inventive architect, whose design is not only unique, but also progressive in its recognition of the malleable nature of concrete—a

material no longer bound by the rectilinear forms of traditional post-and-lintel construction.

In the following century, the Pantheon (FIGS. 6-51 and 6-52) one of the best preserved and most influential buildings in the history of architecture, revealed the full exploitation of concrete both as a building material and as a means for the shaping of architectural space. Here, the builder has created a single, unencumbered, interior space of overwhelming scale, a monumental space scarcely suggested by the exterior. It is a domed rotunda fronted with a rectangular portico. The original effect must have been different, for the building was only partly freestanding, its back and one of its sides hidden by older structures. Moreover, the portico was partly embraced by a no-longer-extant colonnaded court. Built during the rule of Hadrian (A.D. 117–138), it may have been conceived by that versatile emperor.

The Pantheon is of monumental simplicity and great scale. The circular interior is covered by a hemispheric dome 144 feet in diameter, the summit of the dome being the same distance from the floor. The design is thus based on the intersection of two circles (one horizontal, the other vertical), imaginable as sections of a globe of space inscribed within the building. The dome is a shell of concrete that gradually

6-51　The Pantheon, Rome, A.D. 118–125.

OCULUS (UNGLAZED)

4' 0" THICK

thickens toward the base to augment structural strength where it is most needed. The center of the dome is dramatically pierced by the *oculus*, a round opening 30 feet in diameter, which, left unglazed and open to the sky, is the only source of light for the interior. Supporting the dome are piers of immense thickness, formed by alternating rectangular and rounded niches, each covered by a vault that channels pressures exerted by the weight of the dome into solid masonry. The dome is *coffered* (furnished with decorative, sunken panels called "coffers") for the multiple purposes of making a handsome geometric foil of squares within the vast circle, reducing the weight and mass of the dome without weakening its structure, and symbolizing the starry heavens, each coffer having a gilded, bronze rosette at its center. The floor of the building is slightly convex, and drains are cut into the shallow depression in the center (directly under the oculus) to carry off any rain that falls through the opening far above.

Giovanni Pannini's painting of the interior of the Pantheon (FIG. 6-53) exhibits, better than any photograph, the unity and scale of the design, the simplicity of its relationships, and its breathtaking grandeur.

It almost records the experience one has on first entering this tremendous, shaped space—a feeling not of the weight of the enclosing masses, but of the palpable presence of space itself, for the architecture here displayed is first of all an *architecture of space*. In the architectures studied thus far, the form of the enclosed space is determined by the placement of the solids, which do not so much shape as interrupt the space. The solids are so prominent in Egyptian and Mesopotamian architecture that it is the solids we *see*; space is only "negative," simply *happening* between the solids. We think of this as an *architecture of mass*. Greek architecture, also primarily concerned with masses and their relationships and with the shaping of solid units, is designated as *skeletal* or *sculptural architecture*. It is the Roman architects who initially conceived architecture in terms of units of space that could be shaped by enclosures. The interior of the Pantheon, in keeping with this interest, is a single, unified, self-sufficient whole, uninterrupted by supporting solids; it is a whole that encloses visitors without imprisoning them—a small cosmos that opens through the oculus to the drifting clouds, the blue sky, the sun, universal nature, and the gods. To

6-53 GIOVANNI PANNINI, *Interior of the Pantheon, c.* 1740. National Gallery of Art, Washington, D.C. (Samuel H. Kress Collection).

escape from the noise and torrid heat of a Roman summer day into the sudden cool and calm immensity of the Pantheon is an experience almost impossible to describe and one that should be promised oneself. Above all, it is an *architectural* experience.

It should not be forgotten that Roman inventiveness in the construction of great interior spaces depended on engineering knowledge of the properties of solids and of the statics of inert masses. The *arch*, the *vault*, and the *dome* were structural units appropriated and developed by the Romans, with skill unsurpassed in the ancient world and not often since. Basically the problem as the Romans met it was this: how to enclose and roof over a vast space and how to give this space proper illumination while still keeping it open and free of the necessary roof supports. (Compare this approach with the approach embodied in the hypostyle halls of Egypt, shown in FIGS. 3-29 and 3-30.)

The simplest vault used by the Romans was the *barrel vault* or *tunnel* (FIG. 6-54c)—in essence, a deep arch that forms a half-cylindrical roof over an oblong space; the edges of the half-cylinder rest directly on the side walls, which must be either thick enough to support the weight or reinforced by *buttresses*. This

vault was made of concrete by the process of *centering*—using a temporary wooden form the size and shape of the finished vault to hold the fluid concrete until it hardened. The vaulting of the central hall (the "tepidarium") of the Baths *(thermae)* of Caracalla (FIG. 6-55), who ruled from A.D. 211–217, and of the Basilica of Constantine (FIGS. 6-85 and 6-86) was made by intersecting the main barrel vault at right angles with other barrel vaults at regular intervals, thus obtaining what is known as the *cross-barrel vault* (FIG. 6-54d). When the heights of the intersecting and main barrel vaults were the same, the result was a *groin* or *cross vault*, the line of intersection being called the *groin*. (Groin lines can be seen readily in FIG. 6-55). Besides being lighter in appearance than the barrel vault, the groin vault required less buttressing. In the barrel vault, the *thrust* (the downward and outward forces exerted by the vault, like those of the arch) was along the entire length of the wall, requiring a correspond-

6-54 Roman vaulting systems: (a) post-and-lintel construction; (b) round arch; (c) barrel vault; (d) cross-barrel or groin vault; (e) fenestrated sequence of groin vaults. (Arrows indicate direction of thrust.)

6-55 Central Hall ("tepidarium") of the Baths of Caracalla, Rome, c. A.D. 215. (Restoration drawing by G. ABEL BLONET.)

emperors hoped to keep an unruly and indigent populace preoccupied with pleasure, alone covered a large area (roughly 240 yards long and 120 yards wide); and the baths, which were the center of interest, as well as the architectural center of the design, had a capacity of 1,600 bathers. The functions of various parts of the complex are still matters of controversy. The design was symmetrical along a central axis occupied by pools filled with water of different temperatures: the *frigidarium,* the cold-water pool; the *tepidarium,* the central room containing smaller, warm-water pools; and the *calidarium,* a circular, hot-water pool in a domed rotunda. The central buildings also contained steam baths, dressing rooms, lounges, lecture halls, and *palestrae* (exercise rooms). This whole core complex was surrounded by landscaped gardens bordered by secondary buildings that housed shops, restaurants, libraries, gymnasiums, and (perhaps) a stadium. The long side of the entire complex measured almost one-quarter of a mile. Beneath it all was a subterranean world of corridors (some wide enough to accommodate vehicles), store-

ing buttressing; in the groin vault, the thrust was concentrated along the lines of intersection (the groins), and heavy buttressing was needed only at those points at which they met their vertical supports (the walls or piers). Thus, the interior could be kept free of load-carrying walls, and more light could be admitted through the use of clerestory windows located in the free space where buttressing was not needed (in effect, the ends of the cross vaults; FIG. 6-54e). Buttressing was provided by heavy walls perpendicular to the main wall and pierced by arches, forming side aisles to the main hall, and by short wall sections above the aisle roofs that channeled part of the vaults' thrust into the outside walls (FIG. 6-86).

All this was elementary to the builders of the gigantic Baths of Caracalla (FIGS. 6-55 and 6-56), dating from about A.D. 215. The enclosure of great spaces by vaulting was common practice at this time. Although nothing of the covering is left, the baths reveal traces of the vaults that sprang up from the thick walls to heights of up to 140 feet; under them, spread out in unending variety, were spaces designed for the intellectual as well as physical recreation of thousands of leisured Romans—all at the expense of the state. The central buildings of the huge complex, in which the

0 160 320 FEET

0 50 100 METERS

1. Central hall (tepidarium)
2. Calidarium
3. Natatio (frigidarium)
4. Palaestra
5. Lecture halls and libraries
6. Gardens
7. Shops
8. Stadium (?)
9. Aqueduct and reservoirs

6-56 Plan of the Baths of Caracalla, Rome. (After Sir Banister Fletcher.)

rooms, and heating chambers populated by slaves and stokers, for the halls and the water were heated by a system in which hot air was circulated through tubes and hollow bricks beneath the floors, in the walls, and sometimes in the vaults. The water was plentifully supplied by an individual aqueduct.

This enormous dedication of human ingenuity in the service of human ease! For a negligible admission fee, Romans could lounge for a whole day at the baths, in surroundings of the greatest magnificence. In fact, the baths were so lavish, ornate, and luxurious that moralists of the time complained of their wasteful ostentation. In his "Epistula Morales," the Roman philosopher–statesman Seneca, comparing his degenerate times with those of the heroic general Scipio, who bathed in austerely simple surroundings, complained:

> But who in these days could bear to bathe in such a fashion? We think ourselves poor and mean if our walls are not resplendent with large and costly mirrors; if our marbles from Alexandria are not set off by mosaics of Numidian stone, if their borders are not faced over on all sides with difficult patterns, arranged in many colours like paintings; if our vaulted ceilings are not buried in glass; if our swimming pools are not lined with Thasian marble, once a rare and wonderful sight in any temple. . . . What a vast number of statues, of columns that support nothing, but are built for decoration, merely in order to spend money! And what masses of water that fall crashing from level to level! We have become so luxurious that we will have nothing but precious stones to walk upon.

The baths were, of course, not merely as Seneca described them, but social centers in which the whole day could be spent "sweetly doing nothing." And the baths were cultural centers as well, with their libraries and their profusion of magnificent statues. A large number of Roman copies after Greek originals were found in public baths, a few of the most important in the Baths of Caracalla. To the Romans, baths of this type were a natural and indispensable part of "civilization."

SCULPTURE AND MONUMENTAL RELIEF
Sculpture in the Roman empire began under the influence of Augustan Rome's admiration of Hellenic culture and of the emperor's apparent determination to base a cultural renewal of Rome on it. That the Hellenized glorification of the empire was politically motivated is undoubtedly true; we have already seen how Roman architecture was molded to the end of manifesting the Imperial authority. But the Imperial motivation produced the esthetic consequence that work of the highest quality in all the arts bore the seal, as it were, of the Hellenic spirit. The *Augustus of Primaporta* (FIG. 6-57), about 20 B.C., no less than the

Aeneid of Vergil, is an example of the sedate, idealizing manner we have come to recognize as "Augustan." The statue, which once stood in front of the Imperial villa in Primaporta, about ten miles north of Rome, represents Augustus proclaiming a diplomatic victory to the people. The work is of the highest quality and is very likely by a Greek artist. At first glance, it might appear to be in the realistic mode of Republican statues; but on second glance, we find it strongly idealized, made according to Polykleitan proportions and even reminiscent of the *Doryphoros* (FIG. 5-61), especially in the walking pose. The reliefs on the emperor's breastplate are Roman in subject and refer to contemporaneous events—at least in the central theme: a Parthian returning a Roman standard to a Roman soldier. But these historical references are enframed by mythological and allegorical figures representing the sky god, the earth goddess, and the pacified provinces of Spain and Gaul. Together, the figures symbolize the blessings of the new Golden Age that were expected to come with the Augustan peace. They also place, side by side, the idealizing and realistic tendencies in Roman art that would alternate and intermingle throughout Imperial times.

The idealistic and realistic mingle, yet remain distinguishable, in the sculptured figures of the Ara

6-57   *Augustus of Primaporta, c.* 20 B.C. Marble, 6' 8" high. Vatican Museums, Rome.

Pacis Augustae, or Altar of the Augustan Peace (FIG. 6-58). Completed and dedicated in January, 9 B.C., to commemorate pacification of Spain and Gaul in 13 B.C., the altar can stand as a monument to the pacification of the whole Roman empire in the Augustan years following the establishment of the new government in 27 B.C., although presently there is disagreement regarding the meaning of its theme and figures. The actual altar is raised on an interior platform that is surrounded by a nearly square enclosure (35½ feet long and 39 feet wide). The exterior and interior surfaces of the enclosing walls are decorated with reliefs. On the interior walls are garlands suspended from bucrania. On the exterior walls, a lower zone displays a delicately carved, decorative, acanthus-leaf pattern,

arranged in spiral designs. An upper zone depicts a procession of men, women, and children and, on separate panels, allegorical subjects. The wall surfaces are framed by florid, Corinthian pilasters in a composition reminiscent of the second style of Pompeian wall painting.

The *"Tellus" Relief* panel from the Ara Pacis Augustae (FIG. 6-59) may represent the ancient Roman earth mother, Tellus, flanked by personifications of the elements, their draperies blowing about them, seated in a fertile landscape against clouds simulated in low relief. Although we have come to think of the interest in the illusion of landscape as Roman, the poses, style of the draperies, and lateral placement of the figures in a single plane here attest the

6-59 *"Tellus" Relief,* panel from the Ara Pacis Augustae.

6-60 *Procession,* portion of the frieze of the Ara Pacis Augustae. Marble, approx. 63" high.

Greek influence. The whole tableau celebrates the Augustan peace as the source of a new bounty of nature and the new richness and fertility of earth as the foundation of Roman wealth and power.

The *Procession* (FIG. 6-60) on the Ara Pacis Augustae, led by the emperor himself, almost certainly was intended to represent the actual solemnities when the altar was dedicated. The historical particularity of the frieze is characteristic of the Roman feeling for the factual, especially as we have seen it expressed in the portrait bust, in a pragmatic architecture, and, to a degree, in landscape painting. This contrasts with the Greek practice of disguising historical events in the mythological, as in the great frieze of Pergamon, (FIG. 5-79), on which a historical war between Greeks and Gauls becomes a struggle between gods and giants. In some respects, the Roman feeling for narrative bound to actual events resembles more the Assyrian than the Greek approach. Yet the style of the figures of the *Procession* is Hellenizing and may be directly inspired by the Panathenaic frieze of the Parthenon (FIG. 5-52). In the Ara Pacis Augustae, the *Procession* moves in several files. Differences in distance are signified by differences in degree of relief—the nearer the figure, the higher the relief. There is studied differentiation of individual persons; the heads are moderately idealized portraits, and there are "human interest" touches—for example, the clinging, restless children quieted by the adults. The overall demeanor is solemn, as would have befitted the occasion, and the impression is of a quiet concourse of participants behaving in a manner they believe to be appropriate to a quasireligious ceremony. The draperies, the quiet dignity, the ordered deployment within a shallow plane of space echo the older, Classical style, and the Ara Pacis Augustae, with its blend of the real and the ideal, signifies the Augustan style and the style of the empire in general.

The memorializing of actual events in monumental form finds striking expression in the Imperial *triumphal arch*, one of the most popular types of commemorative monument. Essentially, the triumphal arch is an ornamental version of a city gate, moved to the center of the city to permit the entry of triumphal processions into the forum. The Arch of Titus (FIG. 6-61), dated A.D. 81, is located at a point at which the Via Sacra enters the Roman Forum. As a building type, the triumphal arch exerted considerable influence on the architecture of the Renaissance. Closely related to the Colosseum-arch order, it consists of a single arch flanked by massive piers, to which the *Composite* order (a combination of Ionic and Corinthian) has been attached decoratively. Its typical superstructure, the *attic,* bears the commemorative inscription. Occasionally, the flanking piers are also pierced by arches, producing a triple arch like the

6-61   Arch of Titus, Rome, A.D. 81.

Arch of Constantine (FIG. 6-89). The walls of the passageway of the Arch of Titus are decorated with relief panels representing the triumphal return of Titus from the conquest of Jerusalem at the end of the Jewish Wars (A.D. 66–70). In later arches, the sculptural decor moved to the outside surfaces of the structure, as seen in the Arch of Constantine.

One of the archway reliefs shows soldiers of the Roman army carrying *Spoils from the Temple in Jerusalem,* including the seven-branched candelabrum from the Holy of Holies (FIG. 6-62). The panel is much damaged. Beam holes in the upper part date from the Middle Ages, when the family of the Frangipani converted the arch into a private fortress and built a second story into the vault—only one of many examples of later indifference to the esthetic and historic value discovered in recent times in the ruins of Rome. But enough of the relief remains to show that spatial effects aimed at in the Ara Pacis Augustae reach full development here. The illusion of movement is complete and convincing. The marching files press forward from the left background into the center foreground and disappear through the obliquely placed arch in the right background. The energy and swing

6-62   *Spoils from the Temple in Jerusalem,* relief from the Arch of Titus. Marble, approx. 7' 10" high.

of the column suggest a rapid marching cadence and the chant of triumph. The carving is extremely deep. The heads of the forward figures have been broken off, probably because they stood vulnerably free from the block, emphasizing their different placement in space from the heads in low relief, which are intact. The deep relief produces strong shadows and the light and shade quicken the movement and strikingly suggest the ''momentary flash of a passing parade.'' The work brings to mind the experiments with light and space in Imperial painting and architecture.

Across the archway is represented the *Triumph of Titus* (FIG. 6-63), which is more slowly paced, without the thrusting movement of the marching soldiers car-

rying the spoils from the temple and without the spatial experiments found there. The numerous layers of figures do create an illusion of depth, and a bold attempt at representing the overlapping horses turning into the way, drawing the chariot of Titus, persuades us that the sculptor's intentions are alike in both panels. The close correspondence between the event as shown in the panels and as described by Josephus (contemporaneous Jewish soldier, statesman, and historian) points up the Roman bent for the factual:

Most of the spoils that were carried were heaped up indiscriminately, but more prominent than all the rest were those captured in the Temple of Jerusalem—a golden table weighing several hundredweight, and a

6-63   *Triumph of Titus,* relief from the Arch of Titus. Marble, approx. 7' 10" high.

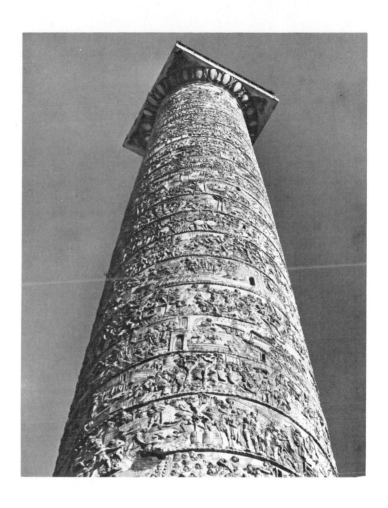

lampstand similarly made of gold. . . . The central shaft was fixed to a base, and from it extended slender branches placed like the prongs of a trident, and with the end of each one forged into a lamp: these numbered seven, signifying the honour paid to that number by the Jews. After these was carried the Jewish Law, the last of the spoils. Next came a large group carrying images of Victory, all fashioned of ivory and gold. Behind them drove Vespasian first with Titus behind him: Domitian rode alongside, magnificently adorned himself, and with his horse a splendid sight.

The Column of Trajan, another kind of commemorative monument, dating from A.D. 113, stood in his forum before the temple of the Trajanic deities (FIGS. 6-64 and 6-65). The column, perhaps the work of Trajan's favorite architect and military engineer, APOLLODORUS of Damascus, was often copied. As late as the nineteenth century, in commemoration of the victories of Napoleon, a column inspired by the Column of Trajan was erected in the Place Vendôme in Paris. The original column is 128 feet high. It was once crowned by a statue of Trajan, which was lost in the Middle Ages and replaced by a statue of St. Peter in the sixteenth century. The square base served as Trajan's mausoleum, and his ashes were deposited there in a golden urn in A.D. 117. The column records Trajan's two successful campaigns against the Dacians, which resulted in the extension of Roman dominion across the Danube into what is now Hungary and Rumania. Under Trajan, the limits of the Roman empire reached their greatest expansion. The marble reliefs, in a 625-foot band that winds the height of the column, represent a continuous record of the campaigns, told in 150 separate episodes with literally thousands of figures. The band increases in width as it moves toward the top of the column (from

6-65 Detail of the two lowest bands of the Column of Trajan. Marble, each band approx. 36" high.

approximately 36 inches to 50 inches) for better visibility from the ground. But recognition of the upper subjects must have been a problem, although the column originally stood in a small courtyard surrounded by two-story buildings, from the upper story or roofs of which the topmost reliefs may have been recognizable.

The carving is of relatively low relief to reduce shadows to a minimum, as they would have tended to impair the legibility of the work. This low relief constitutes a significant reduction in illusionistic depth. The sculptured narrative places much emphasis on military architecture, fortifications, bridges, and the like, to demonstrate Roman technical superiority over the barbarian foe. At the bottom of the column a pontoon bridge is built across the Danube, while the river-god looks on in amazement at the achievement; on the fourth circuit of the column, Trajan is shown speaking to his troops (FIG. 6-65). The emperor's figure is seen many times throughout the narrative, appearing as a kind of major motif. The story of the campaigns is told throughout with objectivity; the enemy is not belittled, and the Roman victories are hard won. But only about a quarter of the reliefs show battle scenes. Much of the balance represents what Rome thought to be her mission—bringing civilization to the benighted. Towns are built, crops harvested, rituals performed, and Imperial speeches given. In short, the reliefs of the column are not only an exaltation of Trajan, but a hymn to *romanitas*.

The Column of Trajan reliefs embody some features of great importance for the art of the Middle Ages. We have already indicated one of them—a *flattening of relief*—and the functional reason for it (better visibility). But the sacrifice of the strong illusionism of the Arch of Titus reliefs, even of the Ara Pacis Augustae reliefs, may have another reason: a desire for completeness of narrative description that required that a great number of actions be shown in a limited space. Thus, *narrative* fact, rather than *visual* fact, is required, and truth to appearance ("illusionism," "realism"), to a greater or lesser degree, can be sacrificed. A very singular and important sacrifice is made in the Column of Trajan compositions, and that is in the representation of space. In the Ara Pacis Augustae and the Arch of Titus, the figures are represented as standing and moving on the same groundline, at the eye level of a presumed observer who occupies an imagined place on the same line; thus, all the heads are approximately on the same level. But the figures of the Column of Trajan are superposed (placed in rows one above the other), a device altogether different from the approximate perspective of illusionism. From a perspective viewpoint, the figures and architecture are entirely haphazard in their arrangement; from a narrative viewpoint, they occur where the story demands. Often relative proportions are sacrificed: soldiers are represented as large as the walls they attack, or (although not visible in our illustrations here) cavalrymen are as large as, or larger than, their horses. We can say that conventions of Medieval art already appear in the sculptures of the Column of Trajan.

These features were not immediately adopted. They appear in the somewhat later Column of Marcus Aurelius, but in a relief of *Marcus Aurelius Sacrificing* (FIG. 6-66), one of three panels surviving from a triumphal arch dedicated to that emperor and carved about A.D. 180, the older illusionism persists, although not to the degree we find in the Arch of Titus. In this relief, the procession was cut up into panels (each a part of a larger whole to be imagined by the viewer), because the narrative requirements were not so demanding. There is much of Hellenic Classicism in the poses of the figures and in their draperies. (The drapery of the figure at the left echoes the Nike on the balustrade of the Temple of Athena Nike on the Acropolis, shown in FIG. 5-59.) Hadrian, Antoninus Pius, and Marcus Aurelius were all Hellenophiles,

6-66 *Marcus Aurelius Sacrificing*, panel from a triumphal arch dedicated to Marcus Aurelius, late second century A.D. Marble, approx. 10' 6" high. Palazzo dei Conservatori, Rome.

and it is in their reigns that perhaps the last powerful influence of Classical Greece was felt in Roman art. The figures in the relief are cut to ideal proportions, but a considerable Roman realism appears in the details and in such illusionistic devices as the perspective of the background architecture and the varying depth of relief to show distance. The bland composure of the faces of the Ara Pacis Augustae does not appear; the times have changed—the end of the Golden Age has come. A kind of brooding solemnity prevails as the grave philosopher–emperor (the sculptor gives us a portrait likeness) prepares the sacrifice that may produce omens of a troubled future for the empire.

PORTRAIT SCULPTURE

Two portrait busts from Republican times (FIGS. 6-14 and 6-15) have already shown us the Roman aptitude for and skill in this art—an expression of the now familiar Roman instinct for the factual. It is scarcely an accident that the historical reliefs just discussed contain portrait figures. Literally thousands of portrait busts have been found from the times of the republic and the empire, and the best are evidence of the important contribution of the Romans to portrait art. Two tendencies of style determine the production of portrait sculpture—the *verism* of the republic, and the Hellenizing *idealism* of the empire; in the later period, the tendencies alternate and sometimes converge. It is significant that members of the lower social classes generally are portrayed realistically in all periods, but that official portraits (of the ruling class, that is) tend to shift between realism and idealism, depending in part on the general style of the period, the preference of the sitters, or the artist's own interest in the psychological probing of personality.

A portrait of the emperor Augustus (FIG. 6-67), a detail of the Primaporta figure (FIG. 6-57), which can be profitably compared with earlier portraits from the republic (FIGS. 6-14 and 6-15), is very subtly idealized without any apparent loss of likeness. The hair, adhering closely to the skull, is reminiscent of the fifth-century B.C. Greek style and reflects Augustus' Classical taste prevailing over Hellenistic realism. We have met the Classicism of the Augustan Age in the Ara Pacis Augustae and have pointed out that Vergil's *Aeneid*, deliberately imitating Homer and commissioned by Augustus himself, reveals in its form the same Classical spirit. Livia, the second wife of Augustus and mother of the emperor Tiberius, is shown in a portrait bust as the shrewd and tough, yet tactful and elegant, woman she is believed to have been (FIG. 6-68). There is the same Augustan idealiza-

6-67 *Head of Augustus* (detail of FIG. 6-57).

tion and the same retention of the likeness. The life-like quality is enhanced by effective use of color, much of which is preserved in the hair, eyes, and lips.

The emperor Vespasian, successor to Nero, the last of the Julio–Claudian line, which began with Augustus, reigned from A.D. 69 to 79. His portrait bust (FIG.

6-68 *Livia* (second wife of Augustus), *c.* A.D. 20. Marble, head approx. 15″ high. Antiquario, Pompeii.

6-69 *Vespasian, c.* A.D. 75. Marble, life-size. Museo
Nazionale Romano, Rome.

6-70 *Portrait of a Lady, c.* A.D. 90. Marble, life-size.
Museo Capitolino, Rome.

6-69) forcefully reveals the veteran general who had
fought successfully in all parts of the empire. Vespasian was a man of simple origin and simple tastes,
who desired to return to Repulican simplicity after
Nero's extravagant misrule. He was a good administrator—honest, shrewd, and earthily humorous, all
of which qualities speak from his portrait. The artist
has attempted no flattery; quite possibly, Vespasian
himself discouraged him from idealizing overmuch,
for he preferred the blunt, rugged aspect of the soldier. From the portrait, we can understand the active
man whose care was restoration of the empire and
who is reported to have said on his deathbed: "An
emperor should die standing." The portrait, although
a little subtler in characterization, is almost Republican in its directness.

The *Portrait of a Lady* from the Flavian period (FIG.
6-70) embracing the reigns of Vespasian and his sons,
Titus and Domitian, is a departure from the usually
rather stern portraits of Roman women. It is a rare
masterpiece in its inimitable union of sensitive
beauty, noble elegance, and lucid intelligence. The
elaborate coiffure stands in striking textural contrast
to the delicate, softly modeled features, and the technique and effort to reproduce the luminosity and
glow of actual flesh recalls the art of Praxiteles. This
truly regal work, exemplar of Roman portrait art at its
height, can be instructively compared with the head
of *Queen Nefertiti* (FIG. 3-37), done in the subtle
Amarna style of Egypt.

Portraits of great persons who exhibit ambivalent
qualities, as of Pompey (FIG. 6-15), are perhaps more
interesting to us than portraits of persons of more

uniform character. This quality of ambivalence was
especially true of the emperor Hadrian (FIG. 6-71). We
approach his portrait informed by the account of his
personality given by an ancient biographer. Hadrian,
beyond all other Roman emperors a lover of Greek art
and culture and himself a skillful artist and architect,
poet, scholar, and writer, is thus described:

6-71 *Hadrian, c.* A.D. 120. Marble, approx. 16" high. Museo
Ostiense, Ostia.

He was grave and gay, affable and dignified, cruel and gentle, mean and generous, eager for fame yet not vain, impulsive and cautious, secretive and open. He hated eminent qualities in others, but gathered round him the most distinguished men of the state; at one time affectionate towards his friends, at another he mistrusted and put them to death. In fact he was only consistent in his inconsistency [*semper in omnibus varius*]. Although he endeavored to win the popular favor, he was more feared than loved. A man of unnatural passions and grossly superstitious, he was an ardent lover of nature. But, with all his faults, he devoted himself so indefatigably to the service of the state, that the period of his reign could be characterized as a "golden age."*

We might bring also to the contemplation of his portrait the poem, long famous, that Hadrian wrote at the end of his life:

> Charming, fleeting, little soul,
> My body's guest and comrade,
> Where now will you go
> Naked, pallid, unmoving
> Never again to play?

In this portrait (FIG. 6-71), *Hadrian* affects the Greek coiffure, in form much like the Early Classical ringlets of the *Apollo* from the Temple of Zeus at Olympia (FIG. 5-40). Perhaps inspired by portraits of Pericles, the artist has also adopted the Greek beard, abandoning the age-old tradition of the clean-shaven face. From this point on, most Roman emperors would be presented bearded. The head is idealized, but with restraint; the features are a little regularized and retouched, perhaps, but not so as to interfere with the likeness. A certain ambiguity and inscrutability shadows the face. But, when we know a little about Hadrian, we are prepared for this.

The last emperor of the great Imperial line that included Trajan and Hadrian was the Stoic Marcus Aurelius. We have touched on his philosophy in looking at the Faiyum portrait of a man from his time (FIG. 6-41)—a man whose serenely gentle and reflective face manifests the emperor's philosophy. A great equestrian, bronze, portrait statue of Marcus Aurelius (FIG. 6-72) has survived from the ancient world, unique in that it *did* survive, for there are no other examples of what must have been a statue type popular with the Roman emperors. (Medieval Christians probably melted the statues down for their bronze, because they were impious images from the pagan, demonic world of the Caesars. It is thought that the Christians mistook the statue of Marcus Aurelius for that of the first pro-Christian emperor, Constantine, and that that is why it escaped destruction.) The emperor, whom we have seen earlier in his role of head priest, *pontifex maximus*, with his toga drawn over his head (FIG. 6-66), is portrayed here exercising

his office as commander of the legions, perhaps passing before the people. His gesture here—magisterial, benignly authoritative, much like a later papal blessing—conveys at once the awesome and universal significance of the Roman *imperium*, the almost god-like presiding of the emperor over the whole world. Yet, at closer view, we see the same features as in the sacrifice panel—those of a man calmly aloof, meditative, a little resigned. The magnificent, high-stepping charger, the war horse mettlesome and impatient with the tameness of the parade, breathes hotly through dilated nostrils. This superb bronze was the inspiration, and sometimes the despair, of Renaissance sculptors. It stands today on the Capitoline Hill, the authentic, ancient centerpiece of Michelangelo's great architectural design (see Chapter 13), representing—as does no other single object—the lost authority of the Roman empire.

After the rule of Marcus Aurelius, the downward course of the empire became precipitous, although not at once; Septimius Severus held it level for a

6-72 Equestrian statue of Marcus Aurelius, Capitoline Hill, Rome, c. A.D. 165. Bronze, over life-size.

*Aelius Spartianus, in *Scriptores Historiae Augustae* (Harvard University Press, Loeb Classical Library, rev. 1985).

6-73 *Caracalla, c.* A.D. 215. Marble, life-size. Vatican Museums, Rome.

6-74 *Philip the Arab,* A.D. 244–249. Marble, life-size, Vatican Museums, Rome.

while. His son Caracalla (FIG. 6-73), under whom the great baths named after him progressed toward completion, was a brutal man, murderer of his own brother. He reigned briefly (A.D. 211–217), and his murder grieved no one. Edward Gibbon writes of him: "Caracalla was the common enemy of mankind." To render his violent traits, the sculptor had to return to realism. We find a burly, suspicious, almost snarling man, more a cut-throat than an emperor, a man who could scarcely be more the opposite of Marcus Aurelius. Significantly for what was to follow—the military anarchy of the third century, when the "barrack emperors" were set up (and pulled down) by the army—Caracalla pursued the tyrant's rule that if one has the loyalty of the army, one need not consider the people. His soldiers, however, were not wary enough to protect him from the dagger of an assassin, and his death was the model death of the tyrant, in form repeated again and again throughout the terrible third century. "Such," writes Gibbon, "was the end of a monster who disgraced human nature." Yet Michelangelo was later to base his noble bust of Brutus on this bust of Caracalla.

Internal unrest combined with attacks on frontiers by the new Sassanian line of Persian kings in the east and German tribes in the north brought the empire to the verge of collapse. In the space of 50 years, some 20 of the barrack emperors were exalted and then assassinated by factions of the army. This created anguish and foreboding throughout the empire, curiously reflected in numerous portraits, including that of a barrack emperor himself, *Philip the Arab* (FIG. 6-74). Philip became emperor after having his predecessor, Gordianus, executed. In considering his por-

trait, it will be useful to know something about the close of his career. An adventurer himself, he knew that he was surrounded by adventurers (especially in the army) who were ready to follow his example. Faced with a revolt, Philip appointed a brave and intelligent aristocrat, Decius, to put it down and to calm the army. The army accepted Decius as its leader on condition that he agree to depose Philip or be put to death himself. Decius then led the best of the army against Philip, who was slain, and became emperor. The portrait of Philip shows the face of a man who knows he is utterly without security. Fear, distrust, and suspicion work the face into a mask of guilt and anxiety. The brow is furrowed; the deep-set eyes shift sideways. The eye pupils are carved, an innovation that focuses on the psychic state. The hair is cropped short; the beard, stubbly. The short, nervous chisel strokes adapt to the nervous mood. (In the works of later sculptors, these strokes would become increasingly abrupt and schematic, leading to the geometric patterning of the fourth century.) But it is the face, with its terrible tensions, that rarely had been seen before in the history of art. From the Archaic masks, we come at last, in the third century A.D., to a face so "modern" in what it reflects of trouble that we experience a shock of recognition. Both the ideal and the real in Roman sculpture have been replaced with something new, *expression,* wherein the artist is concerned first of all with expressing an emotional state—either his subject's or his own, or perhaps both.

The Late Empire

The anarchy of the third century A.D.—when, at one time, as many as 18 claimants struggled for the throne and it seemed as if the empire would be divided into a number of small, weak states—was brought to an end by a vigorous leader, Diocletian, in A.D. 285. Diocletian (A.D. 284–305) saw the impossibility of ruling the vast empire alone, given the continual German and Persian attacks in the north and east and countless revolts in the provinces. He restored political order by dividing authority among four persons, the *tetrarchs*, including himself as prime mover. Diocletian appointed a co-ruler called, like himself, "augustus," and each of the two "augusti" then adopted an assistant of slightly lower rank, the "caesar." One augustus and one caesar ruled in the east; the other pair, in the west. Although political control was restored, a fatal precedent was set: the division of authority within the Roman empire.

Under Constantine (A.D. 324–337), who did away with Diocletian's system and ruled alone, the practice was begun of dividing the empire, like personal property, among the emperor's sons—a crippling, divisive custom that was to last into the Middle Ages. Even more divisive was Constantine's founding of a city named after him (Constantinople, now Istanbul, on the site of the ancient Greek city of Byzantium), which led inevitably to the decline of the city of Rome and the shift of Imperial emphasis to the east. Byzantium gives its name to the later civilization of the eastern Roman empire.

After the reign of Theodosius, at the end of the fourth century, the empire was irreparably divided, although the emperors of the east, at Constantinople, continued for centuries to claim the west. These claims were made in vain; in the fifth century, the barbarians took power in the west—the Ostrogoths in Italy, the Vandals in Africa, the Visigoths in Spain, the Franks and Burgundians in Gaul, the Angles and Saxons in Britain. These Romano–Germanic petty kingdoms succeeded to the once centralized and almost universal power of Rome and became the predecessors of the nations of modern Europe. The eastern half of the empire lived on as the Byzantine

empire for a thousand years, until the conquest of Constantinople by the Turks in 1453.

ARCHITECTURE

Developments in architecture powerfully express the ebbing authority of the Roman empire. In the days of Augustus and Trajan, the "walls" of the empire had been the might of the legions on its remotest borders; behind the bulwark of the legions, a great empire could rest secure. But late in the third century, the emperor Aurelian was forced to girdle the city of Rome itself with walls, turning it into a fortress; Rome became what it had been at the start, a walled city, now dwindling into the ghost of an empire. Aurelian's insecurity was shared by Diocletian, who, unlike Tiberius in the first century A.D., could not afford to retire to the undefended paradise of Capraea (modern Capri) and instead built, for his retirement, a well-fortified palace on the Dalmatian coast at Spalatum (modern Split, in Yugoslavia), about A.D. 300 (FIGS. 6-75 and 6-76). The complex, covering about ten acres, is laid out like a Roman colonial city. The plan is almost identical with the plan of Thamugadis (FIG. 6-44), although its military aspects, such as the fortified walls and tower-flanked gates, are even more dominant on the relatively small scale of a palace. Such a fusion of military and Imperial palace architecture strikingly reflects the changed life style of the Late Imperial period, when increased centralization and standardization infused all levels of Roman society, private and official alike, with mili-

6-76 Plan of the palace of Diocletian, Spalatum (Split). Original Roman masonry is shown in solid black.

6-75 Palace of Diocletian, Spalatum (Split), A.D. 300–305. (Reconstruction by E. HÉBRARD.)

taristic thinking. In architecture, such standards of military behavior as obedience and subordination are reflected in symmetry, axiality, and unity of direction, all apparent in the plan of the Spalatum palace.

The broad, columned street leading toward the palace constitutes a ceremonial axis that dominates the architectural layout. All other architectural features are symmetrically arranged around this avenue, which leads into a large columned (peristyle) court fronting the entrance of the palace proper (FIG. 6-77). Designed as a three-bay Classical portico, the façade is marked by an unusual and quite un-Classical feature: over the central bay, the entablature arches upward into the triangular face of the pediment. Formally, the purpose of this "broken pediment" undoubtedly was to stress the central axis of the design. Symbolically, it became the "gable of glorification," under which the emperor appeared before those who gathered in the peristyle court.

The feature of the broken pediment had appeared earlier, mostly in the eastern provinces of the Roman empire—for example, in the façade of the great temples at Heliopolis (modern Baalbek, Syria). It is, to repeat, an un-Classical device—hardly imaginable in a building like the Parthenon—that represents a tran-sitional stage between the Classical, column-supported, horizontal entablature and the springing of arches directly from column capitals, as is the case in the flanking colonnades of this same peristyle. (There are examples of this direct springing of the arch in Pompeian painting of the first century B.C., as well as in the architecture of Hadrian's villa at Tibur (modern Tivoli). The process of change from the *trabeated* (post-and-lintel) architecture of Greco–Roman antiquity (and earlier) to the *arcuated* (arch-column) architecture of the Middle Ages began in the first century A.D., and we see it here, in the arcade of the Spalatum palace, in its perfected form and on a grand scale. It is interesting to observe the gradual emergence of arcuated architecture from the Roman arch order (FIG. 6-78) and the Roman architect's reluctance to give up the conventional three-part division of the entablature, even once it had become only a block-like fragment, as in the capital from the Baths of Caracalla (FIG. 6-55). Later, Byzantine architects would retain the entablature block but rid it of the old Classical features, geometrizing it into a flat-sided, trapezoidal, "impost" block (FIG. 7-35).

From early in Imperial times, structural changes in Roman architecture continued to be based on Helle-

6-77 Peristyle court, palace of Diocletian.

1	2	3	4	5	6
COLOSSEUM Roman architectural order (c. A.D. 70)	PANTHEON Central niche (c. A.D. 125)	BATHS OF CARACALLA (c. A.D. 215)	SPALATUM Central arch (c. A.D. 300)	SPALATUM Porta Aurea	SPALATUM Street arcade

nistic developments but were accompanied by experiments in nonstructural design. Throughout the empire, purely ornamental combinations of the elements of Classical architecture—often so dramatically elaborate that they have been called "baroque" (see Chapter 19)—could be found. A striking example is Al-Khazneh, the so-called "Treasury," at Petra (FIG. 6-79), in modern Jordan. This rock-cut structure of imposing scale (over 130 feet in height) has a decorative façade in two stories. The lower story contains a six-columned portico, the columns irregularly spaced, with niches for statuary between the outer pairs. The upper level splits the façade and the pediment to make way for a cylindrically shaped, tholos-like element, which stands in sharp contrast to the rectangles and triangles of the design. (Exactly this same feature appeared on a painted wall of the second style in the Room of the Labyrinth at Pompeii as early as 50 B.C.). The rhythmic alternation of deep projection and indentation creates dynamic patterns of light and shade—an effect of restless oppositions of form. The façade of the "Treasury" deliberately seems to contradict the ordered regularity we expect of Classical architecture. Its theatricality reflects, and perhaps was derived from, the scene buildings that backed the stages of Greek and Roman theaters, providing a richly elaborate architectural backdrop for action and spectacle.

Symptomatic of the decline of Rome's central power and authority, major building efforts began to shift toward the provinces. After the division of the Roman empire under Diocletian, who realized that the far-flung empire could no longer be ruled effectively from Rome, Constantius Chlorus, father of Constantine the Great, became caesar of the western empire and established his residence at Augusta Trevirorum (modern Trier, West Germany) on the Moselle river. Augusta Trevirorum became the largest city of the northwestern sector of the empire.

After being sacked by the Franks and Alemanni in

A.D. 275–276, Augusta Trevirorum was largely rebuilt and ringed with defensive walls. The Porta Nigra, or "Black Gate" (FIG. 6-80), which probably dates between this period and about A.D. 310, was never quite completed. Large enough to be converted into a Christian church later on, it is an outstanding example of a Roman city gate, built not only for defensive purposes, but also for the impression it would make

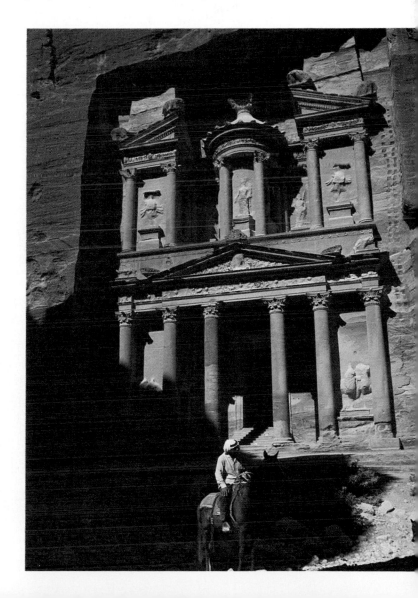

6-79 Al-Khazneh (the "Treasury"), rock-cut mausoleum, Petra, Jordan, second century A.D.

6-80 The Porta Nigra ("Black Gate"), Augusta Trevirorum (Trier, West Germany), c. A.D. 280–310.

on a visitor, manifesting the might of Imperial Rome. The rough, blunt exterior gives it an unintended effect of rustication, partly due to the incompletion of the building. Its defensive function, moreover, scarcely would have permitted refined details, and we find the structure expressing Roman features like the Colosseum arch order with a heavy, provincial accent.

The vast palace complex (some 700 acres), of which the Porta Nigra is the north gate, had, at its center, the audience hall of the palace proper (FIG. 6-81), which dates from about A.D. 310. Its basic design is quite simple: a rectangular hall measuring about 190 feet long and 95 feet wide, covered by a flat, wooden, coffered ceiling some 95 feet above the floor. Added to the short, north side is a semicircular apse, also with a flat ceiling, separated from the main hall by a "triumphal arch." Arch and apse originally were decorated with marble incrustation and mosaics to provide a magnificent environment for, and to set off with proper majesty, the enthroned caesar. The interior was brightly lighted through double rows of large, arched windows.

Significant, and characteristic of much late Roman architecture, is the articulation of the building's exterior with boldly projecting vertical buttresses to create

6-81 The Aula Palatina ("audience hall of the palace"), Augusta Trevirorum (Trier, West Germany), c. A.D. 310.

a pattern of alternating voids and solids; the verticality of the building was originally lessened by horizontal timber galleries, which permitted the servicing of the windows. The exterior was stuccoed in gray–white, with windows framed in color. The interior could be heated through a *hypocaust* system (hot air circulating through tubes built into the walls to a height of 24 feet). The growing taste for large windows was due to the development and increasing use of lead-framed panes of window glass, which offered late Roman builders the possibility of giving life and movement to blank exterior surfaces.

A fascinating monument of the late Roman empire, the villa at Piazza Armerina in Sicily (FIG. 6-82), recalls, on a much smaller scale, the intricate planning of Nero's villa–palace, the Domus Aurea, and shows that patrons of great wealth could still live the opulent life of the caesars of the Golden Age. Excavated and studied in very recent times, the villa is still the subject of scholarly debate regarding its date of construction and its ownership; we may be allowed to place it in time between A.D. 310 and A.D. 350, and to leave to further study whether its owner was Maxentius, the defeated rival of Constantine, or a multi-millionaire with sufficient resources to live in Imperial style. The rambling plan (FIG. 6-82) displays almost every spatial arrangement and building type in the Roman architectural repertory—porticoes, peristyles, tri-lobed and poly-lobed halls, thermae, a basilica, aqueducts—arranged along a variety of axes. There is a contrapuntal play of square, round, and elliptical spaces, yet the effect is quite casual. Many of the elements constitutive of the ecclesiastical architecture of early Christianity are present here in this pagan villa of the late Roman empire.

Perhaps the most exciting feature of the villa is its 7,000 square feet of floor mosaic. Possibly the work of craftsmen from North Africa, the mosaics provide a

6-82 Plan of the Roman villa at Piazza Armerina, Sicily, *c.* A.D. 310–350.

1. Entrance
2. Atrium
3. Imperial shrine
4. Peristyle court
5. Audience hall
6. Living quarters
7. Room with "Bikini" mosaic (FIG. 6-84)
8. Oval court and triconch hall
9. Thermae
10. Aqueducts

N

0   20   50   100 FEET

0   10   20   30 METERS

6-83 *Allegory of Africa*, from the
Roman villa at Piazza Armerina,
early fourth century A.D. Mosaic.

compendium of late Roman themes: the hunt, the
games, wild and domestic animals, river and forest
life, genre scenes, scenes from mythology, allegorical
subjects, and the like. A seated female figure, an *Allegory of Africa* (FIG. 6-83), holds a horn of plenty as she
embraces a sacred tree. She is flanked by animals
symbolic of the tropical orient—an elephant, a tiger,
and the mythical phoenix. A frieze shows briefly at-
tired young women (FIG. 6-84), often referred to as

the "bikini girls," performing vigorous exercise and
displaying trophies. The style of the Piazza Armerina
mosaics is not distinguished; it represents a kind of
commonplace vernacular familiar throughout the
empire. But these mosaics do present an encyclopedia of pagan images drawn from real life or imagination, many of which will survive, in some transformed state, through the Christian period.

Although Constantine moved the center of the

6-84 *Young Women Exercising*, from the Roman villa at Piazza Armerina, early fourth century A.D. Mosaic.

Roman empire to his new city on the site of ancient Byzantium, he completed some important building projects prior to leaving Rome. One of these was the vast basilica begun between A.D. 306 and A.D. 310 by Maxentius, rival of Constantine, and finished by Constantine after A.D. 313 (FIGS. 6-85 and 6-86). All that remains of the building are three barrel-vaulted bays of the north aisle, with brick-faced concrete walls 20 feet thick supporting the coffered vaults. The interior, like that of the Baths of Caracalla (FIG. 6-55), was richly marbled and stuccoed. The ruins, most impressive by virtue of their size and mass, represent only a small part of the original structure, which measured 300 feet long and 215 feet wide and had a groin-vaulted central nave 114 feet high. The reconstruction (FIG. 6-86) shows groin vaults (over the central nave) that permitted lighting of the interior through the ends of the cross vaults, which were left open in a manner similar to clerestory construction. Buttresses reinforced the vault (where the groins join vertical supports) and channeled part of the pressures exerted by the weight of the vault across the aisles and into the outside walls. Remains of the springing of the central vault and of the buttresses can be seen in FIG. 6-85. This late, great building of the ancient world is a monument to the ingenuity of the Roman architects. Exemplar of an architecture of space, it is designed on a grand, Imperial scale—spacious, fully illuminated, uninterrupted by rows of vertical supports, and constructed of a highly malleable, versatile, fireproof material. In this, the Basilica of Constantine fulfills the requirements of architecture in periods of high civilization; not until Hagia Sophia would they be so artfully represented again.

6-86 Reconstruction of the Basilica of Constantine, Rome.

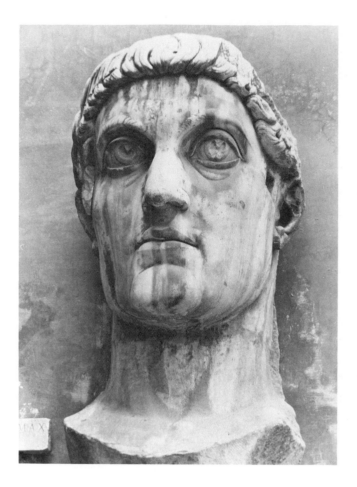

6-87 *Constantine the Great, c.* A.D. 330. Marble, approx. 8' 6" high. Palazzo dei Conservatori, Rome.

although they still turn slightly to the side and upward in the Constantine head, as in certain third-century portraits like that of *Philip the Arab* (FIG. 6-74). Those unchanging qualities of the permanent form—seen in Egypt and Mesopotamia, particularly in the representation of kings—once more make their appearance. The personality of the emperor is lost in the immense image of eternal authority. It is his authority, not his personality or his psychic state, that the sculptor exhibits. The colossal size, the Archaic rigidities, the eyes directed at no thing or person of this world—all combine to produce the formula of overwhelming power appropriate to the exalted position of Constantine as absolute despot, which, by the early fourth century, he had certainly become. It is not surprising that the first of the Christian emperors—in authority, the European equivalent of a Ramses II—should be embodied in colossal form like the giant statues of the Egyptian king at Luxor and (formerly) Abu Simbel (FIG. 3-24).

SCULPTURE AND MONUMENTAL RELIEF

The western apse of the Basilica of Constantine contained a colossal statue of the emperor, a seated figure some 30 feet high, the head of which has been preserved (FIG. 6-87). The figure was composed of a brick core, a wooden torso covered with bronze, and head and limbs of marble. The head alone is 8½ feet high and weighs over eight tons. The characteristics of the earlier busts we have described, in which the real and the ideal alternate or blend, here are no longer dominant. Rather, we note the onset of traits familiar in the earlier, Archaic period: simplification of detail, with a regularizing and a flattening of the features that make the face a rigid mask, uncompromisingly frontal in aspect.* The eyes become enormously large in proportion to the rest of the features,

*The living emperor himself, on formal occasions may have approximated a statue in appearance. H. P. L'Orange quotes the ancient writer Ammianus Marcellinus describing Constantius II, a successor to Constantine, on his entry into Rome: "He looked so stiffly ahead as if he had an iron band around his neck and he turned his face neither to the right nor the left, he was not as a living person, but as an image." L'Orange adds: "This hieratic emperor style, which as divine majesty (*divina maiestas*) in the same way leaves its mark upon palace, image and living reality, can furthermore be traced through Byzantium all the way down to the Holy Russian Empire." *Art Forms and Civic Life in the Late Roman Empire* (Princeton: Princeton University Press, 1965), pp. 124–125.

6-88 *The Tetrarchs, c.* A.D. 305. Porphyry, approx. 51" high. Piazza San Marco, Venice.

6-89　Arch of Constantine, Rome, A.D. 312–315.

The profound changes in style that occurred at an accelerated pace in the fourth century, introducing the epoch of Medieval art, can be seen in the group called *The Tetrarchs*, dating from about A.D. 305 (FIG. 6-88). Although it is an earlier work than the portrait of Constantine, it is a much stronger reflection of the trend toward Archaism. Carved from porphyry (purple marble) in one of the eastern provinces (perhaps Egypt), the group represents the four co-rulers of the empire: Diocletian and Maximian (the augusti) and Galerius and Constantius Chlorus (the caesars). They embrace each other to symbolize their hoped-for, but unrealized, serenity and concord. They seem, even as they embrace, to be huddled in fear and foreboding, facing some impending disaster, in an expression of the already noted prevalent anxiety of the age. Classical features have disappeared; the figures are ill-proportioned, with large heads on squat bodies, giving them a gnome-like appearance. The drapery is schematic; the bodies, shapeless. Here, some 700 years of Greek and Roman idealism and naturalism terminate. No portrait likenesses are attempted; the mask-like faces are the same face in quadruplicate. Individuality and personality already belong to the past.

The waning creative power and technical skill of Rome in the west can be seen in the Arch of Constan-tine (A.D. 312–315) in the city of Rome (FIG. 6-89). It is the last great triumphal arch preserved in the declining city. Dedicated to Constantine by a figurehead Senate, it commemorates the ruler's victory over his rival Maxentius—a victory that made Constantine the Great absolute monarch of the Roman empire. But the occasion failed to stimulate the imagination of his builders. The design of the arch is copied from the Arch of Septimius Severus, of the early third century, and most of its decorative sculpture is taken from the monuments of rulers like Trajan, Hadrian, and Marcus Aurelius.

Beneath two Hadrianic medallions are reliefs belonging to Constantine's own period (FIGS. 6-90 and 6-91), which give us an opportunity to estimate the degree of change from the style of the Early Imperial age to a new style that it is not inappropriate to call Medieval. Constantine, surrounded by his entourage, stands at the center of a rostrum, addressing the people. His central position corresponds here to the frontality of his colossal statue and expresses a new, rigid formality of composition that would increasingly come to depend on the fixed positions of figures instead of on the representation of action. The figures are non-Classical in their lack of proportionality; in this respect, they are like *The Tetrarchs*. Moreover,

6-90　Reliefs from the Arch of Constantine: medallions, A.D. 117–138; frieze, early fourth century A.D. Marble, frieze approx. 40″ high.

6-91　Detail of the frieze shown in FIG. 6-90.

they do not move according to any principle of Classical–naturalistic movement, but rather with the mechanical and repeated stances and gestures of puppets. The relief is flattened back into the block; the forms are no longer fully modeled, and the details are incised. The lines of figures are superposed (a device used in the Column of Trajan, shown in FIG. 6-65); the spatial arrangement is, as noted, not casual, but a careful, head-counting lineup. The gestures are few and, like the uniform heads, reproduced again and again. Here is not so much a historical narrative of action as the labeling of an event frozen into a tableau, so that the ordered groups can quickly be read and labeled as "crowd," "emperor," "servants of the emperor." The artist wished to include all the essential participants without the ambiguity that can accompany the description of particulars. These have been reduced to an absolute minimum and replaced with formal placement and repetition of attitude and gesture.

We began the story of Roman art with two sculptured portraits that define, in different ways, the Roman bent for realism. We can end that story with two portraits stamped on Roman coins (FIG. 6-92)—portraits of emperors whose reigns are separated by two centuries: Hadrian (A.D. 117–138), and the emperor Maximin Daia (A.D. 308–314), tetrarch of the east, in the tetrarchy with Constantine, Licinius, and Galerius at the time of the first Edict of Toleration of the Christians. We have described the portrait and character of Hadrian and, in this bronze medallion, we have a sensitive, classicizing, naturalistic report of the great emperor's features. This Classical naturalism contrasts markedly with the almost startling abstraction of the features portrayed on the gold coin of Maximin Daia, which convey, through both sharp and blunt simplifications of form, the awesome strength of Late Imperial authority. Two centuries have transformed the image of the emperor as a particular man into an image of the emperor as the mask of power. Individual traits are suppressed in the force of the idea and the idea of force. The idea—not the thing—would henceforth dominate in art.

The archaizing of Greek and Roman figurative art in the Constantinian reliefs, *The Tetrarchs*, and the coin portrait of Maximin Daia reflects a transformation in the way the peoples of the late Roman world interpreted the structure of appearance. Underlying this change in interpretation is a mighty spiritual change: the assimilation of Christianity into Greco–Roman civilization—a phenomenon so far-reaching in its influence as to separate the psychologies of two millennia, that of Greece–Rome and that of Medieval Christianity.

6-92   *Left:* medallion of Hadrian (second century A.D.). Bronze, 1.6" in diameter. *Right:* gold coin with portrait of Maximin Daia (A.D. 308–314). Gold, 0.8" in diameter. Both Museo Nazionale, Rome.

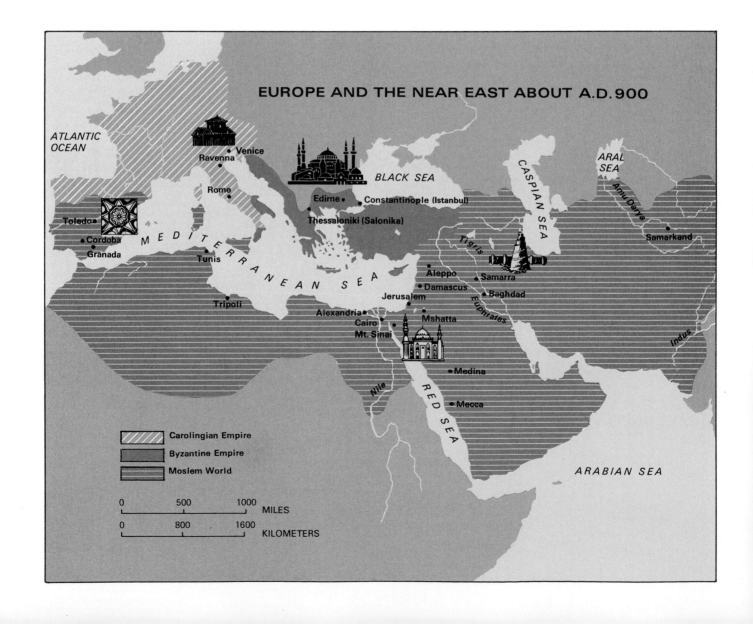

7

EUROPE AND THE NEAR EAST ABOUT A.D.900

ATLANTIC
OCEAN

Ravenna • Venice

Rome

Toledo

• Cordoba
Granada

MEDITERRANEAN SEA

Tunis

Tripoli

BLACK SEA

Edirne • Constantinople (Istanbul)
Thessaloniki (Salonika)

CASPIAN SEA

ARAL
SEA

Amu Darya

Samarkand

Tigris

Aleppo
• Samarra
• Damascus
Baghdad
Euphrates

Indus

Alexandria
Cairo • Mshatta
Mt. Sinai

Jerusalem

Nile

RED SEA

• Medina

• Mecca

ARABIAN SEA

Carolingian Empire
Byzantine Empire
Moslem World

0   500   1000
                              MILES
0   800   1600
                              KILOMETERS

EARLY CHRISTIAN, BYZANTINE, AND ISLAMIC ART

A.D. 100

200

PERIOD OF PERSECUTION

325 Constantine recognizes Christianity

PERIOD OF RECOGNITION

400

Division of Roman empire;
beginning of Byzantine Era 395

Mausoleum of
Galla Placidia

Sant' Apollinare
in Classe, detail
c.526

Theodoric
at Ravenna 493–526

539 Investment
of Ravenna

c.565

Honorius at
Ravenna 402–423

Galla Placidia
at Ravenna 425–450

Fall of Rome to
Visigoths under
Alaric 410

Fall of Ravenna to
Odoacer;
end of western
Roman empire 476

JUSTINIAN
(FIRST FLOWERING)

600

Justinian mosaic
detail, San Vitale

Hagia Sophia

726

ICONOCLASTIC CONTROVERSY

TERRITORIAL LOSSES

c. 800

732
Battle of
Poitiers

711
Conquest
of Spain

Paris
Psalter

637
Conquest of
Jerusalem

622
Moslem era
begins

Great Mosque,
Samarra

MOSLEM ERA

SECOND FLOWERING

Mosque,
Cordoba

843

c. 900

Vladimir
Madonna

1000

Mausoleum of
Sultan Hasan

Crusaders
capture of
Constantinople 1261

St. Mark's
begun
1063

Church of the
Katholikon
c. 1020

1390

1297

THIRD
FLOWERING

D E C L I N E

1453
Ottoman conquest
of Constantinople

The Harrowing
of Hell

Baghdad
captured by
Mongols 1258

c. 1100

Abelard
(1079–1142)

1031
End of Caliphate
of Cordoba

CHRISTIANITY, like many Eastern cults, was a peculiarly persuasive religion of salvation. Its immense success in making converts among the teeming populations of the great Imperial cities brought it to the attention of the Roman authorities. Because Christians refused to acknowledge the state religion, which was the cult of the emperor, and because they refused to participate in its rather perfunctory rites, they were regarded as politically subversive and were bitterly persecuted. Tacitus, reflecting the attitudes of his time, regarded the Christians as believers in a degenerate doctrine and practitioners of obscene and perverse rites that, he felt, were typical of Eastern cults; he refers to the Christians as "a class hated for its abominations." Pliny the Younger, reporting to the emperor Trajan on his investigation of Christian beliefs, writes that he has found only a "depraved and extravagant superstition," although Christian ritual was innocent enough.

The pagan Romans believed in many gods; the Christians, in one. To the educated pagan, the Christian doctrines—the incarnation of a god in the body of a man, and the salvation or redemption of all mankind through the death and resurrection of the god–man Christ—must have seemed absurd to the point of insanity. The Christians exulted in this imputation of absurdity to their faith: *Credo quia absurdum* ("I believe *because* it is absurd") became their slogan. Pagan and Christian had opposed orientations: the pagan, to this world; the Christian, to the next. The religion of the empire, *Romanitas,* based its ritual and practice on imperial dominion; but Christ declared "My kingdom is not of this world . . . ." (John 18:36).

The differences between pagan and Christian were profound, as were the differences between the Judaic world and the Christian church. Further differences would divide the cultures of the Greek-speaking eastern Mediterranean and the Latin-speaking west. These divisions would cut several ways, and deeply. The fundamental opposition between the Eastern and Western spirit proclaimed in Zechariah, "when I have raised up thy sons, O Zion, against thy sons, O Greece . . ." (9:13), rings angrily once again in the words of the early Christian Tertullian: *Quid Athenae Hierosolymis!* ("What is there in common between Athens and Jerusalem? what between the Academy [of Plato] and the Church?"). Although the unmitigated hostility of Tertullian was by no means shared by all Christians, an antagonism between the ancient Semitic east and the Hellenic world that had, for a while, conquered it was inevitable and could not be suppressed.

Greek naturalism and rationalism had become integral to the western Roman world; yet, at the same time, they had been changed through contact with the old civilizations of the Middle East. Although the *mystery cults*—with their suspiciously secret rites, their savior gods, their redemptive messages and occult sciences, their solar and fertility myths—drew heavily on Egypt, Babylon, Persia, and even India, they also borrowed a good deal of the intellectual apparatus of Hellenic philosophy, mysticizing it and making of it a kind of magical formula and a *gnosis*—the privileged knowledge of only an initiated few.

Christianity, based as it was on Jewish teaching and tradition, differed radically from many of the crude cults with which Romans, like Tacitus, confused it. But Christianity also joined with those cults in the long, vast, historical reaction against the Hellenized west—both its world view and that material manifestation of it, the increasingly oppressive Roman empire. To Christians, the empire, with its exactions, cruelties, materialism, wars, and false gods, became *regnum Caesaris, regnum Diaboli* ("the kingdom of Caesar, the kingdom of the Devil"). But the empire would be inherited by the Christians in 325,* when Constantine recognized Christianity; by the end of the century Theodosius, his successor, had made it the official religion of the state.

In the eighteenth century, Edward Gibbon, in his monumental history, *The Decline and Fall of the Roman Empire,* accused Christianity of being the principal cause of that (in his time) calamity. We do not now believe that Christianity had that effect, but, as early as the fifth century, Augustine wrote his *City of God* to defend the Church against the pagan accusation that the sack of the city of Rome (in 410 by the Goths) was a punishment sent by the ancient gods because the city had become Christian. The disintegration of the Roman empire, beginning with its nominal separation into the western and eastern empires toward the end of the third century, was a phenomenon of considerable complexity that cannot be laid at the door of the Christians—or entirely at the door of the "barbarians," those Celtic, Germanic, Slavic, and other peoples who had been pressing slowly into the Mediterranean world for thousands of years. (We have met their predecessors in the great migrations that disturbed Egypt, Mesopotamia, Asia Minor, Crete, and Greece.)

At any rate, from the end of the third century, there was a slow, sometimes hardly perceptible, takeover—not of the unified empire, but of its already fragmented remains. The spiritual and ideological conquest made by the Christians in the politically consequential form of mass conversion paralleled the gradual infiltration and settlement by the "barbari-

*The epoch time designation A.D. will be dropped from now on.

ans," who, for that matter, had long been present in the administrative and military structure as well as in recognized possession of Imperial territories. The subsequent actions of these "barbarians," who were Christianized and in control of the western empire by the end of the fifth century, make up the history of the Middle Ages in the west. The eastern empire, which was actually but not officially severed from the western empire by the beginning of the fifth century, was to go its own continuous way as the Byzantine empire, reverting to its Greek language and traditions, which, to be sure, had become much "Orientalized." The Byzantine world was a kind of protraction of the life of the late Roman empire and the Early Christian culture that filled it. With a quite Oriental conservatism, which reminds us somewhat of the Ancient Near Eastern civilizations, the Byzantine empire remained Greek, orthodox, unchanging for a thousand years, preserving the forms of its origin, oblivious to and isolated from the new.

In the seventh century, Islam, a new spiritual force, erupted from Arabia and swept across the Near East and the southern Mediterranean world with amazing speed. Islam created a new civilization that rivaled Christianity and would have far-ranging influence in Medieval Europe: Arabic translations of Aristotle and other Greek writers of antiquity were eagerly studied by Christian scholars of the twelfth and thirteenth centuries; Arabic love lyrics and poetic descriptions of nature inspired the early French troubadours; Arab scholars laid the foundations of arithmetic and algebra, as they are still taught in our schools, and their contributions to astronomy, medicine, and the natural sciences have made a lasting impression in the Western world. Although Islamic art may not fall within the scope of Western art in the more limited sense, it deserves attention at this point in our survey, particularly because its early monuments, like the Early Christian and Byzantine monuments, derive from earlier Near Eastern and Mediterranean artistic traditions. Most early monuments of Islamic art belong to the succession of Late Roman, Early Byzantine, and Iranian (Sassanian) art, although different social and religious needs would soon transform similar prototypes into quite different forms in the Islamic world than they would take in the Christian world.

EARLY CHRISTIAN ART

The style that we call Early Christian could as accurately be called Late Roman, or, in art-historical usage, Late Antique. Christian works are distinguished from pagan works only by subject, not by style. After all, the Christians of the time were as "Roman" as the pagans; they were trained in the same crafts, were brought up in the same environment, and spoke the same language. The Christian church itself, both in its organization and its philosophy, owed much to the Greco–Roman structure of life. Early Christian art shows the simple transformation of pagan into Christian themes and the freest kind of borrowing of pagan motifs and manners. Hybrid forms are produced throughout the Christianized late empire in the greatest profusion and with the greatest intermingling of regional styles, making it almost impossible to recognize any one style—or even half a dozen—that could definitely be called Early Christian or that could serve as an exclusive exemplar of what we mean by Early Christian.

In the "plastic" arts (sculpture and monuments), Greco–Roman naturalism underwent a kind of "denaturing"—something that began as early as the Column of Trajan (FIG. 6-64) and was well advanced in the reliefs from the Arch of Constantine (FIG. 6-90), the sculpture group *The Tetrarchs* (FIG. 6-88), and the coin portrait of Maximin Daia (FIG. 6-92). Archaizing modes supervene on the old naturalism, and things come to look less and less like the Greco–Roman prototypes from which, ultimately, they derive. This "denaturing" process, variously influenced by barbarian styles, continues well into the western Medieval period. It should by no means be viewed as merely the negation of the Greco–Roman style, or as a clumsy botching of it by men who had lost the sense of it and the necessary manual skill. Rather, it is the product of an entirely new world view—one that inevitably was to bring about the transformation of the naturalistic Classical tradition. Early Christian art shows that transformation in process—already well-begun in the late third century, while the Roman empire was still intact.

The Early Christian era can be divided conveniently into the Period of Persecution (from the establishment of the earliest communities, in the first century) and the Period of Recognition (from 325, when Constantine recognized Christianity, along with other religions of the Roman empire, until about 500, when the western provinces of the empire had come under the sway of barbarian princes). Some authorities would extend the period of Early Christian art to the eighth century, when it was terminated in the east by the Iconoclastic Controversy. In the earlier period, the Christians were, in the Roman view, a troublesome, even dangerous, sect that needed to be curbed. During this time, it is likely that the Christians, shrinking from the kind of attention public shrines might attract, worshiped in the private houses of their wealthier communicants, perhaps in the elaborate atrium houses of the type seen in Pompeii (FIG. 6-24). It is quite possible that the atrium forecourt of the later public churches, the basilicas, derived from their liturgical relationship to the earlier atrium of the private house.

The Catacombs

The most significant monuments of the Period of Persecution are the least conspicuous in Rome; they are entirely underground. The catacombs are vast networks of galleries and chambers, beneath Rome and other cities, that were designed as cemeteries for the burial of the Christian dead, many of them sainted martyrs. From the second through the fourth century the catacombs were in constant use, and it is estimated that as many as four million bodies were accommodated in the Roman catacombs alone. In times of persecution, they could also have served as places of concealment for fugitives; evidence of this function survives in blocked and cut-off staircases, secret embrasures (openings) and passages, and concealed entrances and exits. Undoubtedly, the Christian mysteries must have been enacted here, although the principal function of the catacombs was mortuary.

In Rome, the catacombs were tunneled out of a stratum of granular tufa, the convenient properties of which had been exploited earlier by the Etruscan necropolis builders (FIG. 6-2). After a plot of ground had been selected for the cemetery (Christians were not prevented by Roman law from owning property), a gallery 3–4 feet wide was dug around its perimeter at a convenient level below the surface (FIG. 7-1). In the walls of these galleries, embrasures were opened parallel to the gallery axis to receive the bodies of the dead; these openings, called *loculi*, were one above the other, like shelves (FIG. 7-2). Often, small rooms, called *cubicula*, were constructed in the walls to serve as mortuary chapels, and these were variously vaulted. Once the original perimeter galleries were full of *loculi* and *cubicula*, other galleries were cut at right angles to them; this process continued as long as lateral space permitted. Lower levels would then be dug and connected by staircases, some systems extending as deep as five levels. When adjacent burial areas belonged to members of the same Christian confraternity, or by gift or purchase fell into the same hands, communications were opened between the respective cemeteries, so that they spread laterally and gradually acquired a vast extent. After Christianity received official sanction, the catacombs fell into disuse, except as holy places—monuments to the great martyrs—which were visited by the pious.

Many cubicula were decorated with frescoes that were Late Antique (pagan) in manner and even in subject, as interpreted by the Christians to conform with their own beliefs. The geometric patterning of a ceiling in the catacomb of Saints Pietro and Marcellinus in Rome (FIG. 7-3) becomes akin to the Dome of Heaven (the large circle), which has been inscribed with the basic symbol of the Christian faith, the cross. The arms of the cross terminate in four *lunettes* (semicircular fields) in which are represented the key episodes from the Old Testament story of Jonah, who is thrown from his ship on the left, emerges from the whale on the right, and, safe on land on the bottom, contemplates the miracle of his salvation and the mercy of God. (Jonah, an often-painted figure in

7-1 Plan (*top*) of the catacomb of Callixtus, Rome, second century, and section (*bottom*) through main gallery of oldest region.

1 and 2. Main galleries
3. Collapsed lower floor
4. Cubicula

0 10 20 30 FEET
0 3 6 9 METERS

NOTE: Open rectangles indicate loculi.

Early Christian art, was honored as a prefiguration of Christ, who rose from death as Jonah had been delivered from the belly of the whale.) The compartments between these lunettes are occupied by *orans* figures, arms raised in the attitude of prayer; in the pagan world, from which they derive, they are symbols of piety. The central medallion shows the figure of Christ as the Good Shepherd, whose powers of salvation are underscored by his juxtaposition with the story of Jonah. As a theme, the Good Shepherd can be traced back through Greek Archaic art to Egyptian art—and, in Classical art, the Good Shepard signified the virtue of philanthropy—but here it becomes the symbol for the loyal protector of the Christian flock, who said to his disciples, "Feed my lambs; feed my sheep." It is noteworthy that, during the Period of Persecution, Christ was almost invariably represented in the catacombs either as the Good Shepherd or as a teacher. Only later, when Christianity became the official state religion of the Roman empire, did Christ take on such Imperial attributes as the halo, the purple robe, and the throne, which denoted rulership.

The style of the catacomb painters is most often the quick, sketchy impressionism we have seen in earlier Roman painting of the last Pompeian period, and the execution ranges from good to inferior—most often, the latter. We must take into account that the catacombs were very unpromising places for the art of the mural decorator. The air was spoiled by decomposing corpses, the humidity was excessive, and the lighting (provided largely by oil lamps) was entirely unfit for elaborate compositions and painstaking execution.

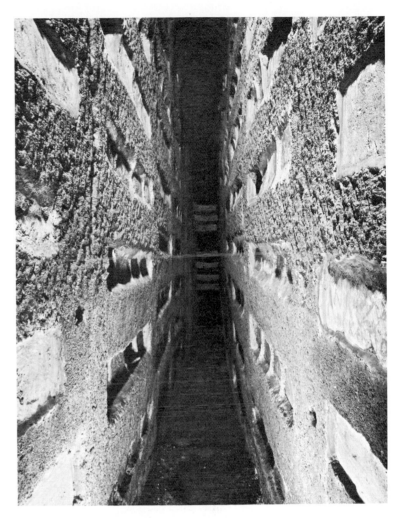

7-2 Gallery and loculi of the catacomb of Pamphilus, Rome, third century.

7-3 Painted ceiling from the catacomb of Saints Pietro and Marcellinus, Rome, fourth century.

For designs on ceilings, arches, and lunettes, the painter was required to assume awkward and tiring poses, and it is no wonder that he proceeded hastily and that often his results were poor.

Architecture

Although some Christian ceremonies were held in the catacombs, regular services were probably held in private houses that were rearranged and partitioned off to make "community" houses, or in simple, columned halls. The latter were destroyed in the last great persecutions under Diocletian and have not survived intact; the remains of one, a kind of rudimentary basilica, dating from 311, have been found beneath the cathedral of Aquileia. Once Christianity achieved Imperial sanction under Constantine, there was suddenly an urgent need to set up buildings that would meet the requirements of the Christian liturgy and would aggrandize the Christian cult. All the architectural ingredients were present: the atrium house, the catacomb chapel, the Roman basilica, and the Imperial audience hall. How these elements were combined into the masterful composition that was to become one of the first Christian church buildings of the new age—Old St. Peter's in Rome (FIGS. 7-4 and 7-6)—we do not know; discussion about the origins of the Christian basilica has not ended. Begun in 333, Old St. Peter's is probably the most important design

in the history of church architecture. Its wide influence was augmented by the belief that it stood where Peter, the first Apostle, had been buried. Its extraordinary dimensions are difficult to realize from the old drawings; the nave was as long, as high, and twice as wide as the nave of a great Gothic cathedral. Its interior was "one of the most spacious, most imposing, and most harmonious . . . ever built, imperially rich in its marbles and mosaics, grandiose yet forthright and large in the best Roman sense of the word."*

The plan of Old St. Peter's (FIG. 7-4) shows a rectangular building entered from the street through the *propylaea*—a gateway building that leads into an open, colonnaded court, the *atrium*; that part of the colonnade joined to the façade functions as an entrance hall, the *narthex*. The body of the church consists of the *nave*, low side *aisles*, *apse*, and transverse aisle, or *transept*, which is placed between the nave and the apse and projects slightly beyond the walls of the nave and aisles. This fundamental arrangement was used in subsequent Christian architecture, although it would be wrong to think that there is some rigid, standardized basilican design; for instance, the transept, an occasional feature of churches in the city of Rome, is often lacking in other churches, especially in the smaller ones.

*Kenneth Conant, *Early Medieval Church Architecture* (Baltimore: Johns Hopkins University Press, 1942), p.6.

7-4   Reconstruction of Old St. Peter's, Rome, *c.* 333. Approx. 215' wide.

1. Nave   4. Apse
2. Aisles   5. Narthex
3. Transept 6. Atrium
         7. Propylaea

7-5 Interior of St. Paul's Outside the Walls, Rome, late fourth century. (Etching by GIOVANNI BATTISTA PIRANESI.)

The cross section (FIG. 7-4) shows a great columned hall that obviously is related to such Roman secular basilicas as the Basilica Ulpia in the Forum of Trajan (FIG. 6-48). Unlike the slightly earlier Basilica of Constantine (FIGS. 6-85 and 6-86), Old St. Peter's was not vaulted, but timber-roofed, as were, traditionally, most Roman basilicas (the vaulted Basilica of Constantine being an exception). The pagan basilica's lateral entrance is moved to the short side of the Christian church. Only one of the multiple apses is retained, and that is placed opposite, and at a dramatic distance from, the entrance. Evenly spaced columns no longer surround, but flank, the central nave. All these modifications of the pagan basilica create a sweeping perspective that converges on the shrine as the focus of the whole design and the place of the principal mystery of the Christian faith.

The old church of St. Peter no longer stands, and it is from an eighteenth-century print by Piranesi of its slightly later stylistic associate, St. Paul's (FIG. 7-5), that we can get some idea of what it looked like—some idea of its great space, scale, and majesty. The "spiritualizing" of the secular Roman design is expressed not only in the realignment of the building's axis (to focus the viewer's whole experience on the ritual climax of the design), but also in its extreme simplicity of structure and the lightness of its bearing walls and columns. Roman mass—huge walls and ponderous weight, sculptured surfaces in relief and recess, and whole populations of statuary—has been lightened, rarefied, smoothed; we could say that it has been "dematerialized" to suit the new orientation toward a spiritual rather than a physical world.

The bird's-eye view of Old St. Peter's in reconstruction (FIG. 7-6), although partly conjectural, shows the Roman stepped podium that we have seen before in

the Temple of "Fortuna Virilis" (FIG. 6-16) and that has Etruscan predecessors; a propylaeum and a forum converted to an atrium are other elements with not only Roman but ancient antecedents. We believe that the exterior of Old St. Peter's was, like Christian basilicas in general, unadorned, reserving the whole decorative enterprise for the interior. It is as if the building imitated the ideal Christian, with grave and plain exterior and a glowing and beautiful soul within.

The rectangular, basilican, church design was long the favorite of the western Christian world. But the Early Christians also adopted another Classical building type—the central plan, a round or polygonal-domed structure—which was later favored in the east, where Byzantine architects developed it to monumental proportions and amplified its theme in numerous, ingenious variations. In the west, the cen-

7-6 Conjectural reconstruction of Old St. Peter's, Rome. (After K.J. Conant.)

7-7   Interior of Santa Costanza, Rome, *c.* 350.

tral-plan building was used generally for structures adjacent to the main basilicas, like mausoleums, baptistries, and private chapels. A highly refined example of the central-plan design is Santa Costanza in Rome (FIGS. 7-7, 7-8, 7-9). Built in the mid-fourth century, it early served as the mausoleum of Constantia, daughter of the emperor Constantine. Its antecedents can be traced to the beehive tombs of the Mycenaeans, (FIGS. 4-26 and 4-27), although its direct inspiration may have been the Pantheon, (FIGS. 6-51, 6-52, 6-53) or the pool-enclosing rotunda of some public baths, like those of Caracalla (FIGS. 6-55 and 6-56). The Pantheon's mass, however, has been metamorphosed, as with the mutation of the pagan into the Early Christian basilica. In Santa Costanza, the circle of paired columns that carries the domed cylinder is well free of the external walls-free enough to leave space for a barrel-vaulted corridor, or *ambulatory*. In fact, it is as if the basilican wall-arcade has been bent around a circle, the ambulatory corresponding to the basilican aisles and, like them, equipped with a high, ample clerestory. The exuberant naturalism of the luxurious mosaics in the vault of the ambulatory (FIG. 7-9) suggests a lingering influence of the pagan spirit.

All the important buildings of the fourth century, including Santa Costanza and the great, longitudinal basilicas, are closely associated with Constantine and his immediate relatives, for it was through their pa-

7-8   Plan (*left*) and section (*above*) of Santa Costanza, Rome.

7-9 Detail of mosaics in the vault of the ambulatory, Santa Costanza.

Mosaic and Painting

As the church-building enterprise under Constantine and his successors was designed to meet the urgent ceremonial needs of Christianity, which had now suddenly become official and public, so wholesale programs of decoration for the churches were also called for. To advertise the new faith in all its diverse aspects—its dogma, scriptural narrative, and symbolism—and to instruct and edify the believer, acres of wall in dozens of new churches had to be filled in the style and medium that would carry the message most effectively. Brilliantly ornamental mosaics—with sparkling tesserae of reflective glass, rather than the opaque, marble tesserae preferred by the Romans—became the standard vehicle of expression almost at once. Mosaics were particularly suited to the flat, thin-walled surfaces of the new basilicas, becoming a durable, tangible part of the wall, a kind of architectural tapestry. The light flooding through the clerestories was caught in vibrant reflection by the mosaics, which produced abrupt effects and contrasts and sharp concentrations of color that could focus attention on the central, most relevant features of a composition. Mosaic, worked in the Early Christian manner, is not intended for the subtle changes of tone that a naturalistic painter's approach would require, although—as we have seen in the Roman mosaics—tonality is well within the mosaicist's reach. But in mosaic, color is *placed*, not blended; and bright, hard, glittering texture, set within a rigorously simplified pattern, becomes the rule. For mosaics placed high on the wall, far above the observer's head, the painstaking use of tiny tesserae, seen in Roman floor mosaics, became meaningless. Early Christian mosaics, designed to be seen from a distance, employed larger stones; the surfaces are left uneven, so that the tesserae's projecting edges can catch and reflect the light, and the designs were kept simple, for optimum legibility. For several centuries, mosaic—in the service of Christian theology—was the medium of some of the supreme masterpieces of world art.

Content and style find their medium; the content of Christian doctrine took centuries to fashion, and, for a long time, even the proper manner of representing the founder of Christianity was in question. Once Christianity became the official religion of the Roman state, Jesus' status changed. In early works, he is shown as teacher and philosopher; in later works, he is imperialized as the ruler of heaven and earth. In the fourth and fifth centuries, artists were hesitant about how to represent Jesus, and variant types of images were produced. After some crucial theological questions on Jesus' nature were resolved, a more-or-less standard formula for his depiction emerged.

In the minds of simple Christians who were only recently converted, Jesus could be easily identified

tronage and supervision, as an expression of the new ideal of the Christian *imperium*, that these buildings were constructed. This close relationship between the Constantinians and Early Christian architecture may explain a certain consistency of design in the apparently diverse basilicas of the fourth and early fifth centuries. It might also partly explain how such apparently contradictory designs as the long church and the central church could be imagined as working together in meeting the requirements of Christian belief and ritual. Given centuries of tradition, it would have been perfectly natural for Constantine to memorialize the place of Jesus' death and burial with a traditional monument, the domed rotunda, as he did in the Church of the Holy Sepulchre in Jerusalem. At the same time, the existing plan of the basilica might have been designed to offer the space needed for the congregations of pilgrims coming to the holiest place in Christendom. For several centuries then, the architectural problem, although never explicitly stated, was how to integrate the long plan and the central plan.

conception far more grandiose than that of the Good Shepherd.

The style, or styles, of Christian art emerged as a transmutation of Greco–Roman art; for the mosaicists, the point of departure was Roman illusionism. This can be seen in the apse mosaic of the church of Santa Pudenziana in Rome (FIG. 7-11), dated about 410, the earliest surviving example in a succession of monumental apse mosaics that extended through the history of Christian art. Although drastically restored in the nineteenth century (almost the whole right half was damaged), enough remains to show the persistence of Roman forms and the assimilation of Roman Imperial attributes to the image of Christ. On an emperor's throne, Christ, clad in Imperial purple and gold, sits within the Heavenly Jerusalem and presides over the Church Triumphant. He is flanked on either side by ascending ranks of apostles, deployed like a Roman emperor's entourage of senators. Behind them, on either side of the throne, stand two women—the personifications of the Church of the Gentiles (New Testament) and the Church of the Synagogue (Old Testament). Above and behind the head of Christ is the jeweled cross that Constantine raised on the site of Christ's crucifixion. Within the goldstreaked, blue sky hover the four symbolic creatures of the visions of Ezekiel and the Book of Revelation, representing the Four Evangelists: the winged Man of St. Matthew (partly obscured by the arch), the Lion of

with the familiar deities of the Mediterranean world, especially Helios (Apollo), the sun god, or his Romanized eastern aspect, Sol Invictus (the Unconquered Sun). The late third-century vault mosaic of a small Christian mausoleum in a pagan cemetery (FIG. 7-10), excavated underneath Old St. Peter's in Rome in the 1940s, shows Jesus as Apollo, driving the horses of the sun chariot through the heavens—a

7-11 *Christ Enthroned in Majesty, with Saints,* apse mosaic, Santa Pudenziana, Rome, 402–417.

St. Mark, the Ox of St. Luke, and (also partly obscured) the Eagle of St. John. (This is an early appearance of these symbols, which we will find commonly represented throughout Medieval art; see, for example, the top of FIG. 7-30.) The background recalls the kind of perspective illusionism and naturalistic depiction of architectural forms found in Pompeian wall paintings, and the buildings may reflect, to some degree, those actually in Jerusalem at that time.

As in Santa Pudenziana, we can witness the union of the old naturalism and the new symbolism in the great mosaic cycle in Santa Maria Maggiore in Rome, which also dates from the early fifth century. The panel representing *The Parting of Lot and Abraham* (FIG. 7-12) tells its story (Genesis 13:5–13) succinctly. Agreeing to disagree, Lot leads his family and flocks to the right, toward the city of Sodom, while Abraham moves toward a building on the left (the church?). Lot's is the evil choice, and the instrumentalities of the evil (his two daughters) are represented in front of him; the figure of the yet unborn Isaac, the instrument of good, stands before his father, Abraham. The cleavage of the two groups is emphatic, and each is represented by a shorthand device that could be called a "head cluster," which will have a long history in Christian art. The figures turn from each other in a kind of sharp dialogue of glance and gesture, and we recognize a moving away from the flexibility of naturalism toward the significant gesture and that primary method of Medieval representation, *pantomime*, which simplifies all significance into body attitude and gesture. The wide eyes turned in their sockets, the broad gestures of enlarged hands, the

7-12 *The Parting of Lot and Abraham*, mosaic from Santa Maria Maggiore, Rome, *c.* 430.

opposed movements of the groups all remind us of some silent, expressive chorus that comments only by gesture on the action of the drama. Thus, the complex action of Roman art stiffens into the art of simplified motion or dumb show, which has great power to communicate without ambiguity and which, in the whole course of Medieval art, will produce the richest kind of variety. Also foreshadowing the character of later Christian art are the facts that the figures of the panel have been moved to the foreground and that the artist takes no great pains to describe either space or landscape setting; the background town and building are symbolic, rather than descriptive. But within this relatively abstract setting, the figures themselves loom with massive solidity. They cast shadows and are modeled in dark and light to give them that three-dimensional appearance that testifies to the artist's heritage of Roman pictorial illusionism. It would require another century and much modification under non-Hellenized Eastern influence before the artist would be able to think of his figures entirely as flat images, rather than as plastic bodies.

The vivid narrative style of the Santa Maria Maggiore mosaic can be contrasted with the monumental stillness of the *orans* figures of martyrs in the great dome (some 74 feet in diameter!) of the Church of St. George at Thessaloniki (Salonika) in northern Greece (FIG. 7-13). These figures, with their architectural backgrounds and enframements, are the only survivors of a magnificent mosaic composition in concentric rings of golden tesserae, which climaxed at the summit of the dome in an apparition of Christ supported by flying angels. A middle zone may have

7-13 *Saint Onesiphorus and Saint Porphyrius*, detail of dome mosaic, Church of Saint George, Thessaloniki, Greece, late fifth century.

contained figures in adoration before the Second Coming, to which the whole composition may have alluded. The formality of pose and the solemn, priestly demeanor of the figures—unvarying features of Byzantine art throughout its centuries of life—will coexist with the narrative approach that is brought into play when events of Scripture are illustrated. The formal style, intended to eternalize a vision of the transcendent mysteries of the faith, was confined principally to the upper levels of the church: the central dome, the apsidal dome, and the immediately lower levels that they command (FIG. 7-13). The elaborate architecture surrounding the St. George figures recalls the paintings on Pompeian walls and the actual "stage-set" architecture of buildings like the "Treasury" at Petra (FIG. 6-79). The Classical tradition persists even while the ethereal, golden splendor of the whole composition dissolves material form into spiritual phantasm. One could say that the dome mosaic of St. George completes the change from the images of the pagan floor mosaic, which are literally under the feet and of this world, to the floating images of a celestial world high above the Christian's wondering gaze. Yet the pagan substance is never entirely transformed.

The Illuminated Manuscript

Santa Maria Maggiore is an early and outstanding example of the complementarity of the new basilican architecture and the detailed mosaics and paintings designed for it. But the earlier art of the catacombs could not have provided the resources for narratives as elaborate as those found at Santa Maria Maggiore; catacomb painting was much too narrow in scope of subject and much too rudimentary in style and technique. Rather, the church decorators must have drawn on a long tradition of pictures in manuscripts going back to pharaonic Egypt and highly developed by the Hellenistic Greeks of Alexandria. Thousands of texts must have been available to the Constantinian artists, richly illustrated with themes—Hebrew, Greek, Christian, and combinations of all three.

Although both Jews and Christians were bound by the Second Commandment against images, the ban was somehow evaded and both sects made use of them. (Mural pictures found in the third-century Jewish synagogue at Dura-Europos in Mesopotamia illustrate themes from the Old Testament.) No Jewish illustrated manuscript has survived from ancient times; yet, it has been suggested that Jewish figural art—and certainly oral tradition—had considerable thematic influence on Christian art. We know that Constantine summoned numerous savants and literati of Alexandria—an intellectual center for both Jews and pagans since Hellenistic times and one of

7-14 Miniature from the *Vatican Vergil,* early fifth century. Approx. 12½″ × 12″. Vatican Library, Rome.

the great episcopal sees of the Christian church—and that he established a library where they gave instruction; we know also that he was a generous donor of manuscripts to the Church. Hence, it is no wonder that Constantinople became a center of traditional and Christian learning that was transmitted by the copying and recopying of manuscripts through the centuries. The dissemination of manuscripts, as well as their preservation, was greatly aided by an important invention in the Early Imperial period. The long manuscript scroll (*rotulus*), used by Egyptians, Greeks, and Romans and made of the fragile papyrus, was superseded by the *codex*, which was made, much like the modern book, of separate pages bound together at one side and having a cover. Papyrus was replaced by the much more durable *vellum* (calfskin) and *parchment* (lambskin), which provided better surfaces for painting than did papyrus. These changes in the durability, reproduction, and format of texts greatly improved the possibility that the records of ancient civilizations could survive long centuries of neglect, even if not in great number.

The sacred texts were copied as faithfully as possible, as were the pictures in them. After the great fathers of the Eastern Church recommended the didactic use of pictures in churches and books, the picture became only slightly less significant than the text from which it drew its authority. The passage from the scroll to the codex (from continuous narrative to a series of individual pictures) can be seen in two manuscripts of different dates, (the later manuscript still reflects the scroll procedure). The *Vatican Vergil* (FIG. 7-14), from the early fifth century and the oldest painted manuscript known, is pagan in content, representing a scene from Vergil's *Georgics*, in which a seated farmer (at the left) instructs two of his slaves in the art of husbandry, while Vergil (at the right) listens and records the instructions. (We are reminded of the Roman idealization of country life and nature.) The style is Late Antique and reminiscent of Pompeian landscapes. The quick, impressionistic touches that suggest space and atmosphere, the foreshortened villa in the background, the small, active figures in their wide, spacious setting are all familiar features of Roman illusionistic painting. We also saw the heavy, black frame isolating a single episode in the late Pompeian styles.

The *Vatican Vergil* can be contrasted in form with the *Vienna Genesis* (FIG. 7-15)—the earliest, well-preserved, painted manuscript we know of that contains Biblical scenes—which employs the continuity of a frieze in a scroll. In a continuous narrative like this, two or more scenes of a story are represented within a single frame; this will become the common form of narrative in Medieval art. In this scene from the Book of Genesis (24:15–61), Rebecca leaves the city of Nahor to fetch water from the well in the first episode. In the second, she gives water to Eliezer and his camels. Her way is marked by a colonnaded avenue; her destination, by a semi-nude, naïvely pert, little personification of the well—a lingering Classical reminder of a pagan river-goddess, as well as a reminder of the persistence of Classical motifs and stylistic modes in Medieval art. The action is presented

with all possible simplicity in an expressive pantomime that includes convincing touches; for example, Rebecca braces herself with her raised left foot on the rim of the well as she tips up her jug for Eliezer. The figures are silhouetted against a landscape that is blank except for the toy-like city. Everything necessary to bare narrative is present, and nothing else. Although the figures have only narrative significance, the page itself becomes sumptuous—a rich, purple ground (the material is vellum) lettered in silver. The luxuriousness of ornament that will become more and more typical of sacred books absorbs the human figure or confines it exclusively to iconic or narrative functions. The spiritual beauty of the text and the material beauty of the vehicle that serves and intensifies it will come to count above all else. The luster of holy objects becomes the intent and the effect of Byzantine art.

Closely related to the *Vienna Genesis* is another manuscript of about the same time, the early sixth century, and perhaps of the same provenance. *The Rossano Gospels* (known also as the *Codex Rossanensis*) is the earliest illuminated book we have that contains illustrations of the New Testament (FIG. 7-16). We can infer from them that, by this time, a canon of New Testament iconography has been fairly well established. Like the *Vienna Genesis*, the text of *The Rossano Gospels* is inscribed in silver on purple vellum; unlike the former, the Rossano artist has attempted, with considerable success, to harmonize his colors with the purple ground. The subject of our miniature, pre-

7-15 *Rebecca and Eliezer at the Well*, from the *Vienna Genesis*, early sixth century. Book illumination painted on purple vellum, 9¾″ × 12¼″. Österreichische Nationalbibliothek, Vienna.

7-16 *Pilate Demanding That the People Choose Between Jesus and Barabbas*, from *The Rossano Gospels*, early sixth century. Book illumination on purple vellum, 11″ × 10¼″. The Diocesan Museum, Archepiscopal Palace, Rossano, Italy.

sented in vigorous pantomime, is the judgment of Jesus by Pilate or, more particularly, the people's choice of Barabbas over Jesus (Matthew 27:2–26). In the fashion of continuous narrative, several different episodes are included. Arranged on two levels separated by a simple ground line, the figures in the upper level represent Pilate presiding over the tribunal, at which the people demand the death of Jesus and Judas returns the 30 pieces of silver—an inaccuracy in the time and place of the episode as it occurs in the text. Jesus and the bound thief Barabbas, between whom Pilate has demanded that the people choose, appear in the lower level. Jesus, at the left, is now distinguished by the cross-inscribed *nimbus* (halo) that signifies his divinity; Barabbas, at the far right, is bending low in the direction of Judas, who hangs himself. The illuminator has assumed that the reader is perfectly familiar with the text being illustrated and has tried to make his composition as inclusive of all relevant episodes as possible, adding labels when he felt they were needed. Here, the artist wants his picture to be as readable as the text; the story is all that counts.

By the sixth century, the canon of Christian sacred texts, as well as the cycles of illustration appropriate to them, had been agreed on. The denaturing of Classical form is well advanced, and a new art is originating. We are now a considerable distance in time from the painting of the Roman Imperial period, with its worldly themes, naturalism, perspective illusionism, modeling in light and shade, graded tonality, and proportionality. There will be little regard for the pagan ideals of beauty in the centuries to come.

Sculpture and Craft Art

The transformations that occurred in architecture in the period of early Christianity—the adaption of the multipurpose pagan basilica to the single purpose of Christian ritual and the "dematerialization" of the heavy materiality of Roman buildings into the screen-like thinness and lightness of Christian structure—are paralleled in the sculpture of the time. We have seen anticipations of the change as early as the second century in the Column of Trajan (FIG. 6-65), and we have seen the change almost completed in early fourth-century reliefs of the Arch of Constantine (FIGS. 6-89 and 6-90). A third-century relief on the so-called *Ludovisi Battle Sarcophagus* (FIG. 7-17) should be interpolated between them. This work, still quite pagan in theme and spirit, representing a struggle between Romans and barbarians, is most instructive as an illustration of the "flattened relief" and the "piled-up" perspective so characteristic of the denaturing of Greco–Roman naturalism and the emerging Medieval style. Although a strong descriptive realism persists in the details of physiognomy, dress, action, gesture, and accessories, *pattern* has taken over from figure composition. The writhing figures are all within the same plane; at the same time, the "foreground" figures (at the base of the pattern) are relatively small, while the "background" figures (at the top of the pattern) are the largest. This *reverse perspective* strengthens the surface into a dense mass with no illusion of space beyond (behind) it. Carving plays a lesser and lesser role, and quick effects of light and dark are achieved by gouging, punching, and drilling the surface. As yet, the formal placement of the fig-

7-17 *Battle Between Romans and Barbarians,* front panel of the so-called *Ludovisi Battle Sarcophagus,* third century. Marble, approx. 56" high. Museo Nazionale, Rome.

ures that we find in the Arch of Constantine has not appeared; of course, the subject does not call for that, and the sarcophagus composition is more a representation of the dissolution of the style of the Trajanic reliefs than of the advent of Constantinian formalism. But the patterning and constriction of surface, the sacrifice of realism of space and proportion, are all present and share the characteristics of Early Christian art.

Toward the end of the fourth century, we find the flattening and patterning process well advanced. *The Good Shepherd Sarcophagus* (FIG. 7-18) has a thick, spaceless surface that is perforated rather than carved, producing a kind of hard lacing of flat darks and lights. This sarcophagus is interesting, too, for what it reveals of the Christian adaptation of pagan material. We have seen that the Good Shepherd theme appears in pre-Christian times and that the Christians chose it to signify Christ. Here, the motif appears three times, possibly in an allusion to the Trinity. Around the Good Shepherd twines a grapevine heavy with grapes, through which busy cupids climb, bringing in the harvest. Three cupids crush the grapes in a wine press; their wine, once sacred to Bacchus, has now become symbolic of the blood of Christ. The cupids themselves, once associated with love and erotic passion (Cupid is the son of Venus), are forerunners of the Christian cherubs. Thus, a purely pagan theme with orgiastic overtones is transmuted, by Christian intention, into a symbol of redemption through the blood of Christ. The figure style, with its stumpy proportions, frontalizing pose, and stereotyping of action, had its predecessor in the reliefs of the Arch of Constantine and is common (with many variations) to a great number of sarcophagi from the fourth, fifth, and sixth centuries.

Despite the great changes in sculpture during the second half of the third century, the Classical tradition was by no means extinguished, even though there seemed to be an almost deliberate turning away from Greco–Roman art to something Archaic, abstract, and bluntly expressive, as in *The Tetrarchs*, the reliefs from the Arch of Constantine, and the coin portrait of Maximin Daia. The tradition lived on through the Middle Ages, if not with entirely discernible continuity, in intermittent revivals, renovations, and restorations, commingled with—or side-by-side and in contrast with—the opposing, nonclassicizing Medieval styles. The end of the Medieval world will be signalized by the rise of Classical art to dominance in the Renaissance. It has been recently observed that the greatest achievement of Early Christian art from the third to the seventh century is that it has "preserved, in the face of vast and cataclysmic changes, basic and essential elements of the Greco–Roman heritage."* As we follow the course of stylistic change throughout the history of Western art, especially in the Middle Ages, the strength of the Classical tradition in its dialogue with competing strains and tendencies of style should always be kept in mind.

Monumental sculpture began to decline in the fourth century and did not recover its place in the history of art until the twelfth century. The Christian tended to be suspicious of the freestanding statue, linking it with the false gods of the pagans. In his *Apologia*, Justin Martyr—a second-century ecclesiast mindful of the admonition of the First Commandment to shun graven images—accused the pagans of worshiping statues as gods. But the Greco–Roman experience was still a living part of the Mediterranean mentality, and, at least in the west, the Semitic ban on images in sacred places was not likely to be adopted. The reasoning of the fathers of the early Church—that the use of pictures and statues could be justified on the grounds that they instructed the illiterate in the mysteries and stories of the faith—was later supplemented by the theological argument that since Jesus was "made flesh and dwelt among us," he had a human nature and human likeness that could be represented in art.

In any event, during the Early Christian and Byzantine periods, sculpture dwindled to craft art and small work: sarcophagus reliefs, commemorative ivory panels, metalwork, church furniture and acces-

*Ernst Kitzinger, *Byzantine Art in the Making* (Cambridge, MA: Harvard University Press, 1977), p. 126.

7-18 *The Good Shepherd Sarcophagus,* from the catacomb of Praetextatus, late fourth century. Museo del Laterano, Rome.

sories, book covers, and the like. Yet, in this great reduction of the scope of the medium, works of exquisite craftsmanship could still be produced that reflected, even in Christian times, the persistence of pagan, Classical ideals of beauty. An ivory plaque (FIG. 7-19), probably produced in Rome toward the end of the fourth century, strikingly exhibits the endurance of Classical form. The ivory, one of a pair of leaves of a *diptych*, (two carved, hinged panels) commemorates the marriage of members of two powerful Roman families of the senatorial class, the Nicomachi and the Symmachi, who remained pagan during this first triumphal period when the emperor Theodosius decreed Christianity to be the only legally recognized religion of the empire. Here, they seem consciously to reaffirm their faith in the old pagan gods; certainly, they favor the esthetic ideals of the Classical past, much as we find them realized in such works as the Parthenon frieze (FIG. 5-52) and the Ara Pacis Augustae (FIG. 6-60). The illustration represents a pagan priestess celebrating the rites of Bacchus and Jupiter; its companion piece shows a priestess honoring Ceres and Cybele. The priestess (FIG. 7-19) prepares a libation at an altar where the sacred fire burns. The precise yet fluent and graceful line, the easy, gliding pose, and the mood of spiritual serenity bespeak an artist practicing within a still vital Classical tradition, to which idealized human beauty is central. That tradition was probably deliberately sustained by the great senatorial magnates of Rome, who resisted the empire-wide imposition of the Christian faith in the later fourth century.

A later work, carved in the eastern empire, perhaps in Constantinople, offers still further evidence of the persistence of Classical form, although there are subtle deviations from its rules. It is an ivory leaf from a diptych dating from the early sixth century, depicting *St. Michael the Archangel* (FIG. 7-20). The prototype of St. Michael must have been a pagan Victory; the flowing Classical yet naturalistic drapery, the delicately incised wings, and the facial type and coiffure are of the pre-Christian tradition. But even so, there are significant divergences—misinterpretations or misreadings of the rules of naturalistic representation. Subtle ambiguities in the relationship of the figure to its architectural setting appear in such details as the placement of the scepter and the feet hovering above the stair without real relationship to it. These matters have, of course, little to do with the striking beauty of the form; they simply indicate the course of stylistic change, as the Greco–Roman world faded into history and the Medieval era began.

We find that change almost completed in the *Diptych of Anastasius* (FIG. 7-21), which represents the emperor Anastasius I, as consul, about to throw down the *mappa* (handkerchief), the signal for the

7-19 *Priestess Celebrating the Rites of Bacchus*, c. 380–400. Leaf of an ivory diptych of the Nicomachi and the Symmachi, 11¾″ × 5½″. Victoria and Albert Museum, London.

games to start. Although the diptych, dated 517, is almost contemporary with the St. Michael ivory, the mutation of Classical naturalism is much further advanced (a reminder that the process does not proceed

7-20 *St. Michael the Archangel*, early sixth century. Leaf of an ivory diptych, approx. 17" × 5½". British Museum, London.

7-21 *Diptych of Anastasius*, 517. Ivory, each leaf 14" × 5". Bibliothèque Nationale, Paris.

evenly along the same historical front or at the same tempo). The figure of the emperor in both panels is elevated above the lively scenes taking place in the arena. He is enthroned in rigid frontality, making a static, suspended gesture, entirely symbolic, the abstraction of his consular authority. His features are mask-like, and his quasidivine status is announced by a halo. The halo, a shell form, would originally have been an architectural feature, part of the pediment of the niche; here—in an excellent example of a misreading of a prototype—it has migrated to its place behind the emperor's head. The details of the architecture are confused and have lost their original significance; the flattening and patterning of the surface is as we have seen it developing earlier. The work is entirely ornamental and symbolic; the living man is lost in the concept—in this case, the concept of supreme and suprahuman authority. Dating 100 years after the *Diptych of Anastasius*, the sarcophagus

of Archbishop Theodore (FIG. 7-22) is not only ornamented with entirely symbolic forms, but the human figure is dismissed altogether. Peacocks, symbolic of eternity, flank a *chi–rho* monogram (XP are the first two letters of "Christ" in Greek). The XP is supplemented in the monogram with the alpha (A) and the omega (Ω)—the first and last letters of the Greek alphabet, representing the words of Christ: "I am the Beginning and the End." The fruiting vines behind the peacocks represent, as we have seen, the source of the redeeming blood of Christ. Set within wreaths on the lid of the tomb, the *chi–rho* monogram appears three times; it had already served as the *labarum* carried on the standards of the Imperial Christian army. Thus, the hope of the deceased archbishop and the guarantee of his salvation are expressed entirely in symbol: eternity; redemption through the blood of Christ, who stands at the beginning and the end of time; and the triumph of Christianity. The accidents

7-22 Sarcophagus of Archbishop Theodore, seventh century, Sant' Apollinare in Classe, Ravenna, Italy. Marble.

and irregularities of figural representation, the busyness of narrative, are replaced by timeless signs of salvation and immortality.

BYZANTINE ART

The transition from Early Christian to Byzantine art is neither abrupt nor definite and, in fact, defies accurate definition. The almost contemporary diptychs of St. Michael (FIG. 7-20) and of Anastasius (FIG. 7-21) are both products of eastern carvers and might well be classified as Byzantine works. Yet *St. Michael the Archangel* is still firmly rooted in the Greco–Roman tradition, and the *Diptych of Anastasius* panels show the Medieval stress on the event rather than on its appearance. In the latter approach, which was essentially Near Eastern or Semitic, forms evolved into decorative symbols placed before a shallow, often neutral background that made little, if any, allusion to optical space.

One point of departure for the abstract, symbolic, Eastern Christian art may be a mural painting (FIG. 7-23) from Dura-Europos—a small garrison town on the west bank of the Euphrates in the heart of ancient Mesopotamia and on the very edge of the Roman empire, already noted as the site of the Jewish synagogue with figural mural paintings (page 258). The mural dates from the second to third century, the time of the Roman occupation. The detail shown here may depict an attendant and priests of a forgotten pagan cult of Parthia or Palmyra (biblical Tadmor). The figures stand with formal frontality in front of (within?) an architectural background. Their drapery is rendered by line, not tone, and their gestures are slow, ceremonial, and grave. Each figure is, in itself, a vertical design entity, isolated from its neighbor.

The bodies hover weightlessly, their feet in ambiguous relationship to the ground and to the architectural setting, reminding us of the St. Michael ivory (FIG. 7-20) carved centuries later. Although the meaning of the enacted ceremony is lost to us, it must have been represented with utmost clarity to initiates, who could read the depicted symbols and gestures like a pictorial script—a script that moved laterally across

7-23 *Priests with Attendant*, detail of a mural from the Temple of the Palmyrene Gods, Dura-Europos, second to third century.

the surface of the painted wall, unobstructed by perspective and other illusionistic devices.

As Christian dogma developed, this form of symbolic interpretation of reality became more favored, and a flat, decorative, abstract, "Byzantine" style, rooted in such Near Eastern works as the Dura-Europos murals, began to dominate Christian art. Although Western illusionism was tenacious and enjoyed repeated revivals, the transition was more-or-less complete by the middle of the sixth century.

Ravenna and Mount Sinai

Early in the fifth century, when the Visigoths, under their king, Alaric, threatened to overrun Italy, Emperor Honorius moved the capital of his crumbling empire to Ravenna—an ancient Roman harbor on Italy's Adriatic coast, some 80 miles south of Venice. There, in a city surrounded by swamps and thus easily defended, his Imperial authority survived the fall of Rome to Alaric in 410. Honorius died in 423, and the reins of government were taken over by his half sister, Galla Placidia, whose biography reads like an outrageously exaggerated adventure story. Galla Placidia died in 450, some 25 years before the last of her weak successors was deposed. In 476, Ravenna fell to Odoacer; eventually, in 493, it was chosen by Theodoric, the Goth's greatest king, to be the capital of his Ostrogothic kingdom, which encompassed much of the Balkans and all of Italy. During the short history of Theodoric's unfortunate successors, the importance of the city declined. But in 539, the Byzantine general Belisarius conquered Ravenna for his emperor, Justinian, and led the city into the third and

most important stage of its history. Reunited with the eastern "empire," Ravenna remained the "sacred fortress" of Byzantium, its foothold in Italy for 200 years, until its conquest successively by the Lombards and then the Franks. Ravenna enjoyed its greatest cultural and economic prosperity during the reign of Justinian, at a time when the "eternal city" of Rome was threatened with complete extinction by repeated sieges, conquests, and sackings.

As the seat of Byzantine dominion in Italy, ruled by Byzantine governors, or *exarchs*, Ravenna and its culture became an extension of Constantinople, and its art, more than that of the Byzantine capital (where relatively little outside of architecture has survived), clearly reveals the transition from the Early Christian to the Byzantine style.

The climactic points of Ravenna's history are closely linked with the personages of Galla Placidia, Theodoric, and Justinian. All left their stamp on the city in monuments that have survived to our day (one might say "miraculously," as the city was heavily bombed in the Second World War) and that make Ravenna one of the most complete repositories of fifth- and sixth-century mosaics in Italy. The monuments of Ravenna, particularly the Justinianic ones, represent ideas that ultimately will determine the forms of the culture, and certainly of the art, of the Middle Ages.

Galla Placidia's own mausoleum (the identity of which has recently been questioned) is a rather small, cruciform structure with a dome-covered crossing (FIGS. 7-24 and 7-25). Built shortly after 425, it was originally attached to the narthex of the now greatly altered basilican palace-church of Santa Croce. Al-

7-24 Mausoleum of Galla Placidia, Ravenna, Italy, 425–450.

7-25 Interior of the mausoleum of Galla Placidia.

though its plan is that of a Latin cross, the cross arms are very short and appear to be little more than apsidal extensions of a square. Thus, all emphasis is placed on the tall, dome-covered crossing, and the building becomes, in effect, a central-plan structure. On the other hand, this small, unassuming building also represents one of the earliest successful fusions of the two basic early church plans, the longitudinal and the central, and introduces us, on a small scale, to a building type that would have a long history in Christian architecture—the basilican plan with a domed crossing.

The mausoleum's plain, unadorned, brick shell encloses one of the richest mosaic ensembles in Early Christian art. Every square inch of the interior surfaces above the marble-faced walls is covered with mosaic decor: the barrel vaults of nave and cross arms, with garlands and decorative medallions reminiscent of snowflakes on a dark blue ground; the dome, with a large, golden cross against a star-studded sky; other surfaces, with representations of saints and apostles; and the lunette above the entrance, with a representation of Christ as the Good

Shepherd (FIG. 7-26). We have seen earlier versions of the Good Shepherd, but none so regal as this. Jesus no longer carries a lamb on his shoulders, but is seated among his flock in splendid isolation, haloed and robed in gold and purple. To his left and right, the sheep are evenly distributed in groups of three. But their arrangement is rather loose and informal (compare FIG. 7-28), and they have been placed in a carefully described landscape that extends from foreground to background and is covered by a blue sky. All forms are tonally rendered; they have three-dimensional bulk, cast shadows, and are disposed in depth. In short, the panel is replete with devices of Roman illusionism; its creator was still deeply rooted in the Hellenic tradition. Some 50 years later, his successors would work in a much more abstract and formal manner.

Around 504, shortly after he settled in Ravenna, Theodoric ordered the construction of his own palace-church, a three-aisled basilica dedicated to the Savior. In the ninth century, the relics of Apollinaris were transferred to this church, which was rededicated and has been known since that time as

7-26 *Christ as the Good Shepherd,* mosaic from the entrance wall of the mausoleum of Galla Placidia, 425–450.

Sant' Apollinare Nuovo. The rich mosaic decorations of the interior nave walls (FIG. 7-27) are arranged in three zones, of which the upper two date from the time of Theodoric. Old Testament patriarchs and prophets are represented between the clerestory windows; above them, scenes from the life of Christ alternate with decorative panels. The lowest zone originally bore subjects of either Arian or political character. Although Christians, Theodoric and his Goths were Arians (followers of the teachings of Bishop Arius)—a sect declared heretical by the Orthodox Church. After the Byzantine conquest of Ravenna, Bishop Agnellus ordered all mosaics that bore reference to Theodoric or to Arianism removed and replaced with the present procession of orthodox saints (male on one side, female on the other). Agnellus had no quarrel with the subjects on the upper two levels, and they were left intact; our example, *The Miracle of the Loaves and the Fishes* (FIG. 7-28), must date from *c.* 500. It well illustrates the stylistic change that has occurred since the decoration of Galla Placidia's mausoleum. Jesus, beardless and in the Imperial dress of gold and purple, faces directly toward us as

he directs his disciples to distribute the miraculously augmented supply of bread and fish to the great crowd to which he has preached. The artist has made no attempt to supply details to the event. Rather, he has emphasized the sacramental character of it, the spiritual fact that Jesus, outstanding in the group, is performing a miracle by the power of God. The fact of the miracle takes it out of the world of time and of incident, for what is important in this scene is the presence of almighty power, which requires nothing but an unchanging presentation in terms of formal, unchanging aspect. The story is told with the bare minimum of figures necessary to make its meaning explicit; these figures have been aligned laterally, moved close to the foreground, and placed in a shallow picture box that is cut off by a golden screen close behind the backs of the figures. The landscape setting, which was so explicitly described by the artist who worked for Galla Placidia, is here merely suggested by a few rocks and bushes that enclose the figure group like parentheses. That former reference to the physical world, the blue sky, is now replaced by a neutral gold, which would be the standard back-

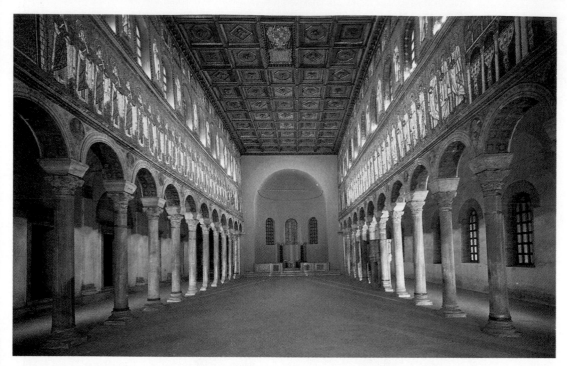

7-27 The nave of Sant' Apollinare Nuovo, Ravenna, c. 504.

7-28 *The Miracle of the Loaves and the Fishes*, mosaic from the nave wall of Sant' Apollinare Nuovo, c. 504.

ground color from now on. Remnants of Roman illusionism are found only in the handling of the individual figures, which still cast shadows and retain some of their former volume. But the shadows of the drapery folds have already narrowed into bars and would soon disappear.

The Ravenna epoch closes with the church of Sant' Apollinare in Classe, where, in the great apse mosaic, the Byzantine style reaches full maturity. Here, until the ninth century (when it was transferred to Ravenna), rested the body of St. Apollinaris, who suffered his martyrdom in Classe, Ravenna's port city. The building itself (FIG. 7-29) is Early Christian in type, a three-aisled basilica with a plan quite similar to that of Theodoric's palace-church in Ravenna. The peculiar design of the apse, which combines a semicircular interior with a polygonal exterior, is typical of Ravenna churches and is probably of Byzantine origin. As usual for the period, the outside of the building is plain and unadorned. (The cylindrical bell tower, or *campanile*, is of a later date.) The interior decoration in this case is confined to mosaics in the triumphal arch and the apse behind it. Of these, the mosaic decorating the semivault above the apse (FIG. 7-30) was probably completed by 549, when the church was dedicated. It shows, against a gold ground, a large, blue medallion with a jeweled cross, (symbol of the transfigured Jesus); this may be the cross Constantine had erected on the hill of Calvary to commemorate the martyrdom of Christ, which we saw at Santa Pudenziana in Rome (FIG. 7-11). Just above, there is the hand of God. On either side, in the clouds, appear the figures of Moses and Elijah, who had appeared before Christ during his transfiguration. Below these two figures are three sheep, the three disciples who accompanied Christ to the foot of the Mount of the Transfiguration. Beneath, in the midst of green fields with trees, flowers, and birds, stands the patron saint of the church, Appollinaris, with uplifted arms, accompanied by twelve sheep, perhaps representing the Christian congregation under the protection of St. Appollinaris and forming, as they march in regular file across the apse, a wonderfully decorative base. On the face of the triumphal arch above, the image of Christ in a medallion and the Signs of the Evangelists are represented in the rainbow-streaked heavens. The twelve lambs are the Twelve Apostles, issuing from the cities of Bethlehem and Jerusalem. The iconographical program is completed by the two palms of Paradise in the narrow spandrels of the arch and by the two archangels below them.

Comparison with the Galla Placidia mosaic (FIG. 7-26) shows how the style and the artist's approach to his subject have changed during the course of a century. In each case, we are looking at a human figure

7-29 Sant' Apollinare in Classe, Ravenna, Italy, c. 533–549.

and some sheep in a landscape. But now, in the mid-sixth century, the artist no longer tries to recreate a segment of the physical world, but tells his story in terms of flat symbols, lined up side by side. All overlapping is carefully avoided in what must have been an intentional effort to omit all reference to the three-dimensional space of the material world and physical reality. Shapes have lost their volume and become flat silhouettes, into which details have been inscribed with lines. The effect is that of an extremely rich, flat, tapestry design that tells its story directly and explicitly without illusionistic devices. The Byzantine style has become the ideal vehicle for the conveyance of the extremely complex symbolism of the fully developed Christian dogma. Our apse mosaic, for example, has much more meaning than first meets the eye. The transfiguration of Christ—here, into the image of the cross—symbolizes his own death, with its redeeming consequences, but also the death of his martyrs (in this case, St. Apollinaris). The lamb, also a symbol of martyrdom, is appropriately used to represent the martyred apostles. The whole scene expands above the altar, where the sacrament of the Eucharist—the miraculous recurrence of the supreme redemptive and transfigurative act—is celebrated. The very altars of Christian churches were, from early times, sanctified by the bones and relics of martyrs. Thus, the mystery and the martydom were joined in one concept: the death of the martyr, in imitation of Christ, is a triumph over death that leads to eternal life. The images above the altar present a kind of inspiring vision to the eyes of believers; the way of the martyr is open to them, and the reward of eternal life is within their reach. The organization of the symbolism and the images is hieratic, and the graphic message must have been delivered to the faithful with overwhelming force. Looming above their eyes is the apparition of a great mystery, ordered in such a

7-30 Apse mosaic from Sant' Apollinare in Classe, *c.* 549.

way as to make perfectly simple and clear the "whole duty of man" seeking salvation. That the anonymous artists, working under the direction of the priests, expended every device of their craft to render the idea explicit is plain enough; the devout could read it as easily as an inscription. The martyr's glorification beneath the cross, inscribed in the starry heavens, presented—in one great tableau—the eternal meaning of Christian life in terms of its deepest mystery.

The Byzantine style, born of the Orientalizing of Hellenistic naturalism, appears in monumental grandeur and ornamental splendor in the mosaics of San Vitale (FIG. 7-31), which, in the high quality they share with the beautiful building itself, symbolize the achievements of the age of the emperor Justinian and are worthy representatives of the First Golden Age of Byzantine art. Begun shortly after Theodoric's death and dedicated by Bishop Maximianus in 547, San

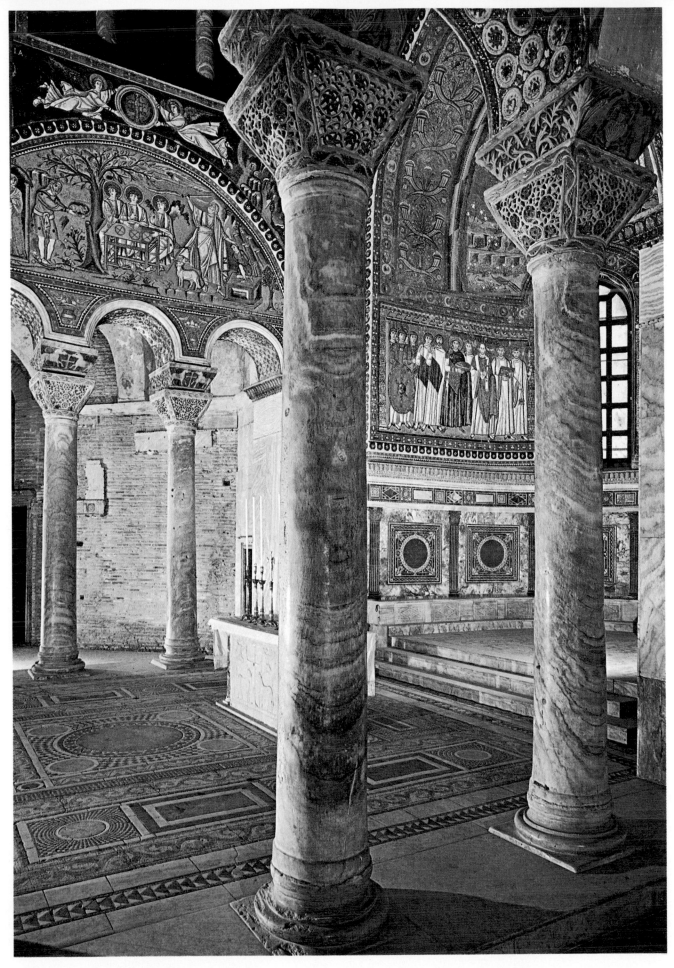

7-31 Sanctuary of San Vitale, Ravenna, 526–547.

Vitale (FIG. 7-32) shares, with the other Ravenna churches, its plain exterior (slightly marred by a Renaissance portal) and the polygonal apse. But beyond these features, it is an entirely different building (FIG. 7-33). The structure is centrally planned and consists of two concentric octagons; the dome-covered inner octagon rises above the surrounding octagon to provide the interior with clerestory lighting. The central space is defined by eight large piers that alternate with curved, columned niches, pushing outward into the surrounding ambulatory and creating, on the plan, an intricate, multifoliate design. These niches effect a close integration between inner and outer spaces that, otherwise, would simply have existed side by side as independent units. A cross-vaulted sanctuary preceding the apse interrupts the ambulatory and provides the plan with some axial stability. This effect is weakened, however, by the unsymmetrical placement of the narthex, the odd angle of which has never been fully explained. (The atrium, which no longer exists, may have paralleled a street that ran in that direction; it has also been suggested that the angle of the narthex might have been intended to force the visitor to reorient himself as he entered the complex arrangement of the main space and, thereby, to experience the transition from the material world outside into the spiritual world of the Church.) The ambulatory (FIG. 7-34) has been provided with a second story, the *gallery*, which was reserved for women and is a typical feature of Byzantine churches. Probably also of Byzantine origin are the so-called *impost blocks*, which have been inserted between the simply profiled, but richly patterned,

ENTRANCE VISIBLE IN FIG. 7-32

7-33 Plan of San Vitale, Ravenna.

column capitals and the springing of the arches (FIG. 7-35). Resembling an inverted, truncated pyramid, these impost blocks appear in most Ravenna churches (compare FIG. 7-27) and may be highly abstracted reflections of the entablature segments in-

7-34 Interior of San Vitale (view facing apse).

serted between column and arch by Late Roman architects (compare FIG. 6-78).

San Vitale's intricate plan and elevation combine to produce an effect of great complexity. Walking through the building, one is struck by the rich diversity of ever-changing perspectives. Arches looping over arches, curving and flattened spaces, and shapes of wall and vault seem to change constantly

7-35 Capital from San Vitale.

with the viewer's position. Light filtered through alabaster-paned windows plays over the glittering mosaics and glowing marbles that cover the building's complex surfaces, producing an effect of sumptuousness that is not Western but Oriental. And, indeed, the inspiration for this design is to be found in Byzantium, rather than Rome. In Constantinople, some 10 years before the completion of San Vitale at Ravenna, a church dedicated to the saints Sergius and Bacchus appears to be a rough preparatory sketch for the later church, in which the suggestions of the earlier plan may be seen developed to their full potential.

Slightly earlier than those of Sant' Apollinare in Classe, but of higher quality, the mosaics that decorate the sanctuary of San Vitale, like the building itself, must be regarded as one of the climactic achievements of Byzantine art. Completed less than a decade after the surrender of Ravenna by the Goths, the decorations of apse and forechoir proclaim the triumph of Justinian and of the Orthodox faith. The multiple panels of the sanctuary form a unified composition, a theme of which is the holy ratification of the emperor's right to the whole western empire, of which Ravenna was now the principal city. The apse mosaics are portrait groups representing Justinian on one wall (FIG. 7-36) and his empress, Theodora, on the other (FIG. 7-37). The monarchs are accompanied by their retinues in a depiction of the offertory procession (the part of the liturgy when the bread and wine of the Eucharist are brought forward and presented). Justinian, represented as a priest–king, carries a vessel containing the bread, and Theodora carries the golden cup with the wine. Images and symbols covering the entire sanctuary express the single idea of man's redemption by Christ and the reenactment of it in the Eucharist. Moses, Melchizedek, Abraham, and Abel are represented as prefigurations of Christ and also as priestly leaders of the faithful, whose offerings to God were declared acceptable to Heaven. In the representation of the Second Coming (FIG. 7-38), Christ, seated on the orb of the world, with the four rivers of Paradise beneath him and rainbow-hued clouds above, extends a golden wreath of victory to Vitalis, the patron saint of the church, who is introduced by an angel. At Christ's left, another angel introduces Bishop Ecclesius, in whose time the foundations of the church were laid and who carries a model of it. The arrangement recalls Christ's prophecy of the last days of the world: "And then shall they see the Son of man coming in the clouds with great power and glory. And then shall he send his angels, and shall gather together his elect from the four winds, from the uttermost part of heaven" (Mark 13:26–27). It appears that Justinian's offering is acceptable, for the wreath extended to St. Vitalis is also extended to him where he stands in a dependent

7-36 *Justinian and Attendants,* apse mosaic from San Vitale, *c.* 547.

7-37 *Theodora and Attendants,* apse mosaic from San Vitale, *c.* 547.

7-38 *Christ Between Angels and Saints (The Second Coming),* apse mosaic from San Vitale, *c.* 547.

mosaic (FIGS. 7-31, and 7-36). Thus, his rule is confirmed and sanctified by these rites, in which—as is so typical of such expressions of the Byzantine imperial ideal—the political and the religious are one:

> In the atmosphere of Byzantium, the Christian emperor appeared as a Christ-like high priest and . . . the principles of his administration seemed to be symbolized in the liturgical rite. In the offertory procession, he appeared like the priest–king Melchizedek, ''bringing forth bread and wine'' on behalf of his people, to propitiate God.*

The laws of the Church and the laws of the state, united in the laws of God, are manifest in the person of the emperor and in his God-given right. The pagan

*Otto von Simson, *Sacred Fortress: Byzantine Art and Statecraft in Ravenna* (Chicago: University of Chicago Press, 1948), p. 35.

emperors had been deified; it could not have been difficult, given that tradition, to accept the deification of the Christian emperor. Justinian is distinguished from his dignitaries not only by his wearing of the Imperial purple but also by his halo—a device emanating from ancient Persia and originally signifying the descent of the honored one from the sun and, hence, his god-like origin and status.

The etiquette and protocol of the imperial court fuse here with the ritual of the liturgy of the Church (see FIG. 7-36). The positions of the figures are all-important; they express the formula of precedence and the orders of rank. Justinian is exactly at center. At his left, is Bishop Maximianus, the architect of his ecclesiastical–political policy and the one responsible for the completion of San Vitale and its consecration in 547. The bishop's importance is stressed by the

7-39 *Justinian and Maximianus* (detail of FIG. 7-36).

label bearing his name, the only identifying inscription in the composition. Between Justinian and Maximianus is Julius Argentarius, the principal benefactor of the church. The figures are in three groups: the emperor and his staff (standing for the Imperial administration); the clergy; and the army, who bear a shield with the *chi–rho* monogram seen on the sarcophagus of Archbishop Theodore (FIG. 7-22). Each group has a leader, one of whose feet precedes (by overlapping) the feet of those who follow. There is a curious ambiguity in the positions of Justinian and Maximianus; although the emperor appears to be slightly behind the bishop, the sacred vessel he carries overlaps the bishop's arm. Thus, symbolized by place and gesture, the imperial and churchly powers are in balance. The paten (the plate holding the bread in the Eucharist) carried by Justinian, the cross car-

ried by Maximianus, and the book and censer carried by his attendant clerics produce a movement that strikingly modifies the rigid formality. There is no indication of a background; the observer is expected to understand the procession as taking place in this very sanctuary, where the emperor will appear forever as participant in the sacred rites and as proprietor of this royal church, the very symbol of his rule of the western empire. The portraits of the empress Theodora and her entourage (FIG. 7-37), on the other hand, are represented within a definite architecture, perhaps the narthex of San Vitale. The empress stands in state beneath an imperial canopy, waiting to follow the emperor's procession and to pass through the curtained doorway into which she is beckoned by an attendant. The fact that she is outside the sanctuary and only about to proceed attests that, in the ceremonial protocol, her rank is not quite equal to that of her consort—even though the representation of the Three Magi on the border of her robe recalls their offerings to the infant Christ and makes an allusive connection between Theodora and the Virgin Mary.

The figure style shows the maturing of conventions of representation that date back to Dura-Europos and earlier. Tall, spare, angular, and elegant, the figures have lost the rather squat proportions characteristic of much Early Christian work. The gorgeous draperies fall straight, stiff, and thin from the narrow shoulders; the organic body has dematerialized, and, except for the heads, we see a procession of solemn spirits, gliding noiselessly in the presence of the sacrament. Byzantine style will preserve this hieratic mood for centuries, no matter how many individual variations occur within its conventions.

We can hardly talk of Byzantine art without using the term "hieratic." Christianity, originating as a mystery cult, kept mystery as its center (one might say that the priest became a specialist in mystery). The priestly supernaturalism that disparages matter and material values prevails throughout the Christian Middle Ages, especially in Orthodox Byzantium. It is that hieratic supernaturalism that determines the look of Byzantine figurative art—an art without solid bodies or cast shadows, with blank, golden spaces, with the perspective of Paradise, which is nowhere and everywhere.

The portraits in San Vitale are individualized, despite the prevailing formality (FIG. 7-39). However, this is true only of the principals; the lesser personages on the outskirts of the groups are treated more uniformly. There can be little doubt that, in these portrait groups memorializing the dedicatory ceremony, the artists intended to create close likenesses of the central characters—the emperor and empress and the high officials of Church and state. Since pagan times, the image of the deified emperor in public and sacred places has been tantamount to his actual presence, for the image and the reality were taken to be essentially one. The setting up of the image of the emperor was "an act which furnished the occasion for the declaration of submission on the part of the people";* those who gazed on the images must have known that they owed them absolute reverence: "In these awe-inspiring images, the sovereigns, though far away in Byzantium, had actually set foot on the soil of Italy."†

Thus, the symbol, the image, and what they represent are most often one and the same. Just as the image of Justinian or Theodora or a saint is venerated

as if it were the person, so are a cross, relics, and mementos. Even vessels associated with holy rites came to be venerated as real presences of sacred powers that can cure not only spiritually but also physically. To the believer, this communion of reality between objects and what they represent is logical enough; if the body of Christ is reproducible through the ritual of the Eucharist, then representations of all holy things ought to be just as real as what they represent. Symbols, images, narratives, sacramental objects—the furniture and accessories of ritual—can all be venerable and spiritually potent in themselves; this is like the magic of the Paleolithic caves, in which the hunter–artists believed they summoned and controlled their animal quarry by the miracle of representation.

In Ravenna, a powerful statecraft under the management of Justinian and Maximianus had been able to combine, in a group of monuments, the full force of Christian belief and political authority. In the process, a model of religious art, sacramental and magical in its power, was created that could work in the service both of the Church and the sanctified imperial state. This model, image, or ideal unity of the spiritual and temporal would strongly influence the Middle Ages in both the east and the west. The hieratic style of Byzantium, matured and exemplified in Ravenna, will remain both the standard and the point of departure for the content and form of the art of the Middle Ages.

Only slightly later than the Ravenna mosaics, the great apse mosaic in the church of the monastery of St. Catherine on Mt. Sinai (on the Sinai peninsula, now under Egyptian control) shows striking divergences from the Ravenna style, although both are likely to have emanated from Justinian's city, Constantinople. Justinian built the fortress monastery of St. Catherine between 548 and 565, which gives us the date of the mosaic; it is unlikely that it could have been done much later than the year of the completion of the church building. In the mosaic (FIG. 7-40), *The Transfiguration of Jesus* (Mark 9:2–8), Jesus appears in a deep blue mandorla, or "glory," flanked by Elijah and Moses, with the disciples John, Peter, and James at his feet; the whole scene is framed by portraits of saints in medallions. The artist has stressed the intense whiteness of Jesus' transfigured, spiritualized figure, from which rays stream down on the disciples. The stately figures of Elijah and Moses and the static frontality of Jesus set off the frantic terror and astonishment of the gesticulating disciples in a contrast of the eternal composure of heavenly beings with the distraught responses of the earthbound. All traces of landscape or architectural setting have been swept away and replaced by a depthless field of gold, on which the figures and their labels are fixed in iso-

---

*Otto von Simson, *Sacred Fortress: Byzantine Art and Statecraft in Ravenna* (Chicago: University of Chicago Press, 1948), p. 28.
†Ibid., p. 39.

7-40 *The Transfiguration of Jesus*, apse mosaic from the Church of the Monastery of St. Catherine, Mount Sinai, *c.* 560.

lation from one another. The gold field is bounded at its base by a rainbow band of colors graduating from yellow to blue, a ground line to which the figures are ambiguously related—sometimes placed behind it; sometimes overlapping it. The bodies cast no shadows even though supernatural light streams over them. We are in the world of mystical vision, where all substance that might suggest the passage of time or motion through physical space is subtracted, so that the eternal and motionless world of religious truth can be contemplated by the devout.

The formal, hieratic style of Ravenna, appropriate to a court church, and the cultic, visionary style of Mt. Sinai, appropriate to a monastery church, although standing in obvious contrast, mark two main kinds of expression in Byzantine art and face toward their common source—Justinian's Constantinople.

Constantinople

Ravenna—the successor to Rome as imperial capital in Italy and then, as the so-called exarchate, the beachhead of Byzantium in the Germanized west—

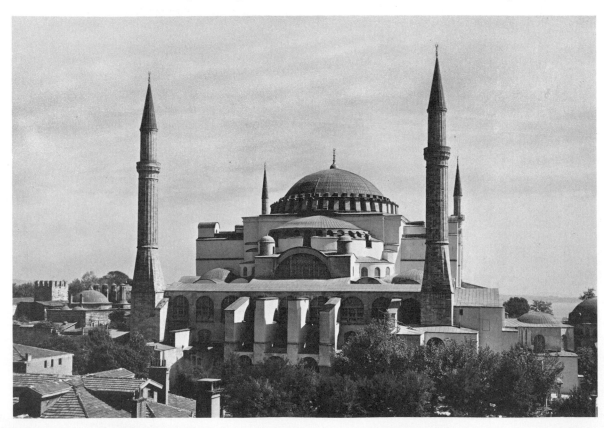

7-41 Anthemius of Tralles and Isidorus of Miletus, Hagia Sophia, Constantinople (Istanbul, Turkey), 532–537 (view from the northwest).

finally passed from Byzantine control. The images of Justinian and Theodora in San Vitale, proclaiming that the empire was still whole, were powerless to make it so. But the east remained firmly in the hands of successions of emperors for a thousand years; Constantinople became the magnificent citadel of Byzantine civilization, and its influence streamed to all points of the compass. At the time that the Imperial presence in Ravenna was being symbolized in architecture and art, the vast church of Santa Sophia, or more properly Hagia Sophia, Church of the Holy Wisdom (FIGS. 7-41, 7-42, 7-43, 7-44), was being built for Justinian in Constantinople by the architects ANTHEMIUS OF TRALLES and ISIDORUS OF MILETUS between 532 and 537. Even today, the church remains one of the supreme achievements in the history of world architecture. Its dimensions alone, formidable for any structure not made of steel, attract our attention. In plan, it is about 270 feet long and 240 feet wide; the dome is 108 feet in diameter, and its crown rises some 180 feet above the pavement. In scale, Hagia Sophia rivals the great buildings we have seen

7-42 Interior of Hagia Sophia. (Engraving from *Aya Sophia* by CHEVALIER FOSSATI, London, 1852.)

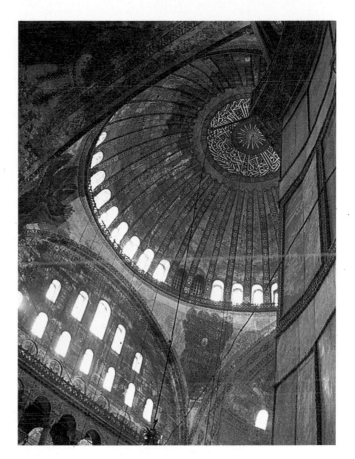

7-43 Vaults of Hagia Sophia.

in pagan and Christian Rome: the Pantheon, the Baths of Caracalla, the Basilica of Constantine. In exterior view, the great dome dominates the structure; but the external aspects of the building are much changed from their original appearance—by huge buttresses added to the original design and by four towering Turkish minarets added after the Ottoman conquest of 1453, when Hagia Sophia became an Islamic mosque. The building was secularized in the twentieth century and is now a museum.

The characteristic Byzantine plainness and unpretentiousness of exterior (which, in this case, also disguise the great scale), scarcely prepare us for the interior of the building (FIG. 7-42). One encounters first the huge narthex, with its many entrances, and then the open, tremendous space above, in which the soaring, canopy-like dome rides on a halo of light provided by windows in the dome's base. The impression made on the people of the time—an impression not lost on us—is carried in the words of the poet Paulus, an usher at the court of Justinian:

About the center of the church, by the eastern and western half-circles, stand four mighty piers of stone, and from them spring great arches like the bow of Iris, four in all; and, as they rise slowly in the air, each separates from the other . . . and the spaces between

7-44 Section (*top*) and plan (*bottom*) of Hagia Sophia Constantinople (Istanbul). (After drawings by Van Nice and Antoniades.)

0 25 50 75 100 FEET
0 10 20 30 METERS

A   A'

------- Not extant

■ Theodosian
□ Justinian intact
▨ " speculative
▤ " foundation remains
▨ " standing remains

BYZANTINE

▨ Later additions
▨ Turkish additions
— · — Reconstruction

0 25 50 75 100 FEET
0 10 20 30 METERS

BUTTRESS

BUTTRESS

MINARET

BAPTISTRY

STAIRWELL

CLOCK TOWER

MINARET

NARTHEX

OUTER NARTHEX

BUTTRESSES

A'

THEODOSIAN FORECOURT

ATRIUM

A

SACRISTY

MINARET

STAIRWELL

BUTTRESS

BUTTRESS

STAIRWELL

MINARET

BUTTRESS

N

them are filled with wondrous skill, for curved walls touch the arches on either side and spread over until they all unite above them. . . . The base of the dome is strongly fixed upon the great arches . . . while above, the dome covers the church like the radiant heavens. . . . Who shall describe the fields of marble gathered on the pavement and lofty walls of the church? Fresh green from Carystus, and many-colored Phrygian stone of rose and white, or deep red and silver; porphyry powdered with bright spots; emerald-green from Sparta, and Iassian marble with waving veins of blood-red and white; streaked red stone from Lydia, and crocus-colored marble from the hills of the Moors, and Celtic stone, like milk poured out on glittering black; the precious onyx like as if gold were shining through it, and the fresh green from the land of Atrax, in mingled contrast of shining surfaces. . . .*

The dome rests on four *pendentives*. In pendentive construction (FIG. 7-47)—developed, apparently after many years of experiment, by builders in the Near East and *the* contribution of Byzantium to architectural engineering—a dome rests on what is, in effect, a second and larger dome, from which have been omitted the top portion and four segments around the rim—the latter forming four arches, the planes of which bound a square. By transferring the weight to piers, rather than to the wall itself, pendentive construction makes possible a lofty, unobstructed interior space, as is particularly evident in Hagia Sophia. In our view of the interior (FIG. 7-42), the arches that bound two of the great pendentives supporting the central dome can be seen converging on their massive piers. The domes of earlier, central-plan buildings, like the Pantheon, Santa Costanza, or even San Vitale, spring from the circular or polygonal bases of a continuous wall or arcade. The pendentive system is a dynamic solution to the problem of setting a round dome over a square or a rectangle, making a union of the central and the long basilican structures possible. Hagia Sophia, in its successful fusion of these two architectural types, becomes a domed basilica—a uniquely successful conclusion to several centuries of experiment in Christian church architecture. However, the thrusts of its pendentive construction make other elements necessary: huge wall piers to the north and south, and, to the east and west, half-domes, whose thrusts descend, in turn, into still smaller domes (FIG. 7-44), covering columned niches that give a curving flow to the design, reminiscent of San Vitale (see FIG. 7-34). And, as in San Vitale, the wandering space, the diverse vistas, and the screen-like, ornamented surfaces all mask the lines of structure. The arcades of the nave and galleries have no real structural function; like the walls they pierce, they are only part of a fragile "fill" between the great piers. Structurally, although Hagia Sophia may seem Roman in its great scale and majesty, it does not have Roman organization of its masses. The very fact that what appears to be wall in Hagia Sophia is actually a concealed (and barely adequate) pier indicates that Roman monumentality was sought as an *effect* and not derived directly from Roman building principles.

Visitors to Hagia Sophia have been struck by the quality of light within the church and the effect it has on the human spirit. The 40 windows at the base of the dome (FIG. 7-43) create the peculiar illusion that the dome is resting on the light that floods through them; an observer of the time thought that it looked as if the dome were suspended by a "gold chain from Heaven." Procopius, the historian of the age of Justinian, wrote: "One would declare that the place were not illuminated from the outside by the sun, but that the radiance originated from within, such is the abundance of light which is shed about this shrine." Paulus observed: "the vaulting is covered over with many little squares of gold, from which the rays stream down and strike the eyes so that men can scarcely bear to look." Thus, we have a vastness of space shot-through with light and a central dome that *appears* to be supported by the light it admits. Light is the mystic element—light that glitters in the mosaics, that shines forth from the marbles, that pervades and defines spaces that, in themselves, seem to escape definition. Light becomes the agent that seems to dissolve material substance and transform it into an abstract, spiritual vision. At Hagia Sophia, the intricate logic of Greek theology, the ambitious scale of Rome, the vaulting tradition of the Near East, and the mysticism of Eastern Christianity combine to create a monument that is at once a summation of antiquity and a positive assertion of the triumph of Christian faith.

Hagia Sophia was a unique hybrid, uniting the western basilican and the eastern central plans into a design without successors. After it, the east forsook the long church for a thousand years or more to develop the central plan, while the basilican plan was consciously being revived in the west in Carolingian times.

LATER BYZANTINE ART

Between the tenth and the twelfth centuries, there occurred, under the auspices of the Macedonian dynasty, what has been called the Second Flowering or Second Byzantine Golden Age, during which Byzantine culture reencountered its Hellenistic sources and accommodated them to the styles inherited from the Age of Justinian, the time of the *First* Flowering.

*In W.R. Lethaby, "Santa Sophia, Constantinople," *Architectural Review* (April 1905), p. 12.

7-45 Monastery churches at Hosios Loukas, Phocis, Greece: Church of the Katholikon, *c.* 1020 (*left*), and Church of the Theotokos, *c.* 1040 (*right*). (View from the east.)

7-46 Plans of the Church of the Katholikon (*bottom*) and the Church of the Theotokos (*top*), Hosios Loukas.

FORMER COURT

FEET
0   10   20   30

0   3   6   9
METERS

Upper level
Closed with masonry

Greece, one can see the form of a domed cross with four equal-length, vaulted cross arms (the "Greek Cross"). Around this unit, and by the duplication of it, Byzantine architectural design developed bewilderingly involved spaces. In the adjacent, larger Church of the Katholikon (FIGS. 7-45 and 7-46), a dome is placed over an octagon inscribed within a square; the octagon is formed by *squinches*—arches, corbeling, or lintels that bridge the corners of the square (FIG. 7-47). This arrangement represents a subtle extension of the older designs, such as Santa Costanza's circular plan (FIG. 7-8), San Vitale's octagonal plan (FIG. 7-33), and Hagia Sophia's dome on pendentives rising from a square (FIG. 7-44). The complex core of the Church of the Katholikon lies

7-47 Domes on pendentives (*left*) and squinches (*right*).

Architecture

In architecture, a brilliant series of variations on the domed central theme began to appear. From the exterior, the typical later Byzantine church building is a domed cube, with the dome rising above the square on a kind of cylinder or drum. (Less often, some other rectangular form, with something other than a square as its base, was used.) The churches are small, vertical, high-shouldered, and, unlike earlier Byzantine buildings, have exterior wall surfaces with ornament in relief. In the Church of the Theotokos (FIGS. 7-45 and 7-46), built about 1040 at Hosios Loukas in

Pendentives   Squinches

7-48 Interior of the Church of the Katholikon (view facing east).

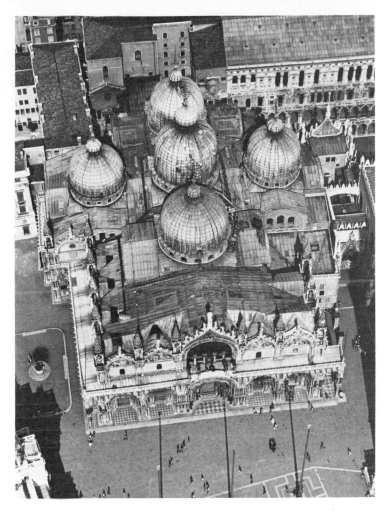

7-49 Aerial view of St. Mark's, Venice, Italy, begun 1063.

within two rectangles, the outermost forming the exterior walls. Thus, in plan, from the center out, a circle–octagon–square–oblong series exhibits an intricate interrelationship that is at once complex and unified.

The interior elevation of the Church of the Katholikon (FIG. 7-48) reflects its involved plan. Like earlier Byzantine buildings, the church creates a mystery out of space, surface, and light and dark. High and narrow, it forces our gaze to rise and revolve: "The overall spatial effect is overwhelmingly beautiful in its complex interplay of higher and lower elements, of core and ancillary spaces, of clear, dim, and dark zones of lighting."* Thus, the aim of Middle and Late Byzantine architecture seems to be the creation of complex interior spaces that issue into multiple domes in the upper levels; these, in exterior view, produce spectacular combinations of round forms that shifting perspectives develop dramatically. The splendid Church of Holy Apostles, built in the time of Justinian and now no longer in existence, is reflected in plan in St. Mark's in Venice, which reproduces it (FIGS. 7-49, 7-50, 7-51). The original structure of St. Mark's, dating from the eleventh century, is dis-

*Richard Krautheimer, *Early Christian and Byzantine Architecture* (Baltimore: Penguin, 1965), p. 244.

guised on its lower levels by Romanesque and Gothic additions. But in plan, or from an aerial view, the domes, grouped along a cross of equal arms (the Greek Cross again), make the Byzantine origins of St.

7-50 Plan of St. Mark's, Venice. (After Sir Banister Fletcher.)

The Tetrarchs of San Marco (Fig. 6-88)

▨▨▨ Additions to original structure

7-51 Interior of St. Mark's (view facing east).

Mark's evident at once. The inner masonry shells are covered with swelling, wooden, helmet-like forms sheathed in gilded copper; these forms not only protect the inner domes, but also make an exuberant composition appropriate to this great community church of the proud Venetian republic. Venice was—like Ravenna, some 80 miles to the south—under strong Byzantine influence, despite the independence it had won early in the Middle Ages and preserved for centuries. The interior of St. Mark's is, like its plan, Byzantine in effect, although its great Justinianic scale and intricate syncopation of domed bays are modified slightly by western Romanesque elements. But, its light effects and its rich cycles of mosaics are entirely Byzantine (FIGS. 7-58 and 7-59).

Byzantine influence was wide-ranging—not only in Italy, but also in the Slavic lands and in the regions of the east into which Islam had expanded. Byzantium brought its script, its religion, and much of its culture to Russia. The "holy" Russia before the revolution of 1917 was largely Byzantine in its traditions and, one might even say, in its mood. Russian architecture, magnificently developed in the Middle Ages, is a brilliant, provincial variation on Byzantine themes.

The ecclesiastical architecture of medieval Russia was, at first, strongly under the influence of Constantinople, if not actually produced by Greeks. The church of St. Dmitri at Vladimir (FIG. 7-52) is built on the typical plan of a square enclosing a Greek cross and crowned with a single dome on a high drum. The church is of stone—a rare building material in Russia, where brick, stucco, and wood are more usual. Wall spaces, which have few openings, are decorated here with moldings. Some of these, rising unbroken from the ground to the roof, divide the wall into panels; others, much shorter, form blind arcadings. The surface within the arcadings is elaborately carved in low reliefs that are peculiarly well-adapted to stone and are close, in subject matter and form, to Sassanian (Persian) and other western Asiatic carvings. The whole composition of St. Dmitri is a masterpiece of simplicity and compactness, with a classic, monumental dignity. Later structures will develop a colorful complexity of plan and elevation. In Moscow, within the walls of the Kremlin, stands the Cathedral of the Annunciation (FIG. 7-53), which dates from the later fifteenth century. The domed-cross plan of Byzantium here receives a most spirited expansion. The cathedral is built on a square plan with eastern apses;

7-52　St. Dmitri at Vladimir, Soviet Union, 1194–1197.

7-53　Cathedral of the Annunciation, Moscow, 1482–1490.

its helmet-like domes, now greatly multiplied, rise in a kind of triumphant crescendo to the climax of the central unit, which is crowned with the typical Russian bulbous "onion" or "beet" dome. The bright metal caps, peaked with crosses like miniature masts, reflect the moody Russian skies and proclaim, as if in architectural polyphony, the glory of the Orthodox faith.

Painting and Sculpture

Although architecture enjoyed a fairly continuous development throughout the Byzantine period, the representational arts (painting and sculpture) suffered a severe setback during the eighth and ninth centuries, when they became the subject of a violent controversy. The Iconoclastic Controversy over the propriety of religious imagery, which raged for more than 100 years (730–843), began with the temporary victory of the image-destroyers (*iconoclasts*), who interpreted the biblical ban against graven images literally. In 730, an imperial edict banned religious imagery throughout the Byzantine empire, and artists were either forced to migrate to the west, where the edict could not be enforced, or, if they chose to remain in Byzantium, to turn their talents to secular subject matter, which was not affected by the ban.

Migrant Byzantine painters worked in Italy in a classicizing style and with religious subject matter. Although little remains of their work, examples can be found in Rome—especially in Santa Maria Antiqua—where, in the eighth century, a succession of Greek popes provided an encouraging atmosphere for the forbidden culture and art of Iconoclastic Byzantium. At Castelseprio in northern Italy, remarkable murals of uncertain date, but probably from the late seventh or early eighth century (FIG. 7-54), are, without doubt, the art of a gifted Byzantine painter whose deft hand and fluent, sweeping style show the enduring illusionistic classicism born in Hellenistic times and destined to recur often in the centuries after the First Golden Age of Byzantine art. This naturalistic manner could exist side by side with the austere and abstract style seen at Ravenna, or could merge with it. When the ban against religious images was lifted in 843 and religious painting was again encouraged in Byzantium, a style of painting emerged that was a subtle blend of the pictorial, classicizing Hellenistic and the later, more abstract and formalistic Byzantine style.

An eleventh-century crucifixion scene on the wall of the monastery church at Daphne in Greece (FIG. 7-55) shows the simplicity, dignity, and grace of classicism fully assimilated by the Byzantine artist into a perfect synthesis with Byzantine piety and pathos. Christ is represented on the cross, flanked by the Vir-

7-54 *The Angel Appearing to Joseph,* detail of wall painting, Santa Maria de Castelseprio, Castelseprio, Italy, early eighth century (?).

gin and St. John. A skull at the foot of the cross indicates Golgotha, the "place of skulls." Nothing is needed to complete the tableau. In quiet sorrow and resignation, the Virgin and St. John point to Christ as if to indicate the meaning of the cross. Symmetry and closed space combine to produce an effect of the motionless and unchanging aspect of the deepest mystery of the Christian religion; the timeless presence is,

as it were, beheld in unbroken silence. The picture is not a narrative of the historical event of the Crucifixion, but a devotional object, a thing sacramental in itself, to be viewed by the monks in silent contemplation of the mystery of the Sacrifice. Although elongated, these figures from the Second Golden Age of Byzantine art (tenth and eleventh centuries) have regained their organic structure to a surprising degree, particularly compared to figures from the Justinian period (compare FIGS. 7-36 and 7-37). The style is a masterful adaptation of classical, statuesque qualities to the linear Byzantine style.

Variations of Byzantine style appeared widely in the twelfth century throughout the Balkan world (Yugoslavia, Bulgaria, Romania) and in Venice, South Italy, and Sicily, where Mediterranean powers were eager to adopt Byzantine art and culture. At Nerezi in Macedonia (Yugoslavia), paintings of astonishing emotional power have been found that contrast dramatically with the almost stern formalism and hieraticism of the Daphne mosaic. The *Lamentation Over the Dead Christ* (FIG. 7-56), from the second half of the twelfth century, is a tableau of passionate grief, the friends of Christ captured in attitudes, expressions, and gestures of quite human bereavement. The artist has striven above all to make his realization of the theme utterly convincing. His stirring staging of the subject points forward to the art of thirteenth-century (Gothic) Italy, when the reception of this mode of emotional realism would carry all before it into the Italian "proto-Renaissance" and the art of Giotto (compare FIG. 15-14).

In the art of the Second Byzantine Golden Age, particularly in its later phase, there is a kind of dialogue between the formal, symbolic, hieratic style of

7-55 *The Crucifixion,* mosaic from the monastery church in Daphne, Greece, eleventh century.

the Daphne mosaic and the intense, emotional, active style of the Nerezi murals—the choice of alternative depending on site and on ecclesiastical, political, and artistic intentions. An example of the hieratic style accommodated to a monumental site is the apse mosaic of the royal church of Monreale in Sicily (FIG. 7-57), part of a total program of ecclesiastical–artistic aggrandizement of and by Roger, the great Norman king of Sicily, who imported the splendor of Byzantium to glorify his reign. Christ, as "Pantocrator," judge of the world, looms menacingly in the vault of the apse—a colossal image of kingly power and authority, whether spiritual or temporal. (The king would have believed that his own sovereign power came directly from the divine.) Below Christ in rank and dignity, the enthroned Virgin and saints are ranged symmetrically. Here, Byzantine formality manifests the very image of heavenly and earthly power: the former, explicitly; the latter, by association. From Sicily, from Venice, from the Byzantine Balkans, the art of Byzantium found its way into the West, stimulating and influencing the art of the periods we call Romanesque and Gothic.

Recent cleaning and restoration on a grand scale have returned the mosaics of the church of St. Mark's in Venice (FIG. 7-51) to their original splendor (FIGS. 7-58 and 7-59). It is now possible to experience, in all its iconographic complexity, the awe-inspiring decorative program of a great Byzantine church and to appreciate to the fullest the radiance of mosaic (some 40,000 square feet of it!) as it covers, like a gold-brocaded and figured fabric, all architectural surfaces—walls, arches, vaults, and domes. Looking up into the central dome (FIG. 7-58), 80 feet above the floor and 42 feet in diameter, one sees Christ, seated on the rainbow (the symbol of reconciliation) and supported by flying angels, ascending into the starry heavens (Acts 1:9–11). On a lower level, the miracle is witnessed by

the disciples of Christ, the Virgin Mary, and two angels (the "two men in white" of the biblical account). Still lower, along the base of the dome, are allegorical figures representing the Theological Virtues (Faith, Hope, and Charity), the Cardinal Virtues (Prudence,

7-57 *The Pantocrator, with the Virgin, Angels, and Saints,* apse mosaic from the royal church of Monreale, Sicily, late twelfth century.

7-58 *The Passion, Resurrection, and Ascension of Christ*, mosaics in vault and central dome, St. Mark's, Venice, late twelfth century.

7-59 *Joseph in Egypt*, mosaic in the dome of the narthex, St. Mark's, Venice, 1255–1260.

Justice, Temperance, and Fortitude), and the Beatitudes. The Four Evangelists (two barely discernible in this perspective) write their gospels, which attest to the truth of the event. Along the curving face of the great arch are scenes from the Crucifixion and Resurrection of Christ. On these page-like, golden surfaces, the figures ("sages standing in God's holy fire"), levitating and insubstantial, are drawn with a flowing, calligraphic line; they project from their flat field no more than the letters of the elegant Latin script that captions them. There is nothing here of the world of matter, of solids, of light and shade, of perspective space; the trees are ornamental standards, furniture of Paradise. We have before us the open book of the heavenly order, its image as solemn and hieratic as the sacred text that reveals it in words. Here, in hierarchical placement, the chief mysteries and narratives of the Christian Church are arrayed to present the supernatural and eternal world to which its dogma refers.

The New Testament is set forth within the church proper. Outside, in the shallow domes of the narthex, the Old Testament is recounted—in particular, the Book of Genesis, which tells the story of the creation and fall of man. One of the domes (FIG. 7-59) depicts the sojourn of *Joseph in Egypt* (Genesis 39, 40, 41, 42): the affair of Potiphar's wife, Joseph imprisoned, his interpretation of the dreams of Pharaoh and the baker. The episodes, with their captions, are arranged in a circle following the curve of the dome, their radial axes converging to an exquisite, star-studded medallion resembling the great rose windows of contemporaneous cathedrals in Gothic France (page 310). The figures, like those of the interior of the church, are rendered in sharp, precise line on a golden ground, with all the clarity and readability of the script that describes them. Again, we have the perfect harmony of architectural surface, figural image, and lettered inscription in a scintillating, rainbow-colored aureole. The mosaicists' masterly control of their medium, their consummate skill in design, their faultless geometric procedure, their subtle color harmonies, their deft, clear and economical draftsmanship make for a perfection almost without parallel in Byzantine art. The great mosaic cycles of St. Mark's would, in themselves, proclaim an artistic "golden age." In them, we find the culmination and confluence of both the hieratic and narrative stylistic currents begun at Santa Maria Maggiore in Rome and at St. George in Thessaloniki (FIGS. 7-12 and 7-13) some eight centuries before.

From the last great period, the Third Golden Age of Byzantine art (thirteenth to late fourteenth century), we have a late example of vigorous, expressive action, related to the drama of the Nerezi painting but with a heightened naturalism that parallels developments in contemporaneous Italian art, and may even lead them in sophistication. A recently uncovered fresco in the vault of a side chapel of the Mosque of the Ka'riye in Istanbul (completed about 1320 and originally the Church of the Blessed Savior of the Chora) represents, although inscribed *Anastasis* ("Resurrection"), *The Harrowing of Hell* (FIG. 7-60). Christ, after his death on the cross, descends into Hell, tramples Satan, and rescues Adam and Eve, while other worthies of the Old Testament stand by awaiting their liberation. The movement of the central figures is highly dramatic. The white-robed, aure-

ole-surrounded figure of Christ is laden with energy as he literally tears the parents of mankind from their tombs. The dynamic postures of the figures are reinforced by swirling draperies, agitated by the winds of a supramaterial force. But we also notice that, here and there, the carefully and precisely drawn drapery folds tend to take on a life of their own, as the Late Byzantine artist often showed delight in creating linear patterns for their own sake. These abstract, decorative, linear patterns tend to obscure the fact that, in its late stages, Byzantine art became increasingly realistic.

The characteristics of Byzantine painting were developed in large-scale mural decorations, but it was through miniatures in manuscripts and small panel paintings, more popularly known as *icons,* that the elements of the style were spread abroad. A fine example of the former is a page from a book of the Psalms of David, the so-called *Paris Psalter* (FIG. 7-61), which reasserts the artistic values of the Classical past with astonishing authority. It is believed to date from the early tenth century—a time of enthusiastic and careful study of the language of ancient Greece as well as its literature, a time when the classics were regarded with humanistic reverence. It was only natural that, in art, inspiration should be drawn once again from the Hellenistic naturalism of the pre-Christian Mediterranean world, especially Alexandria. David, the psalmist, is seated with his harp in a flowering, Arcadian landscape recalling those of Pompeian murals. He is accompanied by an allegorical figure of Melody and is surrounded by sheep, goats, and his faithful dog. Echo ("Spring"?) peers from behind a trophied column, and a reclining male

7-61 *David Composing the Psalms*, page from the so-called *Paris Psalter, c.* 960. Approx. 15″ × 11″. Bibliothèque Nationale, Paris.

figure points to an inscription that identifies him as representing the mountains of Bethlehem. These allegorical figures do not appear in the Bible; they are the stock population of Alexandrian and Pompeian landscape. Apparently, the artist had before him a work from Late Antiquity or perhaps earlier, which he partly translated into a Byzantine pictorial idiom. In the figure of Melody, we find some incongruity between the earlier and later styles. Her pose, head, and torso are quite Hellenistic, as is the light, impressionistic touch of the brush, but the drapery enwrapping the legs is a pattern of hard line. Byzantine illuminations like this will exert their influence again and again on Western painting in the Romanesque and Early Gothic periods.

The devotional panel bearing the portrait of a saint, the icon, was a characteristic type of Byzantine painting. The icon's origins, of great antiquity, derive from the kind of painted Roman portrait we have already seen in the Faiyum type (FIG. 6-41) and the mosaic portrait medallions conspicuous in Byzantine churches, like that of Christ in the triumphal arch of Sant' Apollinare in Classe (FIG. 7-30). A famous example of the icon is *The Vladimir Madonna* (FIG. 7-62), which was probably painted by an artist in Byzantium in the twelfth century, exported to Vladimir, and then taken to Moscow in 1395 to protect that city from the Mongols. As these icons were quickly blackened by incense and smoke from the devotional candles that burned before them, they were frequently repainted, often by inferior artists. In our panel, only the faces show the original surface, but the painting retains its Byzantine characteristics in the typical configuration of the Madonna's face, with its long, straight nose and tiny mouth, and in the decorative sweep of the unbroken contour that encloses the two figures and creates a flat silhouette against a golden background. The deep pathos of the Madonna's expression shows an interest in depicting emotion that would flow into the art of Russia and the West.

7-62 *The Vladimir Madonna,* twelfth century. Painted wood, original panel approx. 30½″ × 21″. State Historical Museum, Moscow.

In Russia, icon painting flourished for centuries, extending the life of the style well beyond the collapse of the Byzantine empire in 1453. The development of the *iconostasis*—the large, icon-bearing screen that shuts off the sanctuary from the rest of the church—into an elaborate structure with more than five tiers had an important effect on icon painting. The purpose of these paintings was to enable the worshiper to read pictorially. Clear, pictorial legibility in wavering candlelight and through clouds of incense required strong pattern, firm lines, and intense color. Hence, the relatively sober hues of the early Byzantine paintings gave way, more characteristically, to the intense and contrasting Russian colors. It was under a renewed Byzantine impulse, after the waning of the Mongol domination, and through the requirements of the iconostasis (just then reaching its highest development), that Russian painting reached a climax in the work of ANDREI RUBLËV (*c.* 1370–1430). *The Old Testament Trinity Prefiguring the Incarnation* (FIG. 7-63) is a work of great spiritual power, as

7-63 ANDREI RUBLËV, *The Old Testament Trinity Prefiguring the Incarnation, c.* 1410. Painted wood, 56″ × 45″. Tretyakov Gallery, Moscow.

well as an unsurpassed example of subtle line in union with intensely vivid color. The three angels who appeared to Abraham near the oaks of Mamre (Genesis 18:2–15) are seated about a table. (The angels are interpreted in Christian thought as a prefiguration of the Holy Trinity after the Incarnation of Christ.) The figures, each framed with a halo and sweeping wings, are suavely, languorously poised within an implicit circle, each, in its way, appearing rapt in meditation on the mystery of the Trinity. The tranquil demeanor of each figure is set off by the light, linear play of the draperies. Forms are defined by color, and areas are frequently intensified by the juxtaposition of a complementary hue. The intense blue and green folds of the cloak of the central figure, for example, stand out starkly against the deep red robe and the gilded orange of the wings. In the figure on the left, the highlights of the orange cloak are an opalescent blue-green. The color harmonics are Oriental in their unmodulated saturation, brilliance, and purity. In Russian painting, the Byzantine tradition was enlivened and enriched by a feeling and a touch that were not Byzantine or native but, rather, a fusion of the two; the same can be said of Russian architecture.

We should not forget, in considering the rich ecclesiastical art of Byzantium and Russia, the indispensable part played by other arts in the ensemble of a church interior: the carvings and rich metalwork of the iconostasis; the finely wrought, jeweled halos and other ornaments on the icons; the candlesticks and candelabra; the miters and ecclesiastical robes stiff with gold, embroidery, and jewels; the illuminated books bound in gold or ivory, inlaid with jewels and enamels; the crosses, croziers, sacred vessels, and processional banners. Each, with its great richness of texture and color, contributed to the total effect. In the life of Orthodox Byzantium, to produce this effect was to honor God and his vicar, the emperor.

Although carved ornament continued to appear in Byzantine churches, monumental stone sculpture was never encouraged to the degree that it was in western Europe. Life-size figures in the round apparently offended the East Christians. Their uneasiness was underlined by the Iconoclastic Controversy; they made an early association between statues and pagan idols. Painted images, on the other hand—particularly given the stylistic conventions that were to develop—created forms that were less directly identified with natural figures. The Byzantine sculptor was called on, however, to carve small statues and reliefs, particularly in ivory, to be used primarily for devotional purposes, although secular themes are also evident. These were used to adorn books, caskets, portable plaques, and venerable images, in much the same manner as the painted icons.

From the Second Byzantine Golden Age, a panel from a small work in ivory, the *Veroli Casket* (FIG. 7-64), testifies to the persistence of Classical form and content in Byzantine art, and to their strong revival in the tenth century. This panel represents a scene at the end of Euripides' play, *Iphigenia in Aulis,* in which Iphigenia, at center, is about to be sacrificed. The characters are all identifiable, and the human types, poses, costumes, and accessories are all from Classical antiquity, although the stunting of the proportions (perhaps partly a consequence of the diminutive space) and the bulbous modeling show the figures at a considerable distance in time and style from their prototypes in the Greco–Roman world.

From about the same time, the *Harbaville Triptych,* a portable shrine with hinged panels (FIG. 7-65), manifests in its figures the hieratic formality and solemnity we have learned to associate with Byzantine art and we have seen as standard in the mosaics of Ravenna. A softer, more fluent technique and the looser stance of the figures mitigates the hard austerity of the customary frontal pose. This may also result from the influential, classicizing spirit of the Second Byzantine Golden Age. Originating in a workshop associated with the imperial palace in Constantinople, the triptych marshals Christ and the saints in such a way as to align the powers of Church and state, of God and emperor. Christ is enthroned between St. John and

7-64 *The Sacrifice of Iphigenia,* panel from the Veroli Casket, tenth or eleventh century. Ivory, whole casket 4½" high, 16" long. Victoria and Albert Museum, London.

7-65 *Christ Enthroned with Saints*, the *Harbaville Triptych*, c. 950. Ivory, central panel 9½″ × 5½″. Louvre, Paris.

the Virgin in the upper central zone. Beneath them are five apostles. In the wings are soldier-saints like George and Theodore and bishop-saints like Demetrius and Procopius. Between the levels are portraits of other saints. Here, we have, in effect, a miniature, sculptured iconostasis, with the sacred personages placed in their celestial ranks of authority, like officials ranked in the Imperial hierarchy.

Portable works like icons and ivories found their way to distant lands as royal gifts, as items of trade, or as plunder, so that the rich and potent religious art of Byzantium became known throughout Europe. Everywhere it had directing influence and, as we have seen, nowhere more than in Russia. For the Medieval west, the art of Byzantium was to inspire, through its steady influence, a return to the principles of Classical humanism and naturalism long implicit in it.

ISLAMIC ART

In 622, Mohammed fled from Mecca to Medinet-en-Nabi ("City of the Prophet," now Medina). From this flight, known as the "Hegira," Islam dates its era.*

During the century that followed, the new faith spread with unprecedented speed from Arabia, where it was first espoused, through the Middle East to the Indus Valley and westward across North Africa to the Atlantic Ocean. By 640, Syria, Palestine, and Iraq had been conquered by Arab warriors in the name of Islam. In 642, the Byzantine army aban-

doned Alexandria, marking the Moslem conquest of Lower Egypt. In 651, Iran was conquered; by 710, all of North Africa had been overrun and a Moslem army crossed the straits of Gibraltar into Spain. A victory at Jerez de la Frontera in 711 seemed to open all of western Europe to the Mohammedans. By 732, they had advanced north to Poitiers in France, where an army of Franks under Charles Martel, the grandfather of Charlemagne, opposed them successfully. Although they continued to conduct raids in France, they were unable to extend their control beyond the Pyrenees. But in Spain, the great Caliphate of Cordoba flourished until 1031, and it was not until 1492, when Granada fell to Ferdinand and Isabella, that Islamic influence and power in the West came to a close. In the East, the Indus River had been reached by 751, and only in Anatolia was stubborn Byzantine resistance able to slow the Moslem advance. But relentless Moslem pressure against the shrinking Byzantine empire eventually caused its collapse in 1453, when the Ottoman Turks conquered Constantinople.

The early lightning successes of Islam were due largely to the zeal and military prowess of Arab warriors who set out to conquer the earth for Allah and who burst on the Near Eastern and Mediterranean worlds when Persian and Byzantine military power was at a low ebb. But the fact that these initial conquests had effects that endured for centuries can be explained only by the nature of the Islamic faith and its appeal to millions of converts.

Many of the features of the Islamic faith are derived from the Judeo–Christian tradition. Its sacred scripture is the Koran, the collection of Mohammed's revelations ordered to be gathered by the caliph Othman (644–656) and unchanged to the present day. Its basic teachings and ethics are similar to those of the Bible,

---

*Islam, "exclusive worship of the one God (Allah)," was Mohammed's name for his new religion. Mohammedan, Muhammadan, Muslim, and Moslem all refer to the same faith.

and the Old Testament prophets, as well as Jesus, are counted among the predecessors of Mohammed. On the other hand, all Moslems believe that they have direct and equal access to God without need for complex ritual or an intervening priesthood. Furthermore, a new social order, quite different from the Christian one, was established by Mohammed in that he took charge of the temporal as well as the spiritual affairs of his community. This practice of uniting religious and political leadership in the hands of a single ruler was continued after Mohammed's death by his successors, the *caliphs*, who based their claims to authority on their descent from the families of the Prophet or those of his early followers.

Architecture and Architectural Ornament

During the early centuries of Islamic history, the political and cultural center of the Moslem world was the Fertile Crescent (Palestine, Syria, Iraq)—that melting pot of East and West strewn with impressive ruins of earlier cultures that became one of the fountainheads of the development of Islamic art. The vast territories conquered by the Arabs were ruled by governors, originally sent out from Damascus or Baghdad, who eventually gained relative independence by setting up dynasties in various territories and provinces: the Umayyads in Syria (661–749) and in Spain (756–1031), the Abbasids in Iraq (749–1258, largely nominal after 945); the Fatimids in Tunisia and Egypt (909–1171); and so on. Despite the Koran's strictures against sumptuousness and license, the caliphs were not averse to surrounding themselves with luxuries commensurate with their enormous wealth and power. This duality is expressed by the two major architectural forms developed during the early Islamic period: the *mosque* and the *palace*.

Moslem religious architecture is closely related to

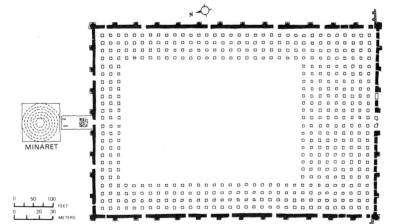

7-66   Plan of the Great Mosque, Samarra.

MINARET

0   50   100
|___|___| FEET
0   20 30
|__|__| METERS

Moslem prayer, the performance of which is an obligation laid down in the Koran for all Moslems. Prayer as a private act requires neither liturgical ceremony nor a special locale; only the *qiblah*—the direction (toward Mecca) in which the prayer is addressed—is important. But prayer also became a communal act for which a simple ritual was established by the first Moslem community. Once a week, the community convened—probably in the Prophet's house, the main feature of which was a large, square court with two *zullahs*, or shaded areas, along the north and south sides. These zullahs consisted of thatched roofs supported by rows of palm trunks; the southern zullah, wider and supported by a double row of trunks, indicated the qiblah. During these communal gatherings, the *imam*, or leader of collective worship, standing on a pulpit known as a *minbar*, near the qiblah wall, pronounced the *khutbah*, which is both a sermon and an act of allegiance of the community to its leader. The minbar thus represents secular authority even as it serves its function in worship. The requirements of this ritual were satisfied by the hypostyle mosque, the origin of which is still in dispute but one prototype of which may well have been the Prophet's house in Medina. Once the Moslems had firmly established themselves in their conquered territories, they began to build on a large scale, impelled perhaps by a desire to create visible symbols of their power that would surpass those of their non-Islamic predecessors in size and splendor; the great size of some of the early mosques, however, may also be explained by the fact that they were intended to contain the entire Moslem population of a given city.

The Great Mosque of Samarra on the Tigris River (FIGS. 7-66 and 7-67), built between 848 and 852 but now ruined, was the largest mosque of the Islamic world, measuring 800 feet long and 520 feet wide. Over half its ten-acre area was covered by a wooden roof carried by 464 supports arranged in aisles around the open central court and leading toward the qiblah wall, the importance of which was emphasized by the greater number of aisles on its side. In the center of the qiblah wall is a niche, the *mihrab*, which became a standard feature in all later mosques. Its origin, purpose, and meaning are still matters of debate; some historians feel that it may originally have honored the place where the Prophet stood in his house at Medina when he led the communal prayers. If the mihrab has this symbolic function, it is unusual, because one of the characteristics of early Islamic art is its concerted avoidance of symbols. In this respect, early Islamic art offers a striking contrast to Medieval Christian art; the avoidance of religious symbolism, in fact, may reflect a conscious rejection of Christian customs and practices.

7-67　Aerial view of the Great Mosque, Samarra, Iraq, 848–852.

On the north side of the Great Mosque of Samarra stands a single, large minaret from which a *muezzin* called the faithful to prayer. Although its shape is reminiscent of the ancient ziggurats of Mesopotamia, it was probably inspired not by them but by a certain kind of spiral tower of unknown purpose found in Sassanian Iran. More numerous were minarets that were square in plan and derived from the towers of Early Christian churches in the Near East. Cylindrical minarets, from which the slender needles so characteristic of later mosques evolved, became popular only in the eleventh century.

The early Moslem hypostyle system, as illustrated by the Samarra mosque, was diffused and, except for the orientation of the building and the position of the qiblah wall, lacked architectural focus and direction. On the other hand, it was a flexible system that per-

mitted enlargement and addition with minimum effort. Its main element was the single support, either a column or a pier, which could be multiplied at will and in any desired direction. A striking illustration of the flexibility of this system is the mosque of Cordoba (FIGS. 7-68 and 7-69), which was begun in 784 and enlarged several times during the ninth and tenth centuries. The additions followed the original style and arrangement of columns and arches, and the builders were able to maintain a striking stylistic unity for the entire building. The 36 piers and 514 columns are topped by a unique system of double-tiered arches that carried a wooden roof, now replaced by vaults. The lower arches are horseshoe-shaped, a form perhaps adapted from earlier Near Eastern architecture or of local Spanish origin and now closely associated with Moslem architecture.

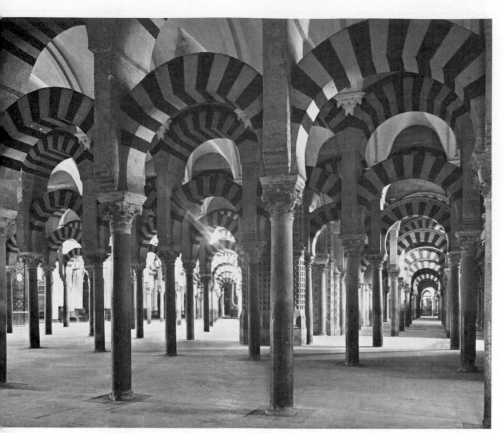

7-68 Interior of mosque at Cordoba, Spain, eighth to tenth century.

7-69 Plan of mosque at Cordoba.

MIHRAB

N

MINARET

Years of Construction

☐ 784 ■ 965-66
☐ 833-48 ▨ 987-88

0 25 50 75 100 FEET
0 10 20 30 METERS

Visually, these arches seem to billow out like sails blown by the wind, and they contribute greatly to the light and airy effect of the mosque's interior.

In areas the builders wished to emphasize, like that near the mihrab (FIG. 7-70), the arches become highly decorative, multi-lobed shapes. Other Early Islamic experiments with arch forms had led to the pointed arch, which, however, was not used to cover variable spaces, as in Gothic buildings. Early Islamic buildings had wooden roofs, and the experiments with arch forms were motivated less by structural necessity than by a desire to create rich and varied visual effects. The same desire for decorative effect seems to have inspired the design of the dome that covers the area in front of the mihrab (FIG. 7-71), one of four domes built during the tenth century to stress the axis leading to the mihrab. Here, the large ribs that subdivide the hemispheric surface of the dome into a number of smaller sections are primarily ornamental. Only in the hands of Gothic builders, centuries later, were ribs, in combination with the pointed arch, to become fundamental structural ingredients of a new and revolutionary architectural vocabulary.

Of the early palaces, there are only scattered remains, and they are of limited historical importance, serving primarily to illustrate the way of life of Moslem aristocrats and to provide us with some notion of the decorative styles of Early Islamic art. Even the purpose of these early palaces is not quite certain.

They were built both in cities and in the open country. The rural palaces, which have been better investigated, seem to have served a function similar to that of the Roman villas. That they reflect an Islamic taste

7-70 Mihrab of mosque at Cordoba.

7-71 Dome before the mihrab of mosque at Cordoba.

7-72 Palace at Ukhaydir, Iraq, late eighth century (view from the southeast).

for life in the desert seems too simple an explanation, although a desire to avoid plague-infested cities may well have been at least a partial motivation of their builders. But these rural palaces probably also served as nuclei for the agricultural development of conquered territories; they may also have been symbols of authority over conquered and inherited lands, as well as expressions of the newly acquired wealth of their owners.

One of the better preserved of these early Moslem palaces is the palace at Ukhaydir in Iraq (FIGS. 7-72 and 7-73), built in the second half of the eighth century. Somewhat larger than most, the palace is a separate entity within a fortified enclosure. From the outside, the high, tower-studded walls look much like those of the Great Mosque of Samarra (FIG. 7-67). This similarity illustrates a flexibility that is characteristic of Early Islamic monuments, as relatively minor changes could convert them from one purpose to another. Differences between a mosque, a palace, or a caravansary were rarely evident from the exterior; the structures tended to share a rather grim, fortified look that belied their military inefficiency. The high walls may have offered safety from marauding nomadic tribes, but—more important to the builders—they may also have fulfilled abstract considerations, like the promise of seclusion for a mosque or, for a palace, privacy for the prince and the symbolic assertion of his power over newly conquered territories.

The plan of the palace at Ukhaydir (FIG. 7-73) expresses its dual residential and official function. An elaborate entrance complex, consisting of a monumentalized gate and a Great Hall between two small, domed rooms, leads onto the large central court, beyond which is a reception hall surrounded by satellite rooms. Flanking this ceremonial axis are four smaller courts, all with three rooms on each of two sides. These grouped rooms appear to be self-contained and probably served as family living units or guest houses. To the right of the entrance hall is a standard feature of these early palaces—a mosque, here incorporated into the main building complex, although sometimes it stood by itself. Most palaces also were provided with fairly elaborate bathing facilities that displayed technical features, such as heating systems, adopted from the Roman tradition of baths. (The baths at Ukhaydir, only recently discovered near the mosque, are not shown on the plan.) Just as in Classical antiquity, these baths probably served more than merely hygienic purposes. Large halls frequently attached to them seem to have been used as places of entertainment. Thus, a characteristic amenity of Classical urban culture that died out in the Christian world survived in Medieval Islamic culture.

7-73 Plan of the palace at Ukhaydir.

7-74 Portion of stone frieze, palace at Mshatta, Jordan, *c.* 743.

large rosette that projects from a field densely covered with curvilinear, vegetal designs; no two triangles are treated the same way, and into some of them, as in FIG. 7-74, figures of animals are introduced. The sources of the various design elements are easily identified as Late Classical, Early Byzantine, and Sassanian Persian, but their combination and arrangement are typically Islamic.

Most of the design elements of Islamic ornament are based on plant motifs, which are sometimes intermingled with symbolic geometric figures and with human and animal shapes. But the natural forms often become so stylized that they are lost in the purely decorative tracery of the tendrils, leaves, and stalks. These arabesques form a pattern that will cover an entire surface, be it that of a small utensil or the wall of a building. (This *horror vacui* is similar to tendencies in barbarian art, although other aspects of Islamic design distinguish it from the abstract, barbarian patterns.) The relationship of one form to another in the Islamic is more important than the totality of the design: the patterns have no function but to decorate. This system offers a potential for unlimited growth, as it permits extension of the designs in any desired direction. Most characteristic, perhaps, is the design's independence of its carrier; neither its size (within limits) nor its forms are dictated by anything but the design itself. This arbitrariness imparts a certain quality of impermanence to Islamic design—a quality that, it has been said, may reflect the Moslem taste for readily movable furnishings, such as rugs and hangings.

Stone carving was only one of several techniques used for architectural decoration. Floor mosaics and wall paintings continued a long Mediterranean tradition. In later periods, colored tile became increasingly important. A magnificent example of a floor mosaic was found in the bath of the palace at Khirbat al-Mafjar near Jericho in Jordan (FIG. 7-76). Set into square and rectangular fields covered with a rich variety of

The decoration of the Ukhaydir palace seems to have been rather sparse and confined to simply molded stucco and occasional decorative brickwork. In this respect, finds made in the western palaces in Syria and Palestine (modern Israel and Jordan) have been much richer. At Mshatta, an unfinished palace in the Jordanian desert, for instance, gate and façade are decorated by a wide, richly carved, stone frieze (FIGS. 7-74 and 7-75). Its design, arrangement, and relation to its carrier serve well to illustrate the major characteristics of Early Islamic decoration.

A long band, almost 15 feet high, is decorated with a series of triangles of the same size framed by an elaborately carved molding. Each triangle contains a

7-75 Reconstruction of façade of the palace at Mshatta. (After Schulz.)

7-76 Floor mosaic, palace at Khirbat al-Mafjar, Jordan, mid-eighth century.

floral and geometric patterns are medallions with extremely intricate abstract designs, some of them creating the illusion of a downward projection of the dome or half-dome under which they are placed.

The use of colored tile has a long history in the Middle East and Iran, reaching back into the Sumerian period. It enjoyed particular favor among the Babylonians (see FIG. 2-33). After periods of neglect, the art was revived by the Abbasids in the ninth century at Samarra, where tiles with a metallic sheen were developed. From there, the fashion spread throughout the Moslem world, reaching the height of its development during the sixteenth and seventeenth centuries in Turkey and Iran. Used as veneer

over a brick core, entire buildings, including their domes and minarets, could be sheathed with tiles. Our example, the Dome of Madrasa-I-Shāh in Isfahan (FIG. 7-77), dates from the early seventeenth century and shows such tilework at its most brilliant. Beautifully adjusted to the shape of the dome, the design of the spiraling tendrils is at once rich and subtle, enveloping the dome without overpowering it. In contrast to the more general Islamic tendency to disguise structure, the design here enhances the dome's form without obscuring it. On parts of the dome and on the minarets, the tiles are curved to conform to the shape of the architecture.

Particularly popular were *stucco reliefs*, a method of decoration that was known, but not common, in pre-Islamic Iran and Iraq. Cheap, flexible, and effective, the basic material (wet plaster) was particularly adaptable to the execution of the freely flowing line that distinguishes Islamic ornament, and it became a favorite technique. Some of the very richest examples of stucco decoration are found in the Alhambra palace in Granada, Spain—the last Moslem stronghold in western Europe in the Middle Ages. In the Court of the Lions and the rooms around it (FIGS. 7-78 and 7-79), stucco decoration runs the gamut of the medium's possibilities and creates an exuberant atmosphere of elegant fantasy that seems to be the visible counterpart of the visions of the more ornate Moslem poets.

The court itself (FIG. 7-78), proportioned according to the Golden Mean, is framed by rhythmically spaced single, double, and triple columns with slender, reed-like shafts that carry richly decorated block-capitals and stilted arches of complex shape. All surfaces above the columns are covered by colored stucco moldings that seem aimed at denying the so-

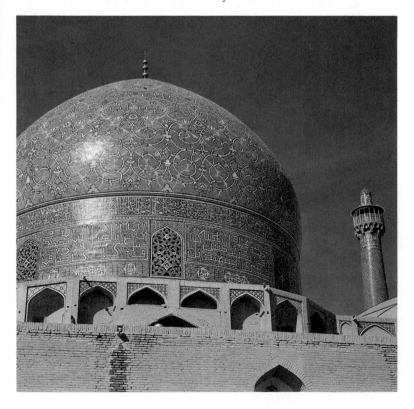

7-77 Dome of Madrasa-I-Shāh, Isfahan, Iran, 1612–1637.

7-78 Court of the Lions, the Alhambra, Granada, Spain, 1354–1391.

7-79 Hall of the Two Sisters, the Alhambra.

lidity of the stone structure that supports them. The resulting buoyant, airy, almost floating appearance of the building is enhanced by the "stalactite" decorations that break up the structural appearance of the arches, transforming them into near-organic forms.

This same tendency to disguise architectural forms is shown even more vividly in the Hall of the Two Sisters (FIG. 7-79), which adjoins the Court of the Lions. Here, all surfaces are covered by a poly chromed lacework of stucco and tile, in which an almost limitless variety of designs is held together by symmetry and rhythmic order. The overall effect of the incredibly rich decoration is that of tapestries suspended from walls and dome, the "stalactites" resembling pendant tassels. In this hall, the Moorish (North African and Spanish) style, heralded in the mosque at Cordoba (FIG. 7-68), has reached its ultimate refinement. Its influence on Spanish art remained strong throughout the Middle Ages and well into the Renaissance, and traces of it may be observed in the art of the Hispanic colonies of America.

A very different architectural concept is expressed in the madrasah and mausoleum of Sultan Hasan in Cairo (FIGS. 7-80 and 7-81). The *madrasah*, a combined school and mosque, was a building type developed in Iran and brought westward by the advancing Seljuk Turks during the eleventh century. It shares with the hypostyle mosque the open central court but replaces the early Islamic forests of columns with austere

7-80 Madrasah and attached mausoleum of Sultan Hasan, Cairo, Egypt, 1356–1363 (view from the southeast).

7-81 Plan of the madrasah and mausoleum of Sultan Hasan, Cairo.

7-82 Taj Mahal, Agra, India, 1632–1654.

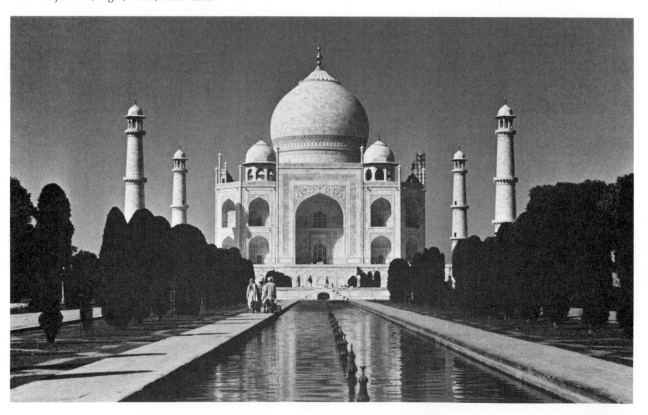

masses of brick and stone. The court is now surrounded by four vaulted halls, the one on the qiblah side being larger than the other three. Crowded into the angles formed by these halls are the various apartments, offices, and schoolrooms of the Moslem educational institution. Decoration of the main building is confined to moldings around the wall openings and a frieze below the crenellated roofline, which serve to accentuate, rather than to disguise, the geometric clarity of the massive structure, presenting a striking contrast to the filigreed elegance of the contemporary Alhambra.

Attached to the qiblah side of the madrasah is the mausoleum, which is a simple cubical structure covered by a dome. Mausoleums (central-plan, domed structures) were adopted either from Iran or from the Antique vocabulary of the Mediterranean, as they had not been a part of the original inventory of Islamic architecture. They were built either as memorials to holy men or for the secular function of commemorating Islamic rulers. By the tenth century, the building type was well established in Iran, from which it spread both east and west; it became especially popular in Egypt, which, of course, had its own age-old tradition of large-scale funerary monuments.

The most famous of all Islamic mausoleums is the fabled Taj Mahal at Agra (FIG. 7-82), which was built by one of the Moslem rulers in India, Shah Jahan, as a memorial to his wife, Mumtaz Mahal. The basic shape of the monument is that of the Cairo mausoleum, but modifications and refinements have converted the massive, cubical structure into an almost weightless vision of cream-colored marble that seems to float magically above the tree-lined reflecting pools. The interplay of shadowy voids with gleaming marble walls that seem paper-thin creates an impression of translucency, and elimination of the Cairo structure's heavy, projecting cornice (which separated the blocky base of the earlier building from its dome) ties all the elements together. The result is a sweeping, upward movement toward the climactic, balloon-shaped dome. Carefully related minarets and corner pavilions introduce, and at the same time stabilize, this soaring central theme. Although the entire monument recalls the fragile elegance of the Alhambra, it far surpasses the latter in subtle sophistication and represents one of the high-water marks of Moslem architecture.

OTTOMAN ARCHITECTURE

A related, yet different, Islamic architecture was developed by the Ottoman Turks. The Turkic people, of central Asian origin, had been converted to Islam during the ninth and tenth centuries. They moved into Iran and the Near East in the eleventh century, and, by 1055, the Seljuk Turks had built an imposing, although short-lived, empire that stretched from India to western Anatolia. It crumbled under the onslaught of the Mongols, led by Genghis Khan, in the 1240s. After its fall, a number of local dynasties established themselves in Anatolia, among them the Ottomans, founded by Osman I (1290–1326). Under his successors, the Ottoman state rapidly expanded over vast areas of Asia, Europe, and North Africa to become, by the middle of the fifteenth century, one of the great world powers.

Ottoman art, like Islamic art in general, expressed itself primarily in terms of architecture. But while other Moslem countries adopted the hypostyle mosque as their standard religious structure (FIGS. 7-67, 7-68, 7-72), Ottoman builders developed a new type of mosque with a square prayer hall covered by a dome as its core. In fact, the dome-covered square, which had been a dominant form in Sassanian Iran, became the nucleus of all Ottoman architecture. The combination, in addition to its appealing geometric clarity, was permeated with religious symbolism. To the Ottomans, a circle set into a square signified Heaven. (The circle, which has neither beginning nor end, symbolized eternity; the square, the four corners of the universe.) At first used singly, the domed units came to be used in multiples—a turning point in Ottoman architecture, because it drew in its wake the desire to create unity of space and form out of conglomerate aggregates. The resultant Ottoman style is geometric and formalistic, rather than ornamental.

When the Ottoman Turks conquered Constantinople (which they renamed Istanbul) in 1453, their architectural code was firmly established. Although impressed by Hagia Sophia (FIGS. 7-41, 7-42, 7-43, 7-44), which, in some respects, conformed to their own ideals, Ottoman builders were not overwhelmed by it. Direct influence of Hagia Sophia was not felt until about 1500, when a second half-dome, opposite the mihrab, was used for the first time.* But the processional way of Hagia Sophia's interior never satisfied Ottoman builders, and Anatolian development moved instead toward the centralized quatrefoil mosque. First examples of this clover-leaf plan, an ideal of Ottoman mosque design, were built in the 1520s—to be eclipsed only by the works of the most famous of Ottoman architects, SINAN THE GREAT (c. 1491–1588), called Koça ("the architect"). A contemporary of Michelangelo and with equal pretensions to immortality, Sinan carried Ottoman architecture to the height of its Classical period. By his time, the use of the basic domed unit was universal. It could be

---

*Ottoman builders had already adopted (from Byzantine architecture) the half-dome-covered apsidal projection for the mihrab, in addition to pendentive construction, although they preferred the Seljuk method of supporting domes with squinches or series of corbels (FIG. 7-47).

the Selimiye Cami (FIGS. 7-83, 7-84, 7-85, 7-86) at Edirne where he created a structure that fully expresses "the earthly squareness of the gathering place of the faithful under the canopy of eternity" and where, at the same time, the mihrab is visible from almost any spot in the building. It is said that the mosque was built for Selim II at Edirne (which had been the capital of the Ottoman empire from 1367 to 1472) because the Sultan could find no adequate space for it in Istanbul. Its massive dome, effectively set off by four slender, pencil-shaped minarets (each over 200 feet high), dominates the city's skyline. Grouped around the mosque are various dependencies. (Most of the important mosques had numerous annexes, including libraries and schools, hospices, baths, soup kitchens for the poor, markets, and hospitals, as well as a cemetery containing the mausoleum for the sultan responsible for the building of the mosque. These utilitarian buildings were grouped around the mosque and axially aligned with it if possible; more generally, they were adjusted to their natural site and linked with the central building by plantings of shrubs and trees.)

The mosque is preceded by a rectangular court covering an area equal to that of the building. This *avlu* (a courtyard forming a summer extension of the mosque) is surrounded by porticoes formed by domed squares. Behind it, the building rises majestically to its climactic dome, which equals that of Hagia Sophia in width. But it is the organization of the interior space of this mosque that reveals the genius of its builder. The mihrab has been recessed into an apse-like alcove deep enough to permit illumination from three sides, which makes the brilliantly colored tile panels of its lower walls sparkle as if with their own glowing light. The plan of the main hall is an ingenious fusion of an octagon with the symbolic dome-covered square. The octagon, formed by the eight massive dome supports, is pierced by the four half-dome-covered corners of the square. The result is a fluid interpenetration of several geometric volumes that represents the culminating solution to Sinan's lifelong search for a monumental, unified, interior space. The square "singing gallery"—a platform for the *muezzins* (criers) that at first may seem like a distracting piece of furniture—punctuates the central space. It restates the basic squareness of the prayer hall and provides an anchoring focus to a design that might seem diffuse without it. Placed under the center of the dome, it marks "the navel of the mosque."

Sinan's building elegantly resolves complicated laws of statics. The Islamic tendency to disguise the structural function of architectural elements (as, for instance, in the Alhambra, FIGS. 7-78 and 7-79) is min-

enlarged or contracted as needed, and almost any number of units could be used together. Thus, the typical Ottoman building of Sinan's time was an assembly of parts, usually erected with an extravagant margin of structural safety. Measures and forms had been standardized, and design and engineering methods tended to be conservative, with little room given to experimentation. But despite such strictures, which might have been stifling to a lesser architect, Sinan constantly searched for solutions to the problems of unifying the additive elements and of creating a monumental, centralized space with ideal proportions.

In his early buildings, Sinan experimented with the clover-leaf plan, as well as with that of Hagia Sophia. In the mosque of Suleiman I in Istanbul, he flanked the central unit—in which the main dome is abutted by two half-domes, north and south—with dome-covered aisles. But where Hagia Sophia isolates the lateral aisles, Sinan, by reducing interior obstructions to a minimum, made every effort to combine them with the central area and to make central and flanking spaces flow into each other through wide and lofty arcades.

Sinan's efforts to overcome the limitations of a segmented interior found their ultimate expression in imized and confined to a "honeycomb" treatment of squinches and to "stalactite" capitals, a form of decoration that was popular from the twelfth century onward. Sinan's forms are clear and legible, like mathematical equations—height, width, and masses being related to each other in a simple but effective ratio of 1:2. The building is generally regarded as the climax of Ottoman architecture. Sinan himself proudly proclaimed it his masterpiece, and, indeed, it encloses one of the most impressive domed spaces ever built.

1. Madrasa
2. Cemetery
3. Darül-Kurra (house for the readers of the Koran)
4. Mosque
5. Avlu (courtyard forming summer extension of mosque)
6. Arasta (covered market)

7-85   Interior of the Selimiye Cami.

0   100   200   300   400   500
                                        FEET
0   30   60   90   120   150
                                        METERS

7-84   Plan of the Selimiye Cami, Edirne.

7-86   Axonometric perspective of the Selimiye Cami, Edirne.

7-87   Carpet from the tomb-mosque of Shah Tahmasp at Ardebil, Iran, 1540.
Approx. 34½′ × 17½′. Victoria and Albert Museum, London.

Object Art and Textiles

The furnishings of the palaces, as well as of the mosques, reflected a love of rich and sumptuous effects. Metal, wood, glass, and ivory were artfully worked into a great variety of objects for use in mosque or home. Basins (often huge), ewers, jewel cases, and writing boxes were made of bronze or brass, chased and inlaid with silver; enameled glass was used with striking effect in mosque lamps; richly decorated ceramics of high quality were produced in large numbers. Islamic potters, experimenting with different methods of polychrome painting of their wares, developed *luster painting,* a new and original technique that gives a metallic shine to a surface. Their designs were based on the motifs found in architectural decoration. This ready adaptability of motifs to various scales as well as to various techniques again illustrates both the flexibility of Islamic design and its relative independence from its carrier.

The most prestigious and highly valued objects of all were textiles, which, in the Islamic world, served more than purely utilitarian or decorative purposes. Produced by imperial factories, they were used not only in homes, palaces, and mosques, but also served as gifts, rewards, and signs of political favor.

The Moslem weavers adopted and developed the textile traditions of Sassanian Iran and the Mediterranean region (the latter were best known through Coptic textiles from Egypt). The art spread across the Islamic world, and, by the tenth century, Moslem textiles were famous and widely exported. The art of carpet-making was developed to a particularly high degree in Iran, where the need for protection against the winter cold made carpets indispensable both in the shepherd's tent and in the prince's palace. In houses and palaces built of stone, brick, plaster, and glazed tile, carpets also provided a contrasting texture as floor and divan coverings and wall hangings.

The carpet woven for the tomb-mosque of Shah Tahmasp at Ardebil (FIG. 7-87) is a large example of the medallion type and bears a design of effectively massed large elements surrounded and enhanced by a wealth of subordinated details. The field of rich blue is covered with leaves and flowers (chiefly peonies, a Chinese influence) attached to a framework of delicate stems that weave a spiral design over the whole field. Great royal carpets like the one from Ardebil were products of the joint effort of a group of weavers, who probably were attached to the court. Pile weaving is a slow process at best, and, because a carpet like the one from Ardebil often has more than 300 knots to the square inch, a skilled weaver working alone would probably have needed more than 20 years to complete it.

Because the Ardebil carpet was made for a mosque, its decoration excludes human and animal figures, although other carpets from Ardebil show that the Koran's strictures against the representation of man and animal were not taken as seriously in secular art. The ban against the worship of idols, however, had practically eliminated the image of man from Islamic religious art, and, even in early secular art, it appeared only occasionally in secluded parts of palaces as royal imagery. For this reason also, large sculpture in the round and mural or panel painting, as developed in Europe and in the Far East, was rather rare in Early Islamic art. Contributing to this lack of interest in monumental plastic art may have been the predilections of the people that made up the Moslem world; many of them—Arabs, Turks, Persians, Mongols—were nomads, who traditionally preferred small, movable objects (the so-called "nomad's gear") to large-scale works of art. And so, perhaps, it should not be surprising that, when painting did develop in later times, it was mainly on the small scale of book illumination.

The Art of the Book

The Arabs had no pictorial tradition of their own, and it seems possible that their interest in book illumination developed almost accidentally, as a byproduct of their practice of translating and copying illustrated Greek scientific texts. In some of the earliest Islamic illuminated manuscripts (only a few dating earlier than about 1200), the illustrations seem to have been drawn by the scribes who copied the texts. Whatever its origins (often Christian and Mediterranean, but also local Iranian and Buddhist), an art of book illustration had developed, mostly in Iraq and Iran, by 1200.

The Persian rulers were lovers of fine books and maintained at their courts not only skilled calligraphers but also some of the most famous artists of their day. The secular books of the Timurids and the Safavids were illustrated by a whole galaxy of painters. Famous among them were BIHZAD (c. 1440–1536), AQA MIRAK, and SULTAN MUHAMMAD, court painters of Tahmasp (1524–1576), a great art patron. Although the rulers were Moslems, orthodox Islamic restrictions regarding depiction of the human figure were rather liberally interpreted by them and did not affect their secular arts. Within the framework of illustrating specific stories, the gay scenes of their life of pleasure—the hunt, the feast, music, and romance—and battle scenes filled the pages of their books. In them, we feel the luxury, the splendor, and the fleeting happiness of Omar.

7-88 AQA MIRAK, *Laila and Majnun in Love at School*, miniature from a manuscript of the Khamsa of Nizami, 1524–1525. Colors and gilt on paper. Metropolitan Museum of Art, New York.

In *Laila and Majnun* (FIG. 7-88), the painter Aqa Mirak has illustrated one of Nizami's romantic poems. The scene represents a school, apparently in a mosque, and deals less with the pleasures than with some of the more earnest aspects of life. Seated on a rug is a turbaned *mullah,* or teacher, rod in hand, listening to a youth reading; around him are other youths studying, all seated on their knees and heels or with one knee raised, the customary sitting postures of the East. Here and there are cross-legged bookrests. In the foreground, one boy is pulling his companion's ear, and at the left, near the large water jar, two boys are playing ball. In the middle distance are the lovers Laila and Majnun, each obviously aware of the other's presence. Although the figures are drawn expressively with delicate, flowing lines, they are flat, with no shading and with only a hint of perspective; the tiles in the court and the rugs on the floor appear to be hanging vertically. The painting is conceived from a point of view concerned not with natural appearance but with pattern and vivid color. To this end, the tones are kept bright and clear. The decorative quality of the miniature is emphasized by the broad margins of the page, which are tinted and flecked with gold.

In its general appearance, the miniature is much more closely related to the Ardebil carpet than to any European painting or, for that matter, to Chinese painting, by which it was certainly influenced. It falls within the general framework of the Islamic decorative style, which, despite early religious restrictions and the constraints that derive from a limited formal vocabulary, became one of the richest and most harmonious decorative styles in the world.

II

THE MIDDLE AGES

The poets of the Augustan Age were singing the glories of "eternal Rome" while Jesus of Nazareth, obscure founder of the religion that was to transform the city of man into the city of God, was born and died. Within three centuries, Christianity had become the official cult of the dying empire and the faith of the new peoples, the barbarians, who were to inherit its remains. While Byzantium, eastern remnant of the Christianized Roman empire, maintained a continuous sovereignty, the empire in the west disintegrated. What had been the imperial provinces broke up into contesting barbarian kingdoms—those of the Franks, Burgundians, Visigoths, Anglo–Saxons, Lombards, and others. Historians have called the ensuing epoch (the thousand years from about 400 to 1400) the "Middle Ages" or the "Dark Ages." For centuries, it was thought that this interval between the passing of

JEAN DE CHELLES, rose window of the north
transept, Notre Dame, Paris, 1240–1250. Stained
glass, stone, bar-tracery, iron, and lead.
Diameter 43'.

311

the Roman empire and the rebirth of its civilization in the Renaissance was rough and uncivilized (in a word, "barbarous")—that between the ancient and the modern world, life was empty, cruel, and "dark," simply a blank between (in the "middle" of) two great civilizations. Even today, the word "medieval" is often used disparagingly.

But since the late eighteenth century, historians have been thoroughly revising this view and, with it, the long-held belief that Medieval art was crude and primitive. The same romantic enthusiasm for past civilizations that motivated the archeological revolution of Heinrich Schliemann's time, and the consequent recovery of the ancient past, sent scholars in quest of the meaning of Medieval culture—the meaning of monuments that existed in great number and, in this case, that were aboveground and visible. Although we now see these centuries with very different eyes, perceiving their innovation and their greatness, the names "Middle Ages" and "Medieval" continue to be used, simply for convenience.

Medieval civilization represents an interrelation of Christianity, Greco–Roman tradition, and the new, energetic spirit of the Celtic–Germanic peoples—the "barbarians," as the Greeks and the Romans had called them. Christianity, firmly established, constituted a unifying force, even in the midst of anarchy and chronic warfare. It mitigated the harsh passions of rough warriors. It kept alive learning and knowledge of the useful arts. Though itself often corrupted, it was just as often reformed. By the thirteenth century, when the Church was at the height of its power, western Europe had evolved into a great and original civilization, constantly stimulated by influences from the Greco–Roman past and from Byzantium and the world of Islam, but ever reworking those influences in novel ways. The Christian Church, with its monopoly on education, also preserved and handed on aspects of the Roman culture not directly related to religion: the Latin language, Roman law, Roman administrative organization and practice, the idea and ideal of the Roman empire—all elements used by the Church but, as the Renaissance would show, susceptible to entirely secular application.

Although the spirit of Christianity was oriented toward the world of the supernatural and although its learning was centered in theology, which regarded questions about the nature of the physical world as both irrelevant to salvation and irreverent in intention, there was, by the thirteenth century, stirring, even within the Church—a new curiosity about man's natural environment that could not be entirely stifled by the prevailing religious disposition. In a thirteenth-century summation of Medieval knowledge—the influential encyclopedia called the *Speculum Majus (Great Mirror)*—Vincent of Beauvais, a Dominican monk, included the "Mirror of Nature," a comprehensive compilation of lore about natural things. By no means an objective or scientific analysis of nature in the modern sense, it was rather a descriptive record of the appearances of things as the reflection of God's glory and beneficence. Within the Medieval setting, notwithstanding its thoroughly religious view of nature, a different impulse was being felt—a secular and intellectual curiosity about the world that was to mature into modern science.

In addition, the period produced technological advances that pointed to consequences far beyond anything the ancient world had known. The invention and development of tools and mechanisms that extended man's powers over his environment and that facilitated manufacture was encouraged not least by the new dignity that the Church's disapproval of slavery conferred on manual labor and skills. The free craftsman—not, as in the ancient world, the slave—was the Medieval agent of production; organized in guilds, he constituted the firm foundation of Medieval urban economy.

Thriving towns, populated by free men, provided a stimulus for commerce and industry, and new towns were founded and flourished. Most of the prosperous European cities of today were established or underwent renovation around the twelfth century. Indeed, Florence, mother city of the modern world, had early laid the foundations of its wealth and, by the fifteenth century, had the spirit and the means to lead Europe into the bold, creative age of discovery we call the Renaissance.

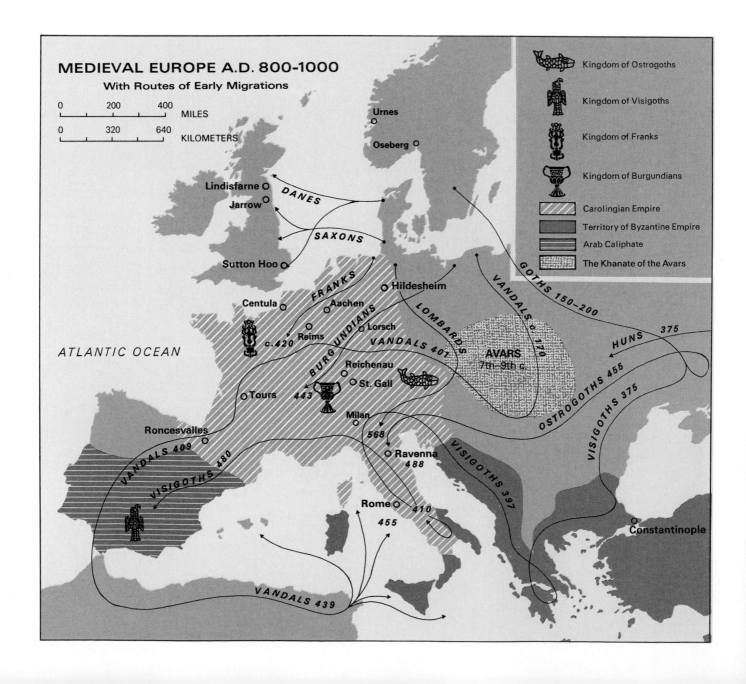

MEDIEVAL EUROPE A.D. 800–1000

With Routes of Early Migrations

0   200   400
MILES

0   320   640
KILOMETERS

Kingdom of Ostrogoths

Kingdom of Visigoths

Kingdom of Franks

Kingdom of Burgundians

Carolingian Empire

Territory of Byzantine Empire

Arab Caliphate

The Khanate of the Avars

ATLANTIC OCEAN

Urnes

Oseberg

Lindisfarne

DANES

Jarrow

SAXONS

Sutton Hoo

FRANKS

Centula

Aachen

Hildesheim

c. 420

Reims

Lorsch

LOMBARDS

BURGUNDIANS

VANDALS 401

AVARS
7th–9th c.

GOTHS 150–200

VANDALS c. 170

HUNS   375

Reichenau

St. Gall

OSTROGOTHS 455

Tours

443

Milan

568

VISIGOTHS 375

Roncesvalles

VANDALS 409

Ravenna
488

VISIGOTHS 480

VISIGOTHS 397

Rome

410

455

Constantinople

VANDALS 439

EARLY MEDIEVAL ART

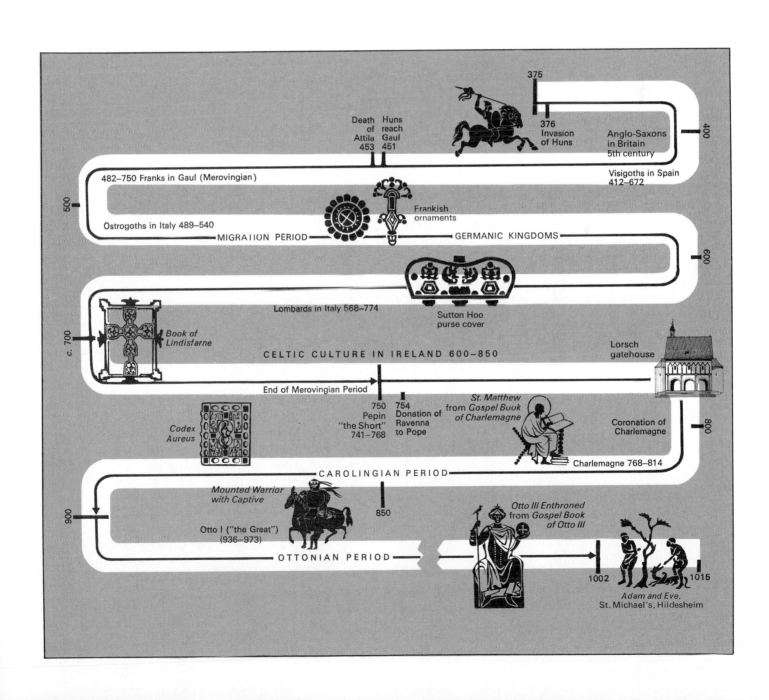

375

Death Huns
of reach
Attila Gaul
453 451

376
Invasion
of Huns

Anglo-Saxons
in Britain
5th century

400

482–750 Franks in Gaul (Merovingian)

Visigoths in Spain
412–672

500

Ostrogoths in Italy 489–540

Frankish
ornaments

MIGRATION PERIOD — GERMANIC KINGDOMS

600

Lombards in Italy 568–774

Sutton Hoo
purse cover

c. 700

Book of
Lindisfarne

CELTIC CULTURE IN IRELAND 600–850

Lorsch
gatehouse

End of Merovingian Period

750
Pepin
"the Short"
741–768

754
Donation of
Ravenna
to Pope

St. Matthew
from Gospel Book
of Charlemagne

Coronation of
Charlemagne

800

Codex
Aureus

CAROLINGIAN PERIOD

Charlemagne 768–814

Mounted Warrior
with Captive

Otto I ("the Great")
(936–973)

850

Otto III Enthroned
from Gospel Book
of Otto III

900

OTTONIAN PERIOD

1002

1015

Adam and Eve,
St. Michael's, Hildesheim

For thousands of years, waves of migrating people moved slowly across the great Eurasian steppes and down into the Mediterranean world; we have met them as the Achaeans and Dorians of Mycenaean times, and again as the Gauls, who invaded Asia Minor and were defeated by Attalus I of Pergamon in the third century B.C.

In the second century A.D., the Goths moved southward from the Baltic region and settled on the north shore of the Black Sea, subjugating the Scythians and Sarmatians, who had inhabited the area for some eight centuries. On their march, the Goths had met and defeated the Vandals, pushing them toward central Europe and setting in motion one of the longest and most infamous migratory treks in history—one that was to end only in the fifth century with the establishment of a Vandal kingdom in North Africa. The Goths themselves split into two groups in the early fourth century: the Ostrogoths (eastern Goths), who remained in Sarmatia, and the Visigoths (western Goths), who moved on into the Danube river basin.

For centuries, these migratory movements had been checked by Roman military might along the Rhine and Danube rivers. Despite constant friction with them since the first century B.C., the Romans had been able to contain the barbarians along their northern frontiers. In the fourth century, however, the eruption of the Huns from the east pressed those tribes and nations against the Roman boundaries, which Rome found more and more difficult to defend. In 376, the Roman emperor Valens allowed the Visigoths, hard-pressed by the Huns, who had already conquered their Ostrogothic cousins, to settle west of the Danube. Maltreated by Roman officials, the Visigoths revolted two years later and, in a battle near Adrianople, killed the emperor and nearly two-thirds of his army. After this, Rome offered little resistance to the different barbarian nations, who crossed into western Europe almost at will. It is the following four centuries of ethnic upheavals in Europe that we refer to as the Migration period.

THE MIGRATION PERIOD

As the name of the period implies, the invasions of Roman territory by barbarian tribes were, in reality, migrations of ethnic groups seeking not to overthrow the Roman empire, for which they often had great admiration, but a place where they could settle peacefully. However, they were seldom allowed to do so, as other tribes and nations would press in behind them and force them to move on. The Visigoths, for example, who moved in and out of Italy and formed a kingdom in southern France, were forced southward into Spain under pressure from the Franks, who had crossed the lower Rhine and established themselves in northern France. The Huns themselves—the force that triggered this chain reaction of ethnic dislocations—reached France and Italy in the mid-fifth century, and only the death of their great leader, Attila, in 453 prevented them from consolidating their vast conquests. As Hunnish power waned, the Ostrogoths shook off their yoke and moved first to Pannonia (junction of modern Hungary, Austria, and Yugoslavia) and then to Italy, where, under Theodoric, they established their kingdom only to have it fall less than a century later to the Lombards.

During this time of upheaval, strife, fear, and uncertainty, the Church, benefiting from the prestige of such early leaders as Augustine and Gregory the Great, constituted the only central authority, political as well as spiritual; the popes had, in effect, succeeded the Roman emperors. It was at this time that the foundations for the later authority of the Church were firmly established. In this connection, we should bear in mind that most of the barbarian tribes entering the Roman empire were already Christian, although of the Arian creed, which had been condemned as heretical by the Orthodox Church. In its contest with the Eastern Orthodox Church for leadership in Christendom, papal Rome was strengthened when the Frankish king, Clovis, was converted to Catholicism. During his reign (481–511) the Franks gained control over the Burgundians (who had moved from the Baltic area into the region around Lake Geneva in the early fifth century), the Visigoths, and other groups in the area that is now France. With the recognition of the pope in Rome by this Frankish kingdom and with the success (in the sixth century) of the later Augustine's mission to England, where he became the first archbishop of Canterbury, Catholicism and the authority of Rome became firmly established in western Europe.

Accounts of the barbarian character vary. Tacitus, pointing up a moral for his Roman contemporaries, praises their courage, good looks, moral purity, fidelity, and good treatment of women, but finds them guilty of drunkenness and a lack of astuteness in matters of money. We get a better picture of the Germanic character from their epics, songs, and sagas, which show a somber pessimism built on a fundamental belief in fate, in the inevitable. Their heroes, like Siegfried and Beowulf, struggle against a pagan world of dreadful monsters. Fierce joy in battle alternates with bragging and carousing; narratives of stoic valor, with expressions of despair. Interpersonal loyalty, which became the basis of feudal ties and feudal law, is glorified in their poetry, as in this fragment of an Anglo–Saxon epic describing the last stand of a band of Saxons against the Danes:

> Remember the times when we spoke over our mead, when we raised up our boasts along the benches, heroes in the hall in anticipation of a hard fight! Now let us see who is brave. . . . Byrhtivold spoke up, an old retainer . . . he taught his warriors their duty: "Mind shall be the harder, heart the keener, courage the greater as our strength grows less."

The imagination of these wandering people teemed with fantastic creatures of all sorts. Their belief that the deep, dark forests of the north virtually swarmed with zoomorphic and demonic populations was widely shared by the nomadic hunters of all tribes. Dragons, like Siegfried's Fafnir and Beowulf's Grendel, symbolize the mysterious and threatening universe of fierce forces that the later Medieval world will picture as the devils and demons of Hell. Medieval man, long after he ceased his wanderings and despite Christianization, remained more than half pagan; his terrors were bound up with his tribal experience and the memory of fiend-filled forests and pagan rites. (Charlemagne, in suppressing the Saxons, decreed against human sacrifice.) Against this background, it is not surprising to find that the Germanic tribes readily adopted an art form that, although foreign, was ideally suited to their imagination—the Eastern "animal style" already encountered in Mesopotamian art.

Craft Art

The original art of the Germanic peoples was abstract, decorative, and geometric and ignored the world of organic nature. It was confined to the decoration of small, portable objects—weapons or items of personal adornment, such as bracelets, pendants, and belt buckles. Most characteristic, perhaps, and produced in considerable numbers by almost all tribes, was the *fibula*, a decorative pin usually used to fasten garments (FIG. 8-1). The fibulae were made of bronze, silver, or gold and were profusely decorated, often with inlaid precious or semiprecious stones. The entire surface of these objects is covered with decorative patterns, reflecting the *horror vacui* so common in the art of primitive cultures. But we also note that the decorative patterns are carefully adjusted to the basic shape of the object they adorn and that they describe and amplify its form and structure, becoming an organic part of the object itself.

This highly disciplined, abstract, and functional type of decorative design was wedded to the animal style during the early centuries of the Medieval era. Probably of prehistoric origin, the animal style had

a

b

8-1 Frankish ornaments, sixth and seventh centuries: (a) looped fibula (4" long), silver gilt worked in filigree, with inlays of garnets and other stones, Musée des Antiquités Nationales, Saint Germain-en-Laye; (b) round fibula (diameter 2¾"), gold with cloisonné work, with inlays of garnets and blue stones, Museo Nazionale di Antichita, Parma. Both ornaments appear actual size.

reasserted itself in the Luristan bronzes (FIG. 2-41) of the ninth and eighth centuries B.C. and was a dominant element of the artistic repertoire of the Scythians, who passed it on to their Gothic overlords in the third century A.D. From that time on, the Goths became the main transmitters of this style, which was readily adopted by many of the other Germanic tribes. But its application was severely controlled by the native Germanic sense of order and design. Abstracted to the point of absolute integration with dominantly geometric patterns, the zoomorphic elements frequently become almost unrecognizable, and one must often examine a fibula (FIG. 8-1) carefully to discover that it contains a zoomorphic form (in this case, a fish).

The art of the Germanic people was expressed primarily in metalcraft. One of their preferred methods of decoration was *cloisonné*, a technique that may be of Byzantine and, ultimately, of Near Eastern origin. In this technique, used in the circular ornament shown in FIG. 8-1b, small metal strips (the *cloisons*), usually of gold, are soldered edge-up to a metal background. An enamel paste (to be subsequently fired) or semiprecious stones, such as garnets, or pieces of colored glass, are placed in the compartments thus formed. The edges of the cloisons remain visible on the surface and are an important part of the design. This cloisonné personal gear was highly prized and handed down from generation to generation. Dispersion of some of the princely hoards at an early date would account for the discoveries of identical techniques and designs in widely divergent areas. Certainly, cloisonné ware must have been given to vassals as gifts and tokens of gratitude; everywhere in barbarian poetry, the name for the prince and lord is "treasure-giver." Other collections or "treasures"

must have been accumulated over time, which could explain the different forms present in the magnificent discovery made at Sutton Hoo in Suffolk, England, one piece from which is shown in FIG. 8-2.

Excavated in 1939, the Sutton Hoo site is now associated with the ship burial of the East Anglian king Anna, who died in 654. The purse lid shown is by no means the best of the pieces found, fine as it is. There are four symmetrically arranged groups of figures. The end groups consist of a man standing between two beasts (he frontal, they in profile)—a heraldic type of grouping that goes back to ancient Mesopotamia (FIG. 2-16), though of course with variation. The two center groups represent eagles attacking ducks, again a familiar predatory motif seen in both Mesopotamian and Egyptian art. The animal figures are adjusted to each other with the cunning design we associate with the whole animal style through centuries; for example, the convex beaks of the eagles fit against the concave beaks of the ducks. The two figures fit together so snugly that they seem at first to be a single, dense, abstract design; this is true also of the man–animals motif. Above these figures are three geometric designs. The outer ones are clear and linear in style; in the central design, an interlace pattern, the interlacements turn into writhing animal figures. Interlacement was known outside the barbarian world but was seldom used in combination with animal figures. It has been suggested that the barbarian fondness for the interlace pattern came from the quite

8-2   Purse cover from the Sutton Hoo ship burial, *c.* 655. Gold and enamel, 7½" long. British Museum, London.

familiar experience of interlacing leather thongs. In any event, the interlace, with its possibilities for great complexity, had natural attraction for the adroit jeweler.

Metalcraft and its vocabulary of interlace patterns and other motifs, beautifully integrated with the animal form, is, without doubt, *the* art of the Early Middle Ages in the West. Interest in it was so great that the colorful effects of jewelry designs were imitated in the painted decorations of manuscripts, in stone sculpture, in the masonry of the early churches, and in sculpture in wood.

Wood is an especially important medium in Viking art. The Vikings (the word means "pirate" in the Norse language) were the pagan, seafaring plunderers from the Scandinavian north, who, from the ninth to the eleventh century, destructively raided the Celtic and Germanic settlements of Christian Europe. Once Christianized, they settled down to become the Normans ("Northmen"), giving their name to that part of France we call Normandy. Striking examples of Viking wood carving have been found in another royal ship buried near Oseberg, Norway. The Oseberg Ship has yielded rich evidence of the quality of Early Viking art, which has now become established, along with Hiberno–Saxon art (with which it interacts), as an original and important artistic development of the Early Middle Ages. The ship has been reconstructed (FIG. 8-3), but we can judge, from such surviving parts as the ornament of the prow, the skill of craftsmen familiar with a tradition of interlace design that was widely dispersed along the routes of the great migrations. The carved bands that follow the gracefully curving lines of the prow are embroidered with tightly interwoven animals, which writhe gripping and snapping, in serpentine and lacertine (lizard-like) interlacement. The convulsive movement is strictly controlled within the continuous margins of the composition.

An animal head that caps a post (FIG. 8-4) expresses, like others in the ship, the fierce, untamed spirit and energy of the pagan sea rovers. It brings together in one composition the image of a roaring beast—eyes protruding, nostrils flaring in predatory excitement—and the deftly carved, controlled, and contained interlacement pattern. As in the carvings of the ship's prow, firm artistic limit is put to wild vigor. As it is, the Oseberg animal head is a powerfully expressive example of the union of two fundamental motifs of barbarian art: the animal form and the interlace pattern.

The inter-patterning of these motifs culminated in the eleventh century with such elegant designs as that on the porch of the "stave" church at Urnes in

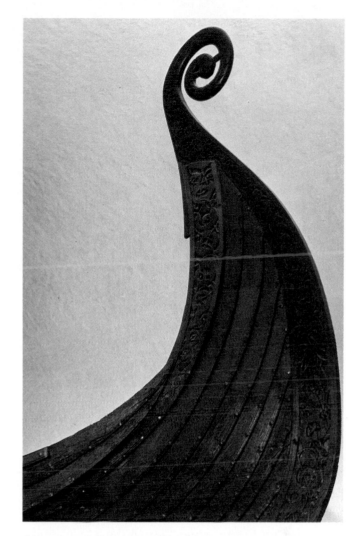

8-3 Prow of the Oseberg Ship, early ninth century. University Museum of National Antiquities, Oslo

8-4 Animal head from the Oseberg ship burial, *c.* 825. Wood, approx. 5" high. University Museum of National Antiquities, Oslo.

8-5 Wood-carved ornament (porch of stave church), Urnes, Norway, early ninth century.

Norway (FIG. 8-5). The church itself is constructed in wood ("staves" are wedge-shaped timbers placed vertically), which gives the wood-carver a special opportunity to show his craft in the embellishment of the architectural features of the building (in this case, the panels of the porch walls). Here, gracefully attenuated animal forms intertwine with flexible stalks and tendrils in spiraling rhythm; the effect of natural growth is astonishing. At the same time, the elaboration is so intricate and refined that the animal-interlace art of design seems to have reached its limit of invention and ingenuity. The Urnes style is the culmination of three centuries of Viking art (from the eighth to the eleventh century), after which it merges with the Romanesque style. During the whole period that it flourished, the art of the Vikings interacted closely with Hiberno–Saxon art and the art of the continent.

Illumination

When we remember that barbarian art essentially was expressed in terms of small portable objects, part of the collection of accessories and instruments that made up the nomad's gear, it is not surprising that monumental art—whether architecture, painting, or sculpture—is not to be found in what the migrating peoples have left. The masterpieces of barbarian art, which show the meeting of its decorative tradition with the art of the Mediterranean world, are illuminations in liturgical books, for with the Christianization of the barbarians, the book became an important vehicle of their art. These books were easy to transport, and we can follow the movements of some of them from place to place; their styles, copied in or from other books, are traceable in sequences of influence.

The complicated interchanges of influences recorded in manuscript illumination from the sixth to the eleventh century are the consequence not only of the restless migration of the new people, but also of the missionary activities of the Church as it sought to stabilize the wandering groups and to establish its authority. Foremost in this activity from the sixth century to the time of Charlemagne was the monastically organized Church of Ireland. Monasticism, a system by which communities of persons lived away from the world and dedicated themselves to the spiritual life, was instituted in the eastern Christian world by Basil in the fourth century and in the west by Benedict in the sixth century. The Celts of Ireland, converted to Christianity in the fifth century, adopted eastern rather than western monasticism and were not firmly connected to the Roman rule or to the papacy. Their independence was strengthened by their historical good luck: they were not invaded by the Germanic migrants. From about 400 to 750, while western Europe sank gradually into conflict, confusion, and ignorance, Ireland experienced a "golden age." Irish monks, filled with missionary zeal, founded monastic establishments in the British islands at Iona, off the west coast of Scotland, and at Lindisfarne, on the Northumbrian (northeastern) coast of Anglo–Saxon England. From these foundations, which became great centers of learning for both Scotland and England, Irish monks, filled with a "wonderful spirit of missionary enterprise," journeyed through Europe, founding great monasteries in Italy, Switzerland, Germany, and France and making the names of "Scot" (the old term for "Irish") and "Ireland" familiar in all western Christendom. The spread of Irish-Christian influence was countered by the Church of Rome, which felt that the Irish, long isolated from Roman Christianity, were tainted by heresy and separatism. The right hand of the papacy in this action was the Anglo–Saxon Winfrid, known to history as St. Boniface, Apostle to the Germans.

This encounter between Irish and Germanic Christianity is curiously reflected in the mingling of design

8-6 Ornamental page from the *Book of Lindisfarne*, Lindisfarne, late seventh century. Illumination, approx. 13" × 10". British Library, London.

elements in the illuminated pages of gospel books produced in Ireland and England between the seventh and ninth centuries. These "Hiberno–Saxon" manuscripts combine Irish and Anglo–Saxon motifs, sharing essentially, but by no means in all details, the same style. An ornamental page (FIG. 8-6)—only one

of several from a gospel book, the *Book of Lindisfarne*— is an exquisite example of Hiberno–Saxon art at its best. Here, the craft of intricate ornamental patterning, developed through centuries and in Viking art, is manifested in a tightly compacted design. Serpentine interlacements of fantastic animals devour each other, curling over and returning on their writhing, elastic shapes. The rhythm of expanding and contracting forms produces a most vivid effect of motion and change—a palpable rippling, as in the surface of a rapids. The inscribed cross, a variation on the stone Celtic crosses familiar in Ireland, regularizes the rhythms of the serpentines and, perhaps by contrast with its heavy immobility, seems to heighten the effect of motion. The motifs are placed in detailed symmetries, with inversions, reversals, and repetitions that must be closely studied with the magnifying glass to appreciate not so much their variety as their maze-like complexity. The zoomorphic forms are intermingled with clusters and knots of line, and the whole design pulses and vibrates like an electromagnetic energy field. The color is rich yet cool; the entire spectrum is embraced, but in hues of low intensity. Shape and color are so adroitly adjusted that a smooth and perfectly even surface is achieved—a balance between an overall, steady harmony of key (color) and maximum motion of figure and line. The discipline of touch is that of a master familiar with long-established conventions; yet neither the discipline nor the convention stiffens the supple lines that tirelessly and endlessly thread and convolute their way through the design. This joy at working on small, infinitely complex and painstaking projects—this goldsmith's, jeweler's, and weaver's craft—will live in northern art throughout the Middle Ages in architectural detail, ivory carving, illumination, stained-glass work, and, ultimately, in panel painting. The instinct and taste for intricacy and precision, propagated in the art of the wandering Celt–Germans, will broaden beyond art into technology and the making of machines. Modern historians make much of Medieval technological invention, declaring that it innovated well beyond Greek and Roman achievement and pointed the way to the technological revolutions of modern times.

The barbarian craft remained, but the Hiberno–Saxon ornamental style, with its gorgeous essays in interlacements, was fated to be replaced by the Mediterranean styles that descended from Early Christian and Late Antique art. Political realities hastened its demise. Irish Christianity lost its influence in Anglo–Saxon England and on the continent; the adherents to the rule of Benedict, the Benedictine order of monks, who wholeheartedly followed the papacy and the Roman version of Christianity, gained the upper hand in power and influence, and although the Irish Church held out for some time, eventually it accepted the Roman form. Even while Hiberno–Saxon art pre-

vailed in Ireland, Scotland, and Northumbria, other monastic foundations in England were copying Mediterranean prototypes. Naturally, the ascendancy of the Roman Church would be expressed in manuscripts from the Mediterranean area, and wherever the Roman orthodoxy was accepted, an orthodox style of manuscript illumination had to follow. The contrast between the two very different styles is particularly striking in juxtaposition. *The Scribe Ezra Rewriting the Sacred Records* from the *Codex Amiatinus* (FIG. 8-7) was copied from an Italian manuscript, the *Codex Grandior of Cassiodorus*, early in the eighth century by an illuminator with Italian training in some Anglo–Saxon monastery, probably Jarrow. The same original must have been seen and "translated" a few years earlier by an artist trained in the abstract Hiberno–Saxon manner; his version appears as the *St. Matthew* figure in the *Book of Lindisfarne* (FIG. 8-8). The Ezra of the *Codex Amiatinus,* as well as the architectural environment, is closely linked with the pictorial illusionism of Late Antiquity. The style is essentially that of the brush; the color, although here and there in flat planes, is blended smoothly to model the figure and to provide gradual transitions from light to dark. This procedure must have been continued in

8-7 *The Scribe Ezra Rewriting the Sacred Records,* from the *Codex Amiatinus,* Jarrow, early eighth century. Approx. 14″ × 10″. Biblioteca Medicea-Laurenziana, Florence.

8-8 *St. Matthew*, from the *Book of Lindisfarne*, Lindisfarne, late seventh century. Approx. 11" × 9". British Library, London.

the Mediterranean world throughout the Early Middle Ages, despite the formalizing into line that we have seen taking place in mosaics. But the Hiberno–Saxon artist of the *Lindisfarne* Matthew, trained in the use of hard, evenly stressed line, apparently knew nothing of the illusionistic, pictorial technique nor, for that matter, of the representation of the human figure. Although he carefully takes over the pose, he interprets the form in terms of line exclusively, "abstracting" the unfamiliar tonal scheme of his model into a patterned figure not unlike what we see in the King, Queen, and Jack of a deck of cards. The soft folds of drapery in the Ezra become, in the St. Matthew, a series of sharp, regularly spaced, curving lines. There is no modeling; no light and shade. The long training in the peculiar linear style of barbarian art made it necessary for the *Lindisfarne* artist to convert the strange Mediterranean forms into the linear idiom familiar to him; he finds before him a tonal *picture* and makes of it a linear *pattern.*

The Medieval artist did not go to nature for his model but to a prototype—another image, a statue, or a picture in a book. His copy might be one in a long line of copies, and, in some cases, we can trace these copies back to a lost original, inferring its former existence. The Medieval practice of copying pictures is of course closely related to the copying of books, especially sacred books like the Scriptures and the books used in the liturgy. The Medieval scribe or illuminator (before the thirteenth century, most often a monk) could have reasoned that just as the text of a holy book must be copied faithfully if the copy is also to be holy, so must the pictures be rendered faithfully. Of course, in the process of copying, mistakes are made; and, while scholars seek to purge the book of these textual "corruptions," "mistakes" in the copying of pictures yield new pictorial styles, or represent the confluence of different styles, as in the relationship of the *Codex Amiatinus* and the *Book of Lindisfarne*. In any event, one should realize that the style of Medieval images, whether in sculpture or in painting, was the result of copying from sources thought to have sacred authority, not from natural models. Thus, one learned what was true from authorities who declared the truth—the Scriptures and the fathers of the Church—and one painted "true" pictures or sculpted "true" statues from authoritative images. To question authority on one's own, to investigate "nature" on one's own, would be to question God's truth as revealed and interpreted. This would be blasphemy and heresy. It would be wrong, however, to leave the impression that dependence on authority in art is characteristic solely of the Middle Ages. In the Renaissance and since—and certainly today—new styles gain sudden authority and win widespread reverence and imitation, even for reasons that differ from those operative in the Middle Ages.

THE CAROLINGIAN PERIOD

The late eighth and the early ninth centuries saw the remarkable historical phenomenon now called "Charlemagne's renovation"—an energetic, brilliant emulation of the art and culture, not to say the political ideals, of Christian Rome. Out of the confusions attendant on the migrations and settlement of the barbarians, Charlemagne's immediate forerunners built, by force and political acumen, a Frankish empire that contained or controlled a large part of western Europe. Charlemagne, wishing, like Constantine, whom he consciously imitated, to create a unified Christendom as a visible empire, was crowned by the pope in Rome in 800 as head of the restored empire; the new entity became the Holy Roman Empire, which, waxing and waning over a thousand years and with many hiatuses, existed as a force in central Europe until its extinction by Napoleon in 1806.

Charlemagne was a sincere admirer of learning and the arts, and so that his empire should be as splendid as that of Rome (he thought of himself as successor to the caesars), he invited to his court at Aachen the best minds and the finest craftsmen of western Europe and of the Byzantine East. Although unlettered and scarcely able to write, he could speak Latin fluently and loved the discourses he frequently held with the learned men he gathered around him. Charlemagne must also have admired the splendid works created in the scriptorium of the school he established in his palace. One of his dearest projects had been the recovery of the true text of the Bible, which, through centuries of miscopying by ignorant scribes, had become almost hopelessly corrupt. Part of the great project, undertaken by the renowned scholar Alcuin of York at the new monastery at Tours, was the correction of the actual script used, which, in the hands of the scribes, had become almost unreadable. The Carolingian rehabilitation of the inherited Latin script produced a clear, precise system of letters; the letters on this page are descended from the alphabet renovated by the scribes of Tours.

Painting and Illumination

Charlemagne, his successors, and the scholars under their patronage imported whole libraries from Italy and Byzantium. The illustrations in these books must have astonished northern painters—some of whom had been trained in the Hiberno–Saxon manner of pattern making, others in the weak and inept Frankish styles of the seventh and eighth centuries. Here, they were suddenly confronted with a sophisticated realism that somehow had survived from the Late Antique amidst all the denaturing tendencies that followed. The famous *Coronation Gospels* (the *Gospel Book of Charlemagne,* formerly in the Imperial Treasury in Vienna) may have been a favorite of Charlemagne himself; an old tradition records that it was found on the knees of the dead emperor when, in the year 1000, Otto III had the imperial tomb at Aachen opened. The picture of *St. Matthew* composing his gospel (FIG. 8-9) descends from ancient depictions in sculpture and painting of an inspired philosopher or poet seated and writing. Its technique is of the same antiquity—deft, illusionistic brushwork that easily and accurately defines the masses of the drapery as they wrap and enfold the body beneath. The acanthus of the frame of the "picture window" recalls the fourth Pompeian style (see FIG. 6-33); the landscape background is thoroughly classicizing, and the whole composition seems utterly out of place in the north in the ninth century. How were the native artists to receive this new influence, so alien to what they had known and so strong as to make their own practice suddenly obsolete?

The style evident in the *Coronation Gospels* was by no means the only one that appeared suddenly in the Carolingian world. A wide variety of styles in all

8-9   *St. Matthew,* from the *Coronation Gospels* (the *Gospel Book of Charlemagne*), *c.* 800–810. Approx. 9″ × 6¾″. Kunsthistorisches Museum, Vienna.

stages of change from Antique prototypes were distributed through the court schools and the monasteries—a bewildering array, one can believe, for the natives, who attempted to appropriate them by copying them as accurately as possible. Thus, Carolingian painting is extremely diverse and uneven, and classification becomes a difficult matter of ascertaining prototypes and the descendants of prototypes. If the *Coronation Gospels* painting is by a Frank, rather than an Italian or a Byzantine, it is an amazing feat of approximation, since, except for the Jarrow copyist, there is nothing to prepare the way for it in the Hiberno–Saxon or Frankish West. Another *St. Matthew,* in a gospel book made for Archbishop Ebbo of Reims (FIG. 8-10), may be an interpretation of a prototype very similar to the one used by the *Coronation Gospels* master, for it resembles it in pose and in brushwork technique. But there the resemblance stops. The Classical calm and solidity have been replaced by an energy that amounts to frenzy, and the frail saint almost leaps under its impulse. His hair stands on end, the folds of his drapery writhe and vibrate, the landscape behind him rears up alive. He appears in frantic haste to take down what his inspiration (the tiny angel in the upper right hand corner) dictates. All fidelity to bodily proportions or structure is forsaken in the artist's effort to concentrate on the act of writing; the head, hands, inkhorn, pen, and book are the focus of

8-10 *St. Matthew,* from the *Ebbo Gospels* (the *Gospel Book of Archbishop Ebbo of Reims*), Hautvilliers (near Reims), c. 816–835. Approx. 10″ × 8″. Bibliothèque Municipale, Épernay.

the composition. This contrasts strongly with the settled pose of the Matthew of the *Coronation Gospels* with its even stress, so that no part of the composition starts out at us to seize our attention. The native power of expression is unmistakable and will become one of the important distinguishing traits of Late Medieval art. Just as the painter of the *Lindisfarne* Matthew (FIG. 8-8) transformed the Ezra portrait in the *Codex Amiatinus* (FIG. 8-7) into something original and strong, translating its classicizing manner into his own Hiberno–Saxon idiom, so the Ebbo artist translated his Classical prototype into a Carolingian vernacular that left little Classical substance. The four pictures should be carefully studied and compared.

Narrative illustration, so richly developed in Early Christian and Byzantine art, was revived by the Carolingians, and many fully illuminated books—some, large Bibles—were produced. One of the most extraordinary and enjoyable of all Medieval manuscripts is the famous *Utrecht Psalter,* written at Hautvilliers near Reims, France, about 830. The text, in three columns, reproduces the Psalms of David and is profusely illustrated by pen-and-ink drawings in the margins. The example shown in FIG. 8-11 depicts figures acting out Psalm 150, in which the psalmist exhorts us to praise the name of God in song and with timbrel, trumpet, and organ. The style shows a vivid animation of much the same kind as the St. Matthew of the *Ebbo Gospels* and may have been produced in the same school. The bodies are tense, shoulders hunched, heads thrust forward. The spontaneity of their actions and the rapid, sketchy technique with which they are rendered convey the same nervous vitality as the figure in the *Ebbo Gospels.* From details of the figures, their dress and accessories, scholars

feel certain that the artist was following one or more manuscripts compiled some 400 years earlier; but his interest in simple human emotions and actions, the pantomimic skill in the variety and descriptiveness of gesture, are essentially Medieval characteristics, although they begin in Early Christian art. Note, for example, how the two musicians playing the pipe organ shout at their helpers to pump air more strenuously. This candid observation of man, often in his unguarded moments, was to lend both truth and charm to the art of the Late Middle Ages.

8-11 *Psalm 150,* from the *Utrecht Psalter,* Hautvilliers (near Reims), c. 830. 4¾″ × 9½″. University Library, Utrecht.

8-12 *Christ in Majesty, Four Evangelists, and Scenes from the Life of Christ,* cover of the *Codex Aureus of St. Emmeram, c.* 870. Gold set with pearls and precious stones, 17″ × 13″. Bayerische Staatsbibliothek, Munich.

Craft Art

To our knowledge, there was little or no monumental sculpture in the Carolingian period. The traditional taste for sumptuously wrought and portable metal objects, which produced the barbarian works we have seen, persisted under Charlemagne and his suc-

cessors and produced numerous precious and beautiful works, like the book cover of the *Codex Aureus of St. Emmeram* (FIG. 8-12). Dating from the second half of the ninth century, it probably originated at either the St. Denis or Reims court of Charles the Bald, a grandson of Charlemagne. Its golden surface is set with pearls and precious jewels. Within the inscribed, squared cross, Christ in Majesty appears in an attitude not far removed from that in the apse mosaic of San Vitale (FIG. 7-38)—an example of the persistence of types and attitudes from Early Christian art into subsequent periods. Around Christ are seated the Four Evangelists, and there are four scenes from the life of Christ. In general, manuscript illumination provides the generative prototypes for ivory and metal work. Here, the style of the figures echoes that of the *Ebbo Gospels* and the *Utrecht Psalter*, although it is modified by influences from other Carolingian schools. There is no trace of the intricate interlace patterns of Hiberno–Saxon art, although the complex and delicate floral filigree clustering about the border jewels and enamels recalls them and

makes a foil for the classicizing figure style. At the center of the Carolingian renovation, the translated, classicizing style of Italy prevails, in keeping with the tastes and aspirations of the great Frankish emperor who fixed his admiring gaze on the culture of the south.

Metalcraft was extended to produce works well beyond the dimensions of the book cover, while maintaining the same principles in terms of materials, methods of production, design, and figure style. An example is the magnificent golden altar (the *Paliotto*) of the church of Sant' Ambrogio in Milan (FIG. 8-13). Shaped like a kind of large tomb, it was designed to contain the bones of St. Ambrose, an early bishop of Milan and one of the fathers of the Latin Church. Its

8-13 Detail of the *Paliotto* (golden altar), Sant' Ambrogio, Milan, early ninth century. Gold, silver, enamel, precious and semiprecious stones; entire altar 3' high, 7' long, 4' deep.

8-14 *Mounted Warrior with Captive* (detail of gold vessel; vessel 8¾" high), from the Nagy-szent-miklós treasure hoard found at Sinicolaul, Romania, probably ninth century. Kunsthistorisches Museum, Vienna.

four sides are ornamented with the lavish detail and jeweler's workmanship that we find in the *Codex Aureus*. Like that work, the *Paliotto* is divided into framed compartments of geometric simplicity and formality. Its gold, silver, and precious and semiprecious stones are set forth in exquisitely worked filigree to honor—in the central panels—the enthroned Christ, the Signs of the Evangelists, and the Twelve Apostles, all wrought in the classicizing figure style of the Carolingian renovation. Inscriptions on the back of the altar, where scenes from the life of Saint Ambrose are found, tell us that the donor was Archbishop Angilbert II, who governed the church in Milan between 824 and 859, which gives us a date for the monument. St. Ambrose places a crown on the bishop's head; he also places a crown on the head of the designer of the altar and its principal artist, a certain "Master Wolvinius," whose name suggests his east Frankish origins and that he may have been trained in the main centers of Carolingian art. Whatever the questions as to its sources, this work of Wolvinius and his fellow craftsmen remains perhaps the supreme masterpiece of the Age of Charlemagne.

Beyond the western regions under Carolingian control, migrations of war-like peoples from the east kept eastern and central Europe in turmoil throughout the ninth century. Mounted nomads rode the great grasslands as the Vikings rode the western seas. Charlemagne managed to repulse the Avars, who had long dominated the Hungarian plain. Like the migrating peoples in general, the Avars were skilled metal-craftsmen, and it is from a hoard of golden vessels left by them (a buried treasure never reclaimed) that we have the vase illustrated here (FIG. 8-14). Made of beaten gold, it bears a medallion with the image of a mounted, armored warrior. Posed both frontally and in profile, an Archaic convention we have seen in ancient art, he carries a spear over his right shoulder, and seizes a disarmed man with his left hand; the thrown-back head of another may belong to a man he has already killed. The dominating bulk of the fierce victor is made larger by the puny stature of his victims, another archaic convention we have seen in the art of Mesopotamia (FIG. 2-21) and Egypt (FIG. 3-41). Here is the very image of the times—when armed, pagan horsemen swept all before them in endless war and depradation. Yet the art of the Avars was influenced by the art of the settled and more civilized nations they came in contact with; the bead and fish-scale molding of the medallion frame and the floral motifs of the shoulder and base of the vessel are derived from Byzantine and Sassanian (Late Persian) art. Whether inspired by the Christian God, or the god of war, the craft art of the Early Middle Ages achieves a rare distinction. The priest and the warrior are the patrons of the craftsman.

Architecture

In his eagerness to reestablish the Imperial past, Charlemagne also encouraged the revival of Roman building techniques; in architecture, as in sculpture and painting, innovations made in the reinterpretation of earlier Roman–Christian sources became fundamental to Medieval designs. Perhaps "importation" is more appropriate here than "revival," as the Mediterranean tradition of stonemasonry could never have been more than an admirable curiosity to northern builders. Although northern Europe was dotted with Roman colonial towns that contained many large and impressive stone structures, the Germanic tribes had always relied on their vast forests to supply them with building materials; northern architecture was a timber architecture and continued to be so well into the Middle Ages. The typical northern European dwelling was a timber-frame structure (FIG. 8-15) that, in its essentials, has survived into our time. Its basic structural unit is the *bay*, which is constructed of four posts placed at the corners of a rectangle and interconnected and braced against each other with horizontal or oblique members. Such a unit is self-sup-

8-15 Conjectural reconstruction of an Iron Age house on foundations excavated at Ezinge, Holland. (After W. Horn.)

///// Reconstruction

0 10 20 30 40 50 60 70 80 90 100		FEET
0 3 6 9 12 15 18 21 24 27 30		METERS

8-16 Restored plan of the Palatine Chapel of Charlemagne, Aachen, West Germany, 792–805.

porting; it can be roofed and, depending on the desired size of the building, multiplied at will. Thus, the interior of such a structure is characterized by a repetition of identical units that move in orderly progression down the length of the building. The plan of such a building is related to the size and proportions of one of its bays in that the bay is the *module*, or basic unit of measurement, and the structure is a multiple of that unit.

Charlemagne's adoption of southern building principles for the construction of his palaces and churches was epoch-making for the subsequent development of the architecture of northern Europe. For his models, he went to Rome and Ravenna: one, the former heart of the Roman empire that he wanted to revive; the other, the long-term western outpost of Byzantine might and splendor that he wanted to emulate in his own capital at Aachen. Ravenna fell to the Lombards in 751 but was wrested from them only a few years later by the Frankish king, Pepin the Short, founder of the Carolingian dynasty and father of Charlemagne. Pepin donated the former Byzantine exarchate to the pope and thus founded the papacy's temporal power, which was to last until the late nineteenth century. In 789, Charlemagne visited Ravenna, and historians have long thought that he chose one of its churches as the model for the Palatine Chapel of his own palace at Aachen. But although its plan (FIG. 8-16) shows a resemblance to that of San Vitale (FIG. 7-33), recent study disproves a direct relationship between the two buildings. Nevertheless, a comparison of the two buildings is instructive. The Aachen plan is simpler; the apse-like extensions reaching from the central octagon into the ambulatory have been omitted, so that the two main units stand in greater independence of one another. This solution may lack the subtle sophistication of the Byzantine building but gains geometric clarity. A view of the interior of the Palatine Chapel (FIG. 8-17) shows that the "floating" quality of San Vitale has been con-

verted into blunt massiveness and stiffened into solid geometric form. The conversion of a complex and subtle Byzantine prototype into a building that expresses robust strength and clear structural articulation foreshadowed the architecture of the eleventh and twelfth centuries and the style we call Romanesque.

8-17 Interior of the Palatine Chapel of Charlemagne.

the final product no longer closely resembles the original, it is due to the fact that it is not a copy but a free and fanciful interpretation of its model.

The models that carried the greatest authority for Charlemagne and his builders were those from the Christian phase of the late Roman empire, and it was the adoption of the Early Christian basilica, rather than the domed, central plan of Byzantine churches, that was crucial to the subsequent development of Western church architecture in general and to the Romanesque style in particular. Several churches of the basilican type were built in northern Europe during the reign of Charlemagne, but none has survived; nevertheless, it is possible to reconstruct the appearance of some of them with fair accuracy. Some appear to have followed their Early Christian examples quite closely, as the abbey church of Fulda (begun in 802), which derives directly from Old St. Peter's and other Roman basilicas with transepts. But in other instances, Carolingian builders subjected the basilica plan to some very significant modifications, converting it into a much more complex organism.

The study of a fascinating Carolingian document, the ideal plan for a monastery at St. Gall, Switzerland (FIG. 8-19), may provide some insight into the motivations of the Carolingian planner. The monasteries were of central importance in the revival of learning. Monasticism held that the most perfect Christian life should be led in seclusion, removed from the temptations of ordinary life. In 526, Benedict had adapted the earlier regulations to the needs of western Europe. The "Benedictine Rule," which won out over Irish monasticism and which demanded, among other things, vows of poverty, chastity, and obedience, provided the basic organization for most western monasteries. Daily life was rigidly controlled, and each monastic community was self-sufficient. About 819, a schematic plan for such a community was copied from a lost original—probably designed by the abbot of Reichenau—and sent to the abbot of St. Gall for use as a guide in his planned rebuilding of that monastery. Near the center, dominating everything, was the abbey church, with the cloister (not unlike the early colonnaded atrium) at one side. Around the cloister were grouped the most essential buildings: chapter house (meeting room), dormitory, refectory, kitchen, and storage rooms. Other buildings— including an infirmary, school, guest house, bakery, brewery, and workshops—were grouped around this central core of church and cloister. That the scheme may have been meant to be more than an ideal and actually to have been built is indicated by Walter Horn's recent discovery that the original plan must have been laid out on a modular base of $2\frac{1}{2}$ feet

Charlemagne's dependence on Roman models is illustrated by a fascinating survival from his time, the Torhalle (gatehouse) of the Lorsch Monastery, which dates from about 800 (FIG. 8-18). Originally built as a freestanding structure in the atrium of the now-lost monastic church, this decorative little entrance gate is a distant relative of the Arch of Constantine (FIG. 6-89) by way of its reinterpretation in Christian terms for the entrance to the atrium of Old St. Peter's in Rome (if, in fact, it resembled the reconstruction shown in FIG. 7-6). To Charlemagne, either one could have been a symbol of Christian triumph over paganism. The triple-arched gateway on the lower level (FIG. 8-18) closely follows the design of Roman triumphal arches, with its column–arch combination, the fairly close copies of Late Roman capitals, and the decorative treatment of the flat wall surfaces with colored inlays of cream and pink stone in imitation of the Roman *opus reticulatum*. However, the columns support a decorative stringcourse instead of a full entablature, and what happens above it on the second level no longer has anything to do with triumphal arches. Instead of bearing the traditional dedicatory inscription, it is articulated with pseudo-Ionic pilasters that carry a zigzag of ornamental moldings, and the *opus reticulatum* has been converted into a decorative pattern of hexagons and triangles that form star shapes. Finally, the steeply pitched, timber roof that shelters a chapel dedicated to St. Michael unmistakably stamps this gatehouse as a northern building. Still, the source of inspiration is clear, and if

8-19 Schematic plan for a monastery at St. Gall, Switzerland, c. 819. (Redrawn after a ninth-century manuscript.)

and by the fact that parts or multiples of this module have been used consistently throughout the plan. Therefore, the width of the nave, indicated on the plan as 40 feet, would be equal to 16 modules; the length of each monk's bed to 2½ modules; and the width of paths in the vegetable garden to 1¼ modules.

Although the church is essentially a three-aisled basilica, it has features not found in any Early Chris-tian churches. Perhaps most obvious is the addition of a second apse on the west end of the building. The origin and purpose of this feature have never been satisfactorily explained, but it remained a characteris-tic regional element of German churches to the elev-enth century. Not quite as evident, but much more important to the subsequent development of church architecture in the north, is the fact that the transept is as wide as the nave. Early Christian builders had not been concerned with proportional relationships; they assembled the various portions of their buildings only in accordance with the dictates of liturgical needs. On the St. Gall plan, however, the various parts of the building have been related to each other by a geometric scheme that ties them together into a tight and cohesive unit. Equalizing the widths of nave and transept automatically makes the area in which they cross (the *crossing*) a square. This feature is shared by most Carolingian churches. But the St. Gall planner also took the subsequent steps that became fundamental to the development of Romanesque architecture: he used the crossing square as the unit of measurement for the remainder of the church plan. The arms of the transept are equal to one cross-

ing square, there is one square between transept and apse, and the nave is $4\frac{1}{2}$ crossing squares long. The fact that the aisles are half as wide as the nave integrates all parts of the church in a plan that is clear, rational, lucid, and extremely orderly.

The St. Gall plan reflects a Medieval way of thinking that is important for Romanesque art and architecture. As a guide for the builder of an abbey, it expresses the authority of the Benedictine Rule and serves as a kind of prototype. In the interest of clarity and orderliness, the "rule" is worked out with systematic care. There is balancing of units and a kind of division and subdivision of the site. (This parallels the Medieval invention of that most convenient device, the division of books into chapters and subchapters.) The neat "squaring" that characterizes the plan—together with the principle of the balance of clearly defined, simple units—will especially dominate Romanesque architectural design. The eagerness of the Medieval mind to explain the Christian faith in terms of an orderly, rationalistic philosophy built on carefully distinguished propositions and well-planned arguments finds visual expression in the plan of St. Gall.

Although the rebuilding project for St. Gall was not consummated, the church of St. Riquier at Centula in northeast France (FIG. 8-20) gives us some idea of what the St. Gall church would have looked like. A monastery church like that of St. Gall, the now-destroyed St. Riquier was built toward the very end of the eighth century and therefore predates the St. Gall plan by approximately 20 years. The illustration, taken from a seventeenth-century copy of a much older drawing, shows a feature not indicated on the plan of St. Gall but most likely common to all Carolingian churches—multiple, integrated towers. The St. Gall plan shows only two towers on the west side of the church, but they stand apart from it in the manner of the Italian campaniles. If we assume a tower above the crossing, the silhouette of St. Gall would have shown three towers rising above the nave. St. Riquier had six towers (not all are shown in the illustration) built directly onto or rising from the building proper. As large, vertical, cubic and cylindrical masses, these towers rose above the horizontal roofline, balancing each other in two groups of three at each end of the basilican nave. Round stair towers on the west end provided access to the upper stories of the so-called *westwork* (entrance structure) and to the big, spired tower that balanced the similar one above the eastern crossing. Such a grouping of three towers at the west, quite characteristic of churches built in the regions dominated by the Carolingians and their successors in German lands, probably foreshadows, in rudimentary form, the two-tower façades that were to become an almost universal stand-

8-20 Monastery church of St. Riquier, Centula, France, *c*. 800. (Engraving made in 1612 after a now-destroyed, eleventh-century miniature.)

ard in Late Romanesque and Gothic architecture. The towered westwork contained, on the second floor, a complete chapel flanked by aisles—a small upper church that could be used for parish services, the main floor of the building being reserved for the use of the clergy. (One must remember that this was a monastery church.) A gallery opened onto the main nave, and from it, on occasion, the emperor and his entourage could watch and participate in the service below. The plan of St. Riquier, as reconstructed (FIG. 8-21), shows an emphatic handling of the crossing square, which has been set apart from the rest of the building by massive arches. The dimensions of the square have been used once for the fore-choir and again for the westwork chapel. But beyond that, the plan is not as fully developed as that of St. Gall. The aisles are only one-third the width of the nave, the transept arms are about two-thirds the crossing square, and the length of the nave is not related to either the crossing square or any other components of the building's plan. However, the St. Riquier design, particularly the silhouette with its multiple integrated towers, was highly influential, especially in Germany.

THE OTTONIAN PERIOD

Charlemagne's empire survived him by less than 30 years. Under his three grandsons, Charles the Bald, Lothair, and Louis the German, the Carolingian empire was partitioned by 843 into western, central, and eastern areas, very roughly foreshadowing the later sections of France, Lorraine, and the Germanies. Intensified incursions of the Vikings in the west helped bring about the collapse of the Carolingians and the suspension of their great cultural effort. The breakup of the empire into weak kingdoms, ineffectual against the invasions, brought a time of darkness and confusion that was perhaps even deeper than the seventh and eighth centuries. The scourge of the Vikings in the west was complemented by the invasions of the Magyars in the east and by the plundering and piracy of the Saracen corsairs in the Mediterranean. Only in the mid-tenth century did the eastern part of the former empire consolidate under the rule of a new Saxon line of German emperors called, after the names of the three most illustrious members of the family, the "Ottonians." The three Ottos made headway against the invaders from the east, remained free

from Viking depredations, and were able to found an empire that, nominally at least, became the successor to Charlemagne's Holy Roman Empire. The culture and tradition of the Carolingian period were not only preserved but advanced and enriched. The Church, which had become corrupt and disorganized, recovered in the tenth century under the influence of a great monastic reform encouraged and sanctioned by the Ottonians, who also cemented ties with Italy and the papacy. When the last of the Ottonian line, Henry II, died in the early eleventh century, the pagan marauders had become Christianized and settled, the monastic reforms had been highly successful, and there were signs of a cultural renewal soon destined to produce greater monuments than had been known since ancient Rome.

Architecture

Ottonian architects followed the direction of their Carolingian predecessors. St. Michael's, the abbey church at Hildesheim (FIG. 8-22) built between 1001 and 1031 by Bishop Bernward, retains the tower groupings and the westwork of St. Riquier, as well as its massive, blank walls. But the addition of a second transept and apse result in a better balancing of east and west units. The plan and section of St. Michael's (FIG. 8-23) clearly show the east and west centers of gravity, the nave being merely a hall that connects them. Lateral entrances leading into the aisles from the north and south are additional factors making for an almost complete loss of the traditional basilican orientation toward the east. More refined and precise than St. Riquier, the marked-off crossing squares have been used as a module for the dimensions of the nave, which is three crossing squares long and one square wide. This fact is emphasized visually by the placement of heavy piers at the corners of each square. These piers alternate with pairs of columns as wall supports, and the resultant "alternate-support system" will become a standard feature of many Romanesque churches in northern Europe. Contrary to one view, the alternate-support system is not related to the development of Romanesque systems of vaulting. It made its first appearance in timber-roofed structures of the tenth century (such as St. Cyriakus at Gernrode, begun in 961) and appears to be the logical outcome of the Carolingian suggestion that the length of a building could be a multiple of the cross-

8-22 Abbey church of St. Michael, Hildesheim, West Germany, *c.* 1001–1031. (Restored.)

8-23 Section (*top*) and plan (*bottom*) of St. Michael's, Hildesheim.

8-24 The nave of St. Michael's. (Restored.)

A view of the interior of St. Michael's (FIG. 8-24) shows the rhythm of the alternating light and heavy wall supports. It shows as well that this rhythm is not yet reflected in the upper nave walls—that in fact it has not yet been carried further than the actual supports. Although its proportions have changed—it has become much taller in relation to its width than a Roman basilica—the nave retains the continuous and unbroken appearance of its Early Christian predecessors. We see a fully developed Romanesque interior only when the geometric organization of the church plan is fully reflected in the elevation of the nave walls and the interior space takes on the appearance of being composed of a number of vertical segments.

Sculpture

St. Michael's is an important and highly refined transitional monument that fills a gap between the Carolingian and Romanesque styles. Its patron, Bishop Bernward, who made Hildesheim a center of learning, was not only skilled in affairs of state, but was also an eager scholar, a lover of the arts, and, according to his biographer, an expert craftsman and bronze-caster. His stay in Rome in 1001 as guest of the emperor, Otto III, whom he had tutored and whose friend he was, must have acquainted him with monuments like the Column of Trajan (FIG. 6-64), which may have influenced the great, column-like, paschal candlestick he set up in St. Michael's; and the wooden doors of an Early Christian church, Santa Sabina, may have inspired the remarkable bronze doors he had cast for his splendid church. The doors were cast in a single piece, the first of their kind since ancient Rome. Carolingian sculpture, like most sculpture since antiquity, had been small art in ivory and metal; the St. Michael's doors anticipated the coming reinstatement of large-scale sculpture in the Romanesque period. The style of the figures on the doors (FIG. 8-25) derives from Carolingian manuscript illumination but has an expressive strength of its own—

ing square. Thus, the suitability of the alternate-support system to some Romanesque vaulting systems is only incidental; it seems to have been adopted not as a structural but as an esthetic device that furnishes visual proof of the geometric organization of the building's plan. It has been suggested that the alternate-support system is an importation from the eastern empire, perhaps from Thessaloniki (modern Salonika). If so, it seems to have been adopted enthusiastically by northern architects, who, it has been lately proposed, may have seen it as an ideal means of converting unbroken basilican interiors into the modular units to which they were accustomed in their native timber architecture (FIG. 8-15).

8-25 *Adam and Eve Reproached by the Lord,* from the bronze doors commissioned by Bishop Bernward for St. Michael's, 1015. Approx. 23″ × 43″.

once again, a case of the form derived from a prototype becoming something new and firmly itself. God is accusing Adam and Eve after their fall from grace. As he lays on them the curse of mortality, the primal condemnation, he jabs his finger with the force of his whole body—the force concentrating in the gesture, the psychic focus of the whole composition. The frightened pair crouch, not only to hide their shame but to escape the lightning bolt of the divine wrath. Each passes the blame—Adam pointing backward to Eve, Eve pointing downward to the deceitful serpent.

8-26 *Doubting Thomas*, from the *Magdeburg Antependium*, *c.* 970–990. Ivory, approx. 9″ × 4″. Staatliche Museen, Berlin.

The setting, the starkly flat ground, throws into relief the gestures and attitudes of rage, accusation, guilt, and fear; once again, the story is presented with all the simplicity and impact of skilled pantomime.

We have seen how the instinct for pantomimic pose and gesture guides the representations and narratives of Medieval art from the very beginning. Such pantomime, emphasized by telling exaggeration, appears in an ivory carving (FIG. 8-26) that surely is among the masterpieces of the art of the Middle Ages. This small panel (only 9 inches high and 4 inches wide) carries a composition of two intertwined figures, beautifully adjusted to the space. The theme is the persuasion of Doubting Thomas when, after the Resurrection, Christ appears to his sorrowing disciples. All believe that he is truly Christ and truly risen except the skeptical Thomas, who demands to feel the bodily wounds of the master he has seen crucified. In the panel, Thomas explores the wound in Christ's side in a kind of climbing, aggressive curiosity. Christ, his right arm raised to reveal his side, bends over Thomas in an attitude that wonderfully combines gentleness, benign affection, protectiveness, and sorrow. The figures are represented entirely within the context of emotion; the concentration on the single act of Christ's revelation to the doubter, the emotional vibrations that accompany the doubt, and the ensuing conversion of Thomas determine every line of the rendering. We are not aware of the presence here of the influence of a prototype; we seem to have before us an original work of great power.

Painting and Illumination

It must be assumed that, by Ottonian times, artists had become familiar enough with the Carolingian figurative modes to work with considerable independence, developing a functional, vernacular style of their own. A supreme example of this is an illumination in the *Lectionary of Henry II* (FIG. 8-27), in which an angel announces the birth of Christ to the shepherds. The angel has just alighted on a hill, his wings still beating, and the wind of his landing agitates his draperies. He looms immense above the startled and terrified shepherds, filling the sky, and bends on them a fierce and menacing glance as he extends his hand in the gesture of authority and instruction. Emphasized more than the message itself is the power and majesty of God's authority. The electric force of God's violent pointing in the Hildesheim doors is felt again here with the same pantomimic impact. Although the figure style may stem ultimately from the Carolingian School at Tours, the painters of the scriptorium of Reichenau (an island in Lake Constance on the German–Swiss border) who

8-27 *The Annunciation to the Shepherds,* from the *Lectionary of Henry II,* 1002–1014. Approx. 17" × 13". Bayerische Staatsbibliothek, Munich.

8-28 *Otto III Enthroned Receiving the Homage of Four Parts of the Empire* (with nobility and clergy), from the *Gospel Book of Otto III*, 997–1000. Approx. 14″ × 10″. Bayerische Staatsbibliothek, Munich.

produced the *Lectionary of Henry II* have made of their received ideas something fresh and powerful; a new sureness in the touch is epitomized by the way in which the draperies are rendered in a hard, firm line and the planes are partitioned in sharp, often heavily modeled shapes. We saw this in Middle and Late Byzantine art, and indeed there was a close connection between the Ottonian and Byzantine spheres. Yet, for the most part, the Ottonian artists went their own way; Ottonian painting was produced for the court and for the great monasteries, for learned princes, abbots, and bishops, and thus appealed to an aristocratic audience that could appreciate independent and sophisticated variations on inherited themes. Although an illumination like *The Annunciation to the Shepherds* could by no means be called Classical, there is a sculpturesque clarity about it—a strong, relief-like projection and silhouette that suggests not a hesitating approximation of misunderstood prototypes from antiquity but a confident, if unconscious, capture of the Antique spirit. At the same time, the powerful means of expression of *The Annunciation to the Shepherds* miniature imply an intensification of Christian spirituality that is perhaps related to the broad monastic reforms of the tenth and eleventh centuries. With that force of expression goes a significantly new manner of fashioning the human figure in art, one that is not slavishly dependent on prototypes even when prototypes are exchanged and studied. Ottonian figurative art reveals a translation of prototypal material into a kind of ready idiom of forms and a native way of drawing. Although there are exceptions, for the most part Ottonian figures have lost the old realism of the *Coronation Gospels* (FIG. 8-9), inherited from the Antique style, and move with an abrupt, hinged, jerky movement not "according to nature" but nevertheless with sharp and descriptive expressiveness. This new manner would be passed on to the figurative artists of the Romanesque period. As the western European spoken and written languages emerged from the polyglot Latin–Germanic of the early centuries into the vernacular tongues we recognize today, so figurative art gradually developed out of the same kind of mixture of Latin, Germanic, and Celtic elements into a new, strong, and self-sufficient vernacular of representation.

A picture from the *Gospel Book of Otto III*, representing the emperor himself (FIG. 8-28), sums up much of what went before and points to what is coming. The emperor is represented enthroned under a canopy (the *baldachin*), holding the scepter and cross-inscribed orb that represent his universal authority. He is flanked by the clergy and the barons (the Church and the State), both aligned in his support. Stylistically remote, the picture still has a clear political resemblance to the Justinianic mosaic in San Vitale (FIG. 7-36). It was the vestigial, Imperial ideal—awakened in the Frankish Charlemagne and preserved for a while by his Ottonian successors in Germany—that had given partial unity to western Europe while the barbarians were settling down. This Imperial ideal, salvaged from ancient Rome and bolstered by the experience of Byzantium, would survive long enough to give an example of order and law to the barbarians; to this extent, ancient Rome lived on to the millennium. But native princes in England, France, Spain, Italy, and eastern Europe would aspire to a sovereignty outside the imperial Carolingian and Ottonian hegemony; staking their claims, they make the history of the Medieval power contests that led to the formation of the states of Europe as we know them. In the illumination (FIG. 8-28), Otto, sitting between the rival Church and State, represents the very model of the Medieval predicament that will divide Europe for centuries. The controversy of the Holy Roman Emperors with the popes will bring the German successors of the Ottonians to bitter defeat in the thirteenth century; and with that defeat, the authority of ancient Rome will come to an end. The Romanesque period that is to follow will, in fact, deny the Imperial spirit that had prevailed for centuries. A new age is about to begin, one in which Rome—an august memory—will cease to be the deciding influence.

9

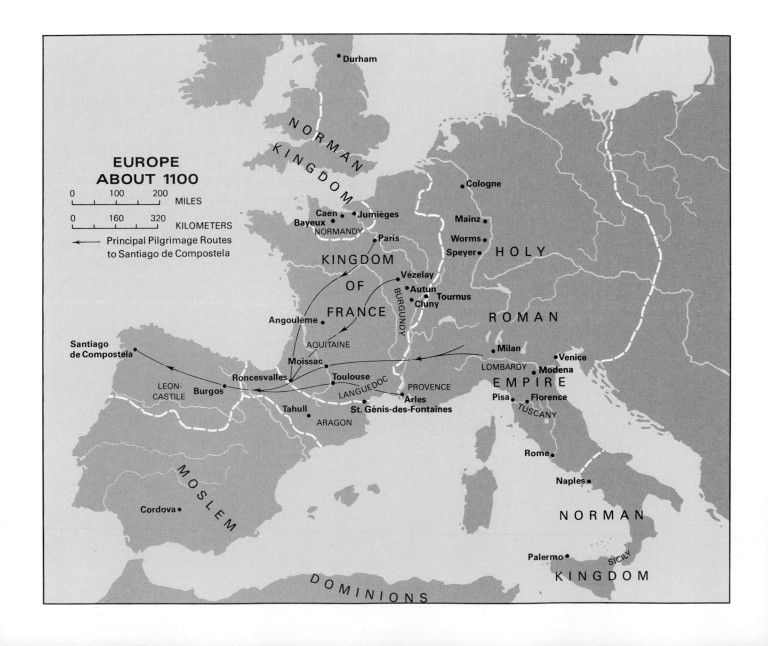

**EUROPE
ABOUT 1100**

0	100	200

MILES

0	160	320

KILOMETERS

← Principal Pilgrimage Routes
to Santiago de Compostela

Durham

NORMAN

KINGDOM

Cologne

Mainz

Caen · Jumièges
Bayeux
NORMANDY

Worms

Paris

Speyer

HOLY

KINGDOM

Vézelay

OF

Autun
Tournus
Cluny

BURGUNDY

FRANCE

ROMAN

Angoulême

AQUITAINE

Milan

EMPIRE

Venice

Santiago
de Compostela

LOMBARDY

Modena

Moissac

Roncesvalles

Toulouse

LEON-
CASTILE

Burgos

LANGUEDOC

PROVENCE

Arles

Pisa

Florence

TUSCANY

Tahull

St. Génis-des-Fontaines

ARAGON

Rome

MOSLEM

Naples

NORMAN

Cordova

Palermo

SICILY

DOMINIONS

KINGDOM

ROMANESQUE ART

Crypt of St. Philibert, Tournus (c. 950)

900 · 1000

FIRST ROMANESQUE

Pisa Cathedral (1053–1272)

Speyer Cathedral (1030)

1030

ROMANESQUE PERIOD

Bayeux Tapestry (1073–1083)

1060

NORMAN CONQUEST OF SOUTH ITALY AND SICILY

1066 Norman conquest of England (Battle of Hastings)

1071 Turkish conquest of Jerusalem

St. George and the Dragon from the *Moralia in Job*

Durham Cathedral (1093)

1090

1101

1095 First Crusade

The Scribe Eadwine from the *Canterbury Psalter*

1120

The Mission of the Apostles, Vézelay (1120–1132)

1147 Second Crusade

The Crusades

c. 1150

THE MID-ELEVENTH CENTURY marks a turning point in European history; Europe *as* Europe begins to emerge. The past was a boiling confusion of barbarian movements, coalescing into settlements and then aggregating into "empires," like the Carolingian and Ottonian, that had their spiritual and political roots in the memory of the Roman *imperium.* Now, although a Latin culture and tradition persist and are still accepted with reverence, the Medieval people are not so retrospective; they have new experiences and take new directions.

After the disintegration of the Carolingian state, when the successors to the imperializing Ottonians had begun to limit their concerns to Italy and the German duchies, numerous feudal political entities—petty and great, within and without the outlines of the old Frankish and Saxon "empires"—pursued their own interests and developed in their own ways. Two institutions gave them a certain coherence: the Christian Church and feudalism. If the descendants of the barbarians had anything in common, it was, above all else, their Christianity. Feudalism, which had its origins both in barbarian custom and in late Roman institutions, preserved a stability, but it was a stability of a local kind, being naturally antagonistic to broad, centralized government.

Essentially, feudalism was an economic system involving a complicated series of interpersonal relationships, obligations, and services based on land tenure. One held a piece of land, a *fief,* and paid for it, not in money, but in service (often military). Feudal obligation led downward from a lord to his vassal to the lower orders of society and ultimately to the serf, who was bound to the land and to the unquestioning service of the lord. The lords or nobles held fiefs in various ways from each other or from an overlord, such as a king. Inevitably, many of them became large landowners and so powerful that they ignored their obligations and defied their king. Their time was spent in petty wars for the purpose of protecting or increasing the extent of their holdings. The *château fort,* or castle, surrounded by walls and moats, was the symbol and seat of feudal authority. Today, the moldering ruins of these castles in the countrysides of Europe recall the modern visitor to an age when government was always visible, singular, personal, and absolute.

The Romanesque baron or knight, still in the heroic tradition of the Germanic hero, was loyal, defiant, and proud. However, being a Christian, he was without the deep barbarian fatalism of the earlier Saxons and Norse and hoped not only for immortal honor in battle (won as much by the power of religious faith as by his own strength and courage) but also for life eternal in Heaven. This was the mood—the psycho-logical "set"—of the aristocratic, warring magnates who led the Crusades and maintained the feudal system.

Monasticism, which reached its peak at the same time as feudalism, provided seclusion from the world, an assurance of salvation, and almost the only means of receiving an education. The history of monasticism, which, as we have seen, began in the Early Middle Ages, is essentially a series of reform movements. Because gifts and bequests to them were potent means of assuring salvation, monasteries grew wealthy. With wealth came luxury and laxness and recurrent reforms to combat them. The reforms led to the formation of new monastic orders. The two great Romanesque orders were the Cluniac and the Cistercian. The former, which especially fostered the arts, was founded early in the tenth century and had its main abbey at Cluny near Mâcon in France. Encouraged by the Ottonian emperors, the Cluniac order owed allegiance only to the pope in Rome and formed, with the vast number of its priories scattered all over Europe, a centrally organized administration in sharp contrast to the decentralizing tendencies of feudalism. The Cluniac reform, based on a liberal interpretation of St. Benedict's original rule, stressed intellectual pursuits, the study of music, and the cultivation of the other arts. The wealth and the vastness of the resources of the Cluniac order soon provoked still another reform—one that emphasized self-denial and the virtues of manual labor and gave rise to the Cistercian order, which also grew rapidly.

Thus, with feudalism and monasticism triumphant and replacing the emperors, the barons and the monastery clergy (the latter often themselves feudal lords) played a peculiarly cooperative role, and the feudal stratification of society into strictly separated classes was given religious sanction. Notwithstanding this cooperation, however, the chief conflict of the time was between the popes and the feudal principals—not over the justice or injustice of the feudal system, but over the question, Who is the supreme feudal lord; who is king?

There was great movement of populations in the endless pilgrimages to innumerable shrines and in the Crusades (the first two of which belong to this period), which saw thousands of people trek from western Europe to the Holy Land. The pilgrimage was a principal feature of Medieval Christian life. Travel to the distant shrine of a saint, whose spiritually powerful relics could there be venerated, was commonly enjoined as a penitential act on which the salvation of the pilgrim depended; of such shrines, that of St. James (Santiago) at Compostela in Spain was the most famous in the West, outside of Rome itself. Travel, extremely dangerous in those turbulent times, became the duty and the hope of thousands.

The Crusades were a militant expansion of the pilgrimages. Crusader and pilgrim were bound by similar vows and hoped not only to expiate sin and win salvation but to glorify God and extend the power of the Church. Most important of the immediate results of the Crusades were the establishment of the Church as a leader of the people and the reopening of commerce with the great trading centers in the Near East.

Pisan ships carried the crusading barons to the Holy Land and brought back their bones. The Pisans prospered, as did the burghers of the towns that the barons left behind them and to whom they had given charters of liberty in return for financing their campaigns. Thus, the Crusades created subcurrents of independence; the towns got their charters, and a middle class of merchants and craftsmen grew up to countervail the power of feudal barons and the great monasteries. A growing city culture was quick to receive new impulses from abroad. The lines of commerce, often the arteries of ideas, conveyed new learning to Europe. The Crusades, destructive as they were, effected a new insight into Greek science and philosophy through contact with Islam, which had assimilated Greek culture much earlier. Within a century, the relatively limited knowledge possessed by the Carolingians and the Ottonians was expanded to an enormous store. It was from this store that men would draw the materials and inspirations for renaissance after renaissance until, in the sixteenth century, a distinction would come to be made between pagan and Christian antiquity. Within this context of an emerging world, unique although shadowed with a tremendous past, Romanesque art appeared in the eleventh and twelfth centuries. It is a confident art, one that does not hesitate among alternatives and is sure even in the midst of its own changes.

ARCHITECTURE

As a term, "Romanesque" was first used in the nineteenth century to designate buildings with round arches and blunt, heavy walls that were supposed to bear some resemblance to ancient Roman architecture, just as the developing "Romance" languages were related to Latin. Although the Romanesque style varies widely and embraces numerous provincial differences within its almost two-century span, architectural historians now regard it as complete within itself and not as the imperfect antecedent of the Gothic style. Thus, despite its variety, Romanesque architecture is readily recognizable as such. An aerial view of the church of St. Sernin at Toulouse in the south of France (FIG. 9-4) shows certain features that appear in Romanesque buildings no matter how their arrangement differs. There is an overall blocky appearance, a grouping of large, simple, easily definable, geometric masses—rectangles, cubes, cylinders, and half-cylinders. The main masses are subdivided by enframing buttresses or colonnettes. Exterior wall surfaces, which had been plain and unadorned through the Ottonian period, now reflect the interior organization of the structure. This enlivening of formerly blank wall surfaces foreshadows the structural translucency that would typify Gothic architecture.

The new demands of a people with religious as well as commercial reasons to travel shaped the new architecture. The building impulse, which became almost a Medieval obsession, was noted by an eleventh-century monk, Raoul Glaber, who wrote:

> . . . there occurred, throughout the world, especially in Italy and Gaul, a rebuilding of church basilicas. Notwithstanding the greater number were already well established and not in the least in need, nevertheless each Christian people strove against the others to erect nobler ones. It was as if the whole earth, having cast off the old . . . were clothing itself everywhere in the white robe of the church.*

Glaber does not mention that a contributing cause of this eleventh-century building "obsession" may have been the widely felt relief and thanksgiving that the millennium (1000) did not bring an end to the world, as had been feared.

Great building efforts were provoked not only by the pilgrimages and the Crusades and the needs of growing cities, but also by the fact (notably in Italy and France) that hundreds of churches had been destroyed during the depredations of the Norsemen and the Magyars. Architects of the time seemed to see their fundamental problem in terms of providing a building that would have space for the circulation of its congregations and visitors and that would be solid, fireproof, well lighted, and acoustically suitable. These, of course, are the necessities of any great civic or religious architecture, as we saw in ancient Rome, but in this case, fireproofing must have been foremost in the builders' minds, for the wooden roofs of the pre-Romanesque churches of Italy, France, and elsewhere had burned fiercely and totally when set aflame by the marauders from north, east, and south in the ninth and tenth centuries. The memory was fresh in the victims' minds; the new churches would have to be covered with cut stone, and the structural problems arising from this need for a solid masonry were to help determine the "look" of Romanesque architecture.

*In E.G. Holt, ed., *Literary Sources of Art History* (Princeton, N.J.: Princeton University Press, 1947), p. 3.

Languedoc–Burgundy

A fascinating building of the so-called "First Romanesque" period, in which a variety of experimental solutions to the vaulting problem are illustrated, is the church of St. Philibert at Tournus on the Saône river in Burgundy (FIGS. 9-1, 9-2, 9-3). The long and complex building history of this church explains, in part, the curious assembly of various vaulting systems found in it. Of the original building, which was begun around 950, only the crypt survived a disastrous fire in 1008. The rebuilt church was consecrated in 1019, although the nave was not vaulted until 1066 and the crossing and choir were not completed until 1120. The new choir was built according to the plan of the crypt below it, but the original westwork was replaced with a two-story narthex.

The unusual variety of vaults resulted when each successive generation of builders addressed the problem of vaulting anew and produced fresh and ingenious solutions. The crypt used small groin vaults over square areas defined by slender, supporting columns; the corridor surrounding the central area was covered by a curving barrel vault. The vaulting of the narthex, which was probably completed by 1019, is more complex. The groin-vaulted square bays of the ground floor's central passage are flanked by aisles slightly less than half as wide as the nave; they had to be covered with shallow barrel vaults, as true groin vaults can only be erected over square areas. Above this entrance hall, on the second level, stands a three-aisled chapel dedicated to St. Michael. Here, the central nave is covered by a longitudinal barrel vault that is buttressed by *quadrant vaults* (half-barrel vaults)

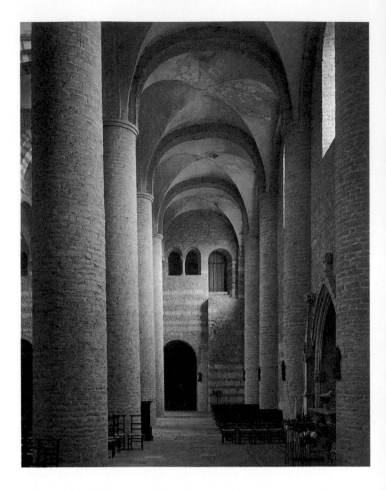

9-1   The nave of St. Philibert, Tournus, France, *c.* 950–1020 and later.

9-2   View into the nave vaults, St. Philibert.

over the flanking aisles. Most remarkable is the main church, where groin-vaulted aisles flank a nave that rises to a series of five parallel, transverse barrel vaults that buttress each other and obviate the massive side walls that a single, longitudinal vault would have required. It also allowed the builders to cut generous clerestory windows into the end walls of the barrels, which have no major supporting function. As a result, the interior is adequately illuminated and light can play with marvelous effect over the simple, curved surfaces of the ceiling and the sturdy, cylindrical columns.

Just about all known vaulting methods, except the dome, were explored in this single building—a ready-to-choose-from collection of solutions for later builders. (As we will soon see, Burgundian masons opted for the longitudinal barrel vault.) But possibly an even more important and influential feature of this unique building is revealed by the plan of the choir (FIG. 9-3), which, if it does not repeat that of the one destroyed by the fire of 1008, does duplicate that of the crypt of 950. The monks' choir is surrounded by an ambulatory from which a series of chapels (and a stairwell) radiate outward. This ambulatory afforded easy circulation for the pilgrims who came to venerate the relics of St. Philibert, without interrupting the monks' obligations. This arrangement, in which subordinate chapels and ambulatories are ingeniously integrated, was to become, with due modifications, a standard feature of later pilgrimage churches.

9-3 Plan and section of St. Philibert, Tournus.

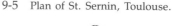

9-4 Aerial view of St. Sernin, Toulouse, France, *c.* 1080–1120 (view from the southeast).

9-5 Plan of St. Sernin, Toulouse.

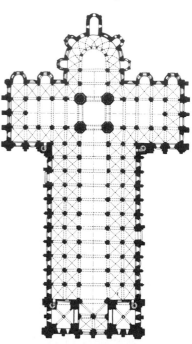

St. Sernin at Toulouse (FIG. 9-4) was one of the churches constructed in the Cluniac–Burgundian style that may have profited from the experiments made at Tournus; it met the requirement of a stone ceiling by using a semicircular barrel vault above which was a timber-roofed loft. Such churches dominated much of southern France and were closely related to those built along the pilgrimage road to Santiago de Compostela in northwest Spain. The plan of St. Sernin (FIG. 9-5) is one of extreme regularity and geometric precision. The crossing square, flanked by massive piers and marked off by heavy arches, has been used as the module for the entire body of the church. In this *square schematism*, each nave bay measures exactly one-half and each square in the aisles measures exactly one-quarter of a crossing square, and so on throughout the building. The first suggestion of such a planning scheme is seen almost three centuries earlier in the St. Gall plan (FIG. 8-19). Although St. Sernin is neither the earliest nor the only (perhaps not even the ideal) solution, it does represent a crisply rational and highly refined realization of the germ of an idea first seen in Carolingian designs. A view of the interior (FIG. 9-6) shows that this geometric floor plan is fully reflected in the nave walls, which are articulated by half-columns that rise from the corners of each bay to the springing of the vault and are continued across the nave as transverse arches. Ever since Early Christian times, basilican interiors had been framed by long, flat walls between arcades and clerestories that enclosed a single, horizontal, unbroken volume of space. Now the aspect of the nave is radically changed, so that it seems to be composed of numerous, identical, vertical volumes of space that have been placed one behind the other, marching down the length of the building in orderly procession. This segmentation of St. Sernin's interior space corresponds with and renders visual the geometric organization of the building's plan and is also reflected in the articulation of the building's exterior walls. The result is a structure in which all parts have been integrated to a degree unknown in earlier Christian architecture.

The grand scale of St. Sernin at Toulouse is frequent in Romanesque churches. The popularity of pilgrimages and of the cult of relics brought great crowds even to relatively isolated places, and large congregations were common at the shrines along the great pilgrimage routes and in the reawakening cities. Additional space was provided by increasing the length of the nave, by doubling the side aisles, and by building, over the inner aisle, upper galleries, or *tribunes,* the latter to accommodate overflow crowds on special occasions. Circulation was complicated, though, as the monks' choir often occupied a good portion of the nave. As seen in St. Philibert at Tournus, an extension of the aisles around the eastern end to make an ambulatory facilitated circulation, and the opening of the ambulatory (and often of the transepts) into separate chapels (as at St. Sernin) provided more space for worshipers and for liturgical processions. Not all Romanesque churches were as large as St. Sernin, however, nor did every one have an ambulatory with radiating chapels; but such chapels are typical Romanesque features, especially when treated as separate units projecting from the mass of the building.

The continuous, cut-stone barrel (or tunnel) vaults at St. Sernin (FIG. 9-6) put constant pressure along the entire length of the supporting masonry. If, as in most instances, including St. Sernin (FIG. 9-5), the nave was flanked by side aisles, then the main vaults rested on arcades and the main thrust was carried to the thick outer walls by the vaults over the aisles. In larger churches, the tribune galleries and their vaults (in cross section, often a quadrant, embracing a 90° arc) were an integral part of the structure, buttressing the high vaults over the nave. The wall–vault system at St. Sernin is successful in its supporting function; its great scale provides ample space, and its squaring-off into cleanly marked bays, as well as the relief of wall and pier, are thoroughly Romanesque. But the system fails in one critical requirement—that of lighting. Due to the great thrust exerted by the barrel vault, a clerestory was difficult to construct, and windows cut into the haunch of the vault would make it unstable. A more complex and efficient type of vaulting was needed; one might say that, structurally, the central problem of Romanesque architecture was the development of a masonry vault system that admitted light.

In working toward this end, Romanesque architectural ingenuity produced numerous experimental consequences that appear as a rich variety of substyles. We have already mentioned that one of the apparently confusing features of Romanesque architecture is the great variety of regional and local building styles—a variety that makes classification, coordination, and interpretation still very difficult for scholars. Ten or more types may be identified in France alone, each with its distinctive system of vaulting and its varying solutions to the lighting of the interior.

Among the numerous experimental solutions, the groin vault turned out to be the most efficient and flexible. The groin vault had been widely used by Roman builders, who saw that its concentration of thrusts at four supporting points would allow clerestory fenestration. The great Roman vaults were made possible by an intricate system of brick-and-tile relieving arches, as well as by the use of concrete, which could be poured into forms and which solidified into a homogeneous mass. The technique of mixing concrete did not survive into the Middle Ages, however, and the technical problems of building groin vaults of cut stone and heavy rubble, which had very little cohesive quality, limited their use to the covering of small areas. But during the eleventh century, Romanesque masons, using cut stone joined by mortar, developed a groin vault of monumental dimensions that, although it still employed heavy buttressing walls, eventually evolved into a self-sufficient, skeletal support system.

Germany–Lombardy

The progress of vaulting craft can best be seen in two regions: Germany–Lombardy and Normandy–England. Speyer Cathedral in the German Rhineland (FIGS. 9-7, 9-8, 9-9) was begun in 1030 as a timber-

9-6 The nave of St. Sernin.

9-7 Speyer Cathedral, West Germany, begun 1030. (Pen-and-ink drawing by WENZEL HOLLAR, c. 1620.) Graphische Sammlung Albertina, Vienna.

roofed structure. When it was rebuilt by the emperor Henry IV, between 1082 and 1106, it was covered with groin vaults. It thus may be one of the earliest, fully vaulted Romanesque churches in Europe. Its exterior preserves the Ottonian tradition of balanced groups of towers east and west, but adds to it a rich articulation of wall surfaces. A great many of the decorative features, such as the arcades under the eaves, the stepped arcade gallery under the gable, and the moldings marking the stages of the towers, may be of Lombard origin. So may be the inspiration for the groin vaults covering the aisles, as groin-vaulting on a small scale had been used by Lombard builders throughout the Early Middle Ages. The large groin vaults covering the nave (FIG. 9-9), however—probably the achievement of German masons—represent one of the most daring and successful vaulting enterprises of the time. (The nave is 45 feet wide, and the crowns of the vaults are 107 feet high.) The plan of the cathedral (FIG. 9-8) shows that the west apse and the lateral Ottonian entrances have been given up, that the entrance has been moved back to the west end, and that the processional axis leading to the sanctuary has been reestablished. The

marked-off crossing, covered by an octagonal dome, has been used as the module for the arrangement of the building's east end. Because the nave bays are not square, the use of the crossing as a unit of measurement is not as obvious. In fact, the length of the nave is almost four times the crossing square, and every third wall support marks off an area in the nave the size of the crossing; the aisles are half the width of the nave. Although the plan has some irregularities and has not been worked out as neatly and precisely as the plan of St. Sernin, the builders' intention to

9-9 Interior of Speyer Cathedral.

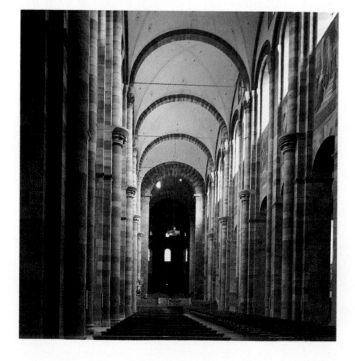

9-8 Plan of Speyer Cathedral.

apply the square schematism is quite clear. Curiously, the alternate-support system, which is now carried all the way up into the vaults (FIG. 9-9), does not seem to reflect the square schematism of the building's plan. This discrepancy may be explained by the fact that the original building of 1030 was a timber-roofed structure and that the walls were articulated by a series of identical shafts that rose to enframe the clerestory windows (FIG. 9-10). The alternate-support system was introduced in the 1080s (when the building was vaulted), perhaps partially to strengthen the piers at the corners of the large vaults and to provide bases for the springing of the transverse arches across the nave. That every other support was chosen to anchor a nave vault may simply have been because the walls were not as stable as the massive piers that carry the crossing dome, so that it would be safer to reduce each area to be vaulted by one-third. The resultant bay arrangement, in which a large unit in the nave is flanked by two small units in each aisle, becomes almost standard in northern Romanesque architecture. Speyer's interior (FIG. 9-9) shows the same striving for height and the same compartmentalized effect shown in St. Sernin. By virtue of the use of the alternate-support system, the rhythm of the Speyer nave is a little more complex—a

9-11 Sant' Ambrogio, Milan, Italy, late eleventh to early twelfth century (view from the northwest).

9-10 Reconstruction of the original nave of Speyer Cathedral, c. 1030–1060.

little richer, perhaps—and because each compartment is individually vaulted, the effect of a sequence of vertical blocks of space is even more convincing.

From Carolingian times, Rhineland Germany and Lombardy had been in close political and cultural contact, and it is generally agreed that the two areas cross-fertilized each other artistically. But no such agreement exists as to which source of artistic influence was dominant: the northern or the southern. The question, no doubt, will remain the subject of controversy until the date of the central monument of Lombard architecture—the church of Sant' Ambrogio in Milan—can be established unequivocally. Dates ranging from the tenth to the early twelfth century have been advanced for the present building (preceded by an earlier church that dated back to the fourth century); the late eleventh and early twelfth centuries apparently are most popular with architectural historians today.

Whether or not it is a prototype, Sant' Ambrogio remains a remarkable building. As shown in FIG. 9-11, it has an atrium (one of the last to be built), a two-story narthex pierced by arches on both levels, two towers joined to the building, and, over the east end of the nave, an octagonal tower that recalls the crossing towers of German churches. Of the façade towers, the shorter one dates back to the tenth century, while the taller north tower was built during the twelfth century. The latter is a sophisticated and typi-

9-12 Plan of Sant' Ambrogio, Milan.

9-13 Interior of Sant' Ambrogio.

cal example of Lombardic tower design; it is articulated by pilasters and shafting and divided, by means of corbel tables (horizontal projections resting on corbels), into a number of levels, of which only the topmost (the bell chamber) has been opened by arches.

In plan (FIG. 9-12), Sant' Ambrogio is three-aisled and without a transept. The square schematism has been applied with greater consistency and precision than at Speyer, each bay consisting of a full square in the nave flanked by two small squares in each aisle, all covered with groin vaults. The main vaults are slightly domical, rising higher than the transverse arches, and the last bay is covered by an octagonal dome that provides the major light source (there is no clerestory) for the otherwise rather dark interior (FIG. 9-13). The geometric regularity of the plan is perfectly reflected in the emphatic alternate-support system, in which the light supports are interrupted at the gallery level and the heavy ones rise to support the main vaults. These ponderous vaults, which have supporting arches along their groins, are sometimes claimed to be the first examples of rib-vaulting; however, in fact, these vaults are solidly constructed groin vaults that have been strengthened by diagonal ribs.

The dating of the Sant' Ambrogio vaults remains controversial. Most scholars seem to feel that they were not built until after 1117, when a severe earthquake caused great damage to the existing building. If so, the Speyer vaults would be earlier than the vaults of Sant' Ambrogio, and the inspiration and technical knowledge for the construction of groin vaults of this size would seem to have come from the north. But such possible influence did not affect the proportioning of the Milanese building, which does not aspire to the soaring height of the northern churches. Sant' Ambrogio's proportions are low and squat and remain close to those of Early Christian basilicas. As we will see, Italian architects never—not even during the height of the Gothic period—accepted the verticality found in northern architecture.

The fame of German architecture rests on its achievements in the eleventh and early twelfth centuries. After the mid-twelfth century, it made no major contribution to architectural design. The architectural statements at Speyer were repeated at Worms and Mainz and other, later churches. German builders were content with refining their successful formula; beyond that, they tended to follow the lead of the more adventurous and progressive Franks and Normans.

Normandy–England

The predatory pagan Vikings settled in northwestern France after their conversion to Christianity in the tenth century and, almost at once, proved themselves skilled administrators and builders. With astounding rapidity, they absorbed the lessons to be learned from Ottonian architecture and went on to develop the most progressive of the many Romanesque styles and the one that was to become the major source in the evolution of Gothic architecture. The church of St. Étienne at Caen in Normandy is generally considered to be the master model of Norman Romanesque architecture. It was begun by William of Normandy ("the Conqueror") in 1067 and must have advanced rapidly, as he was buried there in 1087. The west façade (FIG. 9-14) is a striking design that looks forward to the two-tower façades of later Gothic churches. Four large buttresses divide it into three bays that correspond to the nave and aisles in the interior. There is also a triple division of the towers above their buttresses and a progressively greater piercing of their walls from lower to upper stages. The spires are a later (Gothic) feature. The tripartite division is em-

9-15   Interior of St. Étienne, vaulted c. 1115–1120.

ployed throughout the façade, both vertically and horizontally, organizing it into a close-knit, well-integrated design that reflects the careful and methodical planning of the entire structure. Like Speyer Cathedral, St. Étienne was originally planned to have a wooden roof, but, from the beginning, the walls were articulated in an alternating rhythm (simple half-columns alternating with shafts attached to pilasters) that mirrors the precise square schematism of the building's plan (FIGS. 9-15 and 9-16). This alternate support system was effectively utilized some time after 1110—significantly later than it was used at Speyer—when it was decided to cover the nave with vaults. Its original installation, however, must have been motivated by esthetic rather than structural concerns. In any event, the alternating compound piers soar all the way to the springing of the vaults, and their branching ribs divide the large, square-vault compartments into six sections, making a sexpartite vault (FIG. 9-15). These vaults, their crowns slightly

9-14   West façade of St. Étienne, Caen, France, begun 1067.

9-16   Plan of St. Étienne, Caen.

Eleventh century
Thirteenth century
Fourteenth century

0   25   50   75   100
                              FEET
0   10   20   30
                       METERS

depressed to avoid the "domed-up" effect of those at Sant' Ambrogio, rise high enough to make an efficient clerestory; they are also viewed as some of the earliest true *rib vaults*, in which the diagonal and transverse ribs compose a structural skeleton that partially supports the still fairly massive paneling between them. Rib-vaulting was to become universal practice during the Gothic period, and its development by Norman builders must be rated as one of the major structural innovations of the Middle Ages. Other elements in St. Étienne point to the future. The complex piers, their nuclei almost concealed by attached pilasters and engaged columns, forecast the Gothic "cluster pier," and the reduction in interior wall surfaces that resulted from use of very large, arched openings anticipates the bright curtain walls of Gothic architecture. In short, St. Étienne at Caen is not only a very carefully designed structure but also a highly progressive one in which the Romanesque style begins to merge into the Early Gothic.

The conquest of Anglo–Saxon England in 1066 by William of Normandy began a new epoch in English history; in English architecture, it signaled the importation of Norman building and design methods. Durham Cathedral in northern England, begun around 1093, was apparently designed for vaulting at the outset. Like most Romanesque churches in England, it was subjected to many later alterations that, in this case, fortunately were largely confined to the exterior; the interior (FIG. 9-17) has its original severe

9-18   Plan of Durham Cathedral.

Romanesque appearance. Ambitious in scale—comparable to both St. Sernin at Toulouse and St. Étienne at Caen—its 400-foot length compares favorably with that of the great imperial cathedral of Speyer. With the latter, it also shares a reliance on mass for stability. But unlike Speyer, this building was conceived from the very beginning as a completely integrated skeleton in which the vaults stand in intimate and continuous relation to the vertical elements of the compound piers that support them. At Durham, the alternate-support system is interpreted with blunt power and more emphasis, perhaps, than in any other Romanesque church. Large, simple pillars ornamented with abstract designs—diamond, chevron, and cable patterns descended from the metalcraft ornamentation of the migrations—alternate with compound piers that carry the transverse arches of the vaults. The pier–vault relationship could scarcely be more visible, or the structural rationale of the building better expressed. The plan (FIG. 9-18), typically English in its long, slender proportions and the strongly projecting transept, does not develop the square schematism with the same care and logic we see at Caen. But the rib vaults of the choir (1104) are the earliest in Europe, and, when they were combined with slightly pointed arches in the western parts of the nave (before 1130), the two key elements that would determine the structural evolution of Gothic architecture were brought together for the first time. Only the rather massive construction and the irregular division into seven panels prevent these vaults from qualifying as Early Gothic structures.

Among the numerous regional Romanesque styles of architecture, it was the northern—more specifically, the Norman—style that would indirectly influence the development of Gothic architecture; no other style had as great a potential for evolution.

Tuscany

South of the Lombard region, Italy retained its ancient traditions and, for the most part, produced Romanesque architecture that was less structurally

9-17   The nave of Durham Cathedral, England, begun *c.* 1093 (view facing east).

9-19 Aerial view of the cathedral group of Pisa (baptistry, cathedral, and campanile), Italy, 1053–1272 (view from the southwest).

experimental than that of Lombardy. The buildings of Tuscany seem to adhere more closely than those of any other region to the traditions of the Early Christian basilica. The cathedral group of Pisa (FIG. 9-19) manifests, in addition to these conservative qualities, those of the great Classical "renaissance" of the late eleventh and twelfth centuries, when architects, craftsmen, poets, and philosophers again confronted Classical–Christian prototypes and interpreted them in an original yet familiar way. The cathedral is large, five-aisled, and one of the most impressive and majestic of all Romanesque churches. At first glance, it resembles an Early Christian basilica, but the broadly projecting transept, the dome over the crossing, the rich marble incrustation, and the multiple arcade galleries of the façade soon distinguish it as Romanesque. The interior (FIG. 9-20) also at first suggests the basilica, with its timber roof rather than vault (originally the rafters were exposed, as in Early Christian basilicas), nave arcades, and Classical (imported) columns flanking the nave in unbroken procession. Above these columns is a continuous, horizontal molding, on which rest the gallery arcades. The gallery, of course, is not a basilican feature but is of Byzantine origin. There are other divergences from the basilica, such as the relatively great verticality and, at the crossing, the markedly un-Classical pointed arch, which was probably inspired by Islamic architecture. The striped incrustation, produced by alternating dark green and cream-colored marble, provides a luxurious polychromy, which will become a hallmark of

Tuscan Romanesque and Gothic buildings. The leaning campanile, the result of a settling foundation, tilted from the vertical even while it was being built and now inclines some 21 perilous feet out of plumb at the top. Round, like the Ravenna campaniles, it is much more elaborate; its stages are marked by grace-

9-20 The nave of the cathedral of Pisa (view facing east).

ful, arcaded galleries that repeat the motif of the cathedral's façade and effectively relate the tower to its mother building. Although the baptistry, with its partly remodeled Gothic exterior, may strike a slightly discordant note, the whole composition of the three buildings, with the adjacent Campo Santo (cemetery), makes one of the handsomest ensembles in the history of architecture and expresses dramatically the new building age made possible by the prosperity enjoyed by the busy maritime cities of the Mediterranean.

Another Tuscan church, San Miniato al Monte (FIG. 9-21) in Florence, completed in 1062, recalls Early Christian architecture, although the wall arcading and its elaborate, geometric incrustation in colored marbles make for a rich ornamental effect foreign to the austere exteriors of the earlier buildings. Retrospective as San Miniato may appear externally, the interior (FIG. 9-22) is another matter. Although the church is timber-roofed, as are most Tuscan Romanesque churches, the nave is divided into three equal compartments by *diaphragm arches* that rise from compound piers. The piers alternate with simple columns in a rhythm that recalls St. Michael's in Hildesheim (FIG. 8-24). The diaphragm arches, which appear here for the first time (before 1060), have multiple functional and esthetic purposes. They brace the rather high, thin walls, provide firebreaks within the wooden roof structure, and compartmentalize the basilican interior in the manner so popular with most Romanesque builders. Antique, or neo-Antique, motifs appear in the capitals as well as in the incrustation, expressing again the persistence of the Classical tradition in Tuscany.

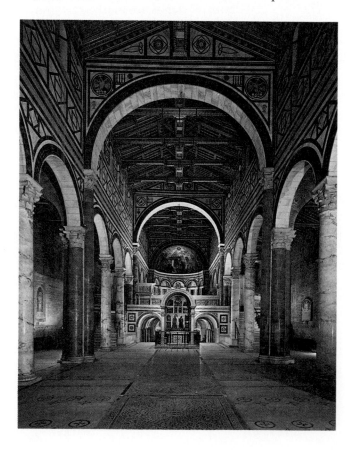

9-22 Interior of San Miniato al Monte (view facing east).

Aquitaine

Influences crisscrossed in Romanesque architecture, helping to diversify it and creating exotic hybrids. In the region of Aquitaine in southwestern France, for instance, it became customary to roof the churches with domes, reflecting the influence of Byzantium, Armenia, and Cyprus—the crusaders' bridge between East and West. Curiously, most of these Aquitanian churches mate the dome with a longitudinal plan to which, at first glance, it seems ill-suited. In the typical Aquitanian church, a longitudinal, aisle-less nave is covered by a sequence of domes, which, in turn, are usually covered by a pitched wooden roof. The result turns out to be highly practical, as the pendentive-supported domes require much less buttressing than, for instance, continuous barrel vaults. Also, the system automatically produces the cherished compartmentalized effect of Romanesque architecture. Although they never aimed at the soaring height of northern Romanesque structures, these Aquitanian domed churches not only represent an almost perfect fusion of geometric plan with elevation, but also are visually most effective, clearly exhibiting the functions of all their structural parts (FIG. 9-23).

9-23 Interior of St. Pierre, Angoulême, France, twelfth century (view facing west).

From about 1050 on, the old dependence of the pre-Romanesque (Carolingian and Ottonian) on Late Antique and Early Christian design concepts fades gradually, although never completely. Romanesque architecture develops a number of clear characteristics: the square schematism, the alternate-support system, and the increased relief and depth of walls and piers as they connect with the vaults above. The Romanesque architect conceives a building in terms of the geometric relation of its parts, a view basically different from that of the Early Christian architect, who never thought of large units as related geometrically and who thought of the wall not as essentially a structural element, but as a surface to receive applied decoration.

SCULPTURE

For Medieval art, the first definite relation of architecture and sculpture appears in the Romanesque style. Figurative sculpture, confined for centuries to small art, flowers again in the new Romanesque churches of the mid-eleventh century. The rich profusion of sculpture and something of its nature may be guessed from Bernard of Clairveaux's famous tirade against it, written in 1127:

> I say naught of the vast height of your churches, their immoderate length, their superfluous breadth, the costly polishings, the curious carvings and paintings. . . . [Men's] eyes are feasted with relics cased in gold, and their purse-strings are loosed. They are shown a most comely image of some saint, whom they think all the more saintly that he is the more gaudily painted. Men run to kiss him, and are invited to give; there is more admiration for his comeliness than veneration for his sanctity. Hence the church is adorned with gemmed crowns of light. . . . candelabra standing like trees of massive bronze, fashioned with marvellous subtlety of art, and glistening no less brightly with gems than with the lights they carry. . . . O vanity of vanities, yet no more vain than insane! The church is resplendent in her walls, beggarly in her poor; she clothes her stones in gold and leaves her sons naked. . . . in the cloister, under the eyes of the Brethren who read there, what profit is there in those ridiculous monsters, in that marvellous and deformed comeliness, that comely deformity? To what purpose are those unclean apes, those fierce lions, those monstrous centaurs, those half-men, those striped tigers, those fighting knights, those hunters winding their horns? Many bodies are there seen under one head, or again, many heads to a single body. . . . For God's sake, if men are not ashamed of these follies, why at least do they not shrink from the expense?*

*In E.G., Holt, ed., *Literary Sources of Art History* (Princeton, N.J.: Princeton University Press, 1947), pp. 17–18.

Stone sculpture had almost disappeared from the art of western Europe during the eighth and ninth centuries. The revival of the technique is one of the most important Romanesque achievements. As stone buildings began to rise again, so did the impulse to decorate parts of the structure with relief carving in stone. It was to be expected that the artists should turn for inspiration to surviving Roman sculpture and to sculptural forms such as ivory carving or metalwork; it is obvious that they also relied on painted figures in manuscripts. But these Romanesque artists developed their own attitude toward ornamental design and its relation to architecture. At first, this was somewhat random and haphazard; one put the sculpture wherever there seemed to be a convenient place. A little later, the portals of the church seemed the appropriate setting, both for religious reasons and for the practical matter of display. As Romanesque sculpture turns into Gothic, the statuary of the

9-24 *Christ in Majesty,* from the ambulatory of St. Sernin, Toulouse, France, late eleventh century.

portals becomes integrated with the design of the whole façade, following the lines of the architecture. An example of the earlier, random placement is the figure of *Christ in Majesty,* set into the wall of the ambulatory of St. Sernin at Toulouse (FIG. 9-24). Clearly, its source is some prototype made of metal, perhaps a book cover like that of the *Codex Aureus of St. Emmeram* (FIG. 8-12). The figure has the bulge of metal hammered out from behind, as in the *repoussé* method, and, even here in stone, one senses the gloss of smooth metal. The Signs of the Evangelists at the four corners square off the book-cover-like design and remind one of the corner screws that fix the plate to the book. As yet, there is no relation between the relief and its architectural setting; it is "portable," like a work of craft art, and could find its place on any wall. In the later mode, the architectural limits of the parts of a portal or the shape of a capital were respected as frames to which the sculptors accommodated their work. A typical Romanesque portal can be seen in the façade of St. Trophime at Arles in the south of France (FIG. 9-34). The architectural elements of such a portal are jambs, lintel, semicircular tympanum (beneath the arches, or archivolts) and, in some instances, a pier, or *trumeau,* in the middle of the doorway.

Before the elements of the Romanesque portal were assembled in a unified design, they were placed in isolation inside or outside the church building, without any apparent scheme of organization. The St. Sernin figure, as we have seen, is set into the ambulatory wall. At St. Génis-des-Fontaines in the extreme south of France, sculpture appears in the lintel over a doorway (FIG. 9-25). Dated 1020 by inscription, the quite primitive style is more-or-less characteristic of what we call "First Romanesque." It is representative of developments in sculptural art common to northeastern Spain, southern France, and northern Italy— an artistically integrated region that can be considered as originative of Romanesque art. On the lintel at St. Génis-des-Fontaines, Christ is enthroned in a lobed mandorla supported by angels and is flanked by apostles in an arcade. The latter motif goes back centuries to Late Antiquity. Some Late Antique or Early Christian sarcophagus—or perhaps some later Carolingian or Ottonian derivative therefrom—may have been the sculptor's prototype. Whatever his source, he has translated its images into his own rudimentary idiom and has similarly adapted the original's ornament in the foliate motifs of the frame.

Almost a century later, the full Romanesque style emerges in the sculptured frieze of the façade of the Modena Cathedral in northern Italy (FIG. 9-26). The sculpture, which extends on two levels across three bays of the façade, represents scenes from Genesis. This segment illustrates the *Creation and Temptation of*

9-25 *Christ in Majesty with Apostles,* lintel over doorway, St. Génis-des-Fontaines, France, *c.* 1019–1020. Marble, 24″ high.

Adam and Eve (Genesis 2, 3:1–8) and, at the far left, Christ in a mandorla held by angels—the theme of the central section of the lintel at St. Génis-des-Fontaines. But the style and execution are far more mature in representational sophistication—the work of a master craftsman, whose name (''Wiligelmus'') is given in an inscription on another relief on the façade. The name is German, and the sculptor is believed to have been a German goldsmith. If so, the close relationship of Germany and Lombardy in architecture is indicated here as well as in sculpture. The figures have broken through the constriction of the arcade to make for a more continuous narrative. They are no longer in flat pattern but are cut in deep relief, some parts almost entirely in the round. The origins of the authoritative style of WILIGELMUS are obscure. His prototypes may have been fragments of Late Antique sarcophagi, Carolingian ivories, or the panels of

9-26 WILIGELMUS, *Creation and Temptation of Adam and Eve,* frieze on the west façade, Cathedral of Modena, Italy, *c.* 1110. Approx. 36″ high.

doors like those at Hildesheim (FIG. 8-25). The rectilinear shape and the arrangement of the frieze suggest that it may have been inspired by sculptured altar frontals; as yet, they are not logically related to the architecture of the facade, as the sculpture of the great Romanesque portals will be. Yet the Modena sculpture of Wiligelmus, whose work the inscription rightly honors, is an outstanding and abrupt introduction of a new artistic style—"High Romanesque."

The stirring of the peoples in Romanesque Europe, the Crusades, the pilgrimages, and the commercial journeyings brought a slow realization that Europeans were of the same religion, even if of different ethnic stock. The reception of hitherto unknown documents of Greek thought and learning strongly influenced theology, bringing to it, along with new and deep challenges, a kind of order and concentration. There can be little doubt that theologians dictated the subjects of the Romanesque portals; it was just as important to have the right subjects carved in the right places as to have the right arguments rightly arranged in a theological treatise. The apocalyptic vision of the Last Judgment, appalling to the imagination of twelfth-century man, was represented conspicuously at the western entrance portal as an inescapable reminder to all who entered.

At Modena, the great frieze recounted the beginning of the human race; in the portal at Moissac, some 25 years later, its end was announced. With new architectural and iconographic organization giving coherence to sculptural design on a grand scale, the vast tympanum that crowns the portal of St. Pierre at Moissac depicts the Second Coming of Christ as King and Judge of the world in its last days (FIG. 9-27). As befits his majesty, Christ is centrally enthroned, reflecting a rule of composition we have seen followed since Early Christian times. The Signs of the Evangelists flank him: on his right side, the Angel of St. Matthew and the Lion of St. Mark; on his left, the Eagle of St. John and the Ox of St. Luke. To one side of each pair of signs is an attendant angel holding scrolls on which to record the deeds of mankind for judgment. The figures of crowned musicians are the 24 music-making elders who accompany Christ as the kings of all this world and make music in his praise; each turns to face him, much as would the courtiers of a Romanesque monarch in attendance on their lord. The central group, reminiscent of the heraldic groupings of ancient Mesopotamian art, is set among the elders, who are separated into three tiers by two courses of wavy lines that symbolize the clouds of Heaven.

9-27   Tympanum of the south portal of St. Pierre, Moissac, France, c. 1115–1135. Diameter 16' 6".

There are as many variations within the general style of Romanesque sculpture as there are within Romanesque architecture, and the figures of the Moissac tympanum constitute no exception. Yet there are elements here familiar in painting and sculpture throughout western Europe in the eleventh and twelfth centuries. The extremely elongated figures of the recording angels, the curious, cross-legged, dancing pose of the Angel of St. Matthew, and the jerky, hinged movement are characteristic in general of the emerging vernacular style of representing the human figure. Earlier Carolingian, Ottonian, and Anglo–Saxon manners diffused and interfused to produce the now sure and unhesitating style-languages of the Romanesque. The zigzag and dovetail lines of the draperies (the linear modes of manuscript painting are everywhere apparent), the band-like folds of the torsos, the bending back of the hands against the body, and the wide cheekbones (reminiscent of the ancient Archaic mask) are also common features of this new, cosmopolitan style.

A triumph of the styles is the splendid figure of *The Prophet Jeremiah* (identified by some as *Isaiah*) carved in the trumeau of the Moissac portal (FIG. 9-28). His position below the apparition of Christ as the apocalyptic Judge is explained by his prophecy (recalled by his scroll) of the end of the world, when "ruin spreads from nation to nation." He is compressed in the mass of the trumeau behind roaring, interlaced lions of the kind familiar not only in barbarian art but also in the art of ancient Mesopotamia and Persia and Islamic Spain. (The totemistic animal was never far from the instinct and imagination of the Medieval artist and was certainly not far from Medieval man in general. Kings and barons were often named by association with animals thought to be the most fiercely courageous—for example, Richard the Lion-heart, Henry the Lion, and Richard III of England, whose heraldic animal was the wild boar. It is not unthinkable that the Medieval artist, with millennia of animal lore and ornament in his background, associated animal strength with architecture—the animal body being thought of as providing support and symbolizing the very forces locked in the architectural fabric. The sphinxes and winged monsters at the palace gates in the ancient world—at Boghazköy, Khorsabad, Persepolis, and Mycenae (FIGS. 2-24, 2-27, 2-35, 4-25)—are the ancestors of the interlaced lions at Moissac.) The figure of Jeremiah is very tall and thin, in the manner of the angels of the tympanum, and, like the Angel of St. Matthew, he executes a cross-legged step that repeats the crisscrossing of the lions. There is as yet no representation of movement in terms of the actual structure of the body or its natural proportions. At this beginning of a new epoch in the history of sculpture, movement is a kind of gro-

9-28 *The Prophet Jeremiah (Isaiah?)* from the trumeau of the south portal of St. Pierre, Moissac. Life-size. *Below:* the head in detail.

tesque, mechanical dance. The placing of the parts of the body depends on the architectural setting, on the sculptor's interpretation of his carved or painted model, or on the vocabulary of the prevailing vernacular styles; the artist's originality might also play a large part, as in this case. The folds of the drapery are incised in flowing, calligraphic lines that ultimately derive from manuscript illumination and here play gracefully around the elegant figure.

A detail of the head and shoulders (FIG. 9-28) reveals the artist's striking characterization of his subject. The long, serpentine locks of hair and beard (familiar in the vocabulary of French Romanesque details) frame an arresting image of the dreaming mystic. The prophet seems entranced by his vision of what is to come, his eyes wide but unseeing the light of ordinary day; the expression is slightly melancholy—at once pensive and wistful. For the man of the Middle Ages, there were two alternative callings: one, to the active life *(vita activa)*; the other, to the religious life of contemplation *(vita contemplativa)*, the pursuit of the beatific vision of God. The sculptor of the Moissac Jeremiah has given us the very image of the *vita contemplativa*. It has been said of Greek sculpture that the body becomes "alive" before the head (as in the *Fallen Warrior* from Aegina, FIG. 5-31); in the epoch that begins in the eleventh century, the head becomes humanly expressive well before the body is rendered as truly corporeal. The Moissac Jeremiah is a remarkable instance of this.

Romanesque sculpture is not confined to the portals at Moissac; it also appears in delightful variety in the carved capitals within the church and in the cloister walk. It was such sculpture that Bernard complained distracted the monks from their devotions; we are distracted, too—by its ingenuity and decorative beauty. The capitals of the Moissac cloister (FIG. 9-29)—some of which are historiated, some purely

decorative—are excellent examples. The capital in the foreground of the view at the left has an intricate leaf-and-vine pattern with volutes, an echo of the Corinthian capital. The abacus carries rosettes, and its upper edge exhibits the fish-scale motif. The capital in the background has figures seated at a table, probably a representation of the Marriage Feast at Cana. The two other capitals shown reveal the richness and color of the Romanesque sculptor's imagination; monsters of all sorts—basilisks, griffins, lizards, gargoyles—cluster and interlace and pass grinning before us. We have the Medieval bestiary in stone.

Yet for all its distinctive stylistic characteristics and exotic look, Romanesque art reveals its debt to ancient Roman, Early Christian, and Byzantine art, and to their Classical heritage. For example, the beautifully carved rosettes on the lintel beneath the tympanum at Moissac (FIG. 9-27) derive from ancient Roman types. It is likely that some very late, still classicizing work, perhaps of the seventh century, served as model for the rosettes. Other rosettes closely resembling those of the Moissac lintel survive. At the same time, there are unmistakable indications of Islamic influence in other decorative motifs of the portal.

The relatives of the monsters of the Moissac capitals appear as the demons of Hell in the awesome tympanum of the church of St. Lazare at Autun in Burgundy (FIGS. 9-30 and 9-31). At Moissac, we saw the apparition of the Divine Judge before he has summoned man; at Autun, the Judgment is in progress. The detail (FIG. 9-31) shows the weighing of souls—the reader may remember this theme from Egyptian art (FIG. 3-43)—while below, in the lintel, the dead are rising, one being plucked from the earth by giant hands. Mankind's pitiful weakness and littleness are distilled in these terror-stricken, weeping dolls, whom an angel with a trumpet summons to Judg-

9-29   Capitals from the cloister of St. Pierre, Moissac.

9-30 GISLEBERTUS, west tympanum of St. Lazare, Autun, France, c. 1130.
11' 4" high, 21' wide at base.

ment. Angels and devils contest at the scales where souls are being weighed, each trying to manipulate the beam for or against a soul. Hideous demons guffaw and roar; their gaunt, lined bodies, with legs ending in claws, writhe and bend like long, loathesome insects. A devil, leaning from the dragon-mouth of Hell, drags souls in, while, above him, a howling demon crams souls head first into a furnace. The resources of the Romanesque imagination, heated by a fearful faith, provide an appalling scene;

9-31 Detail of FIG. 9-30.

we can appreciate the terror the Autun tympanum must have inspired in the believers who passed beneath it as they entered the cathedral.

There is an inscription on the tympanum: ''Master GISLEBERTUS made this.'' This master stone-carver, whose work appears throughout St. Lazare as well as on its portal, is like Wolvinius, who made the *Paliotto* in Sant' Ambrogio, Milan (FIG. 8-13), and Wiligelmus, sculptor of the Modena frieze (FIG. 9-26)—he wants to make sure his work is remembered in association with his name. In the twelfth century, more and more craftsmen–artists, illuminators as well as sculptors, would begin to identify themselves; we have yet to encounter MASTER HUGO (FIG. 9-39) and EADWINE THE SCRIBE (FIG. 9-41). Although many Medieval artists remain anonymous, the trend is now set that will culminate in the self-concerned, ''fine'' artist of the Renaissance, who is preoccupied with his reputation and his fame.

Another great tympanum, this one at the church of La Madeleine at Vézelay, not far from Autun, varies the theme of the apocalyptic Last Judgment, representing *The Ascension of Christ and the Mission of the Apostles* (FIGS. 9-32 and 9-33). As related in scripture

9-32 *The Ascension of Christ and the Mission of the Apostles,* tympanum of the center portal of the narthex of La Madeleine, Vézelay, France, 1120–1132.

(Acts 1:4–9), Christ foretold that the apostles would receive the power of the Holy Ghost and become the witnesses of the truth of the gospels throughout the world. The rays of light emanating from Christ's hands represent the promise of the coming of the Holy Ghost. The apostles, holding the gospel books, receive their spiritual assignment. Christ assigns three specific tasks to the apostles and gives them the power to perform them: to save or to condemn; to preach the gospel to all nations; to heal the sick and drive out devils. The task of saving or condemning is indicated in the central scene and in the lower four compartments surrounding it. The task of preaching the gospel to all nations (some at the very edge of the world) is represented on the lintel. The task of healing the sick and driving out devils is indicated in the upper four compartments. The outer archivolt has a repeated ornamental device; the inner archivolt has medallions with the signs of the zodiac, the seasons, and the works of the months.

The Vézelay tympanum reflects, like a vast mirror, religious and secular writings and the influence of antiquity and the Byzantine East. It is a complete and encyclopedic work, in which the Mission of the Apostles and their power to perform it are merged in a single subject. The theme has its sources in the Acts and in the gospels, in the prophecies of Isaiah, and in writings of antiquity and of the Middle Ages. The crowding, agitated figures reveal wild deformities. We find people with the heads of dogs, enormous

9-33 Detail of FIG. 9-32.

ears, fiery hair, snout-like noses; there are hunch-backs, mutes, blind men, lame men—a whole lexicon of human defects and ailments. Mankind, still suffering, awaits the salvation to come. The whole world is electrified by the promise of the ascended Christ, whose great figure, seeming to whirl in a vortex of spiritual energy, looms above human misery and deformity. Again, as in the Autun tympanum, we are made emphatically aware of the greatness of God and the littleness of man.

Vézelay is more closely associated with the Crusades than any other church in Europe. Pope Urban II had intended to preach the First Crusade at Vézelay in 1095, about 30 years before the tympanum was carved. In 1146, some 15 years after the tympanum was in place, Bernard preached the Second Crusade, and King Louis VII of France took up the cross. In 1190, it was from Vézelay that King Richard the Lion-heart of England and King Philip Augustus of France set out on the Third Crusade. The spirit of the Crusades undoubtedly determined the iconography of the Vézelay tympanum, for it was believed that the Crusades were a kind of "second mission of the apostles" to convert the infidel.

Stylistically, the figures of the Vézelay tympanum display characteristics similar to those of the Moissac and Autun tympanums: abrupt and jerky movement (strongly exaggerated at Vézelay), rapid play of line, wind-blown drapery hems, elongation, angularity, and agitated poses, gestures, and silhouettes. The figure of the Vézelay Christ (FIG. 9-33) is a splendid essay in calligraphic theme and variation and is almost a summary of the Romanesque skill with decorative line. The lines of the drapery shoot out in rays, break into quick, zigzag rhythms, and spin into whorls, wonderfully conveying a spiritual light and energy flowing from Christ over and into the animated apostles. The technical experience of centuries of working with small art—with manuscripts, ivories, and metalcraft—is easily read from this monumental translation of such work into stone.

In Provence, rich in the remains of Roman art and architecture, the vivid linear style of Languedoc (Moissac) and Burgundy (Autun and Vézelay) is considerably modified later in the twelfth century by the influence of the art of antiquity. The quieting influence of this art is seen at once in the figures on the façade of St. Trophime at Arles and in the design of the portal, which reflects the artist's interpretation of a Roman triumphal arch (FIG. 9-34). The tympanum shows Christ surrounded by the Signs of the Evangelists. On the lintel, directly below him, the Twelve Apostles appear at the center of a continuous frieze that depicts the Last Judgment; the outermost parts of the frieze depict the saved (on Christ's right) and

9-34 Portal on the west façade of St. Trophime, Arles, France, late twelfth century.

the damned in the flames of Hell (on his left). Below this, in the jambs and the front bays of the portals, stand grave figures of saints draped in Classical garb, their quiet stance contrasting with the spinning, twisting, dancing figures seen at Autun and Vézelay. The stiff regularity of the figures in the frieze also contrasts with the animation of the great Burgundian tympana and reminds us of the "lining-up" seen in Early Christian sarcophagus sculpture. Their draperies, like those of the large statues below, are also less agitated and show nothing of the dexterous linear play familiar at Moissac, Autun, and Vézelay. Here, the rigid lines of the architecture of the façade as a whole (rather than just an enframing element, such as a tympanum) are now determining the placement and look of the sculpture and the freedom of execution appropriate to small art has been sacrificed to a simpler and more monumental adjustment to the architecture. In the north of France, in the area around Paris, a new system of portal sculpture was developing some 30 years earlier than that at St. Trophime. In the Royal Portals of the cathedral of Chartres (FIG. 10-14), we shall see the expansion of the whole portal design into a magnificent frontispiece, in which the architectural and sculptural elements are balanced, the sculptural style being firmly determined by the lines of the building.

9-35 *Norman Cavalry Charging in the Battle of Hastings,* from the *Bayeux Tapestry,* 1070–1080. Embroidered wool on linen, 20″ high (entire length of fabric 231′). Musée de Peinture, Bayeux.

PAINTING AND ILLUMINATION

We can begin an account of Romanesque painting with a work that is *not* a painting. Nor is the famous and unique *Bayeux Tapestry* a woven tapestry, but rather an embroidered (needle-worked) fabric made of wool sewn on linen (FIG. 9-35). Some 20 inches high and 230 feet long, it is a continuous, frieze-like, pictorial narrative of a crucial moment in the history of England and of the events that led up to it. The Norman defeat of the Anglo–Saxons at Hastings in 1066 brought Saxon England under the control of the Normans, uniting all of England and much of France under one rule; the dukes of Normandy (descendants of the Viking norsemen) became the kings of England. Commissioned by Bishop Odo, the half brother of the conquering Duke William (under whose reign in Normandy St. Étienne at Caen had been begun), the "tapestry" may have been sewn by ladies at the Norman court, although some believe it was the work of English needlewomen in Kent, where Odo had been given lands and influence by Duke William. The *Bayeux Tapestry* is unique in Romanesque art in that it depicts a contemporary event in full detail at a time shortly after it took place—a kind of distant anticipation of modern pictorial reportage; inscriptions accompanying the pictures comment on the action. A section of the embroidered frieze shows a charge of Norman cavalry; the upper and lower margins show various fanciful beasts and birds in heraldic arrangement. Despite the schematic simplification of form, the Archaic flatness without cast shadows, and an entirely neutral background, there is surprisingly exact description of arms and armor, as well as convincing representation of action, pose, and gesture. The work is of great importance—not only as art, but also as a valuable historical document. There is stylistic unity and consistency throughout the whole length of the "tapestry," suggesting a single designer or a small "school" of needleworkers thoroughly trained in a distinctive idiom of representation.

Monumental mural painting, like monumental sculpture, comes into its own once again in the eleventh century. Although we have examples of it from Carolingian and Ottonian times and although there is an unbroken tradition of it in Italy, it blossoms in the Romanesque period. As with architecture and sculpture, mural painting exhibits many regional styles and many degrees of sophistication. Sometimes a provincial style (a style that appears at some distance from its origin, in an artistic "province" rather than at an artistic "capital") can reveal more clearly than its sophisticated source the elements common to both. Such a case is the mural painting in the apse of the little church of Santa Maria at Tahull in Catalonia, in the extreme northeastern corner of Spain. This painting (FIG. 9-36) could be called provincial Byzantine, as, for that matter, could much Romanesque painting. If we compare it with a Byzantine mosaic like the one at Daphne (FIG. 7-55) or the apse mosaic at Monreale (FIG. 7-57), we find that its distance from the Byzantine source—much greater than the distance from Venice or Sicily to Byzantium—results in a loss of subtlety and refinement and some misunderstanding of motifs in the original style. On the other hand, the Tahull painting has a simple and strong directness, even bluntness, that gives it a peculiarly expressive force. One emphatic feature is the partitioning of the draped figures into separate, decoratively modeled segments that almost break the figure itself into independent parts. (Note the similarity to the modulation and articulation of Romanesque architecture.) This is especially well seen in the pattern made by the pipe-like legs and the ladder-like folds between them. This decorative banding of the surface serves to keep the figures flat and contributes to the effect of stiff formality. The drapery, also with decorative partitioning, is scarcely distinguished from the body. Even the hands of the Madonna are subdivided, as are the heads and necks of other figures. This technique, which had begun to appear in Ottonian paint-

9-36 *Adoration of the Magi*, apse fresco from Santa Maria, Tahull, Spain, eleventh century.

ing (FIG. 8-27), is almost universal in Romanesque painting; it may be seen beneath the whirling linear draperies of Autun and Vézelay (FIGS. 9-30 and 9-32) and in the angels of the Moissac tympanum (FIGS. 9-27 and 9-28). Here, the sharp patterning of the figures is assisted by bold coloring, and the whole effect is one of rude strength, not a little of which derives from the architectural planes to which the patterned figures are masterfully adjusted.

The vernacular Romanesque style can be seen almost in exaggeration in a manuscript illumination from northern France illustrating the life of St. Omer (FIG. 9-37). Here, the figures are cut into patterns by hard lines, and the action is remote from even an approximation of organic motion. St. Omer (bound and pulled by the beard) and his captors seem to be performing some bouncing ritual ballet. The frame creates no sense of containment, as it did in Anglo–Saxon and Carolingian manuscripts, and bodies and feet move arbitrarily in, out of, and across it. Locally different from the Tahull mural, the St. Omer illumination shares its fundamental vocabulary.

The vocabulary, richly applied and gracefully modulated, appears in what surely must be one of the masterpieces of Medieval art—a manuscript illuminated in Bernard's great abbey of Citeaux, the motherhouse of the Cistercian order. Citeaux, and its sister abby, Clairvaux, where Bernard was abbot, produced magnificent illuminated manuscripts throughout the twelfth century, among which was Gregory's *Moralia in Job*, painted before 1111. A splendid example of Cistercian illumination, the historiated initial from this manuscript (FIG. 9-38) represents St. George, his squire, and the roaring dragons intricately composed to make the letter "R." St. George, a slender, regal figure, raises his shield and sword against the dragons—distinguished representations of the age-old animal style so often encountered—while the squire, crouching beneath St. George, runs a lance through one of the monsters. (An image of status, the greater and the lesser dragons correspond to the lord and his man.) The ornamented initial goes back to the Hiberno–Saxon eighth century; the inclusion of a narrative within the initial is a practice that would have an important future in Gothic illumination. The banding of the torso, the fold partitions (especially evident in the skirts of the servant), and the dovetail folds—all part of the Romanesque manner—are done here with the skill of a master who deftly avoids the stiffness and angularity that result from less skillful management of the vocabulary. Instead, he makes a virtue of stylistic neces-

9-37 *The Life and Miracles of St. Audomarus (Omer),* eleventh century. Illuminated manuscript. Bibliothèque Municipale, Saint-Omer.

9-38 *St. George and the Dragon,* from the *Moralia in Job,* early twelfth century. Illuminated manuscript, 13¾″ × 9¼″. Bibliothèque Municipale, Dijon.

9-39 MASTER HUGO, *Moses Expounding the Law*, frontispiece of the Book of Deuteronomy of the Bury Bible, the abbey of Bury St. Edmunds, England, early twelfth century. Illuminated manuscript, approx. 20″ × 14″. Reproduced by permission of the Master and Fellows of Corpus Christi College, Cambridge, England.

sity; the partitioning accentuates the verticality and elegance of the figure of St. George, as it does the thrusting action of his servant. The flowing sleeves add a spirited flourish to St. George's gesture. The knight, handsomely garbed, cavalierly wears no armor and aims a single stroke with proud disdain. This miniature may be a reliable picture of the costume of a Medieval baron and of the air of nonchalant gallantry he cultivated.

An illumination of exceeding refinement of execution, exemplifying the sumptuous illustration common to the large Bibles produced in the wealthy Romanesque abbeys, is the frontispiece to the Book of Deuteronomy from the Bury Bible (FIG. 9-39). Produced at the abbey of Bury St. Edmunds in England in the early twelfth century, the work shows two scenes from Deuteronomy enframed by symmetrical leaf motifs in softly glowing, harmonized colors. The upper register shows Moses and Aaron proclaiming the Law to the Israelites; the lower, Moses pointing out the clean and unclean beasts. The gestures are slow and gentle and have quiet dignity; the figures of Moses and Aaron seem to glide. This is quite different from the abrupt emphasis and spastic movement seen in earlier Romanesque painting; here, as the patterning softens, the movements of the figure become more integrated and smooth. Yet the patterning does remain in the multiple divisions of the draped limbs, the lightly shaded volumes being connected with sinuous lines and ladder-like folds; the drapery and body are still thought of as somehow the same. The frame now has a quite definite limiting function, and the figures are carefully fitted within it.

The apocalyptic vision of the Second Coming of Christ, recorded in the Book of Revelation and carved on the great tympanum at Moissac (FIG. 9-27), is represented in the illuminations of the *Apocalypse of Saint Sever* (FIG. 9-40), a book of commentaries on the Apocalypse written by Beatus of Liébana, an eighth-century theologian. The theme of the Second Coming was of such interest that numerous manuscripts of Beatus' commentary were copied and illustrated; with the exception of this book, all were produced in

Spain. The *Apocalypse of Saint Sever*, made in the French monastery of that name, is significant not only as a masterpiece of the illuminator's art but also as a pictorial relative of the Moissac tympanum, for which it—or another book like it—may have served as a prototype. The characters in the drama are essentially the same, only the composition is different. In both cases, the artist has strictly followed the biblical account of the vision of St. John (Revelation 4:6–8, 5:8–9). Christ enthroned in a sapphire aura is surrounded by the Signs of the Evangelists, whose bodies are full of eyes and who are borne aloft by six wings apiece. The 24 crowned and music-making elders offer their golden cups of incense and their stringed rebecks (viols). Flights of angels frame the great circle of the apparition. Color, intense and vivid, is harmonized with great sophistication; the agile figures are fluently drawn. The seated elders are shown in a kind of bird's-eye perspective, in which their figures overlap, and some of them are seen from behind. Within a context of visionary abstraction, these deft touches of realism are still contained by the characteristic patternings of Romanesque figural art.

The transition from the Romanesque vernacular style to something new seems to reach a midpoint in

9-40 *The Revelation to St. John: Enthroned Christ with Signs of the Evangelists and the Twenty-four Elders*, from the *Apocalypse of Saint Sever*, painted in the abbey of Saint Sever, France, *c.* 1050. Bibliothèque Nationale, Paris.

a work of great expressive power, the portrait of *The Scribe Eadwine* in the *Canterbury Psalter* (FIG. 9-41) made in Canterbury about the same time as the Bury Bible. Particularly noteworthy is the fact that the portrait represents a living man, a priestly scribe—not some sacred person or King David, who usually dominated the Psalter. Although it is true that Carolingian and Ottonian manuscripts included portraits of living men, they were of reigning emperors, whose right to appear in sacred books was God-given, like the right of Justinian and Theodora and their court to be depicted in the sanctuary of San Vitale (FIGS. 7-36 and 7-37). Here, the inclusion of his own portrait sanctified the scribe's work, marking a change in attitude that points to the future emergence of the artist as a person and a name. Eadwine has greatly aggrandized his importance by likening his image to that of an Evangelist writing his gospel (FIGS. 8-7, 8-8, 8-9, 8-10) and by lettering along the margins an inscription that identifies the figure as himself and proclaims that he is a prince among writers. He declares that, due to the excellence of his work, his fame will endure forever and that he can offer his book as an acceptable gift to God. The Medieval artist, concerned as he might be for his fame, is not yet aware of the concepts of fine art and fine artist; these will emerge in the Renaissance. As yet, his work exists not for its own sake, but for God's.

The style is related to that of the Bury Bible, but, although the patterning is still firm—notably in the cowl and the thigh—the drapery has begun to fall softly, to wrap about the frame, to overlap parts of it, and to follow the movements beneath. Here, the arbitrariness of the Romanesque vernacular style yields slightly, but clearly, to the requirements of a more naturalistic representation. The artist's instinct for decorative elaboration of his surface remains, as is apparent in the whorls and spirals of the gown, but it is significant that these are painted in very lightly and do not conflict with the functional lines that contain them.

With the distinction of body and drapery finally achieved in the Gothic art of the thirteenth century, an epoch of increasing naturalism will begin. As did Exekias' billowing sail (FIG. 5-7), the Eadwine figure marks a turning point—in this case, in the history of Medieval representation. The Late Romanesque and Early Gothic "feel" of body and drapery as surfaces that interact forcefully implies not only a sense of their materiality but also a sense of depth. That sense will sharpen and deepen into the representational art of the Renaissance.

9-41   EADWINE THE SCRIBE, *The Scribe Eadwine* from the *Canterbury Psalter, c.* 1150, Trinity College, Cambridge, England.

ENGLAND

Gloucester

London

Wells

Salisbury

Rouen

Amiens

Beauvais

Noyon

Paris

St. Denis

Laon

Reims

ILE DE
FRANCE

Chartres

Etampes

Sens

Le Mans

FRANCE

Lyons

Avignon

Toulouse

LEON

NAVARRE

ARAGON

CASTILE

Zaragoza

Barcelona

DOMINION OF THE ALMOHADES

Cologne

Marburg

HOLY ROMAN EMPIRE

Naumburg

Prague

Bamberg

Nuremberg

Strasbourg

Ulm

Basel

Milan

Verona

Venice

Bologna

Lucca

Florence

Pisa

Siena

PAPAL
STATES

Orvieto

Rome

GOTHIC EUROPE ABOUT 1200

0	100	200	300	
				MILES

0	160	320	480	
				KILOMETERS

GOTHIC ART

Laon Cathedral
(c. 1160–1205)

Chartres Cathedral

1140

1194

EARLY GOTHIC PERIOD c. 1140–1194

1200

Louis VII of France (1137–1180)   St. Francis of Assisi (1182–1226)   Third Crusade 1189–1192

Abbot Suger
(1081–1151)
Frederick Barbarossa
(1152–1190)
Henry VI (Hohenstaufen)
(1190–1197)
Norman Kingdom joined to Holy
Roman Empire under Henry VI

Louis IX (St. Louis)
(1226–1270)

Fourth Crusade
(Constantinople) 1204

HIGH GOTHIC PERIOD c. 1194–1300

St. Thomas Aquinas
(c. 1225–1274)
Frederick II
(Hohenstaufen)
(1215–1250)

Franciscan order
founded 1210

Sixth Crusade
1228–1229

Amiens
Cathedral
(1220–1236)

1250

Cologne Cathedral
(begun 1248)

Charles of Anjou conquers Sicily
(end of Hohenstaufen rule in Italy) 1266

Bamberg Rider

Marco Polo in China 1271–1292

Palazzo
Pubblico
(1288–1309)

1300

Doge's Palace
(1345–1438)

Babylonian Captivity of papacy at Avignon

The Black Death 1346–1348

Virgin of Paris

1309

1350

Milan Cathedral

1377

The Great Schism 1378–1417

LATE GOTHIC PERIOD c. 1300–1700

1400

1500

1417

Facade of St. Maclou, Rouen
(c. 1500–1514)

GOTHIC WAS FIRST used as a term of derision by Renaissance critics, who scorned the lack of conformity of Gothic art to the standards of Classical Greece and Rome: "May he who invented it be cursed," wrote one of them. The style, the critics mistakenly thought, had originated with the Goths, who thus were responsible for the destruction of the good and true Classical style. The men of the thirteenth and fourteenth centuries, however, referred to the Gothic cathedrals as *opus modernum* (modern work) or *opus francigenum* (Frankish work). They recognized in these structures that towered over their towns a style of building and of decoration that was original. It was with confidence in their own faith that they regarded their cathedrals as the real image of the City of God, the Heavenly Jerusalem, which they were privileged to build on earth.

There are strong contrasts between the Gothic and the Romanesque environments and points of view. Romanesque society was dominated by the uncertainties inherent in the anarchical tendencies of feudalism. The great barons of the countryside and the great abbeys enjoyed an almost total independence, and the conflict of their claims to privilege led to constant warfare. Gothic society was also feudal, but it was a comparatively ordered feudalism. Here and there, powerful barons had been able to make themselves kings, and monarchy, especially in England and France, asserted itself strongly to limit the independence of lesser lords and the Church. Centralized government was established, and law and order instilled confidence in people of all walks of life. The cities, entirely new or built on the foundations of old Roman ones, began to thrive and to become strong; allied for common defense, they were very often powerful enough to defy kings and emperors. Within their walls, men who had escaped from the land could find freedom: "The air of the city is the breath of freedom," one slogan had it. City life took on a complex but ordered form; craft guilds, resembling strong unions, were formed to give protection and profit to artisans of the same specialties. A middle class, made up of the craftsmen, merchants, and professionals (lawyers, doctors, teachers, and many others) came to constitute a new and powerful force to check and balance the feudal aristocracy. The fear and insecurity that pervaded the Romanesque world was mitigated by the new alignment of economic and social forces, and the Gothic world emerged.

Romanesque society had been dominated by men. In Gothic society, women took on a new importance. Wandering minstrels sang less of the great deeds of heroes in war and more of love, beauty, and springtime. Eleanor of Aquitaine, wife of Louis VII of France and of Henry II Plantagenet of England and mother of Richard the Lion-heart and John, was one of the first to rule over a "court of love," in which respect for the lady was prerequisite and from which the code of chivalry was to emanate that so decided social relationships in the later Middle Ages. The monastic prejudice against women no longer determined the representation of them in art. In the twelfth century, *luxuria*, sensual pleasure, is represented at Moissac as a woman with serpents at her breasts; in the thirteenth century, as a pretty girl looking into a mirror. It is almost with relief that the Gothic upper classes turn from the *chansons de geste* to the new amorous songs and romances, in which the lover adores his lady and in which such immortal lovers as Tristan and Isolde are celebrated. Marie de France, herself a noblewoman, introduced this tale, along with many others of the new Arthurian legends, to northern French feudal society. The poetry of the times nicely illustrates the contrast between Romanesque and Gothic taste and mood: in the Romanesque *Song of Roland*, the dying hero waxes rhapsodic over his sword, but the German minnesinger of the Gothic period, dreaming in a swooning ecstasy of his lady, is "woven round with delight."

The love of woman, celebrated in art and formalized in life, received spiritual sanction in the cult of the Virgin Mary, who, as the Mother of Heaven and of Christ and in the form of Mother Church, loved all her children. It was Mary who stood compassionately between the Judgment seat and the horrors of Hell, interceding for all her faithful. The later twelfth and thirteenth centuries sang hymns to her, put her image everywhere, and dedicated great cathedrals to her. Her image was carried into battle on banners, and her name sounded in the battle cry of the king of France: "Sainte Marie . . . Saint Denis . . . Montjoie!" Thus, Mary became the spiritual lady of chivalry, and the Christian knight dedicated his life to her. The severity of Romanesque themes stressing the Last Judgment yields to the gentleness of the Gothic, in which Mary is represented crowned by Christ in Heaven.

It was not only the new position of women, the lyrical and spiritual exaltation of love, or the cult of the Virgin that softened barbarous manners. In concert with the new mood was the influence of one remarkable man, St. Francis of Assisi, who saw Christ not as the remote and terrible Judge but as the loving Savior who had walked among and had himself been one of the "rejected of men." The series of reform movements that make up the history of Medieval monasticism culminates in St. Francis' founding of the religious order that bears his name, the Franciscans. St. Francis felt that the members of his order must shun the cloistered life and freely walk the streets of the busy cities as mendicants, preaching the original message of Christ—the love of oneself and one's neighbor. Shortly after Francis' death and against his wish that his followers never settle in monasteries, they commenced the great basilica in his name at Assisi. The historical importance of the Franciscan movement lies in its strengthening of religious faith, its stimulating of the religious emotion among people in cities, and its weakening of the power and influence of the old, Romanesque, countryside abbeys. St. Francis could be said to have brought a kind of democracy to religion in Europe at the expense of its feudal establishment.

Courtly love, the development of chivalry, the cult of the Virgin Mary, and the teaching and example of St. Francis could not, of course, nullify, although they could mitigate, the cruel realities of Medieval life. While St. Francis was still living, the Fourth Crusade sacked Christian Constantinople, visiting atrocities on it that would outdo those of the later conquest by the Ottoman Turks. The papacy and king of France collaborated in the annihilation of the peoples of Languedoc and Provence in the south of France, the so-called Albigensians, who were accused of heresy but who also stood in the way of the territorial ambitions of royal France. It was this region that had fostered the new poetry of the troubadours and produced the Romanesque sculpture examined earlier. The Albigensian "crusade" also produced that grim and fateful instrument of heretic-hunting, the Inquisition or "Holy Office," instituted by St. Dominic. The Dominicans, called in fearful derision *Domini Canes* ("dogs of the Lord"), were in many ways rivals of the Franciscans and saw themselves as rooting out unbelievers and heretics and guarding the purity of orthodox dogma. The Dominicans' concern for theology led them to be teachers, and they produced one of the great Christian theologians and philosophers, St. Thomas Aquinas, who, at mid-thirteenth century, was the leading light of the University of Paris.

The institution of the university begins to appear in the early Gothic period in its natural setting: the city. The monastic and cathedral schools of the earlier Middle Ages had sought to keep the learning of the fathers of the Church alive and to reassess these teachings in the light of developing Christian thought. From these schools, the universities, communities of scholars and their pupils, evolved in the twelfth and thirteenth centuries at Bologna and Padua, Oxford, and Paris. The most important study at the university was theology, but several other subjects were taught, among them mathematics, astronomy, music, grammar, logic, law, and medicine. Ancient Greek philosophy, principally that of Aristotle, was recovered from Arabic translations and had an enormously stimulating effect on theology. Here appeared a reasoned, systematic method of argument

and a treasury of lore and observation of natural things. The philosophers set to work to find some way to adjust this new authoritative knowledge to Christian belief; they sought, in short, to rationalize religion. Their method was to arrive at proofs for the central dogmas of the faith by argument, or disputation. This method, taught in the schools and universities, came to be called "scholasticism," and its proponents "schoolmen." Scholastic philosophy is still the official philosophy of the Roman Catholic Church. The greatest exponent of this systematic procedure was St. Thomas Aquinas. Typical of the method is his treatise, the *Summa Theologiae*, which was laid out into Books, the Books into Questions, the Questions into Articles, each Article into objections with contradictions and responses, and, finally, answers to the objections.

Within this framework, the shrewdest and subtlest arguments of the Middle Ages were advanced. The habit of mind it created lasted for centuries, an obstacle to the rise of empirical thought and science; yet much value is still found in it today. It is quite possible that the Scholastic habit of disputation is reflected in the thought processes of Gothic architects, as Erwin Panofsky suggested (see pp. 387–88).

St. Thomas wrote his summary of Christian theology at a time when the great cathedrals were manifesting a kind of architectural "summation" of the Christian universe. At the time, the papacy ruled supreme in Europe, not only spiritually but temporally. At the beginning of the thirteenth century, Pope Innocent III, who took England away from King John, could claim: "Single rulers have single provinces, and single kings single kingdoms; but Peter . . . is pre-eminent over all, since he is the Vicar of Him whose is the earth and the fulness thereof, the whole wide world and all that dwell therein."

The thirteenth century represents the summit of achievement for unified Christendom: the triumph of the papacy; a successful and inspiring synthesis of religion, philosophy, and art; and the first firm formation of the states that will make modern history. The scene of this great but brief equilibrium of forces favoring religion is the Gothic city; within the city, the soaring cathedral, "flinging its passion against the sky," asserts the nature of the Gothic spirit.

EARLY GOTHIC

Architecture

On June 11, 1144, Louis of France, Eleanor of Aquitaine (his queen), members of the royal court, and a host of distinguished prelates, including five archbishops, as well as a vast crowd, converged on the royal abbey of St. Denis, just a few miles north of Paris, for the dedication of the new choir. This choir, with its crown of chapels radiant with stained-glass windows, set a precedent that the builders in the region surrounding Paris, the Île-de-France, were to follow for the next half century.

Two eminent persons were particularly influential in the formation of the Gothic style: Bernard of Clairvaux and Suger, abbot of St. Denis. Bernard held the belief that faith was mystical and intuitive rather than rational. In his battles with Abelard, a contemporary scholastic philosopher whose views were a basis for the dialectical method of Aquinas, he upheld this position with all the persuasiveness of his powerful personality and eloquence and by the example of his own holiness. The Cistercian architecture that was being built under Bernard's influence reflected his

10-1   Ambulatory and radiating chapels of the abbey church of St. Denis (near Paris), 1140–1144.

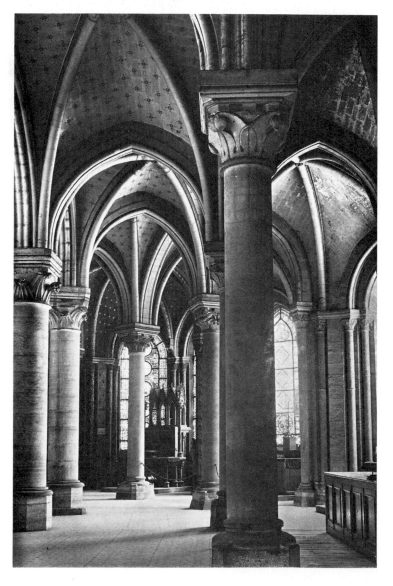

theology, stressing purity of outline, simplicity, and a form and light peculiarly conducive to meditation.

Although Bernard denounced lavish decoration and elaborate architecture, the Gothic style was initiated by a fellow abbot who, accepting Bernard's admonitions to reform his monastery, built his new church in a style that surpassed the Romanesque in splendor. The fellow churchman was the Abbot Suger, who had risen from humble parentage to become the right-hand man of both Louis VI and Louis VII, and, during the latter's absence in the Second Crusade, the regent of France. From his youth, Suger wrote, he had dreamed of the possibility of embellishing the church that had nurtured him, the royal Church of France, within the precincts of which its kings had been buried since the ninth century. It was in fact his intention to confer authority on the claims of the kings of royal France to the territory we recognize as France today, for, in Suger's time, the power of the French king, except for scattered holdings, was confined to an area not much larger than the Île-de-France. Thus, Suger's political role and his building role were one: to construct a kingdom and an architectural expression of it. In 1122, he was elected abbot of St. Denis and, within 15 years, was at work rebuilding the old monastery, which had been in use for almost 300 years. As he made his plans for the new building, he must have recalled many of the churches seen during his travels, and the workmen and artists who labored to raise the church were summoned from many regions. St. Denis, one of the last great abbey churches to be built, became the monastic inspiration for the city cathedrals and is known as the cradle of Gothic art.

Suger described his new choir at St. Denis (FIG. 10-1) as follows:

> Moreover, it was cunningly provided that—through the upper columns and central arches which were to be placed upon the lower ones built in the crypt—the central nave of the new addition should be made the same width, by means of geometrical and arithmetical instruments, as the central nave of the old [Carolingian] church; and, likewise, that the dimensions of the new side-aisles should be the same as the dimensions of the old side-aisles, except for that elegant and praiseworthy extension . . . a circular string of chapels, by virtue of which the whole [church] would shine with the wonderful and uninterrupted light of most luminous windows, pervading the interior beauty.*

The abbot's description is a key to the understanding of Early Gothic architecture. As he says, the major

*Erwin Panofsky, trans., *Abbot Suger on the Abbey Church of St. Denis and Its Art Treasures* (Princeton: Princeton University Press, 1951), p. 101.

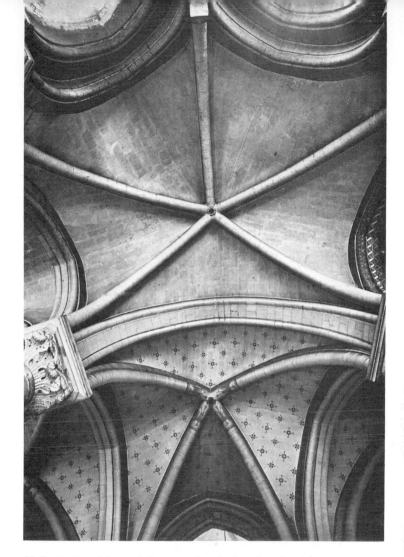

10-2 Plans of the crypt (*top*) and choir (*bottom*) of St. Denis (near Paris). (After Sumner Crosby.)

10-3 Vaults of the ambulatory and radiating chapels of the choir of St. Denis.

dimensions of the structure were dictated by an older church, but it was the "elegant and praiseworthy extension"—the "string of chapels" with "luminous windows"—that proclaimed the new style.

Although the crypt at St. Denis served as a foundation for the choir above it, a comparison of their respective plans and structures reveals the major differences between Romanesque and Gothic building (FIG. 10-2). The thick walls of the crypt create a series of separate volumes—a careful Romanesque "partitioning" into units—whereas the absence of walls in the choir above produces a unified space. The crypt is essentially a wall construction, and it is covered with groin vaults; the choir, on the other hand, is a skeletal construction, and its vaults are Gothic rib vaults (FIG. 10-3).

The ancestors of the Gothic rib vault were found at Caen and Durham. A rib vault is easily identified by the presence of crossed, or diagonal, arches under the groins of a vault. These arches form the armature, which serves as the framework for Gothic skeletal construction. The Gothic vault may be distinguished

from other rib or arched vaults by its use of the pointed, or broken, arch as an integral part of the skeletal armature, by the presence of thinly vaulted webs, or severies, between the arches, and by the fact that usually, regardless of the space to be vaulted, the crowns of all the arches are at approximately the same level—something the Romanesque architects could not achieve with their semicircular arches (FIG. 10-4). Thus, a major advantage of the Gothic vault is its flexibility, which permits the vaulting of compartments of varying shapes, as may be readily seen in the plan of the choir of St. Denis and in many other Gothic choir plans. Moreover, although it does not entirely support the webs, the Gothic armature allows predetermining of the alignment and concentration of thrusts to be buttressed.

Although the Medieval mason unquestionably derived great satisfaction from his mastery of these technical problems and at times must have been preoccupied with them, he did not permit them to be an end in themselves. The ambulatories and chapels at St. Denis are proof that the rib vault was exploited, as

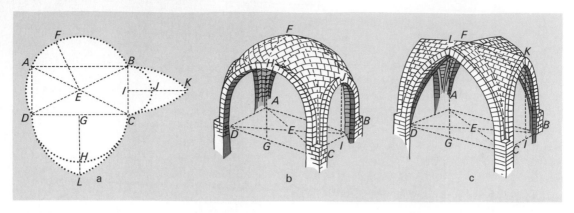

10-4   The Gothic rib vault and the domical vault differ in ways that derive from the fact that they are based on the pointed arch and the semicircular arch, respectively. Diagram a illustrates this: *ABCD* is an oblong bay to be vaulted; *AC* and *BD* are the diagonal ribs; *AB* and *DC*, the transverse arches; and *AD* and *BC*, the wall arches. If semicircular arches (the dotted arcs) are used, their radii, and therefore their heights (*EF, GH,* and *IJ*), will be different. The result will be a domical vault (diagram b), irregular in shape and difficult to light. If pointed arches are used, the points (and hence the ribs) can have the same heights (*IK* and *GL*). The result will be a Gothic rib vault (diagram c), a lighter, more flexible system than the domical vault, affording ample space for large clerestory windows.

Suger wrote, so that the whole church "would shine with wonderful and uninterrupted light." This was, in Medieval terms, the *scientia*—the theory—that motivated the creation of the Gothic style; and it was *ars*—technical knowledge and practical skill—that made it possible. The difference between the two was akin to the difference between modern physics and engineering; when a Medieval architect spoke of the "art of geometry," he meant not the abstract nature of geometric forms, but the practical uses to which mathematical formulations might be put in designing a piece of sculpture or in erecting a building. An understanding of Gothic architecture will not be reached, however, by trying to decide whether it was predominantly concerned with *ars* or with *scientia*, but rather by realizing that the cathedrals were the result of both. And it is in the stones themselves, in the extraordinary sensitivity of the Gothic mason for stone as a building material, that the spirit of Gothic architecture is to be discovered. The fact is that procedure was often hit or miss and rule of thumb; build-

ings often collapsed and were rebuilt with very large margins of safety. There was no one sure way and certainly no fundamental agreement about method. The certainties of modern engineering—themselves sometimes not so certain—were centuries beyond the Gothic reach. Even so, what still stands of Gothic architecture is a monument to the supreme skill, persistence, and vision of the Gothic architects.

It was the *scientia* of light that led Suger to the invention of the Gothic building, the slender, skeletal

10-6   Section through the aisle, gallery, triforium, and clerestory of Laon Cathedral. (After E. Gall.)

10-5   Plan of Laon Cathedral, France, *c.* 1160–1205. Choir extended after 1210. (After E. Gall.)

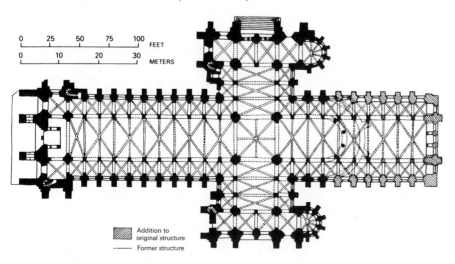

Addition to original structure
------- Former structure

10-7 Laon Cathedral (view into the choir from the gallery of the north transept).

structure that permitted the flooding of the interior with light. This "theory" came from the writings of a fifth-century mystic called "pseudo-Dionysius the Areopagite" because of his claim to be the true Dionysius, a first-century Athenian follower of St. Paul. This "pseudo-Dionysius" had become confused with the patron saint of royal France, St. Denis, making it natural for Suger to take the former's mystical identification of light with the divine as a kind of prescription for any building dedicated to St. Denis. When Suger, steeped in the theology of the Areopagite, envisioned the new St. Denis, he saw it as a mystic radiance. This is another example of the significance of religious authority in the Middle Ages. Not only scripture, but the works of the fathers of the Church, were the key to reality, and things had to be interpreted in terms of their authority.

The evolution of Gothic architecture is a continuing adjustment of scale, proportion, buttressing, vault arrangement, and wall and façade design that, in Erwin Panofsky's image, is like the steps of a complex scholastic argument. Only the choir and narthex of St. Denis were completed in the twelfth century; for a fairly complete view of the Early Gothic style of the second half of the century, one must turn to Laon Cathedral (FIGS. 10-5, 10-6, 10-7, 10-8). Begun about 1160 and completed shortly after 1200, the building retains many Romanesque features but combines them with the new Gothic structural devices of the rib vault and the pointed arch. Shortly after the building's completion, the choir was enlarged and the present plan—relatively long and narrow with a square east end—has a decidedly English flavor. Among the plan's easily discernible Romanesque features are the strongly marked-off crossing square and the bay system, composed of a large unit in the nave flanked by two small squares in each aisle (FIG. 10-5). The nave bays are defined by sexpartite rib vaults and an alternate-support system that, in combination, continue the Romanesque tradition of subdividing the interior into a number of separate compartments. Both features, as well as the gallery above the aisles, have been derived from Norman Romanesque architecture, which enjoyed great prestige in northern France throughout the twelfth century (FIGS. 9-15 and 9-16). A new feature of the interior, however, is the *triforium*, the band of arcades below the clerestory that occupies the space corresponding to the exterior strip of wall covered by the sloping timber roof above the galleries. The triforium expresses a growing de-

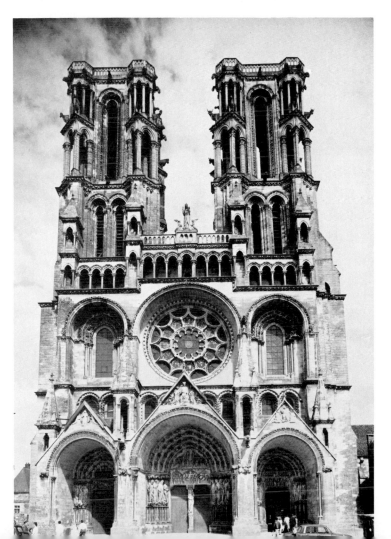

10-8 West façade of Laon Cathedral, begun c. 1190.

sire to break up and eliminate all continuous wall surfaces. Its insertion produces the characteristic Early
Gothic nave-wall elevation of four parts: nave arcade,
gallery, triforium, and clerestory (FIGS. 10-6 and 10-7).

At Laon, the alternate-support system is treated
less emphatically than in other Early Gothic churches
(for example, Sens, Noyon). It is not reflected in the
nave arcade (although colonnettes were added to a
few of the columns as an afterthought), as alternating
bundles of three and five shafts have their origin
above the level of the main wall supports (FIG. 10-7).
It appears that the Laon architect is no longer completely happy with the compartmentalized effect of
Romanesque interiors, which tends to make visitors
pause as they advance from unit to unit. Gothic
builders aim, as yet rather timidly at Laon, to create
an integrated, unified interior space that sweeps un-
interruptedly from west to east. The alternate-support system, hugging the ground in Ottonian times
and rising to dominate nave walls in northern Romanesque, has lost its footing at Laon and, like the
solid masonry of Romanesque walls, is about to evap-
orate.

Important changes in the design of the church exterior were also part of the Early Gothic experience.
At Laon, the doorways, under protective porches,
and the towers have been treated as integral parts of
the mass of the building (FIG. 10-8). The interior stor-

10-9   *Above:* West façade of Notre Dame, Paris, begun *c.* 1215.

10-10   *Below:* South flank of Notre Dame, Paris.

10 11 *Above:* Plan of Notre Dame, Paris. (After Frankl.)

10-12 *Right:* East end and part of the nave of Notre Dame, begun 1163; modified 1225–1250.

ies are reflected in the levels into which the façade is divided. (A noticeable discontinuity between the central and flanking portions of the façade was to be regulated in later designs.) Typically Gothic are the deep embrasures of the doorways and windows and the open structure of the towers. A comparison of the façades of Laon and St. Étienne at Caen (FIG. 9-14) reveals how deep the penetration of the mass of the wall has become. Here, as in Gothic generally, there is operating a kind of principle of reduction of sheer mass by its replacement with intricately framed voids.

Laon has a pair of towers flanking each arm of the transept (only two completed) and a lantern tower over the crossing, which, with the two western towers, gives a total of seven, the perfect mystic number. (Composed of three and four, it represents the Trinity and the Evangelists or the gospels.) This complement of towers was the Early Gothic ideal and continued the German Romanesque tradition of multiple integrated towers. Rarely, however, did building funds suffice for the completion of all towers. Even the façade towers of French cathedrals were seldom finished; most, including those of Laon, lacked the crowning spires planned for them. Eventually, the massed towers of the east end were omitted from building plans, and the Norman two-tower façade became the French High Gothic standard.

Transept towers were not part of the plan for the cathedral of Paris, the renowned Notre Dame (FIG. 10-9). Thus, this essentially Early Gothic building has a High Gothic silhouette in which only the slender crossing spire interrupts the long horizontal roof line that extends eastward behind the massive façade towers (FIG. 10-10). Notre Dame of Paris—begun in 1163, only a few years after Laon—embodies a fascinating mixture of conservative and progressive ideas. Choir and transept were completed by 1182; the nave, by 1225; and the façade, by 1250. The plan (FIG. 10-11) shows an ambitiously scaled, five-aisled structure in which a Romanesque bay system is combined with Early Gothic six-part (sexpartite) nave vaulting. The original transept was short and did not project beyond the outer aisles. The original nave wall had four parts, in the Early Gothic manner, with a triforium in the form of a series of rosettes.

Barely completed, the building was extensively modified. Between 1225 and 1250, chapels were built into the spaces between buttresses, and the transept arms were lengthened in 1250. At the same time— perhaps as the result of a fire (according to Viollet-le-Duc, the cathedral's nineteenth-century restorer), but probably to admit more light into the nave—changes were made in the nave wall (the bays adjacent to the crossing were redone by Viollet-le-Duc), as shown in FIG. 10-12. By this time, the nave of Chartres Cathedral had been completed (FIG. 10-17) and had rendered Early Gothic galleries and four-level wall elevations obsolete. As the galleries had already been built at Paris, the "modernization" of the nave of Notre Dame had to be a compromise. The clerestory windows were lowered to the top of the gallery by suppressing the rosettes of the triforium. This, in turn, required that the gallery roof be lowered and redesigned. The solution—a pitched roof with one of its slopes inclined toward the nave wall—created a difficult drainage problem that was solved only in the nineteenth century, when Viollet-le-Duc designed a single-slope roof to throw the water outward.

Like the interior, the façade of Notre Dame seems to waver between the old and the new (FIG. 10-9). Begun after the Laon façade had been completed, it appears much more conservative and, in the preservation of its "mural presence," more closely related to Romanesque than to High Gothic façades. From the modern observer's point of view, this may be one of its great assets. Less perforated and more orderly than that of Laon, Notre Dame's façade exudes a sense of strength and permanence that is lacking in many contemporary and later designs. Careful balancing of vertical against horizontal elements has achieved a quality of restful stability that makes this façade one of the most satisfying and memorable in Gothic architecture.

While the new Gothic style was developing in northern France, the regional Romanesque style prevailed in the south of France and in most of Europe. We have seen the Romanesque church of St. Trophime at Arles (FIG. 9-34), which, like its neighbor St. Gilles-du-Gard, reflects ancient Roman architectural motifs, such as the gabled portico and triumphal arch. This region of the lower Rhône valley is crowded with remnants of Roman monuments, some very well preserved: the Pont du Gard near Nîmes, (FIG. 6-43), the Maison Carrée at Nîmes, and the triumphal arch at Orange. The classicizing Romanesque style in Italy (FIG. 9-21) can almost be regarded as an anticipation of the classicizing Renaissance style to come.

Sculpture

Gothic sculpture makes its first appearance in the Île-de-France and its environs with the same dramatic suddenness as Gothic architecture and, it is likely, in the very same place—the abbey church of St. Denis. Almost nothing of the sculpture of the west façade of St. Denis remains to be studied, but it was there that sculpture emerged completely from the interior of the church to dominate the western entrances, which were regarded as the "gateways to Heavenly Jerusalem" and as the "royal portals." These royal portals, so called because of the statues of kings and queens on the embrasures flanking the doorways, are typified by the west portals of Chartres Cathedral (FIG. 10-13), carved between 1145 and 1170. This west façade and its portals are the only surviving parts of an Early Gothic cathedral that was destroyed in a disastrous fire in 1194 before it had been completed. The cathedral was reconstructed immediately, but in the

10-13   Royal (west) Portals of Chartres Cathedral, France, c. 1145–1170.

10-14 Detail of the jamb statues, Royal Portals, Chartres Cathedral.

Around the central tympanum are the 24 elders of the Apocalypse, accompanying the Second Coming. Decorating the multiple jambs flanking each doorway are the most striking figures: the great statues of the kings and queens of the Old Testament, the royal ancestors of Christ (FIG. 10-14). It is almost certain that the Medieval observer also regarded them as the figures of the kings and queens of France, symbols of secular as well as of biblical authority. The unity of the triple portal in its message and composition complements the unity of the cathedral itself, which—in its fluent, uninterrupted, vast, and soaring space—compounds earth and heaven in a symbol of the spiritually perfected universe to come.

The jamb statues are among the few original forms of architectural sculpture to have appeared in any age. At first glance, they seem—in their disregard of normal proportions and their rigid adherence to an architectural frame—to follow many of the precepts of Romanesque architectural sculpture. Yet the differences are striking and important. The statues stand out from the plane of the wall; they are not cut back into it. They are conceived and treated as three-dimensional volumes. They move into the space of the observer and participate in it with him. Most significant of all is the first trace of a new naturalism: drapery folds are no longer calligraphic exercises translated into stone; they now either fall vertically or radiate naturally from their points of suspension. Although carefully arranged in regular patterns, these folds suggest that the artist is no longer copying painted images but that actual models have become his guides. This is particularly true of the figures flanking the central doorway (some appear in the left foreground of FIG. 10-14), which are the work of the anonymous HEADMASTER, the artist in charge of the overall design and decoration of the portals. The advanced nature of his style becomes particularly noticeable when his figures are compared with those on the outside jamb of the lateral portal (right background in FIG. 10-14), which evidently were carved by a different, perhaps older, and certainly more conservative artist. The latter's approach is still deeply rooted in the Romanesque tradition. His figures seem more agitated; their silhouettes are curvilinear and broken. The drapery folds are treated decoratively and, here and there, continue to rotate in abstract swirls. Only the windblown lower garment edges, characteristic of much Romanesque sculpture, have come to rest—reluctantly, it seems, and perhaps at the Headmaster's insistence. Even so, the figures fail to adjust themselves as neatly and consequently to their architectural setting as do the Headmaster's statues, which—although they have stepped out of the wall and have become corporeal—are severely disciplined and have been rigorously subordinated to

High Gothic style. The portals, however, constitute the most complete and impressive corpus of Early Gothic sculpture.

The three west portals of Chartres, treated as a unit, proclaim the majesty and omnipotence of Christ. His Birth, the Presentation at the Temple, and Christ in Majesty with his Virgin Mother are shown on the right portal; Christ's Ascension into Heaven is shown on the left portal. Scenes from his life and from the passion are vividly carved on the capitals, which continue as a frieze from one portal to the next. On the central portal is depicted the Second Coming, surrounded by the Signs of the Four Evangelists, with the Twelve Apostles below, seated as representing the corporate body of the Christian Church. The Second Coming—in essence, the Last Judgment theme—remains, as in the Romanesque works we have seen (which are only some 20 years older than the west portals of Chartres), centrally important. Here, however, it has become a symbol of salvation rather than damnation. It is, moreover, combined with other scenes and symbolic figures as part of a larger theme rather than a symbol of the dogma itself. In the archivolts of the right portal are shown the seven liberal arts—the core of Medieval learning and therefore symbolic of man's knowledge, which will lead him to the true faith. The signs of the zodiac and scenes representing the various labors of the months of the year are carved into the left-portal archivolts as symbols of the cosmic and of the terrestrial worlds.

their architectural background. Seen from a distance, they appear to be little more than vertical, decorative accents within the larger designs of portals and façade. And yet, within and despite this architectural straitjacket, the incipient naturalism has softened the appearance of the figures. This is particularly noticeable in their faces, in which can be seen the mask-like features of the Romanesque being converted into human likenesses. Here is the faint beginning of a personalizing naturalism that will become transformed first into idealized portraits of the perfect Christian and finally into the portraiture of specific individuals.

During the early twelfth century, great changes were taking place in Western humanity's view of itself, especially with respect to the relation of body and soul. Previously, the old Augustinian view had prevailed. The essence of the soul was completely unlike that of the body: the soul was spiritual and immortal; the body, material and subject to corruption. With the rediscovery of the main works of Aristotle, it gradually came to be believed that the soul and the body were closely interrelated, that the soul was the *form* of the body, and that, therefore, the body was no longer to be despised as merely the cor-

ruptible prison of the soul from which it is then released when the body dies. One Scholastic philosopher saw the soul and the body as meeting and the combination as responsible for the personality of the individual. Another saw the soul as ruling the body but also cherishing its prison. These views, in which the body is seen as coming into its own, reflected a universally changing outlook. John of Salisbury (*c.* 1110–1180), the great English Scholastic, took the perhaps radical view that the soul is stimulated and acted on by sensations from the world, rather than directly inspired and moved by entirely spiritual principles. He even declared that some of the principal problems of Scholastic philosophy could be solved by psychological examination of the way we think. The West was now speaking with a new voice: souls must be manifested through bodies—the individual bodies of men and women. Thus, the new, individualized heads of Chartres herald an era of artistic concern with the realization of personality and individuality that may only now, in our times, be terminating. The figures of the Royal Portals of Chartres hold a place analogous to the works of Greek artists in the late sixth century B.C.; they turn the corner into a historical avenue of tremendous possibility.

10-15 Chartres Cathedral, begun 1194 (aerial view from the southeast).

10-16 Plan of Chartres Cathedral. (After Frankl.)

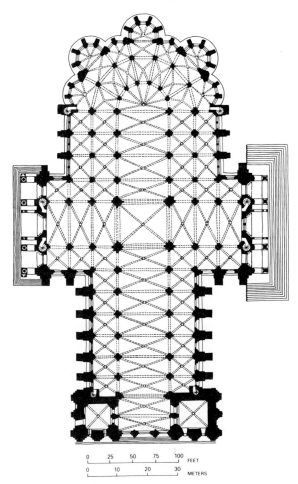

HIGH GOTHIC

Architecture

On June 10, 1194, a great fire consumed the town of Chartres. Its cathedral was again destroyed, except for the crypt, the western towers, and the Royal Portals between them. A new cathedral was begun almost immediately and was completed, for the most part, by 1220. This new cathedral of Chartres is usually considered the first of the High Gothic buildings—the first to have been planned from the beginning for the use of flying buttresses.

The flying buttress, that exceedingly useful and characteristic Gothic structural device, seems to have been employed by about 1180 for the bracing of the nave of Notre Dame in Paris and, shortly thereafter, at Laon. A section through Laon Cathedral (FIG. 10-6) shows how the flying buttress reaches across the lower vaults of aisle and gallery and abuts the nave walls directly at the points at which the vaults exert their major thrusts. Similar methods to strengthen the walls of vaulted naves had already been used in Romanesque architecture, but there the buttresses were concealed under the aisle roofing. Now, they are left exposed in a manner that has been either condemned as "architectural crudity" or praised as "structural honesty." An aerial view of Chartres Cathedral (FIG. 10-15) shows that a series of these highly dramatic devices has been placed around the *chevet* (the east end of the church), thus supporting the vaults with permanent arms, like scaffolding left in place. With the mastery of this structural form, the technical vocabulary of Gothic architecture became complete. The buttress eliminates the need for Romanesque walls and permits the construction of a self-consistent and self-supporting skeletal structure. The Chartres architect was the first to arrive at this conclusion and to design his building accordingly.

At Chartres, after the great fire, the overall dimensions of the new structure were determined by the towers left standing to the west and by the masonry of the crypt to the east. For reasons of piety, but also of economy, the crypt—the repository of the most precious relic of Chartres, the mantle of the Virgin—was used as the foundation for the new structure. The earlier forms did not limit the plan (FIG. 10-16), however; it shows an unusual equilibrium between chevet, transept, and nave, which are almost equal in dimension. More important, perhaps, the plan reveals a new kind of organization. The last remnants of square schematism, still present in Early Gothic churches, have been replaced by a "rectangular-bay system" that will become the High Gothic norm. Now a rectangular unit in the nave, defined by its

10-17   Nave of Chartres Cathedral (view facing east).

own vault, is flanked by a single square in each aisle. This new bay arrangement was accompanied by a change in vault design. The new High Gothic vault, covering a relatively smaller area and more easily braced than its Early Gothic predecessor, has only four panels. The visual effect of these changes is to decompartmentalize the interior (FIG. 10-17); identical units have been aligned so that they are seen in too rapid a sequence to be discriminated as individual volumes of space. The alternate-support system, of course, is gone, and the nave, although richly articulated, has become a vast, continuous hall.

The organic, "flowing" quality of the High Gothic interior was enhanced by a new nave-wall elevation, which admits more light to the nave through greatly enlarged clerestory windows. The use of flying buttresses made it possible to eliminate the tribune gallery above the aisle, which had partially braced Romanesque and Early Gothic naves. The new, High Gothic, tripartite nave elevation—consisting of arcade, triforium, and clerestory—emphasizes the large clerestory windows; those at Chartres are almost as high as the main arcade. A comparison of the elevations of Laon and Chartres (FIG. 10-18) illustrates the radical changes that could be achieved by logical application of the new structural device, the flying buttress, that had been used only tentatively at Laon.

EARLY GOTHIC　　　　HIGH GOTHIC

CLERESTORY

TRIFORIUM

GALLERY

NAVE
ARCADE

10-18　Elevations of the nave walls of the cathedrals of
Laon (*left*) and Chartres (*right*), which is drawn to a
smaller scale than the Laon elevation. (Umschau-Verlag,
Frankfurt/Main.)

Despite the vastly increased size of the clerestory
windows, some High Gothic interiors remain relatively dark, largely due to the light-muffling effects of
their colored glass. Chartres has retained almost the
full complement of its original stained glass, which,
although it dims the interior, sheds a color-shot light
of great beauty that has helped to make Chartres the
favorite church of lovers of Gothic architecture.

Whatever the glory of Chartres, it had a contemporary rival in the cathedral of Bourges (FIG. 10-19),
which, although perhaps lacking the esthetic power

of Chartres, may have been, to a degree, its superior
in structural ingenuity, stability, and economy of
means. The two buildings, begun at about the same
time, were completely different yet satisfactory solutions to the problems of Gothic architectural design.
As such, they offered architects two alternative models: at Amiens and Reims, the design of Chartres was
perfected; and at Beauvais, the first master architect
conceived a kind of synthesis of Chartres and
Bourges.

The plan of Bourges Cathedral is strikingly different from that of Chartres Cathedral, resembling more
the plan of Notre Dame in Paris (FIG. 10-11). At
Chartres, the chevet, transept, and nave are of almost
equal dimension. At Bourges, the plan is continuous
(FIG. 10-20), eliminating the transept entirely, so that
the side aisles continue without interruption from the
western façade around the choir to the east. The
unity and sweeping continuity of the plan is furthered by the unusual elevation (FIG. 10-21). Instead
of one aisle on each side of the nave, there are two—
the inner one being higher and having its own clerestory, triforium, and arcade, all clearly visible through
the nave arcade. The stepping upward of the side
aisles to a climax in the nave vaults and the restatement in the inner aisle (albeit on a smaller scale) of
the three-part nave-wall elevation provide a rhythmic, vertical repetition of the distinctive High Gothic
arrangement. At the same time, windows at three
levels enhance the fluent opening of the space of the
nave into the aisles by saturating the interior with a
form-dissolving permeation of light—the ideal of
Gothic architecture.

The retention of older, Romanesque features—like
the sexpartite vaults, the alternate-support system
(seen in the slight differentiation in the membering of
alternate piers), and the small clerestory—do not reflect structural uncertainty. Modern engineering

10-19　Bourges
Cathedral, France,
1195–1255 (view from
the southeast).

10-20 Plan (*left*) and section (*right*) of Bourges Cathedral.

10-21 Bourges Cathedral, 1225–1250 (view across the nave from the south side).

analyses of wind and dead-load stresses (necessary for the high-rise structures of today) show that the lighter and more open buttresses of Bourges transfer structural forces to the foundations more efficiently than the massive ones at Chartres; a pier buttress at Chartres is estimated to weigh 1,000 tons, versus 400 tons at Bourges, yet the stress levels for high winds have been shown to be equivalent. Nevertheless, the Chartres design, with its balanced, additive, and logical arrangements of plan and elevation, became the more influential of the two. At Bourges, the relationships of the parts were perhaps too elusive and individual to be readily grasped and widely applied as a standard.

Amiens Cathedral (FIGS. 10-22, 10-23, 10-24, 10-25) continued the Chartrian manner and gracefully refined it. Amiens was begun in 1220, according to the designs of ROBERT DE LUZARCHES. The nave was finished in 1236 and the radiating chapels were completed by 1247, but work on the choir continued until almost 1270. The façade (FIG. 10-22)—slightly marred by uneven towers (the shorter dates from the fourteenth century; the taller, from the fifteenth century)—was begun at the same time as the nave (1220). Its lower parts seem to reflect the influence of the Laon façade in the spacing of its funnel-like and gable-covered portals. However, unlike Laon's, the Amiens portals do not project from the façade but are recessed behind the building's buttress-defined frontal plane. The upper parts of the façade, on the other hand, seem to be related to Notre Dame in Paris, the

10-22 West façade of Amiens Cathedral, France, c. 1220–1236; area above the rose window, early sixteenth century.

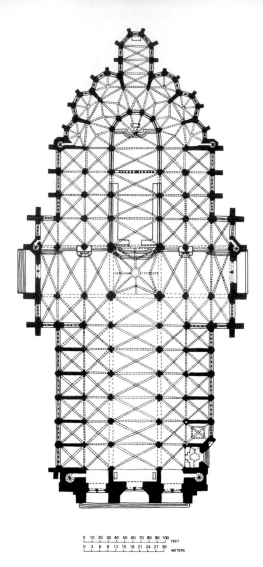

10-23 ROBERT DE LUZARCHES, plan of Amiens Cathedral. (After Frankl.)

rose window (with fifteenth-century tracery) being placed above the "king's gallery" and between double-arched openings in the towers. But the Amiens façade goes well beyond its apparent models in the richness and intricacy of its surface decoration. The deep piercing of walls and towers seems to have left few continuous surfaces to be decorated, to be sure, but the remaining ones have been covered with a network of articulating colonnettes, arches, pinnacles, rosettes, and other decorative stonework that screens and nearly dissolves visually the structure's solid core. Despite its decorative intricacy, the façade retains its monumental grandeur and is one of the first to achieve full integration with the building behind it. The cavernous portals correspond in width and placement to the nave and aisles, and (although in slightly different proportions) the façade's three-part elevation reflects that of the nave, the rose window corresponding to the clerestory.

The plan of Amiens (FIG. 10-23), like the façade, is exemplary of the grand High Gothic style. Derived from Chartres and perhaps even more elegant in its proportions, it reflects the builder's unhesitating and confident use of the complete Gothic structural vocabulary: the rectangular-bay system, the four-paneled rib vault, and a buttressing system that permits almost complete dissolution of the heavy masses and thick bearing walls of the Romanesque style. The concept of a self-sustaining, skeletal architecture has reached full maturity; what remains of the walls has been stretched like a skin between the piers and seems to serve no purpose other than to provide a weather screen for the interior (FIG. 10-24). From a height of 144 feet, the tense, strong lines of the vault ribs converge to the colonnettes and speed down the shell-like walls to the compound piers; almost every part of the superstructure has its corresponding element below, the only exception being the wall rib (the rib at the junction of the vault and the wall). There is an appearance of an effortless strength (that counters the fact of great weight), of a buoyant lightness one would never associate with the obdurate materiality of stone. Viewed directly from below, the vaults of the choir seem like a canopy, tent-like and suspended

10-24 Nave of Amiens Cathedral (view facing east).

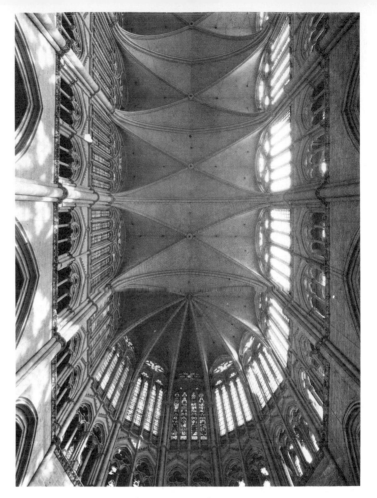

10-25 Choir vault of Amiens Cathedral.

from bundled masts (FIG. 10-25). The light flooding in from the clerestory imparts even more "lift" and, at the same time, blurs structural outlines. The effect is visionary, and we are reminded of another great building, utterly different from Amiens, in which light plays an analogous role—Hagia Sophia in Constantinople (FIG. 7-42). Not only is the physical mass of the building reduced by structural ingenuity and daring, but what remains is further dematerialized visually by light. As with scholastic philosophy, the logic of the structure here is in the service of mystery. Although philosophy might prove the existence of God with reason, the experience of the beatific vision gave the believer a mystical proof, like Dante's experience in Paradise as he gazed, rapt, into the "heart of Light, the heart of Silence."

In examining the interior of Amiens, it may be useful to reconsider Erwin Panofsky's suggestion of a connection between Gothic architecture and Scholastic philosophy and the description of the method as typified in Aquinas' *Summa Theologiae*. Most striking in the propositions of Aquinas and in the structure of Amiens is an insistence on an order and unity made up of clearly distinguished and clearly related parts—the philosopher aiming at logical consistency; the architect, at structural coherence. In neither is the order intended to be less than total. Aquinas' *Summa*

was designed to treat *all* possible questions in which faith and reason touch; in Amiens, all individual elements are subordinated to the whole, unlike the sharply subdivided, often opposed units of Romanesque design. This principle of *manifestatio* ("manifestation," "transparency") determines the look of the philosophic system, as it does the look of the cathedral. As Panofsky wrote:

A man imbued with the Scholastic habit [of thought] . . . would look upon the mode of architectural presentation, just as he looked upon the mode of literary presentation, from the point of view of *manifestatio*. He would have taken it for granted that the primary purpose of the many elements that compose a cathedral was to ensure stability, just as he took it for granted that the primary purpose of the many elements that constitute a *Summa* was to ensure validity.

But he would not have been satisfied had not the membrification of the edifice permitted him to re-experience the very processes of architectural composition, just as the membrification of the *Summa* permitted him to re-experience the very processes of cogitation. To him, the panoply of shafts, ribs, buttresses, tracery, pinnacles, and crockets was a self-analysis and self-explication of . . . architecture, much as the customary apparatus of parts, distinctions, questions, and articles was, to him, a self-analysis and self-explication of reason. . . . the Scholastic mind demanded a maximum of explicitness. It accepted and insisted upon a gratuitous clarification of function through form, just as it accepted and insisted upon a gratuitous clarification of thought through language.*

The other principle Panofsky saw at work in philosophy and architecture is that of *concordantia* ("harmony"), whereby contradictory possibilities are accepted and ultimately reconciled. This is achieved by careful debate, the *disputatio*, in which a possibility is stated, one authoritative view is cited, another authoritative view is cited in objection, the solution (a reconciliation of positions) is given, and finally a reply is given to each of the original arguments now rejected. Panofsky saw this process in the resolution of three "questions" in Gothic architecture: the placement and design of the rose window in the west façade, the design of the interior wall beneath the clerestory, and the conformation of the pier. (Very likely the development of the Gothic plan could also be seen as an evolved "solution" to a "question.") Evidence that the habit of mind reflected in the *disputatio* was not exclusive with the Scholastics in the universities, but was more broadly shared, is found on a page from the "album" of drawings by the thirteenth-century architect Villard de Honnecourt (Introduction FIG. 13 and FIG. 10-36). According to the inscription, Villard and another architect, PIERRE DE CORBIE, arrived at an ideal plan for a chevet after a *disputatio* (discussion).

*Erwin Panofsky, *Gothic Architecture and Scholasticism* (Latrobe, PA: Archabbey Press, 1951), pp. 58–60.

10-26   JEAN DE CHELLES, rose window of the north transept, Notre Dame, Paris, 1240–1250. Stained glass, iron and lead stone-bar tracery, diameter 43'.

THE RAYONNANT STYLE

From the grand style of the first half of the thirteenth century came a period of great refinement, the so-called *rayonnant* ("radiant") style, which dominated the second half of the century and was associated with the royal Paris court of Louis IX (St. Louis), famed throughout Europe for his justice, chivalry, and piety, and the Medieval ideal of the "saint-king." Royal France, growing increasingly wealthy, powerful, and prestigious, radiated its art and culture throughout Europe. The king was lavish in embellishing the realm, especially with religious architecture.

Preeminent examples of *rayonnant* design are the two great rose windows of Notre Dame in Paris, located in the south (FIG. 10-10) and north (page 310 and FIG. 10-26) transept façades. The tremendous north rose window, the work of the master-builder JEAN DE CHELLES, is a masterpiece of architectural ingenuity. Almost the entire mass of wall opens up into stained glass, which is held in place by an intricate armature of stone tracery that practically has the tensile strength of steel. Here, the Gothic passion for light leads to a most daring and successful attempt to subtract all superfluous material bulk just short of destabilizing the structure and to transform hard substance into insubstantial, luminous color. The fact that this vast, complex fabric of stone-set glass has maintained its structural integrity and equilibrium against the disintegrative forces of nature and time for 700 years attests to the master-builder's engineering genius.

The "multifoliate rose" of light, ever-changing in hue and intensity with the hours of the day, seems to turn solid architecture into a floating vision of the celestial heavens—a constellation of radiant, jewel-like stars. Expressive of the Gothic adoration of the Virgin Mary, the concentric circles exalt her as Mother of Christ; she appears at the very center of the design. Around her are figures of the prophets who foretold the Incarnation; in the second circle, are 32 Old Testament kings, the ancestors of Christ; in the outermost circle, are 32 high priests and patriarchs, who further testify to the royal lineage and divinity of Christ. The light of the north rose is predominantly blue, the color of the northern sky, of the heavens, and of the mantle of the Virgin, which she throws protectively around all those devoted to her.

The Gothic architect uses light as a medium, as does the Byzantine, but they use it in opposite ways. In Gothic architecture, light is *transmitted through* a kind of diffracting screen of stone-set glass; in Byzan-

tine architecture, light is *reflected from* myriad glass tesserae set into the hard bed of the wall (FIGS. 7-58 and 7-59). With light, both stained glass and mosaic create an opalescent splendor that transforms solid substance into insubstantial vision—the material world into the spiritual.

If the rose windows of the transepts of Notre Dame demonstrate the wall-dissolving architecture of *rayonnant* design, the Sainte Chapelle in Paris shows the principle of the style applied to a whole building (FIGS. 10-27 and 10-28). The building, joined to the royal palace, was intended to be a repository for relics of the Passion of Christ brought back by Louis IX after the ill-fated Sixth Crusade, so that its resemblance to an intricately carved reliquary is intentional. Here, the dissolution of the wall and the reduction of the bulk of the supports has been carried to the point that more than three-quarters of the structure is composed of stained glass. The supporting elements have been so reduced that they are hardly more than large

10-27 Sainte Chapelle, Paris, 1243–1248 (view from the southwest). The rose window was installed after 1485.

10-28 Interior of Sainte Chapelle (view facing east).

10-29 Beauvais Cathedral, France, begun 1247 (aerial view from the south).

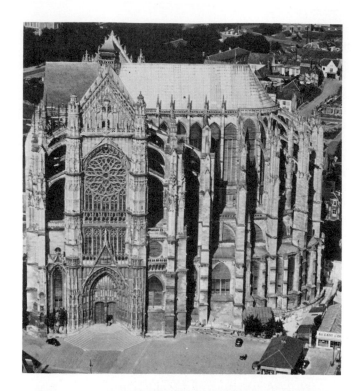

mullions separating the enormous windows, which are approximately 49 feet high and 15 feet wide and are the largest designed up to their time. Although the chapel was heavily restored during the nineteenth century (after being damaged in the French Revolution), it has retained most of its original thirteenth-century glass, which filters the light and fills the interior with an unearthly rose–violet atmosphere. Amid richly colored stone surfaces and shimmering strips of decorative mosaic stand statues of the apostles. Multicolored also, they stand on *soffits* almost independent of the architecture, and their related poses, with multiple axes, foreshadow the graceful rhythms of later thirteenth- and fourteenth-century sculpture. Here are technical and esthetic refinements that would have upset the solemn harmonies and monumentality of the art of the earlier part of the century. The emphasis on the extreme slenderness of the architectural forms and on linearity in general, with exquisite color and precise carving of details, does indeed recall the richly ornamented reliquaries of the time.

Beauvais Cathedral (FIGS. 10-29 and 10-30) was begun in 1247, after plans that had been drawn in the 1230s. As customary, construction was begun at the east end, so that apse and choir would be finished and ready for use while the remainder of the building was being completed. In contrast to monastic churches, which were usually assured of funding before construction began and which were completed in fairly short order, the building histories of urban cathedrals often extended over decades, and sometimes over centuries. Their financing depended largely on collections and public contributions (not always voluntary), and building programs were often interrupted by a lack of funds. Unforeseen events, such as wars, famines, or plagues, could stop construction, which might not be resumed for years, or even decades. The rebuilding of Chartres Cathedral took a relatively short 27 years; the building history of Cologne Cathedral (see FIG. 10-57) extended over six centuries, and Beauvais Cathedral was never completed.

The wisdom of starting at the east end and working westward was proven at Beauvais, where construction stopped around 1500 after a "flamboyant" Late Gothic transept had been added to the choir. Although unfinished, the completed and serviceable part of the building stands to this day as one of the most impressive examples of the Gothic "rush into

10-30 Choir of Beauvais Cathedral, 1272; vaults rebuilt after 1284.

the skies." That skyward impulse, seen first in the height of the nave at Paris (at the turn of the century), became an obsession with French Gothic builders. With their new skeletal frames of stone, they attempted goals almost beyond limit, pushing with ever-slenderer supports to new heights, aiming always at effects of insubstantial visions floating far beyond the reach of man. The nave vaults at Laon had risen to a height of about 80 feet; at Paris, to 107 feet; at Chartres, to 118 feet; and at Amiens, to 144 feet. In 1272, the builders of the choir of Beauvais planned a height of 157 feet.

In 1284, the vaults collapsed; the cause of the failure is still a matter of scholarly debate. The original design of the first master architect had been brilliant, audacious, and stable; the parts of the choir hemicycle completed by him remained standing. Modern engineering analysis, of the kind we have mentioned in the discussion of Chartres and Bourges, indicates that succeeding builders seem to have miscalculated wind and dead-load stresses, particularly those on the external intermediate piers. The choir, rebuilt with a broad margin of safety, has additional piers and old-fashioned, sexpartite vaults, not unlike those at Bourges. Unfortunately, the rebuilt vaults and piers disfigure the original design, for it was exactly those former features of wide-spread piers and slender buttresses that the rayonnant architects had sought in their effort to make an architecture seemingly out of nothing but line and light. Henceforth, the great structural innovations of the High Gothic style and the vast scale in which they were worked out would be things of the past. Late Gothic architecture, born of the linear rayonnant design, would be confined to buildings of quite modest size, conservative in structure and ornamented with restless designs of intricately meshed, pointed motifs.

Sculpture

Sculpture, as it had been since the Romanesque period, was subservient to architecture during the High Gothic period, but rapid changes were taking place. The unity of idea that controls the design of the Royal Portals of Chartres (FIG. 10-13) expanded to embrace the whole cathedral (see the façade of Amiens Cathedral; FIG. 10-22). The sculptural program came to include not only the huge portals but the upper levels of the building as well. The height of Gothic art—the cathedral-building and cathedral-adorning age—lasted from about 1210 to 1260. The range of the iconography of the sculpture is as vast and complex as the building. Most of the carved figures are symbolic, but many, particularly the grotesque gargoyles (used as rain-spouts) and other details of the upper por-

tions, are purely decorative and show the vivacity and charm of the Medieval spirit at this moment, when it was confident in its faith. The iconographic program, no longer (as in Romanesque art) confined almost entirely to the letter of the dogma, is extensive enough to embrace all the categories of Medieval thought. Indeed Émile Mâle showed that many iconographic schemes were based on the *Speculum majus* ("Great Mirror") of Vincent of Beauvais—a comprehensive summary of Medieval knowledge in which accounts of natural phenomena, scriptural themes, and moral philosophy serve a didactic religious purpose.

Nature begins to come forward as important, and man comes forward with it. Two figures from the Porch of the Confessors in the south transept of Chartres Cathedral illustrate how much the incipient realism of the Royal Portals has advanced. The figures, representing *St. Martin and St. Jerome* (FIG. 10-31), date from 1220–1230. Although attached to the architectural matrix, their poses are not determined by it as much as before. The setting now allows the

10-31 *St. Martin and St. Jerome, c.* 1220–1230, from the Porch of the Confessors, Chartres Cathedral, France.

10-32 *Left:* Central portal of the west façade of Reims Cathedral, France, *c.* 1225–1290.

10-33 *Below: The Annunciation* (*left*) and *The Visitation* (detail of FIG. 10-32). Jamb statues over life-size.

figures to communicate quietly with one another, like dignitaries waiting for some solemn procession to begin; they turn slightly toward each other, breaking the rigid vertical lines that, on the Royal Portals, fix the figures immovably. Their draperies are no longer described by the stiff and reedy lines of the figures of the Royal Portals; they fall and lap over the bodies in soft, if still regular, folds.

The faces are most remarkable; they show, for the first time since the ancient world, the features of specifically Western men, with no admixture whatever of the denatured mask passed down over a thousand years. Moreover, they seem to have been taken from particular persons as models, and we have no difficulty characterizing them. St. Martin is tall and ascetic—the intense priest with the gaunt features of the Gothic visionary (compare the spiritually moved but not particularized face of the Moissac Jeremiah or Isaiah in FIG. 9-28). He may have been a saintly canon of Chartres who reluctantly became a bishop; in any event—and another realistic touch—his vestments are the liturgical costume of the time. His companion, St. Jerome, who appears as a humorous, kindly, practical administrator–scholar, holds his Vulgate translation of the Scriptures. Thus, the two men are

not simply contrasted in terms of their poses, gestures, and attributes but, most particularly and emphatically, as *persons*, so that personality, revealed in human faces, makes the real difference—something rare even in Classical art. In another century or so, the identifiable portrait will emerge.

The fully ripened Gothic style can be seen in the west portals of Reims Cathedral (FIG. 10-32), built in the mid-thirteenth century. At first glance, the jamb statues appear to be completely detached from their architectural background. The columns to which they are attached have shrunk into insignificance and in no way impede the free and easy movement of the full-bodied figures. (On the Royal Portals of Chartres, the background columns occupy a volume equal to that of the figures; see FIG. 10-14.) However, two architectural devices limit the statues' spheres of activity and tie them to the larger design of the portal— the pedestals on which they stand and the canopies above their heads. Less submissive than their predecessors from the Royal Portals of Chartres, these Reims figures create an electric tension within the portal design; they were designed for this portal, however, and would look incongruous in any other setting. Gothic portal statues placed in museums to protect them from weathering look, without exception, forlorn and out of place.

On the right jamb of the central portal, four figures (FIG. 10-33) represent *The Annunciation* (left) and *The Visitation* (right). Their different styles reflect the hands of several anonymous masters. The master of the *Visitation* group, quite original in his manner, manifests a classicizing bent startlingly unlike anything seen since Roman times. The group illustrates the impact on its master carver of either actual Classical statuary he had seen or of manuscripts or ivories from Late Antiquity or Byzantium. Whatever the artist's source, the facial types, costumes, and drapery treatment are astonishing approximations of the naturalistic style traits of ancient figure sculpture. He has even tried to represent the Classical contrapposto stance, although the only partially successful result betrays the sculptor's ignorance of human anatomy. The two figures of the *Annunciation* group evidently were carved by different masters. The Virgin is by a sculptor who may have worked at Amiens before he came to Reims and whose style is characterized by a weighty, massive quality. Drapery resembling a thick, flannel-like material heavily falls from the figure's shoulders to her feet and, by stressing mass and verticality, imparts an aspect of grave solemnity.

The angel of the *Annunciation* group differs strikingly from the Virgin. It is tall and slender, animated by a kind of swaying curve, the head quite small, the face bright with a winsome smile. This almost dainty figure, contrasting with the still and somber Virgin, represents the new, courtly style—corresponding to the rayonnant style in architecture—that was ushered in with the reign of Louis IX and the cultural dominance of the Île-de-France after mid-century. The influence of these great cathedral statues must have been widely felt by those who contemplated them. John of Garland, writing in the thirteenth century on how university students should conduct themselves, advised: " . . . regard as models of deportment the graven images of the churches, which you should carry in your mind as living and indelible pictures."

Certainly, their influence on artists must have been great (as, for example, in the case of the painter of the *Psalter of St. Louis;* (see FIG. 10-37). Although the degree and the progress of that influence has not yet been worked out in complete detail, it is certain that, by the fourteenth century, Gothic sculpture was widely naturalized in Italy and elsewhere outside of France. In Italy, by the beginning of the fifteenth century, the native Gothic sense for realism had fused with a new classicizing impulse—partly generated from Byzantine art, partly from the discovery of the art of ancient Rome—to form the first distinctive styles of the Renaissance.

Stained Glass and Illumination

The Gothic accomplishment in architecture and sculpture is matched by the magnificent stained glass of the time, which we have already seen at Notre Dame and Sainte Chapelle in Paris. This medium is almost synonymous with the Gothic style; no other age has managed it with such craft and beauty. The mysticism of light that induced Suger to design an architecture that would allow for great windows is widespread in Gothic theology. "Stained-glass windows," wrote Hugh of St. Victor, "are the Holy Scriptures . . . and since their brilliance lets the splendor of the True Light pass into the church, they enlighten those inside." St. Bernard compared the manner in which light is tinted by a stained-glass window to the process of the Incarnation and virgin Birth of Jesus. The Gothic mood seems to take its inspiration from the Gospel of John: "In him was life; and the life was the light of men. And the light shineth in darkness."

The difference between these words and the sonorous verses of Revelation, which provide the program of the Romanesque "Last Judgments," reflects the difference between the shining walls of colored light, which change with every passing hour or cloud, and the painted walls of Romanesque churches or the shimmering Byzantine mosaics.

Colored glass was used as early as the fourth century to decorate the windows of churches. Perfection of the technique must have been gradual, with the greatest advancements made during the tenth and eleventh centuries. The first accurately dated windows, those of the choir of St. Denis in 1144, show a high degree of skill; according to Suger, they were "painted by the exquisite hands of many masters from different regions," proving that the art was widely known at that time. Yet the stained-glass window may be said to be the hallmark of the Gothic style, particularly in northern Europe, where the almost total dissolution of walls left few surfaces that were suitable for decoration with frescoes.

Imperfections or unexpected results in making colored glass were frequent; yet this was not an art left entirely to chance. The different properties of colors were well understood and carefully controlled. The glass was blown and either "spun" into a "crown" plate of varying thickness or shaped into a cylindrical "muff," which was cut and rolled out into square pieces. These pieces were then broken or cut into smaller fragments and assembled on a flat table, on which a design had been marked with chalk dust. Many of the pieces were actually "painted" with a dark pigment, so that details, as of a face or clothing, could be rendered. The fragments were then "leaded," or joined by strips of lead that were used to separate colors or to heighten the effect of the design

10-34 *Crucifixion*, detail of a window from St. Remi, Reims, France, *c.* 1190. Stained glass, approx. 12' high.

10-35 Detail of the *Good Samaritan* window, Chartres Cathedral, France, early thirteenth century. Stained glass.

as a whole (FIGS. 10-34 and 10-35). The completed window was strengthened with an armature of iron bands, which, in the twelfth century, took the form of a grid over the whole design (FIG. 10-34); in the thirteenth century, these bands were shaped to follow the outlines of the medallions and of the surrounding areas (FIG. 10-35).

The technical difficulties of assembling a large stained-glass window and fixing it firmly within its frame were matched by compositional problems. Illuminated manuscripts—the painter's chief vehicle during the earlier Middle Ages—had little instructional value for artists who not only had to work on an unprecedented scale but who also had to adjust their designs to the larger whole of the church building and its architecture. Sculptors, of course, had already solved these problems, and it is not too surprising to find that painters turned to them for instruction. Certainly, the saints flanking the cross in the St. Remi window (FIG. 10-34) seem vaguely familiar. Their erect poses, the straight, almost unbroken silhouettes, and the rather precarious manner in which they perch on their hilltop pedestals stamp them as not too distant relatives of the jamb statues from the Royal Portals at Chartres. Here, the Romanesque process has been reversed, and the sculptors—the former students who found their inspiration in paintings—have now become the teachers.

Like the architects and sculptors with whom they worked in close collaboration, the stained-glass artists relied heavily on the *ars de geometria* for their designs, layouts, and assemblies. The sketchbook of VILLARD DE HONNECOURT, the mid-thirteenth-century architect, was intended as a text for Villard's students. But in it, he does not confine his instruction to architecture alone. In addition to details of buildings, plans of choirs with radiating chapels, and church towers, he also presents information on lifting devices, a saw mill, and stained-glass windows. Sprinkled liberally throughout the pages are drawings of figures, religious and worldly, and animals—some surprisingly realistic, others purely fantastic. On the page shown here (FIG. 10-36), Villard is evidently informing his students of the usefulness of the *ars de geometria* in designing human heads and animals. In some instances, Villard claimed to have drawn his animals from nature, but even these appear to have been composed around a skeleton not of bones but of abstract geometric figures. It seems likely that the designers of stained-glass windows proceeded in a similar manner. No matter how it was arrived at, the effect of these glowing, translucent paintings, which often seem to be suspended in space, is as spellbind-

10-36 VILLARD DE HONNECOURT, page from a notebook, *c.* 1240. Bibliothèque Nationale, Paris.

ing today as it must have been to the Medieval churchgoer (FIG. 10-26). For the first time in centuries, the art of painting was accessible to the common man—painting in a form so compelling that the desire to have more and more of it, from pavement to vault, may well have influenced the development of Gothic architecture. By the mid-thirteenth century, architectural techniques had advanced to the point that the space of cathedrals seems to be defined by the burning intensity of the stained-glass windows, rather than by the stone structure.

The radiance of stained glass must have inspired the glowing color of illuminated manuscripts; in some cases, glass and book must have been produced by masters in the same shop, or perhaps by one master who was expert in both arts. The *Psalter of St. Louis* is believed to have been one of a number of books produced in Paris in the late thirteenth century for King Louis IX of France ("St. Louis") by craftsmen associated with those who made the stained glass for Sainte Chapelle (FIGS. 10-27 and 10-28). Certainly, the figures in the illuminated Psalter express the same aristocratic elegance as the "court" style of architecture—the rayonnant—favored by royal Paris. The painted architectural setting reflects the pierced, screen-like lightness and transparency of royal buildings like Sainte Chapelle and the new work at St. Denis. The intense colors, especially the blues, emulate glass; the borders resemble glass partitioned by leading; and the gables, pierced by rose windows, are almost portraits of rayonnant architectural features. The subject of the page from the *Psalter of St. Louis* shown here (FIG. 10-37) is *Abraham and the Three Angels*. (See Andrei Rublëv's version of essentially the same theme in FIG. 7-63.) Two episodes are included, separated by the Tree of Mamre: in one, Abraham greets the three angels; in the other, he entertains them while Sarah peers at them from the tent. The figures, compared with those in Romanesque illumination (FIGS. 9-37, 9-38, 9-39, 9-41), are quieter in pose and attitude and have a firmness of stance and a sense of weight suggestive of sculpture. Moreover, the busyness of the drapery lines is greatly subdued, making us less mindful of the flat areas that encourage decorative line-play and more aware of the modeling tones that suggest plastic form and contour.

Although these figures owe much of their color to stained glass works, the influence of sculpture is also evident. The lead angel in the group at the left closely resembles the angel of the *Annunciation* group at Reims (FIG. 10-33); and if we look at the general arrangement of the portal (FIG. 10-32) in which the group appears, we see that the illuminator thinks of the sacred personages as framed, canopied, and backed by architecture and their placement as determined by it—like the actual sculptures of the portal.

10-37 *Abraham and the Three Angels*, illuminated page from the *Psalter of St. Louis*,
1253–1270. Bibliothèque Nationale, Paris.

It may be that the artist's response to the monumental, over-life-size sculptures of the cathedral portals led him to a new sense of the possibilities of representation—the function of light and shade, for example, and of volume, contour, and silhouette. These imposing figures could have had a new, awesome authority not conveyed by the traditional prototypes (ivory carvings, say, or painted pages). The impulse toward naturalism and pictorial illusionism—endemic in the Greco–Roman world, and by no means lost in Early Christian and Byzantine art—could here be receiving a new and powerful impulse from monumental sculpture. The illusionistic effect of sculpture may have caught and held the Gothic artist's attention.

Byzantine artists will go a different way—working within received conventions, disdaining sculpture and the pictorial form built on it, respecting the flat surface, and unfriendly to the more-or-less systematic pursuit of three-dimensional illusionism widely favored in the West from this time till the twentieth century. We read of a Byzantine priest in the sixteenth century rejecting some paintings by Titian, the great Venetian master of the Renaissance (FIGS. 17-61 and 17-62), because "the figures stand quite out from the canvas" and therefore look "as bad as a group of statues."* The Byzantine artist did not find monumental sculpture like that of the Gothic portals in his environment. Would Byzantine painting and mosaic have been different if he had? The Gothic painter could not help but be struck by these majestic figures of great scale. The attention he paid them is evident in the figures of the *Psalter of St. Louis* (FIG. 10-37).

LATE GOTHIC

The collapse of the vaults of Beauvais Cathedral would seem to have brought the great thirteenth-century architectural debate to an unarguable conclusion. Analogously, the followers of Aquinas came to believe that his accommodation of faith and reason was impossible and that both must go their separate ways. This was the beginning of the dissolution of the Medieval synthesis, which would lead to the eventual destruction of the unity of Christendom. The resolution of opposites could not be achieved; the conflict that would reshape western Europe was about to begin.

Villard de Honnecourt left us a record of these years when so much was expected of art because art

had already achieved so much. The search for an ideal solution for a building and the codification of artistic, as well as philosophical, procedures were essentially academic in spirit—conscious evaluations of a style that had already reached and passed its complete definition. For a long time, artistic practice and scholastic method would retrace ground already covered, dealing with elaborations of surface forms, but would no longer attempt grandiose innovations in structure.

By the early fourteenth century, the monumental and solemn sculpture of the High Gothic portals had been replaced by the "court" style developed from the angel in the *Annunciation* group at Reims (FIG. 10-33), a quite rarefied example of which may be seen in the statue of *The Virgin of Paris* within Notre Dame (FIG. 10-38). The curving sway of the figure, emphasized by the blade-like sweeps of drapery that converge to the child, has a mannered elegance that will mark Late Gothic sculpture in general. This is the famed Late Gothic "S-curve" encountered again and again during the fourteenth and fifteenth centuries. Superficially, it may resemble another S-curve seen much earlier—that of Praxiteles in the fourth century

10-38 *The Virgin of Paris*, Notre Dame, Paris, early fourteenth century.

*Edward Gibbon, *Decline and Fall of the Roman Empire*. Quoted with citation in Ernst Kitzinger, *Byzantine Art in the Making* (Cambridge: MA: Harvard University Press, 1977), p. 107.

B.C. (FIG. 5-65). But, unlike its Classical predecessor, the Late Gothic S is not organic (deriving from within the figure) nor is it the result of a rational, if pleasing, organization of the figure's anatomical parts. Rather, it is an artificial form imposed on the figure—a decorative device that may produce the desired effect of elegance but that has nothing to do with the figure's structure. In fact, in our example, the body is quite lost behind the heavy drapery, which, deeply cut and hollowed, would almost deny the figure a solid existence. The ornamental line created by the flexible fabric is analogous to the complex, restless tracery of the "flamboyant" style in architecture, which dominated northern Europe in the fourteenth and fifteenth centuries. The emphasis on ornament for its own sake is in harmony with the artificial prettiness the artist has contrived in the Virgin's doll-like face—large-eyed and tiny-mouthed under her heavy, gem-encrusted crown.

The change from rayonnant architecture to the Late Gothic or *flamboyant* style (so-called because of the flame-like look of its pointed tracery) took place in the fourteenth century; the style reached its florid maturity toward the end of the fifteenth. This period was a difficult one for royal France; long wars against England and Burgundy sapped its economic and cultural strength, and building projects in the royal domain were either halted or not begun. The new style found its most fertile soil in regions outside the Île-de-France. Normandy is particularly rich in flamboyant architecture, and its close ties with England suggest that the Anglo–Norman school of "decorated" architecture may have had much to do with the development of the flamboyant style. The church of St. Maclou (FIG. 10-39), in Rouen, the capital of Normandy, presents a façade that differs widely from the thirteenth-century style. St. Maclou, some 75 feet high and 180 feet long, is almost diminutive compared with the great cathedrals. The five portals, two of them blind, bend outward in an arc and are crowned by five gables, pierced through and filled with sinuous, wiry, flamboyant tracery. Pierced galleries of spidery arcades climb steeply to the center bay, marching along behind the transparent gables. The overlapping of all features, pierced as they are, confuses the structural lines and produces a bewildering complexity of views. It is almost as if the Celtic–Germanic instinct for intricate line, expressed in works like the *Book of Lindisfarne,* (FIG. 8-6), is manifesting itself once again against the form and logic newly abstracted from the traditions of the Mediterranean. Yet the Renaissance is not far off, and, within a generation or two of St. Maclou, France will adopt a new Classical style from Italy.

10-39 West façade of St. Maclou, Rouen, France, c. 1500–1514; *left:* detail of façade.

NON-FRENCH GOTHIC

Around 1269, the prior of a German monastery "hired a skilled architect who had just come from the city of Paris" to rebuild his monastery church. The architect reconstructed the church *opere francigeno* ("in the Frankish manner")—that is, in the Gothic style of the Île-de-France. In 1268, Pope Clement IV, stipulating the conditions for the building of a new cathedral at Narbonne, wrote that the building was "to imitate the noble and magnificently worked churches. . . . which are built in the kingdom of France." The diffusion of the French Gothic style had begun even earlier, but it was in the second half of the thirteenth century that the new style became dominant and that European architecture turned Gothic in many different ways. Because the old Romanesque traditions lingered on in many places, each area, marrying its local Romanesque design to the new style, developed its own brand of Gothic architecture.

England

French Gothic came early to England—in the last quarter of the twelfth century. As was so often the case with the great cathedrals, the new style was inaugurated by a devastating fire in 1174 that swept away an older Romanesque structure in the ancient see of Canterbury, creating a new architectural opportunity. (We know of the fire and what followed from a contemporary chronicler, Gervase of Canterbury, who describes the events in dramatic and informative detail.) WILLIAM OF SENS, a master-builder commissioned to build the new cathedral, brought to it the Early Gothic manner of the cathedral in Sens (his home in France), which was closely related to the design of Laon Cathedral. The choir and choir chapel of Canterbury Cathedral, completed by WILLIAM THE ENGLISHMAN (FIGS. 10-40 and 10-41), resemble those of Sens and Laon (FIG. 10-7) and are essentially French—much more so than most of the mature English Gothic churches to follow, which will retain older Norman features in balance with importations from France. In the end, these churches will be distinctively English.

The characteristics of English Gothic architecture are admirably embodied in Salisbury Cathedral (FIGS. 10-42, 10-43, 10-44, 10-45), built, for the most part, between 1220 and 1260 (the tower and flying buttresses were erected in the fourteenth century). Its location in a park (or *close*), surrounded by lawns and stately trees, contrasts markedly with that of continental churches, around which city dwellings nestle closely. The screen-like façade (FIG. 10-42) reaches beyond and does not correspond to the interior; with its dwarf towers, horizontal tiers of niches, and small entrance portals, the Salisbury façade is emphatically

10-40 WILLIAM OF SENS and WILLIAM THE ENGLISHMAN, choir and Trinity Chapel, Canterbury Cathedral, England, 1179–1184.

10-41 Plan of Canterbury Cathedral. Western portion (second transept and nave) added 1379–1403.

different from the façades of either Notre Dame (FIG. 10-9) or Amiens (FIG. 10-22). Also different is the emphasis on the great crossing tower (*c.* 1320), which dominates the silhouette. The height of Salisbury is modest compared with that of the almost contemporary cathedral of Amiens; as height in the English building is not a decisive factor, the flying buttress is used sparingly—as a rigid prop rather than as an integral part of the armature of arches. The exterior of the building, were it not for its pointed features, would look more like an "additive" Romanesque than a Gothic building.

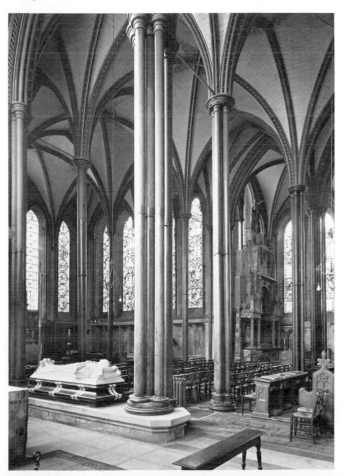

10-43   Plan of
Salisbury Cathedral.

10-42   Salisbury Cathedral, England, begun *c.* 1220 (view
from the southwest).

10-44   Nave of Salisbury Cathedral (view facing east).

10-45   Lady Chapel of Salisbury Cathedral, *c.* 1225 (view
facing southeast).

Equally distinctive is the long rectilinear plan (FIG. 10-43), with its double transept and flat eastern end (the latter a characteristic of Cistercian churches and favored in England since Romanesque times). The interior (FIG. 10-44)—although Gothic in its three-story elevation, in its pointed arches and rib vaults, and in its compound piers (actually a combination of columnar piers with detached monolithic shafts or colonnettes)—shows conspicuous differences from the French Gothic style. The pier colonnettes do not ride up the wall to connect with the vault ribs; instead, the vault ribs rise from corbels in the triforium, producing a strong horizontal emphasis. There is rich detail in the moldings of the arches and the tracery of the triforium, which, enhanced by the contrast of colored stone, gives a peculiarly crisp and vivid sparkle to the interior. The structural craft of the English stonemason is at its best in the Lady Chapel (dedicated to the Virgin Mary) of Salisbury Cathedral (FIG. 10-45). There, incredibly slender piers composed of unattached shafts of Purbeck marble seem to tether the billowing vaults to the ground rather than to support them. Not only is this daring construction, but its linearity and slender forms are analogous to the rayonnant style found on the continent.

Early on, English architecture finds its native language in the elaboration of architectural pattern for its own sake; structural logic, expressed in the building fabric, is secondary. The pier, wall, and vault elements became increasingly complex and decorative in the fourteenth century, and English Gothic architecture of that period has been described as "decorated." The choir of Gloucester Cathedral (FIG. 10-46), built about a century after Salisbury, illustrates the passage from the "decorated" to the last English Gothic style—the *perpendicular* or "Tudor" style, named after the line of English kings beginning with the accession of Henry VII to the throne in 1485.

The characteristically flat east end of Gloucester Cathedral opens into a single, enormous window divided into horizontal tiers of "transom" windows of like shape and proportion, reminiscent of the screen façade of Salisbury. In the nave wall, however, the strong, horizontal accents of Salisbury have been erased, as the vertical-wall elements (the *responds*), lift directly from the floor to the vaulting, pulling the whole elevation into a fluent unity. The vault ribs, which had begun to multiply soon after Salisbury, have now become a dense thicket of entirely ornamental strands having no structural function. This vault, in fact, is no longer a rib vault, but a continuous barrel vault with applied decorations.

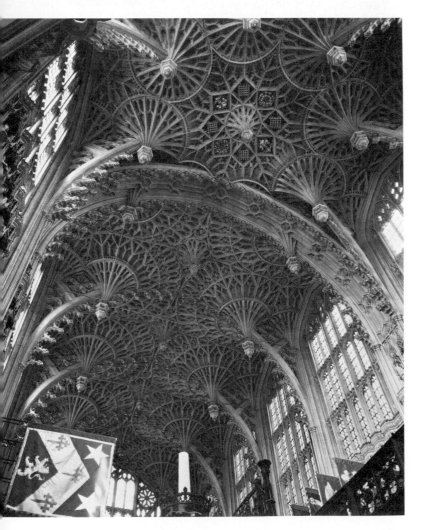

The culmination of the English perpendicular style, and the flowering of the Tudor style, can be seen in the vault of the Chapel of Henry VII (FIG. 10-47), which adjoins Westminster Abbey and was built in the first two decades of the sixteenth century. Here, the linear play of ribs has become a kind of architectural embroidery, pulled into "fan vault" shapes with pendent keystones resembling stalactites. The vault looks like something organic that has been petrified in the process of melting. The chapel represents the dissolution of structural Gothic into decorative fancy; its original lines, released from function, multiply, variegate, and flower into uninhibited architectural virtuosity and theatrics. The perpendicular style in this Tudor structure expresses peculiarly well the precious, affected, even dainty style of life codified in the dying etiquette of chivalry at the end of the Middle Ages. Life was, of course, as violent as ever—indeed, we are at the threshold of the boisterous English Renaissance—but the description and expression of it in art comes in forms that are delicate rather than robust.

Germany

The architecture of Germany remained conservatively Romanesque well into the thirteenth century. The plan and massing of German churches included the familiar Rhenish double-apse system, with towers flanking both apses. In many of these, the only Gothic feature is the rib vault, which is buttressed, however, by the heavy masonry of the walls. By mid-century, though, the French influence became strongly felt, and the great 150-foot-high choir of Cologne Cathedral (FIG. 10-48) is a skillful and energetic interpretation of Amiens (FIG. 10-24). Cologne Cathedral (FIG. 10-57) has one of the longest building histories on record. Begun in 1248, it stood without a nave and with only its chevet, transept, and lower parts of the façade towers completed for some five centuries. Only in the early nineteenth century, when the original designs for the building were discovered, was it decided to finish the structure.

The choir of Cologne Cathedral (FIG. 10-48)—almost as high but narrower than the choir of Beauvais Cathedral (FIG. 10-30)—even more emphatically expresses the Gothic "rush into the skies," and the nave walls (FIG. 10-49) are among the most weightless and translucent designed during the Gothic period. Perhaps it should be repeated here that the nave, although actually built in the nineteenth century, was constructed strictly in accordance with the original thirteenth-century plan, and its walls can be accepted as some of the most refined examples of High Gothic curtain-wall design. Stretched tautly, like skins, between slender vertical

10-48 Choir of Cologne Cathedral, West Germany, thirteenth and fourteenth centuries.

supports, the walls have reached a degree of transparency unmatched in earlier architecture. Their luminous quality is enhanced by the fact that the triforium also has been fenestrated—a feature made possible by the replacement of the traditional, single-sloped shed roofs over the aisles with double-sloped tent roofs. This change created difficult drainage

10-49 Nave wall, Cologne Cathedral, nineteenth century (thirteenth-century design).

problems that appear to have been solved during the second half of the thirteenth century. Now, clerestory and triforium could act together to form an enormous glass wall, held together by a seemingly insubstantial framework of slender piers supported on the outside by an intricate system of vertical and flying buttresses. The impression of weightlessness—of the dematerialization of the building's very substance—is complete here. And yet there is nothing weak or uncertain in the design; all of the lines are crisp and sharply defined, describing forms that seem to have the resiliency of living organic growth.

Despite the cathedral's seeming lack of substance, the structure's stability was effectively proven during the Second World War, when the city of Cologne was subjected to extremely heavy aerial bombardments. The cathedral survived the war by virtue of its Gothic, skeletal design. Once the first few bomb blasts had blown out all of its windows, the structure offered no further resistance to the effects of subsequent blasts, and the skeleton remained intact and structurally sound.

A different type of design, probably of French origin, that met with great favor and was broadly developed in Germany is that of the *Hallenkirche*, or hall church. The term applies to those buildings in which the aisles rise to the same height as the nave (FIG. 10-50). An early and successful example of this type is the church of St. Elizabeth at Marburg (FIGS. 10-51 and 10-52), built between 1233 and 1283. Because the aisles provide much of the bracing for the central vault, the exterior of St. Elizabeth is without the dramatic parade of flying buttresses that circles French Gothic chevets and appears rather prosaic. But the interior (FIG. 10-52), lighted by double rows of tall windows, is more unified and free-flowing (less narrow and divided) than the interiors of other Gothic

10-50 Plan (*below*) and section (*right*) of St. Elizabeth, Marburg, West Germany.

10-51 St. Elizabeth, Marburg, West Germany, 1233–1283 (view from the southeast).

10-52 Interior of St. Elizabeth (view facing west).

churches. The hall church, widely used by later Gothic architects, heralds the age of the Protestant Reformation in Germany, when the old ritual, which focuses on the altar, will be modified by a new emphasis on preaching, which will center attention on the pulpit.

French sculpture, like French Gothic architecture, had its effect abroad. In Germany, the commingled influences of the statuary of the transept portals at Chartres (FIGS. 10 31 and 16 7) and the west façade at Reims (FIG. 10-33) directed the sculptors of the south transept portal at Strasbourg Cathedral (FIG. 10-53).

10-53 *Death of the Virgin*, tympanum, south transept portal, Strasbourg Cathedral, France, *c.* 1230.

10-54 *Ekkehard and Uta, c. 1250–1260*, west choir, Naumburg Cathedral, West Germany.

The sculptured tympanum represents the death of the Virgin Mary. She is surrounded by the Twelve Apostles; at their center, Christ receives her soul (the doll-like figure). Mary Magdalene, wringing her hands in grief, crouches beside the deathbed. The sorrowing figures express emotion in varying degrees of intensity, from serene resignation to gesturing agitation. The group is organized not only by dramatic unification and by pose and gesture but also by the rippling flow of deeply incised drapery that passes among them like a rhythmic, electric pulse. The sculptor's objective is not to produce a timeless tableau presenting some mystery of the faith, but to depict a human event in a particular space and time— an event designed to stir an emotional response in the observer as if he or she were present. In the Gothic world, art is increasingly being humanized and made natural; in the art of the German lands, we will find an increasing and characteristic emphasis on passionate drama.

But the Strasbourg style, with its feverish emotionalism, is balanced and complemented by two stately and reposeful statues from the western choir of Naumburg Cathedral (FIG. 10-54), which depict the quiet, regal deportment of the French statuary of the High Gothic portals, but with a stronger tincture of realism. *Ekkehard and Uta* represent persons of the nobility who, in former times, had been patrons of the church; the particularity of costume and visage almost makes these figures portrait statues, although the subjects lived well before the sculptor's time. Ekkehard, blunt and Teutonic, contrasts with the charming Uta, who, with a wonderfully graceful gesture, draws the collar of her gown partly across her face while she gathers up a soft fold of drapery with a jeweled, delicate hand. The drapery and the body it enfolds are now understood as distinct entities. The shape of the arm that draws the collar is subtly and accurately revealed beneath the drapery, as is the full curve of the bosom. The drapery folds are rendered with an accuracy that indicates the artist's use of a model. We have before us an arresting image of Medieval people—a feudal baron and his handsome wife—as they may well have appeared in life. By mid-thirteenth century, images not only of sacred but also of secular personages had found their way into the cathedral.

The equestrian figure of a Gothic nobleman mounted against a pier in the cathedral of Bamberg (FIG. 10-55) is familiarly known as the *Bamberg Rider*. Like *Ekkehard and Uta*, it has the quality of portraiture;

10-55 *Bamberg Rider*, late thirteenth century, Bamberg Cathedral, West Germany.

10-56 Head of a crucifix, 1301. Wood. St. Maria im Kapitol, Cologne, West Germany.

Italy

Few Italian architects accepted the northern Gothic style, as demonstrated in the Cologne Cathedral (FIG. 10-57), and the question has been raised as to whether it is proper to speak of buildings like Florence Cathedral (FIGS. 10-58, 10-59, 10-60) as Gothic structures. Begun in 1296 by ARNOLFO DI CAMBIO and so large that it seemed to the fifteenth-century architect Leon Battista Alberti to cover "all of Tuscany with its shade," the cathedral scarcely looks Gothic. Most of the familiar Gothic features are missing: no flying buttresses; no stately clerestory windows; walls pierced only here and there by relatively small openings. Like the façades of San Miniato al Monte (FIG. 9-21), the building's surfaces are ornamented, in the old Tuscan fashion, with marble-incrusted geometric designs to match it to the eleventh-century Romanesque baptistry nearby. Beyond an occasional ogival window and the fact that the nave is covered by rib vaults, there is very little that identifies this building as Gothic. The vast gulf that separates this Italian church from its northern European cousins is strikingly evident when the former is compared with a full-blown German representative of the High Gothic style, the cathedral of Cologne (FIG. 10-57).

In Cologne Cathedral, an emphatic stress on the vertical produces an awe-inspiring upward rush of almost unmatched vigor and intensity. The building has the character of an organic growth shooting heavenward—its toothed upper portions engaging the sky, the pierced, translucent stone tracery of the spires merging with the atmosphere. Florence Cathedral clings to the ground and has no aspirations to flight. All emphasis is on the horizontal elements of the design, and the building rests firmly and massively on this earth. Simple, geometric volumes are clearly defined and show no tendency to merge either into each other or into the sky. The dome though it may seem to be rising because of its ogival section, has a crisp, closed silhouette that sets it off emphatically against the sky behind it. But because this dome is the monument with which architectural historians usually introduce the Renaissance (it was built by Filippo Brunelleschi between 1420 and 1436), a comparison of the campanile with the Cologne towers may be somewhat more appropriate. Designed by the painter Giotto di Bondone in 1334 (and completed with some minor modifications after his death), the Florence campanile (FIG. 10-58) stands apart from the cathedral in the Italian tradition. In fact, it could stand anywhere else in Florence without looking out of place; it is essentially self-sufficient. This can hardly be said of the northern towers (FIG. 10-57);

some believe it represents the German emperor Conrad III. The artist has carefully described the costume of the rider, the high saddle, the caparison (cloak) of the horse. The proportions of horse and rider are real, although the anatomy of the animal is not quite comprehended (its shape is rather stiffly schematic). An ever-present pedestal and canopy firmly establish the group's dependence on its architectural setting and manage to hold the horse in strict profile. The rider, however, is turning easily toward the observer, as if presiding at a review of troops, and is beginning to break away from the pull of the wall. The stirring and turning of this figure seem to reflect the same impatience with subordination to architecture found in the portal statues at Reims (FIG. 10-33).

The gradual growth of naturalism during the thirteenth century was modified during the fourteenth century by an impulse toward charmingly ornamental effects and courtly convention, as seen in *The Virgin of Paris* (FIG. 10-38). Also rising was a new intensity of expression—anticipated in the *Death of the Virgin* at Strasbourg (FIG. 10-53)—which concentrated on such themes as the Crucifixion, the Man of Sorrows, and the Sorrows of the Virgin Mary. The head of a crucifix in St. Maria im Kapitol in Cologne (FIG. 10-56), the features wrenched with pain and sorrow, shows the new preference for interpretations of sacred story in terms of human feeling rather than of dogma and mystery. The humanizing that began in the twelfth century is accelerated. The anguish of the suffering Christ is represented with such force that it could not fail to stir the emotions powerfully and to arouse deep empathy in the observer. As motion was introduced into portal sculpture, so motion—read as emotion—here activates the human face. Increasingly, images reach out, not only into the physical space but into the emotions of the observer. The artist presents more than the simple theological tenet in terms of some impersonal symbol; the mystery is brought back to earth once more, incarnate in the image of physical and psychic suffering.

they are essential elements of the building behind them, and it would be unthinkable to detach one of them and place it somewhere else. Heinrich Wölfflin has compared buildings of this kind to a flame, from which no single tongue can be separated.* This holds true for every part of the Cologne structure, down to its smallest details. No single element seems to be capable of an independent existence; one form merges into the next, in an unending series of rising movements that pull the eye upward and never permit it to rest until it reaches the sky. This structure's

*Heinrich Wölfflin, *Classic Art*, 2nd ed. (London: Phaidon, 1953).

beauty is amorphous rather than formal; it is a beauty that speaks to the heart rather than to the intellect.

How different the Italian tower! Neatly subdivided into cubic stages, Giotto's tower is the sum of its clearly distinguished parts. Not only could this tower be removed from the building without adverse effects, but each of the component parts—cleanly separated from one another by continuous, unbroken moldings—seems capable of existing independently as an object of considerable esthetic appeal. This compartmentalization is reminiscent of Romanesque, but it also forecasts the ideals of Renaissance architecture: to express a structure in terms of the clear, logical relationships of its component parts and to produce self-sufficient works that could exist in complete independence. Compared to the northern towers of Cologne, Giotto's campanile has a cool and rational quality that appeals more to the intellect than to the emotions.

From the plan of Florence Cathedral (FIG. 10-59), it would seem that the nave was added to the crossing complex as an afterthought; in fact, the nave was built first, pretty much according to Arnolfo's original plans, and the crossing was redesigned in mid-fourteenth century to increase the cathedral's interior space. In its present form, the area beneath the dome is the focal point of the design, and the nave leads to it, as Paul Frankl says, "like an introduction of slow chords, to a goal of self-contained finality." To the visitor from the north, the nave seems as strange as the plan; neither has a northern European counterpart. The Florence nave bays (FIG. 10-60) are twice as deep as those of Amiens (FIG. 10-24), and the wide arcades permit the shallow aisles to become part of

10-58 South flank of Florence Cathedral, Italy, 1296–1436 (view from the south).

10-59   Plan of Florence Cathedral. (After Sir Banister Fletcher.)

10-60   Nave of Florence Cathedral (view facing east).

10-61   West façade of Orvieto Cathedral, Italy, begun c. 1310.

the central nave. The result is an interior that has an unmatched spaciousness. The accent here, as in the exterior, is on the horizontal elements. The substantial capitals of the piers prevent them from soaring into the vaults and emphasize their function as supports. This interior lacks the mystery of northern naves, and Nikolaus Pevsner has observed that its serene calm and clarity tell the visitor that the Tuscan architects never entirely rejected or forgot their Classical heritage and that it is indeed only here, in central Italy, that the Renaissance could have been born.

The façade of Florence Cathedral was not completed until the nineteenth century, and then in a form much altered from its beginnings. In fact, Italian builders exhibited little concern for the façades of their churches, and dozens remain unfinished to this day. One reason for this may be that the façades were not conceived as integral parts of the structures, but rather as screens that could be added to the fabric at any time. The façade of Orvieto Cathedral (FIG. 10-61) is a typical and handsome example. Begun in the early fourteenth century, it pays the graceful compliment of imitation to some parts of the French Gothic repertory of ornament, especially in the four large pinnacles that divide the façade into three bays. But these pinnacles—the outer ones serving as miniature substitutes for the big, northern, west-front towers— grow up, as it were, from an old Tuscan façade (FIG.

9-21) and, ultimately, from the Early Christian. The rectilinearity and triangularity of the old Tuscan marble incrustation (here enframing and pointing to the precisely wrought rose window) is clearly seen behind the transparent Gothic overlay. The whole effect of the Orvieto façade is that of a great altar screen, its single plane covered with carefully placed carved and painted ornament. In principle, Orvieto belongs with San Miniato al Monte or the cathedral of Pisa, rather than with Amiens or Notre Dame of Paris.

Since Romanesque times, northern European influences had been felt more strongly in Lombardy than in central Italy. When the citizens of Milan decided to build their own cathedral (FIG. 10-62), in 1386, they invited and consulted experts not only from Italy but also from France, Germany, and England. These experts must have carried on a rough *disputatio* about the strength of the foundations and the composition and adequacy of the piers and the vaults—the application of the true geometric *scientia* in working out plan and elevation. The result was a compromise; the proportions of the building, particularly those of the nave, became Italian (that is, wide in relation to height), and the surface decorations and details remained Gothic. But even before the cathedral was half finished, the new Classical style of the Renaissance had been well launched and the Milan design had become anachronistic. The elaborate façade represents a confused mixture of Late Gothic and Classical elements and stands as a symbol of the waning of the Gothic style.

The city churches of the Gothic world were just as much monuments of civic pride as they were temples or symbols of the spiritual and natural world. To undertake the construction of a great cathedral, a city had to be rich with thriving commerce. The very profusion of large churches during the period attests to the affluence of those who built and maintained them, as well as to the general revival of the economy of Europe in the thirteenth century.

The secular center of the community, the town hall, was almost as much the object of civic pride as the cathedral. A building like the Palazzo Pubblico of Siena (FIG. 10-63), the proud commercial and political rival of Florence, must have earned the admiration of Siena's citizens as well as of visiting strangers, inspiring in them respect for the city's power and success. More symmetrical in its design than most buildings of its type and period, it is flanked by a lofty tower, which (along with Giotto's campanile in Florence) is one of the finest in Italy. It served as lookout over the city and the countryside around it and as a bell tower from which signals of all sorts could be rung to the populace. The Medieval city, a political unit in itself, had to defend itself against its neighbor cities and often against kings and emperors; in addition, it had to be secure against internal upheavals, in which the history of the Italian city-republics abounds. Feuds between rich and powerful families, class struggle, even uprisings of the whole populace against the city fathers were constant threats to a city's internal security. The heavy walls and battlements of the Italian town hall eloquently express the frequent need of city governors to defend themselves against their own cit-

10-62   Milan Cathedral, Italy, begun 1386 (view from the southwest).

izens. The high tower, out of reach of most missiles, is further protected by *machicolated* galleries, built out on corbels around the top of the structure to provide openings for a vertical (downward) defense of the tower's base. In many cases, however, the battlements simply symbolize authority or allegiance to a political party (flat-topped merlons indicating adherents of the pro-papacy Guelphs; notched merlons, adherents of the pro-emperor Ghibellines).

The secular architecture of the Italian mainland tends to have this fortified look. But Venice, some miles out in the Venetian lagoon, was secure from land attack and could rely on her powerful navy to protect her against attacks from the sea. Internally, Venice was a tight corporation of ruling families that, for centuries, provided an unshakable and efficient establishment, free from disruptive tumults within. Such a stable, internal structure made possible the development of an unfortified, "open" architecture, exemplified in the Doge's Palace (FIG. 10-64), the seat of government of the Venetian republic. This, the most splendid public building of Medieval Italy, seems to invite passersby to enter rather than to ward them off. In a stately march, the short and heavy columns of the first level support low-pointed arches and look strong enough to carry the weight of the upper structure. Their rhythm is doubled in the upper arcades, where more slender columns carry ogival arches, which terminate in flame-like tips between medallions pierced with quatrefoils. Each story is taller than the one beneath it, the topmost being as high as the two lower arcades combined. Yet the building does not look top-heavy—a fact due in part to the complete absence of articulation in the top story and in part to the delicate patterning of its walls, in cream and rose-colored marbles, which somehow makes them appear paper-thin. The Doge's Palace is the monumental representative of a delight-

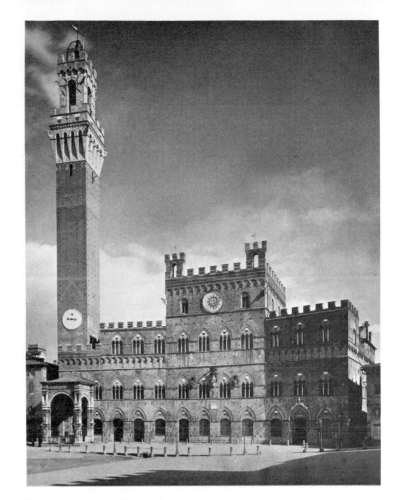

10-63 Palazzo Pubblico, Siena, Italy, 1288–1309.

ful and charming variant of Late Gothic architecture. Its slightly exotic style reminds us of Venice's strategic position at the crossroads of the West and the Orient, where it could synthesize artistic stimuli received from either direction. Colorful, decorative, light and airy in appearance, and never overloaded, the Venetian Gothic is ideally suited to the lagoon city of Venice, which floats between water and air.

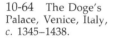

10-64 The Doge's Palace, Venice, Italy, *c.* 1345–1438.

III

THE NON-EUROPEAN WORLD

The art of non-European civilizations is introduced at this point in our survey because much of it is more closely related to the art of the prehistoric period and of the earlier Middle Ages than to the art of the Renaissance and of subsequent times until the twentieth century. In these latter periods, the Western artist moves from a dominantly religious and conceptual approach toward an ever-more secular and perceptual one. This drive toward optical realism and the persistent search for a rational, if not scientific, basis for the objectivization of natural appearances were not shared by the numerous cultures outside the mainstream of European history. Thus, non-European art is more akin to Byzantine and other art of the Middle Ages, although its forms, which are based on non-Western cultural and spiritual precepts, are, of course, very different.

Colossal Heads, from the tower of Bayon, Angkor Thom, Kampuchea (Cambodia), twelfth and thirteenth centuries.

413

There had been sporadic contacts between Africa and the Far East and the West since antiquity. The Phoenicians are said to have circumnavigated Africa as early as 600 B.C., and Alexander the Great—bent on exploration as much as conquest—took his armies beyond the Indus River deep into India. Nomadic peoples from central Asia made repeated incursions into the Near East and Europe; the Huns, under Attila, reached France in the fifth century. In the later Middle Ages, the search for trade routes to the East inspired the exploratory journeys of such enterprising merchants as the Polo brothers, Nicolo and Maffeo, and Nicolo's famous son, Marco, who reached Peking in the late thirteenth century.

Yet all of these contacts were transient and—even when given permanence through the establishment of sea routes during the Renaissance and Baroque periods—served commercial rather than cultural interests. Imported objects were admired as exotic curiosities, and even the eighteenth-century fascination with things Chinese was little more than a superficial and passing fashion. Only toward the end of the nineteenth century, when Western art had exhausted itself in its persistent drive toward realism and was beginning to search for alternative approaches, did non-Western art begin to have a more serious impact on the West.

Even though conquests, colonization, and missionary activity after the Middle Ages carried Christianity well beyond the boundaries of western Europe, we may identify the non-European world as the non-Christian world. This vast region, which dwarfs the area of Europe, produced a great variety of artistic styles and ideas. Of these, the art of Islam has already been surveyed (Chapter 7). The enormous remainder can be roughly subdivided into Oriental art and "Third World" art. The former embraces the art of Southeast Asia, of China, and of Japan; the latter, the essentially tribal arts of the North and South American Indian, of Africa, and of the South Pacific.

The earliest art works from the great Eastern civilizations in India, China, and Japan date from Paleolithic and Neolithic times. Buddhism was the common denominator of the later arts of these different countries, although each developed a distinctive style—or, rather, a series of styles. Indian sculpture, from its beginnings, has been characterized by a pulsating vigor in reproducing the living body. Early Chinese bronzes display amazing technical virtuosity in the use of highly symbolic, though abstract, decorative motifs. In later dynasties, in sculpture and particularly in painting, carefully observed details are lyrically rendered and produce a haunting image of nature. Japanese art, in spite of being subject to recurring waves of foreign influence (especially from China), insistently returns to native traditions. Painting and, above all, architecture show a sensitivity to the relationship between decorative designs and natural forms.

In pre-Columbian Mexico, Central America, and the Andean region of South America, highly cultured peoples, using a Stone Age technology, erected great temple complexes elaborately decorated with reliefs and practiced the crafts of weaving and pottery with great skill. About A.D. 500, the North American Indian began to settle in agricultural communities. Some tribes, such as the Pueblo of the southwest United States, reached a highly developed state in the eleventh, twelfth, and thirteenth centuries. Their stylized arts reflect an extraordinary understanding of the decorative qualities of abstract design.

The peoples native to Africa and the South Sea Islands produced a distinguished and individual art until contact with Europeans either modified it or brought it to a halt. This art, far from being technically or esthetically crude, is sophisticated in its presentation of conceptual rather than naturalistic images and has asserted itself in the West with ever-stronger effect and ever more respectful recognition and appreciation. As we shall see in subsequent chapters, its rhythmical, abstract forms have become a valuable resource and inspiration for many modern artists of great distinction and originality.

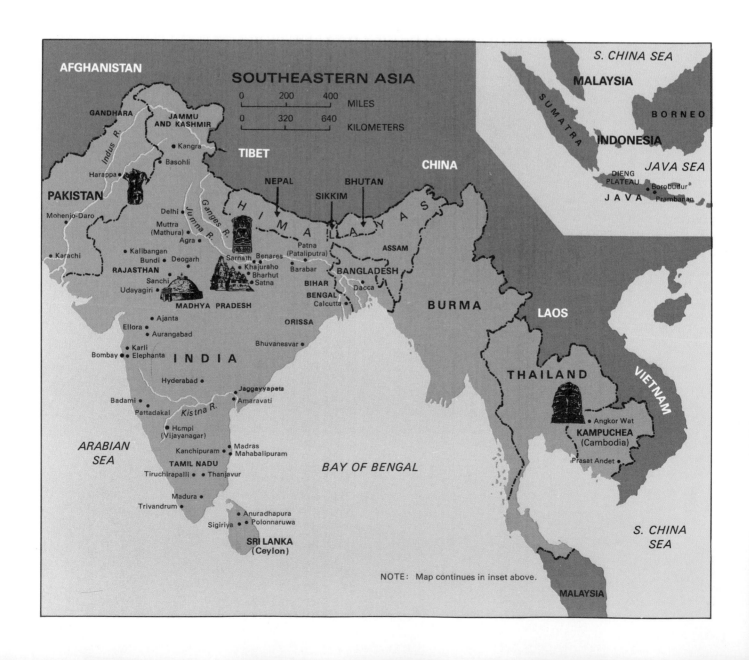

11

SOUTHEASTERN ASIA

0	200	400

MILES

0	320	640

KILOMETERS

AFGHANISTAN

GANDHARA

JAMMU
AND KASHMIR

• Kangra

TIBET

CHINA

• Basohli

Harappa

NEPAL

BHUTAN

SIKKIM

PAKISTAN

H I M A L A Y A S

Mohenjo-Daro

Delhi •

• Karachi

Muttra
(Mathura) •

Agra •

Ganges R.

Patna
(Pataliputra)

ASSAM

• Kalibangan

Jumna R.

Sarnath • Benares

Bundi • Deogarh

Khajuraho

Barabar

BANGLADESH

RAJASTHAN

Sanchi

Bharhut

BIHAR

Dacca •

Udayagiri

• Satna

BENGAL

Calcutta •

BURMA

MADHYA PRADESH

• Ajanta

ORISSA

Ellora •

LAOS

• Aurangabad

Bhuvanesvar •

• Karli

THAILAND

Bombay • • Elephanta

I N D I A

VIETNAM

Hyderabad •

Jaggayyapeta •

Badami •

• Amaravati

Angkor Wat •

Pattadakal •

Kistna R.

KAMPUCHEA
(Cambodia)

ARABIAN
SEA

• Hampi
(Vijayanagar)

• Madras

Prasat Andet •

Kanchipuram • • Mahabalipuram

BAY OF BENGAL

TAMIL NADU

Tiruchirapalli • • Thanjavur

• Madura

Trivandrum •

• Anuradhapura

S. CHINA
SEA

Sigiriya • • Polonnaruwa

SRI LANKA
(Ceylon)

NOTE: Map continues in inset above.

MALAYSIA

S. CHINA SEA

MALAYSIA

S U M A T R A

BORNEO

INDONESIA

JAVA SEA

DIENG
PLATEAU

• Borobudur

J A V A

• Prambanan

THE ART OF INDIA

Harappa torso

c. 3000 B.C.   c. 2000   c. 1800

INDUS–VALLEY CIVILIZATION

ARYAN   INVASIONS

Seated Buddha, Gandhara

Beginnings of Indian influence in Sri Lanka (Ceylon)

Capital, Palace of Asoka

Upanishads evolved (800–600)

30 A.D. B.C.   70   185   322   1500

KUSHAN PERIOD

ANDHRA PERIOD

SUNGA PERIOD

MAURYA (ASOKA) PERIOD

Great Stupa, Sanchi

Birth of Buddha Sakyamuni (c. 563 B.C.)

Indian emigrations to Burma, Cambodia, Java, Thailand, Sumatra

Badami cave temples

c. 600

Stupa, Borobudur, (Java)

c. 750   846

GUPTA PERIOD (North India)

CHALUKYA PERIOD (Central India)

PALLAVA PERIOD (South India)

LATER HINDU DYNASTIES

320

Seated Buddha, Sarnath

Decline of Buddhist art

Temple, Khajuraho

Moslem invasions

Siva as Nataraja

CHOLA KINGDOM

1000

MOSLEM DYNASTIES

NAYAK (HINDU) DYNASTY

VIJAYANAGAR (HINDU) DYNASTY

1736   1565   1420   1336   1173

Bayon, Angkor Thom Kampuchea (Cambodia)

THE SUBCONTINENT OF INDIA, contiguous with the Asian mainland on its northern boundaries, has three distinct geographical areas: the northeast, where the massive Himalayas, the traditional home of the gods, rise as a barrier; the fertile, densely populated area to the northwest and to the south of the Himalayas, where the valleys of the Indus and the Ganges rivers lie; and peninsular India, composed of tropical tablelands separated from the northern rivers by mountains and forests. These areas exhibit great extremes of climate—from tropical heat to perpetual snow and glaciers, from desert conditions to the heaviest rainfall in the world.

The ethnic characteristics and religions of the peoples vary as much as the geography. The most common language of north central India is Hindi, a Sanskrit derivative. Urdu, closely related, is spoken by most of the Moslem population. In the south, several Dravidian languages, unrelated to Sanskrit, are spoken. Hinduism is the main religion of India, as Islam is of Pakistan, but Jainism and Christianity have many adherents and Buddhism and Judaism, a few.

BEGINNINGS

The first major culture of India centered around the upper reaches of the Indus River valley during the late third and early second millennia B.C. Mohenjo-Daro and Harappa in Pakistan were the chief sites. Recently, other important centers of this culture have been found farther south at Kalibangan in Rajasthan, India, and near Karachi, Pakistan.

The architectural remains of Mohenjo-Daro suggest a modern commercial center, with major avenues along a north–south orientation, streets as wide as 40 feet, multi-storied houses of fired brick and wood, and elaborate drainage systems.

Some sculptures from this Indus civilization reflect Mesopotamian influences; others indicate the presence of a thoroughly developed Indian tradition. The latter is exemplified by a miniature torso from Harappa (FIG. 11-1), which, at first glance, appears to be carved according to the precepts of Greek naturalism. (Some question the dating of this piece.) The emphasis given (by polishing) to the surface of the stone and to the swelling curves of the abdomen, however, reveals an interest, not in the logical anatomical structure of Greek sculpture, but in the fluid movement of a living body. This sense of pulsating vigor and the emphasis on sensuous surfaces remained chief characteristics of Indian sculpture for 4,000 years.

Great numbers of intaglio steatite seals, found at Mohenjo-Daro, exhibit a blend of Indian and Near Eastern elements (FIG. 11-2). Indeed, it was the finding of a Mohenjo-Daro seal at a datable Mesopotamian site that enabled scholars to assign dates to the Indus valley cultures. The script on the seals has not been deciphered. Varied devices worked into the stone, such as trees (sometimes associated with animals and humanoid figures), are represented as objects of worship. The beasts most common on the seals are various kinds of bull (including the humped variety), the water buffalo, the rhinoceros, and the elephant. Fantastic animals and anthropomorhic deities are also represented. On one seal, a seated, three-headed figure appears in what is later known as a "yoga position." The heads are surmounted by a trident-shaped device that 2,000 years later was used to symbolize both the Buddhist community and the Hindu deity Siva. Around the deity are various animals, including the bull and the tiger, which were also to become symbols of Siva. Given its date, this seal probably represented a prototype of that god. Such continuity of iconography indicates the deep roots of religious tradition in India. Style, too, shows a continuous tradition. The animals on the Indus valley seals have the flowing contours and sensuous surfaces we see in the Harappa figure, which characterize sculpture throughout most of Indian history. This artistic continuity is remarkable, not only because of the time spanned, but also because, for the period between the disappearance of the Indus civilization (about 1700 B.C.) and the rise of the Maurya empire (third century B.C.), there are virtually no

11-1 *Male Nude*, Harappa, Pakistan, third to second millennium B.C. Red sandstone, 3½" high. National Museum, New Delhi.

11-2 Seals, Mohenjo-Daro, Pakistan, third millennium B.C. Steatite. National Museum, New Delhi.

remains of the visual arts. The Aryan invasions, which began about 1800 B.C., may account for the break in the sequence of Indian art. It is even more amazing, then, in view of the Aryans' profound effect on Indian culture, that so many indigenous traits persisted. Destruction by the invaders, as well as the perishability of the materials used, undoubtedly accounted for the disappearance of many of the objects by which Indian traditions were passed on during the 2,000 years following the collapse of the Indus civilization.

The Aryans brought with them to India the Vedic religion. The term derives from the hymns (Vedas), which have survived to this day. These are addressed to the gods, who are personified aspects of nature. The warrior god Indra is thunder; Surya, the sun; and Varuna, the sky. There are many others. All were worshiped by means of hymns and sacrificial offerings in conformity to strict laws of ritual. There were no temples, but fire altars, built according to prescribed formulas, served as the focus of devotion. So important was the act of ritual that, in time, Agni (the sacrificial fire) and Soma (the sacrificial brew) became personified as gods in their own right. The rather simple form of religion and propitiation so beautifully expressed in the Vedic hymns was greatly elaborated in the *Upanishads* (800–600 B.C.)—a series of treatises on the nature of man and the universe that introduced a number of concepts alien to the simple nature worship of the northern invaders. Chief among the new ideas were those of "samsara" and "karma." *Samsara* meant the transformation of the soul into some other form of life on the death of the body. The type of existence into which the reborn soul entered depended on *karma,* the consequence of actions in all previous lifetimes. A bad karma meant a dark future— rebirth in a hell or in this world as a lower animal (a reptile, for example, or an insect). A good karma meant that the soul might go into the body of a king, a priest, or even a god, for gods also were subject to

eventual death and to the endless cycle of rebirth. The goal of religion therefore became the submersion of individual life in a world soul, which was attainable only after an individual's karma had been perfected through countless rebirths. Penance, meditation, and asceticism were believed to speed the process.

During the sixth century B.C., two major religions developed in India. One, Buddhism, exerted a profound influence on the culture and art of India as a whole from the third century B.C. to the sixth or seventh century A.D. (In some parts, like Bengal and Bihar, it was influential to the eleventh century and, in the south, to an even later date.) Although Jainism, the other major religion, never achieved Buddhism's dominance, it continues to the present day as a small but distinct religion in India, while Buddhism is practically extinct there.

The arts of many Asian countries derive from Indian Buddhism, which began with the birth of the Buddha Sakyamuni about 563 B.C. The son of a king who ruled a small area on the border of Nepal and India, the child, according to legend, was miraculously conceived and sprang from his mother's side. Named Siddhartha, and also known as Gautama, the child displayed prodigious abilities. A sage predicted that he would become a Buddha—an "enlightened" holy man destined to achieve *nirvana.* After a series of confrontations with old age, sickness, and death, Siddhartha renounced courtly luxury. While meditating under a pipal tree in the city of Buddh Gaya, Gautama obtained illumination—the complete understanding of the universe that is Buddhahood. His teaching may be summed up as follows: all existence implies sorrow; the cause of existence is attachment to work and the self; this attachment can be dissolved through the elimination of desires, which also bind the self to a countless succession of rebirths; the cessation of rebirth can be accomplished by following the Eightfold Path, which prescribes simple practices of right thought, right speech, and right action. This initial formulation of Buddhism, in which salvation was achieved by individual efforts, was later known as Hinayana Buddhism.

The religion of Buddhism, so conceived, was not opposed to basic Hindu thought, but was rather a minor heresy deriving from certain speculations in the *Upanishads*. What Buddhism did was to offer a specific method for solving the ancient Indian problem of how to break the chain of existence so that the individual could find ultimate peace.

EARLY ARCHITECTURE AND SCULPTURE: BUDDHIST DOMINANCE

The earliest known examples of art in the service of Buddhism (from the middle of the third century B.C.) are both monumental and sophisticated.

Emperor Asoka (272–232 B.C.), the grandson of Chandragupta, founder of the Maurya dynasty (*c.* 322–184 B.C.), was converted to Buddhism after witnessing the horrors of the brutal military campaigns by which he himself had forcibly unified most of northern India. His palace at Pataliputra (the modern Patna in Bihar) was designed after the Achaemenid palace at Persepolis (FIG. 2-35). Megasthenes, a Greek ambassador at Asoka's court, has left a glowing report of Pataliputra. Only parts of columns, the foundations of buildings, and remnants of a wooden palisade now remain, but we may draw some idea of the architectural details from a series of commemorative and sacred columns that Asoka raised through much of northern India. These monolithic pillars were of polished sandstone, some as high as 60 or 70 feet. The capital of one (FIG. 11-3), now in the Sarnath museum near Benares, typifies the style of the period. It consists of a *lotiform* capital (in the form of a lotus petal), on which rests a horizontal disk sculptured with a frieze of four animals alternating with four wheels. Seated on the disk are four *addorsed* (back-to-back) lions that originally were surmounted by another huge wheel. All of the forms are symbolic. The lotus, traditional symbol of divinity, also connoted man's salvation in Buddhism. The wheel represented the cycle of life, death, and rebirth. This "wheel of life" often had other levels of meaning. In this instance, it was the teaching of Buddha—the "turning of the wheel of the law." The wheel itself (probably developed from ancient sun symbols) and the four animals (the four quarters of the compass) with which it is here associated imply a cosmological meaning in which the pillar as a whole symbolizes the world axis. The lions also had manifold mean-

11-3 Lion capital of column erected by emperor Asoka (272–232 B.C.), Pataliputra, India. Polished sandstone, 7' high. Archaeological Museum, Sarnath.

ings, but here were specifically equated with Sakyamuni Buddha, who was known as the lion of the Sakya clan.

The pillars are noteworthy—not only for their symbolism, but also because they exemplify continuity of style. Although the stiff, heraldic lions are typical of Persepolis, the low-relief animals around the disk are treated in the much earlier, fluid style of Mohenjo-Daro. So, too, are the colossal figures of *yakshas* and *yakshis*, sculptured during Asoka's time or somewhat later. These male and female divinities, originally worshiped as local nature spirits, gods of trees and rocks, were now incorporated into the Buddhist and Hindu pantheons.

The Cave Temple

The Mauryan period also witnessed the beginnings of a unique architectural form—sanctuaries cut into the living rock of cliffs. Parts of the exteriors (and later interiors) of these caves were carved to imitate in accurate detail the wooden constructions of their period. The Lomas Rishi Cave, hollowed out during Asoka's reign, exhibits an entrance type (FIG. 11-4) that will be perpetuated for a thousand years. This faithful replica of a wooden façade has a doorway with a curving eave that mimics a flexible wooden roof bent over rectangular beams. A decorative frieze of elephants over the doorway carries on the indigenous sculptural traditions.

11-4 Entrance to the Lomas Rishi Cave, Barabar Hills, India, third century B.C.

11-5 The Great Stupa, Sanchi, India, completed first century. Shown are the west and south gateways.

The fall of the Mauryan dynasty around the beginning of the second century B.C. led to the political fragmentation of India.

The Stupa

Under the Sungas and the Andhras, who were the chief successors of the Mauryas, numerous *chaitya* (Buddhist assembly halls) and *viharas* (monasteries) were cut into the hills of central India from the west to the east coast. At the same time, the *stupa*, which was originally a small burial or reliquary mound of earth, evolved as an important architectural program. Asoka is supposed to have built thousands of stupas throughout India. By the end of the second century B.C., they had grown to huge proportions. Sculptured fragments from early stupas have been found at Mathura (modern Muttra), at Bharhut (near modern Satna), and elsewhere in India, but the grandeur of this type of structure can be seen best at Sanchi in the state of Madhya Pradesh. There, on a hill overlooking a wide plain, several stupas containing sacred relics were built over a period of centuries. Of these, the Great Stupa (FIG. 11-5), the tallest and finest, was originally dedicated by Asoka. Enlarged and finally completed about the middle of the first century,* it now stands as the culminating monument of an era.

A double stairway at the south side leads from the base to a drum about 20 feet high and permits access to a narrow, railed walk around the solid dome, which rises 50 feet above the ground. Surmounting

the dome is the *harmika*, a square enclosure from the center of which arises the *yasti*, or mast. The yasti is itself adorned with a series of *chatras* (umbrellas). Around the whole structure is a circular stone railing with ornamented *toranas* (gateways, FIG. 11-6) on the north, east, south, and west sides.

The stupa, like most Indian structures, has more than one function. As a receptacle for relics it is an object of adoration, a symbol of the death of the Bud-

11-6 Eastern gateway, the Great Stupa, completed first century.

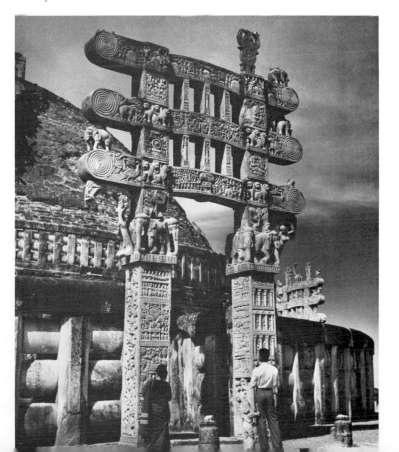

*As a reminder, all dates not designated by the epoch time designation B.C. will refer to the period A.D. Unless required for clarification, especially in Chapters 11–14 where large ranges of time from B.C. to A.D. are being covered, A.D. will no longer be used throughout the text.

covered with Buddhist symbols, deities, and narrative scenes, but the figure of the Buddha never appears. Instead, he is symbolized by such devices as an empty throne, the tree under which he meditated, the wheel of the law, his footprints.

The awe expressed in this iconographic restraint—echoed by the quiet mass of the dome itself—is strikingly and paradoxically contradicted by the sculptural luxuriance that crowds the toranas. Lush foliage mingles with the flowing forms of human bodies, and warm vitality pervades both animal and man. Sensuous yakshis hang like ripe fruit from tree brackets. This almost hedonistic expression is alien to the Buddhist renunciation of life. It is an assertion, rather, of a basic Indian attitude that at all times unites and dominates almost all of Buddhist, Hindu, and Jain art.

As Sanchi is the greatest constructed monument of early Buddhism, so the chaitya at Karli is the finest of the sculptured cave temples. During the second and first centuries B.C., the cave sanctuaries had developed complexities far beyond their simple beginnings in the Lomas Rishi Cave. Splendid façades reproducing wooden architecture in exact detail were given permanence in stone. Around 100, at Karli, in the Western Ghats near Bombay, a cliff was hollowed out and carved into an apsidal temple nearly 45 feet high and 125 feet long. The nave of the hall leads to a monolithic stupa in the apse, and on either side of the nave is an aisle formed by a series of massive columns

dha, or a token of Buddhism in general. Devotion is given the stupa by the believer, who circumambulates its dome. But, in another sense, the stupa is a cosmic diagram, the world mountain with the cardinal points emphasized by the toranas. The harmika symbolizes the heaven of the 33 gods; the yasti, as the axis of the universe, rises from the mountain-dome and through the harmika, thus uniting this world with the paradises above.

The railings and domes of some stupas were decorated with relief sculpture. The toranas at Sanchi are

11-8   Section (top) and plan (bottom) of the chaitya hall at Karli, c. 100.

11-9 *Amorous Couple,* from the entrance of the chaitya hall at Karli, *c.* 100.

crowned with male and female riders on elephants (FIG. 11-7). These great columns follow the curve of the apse thus providing an ambulatory behind the stupa (FIG. 11-8). The inner wall of the narthex, despite some later additions, is almost intact, and today it functions as a magnificent façade. On each side of the entrance, massive elephants, like atlantes, support a multi-storied building, while male and female pairs (related to yakshas and yakshis), flank the central doorway, enhancing the rich surfaces with heroic and voluptuous forms. These undulant figures contrast with the immobile severity of the stupa within and, like the yakshis of Sanchi, speak of life, not death (FIG. 11-9).

THE BUDDHA IMAGE

For some 400 years before the second century, the Buddha was represented only in symbols. At the end of the first century, simultaneously in Gandhara and Mathura, he was suddenly depicted in anthropomorphic form. The explanation is partly to be found in the development of the Buddhist movement, which, during the first century, was divided by two conflicting philosophies. The more traditional believers regarded the Buddha as a great teacher who had taught a method by which man might ultimately attain nirvana. The newer thought, called *Mahayana* (the Great Vehicle) as opposed to the older *Hinayana* (the Lesser Vehicle), deified the Buddha and provided him with a host of divinities (*Bodhisattvas*) to aid him in saving

mankind. According to the older belief, Sakyamuni was the last of seven Buddhas to exist on earth. The Mahayanists peopled the universe with thousands of Buddhas, of whom Amitabha, Lord of the Western Paradise, and Maitreya, a messiah who was to appear on this earth, soon rivaled Sakyamuni in popular favor. Symbols of the Buddha were too cold and abstract to appeal to great masses of people and were not suited to the pageantry of the new faith. In addition, Buddhism had borrowed from a reviving Hinduism the practice of *bhakti* (the adoration of a personalized deity as a means of achieving unity with it), which demanded the human figure as its focus. Thus Buddhism, out of emulation of its rival, produced its most distinct symbol, the Buddha image.

Gandhara, where one of the two versions of the anthropomorphic Buddha appeared, may be loosely taken to include much of Afghanistan and part of modern Pakistan, the westernmost section of northern India. In 327 B.C., Gandhara was conquered by the armies of Alexander the Great. Although the Greek occupation lasted only a short time, it led to continued contact with the Classical West. It is not surprising, then, that the Buddha image that developed at Gandhara had Hellenistic and especially Roman sculpture as its model (FIG. 11-10). Indeed, the features of the Master often suggest those of a marble

11-10 *Seated Buddha,* Gandhara, Pakistan, late third century. Stone, 28¾″ high. Yale University Art Gallery.

11-11 *Seated Buddha,* Mathura, India, second to third century. Red sandstone, 27¼" high. Archaeological Museum, Muttra.

11-12 *Seated Buddha Preaching the First Sermon,* Sarnath, India, fifth century. Stele, sandstone, 63" high. Archaeological Museum, Sarnath.

Apollo, and many details, such as drapery patterns and coiffures, recall successive styles in contemporaneous Roman carving. Although the iconography was Indian, even the distinguishing marks of the Buddha *(lakshanas)* were sometimes translated into a Western idiom. Thus, the *ushnisha,* a knot of hair on the head, took on the appearance of a Classical chignon. At times, even the robe of the Indian monk was replaced by the Roman toga, and minor divinities were transformed into Western water-gods, nymphs, or atlantes.

While this intrusion of Western style was dominating the northwest, the purely Indian version of the anthropomorphic Buddha was evolving 100 miles south of Delhi in the holy city of Mathura. This image derives directly from the yaksha of popular art and, like the yaksha, is draped in a mantle so thin and clinging that, at first glance, it seems to be nude (FIG. 11-11). The Mathura Buddha also has broad shoulders, a narrow waist, and a supple grace. Only such iconographic details as the ushnisha, the *urna* (a whorl of hair between the brows, represented as a dot), the long-lobed ears, and the *mudra* (a symbolic hand gesture) distinguish the Buddha from the earlier yaksha.

By the third century, the two anthropomorphic Buddha types began to coalesce into a form that served as a model for the earliest Chinese versions. But it is the Buddha at Sarnath (FIG. 11-12), from the end of the fifth century, that conveys both the abstract idealism of the religion and the sensuousness of Indian art—the first, in the simplified planes of the face; the second, in the clinging drapery, which reveals the human form.

HINDU RESURGENCE

Architecture and Sculpture

While Buddhism was at its height, Hinduism was slowly gathering the momentum that was eventually to crush its heretical offspring. Buddhism owed its original victory to the clearness of its formula for achieving salvation. About the first or second century B.C., Hinduism's answer appeared in the *Bhagavad-Gita,* a poetic gospel that, ever since, has been fundamental to Hindu doctrine. According to the *Gita,* meditation and reason can lead to ultimate absorption in the godhead; so, too, can the selfless fulfillment of everyday duties. Because the *Gita* also stressed bhakti, which answered a fundamental emotional need, the *Gita* swept Hinduism to final supremacy in the sixth and seventh centuries A.D.

Sporadic examples of Hindu art dating from the last centuries B.C. have been found, but we know of no great monuments before the fourth century A.D. At that time, the Hindus began to emulate Buddhist cave temples, first by carving out monumental icons in shallow niches. One such temple is the *Boar Avatar of Vishnu* (FIG. 11-13)* at Udayagiri near Sanchi. Here, a 12-foot figure of Varaha, a man-like creature with a boar's head, is shown raising the earth goddess from the ocean—an act symbolic of the rescuing of the earth from destruction. The powerful form of Varaha, first formulated by the Kushans, served as a model for innumerable later sculptures of this popular theme. Within a few decades, more developed caves at the same site acquired sculptural doorways, interior columns, and central icons.

During the sixth century, in the rock hillsides at Badami to the south, the Chalukyans carved out rectangular temples that had pillars, walls, and ceilings ornamented with figures of their favorite deities. Porches and interiors were defined by the embellished columns, which were so orderd as to focus attention on the shrine in the center of the rear wall. In a temple dedicated to Siva (with Vishnu, one of the two chief divinities of the Hindu pantheon), the god is shown in his cosmic dance, with numerous arms spread fan-like around his body (FIG. 11-14). Some of the god's hands hold objects; others are represented in prescribed gestures (mudra). Each object and each mudra signify a specific power of the deity. The ar-

*An *avatar* is a manifestation of a deity in which the deity performs a necessary function on earth; the number of avatars varies, Vishnu usually having 10, sometimes 29.

11-13 *Boar Avatar of Vishnu,* Cave V at Udayagiri, India, *c.* 400. Vishnu is 12′ 8″ high.

11-14 *Dancing Siva,* relief from cave temple, Badami, India, sixth century.

rangement of the limbs is so skillful and logical that it is hard to realize that the sculptor conceived of the figure as a symbol and not as an image of a many-armed being.

Perhaps the supreme achievement of Hindu art is at Elephanta, where, in the sixth century, craftsmen excavated a hilltop and carved out a pillared hall almost 100 feet square. On entering this sanctuary, the visitor peers through rows of heavy columns, until, adjusting to the dark, the gigantic forms of three heads can be seen emerging from the end wall (FIG. 11-15). The heads represent Siva as Mahadeva, Lord of Lords and incarnation of the forces of creation, preservation, and destruction. The concept of power

11-15 *Siva as Mahadeva* in rock-cut temple, Elephanta, India, sixth century. Siva is 10′ 10″ high.

is immediately transmitted by the sheer size of the heads, which, rising nearly 14 feet from the floor, dwarf the onlooker. Each of the three faces expresses a different aspect of the eternal. The center one, neither harsh nor compassionate, looks beyond humanity in the supreme indifference of eternal meditation. The other two faces—one soft and gentle, one angry and fearsome—speak of the sequence of birth and destruction that can be ended only by union with the godhead. The assurance of the period is manifest in the guardians of the shrine, who stand tall and relaxed in the certainty of their power. On the surrounding walls, deeply cut panels illustrating the legends of Siva carry on the robust and sensuous traditions of Harappa (FIG. 11-1) and Karli (FIG. 11-9).

During the fourth, fifth, and sixth centuries, Buddhism, in turn, borrowed heavily from Hindu doctrine. Elaborate rituals and incantations, inspired by similar Hindu practices, replaced the simple activities the Buddha had prescribed. Esoteric sects sprouted, and the popular Hindu worship of Sakti, the female power of the deity, was adapted for Buddhist usage. A sixth-century relief in a Buddhist cave temple at Aurangabad depicts worship of the Buddha through music and dance (FIG. 11-16) in a scene that might have been taken from a Hindu temple, for the volatile and rapturous figures of the musicians and the dancer represent an Indian, rather than Buddhist, way of life. With little to distinguish it from Hinduism, Buddhism and its art gradually withered and, within a few centuries, virtually disappeared.

In the same burst of creativity that produced cave temples, other innovative Hindu architects were

11-17 Vishnu temple (SIDE VIEW), Deogarh, India, early sixth century.

building the first structural temples with stone. One of the earliest that remains is the Vishnu temple built in the early sixth century during the Gupta period (320–c. 600) at Deogarh in north central India (FIG. 11-17). All later developments of the Hindu temple were in many ways elaborations on the principles embodied in Deogarh.

The Hindu temple is not a hall for congregational worship; it is the residence of the god. The basic requirement is a cubic cella for the cult image or symbol. This most holy of places, called the *garbha griha*, or womb chamber, has thick walls and a heavy ceiling to protect the deity. A doorway through which the devotee may enter is the only other architectural necessity. Like the stupa, the temple has other meanings, for it is also the symbol of the *purusha*, or primordial man. In addition, in its plan, it is a *mandala*, or magic diagram of the cosmos, and its proportions are based on modules that have magical reference. Thus, the temple itself is a symbol to be observed from the exterior. Contemporary Western theories of architecture as dealing with space-enclosing form within which man carries on his activities do not apply to the Hindu temple, which is to be appreciated as sculpture rather than as architecture.

In early temples such as Deogarh, decoration is limited and restrained and the form is a simple cube, which originally was surmounted by a tower (*sik-*

11-16 Relief with dancers and musicians, Aurangabad, India, sixth century.

hara). All of the walls except the entrance wall are solid but include sculptured panels like false doorways framed in the walls. On these panels, in scenes from Hindu mythology, relaxed and supple figures carry on the Indian tradition of ease and poise.

In striking contrast to the robust plasticity of northern sculpture are the carvings on the Buddhist monuments situated at the mouth of the Kistna River on the Bay of Bengal. The major sites, in chronological

order (dating roughly from the second century B.C. to the third century A.D.), are Jaggayyapeta, Amaravati, and Nagarjunakonda. Little remains from the first, but many reliefs from the other two are extant. These are elaborately ornamented and filled with hosts of figures that, particularly in the later Amaravati scenes (FIG. 11-18), are slender, attenuated, and in graceful movement—rendered almost as if by brush.

The record of Indian art farther to the south begins with a cave temple at Mandagadippattu (early seventh century) that was commissioned by the first great ruler of the Pallavas, Mahendravarman I, and dedicated to the Hindu trinity. Mahendravarman was soon surpassed by his immediate successors at Mahabalipuram, on the coast not far from the city of Madras. Here, near a miscellany of monuments that includes cave shrines, carved cliffsides, and a masonry temple, a unique group of five small, freestanding temples (known as *rathas*) were sculptured, perhaps as architectural models, from some of the huge boulders that litter the area (FIG. 11-19). One of the temples is apsidal; another has a long, vaulted shape with a barrel roof, the ends of which reproduce the bentwood curves of the ancient chaitya halls. The smallest is a square shrine with a pyramidal roof that mimics in stone the thatch of primitive shrines as they appear in reliefs on the rails of early stupas. The

11-19 Rock-cut temples (Dharmaraja in foreground), Mahabalipuram, India, seventh century.

11-20 Muktesvar Temple, Bhuvanesvar, India, *c.* 950

11-21 Visvanatha Temple, Khajuraho, India, *c.* 1000.

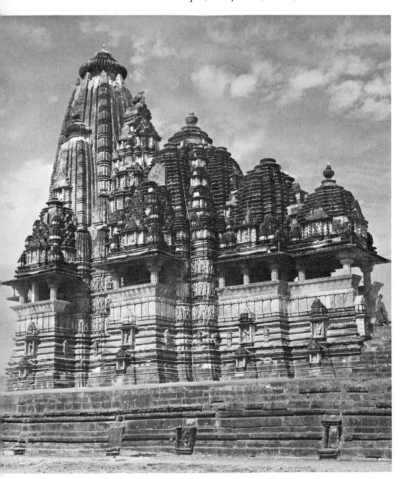

Dharmaraja, largest of the rathas, has a simple cubic cella, as at Deogarh. But the *vimana* (composed of the garbha griha and the sikhara) ascends, in typical southern style, in pronounced tiers of cornices decorated with miniature shrines (foreground, FIG. 11-19). Niches spaced along the walls contain figures of the major deities; these niches will become a regular feature of the southern temple.

The south Indian temple was further developed at the beginning of the eighth century in nearby Kanchipuram and by the artists of the Chalukya dynasty in the Virupaksha Temple (*c.* 740) at Pattadakal near Badami. The vimana here is related to the Dharmaraja ratha, but porches and an assembly hall (*mandapa*) have been added in front of the garbha griha. The interior of this shrine consists of a dimly lighted ambulatory surrounding the cella, which is entered through a large, columned assembly hall, and two subsidiary shrines. Light entering the mandapa through narrow windows and two projecting porches plays over elaborate relief carvings on the columns and walls. The devotee, who entered through an open porch, walked from the blazing light through a cool, softly lighted, and spacious area before reaching, in darkness, the enigma of the garbha griha itself. There, in the austere chamber, he came face to face with the barely visible symbol of his deity. The sense of mystery offered the worshiper was as satisfactory to the Hindu as the soaring exultation of the Gothic cathedral was to the Christian.

In the following few centuries, a different architectural order evolved in northern India, characterized by a smoother integration of halls and porches with the main shrine and tower and by an increased vertical emphasis in all parts. The problem of creating a unified exterior was solved in separate stages. The first step—adding height to the mandapa to mitigate the disparity between the vertical vimana and the horizontal mandapa—is illustrated in the immense Kailasa Temple (*c.* 750), the extraordinary rock-cut monument at Ellora. A second step is exemplified by the lovely Muktesvar Temple at Bhuvanesvar, Orissa (FIG. 11-20), where a high, pyramidal superstructure over the mandapa brought what had been disproportionately horizontal into complete harmony with the tall sikhara. This evolution culminated during the tenth and eleventh centuries at Khajuraho (FIG. 11-21) in north central India. There, the temples, numbering over 20, became larger, more elaborate, and, by virtue of their high plinths, even more prominent. Two and sometimes three mandapa were put before the cella. The greatest esthetic advance was made in the roofs of the mandapa and their pyramidal eaves, which unite with the sikhara to create a rapid and torrential sequence of cascading forms. The lower sections of the building, bound by a series of horizontal registers, are laden with sculptured deities, legends, and erotic scenes. Elongated figures are often set in complex, twisting poses that emphasize the sinuously curved lines of the body. Although the rendering of living forms has become less natural and at times even disturbingly contorted, the sculptures function superbly in leading the eye around the shifting planes of the sides of the temple.

In the year 1000, the first of a series of Moslem invasions sounded the knell of Hindu architecture in northern India. But in the south—first under the Chola kingdom (846–1173) and later under the Hoysala (1022–1342), the Vijayanagar (1336–1565), and the Nayak (1420–1736) dynasties—sculpture and architecture continued to flourish.

Of particular beauty are the small, early Chola temples scattered throughout Tamil Nadu. Many are incomparable in their architectonic order, sensitive detail, and sculpture. A trend toward larger buildings, reflecting the imperial grandeur of the Chola kingdom, led to the great Brihadesvara Temple (*c.* 1000) of Thanjavur, which is 160 feet high and replete with architectural elements and figures. Many deities are represented on its walls, although fewer than at Khajuraho, and most appear in niches spaced with restraint at ordered intervals.

Bronze images were made to grace the shrines and to be carried in processions during important ceremonies. Some of the world's most superb bronzes were produced in the Chola kingdom, where the figures of Siva as Nataraja, Lord of the Dance, reached their high point in the tenth century. The Nataraja (*c.* 1000) at the Naltunai Isvaram Temple at Punjai, Tamil Nadu (FIG. 11-22) shows the god, represented in an ideal human form, dancing vigorously within a flaming nimbus, one foot on the Demon of Ignorance. His flying locks terminate in rearing cobra heads and, on one side, support a tiny figure of the river-goddess, Ganga. One of his four hands sounds a drum, while, from another, a flame flashes. Dancing thus, Siva periodically destroys the universe so that it may be reborn again. Exquisitely balanced, yet full of movement, this bronze is a triumph of three-dimensional sculpture and the art of bronze casting.

Enormous temple compounds grew around the nucleus of earlier temples. The Minakshi Temple at Madura and the Srirangam Temple at Tiruchirapalli eventually covered acres of ground. "Thousand-pillared" halls, built almost one beside the other, have the aspect of a continuous structure, interrupted only by courtyards and sacred water tanks for ritual bathing. Elaborate monolithic columns, carved with high- and low-relief figures, evoke a solemn mood, the stone sculpture having the effect of iron castings. The original walled enclosure came to be surrounded by other walls as the temple expanded, and the gate-

11-22   *Siva as Nataraja* (Lord of the Dance), Naltunai Isvaram Temple, Punjai, India, *c.* 1000. Bronze.

ways (*gopuram*) at each of the four cardinal points grew progressively higher with each additional wall. The fully developed gopuram is multi-storied and crowded with sculpture; as many gopurams are over 150 feet high, they dominate the landscape of southern India.

The spread of Moslem domination gradually sapped the Indian tradition, even in the south. By the seventeenth century, the harmonious proportions of earlier figures had been lost, and even the metal castings had become inferior.

Painting

In India, the art of painting was probably as great as the art of sculpture but, unfortunately, less of it survives. The earliest traces are a few fragments in Cave X at Ajanta that date from approximately the first century B.C. Like the ornamentation on the toranas at Sanchi (FIG. 11-6), to which they are related in style, these fragments illustrate scenes from the past lives of the Buddha.

At Ajanta, again, in Caves I and XVII, we find the next and most magnificent examples of Indian painting. These murals, dating from the fifth, sixth, and seventh centuries, embody all the clarity, dignity, and serenity of Gupta art and must be ranked among

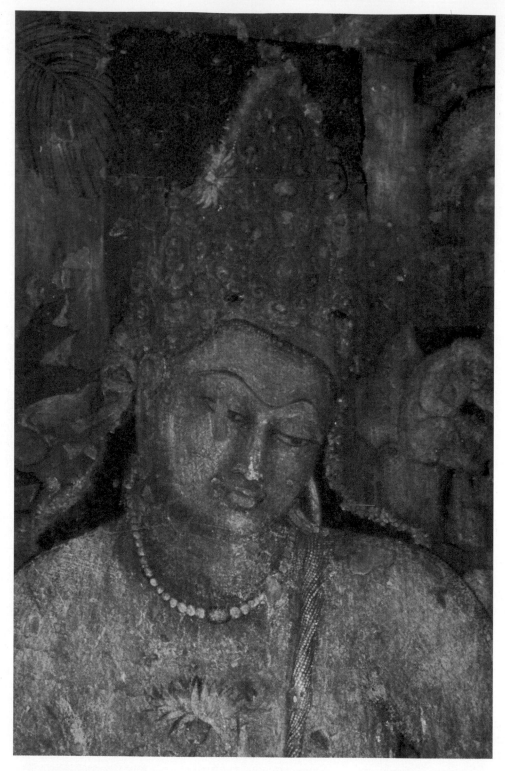

11-23 *Beautiful Bodhisattva Padmapani*, fresco from Cave I, Ajanta, India, *c.* 600–650.

the great paintings of the world. The *Beautiful Bodhisattva Padmapani* in Cave I (FIG. 11-23) moves with the subtle grace of the Deogarh sculptures, while the glow of color imparts an even more spiritual presence. The Ajanta paintings, however, are more than the manifestations of Buddhist devotion. Their genre-like scenes and worldly figures, although illustrating Buddhist texts, reflect a sophisticated and courtly art.

The Ajanta painting tradition, in all its colorful vitality, was continued under the Chola rule, as witnessed by the paintings in the Brihadesvara Temple at Thanjavur. The dancing figures in these paintings, although drawn in the vivacious postures familiar in the Chola bronzes, retain some of the modeling and the soft tonality of the Gupta style.

The Moslem conquests inhibited the evolution of Hindu sculpture and architecture in northern India after the thirteenth century, but revitalized the art of painting. In the sixteenth century—especially under the reign of Akbar, who was sympathetic to Hinduism and Christianity as well as Islam—traditional

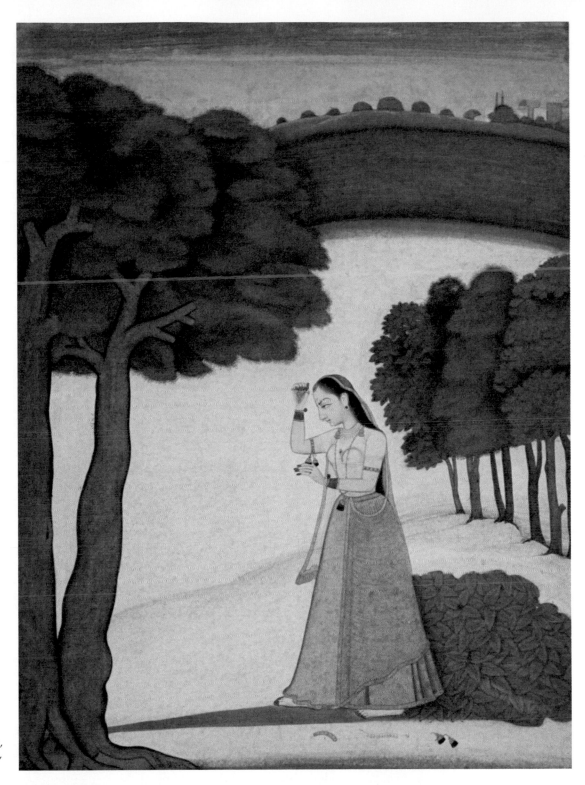

11-24 *The Disappointed Mistress, c.* 1740. Gouache, 8¼" × 6". Private collection, Los Angeles.

Indian painters were exposed to the delicate and conventionalized miniatures of the great Persian artists. During the seventeenth and eighteenth centuries, painting responded vigorously to the interplay between foreign modes at the imperial capital and autochthonous idioms at isolated feudal courts. Many delightful hybrids and innovations resulted—some delicate and lyrical, as at Bundi and Kishangarh (Rajasthan); some stark and bold, as at Basohli in the Himalayan foothills. Among others, the hill schools in Gulcr and Kangra developed their own idiom, emphasizing such subjects as elegant figures in serene landscapes, portraits of rulers, interpretations of musical modes *(ragamalas)*, and religious themes. The joyous exuberance of these new styles was particularly well suited to newer Hindu cults, which were dedicated to the worship of Krishna, an avatar of Vishnu, whose praises were sung in the erotic poetry of the *Gita-Govinda*. The love of the lush and the sensuous, which the earliest Indian sculptures had expressed, thus found an entirely new medium in exquisitely colored, often tender paintings (FIG. 11-24).

THE SPREAD OF INDIAN ART

The vigorous culture that generated the great achievements of art in India overflowed its borders. The great tide of Buddhism in the early centuries of the Christian era carried Mahayana beliefs and Gandhara–Mathura art through Afghanistan, across the desert trade routes of Turkestan into China, and eventually into Japan.

The path of Hinayana Buddhism (see page 417), which was opened in the third century B.C. by the son of the emperor Asoka, led in another direction—south from Amaravati across the straits to Sri Lanka (modern Ceylon). From that time on, Sri Lanka became a "little India"; its arts were influenced first by Amaravati and then, successively, by the Guptas, the Pallavas, and the Cholas. The largest concentrations of art were at two royal centers: Anuradhapura (virtually an extension of Amaravati), where most of what remains is from the second and third centuries and Polonnaruwa (eleventh and twelfth centuries), best known for the colossal 46-foot-long sculpture of the expiring Buddha (FIG. 11-25). Here also are many famous stupas that basically adhere to the Amaravati tradition but are simpler; an innovation is the carvings of guardian figures on steles placed at stupa entrances. Although there are some paintings at Polonnaruwa, the earliest (fifth century) and most exquisite are the heavenly maidens on the escarpment of the fortress at Sigiriya.

By the fifth century, a series of emigrations from India began to bring the impact of Indian culture to Burma, Thailand, Cambodia, (modern Kampuchea), Sumatra, and Java. There, Buddhism and Hinduism continued their struggle for supremacy, with each introducing and fostering its arts. While Buddhism was under siege in India, one of its greatest monuments was rising at Borobudur in Java. There, around 800, a huge stupa (FIG. 11-26), basically square and measuring over 400 feet across the base, was built of stone in nine terraced levels, with a central stairway in each of the four sides. The base and the first four tiers are rectilinear and signify the terrestrial world of sensation; the upper four tiers are circular and symbolize the heavens.

On the base, mostly covered by earth, 160 reliefs depict people trapped in the karmic cycle of life, death, and rebirth. Abundantly decorating the walls along the corridors of the next four tiers are over 1,000 cautionary scenes from the *jatakas* and different *sutras* (scriptural accounts of the Buddha). But above, on the circular terraces, no narratives intrude. Here, ringing the pathways in solitary dignity, are latticed stupas, in each of which, barely visible, is a seated Buddha of gentle beauty (originally, there were 72). A larger stupa, rising at the pinnacle, may have enclosed a single Buddha, symbol of the ultimate.

This architectural orchestration of sculptures is a *mandala*—a cosmic diagram perhaps representing the three spheres of Buddhist cosmology: the Human Sphere of Desire (didactic narratives crowded with figures and foliage); the Bodhisattva Sphere of Form; and the Buddha Sphere of Formlessness, where the simplicity and isolation of the individual stupas effect a serene release. The entire stupa has 505 Buddha figures. In all, it is an eloquent statement of the proto-Esoteric Buddhism that developed from Mahayana in Java.

11-25 *Buddha,* from Gal Vihara, near Polonnaruwa, Sri Lanka, eleventh and twelfth centuries. Stone, whole figure 46' long.

11-26 Stupa, Borobudur, Java, Indonesia, *c.* 800.

The Buddhists in Java also erected *chandis* (temples). Two that are near the stupa of Borobudur and that are of the same date are Chandi Mendut and Chandi Pawon. Their dark sanctuaries, containing colossal Buddhist images, have the same awesome impact on the visitor as the shrines of the Buddhist cave temples in northwest India. Indeed, those caves, as well as other sacred sites throughout India, were well known to Indonesian pilgrims, whose exposure to Indian monuments and texts influenced their island culture.

The Hindus were also active in Java. On the Dieng Plateau, they erected single-celled Siva temples based on south Indian Pallava models. At Prambanan in central Java, where structures and motifs were rapidly Javanized, the tall and narrow Siva temple of Lara Jonggrang (ninth and tenth centuries), is characteristically a studied aggregate of piled-up stones, terraced peaks, and sanctuaries—a symbol of Mahameru, axis of the universe and mountain home of the gods. Reliefs on the temple balustrade illustrate the great Hindu epic *Ramayana*. Naturalistic yet decorative, these dramatic narratives are a harmony of Indian forms and Javenese physical types (FIG. 11-27).

11-27 *Ramayana* scene, Siva temple, Lara Jonggrang, Java, Indonesia, ninth and tenth centuries.

11-28 *Harihara*, Prasat Andet, Kampuchea (Cambodia), seventh century. Stone, 6' 3" high. Musée Albert Sarraut, Phnom Penh.

The mainland, in contact with India by the third century, also reacted to the stimuli of Indian culture. In Thailand, the softly modeled figures of bronze and stucco that were produced during the Dvaravati period (sixth to tenth century) were inspired by the Gupta style. During the pre-Angkor or Early Khmer period (fifth to ninth century), the Cambodians, too, borrowed the flowing planes and sensitive surfaces of Gupta. Around the seventh century, they also worked in the manner of the south Indian Pallavas, as we can see in the figure of *Harihara* (a combined form of Siva and Vishnu) from Prasat Andet (FIG. 11-28). The elegance of the Pallava prototyes at Mahabalipuram has been modified only slightly by

the addition of a taut, almost spring-like tension. Tall, broad-shouldered, full-bodied, and slender-legged, this is an idealized figure, more godly than human. We shall see how the Classical configuration of the pre-Angkor gods was gradually transformed into a distinctly more squat Cambodian type, with a broad face composed of full lips (doubly outlined), continuous eyebrows, and flat nose (FIG. 11-33).

The temple in Cambodia was directly related to the Angkorian concept of kingship. Whereas in India the ideal king was the Universal Lord *(chakravartin)* who ruled through goodness, in Cambodia he was the god–king *(devaraja)* in life and after death. The temple the king built was dedicated to himself as the god. As the kings grew more powerful and ambitious, so grew the size of their temples and the multiplications of architectural and decorative elements.

At Angkor (meaning ''the city'' or ''the capital'' in the Khmer language), in the midst of a fertile plain, a dozen Khmer kings built their successive capitals between the ninth and the thirteenth centuries. Eventually, this agglomoration of capital cities spread across some 75 square miles and comprised a multitude of major brick and stone monuments amid a vast and intricate irrigation system (FIG. 11-29). Only the temples were of stone or brick (materials reserved for the gods); other buildings, including the royal palaces, were of wood and have long since perished. Laid out orthogonally, the network of canals, supported from large reservoirs *(barays)*, served as a means of transportation as well as of irrigation for the fertile rice fields that fed an estimated population of one million. The canals also interconnected and fed the moats surrounding many of the major temples, including the two largest, Angkor Thom and Angkor Wat.

Angkor Wat (a *wat* is a Buddhist monastery; FIG. 11-30) was originally a Hindu temple built between 1113 and 1150. Dedicated to Vishnu by its builder, King Suryavarman II, it is a physical representation of Hindu cosmology. The five central towers represent the peaks of Mount Meru—the Olympus of the Hindu gods and the center of the universe. The outer wall symbolizes the mountains at the edge of the world; the moat, the oceans beyond. Moreover, recent study suggests that the layout had astronomical significance and that the sections of the design were aligned to form a kind of solar calendar by which the summer and winter solstices and the spring and fall equinoxes could be fixed. Sight lines from vantage points within the temple complex can be constructed to show that the varying positions of the sun and moon throughout the year could be systematically observed, predicted, and marked. The dimensions of the complex are enormous. The moat is 2½ miles long, and the circumference of the outer gallery measures

N

Khmer dike
Khmer canal

Siem Reap River

Preah Khan

Neak Pean

Ta Som

Western Mebon
Western Baray (reservoir)

Baphuon

Eastern Mebon
Eastern Baray (reservoir)

The Bayon

Ta-Keo

Ta Prohm

Pre Rup

Angkor Thom

Banteay Kdei

Sras Srang

Phnom Bakheng

Angkor Wat

Siem Reap River

0   5000   10,000   FEET
0 500 1000 2000 3000
METERS

11-29 Overall plan of Angkor site, Kampuchea (Cambodia), twelfth and thirteenth centuries.

11-30 Aerial view of Angkor Wat, Kampuchea (Cambodia).

11-31 Dance relief, Angkor Wat, twelfth century. Musée Guimet, Paris.

half a mile and contains reliefs with literally thousands of figures representing the myths of Vishnu, Krishna, and Rama. The temples comprising this great complex are set at the corners of two concentric walls that gird the central shrine. Each of the eight temple towers repeats the form of the main spire, which rises in the center from a raised platform like the apex of a pyramid. The towers themselves resemble, in outline, the sikhara of northern Indian temples.

The relief carvings express the Cambodian predilection for rhythmic design, the juxtaposition of two, three, or more identical figures, and the repetition of undulating contours. These graceful but stylized forms, thus locked together, move in a harmonious rhythm like their counterparts in Cambodian dance (FIG. 11-31).

The Bayon at Angkor Thom (FIG. 11-32), dating from the twelfth and thirteenth centuries, is, in many ways, the culmination of the Indian temple, particu-

11-32 Bayon, Angkor Thom, Kampuchea (Cambodia), twelfth and thirteenth centuries.

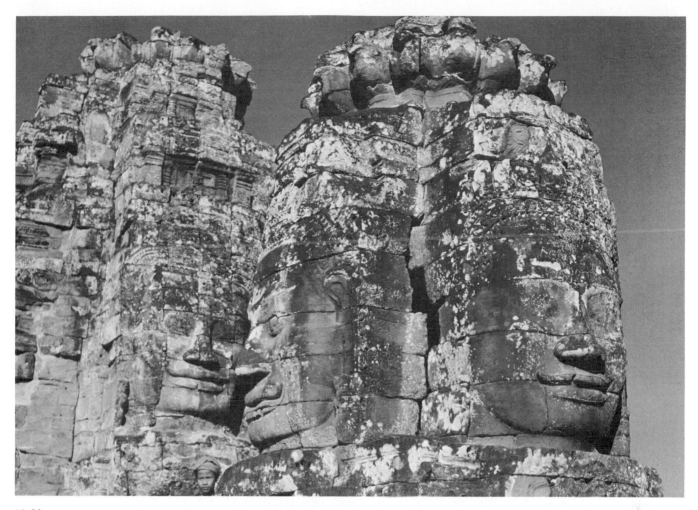

11-33   Tower of Bayon, Angkor Thom, twelfth and thirteenth centuries.

larly in its complete integration of sculpture and architecture. It also illustrates the syncretic relationship
of Hinduism and Buddhism. The long, impressive
approach to the Bayon, a Buddhist temple, is lined in
places with giant gods and demons holding onto the
body of the serpent Vasuki in an enactment of a
Hindu legend, the Churning of the Sea of Milk. But
the uniqueness of the Bayon lies in the size and disposition of the colossal heads, one on each side of the
square towers (FIG. 11-33). These faces, their Cambodian features now fully stylized, smile enigmatically
from a lofty height. They are the faces of the Bodhisattva Lokesvara—god form of the reigning king and
symbol of the infinite powers of the devaraja-Bodhi-
sattva, which extend to all points of the compass. The
Bayon was conceived as the world mountain. On it
and around it, a tropical luxuriance of decorative and
narrative carvings intensifies its magic. The creative
force that had been India left its last great record
abroad in these compassionate faces of Lokesvara,
surveying from eternity the legendary history carved
on the walls below.

12

MANCHOW
(MANCHURIA)

U.S.S.R.

OUTER
MONGOLIA

CHAHAR

JEHOL

LIAONING

SINKIANG
(TURKESTAN)

INNER   MONGOLIA   SUIYÜAN

Tunhwang

KANSU

NINGSIA

Huang R.

Yunkang
Peking

T'ien-lung
Shan

HOPEI
(CHIHLI)

KOREA

TSINGHAI

SHANSI

SHENSI

Huang (Yellow) R.

Anyang

Huang R.

SHANTUNG

KIANGSU

JAPAN

*YELLOW
SEA*

Wei R.

Lungmen

Kaifeng
(Pien–ching)

HONAN

C H I N A

ANHWEI

Nanking Wuhsien
(Soochow)

Shanghai

TIBET

SIKANG

SZECHWAN

HUPEI

Hangchow

CHEKIANG

Yangtze R.

Fowliang
(Chingtehchen)

INDIA

KIANGSI

HUNAN

KWEICHOW

FUKIEN

YUNNAN

Si Kiang R.

KWANGTUNG

Canton

TAIWAN
(FORMOSA)

BURMA

KWANGSI

CHINA

VIETNAM

Macao   Hong Kong

LAOS

THAILAND

0	100	300	500

MILES

0	160	480	800

KILOMETERS

THE ART OF CHINA

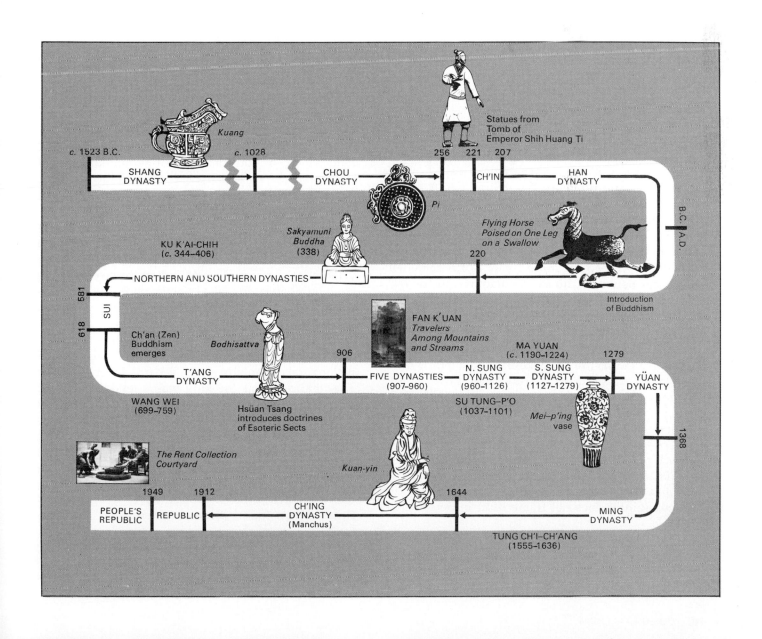

Kuang

Statues from
Tomb of
Emperor Shih Huang Ti

c. 1523 B.C.   *c.* 1028   256 221 207

SHANG
DYNASTY

CHOU
DYNASTY

CH'IN

HAN
DYNASTY

B.C. A.D.

Pi

KU K'AI-CHIH
(*c.* 344–406)

*Sakyamuni
Buddha*
(338)

*Flying Horse
Poised on One Leg
on a Swallow*

220

NORTHERN AND SOUTHERN DYNASTIES

Introduction
of Buddhism

581

SUI

618

Ch'an (Zen)
Buddhism
emerges

Bodhisattva

906

FAN K'UAN
*Travelers
Among Mountains
and Streams*

MA YUAN
(*c.* 1190–1224)

1279

T'ANG
DYNASTY

FIVE DYNASTIES
(907–960)

N. SUNG
DYNASTY
(960–1126)

S. SUNG
DYNASTY
(1127–1279)

YÜAN
DYNASTY

WANG WEI
(699–759)

Hsüan Tsang
introduces doctrines
of Esoteric Sects

SU TUNG-P'O
(1037–1101)

Mei–p'ing
vase

1368

*The Rent Collection
Courtyard*

Kuan-yin

1949   1912   1644

PEOPLE'S
REPUBLIC

REPUBLIC

CH'ING
DYNASTY
(Manchus)

MING
DYNASTY

TUNG CH'I–CH'ANG
(1555–1636)

Of the great non-Western civilizations, that of China was the first to be known and appreciated in Europe. But it is only in the past half-century or so that the achievements of Chinese art and culture have been progressively revealed and systematically studied. Still, many in the West who now realize the extent and continuity of Chinese civilization and who recognize the striking beauty of its art are not fully aware of the complexity of either. Our task here is to identify the spirit of Chinese art and to trace, at least in outline, its major developments and styles.

China is a vast and topographically varied country about the size of the United States. Its political and cultural boundaries have spread, at times, to double that area, encompassing Tibet, Chinese Turkestan (Sinkiang), Mongolia, Manchuria, and parts of Korea. The country includes great stretches of sandy plains, mighty rivers, towering mountains, and fertile farmlands. North China, centered around Peking,* has a dry and moderate-to-cold climate, whereas south China is moist and tropical.

Whereas the spoken language of China varies so much as to be unrecognizable in different areas, the written language has remained uniform and intelligible in all parts of the country, permitting literary, philosophic, and religious traditions to be shared by people thousands of miles apart. Distinct regional styles of art did appear, especially in the early eras and during times of political fragmentation, but a broad cultural unity also permitted an easy flow of artistic ideas and influence throughout China.

The primarily expressive function of Chinese painting during the last millennium has been gradually made more comprehensible to the Western mind, partly by developments in the modern art of the West. We have become more aware of fundamental differences between Chinese secular art and the traditional, premodern art of the West, as determined by differences between the philosophies of nature and man of the two cultures. For the Chinese, man is not dominant in nature; he is a part of it, responding, like all living creatures, to its rhythms. To be happy is to live in accord with nature; to be a painter is to be the instrument through which nature reveals itself. The painter's work is an expression of his immersion in the flow of life and of his attunement to all that changes and grows; in so being, it is also the expression of a personal character refined by the contemplation of nature. Moreover, because nature is not measured and classified according to space and time, the Chinese painter does not frame it off in perspective

boxes with colors scaled in light and shade. He does not attempt to duplicate and fix natural appearances by such means. The asymmetry of growing things, the ceaseless and random movements of nature, the infinity of cosmic happenings—these forbid all enframements, rigid regularities, beginnings and ends. Appearance is always transformed by the artist's passage through it. He becomes part of the total expression of his art, as his art is the total expression of his experience of nature.

This philosophical attitude of the Chinese toward secular painting can be seen even in the artist's almost ritualistic preparation of his medium, his materials. The best ink, for instance, was derived from soot or lampblack mixed with animal glue and pulverized clay, oyster shells or powdered jade, and various fragrances. From these ingredients, each of which had symbolic as well as physical properties, an ink stick (often carved) was formed that was treasured by the artist.

SHANG

A series of Neolithic cultures characterized by a variety of painted wares date back to the fourth millennium B.C. According to traditional Chinese history, this would have been the period of the Hsia. Although the Hsia state is still a matter of legend, the remains of a considerable kingdom, discovered within the last 50 years, have confirmed the existence of the Shang dynasty. As late as 1928, many scholars doubted the existence of the Shang dynasty, but excavations at Anyang in northern China in that year brought to light not only one of the last capitals of the Shang but also evidence of the dynasty's earlier development. Among the astounding discoveries were large numbers of inscribed bones, once used for divination, which tell us much about the Shang people. Their script was basically pictographic but sufficiently developed to express abstract ideas. These fragmentary records, together with other finds from the excavations, reveal an advanced, if barbaric, civilization. They indicate that the king was a feudal ruler and that some of his wives were also his vassals, living in different cities. Warfare with neighboring states was frequent, and cities were protected by surrounding walls of pounded earth. Royal tombs were extensive, and the beheaded bodies of servants or captives accompanied the deceased rulers to the grave. Chariots, trappings of horses buried alive, weapons, and ritual objects found in these graves help us to describe the art of this period.

Although sculpture in marble and small carvings in bone and jade exist, the great art of the Shang dynasty was that of ritual bronze vessels. These bronzes

*In the romanization system called *pinyin*, Peking is presently known as Beijing. This text, however, will use the place–name spellings more commonly recognized prior to the official 1979 adoption of the pinyin spellings for use in all texts in the Roman alphabet.

were made in piece molds. They show a casting technique as advanced as any ever used in the East or West, indicating that this art must have been practiced for some centuries before the period of Anyang. The bronze vessels were intended to hold wine, water, grain, and meat for use in sacrificial rites. The major elements of decoration are zoomorphic, but usually the background and sometimes the animals themselves are covered with round or squared spirals. Conventions, which obviously evolved over a long period, rigidly governed the stylistic representation of animals, so that images or symbols are often involved and difficult to decipher. A major zoomorphic motif is that of an animal divided in half lengthwise, with the two halves spread out on the vessel body in a bilaterally symmetrical design. The two head parts, meeting in the center, can often also be read as a complete frontal animal mask with vestigial bodies at both sides. Such ambiguity of design occurs frequently on Shang vessels, with fragmentary parts of bodies taking on a life of their own.

Such an animal is shown on a covered libation vessel, or *kuang* (FIG. 12-1). In this complex design, the representation (on the vessel's side) may be of the eyes of a tiger and the horns of a ram. (On other such Shang vessels, the eyes may be of a sheep; the horns, of a bull, water buffalo, or deer.) The front of the lid is formed of a horned animal; the rear, of a horned head with a bird's beak in its mouth. Another horned head is on the handle. Fish, birds, elephants, rabbits, and more abstract, composite creatures swarm over the surface against a background of spirals. Specific combinations of such animal motifs may have defined certain concepts; for example, the animal or bird in the mouth of another animal may signify generation.

12-1   *Kuang*, Shang dynasty, twelfth century B.C. Bronze, 6½" high. Smithsonian Institution, Freer Gallery of Art, Washington, D.C.

The multiple designs and their enigmatic fields of spirals are so closely integrated with the form of the vessel that they are not merely an external embellishment but an integral part of the sculptural whole. The tense outline of the bronze compactly encloses the forces symbolized on its surface. These vessels were not only ritual containers but also, in their very form and decoration, a kind of sculptural icon or visualization of the early Chinese attitude toward the powers of nature.

CHOU

About 1027 B.C., the Shang dynasty was overthrown by the Chou, whose dynasty endured until 256 B.C. Although the Chou were a more primitive people from the west, their culture apparently resembled that of the Shang.

The very earliest Chou bronzes are indistinguishable from those of the Shang. Indeed, they were probably made by the same craftsmen. But within a generation, the new and bolder spirit of the conquerors was unmistakably imprinted on the ritual vessels. Where the Shang silhouette had been suave and compact, the Chou was explosive and dynamic (FIG. 12-2). Gradually, this vitality diminished, and, in a hun-

12-2   *Yu*, Early Chou dynasty, *c.* tenth century B.C. Bronze, 20⅛" high. Smithsonian Institution, Freer Gallery of Art, Washington, D.C.

441

dred years, the shapes became more utilitarian and the zoomorphic designs more ornamental. The animal forms were distorted and twisted into interlaces until, by the beginning of the Late Chou period (600–256 B.C.), almost all evidence of the original awesome motifs was lost in an exuberance of playful rhythms over the surface of the bronzes. What had once expressed the power of magic and religion was transformed into a secular display of technical skill and fantasy.

During the sixth century B.C., the Chou empire began to dissolve into a number of warring feudal states. As old values were forgotten, Confucius and other philosophers strove to analyze the troubles of their day. While Confucius urged intelligent and moral action on his followers, his famous contemporary, Lao-tzu, favored meditation, inaction, and withdrawal from society. Neither philosophy, however, was to affect Chinese art for several centuries.

The art of the Late Chou, whether in bronze, jade (FIG. 12-3), or lacquer, was produced to satisfy the elaborate demands of ostentatious feudal courts that vied with each other in lavish display. Popular at this time were bronzes inlaid with gold and silver and mirrors highly polished on one side and decorated with current motifs on the other. About the fourth century B.C., ritual bronzes were embellished with an entirely new system of narrative designs. Scenes of hunting, religious rites, and magic practices, although small, nevertheless reveal subjects and compositions that are probably reflective of paintings lost but mentioned in the literature of the period.

12-3 *Pi* (disc), Late Chou dynasty, sixth to third century B.C. Jade, 6½″ in diameter. Nelson Gallery-Atkins Museum, Kansas City, Missouri (Nelson Fund).

In the Late Chou period, carvings of jade—a stone regarded with special reverence by the Chinese and found in Neolithic tombs—reached a peak of technical perfection in the jewelry and ritual objects entombed with the dead (FIGS. 12-3 and 12-8). At this time, Confucius extolled the virtues of jade, in which, he said, superior men in ancient times "found the likeness of all excellent qualities." It was soft, smooth, and glossy (when polished), like benevolence; fine, compact, and strong, like intelligence; angular, but not sharp and cutting, like righteousness; and (when struck) like music. Like loyalty, its flaws did not conceal its beauty nor its beauty its flaws, and, like virtue, it was conspicuous in the symbols of rank.*

The culture that had produced the great bronzes and jades of the Shang and Chou periods was being transformed. The political turbulence of the Late Chou period, at times called the "period of the Warring States," was accompanied by an intellectual and artistic upheaval that coincided with the rise of conflicting schools of philosophy, and, in art, a new iconography and style combined with vestigial elements from the Shang and Early Chou periods. During the next 400 years, a radically different art was to develop.

CH'IN AND HAN

The political chaos of the last few hundred years of the Chou dynasty was temporarily halted by Shih Huang Ti, ruler of the state of Ch'in (hence, the name "China"), whose powerful armies conquered all rival states. Shih Huang Ti became the first emperor of China, establishing totalitarian control over most of the country between 221–210 B.C. His reign was signalized by the building of the Great Wall and by his attempt to eradicate old traditions by destroying all historical books and burying alive thousands of Confucian scholars.

In 1974, the immense tomb mound of Shih Huang Ti was discovered in Shensi, and its excavation, which is still proceeding, has revealed an astonishing collection of monuments, making this tomb mound one of the great archeological discoveries of modern times. More than 6,000 life-size clay figures of soldiers and horses—and, more recently, bronze horses and chariots—have been found. Replicating the invincible hosts of the emperor, they serve as the immortal imperial bodyguard (FIGS. 12-4 and 12-5), deployed in a vast, underground funerary palace designed to match the fabulous palace occupied by

*From the *Li Chi* attributed to Confucius, translated by James Legge, *The Sacred Books of the East* (New York: Clarendon Press, 1966), Vol. 28, p. 464.

12-4 *Soldiers of the Imperial Bodyguard*, tomb of emperor Shih Huang Ti, Shensi, 221–206 B.C. Painted ceramic, life-size.

the emperor in life. Both palaces were described by the ancient historian Sima Quian (136–85 B.C.), whose account was not taken seriously until these recent discoveries validated it. The statues, originally in vivid color, were arranged in long ranks and files, as if lined up for battle: infantry, cavalry, horses and chariots, archers, lancers, and hand-to-hand fighters. The style of the Ch'in warriors blends Archaic formalism—simplicity of volume and contour, rigidity, frontality—with sharp realism of detail. Set poses are repeated with little or no variation, as if from a single mold, but subtle differences in details of facial features, coiffures, and equipment are delineated. An unarmed warrior assumes the watchful stance of a fighter skilled in hand-to-hand combat, presumably similar to *karate* (FIG. 12-5). He is in line with scores of other figures exactly matching his pose and gesture.

On the death of Shih Huang Ti, the people of Ch'in revolted, and a new dynasty—the Han—was founded in 206 B.C. A powerful, centralized government extended the southern and western boundaries of China. Chinese armies penetrated far into Turkestan, and indirect trade was maintained with distant Rome. Confucianists struggled with Taoists (followers of the mystic philosophy of Lao-tzu) for control of governmental power. The Confucianists eventually won, although the formalized Confucianism that triumphed was far removed from the teachings of the master. The Confucian legends of filial piety and the folklore of Taoism together provided most of the subject matter of Han art.

The Han pictorial style is known from a few extant paintings and many stone reliefs as well as stamped pottery tiles. In some paintings, the outlines of figures are rendered in the characteristic Chinese line, with calligraphic elasticity that conveys not only outline but depth and mass as well. Overlapping of arms and drapery further emphasizes the third dimension, while flat colors, applied within contours, accent the rhythmic relationship between figures. There is no background or any other indication of environment.

Numerous stone reliefs from the Wu family shrines in Shantung (c. A.D. 150) also reflect modes of Han pictorial representation. On the slabs, scenes from history and folklore depict mythological beings associated with Taoism as well as exemplars of Confucian piety. The story unfolds in images of flat polished stone against an equally flat, though roughly striated,

12-5 *Soldier Poised for Hand-to-Hand Combat*, tomb of emperor Shih Huang Ti. Painted ceramic, life-size.

12-6 *Mythological Scenes*, Wu family shrine, Shantung, Late Han dynasty, 147–168. Rubbing of stone relief approx. 60" long.

ground (FIG. 12-6). The rounded figures are related by the linear rhythms of their contours. In addition, buildings and trees now indicate a milieu. Space, however, is conceptual, as in Egyptian painting, and distance is suggested by the superposition of figures, although, curiously enough, chariot wheels overlap. Individuals of importance are shown hierarchically, in larger size than their subordinates. Most interesting are the trees, which are highly stylized as masses of intertwined branches bearing isolated, overlarge leaves. Yet within this schematic form, some accidental variation in a twisted branch or broken bough shows how the designer's generalization derived from the observation of specific trees and how a detail of the particular can individualize the general. It is this subtle relationship between the specific and the abstract that will become one of the most important esthetic attributes of later Chinese painting.

A group of reliefs from Szechwan, although similar to those of the Wu tombs and probably of the same date, are further advanced. Rhythms are more rapid, and space and the environment are more fully stated. Some subjects concern everyday life, in contrast to the earlier preoccupation with mythological or historical themes. There is also a figure of the Buddha—probably the earliest in China and therefore the first reference to the religion that was to dominate Chinese thought for the next 1,000 years.

A superb example of Han bronze craft, in the tradition of the Chinese mastery of that metal since Shang times, is a recently discovered (1969) figure of a horse (FIG. 12-7) from a tomb in Kansu. Although its action

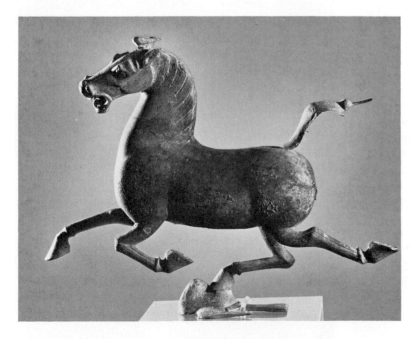

12-7 *Flying Horse Poised on One Leg on a Swallow*, from a tomb at Wuwei, Kansu, Late Han dynasty, second century. Bronze, 13½" high, 17¾" long. The exhibition of archeological finds of the People's Republic of China.

12-8 Funeral suit of the Princess Tou Wan, Mancheng, Hopei, Early Han dynasty, late second century B.C. Jade tablets sewn with gold wire; suit is 68″ long. The exhibition of archeological finds of the People's Republic of China.

is certainly that of a quick trot, it seems to be flying, one hoof lightly poised on a swallow, its single point of attachment to its pedestal. The horse, because it was revered for its power and majesty, has a prominence in Chinese art tantamount to that of the lion or bull in the art of the Near East.

A second-century B.C. Han tomb unearthed in 1968 appears to confirm our knowledge of the use of jade. As noted earlier with respect to the Late Chou *pi* (FIG. 12-3), jade was believed to have had magical properties protective of the dead. The tomb, in Hopei (formerly Chihli), contained the remains of a prince and princess, each of whom had originally been masked and completely outfitted in suits (FIG. 12-8) composed of over 2,000 jade tablets, expertly cut, fitted, and sewn together with gold wire—an extraordinary technical feat.

THREE KINGDOMS
THROUGH SUI

Buddhism (pp. 419–20), whose spirit was profoundly different from the ancient and native philosophies of China, was introduced by the first century of the Christian era. During the last 100 years of Han rule and the succeeding Three Kingdoms period, China, splintered by strife, grasped eagerly at a new ideal by which to live. The Confucian system of ethics had proved unable to adapt itself to the anarchy of the times, and Taoism, having degenerated into magic and superstition, no longer appealed to the philosophic mind. Buddhism offered the Chinese masses the promise of hope beyond the troubles of this world. In addition, its fully developed system of logic—refined to the point of surpassing any previous Chinese system of thought—attracted the intellectuals. Buddhist missionaries from India, working at first with the ruling families, spread their gospel so

successfully that their teachings ran like wildfire through China.

The arts flourished in the service of the imported religion. Following the brief Three Kingdoms period in the third century, China entered an era of political confusion, known as the period of the Northern and Southern dynasties, which fostered many short-lived states. Native Chinese dynasties, centered at Nanking, ruled in the south. Most of the Buddhist art surviving from this period, however, originated in the northern states, which were ruled by barbarian peoples who rapidly adopted Chinese ways and culture. A new esthetic developed in imitation of Indian or central Asian models that was in harmony with the prescribed formalism of Buddhist doctrine. The earliest important Buddhist image—a gilt-bronze statuette of *Sakyamuni Buddha* (FIG. 12-9), dated, by inscrip-

12-9 *Sakyamuni Buddha*, Northern and Southern dynasties, 338. Gilt bronze, 15½″ high, 9⅝″ wide. Asian Art Museum of San Francisco, The Avery Brundage Collection.

tion, in the year 338—is clearly related, in both style and iconography, to the prototype conceived and developed at Gandhara (FIG. 11-10).* The heavy concentric folds of the robe, the *ushnisha* on the head, and the cross-legged position all derived ultimately from the Indian prototype, examples of which had been brought to China by pilgrims and priests who had made the hazardous journey along the desert trade routes of central Asia.

The Chinese artist transformed the basic Indian pattern during the following century or so. These changes may be observed in a series of great cave temples that were carved into the hillsides after the fashion of the early Buddhists in India. At Tunhwang, westernmost gateway to China, over 300 sanctuaries were cut into the loess cliffs, the walls decorated with paintings, and the chambers adorned with images of clay. This site was dedicated in 366, but the earliest extant caves date from the late fifth century. About the same time, in 460, sculptors at Yunkang, near Tatung in northern China, were carving temples in cliffs of sandstone. Although the materials are different, both sites have an Archaic style

*Yet so new was the icon and its meaning that the Chinese craftsman, although endeavoring to make an image faithful to prescription, nevertheless erred in representing the canonical *mudra* of meditation: the Buddha's hands are clasped across his stomach, whereas they should be turned palms upward, with thumbs barely touching (FIG. 11-12).

similar to the sculpture of the sixth century B.C. in Greece and of the early twelfth century in France. Like their Western counterparts, the faces of the cave figures are carved in sharp planes and their drapery is conventionalized into angular patterns; considered as a whole, they too express the intense and noble dignity of a deeply felt religion (FIG. 12-10). The Buddhist concept of divinity may be seen in the caves of Yunkang, where the image of the Buddha—a blend of conventional restraint and religious fervor—became human enough for popular recognition but remained sufficiently idealized to carry the worshiper beyond the image to the abstraction it symbolized.

In 494, the Wei Tatars, staunch Buddhists who had supported the colossal program at Yunkang, moved their court southward to Loyang in Honan. Near there, in the limestone cliffs of Lungmen, another series of caves was started, where the first phase of work continued until the first part of the sixth century. The new carvings reveal elongated body and facial types and a fluid elegance in rendering drapery folds that reflect the influence of native Chinese styles, including those of painting. An air of courtly sophistication appears, especially in some of the secular figures of imperial donors. The new linearity and elongation, combined with pure body volumes and balanced poses, resulted in many images that harmonized religious sincerity with extraordinary grace of design.

While the Lungmen caves were being worked on, the people's imagination was captured by a new form of Buddhism, promoted by various Paradise Sects, that promised rebirth in a Buddhist paradise rich in the material pleasures denied to most in this world. As an idyllic existence in this paradise could be gained merely by faith in the word of the Buddha, many who might have failed to appreciate the goal of nirvana and the ultimate extinction of personality were won over to Buddhism by the more tangible and attractive goal offered by the Paradise Sects. Glories beyond those even of the imperial court were thus offered to every man who put his trust in the Buddha. The pleasant aspirations of these Buddhists were reflected in the greater naturalism of their arts, particularly the humanization of the deity. Thus, it is no wonder that, by the time the Paradise Sects reached their peak in the Sui dynasty, the Buddha had been gradually transformed from an archaic image of divine perfection into a gentle and human savior. The transition is manifest in a gilt-bronze shrine (FIG. 12-11), which also reflects the attenuated

12-10 Colossal Buddha, from Cave XX, Yunkang, Shansi, Northern and Southern dynasties, *c.* 460. Sandstone, 45' high.

12-11 *Prabhutaratna and Sakyamuni,* Northern and Southern dynasties, *c.* 518. Gilt bronze, 10½″ high. Musée Guimet, Paris.

Lungmen style. Prabhutaratna (Buddha of the remote past) listens to the sermon by Sakyamuni, the most recent Buddha. Seated within flame-like aureoles, their graceful, slender figures are almost absorbed into the rhythmic fall and flow of linear drapery that is beginning to acquire the character of cloth. The humanization is manifest in the gentle, suave beauty of attitude and gesture, although the faces retain the characteristics of Archaic formulas.

A comparable development of Buddhist images can be observed in the richly painted walls of the Tunhwang sanctuaries, which were calculated to inspire in the worshiper the splendor of Buddhism and (like Medieval paintings) to instruct the illiterate. Hieratic figures of the Buddha are surrounded by illustrations of stories about past lives (jataka). The formalized patterns of the individual Buddhas are like those of the sculptured images at Yunkang and Lungmen. But the narrative scenes carry on the traditions of Han painting, especially in the cell-like composition, in the leaping rhythms, and in the disproportionate relationship of figures to diminutive, conventionalized settings.

By 539, most traces of central Asian influence had disappeared. Like the sculpture of the time, Buddhist painting responded to the happy credo of the Paradise Sects with increasing naturalism and grace. Although the Buddha groups retained the strict frontality and rigid balance of ritualistic art, the jataka tales expanded haphazardly over the temple walls, their figures—now slim, elegant, and emancipated from their compartmental designs—moving freely over the plane surface. By the end of the century, the abstract environment of the painted figures began to be three-dimensional. Overlapping was used to create depth, and a sense of reality was further heightened by surrounding the celestial groups with such earthly phenomena as trees, pavilions, lotus ponds, and bridges.

It was especially at the courts of the Southern dynasties that painting flourished during this period. Taoist nature cults and a new appreciation of landscape themes in poetry provided the background for the early development of landscape painting. No scrolls from the hands of individual masters have survived from this early era, but descriptive texts indicate that the almost magical potential of landscape painting to re-create and organize the experience of nature or to transport the viewer to an imaginary realm was already well appreciated. When the painter TSUNG PING (373–443), for example, became too old to continue his mountain wanderings, he recreated favorite landscapes on the walls of his studio so that he could take imaginary journeys. Of the representational power of painting, Ping wrote:

Nowadays, when I spread out my silk to catch the distant scene, even the form of the K'un-lun [Mountain] may be captured within a square inch of space; a vertical stroke of three inches equals a height of several thousand feet. . . . By such means as this, the beauty of the Sung and Hua Mountains and the very soul of the *Hsuan-p'in* [Dark Spirit of the Universe] may all be embraced within a single picture. . . .*

Another fifth-century painter, WANG WEI, elaborated on the re-creative potential of landscape painting:

I unroll a picture and examine it, and reveal mountains and seas unfamiliar to me. The wind scatters in the verdant forests, the torrent overflows in bubbling foam. Ah, how could this be achieved merely by the skillful use of hands and fingers? The spirit must also exercise control over it. For this is the essence of painting.†

The painter and essayist KU K'AI-CHIH (c. 344–406) is one of the few individual artists from this period to whom extant paintings have been seriously attributed. In an essay on landscape painting couched in Taoist terms, he describes "crags, fang-like and tapering," and "rocks, split with fissures as though torn by lightning." But for Ku K'ai-chih and others of his time, the crucial aspect of painting was not mere imitation of appearance but transmission of "spiritual quality." Indeed, in the late fifth century the critic Hsieh Ho gave, as the first of the "Six Principles" of painting, "spirit-consonance engendering movement"—a sense of animation through transmission of the vital spirit that pervades both artist and object—which was to remain the cardinal principle for artists and critics until modern times.

Something of this vital spirit appears in a horizontal scroll attributed to Ku K'ai-chih called *Admonitions of the Instructress to the Court Ladies*, perhaps an early copy of a painting of Ku's era. Scrolls in this format were meant to be viewed slowly and in sections; in this case, scenes are illustrated between passages of explanatory text. One of the sections depicts a well-known act of heroism in which the Lady Feng saved the life of her emperor by placing herself between him and an attacking bear (FIG. 12-12). There is no background and only a minimal setting for the scene, but fluid poses and fluttering ribbons of drapery, in concert with individualized facial expressions, convey the quality of animation called for in texts of the period.

*For this and other excerpts from essays on painting quoted subsequently, see Michael Sullivan, *The Birth of Landscape Painting in China* (Berkeley: University of California Press, 1962).

†Ibid.

12-12　Attributed to Ku K'ai-chih (c. 344–406), *Lady Feng and the Bear*, section of the *Admonitions of the Instructress to the Court Ladies*. Horizontal scroll, ink and colors on silk, 7⅝" high. British Museum, London.

T'ANG

The short-lived Sui dynasty (581–618) was followed by the T'ang empire, under which China entered a period of unequaled magnificence. Chinese armies marched to the ends of central Asia, opening a path for the flow of wealth, ideas, and foreign peoples. Arab traders, Nestorian Christians, and other travelers journeyed to the cosmopolitan capital of the T'ang, and the Chinese, in turn, adventured westward. During the middle of the seventh century, Hsüan Tsang, a Chinese monk, visited India, as had some earlier devotees, and returned from the mother country of Buddhism with revolutionizing doctrines of the recently developed Esoteric Sects. It was a critical moment for Buddhism, which was being brought into disrepute by a lax court and a corrupt clergy. Under the notorious Empress Wu, who had usurped the throne, the religion was used as an instrument for political power and as a cloak for personal excesses. The material rewards promised in heaven by the Paradise Sects offered no effective antidote to the troubles of the time. But the elaborate and mysterious rituals of the new Esoteric Sects attracted worshipers by giving them in their daily life many of the sensory pleasures that the Paradise Sects had promised in heaven. As the new cult spread, the Chinese craftsman again looked to India, where he found appropriate models in the sculpture of the time.

The fluid style of art developed during the Gupta period in India (FIGS. 11-13 and 11-14) had already affected Chinese sculpture during the late sixth century, and, by the end of the seventh, Buddhist sculpture in China had lost much of its own character in its borrowing from the sensuous carvings of India. Fleshiness increased even more, and drapery was made to cling, as if wet, against the bodies. The new wave of influence from India brought not only stylistic changes but also the iconography of the Esoteric Sects, which we see in figures with multiple arms and heads, symbolizing various aspects of the deities as described in the new gospels.

The Early T'ang style under Indian influence is admirably exemplified by the *Bodhisattva* (FIG. 12-13). The sinuous beauty of this figure has been accented by the hipshot pose and revealing drapery, as in Gupta sculpture. Executed at almost the same time as the Bodhisattva (around 700) were carvings in the caves of Tien-lung Shan, which anticipated the later T'ang style. These cave figures might seem gross were it not for the graceful postures and the soft drapery that falls in rhythmic patterns over the plump bodies.

Esoteric Buddhism, with its emphasis on detailed and complicated ritual, placed the deity in a formal relationship to the worshiper. The followers of Amitabha Buddha—one of the most important Buddhas of the Paradise Sects—in stressing salvation by

12-13 *Bodhisattva*, Early T'ang dynasty, seventh and eighth centuries. Marble. Private collection of Charles Uht, New York.

faith, visualized a warm and human deity, but, by the ninth century, the arduous discipline of the Esoteric Sects had inspired an austere, heavy-set, almost repellent icon. At times, fleshiness was exaggerated almost to the point of obesity, and yet sufficient restraint lent the figures a somber dignity.*

The westward expansion of the T'ang empire increased the importance of Tunhwang. Here, the desert routes converged and the cave temples profited from the growing prosperity of the people. By the eighth century, wealthy donors to Buddha were

*Few sculptures survived the terrible persecutions of Buddhism during a revival of Confucianism in 845. Many wooden temples were destroyed by fire, and their bronze images were melted down. Fortunately, we are able to reconstruct the style of the period from Buddhist art in Japan, which was then under direct Chinese influence (see FIGS. 13-2, 13-3, 13-4).

demanding larger and more elaborately decorated caves. The comparatively simple Buddha group in paintings of the previous century was enlarged to include crowds of attendant figures, lavish architectural settings, and minor deities who worshiped the resplendent Buddha with music and dance. The opulence of the T'ang style is reflected in the detailed richness of the brilliantly colored *Paradise Paintings* (shown is *Paradise of Amitabha*, FIG. 12-14). Vignettes flanking the Buddha group illustrate incidents from specific *sutras.* These little scenes, like the jataka tales in earlier caves, are usually set in landscapes painted in an altogether different style from that of the hieratic groups. Mountains, for example, are stacked one behind the other and painted in graded washes to give the impression of distance. (Yet, although each mountain is related to the adjacent peak through this device of atmospheric perspective, there is still no continuous perspective to give a sense of recession into the distance.)

The Confucian persecutions of 845 did not affect Tunhwang, which was then under Tibetan rule. Numerous paintings (murals and scrolls) were produced there, but in this region, isolated from the mainstream of Chinese culture, they remained static in style from the middle of the ninth century to the beginning of the eleventh century. Meanwhile, during the seventh and eighth centuries at the T'ang court in Changan (modern Sian)—perhaps the greatest city in the world during this period—a brilliant tradition of figure painting developed that, in its variety and balance, reflected the worldliness and self-assurance of the T'ang empire. Indeed, Chinese historians regard the Early T'ang dynasty as their "golden age" of figure painting. Glowing accounts by poets and critics and a few remaining examples of the paintings themselves permit us to understand this enthusiasm.

Wall paintings from the tomb of the T'ang princess Yung-t'ai (built in 706 near Changan) allow us to view court painting styles unobscured by problems of authenticity and reconstruction. The figures of *Palace Ladies* (FIG. 12-15) are arranged as if on a shallow stage; although there are no indications of background or setting, intervals between the two rows and the grouping of the figures in an oval suggest a consistent ground plane. The women are shown full-face and in three-quarter views from the front and the back. The device of paired figures facing into and out of the space of the picture in a near mirror image—an effective means of creating depth—appears often in paintings attributed to this period. Thick, even, contour lines describe full-volumed faces and suggest solid forms beneath the drapery, all with the utmost economy. This simplicity of form and drawing, along with the measured cadence of the poses, results in an

12-14 *Paradise of Amitabha*, Cave 139A, Tunhwang, Kansu, T'ang dynasty, ninth century. Wall painting.

air of monumental dignity befitting a daughter of the ruling house of the T'ang.

In perfect accord with descriptions of the robust T'ang style are the unrestored portions of *Portraits of the Emperors*, masterfully drawn in line and in colored washes by YEN LI-PEN, celebrated painter and statesman of the seventh century. Each emperor is repre-

sented as standing in undefined space, his eminence clearly indicated by his great size relative to that of his attendants. Yen Li-pen also made designs for a series of monumental and spirited stone horses that once flanked the approach to the tomb of the T'ang emperor T'ai Tsung.

The horse in Chinese art reflected the importance

12-15 *Palace Ladies*, from the tomb of Princess Yung-t'ai, near Changan (Sian), Shensi, T'ang dynasty, 706. Wall painting.

12-16 HAN KAN, *Horse*, T'ang dynasty, eighth century. Album leaf, ink on paper, 11$\frac{13}{16}$" high. Metropolitan Museum of Art, New York.

the emperors placed on the quality of their stables. Even Han emperors had sent missions westward to Bactria for blooded stock. Paintings of the finest among his 40,000 steeds were commissioned by the emperor Ming Huang (713–756), and one of these may be the picture of a tethered horse attributed to HAN KAN, Ming Huang's favorite painter of horses.

The fiery stallion (FIG. 12-16) evokes the dynamic "inner vitality" so stressed by Chinese critics.

Two of the most famous artists of the T'ang period were WANG WEI (699–759), not to be confused with Wang Wei of the fifth century, and WU TAO-TZǔ (active *c.* 725–750), both of whom have become almost legendary figures, although none of their paintings

12-17 T'ang tomb figurines, seventh to ninth century: *left:* Peddler 24$\frac{1}{2}$" high, Portland Art Museum, Portland, Oregon; *middle:* Dancer 10$\frac{3}{4}$" high, Nelson Gallery-Atkins Museum, Kansas City, Missouri; *below:* Horse 14$\frac{1}{4}$" high, Fogg Art Museum, Harvard University, Cambridge, Massachusetts.

has survived. Wang was not only a painter; like so many Chinese artists, he was also a poet. His poems are mellow and lyrical, as his paintings are said to have been. Numerous imitations of his painting style have the peaceful lyricism of his poems. Many of these copies are of snow scenes, a favorite subject of Chinese artists, probably due to its adaptability to monochrome painting, an art of infinite variation and contrast in black and white. Wu's work, according to reports of his time, was very different. He painted with such speed and "ferocious energy" and over such large surfaces that people are said to have watched with awe as astonishingly real images rapidly appeared. His bold brushwork and expansive forms were frequently copied, and rubbings were made from engraved replicas. Later artists looked to Wu's virtuoso brushwork and to Wang's subtle harmonies for their models.

The T'ang rulers embellished their empire with extravagant wooden structures, all of which have disappeared. Judging from records, however, they were of colossal size and colorfully painted. Bronze mirrors with decorations in strong relief added to T'ang luxury and to the furnishings of a court already enriched by elaborate gold and silver ornaments.

The potter met the demand for display by covering his wares with colorful lead glazes and by inventing robust shapes with clearly articulated parts—base, body, and neck. Earlier potters had imitated bronze models, but the T'ang craftsman derived his directly from the character of the clay. Ceramic figures of people, domesticated animals, and fantastic creatures were also made by the thousands for burial in tombs (FIG. 12-17). The extraordinarily delicate grace and flowing rhythms of these figures have a charm and vivacity seldom equaled in ceramic design. Their subject matter, which included such diverse figures as Greek acrobats and Semitic traders, is proof of the cosmopolitanism of T'ang China.

FIVE DYNASTIES AND NORTHERN SUNG

The last century of T'ang rule witnessed the gradual disintegration of the empire. When the dynasty finally fell in 906, China was once more left to the ravages of civil war. Conflicting claims between rival states were not resolved until the country was consolidated under the Sung, whose court was at Pienching (modern Kaifeng in Honan). During the interim of internal strife known as the Five Dynasties (906–960), there was a marked development in the styles and techniques of landscape painting. An analogy with events of the period of the Northern and Southern dynasties may be justified here; that earlier period of political and social turmoil also witnessed a turning away from society toward an involvement with nature and an accompanying development of landscape art.

CHING HAO, who flourished during the first half of the tenth century, left an essay in which he listed his criteria for judging paintings. Under the classification of "divine" he grouped the greatest paintings. In these, he wrote, "there appears no trace of human effort; hands spontaneously reproduce natural forms." In the lowest category, he placed the "skillful" artist who "cuts out and pieces together fragments of beauty and welds them into the pretense of a masterpiece. . . ." "This," he added, "is owing to the poverty of inner reality and to the excess of outward form." Although these ideas were not original with Ching Hao, his restatement of them shows the continuity of thought underlying Chinese painting regardless of changing styles. The artist who painted the truth beneath surface appearances had to be imbued with ch'i, the "divine spirit" of the universe. The man who achieved this had done so through years of self-cultivation. Ching Hao and his equally famous contemporary LI CH'ENG, through the inherent power of their personalities, departed from T'ang landscape formulas, breathing life into every twig and rock they painted. Succeeding generations went to their works for inspiration—great artists, to catch the spirit; lesser painters, to copy tricks for drawing trees and hills.

We know enough about the art of this period to distinguish the styles of some individual masters, such as TUNG YUAN and CHU-JAN, of the mid-tenth century, and FAN K'UAN and KUO HSI, active early and late, respectively, in the eleventh century. Paintings by the latter two artists, which exemplify the maturity of landscape painting styles in the Northern Sung period, express very different personalities and yet exhibit a common feeling for monumentality. A characteristic painting in this style presents a vertical landscape of massive mountains rising from the distance (FIG. 12-18). Human figures, reduced to minute proportions, are dwarfed by overwhelming forms in nature. Paths and bridges in the middle region vanish, only to reappear in such a way as to lead the spectator on a journey through the landscape—a journey facilitated by shifting perspective points. No single vanishing point organizes the entire perspective, as in many Western paintings; as a result, the observer's eye moves with freedom. But to appreciate these paintings fully, one must focus on intricate details and on the character of each line.

The full development of the horizontal handscroll occurred during this period. The scroll, which might measure as long as 50 feet, had to be unrolled from right to left; only a small section could be seen at a

12-18 FAN K'UAN, *Travelers Among Mountains and Streams*, Northern Sung dynasty, early eleventh century. Hanging scroll, ink and colors on silk, 6' 9" × 2' 5". Collection of the National Palace Museum, Taipei, Taiwan.

artist. Representational accuracy was deemphasized, even derided, in favor of learned allusions to Antique styles, sometimes couched in deliberately awkward or naïve forms. Many paintings in this style concentrate on qualities inherent in the medium of brush and ink. In this, they are close to the expressiveness of calligraphy, which depends, for its effects, on the controlled vitality of individual brush strokes and on the dynamic relationships of strokes within a character and among the characters themselves. Training in calligraphy was a fundamental part of the education and self-cultivation of scholars and officials; with Su Tung-p'o and Mi Fu, ranked among the greatest of Northern Sung calligraphers, calligraphic qualities and effects became part of the repertory of many painters as well.

The emperor HUI TSUNG (ruled 1101–1125), an avid collector and patron of art, was himself an important painter. He is known particularly for his meticulous pictures of birds, in which almost every feather is carefully drawn in sharp lines. Lesser artists attached to the imperial court functioned as a sort of academy and, in general, followed the detailed and colorful style of the emperor. Illustrating some lines of poetry in painting often served as an examination for court office. Fans painted by master artists were treasured in albums. But while the court spent its energy on esthetic refinements, less cultured neighbors were assaulting the frontiers of China.

SOUTHERN SUNG

In 1127, as a result of increasing pressure from the Tatars and Mongols in the west and north, the capital of China was moved to the south. From then until 1279, the Southern Sung court lived out its days amid the tranquil beauties of Hangchow. Neo-Confucianism—a blend of traditional Chinese thought and some Buddhist concepts—became the leading philosophy. Accordingly, orthodox Buddhism declined. Buddhist art continued to develop in the north, where a Tatar tribe had established itself as the Chin dynasty, but it stagnated in the south. Buddhist sculpture in the Southern Sung period merely added grace and elegance to the T'ang style. Secular paintings and those associated with Ch'an (a meditative school of Buddhism), however, reflected a new and more intimate relationship between man and nature.

A typical Southern Sung landscape is basically asymmetrical. It is composed on a diagonal and consists of three parts (foreground, middle distance, and far distance), separated from each other by a field of mist. The first is marked by a rock, which, by its position in the foreground, emphasizes the distance of the other parts. The middle distance may be marked by a flat cliff or given over entirely to mist or water,

time and then, properly, by only two or three persons. The organization of these paintings has been compared to the composition of a symphony because of the way in which motifs are repeated and moods are varied in the different sections. The temporal sequence of the scroll involved memory as well as vision; it was an art of contemplation and leisure.

Among the versatile figures clustered around the court at this time was SU TUNG-P'O (SU SHIH, 1036–1101), one of China's greatest poets, a celebrated painter and statesman. Another, LI KUNG-LIN (LI LUNG-MIEN, 1040–1106), was famous for his original Buddhist compositions and for his outline drawings of horses. These, along with the antiquarian and landscapist MI FU (1052–1109), were the leading figures in a group of scholar–gentlemen painters who created an alternative to the emphasis on the skillful representation of nature then prevailing among professional and academy artists. These amateurs of the "literary" school, by contrast, saw painting as primarily expressive of the moods and personality of the

12-19 MA YUAN, *Bare Willows and Distant Mountains,*
Southern Sung dynasty, thirteenth century. Album leaf, ink
and colors on silk, $9\frac{1}{2}'' \times 9\frac{1}{2}''$. Museum of Fine Arts, Boston.

12-20 LIANG K'AI, *The Sixth Ch'an Patriarch Chopping
Bamboo,* Southern Sung dynasty, thirteenth century. Hanging
scroll, ink on paper, $29\frac{1}{4}''$ high. Tokyo National Museum.

and, in the far distance, mountain peaks, which are
usually tinted in pale blue, suggest the infinity of
space. The whole composition illustrates the manner
in which the Sung artists used great voids to hold
solid masses in equilibrium. The technique is one of
China's unique contributions to the art of painting.
To this basic composition, of which there were many
variations, the artist frequently added the figure of a
scholar meditating under a gnarled pine tree and accompanied by an attendant. Such paintings were
expressions of the artist's ideal of peace and pantheistic unity.

The chief painters in the Southern Sung style were
MA YUAN (*c.* 1190–1224) and HSIA KUEI (*c.* 1180–
1230). Ma was a master of suggestion, as demonstrated by a small, fan-shaped album leaf—a picture
of tranquility stated in a few sensitively balanced and
half-seen shapes (FIG. 12-19). Hsia Kuei's misty landscapes were often so like those of Ma Yuan—though
sometimes more delicate and sometimes bolder—
that the Chinese refer to them and to their followers
as the Ma–Hsia School. But the Ma–Hsia tradition,
despite its gentle beauty, could not be maintained. It
perpetuated an ephemeral, classic moment, but the
serenity of its beliefs was soon threatened by political
realities.

As orthodox Buddhism lost ground under the
Sung, the new school of Buddhism—called Ch'an in
China, but better known by its Japanese name, Zen—
gradually gained importance, until it was second
only to Neo-Confucianism. The Zen sect traced its
semi-legendary origins to Bodhidharma, an Indian

missionary of the sixth century. By the time of the
Sixth Patriarch, who lived during the early T'ang period, the pattern of the school was already established, and Zen remains an important religion in
Japan today.

The followers of Zen repudiate texts, ritual, and
charms as instruments of enlightenment. They believe, instead, that the means of salvation lies within
the individual, that meditation is useful, and that direct personal experience with some ultimate reality is
the necessary step to enlightenment. Zen enlightenment is conceived as a sudden, almost spontaneous
act. These beliefs shaped a new art.

LIANG K'AI, a Zen painter of the thirteenth century,
has left us two portraits of Hui Neng, the Sixth Patriarch. In one, the patriarch is a crouching figure chopping bamboo (FIG. 12-20); in the other, he is tearing

12-21 *Mei-p'ing* vase, Sung dynasty. *Tz'u-chou* stoneware, carved black slip over white, 19½″ high, 7¾″ wide. Asian Art Museum of San Francisco, The Avery Brundage Collection.

up a Buddhist sutra. Both are informal sketches that look as though they were caricatures of the revered figure. The brush strokes are staccato and splintery, like the spontaneous process of Zen enlightenment. They probably were painted in a few minutes, but, like enlightenment, they required years of training. Their impact can be a shock, much like the shock of Zen understanding.

Southern Sung artists also produced superb ceramics with monochrome glazes. The most famous of the single-glaze wares are known as *celadon*, (a mat gray–green), *ying-ch'ing* (a subtle pale blue), and *ting* (a fine, white protoporcelain). There was also the heavier *chun* ware, in which a blue glaze, splashed with red and purple, flowed over a stoneware body. A quite different kind of pottery, loosely classed as *tz'u-chou*, is a type of northern Chinese ceramic in which,

during the Sung period, the subtle techniques of underglaze painting and incision of the design through a colored slip were developed. The intricate black-white design of the *mei-p'ing* vase shown (FIG. 12-21) was produced by cutting through a black to a white slip. Here, the tightly twining vine and petal motifs closely embrace the high-shouldered vessel in a perfect accommodation of surface design to vase shape, so common in Chinese pottery in its great periods. These shapes were generally more suave than those of the T'ang period; some, however, reflecting the prevailing interest in archeology, imitated the powerful forms of the Shang and Chou bronzes. Other crafts, particularly jade carving, were also subjected to the influence of archeological or antiquarian interests.

YÜAN

The artistic vitality of Southern Sung was not a reflection of the political condition of the times. In 1279, the Sung dynasty crumbled beneath the continued onslaughts of Kublai Khan. Yüan, the dynasty of the Mongol invaders, dominated China only until 1368, yet it profoundly affected the culture of the country and particularly the art of painting. Many scholar–painters chose exile in the provinces rather than service to the barbarian usurpers in Peking. Forced by their exile to reappraise their place in the world, these artists looked at a landscape no longer as an idyllic retreat but as part of a formidable environment. This new austerity is evident in a painting (FIG. 12-22) by one of the great masters of Yüan, HUANG KUNG-WANG (1269–1354). Here, the misty atmosphere of the Southern Sung landscapes has been replaced by textureful, massive forms. The inner structure and momentum of the landscape is rendered by a rhythmic play of brush and ink.

Another leader of the Yüan scholar–artist movement was CHAO MENG-FU (1254–1322), whose paintings contain knowing allusions to old styles. The landscapes of his grandson WANG MENG (d.1385) reached a high level of dynamic, expressive intensity. Most of these painters rejected the mellow harmonies of Southern Sung as no longer valid; for their sources, they went back to the more monumental works of the tenth century. The degree to which styles could become personalized in this period is shown in the spare, almost brittle landscapes and bamboo-and-rock paintings of NI TSAN (1301–1374), which reveal an aloof and fastidious personality. They contrast with the paintings of WU CHEN (1280–1354), done in a softer and more relaxed manner. Paintings of bamboo (FIG. 12-23), for which Wu Chen is famous, were

12-22 HUANG KUNG-WANG, *Dwelling in the Fu-ch'un Mountains,* Yüan dynasty, 1347–1350. Section of a horizontal scroll, ink on paper, 13″ high. National Palace Museum, Taipei, Taiwan.

particularly favored at this time, for that plant is a symbol of the ideal Chinese gentleman, who, in adversity, bends but does not break. Moreover, the pattern of leaves, like that of calligraphic script, provided an excellent opportunity for the display of brushwork.

The Mongol regime apparently did little to disturb the Chinese potters' increasing mastery of porcelain. A Late Yüan or Early Ming vase of white porcelain (FIG. 12-24), discovered in 1961, exhibits brilliance in the use of the underglaze decoration that was so successful in the Sung period.

12-23 WU CHEN, *Bamboo,* Yüan dynasty, 1350. Album leaf, ink on paper, 16″ × 21″. Collection of the National Palace Museum, Taipei, Taiwan.

12-24 Covered vase (excavated at Peking), Late Yüan or Early Ming dynasty, late fourteenth century. White porcelain with underglaze decoration, 26½″ high. The exhibition of archeological finds of the People's Republic of China.

MING, CH'ING, AND LATER DYNASTIES

In 1368, a popular uprising drove out the hated Mongol overlords, and, from that time until 1644, China was ruled by the native Ming dynasty. Many of the fifteenth-century Ming masters, such as TAI CHIN (1388–1452), reverted to Sung models. The court, where Tai Chin worked, was one center of patronage and activity; local schools of painting, such as those centered in Nanking and in Soochow (modern Wuhsien), also became important. The Soochow School, under the leadership of SHEN CHOU (1427–1509) and WEN CHENG-MING (1470–1559), included a number of highly educated amateur painters who concentrated on refined re-creations of the styles of the masters of the preceding Yüan dynasty. Professional artists, active in Soochow and elsewhere, executed works that displayed great skill and spontaneity.

The distinction between scholar–amateur and academic–professional traditions was codified, rather artificially, in the writings of the influential critic, statesman, and artist TUNG CH'I-CH'ANG (1555–1636) at the end of the Ming period. Tung's glorification of the amateur or literary school reflected his own voracious study and collecting of old paintings. Tung's theories promoted the creation of an orthodoxy in later art that could be stifling, but his own works were true to his ideal of the transformation of old styles, rather than the sterile imitation of them. In Tung's landscapes, there is often a radical reorganization of forms in an attempt to reveal the inner structure and momentum of nature (FIG. 12-25). Ground planes are allowed to tilt or shift; this—and the bold arrangement of rocks and trees to emphasize repeated abstract shapes and textures, heedless of natural scale and surface qualities—may seem arbitrarily distorted, or even crude. What is lost in harmony of surface or representational accuracy, however, is more than made up in qualities of monumentality and power. Paintings by Tung and other masters during the period of social and intellectual readjustment at the end of the Ming dynasty created an atmosphere of artistic freedom; the artists who lived into the next dynasty were its beneficiaries.

The internal decay of Ming bureaucracy permitted another group of invaders, the Manchus, to overrun the country. Established as the Ch'ing dynasty (1644–1912), these northerners quickly adapted themselves to Chinese life. The early emperors cultivated a knowledge of China's arts, but their influence seems merely to have encouraged academic work. While the Yüan style continued to be fashionable among the conservatives, other painters experimented with extreme effects of massed ink or individualized patterns of brushwork. Bold and freely manipulated compositions began to appear that had a new, expressive force.

Two artists with intensely personal styles stand out against a mass of lesser painters of the period. The sketchy brush and wet-ink technique of CHU TA (1625–c. 1705) derived from sixteenth-century forerunners, but his subjects—whimsical animals or petulant birds tensely balanced on an album page—demonstrated his discontent with conventional themes. The theoretical writings of Chu Ta's great contemporary TAO-CHI (1641–c. 1717) called for a return to wellsprings of creativity through use of the "single brush stroke" or "primordial line" that was the root of all phenomena and representation. The figure in a hut in one of his album leaves (FIG. 12-26) is surrounded by the surging energy of free-floating colored dots and multiple, sinuous, contour lines that suggest the vital arteries of an organism. What is depicted is not so much the appearance of the landscape as the animating, molding forces that run through it—the prime focus of Chinese landscape art from the earliest times.

Some twentieth-century artists, such as CH'I PAI-SHIH, have found the free brush expressive and maintained the calligraphic tradition with vitality.

12-25 TUNG CH'I-CH'ANG, *Autumn Mountains*, Ming dynasty, early seventeenth century. Horizontal scroll, ink on paper, $15\frac{1}{8}'' \times 53\frac{7}{8}''$. Cleveland Museum of Art (purchase from the J.H. Wade Fund).

12-26 TAO-CHI, *Landscape*, Ch'ing dynasty, late seventeenth century. Album leaf, ink and colors on paper, 9½" × 11". C.C. Wang Collection, New York.

HSU PEI-HUNG, known for his boldly brushed pictures of horses, has imbued his work with social content, in keeping with China's political developments. The coming decades will reveal whether a popular art can assimilate the traditions of aristocratic painting that have dominated Chinese art for over a thousand years.

In ceramics, the technical ingenuity of the Ming and Ch'ing potters exceeded the skill of even the Sung potters. In general, porcelain was favored over pottery, with the exception of Ming stonewares, which were broadly decorated in "three-color" enamels. More delicate designs were painted on "five-color" wares, with enamels and underglaze painting on fine clay. The celebrated blue-and-white porcelains (FIG. 12-27) owe their quality as much to the distinction of their painted decoration as to the purity of their imported cobalt pigments. Craftsmen also devised a "secret," barely visible decoration that was carved into porcelain as thin as paper.

When the Manchus came into power in 1644, they continued to support the great kilns at Chingtehchen (modern Fowliang), where enormous quantities of excellent porcelains were made until the destruction of the kilns during warfare in the mid-nineteenth century. During the K'ang-hsi period (1662–1722), delicate glazes known as *clair de lune* (a silvery blue) and *peachbloom* (pink dappled with green) vied with

12-27 Vase, Ming dynasty, fifteenth century. Porcelain with blue underglaze decoration. Musée Guimet, Paris.

12-28 *Kuan-yin*, Early Ch'ing dynasty, seventeenth and eighteenth centuries. Fukien ware, white porcelain, 8⅞" high, 6¼" wide. Trustees of the Barlow Collection, University of Sussex, England.

the polychrome wares. Experiments with glazes led to the invention of the superb imperial yellow and oxblood monochromes. A brief revival of Sung simplicity occurred during the reign of Yung Chêng (1723–1735), but under Ch'ien Lung (1736–1795), a reaction against Sung simplicity led to a style that was sometimes more elaborate than artistic.

Fine embroidered and woven textiles, created for lavish court ceremonies, followed the general style of the age, becoming more intricate and, at the same time, more delicate.

During this long period, from the mid-seventeenth to the late eighteenth century, sculpture consisted

primarily of charming but inconsequential porcelain bibelots and jade and ivory carvings of an almost unbelievable technical perfection. An example of this work is the white porcelain *Kuan-yin*, goddess of compassion, from the Early Ch'ing dynasty (FIG. 12-28), which completes that long process of the humanization of the sacred Buddhist images that began even before the T'ang period (see FIG. 12-11). This lovely statuette, reflecting the culmination of the technical achievement of Chinese ceramists, embodies the Bodhisattva's quality of mercy in its softness of form. An easy play of line betrays the influence of painting on ceramics. This "white china ware" (*blanc-de-Chine*) was widely exported to Europe in the eighteenth century, and, in the West to this day, fine ceramic wares, especially porcelain, are called "china."

As the eighteenth century waned, huge workshops, much like our own production-line factories, continued to provide masses of materials for imperial use. Specialists, instead of designer–craftsmen, worked on each stage of manufacture. By the middle of the nineteenth century, this system had drained all vitality from the crafts.

The establishment of the People's Republic of China in 1949 has produced a social realism in art that is familiar to the world of the twentieth century (see pp. 916–17) and that breaks drastically with the Chinese art of tradition. Some carry on creative work based on the old traditions, but for most, the purpose of art now is, as the People's Republic would claim, to serve the people in the struggle to liberate and elevate the masses. In the work shown (FIG. 12-29), a life-sized tableau, the old times are grimly depicted in a scene common enough before the revolution. Peasants, worn and bent by toil, are bringing in their taxes (in the form of produce) to the courtyard of their merciless, plundering landlord. The message is clear: this

12-29 Anonymous team of sculptors, *The Rent Collection Courtyard* (detail of a larger tableau), Ta-yi, Szechwan, 1965. Clay-plaster, life-size.

kind of thing must not happen again. Significantly, the artists who depict the event are an anonymous team. The "name" artist belongs to the past; only collective action, say its theoreticians, can bring the transformations the People's Republic hopes for.

ARCHITECTURE

Little has been said about Chinese architecture, partly because few early buildings exist and partly because Chinese architecture has not displayed distinctive changes in style over the centuries. The modern Chinese building closely resembles its prototype of a thousand years ago. Indeed, the dominating silhouette of the roof, which gives Chinese architecture much of its specific character, may go back to Chou or Shang times. Even the simple buildings depicted on Han stone carvings reveal a style and a method of construction still basic to China. The essentials consist of a rectangular hall, dominated by a pitched roof with projecting eaves supported by a bracketing system and wooden columns. The walls serve no bearing function but act only as screening elements.

Within this limited formula, the Chinese architect has focused his attention on the superstructure. As early as the Han dynasty, combinations of brackets, impost blocks, and columns were devised to support the weight of massive, tiled roofs. The architects gave animation to the exterior by varying the shapes of the brackets. From these simple beginnings, later architects developed very intricate systems of support. Some brackets were placed parallel to the walls; others reached outward to support a beam or other brackets, until the multiplication of units created a rich pattern of light and shade. The effect was intensified by decorations in red and gold lacquer. Function was often subordinated to ornament; complicated bracket systems were sometimes introduced for decoration where only minimal support was required.

On the exterior, the coloristic interplay of the supports formed a pleasing contrast to the uninterrupted sweep of the pitched roof. The overhanging eaves became even wider during the T'ang period, and builders began to turn up the corners. These slightly curving eaves were exaggerated in later buildings, especially in south China, where they produced a riotous fantasy of upswept lines. But in most areas, the gentle curves of the roofs give an air of grace to the otherwise severe rectangular form and rigid symmetry that were imposed by the plans of the buildings. The style was imported by Japan along with Buddhism, and the Phoenix Hall of the Byodoin temple

12-30   Pagoda of the Temple of the Six Banyan Trees, Canton, Kwangtung, 537 (rebuilt 1098). 180' high.

at Ujiyamada, Japan (FIG. 13-12) may serve as a good example. For centuries, the orientation of buildings, even of whole cities, had been ordered on a strict north–south axis. Houses, palaces, temples, and official buildings all fell within one formal pattern. Even the seeming randomness of the varied bridges and pavilions in the informal gardens was carefully devised.

Buddhist architecture contributed a specific form— the *pagoda* (FIG. 12-30)—which, to many, has become a symbol of China. These pagoda towers, which dot the countryside and seem so native to the land, were derived from the Indian stupa (FIG. 11-5). Most of the wooden pagodas, with their multiplicity of winged eaves, bear little resemblance to the solid domes of Sanchi or Amaravati; but their origin, like that of the Chinese Buddha, is to be found in Gandhara, where terraced and towering variants of the stupa had once impressed Chinese pilgrams with their grandeur. So quickly was the stupa structure assimilated by the Chinese that even the earliest pagodas (sixth to eighth century) show only a few traces of their Indian origin. In the Chinese wooden idiom, all that remained of the Indian stupa were the *yasti* and parasols, which crowned that structure. Instead of a circular plan, the Chinese preferred a four-, six-, or eight-sided one, and story was piled on story to form towers as high as 300 feet. Each story was marked by its own projecting eaves, the curved lines of which soared into the sky.

13

JAPAN

MILES		
0	50	100

KILOMETERS		
0	80	160

HOKKAIDO

HOKKAIDO

Otaru • Sapporo

• Hakodate

SEA OF JAPAN

Niigata •

Sendai •

Kanazawa • • Toyama

HONSHU

Fukuoka •

• Hiroshima

Kyoto (Heian-kyo)

• Momoyama

Ashikaga •

• Nagasaki

• Nara

• Nagoya

Tokyo (Edo) •

SHIKOKU

• Ise

Kamakura •

KYUSHU

• Kagoshima

PACIFIC OCEAN

THE ART OF JAPAN

Ise Shrine

c. 3000 B.C.   B.C. A.D.   Imports from Asian mainland

JOMON CULTURE   ARCHAIC PERIOD

Copies of Chinese objects

Kondo

Haniwa figure

897   794   645   552

JOGAN PERIOD

NARA PERIOD   ASUKA PERIOD

Introduction of Buddhism

HEIAN PERIOD

TAKAYOSHI
The Tale of Genji
(c. 1150)

The Sage Kuya Invoking the Amida Buddha

SHUBUN   SESSHU
(1420–1506)

1185   1392

FUJIWARA PERIOD   KAMAKURA PERIOD   ASHIKAGA PERIOD

Lotus Sutra

Zen Buddhism begins rise

1573

MOMOYAMA PERIOD

Uji Bridge

1615

BUSON
(1716–1783)

1868   SOTATSU
(1576–1643)

MODERN JAPAN   TOKUGAWA (EDO) PERIOD

Katsura Palace and gardens
(1615–1663)

HOKUSAI
The Great Wave
(c. 1823–1829)

KIYOTADA
Dancing Kabuki Actor
(c. 1725)

HARUNOBU
(1725–1770)

THE ARTS OF JAPAN have neither the progressive, stylistic continuity of those of India nor the wide variety of those of China. A series of foreign influences sporadically affected the course of Japan's artistic evolution. Yet, no matter how overwhelming the impact of new forms and styles, the indigenous tradition invariably reasserted itself. Hence, the artistic pattern evolved in a rhythmic sequence of marked periods of borrowing, of absorption, and of return to native patterns.

Because Japan and its nearby islands are of volcanic origin, there is little stone suitable for carving or building. In architecture, this lack led to the development of wooden construction carefully devised to withstand the frequent earthquakes and tempests. In sculpture, figures were modeled in clay, which was often left unfired, cast in bronze by the *cire perdue* process familiar to many other cultures, or constructed of lacquer. Although the lacquer technique probably originated in China, Japanese artists excelled in creating large, hollow, lacquer figures by placing hemp cloth soaked in the juice of the lacquer tree over wooden armatures. The surfaces were gradually added to and finished, but the technique remained one of modeling rather than of carving. Such figures were not only light but very durable, being hard and resistant to destructive forces. Hollow lacquer was gradually superseded by sculpture carved in wood, with unusual sensitivity for grain and texture.

NATIVE TRADITIONS

The first artifacts known in Japan are pottery vessels and figurines from a culture designated Jomon, which apparently flourished as early as the fourth

millennium B.C. These objects are associated with Neolithic tools, although they persisted in northern Japan as late as the fourth or fifth century A.D., even while a metal culture was being fully developed in the south.

Japanese objects dating from about the beginning of the Christian era are of three kinds—those imported from the Asian mainland, those copied from imported articles, and those of Japanese invention. There are, for instance, bronze mirrors from Han China, as well as replicas of these mirrors made in Japan. Some of the replicas are adorned with a Japanese innovation—spherical rattles attached to the perimeter. From Korea, another source of continental influence, came a gray pottery known as *sue,* which was soon copied, and small, comma-shaped stones (*magatama*) used in necklaces. A third area, Indo-China, was the source of motifs used on bell-shaped bronzes, known as *dotaku*. The houses and boats depicted on these bronzes are similar to those on contemporaneous drums from Annam (modern Vietnam), in Indo-China.

Within this heterogeneous culture, a specifically Japanese creativity asserted itself in the production of *haniwa*—sculptured tubes made of pottery and placed fence-like around burial mounds, possibly to control erosion or to protect the dead. The upper parts of the haniwa are usually modeled in human form, but sometimes in the shape of a horse (FIG. 13-1), a bird, or even a house. Simple pottery cylinders were used similarly in Indo-China, but the sculptural modeling of haniwa is uniquely Japanese. The arms and legs as well as the mass of the torso, in most instances, recapitulate the cylindrical base of the haniwa. The tube-like character of some later monumental sculpture—and even of a particular wooden doll common in Japan today—may derive from these remote ancestors.

13-1 *Haniwa* figures, horse and peasant, fifth to sixth century. Clay. Horse, Cleveland Museum of Art (gift of The Norweb Collection); peasant, Cleveland Museum of Art (purchase, James Parmelee Fund).

Japanese architecture was first limited to pit dwellings and simple constructions of thatched roofs on bamboo stilts, but we learn from some haniwa that wooden architecture was fully developed by the fifth century; some buildings constructed by that time contained such features as two stories, saddle roofs, and decorative gables. There may have been monumental constructions of wood, but nothing remains from this early period except colossal mounds, which were the tombs of rulers.

ADVENT OF BUDDHISM

The development of native traditions was interrupted in 552 by an event of paramount importance to Japan. In that year, the ruler of Kudara (Korean: Paekche), a kingdom in Korea, sent a gilt bronze figure of the Buddha to Kimmei, emperor of Japan. With the image came the gospels. For half a century, the new religion met with opposition, but at the end of that time, Buddhism and its attendant arts were firmly established in Japan. Among the earliest examples of Japanese art serving the cause of Buddhism is *The Shaka Triad*, a bronze sculpture of Shaka (Sanskrit: Sakyamuni) and attendant Bodhisattvas (FIG. 13-2), made in 623 by TORI BUSSHI, a third-generation Korean living in Japan. Tori's style is that of the mid-sixth century in China. His work proved how tenaciously the formula for a "correct" representation of the icon had been maintained since the introduction of Buddhism almost a century earlier. Yet, at the same time, a new influence was coming from Sui China, which may be seen in the cylindrical form and flowing draperies of the wood sculpture known as the Kudara Kannon (Chinese: Kuan-yin). The two styles were blended, and, in the middle of the seventh century, they coalesced in one of Japan's finest sculptures, the *Miroku* (Sanskrit: Maitreya) of the Chugu-ji (the suffix *-ji* means "temple") nunnery near Nara (FIG. 13-3). In this figure, the Japanese artist combines a gentle sweetness with formal restraint in a manner unknown in Chinese sculpture.

Within a little more than half a century, however, all the archaisms of the fused style (loosely called Suiko, after the empress who reigned from 593 to 628, or Asuka, after the site of the capital) were swept aside by a new influence from T'ang China. The T'ang style, which found its way to Japan at the end of the Hakuho period (645–710), dominated Japanese art during the following periods of Late Nara (710–794) and Early Heian (794–897). Chinese models were followed not only in sculpture and painting but also in architecture, literature, and even etiquette.

The mature T'ang style appeared suddenly in

13-2 TORI BUSSHI, *The Shaka Triad*, Asuka period, 623. Bronze, 69½" high. Horyu-ji Temple, Nara, Japan.

13-3 *Miroku*, Asuka period, mid-seventh century. Wood, 62" high. Chugu-ji Nunnery, Horyu-ji, Nara, Japan.

13-4 *The Amida Triad*, from the *Shrine of Lady Tachibana*, Nara period, early eighth century. Gilded bronze; Amida, 11" high, attendants, 10" high. Horyu-ji Temple, Nara, Japan.

Japan in the bronze *Shrine of Lady Tachibana* (FIG. 13-4). The shrine consists of three full-round figures—the Buddha Amida (Sanskrit: Amitabha) seated on a lotus between the smaller figures of Kannon and Dai Seishi—each standing on a lotus and all three rising

13-5 *Tamamushi Shrine*, Horyu-ji, Nara, Asuka period, seventh century. Lacquer on wood, 7' 8" high. Horyu-ji Museum, Nara.

from a platform representing the stylized waters of the Sukhavati lake in the paradise of the Buddha. Behind them is a threefold screen on which are modeled, in low relief, the graceful forms of *apsaras* (heavenly nymphs) seated on lotuses and the tiny figures of souls newly born into heaven. The upswept scarves of the apsaras and the petals, tendrils, and pads of the lotuses create an exquisite background for the three divinities, while a detached, openwork halo of delicate design frames the head of the Buddha. The ensemble gives us some idea of the glorious T'ang bronzes that were melted down in China during the Buddhist persecutions of 845. It also demonstrates the remarkable adaptability of the Japanese artist, which permitted him to seize a new art form and make it his own.

The development of painting in Japan paralleled that of Buddhist sculpture. Some of the earliest surviving examples are found on the *Tamamushi* ("Beetle-Wing") *Shrine* (so-called because its base was decorated with the iridescent wings of beetles), which dates from the first half of the seventh century (FIG. 13-5). The sides and doors of the shrine, which is a wooden cabinet, are decorated with scenes from the jataka in the style of the Tunhwang caves of a century earlier, as may be seen in the cell-like composition, the crystalline rock formations, the attenuated figures, and the free linear movement. There is also the same delight in surface pattern to the point of disregard of naturalism in scale and spatial relationships.

The many treasured articles in the Shoso-in (storehouse for the belongings of Emperor Shomu after his death in 756) also illustrate the dependence of eighth-century Japan on the arts of China, although the wooden building itself is purely Japanese in style.

This Japanese dependence on China during the seventh and eighth centuries is not confined to sculpture and painting. Buddhist architecture adhered so closely to Chinese models that the lost T'ang style can be reconstructed from such temple complexes as the Horyu-ji or the Todai-ji, which still stand in Japan. The Kondo (Golden Hall) of the Horyu-ji (FIG. 13-6), which dates from shortly after 670, is one of the oldest wooden buildings in the world. Although periodically repaired and somewhat altered (the covered porch was added in the eighth century; the upper railing, in the seventeenth), it retains the light and buoyant quality characteristic of the style of the Northern and Southern dynasties in China.

For a more typically Japanese structure, we must refer to the shrines of Shinto, the indigenous faith of the Japanese people.* These shrines were customarily

---

*Shinto or "the Way of the Gods," was based on love of nature, of the family, and, above all, of the ruling family, as direct descendents of the gods. Nationalistic in character, Shinto was embodied in symbolic forms and shunned pictorial representation.

13-6 Kondo (Golden Hall), Horyu-ji, Nara, Japan, Asuka period, seventh century.

destroyed every 20 years and then replaced by exact duplicates—a process that has been repeated since the third century. Thus, we may assume that such a construction as the Ise Shrine (FIG. 13-7), last rebuilt in 1973, reproduces the original method of building with a great measure of accuracy. This, the greatest of all Shinto shrines, covers an area of 55 by 127 yards and is enclosed by four concentric fences. The Shoden, the main building, rests on piles and has a thatched roof. Massive, golden-hued columns (once the great trunks of cypress trees) and planks of the same wood are burnished to mellow surfaces—their color and texture contrasting with the white gravel that covers the ground of the sacred precinct. In the characteristic manner of the Japanese artist, the thatched roof was transformed from a simple functional element into one that established the esthetic of the entire structure. Browned by a smoking process, the thatch was sewn into bundles and then carefully laid in layers that gradually decreased in number from the eaves to the ridgepole. The entire surface was then sheared smooth, and a gently changing

13-7 Shoden, main building of the Ise Shrine, Japan. Rebuilt in 1973, reproducing third-century type. © Grand Shrine of Ise.

contour resulted. The roof line was further enhanced by decorative elements that once had been structural—the *chigi* or crosspiece at the gables, and cylindrical, wooden weights placed at right angles across the ridgepole. The repeats and echoes of the various parts of the main building and of the related structures are a quiet study in rhythmic form. The shrine, in its setting, is an expression of purity and dignity, effectively emphasized by the extreme simplicity of precisely planned proportions, textures, and architectural forms.

HEIAN PERIOD AND OTHER INDIGENOUS INNOVATIONS

A new style in representation ventured into Japan at the beginning of the ninth century. Under the influence of Esoteric Buddhism (pp. 459–50), a heavier image with multiple arms and heads was introduced—a type that, in China, was then replacing the earlier, classic grace of the T'ang style. The bloated forms of the new style, though they may be repellent, have the merit of somber dignity. In paintings, these bulky figures, often cut off at the sides, give the effect of a mighty force expanding beyond the pictorial format.

From the middle of the ninth century, relations between Japan and China deteriorated so rapidly that, by the end of that century, almost all intercourse had ceased. No longer able to reflect the fashions of China, the artists of Japan began to create their own forms during the Late Heian, or Fujiwara, period (897–1185). At this time, court practices at Heian-kyo (modern Kyoto) were refined to the point of preciosity. A vivid and detailed picture of the period appears in Lady Murasaki's eleventh-century novel, *The Tale of Genji*, a work of superb subtlety. The picture is of a court in which etiquette overwhelmed morality, a society in which poor taste—in such matters as the color of a robe, the paper used in the endless writing of love letters, or the script itself—was considered a cardinal sin. The very essence of this court is reflected in a set of scrolls (illustrating *The Tale of Genji*) attributed to the twelfth-century court artist Takayoshi (FIG. 13-8). Painted in the horizontal-scroll (*makimono*) format, small pictures like this alternate with sections of text. The artist, using a distinctly Japanese technique for representing space, views the scenes from an elevation, removes the ceilings to expose the interiors, and tilts the ground plane sharply toward a high horizon, or one that is often excluded altogether. Thus, the area of representation is expanded in terms of content and abruptly contracted by the resulting diminution of a sense of depth. Flat fields of unshaded color emphasize the painting's two-dimensional character, as do strong diagonal lines, which direct the eye more along the surface than into the picture space. Human figures have the appearance of being constructed of stiff layers of contrasting fabrics, and although they represent specific characters, their features are scarcely differentiated. A formula for

13-8 Takayoshi, detail illustrating *The Tale of Genji*, Late Heian (Fujiwara) period, twelfth century. Scroll, color on paper, 8½″ × 15¾″. Tokugawa Museum, Nagoya.

13-9　*Hokke-kyo* (*Lotus Sutra*), Late Heian (Fujiwara) period, *c.* twelfth century. Fan, ink and color on paper, approx. 19″ wide. Shitenno-ji, Osaka. (National Commission for Protection of Cultural Properties of Japan.)

such aristocratic faces, which produced a depersonalizing effect, called for a brush stroke for each eye and eyebrow, one for the nose, and another (sometimes omitted) for the mouth. Paintings in this purely Japanese style, known as *Yamato-e*,* reflect the sophisticated taste of the Fujiwara nobility for whom they were created.

A series of fan paintings (FIG. 13-9) from about the same period illustrate, with text, the *Hokke-kyo* (*Lotus Sutra*). The high perspective and lavish sprinkling of cut gold and mica to ornament the paper are related to the courtly style of the Genji scrolls. But the scenes of lower-class life and the printing of the underdrawing with wooden blocks suggest that the fans may be an early example of that blending of sophisticated

*Yamato is the area around Kyoto and Nara regarded as the cradle of Japanese culture. The suffix -*e* means "picture."

taste with popular subjects and modes that is one of the great and persistent themes of Japanese art.

A different facet of Yamato-e is represented by the *Shigisan Engi* (the Legends of Mount Shigi), painted at the end of the Fujiwara period. One of the first Japanese scrolls designed as a continuous composition, the *Shigisan Engi* illustrates the story of a Buddhist monk and his miraculous golden bowl. Our episode, called *The Flying Storehouse*, (FIG. 13-10), depicts the bowl lifting the rice-filled storehouse of a greedy merchant and carrying it off to the monk's hut in the mountains of Wakayama. The gaping merchant, his attendants, and several onlookers are shown in various poses—some grimacing, others wildly gesticulating and scurrying about in frantic astonishment. The Fujiwara aristocracy felt that only the crude and ill-bred would display such feelings and that they were

13-10　*The Flying Storehouse*, detail of *The Shigisan Engi*, Late Heian (Fujiwara) period, late twelfth century. Horizontal scroll, ink and color on paper, 12½″ high. Chogosonshi-ji, Nara.

13-11 Attributed to Toba Sojo, animal caricatures, Late Heian (Fujiwara) period, *c.* late twelfth century. Detail of a horizontal scroll, ink on paper, approx. 12″ high. Kozan-ji.

therefore appropriate subjects for humorous caricature. The faces—so unlike the generalized masks in the *Genji* scrolls—are drawn with each feature exaggerated, conforming to a convention of the period to distinguish the lower classes from the nobility. Cartooning of this kind became an important element in Japanese pictorial art.

From the same general period (but of disputed date) are four horizontal scrolls of animal caricatures, painted in monochrome with a free calligraphic brush, which are more typical of Chinese Zen painting than of the refined style of Yamato-e. One of these scrolls, often attributed to the Buddhist Abbot Toba (Toba Sojo), depicts a medley of frogs, monkeys, and hares in a hilarious burlesque of Buddhist practices. In one section (FIG. 13-11), a monkey dressed as a priest pays homage to a Buddha in the shape of a frog seated pompously on a lotus throne

with a nimbus of luxuriant banana leaves. In another, more animated passage, the animals tumble and frolic while washing each other in a river. Throughout this whimsical satire, the Japanese predilection for decoration asserts itself in charming clumps of foliage that play a delicate counterpoint to the vigorous movement of the animals.

A more conservative style of Buddhist art continued through the Late Fujiwara period, but a new subject was added. This subject, known as *raigo*, portrayed the Buddha Amida descending through clouds amid a host of Bodhisattvas, welcoming deceased believers to his paradise. Such paintings, products of the Paradise Sects (pp. 446–48), eased the rigors of religion for the luxurious courtiers in Heiankyo (Kyoto). A remarkable sculptural rendering of the raigo theme is housed at the Hoodo (Phoenix Hall) of the Byodoin temple at Ujiyamada, near Kyoto

13-12 *Below:* Hoodo (Phoenix Hall), Byodoin temple at Ujiyamada, Japan, Heian period, eleventh century. *Right:* Jocho, *Amida* (from the interior of the Hoodo), 1053; gilded wood, 9′ 4″ high.

(FIG. 13-12). The light and sweeping design of the building, suggesting a bird in flight, at once recalls aristocratic palace pavilions and the Chinese architecture depicted in the *Paradise of Amitabha* wall painting at Tunhwang (FIG. 12-14). Inside the hall, the gilded wooden figure of *Amida* (FIG. 13-12) by the sculptor JOCHO embodies a serene grace through the expanding curves of face and torso, stabilized into a triangular composition by the elongated legs below. The smaller figures of angels and celestial musicians, floating on clouds as they accompany Amida Buddha on his descent, complete the impression of courtly elegance.

KAMAKURA REALISM

A series of civil wars led to the downfall of the decadent Fujiwara rulers, and their successful rivals established a new capital at Kamakura, the city that gave its name to the period from 1185 to about 1392. The new rulers, reacting against what they considered to be the effeteness of the Fujiwaras, supported an art that emphasized strength and realism. The style of the Nara period (710–794) was revived by UNKEI (d. 1223), perhaps the greatest sculptor of Japan. Unkei and his followers went even further than the earlier realists, carefully reproducing their observations of every accidental variation in the folds of drapery and using crystal for the eyes of their sculptures. That they were able, nonetheless, to keep a sensitive balance between the spiritual and the realistic is shown in the superb figure of Kuya, a priest who is represented as he walked about invoking the

13-13 *The Sage Kuya Invoking the Amida Buddha*, Kamakura period, thirteenth century. Painted wood, approx. 46". Rokuharamitsu-ji Temple, Kyoto, Japan.

name of Amida Buddha (FIG. 13-13). Not only is every detail meticulously rendered, but six small Buddha images issue from the sage's mouth, as if in a comic strip balloon, to represent the words "Amida, Amida, Amida. . . ." Thus, realism is carried to the point of the sculptor attempting to invest his figures with speech.

Painting during the Kamakura period is most interesting for the advances made in the Yamato-e style, although all types of Fujiwara art were also continued. Perhaps the greatest Yamato-e of this time is *The Burning of the Sanjo Palace* (FIG. 13-14), one of a series of horizontal scrolls illustrating tales of the Heiji insurrection (*Heiji Monogatari*). Here, the artist, perfect-

13-14 *The Burning of the Sanjo Palace*, Kamakura period, thirteenth century. Section of a horizontal scroll, ink and color on paper, 1' 4¼" × 22' 10". Fenollosa-Weld Collection, Museum of Fine Arts, Boston.

ing the symphonic composition of the Chinese land-scape scroll, has added drama with swift and violent staccato brushwork and vivid flashes of color. At the beginning of the scroll (read from right to left), the eye is caught by a mass of figures rushing toward a blazing building—the crescendo of the painting—and is then led at a decelerated pace through swarms of soldiers, horses, and bullock carts, finally, it seems, to be arrested by a warrior on a rearing horse (FIG. 13-14). But the horse and rider are positioned to serve as a deceptive cadence (false ending), for they are a prelude to the single figure of an archer, which picks up and completes the mass movement of the soldiers and so draws the turbulent narrative to a quiet close.

ASHIKAGA: RENEWED CHINESE INFLUENCE

The power of the Kamakura rulers ceased in 1333, after which internal warfare persisted until 1392, when the Ashikaga shoguns (military dictators) imposed a brief peace. Civil war soon broke out again, although the shoguns managed to maintain control amid almost continuous insurrections, and lasted until 1573. The arts, nevertheless, flourished. New painting styles imported from China coexisted with conventional Buddhist pictures and with paintings in the Yamato-e style carried on by artists of the Tosa family. The monochrome landscape style of the thirteenth-century Sung masters Ma Yuan and Hsia Kuei was adopted by the painter–monk SHUBUN at the beginning of the fifteenth century. Shubun created evocative, idealized landscapes, sometimes with subjects and associated poems based on Chinese themes, which reflect the deep involvement with Chinese culture at Japanese monasteries of this period. MINCHO (1352–1431), also known as CHO DENSU, and other painters went directly to Yüan dynasty models. But the most powerful current to come from China was the one that accompanied Zen Buddhism and that accounts largely for the flowering of art despite the troubled times of the Ashikaga period. The new philosophy appealed to the *samurai*, a caste of professional warriors composed of men who held a relatively high position in society and who were supporters of the feudal nobility. They lived by rigid standards that placed high values on such virtues as loyalty, courage, and self-control. The self-reliance required of its adherents made Zen the ideal religion for the samurai.

Because the samurai found Zen attractive, the arts that had been associated with it in China swept Japan. Sculpture, as in China under the influence of Ch'an Buddhism, lost importance, and painting widely imitated the bold brush of the Sung masters of

13-15 SESSHU, *Landscape*, Ashikaga period, 1495. Detail of a hanging scroll, ink on paper, approx. 55" high. Tokyo National Museum.

the Ch'an School. Early in the Ashikaga period, the artist KAO worked in the style of the thirteenth-century Chinese artist Liang K'ai, while his contemporary MOKUAN painted almost indistinguishably from a Chinese predecessor, Mu-ch'i. Of all the Zen artists in Japan at this time, Sesshu (1420–1506) is the most celebrated. He had several different styles, but is best known for paintings in the Ma–Hsia manner (p. 455). Sesshu greatly admired Sung painting and, although he studied in China, he decried the work of contemporary Ming painters. Nevertheless, he was affected by the Ming style, for one of his masterpieces—an ink-splash landscape in the National Museum in Tokyo (FIG. 13-15)—contains elements basic to the Ming as well as to the Sung style. Although the landscape recalls the wet-style characteristic of Ch'an painters of the Sung, the brushwork is more abstract and the tonal contrasts are more startling, after the Ming manner.

The Tea Ceremony

The influence of Zen went considerably beyond painting. It gave rise, during the Ashikaga period, to the *tea ceremony*, a unique custom that, among other things, provided a new outlet for the products of the Japanese artist–craftsman. This ceremony soon became a major social institution of the aristocracy. Its function and purpose is described by Father João Rodrigues (1562–1633), a Portuguese Jesuit who spent more than 30 years in Japan and who was a keen observer of Japanese customs and culture. Everything used in the tea ceremony, he reports, "is as rustic, rough, completely unrefined, and simple as nature made it, after the style of a solitary and rustic hermitage." The purpose of the ceremony was "to produce courtesy, politeness, modesty, moderation, calmness, peace of body and soul, without pride or arrogance, fleeing from all ostentation, pomp, external grandeur and magnificence."

The setting for the tea ceremony was appropriately unpretentious. Special teahouses, small and designed to give the appearance of refined simplicity, were placed into carefully planned and subtly arranged garden settings. The Shokintei (Pavilion of the Pine Lute, named after the sound of the wind in the surrounding trees; FIGS. 13-16, 13-17, 13-18) in the gardens of the Katsura Palace, dating from the early Tokugawa period, is a charming example. Its exterior was carefully planned to blend with the calculated casualness of the gardens (FIG. 13-16). A flagstone path leads past moss-covered stone lanterns to an entrance where the guests washed their hands at a "natural" spring. In a rectangular room, scaled to create a feeling of intimacy and adorned only with a shallow alcove (*tokonoma*) in which a single painting and, perhaps, a stylized flower arrangement might be displayed, the host would entertain his guests. The ritual of tea drinking in this setting imposed a set of mannered gestures and even certain topics of conversation on all participants. Every effort was made to

13-16 The Shokintei, Katsura Palace gardens, near Kyoto, Japan, early 1660s.

13-17 The first room of the Shokintei, Katsura Palace.

prevent any jarring note that might disturb the perfectly planned occasion.

Although often emulated in modern times, originally no two teahouses were alike. According to an old teamaster, "beauty is lost through imitation," and originality was as important an aspect of the design as the perfection of its execution. Visual surprises were highly appreciated; for instance, the bold pattern of blue and white rectangles with which the tokonoma in our example (FIG. 13-17) is papered is an unusual and rather daring departure from the usually neutral and, at best, lightly textured treatment of these alcoves. Important also was the subtlety and finesse with which the building components were treated. Supporting posts were fashioned to keep their natural appearance and often remained rounded and knotty like tree trunks; all surfaces were painstakingly rubbed and burnished to bring out the natural beauty of their grains and textures. Common

13-18   Pond and garden as seen from the second room of the Shokintei, Katsura Palace.

to all teahouses, and expressive of the Japanese love of nature, was the close integration of the building with its natural setting; when their rice-paper-covered, sliding screens (*shoji*) are opened, the rooms become no more than roofed-over extensions of the garden (FIG. 13-18).

Although inspired and developed by Zen monks and subsequently adopted by the high and low aristocracy, the ritual of the tea ceremony, with its refined standards of taste, had a lasting influence on the style of living of the people at large. The studied simplicity, austerity, and understatement of the fifteenth-century teahouse were monumentalized in the Katsura Palace and, from there, filtered down into domestic architecture to become what is now regarded as the traditional Japanese dwelling.

The esthetics of the tea ceremony were found in the beauty of the commonplace, and each object employed in the ceremony was selected with the utmost discrimination. The connoisseur preferred a tea bowl, a flower container, or other ritual utensil that appeared to have been made without artifice. Potteries

13-19   Tea-ceremony water jar, named *kogan* ("ancient stream bank"), Momoyama period, late sixteenth century. *Shino* ware with underglaze design, 7" high. Hatakeyama Memorial Museum, Tokyo.

used in the ceremony were covered with heavy glazes, seemingly applied in a casual manner, belying the skill that had controlled the colors and textures (FIG. 13-19). The irregular, sometimes battered or flawed shapes of many Japanese tea wares provide an extreme contrast to the technical perfection common in Chinese ceramics (FIG. 12-27). Many wares of this type were given individual names based on literary or historical associations of their decor or on the visual and tactile qualities of the entire piece. Conferring such attention and importance on an individual object at this stage foreshadows the entrance into ceramics of major artists, who would sign, paint, and even inscribe poems on their wares as part of the development of a craft into a self-conscious and sophisticated art.

The Tosa and Kano Schools

The artistic understatement of the tea ceremony was counterbalanced by the continuing Yamato-e style of decorative painting. TOSA MITSUNOBU (1434–1525), the foremost exponent of Yamato-e during the Ashikaga period, retained the coloristic patterns of his native style, but also emphasized ink outline after the fashion of Chinese painting. The new manner of painting resulting from this combination is most apparent in pictures of the Kano School. KANO MOTONOBU (1476–1559), who was probably the grandson of the founder of the Kano School, worked so closely in the Sung tradition that some of his paintings have been mistaken for those of Hsia Kuei (p. 455). He had, however, a more personal style, in which we find a new emphasis on brushed outlines and strong tonal contrasts—features that became distinctive of the Kano School. In addition, Motonobu often used Tosa coloring and, at times, even painted in a purely Tosa manner. As a result, the Tosa and Kano schools became less distinguishable after the sixteenth century.

13-20 *Uji Bridge*, Momoyama period, sixteenth to seventeenth century. Six-fold screen, color on paper, 62" high. Tokyo National Museum.

MOMOYAMA AND EDO: THE DECORATIVE STYLE

In the Momoyama period (1573–1615), which followed the stormy Ashikaga, a succession of three dictators finally imposed peace on the Japanese people. Huge palaces were erected—partly as symbols of power, partly as fortresses. The grand scale of the period is typified by the Nagoya Castle, built about 1610. This castle also exemplifies how well the new style of painting suited the tastes of the Momoyama nobility. The sliding doors and large screens within the mammoth structure were covered with gold leaf, on which were painted a wide range of romantic and historical subjects, even exotic portrayals of Dutch and Portuguese traders. Traditional Chinese themes were frequent, as were commonplace subjects of everyday experience. But all were transformed by an emphasis on two-dimensional design and striking color patterns (FIG. 13-20). The anecdotal or philosophical content was almost lost in a grandiose decorative display.

Not every Momoyama artist worked exclusively in the colorful style exemplified by the Nagoya paintings. HASEGAWA TOHAKU (1539–1610), for instance, carried on the Zen manner of Mu-ch'i with brilliant success. His versatility, which was shared by most artists of the time, is evident in a brilliant, monochromatic screen painting, *Pine Trees*, whose strong verticals and diagonals are distinctively Japanese (FIG. 13-21). In Japan, the decoration of screens was especially highly developed and often exemplifies the highest quality of painting.

13-21 HASEGAWA TOHAKU, *Pine Trees*, Momoyama period, sixteenth to seventeenth century. Six-fold screen, ink on paper, 61" high. Tokyo National Museum.

13-22　Eastern façade of the Katsura Palace, near Kyoto, Japan, *c.* 1615–1663.

The Katsura Palace

In 1615, Tokugawa Ieyasu, last of the Momoyama rulers, consolidated his power as shogun of Edo (modern Tokyo) and established the Tokugawa, or Edo, rule, which lasted until 1857. By his time, the emperors had long lost their political power and independence and, under a succession of military dictators, had become little more than ceremonial figureheads. Still, in the hope of legitimizing their rules, the shoguns supported the traditional imperial institutions, and Ieyasu, in a magnanimous gesture, donated some land at Katsura, near Kyoto, to members of the imperial family. There, over a period of some

50 years, and beginning with a modest country retreat (*besso*), successive generations of the Hachijo family developed a country palace that became the admired, but rarely equaled, standard for domestic architecture down to modern times.

The Katsura Palace (*c.* 1615–1663; FIGS. 13-22, 13-23, 13-24) was built at a time when the tea ceremony was enjoying its greatest popularity, and many of its design features and tasteful subtleties can be traced back to the earlier teahouses (FIGS. 13-16, 13-17, 13-18). The straight rooflines of traditional Japanese architecture go back all the way to the Ise Shrine (FIG. 13-7) and stand in striking contrast to the swinging,

13-23　Palaquin Entry, Katsura Palace.

13-24 Interior, Katsura Palace.

curving ridgepoles and eaves of the Buddhist architecture imported from China (compare FIGS. 13-6 and 13-12), which, by this time, had deteriorated to the point that originally structural elements had become overloaded and ostentatious decoration. Here at Katsura, the architectural forms express their function simply and without disguise, and the subtle adjustment of their pleasing proportions to each other and to the whole have produced a building of astonishing beauty. The main entrance to the palace, the so-called Palaquin Entry (FIG. 13-23), is a marvelously rich and subtle composition of juxtaposed solids and voids, of rectangular shapes of varying sizes and proportions, arranged along vertical, horizontal, and sloping planes; lines, planes, and volumes are enriched by a variety of textures (stone, wood, tile, plaster) and by subdued colors and tonal values that build up toward and enframe the composition's focal point—the sliding panels of the doorway.

On the interior (FIG. 13-24), lacquered posts and wooden trim surround painted panels and screens to create settings more sumptuous than those of the teahouse, but just as refined and delicate. Everything is done with the utmost restraint. The rooms are not large by Western standards, but the screens between them can be slid apart, or removed completely, to create sweeping flights of rectangular spaces that can also be opened to the outside to achieve that harmonious integration of building and garden that we have seen already, on a smaller scale, in the teahouse (FIG. 13-18).

GARDENS

In the garden, as in the building, man-made and natural elements are combined to create a sense of balance, proportion, and harmony. Japanese gardens are intended to be retreats in which one can enjoy peaceful seclusion and meditation. They create "landscape pictures" in which waterfalls, streams, lakes, bridges, and teahouses are artfully combined with stones, trees, and shrubs to simulate, in a restricted area, vistas of much larger landscapes. The Katsura gardens skillfully exploit the element of surprise. Long walkways are suddenly blocked by a wall of shrubbery that forces the visitor to turn in the direction of a designed view, such as a single shaped tree dramatically silhouetted against the glittering surface of a pond. Guests are led along carefully designed paths that present charming views of garden and landscape elements at planned intervals. The stepping stones along these paths are small and irregularly spaced, so that visitors must keep their eyes down in order not to stumble. Only here and there, larger stones invite a rest and allow them to lift their heads safely to view their surroundings and appreciate the designed prospect offered to their eyes.

The Katsura gardens cover several acres and are meant to be walked through. Much smaller and intended to be viewed from a fixed position are the Zen rock gardens, which originated in the thirteenth century. They consist of stone groupings in dry landscapes that are symbolic and suggestive of large landscape features. Level ground covered with raked sand or pebbles represents rivers, lakes, or oceans. Scattered over this surface and framing it are rocks, carefully placed singly or in groups: the vertical ones representing islands, cliffs, and mountain ranges; the horizontal ones denoting embankments, bridges, and ships. Peninsulas and islands, carved out by the ocean, or a coastline with mountain ranges may be symbolized. The ensemble is intended to induce and facilitate intense meditation, to encourage the spirit to take off in free flight and transform the limited sphere of a tiny plot of soil into a cosmic universe without man-made boundaries.

13-25 TAWARAYA SOTATSU and HON-AMI KOETSU, *Deer and Calligraphy*, Tokugawa period, early seventeenth century. Section of a horizontal scroll, ink and gold and silver on paper, 12½" high. Seattle Art Museum (gift of Mrs. Donald E. Frederick).

13-26 OGATA KORIN, *White Plum Blossoms in the Spring*, Tokugawa period, late seventeenth to early eighteenth century. Screen, color on gold paper, 62" high. Tokyo National Museum.

Decorative Painting

Screen painting was continued in all its Momoyama magnificence by such artists as KANO SANRAKU (1561–1635), HON-AMI KOETSU (1558–1637), and TAWARAYA SOTATSU (1576–1643), whose lives spanned both periods. Koetsu and Sotatsu also composed numerous scrolls on which pictorial forms of flowers or animals were interlaced with strokes of a free-flowing calligraphy. One such collaborative effort is a deer scroll (FIG. 13-25), in which the shapes of the animals, painted in decorative gold and silver, are repeated with subtle variations in pose and interval to create an almost musical effect.

OGATA KORIN (1658–1716) and his brother OGATA KENZAN (1663–1743) carried the decorative tradition that characterized the Momoyama on into the eighteenth century. Korin was primarily a decorative painter, who also worked as a lacquer designer; Kenzan was a master potter, whose line of "natural" wares is still continued today by the ninth artist to take his name. Korin is famous largely for his dramatic renderings of rocks, tree branches, and waves,

which he combined in elegant and flowing compositions (FIG. 13-26). Both artists harmonized the decorative styles of Momoyama and Early Edo with the studied simplicity required of art in the service of the tea ceremony.

Nanga and Realism

Although the decorative style of the Sotatsu–Korin schools continued to flourish until the nineteenth century, it had to share its popularity with several other trends in later Japanese painting. One, Nanga ("southern school painting"), was inspired by Chinese "literary" school painting of Su Shih, and Mi Fu (p. 454). The Nanga painters transformed the techniques of their Chinese models into a style that combined virtuoso brushwork with decorative pattern and a strong sense of humor. Two outstanding early representatives of this style are IKENO TAIGA (1723–1776) and YOSA BUSON (1716–1783), who jointly illustrated an album entitled *The Ten Conveniences and the Ten Enjoyments of Country Life*. On one of Buson's pages (FIG. 13-27), a bulbous-nosed figure peering

13-27 YOSA BUSON, *Enjoyment of Summer Scenery*, from *The Ten Conveniences and the Ten Enjoyments of Country Life*, Tokugawa period, 1771. Album leaves, ink and color on paper, 7" high. Yasunari Kawabata Collection, Kanagawa.

13-28 MARUYAMA OKYO, detail of *Nature Studies*, Tokugawa period, eighteenth century. Horizontal scroll, ink and color on paper, 12½" high. Nishimura Collection, Kyoto.

from a hut at richly textured summer foliage is shown with wistful humor by this master of the brush.

Another main line of later Japanese painting, which has been called realistic or naturalistic, is represented by MARUYAMA OKYO (1733–1795). His studies of animals, insects, and plants (FIG. 13-28) combine an almost Western objectivity with an unusual handling of the brush to produce a style that follows the observed forms rather than established conventions. This kind of realism may well be due, in part, to Western influence. From the mid-sixteenth century on, Portuguese missionaries and Dutch traders visited Japan, bringing with them paintings that, despite the efforts of the Tokugawa shoguns to bar foreign influences, did not fail to have some effect on Japanese art.

Ukiyo-e and Printmaking

The Tokugawa shoguns maintained a static and stratified society, and, as a result, each class developed its own distinctive culture. The center of the plebeian culture was the Yoshiwara entertainment area of Edo, where the popular idols were the talented courtesans of the teahouses and the actors of the Kabuki theater. Kabuki itself was a popular and lusty form of drama that developed in response to a demand for a more intelligible and more easily enjoyed theater than that of the highly stylized No plays, which were patronized exclusively by the nobility and a small number of the nouveau riche. Kabuki eventually provided endless subjects for a new art form—a style of genre painting (FIG. 21-60) beginning around 1600—that was to have considerable influence on Western art in the nineteenth century. This new art, known as *Ukiyo-e*, or "pictures of the floating (or passing) world," was largely centered in Kyoto. Toward the end of the seventeenth century, the center of production shifted to Edo and the predominant medium became the woodblock print, which reflected the tastes and pleasures of a bourgeoisie emerging in a feudal society.

The woodblock as a device for printing had been invented in China during the T'ang dynasty. The technique was introduced into Japan during the eighth century, when it was employed chiefly to reproduce inexpensive religious souvenirs or charms. In the seventeenth century, Chinese woodblock book illustrations inspired the production of low-priced illustrated guidebooks of the Yoshiwara district.

The art of block printing, as it ultimately developed in the eighteenth century, was a triumph of collaboration. The artist, having been selected and commissioned by a publisher, prepared his design in ink, merely adding color notations. A specialist in woodcutting then transferred the lines to the blocks, and a third man did the printing. The quality of the finished picture depended as much on the often anonymous cutter and printer as on the painter of the original design.

HISHIKAWA MORONOBU (c. 1625–1694) was probably the first to employ the woodblock print to illustrate everyday subjects in books and to make and produce individual prints, which he started to do about 1673. The woodblock quickly evolved as a medium for cheap reproduction and wide distribution. Moronobu's woodblocks were simply in black outline against a plain white paper, as were the prints produced for the next 50 years, but often they were hand-colored by their purchasers. Moronobu's designs of large and simple forms had the exuberance of a young art. The same vitality was expressed in prints of the Torii School by such artists as KIYONOBU I (1664–1729), KIYOMASU I (active 1694–1716), and KIYOTADA (active in the early eighteenth century; FIG. 13-29). These artists specialized in portraying Kabuki actors. (Kiyonobu I was an actor's son.) They worked with a broad rhythmic outline, and, for emphatic pattern, used the bold textile designs of the actors' robes.

At about the same time, members of the Kaiget-sudo family were painting pictures and making de-

13-29 KIYOTADA, *Dancing Kabuki Actor*, Tokugawa period, *c.* 1725. Print, 11¾″ × 6″. Metropolitan Museum of Art, New York (Harris Brisbane Dick Fund, 1949).

signs for woodblocks of elegant courtesans. The Kaigetsudo figures had more grace but somewhat less power than those of the Torii painters. In general, the print style gradually acquired more delicacy during the eighteenth century. The invention of a process of printing in color directly from blocks brought the "primitive" period of Ukiyo-e printmaking to an end by about 1741.

OKUMURA MASANOBU (1686–1764) had experimented with what is called "lacquer technique" in an effort to increase the luster of the ink in his black-and-white prints. Later, he used a new, two-color method for printing in pink and green (*benizuri-e*), in which the dominant pink contrasts with patches of pale green and still smaller areas of black to produce a strong color vibration despite the very limited palette. Coincident with the use of color printing the artists began to work in smaller, more delicate scale. In 1765, a device was introduced that permitted more accurate register and the successful use of even smaller color areas. This led to the development of the *Nishiki-e* or "brocade picture," which was a true polychrome print. The new technique encouraged greater refinement and delicacy, evident in prints by the two leading print masters of the time—the incomparable SUZUKI HARUNOBU (1725–1770) and ISODA KORYUSAI (active 1764–1788). In their work (see FIG. 21-60), a new loveliness replaces the monumentality of earlier

13-30 KATSUSHIKA HOKUSAI, *The Great Wave*, from *Thirty-Six Views of Mt. Fuji*, Tokugawa period, *c*. 1823–1829. Print, 14¾″ wide. Museum of Fine Arts, Boston.

compositions. The figures are of slighter proportions, the colors are more muted, the line is lyric rather than dramatic.

After Harunobu died, prints changed rapidly in style, shape, subject, and color. TORII KIYONAGA (1752–1815) and KITAGAWA UTAMARO (1753–1806) revived the taste for tall, willowy figures. Utamaro, who later concentrated on half-length figures, was fortunate to have the services of craftsmen who were skilled enough in woodcutting to allow him to create extraordinary nuances in color, texture, and line. BUNCHO (active 1766–1790), working in another vein, made many striking portraits of well-known figures. Even more dramatic are the prints of TOSHUSAI SHARAKU, who, active for a brief ten months during 1794 and 1795, was a unique and enigmatic figure among print artists. About 160 of his prints survive— all of them piercing, rather acid, psychological studies of actors, wrestlers, or managers. UTAGAWA TOYOKUNI I (1769–1825) followed in a similar, less biting manner, but the strength of this style was dissipated in the hands of later artists.

Dozens of other artists contributed to the popular art of printmaking, but, during the nineteenth century, KATSUSHIKA HOKUSAI (1760–1849) and ANDO HIROSHIGE (1797–1858) were outstanding. Increasing political and moral censorship, which was to contribute to the decline of this art, led Hokusai to landscape for his Ukiyo-e subjects. His brilliant and ingenious compositions, such as his *Thirty-Six Views of Mt. Fuji*, make use of striking juxtapositions and bold, linear designs (FIG. 13-30). Nature was his primary subject, but, in its setting, he also included genre and anecdote as minor themes. Hiroshige, too, specialized in landscape and, like Hokusai, painted birds, flowers, and legendary scenes. In general, however, his prints did not evoke the sense of grandeur implicit in Hokusai's work.

These prints, although sometimes influenced by European art, show the Japanese attitude toward nature—the regard for natural forms in their utmost simplicity as a point of departure for an interpretation of reality—which, in turn, will lead to abstract pictorial design.

13-31 Interior of a Japanese house.

DOMESTIC ARCHITECTURE

Until recently, the Japanese home—modest or pretentious—has been designed according to basically the same structural and esthetic principles that apply to the teahouse or the Katsura Palace. The traditional Japanese dwelling almost invariably is intimately related to the land around it, and, wherever possible, it is set in a garden closed off by a bamboo fence (a thing of beauty in itself), providing a sense of privacy and intimacy in even the most crowded environment.

The structure is essentially a series of posts supporting a roof. The walls, which are screens rather than supports, slide open from one room into another or onto the outside. Space is treated as continuous yet harmoniously divisible—a concept that revolutionized architectural theory in the West. Uniformity and harmony of proportions are achieved by the use of the conventional straw mat (*tatami*) as a module. Its dimensions (3 feet by 6 feet) determine most measurements of both the plan and the eleva-

tion of the house, so that many of its structural elements can be prefabricated—another feature highly appreciated by Western architects.

In the traditional Japanese house, there is no furniture, except for some low tables and cushions (bedding is rolled up and kept in closets during the day). The various rooms of the house have no specific functions and can be used for any and all purposes. The main room, in which guests are received (FIG. 13-31), is identified by the tokonoma, where works of art from the owner's collection are displayed one at a time. Quite unlike Western collectors, who tend to convert their homes into museums by displaying all of their objets d'art together, their Japanese counterparts rotate the works in their collections, showing a single work in the tokonoma to suit season or mood—an attitude that conforms with the simplicity and architectural understatement of the traditional Japanese dwelling.

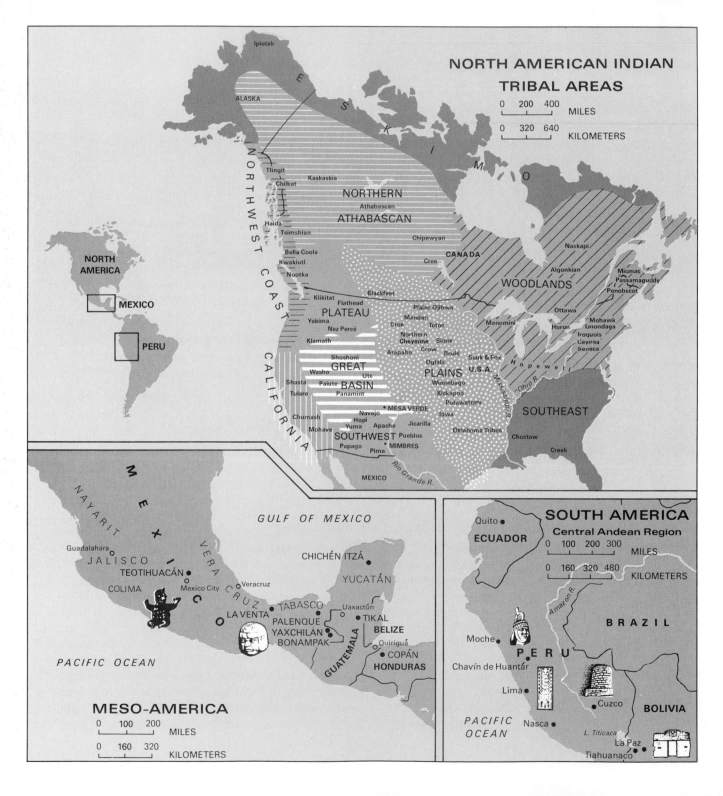

14

NORTH AMERICAN INDIAN
TRIBAL AREAS

| 0 | 200 | 400 | MILES |
| 0 | 320 | 640 | KILOMETERS |

Ipiutak

ALASKA

E S K I M O

NORTHWEST COAST

Tlingit
Chilkat
Kaskaskia
NORTHERN
Athabascan
ATHABASCAN
Chipewyan
CANADA
Haida
Tsimshian
Bella Coola
Cree
Kwakiutl
Nootka
Blackfeet
Klikitat
Flathead
PLATEAU
Yakima
Nez Percé
Klamath
Plains Ojibwa
Mandan
Cree
Northern
Cheyenne
Sioux
Crow
Arapaho
Brulé
Oglala
Shoshoni
GREAT
Ute
BASIN
Washo
Paiute
Panamint
Winnebago
Kickapoo
Potawatomi
Iowa
Oklahoma Tribes
MESA VERDE
Chumash
Navajo
Hopi
Yuma
Apache
Jicarilla
Mohave
SOUTHWEST
Pueblos
Papago
MIMBRES
Pima
CALIFORNIA
Shasta
Tulare

Naskapi
Algonkian
Micmac
Passamaguddy
Penobscot
WOODLANDS
Ottawa
Menomini
Huron
Mohawk
Onondaga
Iroquois
Cayuga
Seneca
Sauk & Fox
U.S.A.
Hopewell
PLAINS
Mississippi R.
Ohio R.
SOUTHEAST
Choctaw
Creek

Rio Grande R.
MEXICO

NORTH
AMERICA

MEXICO

PERU

GULF OF MEXICO

MEXICO

NAYARIT

JALISCO
Guadalajara
TEOTIHUACÁN
COLIMA
Mexico City
Veracruz
VERA CRUZ
CHICHÉN ITZÁ
YUCATÁN
LA VENTA
TABASCO
Uaxactún
PALENQUE
YAXCHILÁN
TIKAL
BONAMPAK
BELIZE
Quiriguá
GUATEMALA
COPÁN
HONDURAS

PACIFIC OCEAN

MESO-AMERICA

| 0 | 100 | 200 | MILES |
| 0 | 160 | 320 | KILOMETERS |

SOUTH AMERICA
Central Andean Region

| 0 | 100 | 200 | 300 | MILES |
| 0 | 160 | 320 | 480 | KILOMETERS |

Quito
ECUADOR
Amazon R.
BRAZIL
Moche
PERU
Chavín de Huantár
Lima
Cuzco
BOLIVIA
Nasca
L. Titicaca
La Paz
Tiahuanaco

PACIFIC OCEAN

THE NATIVE ARTS
OF THE AMERICAS, AFRICA,
AND THE SOUTH PACIFIC

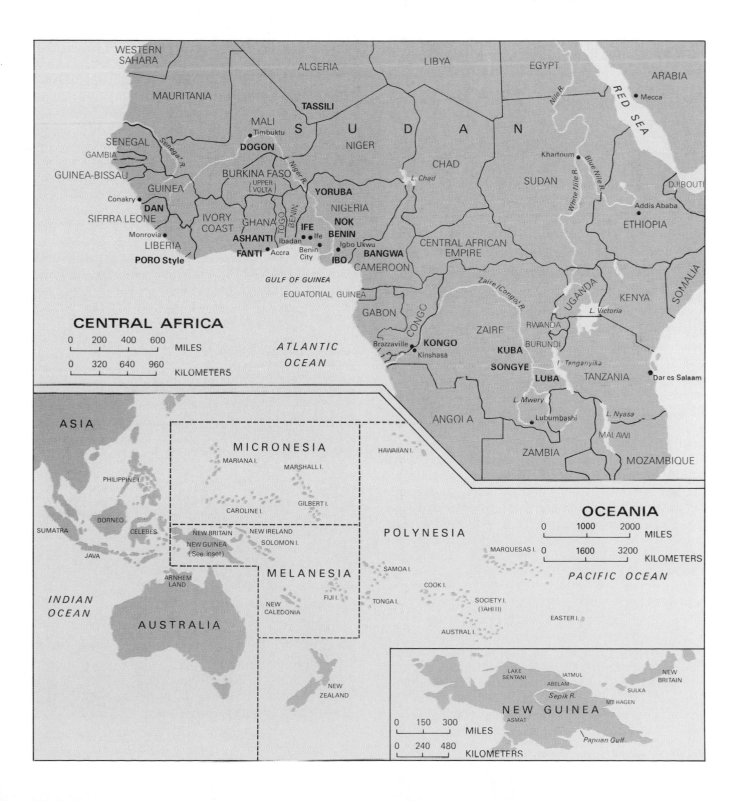

WESTERN SAHARA

ALGERIA

LIBYA

EGYPT

ARABIA

MAURITANIA

TASSILI

MALI

Timbuktu

S U D A N

RED SEA

Mecca

Nile R.

DOGON

NIGER

SENEGAL

Senegal R.

GAMBIA

GUINEA-BISSAU

GUINEA

Conakry

DAN

SIERRA LEONE

Monrovia

LIBERIA

PORO Style

BURKINA FASO
UPPER VOLTA

Niger R.

TOGO

BENIN

YORUBA

NIGERIA

NOK

IFE

BENIN

CHAD

L. Chad

Khartoum

SUDAN

White Nile R.

Blue Nile R.

DJIBOUTI

Addis Ababa

ETHIOPIA

IVORY COAST

GHANA

ASHANTI

FANTI

Ibadan

Ife

Accra

Benin City

Igbo Ukwu

IBO

BANGWA

CAMEROON

CENTRAL AFRICAN EMPIRE

GULF OF GUINEA

EQUATORIAL GUINEA

GABON

CONGO

Zaire (Congo) R.

UGANDA

L. Victoria

KENYA

SOMALIA

CENTRAL AFRICA

| 0 | 200 | 400 | 600 | MILES |
| 0 | 320 | 640 | 960 | KILOMETERS |

ATLANTIC OCEAN

Brazzaville

KONGO

Kinshasa

ZAIRE

RWANDA

BURUNDI

KUBA

SONGYE

LUBA

L. Tanganyika

TANZANIA

Dar es Salaam

L. Mweru

Lubumbashi

L. Nyasa

ANGOLA

MALAWI

ASIA

MICRONESIA

MARIANA I.

MARSHALL I.

HAWAIIAN I.

ZAMBIA

MOZAMBIQUE

PHILIPPINE I.

SUMATRA

BORNEO

CELEBES

CAROLINE I.

GILBERT I.

OCEANIA

| 0 | 1000 | 2000 | MILES |
| 0 | 1600 | 3200 | KILOMETERS |

JAVA

NEW BRITAIN

NEW IRELAND

NEW GUINEA
(See inset)

SOLOMON I.

POLYNESIA

MARQUESAS I.

PACIFIC OCEAN

MELANESIA

SAMOA I.

COOK I.

ARNHEM LAND

INDIAN OCEAN

AUSTRALIA

NEW CALEDONIA

FIJI I.

TONGA I.

SOCIETY I.
(TAHITI)

EASTER I.

AUSTRAL I.

NEW ZEALAND

LAKE SENTANI

IATMUL

ABELAM

Sepik R.

NEW BRITAIN

SULKA

MT HAGEN

NEW GUINEA

ASMAT

Papuan Gulf

| 0 | 150 | 300 | MILES |
| 0 | 240 | 480 | KILOMETERS |

THOUGH RICH AND VARIED and coming from three continents and numerous historical backgrounds of great diversity, the art traditions dealt with in this chapter are more like one another than they are like those of Europe and Asia. An exception is the pre-Columbian art of Central and South America, some phases of which are characterized by monumental architecture, which is not found in the other regions. This, and the preference for working in stone, gives pre-Columbian art a quality of permanence not shared by the art of the other native cultures. (The arts of the North American Indian, of Africa, and of the South Pacific give greater emphasis to transient, impermanent works.) Perhaps the rigidity implied by this preference for enduring materials was partly responsible for the abrupt and complete collapse of Late pre-Columbian cultures under the onslaught of Spanish conquerors. In other parts of the colonized world, native arts tended to survive conquest, declining slowly to extinction or, more frequently, living on to today, albeit in forms modified by Western influence.

In its broadest sense, "pre-Columbian" refers to all the peoples indigenous to the New World as they existed prior to the advent of the Europeans. In practice, however, the term is used to designate the pre-European-contact cultures of Meso-America and South America. Although the Aztec and the Inca are the two groups most commonly associated with the pre-Columbian world, in actuality they represent only a final brief flicker of a flame of cultural development that had been kindled thousands of years before the arrival of Columbus. This development began with a series of migrations—primarily, it seems, via a land bridge from Asia at what is now the Aleutian Island chain. Perhaps as early as 4000 B.C., some of these wandering peoples had developed the food plant maize, and, with agriculture established and a constant food supply assured, these early Americans were able to turn from the time-consuming necessities of hunting and gathering to developing the complex civilizations that were marveled at by the Spanish conquistadors. Their civilizations were impressive not only in grandeur and complexity but in the vastness of time and area in which they developed as well.

MESO-AMERICA

Meso-America (primarily an ethnographic term) includes most of central and southern Mexico and the northern section of Central America. The variety of geographical and climatic conditions one encounters within this vast area (ranging from the temperate central highlands to the hot, humid southern coast of Veracruz) is paralleled in its art styles. In this brief section, we will discuss only four representatives of the many distinct periods and areas of the Meso-American realm.

Olmec

The Olmec were the first to display a number of artistic and social features considered typical of the peoples of Meso-America. For this reason, they are often referred to as the "mother culture" of that region. Although their heartland was principally in the area of La Venta and San Lorenzo (northern Tabasco and southern Veracruz), their influence was felt in many parts of Mexico. La Venta itself was a ceremonial center, with earthen platforms and columns of basalt marking out two large courtyards. Facing out from the courtyard were four huge human heads of basalt (FIG. 14-1). The supple modeling of these heads reflects the ability of the Olmec to manipulate extremely hard materials, such as basalt and jadeite. An equal achievement was the transportation of these huge pieces of stone, the closest known source of which is separated from La Venta by over 60 miles of swampland.

Although the colossal heads may be the best known examples of Olmec stone sculpture, this culture also produced small-scale stone carvings and relief sculpture. The former frequently depicted a crea-

14-1 *Colossal Head,* Olmec, La Venta, Mexico, 1500–800 B.C. Basalt, 8' high, 21' in circumference. © Courtesy National Geographic Society.

14-2 *Important Personage Seated in a Stylized Niche,* Olmec, Chalcacingo, Morelos, Mexico, *c.* 1100–800 B.C. Relief sculpture, approx. 10' high, 9' wide. (Drawing by FRANCES PRATT.)

ture combining the features of a human infant with those of a jaguar. So numerous are these figures that it is believed that the creature was a principal figure in the Olmec pantheon. Numerous relief sculptures on Olmec themes have been found at the highland site of Chalcacingo, apparently an Olmec ceremonial center. One relief (FIG. 14-2) depicts an important personage seated in a stylized niche, while phallic shapes rain downward from clouds above. The scene appears to refer to agricultural fertility and related rites practiced by local Olmec people.

Although there is growing evidence that the Maya may have had an Olmec origin, the sculpture styles of the two cannot be confused. Mayan stone sculpture was predominantly architecture-related, whereas Olmec sculpture emphasized free-standing forms modeled in the full round.

West Mexico

The pre-Columbian peoples of West Mexico produced neither massive architecture nor large-scale stone sculpture and, in general, did not share in the cultural achievements of the central and southern zones of Meso-America. In fact, the West Mexico areas of Jalisco, Nayarit, and Colima have frequently been referred to as cultural "backwaters" relative to the "high" cultures for which Meso-America is most famous.

Yet West Mexico had a long and rich artistic tradi-

tion, principally in the medium of clay sculpture. Effigy figures of humans, animals, and mythological creatures have been encountered in distinctive tombs consisting of shafts (as deep as 50 feet) with chambers at their bottom end. Unfortunately, this area was long neglected by archeologists, and our limited knowledge of the tomb contents derives primarily from the operations of grave robbers.

These large, hollow, ceramic figures exhibit—particularly in the swollen torsos and limbs—a distinct sense of volume. The Colima figures are consistently a highly burnished red–orange, in contrast with the distinctive variegated surfaces of the majority of other West Coast ceramics. The area is also noted for small-scale clay scenes that include modeled houses or temples and numerous solid figurines, the latter shown in a variety of lively activities, some of which have been interpreted as festivals and battles.

It has frequently been observed that the sculpture from this area exhibits a secular quality seldom encountered in the arts of Meso-America. To some degree this viewpoint may have been a result of our inability to discriminate religious from nonreligious objects. Many figures have been identified, for example, as "warriors" or as "shamans." The latter seems to be the correct identification for *The Drinker,* (FIG. 14-3), especially since it is becoming increasingly clear that the arts of this area, with few exceptions, were largely connected with religion and ritual.

14-3 *The Drinker,* seated shaman figure, Colima, Mexico, *c.* A.D. 250. Ceramic, 13" high. Collection of Proctor Stafford, Los Angeles.

Maya

By the early centuries of the Christian era, the Maya Indians, who occupied the moist lowlands of what is now Guatemala, Belize, and the Yucatán Peninsula, had reached a stage of cultural advancement that presupposed development for many centuries. Like all Meso-American cultures, the Maya possessed only tools of stone, wood, and bone, even during their classic period (c. A.D. 250–600), when they erected huge limestone structures with richly carved decorations at such centers as Copán, Tikal, Uaxactún, Yaxchilán, and Palenque. Metal was not used on a large scale in Meso-America until after about 800.

Priests, astronomer–priests, and nobles are believed to have constituted a theocratic government that dominated the mass of the people, who were farmers and artisans. Agricultural activities were probably regulated by religious precept, and people traveled far to visit the ceremonial centers for festivals and markets. The intricate Maya calendar expresses the interaction of such gods as the sun god, the wind god, the maize god, and the death god in astrological combinations for purposes of prophesy and divination.

In building durable stone enclosures, the Maya used a corbeled-vault structure in which the masonry courses projected inward (FIG. 14-4) until they met, producing an interior space with a triangular upper section. Rooms so constructed were never more than about 15 feet wide but might be of any length. Temples constructed in this manner consisted of one or

14-4   Section of a North Maya structure, Chichén Itzá, Mexico, *c.* ninth century: (A) twin corbeled vaults; (B) flying façade; (C) roof comb.

more long, narrow compartments. In some buildings, a pierced roof crest or decorative comb rose above the roof.

A representative temple group (FIG. 14-5) stands at Uaxactún. It was part of a larger assembly of temples and buildings on hilltops, all connected by roadways and covering many square miles. Its base consisted of a series of terraces with stairways leading up to the temple court. The massive temple roofs were sur-

14-5   Temple group, Maya, Uaxactún, Mexico. Carnegie Institute, Washington, D.C. (Reconstruction drawing by T. Proskouriakoff, as of *c.* 700.)

14-6 *Great Dragon*, Maya, Quiriguá, Mexico, sixth century. 7' 3" high.

mounted by ornate and towering roof combs. Both roofs and combs were polished and painted so that their surfaces shone brilliantly.

Wealth of ornament is characteristic of Maya sculpture. This is seen in the stelae, commemorative or calendrical stone shafts 5–25 feet high, erected in the temple plazas. Many bear dates, often recording the day of the erection of the stone. Such stelae were carved from about the first to the seventh or eighth century, so that a stylistic sequence can be accurately charted. Most are crowded with relief carvings, usually consisting of a figure in ceremonial dress surrounded by hieroglyphs and other motifs in low relief.

The huge boulder at Quiriguá, which may have been an altar, is entirely covered with intricate carvings in both high and low relief. The most conspicuous part of the design on the north face is a human figure dressed in rich garments, wearing an enormous, elaborate headdress, and seated in the mouth of a great dragon (FIG. 14-6). Placement of a human figure in the jaws of a reptile is quite common in Maya art and, in view of the fact that serpent forms often symbolize the sky, perhaps indicates the supernatural or god-like character of the human represented.

Maya stone sculpture in the round or in high relief is rare and is usually closely associated with architecture, as in the case of the head and torso of the *Maize God* (FIG. 14-7) from Copán. Sculpture is often found on lintels, jambs, and entire façades.

The work of the Maya painter, like that of the sculptor, was closely coordinated with building and can hardly be considered separately. Most of the reliefs were colored, and most other painting occurs on the inside of temple walls. The painter outlined his figures in red, filled them in with flat colors, and finally outlined the figures again in black.

In the temple discovered in Bonampak in 1947, narrative murals in scenes of rich color cover the walls of the three chambers. In each chamber, lower, middle, and upper registers correspond, respectively, to the

14-7 *Maize God*, Maya, Copán, Honduras, sixth century. Limestone American Museum of Natural History, New York.

14-8 Temple mural of warriors surrounding captives on a terraced platform, Maya, Bonampak, Mexico, *c*. sixth century. Carnegie Institute, Washington, D.C. (Watercolor copy by ANTONIO TEJEDA.)

people, to priests and nobles, and to celestial symbols. The principal scenes deal with preparations for a ritual dance, a raid on a town and the capture of prisoners, sacrifices of prisoners (FIG. 14-8), and the dance.

The records of classic Maya civilization continue to be salvaged by archeology from the dense layers of jungle growth that had concealed them for centuries. Very recently (1984), rich tombs, dating from about 500, were uncovered in northern Guatemala in the area now called Rio Azul. At this writing, they are being carefully studied, and it is believed that the Rio Azul find may be one of the most important of this century. The walls of a crypt, plundered by modern looters, bear vivid pictographs of Maya deities and the insignia of royalty wrought in intricate, crimson, linear patterns. A stirrup-handle pot is adorned with hieroglyphs that may record information about the royal occupants of the tombs. The lid of the pot can be twisted off—surprising testimony to Maya technical knowledge of the principle of the screw, indispensable in modern engineering and unique in the early history of ceramics.

Teotihuacán

Contemporaneous with the period of early classic Maya art was the civilization called Teotihuacán—the name of the great city and ritual center just north of Mexico City. The site was the largest city in the pre-European-contact New World, with a possible population of 100,000 at its height. The builders of its temples were an agricultural people who created a dis-

tinctive art style during the first centuries of the Christian era. They worshiped many nature gods and made innumerable clay figurines of humans to place in their fields, perhaps to ensure fertility.

Teotihuacán ("place of the gods") was laid out so that all of its temples were in symmetrical groupings flanking a broad avenue. The largest and most im-

14-9 Detail of Temple of Quetzalcóatl, Teotihuacán, Mexico, third century (?).

posing temple—the Pyramid of the Sun, a massive pyramidal substructure that once supported a temple—consists of five tiers and one broad stairway, alternately single and double, leading from the ground level to the top. A smaller shrine, the Temple of Quetzalcóatl (a major hero of the Meso-American mythos), lay at the center of a great quadrangle, marked by terraced mounds. Its sculptured panels, because they were covered by subsequent building, are excellently preserved. The temple consists of six terraces, each decorated with massive projecting heads of the feathered serpent Quetzalcóatl, which alternate with heads of the goggle-eyed rain god, Tláloc (FIG. 14-9). Linking these alternating heads are low-relief depictions of feathered serpent bodies and seashells, the latter indicating contact with the coast.

Aztec

The Aztec, a small and war-like tribe from the north, established their capital, Tenochtitlán (now the site of Mexico City), in the Valley of Mexico about 1325. This was to become the center of an extensive empire. The Aztec, as fierce in their religious as in their military life, practiced human sacrifice, believing that as the sun god had sacrificed himself to create man, man was obliged to repay him with the nourishment of human blood. The ritual required not only a splendid temple setting but magnificent costumes and accessories, which, like much of Aztec culture, continued customs already established by predecessors.

Aztec sculpture is famous for its massive, monumental quality, exemplified in the figure of *Coatlicue* (FIG. 14-10), earth goddess and mother of the gods. Her identifying features include a skirt composed of intertwining snakes as well as features symbolic of sacrificial death—a necklace of human hands and hearts, and a skull pendant. The quality of overwhelming monumentality of Aztec sculpture is also present in a variety of realistic, large-scale representations of organic forms, including such diverse entities as snakes, rabbits, grasshoppers, squash, and cacti.

CENTRAL ANDES

Of the three zones (jungle, highlands, and coast) that make up the Central Andean region in South America, two—the coast and the highlands—served as homes for highly developed Andean cultures. The coastal zone is a narrow desert plain transected by fertile valleys; its dryness resulted in the preservation of organic burial offerings to a degree rarely encountered in the New World. The highland zone lies in the Andean Cordillera, where massive ranges are occasionally broken by habitable, high-altitude valleys. Both zones lie in the area composing modern Peru.

Chavín

There is evidence that, in the first millennium B.C., a cult began to grow that, at its height, prevailed over great portions of the coast and highland areas. The cult is called Chavín, after the ceremonial center Chavín de Huantár, which is located in the northern highlands and consists of a number of stone-faced, pyramidal platforms penetrated by narrow passageways and small chambers and associated with a sunken court.

Chavín de Huantár is famed, too, for its stone sculpture. Associated with the architecture and consisting of much sunken relief on panels, lintels, and columns and some rarer instances of sculpture in the round, this sculpture has a linear quality. Free-standing sculpture is represented by an immense cult image in the center of the oldest structure, as well as

14-10 *Coatlicue*, goddess of earth and death, Aztec, fifteenth century. Andesite, approx. 8' 6" high. Museo Nacional de Antropología, Mexico City.

"staff god" (for it is always depicted holding staffs), versions of which have been encountered from Columbia to northern Bolivia, but seldom with the degree of elaboration found at Chavín. In this instance, the squat, scowling deity is depicted with his gaze directed upward. An elaborate headdress dominates the upper two-thirds of the slab. Inverting the image reveals that the headdress is composed of a series of fanged, jawless faces, each emerging from the mouth of the one above it. Snakes abound, extending from the deity's belt, forming part of the staffs, serving as whiskers and hair for the deity himself and the headdress creatures, and, finally, forming a guilloche at the apex of the composition.

The ceramic vessels of the northern Chavín area are easily identified by their massiveness of chamber, spout, and surface relief. The stirrup-spout became popular at this time and continued to be a commonly used north-coast form until the advent of the Spaniards.

Mochica

The great variations occurring within Peruvian art styles are exemplified by two coastal traditions that developed during the period between about 200 B.C. and A.D. 600 in the cultures of the Mochica on the south coast.

The Mochica concern with ritual is clearly reflected in their ceremonial architecture and ceramic vessels. The former consisted of immense, pyramidal, supporting structures for temples that, due to the scarcity of stone, were constructed of sun-dried brick or adobe. Their scale may be surmised from the remains of the Temple of the Sun in the lower Trujillo Valley, which utilized millions of adobes. The temple atop it had already disappeared by the advent of the Spaniards. As a result of persistent treasure-hunting by early colonial residents, only a remnant of the original pyramid remains.

Probably the most famous art objects produced by the ancient Peruvians are the ceramic vessels of the Mochica, which were predomnantly flat-bottomed, stirrup-spout jars, molded without the aid of a potter's wheel and generally decorated with a bichrome slip. (Their abundance can be credited to the ancient Peruvian practice of seeing that the dead were accompanied in the grave by many offerings.) Mochica potters continued to employ the stirrup-spout, making it an elegant tube much more slender than the Chavín prototype. This may be seen in one of the famous

by heads of mythological creatures tenoned into the exterior walls. Although, at first glance, the subject matter of Chavín stone carving appears to exhibit considerable variety, the emphasis is most consistently on composite creatures that combine feline, avian, reptilian, and human features. The Raimondi stone (named after its discoverer) is representative of the late variant of Chavín stone carving (FIG. 14-11). On the lower third of the stone is a figure called the

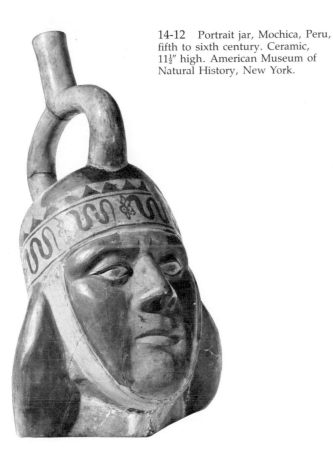

14-12 Portrait jar, Mochica, Peru, fifth to sixth century. Ceramic, 11½" high. American Museum of Natural History, New York.

Mochica portrait bottles (FIG. 14-12), believed to be either a warrior or a priest. In early bottles of this type, the sculptured form was dominant; in time, however, linear surface decoration came to be employed equally. On the top of a Mochica pot (FIG. 14-13) a seated messenger figure is holding the ties of his headdress. Below him, a painted frieze depicts human runners carrying bags. The piece combines realistic modeling with a fine linear style of painting that offers a striking contrast to the bold stylization of the decor on the Nasca vessel shown in FIG. 14-14.

14-13 Messenger and runner figures, Mochica, Peru, fifth to sixth century. Ceramic, 10⅜" high. (Buckingham Fund.) © The Art Institute of Chicago. All rights reserved.

Nasca

Although the Nasca rarely produced ceremonial architecture on a large scale, as was done in the north, they did create a comparable art form in their ceramic vessels, which, unlike their north-coast counterparts, had round bottoms, double spouts connected with bridges, and—most distinctive—smoothly burnished, polychrome surfaces. The subject matter is of great variety, with particular emphasis on plants, animals, and mythological creatures. The initially elegant simplicity of their depiction evolved into a style exhibiting a marked complexity (FIG. 14-14).

14-14 Bridge-spout vessel, Nasca, Peru, c. fifth and sixth centuries. Ceramic with slip, 5⅛" high. Museum of Cultural History, University of California, Los Angeles.

14-15   *Above:* detail of monolithic gateway shown at left, Tiahuanaco, Bolivia, ninth century (?).

Tiahuanaco

The bleak highland country around Lake Titicaca in southeastern Peru contrasts with the warm valleys of the coast. Isolated in these mountains, another culture—named for Tiahuanaco, the principal archeological site on the southern shores of the lake—developed semi-independently of the coastal cultures until 1000, when the style of its art spread to the adjacent coastal area as well as to the highland areas, extending from southern Peru to northern Chile.

At Tiahuanaco, an imposing center was built of massive stones, some of which were joined with copper cramps. The gateway (FIG. 14-15) is monolithic, with a sculptured frieze above the doorway. In the center of the frieze is the image of the "staff god," a deity who was part of the ancient Chavín pantheon. During the Tiahuanaco period, the staff god is frequently associated with smaller-scale, attendant figures—in this instance, rows of winged and sometimes bird-headed men. The importance of the staff god is conveyed not only by the dominance of its scale, but also by its central position and its high relief, which contrast strongly with the low-relief of the attendant figures.

Best known of the Tiahuanaco-style textiles are polychrome tapestries of extremely fine weave, in which the principal motif is frequently a single figure repeated at regular intervals but with varying details (FIG. 14-16). Specific features consistent in this style include a bifurcated "eye" (generally a rounded octagon that is half black and half white), N-shaped canine teeth, and blunt-ended, limb-like forms.

14-16   Textile, Coastal Tiahuanaco style, *c.* 800. Alpaca wool, cotton, 21″ long. Metropolitan Museum of Art, New York.

Inca

The Inca, a small tribe in the southern highlands of Peru, embarked about 1438 on a course of expansion that did not cease until the area from northern Ecuador to central Chile was under their rule.

Although the Inca aimed at imposition of their art style throughout their realm, objects of pure Inca style were confined to areas that came under the power of the southern capital, Cuzco. The Inca were concerned not so much with annihilating local traditions as with subjugating them to those of the empire. Local styles—although they sometimes came to employ a few Inca features—continued to be produced in areas marginal to the centers of Inca power.

Imperial Inca architecture is famous for its dry-masonry techniques. Stone (in the walls of temples or administrative buildings) was occasionally laid in regular horizontal courses, but a dramatic polygonal pattern was more common. One of the most striking aspects of this mortarless masonry is the extreme precision with which stones are fitted together. A prime example of this precision is the Temple of the Sun (FIG. 14-17) in Cuzco, the remains of which now support the apse of a Dominican church.

14-17 Temple of the Sun (now church of Santo Domingo), Inca, Cuzco, Peru, fifteenth century.

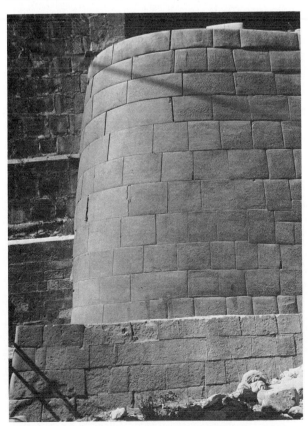

NORTH AMERICAN INDIAN AND ESKIMO

The styles and objects of the North American cultures are well known from the period beginning with prolonged contact with Europeans. However, there is also quite extensive knowledge of much earlier forms and styles. In many parts of the United States and Canada, "prehistoric" cultures have been discovered that reach as far back as 12,000 years, although most of the finer art objects come from the last 2,000 years. "Historic" cultures, designated as such beginning with the earliest date of prolonged contact with Europeans (varying from the sixteenth to the nineteenth century), have been widely and systematically recorded by anthropologists and usually reflect profound changes wrought by the impact of alien tools, materials, and values.

Scholars divide the vast and varied territory involved into a number of areas on the basis of relative homogeneity of language and culture patterns. Both prehistoric and historic art forms from most of these culture areas are discussed briefly in this section.

Prehistoric Era

Eskimo sculpture, often severely economical in the handling of form, is, at the same time, refined—even elegant—in the placement and precision of incised designs, both geometric and representational. A carved ivory burial mask (FIG. 14-18) from the Ipiutak culture (c. 300) is composed of nine carefully shaped

14-18 Set of burial carvings, Ipiutak, c. 300. Ivory, greatest width 9½". American Museum of Natural History, New York.

14-19 Eskimo shaman mask representing a sea-mammal spirit, before 1900. 17" high. Lowie Museum, Berkeley, California.

14-20 Adena pipe, Adena, c. 1000–300 B.C. Stone, 8" high. Ohio Historical Society, Columbus.

14-21 Incised shell gorget, Mississippian culture, Sumner County, Tennessee, c. 1200–1500. 4" wide. Museum of the American Indian, New York.

parts that are interrelated to produce several faces, both human and animal, in the manner of a visual pun. It is a confident, subtle composition in shallow relief, a tribute to the artist's imaginative control over his materials. Over the centuries, Eskimos have also carved hundreds of small figures and animals (usually in ivory) and highly imaginative "mobile" masks (with moving parts) used by shamans (FIG. 14-19) that, due to their fanciful forms and odd juxtapositions of images and materials, were much appreciated by Surrealists in the 1920s.

Early American Indian craftsmen also excelled in working stone into a variety of utilitarian and/or ceremonial objects. The quite realistic handling of the so-called Adena pipe (1000–300 B.C.)—a figural pipe bowl (FIG. 14-20)—provides an interesting contrast to the two-dimensional, more animated composition (FIG. 14-21) found at a Mississippian culture site in Tennessee and dating from the Temple Mound II period (c. A.D. 1200–1500). The incised shell gorget depicts a kneeling personage with an elaborate headdress, carrying a mace in his left hand and a severed human head in his right. The standing pipe figure, although simplified, has naturalistic joint articulations and musculature, a lively, flexed-leg pose, and an alert facial expression—all of which combine to suggest movement. Most Adena and Mississippian objects come from burial and temple mounds and are thought to have been gifts to the dead to ensure their safe, prosperous arrival in the land of the spirits.

14-22 Serpent Mound, Adams County, Ohio. Approx. 1,400' long.

14-23 Cave painting, Chumash (?), Santa Barbara, California.

Other art objects found in such contexts include fine mica and embossed copper cut-outs of hands, bodies, snakes, birds, and other presumably symbolic forms.

One of the larger Indian creations—Serpent Mound (FIG. 14-22) in Adams County, Ohio—is an artistic transformation of the natural environment. Undoubtedly made for spiritual purposes, this monument is a spectacular prehistoric example of the universal practice of creating visually impressive settings for ceremonial activities. The serpent, which has been restored, is about a quarter of a mile long. Other effigy mounds are known, and complex platformed temple mounds have been discovered. The latter, along with small, incised, shell reliefs, such as the Mississippian shell (FIG. 14-21), show strong influence from pre-Columbian Meso-America.

Engravings and paintings on rock are found widely distributed across North America. Many of these are sacred sites and were probably used for communal rituals or the recording of personal spiritual experiences, which were very important in traditional American Indian religions. Rock arts vary from lively naturalistic or schematic renderings of humans and animals to complex, convoluted compositions of as yet undeciphered symbols. Both the symbolic complex in black, white, and red (FIG. 14-23) shown in its cave setting near Santa Barbara, California, and the processions of linear, geometric, human (or spirit) figures (FIG. 14-24) picked into rock surfaces near Dinwoody, Wyoming, have overlays suggesting successive visits, probably for ritual purposes. Precise dating of rock art is often impossible, and, although the examples shown were probably made prior to European contact, others depict horses and guns and have more naturalistic renderings, indicating a later date of execution.

Most Indian art forms (rock painting, pottery, architecture) span great periods of time. Detailed chronological sequences of pottery styles are, in fact, the historian's major tool in dating and reconstructing the cultures of the distant past, especially in the Southwest, where there were no written records.

14-24 Human figures engraved on a sandstone cliff, prehistoric Shoshone (?), Dinwoody, Wyoming. Panel, 8' 2" × 18'.

14-25 Bowl, Mimbres, thirteenth century. Ceramic, 9" in diameter. Peabody Museum, Harvard University, Cambridge, Massachusetts.

Many fine specimens of Southwest ceramics date from before the Christian era until the present day, but pottery became especially fine, and its decoration most impressive, after about 1000.

A thirteenth-century bowl (FIG. 14-25) has an animated, graphic rendering of a warrior with a shield in a composition that creates a dynamic tension between the black figuring and the white ground. Thousands of different compositions are known from Mimbres in the southwest—from lively and often complex geometric patterns to fanciful, often whimsical pictures of humans and animals; almost all are imaginative creations of artists who seem to have been bent on not repeating themselves. Designs are created by linear rhythms balanced and controlled within a clearly defined border. Because the potter's wheel was unknown in the Southwest, countless sophisticated shapes of varied size—always characterized by technical excellence—were built by the coiling method.

In the later centuries of the prehistoric era, Indians of the Southwest constructed many architectural complexes that reflect masterful building skills and impressive talents of spatial organization. Of the many ruins of such complexes, Pueblo Bonito in New Mexico and the "Cliff Palace" at Mesa Verde, Colorado, are among the best known. The Cliff Palace (FIG. 14-26) occupies a sheltered ledge above a valley floor and has about 200 rectangular rooms (mostly communal dwellings) in several stories of carefully laid stone or adobe and timber; 20 larger circular underground structures, called *kivas*, were the spiritual and ceremonial centers of Pueblo life. Pueblo Bonito (FIG. 14-27) contains similar rooms but contrasts with Mesa Verde in its open site and, especially, in its superbly unified plan. The whole complex is enclosed by a wall in the shape of a giant "D." The careful planning suggests it was designed by a single architect or master-builder and constructed by hundreds of workers under a firm, directing hand. Modern ter-

14-26 The "Cliff Palace," Mesa Verde National Park, Colorado, *c.* 1100.

14-27 Pueblo Bonito, New Mexico, *c.* 1100.

14-28 Detail of a kiva painting from Kuaua Pueblo (Coronado State Monument), New Mexico, *c.* 1300–1500. Museum of New Mexico, Santa Fe.

raced pueblos, like Taos in New Mexico, although impressive, reflect neither such unified design nor such a massive, well-organized building effort.

Between 1200 and 1400, long before Europeans arrived in the New World, ancestors of the present-day Hopi and Zuñi decorated their kivas with elaborate mural paintings representing deities associated with agricultural fertility. The detail of the Kuaua Pueblo mural shown (FIG. 14-28) depicts a "lightning man" on the left side, and fish and eagle images (associated with rain) and the partial figure of a "blue corn maiden" on the right side, all of which are associated with the fertility of the earth and the life-giving properties of the seasonal rains.

Historic Era

SOUTHWEST

Obviously, the motivations, functions, and means of art forms from the historic period are better known than those of the art forms from earlier eras. Thus, the complex prehistoric religious murals from the Southwest are hard to interpret, but Navajo sand painting, an art that still survives, is susceptible of detailed elucidation. These highly transient paintings, constructed by artist–priests to the accompaniment of prayers and chants, are an essential part of ceremonies for curing disease. (In the healing ceremony, the patient sits in the center of the painting to absorb the healing, life-giving powers of the gods and their representations.) Similar rites are performed to assure success in hunting and to promote fertility in man and nature alike. The natural materials used (corn pollen, charcoal, and varicolored, powdered stones) play a symbolic role that reflects the Southwest Indians' preoccupation with the spirits and the forces of nature. The paintings, which depict the gods and mythological heroes whose help is sought, are destroyed in the process of the ritual, so that no models exist; still, the traditional prototypes, passed on from artist to artist, must be adhered to as closely as possible, as mistakes can render the ceremony ineffective. Navajo dry-painting style is rigid—composed of simple curves, straight lines, and serial repetition—despite the potential freedom of freehand drawing (FIG. 14-29). Navajo weaving and silver jewelry making are later developments that, until very recently, have met high technical and artistic standards.

Another art form from the Southwest, the Kachina spirit mask, contrasts markedly with the Northwest Coast and Eastern Woodlands masks. The Hopi spirit mask of a rain-bringing deity (FIG. 14-30) is painted in geometric patterns based on rainbow, cloud, and flower forms—quite different from the more expressionistic handling of human physiognomy in the Northwest Coast (FIG. 14-31) and Eastern Woodlands (FIG. 14-39) masks.

14-30 Kachina spirit mask, Hopi, late 1890s. 22" high. Museum of the American Indian, New York.

NORTHWEST COAST

Working in a highly formalized, subtle style, the Indians of the Northwest Coast have produced a wide variety of art objects: totem poles, masks, rattles, chests, bowls, clothing, charms, and decorated houses and canoes. Masks were carved for use by shamans in their healing rites and by others in public reenactments of "spirit quests." The animals and

14-31 Mask, Kwakiutl, c. 1890. Approx. 13¼" high. Denver Art Museum.

14-29 Ceremonial dry painting, Navajo, 1952. Wheelwright Museum of the American Indian, Santa Fe, New Mexico.

14-32 Helmet, Tlingit. Wood, 12″ high. American Museum of Natural History, New York.

14-33 Haida mortuary poles and house frontal poles at Skedans Village, British Columbia, 1878. National Archives, Canada. (After a photograph by George M. Dawson.)

mythological creatures encountered on such quests were, in turn, represented in masks and a host of other carvings. The mask (FIG. 14-31) from the Kwakiutl people owes its dramatic character to the exaggeration of facial parts and to the deeply undercut curvilinear depressions, which give strong shadows. It is a refined, yet forceful carving typical of the more expressionistic styles of the area. Others are more subdued, and some, like a Tlingit helmet (FIG. 14-32), are exceedingly naturalistic, probably actual portraits, almost as if the artist were proving that he could represent whatever he chose to. Inherited motifs and styles were usually preferred, however, above radical new departures. Although Northwest Coast arts have a spiritual dimension, they are more important as expressions of social status, in that the art form one uses and, indeed, the things one may depict, are functions of that status. Haida mortuary poles and house frontal poles (FIG. 14-33), used where totemic crest emblems of clan groups are displayed before the clan chief's house, are striking expressions of this interest in social status.

Another characteristic Northwest Coast art form is the Chilkat blanket (FIG. 14-34), for which male artists provided the designs in the form of pattern boards from which female weavers worked. These blankets, which became widespread prestige items of ceremonial dress during the nineteenth century, display several recurrent characteristics of the Northwest Coast style: symmetry and rhythmic repetition, schematic abstraction of animal motifs (in the blanket illustrated, a bear), eye designs, a regularly swelling and thinning line, and a tendency to round off corners.

14-34 Blanket with bear design, Chilkat. Wild goat's wool and cedar bark in bright colors, approx. 5′ 6″ wide. American Museum of Natural History, New York.

Elegant, precise, and highly accomplished technically, the art of the Northwest Coast is held by many to be one of the sophisticated high points of North American Indian artistic accomplishment.

GREAT PLAINS

Indians of the Great Plains worked in materials and styles quite different from those of the Northwest Coast. Much artistic energy went into decoration of leather garments, first with compactly sewn quill designs and later with beadwork patterns. Tepees, tepee linings, and buffalo-skin robes were painted with geometric and stiff figural designs prior to about 1830; after that, there was a more-or-less gradual introduction of naturalistic scenes, often of war exploits, in styles adapted from those of visiting European artists. The tepee lining illustrated (FIG. 14-35) is of that later style, when realistic action and proportions, careful detailing, and a variety of colors were employed. An example of the earlier type of Plains art is a finely quilled buckskin shirt (FIG. 14-36), which belonged to the Sioux chief Spotted Tail. With attached hair locks and six red and yellow bull's-eye patterns connected by parallel lines, such a garment, especially in motion, would have a dramatic impact.

Because, at least in later periods, most Plains peoples were nomadic, their esthetic attention was focused largely on their clothing and bodies and on other portable objects, such as shields, clubs, pipes, tomahawks, and various containers. Transient but important Plains art forms can sometimes be found in the paintings and drawings of visiting white artists. The Swiss KARL BODMER, for example, accurately portrayed the personal decoration (FIG. 14-37) of Chief Four Bears (Mato-Tope), a Mandan warrior and

14-35 Tepee lining with pictograph of war scenes, Crow, late nineteenth century. Painted muslin, 2' 11" × 7' 1". Smithsonian Institution, Washington, D.C.

14-36 Shirt, Brulé, early nineteenth century. Buckskin with quillwork, beads, and hair locks, 58" arm spread. Museum of the American Indian, Heye Foundation, New York.

14-37 KARL BODMER, *Mandan Chief Mato-Tope*, 1840. Lithograph, 14″ × 10″. Thomas Gilcrease, Institute of American History and Art, Tulsa, Oklahoma.

14-38 Shield, Mandan, North Dakota. Buffalo hide, deerskin, black and green paint, feathers, and bells, approx. 21″ in diameter. Museum of the American Indian, Heye Foundation, New York.

chief. The chief's body paintings and feather decorations, all symbolic of his affiliations and military accomplishments, may be said to be his biography—a composite artistic statement in several media—which could be easily "read" by other Indians. Plains men also made shields and shield covers that were at once art works and "power images." Shield paintings often derive from religious visions; their symbolism, the pigments themselves, and added materials, such as feathers, provided their owners with magical protection and supernatural power. The Mandan example shown (FIG. 14-38) has a central, schematic view of a turtle whose legs, head, and tail radiate outward. This and two smaller motifs are encircled by an undulating line that repeats but varies the round format. The drawing is rough but vigorous.

EASTERN WOODLANDS

Artists of the Eastern Woodlands made quilled and beaded objects and items of clothing, often decorated with curvilinear, floral motifs. The Iroquois also carved compelling, expressionistic masks for use in the False Face Society ceremonies, which healed physical and psychological sickness and cleansed whole communities of destructive impurities (FIG. 14-39). The spirit "faces" portray legendary supernaturals whose exploits are recounted in mythology. Bold in conception, these masks rely on a dramatizing distortion and exaggeration of facial features for their strong effects. Like others used in Africa and Oceania, these masks must be hidden when not in use, lest their power inadvertently cause injury.

Whether secular and merely decorative or spiritual and highly symbolic, the diverse styles and forms of

14-39 ELON WEBSTER, False Face mask, Iroquois, 1937. Wood. (The artist was an Onondaga of the Tonawanda Reservation.) Courtesy of Cranbrook Institute of Science, Bloomfield Hills, Michigan.

North American Indian art testify to the ancient and continuing artistic sensibility of the native Americans. Their creative use of local materials and pigments constitutes an artistic reshaping of nature that, in many cases, reflects the Indians' reliance on and reverence toward the environment that they considered it their privilege to inhabit.

AFRICA

The huge continent of Africa has a population of millions that is subdivided into several racial and linguistic groups. Although nearly all African peoples have produced artists (dancers, musicians, storytellers, rock painters, architects, and adepts at personal decoration), only those peoples dwelling in the vast areas drained by the great Niger and Congo rivers—essentially, tropical Africa—produced the great numbers of sculptures, primarily in wood, that have become deservedly famous as "African art." It is this area that we will survey here.

Africa is as widely varied artistically as it is sociopolitically, geographically, ecologically, linguistically, and racially. Divine rulers head great kingdoms, and groups of elders govern small tribes; forest regions along the coast give way inland to grassy savannas and highlands and, in turn, to the semiarid lands south of the Sahara desert.

Like North America, Africa has hundreds of Neolithic rock painting sites that contain the earliest ex-

14-40 Rock painting, Inaouanrhat, Tassili region, Algeria, c. 3000 B.C.

14-41 Head, Nok, fifth century B.C. to second century A.D. Terra cotta, 9" high. Jos Museum, Nigeria.

amples of its art. These paintings and engravings—considerably more recent than the Paleolithic works found in Spain and southern France—are equally accomplished renderings of humans, animals, and a host of nonrepresentational patterns thought to be symbolic. One very sensitively executed human figure (FIG. 14-40) is a "dancing" woman from Inaouanrhat in the Tassili region of Algeria. She is actively posed and has varied types of body decoration done in several colors and with delicate precision. The dancing figure dates from roughly 3000 B.C., but here, as with many rock paintings, dating is somewhat speculative.

From a number of archeological sites collectively labeled Nok, however, we have more precise radiocarbon dating (c. 500 B.C.–A.D. 200). Here, the earliest African evidence of sculpture in the round was found. Because they are so confidently handled, Nok terra-cotta heads and figures of humans (FIG. 14-41) and animals suggest wooden or other clay prototypes, now lost. No "formative" prototypes are known. Volumes are full and surfaces are smoothly modeled in these terra-cotta sculptures, which some authorities believe to be direct ancestors of Ife terra cottas and bronzes found 150 miles southwest of the Nok area that date from 1000 to 1200.

By about the ninth century, at Igbo Ukwu in tropical Africa, sophisticated *cire-perdue* (lost-wax) casting techniques had evolved (or had been received from

Egypt), and, by the twelfth century, the most naturalistic style known for any tropical African era had appeared. Wood carvings were certainly made in the latter period, too, but no examples have survived. The bronze figure illustrated (FIG. 14-42) is undoubt-

14-42 Ife king figure, Yoruba, tenth to twelfth century. Bronze, 18½" high. Ife Museum, Nigeria.

edly an ancient, divine king of Ife, the city in western Nigeria that is still the spiritual capital of the numerous Yoruba peoples. The king figure, unlike most African wood sculpture, shows flesh-like modeling that attempts a realistic rendering of the human form. The idealized naturalism of the flesh and head in this figure approaches portraiture, although its proportions, which exaggerate the head, are not lifelike. The casting is fine, though somewhat weathered, and accurately records precise details of the costume and jewelry worn by ancient Ife kings.

There are numerous historical and ritual ties between the divine kings of Ife and those who presided over the kingdom of Benin, which was ascendant from the fifteenth to the eighteenth century. Many finely cast, complex bronzes—as well as ivory, wood, terra-cotta, and wrought-iron sculptures—are known from Benin, where bronze casting and ivory carving were royal prerogatives carried out by guilds of highly trained professionals.

An exquisite bronze portrait of a royal lady (FIG. 14-43) shows the Ife–Benin style at its classic height.

14-43 *Queen Mother Head*, early sixteenth century. Bronze, 20″ high. Benin National Museum, Lagos, Nigeria.

14-44 *Altar of the Hand*, 1550–1680, Benin, Nigeria. Bronze, 17½″ high. British Museum, London.

Cast in the *cire-perdue* process, which the Greeks learned from Egypt in the sixth century B.C., the head does seem to be designed on principles of form familiar in Greek idealizing art; the naturalistic traits of the subject are simplified into near-geometric volumes. Of course, no influence from Greek art is to be supposed, although, through the centuries, knowledge of the *cire-perdue* process may have made its way from Egypt across the Sahara desert; or, it may have been independently discovered by native Africans. In any event, the Benin queen and related portraits in clay and bronze do contrast noticeably in their realism of proportion and likeness with the African sculpture we are surveying here. The queenly beauty wears a high, conoid, basket-weave headdress, plaited side curls, and a tight choker; ornamental scars adorn her forehead. The serene and proud composure of her expression is reinforced by the formal control of the elegant surfaces and contours. The perfect unity of form and expression achieved here places this portrait sculpture among the masterpieces of world art.

Much Benin art—like the gilded objects of the Ashanti further west and the altarpiece illustrated (FIG. 14-44)—glorifies the office and trappings of the divine king, who is central and most prominent in this casting, as in many others. As in the Ife king figure (FIG. 14-42), the head is greatly exaggerated, reflecting the view that it is the center of being and the source of power and intelligence. Taken together with the hieratic arrangement of the group, this distortion clearly affirms the importance of symbolism to the artist.

The Ijo Iphri sculpture (FIG. 14-45) manifests the symbolism of power in a less centralized culture than that of Benin. The owner himself is seen sitting atop a monstrous animal (symbolic of his own aggressiveness), holding a fan and libation vessel. This Ijo piece seems more expressionistic in form and freer in invention than the more court-regulated style at Benin (FIG. 14-44).

In understanding the range and quality of African

14-45 Iphri figure, Ijo, Nigeria, nineteenth to twentieth century. Wood, 25½" high. Metropolitan Museum of Art, New York (Michael C. Rockefeller Memorial Collection of Primitive Art, gift of the Matthew T. Mellon Foundation).

14-46 Dancer of the Gelede Society of Meko, Yoruba, Nigeria, 1969.

art, customary definitions must be broadened to include more than monuments, more than objects that can be displayed in museums. This is especially true of the art of masquerade, which depends on music, dance, and costuming for its real vitality. Although many of the wooden masks used in such performances are dramatic carvings in their own right, they should be seen as single, important elements in a complex of interacting artistic media that occupies time as well as space.

The Yoruba Gelede masquerader from Nigeria (FIG. 14-46), photographed in full costume and caught in

14-47 AREOGUN, door from the king's palace at Ikerre, Yoruba, Nigeria, twentieth century. Wood, approx. 6' high. Trustees of the British Museum, London.

Like many African artists, Areogun had a clearly recognizable personal style (his figures are elongated and rather expressionistic), although individuality and personal, idiosyncratic style are of less concern here than, for example, in the modern West.

As the prevalence of the multimedia art of masquerade suggests, dance may be the artistic medium most important and expressive to native Africans. Many sculptures are used in dance contexts, and many others depict people dancing. The vital, energetic figures from the Bangwa kingdom of the Cameroon grasslands (FIG. 14-48) express the vigor of dance in several complementary ways: by active, asymmetrical posing, a thrust-back head with open mouth, constrictions at the joints, which rhythmically energize the figures, and the use of rough textures (surfaces faceted with tool marks). The female figure is believed to portray a priestess and finder of witches. Both stood among dozens of royal carvings depicting ancestors, chiefs, and priests—those, whether living or dead, who were responsible for the continuity of life itself. Such figures—intended to display the wealth, power, and taste of the ruler who presided over them—were gathered for rituals and given food and drink. The importance of artistic display to Cameroon leaders made them major patrons, as well as critics, of the arts.

14-48 Dancing royal couple, Bangwa, Cameroon, nineteenth century, Wood; female 33½" high, male 35½" high. Private collection.

motion, is a case in point. Gelede is a cult devoted to the propitiation and entertainment of powerful senior women and deities associated with witchcraft in Yoruba communities. The masqueraders perform in pairs, their rich, appliqué-panel costumes activated by vigorous dance movements. Theater and ritual combine in the dance, and the masked characters present a bewildering array of traditional and modern types: a motorcyclist, cloth-seller, hunter, leopard, king, white man, prostitute, policeman. Performances involve much social criticism of the community at large, expressed in song, gesture, dance, and in the masks themselves.

The Yoruba—Africa's most prolific artists—have created an abundance of art forms other than masks: cult figures in wood, bronze, terra cotta, and iron, beaded objects and garments, as well as palace houseposts and doors designed to enhance the dignity and prestige of leaders. One such door (FIG. 14-47), which stood at the king's palace at Ikerre, was carved by the master sculptor AREOGUN of Osi. It records the historic visit of an early British colonial, as well as genre scenes and anecdotes of Yoruba life.

14-49 *Mbari* house, Ibo, Ndiama Obube, Nigeria, twentieth century.

Ibo *mbari* houses, like the Yoruba door (FIG. 14-47), are complex works of art. These elaborate, unified complexes—groupings of clay sculptures (often with more than a hundred pieces in one mbari) and paintings in a specially designed architectural setting—are built to honor principal community deities, often the goddess of the earth. In the house shown (FIG. 14-49), the goddess is seated with dignity in the center of the front side, her children close by, her servants, in high relief, standing guard behind. The sculptor has enlarged and extended her torso, neck, and head to express her aloofness and power. She is the apex of a formalized, hieratic composition balanced on either side by seated couples. More informally posed figures and groups are found on the other sides of the house—beautiful, amusing, or frightening figures of animals, humans, and gods taken from history, mythology, and everyday life. The complex, secret mbari construction rituals, as well as the sculptural program, suggest that each house is in fact a cosmic symbol and that the building process itself is a stylized, world-renewal ritual. Ceremonies of opening the house to public view indicate that the god has accepted the offering (of the house) and, for a time at least, will be benevolent. The mbari is never repaired; instead, it is allowed to disintegrate and return to the earth from which it is made and to which it often is dedicated. The mbari, then, is a relatively transient art form, as are the arts of masquerade, personal ornamentation, and festivals. (The last three are best seen on film, which preserves the movement inherent in their design.)

Ancestral or power images from the Belgian Congo (modern Zaire) are more conventional sculptural forms, often carefully preserved by their owners for generations. The commemorative, ancestral mother-and-child carving from the Kongo peoples has a smooth, refined delicacy (FIG. 14-50), whereas the composite power figure from the Songye, a people

14-50 Ancestral figure, Kongo, Zaire, nineteenth to twentieth century. Wood and brass, 16" high. Musée Royal de l'Afrique Centrale, Tervuren, Belgium.

living several hundred miles to the east, deals with the human form more abstractly, in abrupt and forceful carving (FIG. 14-51). The functions of the two are comparable, both being visible manifestations of ancestral power, which can so materially affect people's lives. The Kongo piece, probably a symbolic repository of the soul of a deceased noblewoman, received prayers invoking her continuing care and beneficence; the Songye figure directed (for the benefit of the community) specific ancestral powers activated by (and to some extent contained in) various "medicines" placed inside and on the figure. The most common purposes of such power figures were protection in warfare, promotion of human and crop fertility, curing disease, and ending drought.

The dramatic stylistic contrast between the Songye image and the Kongo mother and child suggests the wide range and variety of carving conventions present in Africa. Indeed, tendencies toward realism or toward abstraction are not easily charted on the African map; deviations sometimes occur between neighboring tribes, within a tribe, and, occasionally, in the

work of a single artist, as is the case among the Dan and related peoples of Liberia, Sierra Leone, and the Ivory Coast. Like many African peoples, the Dan evolved a great variety of masks representing judges, policemen, priests, and a host of other people, both harmful and helpful. In many cases, the role conferred by the mask was functionally real. A person wearing a judge or an executioner mask, for example, actually judged cases or executed criminals. Members of the men's masking society, armed with the power of the bush spirits and clothed in anonymous masking costumes, regulated the behavior of the community. The society also held masked entertainments, impersonating secular personages, whose behavior was held up for public scrutiny, or performing spectacular acrobatic and stilt dances.

Dan woodcarvers, required to make representations of varied spiritual and secular types, became skilled in several contrasting styles. The same man could carve a refined, polished mask depicting a beautiful woman (FIG. 14-52) and a rougher, highly abstracted mask called *kagle* (FIG. 14-53). In fashioning the female mask, the carver has simplified facial planes and brought their smooth surfaces to a high polish, while retaining naturalistic shapes and the placement of features. The carver of kagle, on the other hand, simplifies and abstracts, creating a series

14-51 Power figure, Songye, Zaire, nineteenth to twentieth century. Wood, iron, copper, horn, fibers, cowrie shells, feathers, and glass beads, 35" high. Musée Royal de l'Afrique Centrale, Tervuren, Belgium.

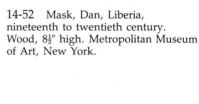

14-52 Mask, Dan, Liberia, nineteenth to twentieth century. Wood, 8½" high. Metropolitan Museum of Art, New York.

14-53 *Kagle* (mask), Dan, Sierra Leone, c. 1775–1825. Wood, 9" high. Yale University Art Gallery, New Haven, Connecticut (gift of Mr. and Mrs. James M. Osborn for the Linton Collection of African Art).

of forceful thrusting and receding positive and negative shapes with great dramatic impact.

The royal Kuba sculptors of the central Congo (Zaire) created an entirely different type of mask to represent a primordial ancestor who helps to oversee the ritual passage of boys into adulthood. (Many other African peoples have masks used in analogous ceremonies.) Several of these, like the *mboom* mask illustrated here (FIG. 14-54), employ a rich combination of beads, feathers, copper, fur, and raffia—all attached to a carved, wooden helmet. Thus, a strong basic head shape with a bulging forehead is overlaid with visually complex, textural effects that are Kuba symbols of royalty.

The seated male and female sculpture shown in FIG. 14-55 is an example of another well-known African style, that of the Dogon people of Mali. Depicting mythical ancestors of the human race, this group is a masterfully integrated composition of vertical forms enclosed by tubular shapes, with geometric incised decorations on the surfaces of both. Rejecting naturalistic rendering in this instance (though he was capable of it), the Dogon sculptor seems here to have dismantled the human body, straightening, simplifying, and distorting its parts before reassembling them. Body parts are present but often sharpened,

attenuated, or reduced to suggestions. Perhaps it was this primordial couple's remoteness from life that prompted the artist to work in such a schematic style. In any case, the group remains one of the great monuments of African creative genius, a strong and complex statement about human values—indeed, about the very origins of the human race itself.

Recent research among the Baule people of the Ivory Coast has led to new information regarding the male and female figures so popular in European and American private and public collections. Figures that represent spirit ''marriage partners'' (*blolo bla*, the male, and *blolo bia*, the female) differ neither formally nor conceptually from figures that represent wild

14-55 *Couple*, Dogon, Mali. Wood, 30" high. Photograph copyright © 1975 by the Barnes Foundation.

14-54 *Mboom* helmet mask, Kuba, Zaire, nineteenth to twentieth century. Wood, brass, cowrie shells, beads, seeds, 13" high. Musée Royal de l'Afrique Centrale, Tervuren, Belgium.

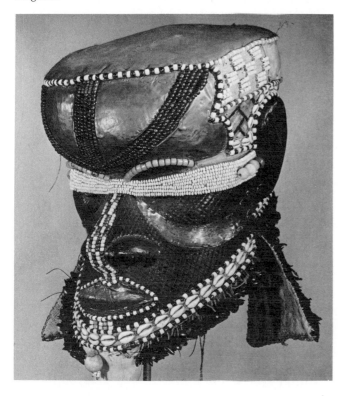

bush spirits (*asie usu*). The main distinction is found in the surface. The asie usu (FIG. 14-56) have a "sacrificial patina"—a surface thickly encrusted with matter accumulated when they are "fed" during sacrificial ritual; the spirit "marriage partners," on the other hand, are rubbed and polished, so that, in time, they acquire a smooth and shiny surface.

African arts also include beautifully decorated, utilitarian objects such as stools, chairs, pipes, and spoons; a host of sculptural as well as decorated buildings; body painting and scarification; miniature objects, such as the well-known Ashanti gold weights; finely crafted textiles and leatherwork; and countless forms of pottery and basketry. Subdivision of the arts into "fine," "decorative," and "craft" is, in

14-56   *Wild Bush Spirit,* Baule, Ivory Coast, nineteenth to twentieth century. Wood, male figure approx. 22″ high. Metropolitan Museum of Art, New York (Michael C. Rockefeller Memorial Collection of Primitive Art, gift of Nelson A. Rockefeller, 1969).

fact, a barrier to the understanding of African artistic sensibilities, for African arts often play a role in everyday affairs, as well as in the life-crisis rituals such as initiations, funerals, and the countless other events that punctuate human existence.

OCEANIA

Relative to the abundant records associated with Western art, there is little historical depth to the arts of Oceania even though archeologists, linguists, and others have gone far in sorting out migration routes, language and racial distributions, and early aspects of Stone Age technology and social organization. The thousands of islands that make up Oceania are conventionally divided into three cultural areas— Polynesia, Melanesia, and Micronesia.

Polynesia was the last area in the world to be settled. Its inhabitants seem to have brought complex sociopolitical and religious institutions with them, and there is a general homogeneity of style (lacking in Melanesia), despite the relative isolation of various island groups during the several centuries prior to European exploration. Polynesian societies are typically aristocratic, with ritual specialists and elaborate political organizations headed by chiefs. Polynesian art forms often serve as a means of upholding spiritual power, *mana,* which is vested in the nobility and channeled by ancestral and state cults.

Melanesia was certainly settled early, and its art forms seem to suggest a variety of overlays of style and symbolism brought with a series of migrations. Art styles are numerous and extremely varied. Typical Melanesian societies are more democratic than Polynesian societies and relatively unstratified. Their cults and art forms address a host of nature and legendary ancestral spirits. Masks, absent in Polynesia, are central in many Melanesian spirit cults, and elaborate festivals, in which masks and other art forms are displayed, occur with some frequency.

Micronesia, in contrast to the other two areas, has little visual material and will not be discussed. The rich arts of Australia, though quite distinct from those of other areas, are often included in discussions of Oceanic art and will be mentioned briefly here.

Polynesia

Polynesian artists excelled in carving figural sculptures in wood, stone, and ivory in sizes ranging from the gigantic fabled stone images of Easter Island to tiny ivory Marquesan ear plugs an inch long. These sculptures were generally full-volumed, monochromatic human figures, often dynamic in pose. Polynesians were also adept in making decorative bark cloth, called *tapa,* and the art of tattoo was highly developed.

Polynesian carving at its most dramatic is represented by the Hawaiian figure of the war god, *Kukailimoku* (FIG. 14-57). Huge wooden images of this deity were erected on stone temple platforms that, in varied forms, were part of the apparatus of all Polynesian state religions. Although relatively small, the figure illustrated here is majestic in scale and forcefully carved to convey vigorous tensions—in short, the ferocity attributed to the deity. Flexed limbs and faceted, conventionalized muscles combine with the aggressive, flaring mouth and serrated headdress to achieve a tense dynamism seldom rivaled in any art. This is the work of a master sculptor supremely confident of his materials and technique—a work that speaks forcefully across cultural barriers.

Even though Polynesians were skillful navigators, various island groups remained isolated enough from one another to allow distinct regional styles to de-velop within a recognizable, general Polynesian style. Thus, the arts of central Polynesia—represented here by the contrasting art forms of a wooden *District God* (FIG. 14-58) and a skeletalized, double-headed male figure from Easter Island (FIG. 14-59)—are quite different from the Hawaiian figures. The highly polished *District God* from the Cook Islands (FIG. 14-58) has a blade-shaped head and schematized features. Instead of a body, numerous tiny, abstracted figures—the god's progeny—are carved in the same geometric, angular style as the head above. Such carvings probably represented clan ancestors, revered for their

14-59 Double-headed male figure (*moai kava-kava*), Easter Island, before 1860. Wood, approx. 16" high. Museum of Natural History, La Rochelle, France.

14-57 *Kukailimoku,* Hawaii. Wood, 30" high. British Museum, London.

14-58 *District God,* Cook Islands, nineteenth century. Wood, approx. 25" high. Peabody Museum, Harvard University, Cambridge, Massachusetts.

14-60　Tattooed Marquesan warrior, nineteenth century. Engraving.

aggressive sculpture of the Hawaiian war god (FIG. 14-57).

Polynesians developed the painful but prestigious art of tattoo more fully than other Oceanic peoples. Nobles and warriors, especially, were concerned with increasing their status, mana, and personal beauty by accumulating such patterns over the years. An early nineteenth-century engraving (FIG. 14-60) shows Marquesan tattoo patterns, with divided and subdivided geometric motifs, covering most of the body. Such a multiplication of small, repetitive, abstract forms—also seen in the "children" on the Cook Islands figure (FIG. 14-58)—is one major tendency in much Polynesian art. The other main tendency—toward bold, full-volume, large-scale figural sculptures—is manifest in the Hawaiian war god (FIG. 14-57).

The highly distinctive arts of the Maori peoples of New Zealand merge these two stylistic currents in images that are at once dynamic and intricate, bold in major forms but with surfaces covered and interconnected by minute curvilinear detailing. The door lintel shown (FIG. 14-61) comes from a council house generously decorated, inside and out, with technically refined, complex imagery. The subjects are real and mythological ancestors, whose advice and protection were sought for the political, war-making, and ritual deliberations that took place in their midst. Countless prestige items and weapons of the Maori nobility displayed this unique style, as did the tattooing on their faces and bodies (Introduction, FIG. 15).

Melanesia

Despite the aggressive poses of the figural art of Hawaii and the lively surface convolutions found in the art of New Zealand, Polynesian art is generally characterized by compactness, solidity, and restraint, as exemplified in the Cook Islands *District God* (FIG. 14-58). Melanesian art, on the other hand, has an insubstantial, colorful, flamboyant aspect, epitomized in bark-cloth masks from the Baining of New Britain

protective and procreative powers. Analogous images from Mangaia in the Cook Islands and Rurutu in the Austral Islands also have multiple figures attached to their bodies. All such images refer ultimately to creator deities, revered for their central role in human fertility. The double-headed male figure (FIG. 14-59) may represent a mythological ancestor or deity of the early inhabitants of Easter Island. Its bent posture and the emphasis on skeletal structure reflect an esthetic quite different from that of the massively

14-61　Door lintel, Maori, New Zealand, late nineteenth century. Wood, 19″ × 45″. Peabody Museum of Salem, Massachusetts.

14-62 Composite day dance helmet and mask, Northwest Baining, New Britain, twentieth century. Bark cloth and bamboo, approx. 9' long. George A. Corbin, New York.

(FIG. 14-62) and in woodcarving from New Ireland (FIG. 14-63). The Baining mask is made of bark cloth and bamboo, painted with charcoal and plant-derived pigments. It is used only once—for a day-long, night-long ceremony to celebrate the harvest and to commemorate the dead—and then discarded. Similar forms are made anew the following year at harvest time, only to be discarded again after use. The black-and-white designs that cover the mask are symbols of the growth of garden plants; the long, protruding, cone-shaped form refers to the growth of coconut trees. The bewildering intricacy of the New Ireland wood carvings (FIG. 14-63)—called *malanggan* and used in display ceremonies of the same name—stems from generous use of openwork and sliver-like projections and from over-painting in minute geometric patterns that further subdivide the image. The result is a "splintered" or fragmented and airy effect. This style is the more remarkable in view of the fact that most of these forms are carved from a single block of wood, a characteristic of all woodcarving considered in this chapter. In the scene shown, several malanggan showpieces are set up in a special house dramatically opened to the public; the associated rituals served both to commemorate ancestors and to ini-

14-63 Malanggan tableau, New Ireland, nineteenth to twentieth century. Bamboo, palm and croton leaves, painted wood, approx. 8' high, 16' 6" wide, 10' deep. Museum für Völkerkunde, Basel, Switzerland.

14-64 Ceremonial Men's House, Abelam, New Guinea.

tiate youths into adulthood. Dancers wearing a variety of intricate masks also performed during these rites.

The Melanesian penchant for color and drama in art is reflected too in the Abelam cult sculptures and paintings found on and inside the monumental Men's Houses in New Guinea (FIG. 14-64). The gable paintings on these buildings show row on row of mythological creatures, intricately painted in contrasting bright colors. This kind of repetition and almost compulsive space-filling, common to many art areas considered in this chapter, can be seen in the

bark-cloth banner from Lake Sentani, near the North Coast of New Guinea (FIG. 14-65). Such banners— display cloths for funeral and other ritual occasions— are painted in a lively and, to us, somewhat whimsical style and illustrate a variety of aquatic creatures and symbols that may well refer to myths.

In other Melanesian art forms, from the Papuan Gulf and Asmat areas of New Guinea's South Coast, the artists distort human forms according to local preferences, which here, as elsewhere, are not attuned to realistic proportions or modeling. The fact that remote spirits (Papuan Gulf, FIG. 14-66) and ancestors (Asmat, FIG. 14-67) are portrayed partially accounts for the lack of naturalism, as do the long traditions of repeating and renewing such spiritual images—a repetition that seems to give rise to highly conventionalized styles in conservative societies. The Papuan Gulf figure is a Melanesian version of the power image, whose in-dwelling spirit is invoked to protect and otherwise benefit its owner. The Asmat pole is erected in ceremonies that prepare the participants to avenge the death of a community member in war. Such poles represent ancestors; the openwork "flags" are penises, exaggerated in a reflection of the Asmat male's aggressive roles in sex and head-hunting.

These and many other Oceanic peoples were head-hunters until early in the twentieth century, and many of their art forms were created for rituals concerned with head-hunting and attendant beliefs about the loss and gain of the life-force. In several cultures, as among the Iatmul of the Sepik River, artists cleaned actual human skulls and reworked them into art objects (FIG. 14-68) by modeling over the skull with a clay-like paste and painting the result with the kinds of flowing facial decoration worn in life, particularly on ritual occasions. These graphic images (a fascinating parallel to the "reconstructed" prehistoric skulls found at Jericho, FIG. 2-2) were believed to contain the life-force or power that men sought to increase by headhunting; the heads were displayed in ceremonies preparing for war or celebrating its success, as well as at funerals.

14-65 Banner, Lake Sentani, New Guinea. Bark cloth, tapa, black and red paint, 52" long. Collection of Paul Wingert, New York.

14-66 Spirit figure, Papuan Gulf, New Guinea. Wood, fibers, bark, red and white paint, 51" long. Tropenmuseum, Amsterdam, Netherlands.

14-68 Skull, Iatmul, New Guinea, nineteenth to twentieth century. Human skull, clay, paint, human hair, cuscus fur, 10" high. Metropolitan Museum of Art, New York (gift of Mr. and Mrs. John J. Klijman).

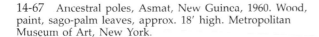

14-67 Ancestral poles, Asmat, New Guinea, 1960. Wood, paint, sago-palm leaves, approx. 18' high. Metropolitan Museum of Art, New York.

Face and body decoration are still important art forms in several parts of New Guinea. Although of course extremely transient, such embellishments can be highly complex, colorful, multimedia assemblages of pigments, feathers, fur, leaves, shells, and other materials, which gain both symbolic significance and artistic impact from their combination. Men and women decorate themselves in this fashion to display their idealized beauty and to compete with rivals similarly embellished.

Varied types and styles of masks were worn in Iatmul ceremonies, as well as in ceremonies of the peoples of New Britain, New Ireland, Abelam, the Papuan Gulf, Asmat, and other areas. Such masks, as in Africa and America, were used in ceremonies to materialize spirits whom man felt the need to entertain and propitiate. Elaborate festivals sometimes included over a hundred such "spirit impersonators," who danced to entertain the human community and, at the same time, to remind it of its obligations to supernatural ancestors and culture-bringers. Many of the same masked spirits played an important role in initiating and educating youths to be fully socialized, productive members of the group. Especially in the design of the heads and bodies of spirits, Melanesian artists seem to have given free rein to their creativity and imagination. A bizarre, flamboyant Sulka mask (FIG. 14-69), but one example, is of a kind made by stretching and sewing vegetable fibers over a light framework. These and other Melanesian masks were quite perishable; indeed, in some areas, the masks were ritually destroyed at the end of a ceremony, an act that banished the spirits until their next "invitation" to intervene in human affairs.

14-69   Mask, Sulka, Melanesia, 1900–1910. Fiber structure covered with pith, feathers, and pieces of wood, 27″ high (without leaf skirt). Übersee-Museum, Bremen, West Germany.

14-70   Canoe-prow figure, Solomon Islands, Melanesia, nineteenth to twentieth century. Wood with mother of pearl, 6½″ high. Museum für Völkerkunde und Schweizerisches Museum für Volkskunde, Basel, Switzerland.

Some Melanesian styles, like that of the Solomon Islands, are more restrained than those just discussed. In the protective canoe-prow carving shown (FIG. 14-70), the emphasis is on strong modeling, the enlargement of facial features, and very precise inlay patterns of seashell fragments that contrast with the solid dark color of the head itself. In several Melanesian areas, styles combine high-contrast, intricate surface patterns with bold sculpture, and, in some, masks are not used—suggesting that these may be transitional cultures between those in which the wilder, less restrained Melanesian style prevails and those in which the Polynesian style, with its more solid, full-volumed sculpture, is dominant.

Australia

A number of varied styles, as well as object types, in Australia bear little relationship to the arts of neighboring New Guinea. Most objects are ceremonial aids used to project the Australian people into the legendary past, called "Dream Time," when their world, its creatures, and its institutions were created. For the native Australian, the fertility of nature and man and the continuity of life itself depended on reenactments of the primordial events of Dream Time. Cosmogonic myths were recited in concert with songs and dances, and many art forms (body painting, decorated stones, carved figures, rock and bark paintings) were essential props in these dramatic re-creations. A bark painting by MUNGARAWAI, entitled *The Djanggawul Sisters* (FIG. 14-71), describes, in schematic form, the birth of the human race along with other mythical episodes from Dream Time, the Djanggawul sisters and brothers being the mythological progenitors of the Yirrkala people of Arnhem Land. Symbolic motifs include trees and pole emblems, the rising and setting sun, a Djanggawul brother, and (top right) the artist himself. The intricate style is representative of the main features of Yirrkala art: rhythmic repetition, subdivision into crowded panels, fine detailing, and lack of a ground line, perspective, or modeling.

Australian art is well known, too, for its "X-ray" style, which simultaneously depicts the insides (backbone, heart, and other organs) as well as the outsides of human beings and animals (FIG. 14-72). This style of painting is common to the area of Arnhem Land called Oenpelli. Our example shows a hunter and his quarry, a black kangaroo, at the moment a spear is about to strike the startled animal. In contrast to the rather static order of the Yirrkala composition, the Oenpelli painting has a fluid and dynamic quality. The figures are large in relation to the surface on which they have been placed and, unlike the distant, "bird's-eye" view of the Yirrkala painting, the immediacy of the depicted action tends to draw the viewer into its orbit.

14-71 MUNGARAWAI, *The Djanggawul Sisters*, Yirrkala, Arnhem Land, Australia. Bark and paint. Art Gallery of New South Wales, Australia.

14-72 *Hunter and Kangaroo,* Oenpelli, Arnhem Land, Australia, *c.* 1913. Paint on bark, 51″ × 32″. National Museum of Victoria, Melbourne, Australia.

Although each area still produces artifacts of various sorts, some of high quality, the advent of modern mechanized life—bringing with it schools, missions, inexpensive clothing, plastic utensils—has changed artistic motivations and needs. Today, one finds "tourist" arts, poor copies of earlier works, and some frankly modern works that draw inspiration from current European styles.

In earlier times, artistic energies were released on countless occasions and for hundreds of reasons, all bearing on the social and spiritual well-being of men and women. Some artifacts took their places in the daily rhythms of existence; others emerged only at climactic individual or community events (initiations, funerals, festivals, for example), when they often served as symbols of higher, guiding powers. In nearly all cases, the wealth and prestige of the people were involved, and the art works were a focus of spiritual energy, activated in performance and display. As in all times and all places, art served to dramatize and intensify life itself, and life without art was virtually unknown.

AFTERWORD: THE PRESENT

The traditional arts of North America, Africa, and Oceania we have surveyed here are, for the most part, not now being practiced, for they no longer have critical roles in cultural continuity and survival. Ironically, only now are we coming to acknowledge the variety and richness of these earlier art traditions—at a time when most of them may no longer be accessible for study and preservation.

IV

THE RENAISSANCE AND THE BAROQUE AND ROCOCO

The Medieval period was once regarded as a thousand dark and empty years separating the "good" eras—Classical antiquity and modern times, the Renaissance being thought of as "early modern." But beginning in the nineteenth century, a more cosmopolitan and tolerant taste and a more discerning and accurate historical method readjusted the view, and to us the Middle Ages are no longer so "dark" as once depicted. In the same way, the

GIANLORENZO BERNINI, *The Ecstasy of St. Theresa*, 1645–1652. Marble, life-size. Cornaro Chapel, Santa Maria della Vittoria, Rome.

Renaissance ("rebirth"), spanning roughly the fourteenth through the sixteenth century, no longer seems, as it was once thought to be, the abrupt onset of the modern world suddenly shining forth in the fifteenth century to illuminate Medieval darkness with the rekindled light of Classical antiquity. Much of the Renaissance has its roots in epochs that long "preceded" the Middle Ages, and much that is Medieval continues in the Renaissance and even much later. Since the mid-nineteenth century, when Jacob Burckhardt wrote his influential and still highly valuable work *The Civilization of the Renaissance in Italy*, the precise dividing line between the Middle Ages and the Renaissance and even the question of whether there ever was a Renaissance have been disputed. Without reopening these issues, it may be useful to examine the Renaissance characteristics that, although originating in the earlier period, seem to have matured and to have become influential during the period from the fourteenth through the sixteenth century.

Medieval feudalism, with its patchwork of baronial jurisdictions and sprawling, inefficient local governments, yielded slowly to the competition of strong cities and city-states, which were increasingly in league with powerful kings, both being the natural political enemies of the countryside barons. The outlines of the modern state, with its centralized administrations, organized armies, aggressive expansionism, and "realistic" politics, began to become firm about this time. The discovery of the world outside Europe—especially the Western Hemisphere and Africa, itself so dramatically expressive of Renaissance expansiveness—brought vast treasures of gold and silver into Europe, beginning its transformation into a money economy, a process already begun in the thirteenth century in the commercial cities of Italy. Increasingly, religion came under the direction of the clergy of the cities, particularly of such orders as the Dominicans and the Franciscans; the claims of the popes to temporal as well as spiritual supremacy were surrendered, and they became merely splendid Italian princes. Eventually, with the upheaval of the Protestant Reformation, which fractured the old Medieval religious unity, religion became almost a branch of the state, with kings and princes well in control of its secular manifestations. Dramatic events in science, like Nicolaus Copernicus' enunciation of the heliocentric theory of the solar system, set the scene for the development of the first successful empirical science—mathematical physics. The opening of the heavens to Western man's scrutiny was attended by the renewed physical exploration of the globe and, until recently, by the increasing subjugation of it to the will of Europe. Technological advances in navigation, metallurgy, mechanics, and warfare helped greatly to that end.

The religious fanaticism that had launched the Crusades—Europe's first extended contact with non-European civilizations—was replaced during the Renaissance by motives of calculated economic interest mingled with the genuine and fruitful curiosity of the explorer. Indeed, the Renaissance was precisely what it has often been called, an "age of discovery," when Europe saw before it an almost fantastic realm of possibility open to all men of merit who could perceive it.

Accompanying the great events that quite clearly set the Middle Ages and the Renaissance apart were subtler changes of human attitude. There was a slow turning away from the ideas and values of a supernatural orientation and toward those concerned with the natural world and the life of man. The meaning of the world and of human life came to be couched in terms that were not exclusively religious. The spirit and dogma of Medieval religion—even its emotional color—were modified as the worldly philosophy of the Greco–Roman tradition revived and took on new strength. But the process of humanization had begun well before the full influence of the pagan tradition was felt; the twelfth century had seen its beginning. In the thirteenth century, the teachings of St. Francis had humanized religion itself and had called man's attention to the beauty of the world and of all things in it, even though he understood the physical beauty he celebrated as a manifestation of the spiritual; nevertheless, his emphasis was clear, and the Franciscan message calls attention to the God-made beauties of the natural order. This message had special significance for the naturalism of proto-Renaissance art. The duty of Medieval man—the focus of his life—was to procure, through the sacred offices of the Church, the salvation of his immortal soul. In the Renaissance, though the obligation and concern remained and the institutions of the Church retained power, nature and the relations among human beings simply became *more interesting* than theological questions. Theology, like institutional Christianity, persisted; so also, for centuries, did fervent Christian devotion. But there can be no doubt that they were affected by a new spirit—the spirit of pagan humanism—which curiously joined with and reinforced the Christian humanism of St. Francis. The intellectual and artistic history of the modern world is as much the history of Christianity's reaction to this new spirit as it is a history of the challenge of that spirit to Christianity. Actually, the challenge and the reaction interacted, modifying each other. The dialogue between the late Greco–Roman world and nascent Christianity commenced again in the Renaissance; since that time, it has been supplemented and amplified by other, even stronger voices, especially those of modern science.

Whereas the veritable face and body of the human being emerged in the transition from Romanesque to Gothic sculpture, Renaissance art brings Western humanity rapidly into full view—a phenomenon that resembles the manifestation of the human figure in Greek art in the sixth and fifth centuries B.C. The Renaissance stresses the importance of the individual, especially men of merit. In life and in art, the focus is sharpened; at last, individuals are real, are solid, and cast a shadow. Medieval man saw himself as corrupt and feeble of will—in fact, capable of acting only by the agency of God's grace. Although many thinkers, both Protestant and Catholic, insisted on this view for centuries, the Renaissance view is different: man may make himself. He is assumed to have a power of agency—God-given, to be sure—that, in the greatest of men, becomes the divine gift of "genius." Thus, in the Renaissance, those who think may overcome the curse of original sin and, in so doing, rise above its devastating load of guilt to make themselves, if they will, what they will. In his *Oration on the Dignity of Man* (the very title of which constitutes a bold new claim), Giovanni Pico della Mirandola, an ingenious and daring Renaissance philosopher, represents God giving the following permission to all in a way that reflects a sharp departure from the Medieval sense of man's natural helplessness:

> The nature of all other beings is limited and constrained within the bounds of laws prescribed by Us. Thou, constrained by no limits, in accordance with thine own free will . . . shalt ordain for thyself the limits of thy nature. We have set thee at the world's center . . . and have made thee neither of heaven nor of earth, neither mortal nor immortal, so that with freedom of choice and with honor . . . thou mayest fashion thyself in whatever shape thou shalt prefer.*

This option would have been almost unthinkable in the Middle Ages: could one really aspire beyond the angels or debase oneself below the beasts and inanimate nature, given one's place in the carefully articulated "chain of being" that God had made permanent?

---

*Giovanni Pico della Mirandola, *Oratio de hominis dignitate* (1485), trans. by E.L. Forbes, in Ernst Cassirer et al., eds., *The Renaissance Philosophy of Man* (Chicago: University of Chicago Press, 1956), pp. 224–25.

Whether or not one could indeed so rise or fall, the leaders of the Renaissance were acutely aware of the new possibilities open to their talents and did not fail to recognize, and often advertise, the powers they were confident they possessed. The wide versatility of many Renaissance artists— like Alberti, Brunelleschi, Leonardo da Vinci, and Michelangelo—led them to experimentation and to achievement in many of the arts and sciences and gave substance to that concept of the archetypal Renaissance genius—*l'uomo universale,* "the universal man." Class distinctions and social hierarchies had loosened, and the ambitious and talented could now take their places even as the friends, companions, and advisers of princes. Such persons could win the award of everlasting fame, and what has been called the "cult of fame" went naturally with the new glorification of individual genius. Indeed, the immortality won through fame may have been more coveted by many great men of the time than the spiritual immortality promised by religion. When the painter Fra Filippo Lippi died in 1469, the town of Spoleto requested that it be allowed to keep his remains on the grounds that Florence, his native city, already had many celebrated men buried within the bounds of its walls.

Petrarch, the great Italian poet and scholar of the fourteenth century, who may fairly be said to have first propounded those peculiarly Renaissance values of versatile individualism and humanism nourished by the study of Classical antiquity, has been called the high priest of the "cult of fame" and, by many, the founder of the Renaissance. Petrarch himself was crowned with the ancient symbol of triumph and fame, the laurel wreath, on the Capitoline Hill in Rome; the occasion was a celebration of his superb sonnets (written in native Italian), which open the age of Renaissance literature. Petrarch, in his development of the "cult of fame," postulated that public recognition is never given to an unworthy work or talent and that, therefore, public glory is proof of excellence. After Petrarch, it would be possible to call both great works and great men "divine," as if they belonged to a kind of religious congregation of a new elect; thus it was with the *Divina Commedia* of Dante and with Michelangelo after his death.

Petrarch's embracement of a new concept of Humanism encouraged the resurrection of the spirit of Classical antiquity from a trove of ancient manuscripts, which were eagerly hunted, edited, and soon to be reproduced in books made by the new process of mechanical printing. With the help of a new interest in and knowledge of Greek (stimulated by the immigration of Byzantine refugee-scholars after the fall of Constantinople to the Turks), the Humanists of the later fourteenth and fifteenth centuries recovered a large part of the Greek as well as the Roman literature and philosophy that had been lost, unnoticed, or cast aside in the Middle Ages. Their greatest literary contribution was, perhaps, the translation of these works, but they also wrote commentaries on them, which they used as models for their own historical, rhetorical, poetic, and philosophical writings. What the Humanists perceived with great excitement in classical writing was a philosophy for living in this world, a philosophy of human focus primarily, that derived not from an authoritative and traditional religious dogma but from reason, which was supposed to be awarded directly to anyone of intelligence and taste. The model, thus, for the Renaissance is no longer the world-despising holy man but rather the great-souled, intelligent man of the world.

Though the Humanism inspired by Petrarch matured and flourished between the late fourteenth and early sixteenth centuries in Renaissance Italy, it was a phenomenon of great complexity, with varying tendencies and emphases, diverging as well as converging doctrines, and personalities often in wordy conflict with one another. Thus, Humanism is not easy to define with comprehensive sureness; the modern philosophy called "humanism," for example, is quite different in many ways from that of the Renaissance. Yet we can say that the early Humanism embraced the ideal of a new kind of practical knowledge, extracted from the literature of Classical antiquity and applied to the problems of secular and civil life prevailing in the city culture of the Renaissance. The Humanists thought of themselves as a new kind of professionals, distinct from the clergy, who could improve the human condition by propagating the new knowledge through education and public service. They were educators, publicists, administrators, secretaries, and advisers to princes just as much as they were philosophers, scholars, historians, and poets—and, as we shall see, important for Renaissance art. Though they prized literature and scholarship for their own sake, they sought not so much to recover Classical antiquity in all its completeness and correctness, but rather to use it as a basis for pointing a new way to the understanding, conduct, and enjoyment of life.

Medieval scholars were in possession of vast learning embodied in the inherited culture of antiquity, but they had viewed this heritage in a different light from that prevalent in the Renaissance. The Medieval scholar, usually a theologian, had valued classical learning mostly for its usefulness in arguing Christian dogma; thus, Aquinas could use Aristotle as the authority for arguments based on scriptural revelation, while others could point to secular classical literature as a tool for tempting souls to damnation through atheism and sensuality. The Renaissance Humanists found inspiration in the heroes of antiquity, especially in the accounts of their careers in Plutarch's *Parallel Lives:* by the fifteenth and sixteenth centuries, even the lives of prominent contemporaries were viewed as appropriate exemplars of life's rule of reason intelligently and nobly followed. The biographies of famous men no longer dealt exclusively with the heroes of antiquity, and artists painted portraits of illustrious contemporaries. The confident, new, "modern" tone rings in Alberti's treatise *On Painting,* in which he congratulates his generation on its achievements:

> And I reveal to you, that if it was less difficult for the ancients, having as they had so very many to learn from and imitate, to rise to a knowledge of those supreme arts that are so toilsome for us today, then so much the more our fame should be greater if we, without teachers or any model, find arts and sciences unheard of and never seen.*

Almost prophetically, Alberti asserts that the moderns will go beyond the ancients; but the ancient example had first to be given—both as a model and a point of departure.

Although the Humanists of the Renaissance received the new message from pagan antiquity with enthusiasm, they did not look on themselves as pagans. It was possible, for example, for the fifteenth-century scholar Lorenzo Valla to prove the forgery of the *Donation of Constantine* (an early Medieval document purporting to record Constantine's bequest of the Roman empire to the Church) without feeling that he had compromised his Christian faith. The two great religious orders founded in the thirteenth century, the Dominicans and the Franciscans, were as dominant in setting the tone of fourteenth- and fifteenth-century Christian thought as they had been earlier, and they continued to be patrons of the arts. Within these established religious orders, Humanist clerics strengthened rather than weakened the reputation of the Church. Humanists, sometimes while members of religious orders, were appointed to important posts in city governments; the Florentine office of chancellor, for example, was held by distinguished men of letters. On the other hand, secular lords like Federigo da Montefeltro, Lord of Urbino—a

*In E.G. Holt, ed., *Literary Sources of Art History* (Princeton, N.J.: Princeton University Press, 1947), p. 109.

skilled general, generous governor of his people, Humanist patron of the arts and letters, and renowned lover of books—chose to die in the arms of the Church after a long and pious spiritual preparation. Here and there, the antagonism between the pagan and the Christian traditions may have manifested itself—and certainly it was bound to continue to exist—but, in general, the Renaissance achieved a natural, sometimes effortless, reconciliation of the two.

Not least among the leaders of the new age were the artists who, it appears to a number of modern historians, were among its most significant producers. Indeed, the products of the plastic arts may have been the most characteristic and illustrious of the Renaissance. Although we now perceive much more of the value of Renaissance literature, philosophy, and science, these branches of human creativity seem, in comparison with the plastic arts, to have been less certain, complete, and developed. But it is noteworthy that the separation of the great disciplines was not as clear-cut as it now is; mathematics and art, especially, went hand in hand, many Renaissance artists being convinced that geometry was fundamental to the artist's education and practice. In *The School of Athens* (FIG. 17-17), Raphael places his portrait and the portraits of his

RAPHAEL, detail of *The School of Athens* (FIG. 17-17). Raphael appears second from the extreme right in the foreground grouping.

colleagues among the mathematicians and philosophers, not among the poets. The Medieval distinction of *ars* and *scientia* is replaced by a concept (becoming current again) that views them as interrelated. Albrecht Dürer will insist that art without science—that is, technique without a theory relating the artist's skills and observations—is fruitless. The careful observations of the optical world made by Renaissance artists and the integration of these observations by such a mathematical system as perspective (derived from Medieval optics) foreshadow the formulations of the natural sciences. The twentieth-century thinker and mathematician, Alfred North Whitehead, believes that the habit and temper of modern science are anticipated in the patient and careful observation of nature practiced by the artists of the Renaissance. The methodical pursuit of a system that could bring order to visual experience may necessarily precede the scientific analysis of what lies behind what we see. Thus, the art of the Renaissance may be said to be the first monument to Western man's later search for order in nature.

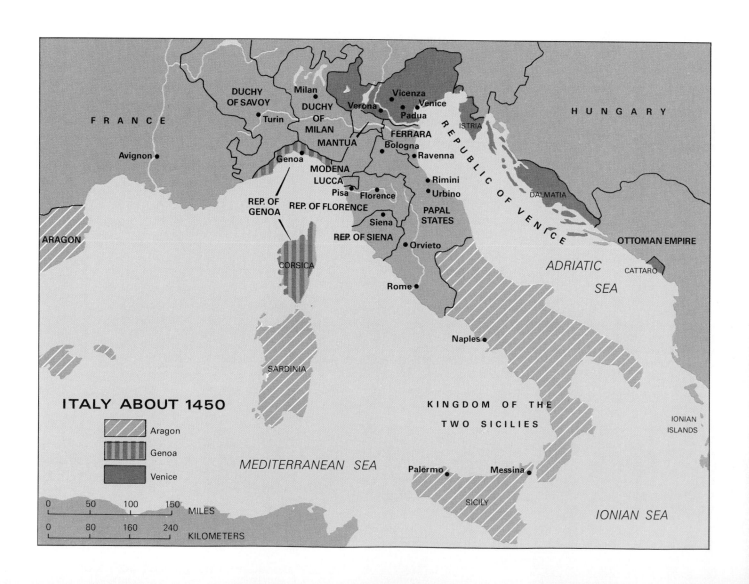

15

ITALY ABOUT 1450

Aragon

Genoa

Venice

| 0 | 50 | 100 | 150 |
| MILES

| 0 | 80 | 160 | 240 |
| KILOMETERS

FRANCE

DUCHY OF SAVOY

Turin

Avignon

DUCHY OF MILAN

Milan

MANTUA

Genoa

REP. OF GENOA

MODENA

LUCCA

Pisa

REP. OF FLORENCE

CORSICA

SARDINIA

ARAGON

Verona

Vicenza

Padua

Venice

FERRARA

Bologna

Ravenna

Rimini

Urbino

Florence

Siena

REP. OF SIENA

PAPAL STATES

Orvieto

Rome

Naples

REPUBLIC OF VENICE

ISTRIA

DALMATIA

HUNGARY

OTTOMAN EMPIRE

CATTARO

ADRIATIC SEA

KINGDOM OF THE TWO SICILIES

MEDITERRANEAN SEA

Palermo

Messina

SICILY

IONIAN ISLANDS

IONIAN SEA

THE "PROTO-RENAISSANCE" IN ITALY

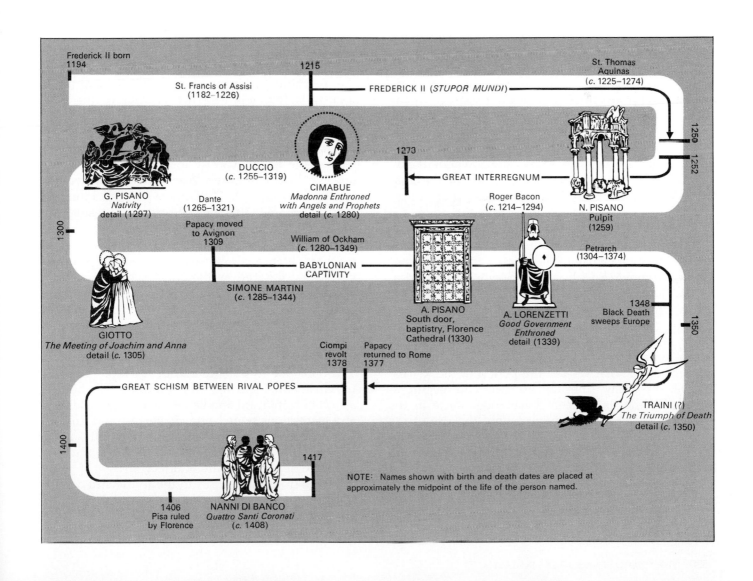

Frederick II born
1194

St. Francis of Assisi
(1182–1226)

1215

FREDERICK II (*STUPOR MUNDI*)

St. Thomas
Aquinas
(*c.* 1225–1274)

1250

1252

GIOTTO
The Meeting of Joachim and Anna
detail (*c.* 1305)

DUCCIO
(*c.* 1255–1319)

CIMABUE
*Madonna Enthroned
with Angels and Prophets*
detail (*c.* 1280)

1270

GREAT INTERREGNUM

Roger Bacon
(*c.* 1214–1294)

N. PISANO
Pulpit
(1259)

G. PISANO
Nativity
detail (1297)

Dante
(1265–1321)

1300

Papacy moved
to Avignon
1309

William of Ockham
(*c.* 1280–1349)

BABYLONIAN
CAPTIVITY

SIMONE MARTINI
(*c.* 1285–1344)

Petrarch
(1304–1374)

A. PISANO
South door,
baptistry, Florence
Cathedral (1330)

A. LORENZETTI
*Good Government
Enthroned*
detail (1339)

1348
Black Death
sweeps Europe

1350

Ciompi
revolt
1378

Papacy
returned to Rome
1377

GREAT SCHISM BETWEEN RIVAL POPES

TRAINI (?)
The Triumph of Death
detail (*c.* 1350)

1400

1417

1406
Pisa ruled
by Florence

NANNI DI BANCO
Quattro Santi Coronati
(*c.* 1408)

NOTE: Names shown with birth and death dates are placed at
approximately the midpoint of the life of the person named.

SCHOLARS HAVE LONG been uncertain about how to classify the art of the late thirteenth and the fourteenth centuries. Most of it still looks quite Byzantine or Gothic; in the countries outside Italy, Gothic traits last into the sixteenth century; but in Italy, a new spirit begins to be felt in art in the late thirteenth. As this new spirit is in fact that of the emerging Renaissance, it is misleading to define its monuments exclusively as "Gothic," even though Gothic traits are obvious in them. (To be sure, Gothic art itself represents a quickening of naturalism, although not the naturalism of the Renaissance; Gothic naturalism is a principal ingredient in the stylistic complex of the Late Medieval world.) What appears in Italy in the thirteenth century is destined to commence a new epoch, one that will have a quite recognizable continuity for centuries—indeed, almost until our own times. To stress the initiative that Italian art takes at this time and to prevent the new epoch from being cut off from its beginnings, we have classified Italian art of the later thirteenth and the fourteenth centuries as "proto-Renaissance." Although it is not until the fifteenth century that Renaissance art makes its not always clear break with the Gothic, one can discern in the "proto-Renaissance" the advance of novel tendencies that will lead to the new era.

Of course, Italy does not come into historical view only with the Renaissance. After the long disorganization of Europe, attendant on the passing of Rome and the age of the migrations, the Italian peninsula held a commanding position in the Mediterranean world, commercially and politically, from the eleventh until the fifteenth century. The power of its city-states on the one hand and of the papacy on the other kept Italy largely independent of the rest of Europe while broadly influencing it; during this time, the country remained politically divided. Economic life as we know it had its beginnings in Italy. Via their fleets, the merchants of Pisa, Genoa, and Venice controlled commerce with Islamic Spain, North Africa, Byzantium, Russia, the Near East, and, overland, with China. The banking houses of Florence and Milan managed the finances of Europe. Southern Italy and Sicily were the site of cosmopolitan civilizations. Indeed, Italy was powerful and influential centuries before what we call the period of the Renaissance. Ironically, the Renaissance had begun to flower at the time when Italian dominance in the Mediterranean was declining before the rise of the Ottoman Turks in the east and of Spain in the west.

French Gothic art had risen and flourished in the regions around Paris under the patronage of the kings of France. In Italy, the art of the Renaissance was supported by the prosperous merchant classes that ruled the cities after ousting the aristocracies. The reconstitution and expansion of city culture, which began as early as the eleventh century, had increasingly broken down old feudal barriers to the advancement of ambitious people of merit from all classes. Communal government (the Italian city-republics were called *communes*) came into the hands of guilds of merchants and bankers. This rule of magnates and their families was not by hereditary right but by the authority of power—a power that, often as not, favored republican institutions; thus, the Medici came to rule in Florence, not as raw tyrants but as a kind of "first among equals." Behind their power was commercial success (their own as well as the city's) and their skill in business government. During the "proto-Renaissance," the growth in wealth and power of many Italian cities corresponded with a rise in their wool trade. Florence, in particular, was noted for finished cloth that was sold all over Europe. As their wealth increased, the guilds, including the powerful wool guild, commanded ever-greater political influence; eventually the city—and, with it, much of the patronage of art—was in their hands. Commercial setbacks or jealousies within the guild coalitions created a highly unstable government, in which authority frequently changed hands overnight.

The Ciompi revolt of 1378 in Florence, when the workmen attempted to wrest the government from the merchant guilds, was only one of many social upheavals that followed the disaster of the great plague (the "Black Death") in 1348, which almost depopulated Europe. All over Europe, there were revolts of peasants in the countryside and of laboring men in the cities. A great and desolating war, destined to last a hundred years, broke out between France and England. The papacy suffered a humiliation that would ultimately destroy its prestige; the popes became puppets of the French monarchy and their residence moved from Rome to Avignon in southern France. Their sojourn there for some 70 years was climaxed by the Great Schism, when the throne of St. Peter was claimed simultaneously by three popes, who excommunicated one another. Christendom was permanently changed by this scandal, which contributed mightily to the advent of the Protestant Reformation in the sixteenth century.

Yet, despite turbulence and devastation, a powerful vitality was stirring, and confusion was but one aspect of significant and beneficial change. Old ideas and institutions were being challenged and, to a degree, discredited, and people of merit—in this age of Petrarch and Giotto—could feel that the times encouraged setting off in new directions.

Events from the twelfth to the fourteenth century constitute a kind of long overture, announcing the advent of full, naturalistic representation in European art. Whether we regard the "proto-Renaissance" as the end of the overture or the raising of the curtain on the first act, the event, especially in painting, is singularly dramatic. The Medieval artist had for centuries depended chiefly on prototypes (pictures and carvings) for representations of the human figure, with an occasional searching glance at objects and persons in the optical world. Now it is the optical world that offers prototype and authority to the artist—though not all at once, of course. Not until the fifteenth century will the "imitation of nature" as an objective give the artist direction, and not until the sixteenth will it become theory and doctrine. In the "proto-Renaissance," the artist's procedure is tentative, as if he were suspicious of an approach involving fleeting appearances and devoid of traditionally authoritative formulations. Nevertheless, as the artist carefully treads the threshold of discovery, his experimental groping and the somewhat unsystematic, yet hopeful and often confident, spirit of the period are unmistakable.

Artists are not philosophers, although in the Renaissance they come very close to sharing in the philosophical enterprise. Certainly, in the fourteenth century, the way was opening to new and tremendous possibilities that would have to be thought through as well as worked through. In many ways, the situation was similar to that of art today: so many possibilities and such diverse directions that, though rich conclusions may be anticipated, the way to them seems confused.

As the Christian Middle Ages evolved out of the disintegration of the Roman empire, so a new way of looking at the world emerged from the disintegration of what might be called the Medieval style of thought. Distinct from and in opposition to the balanced Scholasticism of Aquinas, the new views were only in part products of the Christian humanism of St. Francis and the secular Humanism of Petrarch and the classicizing scholars. The attack on the rationalism of Aquinas made by the *later* Scholastics and theologians led to the discrediting of philosophy as a valid form of knowledge and to the unseating of reason, with its logical method, as the ruling faculty that produces it. The unity of theology and philosophy, which Aquinas had achieved by bringing together Christian dogma and Aristotelian thought, was broken—theology going off in the direction of mysticism and pure faith, and philosophy yielding to skepticism and the first faint manifestation of that inquisitive bent of mind that would later mature into experimental science. If knowledge of God was impossible to achieve through philosophy and pure reason, so also was knowledge of nature and the world, God's crea-

tion. Thus, pure reason came to be despised for its failure to make the mysteries of faith or of the world intelligible. In the fifteenth century, Nicholas of Cusa would disparage philosophy as mere "learned ignorance"; in the sixteenth, Martin Luther would call reason a "whore."

A new approach was needed to understand and explain nature and God, and it is necessary to examine the great changes in the Western view of nature that lie behind and accompany fundamental changes in art. William of Ockham, one of the most subtle and ingenious Scholastics who attacked the rationalism of Aquinas, seemed to be providing such an approach when, on the verge of a great insight, he stressed the importance of the role of intuitive knowledge and individual experience in the process of knowing: "Everything outside the soul is individual . . . [and] knowledge which is simple and peculiarly individual . . . is intuitive knowledge . . . . Abstractive individual knowledge presupposes intuitive knowledge . . . our understanding knows sensible things intuitively."

The placement of intuition before abstraction was common to *both* the mystical and skeptical critics of Aquinas in the fourteenth century and, in effect, put human intuition squarely in front of individual knowledge, whether of God (for the mystic) or of the world (for the skeptic). This elevation of direct human experience constitutes a kind of exaltation of the knowing, human agent. Of course, since Early Christian times and especially since St. Augustine in the fifth century, the tradition of Christian mysticism had been that the experience of God must be personal; knowledge otherwise must be the result of divine illumination. Thus, the fourteenth-century advocacy of intuitive experience is a kind of renewal of the idea that prevailed before the conviction held by Abelard and Aquinas in the twelfth and thirteenth centuries—that truth could be achieved by the intellect only by following rules of rational demonstration. Even in the thirteenth century, the importance of experience in acquiring knowledge had been stressed by the remarkable Roger Bacon, the English philosopher, who bore out his convictions on this point with many astonishingly precocious discoveries and inventions in what now would be called the physical sciences and technology. Calling attention to the existence and necessity of experimental science, he insisted that the experimenter "should first examine visible things . . . without experience nothing can be known sufficiently . . . argumentation [that is, logical rational demonstration in Aquinas' manner] does not suffice, but experience does." In the universities (especially Oxford) of the fourteenth century, the followers of men like Bacon and Ockham discussed questions in physics (the acceleration of freely falling bodies, inertia, the center of gravity, and the like)—anticipating by centuries the age of Galileo.

Particularly noteworthy about the later thirteenth- and fourteenth-century mystical and skeptical thinkers, who emphasized personal intuition and experience in seeking divine and natural knowledge, is the fact that a large majority were Franciscans. In view of St. Francis' humanizing of Medieval religion—making it a matter of intense personal experience and drawing attention to the beauty of natural things, the handiwork of God—it is natural that his successors should inspect nature more closely, with a curiosity that would lead to scientific inquiry. St. Francis' independence and his critical posture toward the religious establishment were passed down to many Franciscans, the more radical of whom were often accused by the Church of association with outright "heretics." The Franciscans—conspicuously, William of Ockham—challenged the papacy itself, especially its claim of secular lordship over all Christendom. In these challenges, there already rings the rebelliousness that will take mature shape in the Protestant Reformation.

What might be called Franciscan "radicalism," then, stresses the primacy of personal experience, the individual's right to know by experiment, the futility of formal philosophy, and the beauty and value of things in the external world. It was in the stimulating intellectual and social environment created in part by the Franciscans that the painters and sculptors of the "proto-Renaissance" began a new epoch—an epoch in which the carved and painted image took its shape from the authority of the optical world and what could be found of that authority in the Classical antique. The individual artist, breaking with the formal traditions of a thousand years, now came to depend on his own inspection of the world before his eyes. Applying the Baconian principle of personal discovery through experience—in the artist's case, the experience of *seeing*—he began to project in painting and sculpture the infinitely complex and shifting optical reticulum that we experience as the world.

SCULPTURE

Many imitations of the art of Classical antiquity may be encountered during the Carolingian, Ottonian, Romanesque, and French Gothic periods. The statues of the *Visitation* group on the west façade of Reims Cathedral (FIG. 10-33) show an unmistakable interest in Late Roman sculpture, even though the modeling of the faces reveals their Gothic origin. However, the thirteenth-century sculpture of NICOLA PISANO (active *c.* 1258–1278), contemporary with the Reims statues, exhibits an interest in the forms of the Classical

antique unlike that of his predecessors—perhaps due in part to the humanistic culture of Sicily under its brilliant king, Holy Roman Emperor Frederick II, who, for his many intellectual gifts and many other talents, was known in his own time as "the wonder of the world." Frederick's nostalgia for the grandeur that was Rome fostered a revival of Roman sculpture and decoration in Sicily and southern Italy before the mid-thirteenth century. It may have been in this environment that Nicola received his early training, although recently it has been suggested that his style continues that of Romanesque Pisa. After Frederick's death in 1250, Nicola traveled northward and eventually settled in Pisa, which was then at the height of its political and economic power and a place where a proficient artist could hope to find rich commissions.

In typically Italian fashion, Nicola's sculpture was not applied in the decoration of great portals; thus, it is quite unlike the French sculpture of the period. Nicola carved marble reliefs and ornament for large pulpits, the first of which he completed in 1260 for the baptistry of Pisa Cathedral (FIG. 15-1). Some elements of the pulpit's design carry on Medieval traditions (for example, the lions supporting some of the columns and the tri-lobed arches), but Nicola is evidently trying to retranslate into Classical terms a Medieval type of structure. The large, bushy capitals

15-1 NICOLA PISANO, pulpit of the baptistry of Pisa Cathedral, 1259–1260. Marble, approx. 15' high.

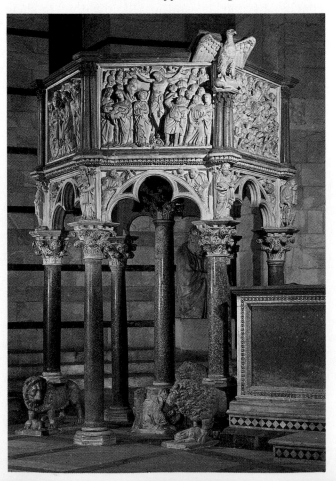

are a Gothic variation of the Corinthian; the arches are round rather than ogival; and the large, rectangular relief panels, if their proportions were slightly altered, could have come from the sides of Roman sarcophagi. The densely packed, large-scale figures of the individual panels seem also to derive from the compositions found on Late Roman sarcophagi. In one of these panels, representing *The Annunciation and the Nativity* (FIG. 15-2), the Virgin of the Nativity reclines in the ancient fashion seen in Byzantine ivories, mosaics, and paintings. But the face-types, beards, coiffures, and draperies and the bulk and weight of the figures are inspired by Classical models and impart a Classical flavor to the relief that is stronger than anything seen in several centuries.

Nicola's classicizing manner was strongly reversed by his son GIOVANNI PISANO (*c.* 1250–1320). Giovan-

ni's version of *The Annunciation and the Nativity* (FIG. 15-3) from his pulpit in Sant' Andrea of Pistoia, finished some 40 years after the one by his father in the Pisa baptistry, offers a striking contrast to Nicola's thick carving and placid, almost stolid presentation of the theme. Giovanni's figures are loosely and dynamically arranged; an excited animation twists and bends them, and their activeness is emphasized by spaces that open deeply between them, through which they hurry and gesticulate. In the Annunciation episode, which is combined with the Nativity (as in the older version), the Virgin shrinks from the sudden apparition of the angel in an alarm touched with humility. The same spasm of diffidence contracts her supple body as she reclines in the Nativity scene. The principals of the drama share in a peculiar, nervous agitation, as if they are all suddenly moved by spirit-

15-2 NICOLA PISANO, *The Annunciation and the Nativity* (detail of FIG. 15-1). Marble, approx. 34″ × 45″.

15-3 GIOVANNI PISANO, *The Annunciation and the Nativity*, 1297–1301, detail of the pulpit of Sant' Andrea, Pistoia. Marble, approx. 34″ × 40″.

ual passion; only the shepherds and the sheep, appropriately, do not yet share in the miraculous event. The swiftly turning, sinuous draperies, the slender figures they enfold, and the general emotionalism of the scene are features to be found not in Nicola's interpretation but in the Gothic art of the north in the fourteenth century. (These deep currents of Gothic naturalism and linear rhythms are evident in most sculpture in Italy throughout the fourteenth century.) Thus, the art of Nicola and of Giovanni show, successively, two novel trends of great significance for Renaissance art—a new contact with the Classical antique and a burgeoning, native Gothic naturalism.

Sculpture seems to have been more actively pursued in centers other than Florence until ANDREA PISANO (*c.* 1270–1348), unrelated to Nicola and Giovanni, was commissioned by the city to make bronze doors for the cathedral baptistry (FIG. 15-4). Each door has 14 panels, each enframing a *quatrefoil*, a motif found in Gothic sculpture and illuminations. Within these, as in *The Visitation* panel (FIG. 15-5), Andrea placed low reliefs with smoothly flowing lines admirably adapted to the complex space of the Gothic frame. The gentle sway of the figures and the blade-like folds of their drapery are quite in the general Late Gothic manner, but Andrea's skill at composition and

15-5 ANDREA PISANO, *The Visitation* (detail of FIG. 15-4). Gilt bronze, approx. 20″ high.

the quiet eloquence of his narrative make him an outstanding master among the fourteenth-century sculptors who followed the earlier Pisani. The simplicity of Andrea's statements, the amplitude of his forms, and their clear placement in shallow space also point to the influence of his great contemporary, the painter Giotto di Bondone.

PAINTING

Maniera Greca

Throughout the Middle Ages, Italian painting was dominated by the Byzantine style. This Italo–Byzantine style, or *maniera greca*, is shown in a panel of the *St. Francis Altarpiece* (FIG. 15-6) and is a descendant of those tall, aloof, austere figures that people the world of Byzantine art. Painted in tempera (a water-base paint using a binder such as glue or egg yolk) on wood panel, the saint, wearing the cinctured canonicals of the Franciscan order, holds a large book and displays on his hands and feet the stigmata—the wounds of Christ imprinted on him as a sign of Heavenly favor. The saint is flanked by two very Byzantine angels and by scenes from his life, the latter very much suggesting that their source is in Byzantine illuminated manuscripts. A detail of the altarpiece represents *St. Francis Preaching to the Birds* (FIG. 15-7). The figures of St. Francis and his two attendants are carefully aligned against a shallow, stage-property tower and wall, a stylized symbol of a town or city from Early Christian times. In front of the saint is another stage-scenery image of nested, wooded hills populated by alert and sprightly birds and twinkling

15-4 ANDREA PISANO, south door of the baptistry of Florence Cathedral, 1330–1335. Gilt bronze, approx. 17′ high.

15-6 BONAVENTURA BERLINGHIERI, panel from the *St. Francis Altarpiece*, 1235. Tempera on wood, approx. 60" × 42". San Francesco, Pescia.

15-7 BONAVENTURA BERLINGHIERI, *St. Francis Preaching to the Birds* (detail of FIG. 15-6).

plants. The strict formality of the composition (relieved somewhat by the sharply observed birds and the lively stippling of the plants), the shallow space, and the linear flatness in the rendering of the forms

are all familiar traits of a long and august tradition, now suddenly and dramatically to be replaced.

BONAVENTURA BERLINGHIERI, artist of the *St. Francis Altarpiece* was one of a family of painters in the Tuscan city of Lucca. It was largely in the busy cities of Tuscany (Lucca, Pisa, Siena, Florence) that the stirrings of the new artistic movement began. Florence was destined to lead the great development toward the new pictorial manner of the Renaissance, just as politically it gradually absorbed the other cities in Tuscany to make the Florentine republic. But during the fourteenth century, its defiant rival, Siena, which had long and stubbornly resisted the encroachment of Florence, was the seat of a splendid school of painting of its own.

Duccio

DUCCIO (Duccio di Buoninsegna, active *c.* 1278–1319) represents the Sienese tradition at its best. Among his large altarpieces, the *Maestà,* so called because it shows the Madonna enthroned in majesty as Queen of Heaven amidst choruses of angels and saints, illustrates the major aspects of his mature style. The front of the seven-foot-high panel (which is painted on both sides) represents the formal, monumental side of Duccio's art, which remains essentially Byzantine. On the reverse side, a series of small panels illustrated scenes from the life of Christ. These little pictures, which show Duccio's power of narration, were dismantled in the sixteenth century and are now scattered throughout the museums of the world. Given their narrative purpose—they were meant to be read, as were the windows of Chartres—Duccio could relax the formalism appropriate to the iconic, symbolic representation of the *Maestà* and could reveal his ability not only as a narrator but as an experimenter with new pictorial ideas. In a synoptic sequence on one of the panels, *The Betrayal of Jesus* (FIG. 15-8), the artist represents several episodes of the event: the betrayal of Jesus by Judas' false kiss, the disciples fleeing in terror, St. Peter cutting off the ear of the high priest's servant. Although the background, with its golden sky and its cheese-like rock formations, remains traditional, the figures before it have changed quite radically. They are no longer the flat, frontal shapes of Byzantine art, but have taken on body; they are modeled through a range from light to dark, and their draperies articulate around them convincingly. Only their relation to the ground on which they stand remains somewhat in doubt, as they tend to sway, glide, and incline with a kind of disembodied instability. Even more novel and striking is the manner in which the figures seem to react to the central event. Through posture, gesture, and even facial expression, they display a variety of emotions,

15-8 DUCCIO, *The Betrayal of Jesus*, detail of the back of the *Maestà Altarpiece*, 1309–1311. Tempera on wood, size of detail approx. 22½″ × 40″. Opera del Duomo, Siena.

15-9 DUCCIO, *The Annunciation of the Death of Mary*, detail of the *Maestà Altarpiece*, 1309–1311. Tempera on wood, size of detail approx. 16″ × 21″. Opera del Duomo, Siena.

as Duccio extends himself to differentiate between the anger of Peter, the malice of Judas (echoed in the faces of the throng about Jesus), and the apprehension and timidity of the fleeing disciples. No longer the abstract symbols of Byzantine art, these little figures have become actors in a religious drama, which, in a lively performance, is interpreted in terms of thoroughly human actions and reactions. In this and similar narrative panels, Duccio takes a decisive step toward the humanization of religious subject matter— an approach that will become an ever stronger undercurrent in the development of painting in the following centuries.

In *The Annunciation of the Death of Mary* (FIG. 15-9) from the same altarpiece, Duccio shows that, in the study of interior space, he is second to none of his contemporaries. Although his perspective is approximate, he creates the illusion of an architectural space that *encloses* a human figure. If we could be sure that the sophisticated ancient Roman painters had not achieved this effect also, we might say that it had never been done before. Certainly, nothing like it is to be found in painting during the 900 years preceding Duccio, and it must be regarded as epoch-making even though it may have been anticipated by the St. Francis master at Assisi and was accomplished in a similar manner by Giotto in the Arena Chapel in Padua (FIG. 15-17) a few years before Duccio painted his *Maestà*. While the angel's position remains ambiguous, the Virgin has been clearly placed in a cubical space that recedes from the picture plane. The illusion is made quite emphatic by the convergence of the three beams in the ceiling, a phenomenon that Duccio observed and recorded. As yet the perspective is not entirely unified, each of Duccio's planes tending to have its own point of convergence. Nevertheless, the illusion is convincing enough and represents the first step in the progressive construction of a true, geometrically ordered, perspective space that will be completed in the next century.

Giotto

Duccio resolved his problems within the general framework of the Byzantine style, which he never really rejected. His great Florentine contemporary, GIOTTO (Giotto di Bondone, *c.* 1266–1337), made a much more radical break with the past. The sources of Giotto's style are still debated, although one must have been the style of the Roman school of painting represented by PIETRO CAVALLINI (active *c.* 1273–1308). As shown in a detail from Cavallini's badly damaged fresco of *The Last Judgment* (FIG. 15-10) in the church of Santa Cecilia in Trastevere, the style is characterized by a great interest in the sculptural rendering of form. Cavallini, perhaps under the influence of Roman paintings now lost, abandons Byzantine linearism for a soft, deep modeling from light to dark and achieves an imposing combination of Byzantine hieratic dignity with a long-lost impression of solidity and strength. Another, perhaps less significant,

formative influence on Giotto may very well have been the work of the man presumed to be his teacher, GIOVANNI CIMABUE (*c.* 1240–1302). A Florentine, Cimabue must have been an older rival of Giotto, as Dante suggests in *Il Purgatorio* (XI, 94–96): "Cimabue thought to hold the field in painting, and now Giotto has the cry, so that the fame of the other is obscured."

Like Cavallini, Cimabue—inspired by the same impulse toward naturalism as Giovanni Pisano and also influenced, no doubt, by Gothic sculpture—pushed well beyond the limits of the Italo–Byzantine style. In an almost ruined fresco of the Crucifixion in San Francesco in Assisi, Cimabue's style can be seen to be—like Giovanni Pisano's—highly dramatic, the figures blown by a storm of emotion. On the other hand, Cimabue is much more formal in his *Madonna Enthroned with Angels and Prophets* (FIG. 15-11), as the theme naturally calls for unmoving dignity and not for dramatic presentation. Despite such progressive touches as the three-dimensional appearance of the throne, this vast altarpiece is a final summing-up of centuries of Byzantine art before its utter transformation. What that transformation looked like in its first phase can be seen in Giotto's version of the same theme (FIG. 15-12).

The art of Cimabue, the art of Cavallini and of the Roman painters like him (whom Giotto must have seen at work in San Francesco), the art of the Gothic sculptors of France (perhaps seen by Giotto himself, but certainly received by him from the sculpture of Giovanni Pisano), and the ancient art of Rome, both sculpture and painting—all must have provided the elements of Giotto's artistic education. Yet no synthesis of these varied influences could have sufficed to

15-10 PIETRO CAVALLINI, *Seated Apostles,* detail of *The Last Judgment,* *c.* 1291. Fresco.* Santa Cecilia in Trastevere, Rome.

*Dimensions for wall paintings will not be given from this point on.

15-11 GIOVANNI CIMABUE, *Madonna Enthroned with Angels and Prophets, c.* 1280–1290. Tempera on wood, 12′ 7″ × 7′ 4″. Galleria degli Uffizi, Florence.

15-12 GIOTTO, *Madonna Enthroned, c.* 1310. Tempera on wood, 10′ 8″ × 6′ 8″. Galleria degli Uffizi, Florence.

produce the great new style that makes Giotto the father of Western pictorial art. Renowned in his own day, his reputation has never faltered. No matter the variety of his materials of instruction, his true teacher was nature, the world of visible things.

Giotto's revolution in painting did not consist only of the final displacement of the Byzantine style, of the establishment of painting as a major art for the next six centuries, and of the restoration of the naturalistic approach invented by the ancients and lost in the Middle Ages. He inaugurated a firm method of pictorial experiment through observation, and, in the spirit of the experimenting Franciscans, opened an age that might be called "early scientific." Giotto and his successors, by stressing the preeminence of the faculty of sight in gaining knowledge of the world—

the visual world must be observed before it can be analyzed and understood—laid the trails that empirical science would follow. Praised in his own and later times for his fidelity to nature, Giotto is more than an imitator of it; he *reveals* nature in the process of observing it and divining its visible order. In fact, he showed his generation a new way of seeing. With Giotto, Western man turns resolutely toward the visible world as the source of knowledge of nature. This new *outward* vision replaced the Medieval *inward* vision that searched not for the secrets of nature but for union with God.

In nearly the same great scale as the Madonna painted by Cimabue, Giotto presents her enthroned with angels (FIG. 15-12) in a work that offers an opportunity to appreciate his perhaps most telling contribution to representational art—sculptural solidity and weight. The Madonna rests within her Gothic throne with the unshakable stability of a marble goddess out of antiquity. The slender Virgins of Duccio and Cimabue, fragile beneath the thin ripplings of their draperies, are replaced by a sturdy, queenly mother, corporeally of this world, even to the swelling of the bosom. The body is not lost; it is asserted. The new art aims, before all else, to construct a figure that will have substance, dimensionality, and bulk—that, like a figure in sculpture, will project into the light and throw a shadow or give the illusion that it does. Thus, in this work the throne is deep enough to contain the monumental figure and breaks away from the flat ground to project and enclose it.

In examining Giotto's work it should be kept in mind that scholars have questioned the attribution of the Assisi frescoes (FIG. 15-13) to Giotto's hand, noting not only a certain inferiority in the execution of the figures and other details but also a crowding or complexity in the composition that is inconsistent with the lucidity and monumentality of his other paintings. All agree that Giotto authored the works at the Arena Chapel (FIGS. 15-14 and 15-17), which must date from about 1304 to 1313, his frescoes in the chapels of Santa Croce in Florence (FIG. 15-15, *c.* 1320), and the *Madonna Enthroned* (FIG. 15-12, *c.* 1310). However, a serious controversy revolves around the great cycle of frescoes depicting the life of St. Francis in the Upper Church of Assisi, traditionally attributed to Giotto and dated about 1300. As written evidence is lacking and opinions are based on stylistic analysis, it is probable that opinions will continue to vary. Current scholarship suggests that the St. Francis cycle was painted in the 1290s, and although the influence

15-13 MASTER OF THE ST. FRANCIS CYCLE, *St. Francis Preaching to the Birds,* c. 1296 (?). Fresco. Upper Church, San Francesco, Assisi.

of Giotto's style is not denied, it is felt that it is better exemplified in other works. Scholars now believe that the Assisi frescoes were most likely done by Florentine artists who were influenced by Giotto or who had a similar background. One of these frescoes, *St. Francis Preaching to the Birds* (FIG. 15-13), is certainly Giottesque in its simplicity of statement, in the reduction of the number of figures to the minimum required for the story, and in the sharp psychological touches—the eloquent gesture of the saint as he bends forward to the birds, almost commanding them to attend his words, and the astonishment of his disciple. The modeling of the figures is strong; their sculptural relief, emphatic. If the picture is compared with Berlinghieri's version of the same theme (FIG. 15-7), the nature of the great stylistic change, happening within little more than half a century, can be appreciated. Its attribution to the MASTER OF THE ST. FRANCIS CYCLE reflects the provisional nature of much of our art-historical knowledge. As the history of art moves into an age of known personalities, the vexatious question of attribution arises with increasing frequency. How can the authorship of a work be verified when documentary evidence is scarce and when the internal evidence (evidence from the study of individual styles) is controversial?

The projection on a flat surface of an illusion of solid bodies moving through space presents a duplex problem. The construction of the illusion of a body requires, at the same time, the construction of the illusion of a space sufficiently ample to contain that body. In Giotto's fresco cycles—and he was primarily a muralist—he is constantly striving to reconcile these two aspects of illusionistic painting. His *Lamentation* from the fresco cycle in the Arena Chapel (Cappella Scrovegni) at Padua (FIG. 15-14) is undisputed and shows us his art at its finest. The theme is the mourning of Christ's mother, his disciples, and the holy women over the dead body of the Savior just before its entombment, in the presence of angels darting about in hysterical grief. Giotto has arranged a shallow stage for the figures, bounded by a thick, diagonal scarp of rock that defines a horizontal ledge in the foreground. The rocky landscape links this scene with the adjoining one of the *Resurrection* and *Noli me tangere* (not shown). Giotto links the framed scenes throughout the fresco cycle, much as Dante joins the cantos in his epic poem, the *Divina Commedia.* Though rather narrow, the ledge provides the figures with firm visual support, while the scarp functions as an indicator of the picture's dramatic focal point at the lower left. The centralizing and frontalizing habits of Byzantine art are here dismissed. The figures are sculpturesque, simple, weighty volumes but are not restrained by their mass from appropriate action. Here, postures and gestures

15-14 GIOTTO, *Lamentation*, *c.* 1305. Fresco. Arena Chapel (Cappella Scrovegni), Padua.

that might have been only rhetorical and mechanical convincingly express a broad spectrum of grief—from the mother's almost fierce despair through the passionate outbursts of Mary Magdalene and John, the philosophical resignation of the two disciples at the right, and the mute sorrow of the two hooded mourners in the foreground. Although Duccio makes an effort to distinguish shades of emotion in *The Betrayal of Jesus* (FIG. 15-8), he does not match Giotto in his stage management of a great tragedy. Giotto has indeed constructed a kind of stage, which will serve as a model for those on which many human dramas will be depicted in subsequent paintings. He is now far removed from the old isolation of episodes and actors seen in art until the late thirteenth century. In the *Lamentation,* a single event provokes a single, intense response within which there are, so to speak, degrees of psychic vibration. This integration of the formal with the emotional composition was scarcely attempted, let alone achieved, in art before Giotto.

The formal design of the *Lamentation* fresco, the way the figures are grouped within the contrived space, is worth close study. Each group has its own definition, and each contributes to the rhythmic order of the composition. The strong diagonal of the rocky ledge, with its single dead tree (the tree of knowledge of good and evil, which withered at the fall of Adam), concentrates our attention on the group around the head of Christ, dynamically off-center in the composition. All movement beyond this group is contained, or arrested, by the massive bulk of the seated mourner in the corner of the painting. The seated mourner to the right establishes a relation with the center group, the members of which, by their gazes and gestures, draw the viewer's attention back to the head of Christ. Figures seen from the back—frequent in Giotto's compositions—emphasize the foreground, helping visually to place the intermediate figures further back in space. This device, the very contradiction of the old frontality, in effect puts the viewer behind the "observer" figures, which, facing the action as spectators, reinforce the sense of stage-craft as a model for paintings with a human "plot." In this age of dawning Humanism, the old Medieval, hieratic presentation of holy mysteries evolved into full-fledged dramas employing a plot. By the thirteenth century, the drama of the Mass was extended first into one- and two-act tableaux and scenes and then into simple shows often presented at the portals of churches. (The portal statuary of the Gothic period suggests a discourse among the represented saints, and the architectural settings serve to enframe and enclose them, as does a stage the movement of its actors.) Thus, the arts of illusionistic painting and of drama were developing simultaneously, and the most accomplished artists of the Renaissance and later periods became masters of a kind of stage rhetoric of their own. Giotto, the first master of the tradi-

tion, was one of the most expert in the matching of form and action; it is difficult to exaggerate his trail-blazing achievement.

For the Franciscan church of Santa Croce in Florence, Giotto painted a St. John cycle and frescoes of the life and death of St. Francis. Shown is the *Death of St. Francis*, as restored in the nineteenth century (FIG. 15-15) and with the restorations removed (FIG. 15-16).* Fortunately, despite the removal of the restora-

*This painting exemplifies another aspect of the problem of attribution and authenticity already mentioned. Until the historically sensitive twentieth century, it had long been the custom to "renew" old pictures by painting over damaged or faded areas. Modern scholars, in their zeal to know the "real" painter, have advocated stripping even where this leaves only fragments that are perhaps esthetically unsatisfactory. The practice remains controversial, and the historian of art, the expert, the connoisseur, and, ultimately, the layman always have before them the question of the authenticity of the given work.

15-15 GIOTTO, *Death of St. Francis, c.* 1320. Fresco. Bardi Chapel, Santa Croce, Florence.

15-16 GIOTTO, *Death of St. Francis*, FIG. 15-15 after removal of nineteenth-century restorations.

tions and the resultant gaps in the composition, there is enough of the original *Death of St. Francis* to give a view of the later style of Giotto. Compared with the *Lamentation,* with which it has considerable spiritual affinity, the St. Francis painting shows significant changes. The Gothic agitation has quieted, and the scene has little of the jagged emotion of the *Lamentation.* It seems, indeed, as if the artist, from off-stage, had watched the solemn obsequies: the saint, at center on his bier, flanked by kneeling and standing monks, the kneeling seen from behind in Giotto's fashion. From left and right come stately processions of friars in profile, as they would be seen in actuality—not frontally, as in a Byzantine procession like that of *Justinian and Attendants* at San Vitale (FIG. 7-36). The figures are carefully accommodated on an architecture-enclosed, stage-like space that has been widened and no longer leaves any doubt that the figures have sufficient room in which to move about. They are taller and have lost some of their former sack-like bulk; Giotto now makes a distinction between the purely form-defining function of the robes and the fact that they are draped around articulated bodies. The impressive solemnity of the procession is enhanced by the omission of the casual and incidental beauties of the world so dear to Sienese and Gothic painters. Giotto sees and records nature in terms of its most basic facts: solid volumes resting firmly on the flat and horizontal surface of this earth. These he arranges in meaningful groups and infuses with restrained emotions, revealed in slow and measured gestures. With the greatest economy of means, Giotto achieves unsurpassed effects of monumentality, and his paintings, because of the simplicity and directness of their statements, belong to the most memorable in world art.

Giotto's murals in the Bardi and Peruzzi chapels of Santa Croce served as textbooks for generations of Renaissance painters from Masaccio to Michelangelo and others later. These later artists were able to understand the greatness of Giotto's art better than his immediate followers, who were never capable of absorbing more than a fraction of his revolutionary innovations. Their efforts usually remained confined to the emulation of his plastic figure description. A good example of a diligent follower is TADDEO GADDI (*c.* 1300–1366), Giotto's foster son and his assistant for many years. The difference between the work of a great artist and that of a competent one is readily apparent if we compare Giotto's *The Meeting of Joachim and Anna* in the Arena Chapel (FIG. 15-17) with Taddeo's version of the same subject in the Baroncelli Chapel in Santa Croce (FIG. 15-18). Giotto's composition is simple and compact. The figures are carefully related to the single passage of architecture (the Golden Gate), where the parents of the Virgin meet in triumph in the presence of splendidly dressed ladies. The latter mock the cloaked servant who refused to believe that the elderly Anna (St. Anne) would ever bear a child. The story, related in the Apocrypha, is managed with Giotto's usual restraint, clarity, and dramatic compactness. Taddeo allows his composition (FIG. 15-18) to become somewhat loose and unstructured. The figures have no clear relation to

15-17 GIOTTO, *The Meeting of Joachim and Anna, c.* 1305. Fresco. Arena Chapel (Cappella Scrovegni), Padua.

15-18 TADDEO GADDI, *The Meeting of Joachim and Anna*, 1338. Fresco. Baroncelli Chapel, Santa Croce, Florence.

the background; the elaborate cityscape, though pleasant in itself, demands too much attention and detracts from the action in the foreground. Gestures have become weak and theatrical, and the hunter (discreetly cut-off and unobtrusive in Giotto's painting) here strides boldly toward the center of the picture—a picturesque genre subject that weakens the central theme. Although his figures retain much of Giotto's solidity, Taddeo weakens the dramatic impact of the story by elaborating its incidental details. Giotto stresses the essentials and, by presenting them with his usual simplicity and forceful directness, gives the theme a much more meaningful interpretation. Yet we must not seem to disparage Giotto's contemporaries and followers. Taddeo presses forward the investigation of perspective, as his cityscape reveals, and the genre figure attests to the development of a keen interest in realism.

Simone Martini

Duccio's successors in the Siena School display even greater originality and assurance. SIMONE MARTINI (*c.* 1285–1344)—a pupil of Duccio and close friend of Petrarch, who praised him highly for his portrait of "Laura"—worked for the French kings in Naples and Sicily and, in his last years, at the papal court at Avignon, where he came in contact with northern painters. By adapting the insubstantial but luxuriant patterns of the French Gothic manner to Sienese art and, in turn, by acquainting northern painters with the Sienese style, Simone became instrumental in the formation of the so-called International style, which swept Europe during the late fourteenth and early fifteenth centuries. It was a courtly style that appealed to the aristocratic taste for brilliant color, lavish costume, intricate ornament, and themes involving splendid processions in which knights and their ladies, complete with entourages, horses, and greyhounds, could glitter to advantage. Simone's own style does not quite reach the full exuberance of the developed International style. But his famous *Annunciation* (FIG. 15-19), with its elegant shapes and radiant color, its play of flowing, fluttering line, its weightless figures and spaceless setting, is the perfect antithesis of the style of Giotto—of whom Simone certainly must have been aware, but whose art just as certainly left him untouched. The complex etiquette of the chivalric courts of Europe dictates Simone's presentation. The angel Gabriel has just alighted, the breeze of his passage lifting his mantle, his iridescent wings still beating, the white and gold of his sumptuous gown heraldically representing the celestial realm whence he bears his message. The Virgin, dropping her book of devotions, shrinks demurely from Gabriel's reverent genuflection, appropriate in the presence of royalty. She draws about her the deep blue, golden-hemmed mantle, the heraldic colors she wears as the Queen of Heaven. Despite the Virgin's modesty and diffidence and the tremendous import of the angel's message, the scene subordinates drama to court ritual and structural experiments to surface splendor.

For the Palazzo Pubblico in Siena, Simone painted a very different kind of composition, a large mural

15-19 SIMONE MARTINI, *The Annunciation*, 1333. Tempera on wood, approx. 10' 1" × 8' 8¾". Galleria degli Uffizi, Florence.

representing a soldier of fortune, Guidoriccio da Fogliano, in the service of Siena (FIG. 15-20). This is the first in a long line of equestrian paintings and statues honoring and commemorating those

freebooting and ambitious professional soldiers (*condottieri*) who led the armies of the Italian states in their endless petty wars and who often took power themselves. Guidoriccio, who recaptured two small

15-20 SIMONE MARTINI, *Guidoriccio da Fogliano*, 1328. Fresco. Palazzo Pubblico, Siena.

Sienese towns from the Pisans, is honored for this solid service to the state by Simone's representation of him cantering in monumental isolation across the barren terrain, his camps to the far right, his banners flying over one city he has just retaken, his resolute and silent course directed toward the hill town at the left still to be conquered. Simone does not concentrate his design around a single episode, as Giotto does, but makes the portrait a kind of sequential description, giving the progress of the general through time. Nor does Simone attempt a single viewpoint; the camp, the towns, and the rider are all seen from different angles. Although this diffuseness is somewhat retrograde, it does not detract from the effectiveness of the great figure on its splendidly caparisoned horse. A quite beautiful touch appears in the diamond pattern shared by horse and rider, which, with the rhythmically fluttering draperies, gives an astonishing illusion of forward motion. The Gothic feeling for line as primarily ornamental is here adroitly employed to produce an illusion of real movement. The subject—a real man in a historically real situation—is itself an innovation and bespeaks the new and irresistible advance of worldly interests into life and art.

Recent scholarly controversy about this great work seems to be leading to a revision of the standard interpretation of it. In the process of its cleaning and restoration, new questions have arisen. Was the figure of Guidoriccio painted later than the landscape? Which cities are represented, and is the one just to the right of the rider not a city but a temporary siege tower? What adjustments of dating must be made? These questions are complicated by the recent discovery of another fresco, just below the larger one of Guidoriccio riding, which represents two figures—the principal one surely Guidoriccio—standing before a captured city. Which city is it? What is its date and significance relative to the equestrian picture? Who was the painter—Duccio, Simone, or some other? Conflicting answers to these questions have been given, and the debate continues. The reader is reminded of how provisional and problematical our art-historical knowledge often is—and of how it is ever-open to revision.

The Lorenzetti

The brothers Lorenzetti, also students of Duccio, share in the general experiments in pictorial realism that so characterize the fourteenth century, especially in their seeking of convincing spatial illusions. PIETRO LORENZETTI (active 1320–1348), going well beyond his master, achieved remarkable success in a large panel representing *The Birth of the Virgin* (FIG. 15-21). The wooden architectural members that divide the panel into three compartments are represented as extending back into the painted space, as if we were looking through the wooden frame (apparently added later) into a box-like stage, where the event takes place. The illusion is strengthened by the fact that one of the vertical members cuts across one of the figures, blocking part of it from view. Whether this architecture-assisted perspective illusion was intentional is problematical; in any case, the full significance of the device of pictorial illusion enhanced by applied

15-21 PIETRO LORENZETTI, *The Birth of the Virgin*, 1342. Tempera on wood, approx. 6' 1" × 5' 11". Museo dell' Opera Metropolitane, Siena.

15-22 AMBROGIO LORENZETTI, *Good Government Enthroned*, from the *Good Government* fresco, 1339. Palazzo Pubblico, Siena.

architectural parts was not realized until the next century. There was no precedent for it in the history of Western art, but there was to be a long, successful history during the Renaissance and Baroque periods of such visual illusions produced by a union of real and simulated architecture with painted figures. Pietro made not just a structural advance here; his very subject represents a marked step in the advance of wordly realism. St. Anne, reclining wearily as the midwives wash the child and the women bring gifts, is the center of an episode that takes place in an upper-class Italian house of the period. A number of carefully observed domestic details and the scene at the left, where Joachim eagerly awaits the news of the delivery, place the scene in an actual household, as if we had slid the panels of the walls back and peered within. Thus, the structural innovation in illusionistic space becomes one with the new curiosity that leads to careful inspection and recording of what lies directly before our eyes in the everyday world.

Pietro's brother, AMBROGIO LORENZETTI (active 1319–1348), elaborated in spectacular fashion the Sienese advances in illusionistic representation, as is shown in his vast mural, the *Good Government* fresco, in the Palazzo Pubblico, in which the effects of good and bad government are allegorically juxtaposed. Good Government (FIG. 15-22) is represented as a majestic figure, enthroned and flanked by the virtues of Justice, Prudence, Temperance, and Fortitude, as well as by Peace and Magnanimity; above hover the theological virtues of Faith, Hope, and Charity. In the foreground, the citizens of Siena advance to do homage to Good Government and all the virtues that accompany it. The turbulent politics of the Italian cities, the violent party struggles, the overthrow and reinstatement of governments would certainly have called for solemn reminders of the value of justice in high places, and the city hall would be just the place for a painting like Ambrogio's. Beyond the allegories

and dedication scene stretches the depiction of the fruits of Good Government, both in the city and the countryside. The *Peaceful City* (FIG. 15-23) is a panoramic view of Siena itself, with its clustering palaces, markets, towers, churches, streets, and walls. Commerce moves peacefully through the city, the guildsmen ply their trades and crafts, and a cluster of radiant maidens, hand in hand, perform a graceful, circling dance. The artist fondly observes the life of his city, and its architecture gives him an opportunity to apply Siena's rapidly growing knowledge of perspective. Passing through the city gate to the countryside beyond its walls, Ambrogio's *Peaceful Country* presents a bird's-eye view of the undulating Tuscan countryside—its villas, castles, plowed farmlands, and peasants going about their seasonal occupations (FIG. 15-24). An allegorical figure of Security hovers above the peaceful landscape, unfurling a scroll that promises safety to all who live under the rule of the law. In this sweeping view of an actual countryside, we have the first appearance of landscape since the ancient world. The difference is that now the landscape—as well as the view of the city—is particularized by careful observation, being given almost the character of a portrait of a specific place and environment in a desire for authenticity. By combining some of Giotto's analytical powers with the narrative talent of Duccio, Ambrogio is able to achieve results beyond those of either of his two great predecessors.

The Black Death may have ended the careers of both Lorenzettis; nothing is heard of them after 1348, the year that brought so much horror to defenseless Europe. In an unusual and fascinating painting relating this common late Medieval theme—*The Triumph of Death* (FIG. 15-25) in the Campo Santo at Pisa, attributed to FRANCESCO TRAINI (active *c.* 1321–1363) and, more recently, to BUONAMICO BUFFALMACCO (active early fourteenth century)—three young aristocrats and their ladies in a stylish cavalcade encounter three

15-23 AMBROGIO LORENZETTI. *Peaceful City*, from the *Good Government* fresco.

15-24 AMBROGIO LORENZETTI, *Peaceful Country*, from the *Good Government* fresco.

corpses in differing stages of decomposition. As the horror of the confrontation with death strikes them, as the ladies turn away with delicate and ladylike disgust and a gentleman holds his nose (the animals, horses and dogs, sniff excitedly), a holy hermit unrolls a scroll that demonstrates the folly of pleasure and the inevitability of death. In another section, the ladies and gentlemen, wishing to forget dreadful realities, occupy themselves in an orange grove with music, gallantries, and lapdogs, while all around them death and judgment occur and angels and demons struggle for souls. The Medieval message is as strong as ever; but gilded youth refuses to acknowledge it. The painting applies all the stock of Florentine–Sienese representational craft to present the most worldly—and mortal!—picture of the fourteenth century. It is an irony of history that, as Western humanity draws both itself and the world into ever-clearer visual focus, it perceives ever more clearly that corporeal things are perishable.

15-25 BUONAMICO BUFFALMACCO OR FRANCESCO TRAINI (?), *The Triumph of Death*, c. 1340. Fresco. Campo Santo, Pisa.

16

FLORENCE

1. Santa Maria del Carmine
2. Santo Spirito
3. Santa Maria Novella
4. Palazzo Rucellai
5. San Lorenzo
6. Palazzo Medici–Riccardi
7. Florence Cathedral
8. Baptistry
9. Or San Michele
10. Santa Croce
11. San Miniato
12. Fortezza da Basso (1536)
13. Pazzi Chapel

NOTE: Darker-toned area
represents
Renaissance Florence.

ARNO

FIFTEENTH-CENTURY ITALIAN ART

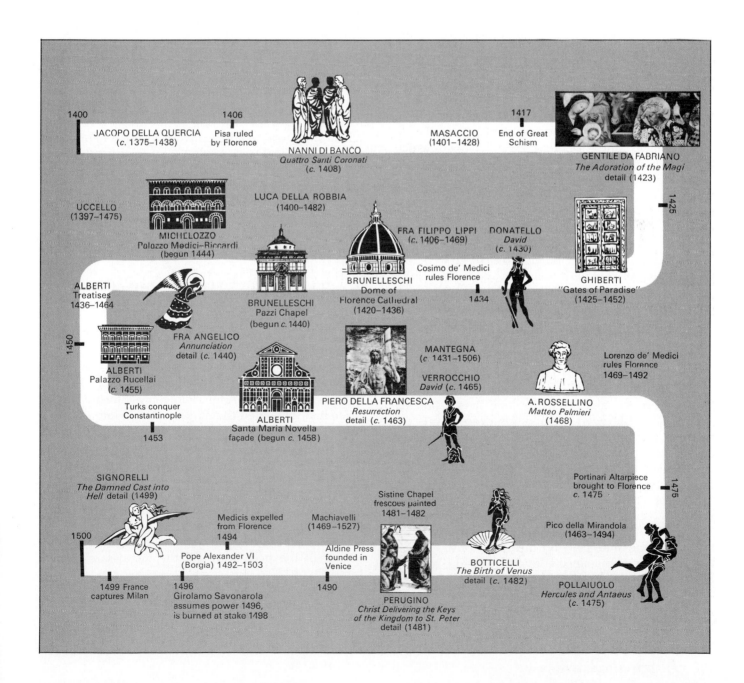

1400

JACOPO DELLA QUERCIA
(c. 1375–1438)

1406 Pisa ruled by Florence

NANNI DI BANCO
Quattro Santi Coronati
(c. 1408)

MASACCIO
(1401–1428)

1417 End of Great Schism

GENTILE DA FABRIANO
The Adoration of the Magi
detail (1423)

UCCELLO
(1397–1475)

LUCA DELLA ROBBIA
(1400–1482)

MICHELOZZO
Palazzo Medici–Riccardi
(begun 1444)

1425

FRA FILIPPO LIPPI
(c. 1406–1469)

DONATELLO
David
(c. 1430)

ALBERTI
Treatises
1436–1464

BRUNELLESCHI
Pazzi Chapel
(begun c. 1440)

BRUNELLESCHI
Dome of
Florence Cathedral
(1420–1436)

Cosimo de' Medici
rules Florence

1434

GHIBERTI
"Gates of Paradise"
(1425–1452)

1450

FRA ANGELICO
Annunciation
detail (c. 1440)

MANTEGNA
(c. 1431–1506)

VERROCCHIO
David (c. 1465)

Lorenzo de' Medici
rules Florence
1469–1492

ALBERTI
Palazzo Rucellai
(c. 1455)

Turks conquer
Constantinople

1453

ALBERTI
Santa Maria Novella
façade (begun c. 1458)

PIERO DELLA FRANCESCA
Resurrection
detail (c. 1463)

A. ROSSELLINO
Matteo Palmieri
(1468)

SIGNORELLI
*The Damned Cast into
Hell* detail (1499)

Medicis expelled
from Florence
1494

Machiavelli
(1469–1527)

Sistine Chapel
frescoes painted
1481–1482

Portinari Altarpiece
brought to Florence
c. 1475

1475

1500

Pope Alexander VI
(Borgia) 1492–1503

Aldine Press
founded in
Venice

Pico della Mirandola
(1463–1494)

1499 France
captures Milan

1496
Girolamo Savonarola
assumes power 1496,
is burned at stake 1498

1490

PERUGINO
*Christ Delivering the Keys
of the Kingdom to St. Peter*
detail (1481)

BOTTICELLI
The Birth of Venus
detail (c. 1482)

POLLAIUOLO
Hercules and Antaeus
(c. 1475)

FLORENCE took cultural command of Italy in the early fifteenth century, inaugurating the Renaissance and establishing itself as the intellectual and artistic capital of southern Europe—a position of dominance it was to retain until the end of the century. According to John Addington Symonds, a nineteenth-century historian of the Renaissance:

> . . . nowhere else except at Athens has the whole population of a city been so permeated with ideas, so highly intellectual by nature, so keen in perception, so witty and so subtle, as at Florence. . . . The primacy of the Florentines in literature, the fine arts, law, scholarship, philosophy and science was acknowledged throughout Italy.*

The power and splendor of Florence had long been building; the fifteenth century marked its perfection. Like the Athenians after the repulse of the Persians, the citizens of Florence (who felt a historical affinity with the Athenians) responded with conscious pride to their repulse of the dukes of Milan, who had attempted the conquest of Tuscany. Like the Athenians also, the Florentines developed a culture that was stimulated and supported by a vast accumulation of wealth; but unlike the Athenians, only a few illustrious families controlled that wealth. The Medici, bankers to all Europe, became such lavish patrons of art and learning that, to this day, the name "Medici" means a generous patron of the fine arts. For centuries, the history of Florence is the history of the House of Medici. Early in the fifteenth century, Giovanni de' Medici had established the family fortune. His son Cosimo, called "father of his country" by the Florentines, secured the admiration and loyalty of the people of Florence against the noble and privileged; with this security, the Medici gradually became the discreet dictators of the Florentine republic, disguising their absolute power behind a mask of affable benevolence. Scarcely a great architect, painter, sculptor, philosopher, or Humanist scholar was unknown to the Medici. Cosimo began the first public library since the ancient world, and it is estimated that in some 30 years he and his descendants expended almost $20,000,000 for manuscripts and books; such was the financial power behind the establishment of Humanism in the Renaissance. The Medici, careful businessmen that they were, were not sentimental about their endowment of art and scholarship; Cosimo declared that his good works were "not only for the honor of God but . . . likewise for my own remembrance." Yet the astute businessman and politician had a sincere love of learning, reading Plato in his old age and writing to his tutor, the Neo-Platonic philosopher Marsilio Ficino, "I desire nothing so much as to know the best road to happiness." This is the very model of the cultivated, Humanist grandee. The grandson of Cosimo, Lorenzo the Magnificent, went, as his name suggests, even beyond his grandfather in munificence. Himself a talented poet, he gathered about him a galaxy of artists and gifted men in all fields, extending the library Cosimo had begun, revitalizing his academy for the instruction of artists, establishing the Platonic Academy of Philosophy, and lavishing funds (often the city's own) on splendid buildings, festivals, and pageants. If his prime motive was to retain the affection of the people and, thus, the power of the House of Medici, he nevertheless made Florence a city of great beauty, the capital of all the newly flourishing arts. His death, in 1492, brought to an end the "golden age" of Florence, and the years immediately following saw the invasion of Italy by—as the Italians called them—the "barbarian" nations of France, Spain, and the Holy Roman Empire. The Medici were expelled from Florence; the reforming, fanatical Girolamo Savonarola preached repentance in the cathedral of Florence; and the Renaissance moved its light and its artists from Florence to Rome. But one of the most prominent patrons of the Roman Renaissance, Pope Leo X, patron of Raphael and Michelangelo, was himself a Medici, the son of Lorenzo the Magnificent. Never in history was there a family so intimately associated with a great cultural revolution. It might safely be said of the Medici that they subsidized and endowed the Renaissance.

THE FIRST HALF OF THE FIFTEENTH CENTURY

Sculpture

The spirit of the Medici and of the Renaissance was nothing if not competitive and desirous of fame. But even before Medici rule, civic competitiveness and pride had motivated the adornment of Florence. The history of the Early Renaissance in art begins with an account of a competition for a design for the east doors of the baptistry of Florence (later moved to the north), the south doors of which Andrea Pisano had designed almost three generations before (FIG. 15-4). LORENZO GHIBERTI (1378–1455), the sculptor who won the competition, describes his victory in terms that reflect the egoism and the "cult of fame" characteristic of the period and of the Renaissance artist himself:

> To me was conceded the palm of the victory by all the experts and by all . . . who had competed with me. To me the honor was conceded universally and with no

*John Addington Symonds, *Renaissance in Italy* (New York: Modern Library, 1935), Vol. 1, p. 125.

exception. To all it seemed that I had at that time surpassed the others without exception, as was recognized by a great council and an investigation of learned men . . . highly skilled from the painters and sculptors of gold, silver, and marble. There were thirty-four judges from the city and the other surrounding countries. The testimonial of the victory was given in my favor by all. . . . It was granted to me and determined that I should make the bronze door for this church. . . .*

This passage also indicates the esteem and importance now attached to art, with leading men of a city bestowing eagerly sought-for commissions and great new programs of private and public works being widely undertaken.

The contestants represented the assigned subject, the Sacrifice of Isaac, within panels shaped like the Gothic quatrefoil used by Andrea Pisano for the south doors of the baptistry. Only those by FILIPPO BRUNELLESCHI and Ghiberti have survived. Brunelleschi's panel (FIG. 16-1) shows a sturdy and vigorous interpretation of the theme, with something of the emotional agitation of the tradition of Giovanni Pisano (FIG. 15-3). Abraham seems all at once to have summoned the dreadful courage needed to kill his son at God's command; he lunges forward, draperies flying, exposing, with desperate violence, Isaac's throat to the knife. Matching Abraham's energy, the saving angel darts in from the left, arresting the stroke just in time. Brunelleschi's figures are carefully observed, and there are elements of a new realism in them. Yet his composition is perhaps overly busy,

*In E.G. Holt, ed., *Literary Sources of Art History* (Princeton, N.J.: Princeton University Press, 1947), pp. 87–88.

and the figures of the two servants and the donkey are not sufficiently subordinated to the main action.

We can make this criticism more firmly when we compare Brunelleschi's panel to Ghiberti's (FIG. 16-2). In the latter, vigor and strength of statement are subordinated to grace and smoothness; little of the awfulness of the subject appears. Abraham sways elegantly in the familiar Gothic S-curve, and seems to feign rather than to aim a deadly thrust. The figure of Isaac, beautifully posed and rendered, recalls ancient Classicism and could be regarded as the first really classicizing nude since antiquity. Ghiberti was trained as both a goldsmith and a painter, and his skilled treatment of the fluent surfaces, with their sharply and accurately incised detail, evidences his goldsmith's craft. As a painter, he shares the painter's interest in spatial illusion. The rocky landscape seems to emerge from the blank panel toward us, as does the strongly foreshortened angel. These pictorial effects, sometimes thought alien to sculpture, are more developed in Ghiberti's later work, a second pair of doors for the baptistry (FIG. 16-10), the execution of which testifies to his extraordinary skill in harmonizing the effects peculiar to sculpture and painting. Here, within the limits of the awkward shape of the panel, Ghiberti achieves a composition that is perhaps less daring than Brunelleschi's but more cohesive and unified, and the jury's choice probably was fortunate for the course of art, despite accusations of collusion by Brunelleschi's biographer, Manetti. One result of the decision was, apparently, to resolve Brunelleschi's indecision about his proper calling. Subordinating sculpture, he became the first great architect of the Renaissance. As for Ghiberti, his conservative style would be greatly modified by the

16-1 FILIPPO BRUNELLESCHI, *The Sacrifice of Isaac*, 1401–1402. Gilt bronze, 21″ × 17″. Museo Nazionale, Florence.

16-2 LORENZO GHIBERTI, *The Sacrifice of Isaac*, 1401–1402. Gilt bronze, 21″ × 17″. Museo Nazionale, Florence.

discoveries of his contemporaries, and their influence on him would be visible in the later east doors of the baptistry.

The artists of Florence in the early Renaissance are sometimes classified as "conservative" or "progressive," depending on whether they cling to the International Gothic style or they take up the new pictorial experimentalism. The classification cannot be applied consistently, however, for some artists who keep to the old conventions still occasionally adopt what they can use from their more experimental contemporaries wherever it may be made consistent with their own styles. Whether conservative or progressive, artists may produce work of the highest quality, and we should not think that their excellence is merely a function of their being up-to-date or avant-garde. In some cases, too fertile and inventive an imagination may outrace the artist's powers to systematize his effort and become detrimental to his development.

JACOPO DELLA QUERCIA (c. 1375–1438), a Sienese sculptor competing for the baptistry commission, was perhaps the only non-Florentine sculptor of first rank in the fifteenth century. In comparison with the early work of Ghiberti, Jacopo's is progressive. His panel, *The Expulsion from the Garden of Eden* (FIG. 16-3), from a series of reliefs enframing the portal of San Petronio in Bologna, is carved in shallow relief and set into the frame in a closely knit pattern of curves and diagonals. The figures are constructed so that they seem capable of breaking out of the confines of the relief. A robust energy animates the powerful, heavily muscled forms and recalls the ideal Classical athletes. The conventional Gothic slenderness and delicacy are

16-3 JACOPO DELLA QUERCIA, *The Expulsion from the Garden of Eden, c.* 1430. Istrian stone, 34″ × 27″. Main portal, San Petronio, Bologna, Italy.

gone, and Jacopo's massive, monumental forms herald the grand style of the Renaissance. Indeed, although his style is without influence in Florence, he was to be rediscovered by Michelangelo at the end of the fifteenth century; the latter's debt to Jacopo is clearly visible in the great Florentine's painting of the same subject in the Sistine Chapel ceiling.

As the Sienese artist turned to the observation of the mechanics of the human body, a Florentine artist, NANNI DI BANCO (c. 1380–1421), began to explore that other popular avenue of Humanistic research, the antique. His life-size figures of four martyred saints, *Quattro Santi Coronati* (FIG. 16-4), represent the patron saints of the Florentine guild of sculptors, architects, and masons. The group, set into the outside wall of the Medieval church of Or San Michele in Florence, is an early near-solution to the Renaissance problem of integrating figures and space on a monumental scale. Here, we are on the way to the great solutions of Masaccio and of the masters of the High Renaissance. The emergence of sculpture from the architectural matrix—seen beginning in such works as the thirteenth-century statues of the west front of Reims Cathedral (FIG. 10-32)—is almost complete in Nanni's figures, which stand in a niche that is *in* but that confers some separation *from* the architecture. This spatial recess permits a new and dramatic possibility for the interrelationship of the figures. By placing them in a semicircle within their deep niche and relating them to one another by their postures and gestures, as well as by the arrangement of draperies, Nanni has achieved a wonderfully unified spatial composition. The persisting dependence on the architecture may be seen in the abutment of the two forward figures and the enframement of the niche and in the position of the two recessed figures, each in front of an engaged half-column. Nevertheless, these unyielding figures, whose bearing expresses—as in Roman art and stoicism—the discipline through which men of passionate conviction attain order and reason, are joined in a remarkable psychological unity. While the figure on the right speaks, pointing to his right, the two men opposite listen and the one next to him looks out into space, meditating the meaning of the words. Such reinforcement of the formal unity of a group with psychological cross-references will be exploited by later Renaissance artists, particularly Leonardo da Vinci.

Nanni has before him the example of the sculpture of antiquity. If we compare his statues with those of the *Visitation* group at Reims (FIG. 10-33) or of Nicola Pisano (FIG. 15-2), we find the Classicism of the older works lacking in authority and, as yet, unsure—hesitant steps in a direction only dimly suspected. The *Quattro Santi Coronati* figures have arrived at a position that, if not identical with the Roman norm, is adjacent to it. The Renaissance artist has begun to

16-4 NANNI DI BANCO, *Quattro Santi Coronati, c.* 1408–1414.
Marble, figures approx. life-size. Or San Michele, Florence.

art and the personality of the sculptor DONATELLO
(1386–1466), who, in the early years of the century,
carried forward most dramatically the search for new
forms capable of expressing the new ideas of the
Humanistic Early Renaissance. Working side by side,
Donatello and Nanni collaborated on sculpture for
the cathedral of Florence and the church of Or San
Michele. They shared the Humanistic enthusiasm for
Roman virtue and form; their innovations in style,
expressive of a new age, are parallel. Donatello's
greatness lies in an extraordinary versatility and
depth that led him through a spectrum of themes
fundamental to human experience and through stylistic variations that express these themes with unprecedented profundity and force.

A principal characteristic of greatness is authority.
The great artist produces work that his contemporaries and posterity accept as authoritative; his work
becomes a criterion and a touchstone for criticism.
Judgments of what is authoritative and "best" will of
course vary with time and place, but the greatest artists seem to survive this relativity of judgment, apparently because they reveal something deeply and
permanently true about man and broadly applicable
to his experience. Shakespeare, for example, seems
miraculously familiar with almost the whole world of
human nature. Similarly, Donatello is at ease not only
with the real, the ideal, and the spiritual, but with
such diverse human forms and conditions as childhood, the idealized human nude, practical men of the
world, military despots, holy men, derelict prelates,
and ascetic old age. Others who follow Donatello in
the school of Florence may specialize in one or two of
these human types or moods, but none commands
them so completely and convincingly. In the early fifteenth century, Donatello defined and claimed as his
province the whole terrain of naturalistic and
Humanistic art.

Early in his career, Donatello took the first fundamental and necessary step toward depiction of motion in the human figure—recognition of the principle of weight shift (*ponderation*). His *St. Mark* (FIG.
16-5), commissioned for Or San Michele, was completed in 1413; with it, Donatello closed a millennium
of Medieval art and turned a historical corner into a
new era. We have seen the importance of weight shift
in the ancient world, when Greek sculptors, in works
like the *Kritios Boy* (FIG. 5-19) and the *Doryphoros* (FIG.
5-61), grasped the essential principle that the human
body is not rigid, but a flexible structure that moves
by continuous shifting of weight from one supporting
leg to the other, the main masses of the body moving
in consonance. An illuminating comparison may be
made between Donatello's *St. Mark* and Medieval
portal statuary, or, for that matter, the sculpture of
Nicola and Giovanni Pisano or even of the early
Ghiberti; in none of these statues except Donatello's

comprehend the Roman meaning, even if he does not
duplicate the Roman form. But duplication is not his
purpose; rather, it is interpretation or commentary in
the manner of the Humanist scholars dealing with
Classical texts.

The Humanist, Roman Classicism expressed in the
sculpture of Nanni was not exclusively of his devising. The whole city of Florence, in its last, fierce war
with the Visconti of Milan at the turn of the century,
modeled itself on the ancient Roman republic. The
Humanist chancellor of Florence, Coluccio Salutati,
whose Latin style of writing was widely influential,
exhorted his fellow citizens to take as their own the
republican ideal of civil and political liberty they believed to be that of Rome, and to identify themselves
with its spirit. To be Florentine was to be Roman;
freedom was the distinguishing virtue of both.

A new realism based on the study of man and nature, an idealism found in the study of Classical
forms, and a power of individual expression characteristic of genius are the elements that constitute the

16-5 DONATELLO, *St. Mark*, 1411–1413. Marble, approx. 7′ 9″ high. Or San Michele, Florence.

16-6 DONATELLO, *St. George*, 1415–1417, from Or San Michele. Marble, approx. 6′ 10″ high. Museo Nazionale, Florence.

has the principle of weight shift been grasped. Now all at once, with the same abruptness with which it appeared in ancient Greece in Early Classical art (FIG. 5-19), it is rediscovered by Donatello. In sculpture and painting, his successors gradually mastered the representation of bodily motion of the most complex kind.

As the body now "moves," so its drapery "moves" with it, hanging and folding naturally from and around bodily points of support, so that we sense the figure as a draped nude, not simply as an integrated column with drapery arbitrarily incised. This further contributes to the independence of the figure from its architectural setting. We feel that *St. Mark* can and is about to move out of the deep niche, as the stirring limbs, the shifting weight, and the mobile drapery suggest. It is easy to imagine the figure as freestanding, unframed by architecture, without loss of any of its basic qualities.

In his *St. George* (FIG. 16-6), also designed for Or San Michele (between 1415 and 1417), Donatello provides an image of the proud idealism of youth. The armored soldier-saint, patron of the guild of ar-

morers, which commissioned the statue, stands with bold firmness—legs set apart, feet strongly planted, the torso slightly twisting so that the left shoulder and arm advance with a subtle gesture of haughty and challenging readiness—as the dragon approaches. His head is erect, turned slightly to the left; the noble features beneath the furrowed brows are intent, concentrated, yet composed in the realization of his power, intelligence, and resolution. In its regal poise and tense anticipation, the figure contrasts strikingly with its earlier Gothic counterpart, *St. Theodore* (FIG. 16-7), from Chartres Cathedral. *St. Theodore* the soldier, essentially weightless, seems in some mystic reverie, removed from the world and unaware of his surroundings. The elements of his body are not coordinated in the unity of action we find in *St. George*. The Medieval figure conveys the *idea* of the chivalric knight but nothing of the *fact* of the soldier confronting his enemy.

Between 1416 and 1435, Donatello carved five statues for the niches on the campanile of Florence Cathedral—a project that, like the figures for Or San Michele, had originated in the preceding century.

16-7 *St. Theodore*, jamb statue, *c.* 1215–1220. South portal, Chartres Cathedral. Stone, over life-size.

16-8 DONATELLO, prophet figure (*Zuccone*), 1423–1425, from the campanile of Florence Cathedral. Marble, approx. 6′ 5″ high. Museo dell' Opera del Duomo, Florence.

The most striking of the five figures—a prophet, generally known by its nickname *Zuccone*, or "Pumpkin-Head" (FIG. 16-8)—shows Donatello's peculiar power of characterization at its most original. All of his prophets are represented with a harsh, direct realism reminiscent of ancient Roman portrait sculpture. Their faces are bony, lined, and taut; each is strongly individualized. The *Zuccone* is also bald, a departure from the conventional representation of the prophets. He is dressed in an awkwardly draped and crumpled toga-like garment with deeply undercut folds. At first view, one might suspect Donatello of simply having draped a gaunt, uncouth assistant, placing him in casual stance, and rendering the subject just as he saw it. The head discloses an appalling personality—instinct with crude power, even violence. The deep-set eyes glare under furrowed brows, nostrils flaring, the broad mouth agape, as if the prophet were in the very presence of the disasters that would call forth his declamation.

In a bronze relief, *The Feast of Herod* (FIG. 16-9), on the baptismal font in the baptistry at Siena, Donatello carries his talent for characterization of single figures

16-9 DONATELLO, *The Feast of Herod*, *c.* 1425. Gilt bronze, approx. 23″ × 23″. Baptistry, San Giovanni, Siena, Italy.

onto the broader field of dramatic groups. Salome (toward the right), still seems to be dancing, even though she has already delivered the severed head of John the Baptist, with which the executioner kneels before King Herod. The actors recoil in horror into two groups: at the right, one figure covers his face with his hand; at the left, Herod and two terrified children shrink back in dismay. The psychic explosion that has taken place drives the human elements apart, leaving a gap across which the emotional electricity crackles. This masterful stagecraft obscures the fact that on the stage itself another drama is being played out—the advent of rationalized perspective space, long prepared for in the "proto-Renaissance" and recognized by Donatello and his generation as a means of intensifying the reality of the action and the characterization of the actors.

"Proto-Renaissance" artists, like Duccio and the Lorenzetti brothers, had used several devices to give the effect of distance, but with the invention of "true" linear perspective (generally attributed to Brunelleschi), early Renaissance artists were given a way to make the illusion of distance mathematical and certain. In effect, they understood the picture plane as a transparent window through which, from a fixed standpoint, the observer looks *into* the constructed, pictorial world, where all orthogonals (lines perpendicular to the picture plane) meet in a single point on the horizon (a horizontal line that corresponds to the viewer's eye level) and where all objects are unified within a single space system—the perspective. This discovery was of enormous importance, for it made possible what has been called the "rationalization of sight"—the bringing of our random and infinitely various visual sensations under a simple rule that can be expressed mathematically. Indeed, the discovery of perspective by the artists of the Renaissance reflects the emergence of science itself, which is, put simply, the mathematical ordering of our observations of the physical world. It is interesting that the artists of the Renaissance were often mathematicians, and a modern mathematician asserts that the most creative work in mathematics in the fifteenth century was done by the artists. The experimental spirit that had animated many Franciscans, like Roger Bacon, now came firmly to earth; indeed, Bacon's essays on optics had large influence on Renaissance theorists like Alberti. The position of the observer of a picture, who looks "through" it into the painted "world," is precisely that of any scientific observer fixing his gaze on the carefully placed or located datum of his research. Of course, the early Renaissance artist was not primarily a scientist; he simply found perspective a wonderful way to order his composition and to clarify it. But there is little doubt that perspective, with its new mathematical authority and certitude, conferred a kind of esthetic legitimacy on painting by making the picture *measurable* and exact. According to Plato, "the excellence of beauty of every work of art is due to the observance of measure." This is certainly expressed in the art of Greece, and now, in the Renaissance—when Plato was newly discovered and eagerly read—the artists once again exalted the principle of measure as the foundation of the beautiful in the fine arts. The projection of measured shapes on flat surfaces now influenced the character of painting and made possible scale drawings, maps, charts, graphs, and diagrams—those means of exact representation without which modern science and technology would be impossible. At this beginning of the modern world, mathematical truth and formal beauty became conjoined in the minds of the artists of the Renaissance. In his relief panel *The Feast of Herod* (FIG. 16-9), Donatello, using the device of pictorial perspective, opens the space of the action well into the distance, showing two arched courtyards and groups of attendants in the background. This penetration of the panel surface by spatial illusion replaces the flat grounds and backdrop areas of the Medieval past. The ancient Roman illusionism returns, but it is now based on a secure principle never possessed by the ancients.

It is worth comparing Donatello's Siena panel with one from Ghiberti's famous east doors of the baptis-

16-10 Lorenzo Ghiberti, east doors ("Gates of Paradise"), 1425–1452. Gilt bronze, approx. 17' high. Baptistry of Florence Cathedral.

try of Florence Cathedral (FIG. 16-10), later declared by Michelangelo to be "so fine that they might fittingly stand as the Gates of Paradise." The east doors (1425–1452) were composed differently from Ghiberti's earlier north doors. There are three sets of doors on the baptistry. The first was made by Andrea Pisano for the east doorway (1330–1335), which faces the cathedral and is the most important entrance. This set of doors was moved to the south doorway to make way for Ghiberti's first pair of doors (1403–1424), which, in turn, was moved to the north doorway so that Ghiberti's second pair of doors, the "Gates of Paradise," could be placed in the east doorway. After 1425, Ghiberti abandoned the pattern of the earlier doors and divided the space into ten square panels, each containing a relief set in plain moldings. When gilded, the glittering movement of the reliefs created an effect of great splendor and elegance.

The individual panels of Ghiberti's doors, such as *Isaac and His Sons* (FIG. 16-11), clearly recall painting in their depiction of space as well as in their treatment of the narrative; some exemplify more fully than painting many of the principles Alberti formulates in his treatise, *On Painting*. In his relief, Ghiberti creates the illusion of space partly by pictorial perspective and partly by sculptural means. Buildings are represented according to the painter's one-point perspective construction, but the figures (in the lower section of the relief, which actually projects slightly toward the viewer) appear almost in the full round, some of the heads standing completely free. As the eye progresses upward, the relief becomes flatter and flatter until the architecture in the background is represented by barely raised lines, creating a sort of "sculptor's aerial perspective" in which forms are less distinct the deeper they are in space. Ghiberti describes the work as follows:

16-11 LORENZO GHIBERTI, *Isaac and His Sons* (detail of FIG. 16-10). Approx. $31\frac{1}{2}'' \times 31\frac{1}{2}''$.

I strove to imitate nature as closely as I could, and with all the perspective I could produce [to have] excellent compositions rich with many figures. In some scenes I placed about a hundred figures, in some less, and in some more. I executed that work with the greatest diligence and the greatest love. There were ten stories, all [sunk] in frames because the eye from a distance measures and interprets the scenes in such a way that they appear round. The scenes are in the lowest relief and the figures are seen in the planes; those that are near appear large, those in the distance small, as they do in reality. . . . Executed with the greatest study and perseverance, of all my work it is the most remarkable I have done and it was finished with skill, correct proportions, and understanding.*

Thus, an echo of the ancient and Medieval past is harmonized by the new science: "proportion" and "skill" are perfected by "understanding." Ghiberti achieves a greater sense of depth than has ever before been possible in a relief. However, his principal figures do not occupy the architectural space he has created for them; rather, they are arranged along a parallel plane in front of the grandiose architecture. (According to Alberti, in his *De re aedificatoria*, the grandeur of the architecture reflects the dignity of events shown in the foreground.) Ghiberti's figure style shows a mingling of Gothic patterning of rhythmic line, Classical poses and motifs, and a new realism in characterization, movement, and surface detail. The Medieval narrative method of arranging several episodes within a frame persists. In *Isaac and His Sons* (FIG. 16-11), the group of ladies in the left foreground attends the birth of Esau and Jacob in the left background; Isaac sends Esau and his hunting dogs on his mission in the central foreground; and, in the right foreground, Isaac blesses the kneeling Jacob as Rebecca looks on (Genesis 25–27). Yet the groups are so subtly placed that there is no crowding or confusion. The figures, in varying degrees of projection, gracefully twist and turn, appearing to occupy and move through a convincing stage space, which is deepened by showing some figures from behind. The Classicism, particularly of the group of visiting ladies, derives from Ghiberti's close study of ancient art. From his biography, we know that he admired and collected Classical sculpture, bronzes, and coins—and their influence is seen throughout the panel. The beginning of the practice of collecting Classical art in the fifteenth century had much to do with the appearance of Classicism in the Humanistic art of the Renaissance.

For a time, Donatello forgot his earlier realism under the spell of Classical Rome, the ruins and an-

---

*In E.G. Holt, ed., *Literary Sources of Art History* (Princeton, N.J.: Princeton University Press, 1947), pp. 90–91.

tiquities of which he studied at some length. His bronze statue of *David* (*c.* 1430–1432) is the first free-standing nude statue since ancient times, and here Donatello shows himself once more to be an innovator (FIG. 16-12). The nude, as such, proscribed in the Christian Middle Ages as both indecent and idolatrous, had been shown only rarely—and then only in biblical or moralizing contexts, like the story of Adam and Eve or descriptions of sinners in Hell. Donatello reinvented the Classical nude, even though, in this case, we have neither god nor athlete but the young David—slayer of Goliath, biblical ancestor and antitype of Christ, and symbol of the Florentine love of liberty. The classically proportioned nude—a balance of opposing axes, of tension and relaxation—recalls, and is perhaps derived from, Roman copies of Hellenic statues. Although the body has an almost Praxitelean radiance and a sensuous quality unknown to Medieval figures, David is involved in a complex psychological drama unknown to Antique sculpture. The glance of this youthful, still adolescent hero is not directed primarily toward the severed head of Goliath, which lies between his feet, but toward his own graceful, sinuous body, as though, in consequence of his heroic deed, he is becoming conscious for the first time of its beauty, its vitality, and its strength. This self-awareness, this discovery of the self, is a dominant theme in Renaissance art.

In 1443, Donatello left Florence for northern Italy to accept the rewarding commission of an equestrian

16-12 DONATELLO, *David,*
c. 1430–1432. Bronze,
approx. 62" high. Museo
Nazionale, Florence.

16-13 DONATELLO, equestrian statue of Erasmo da Narni (*Gattamelata*), *c.* 1445–1450. Bronze, approx. 11' high. Piazza del Santo, Padua, Italy.

statue of the Venetian *condottiere* Erasmo da Narni, called *Gattamelata* ("slick cat"), for the square of San Antonio, Padua (FIG. 16-13). With it, Donatello recovered the Roman grandeur of the mounted leader as it existed in the great equestrian statue of Marcus Aurelius (FIG. 6-72), which he must have seen in Rome. The figure stands high on a lofty, elliptical base to set it apart from its surroundings and becomes almost a celebration of the liberation of sculpture from architecture. Massive and majestic, the great horse bears the amored general easily; together, they make an overwhelming image of irresistible strength and unlimited power. Next to the *Gattamelata,* a Medieval equestrian statue like *The Bamberg Rider* (FIG. 10–55), still attached to the wall, looks positively fragile, even ghost-like. The Italian rider, his face set in a mask of dauntless resolution and unshakable will, is the very portrait of the Renaissance individualist: a man of intelligence, courage, and ambition, frequently of humble origin, who, by his own resourcefulness and on his own merits, rises to a commanding position in the world.

Donatello's ten-year activity in Padua (he received additional commissions for statues and reliefs for the high altar of the church of San Antonio) made a deep and lasting impression on the artists of the region and contributed materially to the formation of a Renaissance style in northern Italy. After his return to Florence in 1453, Donatello's style changes once more. His last period is marked by an intensely personal kind of expression, in which his earlier realism returns, but with purposeful exaggeration and distortion. He turns away from Classical beauty and gran-

16-14 DONATELLO, *Mary Magdalene*, c. 1454–1455. Wood, approx. 6′ 2″ high. Museo dell' Opera del Duomo, Florence.

deur toward a kind of expressionism that seems deliberately calculated to jar the sensibilities; he gives us the ugly, the painful, and the violent. He may, in his last years, have felt religious remorse for such works as *David* and may have set about to achieve a kind of anti-esthetic manner, well exemplified in his *Mary Magdalene* (FIG. 16-14). The repentant saint in old age, after years of wasting mortification, stands emaciated, hands clasped in prayer. Donatello, in what appears to be a rekindling of Medieval piety, here rejects the body as merely the mortal shell of the immortal soul. The beautiful woman has withered, but her soul has been saved by her denial of physical beauty. Donatello's originality, independence, and insight into the meaning of religious experience are asserted here as he reinterprets Medieval material in his own terms. But Medieval as *Mary Magdalene* might first appear, we realize that it was carved by the man who made *David*, and Donatello appears as we first described him—a man with the vast versatility that distinguishes the great artist from the good artist.

Architecture

FILIPPO BRUNELLESCHI (1377–1446)—one of the unsuccessful competitors for the commission to do the doors of the baptistry of Florence in 1401—was trained as a goldsmith, but his ability as a sculptor must have been well known at that time. Although his biographer, Manetti, tells us that Brunelleschi turned to architecture out of disappointment over the loss of the baptistry commission, he continued to work as a sculptor for several years and received commissions for sculpture as late as 1416. In the meantime, however, his interest turned more and more toward architecture, spurred by several trips to Rome (the first in 1402, probably with his friend Donatello), where he too was captivated by the Roman ruins. It may well be in connection with his close study of Roman monuments and his effort to make an accurate record of what he saw that Brunelleschi developed the revolutionary system of geometric, linear perspective that was so eagerly adopted by fifteenth-century artists.

Brunelleschi's knowledge of the principles of Roman construction, combined with an analytical and inventive mind, permitted him to solve an engineering problem that no other fifteenth-century man could have solved—the design and construction of a dome for the huge crossing of the unfinished cathedral of Florence (FIGS. 16-15 and 10-58). The problem was staggering; the space to be spanned (140 feet)

16-15 FILIPPO BRUNELLESCHI, dome of Florence Cathedral, 1420–1436 (view from the southeast).

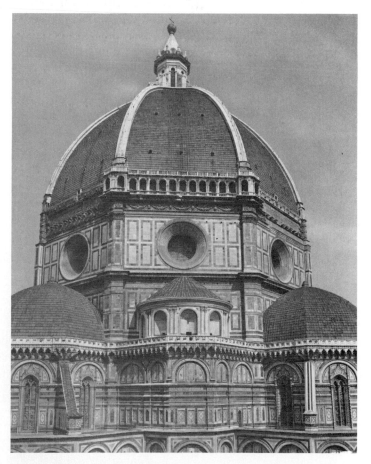

was much too wide to permit construction with the aid of traditional wooden centering. Nor was it possible, because of the plan of the crossing, to support the dome with buttressed walls. Brunelleschi seems to have begun work on the problem about 1417; in 1420, he and Ghiberti were jointly awarded the commission. The latter, however, soon retired from the project and left the field to his competitor. With exceptional ingenuity, Brunelleschi not only discarded traditional building methods and devised new ones but also invented much of the machinery that was necessary for the job. Although he might have preferred the hemispheric shape of Roman domes, Brunelleschi raised the center of his dome and designed it around an ogival section, which is inherently more stable, as it reduces the outward thrust around the dome's base. To reduce the weight of the structure to a minimum, he designed a relatively thin double shell (the first in history) around a skeleton of 24 ribs, the eight major ones being visible on the exterior. Finally, in almost paradoxical fashion, Brunelleschi anchored the structure at the top with a heavy lantern (built according to his design, but after his death). This lantern, although adding to the weight of the dome, has the curious effect of stabilizing the entire structure; without the pressure of its weight, the ribs had a tendency to tilt outward from the center, spreading at the top.

Although the dome of Florence Cathedral is Brunelleschi's most outstanding engineering achievement and although he knew of and admired Roman building techniques, the solution to this most critical structural problem was arrived at by the first acknowledged Renaissance architect through what were essentially Gothic building principles. Thus, the dome does not really express Brunelleschi's own architectural style, which is shown for the first time in a building that he began shortly before he accepted the commission for the dome—the Ospedale degli Innocenti (Foundling Hospital) in Florence (FIG. 16-16). The basic element of its design—a series of round arches supported by slender columns and framed by pilasters that carry a flat, horizontal entablature—appears to have been inspired either by the church of San Miniato al Monte (FIG. 9-21) or by the baptistry of Florence Cathedral, both Romanesque buildings. The latter was mistakenly believed to be a Roman temple in Brunelleschi's time, but even if he had known better, Brunelleschi may well have mistaken it for an Early Christian building of the fourth or fifth century—a style that he associated closely with Classical Roman architecture and that had just as much authority for him. But the hospital expresses quite a different style from that of its possible Medieval prototypes. The stress on horizontals, the clarity of the articulation, and the symmetry of its design—combined with the use of such Classical elements as Corinthian capitals and pilasters, as well as windows topped by pediments—create an impression of rationality and logic that, in spirit at least, relates the Ospedale degli Innocenti more to Classical than to Medieval architecture.

The same clarity of statement is to be found in the two basilican churches that Brunelleschi built in Florence—San Lorenzo and Santo Spirito. Of the two, the later Santo Spirito shows the architect's mature style (FIGS. 16-17 and 16-18). Begun in 1436 and completed, with some changes, after Brunelleschi's death, the cruciform building is laid out on the basis of either multiples or segments of the dome-covered crossing square in a manner reminiscent of Romanesque planning. But this segmentation is not reflected

16-16   FILIPPO BRUNELLESCHI, façade of the Ospedale degli Innocenti, Florence, 1419–1424.

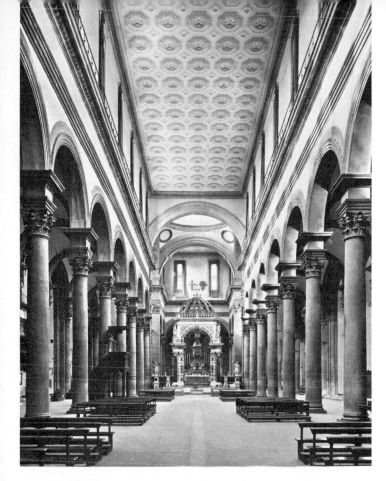

16-17 FILIPPO BRUNELLESCHI, interior of Santo Spirito, Florence, begun 1436 (view facing east).

in the nave, which is a continuous, unbroken space in the tradition of Early Christian basilicas. The aisles—subdivided into small squares covered by shallow, saucer-shaped vaults—run all the way around the flat-roofed central space and have the visual effect of compressing the longitudinal design into a centralized one, because the various aspects of the interior resemble each other, no matter where the observer

16-18 FILIPPO BRUNELLESCHI, early plan of Santo Spirito, Florence (*left*), and plan as constructed (*right*).

0   50   100 FEET
0   15   30 METERS

stands. Originally, this effect of centralization would have been even stronger; Brunelleschi had planned to extend the aisles across the front of the nave as well, as shown on the plan (FIG. 16-18). Because of the modular basis of the design, this would have demanded four (instead of the traditional three) entrances in the façade of the building—a feature that was hotly debated during Brunelleschi's lifetime and changed after his death. The appearance of the exterior walls was also changed later, when the recesses between the projecting, semicircular chapels were filled in to convert an originally highly plastic wall surface into a flat one. The major features of the interior, however, are much as Brunelleschi designed them. Compared with those of the Ospedale degli Innocenti, the forms have gained in volume. The moldings project more boldly, and the proportions of the columns more closely approach the Classical ideal. Throughout the building, proportions in a ratio of 1:2 have been used with great consistency. The nave is twice as high as it is wide; arcade and clerestory are of equal height, which means that the height of the arcade equals the width of the nave; and so on. These basic facts about the building have been delineated for the observer by crisp articulations, so that they can be read like mathematical equations. The cool logic of the design may lack some of the warmth of Medieval buildings, but it fully expresses the new Renaissance spirit that places its faith in reason rather than in the emotions.

Brunelleschi's evident effort to impart a centralized effect to the interior of Santo Spirito suggests that he was intrigued by the compact and self-contained qualities of earlier central-plan buildings, such as the Pantheon and Medieval baptistries. His Old Sacristy, built onto the left transept of San Lorenzo, expresses his admiration of the central plan. He nearly realized his ideal with the Pazzi Chapel (FIGS. 16-19, 16-20, 16-21), begun around 1440 and completed in the 1460s, long after his death. The exterior probably does not reflect Brunelleschi's original design, as the narthex, admirable as it is, seems to have been added as an afterthought, perhaps by sculptor–architect GIULIANO DA MAIANO. Behind this narthex stands one of the first independent buildings of the Renaissance to be conceived basically as a central-plan structure. Although the plan is rectangular, rather than square or round, all emphasis has been placed on the central, dome-covered space; the short, barrel-vault sections that brace the dome on two sides appear to be no more than incidental appendages. The articulation of the interior, with dark pilasters on light walls, reflects a subtle and sophisticated system of modular relationships in both plan and elevation and creates a tight network of geometric patterns that ties all parts of the building together and enhances the effect of compact self-sufficiency.

16-19 FILIPPO BRUNELLESCHI, west façade of Pazzi Chapel, begun *c.* 1440. Santa Croce, Florence.

16-20 FILIPPO BRUNELLESCHI, plan of Pazzi Chapel, Santa Croce, Florence.

16-21 FILIPPO BRUNELLESCHI, interior of Pazzi Chapel (view facing northeast).

Brunelleschi only approximated the central plan in the Pazzi Chapel; he had planned to give it full realization in Santa Maria degli Angeli (FIG. 16-22). Begun in 1434, the project was abandoned, unfinished, in 1437. The plan shows a central octagon, the corner piers of which were undoubtedly intended to carry a dome. Around this core are arranged eight identical chapels (one was to have served as entrance) that are seemingly carved out of the massive masonry that surrounds them. The plastic handling of both exterior and interior wall surfaces recaptures the ancient Roman "sculptured" wall principle and is so far ahead of its time that it does not appear again until

16-22 Plan of Santa Maria degli Angeli, Florence, 1434–1437. (After a sixteenth-century drawing of a design by Filippo Brunelleschi.)

the very end of the fifteenth century. Alberti must have seen the unfinished building and may well have had it in mind when he praised the central plan in his treatise and implanted a taste for it in generations of later architects.

It seems curious that Brunelleschi, the most renowned architect of his time, did not participate in the upsurge of palace-building that Florence experienced in the late 1430s and 1440s and that testified to the soundness of the Florentine economy and the affluence and confidence of its leading citizens. His efforts in this field were confined to work on the Palazzo di Parte Guelfa and to a rejected model for a new palace that Cosimo de' Medici intended to build. Cosimo evidently felt that Brunelleschi's project was too imposing and ostentatious to be politically wise. Instead, he awarded the commission to MICHELOZZO DI BARTOLOMMEO (1396–1472), a young architect who had been Donatello's collaborator in several sculptural enterprises. Michelozzo's architectural style was deeply influenced by Brunelleschi, and, to a limited extent, the Palazzo Medici–Riccardi may reflect Brunelleschian principles (FIG. 16-23). Built for the Medici and later bought by the Riccardi family, who almost doubled the length of the façade in the eighteenth century, the palace is a simple, massive structure; heavy rustication on the ground floor accentuates its strength. The building block is divided into stories of decreasing height by long, unbroken horizontal bands (stringcourses), which give it articulation and coherence. In the upper stories, the severity of the ground floor is modified by dressed stone, which presents a smoother surface with each successive story, so that the building appears progressively lighter as the eye moves upward. This effect is dra-

16-23 MICHELOZZO DI BARTOLOMMEO, Palazzo Medici–Riccardi, Florence, begun 1444.

matically reversed by the extremely heavy, classicizing cornice, which Michelozzo related not to the top story but to the building as a whole. It is a very effective lid for the structure, clearly and emphatically defining its proportions. The palace is built around an open, colonnaded court that most clearly shows

16-24 MICHELOZZO DI BARTOLOMMEO, court of the Palazzo Medici–Riccardi.

Michelozzo's debt to Brunelleschi (FIG. 16-24). The round-arched colonnade, although more massive in its proportions, closely resembles that of the Ospedale degli Innocenti; however, Michelozzo's failure to frame each row of arches with piers and pilasters, as Brunelleschi might have, causes the structure to look rather weak at the angles. Nevertheless, this *cortile* was the first of its kind and was to have a long line of descendants in Renaissance domestic architecture.

Painting

The youngest of the three leading innovators of the early fifteenth century, with Donatello and Brunelleschi, was the painter MASACCIO (Tommaso Guidi, 1401–1428). To understand the almost startling nature of his innovations, we should look again at the International style in painting, which was the dominant style around 1400 and persisted well into the fifteenth century, side by side with the grand new style of Masaccio and his followers. GENTILE DA FABRIANO (*c.* 1370–1427), who was working in Florence at the same time as Masaccio, produced what may be the masterpiece of the International style, *The Adoration of the Magi* (FIG. 16-25). Gentile's purpose is to create a gorgeous surface, spreading across it scores of sumptuously costumed kings, courtiers, captains, and retainers accompanied by a menagerie of exotic and ornamental animals—all in a rainbow of color with much display of gold. Here is all the pomp and ceremony of chivalric etiquette, a picture that proclaims the sanctification of aristocracy in the presence of the Madonna and Child. There is little basic

16-25 GENTILE DA FABRIANO, *The Adoration of the Magi*, 1423. Tempera on wood, approx. 9′ 11″ × 9′ 3″. Galleria degli Uffizi, Florence.

difference between the stylistic apparatus of Gentile and that used in the century following the junction of Gothic and Sienese painting. Into this traditional framework, however, Gentile inserts striking bits of radical naturalism. Animals are seen from a variety of angles and are convincingly foreshortened, as are tilted human heads and bodies. (Note the man removing the spurs from the standing magus in the center foreground.) On the right side of the *predella*, the Presentation scene is shown in a "modern" architectural setting. (The arcade in the right background looks much like Brunelleschi's Ospedale degli Innocenti, FIG. 16-16.) And on the left side of the predella, Gentile paints what may be the very first nighttime Nativity in which the light source is introduced into the picture itself.

Thus Gentile da Fabriano, although dominantly conservative, shows that he is not oblivious to contemporary experimental trends and that, with great skill and subtlety, he is able to blend naturalistic and inventive elements with a traditional composition without sacrificing Late Gothic coloristic splendor.

Masaccio was much less compromising. Although his presumed teacher, MASOLINO DA PANICALE, had worked in the International style, Masaccio moved suddenly, within the short span of only six years, into wide-open, unexplored territory. No other painter in history is known to have contributed so much to the development of a new style in so short a time as Masaccio, whose creative career was so short and whose death at 27 was so untimely. Masaccio is the artistic descendant of Giotto, whose calm, monumental style he revolutionized through a whole new repertory of representational devices that generations of Renaissance painters would study and develop. Masaccio also knew and fully understood the innova-

tions of his great contemporaries Donatello and Brunelleschi and introduced into painting new possibilities for both form and content.

We can see his breakthrough best in his frescoes in the Brancacci Chapel of Santa Maria del Carmine in Florence. In *The Tribute Money* (FIG. 16-26), painted shortly before his death, Masaccio groups three episodes. In the center, Christ, surrounded by his disciples, tells St. Peter that in the mouth of a fish he will find a coin to pay the imperial tax demanded by the collector who stands in the foreground, his back to the spectator. At the left, in the middle distance, St. Peter struggles to extract the coin from the fish's mouth, while at the right, with a disdainful gesture of great finality, he thrusts the coin into the tax collector's hand. Masaccio's figures recall Giotto's in their simple grandeur, but they stand before us with a psychological and moral self-realization that is entirely new. Masaccio realizes the bulk of the figures not through generalized modeling with a flat, neutral light without identifiable source, as Giotto does, but by means of a light that comes from a specific source outside the picture, striking the figures at an angle, illuminating the parts of the solids that obstruct its path and leaving the rest in deep shadow. This placement of light against strong dark gives the illusion of deep sculptural relief. Between the extremes of light and dark, the light is a constantly active but fluctuating force, independent of the figures and almost a tangible substance. As Masaccio and Donatello's generation learn the separation of body and drapery and the functional interrelation of them as independent fabrics, so light, which in Giotto is merely the modeling of a mass, in Masaccio comes to have its own nature, and the masses we see are visible only because of the direction and intensity of the light. We

16-26   MASACCIO, *The Tribute Money*, c. 1427. Fresco. Brancacci Chapel, Santa Maria del Carmine, Florence.

imagine the light as playing over forms—revealing some and concealing others, as the artist directs it. In the creation of a space filled with atmosphere, Masaccio anticipates the achievements of the High Renaissance; few painters between Masaccio and Leonardo da Vinci have so realistically created the illusion of space as a substance of light and air existing between our eyes and what we see.

The individual figures in *The Tribute Money* are solemn and weighty, but they also express bodily structure and function, as do Donatello's statues. We feel bones, muscles, and the pressures and tensions of joints; each figure conveys a maximum of contained energy. Both the stately stillness of Nanni di Banco's *Quattro Santi Coronati* (FIG. 16-4) and the weight-shifting figures of Donatello (FIG. 16-5) are here. The figure of Christ and the two appearances of the tax collector make us understand what the biographer Vasari* meant when he said: "Masaccio made his figures stand upon their feet."

Another important invention, for so we might call it, is the arrangement of the figures. No longer do they appear as a stiff screen in the front planes. Here, they are grouped in circular depth around Christ, and the whole group is shown in a spacious landscape, rather than in the confined stage space of Giotto's frescoes. The foreground space is generated by the group itself, as well as by the architecture on the right, shown in a one-point perspective construction in which the location of the vanishing point coincides with the head of Christ. The foreground is united with the distance by aerial perspective, which employs the diminution in light and the blurring of outlines that come with distance. This device, used by Roman painters, was forgotten during the Middle Ages and rediscovered by Masaccio, apparently independently. Masaccio realized that light and air interposed between ourselves and what we see are part of the visual experience we call "distance." With this knowledge, the world as given to ordinary sight can become for the painter the vast pictorial stage of human action.

In an awkwardly narrow space in the Brancacci Chapel (FIG. 16-27), Masaccio has painted the theme already seen in Jacopo della Quercia's slightly later relief, *The Expulsion from the Garden of Eden* (FIG. 16-3). The representational innovations are all present in Masaccio's work: the sharply slanted light from an outside source, creating deep relief by the placement of lights and darks side by side and acting as a strong unifying agent; the structurally correct motion of the

16-27   MASACCIO, *The Expulsion from Eden, c.* 1425. Fresco. Brancacci Chapel, Santa Maria del Carmine, Florence.

figures; their bodily weight and substantial contact with the ground; the hazed, atmospheric background that gives no locale but suggests a space around and beyond the figures. Masaccio's *Expulsion* is one of the supreme masterpieces of Renaissance art and an interpretation of the tragic scene of man's fall that is perhaps unsurpassed even by Michelangelo's Sistine Chapel ceiling. Adam's feet, clearly in contact with the ground, mark man's presence on earth, and the cry issuing from Eve's mouth voices the anguish of humanity deprived of God. Adam and Eve do not resist; there is no physical contact with the angel, nor are the figures crowded against the frame. Rather, they stumble on blindly, driven by the will of the angel and their own despair. The composition is starkly simple, its message incomparably eloquent.

In *The Holy Trinity* fresco in Santa Maria Novella (FIG. 16-28), the dating of which is still in dispute, Masaccio gives a brilliant demonstration of the organizing value of Brunelleschi's perspective; indeed, so much is it in the Brunelleschian manner that some have thought the great inventor of perspective may have directed Masaccio. The composition is on two

16-28 MASACCIO, *The Holy Trinity*, 1428 (?). Fresco. Santa Maria Novella, Florence.

levels of unequal height. Above, in a coffered, barrel-vaulted chapel, the Virgin Mary and St. John are represented on either side of the crucified Christ, whose arms are supported by God the Father, while the Dove of the Holy Spirit rests on Christ's halo. The donors, husband and wife, kneel just in front of the pilasters that enframe the chapel. Below the altar—a masonry insert in the painted composition—is a tomb containing a skeleton, said to represent Adam. An inscription in Italian reminds the spectator that "I was once what you are, and what I am you will become." Masaccio places the vanishing point, to which all the orthogonals of the perspective converge, at the center of the masonry altar. This is at the eye level of the spectator, who looks up at the Trinity and down

at the tomb. About 5 feet above the floor level, the vanishing point pulls the two views together, creating the illusion of an actual structure, the interior volume of which is an extension of the space in which the spectator is standing. This adjustment of the spectator to the pictured space is a first step in the development of illusionistic painting, which so fascinated many artists of the Renaissance and the later Baroque period. Masaccio has been so exact in his metrical proportions that we can actually calculate the numerical dimensions of the chapel (for example, the span of the painted vault is 7 feet; the depth of the chapel, 9 feet). Thus, he achieves not only successful illusion, but a rational, metrical coherence that, by maintaining the mathematical proportions of the surface design, is responsible for the unity and harmony of this monumental composition. *The Holy Trinity*, standing at the very beginning of the history of Renaissance painting, sums up two principal interests: realism based on observation and the application of mathematics to pictorial organization.

Masaccio's discoveries, like Donatello's, led to further experiments by his contemporaries and successors, who tended to specialize in one of the branches of pictorial science that Masaccio founded. PAOLO UCCELLO (1397–1475), a Florentine painter trained in the International style, discovered perspective well along in his career and became obsessed with it, though he was not always successful in harmonizing the old and the new. In *The Battle of San Romano* (FIG. 16-29), one of three wood panels painted for the Palazzo Medici to commemorate the Florentine victory over the Sienese in 1432, Uccello creates a composition that recalls the processional splendor of Gentile da Fabriano's *Adoration of the Magi* (FIG. 16-25). But the world of Uccello, in contrast with the surface decoration of the International style, is constructed of immobilized, solid forms; broken spears and lances and a fallen soldier are foreshortened and carefully placed along the converging orthogonals of the perspective to create a base plane like a checkerboard, on which the volumes are then placed in measured intervals. All this works very well as far back as the middle ground, where the horizontal plane is met abruptly by the up-tilted plane of an International style background. Beyond that, Uccello's sense of design is impeccable. The rendering of three-dimensional form, used by other painters for representational or expressive purposes, became for Uccello a preoccupation; for him, it had a magic of its own, which he exploited to satisfy his amazingly inventive and original imagination. His fascination with perspective had little in common with the rationality in Masaccio's concern for defining the dimensionality of space. Uccello had an irrational passion for arranging the forms of solid geometry in

16-29 PAOLO UCCELLO, *The Battle of San Romano, c.* 1455. Tempera on wood, approx. 6' × 10' 5". Reproduced by courtesy of the Trustees of the National Gallery, London.

space, and it is perhaps not surprising that he became one of the favorite masters of the Cubists of the early twentieth century.

ANDREA DEL CASTAGNO (*c.* 1423–1457) interested himself both in perspective and in the representation of imposing, strong, structurally convincing human figures. In his *Last Supper* (FIG. 16-30), painted in the late 1440s and covering a wall of the refectory of the convent of Sant' Apollonia in Florence, we see a severity and clarity of form characteristic of this phase of Florentine painting. Christ and the disciples, with Judas isolated at the front of the table in the traditional manner, are painted as static, sculptural solids.

Here, Andrea faced the problem of setting his figures within a space arranged to give (as in Masaccio's *Holy Trinity*) the illusion that the space of the observer is continuous with that of the marble-paneled alcove where the principals are sitting. But the perspective construction is so strict that it serves to limit action; its rigid frame stiffens the figures it controls, and it will not be until Leonardo's famous version of this theme, painted at the end of the century, that the architectural setting will serve the action rather than constrict it.

Andrea is seen at his best in his group of figures of famous people painted in the Villa Pandolfini near

16-30 ANDREA DEL CASTAGNO, *The Last Supper, c.* 1445–1450. Fresco. Museo di Sant' Apollonia, Florence.

16-31 ANDREA DEL CASTAGNO, *Pippo Spano*, c. 1448. Fresco. Galleria degli Uffizi, Florence.

Florence around 1450, and transferred first to the Castagno Museum in Sant' Apollonia and, more recently, to the Uffizi Gallery. One, a portrait of the general called *Pippo Spano* (FIG. 16-31), is the very image of the swaggering commander—his feet firmly planted, "powerful among peers," and bristling with insolent challenge. The figure is meant to be seen as standing in a *loggia*, the space of which is continuous with that of the spectator. The illusion is reinforced by the heavy, armored, foreshortened foot that seems to protrude over a sill of the opening. If Masaccio first "made his figures stand upon their feet," then Andrea followed him faithfully and made the point more emphatically in this splendid figure so alive with truculent energy. And by having parts of his figure appear to project into the space of the viewer, Andrea takes a step beyond Masaccio's *Holy Trinity* in the direction of Baroque illusionism.

Andrea's sometime collaborator DOMENICO VENEZIANO (c. 1420–1461) was born and trained in Venice, but settled in Florence in the late 1430s. The sixteenth-century architect, painter, and biographer Giorgio Vasari tells us that Andrea, in a fit of jealous rage, killed Domenico by hitting him with an iron bar; in fact, Andrea fell victim to the plague some four years before Domenico died. Vasari also claims that Domenico introduced the mixed-oil technique to Florence, but the artist himself seems to have painted in the traditional tempera. Although he fully assimilates Florentine forms, Domenico retains some International-style traits that he may have acquired from northern painters active in Venice. He may also have brought from Venice his sensitivity to color and outdoor light, which goes well beyond that of his Florentine contemporaries; it is in this field that Domenico makes his major contribution to Florentine art of the mid-century. His *St. Lucy Altarpiece* (FIG. 16-32) is one of the earliest examples of a type of painting that will enjoy great popularity from this time on—a *sacra conversazione* (holy conversation), in which saints from different epochs are joined in a unified space to form a company and seem to be conversing either with each other or with the audience. The clarity and precision of the architectural setting and the individualization, weight, and solemn dignity of the figures show Domenico to be a worthy heir to Masaccio and Donatello. The composition recalls Nanni di Banco's *Quattro Santi Coronati* (FIG. 16-4); here, however, the vaulted niche has been converted to an airy loggia open to the sky and flooded with bright, outdoor light. The brilliant local colors and ornate surfaces of the International style are muted by this directed light, which falls into the loggia from the upper right and bathes the scene with atmospheric luminosity. Reflected from the architecture, it lightens the shadows, and the modeling of the figures becomes less harsh than that in Masaccio, to whom effects of relief were more important than those of color. The resultant overall blonde tonality is characteristic of the paintings of Domenico and his followers.

Domenico's most important disciple and his assistant in Florence during the early 1440s was PIERO DELLA FRANCESCA (c. 1420–1492). Piero's art is the projection of a mind cultivated by mathematics and convinced that the highest beauty is found in forms that have the clarity and purity of geometric figures. A skilled geometrician, Piero wrote the first theoretical treatise on systematic perspective toward the end of his long career, after having practiced the art with supreme mastery for almost a lifetime. It is likely that his association with the architect Alberti at Ferrara and at Rimini around 1450–1451 turned his attention fully to perspective (in which science Alberti was an influential pioneer) and helped to determine his later, characteristically architectonic compositions. One can fairly say that Piero's compositions are determined almost entirely by his sense for the exact and lucid structures that mathematics defines. Within this context, he developed Domenico's sophistication in the handling of light and color, so that color became the matrix of his three-dimensional forms, lending them a new density as well as fusing them with the surrounding space.

16-32 DOMENICO VENEZIANO, *The St. Lucy Altarpiece*, center panel, *c.* 1445. Tempera on wood, approx. 6′ 7½″ × 7′. Galleria degli Uffizi, Florence.

A damaged but still beautiful panel, Piero's *The Flagellation of Christ* (FIG. 16-33), is almost a painted exposition of the rules of linear perspective and its inherent pictorial possibilities. The painting has been designed with such precision that modern architects, using the division of the brick floor paneling along the painting's baseline as a module, have been able to reconstruct accurately the floor plans of the depicted court and building and the positions of the figures within them.

The dating of the panel is uncertain; wide-ranging dates from 1445 to 1472 have been advanced. Since the depicted loggia has a distinctly "modern" (that is, Albertian) look, the painting seems to presuppose Piero's contact with the architect Alberti in the early

1450s, so that its date might fall into the middle of that decade. As exact as the architectural rendering of the portico appears to be, its structure has been modified for pictorial reasons. Stalactite-shaped forms at the beam crossings denote the positions from which two interior columns have been removed in order to create a continuous space that encloses the martyr-dom scene and permits a full view of Pontius Pilate, who watches impassively as the executioners raise their whips to chastise Christ. The column to which Christ is tied is topped by a golden statue of a nude man holding a rod in one hand and a ball in the other, attributes that appear on coins of Roman emperors. The meaning of this figure within the context of the flagellation scene is uncertain; apparently a pagan

16-33　Piero della Francesca, *The Flagellation of Christ*, c. 1455 (?). Tempera on wood, 32¾″ × 23⅛″. Palazzo Ducale, Galleria Nazionale delle Marche, Urbino.

symbol, it may represent the pagan power that Christianity had to confront and overcome.

The lighting is not as clearly legible as the perspective rendering. All outdoor forms are illuminated from the left, but the interior of the loggia receives its light from the right, either reflected from the buildings across the court or from a stipulated secondary light source behind the second column of the right colonnade. Even more ambiguous are the identities of the three figures in the right foreground and their relation to the central event, which have given rise to unending speculation. None of many tentative identifications, nor their meanings in relation to the central event, have found universal acceptance, and perhaps we should be content with viewing and experiencing the formal aspects of a masterful painting. In a composition that is at once clear, complex, and marvelously subtle, the perspective design is reinforced by visual cross-references that create a compact, pictorial unity. In the foreground figure group, which, at first glance, seems to have little relation to the depicted event, the pose of the central figure is almost identical to that of Christ. And the relation of the turbaned man with his back to us (Herod?) to the

flagellation scene is the same as that of the viewer of the painting to the foreground figure group. Thus, in a unique and ingenious manner, the artist draws the spectator past the foreground triad toward the main subject in the middle ground. With forms that are essentially static, Piero—by manipulating perspective and the disposition of volumes and voids—creates pictorial tension in a composition that is firmly contained within its frame and, at the same time, highly dynamic. By placing the massed volumes of his three foreground figures off-center into a relatively restricted space, Piero poses the question, How much mass balances how large an empty space? The proportional relationships Piero shows us in this painting provide one possible—and certainly most satisfying—answer.

Piero's most important work is the fresco cycle in the apse of the church of San Francesco in Arezzo, which represents ten episodes from the legend of the True Cross (the cross on which Christ died). Painted between 1452 and 1456, the cycle is based on a thirteenth-century popularization of the Scriptures, the *Golden Legend* by Jacobus de Varagine. The *Annunciation* from this cycle (FIG. 16-34) perhaps best illustrates

16-34 Piero della Francesca, *Annunciation, c.* 1455. Detail of fresco. San Francesco, Arezzo, Italy.

16-35 Piero della Francesca, *The Proving of the True Cross, c.* 1455. Fresco. San Francesco, Arezzo, Italy.

Piero's manner. One of the problems that occupied him all his life was how to establish a convincing architectonic relation between animate and inanimate objects. The key to Piero's solution in this painting is the conspicuously placed column that divides the depicted space into two vertical, cubic sections. The cylindrical shape of the column is echoed in the simplified, solemn, and immobile form of the Virgin. To make his figures conform to the static quality of the architecture that surrounds them, Piero reduces all actions and gestures to the slowest, simplest signals; all emotion is banished. The composition is essentially a cylinder inscribed in a cubic void, and this geometricality of the forms gives the depiction of the event a trance-like and abstract quality.

In the climactic scene of Piero's fresco cycle, *The Proving of the True Cross* (FIG. 16-35), St. Helena, mother of Constantine, accompanied by her retinue, witnesses how the True Cross miraculously restores a dead man (the nude figure) to life. The grouping of the figures is controlled by the architectural background; its medallions, arches, and rectangular panels are the two-dimensional counterparts of the ovoid, cylindrical, and cubic forms placed in front of it. One feels the careful planning behind the placement of each shape and volume; it is almost the procedure of an architect, certainly that of a man entirely familiar with compass and straightedge. As the architectonics of the abstract shapes controls the grouping, so, as in the *Annunciation*, does it impart a mood of solemn stillness to the figures—a quiet rapture shown by unindividualized and emotionless faces, the slow gestures like those of a priest's at an altar. The concourse of all these solid forms yet yields an impression of an otherworldly, mystical and eternally celebrated rite that knows nothing of the passing facts and accidents of this world. We see a union of the unchanging mathematical form with the calm silences of the contemplative spirit.

In addition, of course, Piero's work shows an unflagging interest in the properties of light and color. He suspects that one is the function of the other; he observes that colors turn cool (bluish) in shadow and that they lose intensity with increasing distance from the observer. In his effort to make the clearest possible distinction between forms, he floods his pictures with light, imparting a silver–blue tonality. To avoid heavy shadows, he illumines the dark sides of his forms with reflected light. By moving the darkest tones of his modeling toward the centers of his volumes, he separates them from their backgrounds. As a result, Piero's paintings lack some of Masaccio's relief-like qualities but gain in spatial clarity as each shape becomes an independent unit, surrounded by an atmospheric envelope and movable to any desired position, like a figure on a chessboard.

In the *Resurrection* fresco in the town hall of Borgo San Sepolcro (FIG. 16-36), Piero introduces a compositional device that would enjoy great favor with later Renaissance artists—the figure triangle. To stabilize his composition, Piero arranges his figures in a group that can be circumscribed by a triangle centrally placed in the painting. The figure of the risen Christ, standing with columnar strength and in the attitude of eternal triumph at the edge of the sepulcher, occupies the upper portion of a triangular arrangement that rests on the broad base of the sleeping soldiers in the foreground. This triangular massing of volumes around a picture's central axis gives a painting great compositional stability and is one of the keys to the symmetry and self-sufficiency that Renaissance artists strove for in their work.

Piero was at home with realism and could paint exact and unflattering likenesses of human subjects, quite unlike the generalized heads and features of his customary type. His work summarizes most of the stylistic and scientific developments in painting during the first half of the fifteenth century: realism, descriptive landscape, the structural human figure, monumental composition, perspective, proportionality, and light and color.

But other good artists were active during this period whose style remains rooted in an earlier age and whose interest in the new tendencies remained marginal. One, the Dominican painter–monk FRA ANGELICO (*c.* 1387–1455), was conservative by both training and inclination. Although he was fully aware of what was being done by his more experimentally inclined contemporaries, Fra Angelico adopted only those innovations he could incorporate without friction into his essentially conservative style. While accepting realistic details in anatomy, drapery, perspective, and architecture, he rejected Masaccio's heavy modeling, which would have dulled his bright Gothic coloring. In the *Annunciation* (FIG. 16-37)—one of numerous frescoes with which Fra Angelico decorated the Dominican convent of San Marco in Florence between 1435 and 1445—the Brunelleschian loggia is neatly designed according to the rules of linear perspective, but the fact that the vault is too low to allow the figures to stand would have been unacceptable to a Piero della Francesca. However, such considerations were secondary to Fra Angelico; what he wanted above all was to stress the religious content of his paintings, and he did so by using the means, past and present, that he felt were most appropriate. In our example, the simplicity of the statement recalls Giotto, as does the form of the kneeling, rainbow-winged angel; the elegant silhouette of the sweetly shy Madonna descends from Sienese art, and the

16-37 Fra Angelico, *Annunciation, c.* 1440–1445. Fresco. San Marco, Florence.

flower-carpeted, enclosed garden (symbolic of the virginity of Mary) is a bit of International Gothic. But all these elements have been combined with lyrical feeling and a great sense for decorative effect, so that nothing seems incongruous. Like most of Fra Angelico's paintings, the naïve and tender charm of the *Annunciation* still has an almost universal appeal and fully reflects the character of the artist, who, as Giorgio Vasari tells us, "was a simple and most holy man . . . most gentle and temperate, living chastely, removed from the cares of the world . . . humble and modest in all his works."

A strong—though perhaps somewhat unlikely—contributor to the pictorial humanization of religious subject matter was Fra Filippo Lippi (*c.* 1406–1469). Like Fra Angelico, Fra Filippo was a monk, but there all resemblance ends. From reports, he seems to have been a kind of amiable scapegrace quite unfitted for monastic life, who indulged in misdemeanors ranging from forgery and embezzlement to the abduction of a pretty nun, Lucretia, who became his mistress and the mother of his son, the painter Filippino Lippi. Only the Medici's intervention on his behalf at the papal court preserved Fra Filippo from severe

punishment and total disgrace, and he was, despite all, able to produce important and influential work. An orphan, Fra Filippo was raised in a monastery adjacent to the church of Santa Maria del Carmine, and, when about 18, he must have met Masaccio there and witnessed the decoration of the Brancacci Chapel. Fra Filippo's early work survives only in fragments, but these show that he tried to work with Masaccio's massive forms. Later, probably under the influence of Ghiberti's and Donatello's relief sculptures, he developed a linear style that emphasizes the contours of his figures and permits him to suggest movement through flying and swirling draperies. A fresh and inventive painting from Fra Filippo's later years, a *Madonna and Child with Angels* (fig. 16-38) shows his skill in manipulating line at its very best. Beyond noting its fine contours and modeling, we soon become aware of the wonderful flow of line throughout the picture, making precise yet smooth delineations of the forms, whether of the whole figures or of the details within them. Even without the reinforcing modeling, the forms would look three-dimensional and plastic, as the line is handled in a sculptural rather than in a two-dimensional sense.

16-38 FRA FILIPPO LIPPI, *Madonna and Child with Angels,*
c. 1455. Tempera on wood, approx. 36" × 25". Galleria degli
Uffizi, Florence.

Fra Filippo's skill in the use of line is rarely surpassed;
in the immediate future, only his most famous pupil,
Botticelli, will use it with greater subtlety.

Fra Filippo has interpreted his subject in a surprisingly worldly manner. The Madonna, a beautiful
young mother, is not at all spiritual or fragile, and
neither is her plump bambino, the child Christ, who
is held up to her by two angels, one of whom turns
toward us with the mischievous, puckish grimace of a
boy refusing to be subdued by the pious occasion.
Significantly, all figures reflect the use of models (that
for the Madonna may even have been Lucretia). Fra
Filippo plainly relishes the charm of youth and
beauty as he finds it in this world; he prefers the real
in landscape also, and the background, seen through
the window, has, despite some exaggerations, recognizable features of the Arno river valley. Compared
with the earlier Madonnas by Duccio (FIG. 15-9) and
Giotto (FIG. 15-12), this work shows how far the humanization of the theme has been carried. Whatever
the ideals of spiritual perfection may have meant to
artists in past centuries, those ideals are now realized
in terms of the sensuous beauty of this world.

THE SECOND HALF OF THE FIFTEENTH CENTURY

In the early fifteenth century, Florence led Italy in the
development of the new Humanism; later, the city
shared its leadership. Under the sponsorship of local
rulers, important cultural centers developed in other
parts of Italy and began to attract artists and scholars:
Urbino under the Montefeltri, Mantua under the
Gonzaga, Milan under the Sforza, Naples under the
kings of Aragon, and so forth.

This later period of Humanism is marked by a new
interest in the Italian language and literature, the
beginnings of literary criticism (parallel to the development of theory in art and architecture), the foundation of academies (especially the Platonic Academy of
Philosophy in Florence), and the introduction of the
printing press—and all that these elements could
mean for the dissemination of culture.

The conquest of Constantinople by the Turks in
1453 caused an exodus of Greek scholars, many of
whom fled to Italy, bringing with them knowledge of
ancient Greece to feed the avid interest in Classical
art, literature, and philosophy. That same conquest
closed the Mediterranean to Western shipping, making it necessary to find new routes to the markets of
the East. Thus began the age of navigation, discovery, and exploration.

In art and architecture, a theoretical foundation
could now be placed under the more-or-less "intuitive" innovations of the earlier generation of artists.
We must emphasize again the high value the Renaissance artist placed on *theory.* In his view, if any occupation or profession were to have dignity and be worthy of honor, it must have an intellectual basis. This is
a requirement we still recognize; a "scientific" pursuit
wins utmost respect in our age, and, for somewhat
similar reasons, the "fine" artist today is likely to consider his pursuit superior to that of the "commercial"
artist. The Renaissance artist strove to make himself a
scholar and a gentleman, to associate with princes
and the learned, and to rise above the long-standing
ancient and Medieval prejudice that saw him as
merely a kind of handicraftsman.

Beginning with Alberti's treatises on painting and
architecture, theoretical studies multiplied. The rediscovered text of the ancient Roman architect and
theoretician, Vitruvius, became the subject of exhaus-
tive examination and interpretation (partly because
the text found was only a copy, which, unlike the
original, was not illustrated, rendering passages that
referred to illustrations obscure and subject to varying interpretations). Brunelleschi's invention of perspective and Alberti's and Piero's treatises on the
subject provided the Renaissance artist with the op-

portunity to demonstrate the scientific basis of the visual arts.

The genius and creative energy required to achieve the new social and intellectual status claimed by the artist were available in abundance. The Renaissance ideal of *l'uomo universale* ("the universal man") here finds its realization; indeed, in Leon Battista Alberti (1407–1472), it finds one of its first personifications. Writing of himself in the third person, Alberti gives us a most revealing insight into the mind of the brilliant Renaissance man—his universal interests, broad capabilities, love of beauty, and hope of fame:

> In everything suitable to one born free and educated liberally, he was so trained from boyhood that among the leading young men of his age he was considered by no means the last. For, assiduous in the science and skill of dealing with arms and horses and musical instruments, as well as in the pursuit of letters and the fine arts, he was devoted to the knowledge of the most strange and difficult things. And finally he embraced with zeal and forethought everything which pertained to fame. To omit the rest, he strove so hard to attain a name in modeling and painting that he wished to neglect nothing by which he might gain the approbation of good men. His genius was so versatile that you might almost judge all the fine arts to be his. . . . He took extraordinary and peculiar pleasure in looking at things in which there was any mark of beauty. . . . Whatever was done by man with genius and with a certain grace, he held to be almost divine. . . .*

It is probably no accident that this autobiography sounds like a funeral oration on a great man.

Architecture

Alberti scarcely mentioned architecture as a prime interest. He entered the profession rather late in life, but today we know him chiefly as an architect. He was the first to study seriously the treatise of Vitruvius *(De architectura)*, and his knowledge of it, combined with his own archeological investigations, made him the first Renaissance architect to understand Roman architecture in depth. Alberti's most important and influential theoretical work, *De re aedificatoria*, although inspired by Vitruvius, contains much new and original material. For later architects, some of Alberti's most significant observations were the advocations of a system of ideal proportions, a central-type plan as the ideal Christian church, and the avoidance of the column–arch combination (which had persisted from Spalatum in the fourth century to Brunelleschi in the fifteenth) as incongruous. By arguing that the arch is a wall-opening that should be

*In J.B. Ross and M.M. McLaughlin, eds., *The Portable Renaissance Reader* (New York: Viking, 1953), pp. 480ff.

supported only by a section of wall (a pier), not by an independent sculptural element (a column), Alberti, with a few exceptions, disposed of the Medieval arcade for centuries.

Alberti's own architectural style represents a scholarly application of Classical elements to contemporary buildings. His Palazzo Rucellai in Florence (fig. 16-39) probably dates from the mid-1450s. The façade, built over a group of three Medieval houses, is much more severely organized than that of the Palazzo Medici–Riccardi (fig. 16-23). Each story of the Palazzo Rucellai is articulated by flat pilasters, which support full entablatures. The rustication of the wall surfaces between the smooth pilasters is subdued and uniform, and the suggestion that the structure becomes lighter toward its top is made in an adaptation of the ancient Roman manner by using different articulating orders for each story: Tuscan (resembling the Doric order) for the ground floor, Composite (combining Ionic volutes with acanthus leaves of the Corinthian) for the second, and Corinthian for the third. Here, Alberti has adapted the articulation of the Colosseum (fig. 6-46) to a flat façade, which does not allow the deep penetration of the building's mass so effective in the Roman structure. By converting the plastic, engaged columns of the ancient model into shallow pilasters that barely project from the wall,

16-39 Leon Battista Alberti, Palazzo Rucellai, Florence, *c.* 1452–1470.

Alberti has created a large-meshed, linear net that, stretched tightly across the front of his building, not only unifies its three levels but also emphasizes the flat, two-dimensional qualities of the wall.

The design for the façade of the Gothic church of Santa Maria Novella in Florence (FIG. 16-40) was also commissioned by the Rucellai family. Just as Brunelleschi has done occasionally, Alberti takes his cue from a pre-Gothic Medieval design—that of San Miniato al Monte (FIG. 9-21). Following his Romanesque model, he designs a small, pseudo-Classical portico for the upper part of the façade and supports it with a broad base of pilaster-enframed arcades, incorporating the six tombs and three doorways of the extant Gothic building in the process. But in the organization of these elements, Alberti takes a long step beyond the Romanesque planners. The height of Santa Maria Novella (to the tip of the pediment) equals its width, so that the entire façade can be inscribed in a square. The upper structure, in turn, can be encased in a square one-fourth the size of the main square; the cornice of the entablature that separates the two levels halves the major square, so that the lower portion of the building becomes a rectangle that is twice as wide as it is high; and the areas outlined by the columns on the lower level are squares with sides that are about one-third the width of the main unit. And so, throughout the façade, Alberti defines areas and relates them to each other in terms of proportions that can be expressed in simple numerical relations (1:1, 1:2, 1:3, 2:3, and so on). In his treatise, Alberti uses considerable space to propound the necessity of such harmonic relationships for the design of beautiful buildings. He shares this conviction with Brunelleschi, and it is this dependence on mathematics—the belief in the eternal and universal validity of numerical ratios as beauty-producing agents—that most fundamentally distinguishes both architects from their predecessors.

At San Francesco in Rimini (FIG. 16-41), Alberti once more modernizes a Gothic church—in this case, at the behest of one of the more sensational tyrants of the Early Renaissance, Sigismondo Pandolfo Malatesta, Lord of Rimini. Malatesta wanted a temple in which to enshrine the bones of great Humanist scholars like Gemistus Pletho, who dreamed of a neopagan religion that would supersede Christianity and whose remains Malatesta had brought from Greece. He intended his "temple" also to memorialize his mistress, Isotta. Alberti's thoroughly Roman design is a monument both to the tyrant's love of Classical learning and to his arrant paganism. Alberti redesigned the exterior shell of San Francesco, making a cubic structure, complete within itself, and fronting it with a façade like a Roman triumphal arch. Four massive engaged columns frame three recessed

16-40 LEON BATTISTA ALBERTI, west façade of Santa Maria Novella, Florence, c. 1458–1470.

arches and carry a flat entablature that projects sharply, making a *ressaut*, or "jump," above each capital. Alberti intended the second story, which remains incomplete, to have an arched window framed by pilasters. The heavy relief of this façade contrasts with the flat, band-like elements in most of Alberti's other buildings. The deep, arched niches, rhythmically deployed along the flanks of the building and containing sarcophagi for the remains of famous

16-41 LEON BATTISTA ALBERTI, San Francesco, Rimini, Italy, begun 1451 (view from the northwest).

16-42   LEON BATTISTA ALBERTI, west façade of Sant'
Andrea, Mantua, Italy, designed *c.* 1470.

16-43   LEON BATTISTA ALBERTI, plan of Sant' Andrea,
Mantua.

men, are in keeping with Alberti's conviction that
arches should be carried on piers, not columns.
These, along with the elements of the façade, provide
an effect of monumental scale and grandeur that approaches ancient Roman architecture.

Adjusting the Classical orders to façade surfaces
occupied Alberti throughout his career. In 1470, in his
last years, he designed the church of Sant' Andrea in
Mantua (FIGS. 16-42, 16-43, 16-44) to replace an older
eleventh-century church. In the ingeniously planned
façade, which illustrates the culmination of Alberti's
experiments, he locks together two complete Roman
architectural motifs—the temple front and the triumphal arch. His concern for proportion made him
equalize the vertical and horizontal dimensions of
the façade, which leaves it considerably lower than
the church behind it. This concession to the demands
of a purely visual proportionality in the façade and to
the relation of the façade to the small square in front
of it—even at the expense of continuity with the body
of the building—is frequently manifest in Renaissance architecture, where considerations of visual
appeal are of first importance. On the other hand,
there *are* structural correspondences in Sant' Andrea.
The façade pilasters are the same height as those on
the interior walls of the nave, and the central barrel

vault, from which smaller barrel vaults branch off at
right angles, introduces (in proportional arrangement
but on a smaller scale) the system used on the interior. The façade pilasters, becoming part of the wall
once more, run uninterrupted through three stories—
an early application of the "colossal" or "giant" order
that will become a favorite motif of Michelangelo.

16-44   LEON BATTISTA ALBERTI, interior of Sant' Andrea.

The interior of Sant' Andrea (FIG. 16-44) suggests that Alberti may have been inspired by the tremendous vaults of the ruined Basilica of Constantine (FIG. 6-85). The Medieval columned arcade, still used by Brunelleschi in Santo Spirito, is now forgotten, and the huge barrel vault—supported by thick walls alternating with vaulted chapels and interrupted by a massive dome over the crossing*—returns us to the vast interior spaces and dense enclosing masses of Roman architecture. In his treatise, Alberti calls the traditional basilican plan, in which continuous aisles flank the central nave, impractical, because the colonnades concealed the ceremonies from the faithful in the aisles; hence, his design of a single, huge hall, from which independent chapels branch off at right angles. This break with a thousand-year Christian building tradition was extremely influential in later Renaissance and Baroque planning.

Although Alberti extolls the virtues of the central plan in his treatise, his one attempt to build a church

*It is not known what kind of dome Alberti planned for the crossing; the present dome was added by FILIPPO JUVARA in the eighteenth century.

of this type remains abortive; San Sebastiano in Mantua, begun in 1460, was never completed. To many Renaissance architects and theoreticians, the circle was the ideal geometric figure; without beginning or end and with all points equidistant from a common center, it seemed to reflect the nature of the universe. This is one reason why the central plan was felt to be so appropriate for religious architecture. (Figures that approached the circle, such as polygons, were considered adequate.) But as firm as this conviction of the architects may have been, the clergy was almost as firm in its demands for traditional longitudinal churches, which, of course, are much more practical for Christian religious services. Additional to the main question of how to accommodate the congregation in central-plan churches was the question of where to put the main altar, and architects were permitted to realize their ideal relatively rarely.

A compromise solution, suggested first in Alberti's San Sebastiano in Mantua, was realized by GIULIANO DA SANGALLO (1443–1516) in Santa Maria delle Carceri in Prato (FIGS. 16-45, 16-46, 16-47). Built according to the plan of a Greek cross—with the cross arms so short that the emphasis is on the central, dome-covered square—the building, in fact, very closely approaches the central-plan ideal. Block-like, it is as high as it is wide, the cross arms are twice as wide as they are deep, and the Ionic second story is two-thirds the height of the Doric first floor—in fact, the whole building can be read in terms of the simple numerical relations that Alberti advocates. Interior articulation, however, is much closer to Brunelleschi and resembles that of the Pazzi Chapel (FIG. 16-21).

16-45 GIULIANO DA SANGALLO, Santa Maria delle Carceri, Prato, Italy, 1485 (view from the northwest).

16-46 GIULIANO DA SANGALLO, plan of Santa Maria delle Carceri, Prato.

16-47   Giuliano da Sangallo, interior of Santa Maria delle Carceri (view facing northeast).

The building seems to be a hybrid of the styles of Giuliano's two great predecessors, but it is also a neat and compact near-realization of an ideal central-plan Renaissance church.

Sculpture

Like the work of Alberti in the latter half of the fifteenth century, the sculpture of the Florentine School realizes new triumphs of Humanist Classicism. The successors of Donatello refined his innovating art and specialized in its many forms and subjects. No monument made by the following generation expresses more beautifully and clearly this dedication to the values of pagan antiquity than the tomb of Leonardo Bruni in Santa Croce in Florence (FIG. 16-48). Its sculptor, Bernardo Rossellino (1409–1464)—at one time a resident of Arezzo, like the man whose tomb he built—strove mightily to immortalize the fame of his fellow citizen. The wall tomb has a history that reaches back into the Middle Ages, but Rossellino's version is new and definitive and the expression of an age deliberately turning away from the Medieval past.

Leonardo Bruni was one of the most distinguished men of Italy, and his passing was widely mourned. An erudite scholar in Greek and Latin, a diplomat and apostolic secretary to four popes, and finally a member of the chancery of the city of Florence, Bruni's career sums up the Humanistic ideal. The Florentines particularly praised him for his *History of*

Florence. In his honor, the practice of the funeral oration was revived, as was the ancient custom of crowning the deceased with laurel. It is quite possible that the historic event of the crowning of the dead Humanist gave Rossellino his theme and that the tomb is a kind of memorialization of the laureate scene. The forms of antiquity and the event of their restoration are brought together by the call of fame.

The deceased lies on the catafalque in a long gown, the *History of Florence* on his breast, the drapery of his couch caught up at the ends by Imperial Roman eagles. Winged genii at the summit of the arch hold a great escutcheon; on the side of the sarcophagus, others support a Latin inscription that describes the Muses' grief at the scholar's passing. At the base of the niche are Roman funeral garlands. The only Christian reference is a Madonna and Child with angels in the tympanum. As in Alberti's churches, a Humanist and pagan Classicism controls the mood of the design in an evocation of the ancient Greco–Roman world.

Few could hope for a funeral and tomb like Leonardo Bruni's; but in a Humanistic age, many wanted to see their memory, if not their fame, perpetuated. Also, Renaissance man probably enjoyed seeing likenesses of himself. At the time, Roman portrait busts were being found and preserved in ever-greater numbers; given this model, it was almost inevitable that the Renaissance would develop a similar portrait

16-48 BERNARDO ROSSELLINO, tomb of Leonardo Bruni, *c.* 1445–1450. Marble, approx. 20' high to top of arch. Santa Croce, Florence.

type. The form may have originated in the shop of ANTONIO ROSSELLINO (*c.* 1427–1479), Bernardo's younger brother. An example of Antonio's work is the portrait bust of *Matteo Palmieri* (FIG. 16-49), apostolic delegate for Pope Sixtus IV. Palmieri, who held high rank in Florence, was a learned man and author of a theological poem, *City of Life,* based formally on Dante's work. After his death, parts of the poem were declared heretical because the souls of men were originally represented as fallen angels. However, at the time of his death, Palmieri received a state funeral like Bruni's; his book was placed on his breast and a funeral oration was delivered. Antonio's portrait of Palmieri is extremely realistic but avoids the hardness of Roman Republican visages, which suggest the lifeless exactitude of the death mask—from which, indeed, they must have been made. Palmieri's almost clown-like face, with its enormous nose and endless mouth, is filled with a bright, intelligent animation, and the fine eyes seem those of a man engaged in a quick and subtle dialogue. The unsparing realism in the depiction of the ugly yet beguiling face is not surprising for a subject who probably had little difficulty in detecting flattery and rejecting it.

Donatello has shown the sternly real and the gently idealized in his forms; indeed, realism and idealism are parallel tendencies in the later fifteenth century. DESIDERIO DA SETTIGNANO (1428–1464) specialized in the sensitive reading of the faces of women and children, which he idealized without diminishing character, as we may see in his *Bust of a Little Boy* (FIG. 16-50). The proportions and soft contours of the head are wonderfully understood, as is the psychological set— a wondering innocence—captured by Desiderio in the ambiguous pout and in the uplifted brows and large eyes directed wide at an adult world. The marble has been carved to give a remarkable smoothness to the planes, so that the light will be modulated softly and the impression of living, tender flesh con-

16-49 ANTONIO ROSSELLINO, *Matteo Palmieri,* 1468. Marble, life-size. Museo Nazionale, Florence.

16-50 DESIDERIO DA SETTIGNANO, *Bust of a Little Boy, c.* 1455. Marble, life-size. National Gallery of Art, Washington, D.C. (Andrew W. Mellon Collection).

581

veyed. The subtlety of Desiderio's surfaces and the consequent effect of life they give have long been admired by the Italians, as is evident in their phrase, *il vago Desiderio, si dolce bello* ("the charming Desiderio, so sweetly beautiful"). A whole school of sculptors worked in this manner, and attributions, often quite uncertain, range from Desiderio to the young Leonardo da Vinci. The soft, misty, shadow effects certainly point ahead to the *sfumato* ("smoky" light and shade) in Leonardo's paintings.

Since the thirteenth and fourteenth centuries, the Madonna and Child theme has become increasingly humanized, until, in the fifteenth century, we might almost speak of a school of sweetness and light in which many sculptors attempt to outdo each other, especially in relief, in rendering the theme ever gentler and prettier. In the latter half of the fifteenth century, increasing demand for devotional images for private chapels and shrines (rather than for large public churches) contributed to an increasing secularization of traditional religious subject matter. Luca della Robbia (1400–1482), a sculptor in the generation of Donatello and a leader of the trend toward sweetness and light, discovered a way to multiply the images of the Madonna so that they would be within the reach of persons of modest means. His discovery (around 1430), involving the application of vitrified potters' glazes to sculpture, led to his production, in quantity, of the glazed terra-cotta reliefs for which he is best known. Because they were cheap, durable, and decorative, these works became extremely popular and the basis for a flourishing family business. The tradition was carried on by his nephew Andrea, whose colors tend to become a little garish, and by the latter's sons (Giovanni and Girolamo), whose activity extends well into the sixteenth century, when

16-51 Luca della Robbia, *Madonna and Child, c.* 1455–1460. Terra cotta with polychrome glaze, approx. 6' in diameter. Or San Michele, Florence.

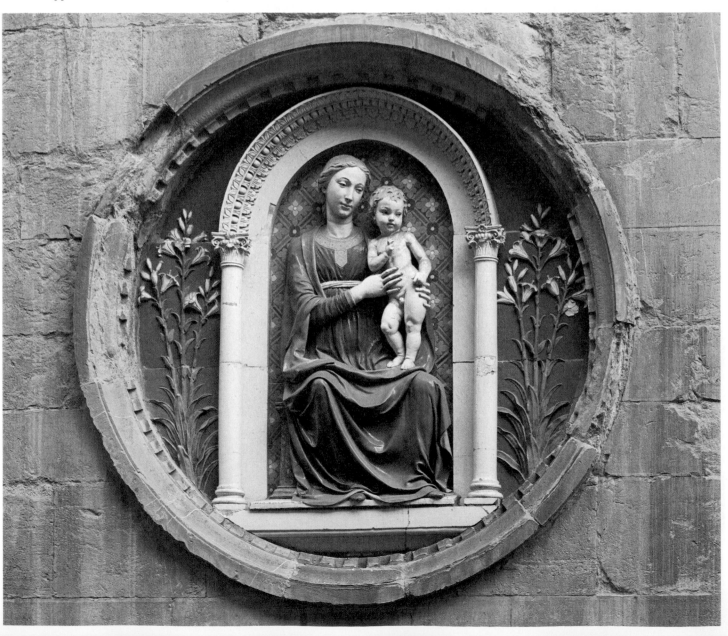

the product tends to become purely commercial; we still speak today of "della Robbia ware." An example of Luca's specialty is the *Madonna and Child* set into a wall of Or San Michele (FIG. 16-51). The figures are composed within a *tondo*, a circular frame that will become popular with both sculptors and painters, particularly the della Robbia family, in the later part of the century. The introduction of high-key color into sculpture adds a certain worldly gaiety to the theme, and the customary light blue grounds (and here the green and white of lilies and the white architecture) suggest the festive season of Easter and the freshness of May, the month of the Virgin. Of course, the somber majesty of the old Byzantine style has long since disappeared. The young mothers who prayed before images like this could easily identify with the Madonna, and doubtless did. The distance between the observed and the observer has vanished.

The most important sculptor of the second half of the century was ANDREA DEL VERROCCHIO (1435–1488). A painter as well as a sculptor, with something of the versatility and depth of Donatello, Verrocchio had a flourishing *bottega* in Florence that attracted many students, among them Leonardo da Vinci. Ver-

16-53 ANDREA DEL VERROCCHIO, *Bartolommeo Colleoni, c.* 1483–1488. Bronze, approx. 13' high. Campo dei Santi Giovanni e Paolo, Venice.

16-52 ANDREA DEL VERROCCHIO, *David, c.* 1465. Bronze, approx. 49" high. Museo Nazionale, Florence.

rocchio, also like the great Donatello, had a broad repertory. He too made a figure of *David* (FIG. 16-52), one that strongly contrasts in its narrative realism with the quiet, esthetic Classicism of Donatello's *David* (FIG. 16-12). Verrocchio's *David*—a sturdy, wiry young apprentice clad in a leathern doubtlet—stands with a jaunty pride, the head of Goliath at his feet. He poses like any sportsman who has just won a game, or a hunter with his kill. The easy balance of the weight, the lithe, still thinly adolescent musculature, in which the veins are prominent, show how closely Verrocchio read the text and how clearly he knew the psychology of brash and confident young men. Although the contrast with Donatello's interpretation need hardly be labored, we might note the "open" form of the Verrocchio *David*, the sword and pointed elbow sharply breaking through the figure's silhouette and stressing the live tension of the still alert victor; Donatello's *David*, on the other hand, has a "closed" silhouette, which emphasizes its Classical calm and relaxation. The description of the anatomy of the two figures—specific in the former, generalized in the latter—puts further accent on the difference between them. Both statues are masterpieces and show how two skillful and thoughtful men approach the same theme from very different angles.

Verrocchio competes with Donatello again in an equestrian statue of another *condottiere* of Venice, *Bartolommeo Colleoni* (FIG. 16-53), who, eager to emulate the fame and the monument of Donatello's

Gattamelata (FIG. 16-13), provided for the statue in his will. Both Donatello's and Verrocchio's statues were made after the deaths of their subjects, so that neither artist knew his subject. The result is a fascinating difference of interpretation—like that between the two *Davids*—of what a professional captain of armies would look like. On a pedestal even higher than that of Donatello's *Gattamelata*, Verrocchio's statue of the bold equestrian general is placed so that the dominating, aggressive figure can be seen above the rooftops, silhouetted against the sky, its fierce authority unmistakably present from all major approaches to the piazza (the Campo dei Santi Giovanni e Paolo). In contrast with the near repose of the *Gattamelata*, the Colleoni horse moves in a prancing stride, arching and curving its powerful neck, while the commander seems suddenly to shift his whole weight to the stirrups and, in a fit of impassioned anger, to rise from the saddle with a violent twist of his body. The group is charged with an exaggerated tautness; the bulging muscles of the animal, the fiercely erect and rigid body of the man unify brute strength and rage. The commander, represented as delivering the battle harangue to his troops before they close with the enemy, has worked himself into a frenzy that he hopes to communicate to his men. In the *Gattamelata*, Donatello gives us a portrait of grim sagacity; Verrocchio's *Bartolommeo Colleoni* is a portrait of savage and merciless might. Machiavelli writes that the successful ruler must combine the traits of the lion and the fox; one feels that Donatello's *Gattamelata* is a little of the latter and that Verrocchio's *Bartolommeo Colleoni* is much of the former.

Closely related in stylistic intention to Verrocchio is the work of ANTONIO POLLAIUOLO (c. 1431–1498). Also important as a painter and engraver, Pollaiuolo infuses the nervous movement and emotional expressiveness of Donatello's late style with a new linear mobility, spatial complexity, and dramatic immediacy. He has a realistic concern for movement in all its variety and for the stress and strain of the human figure in violent action. A good example is Pollaiuolo's small-scale group of *Hercules and Antaeus* (FIG. 16-54); not quite 18 inches high, it embodies the ferocity and vitality of elemental, physical conflict. The group illustrates the legend of a wrestling match between Antaeus (Antaios), a giant and son of earth, and Hercules (Herakles). We have already seen this story represented by EUPHRONIOS on an ancient Greek vase (FIG. 5-9). Each time Hercules threw him, Antaeus sprang up again, his strength renewed by contact with earth. Finally, Hercules held him aloft, so that he could not touch earth, and strangled him around the waist. The artist strives to convey the excruciating moment—the straining and cracking of sinews, the clenched teeth of Hercules, the kicking

16-54 ANTONIO POLLAIUOLO, *Hercules and Antaeus*, c. 1475. Bronze, approx. 18″ high with base. Museo Nazionale, Florence.

and screaming of Antaeus. The figures are interlocked in a tightly wound coil, and the flickering reflections of light on the dark, gouged surface of the bronze contribute to the effect of agitated movement and fluid play of planes.

Painting and Engraving

The twisting of figures through space shows the growing interest in realistic action among this generation of artists. Now an enthusiasm, this interest is further revealed in Pollaiuolo's *Battle of the Ten Nudes* (FIG. 16-55). Pollaiuolo belongs to the second generation of experimentalists, who, in their pursuit of realism, were absorbed in the study of anatomy, and he may have been one of the first artists to perform human dissection. The problem of rendering human anatomy had been rather well solved by earlier artists like Donatello and Andrea del Castagno, but their figures are usually shown at rest or in restrained motion. Pollaiuolo, as in his *Hercules and Antaeus*, takes delight in showing violent action and finds his opportunity in subjects dealing with combat. He conceives the body as a powerful machine and likes to display its mechanisms; knotted muscles and taut sinews activate the skeleton as ropes pull levers. To show this to best effect, Pollaiuolo developed a figure so thin and muscular that it appears *écorché* (as if without skin or outer tissue), with strongly accentuated articulations at the wrists, elbows, shoulders,

16-55 ANTONIO POLLAIUOLO, *Battle of the Ten Nudes, c.* 1465. Engraving approx. 15″ × 23″. Metropolitan Museum of Art, New York (bequest of Joseph Pulitzer, 1917).

and knees. His *Battle of the Ten Nudes* shows this figure type in a variety of poses from numerous points of view. If the figures, even though they hack and slash at one another without mercy, seem somewhat stiff and frozen, it is because Pollaiuolo shows *all* the muscle groups at maximum tension. The fact that only part of the body's muscle groups are involved in any action, while the others are relaxed, was to be observed only some decades later by an even greater anatomist, Leonardo da Vinci.

Pollaiuolo's *Battle of the Ten Nudes* is an *engraving,* a print made by pressing an inked metal plate, into which a drawing has been incised, against a sheet of paper. Developed around the middle of the fifteenth century, probably in northern Europe, engraving proved to be more flexible and durable than the older woodcut, which it gradually replaced during the later part of the century. As numerous prints could be made from the same plate, they were cheap and could be widely circulated, bringing art to the common man and spreading new and stimulating pictorial ideas among artists. Because they were easy to transport, prints were a quick and easy means of inter-artist communication. Italian prints had important influence on such northern painters as Albrecht Dürer, and the prints of that great master of engraving were widely admired among Italian artists.

The versatile Pollaiuolo experimented in painting, especially with the problem of representing figures in a landscape setting. The problem of relating figures to architecture had already been solved by Piero della Francesca, but the landscape setting presented some-

what different requirements, some of which had been met by Masaccio. The panel representing *Hercules and Deianira* (FIG. 16-56), contemporaneous with the sculptured group of *Hercules and Antaeus,* indicates that Pollaiuolo is a master not only of anatomy but also of landscape and light. In this, one of three paintings commissioned by Piero de' Medici for the Medici palace (the subjects of which were the labors of Hercules, the legendary Greek hero), the centaur Nessus has abducted Deianira, the bride of Hercules, and Hercules is in the act of slaying him with a poisoned arrow. The dramatic action and play of muscle and sinew is what we would expect of Pollaiuolo, but here he sets the bounding Nessus, the gesticulating Deianira, and the bow-taut Hercules in a broad landscape, the valley of the river Arno. The winding river takes the viewer's gaze all the way to the horizon, past the city of Florence, dim in the distance. (The cathedral can be seen just beyond Deianira's left hand). Pollaiuolo's observation of deep landscape space and atmospheric effects, like the luminous glaze on the river and the fade-out of the contours of the far distant hills, complements his knowledge of the human figure; the broad, quiet, natural perspective serves to set off the tense movements of the actors. From mid-century on, there is sharply increased interest in the pagan mythologies as subjects for painting and sculpture, an interest that will persist well into the nineteenth century. Here, a mythological subject has been imagined so vividly that it has been made part of the actual Florentine scene. Instead of relating figures and space in a rationally clear

16-56　ANTONIO POLLAIUOLO, *Hercules and Deianira, c.* 1470. Egg tempera and oil (?) on canvas, $21\frac{1}{2}'' \times 31\frac{3}{16}''$. Yale University Art Gallery, New Haven, Connecticut. (University purchase from James Jackson Jarves.)

perspective, abstracted from nature, Pollaiuolo represents human figures in their natural environment. This image of the world is not fixed, like Piero della Francesca's, but fluid and changing.

DOMENICO GHIRLANDAIO (1449–1494) differs in character from Pollaiuolo. Neither an innovator nor an experimenter, Ghirlandaio is rather a synthesizer who, profiting from everything done before, summarizes the state of Florentine art by the end of the century. His works express his times to perfection, and, for this, he enjoyed great popularity among his contemporaries. Ghirlandaio's paintings also show a deep love for his city of Florence, its spectacles and

pageantry, its material wealth and luxury. His most representative pictures—a cycle of frescoes representing scenes from the lives of the Virgin and St. John the Baptist, from which is shown *The Birth of the Virgin* (FIG. 16-57)—are found in the choir of Santa Maria Novella. In the rich interior of a palace room, embellished with fine *intarsia* (wooden mosaic) and sculpture, the mother of the Virgin, St. Anne, reclines, while midwives prepare the infant's bath. From the left comes a grave procession of ladies, led by a member of the Tornabuoni family (the donors of the paintings). This splendidly dressed young woman holds as prominent a place in the composi-

16-57　DOMENICO GHIRLANDAIO, *The Birth of the Virgin*, 1485–1490. Fresco. Santa Maria Novella, Florence.

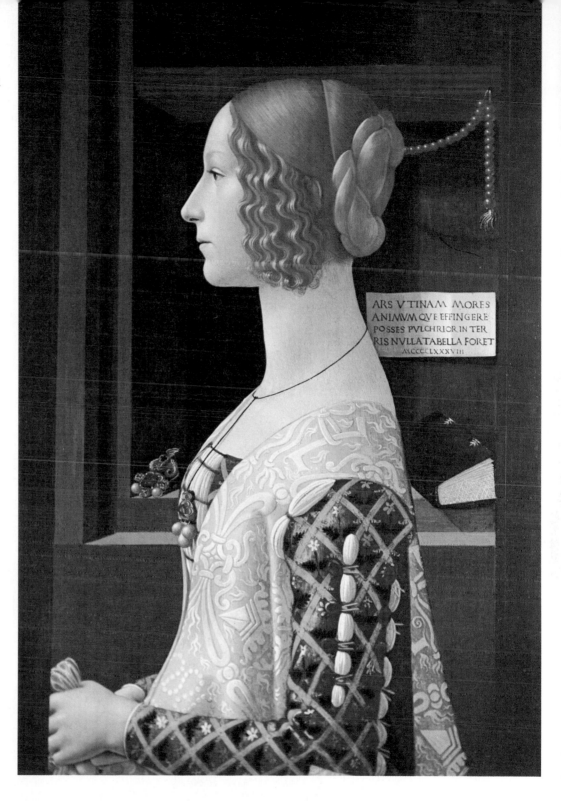

16-58 DOMENICO GHIRLANDAIO, *Giovanna Tornabuoni* (?), 1488. Oil and tempera on wood, approx. 30″ × 20″. Sammlung Thyssen-Bornemisza, Lugano.

ARS VTINAM MORES
ANIMVM QVE EFFINGERE
POSSES PVLCHRIOR IN TER
RIS NVLLA TABELLA FORET
MCCCCLXXXVIII

tion (close to the central axis) as she must have held in Florentine society; her appearance in the painting (a different female member of the house appears in each of the frescoes) is conspicuous evidence of the secularization of sacred themes commonplace in art by this time. Living persons of high rank are now represented not only as present at biblical dramas but, as here, often stealing the show from the saints. The display of patrician elegance absorbs and subordinates the devotional tableau.

The composition epitomizes the achievements of Early Renaissance painting: clear spatial representation; statuesque, firmly constructed figures; and rational order and logical relation among these figures and objects. If anything of earlier traits remains, it is in the arrangement of the figures, which still somewhat rigidly cling to layers parallel to the picture plane.

Giovanna Tornabuoni may be the subject of a portrait by Ghirlandaio (FIG. 16-58), the cool formality of which repeats the lady of the fresco and sets off the proud, sensitive beauty of the aristocratic features. Although the profile pose is not primarily intended to a convey a reading of character, this portrait tells us much about the high state of human culture achieved in Florence, the careful cultivation and prizing of beauty in life and art, the breeding of courtly manners, and the great wealth behind it all.

The profile pose was customary in Florence until about 1470, when three-quarter and full-face portraits began to replace it. From the last quarter of the fifteenth century, we have a three-quarter view, *Portrait of a Young Man* (FIG. 16-59) by SANDRO BOTTICELLI (Alessandro di Mariano dei Filipepi, 1444–1510), the brightest star of the Florentine galaxy in the later part of the century. Earlier in the century, this three-quar-

16-59 SANDRO BOTTICELLI, *Portrait of a Young Man,* late fifteenth century. Oil and tempera on wood, 23″ × 15½″. Formerly in the collection of Sir Thomas Merton, Berkshire, England.

ter view—the head almost full-face, the eyes meeting those of the observer—was made common by the painters of northern Europe. The Italian painters now take it up, perceiving that it greatly increases the viewer's information about the subject's appearance. This almost full view also allows the artist to search and reveal the subject's character, although, for a long while, Italian artists will prefer (and no doubt their sitters would demand) an impersonal formality that presents a calm, undisturbed public face and conceals the private, pyschological man. Thus, Botticelli's young man measures observers with impassive nonchalance, as if expecting them to maintain the proper formal distance.

Botticelli was the pupil of Fra Filippo Lippi, from whom he must have learned the method of "drawing" firm, pure outline with light shading within the contours. The effect is clearly apparent in the explicit and sharply elegant form of the portrait. In the hands of Botticelli, this method will be refined infinitely, and he is known in world art as one of the great masters of line. One of the most important monographs on Botticelli is by a Japanese;* in Botticelli, the Orient recognizes a master from the West.

No discussion of Botticelli can be fully meaningful without some reference to the environment that peculiarly encouraged him—the circle of Lorenzo de' Medici and the Platonic Academy of Philosophy. Here, he studied the philosophy of Plato, or rather of Neo-Platonism, for scholars had not yet developed the critical sense that would distinguish between Plato and the Neo-Platonic mystics of Alexandria, who came centuries after and quite transformed Plato's thought in the direction of a religious system. It was this spiritualized and mystical Platonism that Botticelli absorbed, believing that it was close to Christianity in essence and that the two could be reconciled. He must have heard the Humanists around Lorenzo discourse on these new mysteries in one of the Medici villas, in surroundings highly conducive to reflection. A modern historian writes:

> In a villa overhanging the towers of Florence, on the steep slope of that lofty hill crowned by the mother city, the ancient Fiesole, in gardens which Cicero might have envied, with Ficino, Landino, and Politian at his side, he [Lorenzo] delighted his hours with the beautiful visions of Platonic philosophy, for which the summer stillness of an Italian sky appears the most genial accompaniment.†

Botticelli had the power to materialize the "beautiful visions," and this he did in a number of works for the Medici villas, among them the famous *Birth of Venus* (FIG. 16-60), inspired, it is believed, by a poem

by Politian on that theme. Botticelli is of his generation in his enthusiasm for themes from Classical mythology as well as in his suiting of the ancient pagan materials to a form prepared by the Early Renaissance, a form realistic yet still modified by something of the Medieval past. Competent in all the new representational methods, he seems deliberately to sacrifice them in the interest of his own original manner, rarefying the realism of the Early Renaissance into an inimitable decorative and linear system that generates its own kind of figure and space. Venus, born of the sea foam, is wafted on a cockle shell, blown by the Zephyrs, to her sacred island, Cyprus, where the nymph Pomona, descended from the ancient goddess of fruit trees, runs to meet her with a brocaded mantle. The presentation of the figure of Venus nude was, in itself, an innovation; as we have seen, the nude—especially the female nude—had been proscribed in the Middle Ages. Its appearance on such a scale and its use of an ancient Venus statue of the *Venus pudica* (modest Venus) type as a model could have drawn the charge of paganism and infidelity. But under the protection of the powerful Medici, a new world of imagination could open freely with the new Platonism.

The high priest of the Neo-Platonic cult (for which *The Birth of Venus* could almost have been an altarpiece) was the Humanist Marsilio Ficino, certainly known to Botticelli through Lorenzo de' Medici's circle. Ficino believed that the soul could ascend toward a union with God through the contemplation of beauty, which reveals and manifests the two supreme principles of the Divine: love and light. This kind of mystical approach—so different from the earnest search of the early fifteenth century to comprehend humanity and the natural world through a rational and empirical order—finds expression in Botticelli's strange and beautiful style, which seems to ignore all of the scientific ground gained by experimental art. His style parallels the allegorical pageants in Florence, which were staged as chivalric tournaments but revolved completely around allusions to Classical mythology; the same trend is evident in the poetry of the 1470s and 1480s. Artists and poets at this time did not directly imitate Classical antiquity, but used the myths, with delicate perception of their charm, in a way still tinged with Medieval romance.

In Botticelli's hands, the Classical myth takes on a fresh and fascinating quality. The lovely figure of Venus, strangely weightless and ethereal, is the intellectual or spiritual apparition of beauty, not at all the queen of sensual love whom the Venetian Renaissance will create. The lightness and bodilessness of the Zephyrs move all the figures without effort. Draperies undulate easily in the gentle gusts, perfumed by rose petals that fall on the whitecaps stirred by the Zephyrs' toes. For the Medieval world and for

*Y. Yashiro, *Sandro Botticelli* (London, Boston: 1925, 1929).

†Henry Hallam, in J.A. Symonds, *Renaissance in Italy* (New York: Modern Library, 1935), Vol. 1, p. 477.

16-60   Sandro Botticelli, *The Birth of Venus, c.* 1482. Tempera on canvas, approx. 5′ 8″ × 9′ 1″. Galleria degli Uffizi, Florence.

that of Neo-Platonism, as distinct from the modern scientific view, everything is linked by infinitely complex lines of affinity. Everything is related to everything else; meanings can be read from objects and events, as the ancients read the future from the stars, the entrails of animals, and prodigies. It does not surprise us, then, that any number of interpretations can be made of a picture like *The Birth of Venus*; doubtless, it was intended to mean many things at the same time and to have, so to speak, many layers of significance. For example, a modern scholar sees, beyond the simple depiction of the myth of the birth of Venus, an allegory of the innocence and truth of the human soul, naked to the winds of passion and about to be clothed in the robe of reason. We can be sure that such abstruse interpretations and hyperinterpretations were made of paintings and texts at the time; it has been a long-enduring habit of the Western mind.

Botticelli's style, the sensitive vehicle of an in-

tensely sensitive mind, changed with the fortunes of Florence; as he responded to the Humanist and Neo-Platonic ideas of the circle of Lorenzo de' Medici, so he responded to the overthrow of the Medici, the incursion of the French armies, and especially to the preaching of the Dominican monk Girolamo Savonarola, the reforming priest–dictator who denounced the paganism of the Medici and their artists, philosophers, and poets. Savonarola called on the citizens of Florence to repent their iniquities, and, when the Medici fled, he prophesied the doom of the city and of Italy and took absolute power over the state. Together with a large number of citizens, Savonarola believed that the Medici had been a political, social, and religious influence for the worse—corrupting Florence and inviting the scourge of foreign invasion. Modern scholarship still debates the significance of Savonarola's brief span of power. Apologists for the undoubtedly sincere monk deny that his actions played a role in the decline of Florentine culture at the end of the century. But hc did rail at the Neo-Platonist Humanists as heretical gabblers, and his banishing of the Medici, Tornabuoni, and other noble families from Florence deprived local artists of some of their major patrons. Florence lost its position of cultural leadership at the end of the century and never regained it. Certainly, the puritanical spirit that moved Savonarola—and that was soon to appear throughout Europe in the reforming preachments of the Protestant Reformation—must have dampened considerably the neopagan enthusiasm of the Florentine Early Renaissance.

The sensitive, highly personal, and exotic style of

Botticelli closed the great age of Florentine art on an exquisitely refined note. Artists of his generation outside Florence, but within the circuit of its influence, expanded the experiments of the century. An Umbrian painter, LUCA SIGNORELLI (c. 1445–1523), further developed the interest of Antonio Pollaiuolo in the depiction of muscular bodies in violent action in a wide variety of poses and foreshortenings. In the San Brizio Chapel in Orvieto Cathedral, Signorelli's painted scenes depicting the end of the world include *The Damned Cast into Hell* (FIG. 16-61). Few figure compositions of the fifteenth century have the same awesome psychic impact. St. Michael and the hosts of

16-61 LUCA SIGNORELLI, *The Damned Cast into Hell*, 1499–1504. Fresco. San Brizio Chapel, Orvieto Cathedral, Italy.

Heaven hurl the damned into Hell, where, in a dense, writhing mass, they are tortured by vigorous demons. The figures—nude, lean, and muscular—assume every conceivable posture of anguish. Signorelli's skill at foreshortening the figure is one with his mastery of its action; and although each figure is clearly a study from a model, he fits his theme to the figures in an entirely convincing manner. Terror and rage pass like storms through the wrenched and twisted bodies. The fiends, their hair flaming and their bodies the color of putrefying flesh, lunge at their victims in ferocious frenzy; we can imagine the appalling pandemonium. Not even Pollaiuolo achieves such virtuosity in the manipulation of anatomy for dramatic purpose. Doubtless, Signorelli influenced Michelangelo, who makes the human nude his sole and sufficient expressive motif. In *The Last Judgment* in the Sistine Chapel, Michelangelo shows that he was much aware of Signorelli's version of the theme.

Signorelli's fellow Umbrian, PERUGINO (Pietro Vannucci, c. 1450–1523), was concerned not with the human figure in violent action, as Signorelli was, but with the calm, geometric ordering of pictorial space. Between 1481 and 1483, Perugino and several other famous artists, including Botticelli, Ghirlandaio, and Signorelli, were summoned to Rome to decorate the walls of the newly completed Sistine Chapel with frescoes. Perugino painted *Christ Delivering the Keys of the Kingdom to St. Peter* (FIG. 16-62)—the event on which the papacy had, from the beginning, based its claim to infallible and total authority over the Church. Christ gives the keys to St. Peter at the center of solemn choruses of saints and citizens, who occupy the apron of a great stage space that marches into the distance (stepped off by the parallel lines of the pavement) to a point of convergence in the doorway of a central-plan temple. Figures in the middle distance complement the near group, emphasizing its density and order by their scattered arrangement. At the corners of the great piazza, triumphal arches resembling the Arch of Constantine (FIG. 6-89) mark the base angles of a compositional triangle having its apex in the central building. The group of Christ and Peter are placed on the central axis, which runs through the temple's doorway, within which is the vanishing

16-62 PERUGINO, *Christ Delivering the Keys of the Kingdom to St. Peter*, 1481–1483. Fresco. Sistine Chapel, Vatican, Rome.

point of the perspective. Thus, the composition interlocks both two-dimensional and three-dimensional space, and the central actors are carefully integrated with the axial center. This spatial science provides a means for organizing the action systematically. Perugino, in this single picture, incorporates the learning of generations. His coolly rational, orderly style and the uncluttered clarity of his compositions left a lasting impression on his best-known student, Raphael.

Many Florentine artists worked in northern Italy: Donatello in Padua; Paolo Uccello, Andrea del Castagno, and Fra Filippo Lippi in Venice. Gradually, the International style, which lingered long in the north, yielded to the new Florentine art. Around mid-century, one of the most brilliant talents of the entire Renaissance, ANDREA MANTEGNA (c. 1431–1506) of Padua, appeared in northern Italy; there he must have met Donatello, who greatly stimulated and influenced his art. With Mantegna's frescoes in the Ovetari Chapel in the Church of the Eremitani in Padua (largely destroyed in the Second World War), northern Italian painting falls into line with the Humanistic art of Florence. *St. James Led to Martyrdom* (FIG. 16-63) reveals the breadth of Mantegna's literary, archeological, and pictorial learning. The motifs that appear on the barrel-vaulted triumphal arch are taken from the Classical ornamental vocabulary. The soldiers' costumes are studied from antique models; the painter strives for historical authenticity, much as did the antiquarian scholars of the University of Padua. Mantegna sets himself difficult problems in perspective for the joy of solving them. Here, the observer's viewpoint is set very low, as if looking up out of a basement window at the vast arch looming above. The lines of the building to the right plunge down dramatically. There are, however, significant deviations from true perspective. Mantegna, using artistic license, ignores the third vanishing point

16-63 ANDREA MANTEGNA,
St. James Led to Martyrdom,
c. 1455. Fresco. Ovetari
Chapel, Church of the
Eremitani, Padua, Italy
(largely destroyed, 1944).

16-64 ANDREA MANTEGNA, Camera degli Sposi, 1474. Ducal palace, Mantua, Italy.

(seen from below; the buildings should converge toward the top). Disregarding the perspective facts, he prefers to work toward a unified, cohesive composition in which pictorial elements are related to the picture frame. The lack of perspective logic is partly compensated for by the insertion of strong diagonals in the right foreground (for example, the staff of the banner).

From about 1460 onward, Mantegna worked predominantly for the Gonzaga family of Mantua, who were great art patrons like the Medici but—unlike the Medici (who were the most powerful members of a merchant oligarchy)—hereditary dukes. In the ducal palace at Mantua, Mantegna performed a triumphant feat of pictorial illusionism, producing the first completely consistent illusionistic decoration of an entire room, the so-called Camera degli Sposi ("Room of the Newlyweds," FIG. 16-64). Utilizing actual architectural elements, Mantegna paints away the walls of the room in a manner that forecasts later Baroque

decoration. He represents members of the House of Gonzaga welcoming home a son, a prince of the Church, from Rome. The family members, magnificently costumed, are shown in both domestic and landscape settings and are rendered carefully in portrait realism. The poses are remarkably unstudied and casual, conveying the easy familiarity of a family reunion. The painting is a celebration of fifteenth-century court life and a glorification of the Gonzaga, as well as the century's only major depiction of a current event. The lunettes are filled with garlands and medallions *all' antica* (in the antique manner), motifs that are standard features in northern Italian painting.

Mantegna's daring experimentalism leads him to complete the room's decoration with the first *di sotto in sù* perspective of a ceiling (FIG. 16-65)—a technique later broadly developed by the northern Italian painter, Correggio, and the Baroque ceiling decorators. We look directly up at figures looking down at

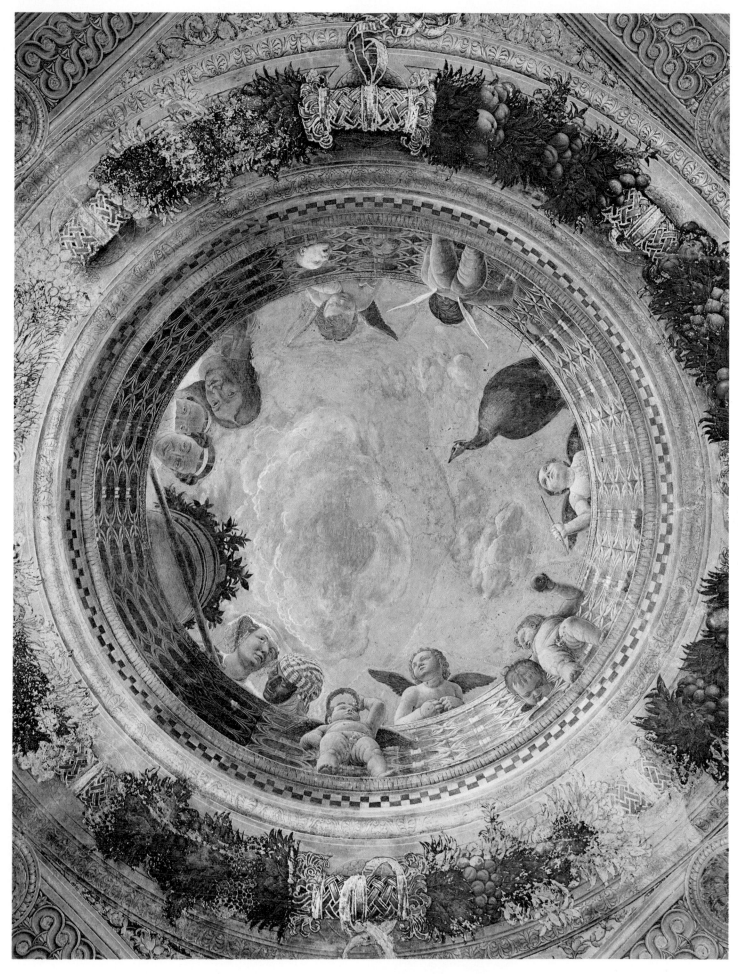

16-65 ANDREA MANTEGNA, ceiling of the Camera degli Sposi, 1474. Fresco. Ducal palace, Mantua.

us. Cupids, strongly foreshortened, set the amorous mood, as the painted spectators smile down on the scene. This *tour de force* of illusionism climaxes almost a century of experiment in perspective.

One of Mantegna's later paintings, *The Dead Christ* (FIG. 16-66), is a work of overwhelming power, despite the somewhat awkward insertion of the two mourning figures on the left. What seems to be a strikingly realistic study in foreshortening, however, is modified by a reduction in size of the figure's feet, which—as every photographer knows and as Mantegna must have known—would cover the body if properly represented. Thus, tempering naturalism with artistic license, Mantegna presents both a harrowing study of a cadaver strongly foreshortened and an intensely poignant presentation of a cosmic tragedy. The harsh, sharp line seems to cut the surface as if it were metal and conveys, by its grinding edge, the corrosive emotion of the theme; one thinks of Ernest Hemingway's "the bitter nail holes in Mantegna's Christ." For Mantegna's presentation is unrelievedly bitter, an unforgiving reproach to guilty mankind. What is remarkable is that all the science of the fifteenth century here serves the purpose of devotion. A Gothic religious sensitivity of great depth and intensity, still lingering in the northern Italian sunset of the Middle Ages, is embodied in an image created by a new science.

Mantegna's influence was great in northern Italy, especially in the school of Ferrara—but also in Venice, where his style had a strong, formative influence on Giovanni Bellini, who may be regarded as the

16-66 ANDREA MANTEGNA, *The Dead Christ, c.* 1501. Tempera on canvas, approx. 26″ × 31″. Pinacoteca di Brera, Milan.

progenitor of Venetian painting (see FIGS. 17-56, 17-57, 17-58, 17-59). Mantegna's influence went even further, however, for he was a great engraver (the line in *The Dead Christ* certainly suggests engraving), and his prints found their way across the Alps to influence Albrecht Dürer, father of the Northern Renaissance.

By itself, the influence of Mantegna might have stunted Giovanni Bellini's development, and the arrival in Venice of an artist with a style very different from Mantegna's probably was most opportune for Bellini's artistic growth. ANTONELLO DA MESSINA (*c.* 1430–1479) is an enigmatic figure about whose background little is known. He was born in Sicily (the only major artist of the fifteenth century to be born south of Rome) and received his early training in Naples, where he must have come in close contact with Flemish painting. The Flemish influence in some of his works is so strong that it has long been assumed that Antonello actually spent some time in Flanders, a possibility that now seems unlikely. It has also been speculated that Antonello may have had direct contact with the Flemish artist Petrus Christus in Milan during the mid-1450s—a most intriguing possibility, as the styles of the two artists have many similarities. But the presence of either man in Milan at that time cannot be definitely proved. In any case, Antonello arrived in Venice in 1475, with a full mastery of the mixed-oil technique, and made a strong impression there during his two-year stay.

How greatly Antonello's style differs from Mantegna's can be seen in one of his later works, *The Martyrdom of St. Sebastian* (FIG. 16-67), which has none of Mantegna's brittle, sometimes harsh linearity. The forms are modeled in broad, simplified planes, reminiscent of the style of Piero della Francesca, whose work Antonello must have studied very closely indeed. Also Pierfrancescan are the crisp clarity of the spatial composition, the subdued emotion, and the solemn calm with which the saint suffers his martyrdom. But Antonello goes even beyond Piero in bathing his painting in atmospheric luminosity, and his colors tend to be warm rather than cool, with golden brown tones dominating. Compared to earlier works, the painting has a "juicy" colorism that is due, in good part, to Antonello's use of mixed oil—a medium more flexible and wider in coloristic range than tempera or fresco. Thus, by combining elements of Piero's style with Flemish painting techniques, Antonello fuses monumental qualities with coloristic effects of unrivaled richness. Giovanni Bellini was one of the first to appreciate the value of Antonello's gift to Venice and to abandon Mantegna's "hard" style, which, within a decade of Antonello's visit to Venice, became hopelessly outdated.

16-67 ANTONELLO DA MESSINA, *The Martyrdom of St. Sebastian,* c. 1475–1477. Oil on wood, approx. 68″ × 34″. Gemäldegalerie, Abt. Alte Meister, Staatliche Kunstsammlungen, Dresden.

ROME

1. Roman Forum
2. Colosseum
3. Pantheon
4. Arch of Constantine
5. Castel Sant' Angelo
6. Baths of Caracalla
7. Circus Maximus
8. Santa Costanza
9. Santa Maria Maggiore
10. St. Peter's
11. Capitoline Hill
12. Tempietto
13. Farnese Palace
14. Il Gesù
15. St. Ivo
16. San Carlo alle Quattro Fontane
17. Triton Fountain
— 16th-century Wall
— Aurelian Wall

NOTE: Darker-toned area represents ancient Rome.

VATICAN

AURELIAN WALL

AURELIAN WALL

PALATINE HILL

TIBER

APPIAN WAY

SIXTEENTH-CENTURY ITALIAN ART

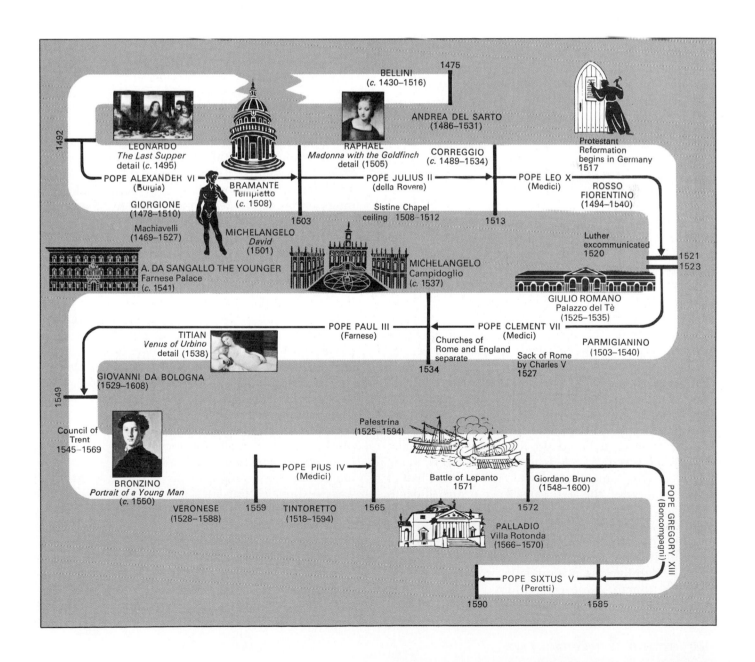

BELLINI
(c. 1430–1516)   1475

ANDREA DEL SARTO
(1486–1531)

1492

LEONARDO
The Last Supper
detail (c. 1495)

RAPHAEL
Madonna with the Goldfinch
detail (1505)

CORREGGIO
(c. 1489–1534)

Protestant
Reformation
begins in Germany
1517

POPE ALEXANDER VI
(Borgia)

BRAMANTE
Tempietto
(c. 1508)

POPE JULIUS II
(della Rovere)

POPE LEO X
(Medici)

ROSSO
FIORENTINO
(1494–1540)

GIORGIONE
(1478–1510)

Machiavelli
(1469–1527)

MICHELANGELO
David
(1501)

Sistine Chapel
ceiling 1508–1512

1503   1513

Luther
excommunicated
1520

1521
1523

A. DA SANGALLO THE YOUNGER
Farnese Palace
(c. 1541)

MICHELANGELO
Campidoglio
(c. 1537)

GIULIO ROMANO
Palazzo del Tè
(1525–1535)

TITIAN
Venus of Urbino
detail (1538)

POPE PAUL III
(Farnese)

POPE CLEMENT VII
(Medici)

PARMIGIANINO
(1503–1540)

Churches of
Rome and England
separate

Sack of Rome
by Charles V
1527

1534

GIOVANNI DA BOLOGNA
(1529–1608)

1549

Council of
Trent
1545–1569

Palestrina
(1525–1594)

POPE PIUS IV
(Medici)

Battle of Lepanto
1571

Giordano Bruno
(1548–1600)

BRONZINO
Portrait of a Young Man
(c. 1550)

VERONESE
(1528–1588)

1559

TINTORETTO
(1518–1594)

1565

1572

POPE GREGORY XIII
(Boncompagni)

PALLADIO
Villa Rotonda
(1566–1570)

POPE SIXTUS V
(Perotti)

1590   1585

BEFORE THE END of the fifteenth century, Florence had lost her unique position of leadership in the arts, and the innovations of her artists had become the property of Italian artists, regardless of local political boundaries. This is not to suggest that Florence no longer produced the artistic giants of an earlier age. Leonardo and Michelangelo called themselves Florentines, even though they spent a great part of their lives outside the city, and the turning point in Raphael's artistic education occurred as a result of his experience of Florentine art. In addition, Florence, with the early work of Leonardo, had already become the source of sixteenth-century style and later shared with Rome the beginnings and growth of Mannerism, a style that was to dominate western Europe during much of the sixteenth century. But Florence was faced with a time of crisis that began with the expulsion of the Medici and the brief and stormy dictatorship of Girolamo Savonarola and ended with the subversion of the Florentine republic by the Spanish and the return of the Medici (a collateral line of the original family) as tyrants under Spanish protection. Finally, in the 1530s, Florentine independence became a thing of the past when the state was made into a grand duchy under the crown of the Hapsburgs.

THE HIGH RENAISSANCE

Between about 1495 and the date of its own invasion and sack in 1527, Rome took the place of Florence and laid claim to its artistic preeminence. A series of powerful and ambitious popes—Alexander VI (Borgia), Julius II (della Rovere), Leo X (Medici), and Clement VII (Medici)—created a new power in Italy: a papal state, with Rome as its capital; and Rome became, at the same time, the artistic capital of Europe. The popes, living in the opulent splendor of secular princes, embellished the city with great works of art, inviting artists from all over Italy and providing them with challenging tasks. In its short duration, this High Renaissance saw works of such authority produced that generations of later artists were instructed by them; the art of Leonardo, Raphael, Michelangelo, and Titian is seen to belong to no school but is, in the case of each, something unique. The masters had of course inherited the pictorial science of the fifteenth century, and they learned from one another. Yet they made a distinct break from the past, occupying new and lofty ground—so lofty as to discourage emulation by their successors.

The High Renaissance not only produced a cluster of extraordinary geniuses, but found in divine inspiration the rationale for the exaltation of the artist–genius. The Neo-Platonists found in Plato's *Ion* his famous praise of the poet: "All good poets compose their beautiful poems not by art, but because they are inspired and possessed. . . . for not by art does the poet sing, but by power divine." And what the poet could claim, the Renaissance artist claimed also, raising visual art to the status formerly held only by poetry. Thus, at the threshold of the modern world, the painter, sculptor, or architect comes into his own, successfully claiming for his work a high place among the fine arts. In the High Renaissance, the masters in a sense created a new profession, having its own rights of expression, its own venerable character, and its own claims to recognition by the great. The "fine" artist today lives—often without realizing it—on the accumulated prestige won by preceding artists, beginning with those who made the first great gains of the High Renaissance.

Leonardo da Vinci

A man who is the epitome of the artist–genius as well as of the "universal man," LEONARDO DA VINCI (1452–1519) has become a kind of wonder of the modern world, standing at the beginning of a new epoch like a prophet and a sage, mapping the routes that art and science would take. The scope and depth of his interests were without precedent, so great as to frustrate any hopes he might have had of realizing all that his feverishly inventive imagination could conceive. We still look with awe on his achievements and, even more, on his unfulfilled promise. His mind and personality seem to us superhuman; the man himself, mysterious and remote. Jacob Burckhardt writes: "The colossal outlines of Leonardo's nature can never be more than dimly and distantly conceived." Although we are here concerned primarily with Leonardo as an artist, we can scarcely hope to do his art credit in isolation from his science; his scientific drawings are themselves works of art, as well as models for that exact delineation of nature that is one of the aims of science. Leonardo's unquenchable curiosity is best revealed in his voluminous notes, liberally interspersed with sketches dealing with matters of botany, geology, zoology, hydraulics, military engineering, animal lore, anatomy, and aspects of physical science, including mechanics, perspective, light, optics, and color. Leonardo's great ambition in his painting, as well as in his scientific endeavors, was to discover the laws underlying the flux and processes of nature. With this end in mind, he also studied the human body and contributed immeasurably to our knowledge of physiology and psychology. Leonardo believed that reality in an absolute sense is inaccessible and that we can know it only through its changing images. Thus, he considered the eyes to be the most vital organs and sight the most essential function, as, through these, the images of reality could be grasped most directly and profoundly. Hence, one may understand Leonardo's insistence, stated many times in his notes, that all his scientific investigations were merely aimed at making himself a better painter.

Leonardo was born near Florence and was trained in the studio of Andrea del Verrocchio. But he left Florence around 1481, offering his services to Ludovico Sforza, Duke of Milan. The political situation in Florence was uncertain, and the Neo-Platonism of Lorenzo de' Medici and his brilliant circle may have proved uncongenial to the empirical and pragmatic Leonardo. It may also be that Leonardo felt that the artistic scene in Milan would be less competitive. He devoted most of a letter to the Duke of Milan to advertising his competence and his qualifications as a military engineer, mentioning only at the end his supremacy as a painter and sculptor:

> And in short, according to the variety of cases, I can contrive various and endless means of offence and defence . . . . In time of peace I believe I can give perfect satisfaction and to the equal of any other in architecture and the composition of buildings, public and private; and in guiding water from one place to another . . . . I can carry out sculpture in marble, bronze, or clay, and also I can do in painting whatever may be done, as well as any other, be he whom he may.*

The letter illustrates the new relation of the artist to his patron, as well as Leonardo's breadth of competence. That he should select military engineering and design to interest a patron is an index, in addition, of the dangerousness of the times. Weaponry had now been developed to the point, especially in northern Europe, that the siege cannon was a threat to the feudal castles of those attempting to resist the wealthy and aggressive new monarchs. When, in 1494, Charles VIII of France invaded Italy, his cannon easily smashed the fortifications of the Italian princes. By the turn of the century, when Italy's liberties and unity were being trampled by the aspiring kingdoms of Europe, not only soldiers and architects, but artists and Humanists, were deeply concerned with the problem of designing a system of fortifications that might withstand the terrible new weapon.

During his first sojourn in Milan, Leonardo painted *The Virgin of the Rocks* (FIG. 17-1)—a group that, although it may derive ultimately from Fra Filippo Lippi, is well on its way out of the older tradition. The old triangular composition now broadens out into three dimensions, making a weighty pyramid. The linear approach, with its musical play of undulating contours and crisp edges, is abandoned, as Leonardo

17-1 LEONARDO DA VINCI, *The Virgin of the Rocks,* c. 1485. Oil on wood, approx. 6' 3" × 3' 7". Louvre, Paris.

returns through the generations of the fifteenth century to Masaccio's great discovery of *chiaroscuro*, the subtle play of light and dark. What we see is the result of the moving together and interpenetration of lights and darks. "Drawn" representations, consisting of contours and edges, can be beautiful, but they are really not true to the optical facts. Moreover, a painting must embody not only physical chiaroscuro but the lights and darks of human psychology as well. Modeling with light and shadow and the expression of emotional states were, for Leonardo, the heart of painting:

> A good painter has two chief objects to paint—man and the intention of his soul. The former is easy, the latter hard, for it must be expressed by gestures and the movement of the limbs. . . . A painting will only be wonderful for the beholder by making that which is not so appear raised and detached from the wall.*

*In E.G. Holt, ed., *Literary Sources of Art History* (Princeton, N.J.: Princeton University Press, 1947), p. 170.

*In Anthony Blunt, *Artistic Theory in Italy, 1450–1600* (London: Oxford University Press, 1964), p. 34.

The figures in *The Virgin of the Rocks* are knit together not only as a pyramidal group but as figures sharing the same atmosphere—a method of unification first seen in Masaccio's *The Tribute Money* (FIG. 16-26). The Madonna, Christ Child, infant John the Baptist, and angel emerge through subtle gradations and nuances of light and shade from the half-light of the cavernous, visionary landscape. Light simultaneously veils and reveals the forms of things, immersing them in a layer of atmosphere between them and our eyes. The ambiguity of light and shade (familiar in the optical uncertainties of dusk) is in the service of the psychological ambiguity of perception. The group depicted, so strangely wrapped in subtle light and shade, eludes our precise definition and interpretation. The figures pray, point, and bless, and these acts and gestures, although their meanings are not certain, visually unite the figures. The angel points to the infant John, who is blessed by the Christ Child and sheltered by the Virgin's loving hand. The melting mood of tenderness, enhanced by the caressing light, is compounded of yet other moods. What the eye sees is fugitive, as are the states of the soul, or, in Leonardo's term, its "intentions."

The style of the High Renaissance fully emerges in a *cartoon* (a full-size drawing) for a painting of *The*

17-2 LEONARDO DA VINCI, cartoon for *The Virgin and Child with St. Anne and the Infant St. John*, 1498 (?). Charcoal heightened with white on brown paper, approx. 54" × 39". Reproduced by courtesy of the Trustees of the National Gallery, London.

Virgin and Child with St. Anne and the Infant St. John (FIG. 17-2). The glowing light falls gently on the majestic forms and on a tranquil grandeur, order, and balance. The figures are robust and monumental, moving with a stately grace reminiscent of the Phidian sculptures of the Parthenon. Every part is ordered by an intellectual, pictorial logic into a sure unity. The specialized depiction of perspective, anatomy, light, and space is a thing of the past; Leonardo has assimilated the learning of two centuries and applies it wholly, in a manner that is Classical and complete. This High Renaissance style, as Leonardo here authoritatively shows it, is stable without being static, varied without being confused, and dignified without being dull. As in the similar case in Greece, this brief, Classical moment inaugurated by Leonardo unifies and balances the conflicting experiences of an entire culture. This style will prove difficult to maintain. In a rapidly changing world, the artist may either repeat the compositions and forms of the day in a sterile, academic manner or revolt against the time by denying or exaggerating its principles. For these reasons, the High Renaissance was of short duration— even shorter than the brief span of the Golden Age of Athens in the fifth century B.C.

For the refectory of the church of Santa Maria delle Grazie in Milan, Leonardo painted *The Last Supper* (FIG. 17-3). Despite its ruined state (in part the result of the painter's own unfortunate experiments with his materials) and although it has often been ineptly restored, the painting is both formally and emotionally his most impressive work.* It is the first great figure composition of the High Renaissance, and the definitive interpretation of its theme. Christ and the Twelve Disciples are seated in a simple, spacious room, at a long table set parallel to the picture plane. The highly dramatic action of the painting is made still more emphatic by the placement of the group in the austerely quiet setting. Christ, with outstretched hands, has just said, "One of you will betray me." A wave of intense excitement passes through the group, as each disciple asks himself and, in some cases, his neighbor, "Is it I?" Leonardo has made a

*Since 1977, the painting has been undergoing painstaking, scientifically controlled restoration (a square inch at a time!). Although much of it is permanently lost, enough has already been recovered and repaired to reveal Leonardo's actual intentions and performance. The restored portions (at this writing, the group of three disciples at the far right)—freed from 500 years dark accumulation of dirt, mold, glue, and overpainting—reveal bright and strong colors and firm and elegant contours. Restoration also shows that Leonardo's style is firmly rooted in the practice of fifteenth-century Italian painting. Beneath the many mistaken overpaintings, the true characters of the disciples emerge from the blurred, murky, out-of-focus forms of the damaged picture. They are vividly realized individuals, of the kind we find in Leonardo's preserved preparatory drawings, who—through attitudes, gestures, personal traits, and facial expressions—compellingly play the roles Leonardo designed for them, consistent with his own highly personal conception of this drama and its protagonists.

17-3 LEONARDO DA VINCI, *The Last Supper*, c. 1495–1498. Fresco. Santa Maria delle Grazie, Milan.

brilliant conjunction of the dramatic "One of you will betray me" with the initiation of the ancient liturgical ceremony of the Eucharist, when Christ, blessing bread and wine, said "This is my body and this is my blood: do this in remembrance of me." The force and lucidity with which this dramatic moment is expressed are due to the abstract organization of the composition. In the center, Christ is in perfect repose, the still eye of the swirling emotion around him. Isolated from the disciples, his figure is framed by the central window at the back, the curved pediment of which (the only curve in the architectural framework, here serving as a halo) arches above his head, which is the focal point of all perspective lines in the composition. Thus, the still, psychological focus and cause of the action is, at the same time, the perspective focus as well as the dead center of the two-dimensional surface. (One could say that the two-dimensional, the three-dimensional, and the psychodimensional focuses are one and the same.) The agitated disciples, registering a whole range of rationally ordered, idealized, and proportionate responses, embracing fear, doubt, protestation, rage, and love, are represented in four groups of three, united among and within themselves by the gestures and postures of the figures. Leonardo sacrifices traditional iconography to pictorial and dramatic consistency by placing Judas on the same side of the table as Jesus and the other disciples. His face in shadow, Judas clutches a money bag in his right hand and reaches his left forward to fulfill the Master's declaration: "Behold, the hand of him that betrayeth me is with me on the table." The two disciples at either end of the table are more quiet than the others, as if to enclose the overall movement, which is more intense

closer to the figure of Christ, whose calm at the same time halts and intensifies it. We know from numerous preparatory studies that Leonardo thought of each figure as carrying a particular charge and type of emotion. Like a skilled stage director (perhaps the first, in the modern sense), he has carefully read the gospel story and scrupulously cast his actors as their roles are described. With him begins that rhetoric of Classical art that will direct the compositions of generations of painters until the nineteenth century. The silence of Christ is one such powerful rhetorical device. Indeed, Heinrich Wölfflin saw that the Classical element is precisely here, for in the silence following Christ's words, "the original impulse and the emotional excitement continue to echo and the action is at once momentary, eternal and complete."* The two major trends of fifteenth-century painting—monumentality and mathematically ordered space at the expense of movement, and freedom of movement at the expense of monumentality and controlled space—are here harmonized and balanced. *The Last Supper* and Leonardo's career leading up to it are at once a synthesis of the artistic developments of the fifteenth century and a first statement of the High Renaissance style of the early sixteenth in Italy.

If Leonardo's *Last Supper* is the world's most famous religious picture, the *Mona Lisa* (FIG. 17-4) is probably the world's most famous portrait. Since the nineteenth century and perhaps earlier, the enigmatic face has been a part of Western folklore. Painted after Leonardo returned from Milan to Florence, the lady, thought by many to be La Gioconda,

*Heinrich Wölfflin, *Classic Art*, 2nd ed. (London: Phaidon, 1953), p. 27.

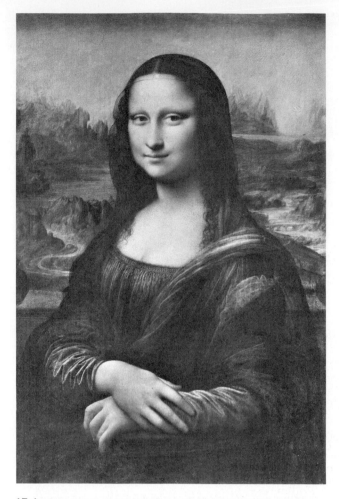

17-4 LEONARDO DA VINCI, *Mona Lisa*, c. 1503–1505. Oil on wood, approx. 30″ × 21″. Louvre, Paris.

wife of the banker Zanobi del Giocondo, was originally represented in a loggia with columns that have been cut from the painting. She is shown in half-length view, her hands quietly folded and her gaze directed at the observer. The ambiguity of the famous "smile" is really the consequence of Leonardo's fascination and skill with atmospheric chiaroscuro, which we have seen in his *Virgin of the Rocks* and *Virgin and St. Anne* groups and which here serve to disguise rather than reveal a human psyche. The light is adjusted subtly enough, but the precise planes are blurred (a useful comparison can be made between the *Mona Lisa* and the portraits by Domenico Ghirlandaio and Sandro Botticelli we saw in Chapter 16) and the facial expression is hard to determine. The romantic nineteenth century made perhaps too much of the enigma of the "smile," without appreciating Leonardo's quite scientific concern with the nature of light and shadow. On the other hand, Leonardo himself must have enjoyed the curious effect he achieved here; it was one of his favorite pictures, one with which he could not bear to part. The superb drawing present beneath the fleeting shadow is a triumph in its rendering of both the head and the hands, the latter exceptionally beautiful. It may well have been the artist's intention to confuse observers or enchant them by allowing them to interpret the secret personality as they pleased.

Leonardo completed very few paintings; his perfectionism, restless experimentalism, and far-ranging curiosity scattered his efforts. Yet an extensive record of his ideas is preserved in the drawings in his notebooks, one of which was discovered in Madrid, Spain, in the 1960s. Science interested him increasingly in his later years, and he took knowledge of all nature (given first to the eye) as his proper province. His investigations in anatomy yielded drawings of great precision and beauty of execution; an example is the *Embryo in the Womb* (FIG. 17-5), which, despite some inaccuracies, is so true to fact that it could be used in medical instruction today. Although Leonardo may not have been the first scientist of the modern world (at least not in the modern sense of "scientist"), he certainly originated the method of scientific illustration, especially cutaway and exploded views. The importance of this has been stressed by Erwin Panofsky: ". . . anatomy as a science (and this applies to all the other observational or descriptive disciplines) was simply not possible without a method of preserving observations in graphic records, complete and accurate in three dimensions."*

Leonardo was well known in his own time as both sculptor and architect, though no sculpture that is certainly by him has survived and no actual buildings can be attributed to him. From his many drawings of central-plan buildings, it appears that he shared the interest of other Renaissance architects in this building type. In Milan, Leonardo must have been in close contact with the architect Bramante, who may well have remembered a drawing by Leonardo when he prepared his original designs for the great church of St. Peter's in Rome (FIG. 17-7).

As for sculpture, Leonardo left numerous drawings of monumental equestrian statues, one of which ripened into a full-scale model for a monument to the Sforza; used as a target, it was shot to pieces by the French when they occupied Milan in 1499. Leonardo left Milan outraged at this treatment of his work and worked for a while as military engineer for Cesare Borgia, who, with the support of his father, Pope Alexander VI, tried to conquer the cities of the Romagna and create a Borgia duchy. At a later date, Leonardo returned to Milan in the service of the French. At the invitation of the king, Francis I, he then went to France, where he died at the château of Cloux in 1519, without leaving any impression on French contemporary art.

*Erwin Panofsky, "Artist, Scientist, Genius," in *The Renaissance*, ed., Wallace K. Ferguson (New York: Harper & Row, 1962), p. 147.

Bramante and His Circle

The most important artist with whom Leonardo came into contact in Milan was BRAMANTE (Donato d' Angelo, 1444–1514). Born in Urbino and trained as a painter (perhaps by Piero della Francesca), Bramante went to Milan in 1481 and, like Leonardo, stayed there until the arrival of the French in 1499. In Milan, he abandoned painting to become the greatest archi-

tect of his generation. Under the influence of Filippo Brunelleschi, Leon Battista Alberti, and perhaps Leonardo, all of whom had been strongly influenced by the Classical antique, Bramante developed the High Renaissance form of the central-plan church. But it was not until after his arrival in Rome in 1499 that Bramante built what was to be the perfect prototype of Classical, domed architecture for the Renaissance and subsequent periods—the Tempietto (FIG. 17-6),

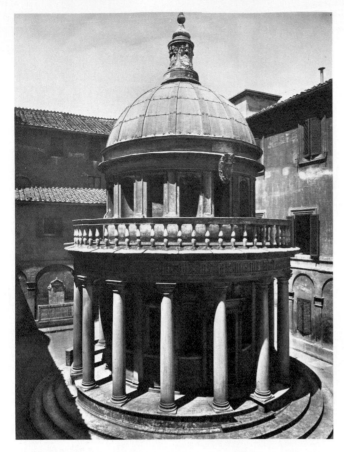

17-6　BRAMANTE, the Tempietto, 1508 (view from the northwest). San Pietro in Montorio, Rome.

so called because it has the aspect of a small pagan temple from antiquity. This building, recently redated to 1508, was to mark the supposed spot of St. Peter's crucifixion and indeed gives the appearance of a solid sculptural reliquary. In fact, it was originally

17-7　BRAMANTE, plan for the new St. Peter's, Rome, 1505.

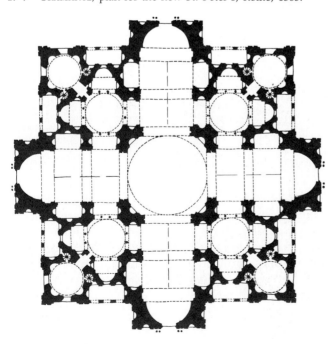

planned to stand, somewhat like a reliquary, in the center of a colonnaded, circular court. All but devoid of ornament, the building relies for its effect on the sculptural treatment of the exterior, which creates a sense of volume in movement (as does High Renaissance sculpture and painting). At first glance, the Tempietto seems unnecessarily formalistic and rational, with its distinct, cool Tuscan order and abstract plan repeated in the colonnade and in the steps of the stylobate. However, Bramante achieves a wonderful harmony among the parts—the dome, drum, and base—and the whole. The balustrade accents, in shorter beats, the rhythms of the colonnade and averts a too-rapid ascent to the drum; the pilasters on the drum itself repeat the ascending motif and lead the eye past the cornice to the ribs of the dome. The strictly regulated play of light and shade around the columns and balustrade and in the alternation of deep-set rectangular windows with shallow, shell-capped niches enhances the experience of the building as an articulated, sculptural mass—a domed cylinder within the wider cylinder of the colonnade.

The significance of the Tempietto was well understood in the sixteenth century. The architect Andrea Palladio, an artistic descendant of Bramante, put it among his survey of ancient temples because "Bramante was the first who brought good and beautiful architecture to light, which from the time of the ancients to his day had been forgotten . . . ." Round in plan, elevated on a base that isolates it from its surroundings, the Tempietto conforms with Alberti's and Palladio's strictest demands for an ideal church, demonstrating "the unity, the infinite essence, the uniformity, and the justice of God."

The same architectural concept guided Bramante's plans for the new St. Peter's, commissioned by Pope Julius II in 1505 to replace the Constantinian basilica, Old St. Peter's (FIG. 7-6). This structure had fallen into considerable disrepair and, in any event, did not suit the taste for the colossal of that ambitious and warlike pope, who wanted to gain sway over the whole of Italy and to make the Rome of the popes more splendid than the Rome of the caesars. As originally designed by Bramante, the new St. Peter's (FIG. 17-7) was to have consisted of a cross with arms of equal length, each terminated by an apse. It was intended as a martyrium to mark St. Peter's grave; Julius also hoped to have his own tomb in it. The crossing would have been covered by a large dome, and smaller domes over subsidiary chapels would have covered the diagonal axes of the roughly square plan. Bramante's ambitious plan called for a boldly sculptural treatment of the walls and piers under the dome. The interior space is complex in the extreme, with the intricate symmetries of a crystal; it is possible to detect in the plan some nine interlocking crosses, five

17-8 CHRISTOFORO FOPPA CARADOSSO, medal showing Bramante's design for the new St. Peter's, 1506. British Museum, London.

17-9 Santa Maria della Consolazione, Todi, Italy, begun 1508 (view from the south).

domed. The scale was titanic; Bramante is said to have boasted that he would place the dome of the Pantheon over the Basilica of Constantine. A commemorative medal (FIG. 17-8) by CHRISTOFORO FOPPA CARADOSSO (1452–1527) shows how Bramante's scheme would have attempted to do just that. The dome is hemispherical, like the Pantheon's, but otherwise the exterior, with two towers and a medley of domes and porticoes, breaks the massive unity, resulting in a still essentially anthropometric design scaled down to human proportions in the Early Renaissance manner. During Bramante's lifetime, the actual construction did not advance beyond the building of the piers of the crossing and the lower walls of the choir. With his death, the work passed from one architect to another and finally to Michelangelo, who was appointed by Pope Paul III in 1546 to complete the building.

After Bramante's Tempietto, the closest realization of the High Renaissance Classical ideals—order, clarity, lucidity, simplicity, harmony, and proportion—is found in the pilgrimage church of Santa Maria della Consolazione at Todi, begun in 1508 (FIGS. 17-9 and 17-10). Its elevated hillside site outside the town makes it visible from far away, and its sturdy, carefully proportioned silhouette offers an attractive goal for the faithful approaching through the valley below. Although the identity of its designer is uncertain, it is quite clearly in the manner of Bramante, and we can call it "Bramantesque." In its plan, the church takes the form of a domed cross, with its lobe-like arms ending in polygonal apses. The interior space, showing a Classical purity of arrangement in which the layout is immediately open to the eye and vol-

umes and spaces are in exquisite adjustment, finds its exact expression on the exterior. Here, each level is carefully marked off by projecting cornices, and there is a steady increase in rhythm from bottom to top. The unfenestrated first story, marked off into blank

17-10 Interior view into the main dome and one of the half-domes, Santa Maria della Consolazione.

panels by pilasters, provides a firm base for the upper structure; the second story is fenestrated, the windows topped by alternating triangular and segmental pediments. The attic story makes a transition to the half-domes, and the half-domes to the balustraded platform that sets off drum and dome as it makes a transition to them. The rhythm of fenestration of the second floor reappears in the drum, where it is quickened by the interpolation of round-headed niches between the windows, like the appearance of a second voice in a fugue. No matter from which side it is seen, the building presents a completely balanced and symmetrical aspect. Like a three-dimensional essay in rational order, all of its parts are in harmonious relation to each other and to the whole, yet each is complete and independent. To appreciate the wide difference between the Medieval and the High Renaissance views of the nature of architecture, one need only recall the design of a typically Gothic building. In both scale and complexity, Santa Maria della Consolazione stands between the Tempietto and the design for the new St. Peter's. More amply than the former, with greater purity than the latter, it expresses the architectural ideals of the High Renaissance. Its spirit is that of Classical antiquity and, though it is modern, it speaks only the Classical language.

17-11 BRAMANTE, Palazzo Caprini (House of Raphael), Rome. (Drawing attributed to ANDREA PALLADIO.)

The palaces designed by Bramante have been preserved only in drawings or engravings. His Palazzo Caprini (FIG. 17-11), bought by Raphael in 1517, was torn down during the rebuilding of the area around St. Peter's. Still, it was one of the most important and influential palace designs of the sixteenth century. In it, Bramante reduced the typical three-story façade of the fifteenth century to two stories, with the strongly rusticated first story serving as a robust support for the elegantly articulated *piano nobile*. This arrangement not only differentiates the two stories, but emphatically puts the residential level of the building above the commercial. (The ground floor was occupied by shops and offices.) The pedimented windows of the second story are flanked by pairs of engaged Tuscan columns supporting an entablature in which the frieze is pierced by the windows of an attic story. The total aspect of the building is of rugged plasticity, and its effect on contemporary and later architects, including Palladio and Inigo Jones, was lasting. With Baroque modifications, Bramante's scheme can be recognized in Claude Perrault's Louvre façade (FIG. 19-65), erected almost two centuries later.

Less plastic, perhaps, than Bramante's design, but equally imposing, is the Farnese Palace in Rome (FIGS. 17-12, 17-13, 17-14), designed by ANTONIO DA SANGALLO THE YOUNGER (1483–1546), which fully expresses the Classical order, regularity, simplicity, and dignity of the High Renaissance. Antonio, the youngest of a family of architects, received his early training from his uncles Giuliano, the designer of Santa Maria delle Carceri in Prato (FIGS. 16-45, 16-46, 16-47), and Antonio the Elder. Antonio the Younger went to Rome around 1503 and became Bramante's draftsman and assistant. As Paul III's favorite architect, he received many commissions that might have gone to Michelangelo. He is the perfect example of the professional architect, and his family constituted an architectural firm, often working up the plans and doing the drafting for other architects. Essentially a developer, Antonio has frequently been criticized as unimaginative; but if this is so, it is only by comparison with Michelangelo. He built fortifications for almost the entire papal state and received more commissions for military than for civilian architecture. Although he may not have invented it, Antonio certainly developed the modern method of bastioned fortifications to a high degree and, in this, demonstrated his ingenuity and originality.

The Farnese Palace, built for Cardinal Farnese, (later Pope Paul III), sets a standard for the High Renaissance palazzo. The sixteenth century saw the beginning of the age of the great dynasties that would dominate Europe until the French Revolution. It was an age of royal and princely pomp, of absolute monarchy rendered splendid by art. The broad, majestic

17-12 ANTONIO DA
SANGALLO THE
YOUNGER, Farnese
Palace, Rome,
c. 1530–1546 (view
from the northeast).

front of the Farnese Palace asserts to the public the exalted station of a great family. This proud frontis-piece symbolizes the aristocratic epoch that followed the stifling of the nascent, middle-class democracy of the European—especially the Italian—cities by pow-erful kings heading centralized states. It is thus sig-nificant that the original, rather modest palace was greatly enlarged to its present form after Paul's acces-sion to the papacy in 1534, reflecting the ambitions of the pope both for his family and the papacy. Unfin-ished at the time of Antonio's death in 1546, the building was completed by Michelangelo.

The façade (FIG. 17-12) is the very essence of princely dignity in architecture. Facing a spacious paved square, the rectangle of the smooth front is framed and firmly anchored by the *quoins* (rusticated building corners) and cornice, while lines of windows (with alternating triangular and segmental pedi-ments, in Bramante's fashion) mark a majestic beat across it. The window casements are no longer flush with the wall, as in the Palazzo Medici–Riccardi (FIG.

17-14 ANTONIO DA SANGALLO THE YOUNGER, courtyard of the Farnese Palace. Third story and attic by MICHELANGELO in 1548.

17-13 ANTONIO DA SANGALLO THE YOUNGER, plan of the Farnese Palace, Rome.

16-23), but project from its surface, so that instead of being a flat, thin plane, the façade becomes a spatially active, three-dimensional mass. Each casement is a complete architectural unit, consisting of a *socle* (a projecting under-member), engaged columns, entablature, and pediment. The variations in the treatment of these units prevent the symmetrical scheme from becoming rigid or monotonous. The rusticated doorway and second-story balcony, surmounted by the Farnese coat of arms, emphasize the central axis and bring the horizontal and vertical forces of the design into harmony. This centralizing feature, not present in the palaces of Alberti or Michelozzo di Bartolomeo, is the external opening of a central-corridor axis that runs through the whole building and continues in the garden beyond; around this axis, the rooms are disposed with strict regularity. The interior courtyard displays stately Colosseum arch-orders on Antonio's first two levels and, on the third, Michelangelo's sophisticated variation on that theme, with overlapping pilasters replacing the weighty columns of Antonio's design.

Raphael

The artist most typical of the High Renaissance is RAPHAEL (Raffaello Santi, 1483–1520). The pattern of his growth recapitulates the sequence of tendencies of the fifteenth century, and although strongly influenced by Leonardo and Michelangelo, Raphael developed an individual style that, in itself, clearly states the ideals of High Renaissance art. His powerful originality prevailed while he learned from everyone; he assimilated what he could best use, and rendered into form the Classical instinct of his age. He worked so effortlessly in the Classical mood that his art is almost the resurrection of Greek art at its height. Goethe, the renowned German poet and critic, said of Raphael that he did not have to imitate the Greeks, for he thought and felt like them. Born in a small town in Umbria near Urbino, Raphael probably learned the rudiments of his art from his father, GIOVANNI SANTI, a provincial painter connected with the court of Federigo da Montefeltro. While still a child, Raphael was apprenticed to Perugino, who had been trained in Verrocchio's shop with Leonardo. We have seen in Perugino's *Christ Delivering the Keys of the Kingdom to St. Peter* (FIG. 16-62) that the most significant formal quality of his work is the harmony of its spatial composition. While Raphael was still in the studio of Perugino, the latter painted a panel of *The Marriage of the Virgin* (not shown), which, in its composition, very closely resembles the central portion of his Sistine Chapel fresco (FIG. 16-62). Perugino's panel, now in the Museum of Caen, probably served as the model for Raphael's *Marriage of the Virgin* (FIG.

17-15   RAPHAEL, *The Marriage of the Virgin*, 1504. Oil on wood, 67″ × 46½″. Pinacoteca di Brera, Milan.

17-15). Although scarcely 21, Raphael was able to recognize and to remedy some of the weaknesses of his master's composition. By relaxing the formality of Perugino's foreground figure screen and disposing his actors in greater depth, he not only provides them with greater freedom of action but also bridges the gap between them and the background building more successfully. The result is a painting that, although it resembles its model very closely, is nevertheless more fluid and better unified.

Four years in Florence, from 1504 to 1508, were greatly stimulating for Raphael. Here, in the home of the Renaissance, he discovered that the style of painting he had so painstakingly learned from Perugino was already outmoded. The two archrivals Leonardo and Michelangelo were engaged in an artistic battle. Crowds flocked to Santissima Annunziata to see the recently unveiled cartoon for Leonardo's *Virgin and Child with St. Anne and the Infant St. John* (FIG. 17-2), the original version of which was done about 1498. Michelangelo responded with the *Doni Madonna*. Both artists were commissioned to decorate the council hall in the Palazzo Vecchio with pictures memorializing Florentine victories of the past. Although only Leonardo completed his task and although only some small preparatory sketches and some small copies survive, the effect on artists in Florence—especially on one as gifted as Raphael—must have been considerable.

Under the influence of Leonardo, Raphael began to modify the Madonna compositions he had learned in Umbria. In the *Madonna with the Goldfinch (Madonna del Cardellino)* of 1506 (FIG. 17-16), Raphael uses the pyramidal composition of Leonardo's *Virgin of the Rocks* (FIG. 17-1). The faces and figures are modeled in subtle chiaroscuro, and Raphael's general application of this technique is based on Leonardo's cartoon for *The Virgin and Child with St. Anne and the Infant St. John* (FIG. 17-2). At the same time, the large, substantial figures are placed in a Peruginesque landscape, with the older artist's typical feathery trees in the middle ground. Although Raphael experimented with Leonardo's dusky modeling, he tended to return to Perugino's lighter tonalities. Raphael preferred clarity to obscurity, not being, as Leonardo was, fascinated with mystery. His great series of Madonnas, of which this is an early member, unify Christian devotion and pagan beauty; no artist has ever rivaled Raphael in his definitive rendering of this sublime theme of grace and dignity, sweetness and lofty idealism.

Had Raphael painted nothing but his Madonnas, his fame would still be secure. But he was also a great

17-16 RAPHAEL, *Madonna with the Goldfinch (Madonna del Cardellino)*, 1505–1506. Oil on wood, 42″ × 29½″. Galleria degli Uffizi, Florence.

muralist, a master in the grand style begun by Giotto and carried on by Masaccio and the artists of the fifteenth century. In 1508, Raphael was called to Rome to the court of Pope Julius II, perhaps on the recommendation of his fellow townsman, Bramante. There, in competition with older artists like Perugino and Luca Signorelli, Raphael received one of the largest commissions of the time: the decoration of the papal apartments in the Vatican. Of the several rooms (*stanze*) of the suite, Raphael painted the first, the Stanza della Segnatura; the others were done mostly by his pupils, after his sketches. On the four walls of the Stanza della Segnatura, under the headings of Theology, Law, Poetry, and Philosophy, Raphael deploys a host of magnificent figures that symbolize and sum up the learning of the West as understood in the Renaissance. His intention was to indicate the four branches of human knowledge and wisdom, while pointing out the virtues and the learning appropriate to a pope. The iconographic scheme is most complex, and it is likely that Raphael received advice from the brilliant company of Classical scholars surrounding Julius. On one wall, Raphael presents a composition that, of itself, constitutes a complete statement of the High Renaissance in its artistic form and spiritual meaning—the so-called *School of Athens* (FIG. 17-17). The setting is not a "school" but rather a concourse of the great philosophers and scientists of the ancient world, who—rediscovered by the Renaissance—hold a convention, where they teach one another once more and inspire a new age. In a vast hall covered by massive vaults that recall Roman architecture and predict the look of the new St. Peter's, the figures are ingeniously arranged around the central pair, Plato and Aristotle. On Plato's side are the ancient philosophers, concerned with the ultimate mysteries that transcend this world; on Aristotle's side are the philosophers and scientists, concerned with nature and the affairs of men. The groups move easily and clearly, with eloquent poses and gestures that symbolize their doctrines and are of the greatest variety. Their self-assurance and natural dignity bespeak the very nature of calm reason, that balance and measure so much admired by Renaissance men as the heart of philosophy. At the lower left, Pythagoras writes as a servant holds up the harmonic scale. In the foreground, Heraclitus (probably a portrait of Michelangelo) broods alone. Diogenes sprawls on the steps. At the right, students surround Euclid, who demonstrates a theorem. This group is especially interesting; Euclid may be a portrait of the aged Bramante. At the extreme right, Raphael includes his own portrait.

Significantly, this great Renaissance artist places himself among the mathematicians and scientists, and certainly the evolution of pictorial science comes

17-17 RAPHAEL, *The School of Athens*, 1509–1511. Fresco. Stanza della Segnatura, Vatican Palace, Rome.

to its perfection in *The School of Athens*. A vast perspective space has been created, in which human figures move naturally, without effort—each according to his own intention, as Leonardo might say. The stage setting, so long in preparation, is complete; the Western artist knows now how to produce the drama of man. That this stage-like space is projected onto a two-dimensional surface is the consequence of the union of mathematics with pictorial science, which yields the art of perspective, here mastered completely. The artist's psychological insight has matured along with his mastery of the problems of physical representation. Each character in Raphael's *School of Athens*, like those in Leonardo's *Last Supper* (FIG. 17-3), is intended to communicate a mood that reflects his beliefs, and each group is unified by the sharing of its members in the mood. The design devices by which individuals and groups are related to each other and to the whole are wonderfully involved and demand close study. From the center, where Plato and Aristotle stand, silhouetted against the

clear blue of the sky within the framing arch in the distance, the groups of figures are rhythmically arranged in an elliptical movement that swings forward, looping around the two forward groups to either side, and then back again to the center. Moving through the wide opening in the foreground along the perspective pattern of the floor, we penetrate the assembly of philosophers and are led, by way of the reclining Diogenes, up to the here-reconciled leaders of the two great opposing camps of Renaissance philosophy. In the Stanza della Segnatura, Raphael reconciles and harmonizes not only the Platonists and Aristotelians, but paganism and Christianity, in the same kind of synthesis manifest in his Madonnas.

Pope Leo X, the son of Lorenzo de' Medici, succeeded Julius II as Raphael's patron, and it was in his pontificate that Rome achieved a splendor it had not known since ancient times. Leo, a worldly, pleasure-loving prince, spent huge sums on the arts, of which, as a true Medici, he was a sympathetic connoisseur. Raphael moved in the highest circles of the papal court, himself the star of a brilliant society—young, handsome, wealthy, and adulated, not only by his followers but by the city of Rome and all Italy. His personality contrasts strikingly with that of the aloof, mysterious Leonardo or the tormented and intractable Michelangelo. Genial, even-tempered, generous, and high-minded, Raphael was genuinely loved. The pope was not his only patron. His friend, the immensely wealthy banker Agostino Chigi, who managed the financial affairs of the papal state, commissioned Raphael to decorate his small but splendid palace on the Tiber, the Villa Farnesina, with scenes from Classical mythology. Outstanding among the frescoes painted there by Raphael is the *Galatea* (FIG. 17-18), which takes its theme from the popular Italian poem by Politian, "La giostra"; Botticelli borrowed the theme for his *Birth of Venus* (FIG. 16-60) from the same work. In Raphael's fresco, Galatea flees from her uncouth lover, the giant Polyphemus, on a shell drawn by leaping dolphins, surrounded by sea creatures and playful cupids. The painting erupts in unrestrained pagan joy and exuberance, an exultant song in praise of human beauty and zestful love. The composition artfully wheels the sturdy figures

17-18 RAPHAEL, *Galatea*, 1513. Fresco. Villa Farnesina, Rome.

around Galatea in bounding and dashing movements that always return to her as the energetic center. The figures of the cupids, skillfully foreshortened, repeat the circling motion. Raphael's figures are sculpturally conceived, and the body of Galatea—supple, strong, and vigorously in motion—should be compared with Botticelli's delicate, hovering, almost dematerialized Venus. Pagan myth presented in monumental form, in vivacious movement, and in a spirit of passionate delight brings back the kernel substance of which the naturalistic art and poetry of the Classical world was made. Raphael revives the gods and heroes and the bright world they populated, not to venerate them but to make of them the material of art. From Raphael almost to the present, Classical matter will hold as prominent a place in art as religious matter. So completely does the new spirit embodied in the *Galatea* take control that it is as if the Middle Ages had never been.

Raphael was also an excellent portraitist. His subjects were the illustrious scholars and courtiers who surrounded Pope Leo X, among them Count Baldassare Castiglione, a close friend of Raphael and memorable for his handbook on High Renaissance criteria of aristocratic behavior. In the *Book of the Courtier*, Castiglione portrays an ideal type of the High Renaissance, a courageous, sagacious, truth-loving, skillful, and cultivated man—in a word, the completely civilized man, a culmination of the line that runs from the rude barbarian warriors who succeeded to the Roman empire through the half-literate knights and barons of the Middle Ages. Castiglione goes on to describe a way of life based on cultivated rationality in imitation of the ancients. In Raphael's portrait of him (FIG. 17-19), Castiglione, splendidly yet soberly garbed, looks directly at us with a philosopher's grave and benign expression, clear-eyed and thoughtful. The figure is in half-length and three-quarter view, in the pose made popular by the *Mona Lisa* (FIG. 17-4), and we note in both portraits the increasing attention paid by the High Renaissance artist to the personality and psychic state of his subject. The tones are muted and low-keyed, as would befit the temper and mood of the reflective, elderly man; the background is entirely neutral, without the usual landscape or architecture. The composition emphasizes the head and the hands, both wonderfully eloquent in what they report of the man, who himself had written so eloquently in *The Courtier* of the way to enlightenment by the love of beauty. Both Raphael and Castiglione, as well as other artists of their age, were animated by such love, and we know from his poetry that Michelangelo shared in this widely held Neo-Platonic belief that the soul rises to its enlightenment by the progressively rarefied experience of the beautiful.

17-19 RAPHAEL, *Baldassare Castiglione, c.* 1514. Oil on wood transferred to canvas, approx. 30¼″ × 26½″. Louvre, Paris.

Michelangelo

MICHELANGELO (Michelangelo Buonarroti, 1475–1564) is a far more complex personality than Raphael, and his art is not nearly so typical of the High Renaissance as Raphael's. Frequently irascible, Michelangelo was as impatient with the shortcomings of others as he was with his own. His jealousy of Raphael, his dislike of Leonardo, and his almost continuous difficulties with his patrons are all well known. Perhaps these personal problems arose out of his strong and stern devotion to his art, for he was always totally absorbed in the work at hand. He identified himself with the task of artistic creation completely, and his reactions to his rivals were often impulsive and antagonistic. In this respect, Michelangelo's character has often been compared with Beethoven's, but the personal letters of both reveal a deep sympathy and concern for those close to them, and a profound understanding of humanity informs their works.

Whatever his traits of character, Michelangelo's career realizes all those Renaissance ideals that we conceptualize as "inspired genius" and "universal man." His work has the authority of greatness we have already attributed to Donatello. His confidence in his genius was unbounded; its demands determined his choices absolutely, often in opposition to the demands of his patrons. His belief that nothing worth preserving could be done without genius was attended by the conviction that nothing could be done without persevering study. Although he was architect, sculptor, painter, poet, and engineer, he thought of himself first as a sculptor, regarding that calling as superior to that of a painter because the sculptor shares in something like the divine power to "make man." In true Platonic fashion, Michelangelo believed that the image produced by the artist's hand must come from the Idea in his mind; the Idea is the reality that has to be brought forth by the genius of the artist. But the artist is not the *creator* of the Ideas he conceives; rather he finds them in the natural world, reflecting the absolute Idea, which, for the artist, is Beauty. In this way, the strongly Platonic strain makes the Renaissance theory of the imitation of nature a *revelation* of the high truths hidden within nature. The theory that guided Michelangelo's hand, though never complete or entirely consistent, appears in his poetry:

> Every beauty which is seen here below by persons of perception resembles more than anything else that celestial source from which we all are come . . .
>
> My eyes longing for beautiful things
> together with my soul longing for salvation
> have no other power
> to ascend to heaven than the contemplation of beautiful things.*

One of the best-known observations by Michelangelo is that the artist must proceed by finding the Idea—the image, locked in the stone, as it were—so that, by removing the excess stone, he extricates the Idea, like Pygmalion bringing forth the living form:

> The best artist has no concept which some single marble does not enclose within its mass, but only the hand which obeys the intelligence can accomplish that . . . . Taking away . . . brings out a living figure in alpine and hard stone, which . . . grows the more as the stone is chipped away . . . .†

The artist, Michelangelo felt, works through many years at this unceasing process of revelation and "arrives late at lofty and unusual things and . . . remains little time thereafter."

Michelangelo did indeed arrive "at lofty and unusual things," for he broke sharply from the lessons of his predecessors and contemporaries in one important respect: he mistrusted the application of mathematical methods as guarantees of beauty in proportion. Measure and proportion, he believed, should be "kept in the eyes." Giorgio Vasari quotes Michelangelo as declaring that "it was necessary to keep one's compass in one's eyes and not in the hand, for the hands execute, but the eye judges." Thus, he would set aside Vitruvius, Alberti, Leonardo, Albrecht Dürer, and others who tirelessly sought the perfect measure, being convinced that the inspired judgment could find other pleasing proportions and that the artist must not be bound, except by the demands made by the realization of the Idea. This insistence on the artist's own authority is typical of Michelangelo and anticipates the modern concept of the right of talent to a self-expression limited only by its own judgment. The license thus given to genius to aspire far beyond the "rules" led Michelangelo to create works in architecture, sculpture, and painting that depart from High Renaissance regularity and put in its stead a style of vast, expressive strength with complex, eccentric, often titanic forms that loom before us in tragic grandeur. His self-imposed isolation (Raphael spoke of him as "lonely as the hangman"), his creative furies, his proud independence, and his daring innovations led Italians to speak of the dominating quality of the man and his works in one word, *terribilità*—the sublime shadowed by the awesome and the fearful.

As a youth, Michelangelo was apprenticed to the painter Domenico Ghirlandaio, whom he left before completing his training. He soon came under the protection of Lorenzo the Magnificent and must have been a young and thoughtful member of the famous Neo-Platonic circle. He studied sculpture under one of Lorenzo's favorite artists, BERTOLDO DI GIOVANNI, a former collaborator of Donatello who specialized in small-scale bronzes. When the Medici fell in 1494, Michelangelo fled from Florence to Bologna, where he was impressed by the sculpture of Jacopo della Quercia (FIG. 16-3). Besides his study of Jacopo—although he claimed that in his art he owed nothing to anyone—Michelangelo made studious drawings after the great Florentines, Giotto and Masaccio, and it is very likely that his consuming interest in representing the male nude both in sculpture and painting was much stimulated by Signorelli (FIG. 16-61).

Michelangelo's wanderings took him to Rome, from which he returned to Florence in 1501, partly because the city might permit him to work a great block of marble, called the Giant, left over from an earlier, abortive commission. With his sure insight into the nature of stone and a proud, youthful confidence that he could perceive its Idea, Michelangelo added to his already great reputation by carving his

*In Robert J. Clements, *Michelangelo's Theory of Art* (New York: New York University Press, 1961), p. 9. © 1961 by Robert J. Clements. Reprinted by permission of the publisher.

†Ibid., p. 16.

17-20 MICHELANGELO, *David*, 1501–1504. Marble, approx. 13' 5" high. Galleria dell' Accademia, Florence.

young David and the large hands and feet, giving promise of the giant strength to come, are not composed simply of inert muscle groups, nor are they idealized by simplification into broad masses. They serve, by their active play, to make vivid the whole mood and posture of tense expectation. Each swelling vein and tightening sinew amplifies the psychological vibration of the monumental hero's pose. Michelangelo doubtless had the Classical nude in mind—Antique statues, which were being found everywhere, were greatly admired by Michelangelo and his contemporaries for their skillful and precise rendering of heroic physique—but if we compare the *David* with the *Doryphoros* (FIG. 5-61), we realize how widely his intent diverges from the measured, almost bland quality of the Antique statue. As early as the *David*, then, Michelangelo's genius, unlike Raphael's, is dedicated to the presentation of towering, pent-up passion rather than calm, ideal beauty. His own doubts, frustrations, and torments of mind passed easily into the great figures he created or planned.

The tomb of Julius II, a colossal structure that would have given Michelangelo the room he needed for his superhuman, tragic beings, became one of the great disappointments of Michelangelo's life when the Pope, for unexplained reasons, interrupted the commission, possibly because its funds had to be diverted for Bramante's rebuilding of St. Peter's. The original project called for a freestanding, two-story

17-21 MICHELANGELO, *Moses*, c. 1513–1515. Marble, approx. 8' 4" high. San Pietro in Vincoli, Rome.

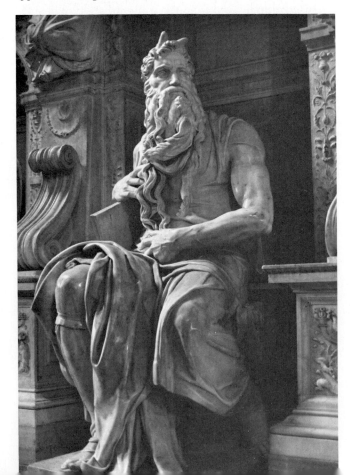

David (FIG. 17-20), still the marvel it was then. The colossal figure again takes up the theme that Donatello and Verrocchio had used successfully, but it reflects Michelangelo's own highly original interpretation of the subject. David is represented not after the victory, with the head of Goliath at his feet, but rather turning his head to his left, sternly watchful of the approaching foe. His whole muscular body, as well as his face, is tense with gathering power. The ponderated pose, suggesting the body at ease, is misleading until we read in the tightening sinews and deep frown what impends. Here is the characteristic representation of energy in reserve that gives the tension of the coiled spring to Michelangelo's figures. The anatomy plays an important part in this prelude to action. The rugged torso and sturdy limbs of the structure with some 28 statues. After the Pope's death in 1513, the scale of the project was reduced step by step until, in 1542, a final contract specified a simple wall tomb with less than one-third of the originally planned figures. The spirit of the tomb may be summed up in the figure of *Moses* (FIG. 17-21), which was completed during one of the sporadic resumptions of the work in 1513. Meant to be seen from below, and balanced with seven other massive forms related in spirit to it, the *Moses* now, in its comparatively paltry setting, can hardly have its full impact. The leader of Israel is shown seated—the tables of the Law under one arm, his other hand gripping the coils of his beard. He may be imagined as resting after the ecstasy of the receiving of the Law on Mount Sinai, while, in the valley below, the people of Israel give themselves up once more to idolatry. Here again,

Michelangelo presents the turned head (as in the *David*), which concentrates the expression of awful wrath that now begins to stir in the mighty frame and eyes. One must study the work in detail to appreciate Michelangelo's sense of the relevance of each detail of body and drapery in forcing up the psychic temperature. The muscles bulge, the veins swell, the great legs begin slowly to move. If this titan ever rose to his feet, says one writer, the world would fly apart. The holy rage of *Moses* mounts to the bursting point, yet must be contained, for the free release of energies in action is forbidden forever to Michelangelo's passion-stricken beings.

Two other figures believed to be intended for the Julius tomb (although this is now doubted by some)—*The Dying Slave* (FIG. 17-22) and *The Bound Slave* (FIG. 17-23), may represent the enslavement of the human

17-22 MICHELANGELO, *The Dying Slave*, 1513–1516. Marble, approx. 7′ 5″ high. Louvre, Paris.

17-23 MICHELANGELO, *The Bound Slave*, 1513–1516. Marble, approx. 6′ 10½″ high. Louvre, Paris.

17-24 Interior of the Sistine Chapel (view facing east). The Vatican, Rome.

17-25 MICHELANGELO, ceiling of the Sistine Chapel, 1508–1512. Fresco. The Vatican, Rome.

soul by matter when the soul falls from Heaven into the prison house of the body. With the imprisoned soul slumbering, our actions, as Marsilio Ficino says, are "the dreams of sleepers and the ravings of madmen." Certainly, the dreams and the ravings are present in these two figures. Originally, there were to be some 20 slaves for the tomb, in various attitudes of revolt and exhaustion. In the two slaves, as in the *David* and the *Moses*, Michelangelo makes each body a total expression of the Idea, so that the human figure serves not so much as a representation of a concept, as in Medieval allegory, but as the concrete realization of an intense feeling. Michelangelo's own powerful imagination indeed communicates itself in every plane and hollow of the stone. The beautiful, Praxitelean lines of the swooning captive present—in their slow, downward pull—the weight of exhaustion; the violent contrapposto of the defiant captive is the image of frantic, impotent struggle. Michelangelo's whole art depends on his conviction that whatever can be said greatly through sculpture and painting must be said through the human figure.

A group of four unfinished slaves, one of which is illustrated in the Introduction (FIG. 10), was probably meant for one of the later versions of the tomb. These figures serve not only as object lessons in the subtractive method of sculpture, but also as revelations of the creative process in which abstract ideas—in effect, encased in blocks of stone—are converted into dynamically expressive, concrete forms. If Michelangelo's slaves indeed symbolize the struggle of the human soul to find release from the bonds of its material body, then this idea can find no fuller expression than in these partly finished figures that, with superhuman effort, struggle to cast off the inert masses of stone that imprison them.

With the failure of the tomb project, Julius II gave the bitter and reluctant Michelangelo the commission to paint the ceiling of the Sistine Chapel (FIG. 17-24). The artist, insisting that painting was not his profession, assented only in the hope that the tomb project could be revived. The difficulties facing Michelangelo were enormous: the inadequacy of his training in the art of fresco; the dimensions of the ceiling (some 5,800 square feet) and its height above the pavement (almost 70 feet); and the complicated perspective problems presented by the height and curve of the vault. Yet, in less than four years, Michelangelo produced an unprecedented work—a one-man master-piece without parallel in the history of world art (FIG. 17-25).* Taking the most august and solemn theme of all—the creation, fall, and redemption of man—he spread a colossal decorative scheme across the vast surface, weaving together more than 300 figures in an ultimate grand drama of the human race. A long corridor of narrative panels describing the creation re-

corded in Genesis runs along the crown of the vault, from God's *Separation of Light and Darkness* to the *Drunkenness of Noah*. On either side, where the vault curves down, are seated the Hebrew prophets and pagan sibyls who foretold the coming of Christ. At the four corner pendentives are four Old Testament scenes with David, Judith, Haman, and the Brazen Serpent. Scores of lesser figures appear: the ancestors of Christ in the triangular compartments above the windows, the nude youths who punctuate the corners of the central panels, and the small pairs of putti in *grisaille* (grey monochrome to imitate sculpture), who support the painted cornice surrounding the whole central corridor. The conception of the whole design is astounding enough in itself; the articulation of it in its thousand details is an achievement little less than superhuman. But Michelangelo *was* human; in the first few months of work, he made mistakes in the technical application of the fresco that spoiled all he had done up to that time. Also, in the first three panels, beginning at the entrance with the *Drunkenness of Noah*, he had not yet estimated the scale properly, and the compositions are crowded, without the simplicity of the panels beginning with the *Temptation and Fall*.

*Like Leonardo's *Last Supper*, Michelangelo's Sistine Chapel paintings are in the process of restoration. Centuries of accumulated grime, overpainting, and protective glue are being removed, and restorers have already revealed much of the artist's original craft in form, color, style, and procedure. The restoration work, part of a 12-year program, began on the lunettes above the windows of the chapel, where the vault curves down on either side. In these semicircular spaces, Michelangelo painted figures representing the ancestors of Christ. These figures, once thought to be purposefully dark, now show brilliant colors of high intensity, brushed on with an astonishing freedom and rapidity. Holes in the walls below the windows are believed to have held trusses that supported a bridge-like scaffold covering half the ceiling at a time; this would seem to verify old accounts that the artist worked from a structure that required no floor supports. The success of the restorers in recovering the freshness and vivacity of Michelangelo's paintings in the lunettes is expected to continue as they begin on the prophets and the narrative scenes along the crown of the vault. By 1988, we should be able to view the great artist's work in all its first splendor. Without doubt, our present knowledge of Michelangelo's art, intentions, and influence will need thorough revision at that time.

17-26 MICHELANGELO, *The Creation of Adam* (detail of FIG. 17-25).

Unlike the case in Andrea Mantegna's Camera degli Sposi in Mantua (FIG. 16-64), the strongly marked, unifying architectural framework is not used to construct "picture windows" through which we may look up into some illusion just above. Rather, our eyes seize on figure after figure, each sharply outlined against the neutral tone of the architectural setting or the plain background of the panels. Here, as in his sculpture, Michelangelo relentlessly concentrates his expressive purpose on the human figure. To him, the body is beautiful not only in its natural form but also in its spiritual and philosophical significance; the body is simply the manifestation of the soul or of a state of mind and character. Michelangelo represents the body in its most simple, elemental aspect: in the nude or simply draped, with no background and no ornamental embellishment, and always with a sculptor's sense that the figures could be tinted reliefs or full-rounded statues.

One of the central panels of the ceiling will evidence Michelangelo's mastery of the drama of the human figure. *The Creation of Adam* (FIG. 17-26) is not the traditional representation but a bold, entirely Humanistic interpretation of the primal event. God and Adam, members of the same race of superbeings, confront each other in a primordial, unformed landscape of which Adam is still a material part, heavy as earth, while the Lord transcends it, wrapped in his billowing cloud of drapery and borne up by his genius powers. Apprehensively curious but as yet uncreated, the female figure beneath his sheltering arm, long held to represent Eve, has recently been interpreted as the Virgin Mary (with the Christ child at her knee). Life leaps to Adam like an electric spark from the extended and mighty hand of God. The communication between gods and heroes, so familiar in Classical myth, is here concrete: both are made of the same substance; both are gigantic. This blunt depiction of the Lord as ruler of Heaven in the Olympian, pagan sense, is an indication of how easily the High Renaissance joined pagan and Christian traditions; we could imagine Adam and the Lord as Prometheus and Zeus. The composition is dynamically off-center, its focus being the two hands that join the great bodies by the energy that springs between the fingers. The bodies themselves are complementary—the concave body of Adam fitting the convex body of the Lord. The straight, architectural axes we find in the compositions of Leonardo and Raphael are replaced by curves and diagonals; thus, motion directs not only the figures but the whole composition. The reclining poses, the heavy musculature, and the twisting contrapposto are all a part of Michelangelo's stock, which he will show again in the sculptured figures of the Medici tombs.

Following the death of Julius II, patron of the Sistine ceiling paintings, Michelangelo went once again into the service of the Medici popes, Leo X and Clement VII. These pontiffs were little interested in perpetuating the fame of their predecessor by letting Michelangelo complete the tomb of Julius; instead, they commissioned him to build a funerary chapel, the New Sacristy, in San Lorenzo in Florence. Brunelleschi's Old Sacristy was off the left transept of San Lorenzo, and Michelangelo built the new addition off the right. He attempted a unification of architecture and of sculpture, designing the whole chapel as well as the tombs. This relationship between the two arts (and, in this case, painting as well) was a common Medieval feature; we think of the sculptured portals and stained glass of the Gothic cathedral. But the relationship had been broken in the fifteenth century, when sculpture fought free of its architectural matrix and asserted its independence—so much so that Brunelleschi could complain that Donatello's architectural and sculptural additions to his Old Sacristy spoiled the purity of his design. This new integration by Michelangelo, though here unfinished, pointed the way to Baroque art, in which the architectural–sculptural–pictorial ensemble will again become standard.

At opposite sides of the chapel stand the tombs of Giuliano, Duke of Nemours, and Lorenzo, Duke of Urbino, son and grandson of Lorenzo the Magnificent. The tomb of Giuliano (FIG. 17-27) is compositionally the twin of Lorenzo's. Both are unfinished; it is believed that pairs of recumbent river-gods were to be placed at the bottom of the sarcophagi, balancing the pairs that rest on the sloping sides. The composition of the tombs has been a long-standing puzzle. How were they ultimately to look? What is their relationship to one another? What do they signify? The present arrangement seems quite unstable; were the sloping figures meant to recline on a flat surface, or were they to be partly supported by the river-gods below them? We can do little more than state some of

17-27 MICHELANGELO, tomb of Giuliano de' Medici, 1519–1534. Marble, central figure approx. 71" high. New Sacristy, San Lorenzo, Florence.

the questions, without attempting to answer them in full. It has been suggested that the arrangement (planned by Michelangelo, but never completed) can be interpreted as the ascent of the soul through the levels of the Neo-Platonic universe. The lowest level, represented by the river-gods, would have signified the underworld of brute matter, the source of evil. The two statues on the sarcophagi would then symbolize the realm of time: the specifically human world of the cycles of dawn, day, evening, and night. Man's state in this world of time is one of pain and anxiety, frustration and exhaustion. At left, the female figure of Night and, at right, the male figure of Day appear to be chained into never-relaxing tensions. Both exhibit that anguished twisting of the masses of the body in contrary directions seen in *The Bound Slave* (FIG. 17-23) and in the Sistine Chapel paintings. This contrapposto is the signature of Michelangelo. Day, with a body the thickness of a great tree and the anatomy of Hercules, strains his huge limbs against each other, his unfinished visage rising menacingly above his shoulder. Night, the symbol of rest, twists as if in troubled sleep, her posture wrenched and feverish. The artist has surrounded her with an owl, poppies, and a hideous mask symbolic of nightmares.

On their respective tombs, the figures of Lorenzo and Giuliano, rising above the troubles of the realm of time, represent the two ideal human types: the contemplative man (Lorenzo) and the active man (Giuliano). They thus become symbols for the two means by which man might achieve union with God: meditation or the active life fashioned after that of Christ. Michelangelo disdained to make portraits of the actual persons; who, he asked, would care what they looked like in a thousand years? What counted was the contemplation of what was beyond the corrosion of time. Giuliano, the active man (FIG. 17-27), his features quite generalized, sits clad in the armor of a Roman emperor, holding the baton of a commander, his head turned alertly, as if in council (he looks toward the statue of the Virgin at one end of the chapel). Across the room, Lorenzo, the contemplative man, sits wrapped in thought, his face in deep shadow. In these works, as in many others, Michelangelo suggests powerful psychic forces that cannot be translated into action but are ever on the verge of it. His prevailing mood is tension and constraint, even in the figures that seem to aspire to the ideal, to the timeless, perfect and unmoving. Michelangelo's style was born to disturb. It brings the serene, brief High Renaissance to an end.

The tensions and ambiguities of Michelangelo's style, which will pass over into the general style called Mannerism, are strongly felt in his architecture. His building activity for the Medici in Florence centered in and around San Lorenzo, and his Laurentian Library, built to house the great collections of the Medici, adjoins it. The building's peculiar layout was dictated by its special function and by its rather constricted site. Michelangelo had two contrasting spaces to work with: the long horizontal of the library proper, and the vertical of the vestibule. In the latter, everything is massive and plastic, but the planes and solids of the reading room are shallow and played down (perhaps so as not to distract the readers). The need to place the vestibule windows high determined the narrow verticality of its elevation (FIG. 17-28).

The vestibule, much taller than it is wide or long, gives the impression of a vertically compressed, shaft-like space. A vast, flowing stairway that almost fills the interior greatly adds to a sense of oppressiveness. Anyone schooled exclusively in the Classical architecture of Bramante and the High Renaissance would have been appalled by Michelangelo's indifference to Classical norms in the use of the orders or in proportion. He uses columns in pairs and sinks them into the walls. He breaks columns around corners. He places consoles beneath columns that are not meant to support them. He arbitrarily breaks through pediments, as well as through cornices and stringcourses. In short, Michelangelo disposes willfully and abruptly of Classical architecture as the High Renaissance knows it. But some features, often called Manneristic, were dictated by structural necessity. The recessed columns, for example, which seem neither to support nor to be supported, have recently been shown to perform a supporting function, in contrast with the standard, applied Classical orders, which are purely decorative. These paired stone columns, due to their greater compressive strength, actually add rigidity to the relatively thin brick walls and support the upper part of the structure. The "ambiguity" of the resulting wall surface is illusory, as the columns clearly have been recessed *into* the wall. In any event, Michelangelo, with his usual trailbreaking independence of mind, has sculptured an interior space that conveys all the strains and tensions we find in his statuary and in his painted figures. But, unlike Mannerist architects—especially his contemporary Giulio Romano in the Palazzo del Tè (FIGS. 17-48 and 17-49)—he never tried to baffle or to confuse. His style in all three arts is wonderfully consistent. The key to that consistency may be found in his own words: "The members of an architectural structure follow the laws exemplified in the human body. He who . . . is not a good master of the nude . . . cannot understand the principles of architecture." His whole inspiration came from the beauty and majesty of the human body: the visible aspect of the human soul.

17-28 MICHELANGELO, vestibule of the Laurentian Library, Florence, begun 1524. Stairway designed 1558–1559.

17-29　MICHELANGELO, the Capitoline Hill (the Campidoglio), Rome, designed *c.* 1537.

In his later years, Michelangelo turned increasingly to architecture. In 1537, he undertook to reorganize the Capitoline Hill (the Campidoglio) in Rome (FIGS. 17-29 and 17-30), receiving from Pope Paul III a flattering and challenging commission. The pope wished to transform the ancient hill, which had once been the spiritual as well as political capitol of Rome, into a symbol of power of the new Rome of the popes. The great challenge of the project was that Michelangelo was required to incorporate into his design two existing buildings—the Medieval Palazzo dei Senatori (Palace of the Senators) on the east, and the fifteenth-century Palazzo dei Conservatori (Palace of the Conservators) on the south—and that these buildings formed an 80° angle. These preconditions might well have defeated a lesser architect, but Michelangelo converted what seemed to be a handicap into the most impressive design of a civic unit of the entire Renaissance.

Michelangelo reasoned that architecture should follow the form of the human body to the extent of disposing units symmetrically around a central and unique axis, as the arms are related to the body or the eyes to the nose. It must have been with arguments like this that he convinced his sponsors of the necessity of balancing the Palazzo dei Conservatori, for which he was going to redesign the façade, with a similar unit on the north side of the square. To achieve balance and symmetry in his design, Michelangelo placed the new building (the Museo Capitolino, originally planned only as a portico with single rows of offices above and behind it) so that it stood at the same angle to the Palazzo dei Senatori as the Palazzo dei Conservatori stood, thus arriving at a trapezoidal rather than a rectangular plan for his piazza (FIG. 17-30). All other elements of the design were subsequently adjusted to this unorthodox but basic feature.

The statue of Marcus Aurelius (FIG. 6-72)—the only one of many equestrian statues of Roman emperors to survive the Middle Ages—became the focal point for the whole design. It was brought to the Capitoline Hill on the pope's orders and against the advice of Michelangelo, who might have preferred to carve his

17-30 MICHELANGELO, plan for the Capitoline Hill, Rome. (Engraving by ÉTIENNE DUPÉRAC, c. 1569).

own centerpiece. The symbolic significance of the statue, which seemed to link the Rome of the caesars with the Rome of the popes, must have appealed to Paul III. To connect this central monument with the surrounding buildings, Michelangelo provided it with an oval base and placed it centrally in an oval pavement design (FIG. 17-30), the twelve points of which may have had ancient or Medieval cosmological connotations. Michelangelo's choice of the oval is significant, as it was considered to be an unstable geometric figure and was shunned by older Renaissance architects. But given the trapezoidal shape of the piazza, the oval, which combines centralizing with axial qualities, was the figure best suited to relate the various elements of the design to one another. It was to become the favorite geometric figure of the Baroque period.

Facing the piazza, the two lateral palazzi have identical, two-story façades (FIG. 17-31). They introduce us again to the giant order, first seen in somewhat timid fashion in Alberti's Sant' Andrea in Mantua (FIG. 16-42). Michelangelo uses it with much greater gusto and authority. The giant pilasters not only tie the two stories of the building together but provide a sturdy skeleton that fully expresses its actual function of being the main support of the structure. Walls have been all but eliminated. At ground level, the transition from the massive bulk of the pilaster-faced piers to the deep voids between them has been softened by the interposed columns. These columns carry straight lintels, in the manner advocated by Alberti, but Michelangelo uses them with even greater logic and consistency than Alberti. The façade

17-31 MICHELANGELO, Museo Capitolino, Capitoline Hill, Rome.

of the third building on the piazza, the three-storied Palazzo dei Senatori, uses the same design elements as the other two palazzi, but in a less plastic fashion. The axial building, with its greater height, thus becomes a distinctive and commanding accent for the ensemble, providing variety within the design without disrupting its unity.

The piazza might have become a room-like enclosure, as Renaissance squares often were and as Alberti, in his treatise, had advised that they be. But again Michelangelo parts with tradition and points to the future. Instead of enclosing his piazza with four walls with entrances leading through their centers, as a room-like enclosure would seem to demand, he left the fourth side open. A fourth wall is merely suggested by a balustrade and a thin screen of Classical statuary that effectively defines the limits of the piazza without obstructing a panoramic view across the city's roofs toward the Vatican. The accidental symbolism of this axis must have pleased the pope just as much as the piazza's dynamic design, and the sweeping vista must have pleased later Baroque planners.

Michelangelo took over the supervision of the building of the new St. Peter's a few years after he had designed the Capitoline Hill; neither project was finished at the time of his death. His work on St. Peter's—after efforts by a succession of architects following the death of Bramante—apparently became a show of dedication, thankless and without pay, on his own decision. Writing in May 1557 to his friend Giorgio Vasari, Michelangelo complains:

> God is my witness how much against my will it was that Pope Paul forced me into this work on St. Peter's in Rome ten years ago. If the work had been continued from that time forward as it was begun, it would by now have been as far advanced as I had reason to hope . . . .*

Among Michelangelo's difficulties had been his struggle to preserve and carry through (with modifications) Bramante's original plan (FIG. 17-7), which he praised even as he changed it:

> It cannot be denied that Bramante was a skillful architect and the equal of any one from the time of the ancients until now. It was he who drew up the original plan of St. Peter's, not full of confusion but clear and straightforward . . . . It was considered to be a fine design, and there is still evidence that it was so: indeed, every architect who has departed from Bramante's plan . . . has departed from the right way . . . .†

*In Robert J. Clements, ed., *Michelangelo: A Self Portrait* (Englewood Cliffs, N.J.: Prentice-Hall, 1964), p. 57.

†In E.G. Holt, ed., *Literary Sources of Art History* (Princeton, N.J.: Princeton University Press, 1947), p. 195.

We have already seen Michelangelo's respect for a good plan in his carrying out of Sangallo's Farnese Palace design with only minor modifications (FIG. 17-14). With Bramante's plan for St Peter's, Michelangelo managed a major concentration, reducing the central fabric from a number of interlocking crosses to a domed Greek cross inscribed in a square and fronting the whole with a Pantheon-like, double-columned portico (FIG. 17-32). Without destroying the centralizing features of Bramante's plan (the nave was lengthened after Michelangelo's death), Michelangelo, with a few strokes of the pen, converted its snowflake complexity into massive, cohesive unity.

The same striving for a unified and cohesive design can be seen in Michelangelo's treatment of the building's exterior. As the front of the church was changed later, his style and intention are best seen on the west (apse) end (FIG. 17-33). The colossal order again serves him nobly, as the giant pilasters march around the undulating wall surfaces, confining the movement without interrupting it. The architectural sculpturing, which Michelangelo began in the Laurentian Library (FIG. 17-28), here extends itself up from the ground through the attic stories and moves on into the drum and the dome, pulling the whole building together into a unity from base to summit. The Baroque architects will learn much from this kind of integral design, which is ultimately based on Michelangelo's conviction that architecture is one with the organic beauty of the human form. The domed west end—as majestic as it is today and as influential as it

0 50 100 FEET
0 15 30 METERS

17-32 MICHELANGELO, plan for St. Peter's, Rome.

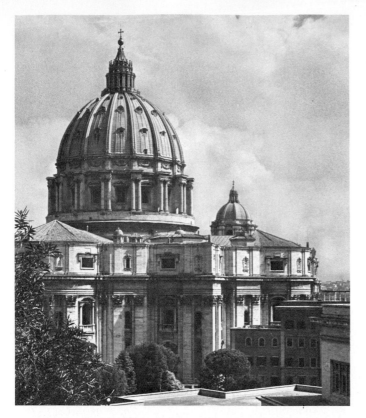

17-33 MICHELANGELO, St. Peter's, Rome, 1546–1564 (view from the northwest). Dome completed by GIACOMO DELLA PORTA in 1590.

has been on architecture throughout the centuries—is not quite as it was intended to be. Originally, Michelangelo had planned a dome with a raised silhouette, like that of the Florence Cathedral. But in his final version he decided on a hemispheric dome (FIG. 17-34), to moderate the verticality of the design of the lower stories and to establish a balance between dynamic and static elements. However, when GIACOMO DELLA PORTA executed the dome after Michelangelo's death, he restored the earlier high design, ignoring Michelangelo's later version. Giacomo's reasons were probably the same ones that had impelled Brunelleschi to use an ogival section for his Florentine dome (FIG. 16-15): greater stability and ease of construction. The result is that the dome seems to be rising from its base, rather than resting firmly on it—an effect that Michelangelo might not have approved. Nevertheless, the dome of St. Peter's is probably the most impressive and beautiful in the world and has served as model to generations of architects down to our own time.

While Michelangelo endured the tribulations of age and the long frustrations of art, his soul was further oppressed by the events that had been erupting around him from the time he fled Florence as a young

17-34 MICHELANGELO, south elevation of St. Peter's, Rome. (Engraving by ÉTIENNE DUPÉRAC, c. 1569.)

man after the fall of the Medici. The liberties of Florence were destroyed; the Medici had returned as tyrants, and Michelangelo felt himself an exile, even while he worked for them. Italy was laid waste by the French and Spanish invasions, and the Protestant Reformation divided Christendom into warring camps. The Catholic Counter-Reformation gained, and Europe was to be racked by religious war for more than a century. The glories of the High Renaissance faded, and the philosophy of Humanism retreated before the resurgence of a religious spirit that was often pessimistic, moralizing, and grimly fanatical, whether Protestant or Catholic. Michelangelo himself turned from his Humanist beginnings to a deep religious preoccupation with the fate of man and of his own soul. His sense that the world had gone mad and that man, forsaking God, was doomed

must have been sharpened by his still vivid memory of Savonarola's foreboding summons of sinners to repent and by his reading of Dante, in whom he was expert. In this spirit, Michelangelo undertook the great *Last Judgment* fresco on the altar wall of the Sistine Chapel (FIG. 17-35). The change from the mood of the ceiling paintings of 20 years before is radical. Fallen man was to have been exalted by the coming of the Redeemer, everywhere announced in the thronging figures of the ceiling. Now, on the altar wall, Christ indeed has come, but as the Medieval judge of the world—a giant whose mighty right arm is lifted in a gesture of damnation so broad and universal as to suggest he will destroy all creation, Heaven and earth alike. The choirs of Heaven surrounding him pulse with anxiety and awe. The spaces below are crowded with trumpeting angels, the ascending just,

17-35 MICHELANGELO, *The Last Judgment,* fresco on the altar wall of the Sistine Chapel, 1534–1541. The Vatican, Rome.

17-36 MICHELANGELO, *St. Bartholomew and "Self-Portrait"* (detail of FIG. 17-35).

and the downward-hurtling damned. On the left, the dead awake and assume flesh; on the right, the damned are tormented by demons whose gargoyle masks and burning eyes revive the demons of the Romanesque tympana (FIG. 9-31). Martyrs who suffered especially agonizing deaths crouch below the Judge. One of them, St. Bartholomew, who was skinned alive, holds the flaying knife and the skin, in which hangs a grotesque self-portrait of Michelangelo (FIG. 17-36). In all this, there is no trace of the old Neo-Platonic aspiration to beauty. The figures are grotesquely huge, violently twisted, with small heads and contorted features. The expressive power of ugliness and terror in the service of a terrible message reigns throughout the composition.

Michelangelo's art began in the manner of the fifteenth century, rose to an idealizing height in the

High Renaissance, and, at the end, moved toward the Baroque. Like a colossus, he bestrides three centuries. He became the archetype of the supreme genius who transcends the rules by making his own. Few artists could escape his influence, and variations on Michelangelo's style will constitute much of artistic experiment for centuries.

Andrea del Sarto and Correggio

The towering achievements of Raphael and Michelangelo in Rome tend to obscure everything else that was done during their time. Nevertheless, aside from the flourishing Venetian School, some excellent artists were active in other parts of Italy during the first part of the sixteenth century. One of these, the Florentine ANDREA DEL SARTO (1486–1531), expresses, in his early paintings, the ideals of the High Renaissance with almost as much clarity and distinction as Raphael. Andrea's *Madonna of the Harpies* (FIG. 17-37) shows the Madonna standing majestically on an altar-like base decorated with sphinxes (misidentified as harpies by Vasari; hence, the name of the painting). The composition is based on a massive and imposing figure pyramid, the static qualities of which are relieved by the opposing contrapposto poses of the flanking saints—a favorite and effective High Renaissance device to introduce variety into symmetry. The potentially rigid pyramid is further softened by the skillful coordination of the figures' poses into an organic movement that leads from St. Francis, on the left, to the Virgin, to St. John the Evangelist, and downward from him toward the observer. This main movement is either echoed or countered by numerous secondary movements brought into perfect formal balance in a faultless compositional performance. The soft modeling of the forms is based on Leonardo but does not affect the colors, which are rich and warm. Andrea's sense of and ability to handle color set him well apart from his central Italian contemporaries; he is perhaps the only Renaissance artist to transpose his rich color schemes from panels into frescoes. Andrea's later compositions tend to be less firmly knit and his color schemes move toward the cool harshness that will become typical of Mannerist painting. Although he was greatly admired in the sixteenth and seventeenth centuries, Andrea's fame has waned; today, he seems to be remembered primarily as the teacher of Jacopo da Pontormo, Rosso Fiorentino, and Vasari and, thus, as one of the forerunners of Mannerism.

Andrea del Sarto may still be firmly placed in the High Renaissance, but his north Italian contemporary, CORREGGIO (Antonio Allegri da Correggio, *c.* 1489–1534), of Parma, is almost impossible to classify.

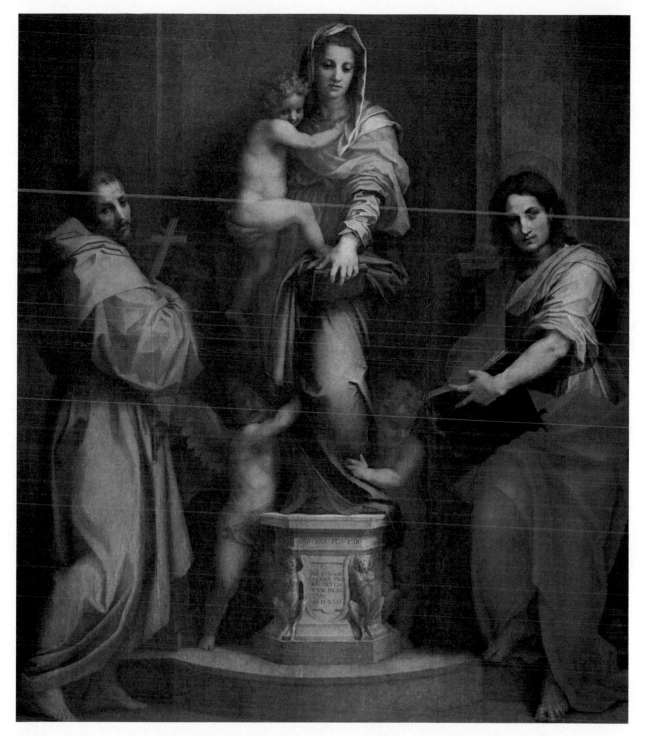

17-37 ANDREA DEL SARTO, *Madonna of the Harpies*, 1517. Oil on wood, approx. 6′ 9″ × 5′ 10″. Galleria degli Uffizi, Florence.

A solitary genius, Correggio brings together many stylistic trends, including those of Leonardo, Raphael, and the Venetians; yet he developed a unique personal style, which, if it must be labeled, might best be called "proto-Baroque." Historically, his most enduring contribution was the development of illusionistic ceiling perspectives to a point seldom sur-passed by his Baroque emulators. At Mantua, Mantegna had painted a hole into the ceiling of the Camera degli Sposi (FIG. 16-65); some 50 years later, Correggio painted away the entire dome of the cathedral of Parma (FIGS. 17-38 and 17-39). Opening up the cupola, the artist shows his audience a view of the sky, with concentric rings of clouds among which hun-

17-38 CORREGGIO, *The Assumption of the Virgin*, 1526–1530. Fresco. Dome of Parma Cathedral, Italy.

dreds of soaring figures perform a wildly pirouetting dance in celebration of *The Assumption of the Virgin*. These angelic creatures, twinkling their rosy toes at the spectators below, will become permanent tenants of numerous Baroque churches in later centuries. Correggio was also an influential painter of religious panels, in which he forecast many other Baroque compositional devices. As a painter of erotic mythological subjects, he had few equals. *Jupiter and Io* (FIG. 17-40) depicts a suavely sensual vision out of the pagan past. The painting is one of a series on the loves of Jupiter that Correggio painted for the Duke of Mantua, Federigo Gonzaga. The god, who assumed many disguises to hide his numerous liaisons from his wife, Juno, here appears as a cloud that embraces the willing nymph. The soft, smoky modeling *(sfumato)*, derived from Leonardo, is fused with glowing color and renders the voluptuous moment with exquisite subtlety. Even Titian, in his mythological paintings, was rarely able to match the sensuous quality expressed here by Correggio. Unlike Andrea del Sarto, Correggio was little appreciated by his contemporaries; only during the seventeenth century did Baroque painters recognize him as spiritual kin.

17-39 CORREGGIO (detail of FIG. 17-38).

17-40 CORREGGIO, *Jupiter and Io, c.* 1532. Oil on canvas, approx. $64\frac{1}{2}'' \times 29\frac{3}{4}''$. Kunsthistorisches Museum, Vienna.

MANNERISM

The term "Mannerism" refers to certain tendencies in the art of the Late Renaissance—the period from the death of Raphael (1520) to the end of the sixteenth century. In its broadest sense, the word means excessive or affected adherence to a distinctive manner, especially in art and literature. In its early application to these tendencies, it also carried the pejorative connotation of the term when applied to a description of individual behavior. Today, we view these styles more objectively and appreciate much that is excellent in them.

The Early Renaissance and the High Renaissance developed their characteristic styles from the studious observation of nature and the formulation of a pictorial science. By the time Mannerism matured (after 1520), all the representational problems had been solved; a vast learning was there to be drawn on. In addition, an age of antiquarianism and archeology was now bringing to light thousands of remnants of ancient Roman art. The Mannerists, instead of continuing the former research into nature and natural appearance, turned for their models to the masters of the High Renaissance, especially Michelangelo, and to Roman sculpture, especially relief sculpture. Instead of nature as their teacher, they took art. One could say that whereas their predecessors sought nature and found their style, the Mannerists looked first for a style and found a manner.

Following Michelangelo's example in one respect, the Mannerists declared the artist's right to his own interpretation of the rules, looking for inspiration to the Platonic Idea—referred to by them as the *disegno interno*—which fired their creative fervor. They saw a roughness in nature that needed refining, and they turned to where it had already been refined in art. From the antique and the High Renaissance, each artist, to the limit of his own ingenuity and skill, abstracted forms that he further idealized, so that the typical Manneristic picture or statue looks like an original essay in human form somewhat removed from nature. As *maniera* (as the style was called by Mannerist theorists) is an art of the human figure almost exclusively, its commonest expression is in paintings of numerous figures performing what appears to be a complicated dance and pantomime, in which the compositions, as well as the fanciful gestures and attitudes, are deliberately intricate. The movements are so studied and artificial that they remind us not of the great stage dramatics of the High Renaissance but of an involved choreography for interpretive dancers. Where the art of the High Renaissance strives for balance, Mannerism seeks instability. The calm equilibrium of the former is replaced by a restlessness that leads to distortions, exaggerations, and bizarre posturings on the one hand and sinuously graceful, often athletic attitudes on the other. The positions and actions of the figures often have little to do with the subject. The Mannerist requirement of "invention" leads its practitioner to the *maniera*, a self-conscious stylization involving complexity, caprice, bizarre fantasy (the "conceit"), elegance, preciosity, and polish. This is an art made for aristocratic patrons by artists who sense that their profession is worthy of honor and the admiration of kings. It is an age when monarchs and grandees may plead for anything from the hands of Raphael and Michelangelo, if only a sketch. The concepts of ''classic'' and ''old master'' are abroad, and artists are being called *divino*. The artist becomes conscious of his own personality, powers of imagination, and technical skill; he acquires learning and aims at virtuosity. He cultivates not the knowledge of nature but the intricacies of art.

In Painting

The Descent from the Cross (FIG. 17-41) by JACOPO DA PONTORMO (1494–1556) exhibits almost all the stylistic features characteristic of the early phase of Mannerism in painting. The figures crowd the composition, pushing into the front plane and almost completely blotting out the setting. The figure masses are disposed around the frame of the picture, leaving a void in the center, where the High Renaissance artists had concentrated their masses. The composition has no focal point, and the figures swing around the edges of the painting without coming to rest. The representation of space is as strange as the representation of

17-41 JACOPO DA PONTORMO, *The Descent from the Cross,* 1525–1528. Oil on wood, approx. 10' 3" × 6' 6". Capponi Chapel, Santa Felicità, Florence.

the figure. Mannerist space is ambiguous; we are never quite sure where it is going or just where the figures are in it. We do not know how far back the depicted space extends, although its limit is defined by the figure at the top. But we do know that the space is really too shallow for what is taking place in it. For example, there is no room in Pontormo's work for the body belonging to the head that appears immediately over Christ's. The centrifugal effect of the positions of the figures is strengthened by the curiously anxious glances that the actors cast out of the picture in all directions. There is an athletic bending and twisting, with distortions (a torso cannot bend at the point at which the foreground figure's does), an elastic elongation of the limbs, and a rendering of the heads as uniformly small and oval. The composition is further jarred by clashing colors, which are unnatural and as dissimilar as possible to the sonorous primary color chords used by painters of the High Renaissance. The mood of the painting is hard to describe; it seems the vision of an inordinately sensitive soul, perhaps itself driven, as are the actors, by nervous terrors. The psychic dissonance of the composition would indeed appear out of tune to a Classical artist.

ROSSO FIORENTINO (1494–1540)—like Pontormo, a pupil of Andrea del Sarto—compresses space in a manner similar to Pontormo but fills it with turbulent

17-42 ROSSO FIORENTINO, *Moses Defending the Daughters of Jethro,* 1523. Oil on canvas, approx. 63" × 46". Galleria degli Uffizi, Florence.

action. Rosso's painting of *Moses Defending the Daughters of Jethro* (FIG. 17-42) recalls the titanic struggles and powerful musculature of Michelangelo's figures on the Sistine Chapel ceiling, but his purpose is not so much expressive as it is inventive of athletic poses. At the same time, although the figures are modeled for three-dimensional effect, they are compressed within a limited space, so that surface is emphasized as a two-dimensional pattern. By 1530, when Francis I of France called him to decorate the palace at Fontainebleau, Rosso had all but forsaken this early furor for more graceful, elongated forms (FIG. 18-51).

Correggio's pupil PARMIGIANINO (Girolamo Francesco Maria Mazzola, 1503–1540), in his best-known work, *Madonna with the Long Neck* (FIG. 17-43), achieves the elegance that is a principal aim of Mannerism. He smoothly combines the influences of his master and of Raphael in a picture of exquisite grace and precious sweetness. The small, oval head of the Madonna, her long, slender neck, the unbelievable length and delicacy of the hand, and the sinuous, swaying elongation of her frame—all are marks of

the aristocratic, gorgeously artificial taste of a later phase of Mannerism. Here is Leonardo distilled through Correggio. To the left is a bevy of angelic creatures, melting with emotions as soft and smooth as their limbs (the left side of the composition is quite in the manner of Correggio). To the right is a line of columns without capitals: an enigmatic setting for an enigmatic figure with a scroll, whose distance from the foreground is immeasurable and ambiguous.

The Mannerists sought a generally beautiful style that had its rules—but rules, as we have seen, that still permitted the artist the free play of his powers of invention. Thus, although all Mannerist paintings have common factors, each artist, as it were, has his recognizable signature. All the points made thus far about Mannerist composition are recognizable in *Venus, Cupid, Folly, and Time,* (or *The Exposure of Luxury,* FIG. 17-44) by BRONZINO (Agnolo di Cosimo, 1503–1572). A pupil of Pontormo, Bronzino was a Florentine and painter to Cosimo I, first Grand Duke of Tuscany. In this painting, he manifests the Mannerist fondness for extremely learned and intricate

17-43 PARMIGIANINO, *Madonna with the Long Neck, c.* 1535. Oil on wood, approx. 7' 1" × 4' 4". Galleria degli Uffizi, Florence.

17-44 BRONZINO, *Venus, Cupid, Folly, and Time (The Exposure of Luxury), c.* 1546. Oil on wood, approx. 61" × 56¾". Reproduced by courtesy of the Trustees of the National Gallery, London.

allegories that often have lascivious undertones; here, we are far from the simple and monumental statements and forms of the High Renaissance. Venus, fondled by her son Cupid, is uncovered by Time, while Folly bombards them with roses; other figures represent Hatred and Inconstancy. The masks, a favorite device of the Mannerists, symbolize falseness. The picture seems to convey that love—accompanied by its opposite, hatred, and plagued by inconstancy—is foolish, and its folly will be discovered in time. But, as in many Mannerist paintings, the meaning is ambiguous, and interpretations vary. The figures are

drawn around the front plane and almost entirely block the space, although there really is no space. The contours are strong and sculptural; the surfaces, of enamel smoothness. Of special interest are the heads, hands, and feet, for the Mannerists considered the extremities to be the carriers of grace and the clever depiction of them evidence of skill in *maniera*.

The sophisticated elegance sought by the Mannerist painter was most often achieved in portraiture, in which the Mannerists excel. Bronzino's *Portrait of a Young Man* (FIG. 17-45) is exemplary of Mannerist portraiture. The subject is a proud youth—a man of

17-45 BRONZINO, *Portrait of a Young Man, c.* 1550. Oil on wood, approx. 37⅝″ × 29½″. Metropolitan Museum of Art, New York (H.O. Havemeyer Collection, bequest of Mrs. H.O. Havemeyer, 1929).

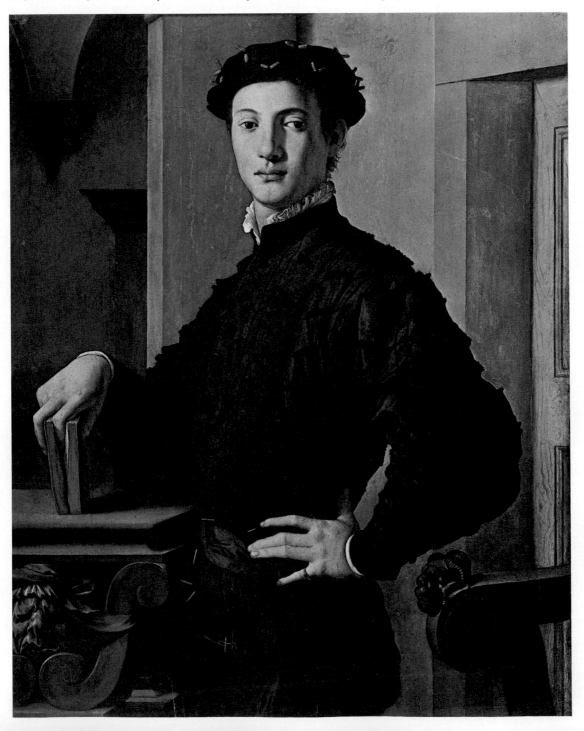

books and intellectual society, rather than a man of action or a merchant. His cool demeanor is carefully affected, a calculated attitude of nonchalance toward the observing world. This austere and incommunicative formality is standard for the Mannerist portrait. It asserts the rank and station of the subject, but not his personality. The haughty poise, the graceful, long-fingered hands, the book, the masks, the severe architecture—all suggest the traits and environment of the high-bred, disdainful patrician. The somber Spanish black of the young man's doublet and cap (this is the century of Spanish etiquette) and the slightly acid olive green walls of the room make for a deeply restrained color scheme—a muted background for the sharply defined, impassive silhouette.

In Sculpture

With Bronzino, Florentine Mannerism in painting passed its high-water mark. But a remarkable person, as Mannerist in his action as in his art, has left us, in his sculpture, the mark of the prevailing style. BENVENUTO CELLINI (1500–1571), perhaps best known for his *Autobiography*, had, to judge by that fascinating work, an awesome proficiency as an artist, statesman, soldier, lover, and many other things. He was, first of all, a goldsmith. The influence of Michelangelo led him to attempt larger works, and, in the service of Francis I, he cast in bronze the *Diana of Fontainebleau* (FIG. 17-46), which sums up Italian and French Mannerism. The figure is derived from the reclining tomb figures in the Medici Chapel (FIG. 17-27), but it exaggerates their characteristics. The head is remarkably small, the torso stretched out, and the limbs elongated. The contrapposto is more apparent than real, for it is flattened out almost into the forward plane, as Mannerist design sense dictates. This

almost abstract figure, along with Mannerist works in paintings by Rosso and others, considerably influenced the development of French Renaissance art, particularly in the school of Fontainebleau.

Italian influence, working its way into France, had strength enough to draw a brilliant, young French sculptor, Jean de Boulogne to Italy, where he practiced his art under the Italian cognomen GIOVANNI DA BOLOGNA (1529–1608). Although his quality and importance have not always been recognized, he is the most important sculptor in Italy after Michelangelo and is the stylistic link between that great master and the Baroque sculptor Gianlorenzo Bernini. Giovanni's *Rape of the Sabine Women* (FIG. 17-47) wonderfully exemplifies the Mannerist principles of figure composition and, at the same time, shows an impulse to break out of the Mannerist formulas of representation. The title was given to the group after it was raised (Giovanni probably intended to present only an interesting figure composition involving an old man, a young man, and a woman). The story, derived from mythic Roman history, tells how the Romans took wives for themselves from the neighboring Sabines. The amateurs, critics, and scholars who flocked around works of art in this age of Mannerism, naming groups in any way they found appropriate, serve to indicate how important and how valued the visual arts had become. The artist himself is learned in his sources; here, Giovanni twice adapts the *Laocoön* (FIG. 5-80) discovered early in the century—once in the figure of the crouching old man and again in the gesture of the woman with one arm flung up. The three bodies interlock on an axis, along which a spiral movement runs; significantly, the figures do not break out of this vortex but remain as if contained within a cylinder. It is necessary to walk around the sculpture to appreci-

17-46 BENVENUTO CELLINI, *Diana of Fontainebleau*, 1543–1544. Bronze, over life-size. Louvre, Paris.

17-47 GIOVANNI DA BOLOGNA, *Rape of the Sabine Women*, completed 1583. Marble, approx. 13′ 6″ high. Loggia dei Lanzi, Florence.

ate that, despite its confinement, the aspect of the group changes radically according to the point from which it is viewed. One reason is that the open spaces that pass through the masses (for example, the space between an arm and a body) have as great an effect as the solids. This is the first large-scale group composed to be seen from multiple points of view since Hellenistic sculpture, which it recalls. But, as yet, the figures do not freely reach out into space and relate to the environment. The fact that they remain "enclosed" prevents our calling them Baroque. Yet the Michelangelesque potential for action and the athletic flexibility of the figures are there. The Baroque period will see the release of the sculptured figure into full action.

In Architecture

Mannerism in painting and sculpture has been studied fairly extensively since the early decades of this century. But only in the 1930s was it discovered that the term could also be applied to much of sixteenth-century architecture. However, the corpus of Mannerist architecture that has been compiled since then is far from homogeneous and includes many works that do not really seem to fit the term "Mannerism." The fact that Michelangelo was using Classical architectural elements in a highly personal and unorthodox manner does not necessarily make him a Mannerist architect. In his designs for St. Peter's he was certainly striving for those effects of mass, balance, order, and stability that are the very hallmarks of High Renaissance design, and even some of the most unusual features in the Laurentian Library (FIG. 17-28) were dictated by structural necessity. Michelangelo never really aimed to baffle or to confuse, but this was the precise goal of GIULIO ROMANO when he designed the Palazzo del Tè, in Mantua (FIGS. 17-48 and 17-49) and, with it, formulated almost the entire architectural vocabulary of Mannerism.

Giulio Romano was born either in 1492, if we accept Vasari's suggestion, or in 1499, if we disallow the possibility of error in a document that states that he died in Mantua in 1546 at the age of 47. If we give credence to the latter birthdate, however, Giulio must have been one of the most precocious young prodigies in the history of world art, as he could then have been little more than 16 when he became Raphael's chief assistant in the decoration of the Vatican stanze. After Raphael's premature death in 1520, Giulio became his master's artistic executor by completing Raphael's unfinished frescoes and panel paintings. In 1524, Giulio went to Mantua, where he found a patron in Federigo Gonzaga, for whom he built and decorated the Palazzo del Tè between 1525 and 1535.

The Palazzo del Tè was intended to combine the functions of a suburban summer palace with those of a stud farm for the duke's famous stables. Originally planned as a relatively modest country villa, Giulio's building so pleased the duke that he soon commissioned his architect to enlarge the structure. In a second building campaign, the villa was expanded to a palatial scale by the addition of three wings, which were placed around a square central court. This once-paved court, which serves both as a passage and as the focal point of the design, has a near-urban character and, with its surrounding buildings, forms a self-enclosed unit to which a large, stable-flanked garden has been attached on the east side. The first impression of the north façade (FIG. 17-48) is that of a fairly standard Renaissance structure with rusticated walls that have been articulated with smooth Doric pilas-

17-48   Giulio Romano, north façade of the Palazzo del Tè, Mantua, Italy.

ters. Closer study reveals a number of startling departures from the Renaissance norm. Most immediately noticeable is the ambiguity of the elevation, which can be read either as a one-story or a two-story system. Other discrepancies gradually reveal themselves. The distances from the central loggia to the corners of the building are unequal; the windows are located eccentrically between pilasters; the pilasters are paired at varying distances from each other; and the voussoirs above the windows and portals are handled in a way that makes them seem to tumble outward from the building. These divergences from convention serve as an overture to a building so laden with structural surprises and contradictions that the whole becomes an enormous parody on the Classical style of Bramante. To be sure, the appreciation of the joke required a highly sophisticated audience, and the recognition of some quite subtle departures from the norm presupposed a thorough familiarity with the established rules of Classical architecture. It speaks well for the duke's sophistication that he accepted Giulio's form of architectural humor.

It has recently been claimed that the irregularities of the north façade were forced on Giulio by the need to adjust its design to the features of the already completed villa behind it. Such impediments, however, rarely kept Renaissance architects from designing regular and symmetrical façades (compare Alberti's Palazzo Rucellai; FIG. 16-39). In any case, Giulio's intent seems to be expressed clearly enough in the palace's garden façade, where the irregularly spaced arches do not have to conform to any preexisting conditions. Even more chaotic is the design of the façades that face the interior courtyard (FIG. 17-49), where keystones (central voussoirs) either have not fully settled or seem to be slipping from the arches. There, massive Tuscan columns carry incongruously narrow architraves; the latter's structural insufficiency is stressed by the fact that they break midway between the columns, evidently unable to support the weight of the triglyphs above. And if this architectural chaos does not suffice to shock the visitor, Giulio delivers the *coup de grace* in the Sala dei Giganti (FIG. 17-50). In a panoramic sequence that covers the

17-49   Giulio Romano, court façade of the Palazzo del Tè.

17-50　Giulio Romano, *The Fall of the Giants* (detail), 1532–1534. Fresco. Sala dei Giganti, Palazzo del Tè.

ceiling and all the walls of this room, Giulio has represented the destruction of the palaces of the rebellious giants by the thunder-bolt-hurling Jupiter, from which visitors cringe involuntarily as the entire universe appears to be collapsing around them in a *tour de force* of pictorial illusionism and wild Mannerist convulsion.

In short, in the Palazzo del Tè, most of the Classical rules of order, stability, and symmetry have been deliberately flouted, and every effort has been made to startle and shock the beholder. This desire to create ambiguities and tensions is as typical of Mannerist architecture as it is of Mannerist painting, and many of the devices invented by Giulio Romano for the Palazzo del Tè will become standard features in the formal repertoire of later Mannerist building.

VENICE

In the sixteenth century, Venetian art became a strong, independent, and influential school in its own right, touched, if at all, only very slightly by the fashions of Mannerism sweeping Western Europe. Venice had long been the proud maritime mistress of the Mediterranean and its coasts; as the gateway to the Orient, it "held the gorgeous east in fee; and was the safeguard of the west." At the height of its commercial and political power during the fifteenth century, Venice saw its fortunes decline in the sixteenth.

Even so, Venice and the papal state were the only Italian sovereignties to retain their independence during the century of strife; all others were reduced to dependency on either France or Spain. Although the fundamental reasons for the decline of Venice were the discoveries in the New World and the economic shift from Italy to the Hapsburg Germanies and Netherlands, other even more immediate and pressing events drained her wealth and power. Venice was constantly embattled by the Turks, who, after their conquest of Constantinople, began to contest with Venice over control of the eastern Mediterranean. Early in the century, Venice also found itself attacked by the European powers of the League of Cambrai, formed and led by Julius II, who coveted Venetian holdings on the mainland. Although this wearing, two-front war sapped its strength, Venice's vitality endured, at least long enough to overwhelm the Turks in the great sea battle of Lepanto in 1571. This time, Europe was on Venice's side.

Architecture: Sansovino and Palladio

Venice was introduced to the High Renaissance style of architecture by a Florentine called Jacopo Sansovino (Jacopo Tatti, 1486–1570). Originally trained as a sculptor under Andrea Sansovino, whose name he adopted, Jacopo went to Rome in 1518, where, under the influence of Bramante's circle, he increasingly turned toward architecture. When he arrived in Venice as a refugee from the Sack of Rome in 1527, he soon established himself as that city's leading and most admired architect; his buildings frequently inspired the architectural settings of the most prominent Venetian painters, including Titian and Veronese (FIG. 17-68).

Sansovino's largest and most rewarding public commissions were the Zecca (Mint) and the adjoining State Library (FIG. 17-51) in the heart of the island city. The Zecca, begun in 1535, faces the Canale San Marco with a stern and forbidding three-story façade; its heavy rustication gives it an intended air of strength and impregnability. This fortress-like look is emphasized by a boldly projecting, bracket-supported cornice reminiscent of the machicolated galleries of Medieval castles.

A very different spirit is expressed by the neighboring State Library of San Marco, begun a year after the Zecca, which Palladio referred to as "probably the richest and most ornate edifice since ancient times." With 21 bays (only 16 of which were completed during Sansovino's lifetime), it faces the Gothic Doge's Palace (FIG. 10-64) across the Piazzetta, a lateral extension of Venice's central Piazza San Marco. The relatively plain ground-story arcade has Doric columns attached to the arch-supporting piers in the manner of the Roman Colosseum (FIG. 6-46). It serves as a sturdy support for the higher, lighter, and much more decorative Ionic second story, which housed the reading room, with its treasure of manuscripts, safe from not-uncommon flooding. On this second level, the stern system of the ground story has been softened by the introduction of Ionic colonnettes that flank the piers and are paired in depth, rather than in the plane of the façade. Two-thirds the height of the main columns, they rise to support the springing of arches, the spans of which are two-thirds those of the lower arcade. The main columns carry an entablature with a richly decorated frieze on which, in strongly projecting relief, putti support garlands. This favorite decorative motif of the ancient Romans is punctuated by the oval windows of an attic story. Perhaps the most striking feature of the building is its roofline, where Sansovino replaces the traditional straight and unbroken cornice with a ballustrade (reminiscent of the one on Bramante's Tempietto, FIG. 17-6) interrupted by statue-bearing pedestals. The spacing of the latter corresponds to that of the orders below, so that the sculptures become the sky-piercing finials of the building's vertical design elements. The deft application of sculpture to the massive framework of the building (there are no visible walls) mitigates the potential severity of its design and gives its aspect an extraordinary plastic richness.

One feature rarely mentioned is the subtlety with which the library echoes the design of the lower two stories of the Doge's Palace (FIG. 10-64) opposite it. Although using a vastly different architectural vocabulary, Sansovino manages to adjust his building to the older one. Correspondences include the almost identical spacing of the lower arcades, the rich and decorative treatment of the second stories (including their balustrades), and the dissolution of the rooflines (by use of decorative battlements in the palace and a statue-surmounted balustrade in the library). It is almost as if Sansovino set out to translate the Gothic architecture of the Doge's Palace into a "modern" Renaissance idiom. If so, he was eminently success-

17-51 JACOPO SANSOVINO, La Zecca (Mint), 1535–1545 *(left)* and State Library, begun 1536, San Marco, Venice.

17-52 ANDREA PALLADIO, Villa Rotonda, near Vicenza, Italy, c. 1566–1570.

ful; the two buildings, although of different spiritual and stylistic worlds, mesh and combine to make the Piazzetta one of the most elegantly framed urban units in Europe.

When Jacopo Sansovino died he was succeeded as chief architect of the Venetian Republic by ANDREA PALLADIO (1508–1580). Beginning as a stonemason and decorative sculptor, Palladio, at 30, turned to architecture, the ancient literature on architecture, engineering, topography, and military science. Unlike the universal scholar, Alberti, Palladio became more of a specialist. He made several trips to Rome to study the ancient buildings at first hand. He illustrated Daniele Barbaro's edition of *Vitruvius* (1556), and he wrote his own treatise on architecture, *I quattro libri dell' architettura (Four Books on Architecture)*, originally published in 1570, which had a wide-ranging influence on succeeding generations of architects throughout Europe. Palladio's influence outside Italy, most significantly in England and in colonial America, was stronger and more lasting than that of any other architect.

Palladio is best known for his numerous villas built on the Venetian mainland, of which 19 still stand; the villas were especially influential on later architects. The same Arcadian spirit that prompted the ancient Romans to build villas in the countryside and that will be expressed so eloquently in the art of the Venetian painter Giorgione, motivated a similar villa-building boom in the sixteenth century. One can imagine that Venice, with its very limited space, must have been more congested than any ancient city. But a longing for the countryside was not the only mo-

tive; declining fortunes prompted the Venetians to develop their mainland possessions with new land investment and reclamation projects. Citizens who could afford it were encouraged to set themselves up as gentlemen farmers and to develop swamps into productive agricultural land. Wealthy families could look on their villas as providential investments. The villas were thus gentleman farms (like the much later American plantations, which were architecturally in-

17–53 ANDREA PALLADIO, plan of the Villa Rotonda, near Vicenza.

fluenced by Palladio) surrounded by service out-buildings that Palladio generally arranged in long, low wings branching out from the main building and enclosing a large, rectangular court area.

Although it is the most famous, Villa Rotonda (FIG. 17-52), near Vicenza, is not really typical of Palladio's villa style; it was not built for an aspiring gentleman farmer, but for a retired monsignor who wanted a villa for social events. Located on a hilltop, Villa Rotonda was planned and designed as a kind of belvedere, without the usual wings of secondary buildings. Its central plan (FIG. 17-53), with four identical façades and projecting porches, is therefore both sensible and functional; each of the porches can be used as a platform from which to enjoy a different view of the surrounding landscape. In this design, the central dome-covered rotunda logically functions as a kind of revolving platform, from which the visitor can turn in any direction for the preferred view. The result is a building with parts that are functional and systematically related to one another in terms of calculated mathematical relationships. Villa Rotonda, like Santa Maria della Consolazione at Todi (FIG. 17-9), thus embodies all the qualities of self-sufficiency and formal completeness of which most Renaissance architects dreamed. In his formative years, Palladio was influenced by Alberti, by Bramante, and, briefly, by Giulio Romano. By 1550, however, he had developed his own personal style, which, in its clarity and lack of ambiguity, was as different from contemporary Mannerism as it was– in its static qualities and rather dry, "correct" Classicism—different from the dynamic style of Michelangelo.

San Giorgio Maggiore (FIG. 17-54), directly across a broad canal from the Piazza San Marco, is one of the most dramatically placed buildings in Venice. Dissatisfied with earlier solutions to the problem of integrating a high central nave and lower aisles into a unified façade design, Palladio solved it by superimposing a tall, narrow, Classical porch on a low, broad one. This not only reflects the interior arrangement of the building, but also introduces the illusion of three-dimensional depth—an effect that is intensified by the strong projection of the central columns and the shadows they cast. Although at first the result seems to be a rigid formalism, the play of shadow across the building's surfaces, its reflection in the water, and its gleaming white against sea and sky create a remarkably colorful effect. The interior of the church (FIG. 17-55) is flooded with light, which crisply defines the contours of the rich wall articulations (pedestals, bases, shafts, capitals, entablatures), all beautifully and "correctly" profiled—the exemplar of what Classical architectural theory means by "rational" organization.

17-54 ANDREA PALLADIO, west façade of San Giorgio Maggiore, Venice, 1565.

17-55 ANDREA PALLADIO, interior of San Giorgio Maggiore (view facing east).

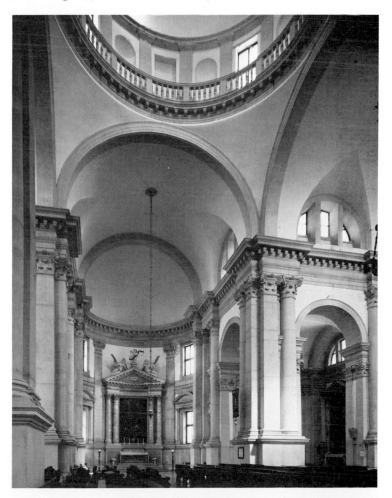

Painting: Giovanni Bellini and Giorgione

The soft, colored light of Venice, which relaxes the severe lines of Palladio's architecture, lives at its fullest in Venetian painting. In the career of GIOVANNI BELLINI (c. 1430–1516), we find the history of that style. In his long productive life, Bellini, always alert to what was new, never ceased to develop artistically and, almost by himself, created what is known as the Venetian style, which will be so important to the subsequent course of painting. Trained in the tradition of the International style by his father, a student of Gentile da Fabriano, Bellini worked in the family shop and did not develop his own style until after his father's death in 1470. His early independent works show him to be under the dominant influence of his brother-in-law, Andrea Mantegna. But in the late 1470s, impressed by the possibilities offered by the new oil technique that Antonello da Messina (FIG. 16-67) introduced during a visit to Venice, Bellini abandoned the Paduan's harsh, linear style and developed a sensuous, coloristic manner that was to become characteristic of Venetian painting.

Bellini is best known for his many Madonnas, which he painted both in half-length (with or without accompanying saints) on small devotional panels and on large, monumental altarpieces of the *sacra conversazione* type (FIG. 16-32). Judging by what appears to have been an unending string of commissions, his half-length Madonnas were especially popular. More than 80 of these are still extant, and, if arranged chronologically, they provide an almost gapless overview of the painter's artistic development. Our example, *Madonna of the Trees* (FIG. 17-56) dates from 1487 (a year or two after Bellini's adoption of the oil technique) and stands about halfway between his early linear, Mantegnesque approach and the fully developed, painterly style of his later years.* Placed before a wide strip of green satin, the grave and pensive Madonna steadies her child's uneasy pose, her somber expression suggesting foreknowledge of the infant's eventual fate. Although firmly modeled, the forms are softly rounded and, combined with warm and luminous colors, instill the painting with a quality of subdued voluptuousness that will become a trademark of much of later Venetian painting.

Despite the large number of similar works he painted, Bellini never repeated himself and always found some new variation on his Madonna theme. In most of his versions, the Madonna is placed behind a low parapet and, quite often, before a hanging drapery—devices that detach without completely isolat-

*The painting suffered some damage during restoration in 1902, when the Madonna's veil was repainted in a style that does not conform with that of the rest of the painting.

17–56   GIOVANNI BELLINI , *Madonna of the Trees, c.* 1487. Oil on wood, 29″ × 22″. Galleria dell' Accademia, Venice.

ing the sacred subject from its worldly surroundings. The Christ child is shown standing or sitting on the parapet, cradled in the Madonna's arms, or seated on her lap; he is shown facing his mother or the viewer. At times, the drapery in back of the figures is moved off-center and its width is varied to show more or less of the background landscape. The drapery may extend into the picture from either the left or the right frame to permit a view into the distance on one side only, creating the kind of asymmetrical composition that will enjoy great favor with Bellini's most illustrious student, Titian. After 1500, the landscape backgrounds become more and more important, to the point that the artist often omits the middle-ground drapery and sometimes changes his format from vertical to horizontal to show a greater expanse of landscape behind his Madonnas—landscapes that take on an increasingly Arcadian character.

If the long series of Bellini's half-length Madonnas reveals the gradual change in his painting style, two of his large altarpieces—the *San Giobbe Altarpiece, c.* 1490 (FIG. 17-57), and the *San Zaccaria Altarpiece,* 1505 (FIG. 17-58)—illustrate not only two stages in the artist's stunning development but also the essential differences between the Early and the High Renaissance treatments of the same subject. In the earlier work, The *San Giobbe Altarpiece* (FIG. 17-57), although the space is large, airy, and clearly defined, the figures seem to be crowded; they cling to the foreground plane and are seen in a slightly forced, Man-

17-57 GIOVANNI BELLINI, *San Giobbe Altarpiece*, c. 1490. Oil on wood, 15' 4" × 8' 4". Galleria dell' Accademia, Venice

17-58 GIOVANNI BELLINI, *San Zaccaria Altarpiece*, 1505. Oil on wood transferred to canvas, approx. 16' 5" × 7' 9". San Zaccaria, Venice.

tegnesque, "worm's eye" perspective. The drawing remains sharp and precise, particularly in that charming Venetian trademark, the group of angel–musicians at the foot of the Madonna's throne. The figures are already arranged in the pyramidal grouping preferred by the High Renaissance, but they tend to exist as individuals rather than as parts of an integrated whole. Seen by itself, the *San Giobbe Altarpiece* is an orderly, well-balanced painting that can hold its own with any produced during the Early Renaissance. But side by side with the subsequent *San Zaccaria Altarpiece* (FIG. 17-58), it suddenly seems cluttered and overly busy. By adding simplicity to the order, balance, and clarity of the earlier painting, Bellini takes the long step into the High Renaissance.

In the *San Zaccaria Altarpiece*, in contrast to his earlier treatment of the theme, Bellini raises the observer's viewpoint and deemphasizes the perspective. The number of figures is reduced, and they are more closely integrated with each other and with the space that surrounds them. Combined into a single, cohesive group, the figures no longer cling to the front of the painting; disposed in depth, they now move in

and out of the apse instead of standing before it. Their attitudes produce a rhythmic movement within the group, but all obvious gestures have been eliminated and former busyness has changed to serene calm. In addition, Bellini's method of painting has become softer and more luminous. Line is no longer the chief agent of form but has been submerged in a sea of glowing color—a soft radiance that envelops the forms with an atmospheric haze and enhances their majestic serenity.

The San Zaccaria Madonna is the mature work of an old man who, in a single lifetime, spanned the development that took three generations in Florence. Departing from the Gothic, Bellini moved through the Early Renaissance and arrived in the High Renaissance even before Raphael and Michelangelo. And, at the very end of his long life, this astonishingly apt artist was still willing and able to make changes in his style and approach to keep himself abreast of his times; he began to deal with pagan subjects.

The Feast of the Gods (FIG. 17-59) represents a feed-back of influence from one of Bellini's own students, Giorgione, who developed his master's landscape

17-59   GIOVANNI BELLINI (and TITIAN ?), *The Feast of the Gods*, 1514. Oil on canvas, approx. 5′ 7″ × 6′ 2″. National Gallery of Art, Washington, D.C. (Widener Collection).

backgrounds into poetic, Arcadian reveries. (In this case, Titian, another of Bellini's pupils, probably completed the right background.) After Giorgione's premature death, Bellini embraced his student's interests and, in *The Feast of the Gods*, developed a new kind of mythology in which the Olympian gods appear as peasants enjoying a heavenly picnic in a shady northern Italian glade. His source is Ovid's *Fasti*, which describes a banquet of the gods. The figures are spread across the foreground. Satyrs attend the gods, nymphs bring jugs of wine, a child draws from a keg, couples engage in love play, and the sleeping nymph at the right receives amorous atten-

tion. The mellow light of a long afternoon glows softly around the gathering, touching the surfaces of colorful draperies, smooth flesh, and polished metal. Here, Bellini announces the delight the Venetian School will take in the beauty of texture revealed by the full resources of gently and subtly harmonized color. Behind the warm, lush tones of the figures, a background of cool, green, tree-filled glades reaches into the distance; at the right, a screen of trees makes a verdant shelter. The atmosphere is idyllic, a floral countryside making a setting for the never-ending pleasure of the immortal gods. The poetry of Greece and Rome, as well as that of the Renaissance, is filled with this pastoral mood, and the Venetians make a specialty of its representation. Its elements include the smiling landscape, eternal youth, and song and revelry, always with a touch of the sensual.

Thus, with Bellini, Venetian art becomes the great complement of the schools of Florence and Rome. The Venetians' instrument is color; that of the Florentines and Romans, sculpturesque form. These two schools run parallel—sometimes touching and engaging—through the history of Western art from the Renaissance on. Their themes are different. Venice paints the poetry of the senses and delights in the beauty of nature and the pleasures of mankind. Florence and Rome attempt the sterner, intellectual themes—the epic of man, the masculine virtues, the grandeur of the ideal, the lofty conceptions of religion as they involve the heroic and the sublime. The history of later Western art can be broadly understood as a dialogue between these two traditions.

The inspiration for Bellini's late Arcadianism is to be found in paintings like the so-called *Pastoral Sym-*

phony (FIG. 17-60) by his illustrious student GIORGIONE (Giorgione da Castelfranco, 1478–1510), a work held by some to be an early Titian. Out of dense color shadow emerge the soft forms of figures and landscape. The theme is as mysterious as the light. Two nude females, accompanied by two clothed young men, occupy the rich, abundant landscape through which a shepherd passes; in the distance, a villa crowns a hill. The pastoral mood is so eloquently evoked here that we need not know (as we do not) the precise meaning of the picture; the mood is enough. The shepherd is symbolic of the poet; the pipes and the lute, of his poetry. The two nymphs accompanying the young men may be thought of as their invisible inspiration, their muses, one turns to lift water from the sacred well of poetic inspiration. The great, golden bodies of the nymphs, softly modulated by the smoky shadow, become the standard Venetian type. It is the Venetian School that resurrects the Venus figure from antiquity, making her the fecund goddess of nature and of love. The full opu-

17-60 GIORGIONE (and/or TITIAN ?), *Pastoral Symphony*, c. 1508. Oil on canvas, approx. 43″ × 54″. Louvre, Paris.

lence of the figures should, of course, not be read according to modern preferences in womanly physique but as poetic personifications of the abundance of nature. Giorgione—himself a pastoral poet in the pictorial medium and one of the greatest masters in the handling of light and color—praises the beauty of nature, music, woman, and pleasure. Vasari reports that Giorgione was an accomplished lutist and singer, and adjectives from poetry and music seem best suited to describe the pastoral air and muted chords of his painting. He casts a mood of tranquil revery and dreaminess over the whole scene, evoking the landscape of a lost but never forgotten paradise. Arcadia and its happy creatures persist in the subconscious memory and longing of mankind. Among the Italians, the Venetians were the first to express a love of nature and a realization of its potentialities for the painter, although they never represent it except as inhabited by man. The ancient spirits, the deities of field and woodland, still inhabit it too, and landscape—manifesting the bounty of Venus and sanctified by her beauty—as yet simply provides the inspiring setting for the poet, without whom it would be incomplete.

Titian

Giorgione's Arcadianism passed not only to his much older yet constantly learning master, Bellini, but also to Tiziano Vecelli, whose name we anglicize into TITIAN (c. 1490–1576). Titian is the most prodigious and prolific of the great Venetian painters. He is among the very greatest painters of the Western world—a supreme colorist and, in a broad sense, the father of the modern mode of painting. An important change that took place in Titian's time was the almost universal adoption of canvas, with its rough-textured surface, in place of wood panels for paintings. It is the painting of Titian that establishes oil color on canvas as the typical medium of our pictorial tradition.

According to a contemporary of Titian, Palma Giovane:

. . . Titian [employed] a great mass of colors, which served . . . as a base for whatever he was going to paint over it . . . I myself have seen his determined brushstrokes laden with color, sometimes a streak of pure earth-red which served him (one might say) as a half-tone, other times with a brushstroke of white lead; and with the same brush colored with a red, black, and yellow, he formed a highlight; and with these rules of technique made the promise of an excellent figure appear in four brushstrokes.

After having laid these important foundations, he then used to turn the pictures to the wall, and leave them—sometimes for as long as several months—without looking at them; and when he wanted to apply his brush to them again, he [examined] them most rigorously . . . whether he could find any defects in them or discover anything which would not be in harmony with the delicacy of his intentions. . . . Working thus, and redesigning his figures, Titian brought them into a perfect symmetry which could represent the beauty of Art as well as of Nature. After this was done, he put his hand to some other picture until the first was dry, working in the same way with this other; thus gradually he covered those quintessential outlines of his figures with living flesh . . . . He never painted a figure all at once, and used to say that he who improvises his song can form neither learned nor well-turned verses. But the final polish . . . was to unite now and then by a touch of his fingers the extremes of the light areas, so that they became almost half-tints . . . at other times, with a stroke he would place a dark streak in a corner; to reinforce it he would add a streak of red, like a drop of blood. . . . in the final phase [he] painted more with his fingers than with his brushes.

Trained by both Bellini and Giorgione, Titian learned so well from them that there is still no general agreement as to the degree of his participation in their later works. He completed several of Bellini's and Giorgione's unfinished works. One of his own

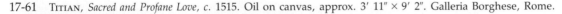

17-61   TITIAN, *Sacred and Profane Love, c.* 1515. Oil on canvas, approx. 3′ 11″ × 9′ 2″. Galleria Borghese, Rome.

early works, *Sacred and Profane Love* (FIG. 17-61), is very much in the manner of Giorgione, with its Arcadian setting, its allegory, and its complex and enigmatic meaning. Two young women—one draped, the other nude—flank a sarcophagus into which a cupid reaches. Immediately behind them is a screen of trees and, to left and right, deep vistas into different landscapes. The two figures may represent the different levels of Neo-Platonic love: the sumptuously draped woman, a kind of allegory of vanity and the love of this world; the nude who holds aloft her lamp, the highest level of love that can be reached (love of the divine, nudity being symbolic of truth). Titian's figures are not suffused with Giorgione's glowing, mysterious tones; they are firmly drawn and boldly and brilliantly colored, and the artist manifests his chief interest in the play of light over the

17-62   TITIAN, *Madonna of the Pesaro Family,* 1519–1526. Oil on canvas, approx. 16' × 9'. Santa Maria dei Frari, Venice.

rich satins and the smooth volumes of the body and glossy flesh. The world given to the eye is a world of color before it is a world of solid forms. And it is this truth that the Venetians were the first to grasp.

On the death of Giovanni Bellini in 1516, Titian was appointed painter to the republic of Venice. Shortly thereafter, he painted the *Madonna of the Pesaro Family* (FIG. 17-62) for the church of the Frari. This great work, which furthered the reputation and established the personal style of Titian, was presented to the church by Jacopo Pesaro, Bishop of Paphos in Cyprus and commander of the papal fleet, in thanksgiving for a successful expedition in 1502 against the Turks during the Venetian–Turkish war. In a stately, sunlit setting, the Madonna receives the commander, who kneels at the foot of her throne. A soldier (St. George?) behind the commander carries a banner with the arms of the Borgia (Pope Alexander VI); behind him is a turbaned Turk, a captive of the Christian forces. St. Peter occupies the steps of the throne, and St. Francis introduces other members of the Pesaro family, who kneel solemnly in the right foreground. The massing of monumental figures, singly and in groups, within a weighty and majestic architecture is, as we have seen, characteristic of the High Renaissance. But Titian does not compose a horizontal and symmetrical arrangement, as does Leonardo in *The Last Supper* (FIG. 17-3) or Raphael in *The School of Athens* (FIG. 17-17). Rather, he places the figures in occult balance on a steep diagonal, positioning the Madonna, the focus of the composition, well off the central axis. Attention is directed to her by the perspective lines, by the inclination of the figures, and by the directional lines of gaze and gesture. The design is beautifully brought into poise by the banner that inclines toward the left, balancing the rightward and upward tendencies of the main direction. This kind of composition is more dynamic than what we have seen so far in the High Renaissance. The forces already moving in it promise a new kind of pictorial design—one built on movement rather than rest. In his rendering of the rich surface textures, Titian gives a dazzling display of color in all its nuances. The human—especially the Venetian—scene is one with the heavenly, as the Madonna and saints find themselves honoring the achievements of particular men in this particular world. A quite worldly transaction is taking place between a queen, her court, and her loyal servants; the tableau is constructed in terms of Renaissance protocol and courtly splendor.

As Praxiteles brought the motif of the feminine nude into ancient Greek art, so Giorgione and Titian re-create it for the art of the modern West. In 1538, at the height of his powers, Titian painted for the Duke of Urbino the *Venus of Urbino* (FIG. 17-63), which gives us the compositional essentials for the representation

17-63　TITIAN, *Venus of Urbino*, 1538. Oil on canvas, approx. 48″ × 66″. Galleria degli Uffizi, Florence.

of a theme that will be popular for centuries. His version, based on an earlier and pioneering one painted by Giorgione, was to become official for paintings of the reclining nude, no matter how many variations would ensue. Venus reclines on a gentle slope made by her luxurious, pillowed couch, the linear play of the draperies contrasting with the sleek, continuous volume of her body. At her feet is a pendant (balancing) figure—in this case, a slumbering lapdog. Behind her, a simple drape serves both to place her figure emphatically in the foreground and to press a vista into the background at the right half of the picture. In the vista, two servants bend over a chest; beyond them, a smaller vista opens into a landscape. The steps backward into space and the division of the space into progressively smaller units are beautifully contrived. All of the resources of pictorial representation are in Titian's hands, and he uses them here to create original and exquisite effects.

Deep Venetian reds set off against the pale, neutral whites of the linen and the warm ivory–gold of the flesh are echoed in the red tones of the matron's skirt, the muted reds of the tapestries, and the neutral whites of the matron's sleeves and the gown of the kneeling girl. One must study the picture carefully to realize what subtlety of color planning is responsible, for example, for the placing of the two deep reds (in the foreground cushions and in the background skirt) that function so importantly in the composition as a gauge of distance and as terminals of an implied diagonal opposed to the real one of the reclining figure. Here, color is used not simply for the tinting of preexisting forms but as a means of organization that determines the placement of forms.

Titian could paint a Virgin Mary or a nude Venus with equal zeal. Neither he nor the connoisseurs of his time were aware of any contradiction. Yet it is significant that the female nude reappears in Western art as Venus, the great goddess of the ancient world, whom Medieval Christianity had especially feared

17-64 TITIAN, *Man with the Glove*, c. 1519. Oil on canvas, approx. 39″ × 35″. Louvre, Paris.

and whom it damned in exalting virginity and chastity as virtues. Now Venus returns, and the great Venetian paintings of her almost constitute pagan altarpieces. The Venetian Renaissance resurrects a formidable competitor for the saints.

Titian was not only a prolific painter of mythological and religious subjects but also a highly esteemed portraitist, and one of the very best. Of the well over 50 portraits by his hand to survive, an early example, *Man with the Glove* (FIG. 17-64), must suffice to illustrate his style. The portrait is a trifle more than half-length. The head is turned slightly away from the observer; the right hand gathers the drapery of a mantle, and the gloved left hand holds another glove. The blade-shaped shirt-front directs attention to the right hand; the subject's gaze controls the left. These dexterous compositional arrangements, creating a kind of "three-spot" relationship among head and hands, had already been made by Leonardo in his *Mona Lisa* (FIG. 17-4). A Titian portrait, as well as many of the Venetian and subsequent schools, generally makes much of the psychological reading of the most expressive parts of the body—the head and the hands. We are not immediately aware that these subtle placements influence our response to the portrait subject. In fact, a portrait must be as skillfully composed as a great figure composition. The mood of this portrait is Giorgionesque—one of dreamy preoccupation. The eyes turn away from us, as if, in conversation, the subject has recalled something that sets him musing in silence. Titian's *Man with the Glove* is as much the portrait of a cultivated state of mind as of a

particular individual. It is the meditative, poetic youth, who is at the same time Baldassare Castiglione's ideal courtier, perfectly poised and self-assured, handsome, gallant, debonair, the "glass of fashion and the mold of form." No portrait gives us so much of the Renaissance manner in a single individual, unless it be Raphael's *Castiglione* (FIG. 17-19).

Honor and glory attached to Titian as he grew older. He was known to and sought after by all the great of Europe. He was painter to and close friend of Emperor Charles V, who made him a knight of the Holy Roman Empire; afterward, he painted numerous pictures for Charles's son, Philip II of Spain. The great Hapsburg painting collections centered around Titian's works, and his fame and wealth recall the success of Raphael. Toward the end of his life, his work became increasingly introspective, and a religious picture like the *Christ Crowned with Thorns* (FIG. 17-65) seems to be a sincerely devotional theme repudiating the paganism of the artist's prime. In this picture, Titian shows Christ tormented by the soldiers of Pilate, who twist a wreath of thorns around his head. The drama is achieved by the limited num-

17-65 TITIAN, *Christ Crowned with Thorns*, c. 1573–1575. Oil on canvas, approx. 9′ × 6′. Alte Pinakothek, Munich.

ber of figures, the concentration on the figure of Christ, and the muted, flickering light that centers the action. The color scheme is almost monochromatic; the light and color play freely within and beyond the contours, making a patchy, confused mixture of lights and darks, in which it is difficult to read the forms with precision. But this only enhances the mystery, the gloomy environment, and the mood of torment. Titian's intention is not so much to stage the event as to present his religious and personal response to it. His very brushstroke—broad, thick, and freely applied—bespeaks the directness of his approach. It melts and scatters solid form to produce the wavering, supernatural glow that encircles spiritual vision. Here Titian's art looks forward to the painting of Rembrandt in the next century.

Tintoretto and Veronese

TINTORETTO (Jacopo Robusti, 1518–1594), claimed to be a student of Titian and aspired to combine the color of Titian with the drawing of Michelangelo. He is usually referred to as the outstanding Venetian representative of Mannerism. He adopts many Mannerist pictorial devices, but his dramatic power, depth of spiritual vision, and glowing Venetian color schemes do not seem to fit the Mannerist mold. We need not settle here the question of whether or not Tintoretto is a Mannerist; we need only mention that he shares some common characteristics with central Italian Mannerism and that, in other respects, he really looks forward to the Baroque. The art of Tintoretto is always extremely dramatic. In his *Miracle of the Slave* (FIG. 17-66), we find some of his typical stageplay. St. Mark hurtles downward to the assistance of a Christian slave, who is about to be martyred for the faith, and shatters the instruments of torture. These are held up by the executioner to the startled judge as the throng around the central action stares. The dynamism of Titian is greatly accelerated, and the composition is made up of contrary and opposing motions; for any figure leaning in one direction, there is another to counter it. At the extreme left a group—two men, a woman, and a child—winds contrapuntally about a column, resembling the later Mannerist twisting of Giovanni da Bologna's *Rape of the Sabine Women* (FIG. 17-47). The main group curves deeply back into space. But the most dynamic touch of all is made by the central trio of the slave, the executioner, and the inverted St. Mark. The three figures sweep together in a great, upward, serpentine curve, the motion of which is checked by the plunging figure of St. Mark, moving in the opposite direction. The entire composition is a kind of counterpoint of motion characteris-

17-66 TINTORETTO, *The Miracle of the Slave*, 1548. Oil on canvas, approx. 14' × 18'. Galleria dell' Accademia, Venice.

tic of Mannerism. The motion, however, is firmly contained within the picture frame, and the robustness of the figures, their solid structure and firm movement, the clearly composed space, and the coherent action have little that is Manneristic. There is nothing hesitant or ambiguous in the depiction of the miraculous event, which is dramatized forcefully and with conviction. Tintoretto's skillful theatricality and sweeping power of execution set him apart from the Mannerists and make him a forerunner of the Baroque, the age of theater and opera. And the tonality—the deep golds, reds, and greens—is purely Venetian.

Toward the end of his life, Tintoretto's art, like Titian's, becomes spiritual, even visionary, as solid forms melt away into swirling clouds of dark, shot through with fitful light. In Tintoretto's *Last Supper* (FIG. 17-67), painted for Palladio's church of San Giorgio Maggiore (FIG. 17-55), the actors take part in a ghostly drama; they are as insubstantial as the shadows cast by the faint glow of their halos and the flame of a single lamp that seems to breed phosphorescent spirits. All are moved by an intense, psychic commotion. The space speeds away into an unearthly darkness peopled by phantoms. Only the incandescent nimbus around his head identifies Jesus as he administers the Sacrament to his disciples. The contrast with Leonardo's *Last Supper* (FIG. 17-3) is both extreme and instructive. Leonardo's composition, balanced and symmetrical, parallels the picture plane in a geometrically organized and closed space; Christ's figure is the tranquil center of the drama and the focus of the perspective. In Tintoretto's painting, Christ is above and beyond the converging perspective lines that race diagonally away from the picture surface, creating disturbing effects of limitless depth and motion. Tintoretto's Christ is located by light flaring beacon-like out of darkness; Leonardo's, by geometric and perspectival centralization. The contrast of the two expresses the direction Renaissance painting takes in the sixteenth century, as it moves away from architectonic clarity of space and neutral lighting toward the dynamic perspectives and dramatic chiaroscuro of the coming Baroque.

17-67 TINTORETTO, *The Last Supper*, 1594. Oil on canvas, 12′ × 18′ 8″. San Giorgio Maggiore, Venice.

The last of the great Venetian masters was VERONESE (Paolo Cagliari, 1528–1588). Where Tintoretto glories in monumental drama and deep perspectives, Veronese specializes in splendid pageantry painted in superb color and set within a majestic, Classical architecture. Like Tintoretto, Veronese painted on a huge scale, with canvases often as large as 20 by 30 feet. His usual subjects, painted for the refectories of wealthy monasteries, afforded him an opportunity to display magnificent companies at table. *Christ in the House of Levi* (FIG. 17-68), originally called *The Last Supper*, is a good example. Here, in a great open loggia framed by three monumental arches (the style of the architecture closely resembles the upper arcades of Jacopo Sansovino's library; FIG. 17-51), Christ is seen seated at the center of splendidly garbed grandees of Venice, while with a courtly gesture, the very image of gracious grandeur, the chief steward welcomes guests. The spacious loggia is crowded not only with robed magnificoes but with their colorful retainers, clowns, dogs, and dwarfs. The Holy Office of the Inquisition accused Veronese of impiety in painting such creatures so close to the Lord, and he was ordered to make changes at his own expense. Reluctant to do so, he simply changed the painting's title, converting the subject to a less solemn one. As Palladio looks to the example of the Classical architecture of the High Renaissance, so Veronese returns to High Renaissance composition, its symmetrical balance, and its ordered architectonics. His shimmering color is drawn from the whole spectrum, although he avoids solid colors for half shades (light blues, sea greens, lemon yellows, roses, and violets), creating veritable flower beds of tone.

Tintoretto and Veronese were employed by the republic of Venice to decorate the grand chambers and council rooms of the Doge's Palace. A great and popular decorator, Veronese shows himself to be a master of imposing, illusionistic ceiling compositions like *The Triumph of Venice* (FIG. 17-69), where within an oval frame, he presents Venice, crowned by Fame, enthroned between two great, twisted columns in a balustraded loggia, garlanded with clouds, and attended by figures symbolic of her glories. This work represents one of the very first modern, pictorial glorifications of a state—a subject that will become very popular during the Baroque period. Veronese's perspective is not, like Mantegna's or Correggio's, projected directly up from below; rather, it is a projection of the scene at a 45° angle to the spectator, a technique that will be used by many later Baroque decorators, particularly the Venetian Tiepolo in the eighteenth century.

It is fitting that we close our discussion of Italian art in the sixteenth century with a scene of triumph, for indeed the century witnessed the triumph of architecture, sculpture, and painting. They achieve the status of fine arts, and a tradition is established by these masters of prodigious genius, whose works inspire all artists who follow but never surpass them.

17-68 VERONESE, *Christ in the House of Levi*, 1573. Oil on canvas, approx. 18′ 6″ × 42′ 6″.
Galleria dell' Accademia, Venice.

17-69 VERONESE, *The Triumph of Venice, c.* 1585. Oil on canvas. Ceiling of the Doge's Palace, Venice.

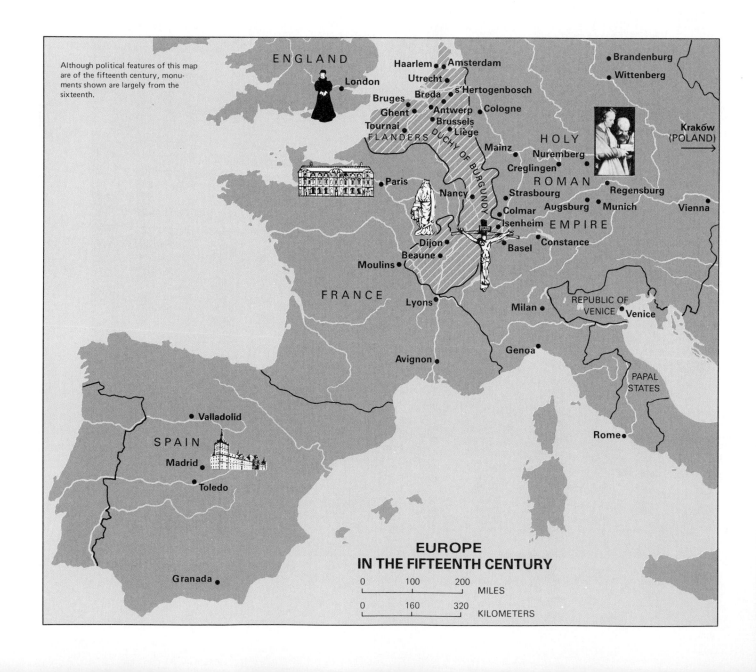

Although political features of this map are of the fifteenth century, monuments shown are largely from the sixteenth.

ENGLAND

London

Haarlem Amsterdam
Utrecht
Breda s'Hertogenbosch
Bruges
Ghent Antwerp Cologne
Brussels
Tournai Liège
FLANDERS DUCHY OF BURGUNDY
Mainz

Brandenburg
Wittenberg

HOLY

Krakôw
(POLAND)

Paris Nuremberg
Creglingen
ROMAN
Nancy Regensburg
Strasbourg
Colmar Augsburg Munich
Isenheim EMPIRE Vienna
Dijon Basel Constance
Beaune
Moulins

FRANCE Lyons

REPUBLIC OF
VENICE
Milan Venice

Avignon Genoa

PAPAL
STATES

Valladolid

Rome

SPAIN

Madrid
Toledo

Granada

**EUROPE
IN THE FIFTEENTH CENTURY**

0   100   200
MILES

0   160   320
KILOMETERS

THE RENAISSANCE OUTSIDE OF ITALY

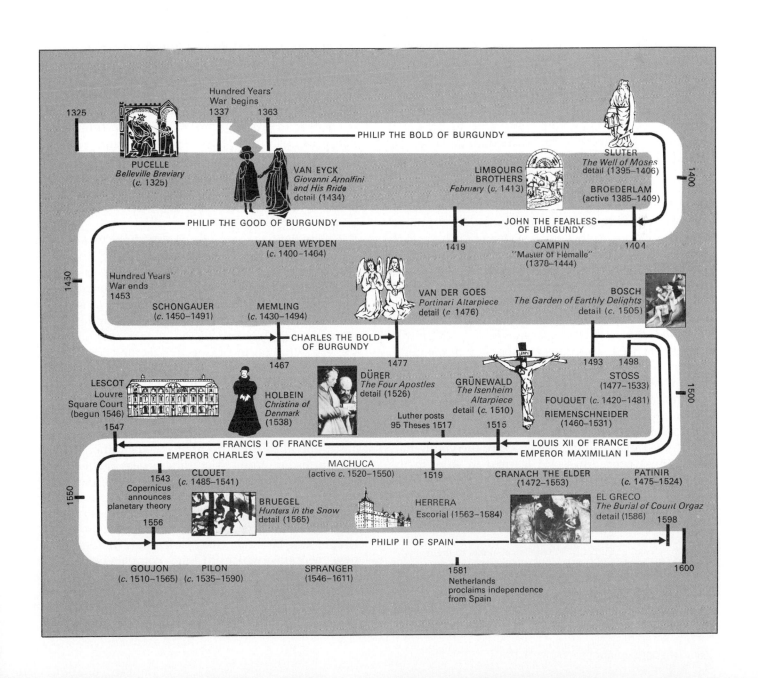

1325

Hundred Years'
War begins
1337   1363

PHILIP THE BOLD OF BURGUNDY

SLUTER
The Well of Moses
detail (1395–1406)

PUCELLE
Belleville Breviary
(*c.* 1325)

VAN EYCK
*Giovanni Arnolfini
and His Bride*
detail (1434)

LIMBOURG
BROTHERS
February (*c.* 1413)

BROEDERLAM
(active 1385–1409)

1400

PHILIP THE GOOD OF BURGUNDY

JOHN THE FEARLESS
OF BURGUNDY

VAN DER WEYDEN
(*c.* 1400–1464)

1419

CAMPIN
"Master of Flémalle"
(1378–1444)

1404

1430

Hundred Years'
War ends
1453

SCHONGAUER
(*c.* 1450–1491)

MEMLING
(*c.* 1430–1494)

VAN DER GOES
Portinari Altarpiece
detail (*c.* 1476)

BOSCH
The Garden of Earthly Delights
detail (*c.* 1505)

CHARLES THE BOLD
OF BURGUNDY

1467

1477

1493   1498

STOSS
(1477–1533)

LESCOT
Louvre
Square Court
(begun 1546)

HOLBEIN
*Christina of
Denmark*
(1538)

DÜRER
The Four Apostles
detail (1526)

GRÜNEWALD
*The Isenheim
Altarpiece*
detail (*c.* 1510)

FOUQUET (*c.* 1420–1481)

RIEMENSCHNEIDER
(1460–1531)

1500

Luther posts
95 Theses 1517

1515

1547

FRANCIS I OF FRANCE

LOUIS XII OF FRANCE

EMPEROR CHARLES V

EMPEROR MAXIMILIAN I

MACHUCA
(active *c.* 1520–1550)

1519

1543
Copernicus
announces
planetary theory

CLOUET
(*c.* 1485–1541)

CRANACH THE ELDER
(1472–1553)

PATINIR
(*c.* 1475–1524)

1550

BRUEGEL
Hunters in the Snow
detail (1565)

HERRERA
Escorial (1563–1584)

EL GRECO
The Burial of Count Orgaz
detail (1586)

1556

1598

PHILIP II OF SPAIN

1600

GOUJON
(*c.* 1510–1565)

PILON
(*c.* 1535–1590)

SPRANGER
(1546–1611)

1581
Netherlands
proclaims independence
from Spain

WHILE THE GREAT artistic events were happening in Renaissance Italy, the lands beyond the Alps were still immersed in the Gothic style that Italy had never really accepted as its own.* Gothicism in architecture persisted well into the sixteenth century in the north, although in the fifteenth century we find the stirring of new artistic forces in sculpture and painting. The north never knew Classical antiquity as the Italians knew it. In Italy, the remains of the Classical world were everywhere, and the Italians believed themselves to be descendants of the ancient Romans. The Gothic International style of the fourteenth century was, for the Italians, only a passing fashion; coming between Giotto and Masaccio, it hardly constitutes more than a brief interruption of a new stylistic movement that will carry along with it the future of European art. In the north, too, the International style will pass, giving way to a powerful realism, which, even without the inspiration of the Classical antique style, will break with the past and point directions of its own.

The northern painter, evolving out of the illuminator, finds, as did the artist in Italy, a new prestige and place. Although coexisting with a development of commerce and wealth almost modern in tone, the social structure of the north in the fifteenth century adhered to the hierarchies of the Middle Ages. The nobles and clergy continued to rule, although the true source of wealth and power was the bourgeoisie. This large middle class, in turn, was still organized and controlled by the guild system that had taken form in the Middle Ages. In the north, the guild dominated the life of the average man to an even greater extent than in Italy. To pursue a craft, a man had to belong to the guild controlling that craft—the painter, for example, to the Guild of St. Luke, which included the saddlers, glassworkers, and mirrorworkers as well. To secure membership in the guild, the aspiring painter was apprenticed in boyhood to a master, with whom he lived as a son and who taught him the fundamentals of his craft: how to make implements; how to prepare panels with gesso (plaster mixed with a binding material); and how to mix colors, oils, and varnishes. Once the youth mastered these procedures and learned to work in the traditional manner of his master, he usually spent several years working as a journeyman in various cities, observing and gaining ideas from other masters.

*Strictly speaking, the term "Renaissance" refers to the revival of ancient Roman ideals and forms in Italian art of the fifteenth century and later and really does not apply to the still Gothic European art outside Italy, where no such revival took place. Nevertheless, strikingly new and promising developments in the Late Gothic centuries contemporaneous with classicizing Italian art invite the use of the term, and it now has wide currency.

He was then eligible to become a master and was admitted to the guild. Through the guild, he obtained commissions; the guild inspected his painting for honest materials and workmanship and secured him adequate payment. The result was the solid craftsmanship that characterizes the best work of Flanders as well as of Italy.

This craftsmanship involved mastery of the new oil medium, which had such great influence on Venetian painters at the end of the fifteenth century; we have spoken of Titian's management of it (p. 646). Traditionally, Jan van Eyck is credited with the invention of oil painting a century before Titian, although the facts surrounding its early history still remain mysterious. Flemish painters built up their pictures by superimposing translucent paint layers, called *glazes*, on a layer of opaque monochrome underpainting, which in turn had been built up from a carefully planned drawing made on a white-grounded panel of wood. The base of the binding medium for the pigments was a fast-drying oil that had been known and used by certain painters in the Late Middle Ages. The secret of the new technique appears to have been an unidentified supplement to the usual composition of the glazes. With the new medium, painters were able to create richer colors, seemingly lit from within, than had previously been possible. As a result, northern painting of the fifteenth century is characterized by a deep, intense tonality, glowing light, and hard, enamel-like surfaces, quite unlike the high-keyed color, sharp light, and rather matte surfaces of Italian tempera.

The brilliant and versatile new medium was exactly right for the formal intentions of the northern painters, who aimed for sharply focused, hard-edged, sparkling clarity of detail in the representation of thousands of objects ranging in scale from large to almost invisible. The Italians were interested primarily in the *structure* behind the appearances given to the eye—that is, in perspective, composition, anatomy, the mechanics of bodily motion, and proportion through measure. The northern painters were intent on rendering the *appearances* themselves—the bright, colored surfaces of things touched by light. Their tradition of stained glass and miniatures made their realism one of radiant, decorative color rather than of sculpturesque form. The differences between the painting of Italy and of northern Europe are emphasized by the fact that, when oil painting spread to Italy after the mid-century, it did not radically affect Italian sensibility to form. Although the color of Italian painting became richer, particularly in Venice, the new medium—which, in time, completely replaced tempera—was exploited in the service of the structural purposes of Italian art. On the whole, until the early sixteenth century, artistic communication between northern and southern Europe seems to have been limited to a relatively few individuals, and both areas tended to develop independently of each other.

The political background against which the development of northern art took place in the fifteenth century was not unlike that of Italy. The commercial free cities that dominated the political scene at the beginning of the fifteenth century gradually fell under the rule of princes until the beginning of the sixteenth century, which saw the emergence of powerful states—France, England, and the Hapsburg empire, comprising Spain, the Germanies, and the Netherlands. As in Italy, the wealth and leisure necessary to encourage the growth of the arts was based on commerce and on the patronage of the powerful princes and rich merchants who controlled it.

THE FIFTEENTH CENTURY

Flanders

The most important of the prosperous commercial cities of the north was Bruges, which, like Florence, derived its wealth from the wool trade and from banking. Until late in the fifteenth century, an arm of the North Sea, now silted up, reached inland to Bruges. Here, ships brought raw wool from England and Spain and carried away the fine manufactured woolen cloth that became famous throughout Europe. The wool trade brought bankers, among them representatives of the House of Medici, and Bruges became the financial clearinghouse for all of northern Europe. In its streets, merchants from Italy and the Near East rubbed shoulders with traders from Russia and Spain. Despite the flourishing economies of its sister cities—Ghent, Louvain, and Ypres—Bruges so dominated Flanders that the Duke of Burgundy chose to make the city his capital and moved his court there from Dijon in the early fifteenth century.

The dukes of Burgundy were probably the most powerful rulers in northern Europe during the first three quarters of the fifteenth century. Although cousins of the French kings, they usually supported England (on which they relied for the raw materials for their wool industry) during the Hundred Years' War and, at times, were in control of much of northern France, including Paris. Through intermarriage with the House of Flanders, they annexed the Low Countries, and, during the height of their power, their lands stretched from the Rhône River to the North Sea. Only the rash policies of the last of their line, Charles the Bold, and his death at the battle of Nancy in 1477 brought to an end the Burgundian dream of forming a strong middle kingdom between France and the Holy Roman Empire. After Charles's death, the southern Burgundian lands were reabsorbed by France, and the Netherlands passed to the

18-1 CLAUS SLUTER, *The Well of Moses*, 1395–1406. Figures approx. 6′ high. Chartreuse de Champmol, Dijon, France.

Holy Roman Empire by virtue of the dynastic marriage of Charles's daughter, Mary of Burgundy, to Maximilian of Hapsburg.

Philip the Bold of Burgundy, who ruled from 1364 to 1404, and his brother John, Duke of Berry, were the greatest sponsors of the arts of their time in northern Europe. Their interests centered on illuminated manuscripts, Arras tapestries, and rich furnishings for their numerous castles and town houses throughout their duchies. Philip's largest artistic enterprise was the foundation of the Chartreuse de Champmol, near Dijon. Intended to receive the tombs of the family, its magnificent endowment attracted artists from all parts of northern Europe. The outstanding representative of this short-lived Burgundian School was the sculptor CLAUS SLUTER (active *c.* 1380–1406).

For the cloister of the Chartreuse de Champmol, Sluter designed a symbolic well in which Moses and five other prophets surround a base that once supported a Crucifixion group. The six prophets of *The Well of Moses* (FIG. 18-1) recall the jamb figures of the Gothic portals, but they far surpass even the most realistic of those (FIG. 10-33) in their intense observation and rendering of minute detail and in their bulk, which manages to contain a wealth of detail that might otherwise be distracting. The life-size figures are swathed in heavy draperies with voluminous folds, characteristic of Sluter's style, and the artist manages to make their difficult, complex surfaces seem remarkably lifelike. This effect is enhanced by the skillful differentiation of textures, from coarse drapery to smooth flesh and silky hair, and by the paint, which is still partly preserved. This fascination with the specific and tangible in the visible world will be one of the chief characteristics of fifteenth-century Flemish painting. But despite its realism, Sluter's *Moses* (FIG. 18-1), compared with Donatello's *St. Mark* (FIG. 16-5), reveals what is still missing in the northern concept of the figure: the principle of interior movement, or weight shift.

The Chartreuse de Champmol must have been furnished with numerous altarpieces, but only a carved altarpiece representing the Adoration of the Magi survives. The odd-shaped wings for this altarpiece were painted by MELCHIOR BROEDERLAM (active 1385–1409), a Flemish painter who had been drawn to Dijon. On the left wing are *The Annunciation* and *The Visitation;* on the right wing (FIG. 18-2), *The Presentation* and *The Flight into Egypt.* The paintings show that Broederlam was a major northern exponent of the International style. His compositional devices—the uptilted plane of the landscape in the *Flight* scene, with its high horizon topped by a castle; the serpentine recession into the background; the elegant silhouettes of the figures, reminiscent of Sienese art—

18-2 MELCHIOR BROEDERLAM, *The Presentation* and *The Flight into Egypt,* 1394–1399. Tempera and oil on wood, approx. 64″ × 51″. Musée des Beaux-Arts, Dijon.

have already been seen in such southern works as Gentile da Fabriano's *Adoration of the Magi* (FIG. 16-25). Also pointing back to Sienese art is Broederlam's modest essay into perspective and the delicate architectural enframement of the *Presentation* scene. All this has been combined with the minutest observation and rendering of realistic details. That Broederlam was not immune to the influence of Sluter is seen in the handling of the voluminous drapery and, near the panel's right border, the strikingly massive figure of Joseph, planted like a tree stump, taking a draft from his cup—and looking like a figure from a painting by Pieter Bruegel some 150 years later.

It is sometimes pointed out that Broederlam's miniaturistic style is ill-suited for the size of the panels, which are some 5 feet high. The reason for this disproportion lies in the fact that, being among the earliest surviving examples of northern panel paintings, these works still reflect some of the long-standing northern painting traditions from which they are a revolutionary departure. For centuries, the characteristic painted surface in the north had been either stained glass or the illuminated manuscript page. Gothic architecture in northern Europe had successfully eliminated solid walls and had left few continuous, blank surfaces that invited painted decorations, contrary to the case in Italy, where climate and architecture favored mural painting in fresco. The northern artist was accustomed to working not only in miniature but with rich, jewel-like color, which, especially in stained glass, has a profound luminosity, the light seeming to irradiate the forms. Thus, he came into the fifteenth century habituated to deep color worked into exquisitely tiny and intricate shapes and patterns. When the northern miniaturist became acquainted, through the International style, with Italian forms and ideas, he saw himself forced to reduce to page size, or smaller, the inventions used in large compositions by Italian wall and panel painters like Duccio, Giotto, Simone Martini, and others. This development, which led to a kind of "perspective naturalism," was inconsistent with the basic function of book illumination—to decorate a page and illustrate part of the written text. Toward the end of the fourteenth century, illuminations began to take on the character of independent paintings, expanding on the page until they occupied it completely. By about 1400, these new forces generated in miniatures seemed to demand larger surfaces, and the shift was made to panel painting.

The first steps toward the illumination's expansion within the text appear in the work of JEAN PUCELLE (active *c.* 1320–1370), a Parisian illuminator who revitalized the stagnating Gothic manner of the Paris School. A page from the so-called *Belleville Breviary, c.* 1325 (FIG. 18-3), shows how the entire page has

18-3 JEAN PUCELLE, page from the *Belleville Breviary*, *c.* 1325. Illumination, approx. 9½″ × 6¾″.
Bibliothèque Nationale, Paris.

become the province of the illuminator. The borders, extended to invade the margins, include not only decorative tendrils and a profusion of spiky ivy and floral ornaments, but also a myriad of insects, small animals, and grotesques. In addition, three narrative scenes encroach on the columns of the next, the graceful postures and flowing draperies of the figures reflecting Sienese influence. One feels that any of these narratives could have been expanded into a full-page illustration or even a panel painting.

Such an expansion has occurred in the calendar pages of a gorgeously illustrated "Book of Hours," made for the Duke of Berry, brother of the king of France and of Philip the Bold of Burgundy. The manuscript, *Les Très Riches Heures du Duc de Berry* (FIGS. 18-4 and 18-5), was completed in 1416 by the three LIMBOURG BROTHERS—Pol, Hennequin, and Herman. Such books became favorite possessions of the northern aristocracy during the fourteenth and fifteenth centuries. As prayer books, they replaced the traditional psalters, which had been the only liturgical books in private hands until the mid-thirteenth century. The heart of the "Book of Hours" is the "Office of the Blessed Virgin," which contains liturgical passages to be read privately at eight set points during the day, from Matins to Compline. This part is usually preceded by an illustrated calendar containing local religious feast days; it is followed by penitential psalms, devotional prayers, litanies to the saints, and other offices, including that of the Dead and of the Holy Cross.

The calendar pictures of *Les Très Riches Heures* are perhaps the most famous in the history of manuscript illumination. They represent the 12 months of the year in terms of the associated seasonal tasks, alternating the occupations of nobility and peasantry. Above each picture is a lunette representing the chariot of the sun as it makes its yearly round through the 12 months and signs of the zodiac; numerical notations designate the zodiacal degree passed through in the course of the year. The picture for the month of *February* (FIG. 18-4), under the signs of Aquarius and of Pisces, displays a snowy landscape, bare trees, a woodsman at work, another driving a donkey laden with faggots to the distant village. A woman blowing on her fingers moves through a farmyard toward the house, where the red-capped master of the domicile and his womenfolk warm themselves before a fire. The high horizon and steep, carefully laid-out landscape, in which the details of the ordinary environment are carefully enumerated and authentically depicted, recall the landscape of Ambrogio Lorenzetti's *Good Government* fresco in Siena (FIG. 15-24); it is possible that one of the Limbourg brothers had seen these works or ones like them. In any event, *February* exemplifies the International style in its northern flowering. Even more representative, perhaps, is the

18-4   THE LIMBOURG BROTHERS, *February*, from *Les Très Riches Heures du Duc de Berry*, 1413–1416. Illumination, approx. 8¾" × 5½". Musée Condé, Chantilly.

colorful *May* from the same series (FIG. 18-5). Here, a cavalcade of patrician ladies and gentlemen, preceded by trumpeters, rides out to celebrate the first day of May, a spring festival observed by the courts throughout Europe. They are clad in springtime green, garlanded with fresh leaves, and sparkle with ornate finery. Behind them is a woodland and the château of Riom. These great country seats, most of which belonged to the Duke of Berry, loom in the backgrounds of most of the calendar pictures and are so faithfully represented that those surviving today are easily recognized. The spirit of the picture is Chaucerian (*The Canterbury Tales* is hardly a generation older)—lightsome, artificial, chivalric, pleasure-loving, and, of course, much in contrast with the peasant mood. The elegant silhouettes, rich colors, and decorative linear effects again recall Sienese art. *February* and *May* were evidently painted by different artists (note especially the differences in figure representation), but it has never been possible to assign specific pictures to the various Limbourg brothers. Nevertheless, although their styles may differ, their

18-5 THE LIMBOURG BROTHERS, *May*, from *Les Très Riches Heures du Duc de Berry*, 1413–1416. Illumination, approx. 8½″ × 5½″. Musée Condé, Chantilly.

main interests were the same. Within the confines of the International style, they represented as accurately as possible the actual world of appearances and the activities of man, peasant or aristocrat, in his natural surroundings at specific times of the year. Thus, the traditional field of subject matter has been expanded to include genre subjects; they are given a prominent place, even in a religious book. Secular and religious subjects remain neatly separated, but they will in-

creasingly encroach on each other during the course of the fifteenth century to produce as thorough a humanization of religious subject matter as we saw in Italy.

Hardly a decade after *Les Très Riches Heures*, an example of the International style at its peak, we have a work of quite different and novel conception, *The Mérode Altarpiece* (FIG. 18-6) by the Master of Flémalle, now identified as ROBERT CAMPIN (*c.* 1378–1444), the

18-6   ROBERT CAMPIN (Master of Flémalle), *The Mérode Altarpiece, c.* 1425–1428. Tempera and oil on wood, center panel approx. 25″ × 25″, wings approx. 25″ × 11″. Metropolitan Museum of Art, New York (Cloisters Collection).

leading painter of the city of Tournai. Here, the aristocratic taste, romantic mood, and ornamental style of the International painters are replaced with a relatively blunt, sober realism in setting and characterization. The old theme of the Annunciation occupies the central panel of the tripytych, and something of Internationalism remains in its decorative line play. But the donors, depicted in the left panel, set the tone. Man and wife, they are of the grave and sedate middle class; unostentatiously prosperous, quietly dressed, they kneel in a little courtyard, the man peering through the door at the mystery taking place. Discreetly set apart from it, they take the mystery as a fact, and factualness determines the artist's whole approach. All the objects in the Annunciation scene are rendered with careful attention to their actual appearance, and the event takes place in an everyday, middle-class Flemish interior, in which all accessories, furniture, and utensils are indicated, lest the setting be incomplete. But the objects represented are not merely that; book, candle, flowers, sink (in the corner niche), fire screen, polished pot, towels, and bench symbolize, in different ways, the Virgin's purity and her divine mission. In the right panel, Joseph has made a mousetrap, symbolic of the theological tradition that Christ is bait set in the trap of the world to catch the Devil. The carpenter's shop is completely inventoried by the painter, down to the vista into a distant city street. Thus, we have a thorough humanizing of a traditional religious theme—a transformation of it in terms of a particular time and place: a middle-class house, courtyard, and shop in a fifteenth-century city of Flanders. So close is the status of the sacred actors to the human level that they are even represented without halos; this does not happen in Italy until the end of the fifteenth century.

We have been tracing the humanization of art from the thirteenth century. The distance between the sacred and the secular has now narrowed to such a degree that they become intermixed. As Johan Huizinga, renowned modern student of the fifteenth century, describes it:

> Individual and social life, in all their manifestations, are imbued with the conception of faith. There is not an object nor an action, however trivial, that is not constantly correlated with Christ or salvation. . . . All life was saturated with religion to such an extent that the people were in constant danger of losing sight of the distinction between things spiritual and things temporal. If, on the one hand, all details of ordinary life may be raised to a sacred level, on the other hand, all that is holy sinks to the commonplace, by the fact of being blended with everyday life . . . the demarcation of the spheres of religious thought and that of worldly concerns was nearly obliterated.[*]

Hence, the realistically rendered, commonplace objects in a Flemish painting become suffused with religious significance and, as such, take on the nature of sacramental things. With this justification for their existence in art, the ordinary things that surround man—and man himself—share the realm of the saints; conversely, the saints now occupy the realm of man. But man, as well as the things of man, will remain when, with the secularization of art, the saints and sanctity have disappeared.

[*]Johan A. Huizinga, *The Waning of the Middle Ages* (Garden City, N.Y.: Doubleday, 1954), p. 156.

JAN VAN EYCK

One of the largest and most admired Flemish altar-pieces of the fifteenth century is *The Ghent Altarpiece* in the church of St. Bavo in Ghent (FIGS. 18-7, 18-8, 18-9). It has also been one of the most controversial ever since the discovery, in 1832, of a partly damaged, four-line Latin poem on the frame of one of the outside panels which, in part, translates: "The painter Hubert van Eyck, greater than whom no one was found, began [this work]; Jan, second in art, completed it at the expense of Jodocus Vyt. . . ." The last line of the quatrain gives the date of 1432.

For more than a century after the discovery of this inscription under a coat of greenish paint, the altar-piece was believed to be the product of a collaboration between JAN VAN EYCK (*c.* 1390–1441) and his older brother HUBERT. But none of the numerous attempts to assign different parts of the many-paneled work to one or the other brother found more than partial acceptance among art historians. Even Erwin Panofsky's tightly argued conclusion that the present altarpiece is the result of an artful combination of

18-7 HUBERT and JAN VAN EYCK, *The Ghent Altarpiece* (closed), completed 1432. Tempera and oil on wood, approx. 11′ × 7′ 3″. St. Bavo, Ghent, Belgium.

three independent works, begun by Hubert and finished by Jan, that originally were not meant to be seen together, left considerable room for doubt and argument.*

An entirely new light was thrown on the controversy with the more recent suggestion that Hubert may not have been a painter at all, but rather a sculptor, who carved an elaborate, now-lost framework for the painted panels. Lotte Brand Philip points out that the damaged word "-ictor" in the inscription, which precedes Hubert's name and had been restored to read "pictor" (painter), could also be read "fictor" (sculptor).† "Second in art" would then not mean that Jan was a less accomplished painter than his brother; instead, it would be a chronological reference to the fact that Jan worked on the altar *after* Hubert. Judging from surviving contracts and commissions of the period, it seems to have been fairly common practice for a painter to begin work on panels after their frames had been completed.

In 1566, the panels were removed from the original frame and hidden, to protect them from Protestant iconoclasts who probably destroyed the frame. The panels were reinstalled in 1587, but without the original framework, which Lotte Brand Philip envisions to have been in the form of a richly carved, two-storied, Gothic reliquary front. Her ingenious theory and imaginative reconstruction would give sole authorship of the paintings to Jan van Eyck and solve the problem of attribution that has vexed art historians for almost a century and a half. It would also tend to explain the disparity of the scale used on the inner panels, which has disturbed some modern observers. If, indeed, the panels were originally more widely spaced and separated by richly carved, Gothic architectural elements, the formal unity of the altarpiece may have been stronger and more cohesive, especially if perspective devices in the lower level created the illusion that the smaller-scale scenes receded and were seen through—and at some distance behind—the architectural screen. On the other hand, it may well be that fifteenth-century viewers paid much less attention to formal unity than we do today and that the spiritual unity of the work was their real concern.

The Ghent polyptych remains an outstanding example of the large, folding altarpiece, typical of the north, that discloses new meanings to the observer as the unfolding panels reveal new subjects in sequence. The very form of the folding altarpiece expresses the Medieval tendency to uncover truth behind natural appearances, to clothe thought in

*Erwin Panofsky, *Early Netherlandish Painting* (Cambridge, MA: Harvard University Press, 1953).

†Lotte Brand Philip, *The Ghent Altarpiece and the Art of Jan van Eyck* (Princeton, N.J.: Princeton University Press, 1972).

18-8 HUBERT and JAN VAN EYCK, *The Ghent Altarpiece* (open). Approx. 11' × 15' 1".

18-9 HUBERT and JAN VAN EYCK, *God the Father* (detail of FIG. 18-8).

allegory, to find "essential" meaning hidden beneath layers of secondary meanings. When closed (FIG. 18-7), *The Ghent Altarpiece* shows the Annunciation and simulated statues of St. John the Baptist and St. John the Evangelist, flanked by the donors, Jodoc Vyt and his wife; above, in the lunettes, are the Prophet Zechariah with the Erythraean sibyl and the Prophet Micah with the Cumaean sibyl. All these are symbolic references to the Coming of Christ. The Annunciation figures are set in a raftered room in which there are both Romanesque and Gothic architectural elements that may symbolize the Old and the New Testaments, respectively. As it does in *The Mérode Altarpiece* (FIG. 18-6), a vista opens on a distant street. The angel and the Virgin are bundled in the heavy flannel draperies of the Burgundian School, resembling those of Sluter's Moses (FIG. 18-1). Although the architecture is spacious, the figures are in ambiguous relation to it and quite out of scale; as yet, there is little concern for a proportioned space adjusted to the human figure.

When opened (FIG. 18-8), the altarpiece reveals a sumptuous, superbly colored representation of the Medieval conception of the redemption of man. In the upper register, God (FIG. 18-9)—wearing the triple tiara of the papacy, with a worldly crown at his feet and resplendent in a deep-scarlet mantle—is flanked on the left by the Virgin, represented as Queen of Heaven, with a "crown of twelve stars upon her head," and on the right by St. John the Baptist. To either side is a choir of angels and, on the right, St. Cecilia at her organ. Adam and Eve are in the far panels. The inscriptions in the arches above the Virgin and St. John extol the virtue and purity of the former and the greatness of the latter as the forerunner of Christ. The particularly significant inscription above the head of the Lord (FIG. 18-9) translates: "This is God, all-powerful in his divine majesty; of all the best, by the gentleness of his goodness; the most liberal giver, because of his infinite generosity." The step behind the crown at the Lord's feet bears the inscription: "On his head, life without death. On his brow, youth without age. On his right, joy without sadness. On his left, security without fear." This is a most concise and beautiful statement of the change from the concept of God as a stern, Medieval judge of mankind to the benevolent Franciscan father of the human race. This Franciscan concept of the benevolent nature of God is reinforced by the pelicans embroidered on the tapestry draped over the back of his throne, for pelicans—then thought to tear open their breasts to feed their starving young with their own blood—were symbols of self-sacrificing love. The entire altarpiece amplifies this central theme; though man is sinful—symbolized by Adam and Eve—he will be saved because God, in his infinite love, will sacrifice his own son for this purpose.

The figures are rendered in a shimmering splendor of color that defies reproduction. Both Hubert and Jan van Eyck were trained miniaturists, and not the smallest detail has escaped their eyes; they amplify the beauty of the most insignificant object as if it were a work of piety as much as a work of art. The soft texture of hair, the glitter of gold in the heavy brocades, the luster of pearls, the flashing of gems—all are given with tireless fidelity to appearance (FIG. 18-.9). The new medium of oil paint—here in its very beginning—shows its marvelous magic.

The panels of the lower register extend the symbolism of the upper. In the central panel, the community of saints comes from the four corners of the earth through an opulent, flower-spangled landscape. They move toward the altar of the Lamb, from whose heart blood flows into a chalice, and toward the octagonal fountain of life into which spills the "pure river of water of life, clear as crystal, proceeding out of the throne of God and of the Lamb" (Revelation 22:1). On the right, the Twelve Apostles and a group of martyrs in red robes advance; on the left, with minor prophets, the Four Evangelists arrive carrying their Gospels. In the right background come the holy virgins; in the left background, the holy confessors.

On the lower wings, other approaching groups symbolize the four cardinal virtues: the hermits, Temperance; the pilgrims, Prudence; the knights, Fortitude; the judges, Justice. The altarpiece celebrates the whole Christian cycle from the fall to the redemption, presenting the Church triumphant in heavenly Jerusalem. The uncanny naturalism and the precise rendering, in the miniaturist tradition, make the great event as concrete and credible as possible to the observer. The realism is so saturated with symbolism that we almost think of it as a kind of superreality or "surrealism," as what is given to the eye is more than the eye alone can report.

Jan van Eyck's matchless color craft is evident in *The Virgin with the Canon van der Paele* (FIG. 18-10), painted in 1436. The figures are grouped in a manner reminiscent of the *sacra conversazione* paintings that appear in Florence about the same time (FIG. 16-32). The architecture, the elaborately ornamented rug, and the figures all lead the eye to the Madonna and Child, who sit in the apse of a church. The rich texture of the Virgin's red robes strongly contrasts with the white surplice of the kneeling Canon van der Paele. A similar contrast plays across the space between the dull glint from the armor of St. George, the patron saint of the canon, and the rich brocades of St. Donatian, the patron of the church for which the painting was commissioned. The incredibly brilliant profusion of color is carefully controlled, so that the forms are clearly distinguished in all detail. The symbolism is as profuse and controlled as the color, incorporating again the complete cycle of the fall and the promise of redemption. The arms of the Virgin's throne and the historiated capitals of the pilasters behind her make reference to the Old Testament prefiguration of the Coming of Christ, so well known in the Middle Ages.

There is evidence in the picture of Van Eyck's use of perspective—not a single perspective that would consistently unify the space, but several. His intention here appears once again to be indirect, the multiple perspectives directing attention to the principal figures. For example, a projection of the line of the column base at the far right leads to the head of the canon; the orthogonals of the floor tiles converge on the midpoint of the figure of the Virgin; and the base of the throne can be projected to the infant Christ. Thus, there is no real spatial unification. The figures do not interrelate as we might expect; each fills its own space with, as it were, its own perspective. Although St. George lifts his helmet to the Virgin, the direction of his gaze goes well beyond her; this disorientation is also true of the other figures. Jan van Eyck and his generation still essentially conceive the organization of the two-dimensional picture surface in terms of shape, color, and symbol; they have not yet

18-10   Jan van Eyck, *The Virgin with the Canon van der Paele*, 1436. Tempera and oil on wood, approx. 48″ × 62″. Musées Communaux, Bruges.

thought of it as a window into a constructed illusion of the third dimension, as the painters of the later Flemish schools will.

The portrait head of Canon van der Paele shows the same nonstructural approach. The heavy, wrinkled visage of the canon is recorded in precise detail, almost to the pores; the artist makes a relief map of his subject, delineating every minute change of the facial surface. Unlike the Italian portraitists, who think first of the structure of the head and then draw the likeness over it, Jan van Eyck works from the outside inward, beginning with the likeness and shaping the head incidentally. This is what gives the mask-like aspect to the canon's face, despite the portrait's fidelity to physiognomy; the surface is all there, but the illusion of three-dimensional mass is only implied.

We have seen three works that included painted portraits of their donors: *The Mérode Altarpiece* (FIG. 18-6), *The Ghent Altarpiece* (FIG. 18-8), and *The Virgin with Canon van der Paele* (FIG. 18-10). These portraits mark a significant revival of a genre unknown since antiquity. A fourth portrait, Jan van Eyck's *Man in a Red Turban* (FIG. 18-11) marks another step in the humanization process. In the Mérode and Ghent altarpieces, the donors were depicted apart from the saints; in the Canon van der Paele portrait, the donor associates with the saints at the throne of the Virgin. In this portrait (possibly of the artist himself) the image of a living individual apparently needs no religious purpose for being—only a personal one; the portrait is simply a record of one's features interesting to oneself or another. These private portraits now begin to multiply, as both artist and patron become

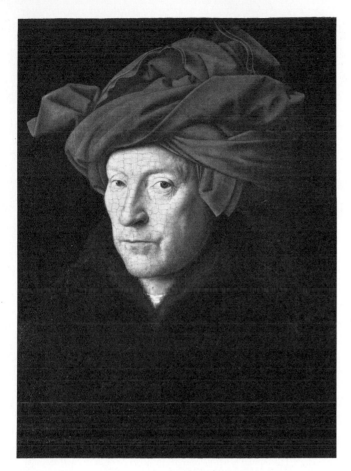

18-11 JAN VAN EYCK, *Man in a Red Turban (Self-Portrait?)*, 1433. Tempera and oil on wood, approx. 10¼″ × 7½″. Reproduced by courtesy of the Trustees of the National Gallery, London.

interested in the reality they reveal, for the painter's close observation of the lineaments of a human face is as revealing of the real world as his observation of objects in general. As man confronts himself in the painted portrait, he objectifies himself as a self, as a person. In this confrontation, the otherworldly anonymity of the Middle Ages must fade away. The *Man in a Red Turban* looks directly at us, or perhaps at himself in a mirror. So far as is known, this is the first painted portrait in a thousand years to do so. The level, composed gaze, directed from a true three-quarter pose of the head, must have impressed observers deeply. There is the illusion that from whatever angle we observe the face, the eyes still fix us. A painting of this kind by the great Rogier van der Weyden must have inspired the writing of *The Vision of God* (1453) by Nicholas of Cusa, who says, in the preface to that work:

> To transport you to things divine, I must needs use a comparison of some kind. Now among men's works I have found no image better suited to our purpose than that of an image which is *omnivoyant* [all-seeing]— its face, by the painter's cunning art, being made to appear as though looking on all around it—for example . . . that by the eminent painter, Roger, in his

priceless picture in the governor's house at Brussels. . . . this I call the icon of God.

Nicholas goes on with a praise of sight and vision that amounts to a sanctification of it:

> Thou, Lord . . . lovest me because Thine eyes are so attentively upon me . . . where the eye is, there is love. . . . I exist in that measure in which Thou art with me, and since Thy look is Thy being, I am because Thou dost look at me, and if Thou didst turn Thy glance from me I should cease to be.

> Apart from Thee, Lord, naught can exist. If, then, Thine essence pervade all things, so also does Thy sight, which is Thine essence. . . . Thou Lord, seest all things and each thing at one and the same time

Nicholas of Cusa is a contemporary of the great Flemish painters, and it is likely that he spoke in a sense they could understand and in a mood they could share. The exaltation of sight to divine status and the astonishing assertion that the essence of God is sight—not being, as St. Thomas tells us—are entirely in harmony with the new vision in painting. As sight and being in God are essentially the same, so the painter's sight, which is instrumental in making likenesses, brings them into being. As the contemplative man achieves union with God by making himself like God, the imitation of objects in the sight of (hence, caused by) God must be a holy act on the part of the painter: seeing what God sees, he achieves the reality of God's vision and reveals it to others. In the light of Nicholas' doctrine, the minute realism of the Flemish painters can be understood. God sees everything, great and small alike, and Nicholas' fundamental doctrine that all opposites and contradictions are resolved and harmonized in God makes God present in the greatest and in the smallest, in the macrocosm and in the microcosm, in the whole earth and in a drop of water. In the whole world of vision *caused* by God's sight, everything is worthwhile because it is seen by God—even the "meanest flower that blows." Nicholas' sanctification of the faculty of sight provides Flemish painters with a religious warrant to apply sight in the investigation of the given world; painters in the north will continue the investigation long after the original religious motive is gone.

Above all, an age had begun in both the Netherlands and Italy in which men gloried in the faculty of sight for what it could reveal of the world around them. The artist now began to show Western man "what things look like," and he took extreme pleasure in recognizing a revelation. The level gaze of the *Man in a Red Turban*, in all its quiet objectivity, is not only the omnivoyant "icon of God"; in its historical destiny, it is the impartial, eternally observant face of science. It is also, significantly, man beginning to confront nature in terms of himself. This is the climax of the slow but mighty process that will bring man's eyes down from the supernatural to the natural world—a process that is expressed with just as much conviction and vigor in the north as it is in Italy.

The humanization of pictorial themes advances another step in Jan van Eyck's double portrait of *Giovanni Arnolfini and His Bride* (FIG. 18-12). The Lucca financier, who had established himself in Bruges, and his lady occupy a scene that is empty of saints but charged with the spiritual. Almost every object depicted is in some way symbolic of the holiness of matrimony. The persons themselves, hand in hand, take the marriage vows. Their shoes have been removed, for the sacrament of matrimony makes the room a holy place. The little dog symbolizes fidelity (the origin of the common canine name, "Fido"). Behind the pair, the curtains of the marriage bed have been opened. The finial of the bedpost is a tiny statue of St. Margaret, patron saint of childbirth; from the finial hangs a whisk broom, symbolic of domestic care (FIG. 18-13). The oranges on the chest below the window may refer to the golden apples of the Hesperides, representing the conquest of death. And the presence of the omnivoyant eye of God seems to be referred to

twice: once in the single candle burning in the ornate chandelier and again in the mirror, in which the entire room is reflected (FIG. 18-13). The small medallions set into the mirror's frame show tiny scenes from the Passion of Christ and represent Van Eyck's ever-present promise of salvation for the figures reflected on the mirror's convex surface. These figures include not only the principals, Arnolfini and his wife, but two persons who look into the room through the door. One of these must be the artist himself, as the florid inscription above the mirror, *Johannes de Eyck fuit hic*, announces that he was present. The purpose of the picture, then, is to document and sanctify the marriage of two particular persons. In this context, man comes to the fore of his own setting; the spiritual is present—but in terms of symbol, not image.

The paintings of Jan van Eyck have a weighty formality that banishes movement and action. His symmetrical groupings have the stillness and rigidity of the symbol-laden ceremony of the Mass; each person and thing has its prescribed place and is adorned as befits the sacred occasion. The long tradition of manuscript illumination accepted that the Holy Book must be as precious as the words it contains; Jan van

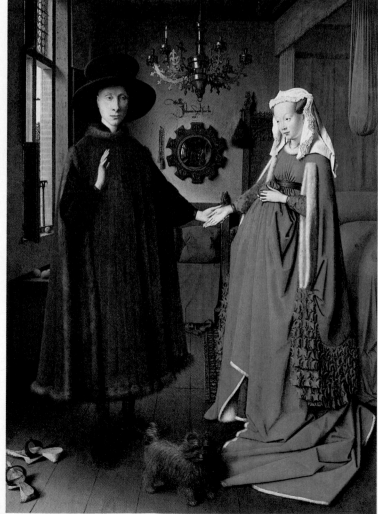

18-12 JAN VAN EYCK, *Giovanni Arnolfini and His Bride*, 1434. Tempera and oil on wood, approx. 32″ × 22″. Reproduced by courtesy of the Trustees of the National Gallery, London.

18-13 JAN VAN EYCK, *Mirror and Chandelier* (detail of FIG. 18-12).

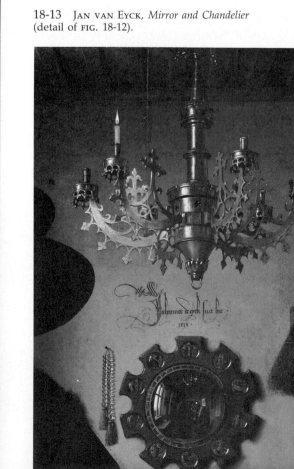

Eyck, himself a miniaturist and illuminator, instinctively created a rich and ornamental style in which to proclaim his optimistic message of human salvation. In their own way, the paintings of Jan van Eyck are perfect and impossible to surpass. After him, Flemish painting looked for new approaches, and Van Eyck had few, if any, emulators.

VAN DER WEYDEN, CHRISTUS, AND BOUTS

The art of ROGIER VAN DER WEYDEN (c. 1400–1464) had a much greater impact on northern painting of the fifteenth century. A student of Robert Campin, Rogier evidently recognized the limitations of Van Eyck's style, although it had not been without influence on his early work. By sweeping most of the secondary symbolism from his paintings, Rogier cleared his pictorial stage for fluid and dynamic compositions stressing human action and drama. He concentrates on themes like the Crucifixion and the Pietà, in which he moves the observer by relating the sufferings of Christ. For Van Eyck's symbolic bleeding lamb, Rogier substitutes the tortured body of the Redeemer and his anguished mother. His paintings are filled with deep religiosity and powerful emotion, for he conceived his themes as expressions of a mystic yearning to share in the Passion of Jesus.

The great *Escorial Deposition* (FIG. 18-14) sums up Rogier's early style and content. Instead of creating a deep landscape setting, as Jan van Eyck might have, he compresses the figures and action onto a shallow stage to concentrate the observer's attention. Here, Rogier imitates the large, sculptured shrines so popular in the fifteenth century, especially in Germany, and the device well serves his purpose of expressing maximum action within disciplined structure. The painting resembles a stratified relief carving in the crisp drawing and precise modeling of its forms. A series of lateral, undulating movements gives the

18-14 ROGIER VAN DER WEYDEN, *The Escorial Deposition*, c. 1435. Tempera and oil on wood, approx. 7' 3" × 8' 7". Museo del Prado, Madrid.

group a unity, a formal cohesion, that is underlined by psychological means—by the desolating anguish common to all the figures. Few painters have equaled Rogier in the rendering of passionate sorrow as it vibrates through a figure or distorts a tear-stained face. His depiction of the agony of loss is the most authentic in religious art; in a painting as bare of secondary symbolism as the *Deposition*, the emotional impact on the observer is immediate and direct. From this single example, we can understand why Rogier's art became authoritative for the whole fifteenth century outside of Italy.

His portraits were no less important than his altarpieces. With Campin, Van Eyck had established portraiture among the artist's principal tasks. Great patrons were ready to have their likenesses painted—and for many reasons: to memorialize themselves in their dynastic lines; to establish their identity, rank, and station by an image far more concrete than a heraldic coat of arms; to represent themselves at occasions of state when they could not be present—even as a kind of photograph, with the families who had arranged their children's marriages exchanging portraits of the betrothed. Royalty, nobility, and the very rich might send painters to "take" the likeness of a prospective bride or groom. It is reported that when a bride was sought for young King Charles VI of France, a painter was sent to three different royal courts to make portraits of the candidates, on the basis of which the king then made his choice.

We are not sure for what specific purpose Rogier's portrait of an unknown young lady (FIG. 18-15) was painted. From her dress and bearing, she was probably of noble rank. The artist is at pains to realize not only a faithful likeness of the somewhat plain features, but to read, with his uncommon perception, her individual character. Her lowered eyes, tightly locked, thin fingers, and fragile physique bespeak a personality reserved, introverted, devout. The unflattering honesty and directness, typical in the Flemish artist's approach, reveals much, despite the formality of pose and demeanor. This style contrasts with the formality of the Italian approach (FIG. 16-58) derived from the profiles common to coins and medallions, which is more stern and admits little revelation of personality. The Italian patron and portraitist will prefer the profile view throughout most of the century, rather than the full-face and three-quarter views favored by the Flemish. Rogier is perhaps chief among the Flemish in his penetrating readings of his subjects, and—great pictorial composer that he is—he makes beautiful use here of flat, sharply pointed angular shapes that themselves so powerfully suggest an "angularity" of this subject's personality. Unlike Jan van Eyck, Rogier lays little stress on minute description of surface detail. Instead, he defines

18-15 ROGIER VAN DER WEYDEN, *Portrait of a Lady, c.* 1460. Oil on wood, 14½″ × 10¾″. National Gallery, Washington, D.C. (Andrew W. Mellon Collection).

large, simple planes and volumes, achieving an almost "abstract" effect, in the modern sense, of dignity and elegance characteristic of his portraiture.

Although evidence that Rogier traveled to Italy is not unequivocal, some of his paintings clearly show his acquaintance with Italian pictorial devices; his religious sincerity and concern with sin and guilt, however, remained undimmed by them. The appearance of these mid-century Italian influences in Rogier's paintings was not an isolated instance in Flemish art. The work of PETRUS CHRISTUS (*c.* 1410–1472) shows so marked an interest in the depiction of space and cubic form that, although the idea is now largely discounted, it was often felt that he too traveled to Italy. Little is known of Christus' life, except that he may have been Van Eyck's student and that he settled and worked in Bruges. Christus' style vacillates between Van Eyck's and Rogier's. Still, his interests are quite different from those of his models. His painting of *The Legend of Saints Eligius and Godeberta* (FIG. 18-16) seems, at first glance, to exhibit all of Van Eyck's miniaturistic traits—from the stitching on the lady's gown to the carefully enumerated attributes that identify the seated saint as a patron of the goldsmith's guild. Even the convex mirror seems to have

18-16 PETRUS CHRISTUS, *The Legend of Saints Eligius and Godeberta*, 1449. Tempera and oil on wood, approx. 39″ × 34″. Metropolitan Museum of Art, New York (the Lehman Collection).

been extracted from Van Eyck's portrait of Arnolfini and his bride (FIG. 18-12), and the two "witnesses" reflected in it suggest that this may also be a wedding picture. But Christus' concept of reality and his approach to it are quite different from Van Eyck's; he is much more concerned with the underlying structure of an object's appearance and, in this respect, is more closely related to the Italian than to the northern approach. The three solidly constructed figures within the cubic void defined by the desk and the room corner represent an essentially southern essay in pictorial form that has been overlaid with Van Eyck's surface realism. Curiously, in his effort to make the structure of his picture clear, Christus resorts to the same kind of simplification of forms seen in the paintings of Paolo Uccello and Piero della Francesca (FIGS. 16-29 and 16-33). Even more striking, perhaps, is the similarity of Christus' "volumetric" portrait heads to those by Antonello da Messina (FIG. 16-67). The speculation that these two artists may have met, either in Flanders or in Italy, remains tempting, despite the lack of solid documentation.

A slightly younger artist with similar temperament and interests, who may have had some contact with Christus, is DIRK BOUTS (*c.* 1415–1475). Rogier may have known about the Italian science of linear perspective, although he apparently did not use it in his paintings. For a long time, the central panel of *The Altarpiece of the Holy Sacrament* by Bouts was believed to be the first northern painting in which the use of a

single vanishing point for the construction of an interior could actually be demonstrated. More recent studies tend to give precedence in this field to Petrus Christus, from whom, in fact, Bouts may have acquired his knowledge. The setting for the altarpiece's *Last Supper* (FIG. 18-17) is probably the refectory of the headquarters of the Louvain Confraternity of the Holy Sacrament, by which the painting was commissioned. All orthogonals of the depicted room lead to a single vanishing point in the center of the mantelpiece above the head of Christ. This is not only the most successful northern fifteenth-century representation of an interior; it is also the first in which the scale of the figures has been realistically adjusted to the space they occupy. So far, however, the perspective unity is confined to single units of space only; the small side room has its own vanishing point, and neither it nor the vanishing point of the main room falls on the horizon of the landscape seen through the windows. The tentative manner with which Bouts solves his spatial problems suggests that he arrived at his solution independently and that the Italian science of perspective had not yet reached the north, except perhaps in fragments. Nevertheless, the works of Christus and Bouts clearly show that, by mid-century, northern artists had become involved with the same scientific, formal problems that occu-

18-17 DIRK BOUTS, *The Last Supper*, 1464–1468. Tempera and oil on wood, approx. 6′ × 5′. St. Peter's, Louvain, Belgium.

pied Italian artists during most of the fifteenth century.

The mood of Bout's *Last Supper* is neutral. The gathering is solemn enough, but it lacks all pathos and dramatic tension—almost as if the artist was more concerned with the solution of a difficult formal problem than with the pictorial interpretation, either personal or traditional, of the sacred event.

VAN DER GOES AND MEMLING

The highly subjective and introspective paintings of HUGO VAN DER GOES (*c.* 1440–1482) seem to express a discontent with the impersonal quality that the artist must have felt was a loss of religious meaning in the paintings of his older contemporaries. Hugo was dean of the painter's guild of Ghent from 1468 to 1475 and an extremely popular painter. At the height of his success and fame, he entered a monastery as a lay brother. While there, he suffered a mental breakdown in 1481 and died a year later. His retirement to the monastery did not immediately interrupt Hugo's career as a painter; he continued to receive commissions and probably completed his most famous work, *The Portinari Altarpiece* (FIG. 18-18), within the monastery's walls. Hugo painted the triptych for Tommaso Portinari, an agent of the Medici, who appears on the wings of the altarpiece with his family and their patron saints. The central panel represents *The Adoration of the Shepherds* (FIG. 18-19). There, on a large surface, Hugo displays a scene of solemn grandeur, muted by the artist's introspective nature. The high drama of the joyous occasion is stilled; the Virgin, Joseph, and the angels seem to brood on the suffering that is to come rather than to meditate on the miracle of the Nativity. On a tilted ground that has the expressive function of centering the main actors, the Virgin kneels, somber and monumental. From the right

enter three shepherds, represented with powerful realism in attitudes of wonder, piety, and gaping curiosity. Their lined, plebeian faces, work-worn hands, and uncouth dress and manner are so sharply characterized as to make us think of the characters in such literature of the poor as *Piers Plowman* and the *Second Shepherd's Play.* The three panels (FIG. 18-19) are unified by the symbolic architecture and a continuous, wintry, northern landscape. Symbols are scattered plentifully throughout the altarpiece: iris and columbine symbolize the Sorrows of the Virgin; the fifteen angels represent the Fifteen Joys of Mary; a sheaf of wheat stands for Bethlehem (the ''house of bread'' in Hebrew), a reference to the Eucharist; and the harp of David, emblazoned over the portal of the far building, signifies the ancestry of Christ. To further stress the meaning and significance of the depicted event, Hugo revives Medieval pictorial devices and casts aside the unities of time and action so treasured by other Renaissance artists, wherein a single episode in time is confined to a single framed piece. Small scenes shown in the background of the altarpiece represent (from left to right across the three panels) the Flight into Egypt, the Annunciation to the Shepherds, and the Arrival of the Magi—the ''prelude and epilogue to the Nativity.'' Also out of the past is the manner in which Hugo varies the scale of his figures to differentiate them according to their importance in relation to the central event. At the same time, he puts a vigorous, penetrating realism to work in a new direction, characterizing human beings according to their social level while showing their common humanity, and the painting becomes a plea for all men to join the Brotherhood of Man.

Portinari placed his altarpiece in the church of Sant' Egidio in Florence, where it created a considerable stir among Florentine artists. Although the painting

18-18 HUGO VAN DER GOES, *The Portinari Altarpiece* (open), *c.* 1476. Oil on wood, center panel 8' 3½" × 10'. Galleria degli Uffizi, Florence.

18-19   HUGO VAN DER GOES, *The Adoration of the Shepherds,* center panel of *The Portinari Altarpiece* (FIG. 18-18).

as a whole must have seemed unstructured to them, Hugo's brilliant technique and what they thought of as incredible realism in representing drapery, flowers, animals, and, above all, human character and emotion made a deep impression on them. At least one Florentine artist, Domenico Ghirlandaio, paid tribute to the northern master by using his most striking motif, the adoring shepherds, in one of his own Nativity paintings a few years later.

Hugo's contemporary, HANS MEMLING (*c.* 1430–1494)—although, like him, esteemed by all, and called, at his death, the ''best painter in all Christendom''—was of a very different temperament. Gentle and genial, he avoided the ambitious, dramatic compositions of Rogier and Hugo, and his sweet, slightly melancholy style fits well into the twilight of the waning fifteenth century. Memling's speciality is the Madonna, of which he has left many. They are slight, pretty, young princesses; the infant Christ, a doll. A good example of his work is the center panel of a triptych, representing *The Mystic Marriage of St. Catherine* (FIG. 18-20). The composition is balanced and serene; the color, sparkling and luminous; the execution, of the highest technical quality (Memling's paintings are among the best preserved from the fifteenth century). The prevailing sense of isolation and the frail, spiritual human types contrast not only with Hugo's monumental and somber forms but also with Van Eyck's robust and splendid ones. The century began, with Van Eyck's sumptuous art, on a note of

18-20 HANS MEMLING,
The Mystic Marriage of St. Catherine,
center panel of *The St. John
Altarpiece*, 1479. Oil on wood,
approx. 69" × 69".
Hospitaal Sint Jan, Bruges, Belgium.

18-21 HIERONYMUS BOSCH,
The Carrying of the Cross,
c. 1510 (?). Oil on wood,
approx. 30" × 32". Musée des
Beaux-Arts, Ghent.

humanistic optimism. It ends with a waning strength of spirit, an erosion of confidence in the moral and religious authority of the Church. Contemporary poetry is filled with dreary pessimism and foreboding, almost in anticipation of another fall of man and the disasters that will lie ahead for Christendom in the Reformation.

HIERONYMUS BOSCH

This time of pessimistic transition finds its supreme artist in one of the most fascinating and puzzling painters in history, HIERONYMUS BOSCH (*c.* 1450–1516). Interpretations of Bosch differ widely. Was he a satirist, an irreligious mocker, or a pornographer? Was he a heretic or an orthodox fanatic like Girolamo Savonarola? Was he obsessed by guilt and the universal reign of sin and death? Certainly, his art is born from the dark pessimism of his age, burdened with the fear of human fate—with the conviction that man's doom is approaching. A contemporary poet, Eustache Deschamps, writes:

> Now the world is cowardly, decayed and weak,
> Old, covetous, confused of speech:
> I see only female and male fools. . . .
> The end approaches . . .
> All goes badly.

In a much copied and imitated series of small panels with half-length figures, Bosch describes the Pas-

sion of Christ. *The Carrying of the Cross* (FIG. 18-21) from this group is a bitter judgment of humanity. Christ is surrounded by hate and evil; his executioners show a sadistic delight in the suffering of their victim. Heedless of spatial effects, Bosch packs the entire surface of his panel with hate-distorted faces. In the upper right corner, a grinning scoundrel in monk's habit exhorts the repentant thief; in the lower right corner, the unrepentant thief grimaces at two leering comrades, forming with them a triad of stupidity, bestiality, and hate. On the lower left, St. Veronica, representing the Church, turns away from Christ and becomes a symbol of vanity. No further interpretation of this panel seems needed; Bosch not only makes his meaning clear but expresses it with unrivaled ferocity.

Much more difficult to understand are Bosch's large altarpieces, which are packed with obscure meaning and symbolism. But even if we may not fully understand his teeming fantasies, we can appreciate the incredible scope of an imagination that makes him the poet of the nightmarish subconscious. The dreaming and waking worlds are one in Bosch, as he draws on the tradition of beast and monster that we have followed from Mesopotamia to the Gothic gargoyle.

His most famous work, the so-called *Garden of Earthly Delights* (FIGS. 18-22 and 18-23), is also his most puzzling, and no interpretation of it is universally accepted. The left wing of the triptych (FIG. 18-22) shows the *Creation of Eve* in the Garden of Eden. However, here Eve is not the mother of mankind, as she is in Van Eyck's *Ghent Altarpiece* (FIG. 18-8), but rather the seductress whose temptation of Adam resulted in the original sin, the central theme of the main panel. Evil lurks even in Bosch's paradise; a central fountain of life is surrounded by ravens, the traditional symbols for nonbelievers and magicians; an owl, hiding in the dark hole in the center of the fountain, represents witchcraft and sorcery. The central panel, *The Garden of Earthly Delights* (FIG. 18-22), swarms with the frail nude figures of men and women sporting licentiously in a panoramic landscape that is studded with fantastic growths of a quasisexual form. Bosch seems to show erotic temptation and sensual gratification as a universal disaster and the human race, as a consequence of original sin, succumbing to its naturally base disposition. The subjects are derived in part from three major sources: Medieval bestiaries, Flemish proverbs, and the then very popular dream books, all mixed in the melting pot of Bosch's astoundingly inventive imagination. In addition, there are frequent allusions to magic and alchemy, and animal and vegetable forms are mingled in the most absurd combinations. Symbols are scattered plentifully throughout the panel: fruit for carnal pleasure, eggs for alchemy and sex, the rat for falsehood and lies, dead fish for memories of past joys. A couple in a glass globe may illustrate the proverb "Good fortune, like glass, is easily broken." We have lost the key to many of Bosch's symbols, but it may be assumed that they were well enough known to his contemporaries. In the right wing, the

fruits of license are gathered in *Hell* (FIG. 18-22). There, sinful mankind undergoes hideous torments to diabolic music, while the hellish landscape burns. This symphony of damnation apparently comments on the wickedness of music, with which the Devil lures souls away from God. In this context, the ears and the musical instruments would represent the erotic, soul-destroying thoughts engendered by music. A man is crucified on a harp; another is shut up in a drum. A gambler is nailed to his own table. A girl is embraced by a spidery monster and bitten by toads. The observer must search through the hideous enclosure of Bosch's hell to take in its fascinating though repulsive details. The great modern poet Charles Baudelaire catches the mood in his *Flowers of Evil*:

Who but the Devil pulls our walking-strings!
Abominations lure us to their side;
Each day we take another step to hell,
Descending through the stench, unhorrified . . .

Packed in our brains incestuous as worms
Our demons celebrate in drunken gangs . . .

. . . in this den of jackals, monkeys, curs,
Scorpions, buzzards, snakes . . . this paradise
Of filthy beasts that screech, howl, grovel, grunt—
In this menagerie of mankind's vice. . . .

The triptych as a whole may represent the false paradise of this world between Eden and Hell, but this is only one interpretation. Another has it that Bosch belonged to a secret, heretical sect, the Adamites, and that the central panel was thought of as a kind of altarpiece symbolically celebrating its rites and practices. Recently, a fairly strong case has been made for an interpretation in terms of contemporaneous alchemical knowledge and practice.* In this connection, it should be pointed out that alchemy, in Bosch's time, was not an illegal and occult art but a practical and legitimate science practiced to make artist's paints, women's cosmetics, herbal cooking preparations, and healing potions. The alchemical science of distillation is basic to modern chemistry, and Philippus Aureolus Paracelsus, an early sixteenth-century physician, stated emphatically that the true and only purpose of alchemy is to heal the sick, not to make gold.

Numerous alchemical treatises circulated during Bosch's time, and some of them may well have been known to our artist. It has long been noted that the triptych is punctuated by forms and shapes similar to diagrams found in distillation texts. Most striking, perhaps, is the beaker-shaped "fountain of life,"

---

* See Laurinda S. Dixon, "Bosch's *Garden of Delights* Triptych: Remnants of a 'Fossil' Science," *The Art Bulletin,* Vol. LXIII, No. 1 (March 1981), pp. 96–113.

18-22 HIERONYMUS BOSCH, *Creation of Eve* (left wing), *The Garden of Earthly Delights* (center panel), *Hell* (right wing), 1505–1510. Triptych, oil on wood, center panel 7′ 2″ × 6′ 5″. Museo del Prado, Madrid.

which appears twice (once in the center of the left wing, and again in the background of the central panel) and which, in form, strongly resembles an alchemical mixing retort. Many other distillation appa-

18-23 HIERONYMUS BOSCH, *The Garden of Earthly Delights*, exterior of closed wings representing *The Third Day of Creation* (?).

ratus appear, especially in the central panel, including glass pipes and lids and transparent globes and funnels. Numerous egg shapes seem to refer to the ovoid mixing vessels in which ingredients were combined to produce the hoped-for transmutations. These vessels, called ''eggs'' in the symbolic language of alchemy, were considered microcosmic models of the world, which contained all the qualities of life and in which ''the four elements [earth, air, fire, water] were perfectly conjoined.'' Egg shapes appear on all three panels of Bosch's altarpiece; the most prominent one, on the right panel (FIG. 18-22), forms the body of a grotesque, human-headed monster. This creature has been called the ''alchemical man,'' and the tiny figures inside his eggshell torso—usually interpreted as embodying the sins of gluttony and lust—are seen as gathered around a table to watch the glow of an alchemical furnace hidden by the broken shell of the egg man's body.

According to this interpretation, the subject and organization of the triptych correspond to the basic (and, at the time, current) alchemical allegory, in which the distillation process—seen as the cyclical and self-perpetuating creation, destruction, and rebirth of the world and its inhabitants—takes place in four stages: ''conjunction'' (the marriage of opposites); ''coagulation'' (the multiplication of Adam and Eve into the peoples of the earth); ''putrification'' (the separation of the opposing elements previously joined in ''matrimony''); and ''cleansing'' (the washing and purifying of the separated ingredients, a process compared to the Christian resurrection and purification of the soul). The final outcome of this entire allegorical distillation—union with God—is symbolized by the circle and the globe.

If interpreted in these terms, the first three stages of the distillation process are symbolically represented in sequence from left to right on the interior of the three altarpiece panels. The fourth and final stage appears on the outside of the closed wings (FIG. 18-23), where a transparent globe containing earth, water, and clouds—painted in *grisaille* (tones of gray)—represents God's creation of the earth, which the alchemists tried to imitate in their operations.

In keeping with the cyclical and self-perpetuating process of distillation, the exterior of the altarpiece can be read either as the beginning or as the end of the cycle depicted on the interior. Placed at the end, it would provide the altarpiece with a comforting conclusion—a consolatory postscript promising that the sufferings of Hell may not be the end of everything after all. Most scholars, however, place the outside panels at the beginning of the sequence. To them, the grisaille represents *The Third Day of Creation*, when dark, light, water, land, and flora—but not the fauna—had been created. The outside thus becomes the natural prelude to the altarpiece's interior, where the remainder of Genesis is recorded on the left wing. On the central panel, the descendants of the first parents abandon themselves to the delights of the flesh, oblivious to the eventual but inevitable consequences recorded on the right wing—the apocalyptic results of the Last Judgement in the form of the fearsome destruction and tortures suffered in Hell. And if we realize how far God—a tiny figure in the upper left corner of the left exterior panel—has been removed from his creation, then Bosch's message seems to become quite clear: humanity, left to its own devices, is destined for damnation. Although far from being universally accepted, this last interpretation of *The Garden of Earthly Delights* appears to conform best with the remainder of the artist's oeuvre. Neither in this, nor in Bosch's other works, does humankind appear to advantage. Abandoned to evil by the fall, humanity merits Hell.

Bosch was a supreme narrative painter, and the visions of his bubbling imagination demanded quick release. His technique is more rapid and spontaneous than the labored traditional Flemish manner. He seemed to have had no time for the customary monochrome underpaintings or careful modeling of figures. His method forecasts the *alla prima* technique of the seventeenth and eighteenth centuries, as he puts down with quick and precise strokes the myriad creatures that populate his panels. His use of *impasto*, which did not require the traditional laborious application of numerous glazes, was ideally suited to the spinning of his mordant fantasies. And if he extends

no hope of salvation for man, he only anticipates Michelangelo, who, in his *Last Judgment* fresco (FIG. 17-35), came to the same conclusion some 30 years later.

France and Germany

The bourgeoisie in France, unlike that in the Netherlands, was not wealthy, localized in strong towns, nor interested in fostering the arts. In France, the Hundred Years' War had wrecked economic enterprise and prevented stability. During the fifteenth century, the anarchy of war and the weakness of the kings resulted in a group of rival duchies. The strongest of these, as we have seen, was the duchy of Burgundy; through marriage and political alliance, it occupied the Netherlands and became essentially Flemish, particularly in art commissioned by the court. In France, artists joined the retinues of the wealthier nobility—the dukes of Berry, Bourbon, and Nemours—and sometimes the royal court, where they were able to continue to develop an art that is typically French despite its regional variations. But no artist of the fifteenth century north of the Alps could escape the influence of the great artists of Flanders; French art accepted it, and works of high quality were produced, although only one really major figure emerged. JEAN FOUQUET (*c.* 1420–1481) is the outstanding French artist of the fifteenth century. During his career, he worked for the king, Charles VII, for the Duke of Nemours, and for Étienne Chevalier, the king's minister of finance. Fouquet's portrait of Chevalier with his patron, St. Stephen (FIG. 18-24), shows, in addition to Flemish influence, the effect of the two years he spent in Italy, between 1445 and

18-24 JEAN FOUQUET, *Étienne Chevalier and St. Stephen, c.* 1450. Tempera on wood, 36½" × 33½". Gemäldegalerie, Staatliche Museen, Berlin-Dahlem.

1447. The kneeling donor with his standing saint is familiar in Flemish art, as are the three-quarter stances and the sharp, clear focus of the portraits. The reading of the surfaces, however, is less particular than in the Flemish practice; the artist is trying to represent the forms underneath the surfaces, in the Italian manner. Also of Italian inspiration are the architectural background and its rendering in perspective. The secularizing tendency advancing so rapidly in the fifteenth century shows in the familiar, comradely demeanor of the two men; nothing whatever distinguishes them as being of different worlds, except possibly that St. Stephen, who holds the stone of his martyrdom, is dressed as a priest.

An isolated masterpiece of great power, painted in the extreme south of France by an anonymous artist, is *The Avignon Pietà** (FIG. 18-25), which has both Flemish and Italian elements. Rogier van der Weyden's great *Escorial Deposition* (FIG. 18-14) comes to mind at once when we see the Avignon work, although the balanced, almost symmetrical massing is of the Italian Renaissance. (The subdued color scheme has also suggested Iberian influence to some writers.) The donor, now familiarly present at the sacred event, kneels at the left. His is a strikingly characteristic portrait—the face gnarled, oaken, ascetic. The group of Christ and saints is united by the splendidly painted figure of Christ and by the angu-

*Now attributed to ENGUERRAND QUARTON (c. 1410–1466), a French artist active in Provence in the south of France.

lar shapes that seem deliberately simplified for graphic emphasis. As in Italian art, surface ornament is suppressed in the interest of monumental form. The luminous gold background, against which the figures are silhouetted and into which the halos are incised, is a strangely conservative feature, contrasting with the detailed background landscape reminiscent of Flemish paintings. No matter what his sources, the painter is deeply sensitive to his theme. Along with Rogier's version, *The Avignon Pietà* is one of the most memorable in the history of religious art.

To an even greater extent than in France, the development of German painting in the fifteenth century was strongly colored by the achievements of Flemish painting. In northern Germany, the influence of Jan van Eyck joined the tradition of the International style to produce the gentle, pictorially ornate world of delicacy and charm of STEPHAN LOCHNER (c. 1400–1451), the leading master of the school of Cologne. Lochner is noted for his compositions on the idyllic theme of the *Madonna in the Rose Garden* (FIG. 18-26), which seems particularly well suited to his sophisticated and refined sensibilities. Sometimes referred to as the "soft" style because of its feminine suavity and curvilinear rhythm, Lochner's manner was very different from the sculptural, blocky, "hard" style of southern Germany as we find it in the work of the Swiss painter CONRAD WITZ (c. 1400–1447). Although *The Miraculous Draught of Fish* (FIG. 18-27) by this remarkable painter also shows Flemish influence, par-

18-25 Attributed to ENGUERRAND QUARTON, *The Avignon Pietà*, c. 1455. Tempera on wood, approx. 5' 4" × 7' 2". Louvre, Paris.

18-26 STEPHAN LOCHNER, *Madonna in the Rose Garden*, *c.* 1430–1435. Tempera on wood, approx. 20″ × 16″. Wallraf-Richartz-Museum, Cologne.

ticularly that of Van Eyck, the painting demonstrates Witz's powerful and original sense of realism. Witz shows precocious skill in the study of water effects: the sky-glaze on the slowly moving lake surface, the mirrored reflections of the figures in the boat, the transparency of the shallow water in the foreground. This is one of the first Renaissance pictures in which the landscape not only predominates over the figures but is also the representation of a specific place—the shores of Lake Geneva, with the town of Geneva on the right and the ranges of the Alps in the distance.

The Late Gothic style is seen to best advantage in the works of German artists, who specialized in the carving of large retables (altar screens) in wood. The sculptor VEIT STOSS (1447–1533) carved a great altar for the church of St. Mary in Kraków, Poland (FIG. 18-28), no element of which is recognizable as Italian Renaissance. Typically, the altar consists of a central, box-like space; the shrine is flanked by hinged, movable wings—an inner pair (shown here) and an outer pair. In the shrine, a composition of huge figures (some 9 feet high) represent *The Death and Assumption of the Virgin* and, in the wings, scenes from the lives of Christ and the Virgin. The altar expresses the intense piety of Gothic culture in its late phase, when every resource of figural and ornamental design from the vocabulary of Gothic art is drawn on to heighten the emotion and to glorify the apparition of the sacred event. The disciples of Christ are gathered about the Virgin, who sinks down in death. One of them

18-27 CONRAD WITZ, *The Miraculous Draught of Fish*, 1444. Tempera on wood, approx. 51″ × 61″. Musée d'Art et d'Histoire, Geneva.

18-28   VEIT STOSS, *The Death and Assumption of the Virgin*, from the Altar of the Virgin Mary, 1477–1489. Painted and gilded wood, triptych (wings open) 43' high, 35' wide. Church of St. Mary, Kraków, Poland.

supports her; another, just above her, wrings his hands in grief; others are posed in attitudes of woe and psychic shock. The sculptor strives for minute realism in every detail. At the same time, he enwraps the figures in an almost abstract pattern of restless, twisting, curving swaths of drapery, which, by their broken and writhing lines, unite the whole tableau in a vision of agitated emotion. The massing of sharp, broken, and pierced forms, which dart flame-like through the composition—at once unifying and animating it—recalls the design principles of Late Gothic, "flamboyant" architecture (FIG. 10-39). Indeed, in the Kraków altarpiece, sculpture and architecture are amalgamated, and their union is enhanced by painting and gilding. The distinction of the different media, familiar in Italian Renaissance art and furthered by it, is as yet unknown to this Late Gothic artist, even though, like the Italian artist, his eye focuses ever more sharply on natural appearance.

In the work of TILMAN RIEMENSCHNEIDER (1460–1531), we find, as we do in the work of Veit Stoss, scarcely a trace of the Italian Renaissance. The canopy of Tilman's *Creglingen Altarpiece* (FIG. 18-29) is an intri-

18-29   TILMAN RIEMENSCHNEIDER, *The Assumption of the Virgin*, center panel of *The Creglingen Altarpiece*, *c.* 1495–1499. Carved lindenwood, 6' 1" wide. Parish church, Creglingen, West Germany.

cate weaving of flamboyant Gothic forms, and the endless and restless line is communicated to the draperies of the figures. The whole design is thus in motion and complication, and no element functions without the rest. The draperies float and flow around bodies lost within them, serving not as descriptions but as design elements that tie the figures to each other and to the framework. The spirituality of the figures, immaterial and weightless as they appear, is heightened by a facial expression common to Tilman's figures and consonant with the age of troubles that is coming—a look of psychic strain. They brood in pensive melancholy, their brows often furrowed in anxiety. A favorite theme in Late Gothic German sculpture was the *Schmerzensmann* (man of sorrows); for Tilman, all his actors were men of sorrow—weary, grave, unsmiling.

With the sculptor–painter MICHAEL PACHER (*c.* 1435–1498), we come to the first important meeting of German art with the Italian Renaissance. Pacher, a Tyrolean, must have journeyed down the Po valley and become familiar with the style of Andrea Mantegna and his school. In his painting *St. Wolfgang Forces the Devil to Hold His Prayerbook* (FIG. 18-30), we find the hard, wiry linearity of Mantegna and a combination of Late Gothic and Mantegna's drapery style. The figure of St. Wolfgang now has the monumental solidity of Italian form. The whole setting is Italian Renaissance. Familiar in northern Italian and Venetian compositions are a perspective down a street—the plunging orthogonals remind us of Mantegna's architecture

in the *St. James Led to Martyrdom* fresco (FIG. 16-63)—and the figures standing on a fretted balcony, which slow the swift recession of the perspective to the horizon. But the gargoylish Devil tells us that the Gothic is still very much in the northern environment.

In Germany, where printing with movable type was developed, we would expect the graphic arts to be well represented by competent masters. And indeed, MARTIN SCHONGAUER (*c.* 1450–14901) was the century's most skilled and subtle northern master of the new metal engraving technique. Printing pictures from woodblocks was developed in Europe around 1400 (the Chinese had known the technique centuries before) and remained popular, especially for book illustration, well into the 1500s. But engraving on metal surfaces—begun, as we have seen, in the 1430s and well developed by 1450—proved a much more flexible technique and, in the second half of the century, widely replaced the woodcut. Schongauer's *St. Anthony Tormented by the Demons* (FIG. 18-31) shows both the versatility of the medium and the artist's mastery of it. Although better known for his gentle Madonnas in a style based on that of Rogier van der Weyden, here Schongauer displays almost the same taste for the diabolical as Hieronymus Bosch; his stoic saint is caught in a revolving thornbush of spiky demons, who claw and tear at him furiously. With unsurpassed skill and subtlety, the artist makes mar-

18-31 MARTIN SCHONGAUER, *St. Anthony Tormented by the Demons,* c. 1480–1490. Engraving, approx. 13″ × 11″. Metropolitan Museum of Art, New York (Rogers Fund, 1920).

18-30 MICHAEL PACHER, *St. Wolfgang Forces the Devil to Hold His Prayerbook,* panel from the Altar of the Fathers of the Church, c. 1481. Tempera and oil on wood, approx. 40″ × 37″. Alte Pinakothek, Munich.

velous distinctions of tonal values and textures—from smooth skin to rough cloth, from the furry and feathery to the hairy and scaly. The method of describing forms with hatching that follows the forms, probably developed by Schongauer, became standard with German graphic artists. The Italians preferred parallel hatching (compare Antonio Pollaiuolo's engraving, FIG. 16-55) and rarely adopted this method, which, in keeping with the general northern approach to art, tends to describe the surfaces of things rather than their underlying structures.

THE SIXTEENTH CENTURY

Germany

The art of northern Europe during the sixteenth century is characterized by a sudden awareness of the advances made by the Italian Renaissance and by a desire to assimilate this new style as rapidly as possible. Many artists traveled to Italy to study the new art first hand; others met it either directly, in the form of Italian artists who came to the north, or indirectly, through the numerous Italian engravings that circulated throughout northern Europe. One of the most prolific Italian engravers, MARCANTONIO RAIMONDI, rarely invented his own compositions but copied those of other artists, particularly Raphael. In this way, many panel paintings and frescoes by Italian Renaissance artists became the common property of all Europe. Naturally, the impact of Italian art varied widely, according to the artist, the time, and the place. Many artists never abandoned existing local traditions; others were frequently content to borrow only single motifs or the general form of a composition. In Germany, the wealthy merchant class maintained close commercial relations with Venice, and German Humanists were in contact with the Neo-Platonic academy of Florence. As a result, Albrecht Dürer frequently illustrated Florentine thought clothed in Venetian and German forms.

During the fifteenth century, painting in the wealthy towns of southern Germany developed along its own expressionistic lines under the dominant influences of Flemish art. Around the turn of the century, it suddenly burst into full bloom. By 1528, with the death of its two greatest exponents, Dürer and Matthias Grünewald, it had spent itself. Thus, its most brilliant period corresponds almost exactly to the High Renaissance in Italy. Its decline around 1530 was just as abrupt as its rise, and the reason for this is uncertain. The almost incessant religious wars devastated the German lands, and puritanism, accompanying the triumph of Protestantism in the north, may have opposed Humanistic paganism in the figurative arts. With the exception of Hans Holbein the Younger, the main representatives of the German School were born within 10 years of one another and were contemporaries of Michelangelo, Raphael, Giorgione, and Titian.

ALTDORFER AND CRANACH

ALBRECHT ALTDORFER (c. 1480–1538) is the primary representative of the *Donaustil* (Danube style), which flourished along the Danube River from Regensburg (Altdorfer's hometown) eastward into Austria. The style is formed around the depiction of landscape and stresses mood, sometimes heightened to passion. Altdorfer's own style is highly personal and only occasionally modified by the influence of Dürer. He was a gifted colorist and observer of atmospheric and light effects. He loved forests and ruins, in which his figure groups are half-submerged. He painted at least one landscape without figures, making *Danube Landscape, Near Regensburg,* (c. 1522, not shown) perhaps the first landscape in Western art painted entirely for its own sake.

His most renowned work, *The Battle of Issus* (FIG. 18-32), bears little resemblance to a Danube setting, although it does give a bird's-eye view of an Alpine landscape. Here, Altdorfer spreads out in awesome detail the battle in which Alexander the Great overthrew the Persian king, Darius (FIG. 6-38); a huge inscription hanging in the clouds relates this. Swarms of warriors from both sides contest on a plain backed by cities, mountains, seas, and the opposed forces of nature: the sun and the moon in an illuminated sky. This sudden opening up of space, with its subordination of the human figure to the cosmic landscape, bespeaks a new view of nature—a view that will see man as an insignificant mote in an infinite universe. We need not suppose that German artists knew of the work of the contemporary astronomer, Copernicus, who was about to revise the age-old view that the earth is fixed and to suggest instead that the earth and the other "fixed" planets revolve about the sun. It is interesting that such high-horizoned, "topographical" landscapes (we might better call them "cosmographical") anticipate the coming cosmic view that the sciences of physics and physical astronomy will open to the Western world. Altdorfer's technique is still that of the miniaturist, yet his setting is no longer a page but a world—one in which his insect-like combatants are all but lost. In this first vision of the immense space and power of the cosmos, Altdorfer seems to suggest what all subsequent philosophers, scientists, and churchmen, as well as artists, will confront—the fact of the littleness of man.

The early works of LUCAS CRANACH THE ELDER (1472–1553) are close to the *Donaustil*, which im-

18-32 ALBRECHT ALTDORFER, *The Battle of Issus*, 1529. Oil on wood, 63" × 46". Alte Pinakothek, Munich.

merses man in the breadth of nature. At Wittenberg, where he was summoned by the elector of Saxony, Cranach became a friend and follower of Luther, and he has been called the outstanding representative of German Protestant painting. His later works are marked by a shift from religious to humanistic subject matter: mythology, history, and portraits. Best known are his figure compositions featuring the nude, which he renders with a charming, provincial naïveté. A good example is *The Judgment of Paris* (FIG.

18-33). Here, Paris and Mercury consult, while three spindly little goddesses show off their pretty contours. One of them bashfully stands on one foot; another coquettishly calls attention to her charms; the third stands by, wearing a fashionable hat. Cranach makes no effort to dress his gods after the antique manner; they wear the functional armor of German knights attached to provincial courts. Doughty and square-faced, they could have just come in from the field of honor. The background landscape reflects

18-33 LUCAS CRANACH THE ELDER, *The Judgment of Paris*, 1530. Oil on wood, approx. 14″ × 9″. Staatliche Kunsthalle, Karlsruhe.

Cranach's earlier *Donaustil* in its meticulous description of foliage. And so far, only Dürer's approach to the nude (FIG. 18-37) is tutored by Italian art.

MATTHIAS GRÜNEWALD

One of the greatest individualists of the Renaissance and an artist of highly original genius is Matthias Neithardt, known conventionally as MATTHIAS GRÜNEWALD (c. 1480–1528). Forgotten until our time, he appears to have had the wide interests of the individualistic Renaissance artists. Working for the archbishops of Mainz from 1511 on as court painter and decorator, he also served them as architect, hydraulic engineer, and superintendent of works. Undoubtedly, he had Lutheran sympathies. He participated in the Peasant Revolt in 1525, and, after its collapse, had to flee to northern Germany, where he settled at Halle in Saxony. The sources of Grünewald's style are not certain. He may have been to Italy, but there is little of Renaissance Classicism in his art. He knew the work of Dürer and perhaps of Bosch. A brilliant colorist, he is not interested in the construction of the monumental, idealized figure in the Italian manner.

His color is characterized by subtle tones and soft harmonies on the one hand and shocking dissonance on the other. Uninterested in natural landscape, he shows us either the celestial or the infernal.

In his appalling *Crucifixion* from *The Isenheim Altarpiece* (FIG. 18-34), Grünewald gives us perhaps the most memorable interpretation of the theme in the history of art. The altar is composed of a carved wooden shrine with two pairs of movable panels, one directly in back of the other. Painted by Grünewald between 1510 and 1515 for the monastic hospital order of St. Anthony of Isenheim, the panels show three scenes, with the *Crucifixion* outermost, when the altar is closed. The dreadful aspect of the painting may be due in part to its placement in a house of the sick, where it may have admonished the inmate that another had suffered more. It may also have had a therapeutic function, in that it offered some hope to the afflicted.* Two saints are represented on the wings flanking the central panels: on the left, St. Sebastian, whose intercession was invoked to ward off disease (especially the plague); on the right, St. Anthony, the patron saint of the order, who was identified with miraculous cure. Together, the saints establish the theme of disease and healing that is reinforced by the paintings on the inner wings.

One of the main illnesses treated at the hospital was ergotism (called "St. Anthony's Fire"), a disease caused by ergot, a fungus that grows especially on rye. Although its cause was not discovered until about 1600, its symptoms (convulsion and gangrene) were well known. The gangrene often compelled amputation, and it has been noted in this connection that the two movable halves of the predella of the altarpiece, if slid apart, make it appear as if the legs of the body of Christ have been amputated. The same observation can be made of the two main panels. Due to the off-center placement of the cross, the opening of the left center panel would "sever" one arm from the crucified figure.

Much of this symbolism may have been dictated by his patrons, but Grünewald's own inflamed imagination produced the terrible image of the suffering Christ. Against the pall of darkness lowered on the earth, the devasted body looms—dead, the flesh already discolored by decomposition and studded with the thorns of the lash. In death, the strains of the superhuman agony twist the blackening feet, tear at the arms, wrench the head to one side, and turn the fingers into crooked spikes. One has only to tense one's fingers in the position of Christ's to experience the shuddering tautness of nerves expressed in every line of the figure. No other artist has produced such

*The following discussion of Grünewald's altarpiece is indebted to Andrée Hayum, "The Meaning and Function of the Isenheim Altarpiece: The Hospital Context Revisited," *The Art Bulletin,* LIX, 4, Dec. 1977, 501–517.

18-34 MATTHIAS GRÜNEWALD, *Crucifixion* from *The Isenheim Altarpiece* (closed), *c.* 1510–1515. Oil on wood, center panel approx. 8′ 10″ × 10′ 1″. Musée Unterlinden, Colmar.

an image of the dreadful ugliness of pain. The sharp, angular shapes of anguish appear in the figures of the swooning Virgin and St. John and in the shrill delirium of the Magdalene. To the other side, the gaunt, spectral form of John the Baptist stands in ungainly pose, pointing with a finger sharp as a bird's beak to the dead Christ and indicating in a Latin inscription Christ's destiny as Redeemer and his own as mere precursor: "It is fitting that he increase and I diminish." The bright, harsh, dissonant colors—black, blood-red, acid-yellow, and the dreadful green of death—suit the flat, angular shapes. Placed in a wilderness of dark mountains, the scene is relieved by a flood of glaring light that holds the figures in a tableau of awful impact.

Death and suffering seem to be the dominant themes shown by the altarpiece in its closed state. Yet they are combined with symbols offering hope and comfort to the viewer. Behind St. John is a body of water (the river Jordan?), which signifies baptism—the healing action of water, which symbolically washes away sin. (It may also refer to the growing contemporary interest in hydrotherapy, as numerous handbooks advertising local thermal and mineral baths were being published around the turn of the ·

century.) The wine-red sky behind the cross evokes the blood of Christ and may symbolize the Eucharist. These references to the sacraments of baptism and the Eucharist offer the viewer the hope of salvation through the sacrifice of Christ, should earthly cures fail.

When we turn from the Good Friday of the *Crucifixion* to the Easter Sunday of the *Resurrection* (FIG. 18-35), an inner panel of *The Isenheim Altarpiece*, the mood changes from disaster to triumph. Christ, in a blazing aureole of light so incandescent that it dissolves his form and overwhelms the guards, rises like a great flame into the starlit heavens. The fluttering Gothic line prevails in the ascending Christ, and something of the awkward angularity of the *Crucifixion* scene shapes the fallen soldiers. The highly expressive light in both scenes is supernatural, not the light of common day. It is certainly not the even, flat light that models Piero della Francesca's *Resurrection* fresco (FIG. 16-36). Indeed, in these two pictures, we find the fundamental differences that set the German School apart from the Italian School in the Renaissance. Piero's *Resurrection* typically represents the event in terms of a static grouping of solidly rendered figures in a completely balanced, measured composi-

18-35 Matthias
Grünewald, *Resurrection*,
detail of the inner right
panel of *The Isenheim
Altarpiece* (open). Approx.
8′ 10″ × 5′.

tion; the central figure of Christ stands solid as a column, one foot placed weightily on the edge of the sarcophagus. Grünewald converts everything into flowing motion; his Christ is disembodied, almost formless, and the composition has the irregularity and free form of a flaming cloud. Color determines everything here—not sculpturesque form and geometric composition, as with Piero. Moreover, Grünewald's intention is to render the supernatural in a bodiless way appropriate to it; Piero makes Christ as massive and corporeal as the stone sarcophagus on which he stands. From the Italian point of view, the visionary flashing and flickering of Grünewald's *Resurrection* must have appeared crude, formless, and utterly devoid of the order that theory, based on the study of nature and measurement, could confer.

ALBRECHT DÜRER

We know that Grünewald's great contemporary ALBRECHT DÜRER (1471–1528) felt this way about much of the art of the north and that, in comparison with Italian art, it appeared to him old-fashioned, clumsy, and without knowledge. In the introduction to an unfinished and unpublished treatise on painting, Dürer writes:

> Now, I know that in our German nation, at the present time, are many painters who stand in need of instruction, for they lack all real art theory. . . . For as much as they are so numerous, it is very needful for them to learn to better their work. He that works in ignorance works more painfully than he who works in understanding; therefore let all learn to understand art aright.

While still a journeyman, Dürer became acquainted with, and began to copy, prints by Mantegna and Pollaiuolo. Fascinated with Classical ideas, as transmitted through Italian Renaissance artists, Dürer became the first northern artist to travel to Italy expressly to study Italian art and its underlying theories at their source. After his first journey in 1495 (he made a second trip in 1505–1506), it became his life mission to bring the modern—the Italian Renaissance—style north and establish it there. Although Dürer did not always succeed in fusing his own native German style with the Italian manner, he was the first northern artist who fully understood the basic aims of the southern Renaissance.

Dürer was also the first artist outside of Italy to become an international art celebrity. Well-traveled and widely admired, he knew many of the leading Humanists and artists of his time, among them Erasmus of Rotterdam and Giovanni Bellini. A man of wide talents and tremendous energy, he became the "Leonardo of the North," achieving fabulous fame in his own time and a firm reputation ever since. Like Leonardo da Vinci, Dürer wrote theoretical treatises on a variety of subjects, such as perspective, fortification, and the ideal in human proportions. Through his prints, he exerted strong influence throughout Europe, especially in Flanders, but also in Italy. Moreover, he was the first northern artist to make himself known to posterity through several excellent self-portraits, through his correspondence, and through a carefully kept, quite detailed and readable diary.

In his own time, Dürer's fame and influence depended on his mastery of the graphic arts, and we

18-36 ALBRECHT DÜRER, *The Four Horsemen of the Apocalypse*, c. 1498. Woodcut, approx. 15¼″ × 11″. Metropolitan Museum of Art, New York (gift of Junius S. Morgan, 1919).

still think that his greatest contribution to Western art lies in this field. Trained as a goldsmith before he took up painting and printmaking, he developed an extraordinary proficiency in the handling of the burin, the engraving tool. This technical ability, combined with a feeling for the form-creating possibilities of line, enabled him to create a corpus of graphic work in woodcut and engraving that has seldom been rivaled for quantity and quality. In addition to illustrations for books, Dürer circulated and sold prints in single sheets, which people of ordinary means could buy and which made him a "people's artist" quite as much as a model for professionals. It also made him a rich man.

An early and very successful series of woodblock prints on 14 large sheets illustrates the Apocalypse, or the Revelation of St. John, the last book of the Bible. With great force and inventiveness, Dürer represents terrifying visions of doomsday, and of the omens preceding it. The fourth print of the series, *The Four Horsemen of the Apocalypse* (FIG. 18-36), represents, from foreground to background, Death trampling a bishop, Famine swinging scales, War wielding a sword, and Pestilence drawing his bow. The human race, in the last days of the world, is trampled by the Terrible Four. Technically, the virtuosity of Dürer's woodcuts has never been surpassed. By adapting to the woodcut the form-following hatching from Schongauer's engravings (FIG. 18-31), Dürer converts the former's primitive contrasts of black and white into a gliding scale of light and shade, achieving a quality of luminosity never before seen in woodblock prints. This dynamic composition retains some Late Gothic characteristics in the angularity of shapes and the tendency of forms to merge one into the other. On the other hand, Mantegna's influence can be found in the plastic and foreshortened poses of the trampled victims in the right foreground and in the head of Famine. But despite such Italicisms, the dramatic complexity of the composition remains essentially northern.

From 1500 on, Dürer became increasingly interested in the theoretical foundations of Italian Renaissance art; an engraving of *Adam and Eve* (FIG. 18-37) represents the first distillation of his studies of the Vitruvian theory of human proportions. Clearly outlined against the dark background of a northern forest, the two idealized figures of Adam and Eve stand in poses reminiscent of the *Apollo Belvedere* and the *Medici Venus*—two Hellenistic statues probably known to Dürer through graphic representations. Preceded by numerous geometric drawings, in which he tried to systematize sets of ideal human propor-

18-37 ALBRECHT DÜRER, *Adam and Eve* (*The Fall of Man*), 1504. Engraving, approx. 10″ × 7½″. Centennial Gift of Landon T. Clay. Courtesy of Museum of Fine Arts, Boston.

tions in balanced contrapposto poses, the final print presents Dürer's 1504 concept of the "perfect" male and female figures. Adam does, in fact, approach the southern ideal quite closely, but the fleshy Eve remains a German matron, her individualized features suggesting the use of a model. Northern also is the elaborate symbolism of the background "accessories" to the main figures. The choleric cat, the melancholic elk, the sanguine rabbit, and the phlegmatic ox represent the four humors of man, and the relation between Adam and Eve at the crucial moment of *The Fall of Man* is symbolized by the tension between cat and mouse in the foreground.

Dürer's *Adam and Eve* shows idealized forms and strongly naturalistic ones in a close combination that, depending on the viewer's attitude, may be regarded as complementing or as conflicting—closely allied ingredients in most of Dürer's works. For he agreed with Aristotle (and the new critics of the Renaissance) that "sight is the noblest faculty of man" and that "every form brought before our vision falls upon it as upon a mirror." "We regard," says Dürer, "a form and figure out of nature with more pleasure than any other, though the thing itself is not necessarily altogether better or worse." This is a new and important idea for artists. Nature holds the beautiful, says Dürer, for him who has the insight to extract it. Thus, beauty lies even in humble, perhaps ugly things, and the ideal, which bypasses or improves on nature, may not be the truly beautiful in the end. There is the hint here that uncomposed and ordinary nature might be a reasonable object of the artist's interest, quite as much as its composed and measured aspect. With an extremely precise watercolor study of a piece of turf (FIG. 18-38), Dürer allies himself to the scientific studies of Leonardo; for both artists, observation yields truth. Sight—sanctified by mystics like Nicholas of Cusa and artists like Jan van Eyck—becomes the secularized instrument of modern knowledge. The "mirror" that is our "vision" will later become telescope, microscope, and television screen. The remarkable *Great Piece of Turf* is as scientifically accurate as it is poetic; the botanist can distinguish each springing plant and variety of grass: dandelions, great plantain, yarrow, meadow grass, heath rush. "Depart not from nature in your opinions," says Dürer, "neither imagine that you can invent anything better. . . . for art stands firmly fixed in nature, and he who can find it there, he has it." The exquisite still life one finds in the northern paintings of the fifteenth century is irradiated with religious symbolism. Dürer's still life is of and for itself; he has found it in nature, and its representation no longer requires religious justification.

As Dürer closely studies floral nature, so he makes his portraits readings of character. The fifteenth-century portrait, like Van Eyck's *Man in a Red Turban* (FIG.

18-38 ALBRECHT DÜRER, *The Great Piece of Turf*, 1503.
Watercolor, approx. 16″ × 12½″. Graphische Sammlung
Albertina, Vienna.

18-39 ALBRECHT DÜRER, *Hieronymus Holzschuher*, 1526. Oil
on wood, approx. 19″ × 14″. Gemäldegalerie, Staatliche
Museen, Berlin-Dahlem.

18-40 ALBRECHT DÜRER, *Melencolia I*, 1514. Engraving,
approx. 9½″ × 7½″. Fogg Museum of Art, Harvard University,
Cambridge, Massachusetts (bequest of Francis Calley Gray).

18-11) or his *Canon van der Paele* (FIG. 18-10), is a
graphic description of features; Dürer's portraits, like
that of *Hieronymus Holzschuher* (FIG. 18-39), are interpretations of personality. It may be, however, that
they are as much projections of Dürer's own personality as they are readings of his subjects', for his portraits of men all show the subject as bold and virile,
square-jawed, flashing-eyed, and truculent. All the
subjects appear intense and intently aware of the observer. This strong psychic relationship to the external world, when the features are precisely particularized, makes for an extremely vivid presence.
Holzschuher, a friend of Dürer's and town councilor
of Nuremberg, fairly bristles with choleric energy and
the burly belligerence of Nuremberg citizens, who,
on many an occasion, had defended the city against
all comers, including the Emperor himself. Leaving
the background blank, except for an inscription, the
artist achieves a remarkable concentration on the
forceful personality of his subject. The portrait in Italy
never really brings the subject into such a tense personal relationship to the observer.

Dürer always found it quite difficult to reconcile his
northern penchant for precise naturalism with his
intellectual, theoretical pursuits and with the demands of southern High Renaissance art for simplified monumentality. This life-long dilemma seems to
be expressed in *Melencolia I* (FIG. 18-40), one of three
so-called "master prints" Dürer made between 1513

and 1514. These works (the other two are *Knight, Death, and the Devil* and *St. Jerome in His Study*)—probably intended to symbolize the moral, theological, and intellectual virtues—carry the art of engraving to the highest degree of excellence. Dürer used his burin to render differences in texture and tonal values that would be difficult to match even in the much more flexible medium of etching, which was developed later in the century. The complex symbolism of *Melencolia I* is based primarily on concepts derived from Florentine Neo-Platonism. About the seated, winged figure of Melancholy, the instruments of the arts and sciences lie strewn in idle confusion; she is the personification of knowledge that, without divine inspiration, lacks the ability to act. Also, according to then current astrological theory, the artist, or any man engaged in creative activity, is the subject of Saturn. As such, he is characterized by a melancholia bordering on madness that either plunges him into despondency or raises him to the heights of creative fury; Michelangelo was regarded as subject to this humor. Like Michelangelo also, Dürer conceived of the artist (and thus of himself) as a genius who struggles to translate the pure Idea in his mind into gross but visible matter. Thus, the monumental image of the winged genius, with burning eyes in a shaded face and wings that do not fly, becomes the symbol for divine aspirations defeated by human frailty and, in a way, a "spiritual self-portrait of Albrecht Dürer."

Only toward the very end of his life, and in one of his very last paintings, was Dürer finally able to reconcile the two opposed tendencies—northern naturalism and southern monumentality—that had struggled for dominance in his entire oeuvre. He painted *The Four Apostles* (FIG. 18-41) without commission and presented the two panels to the city fathers of Nuremberg in 1526 to be hung in the city hall. The work has been called Dürer's religious and political testament, in which he expresses his sympathies for the Protestant cause and warns against the dangerous times, when religion, truth, justice, and the virtues will all be threatened. The four apostles (John and Peter on the left panel; Mark and Paul on the right) stand on guard for the city. Quotations from each of their books, in the German of Luther's translation of the New Testament, are written on the frames. They warn against the coming of perilous times and the preaching of false prophets who will distort the word of God. The figures of the apostles summarize Dürer's whole craft and learning. Representing the four temperaments, or humors, of the human soul—as well as the four ages of man and other quaternities—these portrait-like characterizations of the apostles have no equal in the idealized representations of Italian saints. At the same time, the art of the Italian Renaissance is felt in the monumental grandeur and majesty of the figures, which are heightened by a vivid color and sharp lighting. Here, Dürer unites the northern sense of minute realism with the Italian tradition of balanced forms, massive and simple. The result is a vindication of the artist's striving toward a new understanding—a work that stands with the greatest of the masterpieces of Italian art.

18-41 ALBRECHT DÜRER, *The Four Apostles*, 1526. Oil on wood, each panel 7′ 1″ × 2′ 6″. Alte Pinakothek Munich.

HANS HOLBEIN THE YOUNGER
What Dürer had struggled all his life to formulate and construct was achieved almost effortlessly by his younger contemporary, HANS HOLBEIN THE YOUNGER (1497–1543). Holbein's speciality was portraiture, in which he displayed a thorough assimilation of all that Italy had to teach of monumental composition, bodily structure, and sculpturesque form. He retains the northern traditions of close realism elaborated in fifteenth-century Flemish art. The color surfaces of his paintings are as lustrous as enamel; his detail, exact and exquisitely drawn; and his contrasts of light and dark, never heavy.

Holbein knew Erasmus of Rotterdam in Basel, where Holbein was first active. Because a religious civil war was imminent in Basel, Erasmus suggested that Holbein leave for England and gave him a recommendation to Thomas More, chancellor of Eng-

18-42 HANS HOLBEIN THE YOUNGER, *The French Ambassadors,* 1533. Oil and tempera on wood, approx. 6′ 8″ × 6′ 9½″. Reproduced by courtesy of the Trustees of the National Gallery, London.

land under Henry VIII. Holbein did leave and became painter to the English court. While there, he painted a superb double portrait of the French ambassadors to England, Jean de Dinteville and Georges de Selve (FIG. 18-42). The two men, both ardent Humanists, stand at either end of a side table covered with an oriental rug and a collection of objects reflective of their interests: mathematical and astronomical models and implements, a lute with a broken string, compasses, a sundial, flutes, globes, and an open hymnbook with Luther's translation of *Veni, Creator Spiritus* and of the Ten Commandments. The still-life objects are rendered with the same meticulous care as are the men themselves, the woven design of the deep emerald curtain behind them, and the floor tiles constructed in faultless perspective; not a figure is missing from the astronomical instruments. The

stable, balanced, serene composition is interrupted only by a long, gray shape that slashes diagonally across the picture plane. This is an *anamorphic* image that needs to be viewed by some special means (for example, reflected in a cylindrical mirror) if it is to be recognizable. In this case, the image is of a death's-head, for, like Dürer, Holbein was interested in symbolism as well as in radical perspectives. The color harmonies are adjusted in symphonic complexity and richness. The grave, even somber portraits indicate that Holbein follows the Italian portrait tradition, which gives the face a neutral expression, rather than Dürer's practice of giving it an expression of keen intensity. *The French Ambassadors* exhibits the peculiar talents of Holbein—his strong sense of composition, his subtle linear patterning, his gift for portraiture, his marvelous sensitivity to color, his faultlessly firm technique. This painting may have been Holbein's favorite; it is the only one signed with his full name.

In his later works, Holbein's style underwent a gradual change. He eliminated inventories of objects, confining himself to a simple neutral ground behind the subject. In the portrait of *Christina of Denmark* (FIG. 18-43), his simplification is carried over to the figure itself, to the costume, and to the face. The handsome young widow (of Duke Francesco Maria Sforza), with whom Henry VIII tried unsuccessfully to arrange a marriage, is shown at full length, a format reserved for the most eminent personages (bust portraits or half-lengths sufficed for Holbein's numerous portraits of merchants and court officials). Nothing is shown that might detract from the subject. With flawless draftsmanship, Holbein renders the figure firm and solid; his descriptive line is subtly reinforced

18-43 HANS HOLBEIN THE YOUNGER, *Christina of Denmark*, 1538. Oil on wood, approx. 70″ × 32″. Reproduced by courtesy of the Trustees of the National Gallery, London.

with flat modeling. The complete lack of perspective space may make us think of Mannerism, but we do not feel any ambiguity here; the volume of the figure itself clearly defines the space it occupies. Thus, with utmost restraint and simplicity, Holbein, in his later portraits, is able to achieve the monumental effects of the High Renaissance.

Holbein died prematurely in 1543 and, with him, the great German School of the Renaissance. But in 1532, when he left Basel for England, he had already taken the Renaissance with him. There were no significant successors. German art faded in the uproar of a century of religious war.

The Netherlands

The resurgence of France and the eclipse of the House of Burgundy robbed the Flemish schools of their precedence. The tremendous acclaim of Albrecht Dürer when he visited Antwerp in 1520 indicates a reverse for Flanders; Germany, which had followed, now led developments in the north. The decay of the old Flemish tradition, both in form and content, left a void that was filled by the confusing appearance of Italian ideas, received secondhand through Dürer. As with any new, inspiring, but ill-understood fashion, a number of conflicting mannerisms arose, which, if anything, had in common only their misunderstanding of the principles behind the novel forms. This period is characterized by a great delight in decorative extravagance, in which pedantic allusion to the classics is combined with exotic settings made of piled-up fragments of Italianate ornament. For a generation or so, the north, as it has been said, "simply could not get its Renaissance on straight."

But from all this confusion, new and confident movements could begin. For one thing, remnants of the Medieval tradition had to be swept away, and this happened. The dominance of religious conventions yielded to experiments in subject matter and form; although religious material persisted, it no longer prevailed in art. We have seen how it had been modified by humanization for over a century; now it had to share the artist's interest in portraiture, mythology, landscape, and genre. The structural basis for a new, Humanistic realism had been introduced by the great German painters. It was on this basis that an international, European art, dealing primarily with human interests, had to be built.

Changing views and attitudes were accompanied by a geographical shift in the region's commercial center. Partly due to the silting-up of the Bruges estuary, traffic was diverted to Antwerp, which became the hub of economic activity in the Low Countries after 1510. By mid-century, a jealous Venetian envoy had to admit that more business was transacted in

Antwerp in a few weeks than in a year in Venice. As many as 500 ships a day passed through Antwerp's harbor, and large trading colonies from England and Germany and from Italy, Portugal, and Spain established themselves in the city.

QUENTIN METSYS

Antwerp's growth and prosperity, along with the propensity of its wealthy merchants for collecting and purchasing art, attracted artists to the city—among them, QUENTIN METSYS (c. 1465–1530), who became Antwerp's leading master after 1510. Son of a Louvain blacksmith, Metsys may have been largely self-taught, which would explain, in part, his susceptibility to outside influences and his willingness to explore the styles and modes of a variety of models,

from Van Eyck to Bosch, and from Van der Weyden to Dürer and Leonardo. Yet his eclecticism was subtle and discriminating and enriched by an inventiveness that gave a personal stamp to his paintings and made him a popular as well as important artist. Quentin Metsys represents both the bad and the good aspects of early sixteenth-century Flemish art in its struggle to shed fifteenth-century traditions in favor of a more "modern" Renaissance mode of expression.

Metsys painted *The St. Anne Altarpiece* for the Louvain Brotherhood of St. Anne between 1507 and 1509. Its central panel (FIG. 18-44) shows a stable and orderly grouping of figures before a triple-vaulted loggia, through which a finely painted distant landscape can be seen. The round-arched architecture, complete with tie-rods and a central dome, seems

18-44 QUENTIN METSYS, *The St. Anne Altarpiece*, center panel, 1507–1509. Oil on wood, 7' 4½" × 7' 2¼". Musées Royaux des Beaux-Arts de Belgique, Brussels.

functional enough (except for the rectangular window, which intrudes illogically into the hemispheric dome), but it has little to do with Italian Renaissance architecture, which Metsys evidently tried to emulate. In this respect, he was no more successful than his Romanist contemporaries, whose attempts to provide their paintings with "modern" (Italian Renaissance) settings produced little more than architectural fantasies. On the other hand, the triple loggia effectively unifies the solemn, softly draped figures, whose heads are grouped in three inverted triangles. The compression of the composition may have been inspired by one of the late paintings of Hugo van der Goes, and the calm serenity of the scene evokes memories of Hans Memling's paintings (FIG. 18-20). But these and other possible sources of inspiration are thoroughly assimilated and synthesized by Metsys into a personal style. The regularized composition and the light coloration of his forms produce a tapestry-like effect that is both decorative and memorable.

Metsys' explorations of the past are liberally mixed with forward-looking genre and moralizing subjects to give his oeuvre a highly diversified aspect. The variety of his inventions provides a bridge from the fifteenth into the sixteenth century and makes him an influential inspiration to many of his contemporaries.

JAN GOSSAERT

More single-minded, although no more successful than Metsys in his exploration of Italian Renaissance art, is JAN GOSSAERT (c. 1478–1535), who worked for the later Philip of Burgundy, associated with Humanist scholars, and visited Italy. There, Gossaert (who adopted the name MABUSE, after his birthplace of Maubeuge) became fascinated with the antique and its mythological subject matter. Giorgio Vasari—Italian historian and Gossaert's contemporary—wrote that "Gossaert was almost the first to bring the true method of representing nude figures and mythologies from Italy to the Netherlands," although it is obvious that he derived much of his Classicism from Dürer. The composition and poses in his *Neptune and Amphitrite* (FIG. 18-45) are borrowed from Dürer's *Adam and Eve* (FIG. 18-37), although Gossaert's figures have been inflated, giving an impression of ungainly weight. The artist approximates the Classical stance, but Gossaert seems to have been more interested in nudity than in a Classical, ideal canon of proportions. The setting for the figures is a carefully painted architectural fantasy that illustrates a complete lack of understanding of the Classical style. Yet the painting is executed with traditional Flemish polish, and the figures are skillfully drawn and modeled. Although Gossaert also painted religious subjects in the traditional style, attempting unsuccessfully to outshine the fifteenth-century Flemish masters, his *Neptune*

18-45   JAN GOSSAERT (MABUSE), *Neptune and Amphitrite*, c. 1516. Oil on wood, 7' 2" × 4' 1". Gemäldegalerie, Staatliche Museen, Berlin-Dahlem.

and Amphitrite aligns him firmly with the so-called Romanists, in whose art Italian Mannerism joins with fanciful native interpretations of the Classical style to form a highly artificial, sometimes decorative, often bizarre and chaotic style.

BARTHOLOMEUS SPRANGER

Much more the Romanist than Gossaert, the Netherlandish painter BARTHOLOMEUS SPRANGER (1546–1611) exaggerates the stylistic peculiarities of Italian Mannerism almost to the point of caricature. Spranger traveled widely in Italy and France, studying a variety of pictorial styles from Jacopo da Pontormo and Parmigianino to the painters of the School of Fontainebleau (FIG. 18-51). What he learned from them merged with his earlier training in the Netherlands to form a highly sophisticated and imaginative style. For the connoisseur Emperor Rudolph II, whose court painter he became at Prague, he fashioned such classically learned, intricately composed, and suggestively erotic pictures as *Hercules and Omphale* (FIG. 18-46), much to the taste of his bachelor patron. Hercules was enslaved by the beautiful Om-

18-46 BARTHOLOMEUS SPRANGER, *Hercules and Omphale, c.* 1598. Paint on copper, 9¾″ × 7½″. Kunsthistorisches Museum, Vienna.

phale, who garbed him in the attributes of womanhood. Here, he wears women's satins and jewels and does women's work, spinning with distaff and spindle. His massive wrist is braceleted, and his hand is bent in an effeminate gesture. Behind him, an ugly hag makes the gesture of cuckoldry. The nude Omphale, her form androgynous (the emperor had a penchant for the epicene), smiles coquettishly over her shoulder. She carries Hercules' club and wears his lion's skin teasingly. Spranger's themes, lascivious and pagan, find their appropriate vehicle of expression in Italian Mannerism. The Manneristic traits are all here: the gliding, bending, turning poses; the constricted space; the crowded surface; the bright, decorative colors. Worldly, sensuous and ornamental, his pictures express a luxurious, courtly taste that contrasts markedly with the reverent art of the bourgeois towns in which the Netherlandish master painters worked.

JOACHIM PATINIR

An outstanding representative of a very different trend in sixteenth-century Flemish art is JOACHIM PATINIR (1475–1524)—the first Netherlandish landscape painter and the counterpart of the German Al-

brecht Altdorfer. A highly valued specialist in this field, Patinir often collaborated with other artists, letting them paint figures into his landscapes. Little is known of his background, and, although no definite links can be established between the two artists, Bosch may well have provided the initial inspiration for Patinir's panoramic vistas. Significantly, however, the landscapes in Bosch's paintings are of secondary importance and serve only as broad stages on which his figures perform their fantastic frolics; in Patinir's works, the landscapes take on primary importance, and the figures become mere accessories. In his *Landscape with St. Jerome* (FIG. 18-47), the insignificant figure of Patinir's title saint is almost hidden in the left middle ground. The vast panorama is seen from a mountaintop, and the artist works like a cartographer, building up his landscape in strips or layers parallel to the picture plane. The effect of recession is achieved by the careful diminution of familiar things (houses, trees, figures) and by the emphatic use of aerial perspective, in which the generally warm foreground colors shift to greens in the middle distance and to cool blues in the far distance. Realism is confined to the description of details. Plants are painted with botanical accuracy, and trees and rock forma-

18-47 JOACHIM PATINIR, *Landscape with St. Jerome, c.* 1520 (?). Oil on wood, 30" × 36". Museo del Prado, Madrid.

tions are rendered with great feeling for their textural differences. The rich multiplicity of Patinir's paintings, with activity almost everywhere, is drawn together by a strong design and an extremely effective dark–light pattern. The tiny figures scattered throughout his landscape effectively contrast human frailty and the power of nature.

PIETER BRUEGEL THE ELDER
A similar interest in the interrelationship of man and nature is expressed in the works of the greatest and most original Flemish painter of the sixteenth century, PIETER BRUEGEL THE ELDER (*c.* 1525–1569), whose early, high-horizoned, "cosmographical" landscapes were probably influenced by Patinir. But in Bruegel's paintings, no matter how huge a slice of this world he may show, the activities of man remain the dominant theme. Bruegel was apprenticed to a "Romanist," PIETER COECKE, and, like many of his contemporaries, traveled to Italy, where he seems to have spent almost two years, going as far south as Sicily. But unlike his contemporaries, Bruegel was not overwhelmed by Classical art, and his Italian experiences are only incidentally reflected in his paint-

ings, usually in the form of Italian or Alpine landscape features that he recorded in numerous drawings during his journey. On his return from Italy, Bruegel was exposed to the works of Bosch, and the influence of that strange master, strongly felt in Bruegel's early paintings, must have swept aside any Romanist inclinations he may have had.

Hunters in the Snow (FIG. 18-48) is one of five surviving paintings of a series of six in which Bruegel illustrated seasonal changes in the year. It shows man and landscape locked in winter cold. The weary hunters return with their hounds, wives build fires, skaters skim the frozen pond, the town and its church huddle in their mantle of snow; and beyond the typically Flemish winter scene lies a bit of Alpine landscape. Aside from this trace of fantasy, however, the landscape is realistic and quite unlike Patinir's; it develops smoothly from foreground to background and draws the viewer diagonally into its depths. The artist's consummate skill in the use of line and shape and his subtlety in tonal harmony make this one of the great landscape paintings in history and an Occidental counterpart of the masterworks of classical Chinese landscape.

18-48 Pieter Bruegel the Elder, *Hunters in the Snow*, 1565. Oil on wood, approx. 46″ × 64″. Kunsthistorisches Museum, Vienna.

Bruegel, of course, is not simply a landscapist. In his series of the months, he presents—in a fairly detached manner, occasionally touched with humor—the activities of man at different times of the year. And he chooses for his purpose the social class that is most directly affected by seasonal changes, the peasantry. But usually Bruegel is much more personal as he makes satirical comments on the dubious condition of man. His meaning in specific cases is often as obscure as Bosch's, and he seems to delight in leading us into his pictures through devious paths and confronting us sometimes with mystery, sometimes with an appalling revelation. As a vehicle for his sarcasm, he again chooses the peasant, whom he sees as an uncomplicated representative of humanity—a member of society whose actions and behavior are open, direct, and unspoiled by the artificial cultural gloss that disguises but does not altar the city dweller's natural inclinations. These good countryfolk are shown enjoying themselves in *The Peasant Dance* (FIG. 18-49), which is no mincing quadrille, but a boisterous, whirling, hoedown in which plenty of sweat is shed. One can almost hear the feet stomping to the rhythm of the bagpipe. With an eye much more inci-

sive than any camera lens, the artist grasps the entire scene in its most characteristic aspect and records it in a broad technique that discards most of the traditional Flemish concern for detail. Strong but simplified modeling emphasizes the active, solidly drawn silhouettes, which, combined with strong local colors, give the painting the popular robustness so suited to its subject. From the hilltop that he shared with the *Hunters*, Bruegel descends into the village to look more closely at its life and amusements—and he finds that all is not well in this rustic paradise. A fight is brewing at the table on the left; everyone is turning his back to the church in the background; nobody is paying the least attention to the small picture of a Madonna tacked to the tree on the right; and the man next to the bagpiper is wearing the feather of a peacock—a symbol of vanity—in his cap. And what about the young couple kissing unashamedly in public in the left middle ground? Is Bruegel telling us, like Bosch in his *Hell* (FIG. 18-22), that music is an instrument of the Devil and a perverter of morals? A closer inspection of the painting reveals that Bruegel is telling much more than the simple story of a country festivity. He is showing that a *kermess*, a festival cele-

18-49 PIETER BRUEGEL THE ELDER, *The Peasant Dance, c.* 1567. Oil on wood, approx. 45" × 65". Kunsthistorisches Museum, Vienna.

brating a saint, has become a mere pretext for man to indulge his lust, anger, and gluttony.

Toward the end of his life, Bruegel's commentary on man takes on an increasingly bitter edge. The Netherlands, racked by religious conflict, had become the seat of cruel atrocities, made even more cruel by the coming of the power of Catholic Spain to put down the Reformation. We do not know whether Bruegel took sides; like the great satirist he was, he may have preferred to make all mankind, not just partisans, the object of his commentary. His secret meanings may partly be explained by the danger of too much outspokenness. His biographer, Karel van Mander* (1548–1606), writes:

> Many of Bruegel's strange compositions and comical subjects one may see in his copper engravings . . . he supplied them with inscriptions which, at the time, were too biting and too sharp, and which he had his wife burn during his last illness, because of . . . fear that most disagreeable consequences might grow out of them.

Bruegel knew well how to disguise his intent—so well that in his day he was called ''Peter the Droll,'' because, as Van Mander writes, ''there are very few works from his hand that the beholder can look at seriously, without laughing.''

*Karel van Mander's *Het Schilderboeck (The Painter's Book)* was published in Haarlem in 1604. It contains a section with biographies of Netherlandish and German painters that is the northern equivalent of Giorgio Vasari's *Vite.*

France

Divided and harried during the fifteenth century, France, reorganized under decisive kings, was strong enough to undertake an aggressive policy toward her neighbors by the end of the century. Under the rule of Francis I, the French held a firm foothold in Milan and its environs. The king eagerly imported the Renaissance into France, bringing Leonardo da Vinci and Andrea del Sarto to his court, but they left no permanent mark on French art. It was Florentine Mannerists like Rosso Fiorentino and Benvenuto Cellini who implanted the Italianate style that replaced the Gothic. Francis' attempt to glorify the state and himself meant that the religious art of the Middle Ages was finally superseded, for it was the king and not the Church who now held power. A portrait of *Francis I* by JEAN CLOUET (*c.* 1485–1541), in the Franco–Italian manner, shows a worldly prince magnificently bedizened in silks and brocades, wearing a gold chain, and caressing the pommel of a dagger (FIG. 18-50). One would not expect the king's talents to be directed to spiritual matters, and legend has it that the ''merry monarch'' was a great lover and the hero of hundreds of ''gallant'' situations. The flat light and suppression of modeling give equal emphasis to head and costume, so that the king's finery and his face enter equally into the effect of royal splendor. Yet, despite this Mannerist formula for portraiture, the features are not entirely immobile; there is the faint-

18-50 JEAN CLOUET, *Francis I, c.* 1525–1530. Tempera and oil on wood, approx. 38″ × 29″. Louvre, Paris.

est flicker of an expression that we might read as "knowing."

The personal tastes of Francis and his court must have run to an art at once suave, artificial, elegant, and erotic. The sculptors and painters working to-

gether on the decoration of the new royal palace at Fontainebleau, under the direction of Florentines Rosso and FRANCESCO PRIMATICCIO (1504–1570), are known as the School of Fontainebleau. Rosso became the court painter of Francis I shortly after 1530. In France, his style no longer showed the turbulent harshness of *Moses Defending the Daughters of Jethro* (FIG. 17-42), but became consistently more elegant and graceful. When Rosso and Primaticcio decorated the Gallery of Francis I at Fontainebleau, they combined painting, fresco, imitation mosaic, and stucco sculpture in low and high relief (FIG. 18-51). The abrupt changes in scale and texture are typically Mannerist, as is the composition of the central painting, which shows *Venus Reproving Love* in compressed Mannerist space with elongated grace and mannered poses. The same artificial grace can be seen in the flanking caryatids, and the viewer is jarred by the shift in scale between the painted and the stucco figures. However, the combination of painted and stucco relief decorations became extremely popular from this time on and remained a favorite decorative technique throughout the Baroque and Rococo periods.

It has been said of Francis I that, besides women, his one obsession was building. During his reign, which lasted from 1515 to 1547, several large-scale châteaux were begun—among them the Château de Chambord in 1519 (FIG. 18-52). Reflecting the more peaceful times, these châteaux, developments from the old countryside fortresses, served as country houses for royalty and were usually built near a for-

18-51 ROSSO FIORENTINO and FRANCESCO PRIMATICCIO, *Venus Reproving Love. c.* 1530–1540. Gallery of Francis I, Fontainebleau, France.

est, for use as hunting lodges. The plan of Chambord, originally drawn by a pupil of Giuliano da Sangallo, imposes Italian concepts of symmetry and balance on the irregularity of the old French fortress. There is a central square block with four corridors, in the shape of a cross, leading to a broad, central staircase that gives access to groups of rooms—ancestors of the modern suite of rooms or apartments. The square plan is punctuated at each of the four corners by a round tower, and the whole is surrounded by a moat. From the exterior, Chambord presents a carefully contrived horizontal accent on three levels, its floors separated by continuous moldings. Windows are placed exactly over one another. This matching of horizontal and vertical features is, of course, derived from the Italian palazzo. But above the third level, the lines of the structure break chaotically into a jumble of high dormers, chimneys, and lanterns that recall soaring, ragged, Gothic silhouettes on the skyline.

The architecture of Chambord is still French at heart. During the reign of Francis' successor, Henry II (1547–1559), however, treatises by Italian architects were translated and Italian architects came to work in France; at the same time, the French turned to Italy for study and travel. This interchange brought about a more thoroughgoing revolution in style, although it never eliminated certain French elements that persisted from the Gothic tradition. Francis began the enlargement of the Louvre in Paris (FIG. 18-53) to make a new royal palace, but died before the work was well begun. His architect, PIERRE LESCOT (1510–

1578), continued under Henry II and, with the aid of the sculptor JEAN GOUJON (c. 1510–1565), produced the Classical style of the French Renaissance. Although Chambord incorporated the formal vocabulary of the Early Renaissance, particularly from Lombardy, Lescot and his associates were familiar with the High Renaissance of Bramante and his school. Each story of the Louvre forms a complete order, and the cornices project enough to furnish a strong horizontal accent. The arcading on the ground story reflects the ancient Roman arch-order and is recessed enough to produce more shadow than in the upper stories, strengthening the visual base of the design. On the second story, the pilasters rising from bases and the alternating curved and angular pediments supported by consoles have direct antecedents in several Roman High Renaissance palaces. On the other hand, the decreased height of the stories, the proportionately much larger windows (given the French weather!), and the steep roof are northern. Especially French are the pavilions that jut from the wall. These are punctuated by a feature that the French will long favor—the double columns framing a niche. The vertical lines of the building remain strong; the wall is deeply penetrated by openings and (in un-Italian fashion) profusely sculptured. This French Classical manner—double-columned pavilions, tall and wide windows, profuse statuary, and steep roofs—will be widely imitated in other northern countries, with local variations. The mannered Classicism produced by the French will be the *only*

18-53 PIERRE LESCOT, west façade of the Square Court of the Louvre, Paris, begun 1546.

Classicism to serve as a model for northern architects through most of the sixteenth century. The west courtyard façade of the Louvre is the best of French Renaissance architecture; eventually, the French will develop a quite native Classicism of their own, cleared of Italian Mannerist features.

The statues of the Louvre courtyard façade, now much restored, are the work of Goujon. We can best appreciate the quality of Goujon's style from his *Nymphs* reliefs from the Fountain of the Innocents in Paris (FIG. 18-54). Like the architecture of the Louvre, Goujon's nymphs are intelligent and sensitive French adaptations of the Italian Mannerist canon of figure design. Certainly, they are Mannerist in their ballet-like contrapposto and in their flowing, clinging drapery, which recalls the ancient "wet" drapery of Hellenic sculpture—for example, the figures on the parapet of the Temple of Athena Nike (FIG. 5-59). The slender, sinuous figures perform their steps within the structure of Mannerist space, and it is interesting that they appear to make one continuous motion—an illusion produced by reversing the gestures, as they might be seen in a mirror. The style of Fontainebleau, and ultimately of Primaticcio and Cellini, guides the sculptor here, but Goujon has learned the manner so well that he can create originally within it. The nymphs are truly French masterpieces, with lightness, ease, grace, and something of a native French chic that saves them from being mere lame derivatives of the Italian Mannerist norm.

In France, as in all Europe in the sixteenth century, the influence of Italian art was direct and overpowering. But as the century progressed, native French artists adapted the new elements to the strong Gothic traditions and created a distinctively French expression. An example of this maturing style is seen in the works of the sculptor GERMAIN PILON (c. 1535–1590), who made his reputation with monumental tomb sculpture, especially for the monument of Henry II and Catherine de' Medici in St. Denis, Paris. Like Goujon and other French sculptors, Pilon began in the Fontainebleau style, emphasizing artifice in pose

18-54 JEAN GOUJON, *Nymphs*, reliefs from the Fountain of the Innocents, Paris, 1548–1549.

18-55 GERMAIN PILON, *Descent from the Cross*, 1583. Bronze relief, 19" × 32½". Louvre, Paris.

and gesture and graceful, sinuous contour. Gradually, his style changed as he made contact with the still strong tradition of Late Gothic realism. A bronze relief, *Descent from the Cross* (FIG. 18-55), recalls monumental compositions of Rogier van der Weyden (FIG. 18-14) and the master of *The Avignon Pietà* (FIG. 18-25). Unlike them, Pilon shows the influence of Mannerism in the great, elongated, muscular Christ; like them, he expresses a quiet yet profound pathos that Mannerism could not sincerely convey. The realistic element appears in the very staging of the drama. The Virgin, consoled by a holy woman, is removed from the center of the action; those in authority are at the head and feet of Christ. There is a curiously steady, almost serene reading of the emotions of those present. The curving lines of the draperies have lost the angularity of the Gothic but are not arranged in the contrived patterns of Mannerism. Pilon, from a fusion of the old tradition with the new fashion, has risen to a bold statement of his own—a statement making use of both while transcending them in a moving, personal interpretation of the Medieval theme.

Spain

In some respects, the sixteenth century is the Spanish century. Under Charles V of Hapsburg and his son, Philip II, the Spanish empire dominated a territory greater in extent than any ever known: a large part of Europe, the western Mediterranean, a strip of North Africa, and vast expanses in the newly discovered Western Hemisphere. The Hapsburg empire, enriched by the plunder of the New World, supported the most powerful military force in Europe, which everywhere backed the ambitions and the adventures of the "Most Catholic Kings." Spain defended and then advanced the interests of the Catholic Church in its struggle against the inroads of the Protestant Reformation. What we call the Catholic Counter-Reformation was funded, directed, fought for, and enforced by Spain. By force and influence—by the preaching and the propaganda of the newly founded Spanish order of the Society of Jesus (the Jesuits)— Spain drove Protestantism from a large part of Europe and sponsored the internal reform of the Catholic Church at the great Council of Trent. She humbled France; trampled the Netherlands; reclaimed much of Germany, Poland, and Hungary for Catholicism; and held England at bay (until the end of the century), while she converted the Indian empires of the New World to the Catholic faith and destroyed them in a relentless search for treasure. The material and the spiritual exertions of Spain—the fanatical courage of her soldiers and the incandescent fervor of her great mystical saints—went together. The former became the terror of the Protestant and pagan worlds; the latter, the inspiration of the Catholic. The crusading spirit of Spain, nourished by centuries of war with Islam, engaged body and soul in the formation of the most Catholic civilization of Europe and the Americas. In the sixteenth century, for good or for ill, Spain left the mark of her power, religion, language, and culture on two hemispheres.

Yet Spain, like all of Europe at this time, came under the spell of Renaissance Italy; her architecture especially shows that influence, but not all at once. During the fifteenth century and well into the sixteenth, a Late Gothic style of architecture, the Plateresque, prevailed side by side with buildings influenced by Italy. ("Plateresque" is derived from the Spanish *platero*, meaning silversmith, and is applied to the style because of the delicate execution of its ornament.) The Collegio di San Gregorio in the Castilian city of Valladolid handsomely exemplifies the Plateresque manner (FIG. 18-56). The Spanish were particularly fond of great carved retables, like the German altar screens that influenced them (FIGS. 18-28 and 18-29)—so much so that they made them a conspicuous decorative feature of their exterior architecture, dramatizing a portal set into an otherwise blank wall. The Plateresque entrance of San Gregorio is a lofty, sculptured stone screen that bears no functional relation to the architecture behind it. On the entrance level, ogival, flamboyant arches are hemmed with lace-like tracery reminiscent of Moorish design. Above rises a great screen, paneled into sculptured compartments; in the center, the coat of arms of Ferdinand and Isabella is wreathed by the branches of a huge pomegranate tree (symbolizing "Grenada," the Moorish capital of Spain just recently captured by the "Catholic Kings"). Cupids play among the tree branches, and, flanking the central panel, niches enframe armed pages of the court, heraldic wildmen, and armored soldiers, attesting to the new, proud militancy of the united kingdom of Spain. In typical Plateresque and Late Gothic fashion, the whole design is unified by the activity of a thousand intertwined motifs, which, in sum, create an exquisitely carved panel greatly expanded in scale.

A sudden and surprising Italianate Classicism makes its appearance in the unfinished palace of Charles V in the Alhambra in Granada (FIG. 18-57), the work of the painter–architect PEDRO MACHUCA (active 1520–1550). The circular central courtyard is ringed with superposed Doric and Ionic orders, with continuous horizontal entablatures rather than arches. Ornament consists only of the details of the orders themselves, which are rendered with the simplicity, clarity, and authority we find in the work of Bramante and his school. The lower story recalls the ring colonnade of the Tempietto (FIG. 17-6), although here, of course, the curve is reversed. This pure Classicism, entirely exceptional in Spain at this time, may

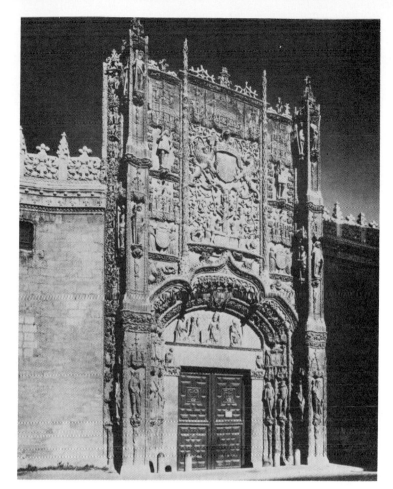

18-56   Portal, Collegio di San Gregorio, Valladolid, Spain, *c.* 1498.

18-57   PEDRO MACHUCA, courtyard of the palace of Charles V, Alhambra, Granada, Spain, *c.* 1526–1568.

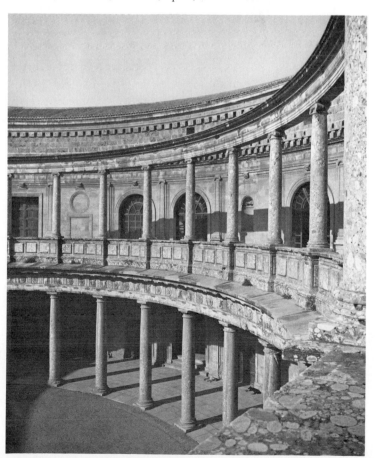

be a reflection of Charles V's personal taste acquired on one of his journeys to Italy. (It should be remembered that the emperor was an enthusiastic patron of Titian.) Machuca himself had sojourned in Italy, and the courtyard may be the consequence of his endeavor to revive this feature of the ancient Classical palace.

But the Spanish spirit of the time would seem to disdain the ideal purity of feature and correctness of proportion sought in Classical design. Something different must be done with what is received from Italy. What could be done is visible in the great fortress–palace–mausoleum–monastery–church complex called the Escorial (FIGS. 18-58, 18-59, 18-60), which was constructed for Philip II by JUAN BAUTISTA DE TOLEDO (?–1567) and JUAN DE HERRERA (1530–1597)—principally the latter. The king, perhaps the greatest in Spanish history, must have had much to do with the design. Certainly, there was close collaboration between Philip and his architects. The whole vast structure is in keeping with his austere and conscientious character, his passionate Catholic religiosity, his proud reverence for his dynasty, and his stern determination to impose his will worldwide.

Philip wrote to Herrera what he expected from him: "Above all, do not forget what I have told you—simplicity of form, severity in the whole, nobility without arrogance, majesty without ostentation." The result is a Classicism of Doric severity, ultimately derived from Italian architecture and with the grandeur of St. Peter's implicit in the scheme, but unique in Spanish and European architecture—a style inimitably of itself, even though later structures will reflect it.

In his will, Charles V stipulated that a "dynastic pantheon" be built to house the remains of past and future monarchs of Spain. Philip II, obedient to his father's wishes, chose a site some 30 miles northwest of Madrid, a rugged terrain with barren mountains. Here, he built not only the royal mausoleum, but a church, a monastery, and a palace above and around it. Legend has it that the grid-like plan for the enormous complex, 625 feet wide and 520 feet deep, was meant to symbolize the gridiron on which St. Lawrence, patron of the Escorial, was martyred.

The long sweep of the severely plain walls is broken only by the three entrances, with the dominant central portal framed by superposed orders topped

18-58   JUAN DE HERRERA, the Escorial (bird's-eye view after an anonymous eighteenth-century painting), near Madrid, Spain, c. 1563–1584.

18-59 JUAN DE HERRERA, the Escorial, façade of church.

18-60 JUAN DE HERRERA, the Escorial, interior of church.

by a pediment in the Italian fashion. The corners of the wall are punctuated by massive square towers. The stress on the central axis, with its subdued echoes in the two flanking portals, forecasts the three-part organization of later Baroque palace façades. Like the whole complex of buildings, the domed-cross church, with similarly heavy towers, is constructed of granite, expressing, in its grim starkness of mass, the obdurate quality of a material most difficult to work. The massive façade of the church (FIG. 18-59) and the austere geometry of its interior, the blocky walls and ponderous arches (FIG. 18-60), dominate the Classical forms, producing an effect of overwhelming strength and weight that contradicts the grace and elegance we associate with much of the Renaissance architecture of Italy.

The Escorial is a monument to the collaboration of a great king and a remarkably understanding architect, who made of it an original expression of a unique idea and personality—the embodiment of the stern virtues of a monarch, a realm, and an age conscious of their peculiar power and purpose. The visitor to the Escorial is awed by the overpowering architectural expression of the spirit of Spain in its heroic epoch and of the character of Philip II, who directed it.

There appear to be two sides to the Spanish genius in the period of the Counter-Reformation: fervent religious faith and ardent mysticism on the one hand and an iron realism on the other. St. Theresa of Avila and St. John of the Cross can be considered representative of the first; the practical St. Ignatius of Loyola, founder of the Jesuit order, of the latter. It is possible for the two tempers to be found in the same persons and works of art, but it is more common to find them apart. Interestingly enough, a painter of foreign extraction was able to combine them in a single picture. Kyriakos Theotokopoulos (c. 1547–1614), called EL GRECO, was born in Crete but emigrated to Italy as a young man. In his youth, he was trained in the traditions of Late Byzantine frescoes and mosaics. While still young, El Greco went to Venice, where he was connected with the shop of Titian, although Tintoretto's painting seems to have made a stronger impression on him. A brief trip to Rome explains the influences of Roman and Florentine Mannerism on his work. By 1577, he had left for Spain to spend the rest of his life in Toledo. El Greco's art is a strong, personal blending of Late Byzantine and Late Italian Mannerist elements. The intense emotionalism of his paintings, which naturally appealed to the pious fervor of the Spanish, the dematerialization of form, and a great reliance on color bind him to sixteenth-century Venetian art and to Mannerism. His strong sense of movement and use of light, however, prefigure the Baroque. El Greco's art is not strictly Spanish, although it appealed to certain sectors of that society,

18-61   El Greco, *The Burial of Count Orgaz*, 1586. Oil on canvas, approx. 16′ × 12′. Santo Tomé, Toledo, Spain.

for it had no Spanish antecedents and had little effect on future Spanish painting.

Nevertheless, the paintings of this hybrid genius interpret Spain for us in its Catholic zeal and yearning spirituality. This is true of his masterpiece, *The Burial of Count Orgaz* (FIG. 18-61), painted in 1586 for the church of Santo Tomé in Toledo. The theme illustrates the legend that the Count of Orgaz, who had died some three centuries before and who had been a great benefactor of the church of Santo Tomé, was buried in the church by Saints Stephen and Augustine, who miraculously descended from heaven to lower the count's body into its sepulcher. The earthly scene is irradiated by the brilliant heaven that opens above it, as El Greco carefully distinguishes the terrestrial and celestial spheres. The terrestrial is represented with a firm realism; the celestial, in his quite personal manner, with elongated, undulant figures, fluttering draperies, cold highlights, and a peculiar kind of ectoplasmic, swimming cloud. Below, the two saints lovingly lower the count's armor-clad body, the armor and heavy draperies painted with all the rich sensuousness of the Venetian School. The background is filled with a solemn chorus of black-clad Spanish grandees, in whose carefully individualized features El Greco shows us that he was also a great portraitist. These are the faces that looked on the greatness and glory of Spain when she was the leading power of Europe—the faces of the *conquistadores,* who brought her the New World and who, two years after this picture was completed, would lead the Great Armada against Protestant England and Holland.

The lower and upper spheres of the painting are linked by the upward glances of the figures below and by the flight of an angel above, who carries the soul of the count in his arms as St. John and the Virgin intercede for it before the throne of Christ. El Greco's deliberate change in style to distinguish between the two levels of reality gives the viewer the opportunity to see the artist's early and late manners in the same work, one above the other. The relatively sumptuous and realistic presentation of the earthly sphere shows a still strong root in Venetian art. But the abstractions and distortions that El Greco uses to show the immaterial nature of the heavenly realm will become characteristic of his later style. Pulling heaven down to earth, he will paint worldly inhabitants in the same abstract manner as celestial ones. His elongated figures will exist in undefined spaces, bathed in a cool light of uncertain origin. For this, El Greco has been called the last and greatest of the Mannerists, but it is difficult to apply that label to him without reservations. Although using Manneristic formal devices, El Greco was not a rebel, nor was he aiming for elegance in his work; he was concerned primarily with emotion and with the effort to express his own religious fervor or to arouse the observer's. To make the inner meaning of his paintings forceful, he developed a highly personal style in which his attenuated forms become etherealized in dynamic swirls of unearthly light and color. There may be some ambiguity in El Greco's forms, but there is none

18-62   EL GRECO, *Fray Félix Hortensio Paravicino,* 1609. Oil on canvas, 44½″ × 33¾″. Isaac Sweetser Fund, Museum of Fine Arts, Boston.

in his meaning—mystical, spiritual, ecstatic devotion.

Toward the end of his life, El Greco painted a portrait of his friend, the theologian, poet, and Trinitarian priest, *Fray Félix Hortensio Paravicino* (FIG. 18-62). It is one of the most distinguished portraits of the age. Father Hortensio, clad in the black-and-white vesture of his order, is represented seated, which, since the time of Raphael, was customary for portraits of ecclesiastics of high rank. He holds books, attributes of intellectual dedication and accomplishment. The vividly contrasting black and white of his canonicals and the square-backed leather chair, with its gilt bronze studs and finials, magnificently set off the pale, ascetic face, accented by the dark hair, eyebrows, and beard. El Greco renders the character of a man, given wholly to other-worldly concerns, as a kind of apparition not quite of this world. The likeness fades into the image of a typical El Greco saint. As is often the case when a great painter makes the likeness of a great-souled subject, the latter becomes more than an individual person. He becomes, as here, generalized into a type, that of the spiritually exalted priest—protagonist in the drama of Spanish history in its great century.

19

EUROPE
AGE OF THE BAROQUE
AND THE RISE OF SCIENCE

Dates for organizations and journals
are of founding; for individuals, of
birth. Names of artists, sculptors,
and architects are capitalized; those
of journals are italicized.

SCOTLAND

**SCIENCE AND
PHILOSOPHY**
Napier 1550

IRELAND

Edinburgh

**SCIENCE AND
PHILOSOPHY**
Boyle 1627

Dublin

**SCIENCE AND
PHILOSOPHY**
Bacon 1561
Harvey 1578
Hobbes 1588
Locke 1632
Newton 1642

ARTS AND LETTERS
Spenser 1552
Marlowe 1564
Shakespeare 1564
Donne 1573
Jonson 1573
JONES 1573
Milton 1608
Dryden 1631
WREN 1632
Purcell 1659

**SCIENCE AND
PHILOSOPHY**
Jansen 1585
Huygens 1629
Leeuwenhoek 1632
Spinoza 1632

ARTS AND LETTERS
Vesalius 1514
RUBENS 1577
HALS 1580
VAN HONTHORST 1590
VAN DYCK 1599
REMBRANDT 1606
KALF 1619
VAN RUISDAEL 1628
VERMEER 1632

Copenhagen

DENMARK

ENGLAND

**ORGANIZATIONS
AND PUBLICATIONS**
Royal Society 1662
Philosophical Transactions 1665

London

Thames

Amsterdam
Leiden
HOLLAND
Antwerp

**ORGANIZATIONS
AND PUBLICATIONS**
Acta Sanctorum 1643
Journal des Savants 1684

Berlin

Vistula

Weser

Elbe

Oder

ARTS AND LETTERS
CALLOT 1592
LE NAIN 1593
DE LA TOUR 1593
POUSSIN 1594
MANSART 1598
LORRAINE 1600
Corneille 1606
LE VAU 1612
PERRAULT 1613
LE NÔTRE 1613
LE BRUN 1619
PUGET 1620
La Fontaine 1621
Molière 1622
de Sévigné 1626
GIRARDON 1628
Perrault 1628
Boileau 1636
Racine 1639
HARDOUIN-MANSART 1646

**ORGANIZATIONS
AND PUBLICATIONS**
French Royal Academy 1635
Academy of Science 1666
Academy of Reims 1677
Academy of Bordeaux 1690

**SCIENCE AND
PHILOSOPHY**
Montaigne 1533
Descartes 1596
Pascal 1623
Bayle 1647

Rouen
Reims
Meuse
Rhine
Leipzig

ARTS AND LETTERS
Kepler 1571
Comenius 1591
Leibniz 1646

**ORGANIZATIONS
AND PUBLICATIONS**
Acta Eruditorum 1682
Leopoldine Academy 1687

Seine
Paris
Nuremberg

HOLY ROMAN EMPIRE

Danube

Vienna

FRANCE

Loire

SWITZERLAND

Bordeaux

Garonne

Lyons

Rhône

Po
Cremona
Venice

HUNGARY

**SCIENCE AND
PHILOSOPHY**
Galileo 1564
Malpighi 1628

Florence

ARTS AND LETTERS
DA VIGNOLA 1507
Palestrina 1526
DELLA PORTA 1537
MADERNO 1556
CARRACCI 1560
Monteverdi 1567
CARAVAGGIO 1571
RENI 1575
DOMENICHINO 1581
IL GUERCINO 1591
GENTILESCHI 1593
LONGHENA 1598
BERNINI 1598
BORROMINI 1599
ROSA 1615
GUARINI 1624
Lully 1633
POZZO 1642
Stradivari 1644

Duero

PORTUGAL

Tagus

Lisbon

Madrid

Ebro

SPAIN

Guadiana

Guadalquivir

Seville

Granada

ARTS AND LETTERS
Cervantes 1547
Lope de Vega 1562
RIBERA 1591
ZURBURÁN 1598
VELÁZQUEZ 1599
Calderón 1600

Tiber

Rome

ITALY

Naples

**ORGANIZATIONS
AND PUBLICATIONS**
Academy della Crusca 1582
Academy dei Lincei 1603
Academy del Cimento 1657
French Academy at Rome 1666
Academy Rossano 1695

0	100	200

MILES

0	160	320

KILOMETERS

BAROQUE ART

MADERNO
Santa Susanna
(1597)

DOMENICHINO
(1581–1641)

Thirty Years'
War begins

VAN DYCK
(1599–1641)

1598   1603   1610   1618   1621

J A M E S   I   O F   E N G L A N D

H E N R Y   I V   O F   F R A N C E   P H I L I P   I I I   O F   S P A I N

GIACOMO DELLA PORTA
Il Gesù façade
(c. 1575)

RUBENS
The Lion Hunt
detail (1617)

1625

French Academy
of Sculpture
and Painting
founded

Blaise Pascal
(1623–1662)

ZURBARÁN
St. Francis in Meditation
(c. 1639)

French Royal Academy
founded

REMBRANDT
(1606–1669)

JONES
Banqueting House
(1619)

1643   1635

P H I L I P   I V   O F   S P A I N   L O U I S   X I I I   O F   F R A N C E

1648

J A M E S   I   O F   E N G L A N D

Thirty
Years'
War ends

HALS
Balthasar Coymans
detail (1645)

BORROMINI
San Carlo alle
Quattro Fontane
(1638–1641)

1633
Inquisition
summons Galileo

1628   William Harvey
discovers blood
circulation

1650

BERNINI
Scala Regia
(1663)

Spanish power
in Europe ends

Great Fire
of London
1666

GIRARDON
Apollo Attended by
the Nymphs
detail (c. 1666)

E N G L A N D   U N D E R
C R O M W E L L   1658   c. 1660   1665

C H A R L E S   I I   O F   E N G L A N D

L O U I S   X I V   O F   F R A N C E

VELÁZQUEZ
Las Meninas
detail (1656)

PERRAULT, LE VAU and LE BRUN
Louvre, east façade (1667–1670)

WREN
St. Paul's
(1675–1710)

GUARINI
Palazzo Carignano
(1679–1692)

Jean Baptiste Racine
(1639–1699)

1675

1702   1689   1688   1685

W I L L I A M   A N D   M A R Y   O F   E N G L A N D
Movement toward parliamentary government begins

◀ J A M E S   I I

Emergence of
Rococo style

KEY: Spanish reigns – – – –   French reigns ——   English reigns – – – –

THE GENERAL PERIOD we have labeled "Renaissance" continues without any sharp stylistic break, unless it be the interrupting episode of Mannerism, into the seventeenth and eighteenth centuries. The art of this later period we call "Baroque," although there is no one Baroque style or set of stylistic principles. The origin of the word is not clear. It may come from the Portuguese word *barroco*, meaning an irregularly shaped pearl. Certainly, the term was originally used in a disparaging sense, especially of post-Renaissance architecture, which nineteenth-century critics regarded as decadent Classical: unstructural, overornamented, theatrical, and grotesque. But the use of "Baroque" as a pejorative has faded, and the term has long been current in art-historical vocabulary as a blanket designation for the art of the period roughly covering 1600 to 1750. Scholars gradually came to see that the Baroque styles were quite different from those of the Renaissance. The Baroque, for example, looks dynamic; the Renaissance, relatively static. This led to the claim that the two are fundamentally in opposition; there is still disagreement about the historical and formal relation of the two stylistic periods, especially since it is clear that the Classicism of the High Renaissance is restored and flourishes in the Baroque. The historical reality lies in the flow of stylistic change, and "Baroque" is a classification useful in isolating the tendencies and products of stylistic change for examination. Traits that the styles of the seventeenth and earlier eighteenth centuries seem to have in common we shall designate as Baroque.

Like the art it produced, the Baroque era was manifold—spacious and dynamic, brilliant and colorful, theatrical and passionate, sensual and ecstatic, opulent and extravagant, versatile and *virtuoso*. It was an age of expansion following on an age of discovery, and its expansion led to still further discovery. The rising national powers colonized the globe. Wars between Renaissance cities were supplanted by wars between continental empires, and the history of Europe could be influenced by battles fought in the North American wilderness and in India.

Baroque expansiveness extended well beyond earth in the conceptions of the new astronomy and physics of Galileo, Kepler, and Newton. The same laws of mechanics were found to govern a celestial body moving at great velocity and a falling apple. Man's optical range was expanding to embrace the macroscopic spaces of the celestial world and the microscopic spaces of the cellular. There is in the Baroque almost an obsession with the space of the unfolding universe. Descartes makes extension (space and what occupies it) the sole physical attribute of being; there exist only mind and extension, the former proving the reality of the latter in Descartes'

famous phrase, *Cogito, ergo sum* ("I think, therefore I am"). Pascal confesses in awe that "the silence of these infinite spaces frightens me." Milton expresses the Baroque image of space in a phrase—"the vast and boundless deep."

The Baroque scientist comes to see physical nature as matter in motion through space and time; the latter two are thought of as the conditions of the first. The measurement of motion is made possible by the new mathematics of analytical geometry and the infinitesimal calculus, and experiment comes to be accepted as the prime method for getting at the truth of physical nature. Time, like space and motion, is a preoccupation of the creative Baroque mind—in art as well as in science. The age-old sense of time, rich with religious, philosophical, psychological, and poetic import, persists alongside the new concept of it as a measurable property of nature. Time—"the subtle thief of youth" that steals away the lives of all of us; that, in the end, reveals the truth, vindicates goodness, and rescues innocence; that demolishes the memory of great empires; and that points to the ultimate judgment of humankind by God—this sense of time pervades the art and literature of the Baroque. The sonnets of Shakespeare dwell on the mutability and brevity of life and on time's destruction of beauty ("that time will come/and take my love away"). The great landscapes of Van Ruisdael suggest the passage of time in hurrying clouds, restless sea, and everchanging light. Painters and sculptors, eager to make action explicit and convincing, depict it at the very moment it is taking place, as in Bernini's *David* (FIG. 19-10). There are countless allegorical representations of time as the fierce old man carrying his scythe or devouring his children. For the Baroque artist, then, time has acquired its new "scientific" connotations of the instantaneous and the infinite, yet without any loss of its significance for each human life.

Scarcely less fascinating to the Baroque mind is light. Light—for thousands of years thought of and worshiped as the god-like sun or the truth of the Holy Spirit—now becomes a physical entity, propagated in waves (or corpuscles) through Pascal's "infinite spaces," capable of being refracted into color by a prism. But, as with time, the new-found materiality of light by no means diminishes its ancient association with spirituality in the religion, poetry, and art of the Baroque. It still stands for inspiration, truth of dogma, the mystical vision of the transcendental world, the presence of the Divine, the "inner light" (page 520). And it can have these associations in a commonplace setting or in one of splendor and magnificence (FIG. 19-9). Yet the age of the new science, adapting the old metaphor of light to the dawn of a new day, would be called the "Enlightenment," signifying that the old, dark, mythical way of reading the world has been given up and that the light of knowledge brings a new day. Alexander Pope, expressing the enthusiasm of his day for the discoveries of Newton, makes them out to be a kind of second revelation:

Nature, and Nature's laws lay hid in night.
God said: "Let Newton be!" and all was Light!

The elements of perception in naturalistic Baroque art are the elements of nature described by Baroque science: matter in motion through space, time, and light. And the ingredients of an increasingly precise method for the scientific study of nature—observation and measurement, representation and experimental testing—are analogous to the naturalistic artist's careful reproduction of natural appearances.

Although the exclusive and exacting report of these elements is a most important enterprise in the age of the Baroque, the mechanical simulation of appearances for its own sake is by no means the naturalistic artist's intention. Although he obviously delights in the achievement of astonishing illusion, his images embody spiritual and metaphysical meanings of nature so persuasively real and present that their significance and truth are strongly reinforced. In this way, he brings before us the reality of the unseen world by means of the seen—the visible objects he regards as symbolic or emblematic of invisible and unchanging truth. Baroque naturalism remains largely religious in content.

While naturalism thrived in Baroque art, Classicism was revised and further developed, and the two styles divided the taste of the age with a third—the dynamic, colorful, sensuous style characteristic of Rubens and Bernini. The differences among these three styles were not so definitive as to disallow exchanges of influence or even occasional collaboration, although the esthetic doctrines or presuppositions of naturalism were fundamentally opposed to those of the other two, and the French Academy could debate the virtues of the Classical (formalistic) Poussin over the coloristic Rubens. Art theory flourished, and most of it was on the side of Classicism. The cause of Classicism was also favored by an increasing antiquarian literature—the fruit of an expanding enthusiasm for ancient civilization and art and an increasingly sophisticated and systematic study of it. The Classical masters of the Baroque took as their models the great artists of the High Renaissance, antique statuary, and nature; artists of whatever stylistic bent were often learned in Classical literature and antiquities. Although the Classical masters' philosophy of art proclaimed the ideal rather than the real as the only worthy subject and form for painting and sculpture, they believed that study of nature was essential to the full and valid realization of the idea in its purity

and perfection. This was manifest in their insistence on the careful observation and depiction of the human figure from life.

Nevertheless, the opposition of Classicism to the dramatic dynamism of painters like Rubens becomes conscious and fixed in the Baroque. This dualism will hold well into the nineteenth and even the twentieth century. Indeed, it reaches through the entire Western tradition, exclusive of the Middle Ages; an ancient statement of this dualism may be seen in the art of Greece and Rome (compare FIGS. 5-52 and 5-79). Classicism in art and thought amounts to calm rationality; we see it in the landscapes of Poussin (FIG. 19-62). Its opposite—turbulent action stirred by powerful passions—(later, we shall call it "Romanticism") appears in the painting of Rubens (FIG. 19-40) and in the sculpture of Bernini (page 520). A central theme of Baroque art and literature is the conflict of reason with passion. The representation of that conflict is, of course, as ancient as Plato and survives as a great dualism in Western thinking about human nature.

Accompanying, quite consistently, the exploration of the elementary structure of physical nature is the exploration of human nature, the realm of the senses and the emotions. The function of the representational arts is to open that realm to full view. The throwing open of the two physical universes of macrocosm and microcosm to human scrutiny did not distract Baroque humanity from the age-old curiosity about the nature of humankind. After all, it was now perceived that if we are one with nature, the knowledge of ourselves must be part of the knowledge of nature. The new resources given to the Baroque artist allow him to render, with new accuracy and authority, the appearances of the world and of the beings that people it. Painting and sculpture, equipped with every device of sensuous illusion now available, provide a stage for the enactment of the drama of human life in all its variety. For Baroque is preeminently the age of theater. Art shares with the actor's stage the purpose (as Shakespeare puts it in *Hamlet*)

To hold, as 'twere, the mirror up to nature, to show virtue her own feature, scorn her own image, and the very age and body of the time his form and pressure. (III:2)

This means to present and analyze the spectrum of human actions and passions in all its degrees of lightness, darkness, and intensity. In this great era of the stage, tragedy and comedy are reborn. At the same time, the resources of music greatly expand, creating the opera and refining the instruments of the modern orchestra. All the arts approve the things of the senses and the delights of sensuous experience. Although here and there the guilty fear of pleasure lingers from the times of Hieronymus Bosch, poetry and literature in all countries acquire a richly expressive language capable of rendering themes that involve the description, presentation, conflict, and resolution of human emotions. In the Catholic countries, every device of art is used to stimulate pious emotions— sometimes, it might be thought, to the pitch of ecstasy. Luxurious display and unlimited magnificence and splendor frame the extravagant life of the courts, cost notwithstanding; the modes of furniture and dress are perhaps the most ornate ever designed. Even in externals, a dramatic, sensuous elaborateness is the rule. However, what people wear and what they do must approach perfection, with the added flourish of seeming effortlessness. Not only courtiers, at one end of Baroque society, and brigands and pirates at the other, but also the men who fashion the arts and the sciences are brilliant performers. They are virtuosi, proud of their technique and capable of astonishing quantities of work.

ITALY

The age of the Baroque has been identified with the Catholic reaction to the advance of Protestantism. Although it extends much more widely in time and place than seventeenth-century Italy and is by no means only a manifestation of religious change, there can be little doubt that Baroque art had papal Rome as its birthplace. Between the pontificates of Paul III (Farnese) from 1534 to 1549 and of Sixtus V (Peretti) in the 1580s, the popes led a successful military, diplomatic and theological campaign against Protestantism, wiping out many of its gains in central and southern Europe. The great Council of Trent, which met in the early 1540s and again in the early 1560s, was sponsored by the papacy in an effort to systematize and harden orthodox Catholic doctrine against the threat of Protestant persuasion. The Council strongly resisted Protestant objection to the use of images in religious worship, insisting on their necessity in the teaching of the laity. This implied separation of the priest from an unsophisticated congregation was to be reflected in architecture as well, the central type of church plan being rejected in favor of the long church and of other plans that maintained the distinction between clergy and laity; an example is the addition of the nave to the central plan of Bramante and Michelangelo for St. Peter's (FIGS. 19-3 and 19-6).

Interrupted for a while, the building program begun under Paul III (with Michelangelo's Capitoline Hill design) was taken up again by Sixtus V, who had greatly augmented the papal treasury and who intended to construct a new and more magnificent Rome, an "imperial city that had been subdued to Christ and purged of paganism." Sixtus was succeeded by a number of strong and ambitious popes— Paul V (Borghese), Urban VIII (Barberini), Innocent X (Pamfili), and Alexander VII (Chigi)—the patrons of Bernini and Borromini and the builders of the modern city of Rome, on which they left their Baroque mark everywhere. The energy of the Catholic Counter-Reformation, transformed into art, radiated throughout Catholic countries and even into Protestant lands, which found a response to it in their own art.

Architecture and Sculpture

The Jesuit order, newly founded (in 1534, in the pontificate of Paul III), needed an impressive building for its mother church. Because Michelangelo was dilatory in providing the plans, the church, called Il Gesù (Church of Jesus), was designed and built between 1568 and 1584 (FIG. 19-1) by GIACOMO DA VIGNOLA (1507–1573), who designed the ground plan, and GIACOMO DELLA PORTA (1537–1602), who is responsible for the façade. Although the church dates from the sixteenth century and stylistically is Late Renaissance, it is transitional to Baroque architecture. Its façade is an important model and point of departure for the façades of Roman Baroque churches for two

19-1 GIACOMO DELLA PORTA, façade of Il Gesù, Rome, c. 1575–1584. Interior by GIACOMO DA VIGNOLA, 1568. (Engraving by JOACHIM VON SANDRART.)

centuries, and its basic scheme is echoed and reechoed throughout the Catholic countries, especially Latin America. It is not entirely original; the union of the lower and upper stories, effected by scroll buttresses, goes back to Leon Battista Alberti's Santa Maria Novella in Florence (FIG. 16-40); its Classical pediment is familiar in Alberti and Andrea Palladio; and its paired pilasters appear in Michelangelo's design for St. Peter's. But the façade is a skillful synthesis of these already existing motifs; the two stories are well unified, the horizontal march of the pilasters and columns builds to a dramatic climax at the central bay, and the bays of the façade snugly fit the nave-chapel system behind them. The many dramatic Baroque façades of Rome will be architectural variations on this basic theme. In plan (FIG. 19-2), a monumental expansion of Alberti's scheme for Sant' Andrea in Mantua (FIG. 16-43), the nave takes over the main volume of space, so that the structure becomes a great hall with side chapels; the approach to the altar is emphasized by a dome. The wide acceptance of the Gesù plan in the Catholic world, even until modern times, seems to attest that it is ritually satisfactory. The opening of the church building into a single great hall provides an almost theatrical setting for large promenades and processions (that seemed to com-

bine social with sacerdotal functions) and, above all, a space adequate to accommodate the great crowds that gathered to hear the eloquent preaching of the Jesuits. The Jesuits had a strong, indirect influence on art and architecture through the teachings of Saint Ignatius of Loyola, their Spanish founder. Loyola, in his *Spiritual Exercises,* advocated that the spiritual experience of the mysteries of the Catholic faith be intensely imagined, so much so as to be visible to the eye. The content of faith was to be visualized, and the sacred objects of the Church were to be venerated as defenses against false doctrine and the powers of Hell. This is still the function and warranty of religious art throughout the Roman Catholic world.

The great Baroque project in Rome was the completion of St. Peter's (FIG. 19-3). Bramante's and Michelangelo's central plan was unsatisfactory to the clergy of the seventeenth century, who thought it smacked of paganism and who felt it was inconvenient for the ever-growing assemblies. Under Paul V, CARLO MADERNO (1556–1629) was commissioned to add three bays of a nave to the earlier nucleus and to provide the building with a façade (FIG. 19-4). Before he received the St. Peter's commission, Maderno had designed the façade of Santa Susanna (FIG. 19-5), concentrating and dramatizing in it the major features of the façade of Il Gesù. Strong shadows cast by the vigorously projecting columns and pilasters of Santa Susanna mount dramatically toward the emphatically stressed central axis; the sculptural effect is enhanced by the recessed niches, which contain statues.

The façade of St. Peter's (FIG. 19-4) is a gigantic expansion of the elements of Santa Susanna's first level. But Maderno overextends his theme, and the compactness of Santa Susanna's façade is lost. The elements are spread too wide, and the quickening rhythm of pilasters and columns from the sides toward the center becomes slack. The role of the central pediment is reduced to insignificance by the façade's excessive width. In fairness to Maderno, it must be pointed out that his design for the façade was never completely executed. The two outside bays are the first stages of two flanking towers, which were never built; their vertical accents might well have visually compressed the central part of the façade. As it stands, this unfinished, watered-down frontispiece is almost universally criticized by artists and historians and has, unfortunately, become the dominant feature of the church's exterior. Lengthening the nave moves the façade outward and away from the dome, and the effect that Michelangelo had planned—a structure pulled together and dominated by its dome—is seriously impeded. When viewed at close range, the dome hardly emerges above the soaring cliff of the façade; seen from farther back, it appears to have no drum. One must go back beyond the piazza to see the

19-2 GIACOMO DA VIGNOLA, plan of Il Gesù, Rome.

0   25   50   FEET

0   10   20   METERS

19-3   Aerial view of St. Peter's, Rome.

19-4   CARLO MADERNO, façade of St. Peter's, 1606–1612.

19-5 CARLO MADERNO, Santa Susanna, Rome, 1597–1603.

dome and drum together and to experience the effect that Michelangelo intended. Today, to see the structure as it was originally planned, it must be viewed from the back (FIG. 17-33).

BERNINI AND BORROMINI

The design of St. Peter's, which had been evolving since the days of Bramante and Michelangelo and had engaged all of the leading architects of the Renaissance and Baroque periods, was completed (except for details) by GIANLORENZO BERNINI (1598–1680). Bernini was architect, painter, and sculptor—one of the most brilliant and imaginative artists of the Baroque era and, if not the originator of the Baroque style, probably its most characteristic and sustaining spirit. Bernini's largest and most impressive single project was the design for a monumental piazza in front of St. Peter's (FIGS. 19-3 and 19-6). Like Michelangelo in the case of the Capitoline Hill, Bernini had to adjust his design to some preexisting structures on the site: an ancient obelisk brought from Egypt and a fountain designed by Maderno. He used these features to define the long axis of a vast oval embraced by colonnades that are joined to the façade of St. Peter's by two diverging wings. Four files of huge Tuscan columns make up the two colonnades, which terminate in severely Classical temple fronts. The dramatic gesture of embrace made by the colonnades

(FIG. 19-3) symbolizes the welcome given its communicants by the Roman Catholic Church. Thus, the compact, central designs of Bramante and Michelangelo are expanded by a Baroque transformation into a dynamic complex of axially ordered elements that reach out and enclose spaces of vast dimension. Where the Renaissance building stood in self-sufficient isolation, the Baroque design expansively relates it to its environment.

The wings that connect St. Peter's façade with the oval piazza flank a trapezoidal space also reminiscent of the Capitoline Hill. But here the latter's visual effect is reversed; as seen from the piazza, the diverging wings counteract the natural perspective and tend to bring the façade closer to the observer. Emphasizing the façade's height in this manner, Bernini subtly and effectively compensates for its excessive width.

The Baroque delight in illusionistic devices is expressed again in the Vatican in the Scala Regia (FIG. 19-7), a monumental stairway connecting the papal apartments and the portico and narthex of the church. Because the original passageway was irregular, dark, and dangerous to descend, Pope Alexander VII commissioned Bernini to replace it. Bernini, like Michelangelo at the Campidoglio, here makes architectural virtue of necessity by using illusionistic techniques characteristic of stagecraft. The stairway, its entrance crowned by a sculptural group of trumpeting angels and the papal arms, is covered by a barrel vault (in two stages) carried on columns that form aisles flanking the central corridor. By gradually reducing the distance between columns and walls as the stairway ascends, Bernini actually eliminates the aisles on the upper levels, while creating an illusion of uniformity of width and continuity of aisle for the whole stairway. At the same time, the space between the colonnades also narrows with ascent, reinforcing the natural perspective and making the stairs appear to be longer than they actually are. To minimize this effect, Bernini made the lighting at the top of the stairs brighter, exploiting the natural human inclination to move from darkness toward light. To make the

19-6 Plan of St. Peter's, Rome, with adjoining piazza designed by GIANLORENZO BERNINI.

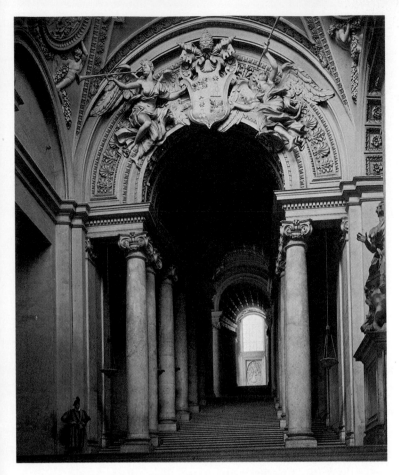

19-7 GIANLORENZO BERNINI, Scala Regia, the Vatican, Rome, 1663–1666.

Indeed, it is this theme of triumph that dictates the architectural as well as sculptural symbolism both inside and outside St. Peter's. Suggesting a great and solemn procession, the main axis of the complex traverses the piazza, slowed by the central obelisk, and enters Maderno's nave. It comes to a temporary halt at the altar beneath the baldacchino, but it continues on toward its climactic destination at another great altar in the apse, the Cathedra Petri (FIG. 19-9), also the work of Bernini. In this explosively dramatic composition, the Chair of St. Peter is exalted in a burst of light, in which the Dove of the Holy Ghost appears amidst flights of angels and billowing clouds. Four colossal figures in gilt bronze seem to support the chair miraculously, for they scarcely touch it. The two in the foreground represent two fathers of the Latin Church, Saints Ambrose and Augustine. Behind them, and less conspicuously, stand Saints Athanasius and Chrysostom, representing the Greek Church. The grouping of the figures constitutes an appeal for unity within Christianity and, at the same time, suggests the subservience of the Eastern Church to the Western. The Cathedra Petri is the quintessence of Baroque composition. Its forms are generated and grouped not by clear lines of structure but by forces that unfold from a center of violent en-

19-8 GIANLORENZO BERNINI, baldacchino for St. Peter's, Rome, 1624–1633.

long ascent more tolerable, he provided an intermediate goal in the form of an illuminated landing that promises a midway resting point. The result is a highly sophisticated design, both dynamic and dramatic, which repeats on a smaller scale, but perhaps even more effectively, the processional sequence found inside St. Peter's.

Long before the planning of the piazza and the completion of the Scala Regia, Bernini had been at work decorating the interior of St. Peter's. His first commission called for the design and erection of the gigantic bronze *baldacchino* above the main altar under the cathedral's dome (FIG. 19-8) to mark and memorialize the tomb of St. Peter. Almost 100 feet high (the height of an average eight-story building), this canopy is in harmony with the tremendous proportions of the new church and is a focus of its splendor. Its four spiral columns recall those of the ancient baldacchino over the same spot in Old St. Peter's. Partially fluted and wreathed with vines, they seem to deny the mass and weight of the tons of bronze resting on them. At the same time, they communicate their Baroque energy to the four colossal angels standing guard at the upper corners and to the four serpentine brackets that elevate the orb and the cross, symbols of the triumph of the Church.

19-9   GIANLORENZO BERNINI, Cathedra Petri, 1656–1666. Gilt bronze, marble, and stucco. St. Peter's, Rome.

19-10   GIANLORENZO BERNINI, *David*, 1623. Marble, life-size. Galleria Borghese, Rome.

ergy. Everything moves, nothing is distinct, light dissolves firmness, and the effect is visionary. The vision asserts the triumph of Christianity and the papal claim to doctrinal supremacy.

Much of Bernini's prolific career was given to the adornment of St. Peter's, where his works combine sculpture with architecture. Although Bernini was a great and influential architect, his fame rests primarily on his sculpture, which, like his architecture, expresses the Baroque spirit to perfection. It is expansive and dramatic, and the element of time usually plays an important role in it. Unlike the states of rest or tension that one finds in the *Davids* of Donatello (FIG. 16-12), Verrocchio (FIG. 16-52), and Michelangelo (FIG. 17-20), Bernini's version (FIG. 19-10) aims at catching the split-second action. His muscular legs widely and firmly planted, *David* is beginning the violent, pivoting motion that will launch the stone from his sling. A moment before, his body was in one position; the next moment, it will be in a completely different one. Bernini selects the most dramatic of an implied sequence of poses, so that the observer has to think simultaneously of the continuum and of this tiny fraction of it. The implied continuum imparts a dynamic quality to the statue that suggests a bursting forth of the energy one sees pent in Michelangelo's figures (FIGS. 17-20 and 17-21). And as the statue seems to be moving through time, so it does through space. This is not the kind of statue that can be inscribed in a cylinder or confined to a niche; its implied action demands space around it. Nor is it self-sufficient in the Renaissance sense, as its pose and attitude direct the observer's attention beyond itself and to its surroundings (in this case, toward an unseen Goliath). For the first time since the Hellenistic era (FIG. 5-76) a sculptured figure moves out into and partakes of the physical space that surrounds it and the observer.

The expansive quality of Baroque art and its disdain to limit itself to firmly defined spatial settings are encountered again in *The Ecstasy of St. Theresa* in the Cornaro Chapel of the church of Santa Maria della Vittoria (FIG. 19-11). In this chapel, Bernini draws on the full resources of architecture, sculpture, and painting to charge the entire area with crosscurrents of dramatic tension. St. Theresa was a nun of the Carmelite order and one of the great mystical saints of the Spanish Counter-Reformation. Her conversion took place after the death of her father, when she fell into a series of trances, saw visions, and heard voices. Feeling a persistent pain in her side, she came to believe that its cause was the fire-tipped dart of Divine love, which an angel had thrust into her bosom and which she described as making her swoon in delightful anguish. The whole chapel becomes a theater for the production of this mystical drama. The niche in which it takes place is a proscenium crowned with a

19-11 GIANLORENZO BERNINI, interior of the Cornaro Chapel, 1645–1652, Santa Maria della Vittoria, Rome. Eighteenth-century painting, Staatliches Museum, Schwerin.

broken Baroque pediment and ornamented with polychrome marble (FIG. 19-11). On either side of the chapel, portraits of the Cornaro family in sculptured opera boxes represent an audience watching the denouement of the heavenly drama with intent piety. Bernini shows the saint in ecstasy, unmistakably a mingling of spiritual and physical passion, swooning back on a cloud, while the smiling angel aims his arrow (page 520). The group is of white marble, and the artist goes to extremes of virtuosity in his management of textures: the clouds, rough monk's cloth, gauzy material, smooth flesh, feathery wings—all are carefully differentiated , yet harmonized in visual and visionary effect. Light from a hidden window pours down bronze rays that are meant to be seen as bursting forth from a painting of Heaven in the vault (FIG. 19-11). Several tons of marble seem to float in a haze of light, the winds of heaven buoying draperies as the cloud ascends. The remote mysteries of religion, taking on recognizable form, descend to meet the world of man halfway, within the conventions of Baroque

19-12 GIANLORENZO BERNINI, Triton Fountain, 1642–1643. Travertine. Piazza Barberini, Rome.

19-13 FRANCESCO BORROMINI, façade of San Carlo alle Quattro Fontane, Rome, 1665–1676.

19-14 FRANCESCO BORROMINI, plan of San Carlo alle Quattro Fontane, Rome, 1638–1641.

art and theater. Bernini had much to do with the establishment of the principles of visual illusion that guided both.

The evident desire of the time to instill designs with dynamic qualities finds expressive release in the design of monumental fountains. The challenge of working with an element that actually *is* in motion fascinated Baroque artists, and it may not be too surprising to find that Bernini was one of the most inventive and most widely imitated designers in this field. It is largely his doing that Rome is a city of fountains. One of his most charming inventions is the Triton Fountain (FIG. 19-12), in which Bernini shows the male counterpart of the mermaid, seated on a shell supported by dolphins, blowing a jet of water toward the sky. The jet falls back into the shell, and the water dribbles in thin rivulets from its corrugated edges into the collecting basin below. The maritime group, risen from the depths of the ocean, is enveloped in rising and falling sprays of water. Sunlight reflected from the constantly agitated surface of the collecting pool around the base of the monument ripples across the stone surfaces of the sculptured group in ever-changing patterns that make the Triton seem alive, his bel-

lows-like chest heaving with the effort of blowing into his shell. For centuries, he has performed his task for Urban VIII, the Barberini Pope, whose emblems (the bees) decorate the fountain's base.

It seems curious that Bernini, whose sculpture expresses the very essence of the Baroque spirit, should remain relatively conservative in his architecture. Frequently planning on a vast scale and employing striking illusionistic devices, Bernini tends to use the Classical orders in a fairly sober and traditional manner, obvious exceptions being his baldacchino in St. Peter's and the St. Theresa altar (FIGS. 19-8 and 19-11). One might call his architectural style academic, in comparison with the unorthodox and quite revolutionary manner of his contemporary FRANCESCO BORROMINI (1599–1667). A new dynamism appears in the little church of San Carlo alle Quattro Fontane (FIGS. 19-13 and 19-14), where Borromini goes well beyond any of his predecessors or contemporaries in the plastic handling of a building. Maderno's façades of St. Peter's and Santa Susanna (FIGS. 19-4 and 19-5) are deeply sculptured, but they develop along straight, lateral planes. Borromini, perhaps thinking of Michelangelo's apse wall in St. Peter's (FIG. 17-33), sets his whole façade in serpentine motion forward and back, making a counterpoint of concave and convex on two levels (note the sway of the cornices), and emphasizes the sculptured effect by deeply recessed niches. This is no longer the traditional, flat frontispiece that defines a building's outer limits; it is a pulsating membrane inserted between interior and exterior space, designed not to separate but to provide a fluid transition between the two. This functional interrelation of the building and its environment is underlined by the curious fact that it has not one but two façades; the second—a narrow bay crowned with its own small tower—turns away from the main façade and, following the curve of the street, faces an intersection. (The upper façade was completed seven years after Borromini's death, and we cannot be sure to what degree the present structure reflects his original intention.)

The interior is a provocative variation on the theme of the centrally planned church. In plan (FIG. 19-14) it looks like a hybrid of a Greek cross and an oval, with a long axis between entrance and apse. The side walls move in an undulating flow that reverses the motion of the façade. Vigorously projecting columns articulate the space into which they protrude just as much as they do the walls to which they are attached. This molded interior space is capped by a deeply coffered, oval dome that seems to float on the light entering through windows hidden in its base. Rich variations on the basic theme of the oval, dynamic relative to the static circle, create an interior that appears to flow from entrance to altar, unimpeded by the segmentation so characteristic of Renaissance buildings.

The unification of interior space is carried even further in Borromini's Chapel of St. Ivo in the courtyard of the College of the Sapienza (Wisdom) in Rome (FIG. 19-15). In his characteristic manner, Borromini

19-15 FRANCESCO BORROMINI, St. Ivo, begun 1642. College of the Sapienza, Rome.

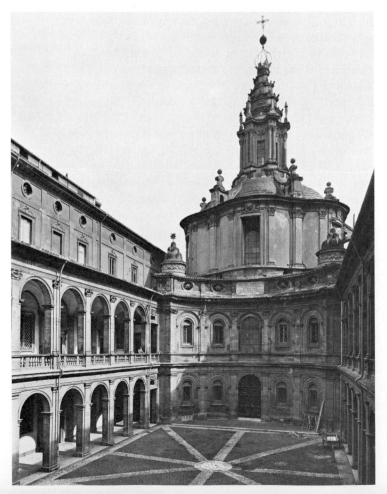

plays concave off against convex forms on the upper level of the exterior of his chapel. The lower stories of the court, which frame the bottom façade, were already there when Borromini began work. Above the inward curve of the façade—its design adjusted to the earlier arcades of the court—rises a convex, drum-like structure that supports the lower parts of the dome. Powerful pilasters restrain the forces that seem to push the bulging forms outward. Buttresses above the angle pilasters curve upward to brace a tall, plastic lantern topped by a spiral that seems to fasten the structure, screw-like, to the sky. The centralized plan (FIG. 19-16) is that of a star, having rounded-off points and apses on all three sides. Indentations and projections along the angled, curving walls create a highly complex plan, all the elements of which are fully reflected in the interior elevation. From floor to lantern, the wall panels rise in a continuously tapering sweep that is halted only momentarily by a single, horizontal cornice (FIG. 19-17). The dome is thus not, as in the Renaissance, a separate unit placed on the supporting block of a building; rather it is an organic part that evolves out of and shares the qualities of the supporting walls, from which it cannot be separated. The complex, horizontal motion of the walls is transferred fully into the elevation, creating a dynamic and cohesive shell that encloses and energetically molds a scalloped fragment of universal space. Few architects have matched Borromini's ability to translate extremely complicated designs into such masterfully unified and cohesive structures as that of St. Ivo.

The heir to Borromini's sculptured architectural style was GUARINO GUARINI (1624–1683), a priest,

19-16 FRANCESCO BORROMINI, plan of St. Ivo, Rome.

19-17 View into the dome of St. Ivo.

block-like wings. This lateral, three-part division of façades, characteristic of most Baroque palazzi, is probably based on the observation that the average human can instinctively recognize up to three objects as a unit; a greater number will require the observer to count each object individually. A three-part organization of extended surfaces thus gives the artist the opportunity to introduce variety into his design without destroying its unity. It also permits him to place added emphasis on the central axis, which Guarini has done here most effectively by punching out deep cavities in the middle of his convex central block. The variety of his design is enhanced by richly textured surfaces (all executed in brick) and by pilasters, which further subdivide his units into three bays each. High and low reliefs create shadows of different intensities and add to the decorative effect a dramatic one that makes this one of the finest façades of the late seventeenth century.

mathematician, and architect who spent the last 17 years of his life in Turin, converting that provincial Italian town into a fountainhead of architectural theories that would sweep much of Europe. In his Palazzo Carignano (FIG. 19-18), Guarini effectively applies Borromini's principle of undulating façades. He divides his long façade into three units, the central one of which curves much like the façade of San Carlo alle Quattro Fontane (FIG. 19-13) and is flanked by two

Guarini's mathematical talents must have been guiding him when he designed the extraordinarily complex dome of the Chapel of the Santa Sindone (Holy Shroud), a small, central-plan building attached to the cathedral of Turin. A view into this dome (FIG. 19-19) reveals a bewildering display of geometric figures that appear to wheel slowly around a circular focus that contains the bright Dove of the Holy Ghost. Here, the traditional dome has been dematerialized into a series of figures that seem to revolve around each other in contrary motion; they

19-18 GUARINO GUARINI, Palazzo Carignano, Turin, Italy, 1679–1692.

19-19   GUARINO GUARINI, Chapel of the Santa Sindone, Turin, Italy, 1667–1694 (view into dome).

19-20   Attributed to BRAMANTE and RAPHAEL, Sant' Eligio degli Orifici, Rome, c. 1509 (reconstructed c. 1600; view into dome).

define it, but they no longer limit the interior space. A comparison of Guarini's dome with that of the church of Sant' Eligio degli Orifici in Rome (FIG. 19-20), attributed both to Bramante and to Raphael and reconstructed about 1600, indicates that a fundamental change has taken place. The static "dome of heaven" of architecture and philosophy has been converted into the dynamic apparition of a mathematical heaven of calculable motions.

The style of Borromini and Guarini will move across the Alps to inspire architecture in Austria and South Germany in the late seventeenth and early eighteenth centuries. Popular in the Catholic regions

in Europe and the New World (especially in Brazil), it will exert little influence in France, where the more conservative style of Bernini will be favored.

In Venice, something of the Late Renaissance Classicism of Andrea Palladio survives, paradoxically, in the very Baroque church of Santa Maria della Salute (FIGS. 19-21 and 19-22), often called simply the "Salute" ("health"). Built by BALDASSARE LONGHENA (1598–1682), the church was commissioned by the

19-21   BALDASSARE LONGHENA, Santa Maria della Salute, Venice, 1631–1648 (consecrated 1687).

19-22   BALDASSARE LONGHENA, plan of Santa Maria della Salute, Venice.

republic in thanksgiving to the Virgin Mary for ridding the city of plague. At the head of the Grand Canal, the main thoroughfare of Venice, the Salute has for centuries dominated it like a gorgeous crown, the admiration of generations of travelers and artists. Longhena knew well the architectural value of the site; the two domes of the Salute harmonize with the family of domes in its vicinity, among them those of St. Mark's (FIG. 7-49) and of the Palladian churches of San Giorgio Maggiore (FIG. 17-54) and Il Redentore ("The Redeemer"). Together, they make a skyline of surpassing beauty, floating above the city or reflected in its waters in ever-changing groupings as the admiring visitor moves.

Central plans were largely foreign to Venice, and it may be that the domes and central plan of St. Mark's suggested the design of the Salute, although Longhena insisted his design had not been done before. The plan of the building (FIG. 19-22) is an octagon with an auxiliary choir. The greater of the two domes is over the octagon; the lesser is over the choir and is flanked by campaniles. Both in plan and elevation, the grouping of the masses and spaces is essentially Renaissance, without the intricacies of Bernini, Borromini, or Guarini. This is especially true of the interior, which has the clear arrangement, the correct orders, and the steady gray–white color of Palladio's wall-and-column features, as in San Giorgio Maggiore (FIG. 17-55). But the exterior elevation is dramatic. The façade-like faces of the octagon play counterpoint with the main façade, and there is the highest excitement of Baroque invention in the great scroll buttresses that seem to open organically from the main body and to sprout statuary (FIG. 19-21). The Salute is a splendid example of an architecture rooted in a native (Venetian) tradition, yet flowering successfully in a new stylistic climate.

The style of Palladio and the Venetian Renaissance could be and was transplanted into a widely different environment. While Longhena was building the Salute, the Palladian style was already being naturalized in the distant north, in England (FIG. 19-76).

Painting

Italian painters of the seventeenth century, with the possible exception of Caravaggio and the later decorators, were somewhat less adventurous than the sculptors and architects. The painters of the High Renaissance had bequeathed to them an authoritative tradition as great as that of Classical antiquity. After the sixteenth century, the artists of Europe drew from both, and the history of painting well into the nineteenth century—that is, well into modern times—is an account of the interpretation, development, and modification of these two great traditions. The three most influential stylistic bequests of the High Renais-

sance were the styles of Raphael, of Michelangelo, and of Titian, with an additional subdominant trend inspired by Correggio. Baroque painting is the consequence of many and varied interchanges among these styles, with the antique sometimes supplementing them and sometimes appealed to against them. Outside the traditions of the antique and of the Renaissance, there rises what might be called "native naturalism"—a style that seems hostile to both authorities and that is based on the assumption that the artist should paint what he sees, without regard for either the antique or the Renaissance masters. This native naturalism appears as a minority style in Italy and France but plays an important role in Spain and a predominant one in the Dutch School.

The Baroque gets well under way in Italian painting around the year 1600, with the decoration of the gallery of the Farnese Palace by ANNIBALE CARRACCI (1560–1609). His generation, weary of the strained artifice of Mannerism, returned for a fresh view of nature, but only after they had carefully studied the Renaissance masters. Annibale had attended an academy of art in his native city of Bologna. Founded cooperatively by members of his family, among them LODOVICO and AGOSTINO CARRACCI, the Bolognese academy is the first significant institution of its kind in the history of Western art. It was founded on the premises that art can be taught—the basis of any academic philosophy of art—and that the materials of instruction must include the antique and the Renaissance traditions, in addition to the study of anatomy and drawing from life. The Bolognese painters were long called academics, and sometimes eclectics, for they appeared to assume that the development of a correct style in painting is learned and synthetic. In any event, we can tell from the gallery of the Farnese Palace that Annibale was familiar with Michelangelo, Raphael, and Titian, and that he could also make clever, illusionistic paintings. The Farnese ceiling (FIG. 19-23) is a brilliant and widely influential revision of High Renaissance painting—restoring its interest in human themes and emotions, renouncing the artificialities of Mannerism to return to the study of nature, and forming a firm bridge between the Renaissance and the Baroque. The style is a vigorous, sensuous, and adroit naturalism, modified by the Classical form inherited from the masters.

The iconographical program of the ceiling is the *Loves of the Gods*, interpretations of the subtle and various stages and degrees of earthly and Divine love (see Titian's treatment of the theme in *Sacred and Profane Love*, FIG. 17-61). Despite the apparent paganism of the subjects, they are found to have Christian overtones. The principal motif is the human nude, as it is in Michelangelo's frescoes and in much of Venetian art. Luxuriantly pagan images from Classical literature, especially Ovid's *Metamorphoses*, throng the

19-23　Annibale Carracci, ceiling frescoes in the Farnese Gallery, 1597–1601. Farnese Palace, Rome.

vault, binding together and filling the composition with exuberant and passionate life (FIG. 19-23).

The scenes are arranged in panels resembling framed paintings on a wall, but here they are on the surfaces of a shallow, curved vault; the Sistine Ceiling (FIG. 17-25), of course, comes to mind, although it is not an exact source. This type of simulation of wall painting for ceiling design is called *quadro riportato*. The great influence of the Carracci will make it fash-

ionable for more than a century. The framed pictures are flanked by seated, nude youths, who turn their heads to gaze at the scenes above them, and by standing giants—motifs taken directly from Michelangelo's Sistine Ceiling. It is noteworthy that the chiaroscuro is not the same for both the pictures and the painted figures surrounding them. The figures inside the pictures are modeled in an even, sculptured light; the outside figures are lit from beneath, as if they

19-24 GUIDO RENI, *Aurora*, 1613–1614. Ceiling fresco in the Casino Rospigliosi, Rome.

were three-dimensional statues illuminated by torches in the gallery below. This interest in illusion, already manifest in the Renaissance, will continue in the grand ceiling compositions of the seventeenth century. In the crown of the vault, a long panel representing the Triumph of Bacchus is a quite ingenious crossing of Raphael and Titian and represents Annibale's adroitness in adjusting their authoritative styles to make something of his own.

Another artist trained in the Bolognese academy, GUIDO RENI (1575–1642), selected Raphael for his inspiration, as we see in his *Aurora* (FIG. 19-24), a ceiling painting conceived in *quadro riportato*. *Aurora*, the dawn, leads the chariot of Apollo, while the Hours dance about it. The fresco exhibits a suave, almost swimming motion, soft modeling, and sure composition, without Raphael's sculpturesque strength. It is an intelligent interpretation of the master's style, but in every sense learned, or "academic." However,

"academic" should not be burdened here with the bad sense it will later acquire as art that is mechanical, imitative, dull, and uninspired. The *Aurora* is a masterpiece of the Bolognese style and of its age. Guido was so much admired in his own day and well into the nineteenth century that he was known as "the divine Guido."

Like Guido, Giovanni Francesco Barbieri, called IL GUERCINO (1591–1666), another member of the Bolognese School, painted a ceiling *Aurora*, but with a very different effect (FIG. 19-25). Guercino abandons the method of *quadro riportato* for that of Veronese, in which the figures are seen from below at a 45° angle (FIG. 17-69). By this method, the subject of the picture is painted as if happening above our heads and seen from beneath; it is not simply a transfer of a painting from wall to ceiling. Taking his cue from the illusionistic figures in the Farnese Gallery and from its central ceiling panel (FIG. 19-23), Guercino converts the ceil-

19-25 IL GUERCINO, *Aurora*, 1621–1623. Ceiling fresco in the Villa Ludovisi, Rome.

ing into a limitless space, through which the procession sweeps past. The observer's eye is led toward the celestial parade by converging, painted extensions of the room's architecture. While the perspective may seem a little forced, Guercino's *Aurora* inspired a new wave of enthusiasm for illusionistic ceiling paintings that culminated in some of history's most stupendous decorations.

Although the Bolognese painters were willing enough to imitate nature as directly as possible, they believed that the Renaissance and the antique masters had already captured much of its essence and that their works would prepare them for the study of nature. Michelangelo Merisi (1571–1610), called CARAVAGGIO after the northern Italian town from which he came, thought very much otherwise. His outspoken disdain for the Classical masters (probably more vocal than real) drew bitter criticism from many painters, one of whom denounced him as the "anti-Christ of painting." Yet many paid him the genuine compliment of borrowing from his innovations.

The unconventional life of this great painter was consistent with the defiant individualism of his art. We know almost as much about Caravaggio from police records as from other documents. Violent offenses and assaults reaching to murder trace his antisocial, tragic career through restless, tormented wanderings, which, nevertheless, did not prevent him from producing a large number of astonishing works. His very association with lowlifes and outcasts may help to account for his unglorified and unfashionable view of the great themes of religion, as well as his indifference to the Renaissance ideals of beauty and decorum. In his art, he secularizes both religion and the Classics, reducing them to human dramas that might be played out in the harsh and dingy settings of his time and place. He employs a cast of unflattering characters selected from the fields and the streets; these, he was proud to declare, were his only teachers—meaning that to paint from them gave him sufficient knowledge of nature.

We can appreciate how startling Caravaggio's methods must have been for his contemporaries when we look at *The Conversion of St. Paul* (FIG. 19-26), which he painted for the Roman church of Santa Maria del Popolo. The scene illustrates the conversion of the Pharisee Saul by a light and a voice from Heaven (Acts 9: 3–9). The saint-to-be is represented flat on his back, his arms thrown up, while an old ostler appears to maneuver the horse away from its fallen master. At first inspection, there is little here to suggest the awful grandeur of the spiritual event that is taking place. We seem to be witnessing a mere stable accident, not a great saint overcome by a great miracle. The saint is not specifically identified; he could be anyone. The ostler is a swarthy, bearded old man, who looks well-acquainted with stables. The horse fills the picture as if it were the hero, and its explicitness and the angle from which it is viewed might betray an irreverence on the part of the artist for this subject. Although Caravaggio found numerous sympathetic patrons in both church and state, some of his works were refused on the ground that they lacked propriety (that is to say, decorum). He sometimes appears to pay no attention to the usual dignity appointed to scenes from scripture and to go too far in dismissing the formal graces of Renaissance figure composition and color.

The fact is that, above all, Caravaggio seeks to create a convincing copy of the optical world as a vehicle of spiritual meanings; his intention in this respect is like Bernini's in the *St. Theresa* (page 520). To this end, he uses a perspective and a chiaroscuro designed to bring viewers as close as possible to the space and action of the scene, almost as if they were participating in it. *The Conversion of St. Paul* is placed on the chapel wall and is composed with an extremely low horizon or eye level, to be on the viewers' line of sight as they stand at the entrance of the chapel. The sharply lighted figures are meant to be seen as emerging from the dark of the background; the actual light from windows outside the chapel functions as a kind of stage lighting for the production of a vision, analogous to the rays in Bernini's *St. Theresa*. Thus, Caravaggio, like Bernini, makes use of the world of optical experience to stage the visionary one. In *The Conversion of St. Paul*, what we see first as merely commonplace is in fact the elevation of the commonplace to the miraculous.

The stark contrast of light and dark was the feature of Caravaggio's style that first shocked and then fascinated his contemporaries. The sharp and sudden relief it gives to the forms and the details of form emphasizes their reality in a way that an even or subtly modulated light could never do. Dark next to light is naturally dramatic; we do not need a director of stage lighting to tell us this. Caravaggio's device—a profound influence on European art—has been called *tenebroso*, or the "dark manner." It goes quite well with material that is realistic. It is another mode of Baroque illusionism by which the eye is almost forced to acknowledge the visual reality of what it sees. Although tenebrism is widespread in Baroque art, it will have its greatest consequences in Spain and the Netherlands.

A contemporary of Caravaggio observed that he had "abandoned beauty and was interested in depicting reality"; and Giovanni Pietro Bellori, the most influential critic of the age and an admirer of the Carracci, wrote: "Caravaggio deserves great praise, as he was the only one who attempted to imitate nature as opposed to the general trend in which painters imi-

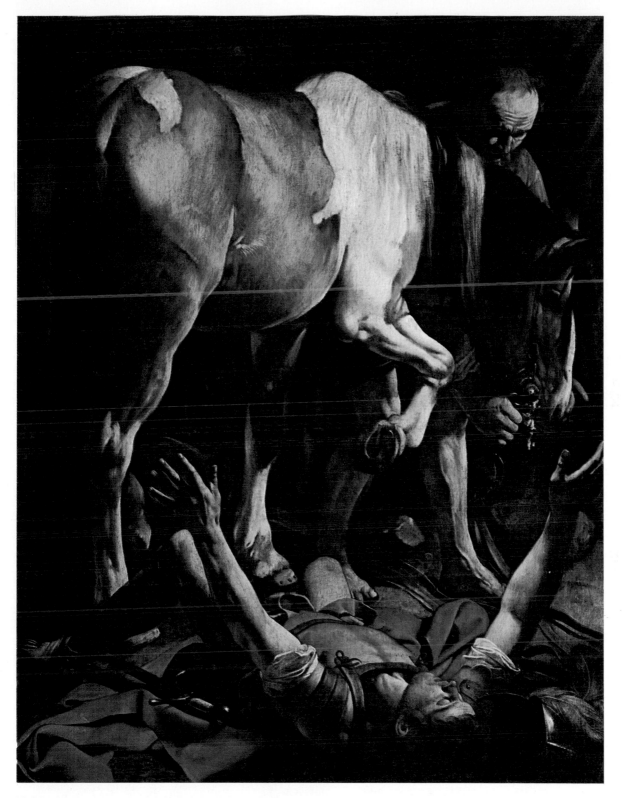

19-26 CARAVAGGIO, *The Conversion of St. Paul, c.* 1601. Oil on canvas,* approx. 7′ 6″ × 5′ 9″. Santa Maria del Popolo, Rome.

*Unless stated otherwise, all subsequent paintings are in oil on canvas.

tated other painters." The instrumentalities of this unorthodox realism find full orchestration in Caravaggio's *Death of the Virgin* (FIG. 19-27). The painting, refused (on the grounds of irreverence) as an altarpiece for Santa Maria della Scala in Rome, rep-resents the Virgin Mary dead, mourned by the disci-ples and friends of Christ. The Virgin is indeed un-ceremoniously laid out in the awkward stiffness of death—her body swollen, limbs uncomposed, and feet uncovered (the last feature considered indecent

19-27 CARAVAGGIO, *Death of the Virgin*, 1605–1606. Approx. 12′ × 8′, Louvre, Paris.

at the time). Contemporaries complained that Caravaggio had used the corpse of a young woman who had drowned as his model for the mother of Christ. Around the dead woman, in attitudes of genuine if uncouth grief, without rhetoric or declamation, are the customary plebeian types that Caravaggio casts in his pictorial dramas of reality. The drawn curtain emphasizes the stage-like setting, into which the grouping of the figures invites the viewer as participant. The harsh light plunges into the space from a single source, shattering the darks into broken areas of illumination that reveal the coarse materialities of the scene. But again—as in *The Conversion of St. Paul*, but in a different way—we can read the artist's interpretation not as diminishing the spiritual import of the theme but rather as informing it with a simple, honest, unadorned piety that is entirely sincere, the very piety that moves the humble watchers of the dead to tears.

One would think that Annibale and Ludovico Carracci and their colleagues at the Bolognese academy would have carefully avoided the dangerous art of

Caravaggio. To the contrary, many borrowed from it (some more than others), unconsciously integrating it into the tradition and into their own work. A painting so typical of the Catholic Baroque—so expressive of the Counter-Reformation and its ideals that we can hardly find its equal as a document of the times—is *The Last Communion of St. Jerome* (FIG. 19-28), painted by another Bolognese disciple, DOMENICHINO (Domenico Zampieri, 1581–1641). In a Renaissance loggia that opens into a Venetian landscape background, St. Jerome, propped up to receive the viaticum (Eucharist), is surrounded by sorrowing friends. The realism of Caravaggio stamps the old man's sagging features, his weakened, once rugged body, and the faces of at least three of his attendants and of the grave old priest. The sharpened darks and lights are also out of Caravaggio; the general composition, the architecture, the floating putti, and the turbaned spectator echo Titian, Correggio, and the mood of the High Renaissance. A painting like this would seem to be, of necessity, an academic pastiche, but all of its borrowed elements are successfully synthesized in a rare, effective unity. Domenichino's *St. Jerome* is a

19-28 DOMENICHINO, *The Last Communion of St. Jerome*, 1614. Approx. 13′ 9″ × 8′ 5″. Vatican Museums, Rome.

successful "school" picture, nourished as it is by all the sources, traditional and contemporary, available to him.

We have already mentioned the spread of Caravaggio's style outside Italy. Of course, he had many followers within its borders also, and they were artists more directly in tune with his message than eclectics like Domenichino. One of the best, whose work is increasingly appreciated by modern critics, is ARTEMISIA GENTILESCHI (1593–1653). Although we have knowledge of women who were painters as far back as the thirteenth century and although they came into their own in the sixteenth, they were few and not prominent. Social conventions, restricted education, and guild rules tended to exclude women from training and practice in the arts. Artemisia Gentileschi was instructed by her artist father, ORAZIO, who was himself strongly influenced by Caravaggio. Her successful career, pursued in Florence, Venice, Naples, and Rome, helped to propagate Caravaggio's manner throughout the peninsula. In her *Judith and Maidservant with the Head of Holofernes* (FIG. 19-29), we find the dark manner (*tenebroso*) and what might be called the "dark" subject matter favored by the *Caravaggisti*, the painters of "night" pictures. The heroism of Judith, often a subject in Italian painting and sculpture, is depicted here. The story, told in an Apocryphal work of the Old Testament, the Book of Judith, relates the delivery of Israel from its enemy Holofernes. Succumbing to the charms of Judith,

19-29 ARTEMISIA GENTILESCHI, *Judith and Maidservant with the Head of Holofernes, c.* 1625. Approx. 6' × 4' 8". Detroit Institute of the Arts (gift of Leslie H. Green).

Holofernes invites her to his tent for the night. When he has fallen asleep, Judith cuts off his head. Here, the act performed, her maidservant is putting the severed head in a sack. The action takes place in a curtained, oppressively closed space. The atmosphere of menace and horror is thickened by the heavy darks, scarcely relieved by the feeble candle, the sole source of light. Yet the light falls on the courtly splendor of the women's raiment and exhibits forms and characters intended by the artist to be convincingly real. The light is interrupted dramatically by Judith's hand, which casts a shadow on her face. This is a favorite device of the night painters: a single source of illumination within the painting—partly or wholly concealed by an object in front of it or, as in this case, intercepted by an object—casting an abrupt shadow. The effect is like opening the shutter of a lantern for a brief moment in a pitch-black cellar where unspeakable things are happening.

The Carracci and Caravaggio powerfully influenced the art of figure painting for two centuries, but the Carracci largely determined the dominant course taken by landscape painting over the same period. In his *Flight into Egypt* (FIG. 19-30), Annibale Carracci created the "ideal" or "classical" landscape. Adopted and developed in France by Nicolas Poussin and Claude Lorraine (FIGS. 19-62 and 19-63), this kind of landscape would come to prevail as the accepted pictorial representation of nature ordered by Divine law and human reason. The roots of the style are in the landscape backgrounds of Venetian paintings of the Renaissance (compare FIGS. 19-30 and 17-60). Tranquil hills and fields, quietly gliding streams, serene skies, unruffled foliage, shepherds with their flocks—all the props of the pastoral scene and mood—expand to fill the picture space. They are regularly introduced by a screen of trees in the foreground, dark against the even light of the sky. Attenuated streams or terraces, carefully placed one above the other, make a compositional direction left or right through the terrain. In the middle ground, there generally appear (as in FIG. 19-30) compositions of architecture, walled towns or citadels, towers, temples, monumental tombs, villas—the constructed environment of idealized antiquity and the idyllic life, undisturbed by the passions. The subjects are drawn from religious or heroic story; here, Mary, with the Christ Child, and St. Joseph wend their slow way to Egypt, after having been ferried across a stream (Matthew 2:13–14). The figures, relative to the landscape, shrink in scale and importance, and are sometimes simply its excuse. For now, in the seventeenth century, landscape comes fully into its own as a major subject for the painter.

But there are landscape types other than the Classical. In dramatic contrast with *Flight into Egypt* is a landscape by SALVATOR ROSA (1615–1673), *St. John the*

19-30 ANNIBALE CARRACCI, *Flight into Egypt*, 1603–1604. Approx. 4' × 7' 6". Galleria Doria Pamphili, Rome.

Baptist in the Wilderness (FIG. 19-31). Rosa's painting, like Annibale Carracci's, has a sacred theme, and the figures in it are subordinate to the landscape; otherwise, the two paintings obviously have nothing in common. Instead of the calm of idealized nature in Annibale's landscape, we have nature in a violent mood, a savage wilderness abandoned by Heaven. A ragged tree, blasted by generations of thunderbolts, writhes before a chaos of barren rocks. For Rosa, nature appears malevolent, the home only of wild beasts, of holy or of desperate men. The broken surfaces, jagged contours, and harsh textures in confused arrangement here should be compared with the smooth volumes and contours and regular placement

of forms that characterize the Classical landscape. The alternative style of Rosa will greatly influence the next century's taste for the "picturesque"—sublime and awesome scenes, filled with terror and foreboding, which will indulge the Romantic temperament and fuel its enthusiasm.

The development of landscape painting was contemporary with that of ceiling painting, the latter being stimulated anew by the large, new churches of Baroque Rome. The problems associated with ceiling painting are, of course, special. Looking *up* at a painting is different from simply looking *at* a painting, for there is an element of awe in the experience of looking at what is above us, particularly when it is at con-

19-31 SALVATOR ROSA, *St. John the Baptist in the Wilderness, c.* 1640. Approx. 5' 8" × 8' 6". Glasgow Art Gallery and Museum.

siderable height. Guercino saw this in his *Aurora* (FIG. 19-25), but apparently Guido Reni did not in his (FIG. 19-24)—or, rather, preferred or was required to use the *quadro riportato* method. The Baroque artist found a ceiling surface high above the ground a natural field for the projection of visual illusion. The devout Christian, thinking of Heaven as "up," must be overwhelmed with emotion when, looking up, he sees its image before his eyes. In the Sistine Ceiling, Michelangelo made no attempt to project an image of the skies opening into heaven; rather, he represented an epic narrative of events of no physical place or time that could be read almost as well from walls as from ceilings. The *illusion* of bodies actually soaring above was of no interest to him; the truth of certain events in the history of Genesis was, and these events and figures could be shut off in their own compartments, self-contained. It is quite otherwise with a Baroque master of ceiling decoration like FRA ANDREA POZZO (1642–1709). A lay brother of the Jesuit order and a master of perspective, on which he wrote an influential treatise, Pozzo designed and executed the vast ceiling fresco depicting *The Glorification of St. Ignatius* (FIG. 19-32) for the church of Sant' Ignazio in Rome. This is indeed the culmination of the *di sotto in sù* experiments of Mantegna (FIG. 16-65) and Correggio (FIG. 17-38). The artist intends to create the illusion that Heaven is opening up above the heads of the congregation— indeed, of the very congregation that fills this church of Sant' Ignazio. For, in painted illusion, Pozzo continues the actual architecture of the church into the vault, so that the roof seems to be lifted off, as Heaven and Earth commingle and St. Ignatius is carried to the waiting Christ in the presence of the four corners of the world. A metal plate in the nave floor marks the standpoint for the whole perspective illusion. Looking up from this point, the observer takes in the celestial–terrestrial scene as one, for the two are meant to fuse in Pozzo's design without the interruption of a boundary. To achieve his visionary effects, the artist employs all means offered by architecture, sculpture, and painting and unites them in a fusion that surpasses even the Gothic effects of total integration.

Sound, as well as light, is a vehicle of ecstasy and vision in the Baroque experience. We know that churches were designed with acoustical effect in mind and can imagine how, in a Baroque church filled with Baroque music, the power of both light and sound would be vastly augmented. Through simultaneous stimulation of both the visual and auditory senses, the faithful might be transported into a trance-like state that would indeed, in the words of Milton, "bring all Heaven before [their] eyes." But this transport would always have to be effected by physical means, for although in the Middle Ages men

19-32 FRA ANDREA POZZO, *The Glorification of St. Ignatius,* 1691–1694. Ceiling fresco in the nave of Sant' Ignazio, Rome.

were able to find the vision within, in the Baroque period they demanded that that mystery be made visible to the outward sight. Thus, to be credible, Heaven must more and more visually resemble the domain of earth; Dante could see Heaven in a dream, but Pozzo wanted to see it unfold above him while he was awake and walking in a church. Medieval man aspired to Heaven; Baroque man wanted Heaven to come down to his station, where he might see it— even inspect it. Vision is the supreme faculty in seventeenth-century art and science.

Baroque expansiveness is expressed not only in the characteristic movement toward the infinite horizontal but in an emphasis on the vertical as well. The heavens are more and more within reach; Galileo and Newton will penetrate them to find the laws of their movement. The clouds of Heaven are not simply the seat of angels; the seventeenth century discovers that they are water vapor. The bright air through which light is propagated has density and weight. As the heavens become physical, so man may dream of taking possession of them someday by flight—not the flight of the soul, but the flight of the body. The Baroque period transforms spirit into matter in motion, as Pozzo's ceiling relates.

SPAIN

In Spain, as in the other countries of Europe, Italianate Mannerism was adopted in the sixteenth century and cast off in the Baroque period. But along with Mannerism, Spain seemed to reject most of what the Italian Renaissance stood for, just as it would reject, for a long time, the scientific revolution and the Enlightenment. Since the Middle Ages, Spain had maintained a proud isolation from the events of Europe—an isolation that has not entirely ended today.

In the art of El Greco, we have seen the mystical side of the Spanish character (FIG. 18-61). The hard, unsentimental realism that is the other side appears in the painting of JOSÉ DE RIBERA (1591–1652), who, because he emigrated to Naples early and settled there, is sometimes called by his Italian nickname, Lo Spagnoletto, "the little Spaniard." The realism of his style—a mixture of a native Spanish strain and the "dark manner" of Caravaggio—gives shock value to his often brutal themes, which express at once the harsh times of the Counter-Reformation and a Spanish taste for the representation of courageous resistance to pain. His *Martrydom of St. Bartholomew* (FIG. 19-33) is grim and dark in subject and form. St. Bartholomew, who suffered the torture of being skinned alive, is being hoisted into position by his executioners. The saint's rough, heavy body and swarthy, plebeian features express a kinship between him and his tormentors, who compose the same cast of characters we found in the painting of Caravaggio and the Neapolitan School. In this painting, Ribera scorns idealization of any kind, and we have the uncomfortable feeling that he is recording rather than imagining the grueling scene. In that age of merciless religious fanaticism on both sides, torture, as a means of saving stubborn souls, was a common and public spectacle.

FRANCISCO DE ZURBARÁN (1598–1664) softens realism with an admixture of the mystical. His principal subjects are austere saints, represented singly in devotional attitudes and usually sharply lighted from the side. He shows us *St. Francis in Meditation* (FIG. 19-34), his uplifted face almost completely shadowed by his cowl, clutching to his body a skull—the *memento mori*, the constant reminder to the contemplative of his own mortality. The bare, unfurnished set-

19-33   JOSÉ DE RIBERA, *The Martyrdom of St. Bartholomew,* *c.* 1639. Approx. 6′ × 6′ 6″. Museo del Prado, Madrid.

19-34   FRANCISCO DE ZURBARÁN, *St. Francis in Meditation,* *c.* 1639. Approx. 60″ × 39″. Reproduced by courtesy of the Trustees of the National Gallery, London.

ting and the stark light and somber dark are the bleak environment of this entranced soul. We see enough to read this as an image of rapt meditation—the parted lips, the tensely locked fingers, the rigid attitude of a devotee utterly unaware of his surroundings and mystically in contact with God. Here, Zurbarán gives us a personification of the fierce devotion of Catholic Spain.

In the Baroque age, visions and the visual go together. It may be that DIEGO VELÁZQUEZ (1599–1660)—an artist who set aside visions in the interest of what is given to the eye in the optical world—stands among the great masters of visual realism of all time. Although he painted religious pictures, he was incapable of idealism or high-flown rhetoric, and his sacred subjects are bluntly real. Velázquez, trained in Seville, early came to the attention of the king, Philip IV, and became the court painter at Madrid, where, save for two extended trips to Italy and a few excursions, he remained for the rest of his life. His close personal relationship with Philip and his high office of marshal of the palace gave him prestige and a rare opportunity to fulfill the promise of his genius with a variety of artistic assignments. In an early work, *Los Borrachos* ("The Drinkers," FIG. 19-35), Velázquez shows his cool independence of the ideals of Renaissance and Baroque Italy in a native naturalism that has the strength and something of the look of Caravaggio. Commissioned to paint Bacchus among his followers, Velázquez makes mock of Classical conventions in both theme and form. He bur-

lesques the stately, Classical Bacchic scenes—making the god a mischievous young *bravo*, stripped to the waist, crowning a wobbly tippler who kneels before him. The rest of the company is of the same type: weather-beaten, shabby roisterers of the tavern crowd, who grin and jape at the event uncouthly, enjoying the game for what it is. Painting the crude figures in strong light and dark that is evenly distributed so as not to obscure them, Velázquez makes sharp characterizations of each person, showing not only his instinct for portraiture but a Baroque interest in human "types." And, typically Spanish, he caricatures, through realism, an Italianate subject that ordinarily would be idealized. Enrique Lafuente, a modern critic, states the Spanish attitude:

> Spain refuses to accept the basic ideas which inspire the Italian Renaissance because they are repugnant to its sense of the life of the Spanish man. The Spaniard knows that reality is not Idea but Life. . . . The supreme value of life is linked with experience and the moral values that are based on personality. Idea, beauty, formal perfection, are abstractions and nothing more. Art, in its turn, is bound to concern itself with realities and not with dreams.*

To Velázquez, as to many Spanish artists, the academic styles of Baroque Italy must have seemed pretentious and insincere, not to say pagan. He turned away from them to the world before his eyes.

*Enrique Lafuente, *Velázquez* (New York: Oxford University Press, 1943), p. 6.

19-35 DIEGO VELÁZQUEZ, *Los Borrachos*, c. 1628. Approx. 5' 6" × 7' 6". Museo del Prado, Madrid.

19-36 DIEGO VELÁZQUEZ, *Juan de Pareja*, 1649–1650. Approx. 33″ × 28″. Metropolitan Museum of Art, New York.

One could hardly find in art a better example of Lafuente's dictum that "reality is not Idea, but Life" than Velázquez's portrait of *Juan de Pareja* (FIG. 19-36). At the height of his powers, Velázquez painted his assistant when they were in Rome together in 1650. He was intending to paint a portrait of Pope Innocent X, a patron of Bernini, and he did the study of Pareja as a kind of trial run. Today, we would probably agree that it is a masterpiece in its own right.

The work was exhibited in the Pantheon and drew the admiration of the many artists in Rome, Italian and foreign alike. They perceived in it an almost incredible knowledge of the structure of appearance, a matchless technique of execution, and an eloquent simplicity of composition that rejected conventional Baroque props and rhetoric. The apparent simplicity of the formal means matches the simplicity of presentation. Placed before an entirely neutral ground, Pareja looks directly at us with a calm dignity and quiet pride, a man perfectly self-contained. His character gives him a natural poise, utterly without arrogance or affectation. His level gaze, the easy gesture of arm and hand, and his erect carriage place him directly in front of us, and Velázquez introduces him.

Velázquez's uncanny power of penetration of the form and meaning before him, though in some ways unique, was not entirely untaught. He had carefully studied the works of other artists and was fully aware of the achievements of the great masters like Michelangelo and the Venetians. He knew the latter from the king's collections, of which he had charge, and he studied them further in Italy, where he journeyed at the suggestion of the great Flemish painter Peter Paul Rubens, whom he met when the older Rubens was copying the Venetians in the collections at the Madrid court. But his studies in Italy did not make a "Romanist" of Velázquez. Their most notable effects were a softening of his earlier, somewhat heavy-handed realism (seen in *Los Borrachos*) and a lighter palette, which gave his paintings brighter and subtler tonality.

Looking at his masterpiece, *Las Meninas* ("The Maids in Waiting," FIG. 19-37), with our experience of his portrait of *Juan de Pareja*, we must view Velázquez as a master of a brilliant optical realism that has seldom been approached and has never been surpassed. The painter represents himself in his studio before a large canvas, on which he may be painting this very picture or, perhaps, the portraits of the king and queen, whose reflections appear in the mirror on the far wall. The little infanta, Margarita, appears in the foreground with her two maids in waiting, her favorite dwarfs, and a large dog. In the middle ground are a duenna and a male escort; in the background, a gentleman is framed in a brightly lit open doorway. The personages present have been identified. On the wall above the doorway and mirror, two faintly recognizable pictures represent the immortal gods as the source of art. Our first impression of *Las Meninas* is of an informal family group (it was long called "The Family" by the Austrian kings of Spain), casually arranged and miraculously lifelike; one could think of it as a genre painting—"A Visit to the Artist's Studio"—rather than as a group portrait.

As first painter to the king and as chief steward of the palace, Velázquez was conscious not only of the importance of his court office but of the honor and dignity belonging to his profession as painter. In this painting, he appears to bring the roles together, asserting their equivalent value. A number of pictures from the seventeenth century show painters with their royal patrons, for painters of the time continued to seek to aggrandize their profession among the arts and to achieve by it appropriate rank and respect. Throughout his career, Velázquez hoped to be ennobled by royal appointment to membership in the ancient and illustrious Order of Santiago, from which, he must have expected, his profession as painter would not disqualify him. Because some of the required patents of nobility were lacking in his background, he achieved this only with difficulty at the very end of his life, and then only through a dispensation from the pope. In the painting, he wears the red cross of the order on his doublet, which was painted there, legend tells us, by the king himself; the truth is that the artist painted it. In Velázquez's mind, *Las Meninas* might have embodied the idea of the

19-37 DIEGO VELÁZQUEZ, *Las Meninas*, 1656. Approx. 10' 5" × 9'. Museo del Prado, Madrid.

great king visiting his artist's studio, as Alexander the Great visited the studio of APELLES in ancient times.

Although Velázquez intends an optical report of the event, authentic in every detail, he also seems to intend a pictorial summary of the various kinds of images in their different levels and degrees of "reality"—the "reality" of canvas image, of mirror image, of optical image, and of the two imaged paintings. The work—with its cunning contrasts of mirrored spaces, "real" spaces, picture spaces, and pictures within pictures—itself appears to have been taken from a large mirror reflecting the whole scene, which would mean the artist has not painted the princess and her suite, but himself in the process of painting

them. In the Baroque period, when artists were taking Leonardo's dictum that "the mirror is our master" very seriously, it is not surprising to find mirrors and primitive camera-like devices used to achieve optimum visual fidelity in painting. *Las Meninas* is a pictorial summary as well as a commentary on the essential mystery of the visual world and on the ambiguity that results when we confuse its different states or levels.

How does Velázquez achieve this stunning illusion? He opens the spectrum of light and the tones that compose it. Instead of putting lights abruptly beside darks—as Caravaggio, Ribera, and Zurbarán would do or as he himself, in earlier works like *Los*

Borrachos (FIG. 19-35), had done—he allows a great number of intermediate values of gray to come between the two extremes. Thus, he carefully observes and records the subtle gradations of tone, matching with graded glazes what he sees in the visible spread of light and dark, using strokes of deep dark and touches of highlight to enliven the neutral tones in the middle of the value scale. This essentially cool, middle register of tones is what gives the marvelous effect of daylight and atmosphere to the painting. Velázquez's matching of tonal gradations approaches effects that the age of the photograph will later discover. His method is an extreme refinement of Titian's. No longer does Velázquez think of figures as first drawn, then modeled into sculptural effects, and then colored. He thinks of light and tone as the whole substance of painting—the solid forms being only *suggested*, never really constructed. Observing this reduction of the solid world to purely optical sensations in a floating, fugitive skein of color tones, one could say that the old, sculpturesque form has disappeared. The extreme thinness of Velázquez's paint and the light, almost accidental touches of thick pigment here and there destroy all visible structure; we examine his canvas closely, and everything dissolves to a random flow of paint. As a wondering Italian painter exclaimed of a Velázquez painting: "It is made of nothing, but there it is!" Painters 300 years later will realize that Velázquez's optical realism constitutes a limit. Their attempts to analyze it and to take it further will lead in an opposite direction to the one taken by the great Spanish master—to the abstract art of our own time.

FLANDERS

In the sixteenth century, the Netherlands came under the crown of Hapsburg Spain when the emperor Charles V retired, leaving the Spanish throne and his Netherlandish provinces to his only son, Philip II. Philip's repressive measures against the Protestants led to the breaking away of the northern provinces from Spain and the setting up of the Dutch republic under the House of Orange. The southern provinces remained with Spain, and their official religion continued to be Catholic. The political distinction between modern Holland and Belgium more or less reflects this original separation, which, in the Baroque period, signalized not only religious but also artistic differences. The Baroque art of Flanders (the Spanish Netherlands) remained in close contact with the Baroque art of the Catholic countries, while the Dutch schools of painting developed their own subjects and styles, consonant with their reformed religion and the new political, social, and economic structure of the middle-class Dutch republic.

The brilliant Flemish master PETER PAUL RUBENS (1577–1640) preceded Bernini in the development and dissemination of the Baroque style. Rubens' influence was international; he drew together the main contributions of the masters of the Renaissance (Michelangelo and Titian) and of the Baroque (the Carracci and Caravaggio) to synthesize in his own style the first truly European manner. Thus, Rubens completes the work begun by Albrecht Dürer in the previous century. The art of Rubens, even though it is the consequence of his wide study of many masters, is no weak eclecticism but an original and powerful synthesis. From the beginning, his instinct was to break away from the provincialism of the old Flemish Mannerists and to seek new ideas and methods abroad. His aristocratic education, his courtier's manner, diplomacy, and tact, as well as his Classical learning early made him the associate of princes and scholars. He became court painter to the dukes of Mantua (descended from the patrons of Mantegna), friend of the King of Spain and his adviser on art collecting, painter to Charles I of England and Maria de' Medici, queen of France, and permanent court painter to the Spanish governors of Flanders. Rubens also won the confidence of his royal patrons in matters of state, being entrusted often with diplomatic missions of the highest importance. In the practice of his art, he was assisted by scores of associates and apprentices, turning out large numbers of paintings for an international clientele. In addition, he functioned as an art dealer, buying and selling works of contemporary art and Classical antiquities. His numerous enterprises made him a rich man, with a magnificent town house and a château in the countryside. Wealth and honors, however, did not spoil his amiable, sober, self-disciplined character. We have in Rubens, as in Raphael, the image of the successful, renowned artist, the consort of kings, and the shrewd man of the world, who is at the same time the balanced philosopher. Rubens more than makes good the Renaissance claim for the preeminence of the artist in society.

Rubens became a master in 1598 and went to Italy two years later, where he remained until 1608. During these years, he formed the foundations of his style. Shortly after his return from Italy, he painted *The Elevation of the Cross* (FIG. 19-38) for Antwerp Cathedral. This work shows the result of his long study of Italian art, especially of Michelangelo, Tintoretto, and Caravaggio. The scene is a focus of tremendous, straining forces and counterforces, as heavily muscled giants strain to lift the cross. Here, the artist has the opportunity to show foreshortened anatomy and the contortions of violent action—not the bound action of Mannerism, but the tension of strong bodies meeting resistance outside themselves. The body of Christ is a great, illuminated diagonal that cuts dynamically across the picture and, at the same time, inclines back into it. The whole composition seethes with a power that we feel comes from genuine exertion, from elastic human sinew taut with effort. Strong modeling in dark and light marks Rubens' work at this stage of his career; it will gradually give way to a much subtler, coloristic style.

The vigor and passion of Rubens' early manner never leaves his painting, although its vitality is modified into less strained and more subtle forms, depending on the theme. Yet Rubens has one general theme—the human body, draped or undraped, male or female, freely acting or free to act in an environment of physical forces and other interacting bodies. There is nothing profoundly tragic in Rubens' con-

ception of the human scene, nor is there anything manneristically intellectual, enigmatic, or complex. His forte is the strong animal body described in the joyful, exuberant motion natural to it. His *Rape of the Daughters of Leucippus* (FIG. 19-39) describes the abduction of two young mortals by the gods Castor and Pollux, who have fallen in love with them. The amorous theme permits departures from realism, especially in the representation of movement and exerted strength. The gods do not labor at the task of sweeping up the massive maidens—descendants of the opulent Venuses of Giorgione and Titian (FIGS. 17-60 and 17-63)—nor do the maidens energetically resist. The figures are part of a highly dynamic, slowly revolving composition that seems to turn on an axis—a

19-39   PETER PAUL RUBENS, *The Rape of the Daughters of Leucippus,* 1617. Approx. 7' 3" × 6' 10". Alte Pinakothek, Munich.

diamond-shaped group that defies stability and the logic of statics. The surface pattern, organized by intersecting diagonals and verticals, consists of areas of rich, contrasting textures: the soft luminous flesh of the women, the bronzed tan of the muscular men, lustrous satins, glinting armor, and the taut, shimmering hides of the horses. And around this surface pattern, a tight massing of volumes moves in space; the solid forms are no longer described simply in terms of the dark–light values of Florentine draftsmanship but are now built up in color and defined by light, as in Venetian painting.

The impact of Rubens' hunting pictures lies in their depiction of ferocious action and vitality. In *The Lion Hunt* (FIG. 19-40), a cornered lion, three lances meeting in his body, tears a Berber hunter from his horse. A fallen man still grips his sword, while another, in a reversed position, stabs at a snarling cat. Horsemen plunge in and out of the picture space, and the falling Berber makes a powerful, diagonal cut across the composition. The wild melee of thrusting, hacking, rearing, and plunging is almost an allegory of the bound tensions of Mannerism exploding into the extravagant activity of the Baroque.

19-40　Peter Paul Rubens, *The Lion Hunt*, 1617–1618. Approx. 8′ 2″ × 12′ 5″. Alte Pinakothek, Munich.

Rubens shared heartily in the Baroque love of magnificent pomp, especially as it set off the majesty of royalty, in which Rubens, born courtier that he was, heartily believed. The Baroque age saw endless, extravagant pageants and festivals produced whenever the great or even lesser dynasts moved. Their authority and right to rule was forever being demonstrated by lavish display; we have seen that the popes themselves, the princes of the Church, made of St. Peter's a permanently festive monument to papal supremacy. And Maria de' Medici, a member of the famous Florentine House of Medici, commissioned Rubens to paint a cycle memorializing and glorifying her career and that of her late husband, the first of the Bourbon kings, Henry IV.

Rubens' imposing, vigorous figure compositions were not his only achievement; he also produced rich landscapes and perceptive portraits. A painting of singular power is Rubens' portrait of *Thomas Howard, Earl of Arundel* (FIG. 19-41). This great nobleman played a leading role in the complicated diplomacy and statecraft of the age of Charles I, when England was verging on the tragic civil war between the Stuart king and the Parliament. He is best remembered, however, as a lover of art, who built a collection of

ancient statuary and other works of art unsurpassed in the Europe of his time. Rubens was a friend of Arundel and an admirer of his taste and learning. Rubens' admiration for the man himself, regarded by contemporaries as the bringer of "true virtu"— knightly gallantry and magnanimity—to England, is clearly expressed in the portrait. The earl is posed in an attitude of regal majesty. He directs a sharp, stern, haughty glance over his shoulder, creating instant distance between *his* rank and that of the observer. The look given by the aquiline features is that of a commander of armies silencing a subordinate; it is full of an authority not to be questioned. Rubens gives us not the sensitive lover of art but the fearless captain; we realize that the earl himself must have stipulated that this aspect of his character and career be shown. To this end, Rubens has garbed him in magnificent ceremonial armor. His gauntleted hand rests on the commander's staff; his plumed helmet, on a table at his side. Behind him, a curtain is drawn aside, showing a severe Classical architecture that echoes his mood. Rubens lavishes all of his rich resources of color tone in the rendering of the splendid accoutrements of high rank and latter-day chivalry. This imperious image speaks for an autocratic age—

19-41 PETER PAUL RUBENS, *Thomas Howard, Earl of Arundel, c.* 1630. Approx. 54″ × 45″. Isabella Stewart Gardner Museum, Boston.

for the great dynasts of the Baroque, whom Rubens knew well and who were his patrons.

Most of Rubens' successors in Flanders had been his assistants. The most famous, ANTHONY VAN DYCK (1599–1641), probably worked with his master on the canvas of *The Rape of the Daughters of Leucippus.* Quite early, the younger man, unwilling to be over-shadowed by the undisputed stature of Rubens, left his native Antwerp for Genoa and then London, where he became court portraitist to Charles I. Al-though Van Dyck created dramatic compositions of high quality, his specialty became the portrait, and he developed a courtly manner of great elegance that would be internationally influential. His style is felt in English portrait painting down to the nineteenth cen-tury. In one of his finest works, *Charles I Dismounted*

(FIG. 19-42), he shows the ill-fated Stuart king stand-ing in a Venetian landscape (with the river Thames in the background!), attended by an equerry and a page. Although the king personates a nobleman out for a casual ride in his park, there is no mistaking the regal poise and the air of absolute authority that his Parlia-ment resented and was soon to rise against. The com-position is exceedingly artful in the placement of the king—off-center, but balancing the picture with a single keen glance at the observer. The full-length portraits by Titian and the cool composure of the Mannerists alike contribute to Van Dyck's sense of pose and arrangement of detail. For centuries, artists who make portraits of the great will keep Van Dyck very much in mind—Thomas Gainsborough, Joshua Reynolds, and John Singer Sargent, among them.

19-42 ANTHONY VAN DYCK, *Charles I Dismounted, c. 1635.*
Approx. 9' × 7'. Louvre, Paris.

HOLLAND

For all intents and purposes, the style of Peter Paul
Rubens is the style of Baroque Flanders; he had few
rivals of significance and a monopoly on commis
sions. The situation is so completely different in Holland that it is difficult to imagine how, within such a
tiny area, two such opposite artistic cultures could
flourish. The Dutch Protestants and the Flemish
Catholics went their separate ways after the later sixteenth century. Although closer in outlook to the
Germans, the Dutch were ethnically the same as the
Flemish, who were, in turn, closer in viewpoint to
their neighbors to the south—the French. A Catholic,
aristocratic, and traditional culture reigned in the
Flanders of Rubens. In Holland, severe, Calvinistic
Protestantism was puritanical toward religious art,
sculptural or pictorial, although there were many
Dutch Catholics, including painters. The churches
were swept clean of images, and any recollection of
the pagan myths, the material of Classicism, or even
historical subjects was proscribed in art. During the
Middle Ages and the Renaissance, religious subjects
and, later, Classical and historical subjects had been
the major stimuli for artistic activity. Divested of
these sources, what remained to enrich the lives of

wealthy Hollanders? For they *were* wealthy! During
the early part of the Spanish rule, the Dutch, like the
Flemish, prospered. The East India Company was
formed, and the discovery of the New World opened
up further opportunities for trade and colonization.
The wars of independence from Spain made Holland
the major maritime country of Europe; its closest rival
was England, another Protestant power in the times
of the Spanish decline. The great Dutch commercial
cities, such as Haarlem and Amsterdam, had been
stimulated and enriched, and civic pride was strong.
Although it was not internationally recognized until
the Peace of Westphalia in 1648, Holland had been
independent from Spain in fact since about 1580 and
was extremely proud of its hard-won freedom. Under
these circumstances, writes the nineteenth-century
French painter EUGÈNE FROMENTIN

> Dutch painting . . . was and could be only the por-
> trait of Holland, its exterior image, faithful, exact,
> complete, with no embellishments. Portraits of men
> and places, citizen habits, squares, streets, country-
> places, the sea and the sky—such was to be . . . the
> program followed by the Dutch School, and such it
> was from its first day to the day of its decline.*

Thus, it came about that the Dutch painters pried into
the pictorial possibilities of everyday life and kept an
eye on their customers, the middle-class burghers,
who wanted paintings to hang on their walls as evidence of their growing wealth and social position.

We have followed the secularization and humanization of religious art since the thirteenth century. In
the Dutch School of the seventeenth century, the
process is completed. A thousand years and more of
religious iconography is dismissed by a European
people who ask for a view of the world from which
angels, saints, and deities have been banished. The
old Netherlandish realism remains, but it no longer
serves religious purposes. The Dutch artists rise to
the occasion, matching the open, competitive, Dutch
society, which is thoroughly middle-class, with an
equally open arrangement of their own, in which the
painter works not for a patron but for the market. He
becomes a specialist in any one of a number of subjects—genre, landscape, seascape, cattle and horses,
table still life, flower still life, interiors, and so on. In
short, he paints subjects that he feels will appeal to
his public and therefore be marketable. This independence from the patron gives the Dutch painter a certain amount of freedom, even if it is only the freedom
to starve on the free-picture market. With respect to
the artist–market relationship, the contrast between

*Eugène Fromentin, *The Masters of Past Time: Dutch and Flemish
Painting from Van Eyck to Rembrandt,* trans. A. Boyle (London:
Phaidon, 1948), p. 130.

Flanders and Holland in the seventeenth century is poignantly reflected in the careers of Rubens and Rembrandt. The former *is* the market in Flanders; his genius determines it. The latter, after finding a place in the market, is rejected by it when his genius is no longer marketable.

The realism of Dutch art is made up of the old tradition, which goes back to Hubert and Jan van Eyck, and of the new "realism of light and dark," brought back to Holland by Dutch painters who had studied Caravaggio in Italy. One of these "night painters" (as they were called), GERARD VAN HONTHORST (1590–1656) of Utrecht, spent several years in Italy absorbing Caravaggio's style. He is best known for merry genre scenes like *The Supper Party* (FIG. 19-43), in which unidealized, human figures are shown in an informal gathering. Although these "merry companies," naturalistically rendered in night settings, were popular and widely produced in the Baroque period, they were not necessarily taken simply as pictures of people enjoying themselves. We must remember the Baroque mental habit of allegorizing and symbolizing even the most realistic images. Here, for example, we may be expected to witness the loose companions of the Prodigal Son (Luke 15:13)—panders and prostitutes, drinking, singing, strumming, laughing. Perhaps, at the same time, we have an allegory of the Five Senses through which sin can enter the soul: taste, touch, sight, sound, scent. Fascinated by nocturnal effects, Van Honthorst frequently places a hidden light source (two, in this case) in his pictures and uses it as a pretext to work with dramatic and violently contrasted dark–light effects. Without the incisive vision of Caravaggio, Van Honthorst is nevertheless able to match, and sometimes to surpass, the former's tenebristic effects.

The Dutch schools were as various as their cities (Utrecht, Haarlem, Leiden, Amsterdam), but all had in common the lesson of Caravaggio interpreted by Dutch "Caravaggisti" like Van Honthorst. FRANS HALS (c. 1580–1666)—the leading painter of the Haarlem School and one of the great realistic painters of the Western tradition—appropriates what he needs from the new lighting to make portraiture (his specialty) an art of acute psychological perception as well as a kind of comic genre. The way light floats across the face and meets shadow can be arranged by the artist, as can the pose and the details of costume and facial expression. Hals shows himself to be a master of all the devices open to a portraitist who no longer need keep the distance required by the strictly formal portrait. The relaxed relationship between the portraitist and his subject is apparent in the engaging portrait of *Balthasar Coymans* (FIG. 19-44), dated 1645. Although the subject is a young man of some importance, the artist seems to be taking a great deal of liberties with his portrait. The young man leans on one arm with a jaunty air of insolence, his hat cocked at a challenging angle, a look of contemptuous drollery in his eyes. The illusion of life is such that we take cues from the subject's expression as if we were face-to-face with him. Hals' genius lies in this capture of the minute, expressional movements by which, in everyday life, we appraise the man across from us. Until now, this

19-43   GERARD VAN HONTHORST, *The Supper Party,* 1620. Approx. 7′ × 4′ 8″. Galleria degli Uffizi, Florence.

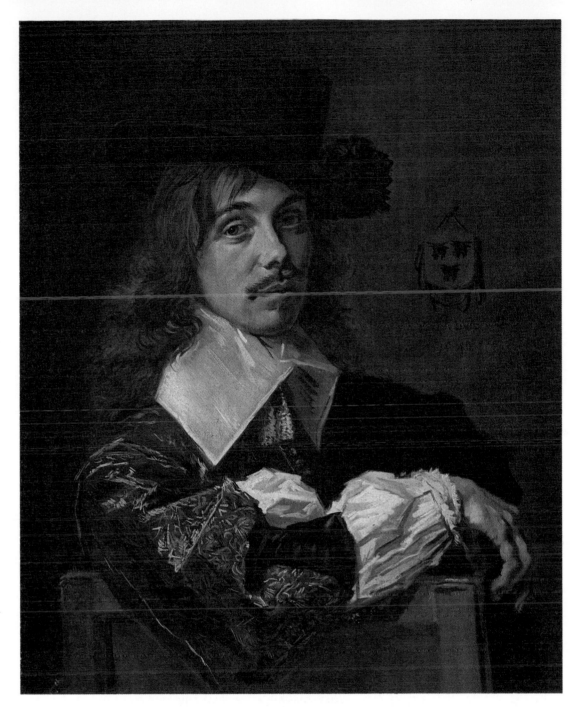

19-44 FRANS HALS, *Balthasar Coymans*, 1645. Approx. 30¼″ × 25″. National Gallery of Art, Washington, D.C. (Andrew W. Mellon Collection).

kind of intimate confrontation had rarely been seen in painting. It is a kind of contradiction of the masks of formal portraiture created in the Renaissance. We are in the presence of an individual without formal introduction; the gap between us and the subject is reduced until we are almost part of his physical and psychological environment. The casualness, immediacy, and intimacy are intensified by the manner in which the painting is executed. The touch of the painter's brush is as light and fleeting as the moment in which the pose is caught; the pose of the figure, the highlights on the sleeve, the reflected lights within face and hand, the lift of the eyebrow—all are

the instant prey of time. Thus, the evanescence of time that Bernini caught in his *David* (FIG. 19-10) is recorded far to the north a few years later in a different subject and a different medium. Both are Baroque.

Frans Hals is a genius of the comic. He had precedents in the gargoylism and grotesquerie of the northern Middle Ages and, in later times, in Hieronymus Bosch and Pieter Bruegel. But Hals' comedy is that of character, rather than situation. He shows us— as Aristotle would demand of comedy—people as they are and somewhat less than they are; this puts us at ease, out of superiority, so that we can laugh at

19-45　Frans Hals, *Malle Babbe, c.* 1650 (?). Approx.
30″ × 25″. Gemäldegalerie, Staatliche Museen, Berlin-Dahlem.

others and ourselves. Hals takes his comic characters, as did Shakespeare, his contemporary, from the depths of society. The *Malle Babbe* ("Mad Babbe," FIG. 19-45), with her owl and her shiny pewter tankard, holds her cackling own in a verbal exchange, doubtless in some cellar tavern. In the Baroque era, as the heavens descend to earth, so Hell rises and becomes familiar in human forms; all the spheres tend to meet. Hals' dashing, *alla prima* brushwork (perhaps more studied than it appears) seems to catch the quick outburst in almost the moment it would take it to be heard. This instant reportage is a development inspired out of the deliberate, almost static method of Caravaggio. No painter, not even among the Impressionists, wanted more than Hals to bring the instantaneous image of life before us.

Good-humored stageplay brightens Hals' great canvases of units of the Dutch civic guard, which played an important part in the liberation of Holland. These companies of archers and musketeers met on their saints' days in dress uniform for an uproarious banquet, giving Hals an opportunity to attack the problem of adequately representing each subject of a group portrait while retaining action and variety in the composition. Earlier group portraits in the Netherlands represent the sitters as so many jugs on a shelf; Hals undertakes to correct this and, in the process, produces dramatic solutions to the problem, like that found in his *Archers of St. Adrian* (FIG. 19-46). Here, the troopers have finished their banquet, the wine has already gone to their heads, and each in his own way is sharing the abundant high spirits. As a

stage director Hals has few equals. In quite Baroque fashion, he balances direction of glance, pose, and gesture, making compositional devices of the white ruffs, broad-brimmed black hats, and banners. Although the instantaneous effect—the preservation of every detail and facial expression—is, of course, the result of careful planning, Hals' vivacious brush seems to have moved spontaneously, directed by a plan in the artist's mind but not traceable in any preparatory scheme on the canvas. The bright optimism of this early period of Dutch freedom is caught in the swaggering bonhomie of the personalities, each of whom plays his particular part within the general unity of mood. This is the gregariousness that goes with the new democracy, as well as the fellowship that grows from a common experience of danger.

With Hals, Baroque realism concentrates on the human subject so intimately that we are forced to relate it to ourselves. We and the subject look at each other, as if in a sharing of mood; there is a confrontation of personalities. Yet it is still mostly a public image that the subject is willing to present; in this respect, Hals has not entirely broken away from the tradition of formal portraiture that goes back to the fifteenth century. The first deep look into the *private* man will be made by Hals' younger contemporary, REMBRANDT VAN RIJN (1606–1669).

Rembrandt's way was prepared spiritually by the Protestant Reformation and the Dutch aspiration to freedom and formally by the Venetian painters, by Rubens, and by Caravaggio and his Dutch imitators. The richness of this heritage, however, cannot alone account for the extraordinary achievement of this artist, one of the very greatest among those geniuses who excel in revealing Western man to himself. Rembrandt used painting as a method for probing the states of the human soul, both in portraiture and in his uniquely personal and authentic illustrations of the Scriptures. The abolition of religious art by the Reformed Church in Holland did not prevent him from making a series of religious paintings and prints that synopsize the Bible from a single point of view— that of a believing Christian, a poet of the spiritual, convinced that the biblical message must be interpreted in human terms for human beings. In Rembrandt, the humanization of Medieval religion is now completed in the vision of a single believer. In the Baroque age, this is roughly parallel to the sighting of a new planet by some single "watcher of the skies."

Rembrandt's pictorial method involves refining light and shade into finer and finer nuances, until they blend with one another. (Caravaggio's "absolute" light has, in fact, many shadows; his "absolute" dark, many lights.) We have seen that Velázquez renders optical reality as a series of values—a number of degrees of lightness and darkness. Thus, the use of abrupt lights and darks gives way in the works of

19-46 FRANS HALS, *Archers of St. Adrian* (*Assembly of Officers and Subalterns of the Civic Guard*), *c.* 1633. Approx. 6′ 9″ × 11′. Frans Halsmuseum, Haarlem.

men like Rembrandt and Velázquez to gradation, and, although the dramatic effects of violent chiaroscuro may be sacrificed, the artist gains much of the truth of actual appearances— for, to the eye, light and dark are not static but are always subtly changing. Changing light and dark can suggest changing human moods; we might say that the *motion* of light through a space and across human features can express *emotion*, the changing states of the psyche.

The Renaissance represents forms and faces in a flat, neutral, modeling light (even Leonardo da Vinci's shading is of a standard kind), just as it represents action in a series of standard poses. The Renaissance painter represents the *idea* of light and the *idea* of action, rather than the actual *look* of either. Light, atmosphere, change, and motion are all concerns of Baroque art, as well as of Baroque mathematics and physics. The difference from what went before lies largely in the new desire to *measure* these physical forces. For example, as the physicist in the seventeenth century is concerned not just with motion, but with acceleration and velocity—degrees of motion— so the Baroque painter discovers degrees of light and dark, of differences in pose, in the movements of facial features, and in psychic states. He arrives at these differences *optically*, not conceptually or in terms of some ideal. Rembrandt found that by manipulating light and shadow in terms of direction, intensity, distance, and texture of surface, he could render the most subtle nuances of character and mood, of persons, or of whole scenes. Rembrandt discovers for

the modern world that differences of light and shade, subtly modulated, can be read as emotional differences. In the visible world, light, dark, and the wide spectrum of values between the two are charged with meanings and feelings that are sometimes independent of the shapes and figures they modify. The lighted stage and the photographic arts have long accepted this as the first assumption behind all their productions. What Masaccio and Leonardo began, the age of Rembrandt completes.

In his early career in Amsterdam, Rembrandt's work was influenced by Rubens and by Dutch Caravaggesque painters like Van Honthorst. Thus, in a work like *Supper at Emmaus*, dating from about 1630 (FIG. 19-47), he represents the subject with high drama—in sharp light and dark contrast—even using the device, familiar among his contemporaries, of placing the source of illumination behind an obstructing form (in this case, the head of Christ). This puts the darkest shadow in front of the brightest light, creating an emphatic, if obvious, dramatic effect. The poses of the two alarmed disciples to whom the risen Christ reveals himself are likewise a studied stage maneuver. Some 18 years later, in another painting of the same subject (FIG. 19-48), the mature Rembrandt forsakes the earlier melodramatic means for a serene and untroubled setting. Here, with his highly developed instinct for light and shade, he gives us no explosive contrasts; rather, a gentle diffusion of light mellows the whole interior, condensing just slightly to make an aureole behind the head of

19-47 REMBRANDT VAN RIJN, *Supper at Emmaus,*
c. 1628–1630. 14½″ × 16⅛″. Musée Jacquemart-André, Paris.

19-48 REMBRANDT VAN RIJN, *Supper at Emmaus, c.* 1648.
Approx. 27″ × 26″. Louvre, Paris.

19-49 REMBRANDT VAN RIJN, *The Return of the Prodigal Son,*
c. 1665. Approx. 8′ 8″ × 6′ 8¾″. Hermitage Museum,
Leningrad.

Christ. The disciples only begin to understand what is happening; the servant is unaware. The Christ is Rembrandt's own interpretation of the biblical picture of the humble Nazarene—gentle, with an expression both loving and melancholy.

The spiritual stillness of Rembrandt's religious painting is that of inward-turning contemplation, far from the choirs and trumpets and the heavenly tumult of Bernini or Pozzo. Rembrandt gives us not the celestial triumph of the Church, but the humanity and humility of Jesus. His psychological insight and his profound sympathy for human affliction produce, at the very end of his life, one of the most moving pictures in all religious art, *The Return of the Prodigal Son* (FIG. 19-49). Tenderly embraced by his forgiving father, the son crouches before him in weeping contrition while three figures, immersed in varying degrees in the soft shadows, note the lesson of mercy. The scene is wholly determined by the artist's inward vision of its meaning. The light, everywhere mingled with shadow, controls the arrangement of the figures—illuminating father and son, largely veiling the witnesses. Its focus is the beautiful, spiritual face of the old man; secondarily, it touches the contrasting, stern face of the foremost witness. There is no flash or glitter of light or color; the raiment is as sober as the characters are grave. Rembrandt, one feels, has put the official Baroque style far behind him and has developed a personal style completely in tune with the simple eloquence of the biblical passage. One could not help but read the Bible differently, given the authority of Rembrandt's pictorial interpretations of it.

Rembrandt carries over the spiritual quality of his religious works into his later portraits by the same means—what we might call the ''psychology'' of light. Light and dark are not in conflict in his portraits; they are reconciled, merging softly and subtly to produce the visual equivalent of quietness. The prevailing mood is that of tranquil meditation, of philosophical resignation, of musing recollection— indeed, a whole cluster of emotional tones heard only in silence. He records the calamities of his own life and the age-old ones of the Jewish people (he had many friends in the Jewish quarter of Amsterdam) in the worn faces of aged and silent men. His study of the influence of time on the human features was one with his study of light; the mood of reflection conveyed by the slow movement of lights and darks complements the appearance of the aged face in slanting light: a sunken terrain crisscrossed with deep lines. In a long series of self-portraits, Rembrandt preserved his own psychic history from the bright alert optimism of youth to the worn resignation of his declining years. These last years, when he was at the height of his artistic powers, cost him much physically if we are to judge from two portraits only eight years apart. The earlier (FIG. 19-50) shows the artist in his maturity—confident, even challenging, confronting the observer as if he would like to see his creden-

tials. Rembrandt hooks his thumbs into the belt of his studio smock, stands on no formality, waits for the observer to declare himself. In its familiarity and lack of formality, the portrait is a radical departure from the Renaissance tradition still alive in Van Dyck. The later portrait is an almost shocking contrast (FIG. 19-51). The light from above and from the artist's left pitilessly reveals a face ravaged by anxiety and care. The pose is that of Raphael's *Baldassare Castiglione* (FIG. 17-19), which Rembrandt had seen in Holland and copied in an earlier self-portrait. The difference between Raphael's and Rembrandt's portraits tells us much about the difference between the approaches of the artists and between the philosophies of their times. In Raphael's subject, the ideal has modified the real; Rembrandt shows himself as he appears to his own searching and unflattering gaze. Here, an elderly man is not idealized into the image of the courtly philosopher; he is shown merely as he is, a human being in the process of dwindling away. For some, the portrait and the self-portrait, which began as a medium for the recording of likeness, came to be painted out of motives of vanity; with Rembrandt, they are the history of Everyman's painful journey through the world.

19-50 REMBRANDT VAN RIJN, *Self-Portrait*, 1652. Approx. 45″ × 32″. Kunsthistorisches Museum, Vienna.

19-51 REMBRANDT VAN RIJN, *Self-Portrait*, c. 1659. Approx. 33″ × 26″. National Gallery of Art, Washington, D.C. (Andrew W. Mellon Collection).

In the group portrait, an area of painting in which Frans Hals excelled, Rembrandt shows himself to be the supreme master. In *Syndics of the Cloth Guild* (FIG. 19-52), representing an archetypal image of the new businessmen, Rembrandt applied all that he knew of the dynamics and the psychology of light, the visual suggestion of time, and the art of pose and facial expression. The syndics, or board of directors, are going over the books of the corporation. It would appear that someone has entered the room and they are just at the moment of becoming aware of him, each head turning in his direction. Rembrandt gives us the lively reality of a business conference as it is interrupted; yet he renders each portrait with equal care and with a studied attention to personality one would expect to be possible only from a long studio sitting for each man. Although we do not know how Rembrandt proceeded, this harmonizing of the instantaneous action with the permanent likeness seems a work of superb stage direction that must have needed long rehearsal. The astonishing harmonies of light, color, movement, time, and pose have few rivals in the history of painting.

Rembrandt's virtuosity also extends to the graphic media—in particular, etching. Here again, he ranks at the summit, alongside the original master, Dürer, who was actually an engraver. Etching, perfected early in the seventeenth century, was rapidly taken up; it was far more manageable than engraving and allowed greater freedom in drawing the design. In etching, a copper plate is covered with a layer of wax or varnish in which the design is drawn with an etching needle or any pointed tool, exposing the metal below but not cutting into its surface. The plate is then immersed in acid, which etches, or eats away, the exposed parts of the metal, acting in the same capacity as the burin in engraving. The softness of the medium gives the etcher greater freedom than the woodcutter and the engraver, who work directly in their more resistant media of wood and metal. Thus, prior to the invention of the lithograph in the nineteenth century, etching was the most facile of the graphic arts and the one that offered the greatest subtlety of line and tone.

If Rembrandt had never painted, he would still be renowned, as he principally was in his lifetime, for his prints. Prints were a major source of income for him, and he often reworked the plates so that they could be used to produce a new issue or edition. The illustration here shows the fourth state, or version, of his *Three Crosses* (FIG. 19-53). In the earlier states, he represents the hill of Calvary in a quite pictorial, historical way, with crowds of soldiers and spectators, all descriptively and painstakingly rendered. In this last state, not the historical but the symbolic significance of the scene comes to the fore. As if impatient

19-52 REMBRANDT VAN RIJN, *Syndics of the Cloth Guild*, 1662. Approx. 6′ 2″ × 9′ 2″. Rijksmuseum, Amsterdam.

19-53 REMBRANDT VAN RIJN, *The Three Crosses*, 1653. Fourth-state etching, approx. 15″ × 18″. British Museum, London.

with the earlier detail, Rembrandt furiously eliminates most of it with hard, downward strokes of the needle, until what appears like a storm of dark lines pours down from Heaven, leaving a zone of light on the lonely figure of the crucified. Here, Rembrandt seems clearly to show that, in the words of theologian William Vischer-T'Hooft, "the entire biblical story is meant to lead us to the cross."

The art of his later years was not really acceptable to Rembrandt's contemporaries (although he occasionally got important commissions, like that for *Syndics of the Cloth Guild*). It was too personal, too eccentric; many, like the Italian biographer Filippo Baldinucci, thought Rembrandt was a tasteless painter, concerned with the ugly and ignorant of color. This prejudice lasted well into the nineteenth century, when his genius was finally acknowledged. We see him now as one of the great masters of the whole tradition, an artist of great versatility, and the unique interpreter of the Protestant conception of scripture. For our time, he stands as the archetype of the modern artist—the isolated and courageous master who finds his own way to new heights of expression, no matter the barriers of misunderstanding raised against him.

The "Little Dutch Masters"

The pictorial genius of the Dutch masters of the seventeenth century surpassed all others in its comprehensiveness of subject, taking all that is given to the eye as its province. The whole world of sight is explored, but especially the things of man in their ordinary use and aspect. In some ways, the old Netherlandish tradition of Jan van Eyck lives on in the rendering of things in the optical environment with a loving and scrupulous fidelity to their appearances. Dutch painters came to specialize in portraiture, genre, interiors, still life, landscape and seascape, and even in more specialized subdivisions of these. With many, the restriction of their professional interest is all to the good; they may not create works of grand conception, but, within their small compass, they produce exquisite art.

The best-known and most highly regarded of these painters, once referred to as the "little Dutch masters," is JAN VERMEER (1632–1675) of Delft, who was rediscovered in the nineteenth century. Vermeer's pictures are small, few, and perfect within their scope. While the fifteenth-century Flemish artists painted interiors of houses occupied with persons who were usually of sacred significance, Vermeer and his contemporaries composed neat, quietly opulent interiors of Dutch middle-class dwellings, in which they placed men, women, and children engaged in household tasks or some little recreation—actions totally commonplace, yet reflective of the values of a comfortable domesticity that has a simple beauty. Vermeer usually composes with a single figure, but sometimes with two or more. His *Young Woman with a Water Jug* (FIG. 19-54) can be considered typical, although we cannot be sure of the precise action or the

19-54 JAN VERMEER, *Young Woman with a Water Jug, c.* 1665. Approx. 18″ × 16″. Metropolitan Museum of Art, New York (gift of Henry G. Marquand, 1889).

19-55 JAN VERMEER, detail of *Young Woman with a Water Jug* (FIG. 19-54).

moment of action. The girl may be opening the window to water flowers in a window box outside. This action is insignificant in itself and only one of hundreds performed in the course of a domestic day. Yet Vermeer, in his lighting and composing of the scene, raises it to the level of some holy, sacramental act. The old Netherlandish symbolism that made every ordinary object a religious sign is gone; but this girl's slow, gentle gesture is almost liturgical. The beauty of humble piety, which Rembrandt finds in human faces, is here extended to a quite different context. The Protestant world, renouncing magnificent churches, finds a sanctuary in a modest room illuminated by an afternoon sun. Yet the light is not the mysterious, spiritual light that falls on the face in a Rembrandt portrait, an outward manifestation of the "inner light" of grace stressed in Protestant mysticism; it is ordinary daylight, observed with a keenness of vision unparalleled—unless we think of Velázquez—in the history of art.

Vermeer is master of pictorial light and so comprehends its functions that it is completely in the service of the artist's intention, which is to render a lighted depth so faithfully that the picture surface is but an invisible glass through which we look immediately into the constructed illusion. We know that Vermeer made use of mirrors and of the *camera obscura*—an ancestor of the modern camera in which a tiny pinhole, acting as a lens, projected an image on a screen or the wall of a room (or, in later versions, on a ground-glass wall of a box, the opposite wall of which contained the pinhole). This does not mean Vermeer merely copied the image; these aids helped him to obtain results that he reworked compositionally, arranging his figures and the furniture of the room in a beautiful stability of quadrilateral shapes that gives his designs a matchless Classical calm and serenity. This quality is enhanced by a color so true to the optical facts and so subtly modulated that it suggests Vermeer was far ahead of his time in color science. A detail of the picture (FIG. 19-55) shows, for one thing, that Vermeer realized that shadows are not colorless and dark, that adjoining colors affect one another,* and that light is composed of colors. Thus, the blue drape is caught as a dark blue on the side of the brass pitcher, and the red of the carpet is modified in the low-intensity gold hue of the basin. It has been recently suggested that Vermeer also perceived the phenomenon photographers call *circles of confusion*, which appear on out-of-focus films; Vermeer could have seen them in images projected by the primitive

lenses of the *camera obscura*. These he approximates in light dabs and touches that, in close view, give the impression of an image slightly "out of focus"; when we draw back a step, however, as if adjusting the lens, the color spots cohere, giving an astonishingly accurate illusion of a third dimension. All of these technical considerations reflect the scientific spirit of the age, but they do not explain the exquisite poetry of form and surface, of color and light, that could come only from the sensitivity of a great artist. In Marcel Proust's *Swann's Way*, the connoisseur hero, trying unsuccessfully to write a monograph on Vermeer, admits that no words could ever do justice to a single patch of sunlight on one of Vermeer's walls.

The "little Dutch masters" treat the humblest objects, which receive their meaning by their association with human uses, as reverently as if they were sacramentals. The Dutch painters of still life isolate these objects as profoundly interesting in themselves, making of their representation both scientific and poetic exercises in the revelation of the functions and the beauties of light. There are many fine examples of Dutch still life, all of which are done with the expertness of the specialist in analytical seeing. A still life by WILLEM KALF (1619–1693) can serve as exemplary of the school (FIG. 19-56). Here, against a dark ground, the artist arranges glass goblets, fruit, a silver salver, and a Turkish carpet, making a rich, luminous counterpoint of absorptive and reflective textures. The glossy, transparent shells of the goblets gleam like night skies with galaxies of sparklets and light filaments, contrasting with the duller highlights that edge the rim of the salver. There is a textural gradation from the glass to the silver, from a lemon to a pomegranate to the muted glow of the light-absorbing Turkish carpet. The luminous flesh of the peeled lemon gleams as if lighted from within. (Oranges, emblem of the ruling House of Orange, occur more frequently in Dutch still life than do lemons.) This little masterpiece shows how this age of seeing must have taken pleasure in the infinite variety of the play of light in the small universe as well as the large. This is not dull imitation; it is revelation of what can be seen if the eye will learn to see it.

The Baroque world discovers the infinite, whether it is the infinitely small or the infinitely great. The spark of light that lifts the rim of a glass out of darkness becomes, when expanded, the sunlit heavens. The globule of dew on a leaf in a Dutch flower painting becomes the aqueous globe of Earth itself. The space that began to open behind the figures of Giotto (FIG. 15-15) now, in Dutch landscape, takes flight into limitless distance, and man dwindles to insignificance—"his time a moment, and a point his place." In some of the works of JACOB VAN RUISDAEL (1628–1682), the human figure does not appear or appears

*Due to the phenomenon of *complementary afterimage*, in which, for example, the eye retains briefly a red image of a green stimulus; thus, a white area adjoining a green will appear "warm" (slightly pink), and a blue adjoining the same green will shift toward violet (blue plus the afterimage red).

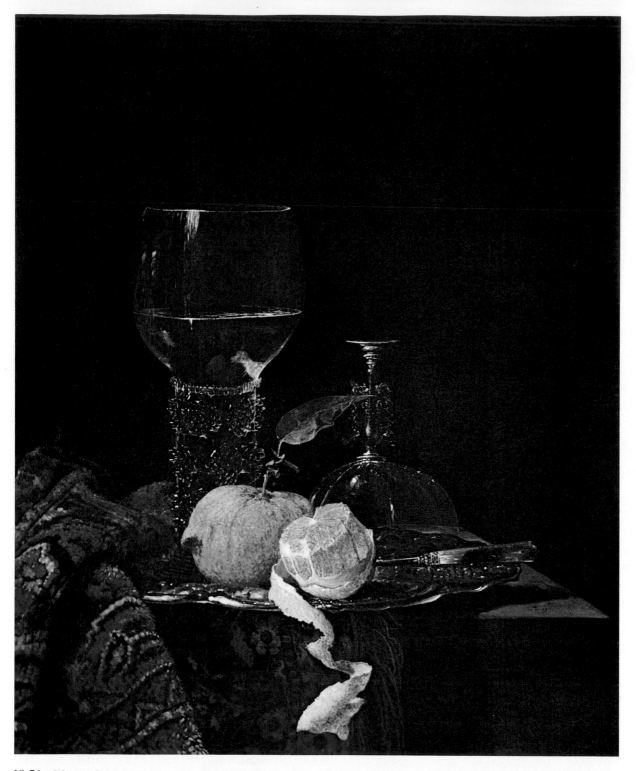

19-56 WILLEM KALF, *Still Life*, 1659. Approx. 20" × 17". Royal Picture Gallery (Mauritshuis), the Hague.

only minutely. In *View of Haarlem from the Dunes at Overveen* (FIG. 19-57), he gives us almost a portrait of the newly discovered, infinite universe, allowing the sky to take up two-thirds of the picture space. One of the great landscape painters of all time, Van Ruisdael turns to the vast and moody heavens that loom above the flat dunelands of Holland. His sullen clouds, in great droves never quite scattered by the sun, are herded by the winds that blew the fortunes of Hol-

land's fleets as well as the disasters of the invading sea. Storms are always breaking up or gathering; the earth is always drenched, or about to be. As Rembrandt reads the souls of men in their faces, so Van Ruisdael reads the somber depths of the heavens. No angels swoop through his skies or recline on his clouds, for clouds now are simply water vapor. Like Rembrandt's, his is a "Protestant" reading of nature. The difference between northern and southern Ba-

19-57 JACOB VAN RUISDAEL, *View of Haarlem from the Dunes at Overveen*, c. 1670. Approx. 22" × 25". Royal Picture Gallery (Mauritshuis), the Hague.

roque is evident at once and completely in a comparison of Pozzo's *Glorification of St. Ignatius* (FIG. 19-32) and Van Ruisdael's *View of Haarlem*. It is the difference between the heavens of Jesuit vision and the heavens of Newton and Leibniz.

FRANCE

In the second half of the seventeenth century, the fortunes of both Holland and Spain sank before those of France, whose "Sun King," Louis XIV, dominated the period of European history between 1660 and 1715. The age of Louis XIV saw the ascendancy of French power in Europe, politically and culturally, and the achievement of an international influence in taste that France has still not entirely lost. The French regard this period as their "golden age"—when Paris began to replace Rome as the art center of Europe; when the French language became the polished instrument of discourse in diplomacy and in the courts of all countries; and when French art and criticism, fashion and etiquette, were imitated universally. Art and architecture came into the service of the king, as once they had been in the service of the Church, and the unity of style so conspicuous in them is the result of the taste of Louis XIV himself—imposed on the whole nation through his able minister Jean Baptiste Colbert and through the new academies Colbert set up to regularize style in all the arts.

The king's taste and, therefore, the taste of France favored a stately and reserved Classicism in place of the lavish and emotional Baroque of Italy and most of the rest of Europe. The severe Classical regularity of form—in the plays of Pierre Corneille and Jean Baptiste Racine, in the Corinthian colonnade of the Louvre (FIG. 19-65), and in the paintings of Nicolas Poussin (FIGS. 19-61 and 19-62)—is exceptional in the age of the Baroque. Even though we can find much that is Baroque in the "Classical" art produced in the time of *le Roi Soleil*, Classicism came to be thought of as standard by the French, and continued to be so for centuries.

Painting

The earlier part of the seventeenth century saw the slow recovery of France from the anarchy of the religious wars. While Cardinals Richelieu and Mazarin painfully rebuilt the power and prestige of the French throne, French art remained under the influence of Italy and Flanders. Even so, artists of originality emerged—for example, GEORGES DE LA TOUR (1593–1652), a painter who learned of Caravaggio possibly through the Dutch School of Utrecht. Much as De la Tour uses the devices of the northern "Caravaggisti," his effects are strikingly different from theirs. His *Lamentation Over St. Sebastian* (FIG. 19-58) shows us the type of night scene favored by that school, as we have seen it in Van Honthorst (FIG. 19-43). However, De la Tour places the source of illumination (the flaming torch) within the picture and does not shield it. His strong light falls on greatly simplified, almost abstract forms, with no complication of surface, drapery, or texture to deflect or splinter the light and shade. This geometric simplicity of light falling on smooth volumes gives a kind of Classical stability and a calm stillness that—in another place and time—belongs especially to the art of Piero della Francesca (FIG. 16-34). In the *St. Sebastian*, only the light is dramatic; the gestures and attitudes of the figures are coolly understated.

LOUIS LE NAIN (*c.* 1593–1648) bears, with his contemporary, De la Tour, comparison with the Dutch. Subjects that in Dutch painting are an opportunity for boisterous good humor are managed by the French

19-58   GEORGES DE LA TOUR, *The Lamentation Over St. Sebastian, c.* 1630 (copy?). Approx. 63″ × 51″. Gemäldegalerie, Staatliche Museen, Berlin-Dahlem.

with a cool stillness. *Family of Country People* (FIG. 19-59) expresses the grave dignity of a family close to the soil, one made stoic and resigned by hardship. Obviously, Le Nain sympathizes with his subjects and seems here to want to emphasize their rustic virtue, far from the gorgeous artificiality of the courts. Stress on the honesty, integrity, and even innocence of un-

19-59   LOUIS LE NAIN, *Family of Country People, c.* 1640. Approx. 44″ × 62″. Louvre, Paris.

corrupted country folk in the following century will become sentimentality. However, Le Nain's objectivity permits him to record a group of such genuine human beings that the picture rises above anecdote and the picturesqueness of genre. These still, sombre country folk could have had little reason for merriment. The lot of the peasant, never easy, was miserable during the time Le Nain painted. The terrible conflict we call the Thirty Years' War (1618–1648) was raging. The last and most devastating of the wars of religion between Protestants and Catholics, which had begun a century before, spread atrocity and ruin throughout France, Italy, and the Germanies. The anguish and frustration of the peasantry, suffering from the cruel depredations of unruly armies living off the country, often broke out in savage revolts that were savagely put down.

A record of the times appears in a series of etchings by JACQUES CALLOT (1592–1635) called *Miseries of War*. Callot, the first great master of the art of etching, a medium to which he almost exclusively confined himself, was widely influential in his own time and since; Rembrandt was among those who knew and learned from his work. Callot perfected the medium and the technique of etching, developing a very hard surface for the copper plate, to permit fine and precise delineation with the needle. In one small print, he may assemble as many as 1,200 figures, which only close scrutiny can discriminate. His quick, vivid touch and faultless drawing produce a panorama sparkling with sharp details of life—and death. In the *Miseries*, he observes these coolly, presenting without comment things Callot himself must have seen of the wars in his own country, Lorraine. In one etching, he depicts a mass execution by hanging (FIG. 19-60). The unfortunates may be war prisoners, or defeated peasant rebels. The event takes place in the presence of a disciplined army, drawn up on parade, with banners, muskets, and lances, their tents in the right background. Hanged men sway in clusters from the branches of a huge, cross-shaped tree. A monk climbs a ladder, holding up a crucifix to a man, around whose neck the noose is being adjusted. At the foot of the ladder, another victim kneels to receive absolution. Under the tree, men roll dice on a drumhead for the belongings of the executed. (This may be an allusion, in the Baroque manner, to the soldiers who cast lots for the garments of the crucified Christ.) In the right foreground, a bound man is consoled by a hooded priest. Callot's *Miseries* are the first realistic, pictorial record of the human disaster of war. They look ahead to Goya's great prints on the same theme (FIG. 21-11).

The brisk animation of Callot's manner contrasts with the quiet composure in the art of De la Tour and Le Nain, his exact contemporaries. Yet although there is calm simplicity and restraint in the latter two, in comparison with other northern painters inspired by Caravaggio, and although these qualities suggest the Classical, it remains for another contemporary, NICOLAS POUSSIN (1594–1665), to establish Classical painting as peculiarly expressive of French taste and genius in the seventeenth century. Poussin, born in Normandy, spent most of his life in Rome. There, inspired by its monuments and the landscape of the Campagna, he produced his grandly severe and regular canvases and carefully worked out a theoretical explanation of his method. He worked for a while under Domenichino but shunned the exuberant Italian Baroque; Titian and Raphael were the models that he set for himself. Of his two versions of a single theme—titled *Et in Arcadia Ego* ("I, too, in Arcadia" or

19-60   JACQUES CALLOT, etching from the *Miseries of War* series, 1621. Bibliothèque Nationale, Paris.

"Even in Arcadia, I [am present]")—the earlier is strikingly Titianesque, with all the warm, rich tonality of the Venetian master and the figure types familiar in Titian's idyllic "bacchanals." But, in the end, the rational order and stability of Raphael proved most appealing to Poussin. His second version of *Et in Arcadia Ego* (FIG. 19-61) shows what he learned from Raphael, as well as directly from antique statuary; landscape, of which Poussin became increasingly fond, expands in the picture, reminiscent of Titian but also indicative of Poussin's own study of nature. The theme is somewhat obscure and of interest to modern scholars. As three shepherds living in the idyllic land of Arcadia spell out an enigmatic inscription on a tomb, a stately female figure quietly places her hand on the shoulder of one of them. She may be the spirit of death, reminding these mortals, as does the inscription, that death is found even in Arcadia, where naught but perfect happiness is supposed to reign. The compact, balanced grouping of the figures, the even light, and the thoughtful, reserved, elegiac mood set the tone for Poussin's art in its later, Classical phase.

In notes for an intended treatise on painting, Poussin outlines the "grand manner" of Classicism, of which he became the leading exponent in Rome. One must first of all choose great subjects: " . . . the first requirement, fundamental to all others, is that the subject and the narrative be grandiose, such as bat-tles, heroic actions, and religious themes." Minute details should be avoided, as well as all "low" subjects, like genre ("Those who choose base subjects find refuge in them because of the feebleness of their talents"). This rules out a good deal of both the decorative and realistic art of the Baroque, and will lead to a doctrinaire limitation on artistic enterprise and experiment in the rules of the French Royal Academy, which, under Charles le Brun in the 1660s, will take Poussin as its greatest modern authority. Although Poussin can create with ease and grandeur within the scope of his rather severe maxims, his method can become wooden and artificial in the hands of academic followers.

Poussin represents that theoretical tradition in Western art that goes back to the Early Renaissance and that asserts that all good art must be the result of good judgment—a judgment based on sure knowledge. In this way, art can achieve correctness and propriety, two of the favorite categories of the classicizing artist or architect. Poussin praises the ancient Greeks for their musical "modes," by which, he says, "they produced marvelous effects." He observes that "this word 'mode' means actually the rule or the measure and form which serves us in our production. This rule constrains us not to exaggerate by making us act in all things with a certain restraint and moderation." "Restraint" and "moderation" are the very essence of French Classical doctrine; in the age of

19-61 NICOLAS POUSSIN, *Et in Arcadia Ego, c.* 1655 (?). Approx. 34″ × 48″. Louvre, Paris.

Louis XIV, we find it preached as much for literature and music as for art and architecture. Poussin tells us further that

> The Modes of the ancients were a combination of several things . . . in such a proportion that it was made possible to arouse the soul of the spectator to various passions. . . . the ancient sages attributed to each style its own effects. Because of this they called the Dorian Mode stable, grave, and severe, and applied it to subjects which are grave and severe and full of wisdom.*

Poussin's finest works, like *The Burial of Phocion* (FIG. 19-62), are instances of his obvious preference for the "Dorian Mode." His subjects are chosen carefully from the literature of antiquity, where his age would naturally look for the "grandiose," and it is with Poussin that the visual arts draw closer to literature than ever before. Here, he takes his theme from Plutarch's life of Phocion, an Athenian hero who was unjustly put to death by his countrymen but then given a public funeral and memorialized by the state. In the foreground, Poussin represents the body of the hero being taken away, his burial on Athenian soil having at first been forbidden. The two massive bearers and the bier are starkly isolated in a great landscape that throws them into solitary relief, eloquently

*In E.G. Holt, ed., *Literary Sources of Art History* (Princeton: Princeton University Press, 1947), p. 380.

expressive of the hero abandoned in death. The landscape is composed of interlocking planes that slope upward to the lighted sky at the left, carefully arranged terraces that bear slowly moving streams, shepherds and their flocks, and, in the distance, whole assemblies of solid geometric structures (temples, towers, walls, villas). The skies are untroubled; the light, even and form-revealing. The trees are few and carefully arranged, like curtains lightly drawn back to reveal a nature carefully cultivated as a setting for a single human action. For, unlike Van Ruisdael's *View of Haarlem* (FIG. 19-57), this is not the scene of a particular place and time; it is the construction of an *idea* of a noble landscape to frame a noble theme, as we have seen it in Annibale Carracci's Classical landscape (FIG. 19-30). The *Phocion* landscape is nature subordinated to a rational plan, much like the gardens of Versailles (FIG. 19-67); it is eminently of the "age of reason."

The disciplined, rational art of Poussin, with its sophisticated revelation of the geometry of landscape, is modulated in the softer style of Claude Gellée, called CLAUDE LORRAINE (1600–1682) and sometimes only Claude. Unlike Poussin's pictures, Claude's are not "Dorian." The figures in his landscapes tell no story, point out no moral, praise no hero; indeed, they often appear added as mere excuses for the radiant landscape itself (FIG. 19-63). For Claude, there is essentially one theme: the beauty of a

19-62 NICOLAS POUSSIN, *The Burial of Phocion*, 1648. Approx. 47″ × 70″. Louvre, Paris.

broad sky suffused with the golden light of dawn or sunset that makes its glowing way through a hazy atmosphere. The setting may be a seaport, a wooded dell, watered plains; generally, there are screens of dark trees to the left or right and sometimes at the center, making stage-like wings that intensify the central light. Occasionally, a Classical temple will appear in the cool shadows, and some little idyll will play itself out inconspicuously in the foreground. In essence, Claude seeks to capture the mood of the Italian landscape; like Poussin, he was a French expatriate in Italy and a lover of the broad Campagna, with its romantic ruins. Claude's own pensive and nostalgic mood blends with his setting, and it is his stress on the subjective side of nature that will make his work so popular with the early Romantics at the end of the eighteenth century.

The softening of Poussin's manner (FIG. 19-62) in Claude (FIG. 19-63) is similar to what appears in the work of other painters of the time, who reacted against the severe rules and regulations of the French Royal Academy, under the dictatorial administration of Le Brun. Established in 1648, the Academy had been intended to free artists from the constraints of the old guild system of art training, to improve the social status of painters and sculptors as more than mere handicraftsmen, to regularize instruction in the arts, and to centralize art production in the interest of the absolute monarchy. Above all, the institution of the Academy was to develop and propagate a Classi-

cal taste, based on the study and imitation of ancient works of art and such classicizing modern masters as Raphael, the Carracci, and Poussin himself. Students were taught the supremacy of drawing over coloring, of sculpturesque form over painterly tonality, of symmetrical and closed composition over the dynamic and open—in short, the superiority of Poussin over Rubens. Yet well before the end of the century, the painting of Rubens was increasingly admired, and his influence would weaken the doctrine of the Academy and shape the taste of eighteenth-century Rococo.

Architecture and Sculpture

In architecture, as in painting, France maintained an attitude of cautious selectivity toward the Italian Baroque. The Classical bent early asserted itself in the work of FRANÇOIS MANSART (1598–1666), as seen in the Orléans wing of the Château de Blois (FIG. 19-64), built between 1635 and 1638. Here are the polished dignity and sobriety that will become the hallmarks of French "classical-baroque," in contrast with the more daring, excited, and fanciful styles of the Baroque in Italy and elsewhere. The strong, rectilinear organization and a tendency to design in terms of repeated units remind us of Italian Renaissance architecture, as does the insistence on the purity of line and sharp relief of the wall articulations. Yet the emphasis on a focal point—achieved through the curving colonnades, the changing planes of the walls, and the

19-64   FRANÇOIS MANSART, Orléans wing of the Château de Blois, France, 1635–1638.

concentration of ornament around the portal—is characteristic of Baroque architectural thinking in general.

The formation of the French Classical style accelerated with the foundation of the Royal Academy of Painting and Sculpture in 1648, of which Poussin was a director, and with the determination of Louis XIV and Colbert to organize art and architecture in service of the state. No pains were spared to raise great symbols and monuments to the king's absolute power and to regularize taste under the academies. The first project undertaken by the young king and Colbert

was the closing of the east side of the Louvre court, left incomplete by Lescot in the sixteenth century. Bernini, as the most renowned architect of his day, was summoned from Rome to submit plans, but he envisioned an Italian palace on a monumental scale that would have involved the demolition of all previous work. His plan rejected, Bernini returned to Rome in high indignation. The east façade of the Louvre (FIG. 19-65) is the result of a collaboration between CLAUDE PERRAULT (1613–1688), LOUIS LE VAU (1612–1670), and CHARLES LE BRUN (1619–1690), with Le Vau probably taking a preponderant part, and is a

19-65   CLAUDE PERRAULT, LOUIS LE VAU, and CHARLES LE BRUN, east façade of the Louvre, Paris, 1667–1670.

brilliant adjustment of French and Italian Classical elements, culminating in a new and definitive formula. The French pavilion system is retained; the central pavilion is in the form of a Classical temple front, and a giant colonnade of paired columns, resembling the columned flanks of a temple folded out like wings, is contained by the two salient pavilions at either end. The whole is mounted on a stately basement, or podium; an even roof line, balustraded and broken only by the central pediment, replaces the traditional French pyramidal roof. All memory of Gothic verticality is brushed aside in the emphatically horizontal sweep of this façade. Its stately proportions and monumentality are both an expression of the new official French taste and a symbol for centrally organized authority.

Work on the Louvre had hardly begun when Louis XIV decided to convert a royal hunting lodge at Versailles, a few miles outside Paris, into a great palace. A veritable army of architects, decorators, sculptors, painters, and landscape architects was assembled under the general management of former Poussin student Le Brun, the king's impresario of art and dictator of the Royal Academy. In their hands, the conversion of a simple hunting lodge into the Palace of Versailles became the greatest architectural project of the age (FIGS. 19-66 and 19-67).

Planned on a gigantic scale, the project called not only for a large palace facing a vast park but also for the construction of a satellite city to house court and

government officials, military and guard detachments, courtiers, and servants. This town is laid out to the east of the palace along three radial avenues that converge on the palace; their axes, in a symbolic assertion of the ruler's absolute power over his domains, intersect in the king's bedroom. (As the site of the king's morning levée, this bedroom was actually an audience room, a state chamber.) The palace itself, over a quarter of a mile long, is placed at right angles to the dominant east–west axis that runs through city and park. Its most impressive feature is the garden façade (FIG. 19-68), begun by Le Vau and continued in his style by JULES HARDOUIN-MANSART (1646–1708), a great-nephew of François who took over the project after Le Vau's death in 1670. In typical Baroque fashion, the vast lateral extension of the façade has been broken up into units and subunits of threes, an effective organizational device even on this scale.

Careful attention has been paid to every detail of the extremely rich decoration of the palace's interior; everything from wall paintings to doorknobs was designed in keeping with the whole and executed with the very finest sense of craftsmanship. Of the literally hundreds of rooms within the palace, the most famous is the Galerie des Glaces, or Hall of Mirrors (FIG. 19-69), which overlooks the park from the second floor and extends along most of the width of the central block. Although deprived of its original sumptuous furniture, which included gold and silver chairs and bejeweled trees, it retains much of its

19-66   Aerial view of the Palace of Versailles and a small portion of the surrounding park. The white trapezoid in the lower part of the plan (FIG. 19-67) outlines the area shown here.

19-67 Plan (after a seventeenth-century engraving by FRANÇOIS BLONDEL) of the Palace of Versailles and related buildings, ANDRÉ LE NÔTRE's vast surrounding park (1661–1668), and a portion of the town of Versailles. The area outlined in the white trapezoid (lower center) is shown in FIG. 19-66.

19-68 LOUIS LE VAU and JULES HARDOUIN-MANSART, garden façade of the Palace of Versailles, France, 1669–1685.

19-69   Jules Hardouin-Mansart and Charles le Brun, Galerie des Glaces, Palace of Versailles, *c.* 1680.

splendor today. Its tunnel-like quality is alleviated by hundreds of mirrors, which, set into the wall opposite the windows, illusionistically extend the width of the room. The mirror, that ultimate source of illusion, was a favorite element of Baroque interior design; here, it must have harmonized as it augmented the flashing splendors of the great festivals of which Louis XIV was so fond.

The enormous palace might appear unbearably ostentatious, were it not for its extraordinary setting in the vast park to which it becomes almost an adjunct. The Galerie des Glaces, itself a giant perspective, is dwarfed by the sweeping vista (seen from its windows) down the park's tree-lined central axis and across terraces, lawns, pools, and lakes toward the horizon. The park of Versailles (FIG. 19-67), designed by André le Nôtre (1613–1700), must rank as one of man's greatest works of art—not only in size, but also in concept. Here, an entire forest has been transformed into a park. Although the geometric plan may appear stiff and formal, the park, in fact, offers an almost unlimited variety of vistas, as Le Nôtre utilized not only the multiplicity of natural forms but also the slightly rolling contours of the terrain with

19-70   Jules Hardouin-Mansart, Royal Chapel of the Palace of Versailles, 1698–1710. (Ceiling decorations by Antoine Coypel.)

stunning effectiveness. A rational transition from the frozen forms of the architecture to the living ones of nature is provided by the formal gardens near the palace. Here, tightly designed geometric units are defined by the elegant forms of trimmed shrubs and hedges, each one different from its neighbor and having a focal point in the form of a sculptured group, a pavilion, a reflecting pool, or perhaps a fountain. Farther away from the palace, the design becomes looser as trees, in shadowy masses, screen or frame views into bits of open countryside. All vistas are carefully composed for maximum effect. Dark and light, formal and informal, dense growth and open meadows—all are played off against each other in unending combinations and variations. No photograph or series of photographs can reveal the full richness of the design; the park unfolds itself only to the person who actually walks through it. In this respect, it is a temporal work of art; its aspects change with time and with the relative position of the observer.

As a symbol of the power of absolutism, Versailles is unsurpassed. It also expresses, in the most monumental terms of its age, the rationalistic creed, based on the mathematical philosophy of Descartes, that all knowledge must be systematic and all science must be the consequence of the imposition of the intellect on matter. The whole stupendous design of Versailles proudly proclaims the mastery of human intelligence over the disorderliness of nature.

On the garden façade of Versailles, Hardouin-Mansart follows the style of his predecessor, Le Vau. When commissioned to add a Royal Chapel to the palace in 1698, he was in a position to give full play to his talents. The interior of the chapel (FIG. 19-70) is a masterful synthesis of Classical and Baroque elements. It is essentially a rectangular building with an apse as high as the nave, which gives the fluid central space a curved Baroque quality. But the light entering through the large clerestory windows lacks the directed, dramatic effect of the Italian Baroque and illuminates the precisely chiseled details of the interior brightly and evenly. Pier-supported arcades carry a majestic row of Corinthian columns that define the royal gallery, the back of which is occupied by the royal pew, accessible directly from the king's apartments. The decoration is restrained and, in fact, only the illusionistic ceiling decorations, added in 1708–1709 by ANTOINE COYPEL, can be called Baroque without reservation. Throughout the architecture, Baroque tendencies are severely checked by Classicism.

Although checked, they are not entirely suppressed in Hardouin-Mansart's masterwork, the Église de Dôme, Church of the Invalides in Paris (FIGS. 19-71 and 19-72). An intricately composed domed square of great scale, it is attached to the veterans' hospital set

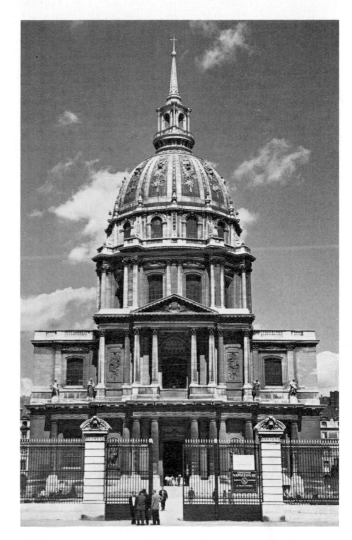

19-71 JULES HARDOUIN-MANSART, Église de Dôme, Church of the Invalides, Paris, 1676–1706.

up by Louis XIV for the disabled soldiers of his many wars. The frontispiece is composed of two firmly separated levels, the upper pedimented; the grouping of the orders and the bays they frame is not unlike that in Italian Baroque. The compact façade is low and narrow in relation to the vast drum and dome, for which it seems to serve simply as a base. The overpowering dome, conspicuous on the skyline of Paris, is itself expressive of the Baroque love for dramatic magnitude. The way that its design aims for theatrical effects of light and space is especially Baroque. The dome is built of three shells, the lowest cut off so that the visitor looks up through it to the next above, which is painted illusionistically with an apotheosis of St. Louis, patron of France. This second dome—filled with light from hidden windows in the third, outermost dome—creates an impression of the open, limitless space and brightness of the heavens. Below, the building is only dimly illuminated and is de-

19-72　Jules Hardouin-Mansart, interior of the Église de Dôme, Church of the Invalides.

signed in a Classicism only less severe than that of the Escorial (fig. 18-58). The rapid vertical gradation from the austerely membered masses below to the ethereal light and space above is Baroque through and through. Yet we feel here the dominance of the Classical style in substance, despite the soaring illusion for which it serves as a setting.

The stylistic dialogue between Classicism and the Italian Baroque in seventeenth-century French sculpture also ends with the former's victory. The strained dramatic and emotional qualities in the work of Pierre Puget (1620–1694) were not at all to the taste of the court. His *Milo of Crotona* (fig. 19-73) represents the powerful ancient hero, his hand trapped in a split stump, helpless before the attacking lion. There is nothing here of heroic idealism; with physical and psychic realism, Puget presents a study of immediate and excruciating agony. This ran counter to the official taste dictated by the king and Le Brun, and, although Puget was very briefly in vogue, the most original French sculptor of his time never found acceptance at the court.

Much more fortunate was François Girardon (1628–1715), who admirably adjusted his style to the taste of his sponsors. His *Apollo Attended by the Nymphs* (fig. 19-74) was designed as a tableau group for the Grotto of Thetis in the gardens of Versailles. (The arrangement of the figures was slightly altered when the group was moved to a different grotto in the eighteenth century.) Both stately and graceful, the nymphs have a compelling charm as they minister to the god–king at the end of the day. The style of the figures is heavily conditioned by the artist's close study of Hellenistic sculpture, the central figure imitating the ancient Apollo Belvedere in the Vatican; the arrangement is inspired by Poussin's figure compositions (fig. 19-61). And if this combination did not suffice, the group's rather florid reference to Louis XIV as the "god of the sun" was bound to assure its success at the court. Girardon's style and symbolism were found to be ideally suited to the glorification of royal majesty.

19-73　Pierre Puget, *Milo of Crotona*, 1671–1682. Marble, approx. 8' 10" high. Louvre, Paris.

19-74 FRANÇOIS GIRARDON, *Apollo Attended by the Nymphs*, c. 1666–1672. Marble, life-size. Park of Versailles, France.

ENGLAND

English art has been mentioned little since the Middle Ages because, except for its architecture, England is outside the main artistic streams of the Renaissance and the Baroque periods. It is as if the English genius were occupied enough with its prodigious creation in dramatic literature, lyric poetry, and music, and not, after all, particularly suited to the purely visual arts. Not until the eighteenth century does England develop an important native school of painting and extend its distinguished architectural tradition.

Gothic practices lived on in English, as in French, building, long after Renaissance architects in Italy struck out in new directions. During the sixteenth century, the English made minor concessions to Italian architectural ideas. Classical ornament appeared frequently in the decoration of buildings, and there was a distinct trend toward more regular and symmetrical planning. But not until the early seventeenth century did England wholeheartedly accept the prin-

ciples that govern Italian architectural thinking. The revolution in English building was primarily the work of one man, INIGO JONES (1573–1652), surveyor (architect) to James I and Charles I. Jones spent considerable time in Italy. He disliked Michelangelo's work as intensely as he admired Palladio's, whose treatise on architecture he studied with great care. From the stately palaces and villas of Palladio, Jones selected certain motifs and systems of proportions to use as the basis of his own architectural designs. The nature of his achievement is evident in the Banqueting House at Whitehall (FIG. 19-75). The structure, a symmetrical block of great clarity and dignity, superimposes two orders in the form of columns in the center and pilasters near the ends. The balustraded roof line, uninterrupted in its horizontal sweep, anticipates the Louvre façade (FIG. 19-65) by more than 40 years. There is almost nothing here that Palladio would not have recognized and approved, but the

19-75 INIGO JONES, Banqueting House at Whitehall, London, 1619–1622. British Crown Copyright.

building as a whole is no copy. While working within the architectural vocabulary and syntax of the revered Italian, Jones retains his own independence as a designer, and, for two centuries, his influence will be almost as authoritative in English architecture as Palladio's. It is noteworthy that Jones' interior at Whitehall is adorned with paintings by Rubens, in a fruitful collaboration recalling the combination of painting by Veronese and architecture by Palladio in northern Italian villas.

Until almost the present day, the dominant feature of the London skyline has been the majestic dome of St. Paul's (FIG. 19-76), the work of England's most renowned architect, CHRISTOPHER WREN (1632–1723). A mathematical genius and skilled engineer, whose work won the praise of Isaac Newton, Wren began as a professor of astronomy and took an amateur's interest in architecture. Asked by Charles II to prepare a plan for the restoration of the old Gothic church of St. Paul, he proposed to remodel the building "after a good Roman manner" rather than "to follow the

Gothic rudeness of the old design." Within a few months, the Great Fire of London in 1666, which destroyed the old structure and many churches in the city, gave Wren his opportunity. He built not only the new St. Paul's but numerous other churches as well. Wren was a Baroque virtuoso of many talents, the archetype of whom we see in Bernini. He was strongly influenced by the work of Jones, but he also traveled in France, where he must have been much impressed by the splendid palaces and state buildings being created in and around Paris at the time of the competition for the Louvre design. Wren must also have closely studied prints illustrating Baroque architecture in Italy, for Palladian, French, and Italian Baroque features are harmonized in St. Paul's. In view of its size, the cathedral was built with remarkable speed—in a little over 30 years—and Wren lived to see it completed. The form of the building was constantly refined as it went up, and the final appearance of the towers was not determined until after 1700. The splendid skyline composition, with the two fore-

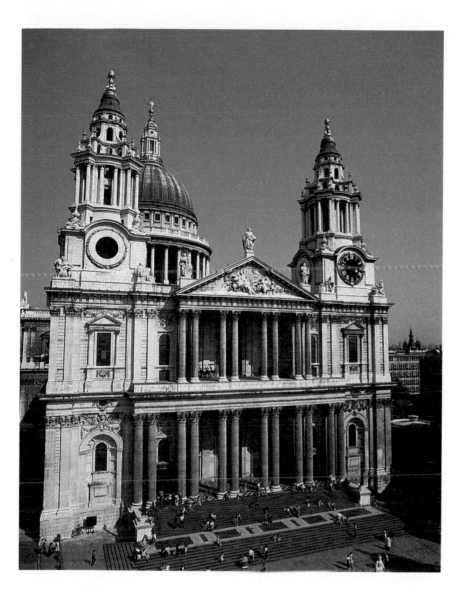

ground towers acting so effectively as foils to the great dome, must have been suggested to Wren by similar schemes devised by Italian architects to solve the problem of the façade–dome relation of St. Peter's in Rome (FIGS. 17-34 and 19-4). Perhaps Borromini's solution at Sant' Agnese in Piazza Navona influenced him. Certainly, the upper levels and lanterns of the towers are Borrominesque, the lower levels are Palladian, and the superposed, paired columnar porticoes remind us of the Louvre façade. Wren's skillful eclecticism brings all of these foreign features into a monumental unity.

Wren's designs for the city churches are masterpieces of Baroque planning ingenuity. His task was never easy, for the churches often had to be fitted into small, irregular areas. Wren worked out a rich variety of schemes to meet awkward circumstances. In designing the exteriors of the churches, he concentrated his attention on the towers—the one element of the structure that would set the building apart from its crowding neighbors. The skyline of London, as left by Wren, is punctuated with such towers, which will serve as prototypes for later buildings both in England and in colonial America.

20

1. Chiswick House
   Osterley Park House
   Strawberry Hill
2. Blenheim Palace
3. Panthéon (Paris)
   (Ste. Geneviève)
   Hôtel de Soubise
4. Vierzehnheiligen
5. Rohr
6. Amalienburg (Munich)
7. Superga (Turin)
8. Hagley Park
   (Worcestershire)

SCOTLAND

NORTH SEA

GREAT BRITAIN

WALES

⑧ ⑧ ②

London ①

Amsterdam

DENMARK

BALTIC SEA

LATVIA

HANOVER

BRANDENBURG

Berlin

PRUSSIA

Vistula

POLAND

Brussels

AUSTRIAN NETHERLANDS

FLANDERS

PICARDY

NORMANDY

BRITTANY

Versailles ③ Paris

Seine

Loire

NIVERNAIS

Dijon

FRANCE

AUVERGNE

Garonne

Tarn

Toulouse

LANGUEDOC

Rhône

Avignon

SAVOY

⑦ Turin

PIEDMONT

LOMBARDY

Po

SWITZERLAND

Cologne HESSE

HOLY

ROMAN

EMPIRE

LORRAINE

Rhine

④

Dresden

SAXONY

SILESIA

BOHEMIA

MORAVIA

AUSTRIA

⑤

BAVARIA

⑥ Munich

Danube

Vienna

TYROL

STYRIA

CARINTHIA

Buda • Pest

HUNGARY

Venice

REPUBLIC

OF

VENICE

OTTOMAN EMPIRE

Florence

TUSCANY

PAPAL STATES

Rome

ITALY

Ebro

ARAGON

Madrid

CATALONIA

SPAIN

MEDITERRANEAN SEA

SARDINIA

EUROPE AFTER 1720

0 50 100 150 200 250 300   MILES

0   100   200   300   400   500   KILOMETERS

SICILY

THE EIGHTEENTH CENTURY: ROCOCO AND THE RISE OF ROMANTICISM

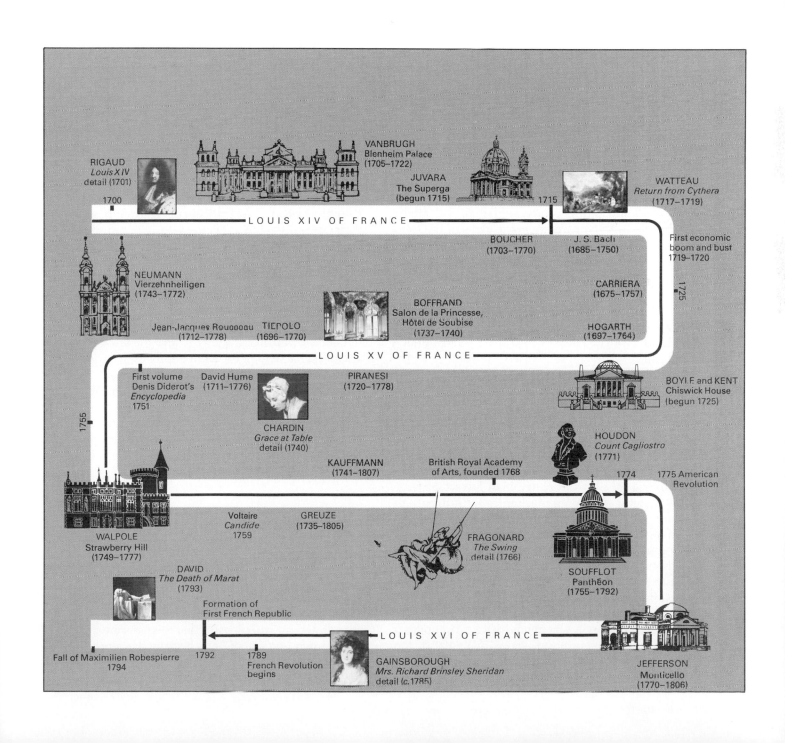

RIGAUD
Louis XIV
detail (1701)

1700

VANBRUGH
Blenheim Palace
(1705–1722)

JUVARA
The Superga
(begun 1715)

1715

WATTEAU
Return from Cythera
(1717–1719)

LOUIS XIV OF FRANCE

BOUCHER
(1703–1770)

J. S. Bach
(1685–1750)

First economic
boom and bust
1719–1720

NEUMANN
Vierzehnheiligen
(1743–1772)

CARRIERA
(1675–1757)

1725

Jean-Jacques Rousseau
(1712–1778)

TIEPOLO
(1696–1770)

BOFFRAND
Salon de la Princesse,
Hôtel de Soubise
(1737–1740)

HOGARTH
(1697–1764)

LOUIS XV OF FRANCE

First volume
Denis Diderot's
Encyclopedia
1751

David Hume
(1711–1776)

PIRANESI
(1720–1778)

BOYLE and KENT
Chiswick House
(begun 1725)

1755

CHARDIN
Grace at Table
detail (1740)

HOUDON
Count Cagliostro
(1771)

KAUFFMANN
(1741–1807)

British Royal Academy
of Arts, founded 1768

1774

1775 American
Revolution

WALPOLE
Strawberry Hill
(1749–1777)

Voltaire
Candide
1759

GREUZE
(1735–1805)

FRAGONARD
The Swing
detail (1766)

SOUFFLOT
Panthéon
(1755–1792)

DAVID
The Death of Marat
(1793)

Formation of
First French Republic

LOUIS XVI OF FRANCE

Fall of Maximilien Robespierre
1794

1792

1789
French Revolution
begins

GAINSBOROUGH
Mrs. Richard Brinsley Sheridan
detail (c.1785)

JEFFERSON
Monticello
(1770–1806)

THE EIGHTEENTH CENTURY has a dual character; its two parts correspond chronologically to an earlier and a later stage. The earlier is a simple continuation of the Baroque seventeenth century, with a number of distinctive differences; the later, a more-or-less abrupt break onto a new scene. The new scene belongs to the modern world and may be regarded as a kind of overture to it. The present chapter, in its title and arrangement, reflects this division. However, a brief view of the century as a whole can be useful.

The political world takes new shapes in the eighteenth century. This is the century of the rise to great power of the maritime British empire and its disputes with France over the continent of North America and the subcontinent of India. Against the awkward and shaky Holy Roman (later Austrian) Empire rises the small but aggressive state of Prussia, soon to become a significant military power. Farther to the east looms the unsuspected might of half-Asiatic Russia, accelerating its slow turn toward the West under Peter the Great. Spain is sunk in decadence; Italy, a jumble of properties owned by the great powers. The real domain of the once-universal Church is confined to a narrow strip of territory in Italy called the "States of the Church"; elsewhere the State controls, and the Church is subordinate to the sovereign.

New ideas are being propagated that will attack both Church and State—democratic ideas of the freedom and equality of all men. "Enlightened" monarchs cultivate outspoken men like Voltaire, who call for reforms of old abuses and for limitations on the privileges of monarchy, aristocracy, and clergy. Reason and common sense are put forth as the real remedies of human ills; progress, as a law of human development. In France, Diderot and the "philosophes" publish an *Encyclopedia* of human knowledge to instruct all mankind. In the eighteenth century, it is as if all Europe is waiting breathlessly for the tremendous revolutions to come. For the great changes that will make the modern world are in preparation—not only the political, social, and economic revolutions, but, perhaps of even greater importance for the entire globe, the technological and industrial revolutions. Following rapidly on the Newtonian laws that reinterpret physical nature as mechanically (rather than spiritually or organically) constituted, come important advances from the emerging natural sciences concerning the nature of such phenomena as electricity, combustion (and, as a concomitant, oxygen), and living matter. But most important (for its immediate application) is the development of steam power and its enormous significance as a substitute for human labor. The invention of steam engines for production and, later, for transportation begins in England, the scene of the primitive phase of the still-expanding machine age. The environment of England, and then of Europe, will be utterly transformed in this age of steam, of coal and oil, of iron and steel.

The political, economic, and social consequences will be tremendous. The era of industrial capital and labor will be born. The system of production in factories, where the new steam engines are housed, will create an urban working class and, with it, the social antagonisms of the nineteenth century. The merchant rich will become the captains of industry, demanding production and trade free of government regulation, as well as participation in the fiscal decisions of government. Later in the century, democracy and free trade will be the animating principles of political revolutions. Ideas and institutions originating at this time (around 1750) are still with us; the era we call "modern" begins.

While these great forces of change are gathering momentum, older patterns of life and society are obscuring their emergence. Between the death of Louis XIV (1715) and about 1750 is a period of relative relaxation after the exhausting "world" wars waged by the great kings; although wars continue to be fought, they are of the nature of balancing maneuvers among the various states and are waged by professionals with a kind of chessboard formality. The ruling aristocracies, as if conscious of their waning historical significance, gradually abandon their administrative—even executive—functions to men of the ambitious "third estate"—the increasingly wealthy and influential middle class. Without fully realizing it, royalty and nobility are slowly becoming obsolete, although the latter, stubbornly insisting on their ancient privileges, will help to precipitate the French Revolution. Still, in this time, they remain the patrons of the arts, and the arts express to a remarkable degree the philosophy of the aristocracy in decline. Life for the aristocracy is simply the pursuit of pleasure, the escape from boredom. Art is luxurious, frivolous, sensual, clever; the great religious and Classical themes of the Baroque, presented in the grand manner of the masters, are forgotten. Intricate and witty artifice is the objective in all the arts—drama, music, painting, sculpture.

EARLY EIGHTEENTH CENTURY: LATE BAROQUE AND ROCOCO

All Europe breathed a sigh of relief at the death of Louis XIV in 1715. The court of Versailles was at once abandoned for the pleasures of town society, and the *hôtels* (town houses) of Paris became the centers of the style we call Rococo—the reaction to the style of

20-1 HYACINTHE RIGAUD, *Louis XIV*, 1701.
Approx. 9' 2" × 6' 3". Louvre, Paris.

20-2 ANTOINE WATTEAU, *L'Indifférent*, c. 1716.
Approx. 10" × 7". Louvre, Paris.

Louis XIV. With respect to this change, it has been well said that the seventeenth century ends with a portrait of a king and the eighteenth century begins with a portrait of a clown. HYACINTHE RIGAUD's portrait of *Louis XIV* (FIG. 20-1) set side by side with ANTOINE WATTEAU's *L'Indifférent* (FIG. 20-2) illustrates the contrast of the periods exactly. On the one hand is pompous majesty in slow and stately promenade, as if reviewing throngs of bowing courtiers at Versailles; on the other is a languid, gliding dancer, whose mincing minuet might also mimic the monarch's solemn pacing. In the first, stout architecture, banner-like curtains, flowing ermine, and fleur-de-lis exalt the king, while fanfares of trumpets blast; in the second, the dancer, to the silken sound of strings, moves in a rainbow shimmer of color from the wings onto the stage of the comic opera. The portrait of the king is very large, the "portrait" of the "clown," quite small. The first is Baroque; the second, Rococo.

Architecture

Late Baroque and Rococo overlap and interpenetrate in the early decades of the century, although Rococo has distinctive features of its own. The scale and grandeur of Baroque architecture, its spatial dynamism, persisted in an age when the grandees of Europe were emulating Versailles in palace architecture and when splendid churches continued to be built and dedicated by royalty. One of the finest of these, the Superga, near Turin in northwestern Italy (FIG. 20-3), was built by FILIPPO JUVARA (1678–1736) for Victor Amadeus II, king of Savoy, to commemorate his victory over the French in 1706. This was during

20-3 FILIPPO JUVARA, the Superga, near Turin, Italy, 1715–1731.

the War of the Spanish Succession, when the "Sun King," Louis XIV of France, suffered his final eclipse. Juvara, the royal architect, began his career in the lavish Baroque manner of his predecessor at Turin, Guarino Guarini (FIGS. 19-18 and 19-19), but study at Rome turned him toward the enduring Classical style. Even so, the setting of the Superga, in itself, is entirely Baroque. Placed on a lofty hill some 2,000 feet above the city of Turin, the church and the monastery, of which it is the frontispiece (an arrangement similar to that of the Church of the Invalides in Paris, FIG. 19-71), command a sweeping view of the city and the surrounding countryside. Close to the dimensions of the Invalides, the great dome and drum of the Superga may reflect Juvara's knowledge of that building. At the same time, there is a Palladian Classicism in the deep, four-columned portico surmounted by a balustrade, which continues around the building, and the relation of the portico to the rotunda-like structure behind it recalls the ancient Pantheon. The severity of the portico and of the colossal orders that articulate the walls is offset by the light, fanciful bell towers that flank the dome. In its adroit adjustment of Classical feature and Baroque grouping, the building is an impressive example of Juvara's intelligent eclecticism.

The victory that occasioned the building of the Superga was won by a great general of the time, Prince Eugene of Savoy. Victories over the forces of Louis XIV, won by Eugene's famous partner in arms, John Churchill, Duke of Marlborough, were also commemorated. In his honor, the government of Great Britain commissioned the building of the vast palace of Blenheim for his residence (FIG. 20-4). Blenheim is not a unique instance of English building, but it is of uncommon scale. Beginning with England's prosperous expansion into the New World, most particularly in the latter half of the seventeenth century, a demand arose for fine mansions on great estates, and the country houses of England in the eighteenth century, both in number and quality of design, are outstanding in European architecture. In the hands of a small group of architects associated with the aging Wren, the Baroque briefly triumphs over the accepted Palladian Classicism of Inigo Jones. The best known of this group, and the designer of Blenheim, was JOHN VANBRUGH (1664–1726), who began as a writer of witty and popular comedies and as the builder of a theater in which to produce them. Certainly, his architecture tends toward the theatrical on a mighty and extravagant scale. The picturesque silhouette of Blenheim, its massing, and its inventive architectural detail are all thoroughly Baroque. The design shows a love of variety and contrast, tempered by a desire for focus found so frequently in the architecture of the seventeenth century. The tremendous forecourt,

hugely projecting pavilions, and extended colonnades simultaneously recall St. Peter's and Versailles. Vanbrugh was not the only Baroque artist to sacrifice convenience to dramatic effect (as, for example, in placing the kitchen at Blenheim some 400 yards from the dining salon), but even in his own time, his piling up of colossal masses of masonry was ridiculed. Great as Blenheim is as scenic art, Voltaire could remark that if the rooms had only been as wide as the walls were thick, the palace would have been convenient enough. Vanbrugh's Baroque architecture did not please his patrons long; before Blenheim was completed, there was criticism of what contemporaries considered its ponderous and bizarre qualities.

This criticism, as it sharpened, came to extend to Baroque architecture as such. For English taste in the eighteenth century, the exaggerations of Blenheim came to be thought of as the general defects of Baroque style. Pomp and magnificence, great space-dominating scale, theatrical effects, irregular forms, exuberant details, grandiose rhetoric—all should be banished as irrational, unnatural, and artificial. "Good sense" should reign instead in simplicity, harmony, and utility of design. Doubtless Baroque was also thought to be the obnoxious art of absolute monarchical pride and display—something to be played down in parliamentary England. In English architecture, the instinct for an unostentatious and commonsensical style led straight to the authority of Vitruvius, Andrea Palladio (FIG. 17-52) and Inigo Jones (FIG. 19-75). Alexander Pope, in his "Fourth Moral Epistle" (1731), addresses his friend, the statesman and architectural amateur RICHARD BOYLE, Earl of Burlington (1695–1753):

> You, too, proceed! make falling arts your care,
> Erect new wonders, and the old repair;
> Jones and Palladio to themselves restore
> And be whate'er Vitruvius was before.

Lord Burlington strongly restated the Palladian doctrine of Inigo Jones and generously endowed the new style that resulted. With the talented professional WILLIAM KENT (1685–1748), Burlington built Chiswick House (FIG. 20-5) on the outskirts of London. The way had been paved for Burlington by, among others, the influential esthetic philosophy (succinctly echoed in Pope's epistle) of the third Earl of Shaftesbury and by Colin Campbell's *Virtuvius Britannicus* (1715), three volumes of engravings of ancient buildings in Britain prefaced by a denunciation of Italian Baroque and praise of Palladio and Inigo Jones.

Chiswick House is a free variation on the theme of Palladio's Villa Rotonda (FIG. 17-52). It was doubtless intended to be a "rational" answer to the colorful splendors of Versailles. Although, in its simple symmetry, unadorned planes, right angles, and stiffly

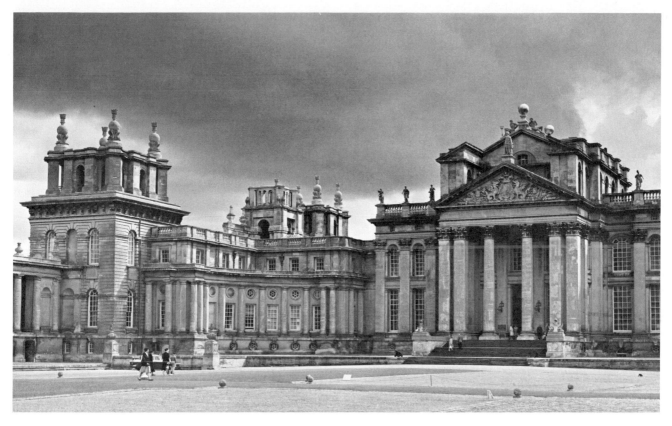

20-4   John Vanbrugh, Blenheim Palace, Oxfordshire, England, 1705–1722.

20-5   Richard Boyle (Earl of Burlington) and William Kent, Chiswick House, near London, begun 1725.
British Crown Copyright.

wrought proportions, Chiswick looks very Classical and "rational," it, like so many Palladian villas in England, is set within informal gardens, where a charming irregularity of layout and freely growing, uncropped foliage dominate the scene. The development of the "English garden" as a rival to the formality of the continental garden is an important chapter in the history of eighteenth-century taste, and we shall return to it. As irregularity was cultivated in landscaping surrounding the Palladian villa, so the interior of the villa was sometimes ornamented in a more-or-less reserved version of the Rococo style fashionable on the continent, belying the severity of the Classical exterior. At Chiswick, the Late Baroque of Kent's interior design is a luxurious foil to the stern symmetry of the exterior and the plan. But, in general, Rococo was never widely known or accepted in England.

Palladian Classicism prevails in English architecture until about 1760, when it begins to merge into what we will call Neoclassicism. This is quite different from what happens on the continent, where, during the same period (roughly 1710–1760), the Rococo style flourishes.

Rococo, in its French manifestation, appears around 1710 as a style primarily of interior design. As with English architecture, the French exterior is most often simple, even plain; Rococo takes over the interior. The sparkling gaiety cultivated by the new age, associated with the regency that followed on Louis XIV's death and with the reign of Louis XV, finds perfectly harmonious expression in Rococo. The word "Rococo" comes from the French *rocaille,* which literally means "pebble," but which refers especially to the small stones and shells used to decorate the interiors of grottoes. Such shells or shell forms are the principal motifs in Rococo ornament. The Rococo is a style preeminently of small art; furniture, utensils, accessories—objects of all sorts, useful and otherwise—are exquisitely wrought in the characteristically delicate, undulating Rococo line. A typically Rococo room is the Salon de la Princesse (FIG. 20-6) in the Hôtel de Soubise in Paris, decorated by GERMAIN BOFFRAND (1667–1754). If we compare it with the Galerie des Glaces at Versailles (FIG. 19-69), we see the fundamental difference at once. The strong architectural lines and panels of the earlier style are softened here into flexible, sinuous curves. The walls melt into

20-6   Salon de la Princesse, Hôtel de Soubise, Paris, 1737–1740. Decorations by GERMAIN BOFFRAND. British Crown Copyright.

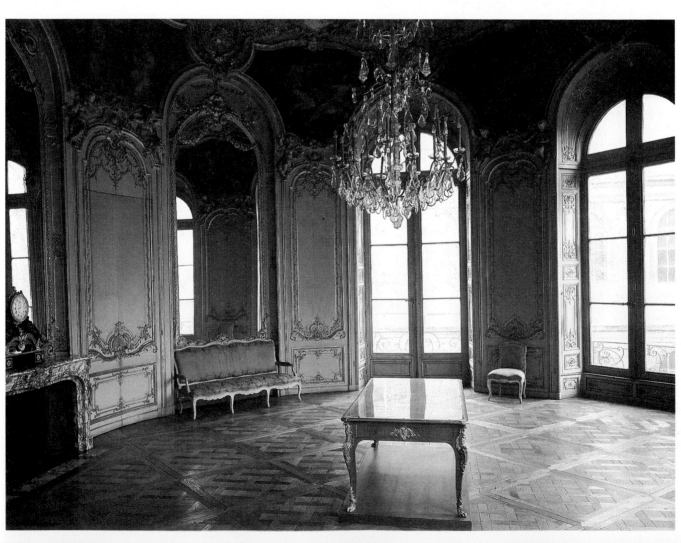

the vault; the cornices are replaced by irregular shapes that are painted, surmounted by sculpture, and separated by the typical shells of *rocaille*. Painting, architecture, and sculpture make a single ensemble. The profusion of curving tendrils and sprays of foliage combine with the shell forms to give an effect of freely growing nature and to suggest that the Rococo room is permanently decked for a festival. Such rooms, with their alternating gilded moldings, vivacious relief sculpture, and daintily colored ornament of flowers and garlands, must have harmonized with the chamber music played in them, with the elegant and elaborate costumes of lustrous satins and brocades, and with the equally elegant etiquette and sparkling wit of the people who graced them.

The Rococo salon was the locale of Parisian society, and Paris was the social capital of Europe in the eighteenth century. Wealthy, ambitious, and clever society women vied with one another to attract the most famous, the wittiest, and most accomplished people to their salons. The medium of social intercourse was conversation spiced with wit, repartee as quick and deft as a fencing match. The feminine look of the Rococo style suggests that the age was dominated by the taste and the social initiative of women—and, to a large extent, it was. Women held the highest places in Europe—Madame de Pompadour in France, Maria Theresa in Austria, Elizabeth and Catherine in Russia—and female influence was felt in any number of smaller courts. The masculine heroics and rhetoric of

the Baroque were replaced by dainty gallantries and pointed sallies of wit. Artifice reigned supreme, and it was considered in bad taste to be "original" or "enthusiastic," eccentric or sincere. The spirit of the age is expressed perfectly in Lord Chesterfield's *Letters to His Son*, instructing him in the manners of the Rococo salon. The honest Dr. Johnson, when he complained that the letters taught "the manners of a dancing master and the morals of a whore," may have been indicting the whole age.

The Rococo in architecture quickly became an international style during the early eighteenth century. There had been indications throughout late-seventeenth-century Europe of a general shift toward a lighter, gayer, more decorative type of expression, and the great prestige enjoyed by France gave impetus to this development.

A brilliant example of French Rococo abroad is the Amalienburg (FIGS. 20-7 and 20-8), a small lodge built by FRANÇOIS DE CUVILLIÉS (1698–1768) in the park of the Nymphenburg Palace in Munich. Although we think of Rococo as essentially interior design, the Amalienburg beautifully harmonizes the interior and the exterior elevations, the curving flow of their lines and planes cohering in a plastic unity of great elegance. The *bombé* (outward-bowed) shape of the central bay commonly occurs in Rococo furniture design; indeed, in its compactness, diminutive scale, graceful lines, and exquisite detail, Amalienburg is a kind of precious furnishing set down on the greens-

20-7   FRANÇOIS DE CUVILLIÉS, the Amalienburg, Nymphenburg Park, Munich, West Germany, 1734–1739.

20-8   FRANÇOIS DE CUVILLIÉS, Hall of Mirrors, the Amalienburg.

ward of the park. Within the structure, the circular Hall of Mirrors (FIG. 20-8)—a silver and blue ensemble of architecture, stucco relief, silvered-bronze mirrors, and crystal—dazzles the sight with myriad scintillating motifs, forms, and figurations from the full Rococo repertory of ornament. This is the ''high noon'' of the style. Facets of silvery light, multiplied by windows and mirrors, sharply or softly delineate the endlessly proliferating shapes and contours that weave rhythmically around the upper walls and the coves of the ceiling. Everything seems organic, growing and in motion, an ultimate rarefaction of illusion. And everything is created with virtuoso flourishes by artists magically in command of all the resources of their media.

One of the most distinctive variants of Rococo architecture developed, side-by-side with French designs like that of Cuvilliés, in an area of southern Germany and Austria that had lain dormant artistically during the seventeenth century. Here, in a great wave of church building in the eighteenth century, the new style is not confined to interiors but appears in exteriors and plans as well. The chief influence, moreover, is not French but stems from the architecture of Francesco Borromini and Guarini, so that it is

perhaps more accurate to think of it as Late Baroque with strong stylistic affinities to Rococo. One of the most splendid of the German buildings is the pilgrimage church of Vierzehnheiligen (Fourteen Saints) by BALTHASAR NEUMANN (1687–1753). The rounded corners and the undulating center of the façade (FIG. 20-9) recall Borromini without approaching his dramatic intensity. Numerous large windows in the richly articulated but continuous walls flood the interior with an even, bright, and cheerful light. The interior (FIG. 20-10) exhibits a vivacious play of architectural fantasy that retains the dynamic but banishes all the dramatic qualities of Italian Baroque. The features pulse, flow, and commingle as if they were plastic ceaselessly in the process of being molded. The fluency of line, the floating and hovering surfaces, make us reach for the analogy of music; indeed, in this great age of music, the intricacy of the voices in a Bach fugue are brought to mind by the interwoven spaces and dematerialized masses of a structure that is the image of ''frozen music.'' The complexity of Vierzehnheiligen is readable in its ground plan (FIG. 20-11), which has been called ''one of the most ingenious pieces of architectural design ever conceived.'' The straight line seems to have been deliberately ban-

20-10 Interior of Vierzehnheiligen.

ished. The composition is made up of tangent ovals and circles, so that, within the essential outlines of the traditional Gothic church (apse, transept, nave, and western towers), a quite different interior effect is achieved—an undulating space in continuous motion, creating unlimited vistas bewildering in their variety and surprise effects. We must think of this kind of church as a brilliant ensemble of architecture, sculpture, music, and painting, in which the boundaries of the arts dissolve in visionary unity.

Painting and Sculpture

The ceiling decorations of Vierzehnheiligen, like those of most German Rococo churches, are inspired by the last great Italian painter to have an international impact, GIAMBATTISTA TIEPOLO (1696–1770). Of Venetian origin, Tiepolo worked for patrons in Austria, Germany, and Spain, as well as in Italy, leaving a strong impression wherever he went. His bright, cheerful colors and his relaxed compositions are ideally suited to Rococo architecture. *The Apotheosis of the Pisani Family* (FIG. 20-12), a ceiling fresco in the Villa Pisani at Stra in northern Italy, shows airy populations fluttering through vast sunlit skies and fleecy clouds, their figures making dark accents against the brilliant light of high noon. While retaining the illu-

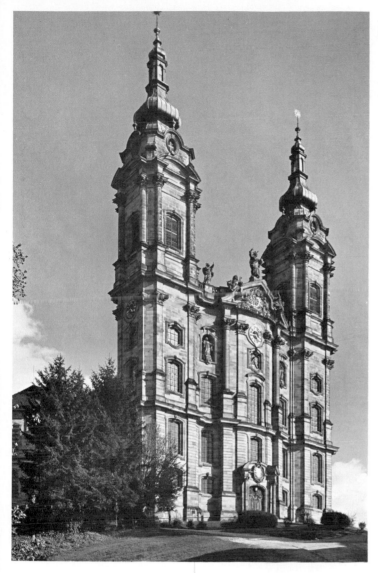

20-9 BALTHASAR NEUMANN, façade of the pilgrimage church of Vierzehnheiligen, near Bamberg, West Germany, 1743–1772.

20-11 BALTHASAR NEUMANN, plan of Vierzehnheiligen, near Bamberg.

20-12 GIAMBATTISTA TIEPOLO, *The Apotheosis of the Pisani Family*, 1761–1762. Ceiling fresco in the Villa Pisani, Stra, Italy.

sionistic tendencies of the seventeenth century, Tiepolo discards all rhetoric to create gay and brightly colored pictorial schemes of great elegance and grace, which, for sheer effectiveness as decor, are unsurpassed.

Pictorial embellishment of the churches of the Germanies and Austria, whether by Italian or native painters, was supplemented by sculpture often contrived to produce entirely pictorial effects. In the group of the *Assumption of the Virgin* (FIG. 20-13) above the altar in the monastery church at Rohr, EGID QUIRIN ASAM (1692–1750) carries Baroque illusionism to its limit. Here, as in Bernini's *St. Theresa* (page 520), the miraculous is made real before our eyes, a spiritual vision materially visible. The Virgin, effortlessly borne aloft by angels, soars to the glowing paradise above her while the apostolic witnesses below gestic-

ulate in astonishment around her vacant tomb. The figures are colored to simulate life. The setting is a luxuriously ornamented theater; the scene itself, pure opera—an art that was perfected and became very popular in the eighteenth century. One can imagine the Virgin as protagonist in an operatic production: singing the climactic aria with all appropriate gestures, an excited chorus in accompaniment, while a virtuoso designer directs the stagecraft. Sculpture dissolves into painting, theater, and music—its mass rendered weightless, its natural compactness of composition broken up and diffuse. Here, the art of the sculptor is, paradoxically, to disguise its substance and function, its weight and tactility, in the interest of eye-deceiving illusion. Baroque sculpture could go no further, and the later eighteenth century will experience a strong reaction to it in Neoclassicism.

The painters of France in the eighteenth century give the Rococo its earthly setting (the salon, the theater, and the boudoir) and create its sensuous moods and luxuriant intimacy. The painter above all others whom we associate with the Rococo is ANTOINE WATTEAU (1684–1721), whose *L'Indifférent* (FIG. 20-2) we have already cited to exhibit what is typical of the Rococo in painting. His masterpiece (he made two versions of it) is *Return from Cythera* (FIG. 20-14), which he painted between 1717 and 1719 as his acceptance piece for admission to the French Royal Academy. Watteau was Flemish, and his style is a beautiful derivative from that of Rubens—a kind of rarefaction and refinement of it. At the turn of the century, the Academy was rather sharply divided between two doctrines. One stated what Le Brun had derived from the art and writings of Nicolas Poussin—

that form is the most important element in painting and that, as Poussin asserts, "the colors in paintings are, as it were, blandishments to lure the eyes," merely something added for effect, and not really essential. The other doctrine, with Rubens as its apostle, proclaimed the supremacy of color as natural and the coloristic style as the proper guide to the artist. Depending on which side they took, members of the Academy were "Poussinistes" or "Rubénistes." With Watteau, the latter carried the day, and the Rococo style in painting was established on the colorism of Rubens and the Venetians.

Return from Cythera represents a group of lovers preparing to depart from the island of eternal youth and love, sacred to Aphrodite. Young and luxuriously costumed, they perform, as it were, an elegant, tender, graceful ballet, moving from the protective

20-14   ANTOINE WATTEAU, *Return from Cythera*, 1717–1719. Approx. 4′ 3″ × 6′ 4″. Louvre, Paris.

shade of a woodland park, peopled with amorous cupids and voluptuous statuary, down a grassy slope to an awaiting golden barge. The attitudes of the figures are carefully studied; Watteau has never been equaled for his distinctive poses, which so beautifully combine elegance and sweetness. He composed his generally quite small paintings from albums of superb drawings, which are still preserved and in fine condition. In these, we find him observing slow movement from difficult and unusual angles, obviously with the intention of finding the smoothest, most poised, and most refined attitudes. As he seeks nuances of bodily poise and movement, so Watteau strives for the most exquisite shades of color difference, defining in a single stroke the shimmer of silk at a bent knee or the iridescence that touches a glossy surface as it emerges from shadow. Here, the color craft of the Venetians and Rubens is exquisitely specialized in the hands of a master of the nuance. It has long been noted that the theme of love and Arcadian happiness in Watteau's pictures (which we have seen since Giorgione and which Watteau may have seen in

works by Rubens) is slightly shadowed with wistfulness, even melancholy, as if Watteau, despite his own short life, had opportunity to meditate on the swift passage of youth and pleasure. Although his mood is never easily described, it is caught in a contemporary work, not of painting but of poetry— Alexander Pope's *Rape of the Lock.* This extraordinary passage from that work shows how widespread the Rococo was in the arts:

But now secure the painted vessel glides,
The sunbeams trembling on the floating tides;
While melting music steals upon the sky,
And softened sounds along the waters die . . . .
The lucid squadrons round the sails repair:
Soft o'er the shrouds aërial whispers breathe,
That seemed but zephyrs to the train beneath.
Some to the sun their insect wings unfold,
Waft on the breeze, or sink in clouds of gold;
Transparent forms, too fine for mortal sight,
Their fluid bodies half dissolved in light,
Loose to the wind their airy garments flew,
Thin glittering textures of the filmy dew,

Dipped in the richest tincture of the skies,
Where light disports in ever-mingling dyes,
While every beam new transient colors flings,
Colors that change whene'er they wave their wings.

The poet's and the painter's language are in perfect harmony. The haze of color, the subtly modeled shapes, the gliding motion, the air of suave gentility— all are the objective and achievement of the Rococo artist and all are to the taste of his aristocratic patronage in its last age. The unifying power of that taste draws the arts together. The titles as well as the mood of many musical compositions by Watteau's exact contemporary, Jean Philippe Rameau, are perfectly suited to Watteau's pictures.

20-15 FRANÇOIS BOUCHER, *Cupid a Captive*, 1754. Approx. 66″ × 34″. Reproduced by permission of the Trustees of the Wallace Collection, London.

The successors of Watteau never quite match his taste and subtlety. Their themes concern love artfully and archly pursued, erotic frivolity, and playful intrigue. After Watteau's untimely death, his follower FRANÇOIS BOUCHER (1703–1770), painter to Madame de Pompadour, rose to the dominant position in French painting. Although he was also an excellent portraitist, Boucher's fame rests primarily on his gay and graceful allegories, in which Arcadian shepherds, nymphs, and goddesses cavort in shady glens, engulfed in pink and sky-blue light. The *Cupid a Captive* (FIG. 20-15) presents the viewer with a rosy pyramid of infant and female flesh, set off against a cool, leafy background, the figures' nudity both hidden and revealed by fluttering draperies. Boucher uses all of the Baroque devices to create his masterly composition: the dynamic play of crisscrossing diagonals, curvilinear forms, and slanting recessions. But powerful Baroque curves are dissected into a multiplicity of decorative arabesques, and Baroque drama dissipates into sensual playfulness. Gay and superficial, Boucher's artful fantasies were the mirrors in which his patrons, the French aristocracy, saw the cherished reflections of their own ornamental decadence.

Boucher's student JEAN HONORÉ FRAGONARD (1732–1806) was a first-rate colorist whose decorative skill almost surpassed his master's. An example of his manner can stand as characteristic not only of him, but of the later Rococo in general. *The Swing* (FIG. 20-16) is a typical "intrigue" picture. A young gentleman has managed an arrangement by which an unknowing, friendly old bishop swings the gentleman's pretty sweetheart higher and higher, while he himself, strategically placed, ardently admires her. The young lady is quite aware of his presence and boldly kicks off her shoe at the little statue of the god of discretion, who holds his finger to his lips. The landscape setting is out of Watteau—a luxuriant perfumed bower in a park that very much resembles a stage scene for the comic opera. The glowing pastel colors and soft light convey, almost by themselves, the sensuality of the theme.

The medium of pastel is especially associated with the art of the Rococo, although it will be popular again with the Impressionists of the late nineteenth century. Pastels are chalk-like crayons, made of ground color pigments mixed with water and a binding medium. They lend themselves to quick execution, particularly of portraits, and provide the artist with a very wide range of colors and subtle variations of tone, suitable for rendering nuances of value and fleeting expressions of feature. The Venetian painter ROSALBA CARRIERA (1675–1757), working almost exclusively with pastels, pioneered the medium, and, in the 1720s and 1730s, made an international reputation for herself with pastel portraits of the gentry, nobility, and royalty of Europe. Her art became the

20-16　Jean Honoré Fragonard, *The Swing*, 1766. Approx. 35″ × 32″. Reproduced by permission of the Trustees of the Wallace Collection, London.

fashion in Paris, and she had more commissions than she could handle. Her pastel of *Cardinal de Polignac* (FIG. 20-17), diplomat and collector of ancient art, shows her new portrait method. Essentially informal, the composition includes only the head and bust, eliminating all details not needed to record the features and status of the subject. The design is simple; the pose and presentation, forthright and unpretentious. The pomp and rhetorical flourishes of the Baroque (FIG. 20-1) are missing. Typically for the pastel medium, the colors are high-keyed and luminous, shading is minimal, and the cardinal's grave features are modulated by a slightly hazed, soft focus, suggestive of sunlit atmosphere.

20-17 ROSALBA CARRIERA, *Cardinal de Polignac*, 1732. Pastel. Gallerie dell' Accademia, Venice.

A host of pastelists followed Carriera's example. One of the best of them, QUENTIN DE LA TOUR (1704–1788), gives us, in his *Self-Portrait*, the very type of the Enlightenment personality (FIG. 20-18). In his own features and expression, in the sidelong glance and

20-18 QUENTIN DE LA TOUR, *Self-Portrait*, c. 1751. Pastel. approx. 25" × 21". Musée de Picardie, Amiens.

almost jaunty pose, we find the kind of poise and suave elegance characteristic of the age—the *esprit* of Enlightenment society. In striking contrast with the solemn portrait of the Cardinal, the face is open and lively, with a bright look of amiable and active intelligence. Here is the optimistic (if slightly sardonic) believer in human progress—a man of good sense and good taste, conversant with the ideas of the "age of reason." He is critical of ancient privilege, prejudice, and superstition, a reader of Locke, Montesquieu, Voltaire, Rousseau, and the other "philosophes," whose principles will rationalize the American and French Revolutions. The smile on his face, familiar in many portraits of the time, has been called "the smile of the eighteenth century" confident, interested, amused, slightly mocking. It is the face one wears to the salon to confront the brilliant society of the *beau monde*.

Along with the sensuous style of the Rococo, patronized by such "first ladies" of Louis XV as Madame de Pompadour and Madame du Barry, a different taste developed—one much more likely to appeal to the middle classes of Paris, who disapproved of the licentious gallantries of Fragonard. JEAN BAPTISTE SIMÉON CHARDIN (1699–1779), briefly Fragonard's teacher, made a specialty of simple interiors and still life, which he painted masterfully in his own mode, rivaling the Dutch masters of the previous century. In *Grace at Table* (FIG. 20-19), Chardin gives us an unpre-

20-19 JEAN BAPTISTE SIMÉON CHARDIN, *Grace at Table*, 1740. 19" × 15". Louvre, Paris.

tentious room in which a mother and her small daughters are about to dine. The mood of quiet attention is at one with the hushed lighting and mellow color and the closely studied still-life accessories, with worn surfaces that tell their own humble domestic history. In his own way, Chardin is the poet of the commonplace and the master of its nuances. A gentle sentiment prevails in all his pictures—not contrived and artificial, but born of the painter's honesty, insight, and sympathy.

The taste of the newly prosperous and confident middle classes of England found expression in the art of WILLIAM HOGARTH (1697–1764), who satirized contemporary life with comic zest and with only a modicum of Rococo "indecency." With Hogarth, a truly English style of painting emerges. England had had no painters or sculptors to match its architects; traditionally, painters were imported from the continent (Holbein, Rubens, Van Dyck). Hogarth waged a lively campaign throughout his career against the English feeling of dependence on and inferiority to continental art. Although Hogarth himself would have been the last to admit it, his own painting owes

much to the work of his contemporaries across the channel in France, the artists of the Rococo. He uses the same bright, opaque colors, applied with dash and virtuosity. Yet his subject matter, frequently moral in tone, is distinctively English. It was the great age of English satirical writing, and Hogarth—who knew and admired this genre and included Henry Fielding, author of *Tom Jones*, among his closest friends—clearly saw himself as translating it into the visual arts:

> I therefore turned my thoughts to . . . painting and engraving modern moral subjects. . . . I have endeavored to treat my subjects as a dramatic writer; my picture is my stage, and men and women my players, who by means of certain actions and gestures, are to exhibit a dumb show. . . .

Hogarth's favorite device was to make a series of narrative paintings and prints, in a serial sequence like chapters in a book or scenes in a play, that follow a character or group of characters in their encounters with some social evil. He is at his best in pictures such as the *Breakfast Scene* (FIG. 20-20) from the *Marriage à la*

20-20 WILLIAM HOGARTH, *Breakfast Scene,* from *Marriage à la Mode, c.* 1745. Approx. 28″ × 36″. Reproduced by courtesy of the Trustees of the National Gallery, London.

Mode, in which the marriage of the young viscount, arranged through the social aspirations of one parent and the need for money of the other, is just beginning to founder. The bright, gay character of the anglicized Rococo style is admirably suited to the situation. The situation, however, must be read completely from its large inventory of detail if we are to enjoy it fully. It is past noon. Husband and wife are very tired after a long night spent in other company. The young nobleman keeps his hat on in his wife's presence. His hands are sunk deep in his pockets, emptied by gambling, and the little dog sniffs suspiciously at a lace cap that protrudes from a pocket. The broken sword suggests that the master has been in a fight; an overturned chair signifies that the previous evening has been somewhat spirited. A steward, his hands full of unpaid bills, raises his eyes to heaven in despair at what this family is coming to. The setting is overly grand. Hogarth pokes fun at the style of interior decoration and mocks the Classical taste in the bust on the mantelpiece. There is a great deal more; typically, Hogarth proceeds as a novelist would, elaborating on his subject with carefully chosen detail, which, as we continue to discover it, heightens the comedy.

LATE EIGHTEENTH CENTURY: THE RISE OF ROMANTICISM

The second half of the century quickens in tempo and changes in mood as the course of history sweeps toward the climax of the revolutions that will open the modern epoch. An uneasiness and then an impatience with the status quo breeds a new and restless spirit of criticism that, here and there, edges toward rebellion. Against what was thought to be the wanton lavishness and profligacy of the Rococo, an impulse toward the simple, the earnest, and the moral begins to rise. It is the time of Rousseau, the "age of sensibility," that preaches sincere feeling and natural human sympathy over artful reason and the cold calculations of courtly societies. The slogan of Sensibility is "Trust your heart rather than your head," or, as Goethe puts it, "Feeling is all!" Werther, the young Goethe's archetype of Romantic sensibility, cries: "We desire to surrender our whole being, that it may be filled with the perfect bliss of one glorious emotion!" All that is false and artificial must be banished as the enemy of honest emotion.

Sensibility is swiftly overtaken by the heroic emotions of the revolutionary age. Models of self-sacrificing virtue are summoned from the Greek and Roman past and from the rebellious present—heroes like Cato and Washington, Regulus and Marat—to inspire thoughts and deeds of civic idealism. And contemporary with both the sentimental and the heroic comes the taste for the sublime in art and nature. The sublime inspires feelings of awe mixed with terror, what is felt when we look on vast, impassable mountain peaks or great storms at sea. Accompanying the taste for the sublime is the "gothick" taste for the fantastic, the occult, the grotesque, the macabre—for the adventures of the soul voyaging into the dangerous reaches of consciousness.

Whatever moves the artist and the audience in this period—the sentimental, the heroic, the sublime, the "gothick," or combinations of them, there is a marked shift in emphasis from reason to feeling, from calculation to intuition, from objective nature to subjective emotion. Here, that attitude of the modern mind we call Romanticism first emerges.

For almost two centuries, scholars have debated the definition and the historical scope of Romanticism; neither the scholarship nor the controversy has ended. The very widest definition—say, Baudelaire's—would equate Romanticism and Modernism, making Romanticism the mood of the modern world and coextensive with its history. More narrowly, Romanticism is a phenomenon beginning around 1750 and ending about 1850. Still more narrowly, Romanticism is just another of a miscellany of styles that rise and decline in the course of modern art. In this view, Romanticism flourishes from about 1800 to 1840, coming between Neoclassicism and Realism.

The term itself originated toward the end of the eighteenth century among German literary critics, who aimed to distinguish peculiarly "modern" traits from the "Classical" traits that had advanced once more against the Baroque and Rococo. "Romance," which can refer as much to the novel, with its sentimental hero, as it does to the old Medieval tales of fantastic adventure written in the "romance" languages, has never quite fitted with the broader term "romantic," nor has "romantic" ever covered snugly all we seem to understand by it. J.P. Eckermann's *Conversations with Goethe* throws a strong, revealing light on Romanticism, especially on its supposed opposition to Classicism. There, Goethe is recorded as declaring:

> The distinction between Classical and Romantic poetry, which is now spread over the whole world and occasions so many quarrels and divisions, came originally from Schiller and myself. [Goethe is recalling some 40 years after the time.] I laid down the maxim of objective treatment in poetry, and would allow no other; but Schiller, who worked quite in the subjective way, deemed his own fashion right, and to defend himself against me, wrote the treatise upon *Naive and Sentimental Poetry*. He proved to me that I, against my

will, was romantic, and that my *Iphigenia*, through the predominance of sentiment, was by no means so much in the antique spirit as some people supposed. The Schlegels took up this idea, and carried it further, so that it has now been diffused over the whole world; and everybody talks about Classicism and Romanticism—of which nobody thought 50 years ago.*

It will be seen that Goethe wants his play to be in the antique spirit and, "against his will," discovers that he has been romantic all the time. This is probably the case with artists throughout the era of Romanticism. The break with tradition forces the artist to look at tradition historically; if he prefers Classical art, then he will have to assume or *affect* a "classic" bent of mind—but he will be *representing* Classical form, not *creating* it. In the end, it is his response to Classical form that counts, and that response is emotional; the emotional response to Classical form will be precisely Romantic!

We treat Romanticism here as a broad generality, finding that it comprehends a number of styles, including Neoclassicism, prevalent throughout the late eighteenth and the nineteenth centuries. Although these styles differ formally, the artists and architects who work within them share a common Romantic attitude. The underlying attitude broadens, deepens, and clarifies in the nineteenth century, and we shall consider it further then. For the moment, it is only necessary to point out that renewed interest in the historical styles (Classic, Gothic, Egyptian, and Chinese among them), as part of a rising eclecticism of taste, is all part of the new Romantic view of nature and of art.

Architecture

In England, where Romanticism was born, the revolt against the "regularity" of Classical architecture stirred early. The late seventeenth century witnessed the beginning of an enthusiasm for Chinese art—in particular, the Chinese garden. An English critic of the time, Sir William Temple, comparing the Chinese garden with the symmetry and uniformity of the European garden, described the beauty of the former as "without . . . order or disposition of parts that shall be commonly or easily observed. . . ." The Chinese term for this quality is defined as "being impressive or surprising through careless or unorderly grace." Within a generation of Temple's observation, English gardens were being designed along Oriental lines. In the eighteenth century, the English garden became a vogue throughout Europe, and the formality of such gardens as those at Versailles was thought unnatural.

Thus, "naturalness," rather than formal order, in architecture came to be the quality in demand, and

"natural" styles like Gothic, which had never entirely died out in England, became very popular. In 1718, John Vanbrugh, the architect of the Baroque Blenheim Palace (FIG. 20-4), designed his country house to look like a Gothic castle to give it a "masculine" (an unaffected or "natural") appearance. The picturesque qualities of the Gothic style had already begun to be appreciated when the Earl of Burlington was building Chiswick House (FIG. 20-5).

The contradiction between the formal villa and its informal gardens was apparently not felt at once; for one thing, the meaning of "nature" had not yet been agreed on in the early eighteenth century. Was it, in the Classical sense, a regularity of proportion, or, in the newer sense, the irregularity of growing things, with their wildness and accidents—in a word, their picturesqueness, or even their primitiveness? In the end, it would be decided that *all* historical styles are "natural," as they evolve historically from the artistic instinct of peoples, who are, after all, part of nature.

Thus, we see a number of "revivals" of styles almost simultaneously parading the romantic past before the eyes and imaginations of the romantically inclined public. Lord Burlington's Palladian revival was on course, having been made current and popular by the designs of William Kent, who was also a pioneer of the picturesque garden. HORACE WALPOLE (1717–1797) a wealthy architectural dilettante, renovated his villa at Twickenham in the rising "gothick" fashion, converting it into a sprawling "castle" with turrets, towers, battlements, galleries, and corridors, "whose fretted roofs, carved panels, and illuminated windows," as Sir Walter Scott describes, "were garnished with the appropriate furniture of escutcheons, armorial bearings, shields, tilting lances, and all the panoply of chivalry." Indeed, at Strawberry Hill (FIG. 20-21), Walpole's villa in Twickenham, the master could enjoy his favorite pastime, which was "to gaze on Gothic toys through Gothic glass." The features of the structure are, of course, pseudo-Gothic, the kind of fairy-tale vision raised in our own times by the late Walt Disney. But Walpole's trifling with Gothic architecture will be as influential as his Gothic novels.

The thrill produced by contemplation of the vanished past was cultivated by garden designers in England, who, when the opportunity offered, decorated the irregularities of random copses of trees, little rustic bridges, and winding streams with replicas of period architecture. Sometimes a single garden would boast four or five different styles. Typical are the gardens at Hagley Park, where a sham Gothic ruin of 1747 (FIG. 20-22) stands near a Doric portico built in 1758 (FIG. 20-23). The latter is of special interest as the work of JAMES STUART (1713–1788), who, with Nicholas Revett, introduced to Europe the splendor and originality of Greek art in the enormously influential *Antiquities of Athens*, the first volume of which was

*John Oxenford, trans., and J.K. Moorehead, ed., *Conversations of Goethe with Eckermann*, (New York: Dutton, 1935), p. 366.

20-21 HORACE WALPOLE, Strawberry Hill, Twickenham, near London, 1749–1777.

published in 1762. These volumes firmly distinguished Greek art from the "derivative" Roman, which had served as the model of Classicism since the Renaissance. Stuart's efforts were greeted with enthusiasm by those who had no use for the Rococo, the Chinese, the Gothic, or any of the "irregular" manners in art. A contemporary journal hoped that Stuart's writings and Robert Wood's magnificently illustrated *Ruins of Palmyra* (1753) and *Ruins of Baalbek* (1757) would "expel the littleness and ugliness of the Chinese, and the barbarity of the Goths, that we may see no more useless and expensive trifles; no more dungeons instead of summer houses."

By mid-century, the rediscovery of Greek art and architecture had turned the romanticizing taste of Europe in a new direction and inaugurated the style we call Neoclassicism, which reembraces the idea of a changeless generality that supposedly transcends the accidents of time. Neoclassicism, once thought of as

in opposition to Romanticism, is now understood as simply one of the many fashions within that general movement but in opposition to the "irregularity" of Romantic styles, like Neo-Gothic and Chinese. By 1763, the German critic Friedrich Grimm could write that "everything is being done today in the Greek mode." Earlier, in 1755, Johann Winckelmann, the first modern historian of art, published his *Thoughts on the Imitation of Greek Art in Painting and Sculpture*, in which he uncompromisingly designated Greek art as the most perfect from the hands of man and the only model to be followed, for doing so would confer "assurance in conceiving and designing works of art, since they [the Greeks] have marked for us the utmost limits of human and divine beauty."

Winckelmann characterizes Greek sculpture as manifesting a "noble simplicity and quiet grandeur," and, in his *History of Ancient Art* (1763), he undertook to describe each monument as an element in the de-

20-22 SANDERSON MILLER, sham Gothic ruin, Hagley Park, Worcestershire, England, 1747. Copyright, *Country Life*, London.

20-23 JAMES STUART, Doric portico, Hagley Park, Worcestershire, England, 1758. Copyright, *Country Life*, London.

velopment of a single grand style. Before Winckelmann, the history of art had been a matter of biography, as with Giorgio Vasari; Winckelmann initiates the modern method of classification and description on the basis of general stylistic traits that change over time. Winckelmann, strangely enough, did not know much about original Greek art—at least not much beyond the *Laocoön* group (FIG. 5-80) and other late Greek works in the Vatican collections, of which he was custodian. For the most part, he had only late Roman copies for study, and he never visited Greece, where he might have seen the genuine thing. Despite the obvious defects of his work, however, its pioneering character cannot be overlooked. Winckelmann had wide influence, and his writings laid a theoretical and historical foundation for Neoclassicism.

Within Neoclassicism's admiration for the art of Greece, sentiment for the art of Rome arose again; "the glory that was Greece / And the grandeur that was Rome" summarized the conception of a noble Classical world. The first great archeological event of modern times—the discovery and initial excavations of the ancient buried Roman cities of Pompeii (FIG. 6-21) and Herculaneum in the 1730s and 1740s—

startled and thrilled all Europe. This was the veritable resurrection of the ancient world, not simply a dim vision of it inspired by a few moldering ruins; historical reality could now replace fancy with fact. The wall paintings and other artifacts of Pompeii (FIGS. 6-23, 6-25, 6-27) inspired the slim, straight-lined, elegant "Pompeian" style that, after mid-century, almost entirely displaced the curvilinear Rococo. In France, the new manner was associated with Louis XVI; in England, it took the name of its most artful practitioner, ROBERT ADAM (1728–1792), whose interior architecture was as influential in Europe as the English garden. The Etruscan Room in Osterley Park House (FIG. 20-24), begun in 1761, compared with the Rococo salon of the Hôtel de Soubise (FIG. 20-6) and the Amalienburg (FIG. 20-8), shows how completely symmetry and rectilinearity have returned, but with great delicacy and none of the massive splendor of the style of Louis XIV. The decorative motifs (medallions, urns, vine scrolls, paterae, sphinxes, and tripods) are taken from Roman art and, as in Roman stucco work, are arranged sparsely within broad, neutral spaces and slender margins.

Adam was an archeologist as well as an architect

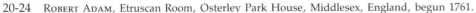

20-24 ROBERT ADAM, Etruscan Room, Osterley Park House, Middlesex, England, begun 1761.

and had explored and written accounts of the ruins of the palace of Diocletian at Spalatum (FIG. 6-77). His Kedleston House in Derbyshire, Adelphi Terrace in London, and many other structures show the influence of Spalatum on his work.

The Romantic fascination with ruins is blended with archeological curiosity about the facts. In Rome, in the late 1740s, Giovanni Battista Piranesi began his *Views of Rome* (FIG. 7-5)—some 135 prints that romantically present the eternal city's majestic ruins and that have served for generations as the standard image of Roman grandeur. Edward Gibbon wrote his monumental *Decline and Fall of the Roman Empire,* which matches in words the stately and august subjects of Piranesi's *Views.* The Roman ruins at Baalbek in Syria, especially a titanic colonnade, inspired the Neoclassical portico of the church of Ste. Geneviève (FIG. 20-25), now the Panthéon, in Paris, designed by JACQUES GERMAIN SOUFFLOT (1713–1780). The columns, reproduced with studied archeological exactitude, are the first revelation of Roman grandeur in France. The walls are severely blank, except for a repeated garland motif in the attic level. The colonnaded dome—a Neoclassical version of the domes of St. Peter's in Rome, the Church of the Invalides in Paris, and St. Paul's in London (FIGS. 17-34, 19-71, 19-76)—rises above a Greek-cross plan, and both vaults and dome rest on an interior grid of splendid, freestanding Corinthian columns, as if the colonnade of the portico were continued within. Although the whole effect—inside and out—is Roman, the structural principles employed are essentially Gothic. Soufflot early maintained that Gothic engineering was highly functional structurally and could be applied

20-25 JACQUES GERMAIN SOUFFLOT, the Panthéon (Ste. Geneviève), Paris, 1755–1792.

in modern building. In Soufflot, we have the curious, but not unreasonable conjunction of Gothic and Classical—not in mere decorative juxtaposition, as they appear at Hagley Park (FIGS. 20-22 and 20-23), but in structural integration. Thus, Soufflot anticipates the nineteenth-century admiration of Gothic engineering that will result in a firmer and more authentic Gothic manner than the stage sets favored by Walpole.

International Neoclassicism will extend across continent and ocean, from the Russia of Catherine the Great to the new American republic. THOMAS JEFFERSON (1743–1826), a gifted amateur, shows in his design for his country house at Monticello (FIG. 20-26) how well acquainted he was with Palladio and his

20-26 THOMAS JEFFERSON, Monticello, Charlottesville, Virginia, 1770–1806.

20-27 THOMAS JEFFERSON, State Capitol, Richmond, Virginia, designed 1785–1789. (The wings are a later addition.)

eighteenth-century English adherents. Monticello is a kind of Villa Rotonda (FIG. 17-52) or Chiswick House (FIG. 20-5)—developed out of the pleasant provincial architecture of Virginia, with the setting of green lawns and the red brick walls and white facings of American Colonial architecture. Even before it was finished (Monticello was built in two stages), Jefferson's experience of Classical art in Europe convinced him that a strictly Classical manner, if not always appropriate for private dwellings, was certainly so for public buildings. He showed his feeling for the Classical past by going beyond those architects who incorporated only elements of ancient architecture in their buildings and taking the complete Roman temple form as his model for the Virginia statehouse at Richmond (FIG. 20-27). He had seen the Roman temple at Nîmes called the Maison Carrée (which resembles the Temple of "Fortuna Virilis," FIG. 6-16) while serving in France as American ambassador. Jefferson's choice was based on the admiration he felt for the original, both as an embodiment of the pure beauty of antiquity and as a symbol of idealized Roman Republican government.

Thus, in a single career, we witness the passage from Palladian Classicism to the stricter Neoclassicism of the end of the eighteenth century. Selection of the Roman model reflects as well the attempt, also found in the thought of Jefferson's contemporary French revolutionaries, to rediscover in antiquity certain lofty principles of life that had presumably been distorted during the intervening centuries. The young United States adopted many Roman symbols: the eagle; the lictor's ax and rods; "Columbia," the allegorical figure of the nation (as a kind of new "Roma"). Its national motto was in Latin: *e pluribus unum;* Washington was honored as a new Cincinnatus, who, after liberating his country, retired to his farm when he could have been king; the upper house

of Congress was named after the Roman Senate. The official architecture of Washington has long been Neoclassical, and the Capitol itself is named after the ancient Roman hill.

Sculpture and Painting

In sculpture, as in the architecture of Jefferson, we can find a similar passage from the less to the more formal—in this case, from the Rococo to the threshold of Neoclassicism. The small group *Nymph and Satyr* (FIG. 20-28) by CLODION (Claude Michel, 1738–

20-28 CLODION, *Nymph and Satyr, c.* 1775. Terra cotta, approx. 23" high. The Metropolitan Museum of Art, New York (bequest of Benjamin Altman, 1913).

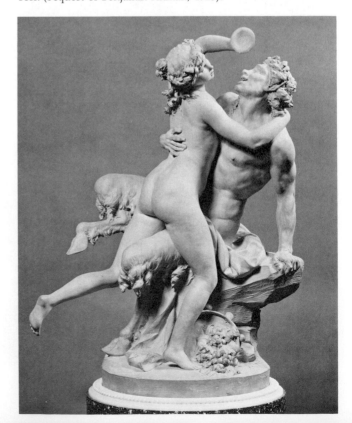

1814) is witness to the fact that the Rococo taste is not altogether passé in the later eighteenth century. The erotic playfulness of Boucher and Fragonard, in an open and vivid composition faintly echoing Gianlorenzo Bernini, energizes the eager nymph and the laughing satyr, into whom she pours a cup of wine. The sensual exhilaration of the Rococo is caught in diminutive scale and fragile terra cotta; as with so many of its artifacts, and most of Clodion's best works, the group is designed for a tabletop.

In sharp contrast, the *Diana* (FIG. 20-29) of JEAN ANTOINE HOUDON (1744–1828) is a bronze statue almost 7 feet high. The fleet goddess of the hunt is caught in one swift moment, elegantly poised. The suavely modeled volumes, the supple contours, and the compact silhouette contribute to her cool simplicity and dignity. All traces of Rococo complexity,

asymmetry, and restlessness have vanished. We cannot yet call the *Diana* Neoclassical (it reflects something of the French Mannerism of the sixteenth century), but it surely represents a *détente* of the Rococo and anticipates Neoclassical formalism.

Houdon was not only a master sculptor of the figure, but the greatest and most successful portraitist of his time. Throughout his long life, Houdon had the opportunity to have as his subjects some of the greatest men of the age: Voltaire, Rousseau, Franklin, Washington, Jefferson, Lafayette. His art comes between the mannered Rococo and the mannered Neoclassicism of the Napoleonic period. Houdon's strong, perceptive realism penetrates at once to personality, catching its most subtle shade. For his *Count Cagliostro* (FIG. 20-30), Houdon had a subject not so much great as notorious. Cagliostro (the name was an alias)—one of the most successful confidence men in history, a brilliant fake, mountebank, quack, and impostor—charmed European society (especially the ladies) even as he swindled it. Houdon renders him in open-necked, romantic *déshabillé*, turning a large-eyed, innocent gaze heavenward, as if in protestation of the purity of his motives and of his love and sympathy for credulous mankind. Houdon's *Cagliostro*, like Molière's earlier *Tartuffe*, presents with exquisite acuteness the character of the sanctimonious fraud.

20-29 JEAN ANTOINE HOUDON, *Diana,* 1790. Bronze, 6′ 11″ high. Louvre, Paris.

20-30 JEAN ANTOINE HOUDON, *Count Cagliostro* (Giuseppe Balsamo), 1771–1789. Marble, approx. 25″ high (without base). National Gallery of Art, Washington, D.C. (Samuel H. Kress Collection).

Hogarth believed that portraiture, rather than his own genre, was the forte of the English School of painting. The accumulating fortunes of both the English nobility and merchants in the eighteenth century led, in the first days of the British empire, to the demand not only for fine buildings but also for fine portraits. The tradition of Van Dyck still flourished and was taken up again by a whole school of painters, who gradually modified it for the more modern taste. THOMAS GAINSBOROUGH (1727–1788)—who began as a landscape painter and always preferred landscape to portrait—gives us, in *The Honourable Mrs. Graham* (FIG. 20-31), the very essence of the early preferred Van-Dyckian manner. Dressed in the Rococo flamboyance of feathers and brocade, silver and crimson, the young gentlewoman poses haughtily by a great column and against a deep Venetian background of dark russet. The pride of birth and station is announced in every detail. Full-length, life-sized canvases like this were intended to decorate the grand

20-31 THOMAS GAINSBOROUGH, *The Honourable Mrs. Graham,* 1775. 7' 9½" × 5' ¾". National Gallery of Scotland, Edinburgh.

stairways of the great country houses of affluent England. But there is a different intention and result in Gainsborough's portrait of *Mrs. Richard Brinsley Sheridan* (FIG. 20-32). The lovely lady, dressed informally, is seated in a rustic landscape faintly reminiscent of Watteau in its soft-hued light and feathery brushwork. (The artist had intended to give the picture "an air more pastoral than it at present possesses" by the addition of sheep, which he did not live to paint in.) Gainsborough intends to match the unspoiled beauty of natural landscape with the natural beauty of the subject, whose dark brown hair blows freely in the slight wind and whose clear, unassisted "English" complexion and air of ingenuous sweetness are in sharp contrast with the pert sophistication of continental Rococo portraits. The Romantic view of life and nature, already manifest in the transitional "age of sensibility," as we have seen, is pretty much the creation of England. That view is rooted in the concept of naturalness, against the artificiality of the Baroque and the Rococo, at least in their official guise.

The vogue of naturalness easily crosses the channel. The ingenuous, quite charming *Self-Portrait* (FIG. 20-33) by ÉLISABETH LOUISE VIGÉE-LEBRUN (1755–1842), a fashionable portraitist for whom Marie Antoinette, queen of France, sat on several occasions, shows us the new, more natural manner, freed of the frills of the Rococo. The lady—dressed simply in the "Republican" mode and proud of her profession of artist—poses with palette and brushes in the act of painting the portrait of the queen. With a slightly coy, quite excusable vanity, she represents herself younger than she was at the time. In her memoirs, written toward the end of a long and productive life, she cannot help recording how well this portrait was received by the art world of Florence. The vivacious subject renders her likeness with a naïve, unaffected enthusiasm that is quite compelling. One of the finest portraits of the eighteenth century, it expresses all we can mean by "naturalness."

For a type of realistic and revealing portrait of participants in the great events that usher in modern times, we turn to SIR JOSHUA REYNOLDS (1723–1792)—rival of Gainsborough and president of the British Royal Academy of Arts from its foundation in 1768—who, in theory, kept very close to the academic Baroque, as we can read in his *Discourses*. There he expounds a doctrine from which, luckily, he often deviated in practice—that "general" nature, as represented by the Carracci and others, is always superior to "particular" nature, as rendered by the Dutch. Yet he showed himself capable of sturdy, characterful portraits, like that of *Lord Heathfield* (FIG. 20-34). Accustomed to highly formal portraits in the tradition of Van Dyck, Reynolds seems almost relieved when he can turn to a subject like this burly, brandy-flushed English officer, commandant of the fortress of Gibralter during the American Revolution. Lord Heathfield doggedly defended the great rock against the Spanish, and his victory is symbolized by the key of the fortress, which he holds so casually. The heavy, honest, unidealized face belongs to a different world from that of Quentin de la Tour (FIG. 20-18). This is a world of camps, battles, and wars

and of revolutions now taking shape in deadly earnest, as the old regime, with all its esthetic artifice, fades into the past.

The commotion attendant on the emerging modern world is dramatized by the American painter BENJAMIN WEST (1738–1820) in a work pioneering a type of painting based on particular historical events. Born in Pennsylvania, on what was then the colonial

20-33 Élisabeth Louise Vigée-Lebrun, *Self-Portrait*, 1790. 8' 4" × 6' 9". Galleria degli Uffizi, Florence.

20-34 Sir Joshua Reynolds, *Lord Heathfield*, 1787. Approx. 56" × 45". Reproduced by courtesy of the Trustees of the National Gallery, London.

frontier, West was sent to Europe early in life to study art, and then to England, where he had almost immediate success. He was a cofounder of the Royal Academy, and succeeded Sir Joshua Reynolds as its president. He became painter to George III and remained so during the strains of the American Revolution. In *The Death of General Wolfe* (FIG. 20-35), West depicts the mortally wounded young English commander, who has just defeated the French under Montcalm in the decisive battle of Quebec (1759), which gave Canada to Great Britain. Recalling the traditional Pietà theme (FIG. 18-25) in religious painting, the composition, still essentially Baroque, replaces Christ with the modern hero, who swoons to death among his grieving officers on the field of victorious battle. The figures are represented in contemporary military garb (not entirely accurately), rather than in the conventional Classical draperies—a startling innovation that would catch on and last through the nineteenth century. The Anglo-American School of history painting is the leader in the development of the genre.

Born of a general enthusiasm for a new, moral seriousness, the later eighteenth century is preoccupied with themes of heroism and virtuous action sharply antagonistic to the hedonism and escapism of the Rococo style. The sober telling of stories with a moral comes suddenly into fashion in the 1760s. The work of JEAN BAPTISTE GREUZE (1735–1805) became widely popular as the Rococo style faded. Greuze's art expresses perfectly the transition of taste from the Rococo to nineteenth-century Romanticism—his vogue coming in the interim period, the "age of sensibility." Almost overnight, France—and Europe—abandoned the wanton frivolity and luxuriance of the Rococo and became not only serious and moralistic but especially "sensible" and "feeling," which is to say *emotional*. Against what he saw as the cold, heartless, selfish culture of courts, Jean Jacques Rousseau, one of the most influential writers of modern times, called for the sincere expression of sympathetic and tender emotions. He exalted the simple life of the peasant as the most "natural" and set it up as a model to be imitated. The joys and sorrows of uncorrupted "natural" people, now described everywhere in novels, soon drowned Europe in a flood of tears; it became fashionable to weep, to fall on one's knees, to swoon, and to languish in hopeless love. This kind of contrived and melodramatic emotion, this *sentimentality*, has been a fundamental ingredient of popular art from the time of its appearance in the eighteenth century until the present. Greuze won wide acclaim with paintings entitled the *Father of the Family Reading the Bible to His Children*, the *Village Bride*, and the *Father's Curse*, in all of which he pointed a moral and sentimentalized his characters. In his *Return of the Prodigal Son* (FIG. 20-36) the theme is plain enough and the action is rather crudely obvious. Yet his moralizing

20-35 BENJAMIN WEST, *The Death of General Wolfe*, 1771. Approx. 5′ × 7′. National Gallery of Canada, Ottawa (gift of the Duke of Westminster, 1918).

does look forward to that of Jacques Louis David and Neoclassicism, and we may credit Greuze with a kind of pioneer work in a type of subject and expression that meets with more general acceptance at present, when his reputation, suffering from later criticism, has been restored to a degree.

It is noteworthy that Denis Diderot, the great philosophe and scholar, advanced the cause of Greuze for a while but afterward acknowledged his artificiality. In *Salon of 1765*, Diderot describes a sketch for *The Return of the Prodigal Son:*

This is the sight which meets the eyes of the ungrateful son. He comes forward, he is on the threshold. . . . His mother meets him at his entrance; she is silent, but with her hand points to the corpse as if to say: "See what you have done."

The ungrateful son is struck with amazement; his head falls forward, and he strikes his forehead with his hand. What a lesson is here depicted for fathers and children! . . . I do not know what effect this short and simple description . . . will produce on others, but for my own part I could not write it without emotion.*

We feel today that the attitudes and gestures of Greuze's figures are somewhat inauthentic and forced; in fact, they are drawn from the stock vocabu-

*See E.G. Holt, *A Documentary History of Art* (Princeton, N.J.: Princeton University Press, 1958), Vol. 2, p. 319.

20-36 JEAN BAPTISTE GREUZE, *The Return of the Prodigal Son*, 1777–1778. Approx. 51″ × 65″. Louvre, Paris.

lary of the academic tradition and will be repeated even more provincially in melodramatic stageplays throughout the nineteenth century.

With the approaching French Revolution, the temper of the times becomes more severe and the type and quality of emotion changes. Following the "age of sensibility," the values of moral virtue, civic dedication, heroism, and self-sacrifice, rather than gentleness and tenderness, now demand expression. The change of interest is from the private to the public theater of action, where the *naturally* noble attributes of human nature are supposed to emerge, cleansed of those past and present corruptions denounced by Rosseau. Naturalness—formerly associated, whether by Rosseau or by Greuze, with the simple people of the French countryside—comes to be identified with the heroes of Classical Greece and Rome, who are understood as the paragons of all goodness, truth, and beauty. "Natural" and "Classical" are identical in Neoclassical thinking.

In the art of ANGELICA KAUFFMANN (1741–1807), the "naturalness" of Greuze's figure types, situations, and contemporary settings is replaced by a Neoclassicism still suggestive of the Rococo. Born in Switzerland and trained in Italy, Kauffmann spent many of her productive years in England. A protégée of Sir Joshua Reynolds and a decorator of the interiors of houses built by Robert Adam, she was a founding member of the British Royal Academy of Arts, and enjoyed a fashionable reputation. Her *Cornelia, Mother of the Gracchi* (FIG. 20-37) is a kind of "set piece" of early Neoclassicism; its subject is an *exemplum virtutis* (example or model of virtue) of the didactic kind, drawn from the history and literature of Greece and Rome. This turning away from the frivolous and sensuous subjects of the Rococo to themes thought to be noble and elevating becomes general in the late eighteenth century. Greuze's moralizing pictures already mark a change in taste; but whereas he stages idealized rustics in peasant cottages, Kauffmann clothes her actors in ancient Roman garb, poses them in classicizing Roman attitudes, and places them in Roman interiors. Her theme here is the virtue of Cornelia, mother of the future political leaders Tiberius and Gaius Gracchus, who, in the second century B.C., attempted to reform the Roman republic. When a lady visitor, boasting of her fine jewels, asks Cornelia to show hers, Cornelia—praised for her gentle and wise education of her children—brings them forward, saying "*These* are my jewels!" The architecture is severely Roman, with not a Rococo motif in evidence, and the composition and drawing have the simplicity and firmness of bas-relief. Yet the charm and grace of Rococo lingers, moderated by Kauffmann's own bland, tranquil manner.

Greuze's philosophy of sentiment and Kauffmann's sentimental Neoclassicism harden into the public, programmatic stoicism of JACQUES LOUIS DAVID (1748–1825), the painter—ideologist of the Neoclassical art of the French Revolution and the Napoleonic empire.

20-37 ANGELICA KAUFFMANN, *Cornelia, Mother of the Gracchi, c.* 1785. 40″ × 50″. Museum of Fine Arts, Richmond, Virginia.

We have noted that Neoclassicism is only one of the revival styles of Romanticism. The fact is, too, that Classical art had a long tradition in Europe and France before the time of David and that academies had long based their existence on the principle that the elements of art can be taught according to rules taken from the ancients and the great masters of the Renaissance. In his own quite individual and often non-Classical style, David reworks the Classical and academic traditions. He rebels against the Rococo as an "artificial taste" and exalts Classical art as, in his own words, "the imitation of nature in her most beautiful and perfect form." He praises Greek art enthusiastically, although he, like Winckelmann, knew almost nothing about it firsthand: "I want to work in a pure Greek style. I feed my eyes on ancient statues; I even have the intention of imitating some of them. . . ." But David's doctrine of the superiority of Classical art is not based on an isolated esthetic; believing, as he writes, that "the arts must . . . contribute forcefully to the education of the public," he was prepared both as artist and politician when the French Revolution offered the opportunity to create a public art, an art of propaganda.

David was active in the French Revolution as a Jacobin friend of the radical Maximilien Robespierre, as a member of the National Convention that voted for the death of the king, Louis XVI, and as quasi-dictator of the Committee on Public Education, where he directed the art programs of the new republic. He joined scholars and artists in soliciting the revolutionary government to abolish the old French Royal Academy and to establish in its place panels of experts to guide the reformation of taste. His position of power made him dominant in the transformation of style, and his own manner was the official model for many years.

Although painted in 1784, before the French Revolution, David's *Oath of the Horatii* (FIG. 20-38) reflects his politically didactic purpose and his doctrine of the educational power of Classical form, as well as his method of composing the Neoclassical picture. Most important of all to David, as artistic descendant of the old Academy, is the choice of subject matter: It must have grandeur and a moral. If effectively presented, David writes, the "marks of heroism and civic virtue offered the eyes of the people will electrify its soul, and plant the seeds of glory and devotion to the fatherland." For this *Oath*, David selected a story from pre-Republican Rome—the heroic phase of Roman history that had been pushed to the foreground of public interest by the sensational archeological discoveries made at the time at Herculaneum and Pompeii. The subject, a conflict between love and patriotism, is based on a play by Pierre Corneille that had been performed in Paris several years earlier and thus was known to the Parisian public. According to the story, first told by Livy, the leaders of the Roman and Alban armies, poised for battle, decide to resolve their conflicts in triple combat among three representatives from each side. The Roman choice falls on the three Horatius brothers; that of the Albans, on the three sons of the Curatius family. A sister of the Horatii, Camilla, is the bride-to-be of one of the Curatius sons.

David's painting shows the Horatii as they swear on their swords to win or die for Rome, oblivious to the anguish and sorrow of their sisters. The theme is

20-38 JACQUES LOUIS DAVID, *Oath of the Horatii*, 1784. Approx. 11' × 14'. Louvre, Paris.

stated with admirable force and clarity. The rigid and virile forms of the men effectively eclipse the soft, curvilinear shape of the mourning women in the right background. Such manly virtues as courage, patriotism, and unwavering loyalty to a cause are emphasized over the less heroic emotions of love, sorrow, and despair symbolized by the women. The message is clear and of a type with which the prerevolutionary French public could readily identify. The picture created a sensation when it was exhibited in Paris in 1785, and although it had been painted under royal patronage and was not at all revolutionary in intent, its Neoclassical style became the semiofficial voice of the revolution. David may have been painting in the academic tradition, but he makes of it something new—a program for arousing an audience to patriotic zeal. From David's *Oath* onward, art will become political—if not often in the sense of serving a state or party, then in its division into trends, movements, and ideologies.

In its form, *Oath of the Horatii* is a paragon of Neoclassical academicism. In a shallow picture box, defined by a severely simple architectural framework, statuesque and carefully modeled figures are deployed laterally and close to the foreground in a manner reminiscent of ancient relief sculpture. But caught up in the general mid-eighteenth-century enthusiasm for the archeological recovery and study of great civilizations, David's goal is the precise description of the monuments and personages of the historical past. This almost pedantic dedication to historical reality (he once complained that Raphael, that paragon of Classicism, erred by putting people of different periods into the same picture) compels David to modify his Neoclassical formula. In later work, he seeks to avoid such changes in formula and even stiffens his style in keeping with his concept of the antique manner, but in a painting like *The Death of Marat* (FIG. 20-39), the Classical elements of closed outline and compact composition, though present, are made to serve the ends of a dramatic realism of strong, psychic impact. The cold, neutral space above the densely organized figure composition makes for a chilling oppressiveness. Here, the scene is shaped by historical fact, not Neoclassical theory; and the "stele"-like composition reveals that David has closely studied Michelangelo, especially the Christ of the *Pietà* in St. Peter's. Marat, a personal friend of David and a revolutionary radical, was stabbed to death in his bath by Charlotte Corday, a political enemy. Narrative details—the knife, the wound, the blood, the letter by which the young woman gained entrance—are vividly placed to sharpen the sense of pain and outrage, but above all to confront the viewer with the scene itself. *Marat*, given David's personal involvement, is a poignantly felt theme, realized with almost painful sincerity. It is convincingly *real*, yet it

20-39 JACQUES LOUIS DAVID, *The Death of Marat*, 1793. Approx. 63″ × 49″. Musées Royaux des Beaux-Arts de Belgique, Brussels.

loses nothing of pose, composition, and rendering of light and shadow in David's astonishingly calm execution.

From modernizing Classical antiquity in the quasi-Realism of the *Oath of the Horatii*, David eventually moves to the point where he is classicizing the modern, as in his *Madame Récamier*, in which a Parisian socialite, dressed and coiffed *à la greque*, reclines on a Pompeian couch in a severely formal setting. The corner is turned, and we are now exposed to the staged, rather than the real, Classicism—much like a modern motion picture concerned with historical events. This is the consequence of David's mobilization of the Classical manner in the service of contemporary political struggles. However, even before David's time, it had been discovered that Classical philosophy and art *were* historical and that they did, after all, belong to a particular time and place.

Thus, for all his loyalty to Classical theory, David turns out not to be a Classicist at all, and his pupils will either drop his program altogether or change Classicism into a decorative, contour manner valued not for its idealism or truth but for its purely visual qualities. David's avowed purpose was to "electrify the soul," but he believed that art must be "of the reason, and rise above the passions." This contradiction—symptomatic of the turbulent change from the "age of reason" to the "age of revolution"—makes

20-40 JOHN FLAXMAN, *Electra Leading the Procession to Agamemnon's Tomb* (from the *Choephoroe*), 1795. Engraving.

his art inconsistent. His followers, although they will agree with the romantic aim to "electrify the soul," will break it into different combinations and directions, using a variety of stylistic means—for all the styles of past times and distant places are now becoming available to the artist.

Neoclassicism, treated in a confused and ambivalent fashion by David and his school, finds clear and simple expression in the influential art of the sculptor and draughtsman, JOHN FLAXMAN (1755–1826), whose style inspired Ingres, David's greatest pupil. Flaxman, creating the extreme limit of withdrawal from the intricacy and sensuality of the Rococo, which he loathed, reduces his forms to bare, linear outlines, without color or chiaroscuro, and his content to themes of an almost ascetic purity and severity (FIG. 20-40). His models were taken from Greek and Etruscan vase painting (FIGS. 5-8, 5-9, 5-10, 5-11) and Greek sculpture (FIGS. 5-52 and 5-57). He chose his subjects from Homer, Hesiod, Aeschylus, Dante, and other great classics of the West, and his illustrations of them were immensely popular, both in Europe and America. Shown here is the opening scene of the *Choephoroe* of Aeschylus, in which Electra and her mourning women move slowly to the tomb of her murdered father, Agamemnon. There, she will meet her brother Orestes and swear with him to revenge their father's death on their hated mother, Clytemnestra, his murderer. Flaxman renders the procession with epic spareness; indeed, his interpretations of the Classical themes were thought worthy of Homer. The drooping figures of the sorrowing women lose nothing of majesty; they have a columnar strength reminiscent of the caryatids of the Erechtheum (FIG. 5-57). At the same time, there is a slow, steady, rhythmic motion, as of some solemn dance interpretive of grief. The disciplined delineation in pure, unaccented line loses nothing of this sense of movement; it does not become immobilized into rigidity. For more than

a generation, Flaxman's style was considered the perfection of the Neoclassical ideal.

The contrast between Flaxman and his older contemporary, HENRY FUSELI (1741–1825), could not be a more startling illustration of the abrupt conflict and contradiction between styles within the same time and place, even within an artist's own development. The stylistic pluralism, the multiplicity of stylistic options characteristic of the nineteenth century, is manifest here. Fuseli, Swiss by birth, settled in England and eventually became a member of the Royal Academy and an instructor there. Largely self-taught, he contrived a distinctive manner, compounded of Michelangelo, the antique style, and his own extravagant invention. He specializes in night moods of horror and in "gothic" fantasies—in the demonic, the macabre, often the sadistic. The twisted poses and frantic gestures of his figures go well beyond exaggeration and often suggest the influence of Italian Mannerism. *The Nightmare* (FIG. 20-41) is the first of four versions of this terrifying theme. The beautiful young woman, tormented by some terrible dream and still not awake, has thrown herself partly from her couch. Her attitude shows her helpless beneath the incubus that squats malignantly on her body, as a horse with flaming eyes bursts into the scene from beyond the curtain. The Romantic vein of violent emotion and of perverse and tragic action will be heavily mined in the nineteenth century. Fuseli's art is near the start of an enterprise that will lead to the uncovering of the dark terrain of the human subconscious.

The later eighteenth century sees the calm weather of romantic Neoclassicism alternate with the storm and stress of emotional Romanticism. This alternation appears almost randomly in the art of WILLIAM BLAKE (1757–1827), the visionary poet and engraver. A friend of both Flaxman and Fuseli, Blake can manage their contradictory moods as if he were merely

20-41 HENRY FUSELI, *The Nightmare,* 1781. Approx. 40″ × 51″. The Detroit Institute of the Arts (gift of Mr. and Mrs. Bert L. Smokler and Mr. and Mrs. Lawrence A. Fleishman).

changing the content of his own dreams. He draws on Flaxman for Neoclassical effects, and exchanges subjects with Fuseli. There is a curious thematic and compositional resemblance between Blake's *Pity* (FIG. 20-42) and Fuseli's *Nightmare* (FIG. 20-41), but the mood and atmosphere are completely different. Blake's is serene; Fuseli's, dark and tormented. In Blake's picture, the soul of the dying woman is snatched up by angels of death, who sweep by on spectral white horses. The gesture of the near angel is benign, almost loving, in contrast with the malignancy of the incubus in Fuseli's picture. The sculptural relief and linearity, as well as the almost total

suppression of color, relate, at some distance, to the manner of Flaxman.

In the work of a great master in the art of etching, GIOVANNI BATTISTA PIRANESI (1720–1778), the Classical world and a world of pure, romantic fantasy coexist, reconciled in a single mood, style, and technique. We have already met Piranesi as the artist whose etched prints spread the monuments of ancient Rome before the eyes of Europe and who took a leading part in stimulating the enthusiasm for the Classical style. But he could also take an utterly different tack— his powerful imagination conjuring up awe-inspiring visions of bafflingly complicated architectural masses, piled up and spread out through gloomy spaces. In such pictures, vistas are multiplied and broken by a seeming infinity of massive arches, vaults, piers and stairways, through which move human figures small as insects. Despite wandering, soaring perspectives, there is a suffocating sense of enclosure; the spaces are locked in, and there is no exit. These grim places are, in fact, prisons *(carceri),* filled with brooding menace and hopelessness. Piranesi etched a series of them, often darkening subsequent editions to make them even more sinister. Our picture (FIG. 20-43) is one of these. In a different way from Fuseli and Blake, Piranesi creates oppressive dreams, and his *Carceri 14* will haunt the night imaginings of many a Romantic poet.

The eighteenth century, as the "age of reason," seems to have found the rational ideal in Neoclassical art (Romantic Classicism)—for example, in a Jefferson or a Flaxman. But Fuseli and Blake and Piranesi show that the equation of reason and nature in Neo-

20-42 WILLIAM BLAKE, *Pity, c.* 1795. Watercolor, approx. 17″ × 21″. Tate Gallery, London.

20-43 GIOVANNI BATTISTA PIRANESI, *Carceri 14, c.* 1750. Etching, second state, approx. 16″ × 21″.
Ashmolean Museum, Oxford.

classicism can be false, or at least insufficient to do
justice to the human reality. Imagination may reach
farther than reason and find, by suprarational intuition and enkindled emotion, a higher and a deeper
experience. The worlds of dream and vision may provide more valid materials for the soul of the artist
liberated from the rules of reason; Blake writes: "I will
not reason and compare, my business is to create."
Feeling, emotion, and passion at full intensity may be
surer guides than reason in the quest for meaning;
Blake again: "The road of excess leads to the palace of
wisdom." Yet there are grave risks. Raw feeling could
lead the soul astray, perhaps beyond the limits of
sanity. The "age of reason" leaves a warning for the
"age of romanticism" and its offspring, the modern
world, in a print by the Spanish master FRANCISCO
GOYA, whom we shall soon consider in some detail.
In a print from a series called *Los Caprichos* (FIG.
20-44), Goya depicts the artist asleep, while around
him throng winged monsters and demons—the
nightmare brood that peoples his dreams (again, the
nightmare!). Goya captions the print: "The Dream
of Reason Produces Monsters."

20-44 FRANCISCO GOYA, *"The Dream of Reason,"* from *Los
Caprichos, c.* 1794–1799. Pen-and-sepia drawing, approx.
8″ × 5″. Museo del Prado, Madrid.

2 enfants sont menacés par un rossignol /M. ernst.

V
THE MODERN WORLD

Our era, the "modern" era, differs from the past as a result of several fundamental revolutions that have radically changed—and are continuing to change—the world. Least dramatic in its arrival, but by far the most fateful for mankind, was the Industrial Revolution: the revolution that introduced the age of the machine. To match the importance of the Industrial Revolution, we would have to go back thousands of years to the development of agriculture. For, in two centuries (an extremely short span of historical time), we have

MAX ERNST, *Two Children Are Threatened by a Nightingale*, 1924. Oil on wood with wood construction, 27½" high, 22½" wide, 4½" deep. Museum of Modern Art, New York (purchase).

created a universe of machines that replaces physical labor and extends the powers of the brain enormously, bringing changes in the conditions of life with such speed that we find it difficult to adjust to them. Human knowledge, dawning in the Old Stone Age, reaches "high noon" in our own times. Control of nature is now widespread and tenacious; science has become our most authoritative source of natural knowledge, and the application of it in technology and industry has become the characteristic activity or ambition of modern societies.

As science and technology challenged old views of the physical world, so political revolution, beginning in the late eighteenth century, challenged the old absolutisms of Church and Realm, setting up such new aims and values as democracy, nationalism, and social justice. Subsequent revolutions have transformed the social and economic organization of vast areas of the world; regions colonized by Europe since the Renaissance have risen against her to the call of her own revolutionary slogans. As Europeans conquered and colonized the non-European world, they unwittingly began an exchange not only of goods, but of ideas and cultures. In the twentieth century, European colonial empires decline or vanish, and non-European nations rise in their place. The trend appears to be away from separate civilizations and toward a *world* civilization, and the peculiarly European traits that took form in the Renaissance lose their distinctive character. In all sectors of Western culture, the Humanist's image of man, created in the Renaissance, is being blurred and, here and there, effaced. In the modern view, man has been displaced from the commanding position the Renaissance assigned him as master of the Nature that God created for him. Now, though man holds greater control than ever before over his environment, he is seen to be as much the despoiler and victim of it as he is its master. Within Western nations, established values and institutions are being challenged on all sides. In fear and mistrust of what the West has created—great evil that seems to outweigh great good—many are turning to non-Western cultures to find fresh and alternative interpretations of life. For many thoughtful persons, there is the poignant feeling that the West has had its day and that its fundamental assumptions about human values have been discredited. They hear, with André Malraux, voices clamoring for the abdication of the West.

The revolutionary changes of the modern world on all fronts—scientific, technological-industrial, political, social, economic, and cultural—make for the characteristic temper of our age: a mixture of restlessness, obsession with progress and novelty, and a ceaseless questioning, testing, and challenging of authority. Old certainties give place to new, and the new give place to still newer. Scarcely a traditional value, system, institution, or rule in the modern world has escaped relentless critical analysis. At the same time, discovery and invention, proceeding at an always accelerating pace, are making the once impossible both possible and actual; today's "nonsense," as Alfred North Whitehead puts it, may be demonstrated truth tomorrow. The rapid obsolescence of ideas and things gives life a tentative and temporary quality and makes confusion a constant in its ever-changing patterns.

It is little wonder, then, that art in this period is a sequence and medley of competing "movements"—each seeking to establish its authority, each having its own ideology, and each subject to displacement in the bewilderingly rapid process of stylistic turnover. We describe these movements in terms (rarely precise) that aim to define their artistic content, form, and intention: "Romanticism," "Realism," "Impressionism," and the like.* Implicit in such words is the notion of doctrine; certainly, the principles and issues of these movements, hotly and widely argued in their time, ultimately spread beyond territorial and national boundaries. Appropriately enough for an age that sees the making of a world civilization, modern art, in all its component movements, tends to be international, like modern science, technology, industry, and politics.

*Terms like these, which we will now encounter more frequently, designate stylistic trends, movements, philosophies, and periods. Where they are so used, we will capitalize them as nouns and also as adjectives. When such terms are used in their broader senses, they will not be capitalized. Realism, for example, can be, on the one hand, the narrower, specific reference to the nineteenth-century movement of that name and, on the other, the wider, more general reference to art that emphasizes the literal reproduction of the facts of appearance, no matter the period, as in the painting of Velázquez, Vermeer, and many others (in the latter case, our choice is "realism" and "realistic.") Any rule for capitalization is arbitrary and sometimes inconsistent; it can, however, be useful in defining trends and influences and as a mnemonic device.

21

Architectural Sites

1 Tour Eiffel
2 Arc de Triomphe
3 Opéra
4 Church of the Invalides
5 Louvre
6 Sainte Chapelle
7 Notre Dame
8 Panthéon
9 Place de la Bastille

MONTMARTRE

PARIS

MONTPARNASSE

SEINE

NINETEENTH–CENTURY CITY LIMIT

Ateliers of Major Artists

A	Cezanne	H	David
B	Manet	I	Delacroix
C	Degas	J	Courbet
D	Moreau	K	Daumier
E	Gericault	L	Seurat
F	Rodin	M	Rousseau
G	Ingres		

THE NINETEENTH CENTURY: PLURALISM OF STYLE

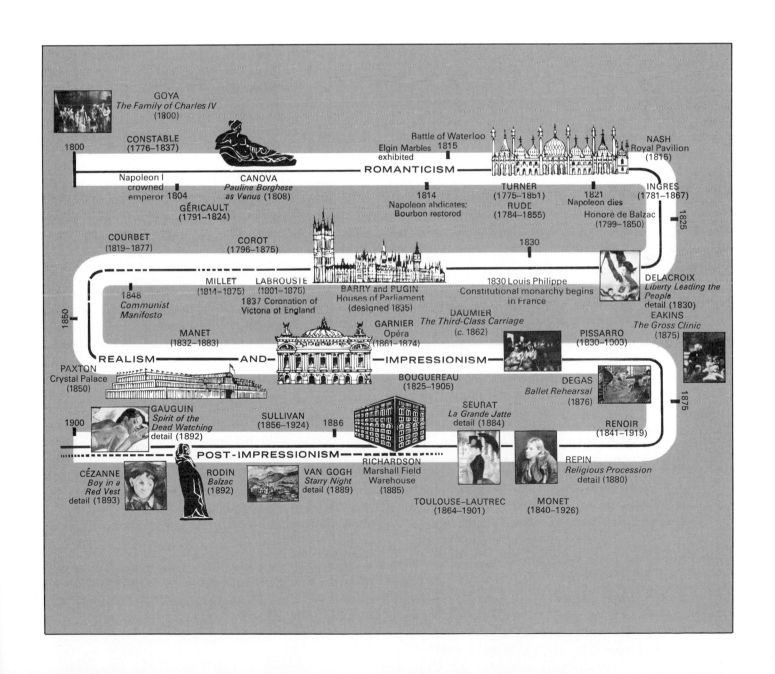

GOYA
The Family of Charles IV
(1800)

CONSTABLE
(1776–1837)

1800

Battle of Waterloo
Elgin Marbles 1815
exhibited

NASH
Royal Pavilion
(1815)

ROMANTICISM

Napoleon I
crowned
emperor 1804

CANOVA
*Pauline Borghese
as Venus* (1808)

1814
Napoleon abdicates;
Bourbon restored

TURNER
(1775–1851)
RUDE
(1784–1855)

1821
Napoleon dies

INGRES
(1781–1867)

1825

GÉRICAULT
(1791–1824)

Honoré de Balzac
(1799–1850)

COURBET
(1819–1877)

COROT
(1796–1875)

1830

DELACROIX
*Liberty Leading the
People*
detail (1830)

MILLET
(1814–1875)

LABROUSTE
(1801–1875)

BARRY and PUGIN
Houses of Parliament
(designed 1835)

1830 Louis Philippe
Constitutional monarchy begins
in France

EAKINS
The Gross Clinic
(1875)

1850

1848
*Communist
Manifesto*

1837 Coronation of
Victoria of England

DAUMIER
The Third-Class Carriage
(c. 1862)

MANET
(1832–1883)

GARNIER
Opéra
(1861–1874)

PISSARRO
(1830–1903)

REALISM ——— AND ——— IMPRESSIONISM

PAXTON
Crystal Palace
(1850)

BOUGUEREAU
(1825–1905)

DEGAS
Ballet Rehearsal
(1876)

1875

1900

GAUGUIN
*Spirit of the
Dead Watching*
detail (1892)

SULLIVAN
(1856–1924)

1886

SEURAT
La Grande Jatte
detail (1884)

RENOIR
(1841–1919)

POST-IMPRESSIONISM

RICHARDSON
Marshall Field
Warehouse
(1885)

REPIN
Religious Procession
detail (1880)

CÉZANNE
*Boy in a
Red Vest*
detail (1893)

RODIN
Balzac
(1892)

VAN GOGH
Starry Night
detail (1889)

TOULOUSE–LAUTREC
(1864–1901)

MONET
(1840–1926)

FOR EUROPE, the nineteenth century was an age of radical change during which the modern world took shape. In a world experiencing a population explosion of unprecedented magnitude, revolution followed on revolution, punctuated by counterrevolution and conservative reaction. Authority was ceaselessly challenged and reaffirmed in all areas of experience. In the political world, democratic governments were demanded, and the demand was resisted. Social and economic struggle pitted industrial capitalism and the bourgeoisie against the teeming and widely impoverished industrial masses. Reform was everywhere urged and often adopted. The technological transformation of the environment that began in the eighteenth century pushed forward with immense speed and made possible European colonization of the globe. The formation of empires abroad was backed by the enthusiasm of popular nationalism at home, and patriotism and imperialism went hand in hand. Improvements in transportation and communication quickened the exchange of ideas and the dissemination of information, propaganda, and opinion. These, in turn, incited competition and conflict among interests and values, theories and practices, programs and policies in all spheres of action—not the least in the arts.

A profound sense of history pervaded the century. The past was rapidly receding, and a unique present was asserting its originality—as decisively as the Early Christian world asserted *its* new value against the defeated and devalued pagan past. The new age, created by the great revolutions, was *modern,* and modern, for many, was good. What was not modern was rejected, for what was to come would be better. This was the doctrine of Progress, which maintained the permanency of change for the better. As early as 1750, Turgot had predicted that the doctrine of Progress would replace that of the will of God.

Many in the nineteenth century did not accept the doctrine of Progress, or did so with reservations—often with grave misgivings. They saw much of value being lost through change and feared for the traditions, institutions, customs, and mores that knit society together and gave meaning to life. They could accept neither the depreciation of human value implicit in scientific explanations of human nature nor the alienation and degradation of human beings by a mechanized and impersonal industry. They had special distaste for the type of modern society built by new wealth, with all its ostentatious materialism. Many who objected to the vulgarity and banality of taste of that society were artists—some of them, the best artists of the century. In a moment, we shall describe their predicament.

The liberal belief in progress is a belief that the course of history can be changed by thought and action, as long as people are not impeded by authority. The great debate of the nineteenth century was about authority: what should be believed, respected, defended, conformed to? Revolutionary shake-ups of authority reverberated throughout the century, carrying the hope of peoples for something newer, better, truer, and purer. Humanity was thought to be perfectible, and the principle of utility—calling for the greatest good of the greatest number—was advocated for law, government, and economic life. But confusion arose over the means to these ends, a confusion that produced a wide multiplicity of philosophies rationalizing change and the reactions to change. These ideologies, which provided the maxims and slogans of the countless movements that agitated the century and remain current, are the "isms": liberalism, radicalism, socialism, communism, conservatism, nationalism—all coinages of the nineteenth century. We will presently meet their counterparts in the world of art: Romanticism, Realism, Naturalism, Impressionism, and the rest.

What all of these ideologies have in common is dissatisfaction with a status quo, in which the past lingers, and disagreement about how it should be corrected—that is, modernized. For the arts, this means continuing debate over the relative values of the "traditional" and the "modern"—a debate restimulated as each new style is itself rapidly superseded by yet a newer one. This rapid appearance and obsolescence of a variety of artistic styles (analogous to the concurrent rapid turnover in types of mechanically produced commodities and to the quick progression of scientific and technological discoveries and inventions) transforms painting, the graphic arts, sculpture, and architecture so radically that the transformations amount to a dismantling of tradition altogether and the appearance of something utterly novel. This is the reverse of the development of science, which builds on its tradition in largely unbroken continuity within the expanding language of mathematics.

The nineteenth-century artist had to face formidable changes on all sides. As sources of artists' commissions, the Church and the secular nobility were replaced by the triumphant middle class (the bourgeoisie), the national state, and national academies. The new, uncultivated taste of large publics—concerned, above all, with money and property and guided and manipulated by the new profession of public critics writing in the press—created an uncertain and risky market for the artist working alone, like a preindustrial handicraftsman. Competition (their number had more than doubled since the end of the previous century) forced crowds of artists, influenced by the fluctuations of fashion and by their natural desire for success, to bid for the public's attention by flattering its taste. Like small, independent capitalists with their own stocks and stores, artists took chances in the market, aiming to please. Where they did not, they risked the suspicion and the hostility of the public. Thus, the century witnessed the gradual alienation of the artists and the emergence of their problematic situation in modern society.

Artists who were dissatisfied with standards of public taste and the professional performances designed to satisfy it protested, in their own work and through that of friendly critics, what they called the degeneration of art into shallow entertainment. Highly individualistic and imbued with the romantic ideals of self-expression, they called for a new vision—original and sincere, free from the sentimentalities, trivialities, and hypocrisies of conventional taste. Rejecting the authority of prevailing taste and of the institutions backing it, they claimed the right to an authority of their own, often with a sense of mission not unlike that of the seer and prophet: to restore or re-create art. These artists tended to group or be grouped into parties or "movements," analogous to those in political life and recognizable by their opposition to the status quo. Whichever side they occupied in the complex, stylistic dialogues that took place, they were, in fact, debating in a new way the very nature of art and the function of the artist. As it turns out, they were dealing with the question of a *modern* art, one fundamentally different from that of the past even though it might be constructed out of the "tradition" to greater or lesser degree.

The Tradition, as we will refer to it, was the whole corpus of art acknowledged to be good or great: the art of Greece and Rome, of the Renaissance, and of the Baroque. These occupied a stylistic spectrum from "classical idealism" to "optical realism" that seemed to exhaust the physical possibilities of the media as well as their thematic content. The Tradition was first challenged and, by the end of the century, rejected for an art "of our own times," a *modern* art. In the course of the century, challenge was met by response, and response by new challenge, so that the modes of traditional and modern were interwoven, combined, recombined, and separated by independent artists, producing a bewildering plurality of individual styles that are not easily categorized. Although we will use the conventional categories of art history—"Romanticism," "Realism," "Impressionism," and so on—as markers, these terms cannot help but be indefinite and often misleading. What we *do* perceive by mid-century is a bifurcation of the pictorial arts not heretofore seen. It is a bifurcation of specialty and purpose: one branch, optical realism, leading to the photograph and the motion picture; the other, imaginative figuration, leading to the abstract art of the twentieth century. The former is di-rected to the public and popular taste; the latter, for the most part, to a select, specially trained audience.

It is necessary, finally, to point out the factors that contributed to this historical division. Painters in the nineteenth century were confronted by three innovations that fatefully affected their craft: the camera, the mass-produced print, and the printed reproduction. The almost infinite proliferation of the products of these new media flooded the world with images that became formidable rivals of the unique picture made by hand. In a way, the nineteenth-century artist was technologically displaced, as the manuscript illuminator was by the printer in the sixteenth century. Moreover, the collective techniques of an industrial age forced the artists, as individual craftsmen, to analyze their function and to study closely the physical nature of their medium—paint on a flat surface. Mechanically produced images sap the iconic function of painting insofar as painting replicates, through tone-matching, the optical world of human experience. Toward the end of the century, artists will find themselves with canvas and paint, using the elements of line, shape, and color to represent their private world, the realm of imagination and feeling. The functions of the artist and of the artist's medium will be decisively transformed by the modern world, and the art of that world is sundered from the Tradition.

THE FIRST HALF OF THE NINETEENTH CENTURY: THE PREDOMINANCE OF ROMANTICISM

The revolutions that usher in the modern world are accompanied by a widespread agitation of spirit—a kind of collective *mental* revolution, the emotional response to accelerating change. We have already met Romanticism in the eighteenth century, noting its rise and the problems of its definition and its period. It continues and sharpens the eighteenth-century concern for human freedom and equality, for liberty of thought and expression, for the abrogation of traditions, institutions, and privileges that have held back human progress. Romanticism as a view of life, as well as a state of mind, inherits the Enlightenment's admiration of nature and the natural, over convention and artifice, and continues to uncover history as a store of natural lessons for correcting the defects of the present.

The emphasis on human rights in the public sphere is accompanied by the assertion of the value of feeling and emotion in private experience. Truth can be sought and found inwardly more surely than in doctrines of religion or rules of reason; for Romanticism's orientation is subjective, and the intensity of the religious and mystical emotions associated with traditional Christianity could live on in the individual, with or without reference to specific creeds. The ardor of Romanticism is religious, as is its soul-searching and truth-seeking through feeling and vision. The pantheistic union of the soul with nature—nature, for many, replacing the Christian God—is part of the Romantic ritual and excitement. T.E. Hulme defines Romanticism as "spilled religion": the old doctrinal vessels are broken, and their volatile contents spread widely and indefinitely.

Indefinitely—because there are really no fixed doctrines for Romanticism; in a world of critical change, where all that is fixed, dogmatic, and categorical is challenged, how could there be? On issues of the day, we can find Romantic spirits on opposing sides: progressive and conservative, democratic and monarchist, religious and agnostic, hoping and despairing, satanic and angelic. The world of history, for example, now being systematically recovered, could be valued as serving the hopes of new nations by showing them the heroic past, by supplying them with an identity. Or it could be regarded as a nightmare from which the present is trying to wake; "The world," wrote Percy Bysshe Shelley, "is weary of the past / O might it die, or rest at last!"

Romanticism—protean as the modern world it reflects and, like the modern mind, incorrigibly romantic—has one firm conviction at its center: the identity of reality is rooted in the self, not in the external, man-made world. The search for this identity—the revelation and expression of it in art and life—is the objective and meaning of personal existence. Jean Jacques Rousseau preaches the religion of the value of the individual in a single assertion: "I may be no better than anyone else; at least I am different." For the Romantic, it is the difference that counts.

Despite the plurality of styles in the nineteenth century, the artist's claim of autonomy is a constant, and this individualism can sometimes result in alienation. The right to be an individual authority justifies this procedure, even when an artist chooses to accept the authority of, say, the academies. The broad right to choose a mode of expression is then matched by the broad range of materials supplied by the Tradition—from which the artist chooses, or chooses to turn aside. The artist's motives may be various: to stir an audience with drama or melodrama; to reconstruct historical incident; to exhibit the beauty of the human figure, landscape, still life, and other traditional subjects; to present the genre of modern life; to paint the inventions of a fertile imagination; to externalize dreams as images, private and strange. The subjects, modes of representation, and techniques of the artists of the nineteenth century, various as they may be, are all derived from a common attitude and claim of autonomy.

In this earlier century of the modern era, then, the subject matter of art is predominantly "romantic," in that the artist stresses dramatic emotion or ideal beauty, or combinations of these with other material. "Romantic" artists will discover their themes in history, literature, religion—the exotic and the esoteric—and draw on the pictorial modes of the Tradition, the Classical, the Renaissance, and the Baroque. "Romantic" architects will recover the historical styles of Western architecture and the non-European world and parade them dramatically. Historical and literary material, often produced with a photographic realism, will predominate. It is this retrospective subject matter, seeming apart or escaping from the specifically modern scene, that, in part, invites the use of the term "romanticism." Yet we shall see that Romanticism is a vital principle that survives into the twentieth century and that much of contemporary art is also, in essence, subjective—an intellectual and emotional reflection of always accelerating and demanding change.

Architecture

The Romantic Neoclassical taste for the more-or-less exact replication of Greek and Roman buildings, as we have seen it expressed in Thomas Jefferson's statehouse (FIG. 20-27), spread throughout Europe and America. From Virginia to Munich, from Paris to St. Petersburg, Neoclassicism could be romantically associated with revolutionary aspirations to primitive democratic purity or with imperial ambitions for unshakable authority. Begun in 1808, at the zenith of Napoleon's power, La Madeleine in Paris (FIG. 21-1) was intended to be a temple of honor for Napoleon's armies and a monument to the newly won glory of France; it was converted to a church before its completion in 1842. Designed by PIERRE VIGNON (1763–1828) as an octastyle peripteral temple, its high podium and the broad flight of stairs leading to a deep porch simulate the buildings of the time of the first caesars, making La Madeleine a symbolic link between the Napoleonic and Roman empires. A curious feature of the building is the fact that its Classical shell surrounds an interior that is covered by a sequence of three domes; a feature found in Byzantine or Aquitanian Romanesque churches has been clothed in the costume of Pagan Rome.

While Romantic Neoclassicism flourished, the Romantic Gothic taste by no means died; it paralleled the former and took on new significance, a religious and national one. In 1802, Chateaubriand published his influential *Genius of Christianity*—a defense of religion (against the skeptical rationalism of the Enlight-

21-1 Pierre Vignon, La Madeleine, Paris, begun 1808.

enment and the French Revolution) on the grounds, not of its truth, but of its beauty and mystery. "There is nothing," Chateaubriand says, "of beauty, sweetness, or greatness in life that does not partake in mystery." This is a significant contradiction of "Be thou clear!"—the classical injunction from the "age of reason." Christian ritual and Christian art, born of mystery, move adherents by their strange and ancient beauty. Gothic cathedrals, according to Chateaubriand, are translations into stone of the sacred groves of the Druidical Gauls and must be cherished as manifestations of France's holy history. In his view, the history of Christianity and that of France merged in the Middle Ages. As the nineteenth century gathered the documentary materials of European history in a stupendous historiographic enterprise, each nation came to value its past as evidence of the validity of its ambitions and claims to greatness. The art of the remote past was now appreciated as a product of racial and national genius. In 1773, Goethe, praising the

Gothic cathedral of Strasbourg in *Of German Architecture*, declares that the German art scholar "should thank God to be able to proclaim aloud that it is German architecture, our architecture . . ."; he bids the observer "approach and recognize the deepest feeling of truth and beauty of proportion emanating from a strong, vigorous German soul . . . ." This was at a time when Gothic architecture, even though enjoyed as picturesque, was generally disparaged as a style inferior to Classical architecture.

Modern nationalism thus brought about a new evaluation of the art in each country's past. In London, when the old Houses of Parliament burned in 1834, the Parliamentary Commission decreed that designs for the new building should be either "Gothic or Elizabethan." Charles Barry (1795–1860), with the assistance of A.W.N. Pugin (1812–1852), submitted the winning design in 1835, and the work was carried on from the 1840s into the 1860s (fig. 21-2). By this time, style had become a matter of selection from

21-2 Charles Barry and A.W.N. Pugin, Houses of Parliament, London, designed 1835.

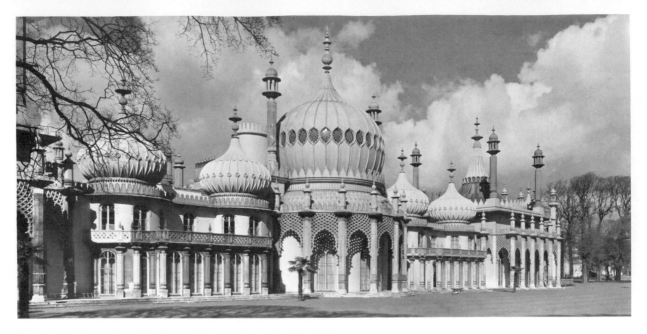

21-3 JOHN NASH, Royal Pavilion, Brighton, England, 1815–1818.

the historical supply. Barry preferred the Classical, but Pugin influenced him successfully in the direction of English Late Gothic. Pugin was one of a group of English artists and critics that included WILLIAM MORRIS and John Ruskin, who saw moral purity and spiritual authenticity in the religious architecture of the Middle Ages and glorified the careful Medieval craftsmen who had produced it. The Industrial Revolution was now flooding the market with cheaply made and ill-designed commodities; handicraft had been replaced by the machine, and men like Pugin believed in the necessity of restoring the old craftsmanship, which had honesty and quality. The design of the Houses of Parliament, however, is not genuinely Gothic, despite its picturesque tower group-

ings. It has a formal axial plan and a kind of Palladian regularity beneath its Tudor detail. Pugin himself is reported to have said of it: "All Grecian, sir, Tudor details on a classic body."*

Neoclassical and Gothic architecture dominate the early nineteenth century, but exotic styles of all sorts, with fancifully mixed ingredients borrowed from the East, began to appear, especially in connection with places of recreation. At Brighton, England—the shore resort fashionable during the reign of the prince regent, later George IV—JOHN NASH (1752–1835) built the Royal Pavilion (FIG. 21-3) from 1815 to 1818. A confection of Islamic domes, minarets, and

*In Nikolaus Pevsner, *An Outline of European Architecture* (Baltimore: Penguin, 1960), p. 627.

21-4 J.L. CHARLES GARNIER, the Opéra, Paris, 1861–1874.

screens, this "Indian Gothic" structure, an appropriate enough backdrop for gala throngs pursuing pleasure by the seaside, served as the prototype of any number of playful architectural exaggerations that can still be found at European and American resorts.

By mid-century, Renaissance and Baroque had been added to the stylistic repertory. France under Napoleon III, the "Second Empire," expanded its vast holdings in Africa and Asia, and its businessmen obeyed the statesman Guizot's patriotic admonition—made early in the previous reign of Louis Philippe—to get rich. The opulence of the period is mirrored in the Paris Opéra (FIG. 21-4), designed by J.L. CHARLES GARNIER (1825–1898). Built between 1861 and 1874, the Opéra parades a festive and spectacularly theatrical front that should be compared with the façade of the Louvre (FIG. 19-65), which it mimics to a degree. The interior is ingeniously planned for the convenience of human traffic. Intricate arrangements of corridors, vestibules, stairways, balconies, alcoves, entrances, and exits facilitate easy passage throughout and provide space for entertainment and socializing at intermissions. The Baroque grandeur of the layout and of the ornamental appointments of the opera house proclaim and enhance its function as a gathering place for glittering audiences in an age of conspicuous wealth. Until the First World War, theaters and opera houses will reflect the Paris Opéra design.

Sculpture

As in architecture, there are several Romantic styles in nineteenth-century sculpture, but their sequence and character are naturally closer to those of painting. A Romantic Classicism is strongly determinative of the work of ANTONIO CANOVA (1757–1822). His reclining portrait-figure of *Pauline Borghese as Venus* (FIG. 21-5) shows him to be learned in the traits of Classicism—drapery, pose, form, and feature. That he adroitly draws the likeness of his subject within the

21-5 ANTONIO CANOVA, *Pauline Borghese as Venus*, 1808. Marble, life-size. Galleria Borghese, Rome.

almost standard outlines of a Classical statue shows that he is not slavishly bound by Neoclassical doctrine. At the same time, with quite remarkable discretion, Canova creates a daring image of seductive charm that is generalized enough to personify the goddess of love rather than to exhibit the living person. Both the voluptuousness and the tact with which he veils it recall the earlier Rococo, when esteemed ladies were often represented as seminude goddesses. The realism of the couch and its drapery, however, almost betray Canova into a too graphic presentation. Despite a lingering Rococo charm and realistic accessories, Canova is firmly Neoclassical in his approach. Considered the greatest sculptor of his time, he has suffered greatly in reputation since. Present criticism has restored him a little, although he still carries, as the most typical of Neoclassicists, something of the burden of negative criticism laid on that often doctrinaire and artificial style. Its defects can be seen well enough in a statue of *George Washington* (FIG. 21-6) by the American sculptor HORATIO GREENOUGH (1805–1852). Here the sculptor aims at monumental majesty, perhaps with a Classical Zeus in mind; but whether his subject was not susceptible of deification or whether the Realistic temper of the period simply could not bring the concepts of ancient god and modern man together, the statue was considered a failure in Greenough's time; today, it is

21-6 HORATIO GREENOUGH, *George Washington*, 1832–1841. Marble, approx. 11' 4" high. Smithsonian Institution, Washington, D.C.

21-7 FRANÇOIS RUDE, "La Marseillaise," Arc de Triomphe, Paris, 1833–1836. Approx. 42' × 26'.

more highly regarded. The father of his country, wearing his eighteenth-century wig and with ancient drapery and nude torso, approximates the period's image of a majestic law-giver. The statue manifests, more than many of its Neoclassical age, the contradictions that sometimes develop when idealization and realistic illusionism meet. Canova appears to harmonize these two trends; Greenough puts them in opposition. Most nineteenth-century monumental sculpture, especially in the Neoclassical mode, seems stiff, cold, or simply unconvincing. Nevertheless,

Greenough's statue has an imperious majesty appropriate to the national memory of its subject.

One monumental group, however, done between 1833 and 1836 and recalling the Baroque, still moves us—the so-called "La Marseillaise" (FIG. 21-7) by FRANÇOIS RUDE (1784–1855). The colossal figures, in bold relief against the Arc de Triomphe in Paris, represent French volunteers leaving to defend the borders of France against the foreign enemies of the revolution in 1792. They are dressed in Classical armor, and the Roman war goddess, Bellona (who may be thought of here as La Marseillaise, or the Goddess of Liberty), shouts the battle cry as she rallies the militia forward. The Classical accessories do not disguise the essentially Baroque qualities of the group—the densely packed masses, jagged contours, violence of motion. If we were to think here of the Classical at all, it would be of the "post-classical baroque" of Hellenistic works like the great frieze at Pergamon (FIG. 5-79).

This explosive style, here effective enough in sculpture, finds its natural medium in Romantic painting. Stormy emotion and untamed nature, those obsessions of Romanticism, require a style full of movement and color; and, to make them sharply convincing to the spectator, they require as realistic a representation as possible. Animal ferocity, which nineteenth-century taste generally does not permit to be shown at full in human beings, Romanticism describes in brute beasts. ANTOINE LOUIS BARYE (1795–1875) was a specialist in such depiction. His *Jaguar Devouring a Hare* (FIG. 21-8), painful as the subject is, draws us irresistibly to it by its fidelity to brute nature; the belly-crouching cat's swelling muscles, hunched shoulders, and tense spine—even the switch of the tail—tell of Barye's long sessions of observing the beasts in the Jardin des Plantes in Paris. The work tells, too, of the influence of the vast, exotic world of animal life—a geography opening before the naturalistic eyes and temper of the nineteenth century, from which artists, novelists, and poets, as well as scientists, would draw increasing knowledge and inspiration.

21-8 ANTOINE LOUIS BARYE, *Jaguar Devouring a Hare*, 1850–1851. Bronze, approx. 16" × 37". Louvre, Paris.

Painting

GOYA

Painting in the nineteenth century, touched strongly by the spirit of Romanticism, proves to be a far more sensitive medium for the kind of personal expression we would expect from the Romantic subjectivity of the time. At the very beginning of the modern period stands the imposing figure of FRANCISCO GOYA (1746–1828), the great independent painter of Spain. Founder of no school and acknowledging indebtedness to Diego Velázquez, Rembrandt van Rijn, and "nature," Goya takes his place as a giant of the Romantic age. He ranges from the Late Venetian Baroque of Giambattista Tiepolo through a brilliant Impressionistic Realism of his own, to a Late Expressionism in which dark and powerful distortions anticipate much of the violence, pain, and psychic upheaval in the art of the twentieth century. Goya is a great transitional figure, who changes the tradition while he manifests the present and prophesies the future of pictorial art. From a much higher vantage point than most of his contemporaries, he often depicts, in a bitter and unsparing revelation, the capacity of man for evil. Great Spanish painting is rarely sentimental; it insists, often with ruthless honesty, on the cruel facts of life. The art of Goya is no exception; it is for the strong-minded and the strong-nerved.

Little of the grim account of humanity foreshadowed in "The Dream of Reason" (FIG. 20-44) can be seen in Goya's early, vivacious manner, brilliantly adapted from Tiepolo. At the royal court in Madrid, where his precocious talent had brought him early in his career, Goya produced a series of genre paintings designed to serve as models for tapestries. Their prevailing mood of gaiety is the mood of the Rococo. But the noonday blitheness of Goya's early style soon wanes.

His experiences as painter to Charles IV, at whose sensationally corrupt court he lived, must have fostered his unsentimental, hard-eyed realism. In his large painting of *The Family of Charles IV* (FIG. 21-9), probably inspired by Velázquez's *Las Meninas* (FIG. 19-37), Goya presents, with a straight face, a menagerie of human grotesques who, critics have long been convinced, must not have had the intelligence to realize that the artist was caricaturing them. This superb revelation of stupidity, pomposity, and vulgarity, painted in 1800, led a later critic to summarize the subject as the "grocer and his family who have just won the big lottery prize." The painter, by his canvas, is dimly discernible at the left; his features impassively ironical, he looks beyond his subjects to the observer. Here, Goya exhibits his extraordinary skill as a colorist and manager of the oil medium. The colors float with a quiet iridescence across the surface, and the paint is applied with deft economy. Great solidity is suggested by the most transparent tones. A magician of optical pictorialism, Goya uses the methods of his great predecessor Velázquez.

Goya sharpened his criticisms of human vanity and vice in a series of satirical paintings and prints done between 1794 and 1799 called *Los Caprichos*, "The Caprices" (FIG. 20-44), in which monsters, grotesques, and caricatured men and women represent the repulsiveness of stupidity and folly. But the intervention of Napoleon Bonaparte in Spain in 1808 and the ensuing conflict gave Goya a new subject: not the foolishness of human ways, but the horror of war. In paintings and etchings, without national bias (although he was a patriot) and without mercy for the viewers' sensitivities, Goya exhibits the atrocities men visit on one another—no matter the issues, no matter the persons involved. His is a peculiarly modern vision; Picasso, in his *Guernica* (FIG. 22-16), which

21-9 FRANCISCO GOYA, *The Family of Charles IV*, 1800. Approx. 9' 2" × 11'. Museo del Prado, Madrid.

21-10   FRANCISCO GOYA, *The Third of May, 1808*, 1814. Approx. 8′ 8″ × 11′ 3″. Museo del Prado, Madrid.

he calls "brutality and darkness," gives us Goya's vision once again, translating his truth into a different formal language.

In *The Third of May, 1808* (FIG. 21-10) a French firing squad butchers citizens of Madrid by lamplight after the fall of the city. Unlike the subtle, even suave, realism of *The Family of Charles IV*, Goya's method here is coarse and extreme in its departure from optical fact. The postures and gestures of the figures are shockingly distorted to signal defiance, hatred, and terror. In keeping with the distortions of the figures, the color is acid and harsh, wrenched out of any normal harmony. Violent suffering and death can be rendered only in painful dissonances of shape and color. It is recorded that Goya visited the site of the event and made sketches.

Goya's perception of the insignificance of human life, of death and suffering in war, and of the obscen-

ity of human wreckage is vented bitterly in a series of aquatint etchings entitled *The Disasters of War*. A print in that series, *Tampoco*, or "Neither Nor" (FIG. 21-11),

21-11   FRANCISCO GOYA, *Tampoco*, 1810. Aquatint etching, from *The Disasters of War*. Courtesy of The New York Public Library (Astor, Lenox, and Tilden Foundations).

21-12 FRANCISCO GOYA, *Saturn Devouring His Children*, 1819–1823. Detail of a detached fresco on canvas, full size approx. 57″ × 32″. Museo del Prado, Madrid.

Employing an overriding irony and ingenious compositions, his refined art serves as a scourge of human complacency. Goya's strength as a graphic artist lies in his astonishing economy of means. Like a master of pantomime, he gives us only a few cues, strengthening the force and meaning of gestures by abbreviating and simplifying them. He reduces all to the essential. It is this that recommends Goya to the painters and graphic artists who follow him, like Honoré Daumier.

The folly and brutalities he witnessed and his own increasing infirmities, including deafness, combined to depress Goya's outlook and led to his late "dark style." In ominous midnight colors, he creates a whole population of subhuman monsters who worship the devil and swarm in nightmares. *Saturn Devouring His Children* (FIG. 21-12) is one product of this pessimistic and misanthropic style. Saturn (Time), glaring in lunatic frenzy, is devouring part of a small body clutched in his hands. The forms are torn and jagged; the colors, raw. Life is in time, and time devours us all. Goya's horror is not merely of man's inhumanity to man, but of life itself. This appalling work came from a supreme artist who had evidently become convinced that "The Dream of Reason Produces Monsters" (FIG. 20-44).

GIRODET, BARON GROS, GÉRICAULT

In France, Jacques Louis David demanded that his pupils select their subjects from Plutarch, ancient author of the *Lives of the Great Greeks and Romans* and principal source of standard Classical subject matter. But often they found their subjects elsewhere. ANNE LOUIS GIRODET-TRIOSON (1767–1824) turned to a popular novel by Chateaubriand, *Atala*, to produce his *Burial of Atala* (FIG. 21-13), a picture that could be a set

shows a French soldier brutalized by his profession to the point of utter indifference to the death of others, lounging in a grove of hanged Spanish peasants and gazing with vague boredom at a miscellaneous victim. Goya, one of the greatest masters of the graphic arts, is at his very best in the *Disasters* series, as he sets out—in the most striking simplicity of sharp shapes, light and dark—the ghastly tableau of death.

21-13 ANNE LOUIS GIRODET-TRIOSON, *The Burial of Atala*, 1808. Approx. 6′ 11″ × 8′ 9″. Louvre, Paris.

21-14 Antoine Jean Gros, *Pest House at Jaffa*, 1804. Approx. 17′ 5″ × 23′ 7″. Louvre, Paris.

piece for Romanticism. Atala, sworn to lifelong virginity, falls passionately in love with a wild, young savage of the Carolina wilderness. Rather than break her oath, she commits suicide and is buried in the shadow of the cross by her distracted lover; the Holy Church is represented in the person of a gentle priest. Thus, Girodet daringly puts religion and sexual passion side by side, binding them with the theme of death and burial. Hopeless love, perished beauty, the grave, the consolation of religion, the purity of primitive life—these are some of the thematic constants of Romanticism that Girodet successfully interweaves. The picture's composite style combines classicizing contours and modeling with a dash of the erotic sweetness of the Rococo and the dramatic illumination of the Baroque. The appeal is to the viewer's private world of fantasy and emotion, unlike David's appeal to the feelings that manifest themselves in public action. If David's purpose is to "electrify the soul," Girodet's is, in the language of Rousseau, to "wring the heart." In either case, the artist speaks to our emotions, rather than inviting philosophical meditation or revealing some grand order of nature and form. The Romantic artist, whether David, Girodet, or any other, wants to excite his audience.

Another pupil of David, the Baron ANTOINE JEAN GROS (1771–1835), deviates from his master's teachings quite as much as—and much more influentially

than—Girodet. In his *Pest House at Jaffa* (FIG. 21-14), painted in 1804, he takes a radically independent tack, sorting through and selecting numerous Baroque pictorial devices of light, shade, and perspective to stage, as dramatically as possible, a tableau testifying to the superhuman power and glory of Napoleon Bonaparte. A comparison of the *Oath of the Horatii* (FIG. 20-38) with the *Pest House* illustrates Gros' departure from David. The works are similar in that they stage an action within an architectural enframement, the figures being deployed before an arcade; but David's arcade is Roman and Gros' is Moorish, and the vista through Gros' arcade is of a distant landscape, a fortress, and the tricolor flag of the revolution. Time has changed the setting, and the painter's means have changed to suit the present. Gros, using every device to focus the viewer's attention on the central figure of the hero, dismisses most theoretical considerations of Classical balance and modeling and poses Napoleon as a stage director would, making the fullest use of stage lights and dramatic darkness to center the figure of the chief protagonist. His purpose is to elevate a historical event to an act of almost religious significance and solemnity, in which Napoleon, the messiah of democracy, plays simultaneously the roles of Alexander, Christ, and Louis XIV. Bonaparte, the First Consul, not yet Emperor Napoleon I, at the end of the disastrous Egyptian campaign, has retreated up the coast of Palestine (modern Israel). His army is stricken with the plague, and he is shown visiting his sick and dying soldiers in a hospital in the ancient city of Jaffa. There in the midst of the dead and dying, the fearless genius of the New Order touches the plague sores of a sick soldier, who stares at him in awe, as if he were the miracle-working Christ. The staff officers stop their noses against the stench of the place, but the general is calm and unperturbed, like the king curing by the King's Touch. In the left foreground, men brood, crouch, and sprawl in a gloom of misery and anguish; these figures will be of special interest to later Romantic artists, like Théodore Géricault and Eugène Delacroix. The whole scene is wrapped in the glamor of its Near Eastern setting: the turbaned Moslem physician and his assistants, the Moorish arches, the exotic landscape. As with Girodet, we have identifiable, if not identical, themes: suffering and death, faith and personal heroism, the lure of distant places, patriotism—all that can appeal to the modern need for emotional stimulation; in a word, Romanticism.

With THÉODORE GÉRICAULT (1791–1824), the programed Classicism of the Davidian school fades and David's sharp light and shade and his insistent accuracy in rendering from nature come to the fore. This maturing of the naturalistic element present in David and his successors is, in Géricault's masterpiece, *Raft of the Medusa* (FIG. 21-15), quickened by the catalytic influences of Michelangelo and Peter Paul Rubens. David and Gros have already initiated the trend toward the dramatic presentation of contemporary events on huge canvases. Géricault takes for his theme the ordeal of the survivors of the French ship Medusa, which foundered off the west coast of Africa, laden with Algerian immigrants. The incident, a result of tragic mismanagement, caused a scandal, and Géricault's depiction of the anguish of the survivors on the raft was construed by the government as a political attack. Géricault chooses the most dramatic moment of the episode, when the frantic castaways attempt to attract the attention of a distant ship. The figures are piled on one another in every attitude of suffering, despair, and death, recalling the foreground figures in Gros' *Pest House at Jaffa* (FIG. 21-14). Powerful light and dark contrasts suit the violence of the twisting and writhing bodies. Although Baroque devices are everywhere present, Géricault's use of shock tactics that stun the viewer's sensibilities amounts to something new—a new tone and intention that distinguish the second and "high" phase of Romanticism. In this phase, an instinct for the sublime and the terrible—qualities already celebrated by the esthetic theory of the mid-eighteenth century—finds sharpest expression in the method of reportorial accuracy already noted in certain pictures by David (FIG. 20-39). Géricault, like a painstaking reporter out to "get the facts," interviewed survivors of the Medusa and made careful studies of dying men and dead bodies in preparation for his work.

His *Mounted Officer of the Imperial Guard* (FIG. 21-16), painted in 1812, shows the Romantic's admiration for

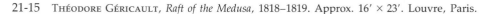

21-15 THÉODORE GÉRICAULT, *Raft of the Medusa*, 1818–1819. Approx. 16' × 23'. Louvre, Paris.

21-16 Théodore Géricault, *Mounted Officer of the Imperial Guard*, 1812. Approx. 9' 7" × 6' 4". Louvre, Paris.

21-17 Théodore Géricault, *Insane Woman* (*Envy*), 1822–1823. Approx. 28" × 21". Musée des Beaux-Arts, Lyons.

fierce power. Géricault's generation is born of the French Revolution and the Napoleonic Wars, in the midst of the thunder of cannon and cavalry. Military splendor, the glamor and pomp of war, its valor and terror—all are natural themes of the times; and pictures by Géricault and his contemporaries celebrate war's furious excitement rather than its horror and degradation. In his *Officer*, man and horse are as if one—part man, part beast. The Romantic obsession with the forces of nature extends to the subhuman in man and the "innocent cruelty" of beasts of prey. Here, Géricault throws his horse and rider into exaggerated gyrations in an effort to create an illusion of explosive action. His color and "open" form recall Rubens, but his intent is to thrill the viewer with the contemporary apparition of fury as he exalts the idea of the Napoleonic hero.

An interest in mental aberration, which contributed to the development of modern psychopathology later in the nineteenth century, is part of the Romantic fascination with the irregular and the abandoned. The inner storms that overthrow rationality could hardly fail to be of interest to the rebels against the "age of reason." Géricault, like many of his contemporaries, studied the influence of mental states on the human face and believed, as they did, that a man's face accurately reveals his character, especially in madness and at the instant of death. He made many studies of inmates of hospitals and institutions for the criminally insane (indeed, he spent some time as a patient in such places) and he studied the severed heads of victims of the guillotine. Scientific and artistic curiosity are not easily separated from the morbidity of the Romantic interest in derangement and death. Géricault's *Insane Woman* (*Envy*) (FIG. 21-17)— her face twisted, her eyes red-rimmed—leers with paranoid hatred in one of several "portraits" of insane subjects that have a peculiar hypnotic power and present the psychic facts with astonishing authenticity. The *Insane Woman* is only another example of the increasingly realistic core of Romantic painting. The closer the Romantics become involved with nature, sane or mad, the more they hope to get at the truth. For painting, this will increasingly come to mean the *optical* truth, as well as the truth to "the way things are." Meanwhile, for the Romantic, the real is nature, wild and untamed. In Géricault's paintings, suffering and death, battle frenzy, and madness amount to nature itself—for nature, in the end, is formless and destructive.

DELACROIX

It is evident that nature cares very little whether man has a mind or not. The real man is the savage; he is in accord with nature as she is. As soon as man sharpens his intelligence, increases his ideas and the way of expressing them, and acquires need, nature runs counter to him in everything.*

In these words Eugène Delacroix (1798–1863) succinctly gives us a clause from the Romantic's testament of nature and of man in nature.

*See *The Journal of Eugène Delacroix,* Walter Pach, trans. (New York: Grove Press, 1937, 1948).

We have seen that the qualities of the sublime and the terrible, and the emotions of awe and admiring wonder they produce, are most sought after by the Romantic poet and artist. As Delacroix writes in his famous journal: "Baudelaire* . . . says that I bring back to painting . . . the feeling which delights in the terrible. He is right. . . ." Delacroix, who knew and admired Géricault, greatly expands the expressive possibilities of Romantic art, developing its themes and elaborating its forms in the direction of ever-greater emotional power—in Romantic parlance, "sublimity." Literature of like power supplied him his subjects, and, as Baudelaire remarks in this regard, he "inherited from the great Republican and Imperial school [of David] a love of the poets and a strangely impulsive spirit of rivalry with the written word. David, Guérin, and Géricault kindled their minds at the brazier of Homer, Vergil, Racine, and Ossian. Delacroix was the soul-stirring translator of Shakespeare, Dante, Byron, and Ariosto. . . ." Since David, literature and art had been developing an ever-more intimate association. Their relation had already been established in the Renaissance. But in the Romantic age, much painting could almost be said to be "programed" by literature, as could most music (for example, Berlioz's *Harold in Italy*, after Lord Byron's *Childe Harold*). As we speak of "program" music, we can also speak of "program" art, and it is the "story picture" produced by this art that will evolve into the genre of the motion picture—a

*Charles Baudelaire (1821–1867), one of the nineteenth century's finest and most influential poets, was also a perceptive art critic.

composite of drama, narrative, sound, and pictures. In Delacroix, what starts with David culminates in the literature-inspired staging of exciting and disturbing human events, real or imaginary, and in a concern for the most accurate visual means of conveying them. From David to Delacroix, and in their lesser followers, the belief is that the purpose of pictorial art is to stir, to "electrify," and to render accurately and sympathetically the modern spirit in a modern look. This art is aimed at large publics—to move and to appeal to the new, populous democratic society. With the great, programmatic pictorialism of the Romantic period, we begin the truly modern and familiar experience of public spectacular drama—the production of thrilling stories, thrillingly staged.

Although the faculty of mind most valued by the Romantic is imagination, Delacroix realized that skill and restraint must go along with it. "In his eyes," Baudelaire writes of Delacroix, "imagination was the most precious gift, the most important faculty, but [he believed] that this faculty remained impotent and sterile if it was not served by a resourceful skill which could follow it in its restless and tyrannical whims." Delacroix's picture dramas are products of his view that the power of imagination—nourished and continually kindled by great literature, art, and music—will synthesize works that will catch and inflame the imagination of the observer. To be intensely imaginative is to be intensely alive.

An example of pictorial grand opera on a colossal scale is *The Death of Sardanapalus* (FIG. 21-18), which he painted in 1826. Undoubtedly, Delacroix was in-

21-18 EUGÈNE DELACROIX, *The Death of Sardanapalus*, 1826. Approx. 12' 1" × 16' 3". Louvre, Paris.

21-19 Eugène Delacroix, *Liberty Leading the People*, 1830. Approx. 8′ 6″ × 10′ 8″. Louvre, Paris.

spired by Lord Byron's narrative poem *Sardanapalus* and perhaps by other ancient sources, but here he relates the last hour of the ancient king in a much more tempestuous and crowded setting than Byron describes. Hearing of the defeat of his armies and the enemies' entry into his city, the king orders all of his most precious possessions—his women, slaves, horses, and treasure—destroyed in his sight while he watches gloomily from his funeral pyre, soon to be set alight. The king presides like a genius of evil over the panorama of destruction, most conspicuous in which are the tortured and dying bodies of his Rubenesque women; the one in the foreground is dispatched by an ecstatically murderous slave. This carnival of suffering and death is glorified by superb drawing and color, the most daringly difficult and tortuous poses, and the richest intensities of hues and contrasts of light and dark. The king is the center of the calamity, the quiet eye of a hurricane of form and color. It testifies to Delacroix's art that his center of meaning is placed away from the central action yet entirely controls it.

Generally, Delacroix chose his stories from either pre- or post-Classical periods and literature, but sometimes he dealt with a Greek subject that moved

him. Other sources of subjects were the events of his own time, notably popular struggles for freedom: the ill-fated revolt of the Greeks against Turkish rule in the 1820s; the Parisian revolution of 1830, which overthrew the restored Bourbons and placed Louis Philippe on the throne of France. In *Liberty Leading the People* (FIG. 21-19), done in 1830, Delacroix makes no attempt to represent a specific incident seen in actuality. Instead, he gives us an allegory of revolution itself. Liberty—a partly nude, majestic woman, whose beautiful features wear an expression of noble dignity—waves the people forward to the barricades, the familiar revolutionary apparatus of Paris streets. She carries the tricolor banner of the republic and a musket with a bayonet and wears the cap of Liberty. Her advance is over the dead and dying of both parties—the people, and the royal troops. Arrayed around her are bold Parisian types: the street boy brandishing his pistols, the menacing *prolétaire* with a cutlass, the intellectual dandy in plug hat and with sawed-off musket. The towers of Notre Dame rise through the smoke and clamor, witnessing the ancient tradition of liberty cherished by the people of Paris throughout the centuries. The *Liberty*, a document of the intimate union of revolution and Roman-

21-20 EUGÈNE DELACROIX, *Tiger Hunt*, 1854. Approx. 29" × 36". Louvre, Paris.

ticism, conveys the political temper of revolutionary Europe more powerfully than any other early nineteenth-century painting.

In terms of form, the *Liberty* still reflects the strong impression made on Delacroix by the art of Géricault, especially *Raft of the Medusa* (FIG. 21-15); the fact that Delacroix makes an allegory of *Liberty* shows that he was familiar with traditional conventions. The clutter of sprawling bodies in the foreground provides a kind of base to support the pyramiding figures in the central ground, building up to frantic energy from the heavy and the inert. The light flashes like the fire of guns, and the darks mingle freely with the lights, like drifting smoke roiled by cannon fire. The forms are generated from the Baroque, as they are in Géricault, but Delacroix's sharp agitation of them creates his own special brand of tumultuous excitement.

Delacroix, who could assert that "style can result only from great research," was ever studying the problems of his craft and ever searching for fresh materials to supply his imagination. He was able to visit North Africa in 1832, and what he found there shocked his imagination with impressions that would

last throughout his life. He discovered, in the sun-drenched landscape and in the hardy and colorful Arabs dressed in robes reminiscent of the Roman toga, new insights into a culture built on proud virtues—one that he believed to be more Classical than anything European Neoclassicism could conceive. "The Greeks and the Romans," he writes to a friend, "they are here, within my reach. I had to laugh heartily about the Greeks of David." Their gallantry, hardihood, valor, and fierce love of liberty made them, in Delacroix's eyes, "nature's noblemen"—unspoiled heroes, uninfected by European decadence.

The Moroccan journey renewed Delacroix's Romantic conviction that there is beauty in the fierceness of nature, natural processes, and natural beings, especially animals. After Morocco, more and more of Delacroix's subjects involved combats between beasts, and men and beasts (FIG. 21-20). He painted snarling tangles of lions and tigers, battles between horses, and clashes of Arabs with great cats in swirling hunting scenes. In these, what he had learned from the hunting pictures of Rubens (FIG. 19-40) mingles in explosive combination with his own visions, reinforced by his memories of the North African scene.

What Delacroix learned about color he passed on to later painters of the nineteenth century, most particularly to the Impressionists. He observed that pure colors are as rare in nature as lines, that color appears only in an infinitely varied scale of different tones, shadings, and reflections, which he tried to re-create in his paintings. He recorded his observations in his *Journal*, which became a veritable corpus of pre-Impressionistic color theory, acclaimed as such by the Neo-Impressionist painter PAUL SIGNAC in 1898–1899. Delacroix anticipates the later development of Impressionist color science, but that science had to await the discoveries by Michel Eugène Chevreul and Hermann von Helmholtz of the laws of light decomposition and the properties of complementary colors before its problems could be properly formulated. Nevertheless, Delacroix's observations are significant: "It is advisable not to fuse the brushstrokes," he writes, "as they will [appear to] fuse naturally at [a] . . . distance. In this manner, color gains in energy and freshness." This observation, suggested to him by his examination of a group of landscapes by John Constable, the great English landscape painter (FIG. 21-30), had strongly impressed Delacroix even before his color experiences in Morocco. He writes:

> Constable said that the superiority of the green he uses for his landscapes derives from the fact that it is composed of a multitude of different greens. What causes the lack of intensity and of life in verdure as it is painted by the common run of landscapists is that they ordinarily do it with a uniform tint. What he said about the green of meadows can be applied to all other tones.

Although these are primarily matters of technique and execution, Delacroix expresses his radical colorism most forcibly in the following statement: "Speaking radically, there are neither lights nor shades. There is only a color mass for each object, having different reflections on all sides." These observations were stimulated by Delacroix's Moroccan visit and do not consistently apply to his early works done under the influence of Géricault. This conception of the optical world as planes of color will find a new realization in the art of Paul Cézanne, who will make color planes serve a structural purpose in locking the composition together.

No other painter of the time explores the domain of Romantic subject and mood as thoroughly and definitively as Delacroix, and none matches his style and content. Delacroix's technique—impetuous, improvisational, instinctive, rather than deliberate, studious, and cold—epitomizes Romantic painting, catching the impression at the very beginning and developing it in the process of execution. We know how furiously Delacroix worked once he had an idea, keeping the whole painting progressing at once. The fury of his attack matches the fury of his imagination and his subjects. He is indeed the artist of passion. Baudelaire sums him up as "passionately in love with passion . . . an immense passion, reinforced with a formidable will—such was the man." In the end, his friend Silvestre, in the language of Romanticism, delivered a eulogy that amounts to a definition of the Romantic artist:

> Thus died, almost with a smile on August 13, 1863, that painter of great race, Ferdinand Victor Eugène Delacroix, who had a sun in his head and storms in his heart; who for forty years played upon the keyboard of human passions and whose brush—grandiose, terrible, or suave—passed from saints to warriors, from warriors to lovers, from lovers to tigers, and from tigers to flowers.

INGRES

The history of nineteenth-century painting in its first 60 years has often been interpreted as a contest between Delacroix, the colorist, and Ingres, the draftsman. They reach back to the end of the seventeenth century to revive the quarrel between "Poussinistes" and "Rubénistes," which pitted the conservative defenders of academicism, who held that drawing was superior to color, against the "Rubénistes," who proclaimed that color was not only more important to a painting than drawing, but had wider appeal than the more intellectual, and thus restrictive, quality of line. Even so, in the art of Delacroix and of his great rival Ingres, we must see the two as complementary rather than contradictory. They are part of the Romantic dialogue.

JEAN AUGUSTE DOMINIQUE INGRES (1781–1867) came to David's studio after Gros and Girodet had left to establish themselves as independent artists. But he did not stay very long, for he broke with David on matters of style. Ingres, feeling that David's art relied too heavily on nature, adopted a manner based on what he believed to be the true and pure Greek style: flat and linear figures approximating those in Greek vase paintings. This early manner was severely criticized as "primitive," even "Gothic," and one critic ridiculed Ingres' work as being the vision of "a Chinaman wandering through the ruins of Athens." Ingres' departure, both in form and content, from David and the French Royal Academy made him a kind of rebel, and the critics did not cease their attacks until the mid-1820s, when an even greater enemy of the official style, Delacroix, appeared. The critics then suddenly perceived that Ingres' art, despite its innovations and deviations, contained many elements that adhered to the official Classicism; he

21-21 JEAN AUGUSTE DOMINIQUE INGRES, *Oedipus and the Sphinx*, 1808. 6' 2" × 4' 8". Louvre, Paris.

was soon to become the leader of the academic forces in their battle against the "barbarism" of Géricault, Delacroix, and their party. Gradually, Ingres warmed to the role in which he was cast by the critics and came to believe himself to be the conservator of good and true art, protecting its principles from those advanced by the "destroyers" of art.

Ingres' *Oedipus and the Sphinx* (FIG. 21-21), painted in 1808, shows his avowed attempt to get at the reality of Greek art instead of the academic myth. He gives us the wise hero, Oedipus, answering the three fatal questions of the Sphinx—a winged, taloned

female monster who terrified the city of Thebes, killing all passersby who could not answer her questions. Oedipus answered, slew the Sphinx, delivered the city, and was made king of Thebes by the grateful citizens; his subsequent tragic history is related in one of the most magnificent dramatic works of ancient Greece, Sophocles' *Oedipus the King*. In Ingres' work, the figure is placed in the foreground, like a piece of low-relief sculpture. The pose is stable, even rigid; the gestures, a kind of pantomime of asking and answering. The value Ingres places on the flow of the contours is characteristic, not only in his early period, but for the rest of his career. For contour, which is simply shaded line, is all there is for Ingres, and drawing is the means of creating contour. Ingres has been credited with the famous slogan, the battle cry of his school, "Drawing is the probity of art," as well as with the statement—which places him squarely against Delacroix and resolutely for the view that the past must provide the model for the present— "Never a color too warm! It is antihistorical!" But Ingres is not always consistent in following his own doctrine—that is, to improve on nature as the Greeks did. Some years after painting the *Oedipus*, he angrily denied that he had "idealized" his model, insisting that the figure was the very image of his model, whom he had copied as faithfully as he could; Ingres is not always sure whether he is following the Greeks or his own often quite naturalistic bent in his search for beautiful form.

Although the *Grande Odalisque* (FIG. 21-22), painted in 1814, drew acid criticisms ("she has three vertebrae too many," "no bone, no muscle, no life"), it seems today to sum up Ingres' artistic intentions. But it also illustrates the rather strange mixture of Ingres' artistic

21-22 JEAN AUGUSTE DOMINIQUE INGRES, *Grande Odalisque*, 1814. Approx. 35" × 64". Louvre, Paris.

21-23 JEAN AUGUSTE DOMINIQUE INGRES, *François Marius Granet*, 1807. Approx. 28″ × 24″. Musée Granet, Aix-en-Provence.

allegiances. His subject, the reclining nude figure, is traditional, going back to Giorgione and Titian; but by converting her into an odalisque (an inhabitant of a Turkish harem), he makes a strong concession to the contemporary Romantic taste for the exotic. Ingres treats the figure in his own "sculpturesque" style: polished surfaces and simple rounded volumes controlled by rhythmically flowing contours. The smoothness of the planes of the body is complemented by the broken, busy shapes of the drapery. His admiration for Raphael is shown in the borrowing of that master's type of female head and headdress and in the inclination of the head, as seen in Raphael's *Madonna of the Chair* (not shown) in the Pitti Palace in Florence. But Ingres is drawing not only from the High Renaissance; his figure's languid pose and her proportions (small head, elongated limbs) betray his debt to such Mannerists as Parmigianino (FIG. 17-43), as does the generally cool color scheme.

Often criticized for not being a colorist, Ingres, in fact, had a superb color sense. It is true that he did not seem to think of his paintings primarily in terms of their color, as did Delacroix, but he did far more than simply tint his drawings for emphasis, as recommended by the Academy. In his best paintings, Ingres creates color and tonal relationships so tasteful and subtle as to render them unforgettable.

Although he always aspired to become a history painter in the academic sense, Ingres never really was successful with multifigured compositions. He is at

his best when he paints single figures and portraits; as a portraitist, he must be ranked among the greatest masters—one of the last in a field that will soon be dominated by the camera. Although the portrait of *François Marius Granet* (FIG. 21-23) is not, by itself, sufficient to demonstrate Ingres' great distinction in this field, it does show the artist's stagecraft in arranging the pose and adjusting the costume to bring out Granet's amiability, self-confident poise, and ever-so-slight swagger. Never insisting on likeness for its own sake, Ingres rarely fails to produce a striking characterization and—analogously to the smooth, formal treatment he gives his nudes—never fails to impart to both characterization and setting an air of suave elegance. In his portraits, as with his nudes, Ingres contrasts the simple and regular volume of the head with the broken, irregular, and complicated folds of the drapery and costume. His apparently cool detachment from his models and his search for "pure form" commend him to the twentieth-century taste for the "abstract."

A comparison of Ingres' pencil portrait of the great violin virtuoso Nicolò Paganini (FIG. 21-24) with Delacroix's version of the same personality (FIG. 21-25) discloses the difference in approach that separates the two artists. Both painters were passionately fond of music, and Ingres was a creditable violin amateur who knew Paganini personally. His version, executed with that marvelously crisp precision of descriptive line that we find in his pencil portraits, is quite literal, relative to Delacroix's. He gives us the man's appearance and public deportment—one

21-24 JEAN AUGUSTE DOMINIQUE INGRES, *Paganini*, 1819. Pencil drawing, approx. 12″ × 8½″. Louvre, Paris.

might say his official likeness—enhanced by Ingres' powers of suggestive characterization and sense of setting. Paganini, sharing with violin and bow a certain delicacy—both being fragile and supple—seems about to make his introductory obeisance to his audience. Above all, Ingres' portrait is *formal,* as is his subject, face-to-face with the public world; but it is a graceful, not a stiff formality. Delacroix's *Paganini* presents a likeness not of the virtuoso's *form* but of his *performance.* Forgetting his audience, no longer in formal confrontation with his listeners, Paganini yields himself completely to the whirlwind of his own inspiration, which envelopes his reed-like frame, making it vibrate in tune to the quivering strings of his instrument. Delacroix tries to give us the portrait, as it were, of Paganini's music, as it plays to his own ear and spirit. Ingres gives us the outward aspect of his subject; Delacroix, the inner substance. With Delacroix, the musician is transformed by his music, as is Delacroix himself. Ingres tries to perfect the form as given to the eye; Delacroix, to realize the truth as given to the imagination.

Critics now regard both masters as equally great, but, in the end, Delacroix may have been more generously endowed with imagination—that faculty of supraperception that catches the essential in experience and unifies its multiplicity of particulars, giving it a force and coherence that mundane experience

cannot have. Delacroix called the art of Ingres "the complete expression of an incomplete intellect." Yet he found much to admire in Ingres, especially in his drawings, and although it was necessary that they go their separate ways in theory and practice, it is pleasant to hear that their personal antagonism eventually may have softened. The painter PAUL JOSEPH CHENAVARD relates how he and Delacroix accidentally encountered Ingres on the steps of the French Institute, at a time late in the lives of both great artists. Although Ingres had been instrumental in preventing Delacroix's election to the Académie des Beaux Arts until 1857, he, after an awkward pause, impulsively extended his hand to Delacroix, who shook it sincerely.

SOME EPIGONES: CHASSÉRIAU, COUTURE, GÉRÔME

"Epigones" are artists of a succeeding and less distinguished generation. Although the artists named above are contemporaneous with Ingres and Delacroix, they follow them at some distance. Paul Delaroche and Jean Léon Gérôme were regarded by nineteenth-century critics as the last great painters of the Tradition—the line of the masters of the Renaissance and Baroque. Aware of an ever-deepening and widening rift separating the past from the present, the Tradition from modern times, the most intelligent critics sensed the necessity of coming to grips with "modernity" and the problem of creating an art "for one's own time." The issue will become serious and urgent by mid-century. A leading critic, Théophile Gautier, could exclaim: "It is well known that something must be done, but what?" And Charles Baudelaire, reviewing the Paris Salon (an annual, government-sponsored exhibition) of 1846, wrote: "It is true that the great tradition has been lost, and that the new one is not yet established. But what *was* this great tradition . . . ?" Almost in answer to this question, the "great tradition" will be analyzed away and replaced with the art we call "modern."

The epigones of Ingres and Delacroix studied with them or were strongly influenced by them; they can be said to have carried on the Tradition, with often unintentional revisions. THÉODORE CHASSÉRIAU (1819–1856), Ingres' favorite pupil, was irresistibly drawn to the style of Delacroix, so much so that he was accused of plagiarizing him. That, in fact, he made his own quite original—if not deliberate—synthesis of Ingres and Delacroix is evident in *Esther Adorning Herself* (FIG. 21-26). Esther (like Judith, a heroine of Israel), adorns herself for King Ahasuerus, through whom she will save her people (Book of Esther, 2:8–17). She is represented seminude, attended by the women sent to serve her. Her torso and upraised arms recall poses of figures by Ingres, and Chassériau certainly learned his faultless drawing from that master. But the softer, more coloristic tonal-

21-25 EUGÈNE DELACROIX, *Paganini,* c. 1832. Approx. 17" × 11½". The Phillips Collection, Washington, D.C.

21-26 THÉODORE CHASSÉRIAU, *Esther Adorning Herself*, 1841. 18" × 14". Louvre, Paris.

ity indicates that he looked carefully, too, at the painting of Delacroix. The compression of the space puts the figures into the forward plane, so that they compose gracefully ornamental shapes, creating a kind of surface arabesque that will appear in the designs of artists like Pierre Puvis de Chavannes and Gustave Moreau later in the century and, ultimately, in Art Nouveau. Esther's pensiveness and an atmosphere of gentle mystery are characteristic features of the intensely personal style of Chassériau, itself distinctive in the art of his times.

An early specimen of the kind of art that will be called "academic," which had the admiration of the public and the support of the government, is the so-called *Romans of the Decadence* (FIG. 21-27) by THOMAS COUTURE (1815–1879), a pupil of both Gros and Delaroche. Later on, we shall say more about the "academic" style and the Academy. In fact, Couture was not an Academician and loathed the institution. Yet this vast picture is of the kind praised and patronized by the Academy. It marks a stage in Romanticism's revitalization of pictorial drama, and its type flourishes throughout the nineteenth century. Couture's *Romans* directly solicits the public's attention with its historical references (vague, to be sure), its sensational setting, and its somewhat sardonic moralism. It is, in fact, an allegory of the decadence of the July Monarchy of 1830; the picture is dated 1847 and was

exhibited just a year before the fall of that government in the Europe-wide revolutions of 1848. We are shown a drunken orgy of Romans of the late empire who have strayed from the severe morality of their forefathers, whose stern statues here frown their disapproval. How this painting differs from David's heroic *Oath of the Horatii* (FIG. 20-38) or the epic stance of Napoleon in Gros' *Pest House at Jaffa* (FIG. 21-14)! Couture knew both pictures well enough; but for his different purpose, he looks back to the huge banquet pieces of Veronese (FIG. 17-68). Taking many cues from the Venetian master, but not his religious content, Couture constructs a luxurious, architecturally strengthened setting for a multitude of figures, nude and draped, posed in attitudes of sensual indulgence and indolence.

Couture's painting is a fanciful reconstruction of the Roman past—significantly, in its decadence rather than in its primitive heroism. Moreover, its disparagement of Rome would seem in defiance of the proprieties of the Tradition, which insisted on the nobility of the ancients. Nevertheless, the design of the *Romans* is certainly traditional; sculptural figures are arranged horizontally in balancing groups, and the setting is so generalized that time and place are not specified. "History painting," as it had been known since the Renaissance, was supposed to depict elevating scenes from Christian and Classical story, with settings, costumes, poses, and accessories left in a more-or-less indefinite and conventional mode. Although actual historical events have been depicted before, notably by Velázquez, it is Benjamin West's *Death of General Wolfe* (FIG. 20-35) that heads a series of history paintings that, unlike those of the Tradition, aim at reporting actual historical events in more-or-less authentic circumstances of time and place.

This new kind of history painting matures in the nineteenth century, at a time when the foundations are being laid and the materials are being gathered for the modern science of historiography. The aim of historical scholarship is to recover and present the past in all accurate detail. Not only the scholars, but poets, artists, and the educated public began to read history; the period became obsessed with it. We have already seen this in architecture; and, as in architecture, so also in art and literature (this is the century of the historical novel) can the reconstruction of the past be imaginary, arbitrary, often inaccurate, often simply wrong. For example, Couture's *Romans* can hardly be taken as evidence that the great empire fell because its citizens became orgiastic.

On the other hand, painters can be as careful as scholars about the truth of the historical events they describe (although, being concerned with the dramatic essence of an event, painters may exaggerate in

21-27 Thomas Couture, *Romans of the Decadence*, 1847. Approx. 15′ 1″ × 25′ 4″. Louvre, Paris.

the interest of excitement). For it now becomes the history painter's function to produce, as on a stage, a convincing reenactment of an incident out of the past that will appeal both to his audience's sense of drama and to its knowledge of history. His goal is to neutralize the intrusion of his personality to produce effects entirely independent of it. He is after an illusion so objective, complete, and immediate that the spectator will think: "It might have looked this way, it might not have looked this way, but it *could* have looked this way." The value of the history painter's picture lies in its presumptive truth—not simply to life, but to life at

a particular time and place, and *as once lived*. This is a new genre, unknown to the Tradition, born of the age of West and David, that will develop well beyond the limits they may have appeared to set for it.

With Paul (Hippolyte) Delaroche (1797–1856)—a pupil of Delacroix, who himself painted many historical pictures—traditional subject matter begins to take on a more and more photographic appearance. This can be seen in the work of Delaroche's pupil Jean Léon Gérôme (1824–1904). In his painting *Thumbs Down!* (*Pollice Verso*) (fig. 21-28), Gérôme moves far from Couture and the Tradition; the inher-

21-28 Jean Léon Gérôme, *Thumbs Down!* (*Pollice Verso*), *c.* 1874. 40″ × 69″. Phoenix Art Museum purchase.

829

ited formulas have been almost entirely transformed. The time and place specifications are as exact as they can be. Although we do not know the day, month, and year of the event, nor the names of the principals involved, we recognize it for what it is and where it is happening; we can even guess the time of day. Gladiatorial combats were part of the Roman imperial games held regularly in great arenas or amphitheaters like the one pictured—the Colosseum at Rome (FIG. 6-45). The incident represented must have happened countless times, and its very ordinariness makes it dramatic and factual. A triumphant gladiator bestrides his fallen opponent and looks toward the box where the Vestal Virgins are seated. The fallen man gestures for mercy. The Vestals deny his appeal by turning their thumbs down; he will be killed on the spot.

Gérôme authenticates the scene to the last detail: the Vestals, the emperor's party (in the box fronted with columns and trophies), the streaks of light (clue to the time of day) thrown on the tapestried barrier walls by chinks in the great awnings overhead, the texture of the bloodstained sand, and, conspicuously, the fantastic garb of the gladiators, their splendid helmets replicating originals found at Pompeii. The scenic illusion is produced by a smooth continuum of tone that runs through the whole scale of values. There is scrupulous fidelity to optical fact. Evidence of brush strokes is suppressed in an exquisitely finished glassy surface. The effect is photographic; the brush stroke is intended to be invisible. In this way, the artist reduces to the barest minimum interference by his own imagination or feeling, or even by the agent of that feeling—his "hand." Like a director in the theater, he expects to be judged on his interpretation—manifest in the characterizations he elicits, in the species of action, scene design, and authenticity of detail. Gérôme makes use of an off-centered, dynamic placement of his figures, to make us spectators at a *real* event, which we witness from *within* the framed space of the action. The curving wall sweeps toward us, and we can feel that our own vantage point is continuous with that of the Vestal Virgins. Gérôme thus brings us onto the stage; with Couture and the Tradition, we are still out in front of it. This radical narrowing of the space between the spectator and the event being watched is a device of great importance in nineteenth-century pictorial technique.

What we are seeing here is an instance of the century's increasing appetite for the optically real in art. Real events (in the cases presented thus far, events verified by history) become subjects for artists who are willing to report or to reconstruct them in visual modes faithful to appearance. These artists paint, for receptive audiences, images that invite comparison with everyday optical experience in life. This criterion of simple recognition is appealed to in paintings like that of Gérôme, with subjects taken from the historical past. But how does one represent the historical present? Will the same modes be as suitable for representations of current events, in which one is a participant, as they are for past events, which must be reconstructed and of which one can only be a spectator?

At this moment in time, a technological device of immense consequence for modern experience was invented: the camera, with its attendant art of photography. We are all familiar with what the camera equips us to do—report and record optical experience at will. We assume that there is a very close correspondence between the photographic image and the fragment of our visual world that it records. The evidence of the photograph is evidence that what we think we see is really there. In other words, the camera report can be a check of what is "real," "true," or "fact" in our visual experience. Naturally, the invention of the first practical photographic process by LOUIS J.M. DAGUERRE in 1839 must have suggested answers to the great debate about what is real and how to represent the real in art. The improvement of the process through daguerreotype, calotype, wet plate, dry plate, and film to snapshot and motion picture is a story that properly belongs to the history of photography. But from its beginnings, the new medium was celebrated as embodying a kind of revelation of visible things. We already find, in the paintings by Delaroche and Gérôme, just such astonishing, cohering aggregations of optical information. Here, then, was a mechanism that could displace the painstaking artist who busied himself with such matters in the interest of truth to his subject. Delaroche is said to have exclaimed, on hearing of Daguerre's invention, "From this day, painting is dead!" And at the end of the century (in 1900), the Fauve-painter-to-be Maurice de Vlaminck declares: "We [painters] hate everything that has to do with the photograph." Yet, as a helpful auxiliary to painting, the photograph was welcomed by Ingres, Delacroix, Gustave Courbet, Edgar Degas and many other leading masters. It is doubtful they could have foreseen the enormous monopoly photography would win in the modern enterprises of image-making and the accumulation of visual information.

Ingres and Delacroix were still living while the Tradition, especially in the hands of Delaroche and Gérôme, was being changed—in substance and direction, in subject matter, in form and technique—to a new concern for the optically real. In the interest of what is real, painting and photography, whether in collaboration or opposition, were destined to replace the Tradition altogether.

Landscape Painting: England and America

Romanticism lifts landscape painting to the level of first importance—the level once occupied exclusively by figure painting. It encourages the expression of moods and feelings animated by experiences of nature undominated by man, experiences into which one can release oneself and with which one can join one's life. In England, as early as the 1740s, a school of poetry began that would reach its height in the early 1800s; its practitioners are the contemporaries of the early Romantics we have seen in architecture and art. These poets, absorbed in describing the look and temper of nature in all its variations, read the landscape closely and sympathetically, from the sublime to the familiarly beautiful. They came to see it almost as the projection of themselves. In a word, they subjectivized it.

There is no better introduction to the English school of landscape painting, so widely influential in the Romantic movement, than the works of these poets. Nature, emotionalized in both its grand and minute manifestations, lives in the canvases of the English School. As literature and history are keys to the art of the French Romantics, so is poetry to the English landscapists.

In the works of JOSEPH MALLORD WILLIAM TURNER (1775–1851), we find readings of nature in its terror and grandeur somewhat more often than in its peace and serenity, although Turner was capable of realizing all of nature's emotions. The brilliant and influential critic, John Ruskin, the first to really understand and call attention to the art of Turner, wrote, in his *Modern Painters* (1846), of the work illustrated here (FIG. 21-29):

> But I think the noblest sea that Turner has ever painted, and if so, the noblest certainly ever painted by man, is that of *The Slave Ship*, the chief Academy picture of the exhibition of 1840. . . . I believe, if I were reduced to rest Turner's immortality upon any single work, I should choose this.

Turner began in the Tradition, an admirer of Claude Lorraine, whose glowing, tranquil, idyllic landscapes (FIG. 19-63) never ceased to move him. But he powerfully wrenches the Tradition in *The Slave Ship*, where he transforms a Claudian sun into an incandescent comet amid flying, scarlet clouds that burst above a sea choked with the bodies of slaves

21-29 JOSEPH MALLORD WILLIAM TURNER, *The Slave Ship*, 1840. 36″ × 48″. Museum of Fine Arts, Boston.

jettisoned from the ship by a ruthless master. Ruskin's masterly prose describes it:

> Between [these] two ridges the fire of the sunset falls along the trough of the sea, dyeing it with an awful but glorious light, the intense and lurid splendor of which burns like gold and bathes like blood. Along this fiery path and valley the tossing waves by which the swell of the sea is restlessly divided lift themselves in dark, indefinite, fantastic forms, each casting a faint and ghastly shadow behind it along the illumined foam. They do not rise everywhere, but three or four together in wild groups, fitfully and furiously, as the under-strength of the swell compels or permits them; leaving between them treacherous spaces of level and whirling water, now lighted with green and lamp-like fire, now flashing back the gold of the declining sun, now fearfully dyed from above with the undistinguishable images of the burning clouds, which fall upon them in flakes of crimson and scarlet and give to the reckless waves the added motion of their own fiery flying. Purple and blue, the lurid shadows of the hollow breakers are cast upon the mist of night, which gathers cold and low, advancing like the shadow of death upon the guilty ship as it labors amidst the lightening of the sea, its thin masts written upon the sky in lines of blood, girded with condemnation in that fearful hue which signs the sky with horror and mixes its flaming flood with the sunlight, and, cast far along the desolate heave of the sepulchral waves, incarnadines the multitudinous sea.

Ruskin's impassioned language matches Turner's turbulent emotion. It is important to note that the particulars of the incident are almost lost in the boiling colors—just as they are almost eliminated from Ruskin's description, which itself is all color. Turner is a great innovator, who releases color from defining outlines to express its nature, as well as the painter's emotion, in storms and calms of its own. The reality of color is one with the reality of feeling. Turner's painting will have an incalculable influence on the development of modern art. His discovery of the esthetic and emotive power of pure color (the most fundamental element of the painting medium), as well as his pushing of the fluidity of the medium to a point at which the subject is almost manifest through the paint itself, points the way to an art that could dispense with shape and form altogether—and the Tradition along with them.

JOHN CONSTABLE (1776–1837), Turner's great contemporary, takes a different route away from the Tradition in his quest for the real. His landscapes—for the most part, placid, untroubled views of the English (Suffolk) countryside—are careful studies of nature in the local colors of woodland, meadow, pond and stream, hill and sky, interspersed with the architecture of mill, cottage, and country church. All these, Constable's favorite subjects, he observes as lighted by a mild sun or shadowed briefly by a changing cloud, bathed in an atmosphere fresh with dew or rain, moved by soft winds. There is no heroic action, nor is the landscape constructed to stage it. In *The Haywain* (FIG. 21-30)—a great success at the Paris Salon of 1824—a farmer in a cart fords a stream. Living nature includes him as it does the dog, the cottage, the stream, the copse, the distant park, the scudding clouds. Here is the oneness with nature sought by the Romantic poets; man is not the observer, but a participant in the landscape's being. But this is not the creation of a dream vision. Constable insists on the reality of the landscape as given to the eye and rendered with the brush: "I hope to show that our profession as painters is *scientific* as well as *poetic*; that imagination never did, and never can, produce works that are to stand by comparison with *realities*" (emphasis added). The reality of the landscape is especially the texture given it by atmosphere (the climate, the weather, which delicately veils what we see) and that atmosphere—constantly *changing* through the hours of the day, the shifts of the weather, and the seasons of the year—is shown by Constable to be the ultimate semblance of nature in its ceaseless process. His use of tiny dabs of local color, stippled with white, creates a sparkling shimmer of light and hue across the surface of the canvas, the vibration itself suggestive of movement and process. The word "fresh" peculiarly denotes Constable's technique and its effects. In speaking of the qualities he intended in his pictures, he mentions: "light—dews—breezes—bloom—and freshness, not one of which . . . has yet been perfected on the canvas of any painter in the world." These are the qualities that we sense in the fleeting states of changing nature—the qualities that startled the young Delacroix when he saw *The Haywain* in the Paris Salon of 1824. In his search for the reality of landscape, Constable studied it like a meteorologist (which he was by avocation). His certainty that the painting of nature partakes of science was his challenge and bequest to Delacroix and the Impressionists.

Less concerned than either Turner or Constable with pioneering advances in color and technique, the American painter THOMAS COLE (1801–1848) typifies the landscape of reflection and mood so romantically appealing to the public, especially in the English-speaking world. Although best known as the leading painter of the Hudson River School, whose members drew their subjects from the still uncultivated regions of the Hudson Valley and the Adirondacks, Cole himself favored more heroic subjects, like *The Course of Empire: Desolation* (FIG. 21-31). The picture describes the final episode in the presumed cycle of the rise, decline, and fall of all the empires of this world. In a setting and atmosphere reminiscent of Claude Lor-

21-30 JOHN CONSTABLE, *The Haywain*, 1821. 4′ 3″ × 6′ 2″. National Gallery, London.

raine, Cole places a giant column embraced by rough vines—all that remains of some colossal temple—in the left foreground. Vegetation runs wild around the silent ruins; the desolation is only partly revealed by a sad moon. Here is the mood of nostalgic moralizing on the fate of empires that dominates Lord Byron's *Childe Harold's Pilgrimage*, the Romantic work that made him famous throughout Europe. Here, as in the poem, we presume that some melancholy, "self-exiled" outcast has stumbled on the scene and somberly

21-31 THOMAS COLE, *The Course of Empire: Desolation*, 1836. Approx. 39″ × 63″. New York Historical Society.

contemplates its meaning for human history. From his viewing point, we see that

> . . . some solitary column mourns
> Above its prostrate brethren of the cave.
> . . . far and wide
> Temple and tower went down, nor left a site:—
> Chaos of Ruins! who shall trace the void,
> O'er the dim fragments cast a lunar light,
> And say, "here was, or is," where all is doubly night?

The tone of Cole's painting is exactly the tone of Byron's lines, and a wide public praised the feelings elicited by both. Indeed, we have in the two works an almost standard blend of familiar Romantic feelings— the melancholy, loneliness, and proud isolation of the contemplative wayfarer, sensitive to the pathos of the distant past and the never-again, to the overtones of the sublime and the flourishes of the picturesque.

Cole may have been thinking that the decay of Europe would be followed by the new promise of youthful America, and that—through its unspoiled experience and pristine virtue—his adopted country (Cole was English-born) might avoid the fateful cycle that dooms great empires. The thoroughly Romantic myth of the innocence of America in contrast to the corruptions of Europe was widely believed on both sides of the Atlantic in the nineteenth century; Cole's colleague, ASHER DURAND, declares America innocent of European "pollution."

Landscape Painting in Germany

Most landscape painting and poetry in the earlier nineteenth century to some degree expresses the Romantic, pantheistic view of nature as a "being" that includes the totality of things in organic unity and harmony; in Goethe's phrase, nature is "the living garment of God." Within nature, man is a sensitive corpuscle that can, by mystical intuition and creative power, reveal the truth of nature, of which humanity is the highest form. In Germany in particular, this view is enspirited with religion. As we saw with Chateaubriand in France, against the materialism, mechanism, and rationalism of the Enlightenment and the Revolution, religion rises once again to regain its lost prestige. But it is not the older, dogmatic, orthodox and institutional religion that returns; rather, it is a religion of nature—Wordsworth's "natural piety," a profoundly personal religion of esthetic emotion. In the thought of the Idealist philosopher Schelling, who made a great impression on the philosophy of art, the artist is a kind of priest; in the act of esthetic creation, he duplicates—or becomes one with—the creative power of nature itself and resolves the contradictions of the inner (subjective) and the outer (objective) worlds. The landscape reveals the divine being of nature to the artist who is prepared by innocence, sincerity, and intuitive insight to

21-32 PHILIPP OTTO RUNGE, *The Times of Day: Morning* (large version), 1809. Approx. 60″ × 45″. Kunsthalle, Hamburg.

receive the revelation. As all nature is mysteriously permeated by "being," the landscape painter has the task of interpreting the signs, symbols, and emblems of universal "spirit" disguised as the material things he sees. He is no longer a beholder of natural landscape, but a participant in its "spirit"; he no longer paints mere things, but the transcendent meaning of them arrived at through his own inspired feelings.

In the art of PHILIPP OTTO RUNGE (1777–1810) landscape becomes religious revelation. Runge declares that true art can be understood only through the deepest mystical experience of religion. In words, as well as images, he celebrates

> . . . the feeling of the whole universe with us; this united chord which in its vibrations touches every string of our heart; the love which keeps us and carries us through life. . . . each leaf and each blade of grass teems with life and stirs beneath me, all resounds together in a single chord. . . . I hear and feel the living breath of God who holds and carries the world, in whom all lives and works; here is the highest that we divine—God!*

Nature is so much a part of God, and we of nature, that, Runge says, "Once we see in all of nature only our own life, then it follows clearly, the right land-

*From letters translated in R.M. Bisanz, *German Romanticism and Philipp Otto Runge* (Dekalb: Northern Illinios University Press, 1970), pp. 48–51.

21-33 CASPAR DAVID FRIEDRICH, *Cloister Graveyard in the Snow*, 1810. Approx. 47" × 70". (Painting destroyed during World War II.)

scape can come about." In *Morning* (FIG. 21-32), from his four-part series *The Times of Day*, Runge gives us an allegory of dawn enriched with his personal flower and color symbolism. All plants descend from Paradise and are emblematic of the states of the human soul, as are colors and musical harmonies. The image of the great lily floating in the sky is the floral manifestation of light and the symbol of Divine knowledge and purity. The morning star, Venus, glows above, under the arc of the earth; below it, on the central axis, is the graceful figure of the goddess herself in the guise of Aurora. On the ground below, the supine figure of an infant is an allusion to the Christ child, as well as a symbol of regeneration and redemption and all the promise of the newborn day. The composition has the symmetry and formality of traditional religious painting and the mood of supernatural mystery. But the careful, quite objective study of color tone—the actual hues of dawn, with its tincture of rose turning to radiance—shows Runge's concern for the truth of appearance as the vehicle of symbolic truth. Crossing the empirical world with the transcendental, he gives us an apparition of the supernatural in a natural sky. Like Blake, whose work he must have known, Runge was a religious visionary who believed in angels; unlike Blake, he revered nature as given to the eye. It is interesting that *The Times of Day* were designed as sacred pictures for a chapel dedicated to a new religion of nature.

It is believed that the ideas of Runge influenced the art of his great contemporary, CASPAR DAVID FRIEDRICH (1774–1840); in the work of both, as Robert Rosenblum remarks, "the experience of the supernatural has . . . been transposed from traditional religious imagery to nature."* Nature, as immanent

God, requires no personifications, other than its organic and inorganic subjects and objects—its things visible to the eye, which symbolically express through their forms the truth of nature, which is to say, Divine truth. For Friedrich, landscapes are temples; his paintings themselves, altarpieces. His reverential mood demands the silence appropriate to sacred places filled with the Divine presence. In *Cloister Graveyard in the Snow* (FIG. 21-33) Friedrich gives us a solemn requiem. Under a winter sky, through the leafless oaks of a snow-covered cemetery, a funeral procession bears a coffin into the ruins of a Gothic chapel. The emblems of death are everywhere: the desolation of the season, leaning crosses and tombstones, the black of mourning worn by the grieving and by the skeletal trees, the destruction wrought by time on the chapel. The painting is a kind of meditation on human morality, as Friedrich himself remarks: "Why, it has often occurred to me to ask myself, do I so frequently choose death, transience, and the grave as subjects for my paintings? One must submit oneself many times to death in order some day to attain life everlasting."* Yet the sharply focused rendering demonstrate's the artist's keen perception of the physical environment in all the detail relevant to his message. In Friedrich, we find a balance of inner and outer experience. "The artist," he writes "should paint not only what he sees before him, but also what he sees within him. If, however, he sees nothing within him, then he should also refrain from painting that which he sees before him." It is interesting that these landscapists, whether a Turner or a Friedrich, insist on the necessity of feeling and of truth to appearance simultaneously, even if their means and emphases seem to differ widely.

---

*Robert Rosenblum, *Modern Painting and the Northern Romantic Tradition: Friedrich to Rothko* (New York: Harper & Row, 1975), p. 22.

*In H. Börsch-Supan, *Caspar David Friedrich* (New York: Braziller, 1974), p. 7.

THE SECOND HALF OF THE NINETEENTH CENTURY: THE PREDOMINANCE OF REALISM

We have already seen realism in the first half of the century, particularly in the art of Delaroche and Gérôme, and we have seen realistic images mechanically produced by the camera. For that matter, realism, in different degrees of focus, has been ingredient in Western art for centuries, from Van Eyck to Velázquez and Vermeer and beyond. The nineteenth-century kind of realism can be described technically and iconographically—technically, as replication of an optical field by matching its color tones on a flat surface, whether or not the subject matter has or could have been seen by the artist; iconographically, as the subject matter of everyday, contemporary life as seen or seeable by the artist, whether recorded photographically or by other modes of visual report. The quarrel between Realism and Romanticism at mid-century is primarily over subject matter. Realism disapproves of traditional and fictional subjects on the grounds that they are not real and visible and are not of the present world. Realism argues that only the things of one's own times, the things one can see, are "real." The Realist vision and report make for a *modern* style—one, by definition, cut off from the past.

The Realist position in art and literature was strengthened by the scientific and technological achievements of the century. Scientific positivism asserted that only scientifically verified fact was "real" and that the "scientific method" was the only legitimate means of gaining knowledge; the others—religion, revelation, intuition, imagination—produced only fictions and illusions. Writing in 1892, Karl Pearson insists confidently that "science claims for its heritage the whole domain to which the word knowledge can be legitimately applied. . . . It refuses to admit any coheirs to its possession." Modern science was indeed the most prestigious of all nineteenth-century intellectual enterprises; its authority rose from its triumphs. Its rigorous practicality, its search for the facts, necessarily served as an example to artists searching for a modern truth and a modern style free from fable and fantasy.

Numerous Realist artists—foremost among them, Gustave Courbet and Édouard Manet—record the life of their times in factual images of it; yet their styles have little in common. At the same time, many artists embody imaginative subject matter in strikingly realistic forms. Indeed, there is a dialogue throughout the century between Realism and Romanticism, and, although technical Realism seems predominant during the latter half of the century, Romantic subject matter and arbitrary formal experiment persist—and, by the end of the century, appear to carry the day for pure artistic subjectivity.

The realism of Manet, which became the realism of the Impressionists, reveals a striking paradox of Realism. To catch the entire optical field spread before him, the artist must paint it just as he sees it. But to record this instantaneous impression, the artist must work swiftly in a sketch-like execution that blurs the visual field as it increasingly emphasizes the brush stroke and the blot of color. The wholeness of the field disintegrates into a plurality of color functions. The scientist would say that the artist is not painting the world, but only his visual sensations of it. As his sensations belong to his private world, the Realist artist finds that the external reality he has sought is *really* only his own inescapable subjectivity.

Transition: Corot, Millet, Daumier

An early turn toward Realism is made in France by the most prominent landscape painter before the Impressionists, JEAN BAPTISTE CAMILLE COROT (1796–1875). In his *Harbor of La Rochelle* (FIG. 21-34), we can see the artist's interest in the full tonal spread, the careful arrangement of dark and light values, which the new device of photography was automatically achieving. Corot's method is to be as faithful as possible to the scale of light to dark. His procedure is interesting. He writes in his notebooks:

> The first two things to study are form and values. For me, these are the bases of what is serious in art. Color and finish put charm into one's work. In preparing a study or a picture, it seems to me very important to begin by an indication of the darkest values . . . and continue in order to the lightest value. From the darkest to the lightest I would establish twenty shades. . . .

In *La Rochelle*, we can appreciate these careful gradations of tone. At the same time, the composition is not the random one of a snapshot; the forms are carefully placed, and the general ordering of them recalls the Classical landscape tradition of Nicolas Poussin (FIG. 19-62). Indeed, there is such firm definition of the forms and such gradation of the half-tones that Corot was said to "Ingres-ize" the landscape. Both

21-34 Jean Baptiste Camille Corot, *The Harbor of La Rochelle*, 1851. Approx. 20" × 28". Yale University Art Gallery, New Haven, Connecticut (bequest of Stephen Carlton Clark, B.A., 1903).

Constable and Corot point toward the Impressionists, but in different ways: Constable, in his brilliant freshness of color and divided brush stroke; Corot, in his concerns for the rendering of outdoor light and atmosphere in terms of values.

Corot painted in close association with members of the "Barbizon School," a group of landscape and figure painters who settled near the village of Barbizon in the forest of Fontainebleau. Chief among these was Jean François Millet (1814–1875). Of peasant stock, Millet undertook to glorify the humble country folk of France. In *The Gleaners* (FIG. 21-35), done in 1857, he characteristically poses his peasants as monumental figures against the flat, dull land and sky. The quiet design of Millet's paintings accents his scrupulous truth of detail and contributes to the dignity he gives to even the simplest rural tasks. The solemn grandeur with which Millet invests the poor causes him to be identified with a kind of socialism that was prevalent in his lifetime. Actually, it is a late echo of the Romantic intuition, held by such men as Wordsworth, which found a touch of nobility in the humblest lives. The objective, carefully realistic landscapes of other painters of the Barbizon School, like Théodore Rousseau, Charles François Daubigny, and Narcisse Virgile Diaz, will powerfully influence the Impressionists and Post-Impressionists.

Corot and his friends in Barbizon were little concerned with the course of events in Paris, where the rapid development of an urban industrial civilization was creating acute political and social unrest. But in a Parisian studio only a few steps from Notre Dame, the lithographer and painter Honoré Daumier (1808–1879) was in close touch with this social ferment. For 40 years, from the July Monarchy of 1830 through the Second Empire, he contributed satirical lithographs to the leading humor journals. In this prodigious output of some 4,000 prints, Daumier's keen insight,

21-35 Jean François Millet, *The Gleaners*, 1857. Approx. 33" × 44". Louvre, Paris.

21-36 HONORÉ DAUMIER, *Rue Transnonain*, 1834.
Lithograph, approx. 12″ × 17½″. Philadelphia Museum of Art.

coupled with his sympathy for human beings, was constantly expressed in superb draftsmanship. The sharpness of his political criticism often put him into conflict with the government, as one would expect in view of such prints as *Rue Transnonain* (FIG. 21-36). Soldiers, fired on from a building on the Rue Transnonain in the working quarter of Paris, entered the building and massacred the inhabitants. Daumier, with the power of Goya, gives us a view of the atrocity from a sharp, realistic angle of vision, almost as if we ourselves are among the felled victims. The broken, scattered forms, lying in the midst of violent disorder, are reported as they were found; Daumier uses every available device of his skill to make the situation real. Long before the age of the police photographer, a great artist snaps the picture of a brutal crime committed at a certain place at a certain time. The harsh fact speaks for itself; the artist does not

have to interpret it for us. The print's significance lies in its *factualness;* the artist is becoming concerned with fact as his subject and with the optical realization of fact as his method. Not that Daumier uses the tonal realism of the new medium of photography; he does not. His manner is rough and spontaneous and carries the strong mark of caricature, exaggeration, and dash; this is part of its remarkable force. Thus, Daumier is true to life in content, but his style is uniquely personal.

Although known principally for his lithographs during his lifetime, Daumier was also a very powerful painter and, after 1848, was acclaimed as such. His unfinished *Third-Class Carriage* (FIG. 21-37) gives us a glimpse into the rude railway compartment of the 1860s, in which sit the poor, who can afford only third-class tickets. The disinherited masses of nineteenth-century industrialism were Daumier's indignant concern, and he makes them his subject over and over again. He does not set them off with the sometimes Romantic idealism of Millet; he simply shows them to us in the unposed attitudes and unplanned arrangements of the millions thronging through the modern city—anonymous, insignificant, dumbly patient with a lot they cannot change. Not only is Daumier's subject real, but so is his view of it; he sees people as they ordinarily appear, their faces vague, impersonal, blank—unprepared for any observer. The artist, in a novel approach, tries to achieve the real by isolating from the continuum of ordinary vision an entirely unrehearsed collection of random aspects of human existence. This is prophetic of the candor that will be introduced into the visual arts by use of the modern surreptitious camera.

21-37 HONORÉ DAUMIER, *The Third-Class Carriage*, c. 1862. 25¾″ × 35½″. Metropolitan Museum of Art, New York (Havemeyer Collection, bequest of Mrs. H.O. Havemeyer, 1929).

Realism—The Theme: Courbet and Manet

To be able to translate the customs, ideas, and appearances of my time as I see them—in a word, to create a living art—this has been my aim. . . . The art of painting can consist only in the representation of objects visible and tangible to the painter . . . , [who must apply] his personal faculties to the ideas and the things of the period in which he lives. . . . I hold also that painting is an essentially *concrete* art, and can consist only of the representation of things both *real* and *existing*. . . . An *abstract* object, invisible or nonexistent, does not belong to the domain of painting. . . . Show me an angel, and I'll paint one. . . . *

From fragmentary observations like these, made by GUSTAVE COURBET (1819–1877), we get some general idea of Realism as the Realists and their friendly critics understood it. Courbet has long been regarded as the father of the Realist movement in nineteenth-century art; certainly, he used the term "realism" in exhibiting his own works, even though he shunned labels. "The title of Realist," he insists, "was thrust upon me, just as the title of Romantic was imposed upon the men of 1830. Titles have never given a true idea of things." In and since Courbet's time, there has been confusion about what Realism *is*. Writing in 1857, Champfleury, one of the first critics to recognize and appreciate Courbet's work, declares: "I will not define Realism. . . . I do not know where it comes from, where it goes, what it is. . . . The name horrifies me by its pedantic ending; . . . there is enough confusion already about that famous word." There still is confusion, or at least disagreement, about Realism among historians of nineteenth- and, for that matter, twentieth-century art. Yet from Courbet's own brief statements, we gather that he wishes to be only of his own time and to paint only what it makes visible to him. Although Courbet himself started as a painter more or less in the manner of the Barbizon School, there is here a sharp iconographical break with Romanticism and the Tradition; all mythological, religious, fantastic, purely imaginative subjects are ruled out as they are not visible to the modern eye. The critic Jules Antoine Castagnary, writing in 1863, says of Courbet: "[His] great claim is to represent what he sees. It is, in fact, one of his favorite axioms that everything that does not appear upon the retina is outside the domain of painting." But what of pictures like those of Delaroche and Gérôme (FIG. 21-28)? The Realist would reply that Delaroche and Gérôme never saw these events, that they are documenting only illusions, no matter how eye-fooling—for the eye can see only what is present, and what we cannot see, we cannot paint. The modern painter, if

he is free, sincere, and honest, rejects fictions and refuses to create them. What is *real*, then, is *modern*; and the true modern style is Realism. Champfleury writes in 1857: "M. Courbet is a Realist. . . . M. Courbet is a new man." Critics looking for an expressly modern art could find their hero in Courbet.

A man of powerful personality, Courbet was indeed cut out to be the truculent champion of the Realist cause, defying alike public taste and the art juries that rejected two of his major works for the Paris International Exhibition in 1855 on the grounds that his subjects and figures were too coarsely materialistic (so much so as to be plainly "socialistic") and too large. Plain people of the kind Courbet shows us in *Burial at Ornans* (FIG. 21-38) were considered (by the public) unsuitable for artistic representation and were linked in the middle-class mind with the dangerous, newly defined working class, which was finding outspoken champions in men like Marx, Engels, and Proudhon and in the work of novelists like Balzac, Flaubert, Zola, Dickens, and others. Courbet, rejected by the exhibition jury, set up his own gallery outside the grounds, calling it the Pavilion of Realism.

Courbet's Pavilion and his utterances amounted to the manifestoes of the new movement. Although he maintained that he founded no school and was of no school, he did, as the name of his Pavilion suggests, accept the term "realism" as descriptive of his art. With the unplanned collaboration of Millet and Daumier, Courbet challenged the whole iconographic stock of the Tradition and summoned public attention to what Baudelaire calls the "heroism of modern life," which he felt should replace all the heroism of traditional subject matter. For the public, it was a contest between the painters of the "ugly" (Courbet) and the painters of the "beautiful" (those who opposed Courbet)—as the public understood those qualities.

But Courbet's bold, somber palette is essentially traditional—even though his subject is "new"—and certainly in harmony with his subject matter. Lights and darks converge abruptly along the edges of simplified planes, and a surface richness results from the way in which he used his pigments. To Courbet's contemporaries, his intentionally simple and direct methods of expression, in composition as well as in technique, seemed unbearably crude, and he was called a primitive. Courbet made much use of the palette knife, with which large daubs of paint could be quickly placed and unified, producing a roughly wrought surface. His example inspired the young men who worked with him (later Impressionists like Édouard Manet, Claude Monet, and Auguste Renoir), but the public accused him of carelessness and the critics wrote of his "brutalities." Courbet insisted that he wished to paint only the life of his own times

*Robert Goldwater and Marco Treves, eds., *Artists on Art*, 3rd ed. (New York: Pantheon, 1958), pp. 295–97.

21-38 GUSTAVE COURBET, *Burial at Ornans*, 1849. Approx. 10' × 22'. Louvre, Paris.

in the costumes of the day, and, toward this end, he "studied without prejudice the art of the old and modern masters." But to the public, which believed that only the ideal or imaginary subject was suitable for major paintings, Courbet's assertion that he could not paint an angel because he had never seen one sounded blasphemous.

Burial at Ornans represents a funeral in a bleak, provincial landscape, attended by obscure persons "of no importance," the kind of people presented by Balzac and Flaubert. Garbed in rusty black, they cluster dumbly around the excavation, while the officious clergyman reads the Office of the Dead. Their faces register all degrees of response to the situation, a gallery of funereal expressions and faithful portraits of the poor—some of them sat for by friends of the artist. Courbet monumentalizes a theme that could hardly have been of less concern to the Salon-going public of Paris but that promises to show full and wide development in all avenues of nineteenth-century life and art: humanitarianism and concern for social reform. The heroic, the sublime, and the terrible are not here—only the drab fact of undramatized life and death. In 1857, Champfluery writes of *Burial at Ornans* ". . . it represents a small-town funeral and yet reproduces the funerals of *all* small towns." What the artist now finds interesting is in his own environment; it is people—not as superhuman or subhuman actors on a grand stage, but as themselves, moved by the ordinary rhythms of modern life.

Although Courbet was often embattled with the critics over the spirit and the form of Realism, he had secure official backing from 1855 onward, and, in his later years, he painted with greater intention to please the public. Indeed, the mode of these later pictures recalls the Baroque, with dark underpainting, heavy chiaroscuro, and subject matter familiar in the popular Salon. This conservatism disappointed the younger artists, who had come to rely strongly on Courbet's vigorous style and technique and on his courageous individualism. Most of the Impressionists had associated and exhibited with him in their early years, but Courbet failed to catch the drift of the new style that was emerging in their work. He spoke disparagingly of Manet's *Olympia*, a reclining nude, as "flat"—that is, without a strong chiaroscuro. He still used dark underpainting after Manet and Monet began to paint on a white surface for greater luminosity. As close to the new generation of painters as he had been, he could say of Manet, in 1867, when the curtain had already risen on a new act: "I myself shouldn't like to meet this young man . . . I should be obliged to tell him that I don't understand anything about his paintings, and I don't want to be disagreeable to him." But the Impressionists could not deny, nor could history itself, the impetus that Courbet's art had given the movement toward a modern style based on observation of the modern environment.

Courbet's art had hardly established one kind of realism before a different version, leading away from Courbet, took its place. In the fall of 1864, the English painter DANTE GABRIEL ROSSETTI wrote home about French Realism, as he had seen it in visits to the studios of Courbet and Manet: "There is a man named Manet . . . whose pictures are for the most part mere scrawls, and who seems to be one of the lights of the Realist School. Courbet, the head of it, is not much better." This comment, though a priggish dismissal of them, does link the two great Realists (who, as we have seen, had little use for one another's work).

With Édouard Manet (1832–1883), the course of modern painting shifts into a new phase, accelerating its move toward that point at the end of the century when the major transformation of the great tradition that began with Giotto will occur.

In 1863, following the protests of angry artists, an exhibition—the Salon des Refusés—was held to accommodate the exceptionally numerous works rejected by the jury for the Salon that year. (The Salons were government-subsidized "warehouses," as Zola called them, where, yearly, the artists of France exhibited canvases by the thousands. Prizes or recognition at the Salon could ensure professional success; refusal or rejection, neglect and failure. In the nineteenth century, at least until the 1880s, the Salon was the field of intense professional competition among artists and the battleground of "modern" versus "traditional.") It was at the Salon des Refusés that Manet shocked the public with his *Déjeuner sur l'herbe*, "Luncheon on the Grass" (FIG. 21-39)—originally titled simply "The Bath." Manet may have been "a child of the century," as Zola called him in praise of his daring modernity, but he did not care to isolate himself as such. He wished to shine in the Salon with a work as strong as the masterpieces of the Tradition, preferably a figure painting. We know that at first he had Giorgione's (and Titian's?) *Pastoral Symphony* (FIG. 17-60) in mind as a source, but that, for the actual composition, he used an engraving by Marcantonio Raimondi, a pupil of Raphael. Manet must also have been mindful of Baudelaire's observation (made as early as 1845): "We are surrounded by the heroism of modern life, [but there is as yet no painter] . . . who will know how to tear out of actual life its epic side and make us see, with color or drawing, how grand we are in our neckties and varnished boots!" Baudelaire may have been smiling ironically when he wrote that; nevertheless, the age, or at least thoughtful artists like Manet, took it seriously—or could have. We have already noted Gautier's query: "It is well known that something must be done [in art], but what?"—an especially urgent question for those who believed, with historian Hippolyte Taine, that the age of heroism was past, or, with Eugène Fromentin, that "Great painting is dead. That is understood." In the *Déjeuner*, Manet does not attempt to revive "great painting," but to speak in a new voice and with an authority equal to his celebrated predecessors. He

21-39   Édouard Manet, *Le Déjeuner sur l'herbe*, 1863. Approx. 7' × 8' 10". Galerie du Jeu de Paume, Paris.

takes the theme of a pastoral paradise, familiar in painting from Giorgione to Antoine Watteau, and embodies it in living, identifiable people: his model Victorine Meurend, his brother Gustave (with cane), and the sculptor Leenhof. This is what outraged the public; the pastoral brought up to date—the promiscuous present in a Paris park—was more the concern of the police than of lovers of art. It is worth quoting a hostile critic of the painting—the voice, no doubt, of public opinion:

> A commonplace woman of the *demi-monde*, as naked as can be, shamelessly lolls between two dandies dressed to the teeth. These latter look like schoolboys on a holiday, perpetrating an outrage to play the man. . . . This is a young man's practical joke—a shameful, open sore.*

Manet's work would have been accepted had he shown men and women as nymphs and satyrs in Classical dress or undress, as did his contemporary, the Academician Adolphe William Bouguereau (FIG. 21-52), ten years later, or as did Giorgione (and Titian?) in *Pastoral Symphony* (FIG. 17-60). But here Manet raises the veils of allusion and reverie and bluntly confronts the public with reality (demonstrating, incidentally, the incompatibility of myth and realism). This masterpiece has the force of tradition without its form; the *Déjeuner* is the valedictory of the world of present fact to the world of the mythic past. The public expected the latter world and was overwhelmed by the former; defeated expectation is part

of the shock tactics of modern art in its unceasing effort to force the public to face a reality that modern art defines for it.

Throughout almost his entire career, Manet suffered the hostility of the critics as surrogates of the public. He never understood their animosity and most often sought their approval, but the doses of the real that he administered were too harsh. His contemporary, the philosopher and historian Ernest Renan, may have been expressing what the public feared from the new realism in art when he said:

> It is possible, then, that the ruin of idealistic beliefs is destined to follow the destruction of supernatural beliefs, and that a real abasement of human morality dates from *the day it saw the reality of things.* [emphasis added.]*

Hardly less than the subject, the public and the critics disliked the new method Manet used to present his figures. His light is photographic, but in a novel way, throwing a harsh, strong illumination directly on the figures to produce a kind of flashbulb effect, similar to that seen in newspaper photographs of night scenes. The middle values, so carefully observed and recorded by Corot, are blotted out; there is a "crowding of the lights" and a compensating "crowding of the darks," whereby many values are summed up in one or two lights or darks. The effect is both to flatten the form and to give it a hard, snapping presence. A detail (FIG. 21-40) shows Manet's procedure, learned partly from Couture, under

*In G.H. Hamilton, *Manet and His Critics* (New Haven: Yale University Press, 1954), p. 45.

*In J.C. Sloane, *French Painting Between the Past and the Present* (Princeton, N.J.: Princeton University Press, 1951), p. 57.

whom he studied, but mostly from Velázquez and Frans Hals. A single high tonality for the flesh is brushed boldly in strokes that create the form. Into this bright tone Manet places abruptly, and without transitions, the strong darks of the eyes and the shadow accents of nose and fingers. The closeup effect is of a blocked-out first or second sketch, but, at a distance, the roughly juxtaposed light and dark cohere. The paint directly reports what is given to the eye, without any presuppositions of form, structure, or contour. Henri Matisse, himself a master of modern art, said of Manet: "He was the first to act by reflex and thus to simplify the painter's task . . . expressing only what immediately touched his senses." He could have added that Manet thereby eliminates painting based on form drawing and sculpture. Form, no longer a matter of line, is only a function of paint and light. Manet himself declared that the chief actor in the painting is the light; *what* the light reveals becomes incidental. The public and the critics, guardians of public taste, knew nothing of this. They saw only a crude sketch without the customary "finish."

One of the byproducts of Manet's new technique is impersonality. The artist, reflexively recording with trained eye and hand, is more or less indifferent to his subject matter, except as it gives him an opportunity to arrange his light sensations in a new way; he creates pictures in which his feelings seem utterly uninvolved. Manet offers the same impersonality and "scientific" detachment in works reporting contemporary events, although we are coming to realize that his subjects meant more to him than was first thought. Without perhaps realizing it, he has given us a representation of man the automaton and man

the disposable object—not the rational animal, the immortal soul, the hero, the darling of nature and the universe, but an ever-changing physical datum whose value is primarily statistical. In this product of the nineteenth-century successes of the biological and social sciences, man is a mere adaptive mechanism, an insignificant unit that blends its biological, political, and social backgrounds. Manet's masterpiece, *Bar at the Folies-Bergère* (FIG. 21-41), painted in 1882, reflects an analogous absorption of the human figure into the pictorial context. The surface of the canvas vibrates with the reflections of light spilling from the gas globes onto the figures and the brilliant still life of fruit and bottles on the counter. In this study of artificial light, both direct and reflected in the mirror background, the subject matter has lost its earlier importance. Manet tells us little about the barmaid and less about her customers, but much about his optical experience of this momentary pattern of light, in which the barmaid is only another *motif*— a larger still life amid the glittering bottles. There is no story, no moral, no plot or stage direction; there is simply an optical event, an arrested moment, in which lighted shapes of one kind or another participate. One is reminded of the novels of Manet's friend Zola, especially of *Nana*, whose heroine is nothing but a meaningless human consequence of an intersection of social forces that create and destroy her. The barmaid in Manet's painting is nothing more than a compositional device—automatic and nonpersonal.

The *Folies-Bergère* illustrates another quality that was to loom with increasing importance in the works of later painters, and that first made its appearance in *Le Déjeuner sur l'herbe*. Although the effect was per-

21-41 ÉDOUARD MANET, *Bar at the Folies-Bergère*, 1882. Approx. 37" × 51". Courtauld Institute Galleries, London.

haps unplanned, Manet's painting made a radical break with tradition by redefining the function of the picture surface. Ever since the Renaissance, the picture had been conceived as a "window" and the viewer as looking *through* the painting's surface at an illusory space developed behind it. Manet, by minimizing the effects of modeling and perspective, forces the viewer to look *at* the surface and to recognize it once more as a flat plane covered with patches of paint. This "revolution of the color patch," combined with Manet's cool, objective approach, points painting in the direction of abstraction, with its indifference to subject matter and its emphasis on optical sensations and the problem of organizing them into form. In the twentieth century, not only the subject matter, but even its supposed visual manifestation in the external world, will disappear.

As we have seen in the cases of Courbet and Manet, the modern movement called Realism met powerful resistance. The public found it "ugly," and the critics who explained art to the public in the press mostly agreed, as did many artists; Couture represented the Realist seated on a fragment of Classical statuary, painting the portrait of a pig. Although the government, the greatest patron of art, was often quite tolerant, the Academy (composed of recognized "official" artists who were members of the Institute of France) was largely hostile; so were the juries of the annual Salons and the instructors of the École des Beaux-Arts, the official art school. The conflicts of the Salon are reflected in the ideological wars fought in the newspapers and in reviews, where strident journalistic criticism exhorted the public to admire or despise this or that artist exhibited at the Salon.

It is noteworthy that the press had (and has today) a fundamental role in shaping and sustaining modern movements in art. Whether attacking or defending new movements, the art press, through its heated polemics, has often made esthetic controversy into something resembling the strife of parties in political life, and artistic dogmas have been labeled with the essentially political suffix "-ism": Realism, Romanticism, Impressionism, and so on. The polemics entailed a rhetoric of value opposites—good and bad, right and wrong, true and false. With the triumph of Realism, the defeated opposition (the defenders of the Tradition) came to be disparaged as "academic"— meaning at best, reactionary; at worst, the makers of false art or non-art. Fortunately, contemporary art-historical scholarship has mitigated the harshness and distortions of long-standing partisan criticism, which—although it may have been historically necessary to promote the advance and the reception of modern art—was indiscriminate and misleading in its destruction of artists' reputations and in its deval-

uation of works that may have both a place in history and quality as art.

In what follows, as well as what has already been said, the reader should keep in mind the intensely competitive and contentious environment in which new art has appeared in the West during the last century and a half. This environment has all the temper of the great revolutions that encompass it and shares the prevailing instinct for restless, impatient, often intemperate controversy. Yet an objective account must attempt to show the personalities and the developments involved, without recourse to any scenario of heroes and villains struggling for the honor or dishonor of art. Painters like the epigones of Ingres and Delacroix need no longer be dismissed as the enemies of artistic progress or the producers of inferior or tasteless works. They, and others like them whom we have yet to study, have made contributions, greater or smaller, to the history of modern art, which it is our business to trace and to fill in without old prejudice and special pleading.

Some Variations on the Theme of Realism

Independent Realism was not exclusively French. In the second half of the century, it is international, although French artists and writers take the lead in promoting it—especially the idea that Realism is and should be the depiction of scenes of modern life. Realistic painting of historical and literary anecdote, as in the work of Delaroche, Gérôme, and many others, continued to be official and popular, while "modern" Realism mostly was not. Yet the latter appeared in all countries and was taken for granted by the end of the century.

Manet had been the pupil of the history painter Couture. The American painter THOMAS EAKINS (1844–1916) studied under Gérôme in the École des Beaux Arts for three years. The generational descent of modern Realism from what might be called Romantic Realism can be seen in the sequences of Delaroche–Gérôme–Eakins, and, much more abruptly, of Couture–Manet, the latter's break with his predecessor being far more marked than Eakins' with his. Eakins, along with Winslow Homer (FIG. 21-47), was a leader of the American School. Like Manet, Eakins had difficulty with the public and the critics. His early masterpiece, *The Gross Clinic* (FIG. 21-42), rejected by the art jury for the exhibition in Philadelphia that celebrated the first century of American independence, was denounced as brutally realistic. It represents the renowned surgeon Dr. Samuel Gross in the operating amphitheater of the Jefferson Medical College in Philadelphia, where the painting now hangs. The surgeon is accompanied by colleagues, all of whom have been identified, and by the patient's mother, who covers her face. Dr. Gross, with bloody fingers and scalpel, lectures on his procedure. It is indeed an unsparing description of a contemporary event, with a good deal more reality than many could endure: "It is a picture," according to one critic, "that even strong men find it difficult to look at long, if they can look at it at all." True to the program of "scenes from modern life," Eakins puts the modern surgeon in the context of his business, as Manet puts the bargirl in the context of hers (FIG. 21-41) and as Courbet, in his *Atelier* (not illustrated), shows himself at work in his studio. Although Eakins' surgeon is certainly of his time and particular place, the subject and its form recall the great group portraits of surgeons painted by Rembrandt—which doubtless were Eakins' inspiration. The lighting is Rembrandtesque, as is something of the feeling. And in his manipulation of the traditional form and technique, Eakins is closer to Courbet than he is to his own master, Gérôme.

He is also much closer to Courbet than he is to Manet. Instead of the quick, "reflexive" report of visual impressions, Eakins preferred a slower, more deliberate method, with long conceptual preparation and the cooperation of visual memory. Knowledge was a prerequisite always—and, where relevant, *scientific* knowledge. Eakins was an expert in mathematics and perspective and taught human anatomy at the Jefferson Medical College. His concern for anatomical correctness led him to investigate human motion with the camera; a skillful and inventive photographer, he made what is thought to be the first rapid-exposure sequence of photographs (with a single camera) of a continuous action. His collaboration with Eadweard Muybridge in the photographic study of human action drew favorable attention in France, especially from Degas, and anticipated the motion picture.

This is not the place to do more than state the vast importance of the photograph as a record of the modern environment. The medium, of considerable value to many painters and especially admired in America, went far beyond the function of a simple auxiliary to painting. Its challenge, historically and technologically, amounted to an expropriation of the realistic image, the property of painting for many centuries. Within three generations or less from the invention of photography, painting was to lose the realistic image to abstraction. This fact is too often disregarded by the historian of art. The reader should keep in mind the steady presence of the camera in the modern environment and its overpowering influence on the way we modern beings see. Although we cannot here do justice to the subject, we can assert that photogra-

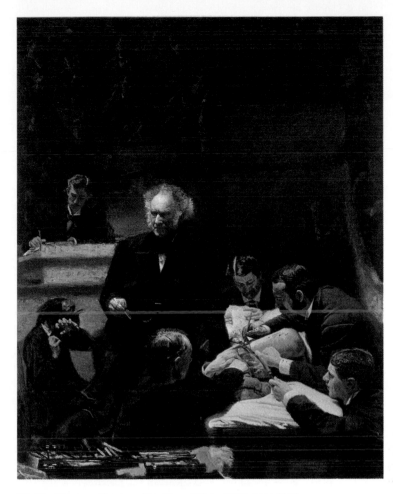

21-42 THOMAS EAKINS, *The Gross Clinic*, 1875. 8' × 6' 6". Jefferson Medical College, Philadelphia.

phy seems to capture the essence of what Realism calls for—objective representation of modern life.

To represent modern life authentically and in all its variety, artists of Realist bent expanded and diversified their subject matter to embrace all classes and levels of society, all types of people and of environment: the working class, urban and rural, the denizens of the big city, the burghers of the small town, the leisure class at its resorts, the rustics of the provinces. Added to the social sympathies we find in Millet, Daumier, and Courbet were other motives—of an anthropological kind, reflecting interest in national and regional characteristics, folk customs and culture, the quaintness and picturesqueness of local color. WILHELM LEIBL (1844–1900), perhaps the most important Realist painter of Germany in the later nineteenth century, is a master of this latter kind of subject. Influenced by Courbet, but lacking his breadth and depth, Leibl exemplifies the Realist credo. His masterpiece, *Three Women in a Village Church* (FIG. 21-43), is the record of a moment sacred in the life of these country women of three generations—the moment of prayer. Dressed in rustic costume, their Sunday best, they pursue their devotions unselfconsciously, their prayer books held in big

21-43 WILHELM LEIBL, *Three Women in a Village Church*, 1878–1881. Approx. 29" × 25". Kunsthalle, Hamburg.

21-44 JAMES TISSOT, *The Ball on Shipboard*, 1874. Approx. 33" × 51". Tate Gallery, London.

hands roughened by work. Their manners and their dress proclaim them innocent of the affectations and refinements of the metropolis, which they have probably never seen. Leibl chooses to show their natural virtues: simplicity, honesty, steadfastness, patience. He could subscribe, doubtless, to the words of a poet from another country and another time: "Far from the madding crowd's ignoble strife / they kept the noiseless tenor of their way."* Leibl himself writes in a letter: "Here in the open country and among those who live close to nature, one can paint naturally." For three years, he worked from his peasant models in the little church, often under impossible conditions of lighting and temperature.

The light in the picture is hard and neutral, without cast shadows and with only the slightest modeling. The focus is sharp, the forms and space flattening out into pattern. We are aware of the documentary power of the photograph-like approach. Yet, for all its objectivity, the picture is a moving expression of the artist's intelligent sympathy with his subjects, a reading of character without a trace of sentimentality, rare for a subject like this.

One could hardly find more different subjects or better examples of the anthropologizing interests of Realism than the earlier work of JAMES TISSOT (1836–1902), who was born in France but worked for many years in England. His *Ball on Shipboard* (FIG. 21-44) is a

*Thomas Gray, from *Elegy Written in a Country Churchyard*.

21-45 ILYA REPIN, *A Religious Procession in the Kursk District, c.* 1880. Tretyakov Gallery, Moscow.

pageant of Victorian high society in an age of great opulence, when the yachts of millionaires served as stages for the exhibition of leisured wealth. The setting is a splendid private cruiser anchored on the Thames, probably downstream at Greenwich. The upper, promenade deck, canopied with flags of the great nations and abloom with the brilliant gowns of society belles, is apparently intended for relaxing and socializing; the companionway at the right leads to the main event on the deck below.

The painter carefully observes the lighting peculiar to the scene; it comes from either side of the ship and from far astern, leaving bright areas left and right, with the center zone shaded by the flag canopy. This obliqueness of light direction makes for a most complex tonality. The dominant shade permits no cast shadows, rather a subtle halftone with subdued hues. A tonal neutrality prevails, setting off the sharply contrasting blacks and whites of the gowns, flattening form into pattern, as in Leibl's painting. In both paintings, the artist intends not only to represent the human types objectively in their characteristic environment, but also to light that environment characteristically, whether it be a country church or a rich man's yacht. Moreover, in Tissot's painting particularly, the perspective space progresses beyond the cropping limit of the frame to include the observer and his viewpoint. And the off-center (eccentric) arrangements of figures, with numerous overlappings and directions of glance, show that the painter is concerned above all with rendering the scene as if it is occurring at an instant in time—spontaneous, unposed, natural. The effect is photographic, as John Ruskin recognized.

The literature of nineteenth-century Russia has long received the attention it deserves; not so its art. We need not argue the value of Russian art of that time, but only recognize the achievement of ILYA REPIN (1844–1930), a master too often passed over in histories of modern art. His painting *A Religious Procession in the Kursk District* (FIG. 21-45), simultaneously drama and document, is a Realistic work of extraordinary power. From the viewing point of the artist, we are witness to a dense throng of people in slow, straggling march behind shrines carried on the shoulders of monks. There are priests, peasants, burghers, provincial officials and bureaucrats, students, soldiers, police—all rallying to the bunting-bedecked shrines and the icon banners of some saint on his feast day. It is a multitude that, in itself, characterizes the society of "Holy Russia" as it was before the revolutions of the twentieth century. The throng tramps along a country road, raising clouds of dust in the heat of noon, in a featureless Russian landscape where trees have been recently hacked down. Closer inspection reveals two files of mounted riders—some in uniform, some priestly in appearance—coming slowly forward through the crowd, their way being cleared by men who savagely ply whips and cudgels to open a path. In the left foreground a boy on a crutch has just been struck heavily by a staff in the hands of a priest. We can read in the crowded details of Repin's *Procession* the sullen poverty and misery, the dogged, almost primitive religion, the officious arrogance, the pitiless harshness of the old Russian scene, almost exactly as in the novels of Dostoevsky (*Procession* and *The Brothers Karamazov* are contemporary). One need suspect no interinfluence; painter and novelist are simply confronting the same realities. In a way, moreover, the *Procession* is a kind of

21-46   JOHN SINGER SARGENT, *The Daughters of Edward Darley Boit*, 1882. 7′ 3″ × 7′ 3″. Museum of Fine Arts, Boston.

Russian *Burial at Ornans* (FIG. 21-38); both Repin and Courbet reveal a society through real images of its people.

Repin's painting expands the program of Realism formulated in his time. It is a scene directly from modern life, at a particular place and time, objectively recorded without Romantic tone and with little of the artist's comment, unless a touch of sad irony or protest. The artist, using his acute visual memory, reconstructs the scene, perhaps from sketches but certainly close to the way he saw it—similar to Eakins' method. The space is fluent and is assumed to continue, along with the action, beyond the frame. The light is out-of-doors, rather than of the studio, and

the color—with its myriad modulations and accents—is suited to the time of day and the local color of landscape and dress. A motion-picture camera set up at the artist's viewpoint would probably record the scene much as we see it here. Indeed, in Repin's *Procession*, we are not far, either in subject or form, from the work of the great directors of the Russian cinema.

The versatility of the Realist approach and the diversity of style it allows are evident when we move across the world from Repin to the work of the American painter JOHN SINGER SARGENT (1856–1925), a younger contemporary of Repin and also of Eakins, Leibl, and Tissot. Sargent was born in Florence of expatriate Bostonians, studied art in Paris, and eventually settled in London—a polished cosmopolitan in culture and a facile and fashionable painter of portraits. His remarkably easy brushing of paint in thin films and his effortless achievement of quick and lively illusion are learned from his study of Velázquez. Sargent may have had in mind the latter's masterpiece, *Las Meninas* (FIG. 19-37), when he painted his own version of a family group portrait, *The Daughters of Edward Darley Boit* (FIG. 21-46). Sargent paints the girls (children of a close friend) in their Paris home, their natural environment, grouped casually within a hall and small drawing room. The informal, eccentric arrangement of their slight figures suggest how much at ease they are within this familiar space and with objects like the monumental Japanese vases, the red screen, and the fringed rug. (The size of the objects, moreover, subtly emphasizes the girls' diminutive stature.) Sargent must have known the Boit children well, and liked them; certainly, they seem comfortable in his presence, being on home ground and not in a studio. Relaxed and trustful, they give Sargent an opportunity to record sensitively a gradation of young innocence—from the naive, wondering openness of the little girl in the foreground, to the grave artlessness of the ten-year-old, to the slightly self-conscious poise of the adolescents. From the positioning of the figures and the continuity of the space of hall and room (made so by the lighting), we sense how spontaneously they move through their element. They seem to be attending momentarily to an adult who has asked them to interrupt their activity and "look this way." Here is a most

effective embodiment of the Realist belief that the business of the artist is to record the modern being in modern context. In this case, the persons and their environment are sharply specified. The Realist painter increasingly moves into the space of the painting, regulating the distance of his standpoint from the objects he is representing, so that he seems to share the space with them and to participate in the action or in the environment of the action.

The Realist's manipulation of distance, whereby the artist is placed in the locale of the subject's action, is evident in a painting by WINSLOW HOMER (1836–1910), who, with Eakins, was a leading representative of the American School. As if equipped with a modern telephoto lens, Homer, in *The Fox Hunt* (FIG. 21-47), witnesses and reports a poignant event in the nonhuman world of nature. A fox, bogged down in heavy winter snow, is attacked by crows made fierce by starvation; trapped, its fate is sure. The double irony of the title is clear. A fox is hunted for sport by the mounted hunter, who has no intention of devouring it; it is not normally hunted by crows. In this case, the swift and elusive fox is caught by a shift of circumstances, and the hungry crows find unaccustomed prey. The fox once hunted birds; now birds hunt the fox. Homer expresses the impersonal, cruel competition of natural species—asserted as a rule of life in the Darwinian–Spencerian theory of the survival of the fittest and appearing in the writers of the time, notably in Jack London's *Call of the Wild*. The Realist factually conveys the Romantic mood of struggle and death in nature. Homer's method is objective

21-47 WINSLOW HOMER, *The Fox Hunt*, 1893. 38" × 68½". The Pennsylvania Academy of the Fine Arts, Philadelphia (Temple Fund Purchase).

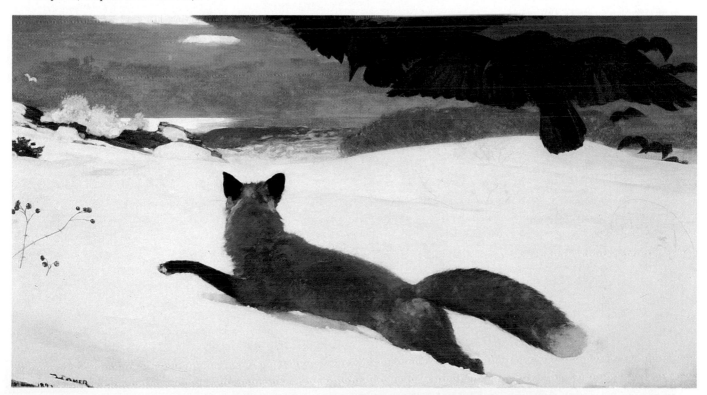

and simple. The figure of the fox is silhouetted against the flat white of the snowy ground; above, the dark shapes of the crows fill the dark sky, overshadowing and overwhelming the fox. The color areas are sharp-edged and icy cold, except for the faintly warm tonality of the fox's vulnerable coat. Form and color convey the grim mood of the scene in reinforcement of what the images literally present. The artist is "present" but powerless to intervene. In any event, this is a fact of nature.

Romantic Responses to Realism

Realism stands for what the eye can see in the modern world—for actuality in all subject matter and verisimilitude in all images. Works of imagination based on subjects from myth and history are believed false. About art, the philosopher Friedrich Nietzsche, reflecting the Realist credo, writes: "We do not demand beautiful, illusory lies from it. . . . Brutal positivism reigns, recognizing facts without becoming excited." The Realist artists, then, confine their subject to what is optically present in the contemporary environment. (Yet, by the end of the century, the realistic recording of modern life will seem hopelessly trivial and will be largely abandoned for wholly subjective, nonrealistic styles.) Like the positivists of science, the Realists believe in the supremacy of cold fact, the enemy of all fictions and illusions, and make it the basis of esthetic truth and personal honesty.

But wasn't this doctrine arbitrary and severely restrictive of that play of artistic imagination long honored in the Tradition? Some artists who subscribed to this view refused to be restricted to the contemporary scene; they painted fictional, fanciful, and historical subjects—realistically. In England, JOHN EVERETT MILLAIS (1829–1896), whom Baudelaire called "the poet of meticulous detail," used the Realistic technique to render religious, historical, and literary subjects. Painstakingly careful in his study of visual fact closely observed from nature, he was a founder of the so-called Pre-Raphaelite Brotherhood in 1848, a group of young English artists who wished to create an art fresh, sincere, and free from what they considered to be the tired and artificial manner propagated by the successors of Raphael in the academies. Millais' method is seen to advantage in his *Ophelia* (FIG. 21-48), which he exhibited in the Universal Exposition in Paris in 1855, where Courbet set up his Pavilion of Realism. The subject, from Shakespeare's *Hamlet*, is the drowning of Ophelia, who, in her madness, is unaware of her plight:

> Her clothes spread wide,
> And mermaid-like awhile they bore her up;
> Which time she chanted snatches of old tunes.
>
> (IV:3)

21-48 JOHN EVERETT MILLAIS, *Ophelia*, 1852. 30″ × 44″. Tate Gallery, London.

Concerned to make the pathos of the scene visible, Millais becomes a faithful and feeling witness of it in every detail, as if it were indeed before his eyes, reconstructing it with a circumstantial stagecraft worthy of the original poetry.

Millais' technique is Realistic, but the orthodox Realist would complain that the subject is not—that it is playacting. Yet it is unlikely that an impartial observer of the painting who is also familiar with *Hamlet* will object that, as the subject is not from the artist's time and place, it is, of necessity, deficient in truth— certainly not deficient in truth to appearance. It may be that this conflict between the *seen* (in everyday experience) and the *seeable* (in plausible reconstructions of past events or fictions) is resolved in modern cinema. The kind of picture drama we have in *Ophelia*—in bringing before our eyes with all optical fidelity the fictive action of a nonpictorial medium, literature—is an anticipation of the motion picture, in which fictions and facts are presented to the eye as equally real. Nineteenth-century Realists like Courbet and Manet might have objected that the picture-drama was not painting, but stage production, and could only be judged as such. The German painter HANS THOMA remarked that many history paintings looked as though they had been made by theater directors, and they were often referred to disparagingly as "costume pieces."

In any event, there were also many painters during this period who did not accept Realism either in terms of subject or technique. Among them was EDWARD BURNE-JONES (1833–1898), a friend and protégé of John Ruskin and (in a later circle of the Pre-Raphaelite Brotherhood) an associate of William Morris and Dante Gabriel Rossetti, who, earlier, had slurred the work of Courbet. Burne-Jones agreed with their distaste for the materialism and ugliness of the contemporary, industrializing world and with their appreciation of the spirituality and idealism, as well as the art and craftsmanship, of past times, especially the Middle Ages and the Early Renaissance. Burne-Jones drew his subjects from literature and depicted them in a soft, languid style much influenced by Sandro Botticelli (FIG. 16-59). His *King Cophetua and the Beggar Maid* (FIG. 21-49) illustrates a little poem of that name written by Alfred Tennyson in 1842, a modern reworking of an ancient and popular ballad. The situation is given in the last lines:

So sweet a face, such angel grace
  In all that land had never been.
Cophetua sware a royal oath:
  "This beggar maid shall be my queen!"

The king, in grave reverie, contemplates the maiden, who sits serenely above him, like some pedestaled perfection oblivious to mortal presence. Burne-Jones

21-49 EDWARD BURNE-JONES, *King Cophetua and the Beggar Maid*, 1884. Approx. 9' 7" × 4' 5". Tate Gallery, London.

is certainly no Realist; although he insisted he wanted the maiden to look like a beggar, she looks anything but. Like the atmosphere, she belongs to the world of trance and dream, in which images arise from some lost age of beauty and innocence. The composition, planar and still, recalls the mural tableaux of the Ren-

21-50　Anselm Feuerbach, *Medea*, 1870. 6′ 6″ × 13′. Bayerische Staatsgemäldesammlungen, Munich.

aissance, the suspended action of stained glass and tapestry. (For the manufacture of works in the latter two media, in fact, Burne-Jones supplied the shop of William Morris with many designs.) His dreamy, abstract, decorative manner perfectly suits the somewhat precious, estheticizing taste of the later nineteenth century. We can appreciate how far we are here from Realism, as well as the great diversity of style at the time, if we compare Burne-Jones' beggar maid with Manet's barmaid (FIG. 21-41). Only two years separate the dates of the paintings.

In the age of Courbet and Manet, the authority of the Tradition could still command artistic obedience. Only slightly touched by the influence of Courbet in Paris, Anselm Feuerbach (1829–1880) found in Italy, as did so many of his German compatriots, the age-old inspiration of the Renaissance and Classical antiquity. A long resident of Rome, he was under the spell of Raphael when he painted the *Medea* (FIG. 21-50). Here, Feuerbach gives us not the climax of the tragedy, but its quiet prologue. Jason and his argonauts

set out to find the Golden Fleece, while Medea, not foreseeing his faithlessness, embraces the children whom she will later kill. The grieving nurse has a premonition of the disaster to come. Yet nothing disturbs the calm of the composition, in which the Classicism of Raphael is enhanced by Feuerbach's study of ancient sculpture. The conception of the figure of Medea is in the spirit of the reclining goddess from the east pediment of the Parthenon (FIG. 5-48). In this picture, more than in any of his others, Feuerbach realizes his stated ideal: a "truly majestic, forbidding tranquility," a Classicism aristocratic and aloof.

This altogether turning away from Realism and, indeed, the modern world that called for it, is also to be seen in the work of Pierre Puvis de Chavannes (1824–1898). Again it is Classical mood and form that the artist seeks to adapt to his own esthetic ends—an art ornamental and reflective, removed from the noisy world of Realism. Puvis had been a pupil of Chassériau, who, early on, pointed the way of retreat into an art of beauty for its own sake, an art uncom-

21-51　Pierre Puvis de Chavannes, *The Sacred Grove*, 1884. 2′ 11½″ × 6′ 10″. (Potter Palmer Collection)

pelled by the dictates of Realism and of modern pragmatism. In his *Sacred Grove* (FIG. 21-51), Puvis deploys statuesque figures in a tranquil landscape with a Classical shrine—their motion suspended in timeless poses, their contours simple and sharp, their modeling as shallow as bas-relief. Puvis, primarily a mural painter, is obedient to the requirements of the wall surface, neutralizing and restraining color, banishing pictorial illusionism with its perspective and tone matching. The calm, almost bland atmosphere suggests some consecrated place, where all movements and gestures, undisturbed by the busyness of life, have a perpetual, ritual significance. The stillness and simplicity of the forms, the linear patterns created by their rhythmic contours, and the suggestion of their symbolic import amount to a kind of program of anti-Realism that impressed younger painters like Paul Gauguin and the Symbolists, who saw in Puvis the prophet of a new style that would replace Realism. Puvis had a double reputation: he was accepted by the Academy and the government for his Classicism, and he was revered by the avant-garde for his vindication of imagination and artistic independence from the world of materialism and the machine. Puvis asks a question significant for artists of his time and later: "What will become of us artists in the face of this invasion of engineers and mechanics?"

In the painting of ADOLPHE WILLIAM BOUGUEREAU (1825–1905), we find a point of view diametrically opposed to that of Puvis. Although he uses a Classical, mythological subject, as Puvis commonly does, Bouguereau renders his *Nymphs and Satyr* (FIG. 21-52) with an optical realism of high finish—scrupulously matching and blending values to achieve, through tonal gradation and continuity, a startling illusion. A painting like this presses the question: Can the subjects of myth, fancy, and fiction be painted with the modern tonal simulation we associate with the camera, without evoking incredulity and, perhaps, a sense of absurdity in the observer? We have raised the question earlier; it is the Realist's. Here, Bouguereau gives us not the tranquil, disassociated vision of Puvis, which is rendered in an almost abstract form, but a heated, orgiastic struggle, which, were it not veiled by Classical allusion, would make us think of those similar, but openly titillating tableaux produced in certain photographers' studios in the later years of the century. What is at question is the appropriateness of the subject in relation to the technique of representation. Do they belong together? *Can* they appear together without contradiction that promotes disbelief? For the Classicist, this picture would fail to fulfill a longing "for nothing more than the moment in which conception and representation will flow together." The Realist, would find the picture false, due to the incongruence of its form and content and the unrealistic nature of its subject.

21-52 ADOLPHE WILLIAM BOUGUEREAU, *Nymphs and Satyr*, 1873. Approx. 8′ 6″ high. Clark Institute, Williamstown, Massachusetts.

The obvious conflict of conception and representation in many of Bouguereau's pictures, as well as in those of other recognized artists of the time, did not displease the public. Bouguereau was immensely popular, enjoying the favor of state patronage throughout his career. His reputation has fluctuated violently; the moderns of his century damned him as the very archetype of the official painter, but critics of our own day acknowledge his love of beauty and his undeniable painterly skills, if not always his esthetic wisdom and taste.

Much of the reputation of the popular, "official," "academic" art of the century stood, fell, and rose again—rehabilitated with Bouguereau and his colleague Gérôme, considered earlier. There were painters, touched lightly or heavily by Realism, who borrowed from it or compromised with it but remained independent of its principal dogma—that the artist must see and represent modern life in a modern way. We need mention only two of a very large number of these to exemplify further the stylistic pluralism of the age.

ROSA BONHEUR (1822–1899), a winner of many

21-53   ROSA BONHEUR, *The Horse Fair*, 1853. 8′ ¼″ × 16′ 7½″. Metropolitan Museum of Art, New York (gift of Cornelius Vanderbilt, 1887).

prizes at the Paris Salon, was very popular in England. Her monumental canvas *The Horse Fair* (FIG. 21-53) displays a scientific naturalist's knowledge of equine anatomy and motion, in combination with an honest love of and admiration for brute beauty and strength. To pictorialize her theme, she makes use of the results of her own sure observation of horses, but a familiarity with Rubens, and especially the compositions of Gericault and Delacroix, also seems likely to have been a factor. The horses and their grooms make the circuit of the exhibition ring of the fair; the excitement of the action generates tensions among men and animals. Horses, some not quite broken, rear up; others plod or trot, guided on foot or ridden by their brawny keepers. The uneven line of march, the tread and tramp, the thunderous pounding of the heavy-weight percherons, the overwhelming power partly breaking out—all are orchestrated by the artist visually, yet almost aurally as well. The great Baroque arc of the painting's space, across which roll and

21-54   JULES BASTIEN-LEPAGE, *Joan of Arc*, 1880. 8′ 4″ × 9′ 2″. Metropolitan Museum of Art, New York (gift of Erwin Davis, 1889).

surge the curving, muscular forms, determines the whole composition. Although she had in mind the horses of the Parthenon frieze (FIG. 5-51), the artist seems to have settled on this structure, quite instinctively, as the shape of the motion of powerful masses. Without deliberate intention, Bonheur strongly restates the Baroque in a painting that is, nevertheless, one of the most original of the nineteenth century.

In a balance of Realist style and Romantic subject, JULES BASTIEN-LEPAGE (1848–1884) makes the perfect compromise. His *Joan of Arc* (FIG. 21-54) represents the inspired heroine of France in the garden of her parents' humble cottage. She hearkens, entranced, to her hovering saints—Michael, Catherine, and Margaret—who announce her mission to save her country from the English enemy. The saints appear as dim apparitions in the trees at the upper left; Joan is off-center at the right. The informal arrangement—the continuing, inclusive space cropped accidentally by the frame—is, as we shall presently see, characteristic of Impressionist composition, which seeks to catch the casual, the informal, the unposed "snapshot." It is as if we have come on the saint suddenly and unannounced. Although the figure is farther away from us and the optical manifold (all the details within the frame) is more sharply focused than in Manet's *Bar at the Folies-Bergère* (FIG. 21-41), the profusion of evenly stressed detail, spread flatly across the picture plane, is closely comparable. If the saints were eliminated and the situation and dress made contemporary, the Realist would have little to complain of. In Bastien-Lepage's *Joan of Arc*, the stylistic paths of Romanticism and Realism run together; the disagreement could only be about the subject: is it "modern" or not? Here, the dialogue-like exchanges between Romanticism and Realism seem to end, at least, in an agreement about form. But do they? We have seen that many artists rejected Realism altogether, and some compromised with it. Still others will follow the Realist premise to its conclusion. These are the Impressionists, and their point of departure is the art of Manet.

Impressionism

Although the term "Impressionism" was first used in 1874 (by a journalist ridiculing a landscape by Monet called *Impression—Sunrise*), the controversy that raged for 20 years over the merits of Impressionism began 11 years earlier with Manet's *Le Déjeuner sur l'herbe* (FIG. 21-39).

From the middle of the 1860s, such Impressionist painters as Monet, Camille Pissarro, Renoir, and Degas followed Manet's lead in depicting scenes of contemporary life and landscape. Their desire for a more modern expression led them to prize the imme-

diacy of visual impression and persuaded the landscapists, especially Monet and Pissarro, to work out of doors. From this custom of painting directly from nature came the spontaneous revelation of atmosphere and climate so characteristic of Impressionist painting. Their rejection of idealistic interpretation and literary anecdote was paralleled by their scrutiny of color and light. Scientific studies of light and the invention of chemical pigments increased their sensitivity to the multiplicity of colors in nature and gave them new colors with which to work. Most of their eight cooperative exhibitions, held between 1874 and 1886, irritated the public. But their technique was actually less radical than it seemed at the time; in certain respects, they were simply developing the color theories of Leonardo and the actual practice of Rubens, Constable, Turner, and Delacroix.

The Impressionists sought to create the illusion of forms bathed in light and atmosphere. This required an intensive study of outdoor light as the source of our experience of color, which revealed the important truth that local color—the actual color of an object— is usually modified by the quality of the light in which it is seen, by reflections from other objects, and by the effects produced by juxtaposed colors. Complementary colors, for example, if used side by side over large enough areas, intensify each other. In small quantities or mixed, though, they fuse into neutral tone. Shadows do not appear gray or black, as many earlier painters had thought, but seem to be composed of colors modified by reflections or other conditions. (Jan Vermeer evidently observed this.) Furthermore, the juxtaposition of colors on the canvas for the eye to fuse at a distance produces a more intense hue than the mixing of the same colors on the palette. Although it is not strictly true that the Impressionists used only primary hues, juxtaposing them to create secondary colors (blue and yellow, for example, to produce green), they did achieve remarkably brilliant effects with their characteristically short, choppy brush strokes, which so accurately caught the vibrating quality of light. The fact that the surfaces of their canvases look unintelligible at close range and their forms and objects appear only when the eye fuses the strokes at a certain distance accounts for much of the early adverse criticism—such as the conjecture that the Impressionists fired their paint at the canvas with a pistol.

Of the Impressionists, CLAUDE MONET (1840–1926), whose *Impression—Sunrise* we just mentioned, carries the method furthest, especially in a series of paintings of the same subject. He painted 16 views of Waterloo Bridge in London and some 40 views of Rouen Cathedral (Introduction FIG. 5 and FIG. 21-55). In each case, the cathedral is observed from the same point of view, but at different times of day and under various

21-55   CLAUDE MONET, *Rouen Cathedral* (façade), 1894. Approx. 39″ × 26″. Metropolitan Museum of Art, New York (Theodore M. Davis Collection, bequest of Theodore M. Davis, 1915).

climatic and atmospheric conditions. Monet, with a scientific precision, gives us an unparalleled and unexcelled record of the passing of time as seen in the movement of light over identical forms. Later critics accused Monet and his companions of destroying form and order for the sake of fleeting atmospheric effects. But we may feel that light is properly the "form" of Monet's finest paintings, rather than accept the narrower definition that recognizes "formal" properties only in firm, geometric shapes. The Impressionist artist does not paint the world we presumably "see"—the world of Corot's "values," of graduated tones of lights and darks; rather, he records his own sensations of color, and the outlines and solidities of the world interpreted by common sense melt away.

The *Place du Théâtre Français* (FIG. 21-56) by CAMILLE PISSARRO (1830–1903) shows the same qualities. The artist's visual sensations of a crowded Paris square, viewed from several stories above street level, yield a panorama of blurred, dark accents against a light ground. Like Monet, Pissarro is after the most fugitive effects of movement; but, unlike Monet, the movements are not so much of light as of the life of the street. He achieves a deliberate casualness in the arrangement of his figures—the effect a single glance from a window would provide if it were prolonged only a few seconds. Ceaseless change of position and ceaseless change of color are the new order of the painter's experience. There is no longer a standard of unchanging optical truth, just as there is no longer a standard way of seeing. The artist's subjective experience is all he has to deal with, and, for him, "nature" is simply the source of his sensations. When Pissarro writes, in a letter to his son Lucien, "we have to approach nature sincerely, with our own modern sensibilities," we should understand him to mean not the "nature" of the great landscape tradition but "nature" precisely as it is revealed to our modern senses. For the Impressionist, the modern sensibility gets at what is *real* in nature—namely the color stimuli it reveals to the analytic eye of the modern painter.

In the later nineteenth century, artists are not alone in emphasizing the prime reality of sensation in the process of apprehending nature or the world. Scientists, philosophers of science, and psychologists in great number begin to assert that reality *is* sensation, or that knowledge can be based only on the analysis of our sensations. Indeed, the Austrian physicist Ernst Mach could hold that the *sole* reality is sensation and that all the laws and principles of physics are only a kind of shorthand referring to complex linkages of the data of sense. And modern experimental psychology, of course, begins with the measurement of sense experience.

What we might call "color sensationism" and fugitive effects of light and motion are what link the Impressionist artists; for on closer view, each has very much his own manner, despite the more-or-less fundamental agreements. For example, AUGUSTE RENOIR (1841–1919) is a specialist in the human figure, a sympathetic admirer of what is beautiful in the body and what is pleasurable in the simple round of human life. The bright gaiety of *Le Moulin de la Galette* (FIG. 21-57), where a Sunday throng enjoys a popular Paris dance hall, is a characteristically Renoir celebration of vivacious charm. People crowd the tables and chatter, while others dance energetically. The whole scene is dappled by sunlight and shade, artfully blurred into the figures themselves to produce just that effect of floating and fleeting light so cultivated by the Impressionists. The casual, unposed place-

21-56   CAMILLE PISSARRO, *Place du Théâtre Français*, 1895. Approx. 28½" × 36½". Los Angeles County Museum of Art (the Mr. and Mrs. George Gard De Sylva Collection).

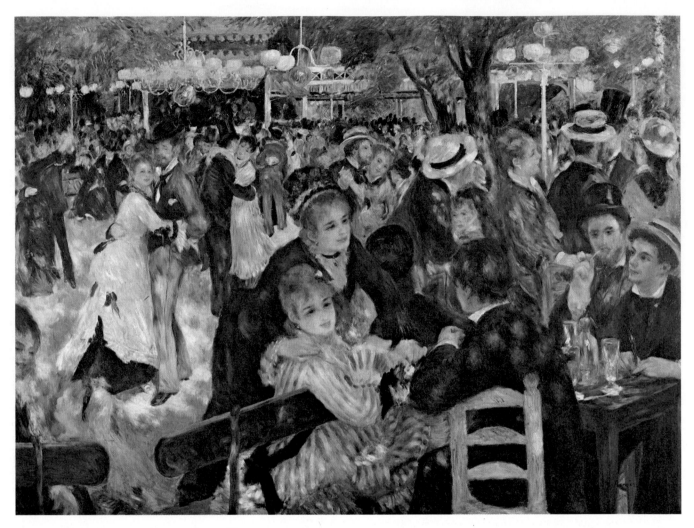

21-57 AUGUSTE RENOIR, *Le Moulin de la Galette*, 1876. Approx. 51″ × 68″. Louvre, Paris.

ment of the figures, and the suggested continuity of space spreading in all directions and only accidentally limited by the frame introduce us, as observers, into the very scene. We are not, as with the Tradition, observing a performance on a stage set; rather, we ourselves are part of the action. Renoir's subjects are quite unconscious of the presence of an observer; they do not pose but merely go about the business of the moment. In his search for the real, Renoir not only analyzes his own visual sensations but attempts to capture the process of events, to catch nature utterly unawares, to find some unique and particular aspect of it that will never recur in quite the same way. As Classical art seeks the universal and typical, Realistic art seeks just the opposite—the incidental, momentary, and passing.

EDGAR DEGAS (1834–1917) is usually included in any discussion of Impressionism. Although actively sympathetic with the Impressionists, he stood somewhat apart from them, an independent talent of great power. In his earlier work, he shares the Realist intentions of Manet, BERTHE MORISOT (1841–1895), and

other Realists not connected with the Impressionist movement. As a Realist, Degas observes and records modern life in its modern settings, whether at a distance or immediately at hand.

A painting of his early middle period, *Intérieur (Le Viol)* (FIG. 21-58), exhibits a penetrating Realism that invades the very bedroom of a newly married couple already in unhappy conflict. This is a time when literature and the stage, as well as art, sought to analyze and present the peculiarly modern problems of human relationships, especially the tensions between the sexes; we think of the plays of Ibsen and the novels of Flaubert, De Maupassant, and Zola, among many others. A novel by Zola, *Thérèse Raquin* (1867), is believed to have provided the program of the picture. The positions and attitudes of man and woman, the latter's gown, the accessories of the room, the play of shadows cast by the fireside and lamp—all are noted by Degas as they appear in the novel. Like Manet, Degas was a cultivated man of the world, conversant with the ideas of the day; like both Manet and Zola, he would be interested in the influences

21-58 Edgar Degas, *Intérieur* (*Le Viol*), *c.* 1868–1870. Approx. 32″ × 46″. Collection of Henry P. McIlhenny, Philadelphia; photo: Philadelphia Museum of Art.

that positive science now saw as determining human behavior—biological, sociological, and psychological forces active in the heredity and environment of every human individual. Human emotions, in Zola's and, presumably, Degas' views, are akin to physiological or even pathological symptoms; love, hate, desire, anxiety, frustration, alienation, and despair are the results of hidden, psychic mechanisms of an irrational or subrational nature. In light of these concepts, which foreshadow the epoch-making teachings of Sigmund Freud, the Realist studies human subjects dispassionately, like a clinician in a laboratory, seeking to describe and interpret their actions in terms of their hidden motivations. The persons in *Intérieur* are entirely unaware that they are being observed. This is the case in almost all of Degas' works.

In this painting, Degas explores the pictorial values of artificial light; later, in association with the Impressionists, he will brighten his palette to daylight hues, although he would never approve of out-of-doors (*plein-air*) painting. He abandons staged space and paused action for cropped spaces produced by acci-

dental or unusual angles of sight. Figures move swiftly into, within, and out of these irregular spaces.

More than any of his contemporaries, Degas studied the infinite variety of particular movements that make up continuous motion. Ballerinas in arrested movements—a split-second pose cut from the sequence of their dance—are one of his favorite subjects. In *Ballet Rehearsal (Adagio)* (fig. 21-59), Degas uses several devices to bring the observer to the pictorial space. The frame cuts off the spiral stair, the windows in the background, and the group of figures in the right foreground; the rapid diagonals of the wall bases and floorboards carry us into and along the directional lines of the swift dancers; the figures are uncentered and "accidental" in arrangement; and, as is customary in Degas' ballet pictures, a large, off-center, empty space creates the illusion of a continuous floor that connects us with the pictured figures. By standing on the "same" surface with them, we seem to be drawn into their space. This cunning spatial projection derives from careful observation and may have been inspired by hints from Japanese prints

21-59   EDGAR DEGAS, *Ballet Rehearsal* (*Adagio*), 1876. 23″ × 33″. Glasgow Art Galleries and Museum (Burrell Collection).

21-60   SUZUKI HARUNOBU, *The Evening Glow of the Andon*, 1765. 11¼″ × 8½″. (Clarence Buckingham Collection)

(FIG. 21-60), in which diverging lines not only organize the flat shapes of the figures but function as lines directing the viewer's attention into the picture space. The Impressionists, familiar with these prints as early as the 1860s, greatly admired their spatial organization, the familiar and intimate themes, and the flat, unmodeled color areas and drew much instruction from them. It is the popular Japanese print of the eighteenth century, "discovered" by European artists in the mid-nineteenth, that has the first definitive non-European influence on European pictorial design. Earlier borrowings from China, India, and Arabia had been superficial.

Degas' *Viscount Lepic and His Daughters* (FIG. 21-61), painted in 1873, summarizes what he learned from his own painstaking research and what his generation in general learned from the Japanese print: the clear, flat pattern; the unusual point of view; the informal glimpse of contemporary life. Whatever his subject, Degas—mindful of Ingres, whose work he greatly admired—sees it as a clear line and pattern, observed from a new and unexpected angle. In the divergent movement of the father and his small daughters, of the man entering the picture at the left, and of the horse and carriage passing across the background, we have a vivid pictorial account of a moment in time at a particular position in space, much as Monet, in his own way, defines such space and time in landscape painting. In another instant, there would be no picture, for each of the figures would move in a different direction, and the group would dissolve. Here again, Degas makes clever use of the empty space of the street to integrate the viewer into the space containing the figures. Actually, the painter seems to be taking into account the range of the sweep of our glance—what we would see in a single split-second inspection; indeed, the picture resembles a snapshot made with a hastily aimed camera.

When Degas was a very young man and about to enter on a career as painter, he met Ingres, who advised him: "Draw lines, young man, many lines, from memory or from nature; it is this way that you will become a good painter." Degas, faithful to the old linearist's advice, became a superb master of line, so much so that his identification as an Impressionist—in the sense that Monet, Pissarro, and Renoir are Impressionists—often seems mistaken to many critics. Certainly, his designs do not cling to the surface of the canvas, as do Manet's and Monet's; they are developed in depth and take the viewer well behind the picture plane; and we are always aware of the elastic strength of his firmly drawn contours. However, Degas does specialize in studies of figures in rapid and informal movement, recording the quick impression of arrested motion, and he does use the spectral color—the fresh, divided hues of the Impressionists—especially when he works in his favorite medium, pastel. These dry sticks of powdered pigment cannot be "muddied" by mixing them on a palette, so that they produce, almost automatically, those fresh and bright colors so favored by the Impressionists. All this is seen in *The Morning Bath* (FIG. 21-62), which is like Renoir's treatment of the same subject in its informality and intimacy but totally unlike Renoir in the indifference to either formal or physical beauty. Degas' concern is with the unplanned realism of the purely accidental attitude of the human figure, seen in an awkward yet natural enough moment. The broken volume of the nude

body twists across "Japanese" angles, flat planes, and patterns. It is the verity of motion that Degas seeks above all. Mingling the method of Ingres with that of the Impressionists, Degas makes an entirely un-"academic" picture that is appropriate to and consistent with the dawning age of the motion picture.

In the Paris Salon of 1874, Degas admired a painting by a young American artist, MARY CASSATT (1845–1926), the wealthy daughter of a Philadelphia banker.

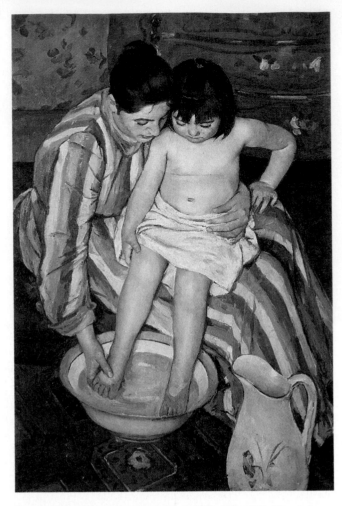

21-63 MARY CASSATT, *The Bath*, c. 1892. 39″ × 26″. The Art Institute of Chicago.

"There," he remarked, "is a person who feels as I do." Cassatt was befriended and influenced by Degas and exhibited regularly with the Impressionists. The compositional devices of Degas and of the Japanese print are equally evident in paintings like *The Bath* (FIG. 21-63), but they do not impair Cassatt's own strong originality and firmness of design. Degas is said to have observed that it was impossible for a woman to draw that well, but he seemed satisfied enough to be proven wrong. Cassatt's subjects are principally women and children, whom she presents with a quite inimitable conjunction of cool objectivity and genuine sentiment. Gauguin's estimate hits it exactly: "Mary Cassatt has charm, but she also has force."

Almost at the moment when the Realists began to discard Romantic subject matter to represent what they saw around them, Manet, in his later works, and the Impressionists seemed to raise the question of whether *what* we see is not ultimately a matter of *how* we see it. What is more "real"—a world of solid objects moving in space, or one's optical sensations of light and color in fleeting patterns? In a sense, Realistic Impressionism continues the Romantic preoccupation with the *self* of the artist, except that artists now consult not so much their feelings and imagination as their purely visual sensations. The world out there is no longer a given order of masses in space. Rather, it is the source of sensations of light and color with no fixed order whatsoever; the only order is the one artists create from their own optical experience, the record of the stimulation of the optic nerve by light.

Thus, there is a paradox in Impressionism. Seeking, through realism, to capture the look of the modern, public world, Impressionist artists rely on an increasingly private vision of it. They do not render the optical world so much as they record their visual sensations of it. They analyze the tonal continuum away and replace it with discontinuous spots of color, the quality and placement of which depend on their *personal choice* in the technical process of painting. The public world is only a stimulus for the reflexive, unreflecting Impressionist response. The way the world looks is not given; it becomes the decision—in a way, the invention—of the artist. Searching for reality, the artist comes to find it in himself. Nothing could be more romantic!

In what follows, we trace the astonishing artistic sequences that complete the transformation of the old pictorial Tradition and produce the prevailing anti-Realism of the first 50 years of twentieth-century art.

Responses to Impressionism

By 1886, the Impressionists were accepted as serious artists by most critics and by a large segment of the public. But just at the time when their gay and colorful studies of contemporary life no longer seemed crude and unfinished, the painters themselves and a group of young followers came to feel that too many of the traditional elements of picture-making were being neglected in the search for momentary sensations of light and color. A more systematic examination of the properties of three-dimensional space, of the expressive qualities of line, pattern, and color, and of the symbolic character of subject matter was undertaken by four men in particular: Georges Seurat, Paul Cézanne, Vincent van Gogh, and Paul Gauguin. Because their art diverges so markedly from earlier Impressionism, although each painter at first accepted the Impressionist methods and never rejected the new and brighter palette, they and others sharing their views have come to be known as the Post-Impressionists—a classification that simply signifies their chronological position in nineteenth-century French painting. A sound understanding of their individual styles and achievements is necessary to comprehend twentieth-century art fully.

SEURAT

At the eighth and last Impressionist exhibition in 1886, GEORGES SEURAT (1859–1891) showed his *Sunday Afternoon on the Island of La Grande Jatte* (FIG. 21-64), which set forth the Impressionist interest in holi-

21-64 GEORGES SEURAT, *Sunday Afternoon on the Island of La Grande Jatte*, 1884–1886. Approx. 6′ 9″ × 10′. (Helen Birch Bartlett Memorial Collection) © The Art Institute of Chicago, all rights reserved.

day themes and the analysis of light in a new and monumental synthesis that seemed strangely rigid and remote. Seurat's system of painting in small dots that stand in relation to each other was based on the color theories of Delacroix and the color scientists Helmholtz and Chevreul. (The method, called "divisionism" by Seurat, was often confused with "pointillism," in which dots of color are distributed systematically on a white ground that remains partially exposed and hence visually functional.) It was a difficult procedure, as disciplined and painstaking as the Impressionist method had been spontaneous and exuberant.

Seurat is less concerned with the recording of his immediate color sensations than he is with their careful and systematic organization into a new kind of pictorial order. The free and fluent play of color is disciplined into a calculated arrangement by prior rules of design accepted and imposed by the artist. The effect is ambiguous, as it produces both a surface pattern and a perspective depth. The apparent formlessness of Impressionism hardens into severe regularity. The pattern in *La Grande Jatte* is based on the verticals of the figures and trees, the horizontals in the shadows and the distant embankment, and the

diagonals in the shadows and shoreline, each of which contributes to the pictorial effect. At the same time, by the use of meticulously calculated values, the painter carves out a deep rectangular space. In creating both pattern and suggested space, he plays on repeated motifs: the profile of the lady, the parasol, and the cylindrical forms of the figures, each so placed in space as to set up a rhythmic movement in depth as well as from side to side. The picture is filled with sunshine, but not broken into transient patches of color. Light, air, people, and landscape are fixed in an abstract design in which line, color, value, and shape cohere in an organization as precise as a machine.

This is a severely intellectual art, of which Seurat himself said: "They see poetry in what I have done. No, I apply my method, and that is all there is to it." There is in this statement something of the scientific attitude we have found manifesting itself throughout nineteenth-century painting. On the other hand, there is something of Renaissance geometric formalism also; the stately stage space, with its perspective and careful placement of figures, is reminiscent of an art, descended from Paolo Uccello and Piero della Francesca, that moves us by its serene monumentality. Manet, in *Le Déjeuner* (FIG. 21-39), uses a Renaissance composition to manifest new techniques; Seurat, in *La Grande Jatte*, turns traditional pictorial stage space into pattern by applying a color formula of which space is only a fairly unimportant variable. For our optical experience of space can only be a function of color. Whereas, in the tradition of Giotto and Raphael, the reality was space, with color something superadded, now with Seurat (and, as we shall see, with Cézanne), color is the reality and spaces and solids are merely figments. Having found the formula of color relationships, the artist need no longer rely on the dubious evidence of his impressions. Paul Signac, Seurat's friend and collaborator in the design of the "neo-impressionist" method, describes it with bland confidence:

> By the elimination of all muddy mixtures, by the exclusive use of the optical mixture of pure colors, by a methodical divisionism and a strict observation of the scientific theory of colors, the Neo-Impressionist ensures a maximum of luminosity, of color intensity, and of harmony—a result that has never yet been obtained.*

We remember Constable's assertion that landscape painting is a natural science! We also remember that the formulas of optical science of the nineteenth century develop into those of the twentieth century and that what is scientific can have technological application. In one respect—the breaking of mass into discrete particles (and color into dots of component colors)—Seurat's *Grande Jatte* may be said to have been the forerunner of the modern techniques of photoengraving and color reproduction.

CÉZANNE

In a conversation with the influential art dealer Ambroise Vollard about 1883, Renoir said: "I had wrung Impressionism dry, and I finally came to the conclusion that I knew neither how to paint nor how to draw. In a word, Impressionism was a blind alley, as far as I was concerned. . . ." This conviction had probably come to other Impressionists; certainly, it must have come early to PAUL CÉZANNE (1839–1906). Although a lifelong admirer of Delacroix, he allied himself with the Impressionists, especially Pissarro, and at first accepted their theories of color and their faith in subjects chosen from everyday life. Yet his own studies of the old masters in the Louvre persuaded him that Impressionism lacked form and structure. As he said: "I want to make of Impressionism something solid and lasting like the art in the museums."

The basis of Cézanne's art is his new way of studying nature (FIG. 21-66). Of course, this could be said of all nineteenth-century landscapists from Constable on; however, each artist's concept of what *is* is different. Cézanne's aim is not truth to appearance, especially not photographic truth, nor is it the "truth" of Impressionism. Rather, he searches for a lasting *structure* behind the formless and fleeting screens of color the eye takes in. If all that we see is color, then color must fulfill the structural purposes of the old perspective and the old light and shade; color alone must give depth and distance, shape and solidity. But if color is only optical sensation, as the Impressionists show, then the structure sought in the optical world is, after all, the structure of one's own sensation. Face-to-face with nature, Cézanne attempts to bring an intellectual order, rather than the random approach of the Impressionists, into his sensations of it, constantly and painfully checking with that part of the scene—he calls it the "motif"—that he is studying. When he says, "We must do Poussin over again, this time according to nature," he apparently means that Poussin's effects of distance, depth, and solidity must be achieved not by perspective and chiaroscuro but entirely in terms of the color-relief maps provided by our analysis of nature.

The old tonal coherence lost, Cézanne sets out to find a new one. Although he never reduces natural objects to geometric abstractions—this will be the work of the Cubists—the monumentality of his forms suggests that they have been stripped of the accidental variations of individual appearance. In this sense, we can read his famous remark to a young follower—that the painter should "treat nature in terms of the cylinder, and the sphere, and the cone"—as an injunction to present natural forms in terms of their simplest and broadest dimensions, rather than to replace them with geometric constructions.

Cézanne's method is to use his intense powers of visual concentration to observe the motif, sustaining the process of minute inspection through days, months, and even years. He resembles the contemporary scientist who proves his hypothesis with repeated tests. With special care, he explores the properties of line, plane, and color, and their interrelationships: the effect of every kind of linear direction, the capacity of planes to create the sensation of depth, the intrinsic qualities of color, and the power of colors to modify the direction and depth of lines and planes. Through the recession of cool colors and the advance of warm ones, he controls volume and depth. Having observed that saturation (or the highest intensity of a color) produces the greatest effect of fullness of form, he would paint an object chiefly in one hue—apples, for example, in green—achieving convincing solidity by the control of color intensity alone, in place of the traditional method of modeling in light and dark.

---

*Robert Goldwater and Marco Treves, eds., *Artists on Art*, 3rd ed. (New York: Pantheon, 1958). p. 378.

21-65 PAUL CÉZANNE, *Still Life*, c. 1894. Approx. 26″ × 32″. National Gallery of Art, Washington, D.C. (Chester Dale Collection, 1962).

In *Still Life*, painted in 1890 (FIG. 21-65), Cézanne's method may be seen at its best. The individual forms have lost something of their private character as bottles and fruit and approach the condition of cylinders and spheres. A sharp clarity of planes and the edges of planes sets forth the objects as if they had been sculptured. Even the highlights of the glassware are as sharply defined as the solids. The floating color of the Impressionists has been arrested, held, and analyzed into interlocking planes. Cézanne gives us here what might be called, paradoxically, an architecture of color.

The still life was the ideal vehicle for Cézanne's experiments, as a limited number of selected objects can be arranged by the artist to provide a well-ordered point of departure. The landscape does not afford the artist this advantage; the problems of representation are complicated by the need to select from the multiplicity of disorganized natural forms those that seem most significant and to order them into pictorial structure that will have cohesive unity. To apply his methods to the painting of landscapes was one of Cézanne's greatest challenges. Thus, just as landscape had been the principal mode of Impressionist theory and experiment, so it became the sub-

ject for Cézanne's most complete transformation of Impressionism.

La Montagne Sainte-Victoire (FIG. 21-66), done around 1886, is one of the many views that Cézanne painted of the mountain near his home in Aix-en-Provence. In it, we can see how the transitory effects of changing atmospheric conditions, effects that occupied Monet, have been replaced by a more concentrated, lengthier analysis of large, lighted spaces. This space stretches out behind and beyond the plane of the canvas (emphasized by the pattern of the pine tree in the foreground) and is made up of numerous small elements, such as roads, fields, houses, and the aqueduct at the far right, each seen from a slightly different point of view. Above this shifting, receding perspective rises the largest mass of all, the mountain, with an effect—achieved by stressing background and foreground contours equally—of being simultaneously near and far away. This is close to the actual experience a person observing such a view might have when the forms of the landscape are apprehended piecemeal and the relative proportions of objects vary, rather than being fixed once and for all by a strict one- or two-point perspective, as a photograph normally shows. Cézanne immoblizes the

21-66 PAUL CÉZANNE,
La Montagne Sainte-Victoire,
c. 1886–1888. Approx.
26″ × 35½″. Courtauld Institute
Galleries, London.

shifting colors of Impressionism, creating a kind of façade of color that is divided into an array of clearly defined planes. Further analyses of these color planes by the Cubists will give them an independent existence, in which there is little reference to the full optical range of nature.

The *Boy in a Red Vest* (FIG. 21-67) shows Cézanne's application of his method to the human figure. Here, the breaking up of the pictorial space, the volumes of the figure, and the drapery into emphatic planes is so advanced that the planes almost begin to take over the picture surface. The geometric character of the color area pushes to the fore, and we at once become aware of the egg-like shape of the head and the flexible, almost metallic shapes of the prominent planes of the body and drapery. The disproportionally long left arm is obvious, for the distortions and rearrangement of natural forms that may go unnoticed in landscape and still-life paintings are immediately apparent in the human figure and often disturbing to the viewer. Still, we may be sure that Cézanne's distortions—and they occur in most of his figure paintings—are not accidental. What Cézanne does, in effect, is to rearrange the parts of his figure, shortening and lengthening, them in such a way as to make the pattern of their representation in two dimensions conform to the proportions of his picture surface. Thus, Cézanne draws the first conclusion from the Impressionists: deemphasis of subject matter. However, although the depicted object is primarily a light-reflecting surface to the Impressionists, to Cézanne it becomes a secondary aid in the organization of the picture plane. By further reducing the importance of subject matter, Cézanne automatically enhances the value of the object he is making—the picture, which has its

own independent existence and must be judged entirely in terms of its own inherent pictorial qualities. In Cézanne's works, the simplification of the shapes and their sculpture-like relief and weight give that peculiar look of stable calm and dignity that reminds one of the art of the fifteenth-century Renaissance and that has led modern criticism to find in Cézanne some vestige of that ancient Mediterranean sense of

21-67 PAUL CÉZANNE, *Boy in a Red Vest*, 1893–1895.
35¼″ × 28½″. National Gallery, Washington, D.C. (collection of Mr. and Mrs. Paul Mellon).

monumental and unchanging simplicity of form that produced Classical art.

VAN GOGH

Unlike Seurat and Cézanne—who, in different ways, sought, by almost scientific investigation, new rules for the ordering of the experience of color—VINCENT VAN GOGH (1853–1890) impetuously and arbitrarily exploits the new color to express his emotions as he is confronted by nature. A Hollander by birth, son of a Protestant pastor, Van Gogh believed that he had a religious calling and did missionary work in the slums of London and in the mining districts of Belgium. Repeated failures exhausted his body and brought him close to despair. Only after he turned to painting and mastered the Impressionist technique did he find a means to communicate his experience of the sun-illuminated world of so many of his landscapes, which he represented pictorially in terms of his favorite color, yellow. His insistence on the expressive values of color led him to develop a corresponding expressiveness in his very application of the paint. The thickness, shape, and direction of his brushstrokes create a tactile counterpart to his intense color schemes. Now a thickly loaded brush moves vehemently back and forth or at right angles, giving a

textile-like effect; now the tube squeezes dots or streaks on the canvas. This bold, almost slapdash attack might have led to disaster had it not been controlled by Van Gogh's sensibility.

A rich source of Van Gogh's thought on his art is left in the letters he wrote to his brother, Theo. In one of these, he says: "Instead of trying to reproduce exactly what I have before my eyes, I use color more arbitrarily so as to express myself forcibly. . . ." In another letter, he explains that the color in one of his paintings is "not locally true from the point of view of the stereoscopic Realist, but color to suggest any emotion of an ardent temperament." This sounds like Delacroix, and indeed Van Gogh writes: "And I should not be surprised if the Impressionists soon find fault with my way of working, for it has been fertilized by the ideas of Delacroix rather than by theirs," by which he seems to mean that he took his color method from Delacroix directly rather than from the Impressionists.

The Night Café (FIG. 21-68), as Van Gogh writes, is meant to convey an oppressive atmosphere of evil, through every possible distortion of color. The scene, a café interior in a dreary provincial town, is supposed to be felt, not simply observed. The slumped denizens are the very color of the mood in which they

21-68　VINCENT VAN GOGH, *The Night Café*, 1888. Approx. 28½″ × 36″. Yale University Art Gallery, New Haven, Connecticut (bequest of Stephen Carlton Clark, B.A., 1903).

21-69 Vincent van Gogh, *Starry Night*, 1889. Approx. 29″ × 36″. Collection, Museum of Modern Art, New York (bequest of Lillie P. Bliss).

drown—a melancholy green. The ceiling is a poisonous green, in dizzying contrast with the febrile red walls. The floor is an acid yellow; the shadow of the billiard table, green. The yellow halos of light are like accumulations of mephitic gases. The proprietor, the pale demon that rules over the place, rises like a specter from the edge of the billiard table, itself in a steeply tilted perspective that suggests the spinning, vertiginous world of nausea.

Even more illustrative of this "expressionist" method is *Starry Night* (FIG. 21-69), painted in 1889. In it, Van Gogh does not envision the sky as we see it when we look up on a clear dark night—as a spangling of twinkling pinpoints of light against a deep curtain of blue. Rather, he feels the vastness of the universe, filled with whirling and exploding stars and galaxies of stars, beneath which the earth and men's habitations huddle in anticipation of cosmic disaster. Mysteriously, a great cypress is in the process of rapid growth far above the earth's surface and into the combustion of the sky. The artist does not seek or analyze the harmony of nature here. Instead, he transforms it by projecting on it a vision that is entirely his own.

GAUGUIN

A similar rejection of objective representation in favor of subjective expression is found in the work of PAUL GAUGUIN (1843–1903). Gauguin writes disparagingly of Impressionism:

The Impressionists study color exclusively, but without freedom, always shackled by the need of probability. For them the ideal landscape, created from many different entities, does not exist. Their edifice rests upon no solid base and ignores the nature of the sensations perceived by means of color. They heed only the eye and neglect the mysterious centers of thought, so falling into merely scientific reasoning. When they speak of their art, what is it? A purely superficial thing, full of affectations and only material. In it thought does not exist.*

Gauguin also uses color in new and unexpected combinations, but his art is very different from Van Gogh's. It is no less tormented, perhaps, but more learned in its combination of rare and exotic elements and more broadly decorative. Gauguin had painted as an amateur, but after taking lessons with Pissarro, he resigned from his prosperous brokerage business in 1883 to devote his time entirely to painting. Although his work did not sell and he and his family were reduced to poverty, he did not abandon his art, for he felt that, despite ridicule and neglect, he was called to be a great artist. In his search for provocative subjects, as well as for an economical place to live, he stayed for some time in small villages in Brittany and visited the tropics (Martinique). Thus, even before he settled in Tahiti in 1891, tropical color and subjects drawn from primitive life had entered his art. In his attitude toward color, Gauguin broke with the Impressionist studies of minutely contrasted hues. As he says: "A meter of green is greener than a centimeter if you wish to express greenness. . . . How does

*Robert Goldwater and Marco Treves, eds., *Artists on Art*, 3rd ed. (New York: Pantheon, 1958), p. 373.

868 THE NINETEENTH CENTURY: PLURALISM OF STYLE

that tree look to you? Green? All right, then use green, the greenest on your palette. And that shadow, a little bluish? Don't be afraid. Paint it as blue as you can." His influence was especially felt by members of the younger generation, such as Parisian artist MAURICE DENIS, who writes in *Definition of Neo-Traditionalism* in 1890:

> Gauguin freed us from all the restraints which the idea of copying nature had placed upon us. For instance, if it was permissible to use vermilion in painting a tree which seemed reddish . . . why not stress even to the point of deformation the curve of a beautiful shoulder or conventionalize the symmetry of a bough . . . ?

Gauguin's art, too, can be understood as a complex mixture of Eastern and Western elements, of themes common to the great masters of the European Renaissance treated in a manner based on his study of earlier arts and of non-European cultures. In Tahiti and the Marquesas, where he spent the last 10 years of his life, he expressed his love of primitive life and brilliant color in a series of magnificent, decorative canvases. The design is often based, although indirectly, on native motifs, and the color owes its peculiar harmonies of lilac, pink, and lemon to the tropical flora of the islands. But the mood of such works is that of a sophisticated, modern man interpreting an ancient and innocent way of life already threatened by European colonization. Although the figure and setting in *Spirit of the Dead Watching* (FIG. 21-70) are Tahitian, the theme of a reclining nude with a pendant, watching figure—that is, a matching or balancing figure—belongs to the Renaissance and after. The simplified linear pattern and broad areas of flat color recall Byzantine enamels and Medieval stained glass, which Gauguin admired, and the slight distortion of the flattened forms is not unlike similar effects in Egyptian sculpture. Romantic art began with the admiration of "exotic" lands (and peoples) peripheral to Europe; with Gauguin, a kind of adaptation of their very style begins. He represents a new rebelliousness—not only against the artistic tradition, but against the whole of European civilization. According to Gaugin, "civilization is what makes you sick." The search for vitality in new peoples and new life styles, begun in the eighteenth century, now quickens. The twentieth century will draw artistic inspiration from Japan, from the Pacific islands, and from much of the non-European world.

21-70   PAUL GAUGUIN, *Spirit of the Dead Watching*, 1892. Oil on burlap mounted on canvas, 28½" × 36⅜". Albright-Knox Art Gallery, Buffalo (A. Conger Goodyear Collection, 1965).

TOULOUSE-LAUTREC

A dissatisfaction with civilization, an anxious awareness of the psychic strains it imposes, and a perception of the banality and degradation it can bring with it color the mood of the artist toward the end of the century and during the years before the First World War. This is the period of the *fin de siècle,* "the end of the century," when art and literature languish in a kind of malaise compounded of despondency, boredom, morbidity, and hypersensitivity to the esthetic. From recording the contemporary scene, with all its variety and human interest, as the Impressionists had done, painters influenced by Gauguin and Van Gogh now often interpreted it in bitter commentary communicated in harsh distortion—both of form and of color. In the work of HENRI DE TOULOUSE-LAUTREC (1864–1901), who deeply admired Degas, the old master's cool scrutiny of contemporary life is transformed into grim satire and mordant caricature. Lautrec's art is, to a degree, the expression of his life.

He was a dwarf, self-exiled from the high society that his ancient, aristocratic name would have entitled him to enter. He became a denizen of the night world of Paris, consorting with a tawdry population of entertainers, prostitutes, and other social outcasts. His natural environment became the din and nocturnal colors of cheap music halls, cafés, and bordellos. In his *At the Moulin Rouge* (FIG. 21-71), the influence of Degas and the Japanese print can be seen in the oblique and asymmetrical composition, the spatial diagonals, and the strong patterns of line to which Lautrec added dissonant color. But each element, although closely studied in actual life and already familiar to us in the work of the older Impressionists, has been so emphasized or exaggerated that the tone is new. Compare, for instance, the mood of this painting with the relaxed and casual atmosphere of Renoir's *Moulin de la Galette* (FIG. 21-57). Lautrec's scene is night life, with its glaring artificial light, brassy music, and assortment of corrupt, cruel, and

21-71 HENRI DE TOULOUSE-LAUTREC, *At the Moulin Rouge,* 1892–1895. Approx. 48″ × 55″. (Helen Birch Bartlett Memorial Collection) © The Art Institute of Chicago, all rights reserved.

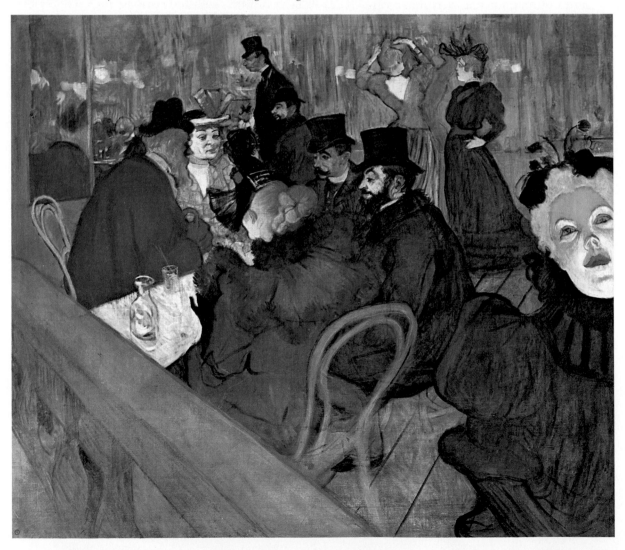

mask-like faces. (He includes himself in the background: the tiny man with the derby accompanying the very tall man, his cousin.) Such distortions by simplification of the figures and faces anticipate the later Expressionism, when artists will become ever more arbitrary in altering what they see (in translation onto canvas) to increase its impact on the observer. Lautrec and his contemporaries are transitional from Impressionism to a highly subjective strain in twentieth-century art.

Persisting Romanticism: Symbolism, Estheticism, Primitivism

That subjective strain is, precisely, Romantic and persists throughout the whole of the nineteenth century and into the twentieth. It could be argued that what seem to be antagonistic movements—like Realism, Impressionism, and Post-Impressionism—are only so many permutations of Romanticism, changing its earlier iconography, but always putting artistic autonomy at the center of the argument, no matter the subject or the technique. Artistic freedom remains all-in-all. Nature as given to the eye was early transformed by the artist's emotion and sensation and, in the end, comes to be completely subjectivized, to the point that the artist does not *imitate* nature but *creates* it by free interpretations of it. The optical world as "given" is rejected in favor of a world of fantasy, of forms conjured up and produced by the artist's free imagination, with or without reference to things conventionally seen. His technique comes to be his own, as well as his ideas. Color, line, and shape, separated from conformity to the optical image, may be used as he pleases, as symbols of his emotions in transaction with the world. He recognizes no requirement other than that he express himself in sincere accord with his spirit and intuition. If he is often not understood, that is because he chooses to stand outside of conventional meanings, as he does outside of conventional images, and speak, like a seer or prophet, in signs and symbols. In the words of the critic Konrad Fiedler, writing in 1876:

> The artist is called upon to create another world beside and above the real one, a world freed from earthly conditions, a world in keeping with his own discretion. This realm of art opposes the realm of nature. . . . Artistic activity begins when man finds himself face-to-face with the visible world as with something immensely enigmatical. . . . What art creates is the world, made by and for the artistic consciousness. . . . It is not the artist who has need of nature; nature much more has need of the artist. . . . By comprehending and manifesting nature in a certain sense, the artist does not comprehend and manifest anything which could exist apart from his activity. . . .

Only through artistic activity does man comprehend the visible world.*

Thus the unceasingly romantic artist, becomes not an imitator of nature, but an arbitrary interpreter of it, trusting absolutely to his own vision. Romanticism, in fostering this view of the artist, presides over the proliferation of individual styles, which, within the broad realm of their variation, can be thought of as Romantic in intention, method, and effect.

We have already met artists, often referred to as "Post-Impressionists," who revised or broke entirely away from Realism and Impressionism. Many others adopted an approach to subject matter and form that associates them with a general European movement called "Symbolism." The term has application to both art and literature, which, as critics in both fields noted, were in especially close relation at this time. A manifesto of literary Symbolism appeared in Paris in 1886, and, in 1891, the critic Albert Aurier applied the term to the painting of Gauguin and Van Gogh. Symbolism disdains the "mere fact" of Realism as trivial and asserts that fact must be transformed into a symbol of the inner experience of that fact. Fact is thus nothing in itself; mentally transformed, it is the utterance of a sensitized temperament responding in its own way to the world. In Symbolism, the subjectivity of Romanticism becomes radical; it will continue to be so in the art of the twentieth century. The artist's task is not to *see* things but to see *through* them to a significance and reality far deeper than what is given in superficial appearance. In this function, the artist, as the poet Arthur Rimbaud insists, becomes a seer, a being of extraordinary insight. (One group of Symbolist painters, influenced by Gauguin, called itself *Nabis*, the Hebrew word for prophet.) Rimbaud, whose poems had great influence on the artistic community, goes so far as to say, in his *Lettre du Voyant*, that to achieve the seer's insight, the artist must become deranged or, in effect, must systematically unhinge and confuse the everyday faculties of sense and of reason, which serve only to blur his vision. The objects given us in our commonsense world must be converted by the artist's mystical vision into symbols of a reality beyond it, and, ultimately, a reality from within himself.

The extreme subjectivism of the Symbolists led them to cultivate all the resources of fantasy, all the regions of imagination, no matter how recondite and occult. Moreover, it led them to urge the exclusiveness, not to say the elitism, of the artist against the vulgar materialism and conventional mores of industrial and middle-class society. Above all, by their phi-

*Linda Nochlin, *Realism and Tradition in Art* (Englewood Cliffs, N.J.: Prentice-Hall, 1966), pp. 168–76.

losophy of *estheticism*, the Symbolists wished to purge art of anything utilitarian, to cultivate an exquisite esthetic sensitivity, and to make the slogan "art for art's sake" into a doctrine and a way of life. As early as 1856, Gautier writes:

> We believe in the autonomy of art; art for us is not the means but the end; any artist who has in view anything but the beautiful is not an artist in our eyes. . . .

And Walter Pater, an English scholar and esthete, advances the same point of view in 1868 in the conclusion to his work *The Renaissance*:

> Our one chance lies in expanding that interval [of our life], in getting as many pulsations as possible into the given time. Great passions may give us this quickened sense of life. . . . Only be sure it *is* passion—that it does yield you this fruit of a quickened, multiplied consciousness. Of such wisdom, the poetic passion, the desire of beauty, the love of art for its own sake has most. For art comes to you proposing frankly to give nothing but the highest quality to your moments as they pass, and simply for those moments' sake.

The subject matter of the Symbolists, determined by this worshipfulness toward art and exaggerated esthetic sensation, becomes increasingly esoteric and exotic, weird, mysterious, visionary, dream-like, fantastic. (It is noteworthy that, contemporary with the Symbolists, Sigmund Freud, the founder of psychoanalysis, begins the new century and the age of psychiatry with his *Interpretation of Dreams*, and introduction to the concept and the world of unconscious experience.)

GUSTAVE MOREAU (1826–1898) seeks a form to suit the content of his fantasies, but not disdaining reference to the facts of the optical world when he needs them. A pupil of Chassériau and influential teacher of Henri Matisse and Georges Rouault, Moreau expanded his master's love of sensuous design to embrace gorgeous color, intricate line, and richly detailed shape. Like Chassériau also, Moreau preferred subjects arising from dreaming solitude, remote as possible from waking commonplaces—subjects that could be submerged in all the glittering splendor that imagination could envision and painterly ingenuity could supply. His *Jupiter and Semele* (FIG. 21-72), one of his rare finished works, demonstrates the full orchestration of his instruments in an opera-like setting. (Moreau was a lover of the music of Wagner and, like him, dreamed of a grand synthesis of the arts.) The grandiose theme is presented within an architecture of towering opulence, the royal hall of Olympus, shimmering in iridescent color, with tiers and tabernacles filled with the glowing and flashing shapes that enclose the icon of Jupiter like encrusta-

21-72 GUSTAVE MOREAU, *Jupiter and Semele*, c. 1875. Approx. 7′ × 3′ 4″. Musée Gustave Moreau, Paris.

tions of gems. The color of Delacroix is harmonized with the exotic hues of Medieval enamels, Indian miniatures, Byzantine mosaics, and the designs of exotic wares now coming into the ornamental repertories of modern artists. Semele, in the lap of Jupiter, is overwhelmed by the apparition of the god, crowned with a halo of thunderbolts. Her languorous swoon and the suspended motion of all the entranced figures show that "beautiful inertia" which Moreau said he wished to render with all "necessary richness." His cherishing of the enigmas of fable, myth, vision, and dream caused Manet to remark of him: "I have a lively sympathy for him, but he is taking a bad road. . . . He takes us back to the incomprehensible,

21-73 ODILON REDON,
The Cyclops, 1898. 25″ × 20″.
Kroeller–Moeller Rijksmuseum,
Otterloo, Netherlands.

while we wish that everything be understood." And Degas said, unsympathetically, "He puts watch chains on the gods." Two Realists confronting Symbolism!

The sharp difference of artistic intention expressed in these comments is even more striking in any comparison of the work of ODILON REDON (1840–1916) and of Monet, who were born in the same year. Redon, the foremost Symbolist painter, uses the Impressionist palette and stippling brush stroke for a very different purpose. In *The Cyclops* (FIG. 21-73), he does not record a fleeting impression of a one-eyed giant in love; rather, he projects a figment of the imagination as if it were seeable, coloring it whimsically—in fresh hues, in full saturation, and in rich profusion—in harmony with the mood he feels befits the subject. The fetal head of the shy, simpering Polyphemus, with its huge, loving eye, rises balloon-like above the sleeping Galatea. The image born of

the dreaming world and the color analyzed and disassociated from the waking world here come together at the will of the artist. As Redon himself observes: "My originality consists in bringing to life, in a human way, improbable beings and making them live according to the laws of probability, by putting—as far as possible—the logic of the visible at the service of the invisible." In the poetry of Redon's friend and contemporary, the Symbolist Stéphane Mallarmé, words and their meanings often lose contact, drift apart, and enter into mystifying relationships with other words and other meanings.

Symbolism had a wide appeal for the so-called "decadents" of the *fin de siècle*, who shunned action for esthetic passivity and who sought escape in art from the ugliness and brutality of a materialistic world on its way to war. Although not strictly speaking a Symbolist, AUBREY BEARDSLEY (1872–1898) was one of a circle of English esthetes that included the

21-74 AUBREY BEARDSLEY, *The Peacock Skirt*, 1894. Pen-and-ink illustration for Oscar Wilde's *Salomé*.

brilliant wit, Oscar Wilde, whose close friend he was and whose controversial books and plays he illustrated. For one of them, *Salomé*, Beardsley drew *The Peacock Skirt* (FIG. 21-74), a dazzlingly decorative composition perfectly characteristic of his influential style. The influence of the Japanese print is obvious, although Beardsley has assimilated it into his own unique manner. Banishing Realism, he confines himself to line and to patterns of black and white, eliminating all shading. His tense, elastic line encloses sweeping, curvilinear shapes that lie flat on the surface—some left almost vacant, others filled with swirling complexes of mostly organic motifs. His mastery of calligraphic line is supported by his unfailing sense of linear rhythms and harmonies. In his short lifetime—he died at 26—he expressed in both his life and art the esthete's ideal of "art for art's sake." Beardsley's work exhibits its own beauty; it has no other message. It reflects and will strongly influence the design principles of Art Nouveau (FIG. 21-91).

Symbolism, although suitable to the withdrawn fancy of artist–esthetes, could also provide the means for a telling criticism of the workaday world they scorned. To produce his corrosive pictures of the declassed denizens of Paris (FIG. 21-71), Lautrec still worked with his human models in their actual setting, having them always before his eyes, in the manner of the Realist. Given the permissiveness of Symbolism, the Belgian painter JAMES ENSOR (1860–1949) creates a spectral and macabre world in which grotesques, masked skeletons, and hanged men populate sideshows, carnivals, and city streets. His best-known work, severely criticized at the time for blasphemy, is *Christ's Entry into Brussels* (FIG. 21-75). In spirit, it recalls the demonizing, moralizing pictures of Hieronymus Bosch (FIG. 18-21) and Pieter Bruegel that represent Christ surrounded by false and ugly creatures utterly unworthy of his mission. But here, in modern fashion, the human creatures are masked "hollow men" who have no real substance, no genuine identity, but are only "images." This is a theme often sounded in modern criticism of modern civilization. Ensor's color is hard, strident, and spotted—a tonal cacophony that matches the sound of the repulsive crowd.

21-75 JAMES ENSOR, *Christ's Entry into Brussels*, 1888. Approx. 8' 5" × 14' 1". Kunsthaus Zurich.

Linked in spirit to Ensor is the Norwegian painter and graphic artist EDVARD MUNCH (1863–1944), also a moralizing critic of modern man. Munch's chief themes are pain, death, and perverse love. In *The Scream* (FIG. 21-76), he gives us quite a disturbing vision of neurotic panic breaking forth in a dreadful but silent scream—the scream heard within the mind cracking under prolonged anxiety. Like his friend,

21-76 EDVARD MUNCH, *The Scream*, 1893. Approx. 36" × 29". Oslo Kommunes Kunstsamlinger Munch-Museet.

the dramatist August Strindberg, Munch presents almost unbearable pictures of the tensions and psychic anguish that beset modern men and the ultimate loneliness that, according to the modern philosophy of existentialism, is the inescapable lot of us all. Influenced by the strong patterns and color of Gauguin, as well as by Gauguin's use of the print medium, Munch transmitted the influence through his own work to the German Expressionists of the early twentieth century.

Protest against the disease of civilization sent Gauguin to the South Seas in search of primitive innocence. HENRI ROUSSEAU (1844–1910) was a "primitive" without leaving Paris—an untrained amateur painter who held a post as customs collector (hence, his sobriquet, *le douanier*). Rousseau produces an art of dream and fantasy in a style that has its own sophistication and makes its own departure from the artistic currency of the *fin de siècle*. His apparent visual, conceptual, and technical naïveté are compensated by a natural talent for design and an imagination teeming with exotic images of mysterious, tropical landscapes. In perhaps his best-known work, *The Sleeping Gypsy* (FIG. 21-77), a desert world, silent and secret, dreams beneath a pale, perfectly round moon. In the foreground, a lion—like a stuffed but somehow menacing animal doll—sniffs at the gypsy. A critical encounter impends, one that is not possible for most of us in the waking world but that is all too common when our vulnerable, subconscious selves are menaced in uneasy sleep. Rousseau early mirrors the landscape of the subconscious, and we may regard him as the forerunner of the Surrealists in the

21-77 HENRI ROUSSEAU, *The Sleeping Gypsy*, 1897. 4' 3" × 6' 7". Museum of Modern Art, New York (gift of Mrs. Simon Guggenheim).

twentieth century, who will attempt to represent the ambiguity and contradiction of waking and dreaming experiences taken together.

The art of the American painter ALBERT PINKHAM RYDER (1847–1917) is made up of dream that never wakes. It is the very essence of Romantic inwardness and is witness to the persistence of Romanticism and its seemingly endless variety of utterance. A recluse, shut away by choice from the world, Ryder found a depthless reservoir of subject solely in his own imagination, from which arose images uniquely private yet often universal. Such is his *Death on a Pale Horse* (FIG. 21-78). The scythe-bearing specter speeds on its ceaseless round through a dead landscape that bears only a withered stalk of a tree. In the foreground, a malignant cobra with glowing eyes undulates. No

21-78 ALBERT PINKHAM RYDER, *Death on a Pale Horse*, c. 1910. Approx. 28" × 35". The Cleveland Museum of Art (purchased from the J.H. Wade Fund).

one remains on earth but Death and the serpent, the symbol of primordial evil. The utter simplicity of the conception and the execution require none but the barest reference to things outside the mind. Blank zones of dark and sombre light are traced through by the faint streaks of the rails, which remain undisturbed by the passage of the phosphorescent wraith. Ryder's indifference to the material world unfortunately extended to his material medium and technique. He painted in thick layers with badly prepared or nonfunctional pigments, and many of his works have suffered serious deterioration.

By the end of the nineteenth century, the Western artist's vision of reality had changed. Attitudes stemming from the rise of experimental science could not help but stimulate the artist's interest in the distinction between *what* is seen and *how* it is seen. A curiosity about and a taste for experiment with the tools of the artist's trade—new pigments and new theories of light and color—was aroused, which markedly influenced the procedure of Impressionists and Post-Impressionists alike. At the same time, the invention of photography profoundly affected the pictorial mode and the artist's manner of expression, offering a mechanical means of recording the spectrum of values of light and shade and of achieving the utmost fidelity to appearance. The pictorial artist—until then the sole maker of flat images and revealer of the structure of appearance—seemed suddenly to be technologically displaced, much as the Medieval scribe was displaced by the invention of the printing press. Artist's then, had to look for new purposes and new means for their craft. These searches would ultimately lead them to break altogether with the long tradition of imitative painting based on the optical check of nature. In the twentieth century, the separation between art and natural appearance is stated by Pablo Picasso: "Nature and art, being two different things, cannot be the same thing. Through art we express our conception of what nature is not."

By mid-century, the nineteenth-century painter was replacing the thematic material of Romanticism with scenes from the modern public world. This new interest paralleled widespread scientific curiosity about human society and group behavior. The artist's method, like the photographer's or the sociologist's, was at first descriptive; but, in the latter part of the century, this was gradually replaced by analysis and expression, and the artist came to realize that his activity is a function of his tools and materials. He discovered that his canvas is not a transparent window opening onto the optical world of nature, but a tangible surface on which pigments are arranged in a variety of ways. This is now the reality he confronts. Whether the artist, like Cézanne, examines color sensations to devise a system of color use or, like Van Gogh, regards the surface and colors simply as means for expressing emotional states, the artist is finally separated from the pictorial tradition that began with Giotto.

The testament of Seurat and Cézanne, Van Gogh and Gauguin is presented to the twentieth-century artist by Denis, in his famous positivist definition of painting: "Remember that a picture—before being a war horse, a nude woman, or some anecdote—is essentially a plane surface covered with colors assembled in a certain order."

In the Romantic painter's long search for the real, he discovers reality in himself and in the physical medium with which he works. But the long relied on optical world of common experience, lost in the radical transformation of traditional art, is rediscovered and preserved in the domain of the photograph and the motion picture. At the turn of the century, the current of art history in the West is divided sharply and fatefully around the problems of reality and of the nature and function of art in relation to it.

Sculpture in the Later Nineteenth Century

The three-dimensional art of sculpture is not readily adaptable to the optical realism favored by many painters and the public in the nineteenth century. Its very nature requires the sense of its permanence as an enduring form, a palpable mass sufficient unto itself. The timeless ideal, not the evanescent real, best suits it. The space it occupies is abstract, not descriptive of some particular locale it does not occupy; certainly, sculpture is not the apt medium for representing the passing season or time of day, fleetingly observed and fleetingly recorded. Thus, sculpture is not really suitable for the description either of historical events or of scenes from contemporary life, although it was often required to do both in the nineteenth century.

Classical or Baroque form limits optical realism; it does not break into the modern scene with the dissembling illusionism of the stage or the trivialities of the street. AUGUSTUS SAINT-GAUDENS (1848–1907), an American sculptor trained in France, used realism efficiently in a number of his portraits, where realism is most appropriate. For the design of a memorial monument of Mrs. Henry Adams, wife of the historian (FIG. 21-79), he chose a Classical mode of representation, which he freely modified, as Puvis had done in painting (FIG. 21-51). Of course, he had no need to specify a particular character; he wanted to represent a generality outside of time and place. A woman of majestic bearing sits in mourning, her classically beautiful face partly shadowed by a sepulchral

21-79 AUGUSTUS SAINT-GAUDENS, Adams Memorial, 1891. Bronze, 70" high. Rock Creek Cemetery, Washington, D.C.

21-80 JEAN BAPTISTE CARPEAUX, *Ugolino and His Children*, 1865–1867. Marble, 6' 5" high. Metropolitan Museum of Art, New York (Josephine Bay Paul and C. Michael Paul Foundation, Inc., and the Charles Ulrick and Josephine Bay Foundation, Inc., gifts, 1967).

drapery that voluminously enfolds her body. The immobility of her form, set in an attitude of eternal vigilance, is only slightly stirred by a natural, yet mysterious and exquisite gesture. Saint-Gaudens' masterpiece is a work worthy of the grave steles of Classical Athens (FIG. 5-58).

The inspiration of the Baroque and of Michelangelo, both in form and content, show in the art of JEAN BAPTISTE CARPEAUX (1827–1875), a precursor of Auguste Rodin. The theme of his group *Ugolino and His Children* (FIG. 21-80) is grim, even repulsive. Based on a passage in Dante's *Inferno* (xxxiii, 58–75), it shows Count Ugolino with his four sons shut up in a tower to starve to death. In Hell, Ugolino relates to Dante how:

> I bit both hands for grief. And
> they, thinking I did it for hunger,
> suddenly rose up and said, "Father" . . .

and offered him their own flesh as food. The powerful forms—twisted, intertwined, and densely concentrated—suggest the self-devouring torment of frustration and despair that wracks the unfortunate Ugolino. A careful student of the male figures of Mi-

chelangelo, Carpeaux also said that he had the *Laocoön* group (FIG. 5-80) in mind—presumably not so much the precise image, as the predicament, mood, and action. Certainly, the storm and stress of the *Ugolino* would recall the Hellenistic "baroque" not only of that group but of others, like the battle of the gods and giants on the frieze of the Pergamon altar (FIG. 5-79).

For the leading sculptors of the nineteenth century, the influence of Michelangelo was decisive. ANTOINE AUGUSTE PRÉAULT (1810–1879) supplemented his study of that great artist with close reference to sculptors of the French Renaissance. Baudelaire heard him say: "I am a connoisseur of Michelangelo, of Jean Goujon, of Germain Pilon . . ." (see FIGS. 18-54 and 18-55). Certainly, the influences of the latter two are visibly commingled in Préault's superb *Ophelia* (FIG. 21-81). Taking the same Shakespearean theme that Millais did for his painting (FIG. 21-48), Préault creates a pattern of swirling, rippling line that simulates both the clinging, drenched drapery and the rushing water. The body of the drowning heroine makes a

21-81　Antoine Auguste Préault, *Ophelia*, 1876 (original 1843). Bronze, 6′ 7″ long. Musée de Longchamps, Marseille.

beautiful, buoyant curve, expressive of the undulating current in which she is suspended and which is sucking her down. She is one of Goujon's fountain nymphs, tragically overwhelmed by the flooding waters she has poured. The sweep and play of curving line are both passionate and decorative; they look forward to the intricate, abstract style of Art Nouveau and its esthetic ideal of graceful, curvilinear ornament.

It is in the art of Auguste Rodin (1840–1917) that sculpture regains the artistic preeminence it had lost to the pictorial media in the nineteenth century. Rodin ably assimilates and manages the century's concurrent esthetic forces and forms—Romanticism, Realism, Impressionism, and Symbolism—and generates in the process a unique personal style that anticipates the Expressionism of the next century. He studied sculpture from the start, as it were, investigating the peculiarities of its materials and form. Avoiding the stilted formulas of the Academy, he studied—as Carpeaux had done—the sculpture of Michelangelo and of Pierre Puget (FIG. 19-73) as well, learning from them to appreciate the unique possibilities of the art for expressive bodily pose and gesture. As a contemporary of the Impressionists, Rodin embraces an esthetic based on a similar acceptance of the world of appearances revealed through light on surface. A modeler of soft material rather than a carver of hard, Rodin could work his surfaces with fingers sensitive to the subtlest variations of plane, catching the fugitive play of living motion as it changes fluidly under light. His touch is analogous to that of the deft Impressionist brush stroke. But, although Rodin's technique and formal sense aligned him with Impres-

sionism, his subjects were still in the Romantic vein, and his Realism bent strongly toward Expressionism as he searched for new forms in which to cast his Romantic themes. Without resorting to the repertory of historical styles, he found fitting and powerful forms for his subjects out of his own exercise of a kind of "impressionist realism." A splendid example is the group of life-size figures, *Burghers of Calais* (FIG. 21-82), commemorating a heroic episode of the Hundred Years' War, when the leading citizens of Calais, which had been taken by the English, offered their lives in return for those of all their fellow citizens. Each of the individual figures is a convincing study of despair, resignation, or quiet defiance. The psychic effects, the result of the technical management, are achieved through the movement of a few simplified planes, the rugged surfaces of which catch and disperse the light. But moving though the work is, it is difficult to believe that Rodin visualized the group as a unit; indeed, the separate figures were conceived as individual pieces and then shifted about until their relationship was considered satisfactory.

Rodin's mastery of dramatic gesture, so evident in the eloquent pantomime of *Burghers*, finds expression in a very different theme in *The Kiss* (FIG. 21-83). Intended to be only one of a number of groups composing the monumental Gates of Hell (including the famous *Thinker*; Introduction, FIG. 2), which was never finished, *The Kiss* is a subtle, if explicit, essay in a contrast of ardent approach and clumsily shy response, the attitude of the figures suiting the artist's poetic conception of the event perfectly. The group was meant to represent sensual love absorbed in self and rooted in matter. The artist may have carried in

21-83 AUGUSTE RODIN, *The Kiss*, 1886–1898. Marble, over life-size. Musée Rodin, Paris.

his mind a memory of Michelango's *Temptation of Adam and Eve*, one of the masterpieces of the Sistine Ceiling. Rodin, who declared that his encounter with the art of Michelangelo had been decisive in the formation of his style, was struck by that master's many uncompleted sculptures and admired the half-finished figures left in the rough block, as here (see Introduction, FIG. 10). The lovers' figures are modeled to a smoothness that suggests the supple surfaces and texture of living bodies. We recall the *sfumato* of Correggio (FIG. 17-40), which melts all harshness and angularity and which here contrasts with the rugged stone from which the figures emerge.

Incompleteness of figure becomes both a means and an end for Rodin. Most of his projects remain unfinished, or are deliberate fragments. Seeing the esthetic and expressive virtue of it, modern sculpture has taken this mannerism from Rodin. The half-completed, the fragment, the vignette lifted out of context, the sketch—all have the power of suggestion and understatement. Rodin's *Balzac* (FIG. 21-84) reveals the method most successfully. Features are not carved but are only suggested by indefinite surfaces that variegate the light and dark in deft blurs and smudges, producing a sketch-like effect. Contours melt away; volumes are not permitted to assert themselves. The great novelist, who surveyed mankind in his *La Comédie Humaine (The Human Comedy)*, draws himself up to a towering height. Wrapped in what seems to be an enormous cloak, he surveys again, from the lofty standpoint of immortality, the little-

21-84   AUGUSTE RODIN, *Balzac*, 1892–1897. Plaster, approx. 9' 10" high. Musée Rodin, Paris.

ness of man. It is characteristic of Rodin's art that, though we feel its power, we cannot quite describe what traits make us feel it. His Impressionist methods, through daring emphasis and distortions, achieve an overwhelmingly Expressionist effect.

Rodin's personal passage from Impressionism to Expressionism was a historical one. While he was still living, sculpture was firmly set on the base he had constructed.

Architecture: The Beginnings of a New Style

The epoch-making development in international architecture that paralleled pictorial Realism could well be called Realistic—or just as well, rational, practical, or functional. For the nineteenth-century architect gradually comes to abandon sentimental and Romantic designs from the historical past in the interest of an honest expression of the building's purpose. Since the eighteenth century, inconspicuous utility architecture—factories, warehouses, dockyard structures, mills, and the like—had often been built simply and without historical ornament, sometimes out of the new, convenient material, cast iron. Iron, along with

other materials of the Industrial Revolution, permitted engineering advancements in the construction of larger, stronger, and more fire-resistant structures. The tensile strength of iron (and especially of steel, available after 1860) allowed new designs involving vast enclosed or spanned spaces, as in the great train sheds of railroad stations and in exposition halls.

The Bibliothèque Ste. Geneviève (1843–1850), built by HENRI LABROUSTE (1801–1875), shows an interesting adjustment of the revived Romantic style—in this case, Renaissance—to a Realistic interior, the skeletal elements of which are cast iron (FIG. 21-85). The row of arched windows in the façade recalls the flank of Alberti's San Francesco at Rimini (FIG. 16-41), yet the division of its stories distinguishes the levels of the interior—the lower, reserved for stack space; the upper, for the reading rooms. The latter consist essentially of two tunnel-roofed halls, roofed in terra cotta, separated by a row of slender cast-iron columns on concrete pedestals. The iron columns, recognizably Corinthian, support the iron roof arches, which are pierced with intricate vine-scroll ornament out of the Renaissance architectural vocabulary. One could scarcely find a better example of how the forms of traditional masonry architecture are esthetically transformed by the peculiarities of the new structural material. Nor could one find a better example of how reluctant the nineteenth-century architect was to surrender traditional forms even when fully aware of the new possibilities for design and construction. For many years, architects would scoff at "engineer's ar-

21-85   HENRI LABROUSTE, reading room of the Bibliothèque Ste. Geneviève, Paris, 1843–1850.

21-86   JOSEPH PAXTON, Crystal Palace, London, 1850–1851. Iron and glass. (Contemporary print.)

chitecture'' and clothe their steel and concrete structures in the Romantic ''drapery'' of a historical style. Many great railroad stations juxtaposed the Romantic with practical, ''undraped'' construction in steel—historically decorated ticket concourses contrasting with open steel sheds just behind them.

Standardization and prefabrication of structural members permitted JOSEPH PAXTON (1801–1865) to construct the exposition building in London called the Crystal Palace (FIG. 21-86), a work almost wholly of iron and glass, in the unheard-of time of six months from 1850 to 1851. But the climax of nineteenth-century enterprise in wide-span construction was the 375-foot span of the 1,365-foot-long Galerie des Machines (FIG. 21-87), erected at the Paris Exhibition of 1889. The building had no encumbering inte-

21-87   Galerie des Machines, Paris International Exhibition, 1889. Steel and glass.

rior supports, so that as many as 100,000 visitors could circulate daily through its vast interior, their movement facilitated by a great rolling bridge from which they could look down at the panorama of operating machines far below. The structural scheme was composed of hinged (at apex and bases), nearly parabolic metal arches that supported a framework on which broad sheets of glass rested. Alexander Eiffel's daring tower, symbol of modern Paris, was also built at this time, and these two feats of engineering jolted some of the architectural profession into a realization that the new materials and new processes might contain the germ of a completely new style—something that picturesque, historical Romanticism had failed to produce.

The desire for greater speed and economy in building, as well as a reduction in fire hazards, encouraged the use of cast and wrought iron for many other building programs, especially commercial ones. Both England and America enthusiastically developed cast-iron architecture until a series of disastrous fires in the early 1870s in New York, Boston, and Chicago demonstrated that cast iron by itself was far from impervious to fire. This led to the practice of encasing the metal in masonry, combining the strength of the first with the fire-resistance of the second.

In cities, convenience required buildings to be closely grouped, and increased property values forced architects literally to raise the roof. Even attics could command high rentals if the newly invented elevator was also provided, as it was for the first time in the Equitable Building in New York (1868–1871). Metal could support such tall structures, and the American skyscraper was born. It was with rare exceptions, however, as in the work of Louis Sullivan (FIGS. 21-89 and 21-90), that this original type of building was treated successfully and produced distinguished architecture.

Sullivan's predecessor, HENRY HOBSON RICHARDSON (1838–1886), frequently used heavy round arches and massive masonry walls, and because he was particularly fond of the Romanesque architecture of the Auvergne in France, his work was sometimes thought of as a Romanesque revival. This designation does not do credit to the originality and quality of most of the buildings Richardson designed during the brief 18 years of his practice. Although Trinity Church in Boston and his smaller public libraries, residences, railroad stations, and court houses in New England and elsewhere best demonstrate his vivid imagination and the solidity—the sense of enclosure and permanence—so characteristic of his style, his most important and influential building was the Marshall Field Warehouse (now demolished) in Chicago (FIG. 21-88), which was begun in 1885. The vast building, occupying a city block and designed for the most

21-88 HENRY HOBSON RICHARDSON, Marshall Field Warehouse, Chicago, Illinois, 1885–1887.

practical of purposes (storage) recalls historical styles without being at all in mere imitation of them. The tripartite elevation of a Renaissance palace or of the aqueduct near Nîmes (FIG. 6-43) may have been close to Richardson's mind, but he uses no Classical ornament, makes much of the massive courses of masonry, and—in the strong horizontality of the window sills and in the interrupted courses that define the levels—stresses the long sweep of the building's lines as well as its ponderous weight.

Although the structural frame still lies behind and in conjunction with the masonry screen of the Marshall Field Warehouse, the great glazed arcades, in opening up the walls of a large-scale building, point the way to the modern, total penetration of the wall and the transformation of it into a mere screen or curtain that serves to express the structural grid and protect it from the weather.

LOUIS SULLIVAN (1856–1924), who has been called the first truly modern architect, recognized Richardson's architectural suggestions early in his career and worked forward from them to his new "tall buildings," especially in the Guaranty (Prudential) Building in Buffalo, New York, built between 1894 and 1895 (FIG. 21-89). Here, the subdivision of the interior is expressed on the exterior, as is the skeletal (as opposed to the bearing-wall) nature of the supporting structure, with nothing more substantial than

21-89 Louis Sullivan, Guaranty (Prudential) Building, Buffalo, New York, 1894–1895.

21-90 Louis Sullivan, Carson, Pirie, Scott Building, Chicago, Illinois, 1899–1904.

windows occupying most of the space between the terra-cotta-clad vertical members. In Sullivan's designs, one can be sure of an equivalence of interior and exterior design, as one cannot in Richardson's warehouse (FIG. 21-88) or in Labrouste's library (FIG. 21-85). Yet something of old habits of thought hangs on; the Guaranty Building has a base and cornice. The base, however, is penetrated in such a way as to suggest the later free supports of modern architecture.

The form of the building, then, is beginning to express its function, and Sullivan's famous "form follows function"—long the slogan of early twentieth-century architects—finds its illustration here. It is important to note that Sullivan did not mean by this slogan that functional building is automatically beautiful; nor did he advocate a rigid and doctrinaire correspondence between external and interior design. Rather, he espoused a free and flexible relationship—one that his great pupil Frank Lloyd Wright will later describe as like that between the bones and tissue of the hand.

Sullivan takes a further step in the unification of exterior and interior design in his Carson, Pirie, Scott Building in Chicago, Illinois (FIG. 21-90), built between 1899 and 1904. A department store, this building required broadly open, well illuminated display

spaces. The structural steel skeleton, being minimal, permits the singular achievement of this goal. The relation of spaces and solids here is so logical that nothing in the way of facing need be added, and the skeleton is clearly revealed in the exterior. The deck-like stories, faced in white ceramic slabs, seem to sweep freely around the building and show several irregularities (notably the stressed bays of the corner entrance) that help the design to break out of the cubical formula of Sullivan's older buildings. In the general search for a new style at the end of the century, Sullivan was a leader. He gave as much attention to finding new directions in architectural ornament as in architecture itself. In this respect, he is an important figure in the movement called Art Nouveau, which will seek an end to all traditional ornamental styles—indeed, to the whole preoccupation with historical style that has been postponing the true advent of a modern method in the arts of form. The lower two levels of the Carson, Pirie, Scott Building are given over to an ornament (of Sullivan's invention) made of wildly fantastic motifs that bear little resemblance to anything traditional architecture could show.

Yet designs of interiors in the later century could still exhibit taste for the historical and the exotic—an eclectic estheticism that would linger on until finally purged by the puritanism of an austere new architec-

21-91 JAMES A. McNEILL WHISTLER, Peacock Room from the home of F.R. Leyland, 1876–1877. Freer Gallery of Art, Washington, D.C.

tural style. The renowned Peacock Room (FIG. 21-91) is a superb example of architectural "art for art's sake." Designed as a dining room for F.R. Leyland of London by THOMAS JECKYL, it was decorated by JAMES A. McNEILL WHISTLER (1834–1903), an American artist who exhibited with the Impressionists and who was strongly influenced by Japanese decorative art, as was Aubrey Beardsley (FIG. 21-74). The room was intended as a showcase for Leyland's collection of Japanese porcelain, as well as for Whistler's own "Japanified" painting, *The Princess of Porcelain Land*.

Although Whistler painted peacocks in blue and gold to heighten the "Japanese" atmosphere, the general design and its details are more Tudor English than Japanese. In their deft elegance, the painted and hand-crafted elements and accessories of the ensemble constitute a kind of manifest transition to Art Nouveau. Although experiment with ornament will have its brief vogue in Art Nouveau, it is the twentieth century that will sweep away the traditional systems and discover its own ornament, as it will discover its own principles of design.

Movie camera patented
1891

Freud's first psychoanalytic work
1895

ARCHIPENKO
Woman Combing Her Hair
(1915)

DUCHAMP
To be looked at, etc.
(1918)

LIPCHITZ
Man with Mandolin
(1917)

ROUAULT
The Old King
detail (1916)

LÉGER
(1881–1955)

MAN RAY
(1890–1976)

BRAQUE
(1882–1963)

D A D A / D E S T I J L / F U T U R I S M

CHAGALL
(1887–1985)

1918
Bauhaus founded

Russian Revolution

Dada movement

1914–1918
World War I

PICASSO
Three Musicians
detail (1921)

1922

BECKMANN
(1884–1950)

RIETVELDT
Schroeder House
(1924)

SCHWITTERS
(1887–1948)

BARLACH
*War Monument,
Güstrow Cathedral*
(1927)

BRANCUȘI
Bird in Space
(c. 1927)

GROSZ
(1893–1959)

KLEE
Twittering Machine
detail (1922)

C U B I S M / S U R R E A L I S M /

1924
Surrealist Manifesto

GROPIUS
Shop Block,
the Bauhaus (1925)

1927
Lindbergh flies over the Atlantic

1929
Stock market crash

LE CORBUSIER
Notre Dame
du Haut
(1950–1955)

GABO
Linear Construction
(1950)

GIACOMETTI
City Square
(1948)

POLLOCK
Lucifer
detail (1947)

A B S T R A C T   F O R M A L I S M

A B S T R A C T

BACON
Number VII etc.
(1953)

1954

WYETH
Christina's World
detail (1948)

NEVELSON
(b. 1900)

LICHTENSTEIN
Blam!
detail (1962)

TINGUELY
(b. 1925)

O P / P O P

MIES VAN DER ROHE and JOHNSON
Seagram Building
(1956)

1957

JOHNS
Painted Bronze
(1960)

1959

KLINE
Painting 1952
(1955)

NERVI
Palazzetto dello Sport
(1958)

TANSEY
*Triumph of the
New York School*
detail (1984)

P O S T - M O

1985

THE TWENTIETH CENTURY

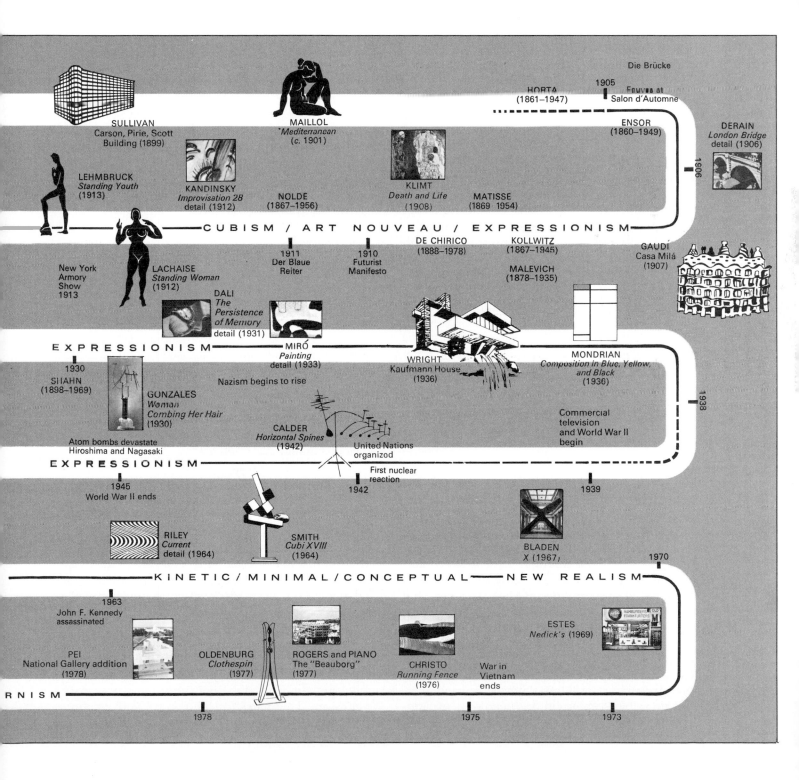

Die Brücke

HORTA
(1861–1947)

1905
Fauves at
Salon d'Automne

ENSOR
(1860–1949)

SULLIVAN
Carson, Pirie, Scott
Building (1899)

MAILLOL
Mediterranean
(c. 1901)

DERAIN
London Bridge
detail (1906)

LEHMBRUCK
Standing Youth
(1913)

KANDINSKY
Improvisation 28
detail (1912)

NOLDE
(1867–1956)

KLIMT
Death and Life
(1908)

MATISSE
(1869–1954)

1906

CUBISM / ART NOUVEAU / EXPRESSIONISM

New York
Armory
Show
1913

LACHAISE
Standing Woman
(1912)

1911
Der Blaue
Reiter

1910
Futurist
Manifesto

DE CHIRICO
(1888–1978)

KOLLWITZ
(1867–1945)

MALEVICH
(1878–1935)

GAUDÍ
Casa Milá
(1907)

DALI
*The
Persistence
of Memory*
detail (1931)

EXPRESSIONISM

MIRÓ
Painting
detail (1933)

WRIGHT
Kaufmann House
(1936)

MONDRIAN
*Composition in Blue, Yellow,
and Black*
(1936)

1930
SHAHN
(1898–1969)

GONZALES
*Woman
Combing Her Hair*
(1930)

Nazism begins to rise

1938

Commercial
television
and World War II
begin

CALDER
Horizontal Spines
(1942)

United Nations
organized

Atom bombs devastate
Hiroshima and Nagasaki

EXPRESSIONISM

First nuclear
reaction

1945
World War II ends

1942

1939

RILEY
Current
detail (1964)

SMITH
Cubi XVIII
(1964)

BLADEN
X (1967)

1970

KINETIC / MINIMAL / CONCEPTUAL — NEW REALISM

1963
John F. Kennedy
assassinated

ESTES
Nedick's (1969)

PEI
National Gallery addition
(1978)

OLDENBURG
Clothespin
(1977)

ROGERS and PIANO
The "Beauborg"
(1977)

CHRISTO
Running Fence
(1976)

War in
Vietnam
ends

RNISM

1978

1975

1973

BECAUSE we are in the midst of it and, hence, still being shaped by it, the twentieth century is perhaps more difficult to characterize than any in history. It has been said that the Renaissance died finally in the holocaust of World War I; it is certain that this century has brought to a close an epoch of a thousand years—from the dim time in the Romanesque era, when Europe began a new life, until now, when European civilization is blending into a world civilization. This century is in a continuing crisis; we are making ourselves into something different from what we have been, at a cost we cannot yet estimate and with consequences we cannot guess. Our historical knowledge has already placed our abandoned traditions an unbridgeable distance behind us and left us self-conscious and isolated in the stream of time, confronted with tremendous possibility or appalling disaster. Science has utterly changed our picture of the physical world and of ourselves. Our technology has provided unique experiences: high-speed flight, instantaneous communication over great distances, expanded ranges of sensory perception, and—for a minority, as yet—conditions of physical ease never before imaginable. But the new patterns of life that are separating us so decisively from the past are also confronting us with new and difficult problems of adjustment. The passing of old traditions and beliefs has robbed us of assurances and securities; we are often doubtful of the meaning and purpose of life and of the very source and nature of our own identity. We hear much of modern man's "alienation," his sense of strangeness and loneliness in the world, where he is, like the figures in Alberto Giacometti's *City Square* (FIG. 22–54), only an aimless unit in a "lonely crowd."

This problematic quality of modern life is the result of the constantly shifting grounds of our beliefs; an axiom for our time could well be "where nothing is certain, everything is a question," the fundamental question being: What is "real"? The twentieth century seems chronically and constitutionally skeptical about all answers to this question, especially the traditional ones. But of one thing it appears to be certain: "reality" is infinitely complex, perhaps ultimately elusive, and by no means given to us in our everyday, conventional, commonsensical experience. "Seeing" is certainly no longer ground for "believing." The world of common sense is simply not what it seems. The quantum theory and the theory of relativity—new theories in physics set forth at the beginning of the century—describe subsensible and suprasensible universes of electrical fields in which there is no absolute space or time and in which all motion is relative to systems themselves in motion. There is no stable "center" in this headlong, expanding universe swarming with electronic and galactic events—no absolute standpoint that can certify our measurements of space and time. A principle of "indeterminacy" reigns in the world of the electron and of outer space, where the speeds of events approach the speed of light. The world of familiar solids and spaces thus dissolves, on physical analysis, into a "dance of atoms"; their configurations apparently have little relation to what we see and feel as "real." In such a world picture, the stature of man, so elevated in the Renaissance, shrinks to infinitesimal dimensions.

If physical science's picture of the world drastically reduces our central role in the old, classical Christian cosmos, modern biology has done little to restore it. In the nineteenth century, the privileged status of human beings in nature had been questioned by the hypothesis that we evolved from lower forms of life. In the newly developed social sciences, biological concepts were adapted to explanations of human culture and of individual differences, and the human individual came to be seen as a resultant of the interacting factors of heredity and environment. Thus, life may be determined rather than free—and man, in the collective, comes to be studied statistically, like the subatomic particles of physics.

A further blow to age-old beliefs was delivered in the twentieth century by the new psychology, associated in its early development with Freud. Although it is deeply rooted in Romanticism, this restatement of our essential irrationality struck at a thousand years of explanations of human conduct and may be seen as a modern revision of the theme of original sin. In the new view, our actions are seen as largely determined by motives operating beneath consciousness at an unconscious or "subconscious" level.

A further modern development, which we might call the information–communication crisis, contributes to uncertainty and the uneasiness that accompanies it. Literacy has been widespread in the Western world since the end of the nineteenth century, and printing has been supplemented by radio, television, and electronic telecommunication. The resulting expansion in communication services has been accompanied by a diminution in credibility and belief; thus, although technical competence has increased, its application may have little relevance to deeper human concerns. From about 1950, a new technological revolution, associated with the development of computer science, has been converting the data of our experience into the language of number. Such "artificial intelligence" augments and may even replace natural intelligence in many of its functions, and this may lead to the automation of the human environment. The consequences of these new instruments and languages for the control and manipulation of our lives can only be imagined. They aim at rigorous solutions to problems and unambiguous definitions; but life and art are rich in ambiguity, and to eliminate it could impoverish and trivialize both.

In our time, "meaning" and "truth" join "reality" as problematic and relative terms. The reduction of truth from absolute, transcendental, and eternal to public, relative, and debatable makes our acquisition of it conditional on language. And ordinary verbal language is ambiguous.

The success of experimental science has had everything to do with making meaning and truth into functions of instruments and languages. Our knowledge of the physical world is obtained by the manipulation of instruments, and the specialized language of mathematics mediates that knowledge. Thus, the meaning, truth, and reality of scientific experience— that is, scientific knowledge—are contained in its media and inseparable from them. This is true also of the arts in this age of science and mechanism. As we saw in Chapter 21, Maurice Denis insists that before a picture is *of* anything it is simply a flat surface covered with colors arranged in a certain way. By a similar reduction, a poem is only a sequence of words or word-images, and a piece of music is only a sequence of sounds. A dominant modern view defines art as consisting of the free manipulation of such elements in arrangements that need not refer to anything outside themselves—that need not *represent* anything. The arrangement is complete and self-contained; one cannot find its message by demanding that it point to something recognizable beyond itself. The modern artist, like the scientist, "experiments" with his medium, investigates its possibilities, and discovers or invents new forms. But unlike the scientist, who searches for new uniformities and regularities, most modern artists seek the singular and the unique; JUAN GRIS, one of the best Cubist painters, remarks: "My aim is to create new objects which cannot be compared to any object in actuality." The task of projecting the optical order of the world onto a flat surface— the task of generations of painters since Giotto—is given up. For, given the new view of the world, the optical "look" of it is problematic and to make pictures that copy it is futile or trivial. New forms must be discovered or created out of the possibilities of the physical medium itself so that new and profound reality can be expressed. Paul Klee, one of the great masters of modern art, puts it this way:

> We used to represent things visible on earth. . . . Now we reveal the reality of visible things, and thereby express the belief that visible reality is merely an isolated phenomenon latently outnumbered by other realities. Things take on a broader and more varied meaning, often in seeming contradiction to the rational experience of yesterday. . . . In the end, a formal cosmos will be created out of purely abstract elements of form quite independent of their configurations as objects, beings, or abstract things like letters or numbers.*

In other words, the reality of visible things is now no longer merely their visibility. The visible state of a thing, given in a single perspective as in traditional art, is an extremely limited account of it; the reality is much more than that. Klee provides an example: "An apple tree in bloom is in effect a complex of stages of growth, its roots, the rising sap, its trunk, the cross section with the annual rings, the blossom, its structure, its sexual function, the fruit, the core with its seeds." Klee wants to express this complexity of parts as a whole that is, in effect, more than the sum of its parts—as a whole that has a meaning that cannot be apprehended by the analysis of the apple tree into parts and phenomena. Thus, the ambiguity that scientists try to eliminate from their procedures, findings, and communicated information is the very essence of the reality the artist deals with. Klee continues:

> In the highest sense, an ultimate mystery lies behind the ambiguity which the light of the intellect fails miserably to penetrate. Yet one can to a certain extent speak reasonably of the salutary effect which art exerts through fantasy and symbols. Fantasy, kindled by instinct-born excitements, creates illusory conditions which can rouse or stimulate us more than familiar, natural, or supernatural ones. Symbols reassure the mind that we need not depend exclusively upon mundane experience. . . .†

The mystery that modern science tries to dispel, modern art cultivates as if it were at the heart of our human experience of reality. The union of art and science in the Renaissance, made on the basis of Humanistic reason, is dissolved in the twentieth century. Even though the arts in one respect—the experiment with forms and materials—have paralleled modern logic and mathematics and have often been close to technology, their intention and their results have led them in the precisely opposite direction. The artist–experimenter is at the same time the artist–prophet. Working ceaselessly at the possibilities of his physical medium, he seeks a reality behind the screen of the conventional world. His search depends not on a general, public agreement about reality or on a general pictorial language for communicating it, but on his own instincts, insight, inner experience, which he expresses as a kind of personal vision—strange, ambiguous, mystifying, impossible to communicate in words. It is little wonder that, as modern art has

*In Margaret Miller, ed., *Paul Klee* (New York: Museum of Modern Art, 1946), p. 12.

†*Ibid.*, p. 13.

developed in its many movements, the general public has been most often hostile to it. Undoubtedly, the artist most often invites that hostility, for almost from the beginning it has been his intention to *épater le bourgeois*—to shake up stodgy citizens and make them see and think in a new way. Picasso insists that art, in this respect, must be subversive, essentially revolutionary. The modern artist, in this view, must live in the avant-garde of society, and his very life must be a model of defiant freedom from spirit-destroying convention.

What has been said by way of background to the ensuing discussion of the art of the twentieth century is, of course, a simplification and it should be viewed only as a partial and uncertain explanation of the central fact—that modern art looks very different from the art of the past. We have generalized modern art and the modern artist, and particular cases escape generalization; what remains unequivocal is the picture of the artist in a dangerous, confused world, experimenting to find a free means of expression of his insights. The modern-artist's task is to reconstruct reality from private experience.

PAINTING BEFORE WORLD WAR II

Symbolism and Art Nouveau

Two movements discussed or anticipated in Chapter 21, continue from the late nineteenth century: Symbolism and Art Nouveau. We have seen that the Symbolists carried the subjectivity of Romanticism to new extremes. In doing so, they turned from the common nineteenth-century stock of historical, mythological, and anecdotal themes to the relatively unfamiliar ones of the Orient, Oceania, Byzantium, Persia, the Early Middle Ages, and the Early Renaissance.

It is in these uncommon sources that the Symbolists search for new forms. The picture-box of the pictorial tradition is replaced by flat surfaces, decoratively embellished with figures that are not modeled or, if modeled, that are often contrasted with flat patterns. An example of this experimental adjustment of planar shapes and plastic forms is the painting *Death and Life* (FIG. 22-1) by the Viennese artist GUSTAV

22-1 GUSTAV KLIMT, *Death and Life*, 1908 and 1911. 5′ 10″ × 6′ 6″. Collection of Marietta Preleuthner, Salzburg.

KLIMT (1862–1918). In 1903, Klimt visited Ravenna and saw its great mosaics. Although Byzantine art had begun to be appreciated in the early nineteenth century, Klimt approaches it here not as critic, historian, or connoisseur, but as an artist open to fresh inspiration, ready and competent to assimilate form from outside his own tradition to express a modern mood. The painting is quite typically Symbolist in both content and form. Bright colors, mosaic-like or enamel-like, stud the surfaces that enwrap the voluptuously somnolent figures in the *Life* group, in which intertwined images of infancy, youth, maturity, and old age celebrate life as bound up with love. Outlined shapes are modeled to the extent needed to show the softness of flesh and the firmness of sinew. It is characteristic of Klimt to contrast often quite realistically modeled forms with flat patterns. The tableau of defenseless sleep is set off against the specter of Death, the nocturnal assassin, who advances threateningly upon it. The shroud of the fleshless Death is appropriately dark as night, only dimly decked with funereal black crosses and chiromantic symbols. While Life, sated with love, sleeps, its enemy, Death, wakes. The grim interval between Life and Death will soon be crossed.

In this and other Symbolist works, the ornamental flatness of the drapery, the organic, undulating contours, and the arbitrary placement of the figures, so that they seem to float and hover as they would in a dream, contradict the presuppositions of realistic representation. From this contradiction and from the example of art outside the Western tradition arose new possibilities of form independent of pictorial Realism that produced an international style, Art Nouveau, which dominated the arts from 1890 to World War I. Art Nouveau, primarily an ornamental style, was a protest not simply against a sterile Realism, but against the whole drift toward industrialization and mechanization and the unnatural artifacts they produced. The forms of nature—growing, sinuous, and graceful—were set against the blunt, ugly masses of the encroaching machine. Art Nouveau called for the renovation of a taste corrupted by mass-produced objects and cluttered urban environments, which seemed to be assuming dominance in the name of unesthetic utility.

The sources of Art Nouveau, as of Symbolism, lay in the arts and crafts of other cultures and times and in the exotic styles cultivated by innovative artists like Paul Gauguin (FIG. 21-70), Vincent Van Gogh (FIG. 21-69), and their contemporaries. The Japanese print played an important part (FIGS. 13-29 and 21-60), as did the movement led by John Ruskin and William Morris, who, as we have seen, extolled careful craftsmanship in all the arts, stressing the moral as well as the esthetic value of honest, individual craft. Art Nouveau, especially effective in architecture and the handicrafts (FIG. 22-55) decisively influenced the figural arts; and most of the great modern painters of the early twentieth century participated in or were touched by the movement at the beginning of their careers.

The Fauves and Expressionism

The first signs of a new and specifically twentieth-century movement in painting appeared in Paris in 1905. In that year, at the third Salon d'Automne, a group of younger painters, independent of the French Royal Academy and the "official" Salon and under the leadership of Henri Matisse, exhibited canvases so simplified in design and so shockingly brilliant in color that a startled critic described the artists as *fauves* ("wild beasts"). The influence of the non-European cultures of the new colonial dominions was everywhere apparent. The "Fauves" were encouraged by the newly discovered exotic arts to seek more personal forms of expression than had been known in the West. In African fetishes, in Polynesian decorative wood carvings, and in the sculptures and textiles from the ancient cultures of Central and South America, they saw unexpected shapes and colors that suggested new ways of communicating emotion. This led them individually into various paths of free invention and took them once and for all out of the traditions of the Renaissance. Deft, spirited painters, they produced canvases of great spontaneity and verve, with a rich surface texture, lively linear patterns, and boldly clashing effects of primary colors. Their subject matter was as varied as their methods of painting, although many subjects familiar in Impressionist and Post-Impressionist painting—such as landscapes, still lifes, and nude figures—still appeared. Thus, the Fauves carried on and expanded the trends begun by Van Gogh and Gauguin, whose works had become better known through extensive retrospective exhibitions held in Paris in 1901 and 1903.

The Fauves brought color to a new intensity with startling discords of vermilion and emerald green, cerulean blue and vivid orange held together by sweeping brush strokes and bold patterns. Relationships to the past and contributions to the present can be seen in a painting like the one exhibited in the 1905 Salon d'Automne entitled *London Bridge* (FIG. 22-2) by ANDRÉ DERAIN (1880–1954), whose Fauve work remains among his finest. We can judge how thoroughly the Fauve painters have broken with most of the art of the late nineteenth century when we recall that Claude Monet had completed his series of views of Waterloo Bridge in London only three years before. Derain entirely rejects the subtle harmonies of Im-

22-2 André Derain, *London Bridge*, 1906. Approx. 26″ × 39″. Museum of Modern Art, New York (gift of Mr. and Mrs. Charles Zadok).

pressionism, so expressive of atmospheric and climatic conditions, in favor of a distorted perspective emphasized by clashing yellows, blues, greens, and reds against the black accents of the arches. Implicit in such work is the philosophy already adopted by Van Gogh and Gauguin (pages 867–69) and fundamental to Expressionism: the artist's presentation of his emotional reaction to the subject in the boldest color and strongest linear pattern is more important than any attempts at objective representation. In this way, the Fauves freed color from its traditional role as the description of the local tone of an object and helped to prepare both artists and public for the use of color as an expressive end in itself. In a sense, color became the "subject" of the picture.

The Fauve movement, never an official organization of painters, was short-lived; within five years, most of the artists had modified their violent colors and found their own more personal treatment of the medium.

The artist who remains most faithful to the Fauve principles yet, through his extraordinary sensitivity for color, transforms them into one of the strongest

and most influential personal expressions in modern art is Henri Matisse (1869–1954). Throughout his long life, his gift for combining colors in unsuspected ways and for inventing new combinations never flagged. He preferred working in two dimensions but, by the subtlest of color accents, his surfaces, no matter how apparently flat, convey effects of three-dimensional space.

Studying his *Red Room (Harmony in Red)*, shown in fig. 22-3, we find that Matisse uses the color craft of Gauguin and Paul Cézanne for his own decorative–expressive purpose. The composition is an essay in the contrast of warm and cool colors and curving and straight lines. Although the planes of the picture seem to resolve into a single, flat spread, directional lines and the variation in the strength of color suggest a front and back, but in a kind of contrived spatial ambiguity. Matisse himself tells us that his procedure is one of continuous adjustment of color to color, shape to shape, and color to shape until the exactly right "feel" is achieved and the painting is completed. He puts the matter of Expressionism very succinctly:

22-3 HENRI MATISSE, *Red Room (Harmony in Red)*, 1908–1909. Approx. 5′ 11″ × 8′ 1″. State Hermitage Museum, Leningrad.

What I am after, above all, is expression. . . . I am unable to distinguish between the feeling I have for life and my way of expressing it. . . . The whole arrangement of my picture is expressive . . . everything plays a part. Composition is the art of arranging in a decorative manner the various elements at the painter's disposal for the expression of his feelings. . . . All that is not useful in the picture is detrimental.*

This way of letting the picture "emerge" out of deep, even unconscious, feeling, letting one's artistic sensitivity and instinct be one's guide, is common in the practice not only of Expressionism but of modern art in general.

Much modern art is based on severely intellectual doctrines (frequently proclaimed in manifestos) and, to be enjoyed, may require some understanding of the artist's relation to contemporary currents of thought. Although Matisse intellectualizes painting, as his *Notes of a Painter* reveals, his art reflects a great love of nature, of color, and of joyous subjects. He

*In Robert Goldwater and Marco Treves, eds., *Artists on Art* (New York: Pantheon, 1945), pp. 409–10.

once observed that he did not care for weighty themes and moods and that art should be as restful as a comfortable chair after a hard day. For this reason, his art is sometimes disparaged as too decorative and lacking in profundity. But this is to overlook its very special and very French qualities, those that an early critic of Matisse expresses as "simplicity, serenity, and clarity." It is significant that these qualities, so evident in Classicism, are manifest in Matisse's subjects as well as his forms; he concerned himself almost exclusively with figure painting.

In a vein very different from that of Matisse, GEORGES ROUAULT (1871–1958) treats themes of grave social and religious import. His studies of sad clowns and broken prostitutes and his long series of religious paintings are Fauve in their simplified designs. They are constructed with black outlines like the leads in Medieval stained glass, which Rouault, who had worked as a glassmaker's apprentice in his youth, had always admired. These strongly effective black bar-like divisions and the somber tonalities he preferred—the glowing reds, greens, and midnight blues of stained glass—are harmonized in Rouault's

22-4 GEORGES ROUAULT, *The Old King*, 1916–1938. Approx. 30″ × 21″. Museum of Art, Carnegie Institute, Pittsburgh (Patrons Art Fund).

powerful evocation of *The Old King* (FIG. 22-4). The fierce aquiline features, dark complexion, and thick black hair and beard recall some ancient Assyrian despot in brooding reverie, almost an icon of absolute and pitiless authority. The sharp and rugged simplification of the forms and the harsh, hacked-out edges convey, with blunt force, an aspect of monarchic vengefulness.

The influence of the Fauves was almost immediately felt outside of France, coalescing with that of James Ensor (FIG. 21-75) and Edvard Munch (FIG. 21-76) in the German schools of the early twentieth cen-

22-5   Oskar Kokoschka, *The Bride of the Wind*, 1914. 5' 11½" × 7' 2½". Kunstmuseum, Basel.

tury. Here, the element of immediate personal expression, especially characteristic of Fauve painting, appealed to groups of German painters who had organized into movements: *Die Brücke* ("the Bridge," symbolizing the unity of nature and emotion) in Dresden and *Der Blaue Reiter* ("the Blue Rider," after a picture of that name by Vasily Kandinsky) in Munich. These painters carried the tendencies in the work of Derain and Matisse even further. In Germany, there was less concentration than in France on purely formal problems. German Expressionism was a manifestation of subjective feeling toward objective reality and the world of imagination. With bold, vigorous brushwork, emphatic lines, and bright color, the German painters produced splendid, almost savagely powerful canvases, particularly expressive of intense human feeling. A striking example is *The Bride of the Wind* (FIG. 22-5) by OSKAR KOKOSCHKA (1886–1980), a Viennese painter early influenced by Klimt. The theme of the painting has its roots far back in the peak of the Romantic period and (even farther back) in the pathetic story of Paolo and Francesca told by Dante in his *Inferno* (V, 73–142), although it may also be Kokoschka's response to a poignant love af-

fair. Two lovers are swept by turbulent winds through a nightmare landscape, neither they nor the winds ever to be at rest. The anguish of love—its lacerating power, not its delight and ecstasy—is expressed in the violence of shredded contours, alternating cold and lurid color, and painfully agitated brushwork. The painting is a passionate expression of the state of two souls who embrace not in joy but in unmitigated sorrow. Here, Kokoschka gives us a clear instance of the transition from Symbolism to Expressionism.

German Expressionism is in the direct line of descent from earlier German painting and engraving, especially in its strong color, linear pattern, emphasis on subject matter of a highly emotional character, and frequent transcendental overtones. These elements appear most effectively in the work of EMIL NOLDE (1867–1956), and an especially good example is *St. Mary of Egypt Among Sinners* (FIG. 22-6). Although he learned much from the masks of Ensor and the color of Matisse, Nolde's painting has an original force of its own, reminiscent of Matthias Grünewald (FIG. 18-35) and Hieronymus Bosch (FIG. 18-21) in its expressive violence. Mary, before her conversion, entertains

22-6   EMIL NOLDE, *St. Mary of Egypt Among Sinners*, 1912. Left panel of a triptych, approx. 34" × 39". Kunsthalle, Hamburg.

22-7   MAX BECKMANN, *Departure*, 1932–1935. Triptych, center panel 7' ¾" × 3' 9⅜". Museum of Modern Art, New York (given anonymously).

lechers whose brutal ugliness is magnified by their lust. The distortions of form and color (especially the jarring juxtapositions of red and green) work to the same end—an appalling tableau of subhuman and depraved passion in which evil wreaks its visible consequence in the repulsive faces and gestures.

MAX BECKMANN (1884–1950), an independent and forceful Expressionist, has left some of the most memorable works of the German schools. His art was elicited by some of the darkest moments of the twentieth century, when Nazi tyranny threatened European civilization. While his message is bitter, its reference is not specific to one time or place but concerns human cruelty and suffering in general. In perhaps his best-known painting, a triptych entitled *Departure* (FIG. 22-7), he organizes figures rendered in caricature-like distortion and simplification, their sculptural relief accentuated by hard, black line. In the left panel is a scene of torture prophetic of the death camps: a bound man stands in a barrel of water; another's hands have been severed; a trussed woman crouches in the foreground; the executioner wields his ax. The horror is continued in the right panel, partly staged as a mad carnival. In striking contrast, the central panel represents a royal family in calm daylight, the figures resigned and serene, departing the terrors of night in what may be an allusion to Beckmann's own flight from Nazi Germany after his work, along with that of most of the Expressionists, had been condemned and banned by Hitler as "degenerate." The hard, bright color, beautifully harmonized, carries in itself a large burden of the meaning.

Beckmann's visions of human disaster were shared by many artists of his generation who had witnessed at first hand the carnage of the battlefields of France and the shattered and corrupted society of postwar Germany. Sensitized by their experience, they often made works that were in an almost prophetic strain. *Punishment* (FIG. 22-8) by GEORGE GROSZ (1893–1959) is both a recollection of the destruction of Sodom and Gomorrah and a premonition of the apocalyptic obliteration of the world by bombs. A wildly free brush configures blazing explosions, thunderclouds of smoke, and the cascading debris of buildings in a furious image of man-made hell where no figure of man survives. Curiously, Grosz's picture is but a step from the total nonobjectivity of Kandinsky's *Improvisations* (FIG. 22-10), in which coherent images are lost in an apparent chaos of shape and color.

The emotional range of German Expressionism varies greatly—from the terror and indignation of artists like Nolde, Beckmann, and Grosz to the poignantly expressed pity for the poor in the moving prints of KÄTHE KOLLWITZ (1867–1945). The graphic art of Gauguin and Munch stimulated a revival of the print medium in Germany, especially the woodcut,

22-8 GEORGE GROSZ, *Punishment*, 1934. Watercolor, approx. 27¼" × 20¼". Museum of Modern Art, New York (gift of Mr. and Mrs. Erich Cohn).

and the forceful block prints cut in the days of the German Reformation proved inspiring models. The harsh, black, splintered lines of the woodblock print were ideal for the stark forms and blunt emphasis of message prized by the German Expressionists. In her *Memorial to Karl Liebknecht* (FIG. 22-9), Kollwitz produces a classic of the Expressionist print. The compo-

22-9 KÄTHE KOLLWITZ, *Memorial to Karl Liebknecht*, 1919. Woodcut. (Location unknown.)

sition is both a masterful presentation of mute sorrow at the bier of a lost leader and a strong political protest. We have seen to what effective political use Honoré Daumier put the graphic medium. Regrettably, modern methods of reproduction have largely usurped the public role of the graphic arts.

The emphasis on color by the Fauves and the German Expressionists made it almost logical that color by itself, without any figurative material, could come to constitute the full "content" of a picture. In the Blue Rider group, the Russian painter VASILY KANDINSKY (1866–1944) carried his research into the emotional and psychological properties of color, line, and shape to the point that subject matter and even representational elements were entirely eliminated. Now that abstract art has become so much a part of our experience, we tend to forget the courage such a step required and the creative imagination needed to undertake such a completely new direction in the art of painting. By 1914, Kandinsky had perfected his methods and established, in two groups of works, two principal kinds of painting. He called one kind *Compositions*, the title for this group implying that

such arrangements of geometric shapes were consciously planned and intellectually ordered; on the other hand, in his *Improvisations* (an example of which is shown in FIG. 22-10), he approached the canvas with no preconceived theme but allowed the colors to come as they would, prompted by subconscious feelings. In these works, the brilliant colors flow across the canvas with as little conscious order or control as possible on the artist's part. In utilizing subconscious sensations, Kandinsky uncovered an area soon to be exploited by other artists, notably the Surrealists. Kandinsky describes his methods and the philosophical connotations of his art in his influential treatise *Concerning the Spiritual in Art* (1912),* in which he proclaims the independence of color and the spiritual value inherent in it. In Kandinsky's view, colors have deep-seated, psychic correlations and the artist's being is revealed in the prerational, utterly uninhibited expression of them. The "rational" world, given to ordinary vision, is hopelessly deceptive, and we must set aside reasoned "seeing" and planning so

*M.T. Saddler, trans., *Concerning the Spiritual in Art* (Mineola, N.Y.: Dover, 1977).

22-10 VASILY KANDINSKY, *Improvisation 28*, 1912. Approx. 44" × 63¾". Solomon R. Guggenheim Museum, New York.

that the deeper reality of ourselves, living in the instinctual world of the subconscious, may rise into sight. This view harmonizes with Freud's conclusions concerning the subconscious and with Arthur Rimbaud's claim that the true artist is a visionary.

Cubism and Its Derivatives

Just as Expressionism, with its emphasis on subjective experience, can be traced back through all its branches to Van Gogh and Gauguin, so two other important currents in modern art—Cubism and Constructivism—can be shown to have vital connections with the Post-Impressionist, Paul Cézanne. Although Matisse and other members of the Fauve group were familiar with Cézanne's work, they admired it chiefly for the color and expressive linear distortions. Cézanne's death in 1906, the retrospective exhibition of his work (held the following year at the Salon d'Automne), and especially the publication by Émile Bernard that year of Cézanne's famous letter, in which he wrote of treating nature in terms of the cylinder, sphere, and cone, enabled the younger painters for the first time to recognize Cézanne's principal intention—to establish substantial forms within a space in which the actual properties of the two-dimensional picture surface and the illusionary effects of three dimensions are consciously and subtly adjusted. Beginning with Cézanne, this adjustment of new sensations of color and form to the physical medium became the common task.

This aspect of Cézanne's practice and theory became the chief concern of a group of younger French painters soon to be known as the Cubists. They drew encouragement from the remarkable personality and achievements of the Spanish painter PABLO PICASSO (1881–1973), whose adult life was spent in France and whose works are inseparably connected with the history of modern French art. From his earliest studies in the Barcelona Academy of Art, Picasso showed precocious ability. At an age when others have learned only the rudiments of their art, Picasso had already mastered all aspects of late nineteenth-century Realist techniques. For one so greatly gifted, not only in manual dexterity but also in powers of pictorial visualization, there was no question of quietly following conventional methods of painting, and it is not surprising that Picasso investigated more than one aspect of picture-making. Even so, the public was ill prepared for the astonishing variety of his "styles" and "periods." Picasso is characteristic of the modern age in his constant experimentation, in his sudden shifts from one kind of painting to another, and in his startling innovations in painting and even sculpture. He is said to have been amused at the attempts of critics and historians to "explain" him and to follow the bewildering turns of his development. But it is a

fact that his work over such a long lifetime manifested most of the significant modern trends in art that have prevailed from the beginning of the period through World War II.

When Picasso settled permanently in Paris in 1904, his work had evolved from the sober Realism of Spanish painting, through a brightening of color in an Impressionistic manner (for a while he was influenced by the early works of Toulouse-Lautrec), and into the so-called Blue Period (1901-1905), in which he painted worn, pathetic, alienated figures in the pessimistic mood of the *fin de siècle*—a "blue" mood conveyed, appropriately, in a predominantly blue tonality. Around 1905 or 1906, Picasso became aware almost simultaneously of the importance of the art of Cézanne, of the primitive art of Africa and Oceania, and especially of the sculpture of ancient Iberia. He detected in them a way of organizing formal elements that differed from anything in Western tradition—a way of giving them esthetic independence from pictorial Realism and a new and vivid value of their own. In *Portrait of Gertrude Stein* (FIG. 22-11), Picasso approximates Cézanne's method, carefully analyzing forms into simple planes, making contours strong and precise, and, particularly in the face, assuming different viewpoints, which makes for an ambiguous

22-11 PABLO PICASSO, *Portrait of Gertrude Stein*, 1906. 39⅜" × 32". Metropolitan Museum of Art, New York (bequest of Gertrude Stein, 1946).

perspective. The two sides of the mask-like face do not fit; the near side reads almost as a profile (a favorite trick of Picasso's). This breaking-up of smoothly continuous volumes into separate but interlocking planes leads sharply away from Realism toward a concept of design independent of nature. African works like the mask shown in FIG. 14-53 must have given Picasso many a lead as to the direction his abstraction from nature could take. A painting that shows the painter well on the path of the reduction of visual fact to abstract form is the startling *Les Demoiselles d'Avignon* (FIG. 22-12), "Avignon" being the name of a street in Barcelona's red-light district. Instead of representing his figures as continuous volumes in motion, the volumes in *Les Demoiselles* are fractured and the jagged planes that result are slipping well beyond the bodies' contours. The images are disintegrating into their planes. Picasso takes this process, begun in the landscape and figures of Cézanne, to the threshold of a radically new kind of painting. Not only does he challenge the traditional concept of an orderly, constructed, unified pictorial space that mirrors the world, but he also dismisses the idea of the human figure as a dynamic unity and, especially in the two figures at the right, twists and breaks it into grotesque dislocations. Three of the heads are adaptations of African masks. Indeed, it was in the abrupt dislocations of African and Iberian sculpture, as well as in the art of Cézanne, that Picasso found a hint of how to dissect natural forms into their essential planes and volumes—a task that was to occupy him for the next few years.

By 1910, Picasso and his experimenting colleague Georges Braque had laid the basis for this new kind of painting, which was soon nicknamed "Cubism" by a critic who was amused by the approximately geometric forms in many of their works.* The name was soon accepted by the painters and their critics, but it suggests very little of the seriousness and originality of the Cubist achievement. Very simply, this consists of the discovery of a new kind of pictorial space, which replaces the one that had been developing since the time of Giotto. Like Cézanne's, this space is based on the principle of basic, simplified forms and a shifting point of view, but the viewpoint is expanded to the point that the Cubists present an object as if from several markedly different angles.

From the time of Masaccio, painting had been assumed to give, in one- or two-point perspective, a fixed and complete "view," in which everything in one plane appears simultaneously with everything

*At present, historians of twentieth-century art are crediting Braque with the first stylistic transformations that produced Cubism. By 1908, working directly from the principles of design found in the late paintings of Cézanne, Braque had produced work that led directly—almost logically—from Cézanne's premises to Cubism. Almost at once, Picasso perceived the importance of Braque's discovery, changed his own direction, and worked concordantly with Braque to develop the new style.

22-12 PABLO PICASSO, *Les Demoiselles d'Avignon*, 1907. 8' × 7' 8". Museum of Modern Art, New York (bequest of Lillie P. Bliss).

22-13 PABLO PICASSO, *Accordionist*, 1911. Approx. 51" × 35". Solomon R. Guggenheim Museum, New York.

else. But this is neither true to visual fact (the fact of seeing the objects rendered) nor to the way we see the picture of these objects, our view of the picture being the result of a great number of eye movements that we make as we take it in. In essence, this is the basis of Cézanne's innovation with respect to a shifting viewpoint. The Cubists, however, go beyond this purely optical reason for using multiple viewpoints. They wish to present the total essential reality of forms in space, and because objects do not appear only as they are seen from one viewpoint at one time, it becomes necessary to introduce multiple angles of vision and simultaneous presentations of discontinuous planes. This, of course, shatters the old continuity of single-viewpoint composition imposed by the Renaissance. The Cubist painter believes that "in order to discover one true relationship it is necessary to sacrifice a thousand surface appearances."*

The concept of reality thus becomes separated from that of appearance, and the resemblance of essential form to ordinary vision is no longer important. The assumption, beginning in the Renaissance, that what we see in nature should find correspondence in the forms that the artist paints is given up, and the epoch that began with Giotto and Masaccio comes to an end in the twentieth century.

Cubism's break with the world of ordinary vision was not simply a matter of esthetic fashion, random experiment, or quixotic exhibitionism, although it has been denounced as all these things and worse: "Cubists," claimed the *New York Times* on the occasion of the 1913 Armory show in that city, "are making insanity pay." However, affinities of thought and imagination give a certain coherence to historical periods; seen within the context of the new Einsteinian vision of the physical world, the new art seems less strange. It has been said that Cubist pictorial space suggests the addition of the dimension of time to spatial dimensions, because objects are represented in temporal sequence, not as they are seen at any one moment. To perceive the many views of the object as given would require movement by the viewer (or at least the viewer's eyes) through some temporally sequential positions. In Einstein's description of the physical world, there is a similar merger of space and time. Time is "assimilated" to the three dimensions of space in such a way that measurements of space and time, especially when astronomical distances are involved, are functions of each other and are never independent. This is decisively different from the Baroque, Newtonian concept of space and time, where both are absolute and independent and where, no matter the distance between two events, it is possible for them to be simultaneous. By extension, si-

multaneous events presuppose a continuous space that is invariant with respect to them. But in the space–time of Einstein's relativity, it is impossible to prove that two physical events at an astronomical distance are actually simultaneous, because time elapses in the very process of their measurement.

Perspective space in Western painting since Masaccio assumes a continuous, unbroken space fixed from a single point of view. We can say of this rigid, geometric space that all the represented objects in it are *simultaneous*; the single *scene* constitutes a single *event*. Cubism, with its new kind of simultaneity—the simultaneity of different viewpoints—destroys consistency of image and appearance and replaces it with "abstract" form. This process is well begun in Picasso's *Les Demoiselles d'Avignon.*

Thus, the recognition and involvement of time in the very pictorial process destroys the structure of appearance constructed over centuries. It replaces appearances with the unlimited possibilities of form. No longer restricted to a single viewpoint, the artist may see any given object in the world not as a fixed appearance or shape, but as a universe of possible lines, planes, and colors. The world of appearance can be analyzed into a world of patterns that is open to endless exploration and adjustment. The shattering of the rigid Renaissance structure of appearance comes to be regarded as a means by which art can be returned to its fundamental functions.

Analysis of these functions is a process that gives its name to the earlier phase of Cubism—the "analytic" phase. A striking example of this style, Picasso's *Accordionist* (FIG. 22-13), is a construction of large, intersecting planes that suggests the forms of the man and his instrument. Hosts of smaller shapes—each probably a simplification of some aspect of the original subject—hover in and interpenetrate the large planes. The total effect is that of a new kind of pictorial reality. We are no longer obliged to contemplate merely a man playing an accordion; we can let our eyes set out on another kind of adventure as they probe the manifold aspects of an object that has been disintegrated, so to speak, and then reintegrated to offer us a great variety of views from different angles.

Picasso's experiments work a still more radical change in what can be called pictorial "reality." From 1908 on, he occasionally attached extraneous materials to the canvas in a technique called *collage*. In his *Still Life with Chair-Caning* (FIG. 22-14), Picasso combines an oilcloth replica of a caned chair seat with elements recovered from disintegrations of pictorial form such as we see in *Accordionist*. This produces a startling confrontation—or juxtaposition—of a commonplace, manufactured surface familiar in everyday experience and the painted abstract shapes. The composition not only introduces violent contrasts of texture but presupposes the painting surface in itself to

*Albert Gleizes and Jean Metzinger, "Cubism," in R.L. Herbert, *Modern Artists on Art* (Englewood Cliffs, N.J.: Prentice-Hall, 1964), p. 3.

22-14 PABLO PICASSO, *Still Life with Chair-Caning*, 1911–1912. Oil and pasted paper simulating chair-caning on canvas, 10⅝″ × 13¾″. Musée Picasso, Paris.

serts that the painting is not a "picture," as it were, but a flat area that can receive almost any kind of application of apparently unrelated substances. Here, pictorial art takes a step toward becoming relief sculpture—an effect intensified by the rope frame. Collage has great importance for later Russian Constructivism and Dada, as well as for various movements today, in which there is a studied ambiguity in the relation of sculpture and painting. Picasso's and Braque's experiments with this new medium marked the end of the "analytic" phase of Cubism.

The premises of "analytic" Cubism are so rational, and the artists' application of their theories so intellectual and logical, that the styles of different painters in the "school" began to become almost indistinguishable. The similarity of the products of "analytic" Cubism became even more apparent when the artists, in their excessive concern with matters of pure form, began to neglect color, so that their paintings became almost monochrome. When the artists recognized this defect—and the fact that they had placed a stylistic straitjacket on themselves—"analytic" Cub-

be an object given to touch as well as sight, a plane surface on which materials other than paint can be placed. This texturing of the surface is new and as-

22-15 PABLO PICASSO, *Three Musicians*, 1921. Approx. 6' 7″ × 7' 3¾″. Museum of Modern Art, New York (Mrs. Simon Guggenheim Fund).

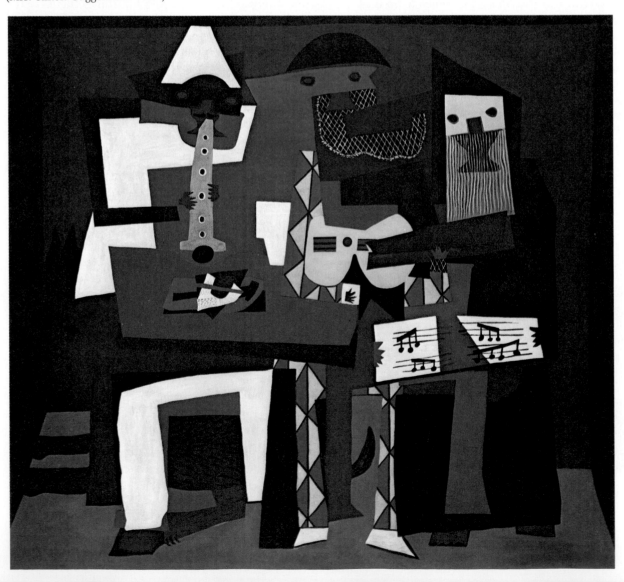

ism yielded to "synthetic" Cubism, which uses stronger colors and allows greater freedom of expression. Again, Picasso led the way by developing a style in which a more limited number of views of an object are selected for their decorative rather than their exclusively spatial significance. The mingling of forms became more spontaneous, their colors stronger, their textures more varied. In an early and superbly decorative example of this aspect of Picasso's work, *Three Musicians* (FIG. 22-15), the space is much flatter, scarcely deeper than a series of planes laid like playing cards one on another, as if different parts, the consequence of multiple views, have been reassembled before a single viewpoint. There is a strong tendency to reduce each form to a simple rectangular shape, but for all that, the figures of the clown, the Harlequin, and the monk, their instruments and music, and the table at which they are sitting can be detected without effort. The broken shapes, filled with flat, bright color against dark tonal variations, move with a syncopated rhythm and vivid dissonance analogous to those of modern music.

Although the development of Cubism must be considered one of Picasso's greatest achievements, he was never content to work for long in any one mode. While still painting "synthetic" Cubist pictures, he also made "Ingres-like" drawings and painted figure subjects in a broadly Realistic manner often influenced by Antique sculpture. In the late 1920s, he created, with heavy swirling lines and rich color, visual distortions that seemed related to contemporary Expressionism. The climax of this personal style came in

1937 in his large mural *Guernica* (FIG. 22-16), painted for the Spanish pavilion of the Paris International Exposition of that year to protest the bombing of the open town Guernica during the Spanish Civil War. In this allegorical presentation of the plight of his native country, where brute force seems momentarily triumphant, Picasso uses all the resources of his Cubist experience. The severe colors—the blacks, whites, and grays—emphasize the marvelously complex design of interpenetrating planes; unexpected and violent linear distortions communicate the horror of the event. In the figures of the dead warrior, the dying horse, and the bellowing bull, Picasso creates impressive and public symbols for the plight of his native country; in his own words, he expresses here an age of "brutality and darkness." The contention that modern forms of expression in art are unequal to the task of interpreting the humanistic values of modern society is contradicted by this painting, for in it Picasso sets forth in masterly terms an indictment of the evils of modern totalitarianism and his conviction that art is the most effective means of affirming the preeminent worth of individual human beings.

In contrast to Picasso's violence of form as well as of expression, GEORGES BRAQUE (1882–1963), the pioneer and master of Cubism per se, works in a more lyrical and even, one might say, more French manner. The rhythmic effect of *The Table* (FIG. 22-17) reveals his admiration for the great masters of French decorative painting; such a work, although entirely contemporary, would not be out of place in an eighteenth-century drawing room. Much of the effect of

22-16 PABLO PICASSO, *Guernica*, 1937. Mural, approx. 11′ 6″ × 25′ 8″. Museo del Prado, Madrid.

Braque's work depends on his mastery of two-dimensional design, for he maintained that a painting is a flat surface and should remain a flat surface, animated by line, color, and texture. He works within a narrow range of restrained but subtly related colors, often using grays and whites to advantage, with frequent unexpected passages of modulated textures. According to Braque:

> The aim of painting . . . is not to reconstruct an anecdotic fact, but to constitute a pictorial fact. . . . We must not imitate what we want to create. The aspect of things is not to be imitated, for the aspect of things is the result of them.*

FERNAND LÉGER (1881–1955) was a friend to and, in his approach to painting, derives from the original Cubists. His works have the sharp precision of the machine, the beauty and quality of which Léger was one of the first to discover. A modern composer, George Antheil, composed a score for a Léger film, *Ballet Méchanique*; it is significant that the work included the sound of an airplane engine. Léger is preeminently the painter of modern urban life, incorporating into his work the massive effects of modern posters and billboard advertisements, the harsh flashing of electric lights, the noise of traffic, the robot-like movements of mechanized people. An early work in which these effects appear— modulated, however, by the esthetic of "synthetic" Cubism—is *The City* (FIG. 22-18). Its monumental scale proves that Léger, had he been given the opportunity, would have been one of the great mural painters of our age. In a definitive way, he presents the mechanical commotion of the contemporary city.

Outside of France, Cubism received its most significant reception in the Italian school of Futurism, inaugurated in 1909 by the manifesto of the poet Filippo Marinetti. Enraptured by the machine age, Marinetti proclaimed a new art of "violence, energy, and boldness," which went along with an extreme dislike of all traditional art and an uncompromising demand for modernism. In the words of the Futurist Umberto Boccioni:

> We propose . . . to sweep from the field of art all motifs and subjects that have already been exploited . . . to destroy the cult of the past . . . to despise utterly every form of imitation . . . to extol every form of originality . . . to render and glorify the life of today, unceasingly and violently transformed by victorious science.†

In principle, the Futurist painters attempt to present aspects of modern mechanized society seen in

*In Maurice Raynal, *Modern French Painting*, trans. Ralph Roeder (New York: Brentano's, 1928), pp. 51–52.

†In Robert Goldwater and Marco Treves, eds., *Artists on Art* (New York: Pantheon, 1945), pp. 409–10.

22-18   FERNAND LÉGER, *The City*, 1919. Approx. 7′ 7″ × 9′ 9½″. Philadelphia Museum of Art
(A.E. Gallatin Collection).

moments of violently energetic movement. In practice, they adopt the Cubist analysis of space; but by repetition of forms across the plane of the canvas, they attempt to impart movement to the static Cubist compositions. Movement and time obsessed the Futurists. Boccioni's manifesto of 1910 rings with a new recognition of universal process:

Everything moves, everything runs, everything turns swiftly. The figure in front of us never is still, but ceaselessly appears and disappears. Owing to the persistence of images on the retina, objects in motion are multiplied and distorted, following one another like waves through space. Thus, a galloping horse has not four legs; it has twenty, and their movements are triangular.*

A method accommodating observations like these was devised from the example of photography by the French painter MARCEL DUCHAMP (1887–1968) in his *Nude Descending a Staircase #2* (FIG. 22-19). The effect is that of a closely spaced series of "still" photographs of an action, although Duchamp analyzed the figure first into planes in the manner of Cubism (which was natural enough, considering that Duchamp and his brother, the sculptor RAYMOND DUCHAMP-VILLON, experimented early with Cubist analysis, perhaps

even before Picasso and Braque). About this time, of course, the motion picture was being developed; this would give the illusion of movement not through the analysis of forms within a single framed space, but through the rapid (relative to the eye's ability to retain an image briefly) projection of a sequence of still photographs (or "frames") of an action. Futurism reaches the limits of the traditional static picture's ability to yield a visual impression of motion. The best Futuristic work is done in sculpture, notably that of Boccioni (FIG. 22-44).

It seems inevitable, once Cubism had broken the Renaissance structure of fixed appearance into a limitless world of forms, that the questions should repeatedly arise: How may these forms be recognized, invented, appropriated, arranged? Assuming the need for completely new principles of pictorial design (or restoration of the old, fundamental ones), how is this to be achieved? The many answers to these questions have produced the many schools and "isms" of modern art. Cubism had hardly made its crucial point when criticisms of it were voiced by artists who wanted to go beyond it to an even more abstract, "purer" formalism. The special effect of Cubist painting is found in the balance maintained between the appearance of the original object or figure, as the viewer may remember it, and the degree of abstraction with which it has been transformed into a work of art. That Cubist technique would almost inevitably

*In Robert Goldwater and Marco Treves, eds., *Artists on Art* (New York: Pantheon, 1945), pp. 409–10.

22-19 MARCEL DUCHAMP, *Nude Descending a Staircase #2,* 1912. Approx. 58″ × 35″. Philadelphia Museum of Art (Louise and Walter Arensberg Collection).

lead to a greater and finally to an absolute degree of abstraction is implicit in Juan Gris's remark:

> Cézanne turns a bottle into a cylinder, but I begin with a cylinder and create an individual of a special type: I make a bottle—a particular bottle—out of a cylinder. Cézanne tends towards architecture; I tend away from it. That is why I compose with abstractions (colors) and make my adjustments when these colors have assumed the form of objects.*

But what would happen if one started with the geometric shape and did not develop the resemblance, no matter how remote, to any actual object? Such was the proposal of the Dutch painter PIET MONDRIAN (1872–1944), who felt that "Cubism did not accept the

*In D.H. Kahnweiler, *Juan Gris, His Life and Work,* trans. Douglas Cooper (New York: Valentin, 1947), p. 138.

logical consequences of its own discoveries; it was not developing abstraction toward its ultimate goal, the expression of pure reality."

Mondrian himself, influenced by his most famous countryman, Van Gogh, began painting as an Expressionist. But after studying in Paris, just before World War I, he turned toward a stricter conception of pictorial design. When hostilities began, he was obliged to return to Holland, where he remained during the war, meditating on the theories of Cubist painting and continuing his own research into the absolute properties of artistic order. His investigations led him to renounce all representational elements and to concentrate on a severely limited vocabulary of colors and shapes: black, white, and the primaries (red, yellow, and blue) and straight lines, squares, and rectangles. With these elements, Mondrian constructed two-dimensional designs arranged in such subtle asymmetrical balances of line, color, and area that even slight changes destroy the composition. His rectilinear purism is closely related to the architecture of the De Stijl movement (a group of Dutch artists, essentially disciples of Mondrian), as is evident in Gerrit Rietveldt's Schroeder House in Utrecht (FIG. 22-60). In his *Composition in Blue, Yellow, and Black* (FIG. 22-20), Mondrian has adjusted the design so carefully that no single portion of the surface is more important than any other; the tension between the rectangles is maintained to the very edges. The power of the colors to hold the viewer's attention is subtly equivalent to the attraction exercised by the much larger blank areas, and the proportions of each of these areas are cunningly varied to avoid a mechanical uniformity of the general equilibrium. Mondrian held the firm belief that

> true reality is attained through dynamic movement in equilibrium. Plastic art affirms that equilibrium can only be established through the balance of unequal but equivalent oppositions. The clarification of equilibrium through plastic art is of great importance for humanity. . . . It is the task of art to express a clear vision of reality.*

To compare Mondrian with the Kandinsky of the *Improvisations* (FIG. 22-10) is to become aware of the range of experimentation within which the search for a new basis for the arts of design took place (although it must be acknowledged that Kandinsky's *Compositions* have much of the "hard-edge" quality of Mondrian's work).

The resources of abstraction opened up by Cubism could be drawn on by artists not directly influenced by it. The American painter GEORGIA O'KEEFFE (1887–1986), in place of reductive analysis of form into frac-

*Piet Mondrian, *Plastic Art and Pure Plastic Art* (New York: Wittenborn, 1951), p. 10.

22-20 PIET MONDRIAN, *Composition in Blue, Yellow, and Black*, 1936. Approx. 17″ × 13″. KUNSTMUSEUM, BASEL (Emmanuel Hoffman-Stiftung).

tured shapes, gives us, in *Jack-in-the-Pulpit IV* (FIG. 22-21), an expanded, sharply focused close-up view of the handsome plant. Exhibiting the natural flow of curved plane and contour, she takes the abstraction almost to the limit of the flower's identity; it might, at first sight, be something exfoliating on some unknown planet or in the cellular world of our bodies. The fluid planes unfold like undulant petals from a subtly placed axis—the white, jet-like streak—in a vision of the slow, controlled motion of growing life.

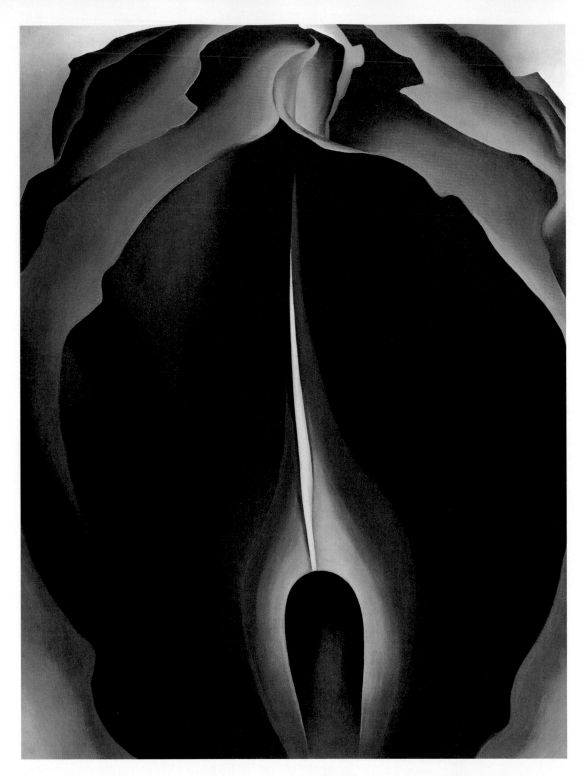

22-21 GEORGIA O'KEEFFE, *Jack-in-the-Pulpit IV*, 1930. 40″ × 30″. Collection of Georgia O'Keeffe.

O'Keeffe's painting, in its graceful, quiet poetry, reveals the organic reality of the object by abstracting and strengthening its characteristic forms, in striking contrast with either Kandinsky's explosions or Mondrian's rectilinear absolutes.

In Russia, the influence of Cubist painting led to a somewhat similar concern with basic design elements. Before 1914, Cubist and even Futurist paintings were exhibited in Moscow and St. Petersburg, and Russian artists of the younger generation were anxious to contribute to the modern movement. KASIMIR MALEVICH (1878–1935), after working in the Cubist and Futurist manners, created what he called Suprematist paintings, in which his intention was the expression of nonobjectivity—a form of expression removed as far as possible from the world of natural forms. In this way, he arrived at what he calls "the supremacy of pure feeling or perception," for "the essential thing [in pictorial art] is feeling—in itself and completely independent of the context in which

22-22 KASIMIR MALEVICH, *Suprematist Composition: White on White*, c. 1918. Approx. 31¼″ × 31¼″. Museum of Modern Art, New York.

it has been evoked." The most nonobjective of Malevich's works is his famous *Suprematist Composition: White on White* (FIG. 22-22). Here, color, shape, and line are reduced to the elements of an off-white square superimposed on a larger off-white square. The two shapes are differentiated only by their size, their angle of inclination, and slight modulations in texture and "color" (one is cool in tone; one, warm).

The other important movement descending, with Cubism, from Cézanne's "geometric" view of nature is Constructivism. Its principles, as stated by the Russian artist Antoine Pevsner and his brother, Naum Gabo (see p. 923), are manifested in painting by a lithe austerity of line and a formal geometricity. Pevsner's belief that art must express contemporary culture led to the use of "modern" materials (sheet metal, plastics, wire), which were particularly suited to the expression of the dynamic character of the emerging industrial culture of the time. Constructivist artists strove for an effect of interpenetration and simultaneity, which was more readily achieved in "constructions" and sculpture. Emotion—apart from a purely esthetic one—was largely secondary in their work.

Dada to Surrealism

The purist artists, Constructivist and Suprematist, tried to create a new art of clarity and order; elsewhere other attitudes toward the times led to a basically destructive artistic expression. In several places and at nearly the same time—in Zurich, Barcelona, and New York in 1916 and 1917—a number of artists independently stated their disgust with the war and life in general by making works of nonart. This movement was early christened Dada, a nonsense or baby-talk term indicative of the conviction that European culture had lost any real meaning. Those who professed to respect the art of the past had been unable

to prevent the outbreak of the holocaust and were now eagerly destroying one another. The artists, refugees from the war, set out in their bitterness to mock all the values of what they believed to be a culture gone mad. "Dada," said one of its historians, "was born from what it hated." Because the Dadaists' intentions were fundamentally nihilistic, Dada works are difficult to interpret and are best approached with their creators' avowed spirit of nonart, or even antiart, in mind: "Dada is against everything, even Dada"—that is, against all that has become organized and formalized. In this sense, the works may be considered destructive criticisms of artistic expression of the present and recent past. Such a critical attitude appears in Duchamp's famous photograph of the *Mona Lisa*, on which he drew a mustache as if defacing a billboard. The public was shocked—as Duchamp intended it to be—and interpreted the defacement as an outrage on the *Mona Lisa* itself. However, we can now see that Duchamp's intention was rather an indirect and witty attack on those he felt had betrayed the Humanistic ideals of the Renaissance, of which the *Mona Lisa* remains one of the noblest expressions. Modern artists did not escape; in 1920, a Dadaist, FRANCIS PICABIA, exhibited a toy monkey nailed to a door and called it *Portrait of Cézanne*. After 1918, Dada spread quickly through Europe, especially France and Germany, where it appealed to the respective national moods of disillusion in the Pyrrhic victory and despair in defeat.

Since the Dadaists claimed that they were not creating art, it is perhaps unfair to examine their works in a critical spirit. Nevertheless, certain positive contributions emerged from their intentionally negative attitude. Among these are the collage compositions by the German artist KURT SCHWITTERS (1887–1948), which he called by the meaningless name of *Merz Pictures*. Although put together from the contents of the gutter and the trash basket (*merz*, a syllable of the German word for "commercial," caught Schwitters' fancy while he was cutting the word into pieces), the *Merz Pictures* always show Schwitters' sensitivity to texture and design (FIG. 22-23). The typical Dada disdain for conventional techniques accounts for the materials used, but truly artistic feeling for color and form endows these works with appeal beyond their historical significance.

In Duchamp, whom we have already seen as a Futurist, the Dada movement found its most provocative and witty champion, as well as its most eloquent philosopher. Duchamp's philosophy and influence continued in the 1970s and 1980s until he has become almost a legend among younger artists. Dada, according to Duchamp, was "a metaphysical attitude . . . a sort of nihilism . . . a way to get out of a state of mind—to avoid being influenced by one's immediate environment, or by the past: to get away from *clichés*—

22-23 KURT SCHWITTERS, *Merz Picture 19*, 1920. Collage, approx. 7¼″ × 5⅞″. Yale University Art Gallery, New Haven, Connecticut (Collection, Société Anonyme).

22-24 MARCEL DUCHAMP, *To be looked at (from the other side of the glass), with one eye, close to, for almost an hour*, 1918. Framed double-glass panel, with oil paint, collage of paper, lens, etc., 20⅛″ high, 16⅝″ wide, 1⅜″ deep. Museum of Modern Art, New York (bequest of Katherine S. Dreier).

to get free.'' This escape from conventional forms and modes of expression can be seen in Duchamp's glass constructions. Unlike the painting and sculpture of the Russian Constructivists, who had a proud sense of public responsibility, Duchamp's painted glass is his own private jest about the world and art. And if its meaning is inseparable from its nonmeaning—as in the title of *To be looked at (from the other side of the glass), with one eye, close to, for almost an hour* (FIG. 22-24)—at least we can admire the perfection with which he has designed and painted the geometric shapes in such irrational perspective on the sheet of plate glass. Not the least perplexing aspect of Duchamp's work is his scrupulous regard for craftsmanship combined with apparently quite irrelevant subject matter. When, at a later date, this and other glass objects by Duchamp were accidentally cracked, Duchamp insisted that the unexpected pattern of fractures completed his original design.

Although much Dada work is intentionally ephemeral (the movement came to a sudden end in 1922), it has important consequences for later art—reinforcing a trend away from the reasoned, formal aim and cool disciplinary requirements of Cubism and abstract art toward a spontaneous, intuitive expression of the whimsical, fantastic, humorous, sardonic, and absurd. Those aspects of experience, expressed in earlier art, were neglected by Cubism and Constructivism. Now a whole new realm of artistic possibility opens, in which the remnants of the optical world,

shattered by compositional analysis, can return in whole and in part to play new, expressive roles. Without the demand that they function in exactly the old context, perspective and chiaroscuro reappear, and their purposes are entirely at the command of the artist. The artist's free imagination now draws on materials lying deep in his consciousness, and his act of expression is the proclamation of new realities that are no less real because they are psychic. In the psychoanalytic view of Freud and others, developing contemporaneously, art is a powerfully practical means of self-revelation and catharsis, and the images that rise out of the subconscious have a truth of their own that is independent of the world of conventional vision. Dreaming fancy demands its own stage and its own means of production in the new, fantastic painting that arises almost at the same time as Cubism but that diverges from it. The historical past as well as the dynamic present can provide inspiration. In the early work of the Greco–Italian painter GIORGIO DE CHIRICO (1888–1978), the squares and palaces of Roman and Renaissance Italy are visualized in a mood of intense and mysterious melancholy. In *The Delights of a Poet* (FIG. 22-25), De Chirico gives us a strange, tilted perspective of a street with arcades, a fountain, a wraith, a distant train, a clock, a blank sky. The hard light fills the emptiness with sharp shadows; there is a foreboding sense of depar-

22-25 GIORGIO DE CHIRICO, *The Delights of a Poet*, c. 1913. Approx. 27⅞" × 34". Collection of Helen and Leonard Yaseen, New York.

ture and of a time long past yet always present, as in T. S. Eliot's "The Hollow Men":

In death's dream kingdom
. . . .
There, the eyes are
Sunlight on a broken column
There, is a tree swinging
And voices are
in the wind's singing
More distant and more solemn
Than a fading star.

Delights is not only visually disturbing, with its sharp inclinations of space and shadow, but so philosophically puzzling that De Chirico's works between 1911 and 1919 are considered to belong to the short-lived school of the *pittura metafisica* in modern Italian art. De Chirico himself has supplied some evidence for a philosophical interpretation by remarking that he was inspired to paint such architectural scenes by Nietzsche's poetic interpretation of autumn afternoons in northern Italian cities. Although such "metaphysical painting" does not, strictly speaking, introduce supernatural elements, it does communicate a feeling of reality very different from our ordinary experience. For this reason, De Chirico is considered to have been a source of inspiration for those artists who created the Surrealist movement in the early 1920s.

The Surrealists' intention is to discover and explore the "more real than real world behind the real"—in other words, the world of psychic experience as revealed by psychoanalytic research, especially that of Freud. In 1924, in his *Surrealist Manifesto*, the French poet André Breton formulated this intention to resolve "conscious" and "subconscious" reality into a new and absolute reality—a superreality (*surréalité*)—

and so "to reestablish man as psychology instead of anatomy." Thus, the dominant motivation of Surrealist painting and construction is to bring together into a single composition aspects of outer and inner "reality," in much the same way that seemingly unrelated fragments of life combine in the vivid world of dreams. The projection in visible form of this new conception required new techniques of pictorial construction. At first, the Surrealists adopted some Dadaist devices, but with new purposes. They used automatic writing and various types of planned "accidents" not so much to reveal a world without meaning as to provoke reactions closely related to subconscious experience. And as Surrealism appeared so soon after the formulations of the principles of abstract and nonobjective art,* the techniques of the latter and even some of its adherents were enlisted in the cause.

Originally a Dada activist in Cologne, MAX ERNST (1891–1976), became one of the early adherents of the Surrealist circle around André Breton, the formulator of the manifesto of Surrealism. The chance association of things and events, the dislocation of images and meanings, the scrambling of conventional contexts, the exploration of the subconscious, the radical freedom of artistic choice, which together make up the creative bases of Surrealism, are all manifest in Ernst's *Two Children Are Threatened by a Nightingale* (page 802 and FIG. 22-26). The heavy frame and the house and gate in actual relief give a concreteness to the dream-like vision while forcing a shock of contrast between representation and the actual. Ernst

---

* An *abstract* work has been "abstracted" from natural appearance, and vestiges of figures or objects may still be detected in it, as in Cubist paintings. A *nonobjective* work has no reference, in conception or execution, to natural appearance, as in the later paintings of Kandinsky and Mondrian.

22-26 MAX ERNST, *Two Children Are Threatened by a Nightingale*, 1924. Oil on wood with wood construction, 27½" high, 22½" wide, 4½" deep. Museum of Modern Art, New York (purchase).

himself writes revealingly of the Surrealist artist's management of subject matter: "He never imposes a title on a painting. He waits until a title imposes itself.

Here however the title existed *before* the picture was painted." A line from an earlier poem written by the artist provided the title. Its subject found, the picture simply happened. In Ernst's later work, he experimented with the texture of the picture surface, leaving surface effects much to the laws of chance. His procedures were widely adopted and influential.

Loosely related or allied to Surrealism, the abstract paintings of Spaniard JOAN MIRÓ (1893–1983) incorporate aspects of organic imagery that lend them a weird and disturbing humor. Intensive work in collage in various mediums led Miró to a greater simplification of shapes, with stress on curved lines and amoeba-like organisms that seem to float in an immaterial space. In *Painting* (FIG. 22-27), black shapes—solid or in outline and with dramatic accents of white and vermilion—appear against a dark background of closely related reds, blues, and greens. These elements give the canvas, which is quite large, a handsome, decorative quality. Several figures are recognizable, including a dog and an ox. But as Miró often attempted to work automatically, moving his brush over the surface with as little direction as possible from his conscious mind (as in automatic writing), he himself could not always explain the meanings of his pictures. They are, in the truest sense, spontaneous and intuitive expressions of the little-understood, submerged, unconscious life.

A new interest in subject matter was perhaps the most important contribution of the Surrealists to modern painting. Miró has said:

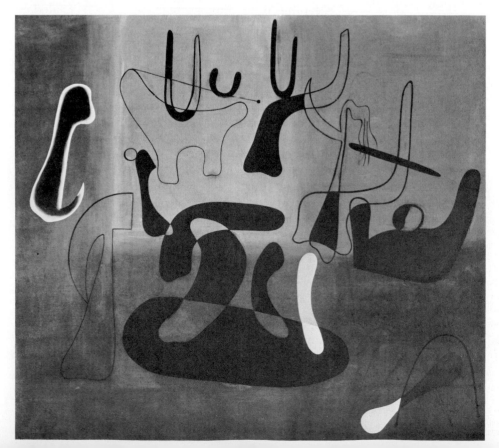

22-27 JOAN MIRÓ, *Painting*, 1933. Approx. 5' 8½" × 6' 5¼". Museum of Modern Art, New York (gift of the Advisory Committee).

I am attaching more and more importance to the subject matter of my work. To me it seems vital that a rich and robust theme should be present to give the spectator an immediate blow between the eyes before a second thought can intervene. In this way, poetry pictorially expressed speaks its own language.*

It is important to note that the title announcing the subject matter often plays an important role in modern art. Most often, it is ambiguous and seems to have little relation to what the spectator sees; there may be an apparent conflict between it and the picture's meaning, which the spectator must struggle to resolve. Indeed, this sense of contradiction of title and picture is like an "immediate blow between the eyes," and the spectator is knocked off balance, expectations defeated and preconceptions challenged. Much of the impact of a work of modern art begins with the viewer's sudden intuition of the incongruous and the absurd.

Nowhere is the tension of divergent title and image so evident as in Surrealist works using dream imagery. Of all forms of nonconscious experience, dream imagery is the most common and the most vivid, but its presentation requires more than a mastery of abstract design. To project the world of dreams as convincingly as possible, the Catalan painter SALVADOR DALI (b. 1904) restudied the masters of seventeenth-century realism, especially the Dutch masters of genre. As, in dreams, objects and situations collide and interpenetrate in ceaseless metamorphoses, Dali uses multiple images of multiple symbolic meanings to suggest evocations from his subconscious. He has also developed a fundamental

*In James T. Soby, *Joan Miró* (New York: Museum of Modern Art, 1959), p. 13.

Surrealist method—the juxtaposition of seemingly irrelevant and certainly unrelated objects in unexpected situations. This method was suggested to the Surrealists by a metaphor originated by one of their spiritual predecessors, the somewhat obscure nineteenth-century French poet Isidore Ducasse (known as the Comte de Lautréamont), who, in his *Maldoror*, speaks of a situation as "beautiful as the encounter of an umbrella and a sewing machine on a dissecting table." The surprise effect of Dali's work depends on his presentation of such incongruities in a meticulous, miniature-like technique.

All of these aspects of Dali's style can be seen in perhaps his most familiar work, *The Persistence of Memory* (FIG. 22-28). Here, he creates his most haunting allegory of empty space in which time is at an end. The barren landscape, without horizon, drifts to infinity, lit by some eerie, never-setting sun. An amorphous creature sleeps in the foreground, draped with a limp watch. Another such watch hangs from the branch of a dead tree; yet another hangs half over the edge of a rectangular form. The watches are visited by ants and a fly, as if they were decaying, organic life, soft and viscous. Here is the impact of contradiction at its sharpest. The watch—a metallic, intricate, and precise instrument—is metamorphosed into an object devourable by busy ants. We recognize the impossible landscape and its impossible contents as perfectly possible in the dream world.

In painting dream images, the artist is handicapped by the fact that each dream is the experience of a single individual and depends for its meaning on the events in the private life of that one person; the clearer and more detailed its description, the less likely that it will be comprehensible to others. Thus, Surrealist art almost inevitably presents feelings so

22-28 SALVADOR DALI,
The Persistence of Memory, 1931.
9½" × 13". Museum of
Modern Art, New York
(given anonymously).

private that communication with an audience of any appreciable size is difficult, if not impossible, except when the artist, through the choice of familiar symbols, describes experiences common to groups of people. Such a broadened use of symbol and fantasy occurs in the work of MARC CHAGALL (1887–1985), who was born in Russia and studied and worked in Paris, Berlin, and New York. Although he accepted many aspects of the most sophisticated theories and practices of the times—Expressionism, Cubism, Fauvist color—Chagall never forgot his early life in an obscure Russian village. Themes from his childhood return as if in dreams and memories. Some, gay and fanciful, suggest the simpler pleasures of folk life; others, somber and even tragic, recall the trials and persecutions of the Jewish people. In his *Crucifixion* (FIG. 22-29), the terror of wars and pogroms is suggested by the pitiful little figures and the village in the background, while resignation and hope are expressed in the flying angel, the Torah scroll, and the rabbi–Christ figure on the cross. The work is a moving portrayal of the artist's feeling that faith is important in a world of war and brutality. Although the very free, floating composition—with unexpected juxtapositions of the actual and the unearthly—is Surrealist in the sense that it perpetuates the fantastic content of a dream, the individual symbols refer to much more than Chagall's personal psychic life. A

comparison of Chagall's interpretation of war with Picasso's (FIG. 22-16) illuminates the broad scale of expressive emotion on which art can play.

The most subtle and one of the most influential of all the masters of fantasy was the German–Swiss artist PAUL KLEE (1879–1940). In his contempt for illusionistic art, which (as a member of the Blue Rider School) he believed to be superseded, he turned to the art of children and primitives for a new kind of brevity, simplicity, and primeval significance unknown to civilized conventions and rational modes of thought. With this inspiration, Klee was able to make, in exquisite line and color, pictorial records of his own sensitive and perceptive reaction to the modern world. His wry whimsy uses strangely delineated figures of men, animals, and fantastic creatures as commentary on human weakness and folly, but his tone is almost always gentle and his irony subdued. Although his paintings and drawings are usually very small and seem at first to be the most private of visual communications, they are charged with meaning that gradually becomes clearer to the imaginative spectator. His *Twittering Machine* (FIG. 22-30), in its title and execution, at first compels a smile. Primitive, flimsy bird "mechanisms" stand on or are attached to an equally flimsy crankshaft. We assume that the shaft can be turned and that, when it is, the "birds" twitter. Here, most effectively, is the cooperative tension of title and design. We do not usually think of machines and birds in association, or of machines as ludicrous, hand-driven works made of bent picture wire. Out of these forced associations and distortions, a new entity seems to emerge that slyly spoofs

22-29 MARC CHAGALL, *Crucifixion*, 1943. 55⅛″ × 39¾″. Collection of the artist, Pierre Matisse Gallery, New York.

22-30 PAUL KLEE, *Twittering Machine*, 1922. Watercolor and pen and ink, approx. 16¼″ × 12″. Museum of Modern Art, New York (purchase).

the "machine age"; although the device "works," it has no real purpose, unless it is to twitter, and birds do this much better. It has recently been suggested that the sly humor of the work may conceal a mordant comment on man's mortality. The heads of the creatures, each carefully distinguished as one of the four temperaments, resemble metallic lures capable of trapping real birds. Below them is a rectangular trough on short legs—perhaps a death trap. The lures and death trap could symbolize the entrapment of all of us by existence. Perhaps no other artist of the twentieth century matches the subtlety of Klee as he adroitly plays with sense, making an artistic means of ambiguity and understatement.

Klee shared the widespread modern apprehension concerning the rationalism behind a technological civilization that could be as destructive as it was constructive. As do some psychologists, he sought clues to man's deeper nature in primitive shapes and symbols. Like his compatriot, the psychologist Carl Jung, Klee seems to have accepted the existence of a collective unconscious that reveals itself in archaic signs and patterns going back to prehistoric times and is everywhere evident in the art of primitive peoples. His *Death and Fire* (FIG. 22-31) manifests his interest in the ideogram—the simple, picture-like sign filled with implicit meaning. A white death's-head, heavily outlined, dominates the work and seems to rise toward a glowing sun. A figure moving left is preceded by three bars of color. The features of the skull could be letters perhaps *tod* ("death"). It has been suggested that the pale green, so definitely harmonized

22-31 PAUL KLEE, *Death and Fire*, 1940. Approx. 18″ × 17″. Paul Klee-Stiftung, Bern.

with the chords of red, could suggest the element of water reconciled with fire in the ever-changing alternation of life and death. The eerie color, the primitive starkness of the images, and the mysterious arrangement convey an almost religious sense of awe, as if one were in the presence of a totem having magical powers. Enigmatic as the subject is, we feel its sources in the religious experience—an experience probably as old as human history.

Social Realism and Commentary

It is noteworthy that a conservative Realism—a Realism most often enlisted in the service of social and political movements—persisted alongside the busy experimentalism in Western art and was only slightly affected by it. This "Social Realism," as it may be called, is an international phenomenon—a genre in which the environment, the labors, and the struggles of the working classes are sympathetically described and exalted. In the West, this kind of art flourished in the 1930s—especially in Mexico and the United States, frequently with overtones critical of "the Establishment."

In the influential Mexican School, José Clemente Orozco (1883–1949) excelled in mural painting dynamically expressive of the spirit of social criticism and revolution that agitated both hemispheres in the earlier twentieth century. Although not himself an ideologue urging a particular political program, his powerful, graphically blunt art sufficiently declares his sympathies. Orozco lived in the United States between 1927 and 1932, during which time he completed several important commissions. In one of his finest mural cycles at Dartmouth College, he depicts the history of ancient and modern Mexico (FIG. 22-

22-32 José Clemente Orozco, *Hispano–America, c.* 1933. Mural. Baker Memorial Library, Dartmouth College, Hanover, New Hampshire.

32). Here, he shows the dauntless Mexican peasant of the revolutionary days, armed and resolute, pressed on all sides by bankers and soldiers—the enemies, as Orozco sees them, of the common people. Money-grubbers pour hoards of gold before the incorruptible *peón*, cannon threaten him, and a bemedalled general raises a dagger to stab him in the back. The allegory is easy to read, for Orozco's training as a maker of political prints and as a newspaper artist taught him the rhetorical strength of graphic brevity and simplicity. At the same time, his training as an architect gave

22-33 Ben Shahn, *Handball*, 1939. Tempera on paper mounted on composition board, approx. $22\frac{3}{4}'' \times 31\frac{1}{4}''$. Museum of Modern Art, New York (Abby Aldrich Rockefeller Fund).

him a sense of the framed wall surface, which he easily commands, projecting these quickly grasped figurations of the newspaper cartoon onto the solid mural plane in monumental scale. Thus, he combines the effects of the graphic and mural media to give his work an originality and force rarely seen in mural painting after the Renaissance and Baroque periods.

Like Orozco, the American painter BEN SHAHN (1898–1969) was a trained graphic artist and muralist. A political and social commentator of great force, Shahn came to attention with his unforgettable series of 23 prints on the controversial Sacco and Vanzetti case of the 1920s, in which, using flat intense color, he denounces injustice in a sharp, dry, angular manner. Shahn adapted and developed the visual idioms of commercial art, at which he worked throughout his life, using its concise and abrupt method to convey his own highly individual messages. He was engaged to do numerous murals in public buildings, and worked with Mexican painter DIEGO RIVERA on the never completed murals of Rockefeller Center in New York. The loneliness of city streets fascinated him, and he made numerous photographic studies of them. *Handball* (FIG. 22-33), although obviously checked with the photographic record, is a skillfully eclectic work. It at once recalls the geometry of Cubism, the haunted space of Surrealism, with its weird vacancy, the still perspectives of Italian painting in the fifteenth century, and the quick, accidental poses and changes of scale of the candid photograph.

Another painter of the American scene, EDWARD HOPPER (1882–1967) shows it through a very personal brand of realism, untouched by the experiments in abstraction carried on by his generation. His cross sections of city life are curiously muted, still, often

empty; motion is stopped and time is suspended, as if the artist is recording a completed and unalterable memory to the last detail in all the original poignancy of the scene remembered. His *Eleven A.M.* (FIG. 22-34) combines precise inventory and delineation with ambiguity of situation to create a mood of unmitigated loneliness. The nude, young woman is seated staring out of a hotel window (we see its sign partly blocked by the stone courses of the outer wall), her face concealed by long, luxuriant hair that falls below her shoulders. She is the forlorn heroine of many a naturalistic American novel and short story. The cold light of one more common day falls without luster on the plain, hard, architectural features and nondescript furnishings of the dismal room. In *Preludes, II,* written a few years before Hopper's painting, the poet T. S. Eliot might have been setting the scene:

The morning comes to consciousness
. . . .
With the other masquerades that time resumes,
One thinks of all the hands
That are raising dingy shades
In a thousand furnished rooms.

Hopper's woman is even more anonymous than Édouard Manet's bargirl (FIG. 21-41) or Edgar Degas' bather (FIG. 21-62), to whom she should be compared (Hopper greatly admired Degas); and a comparison with Titian's *Venus of Urbino* (FIG. 17-63) should remind us of the mighty changes in the interpretation of the nude that have taken place since the Renaissance. In any event, with Hopper, the Realism of the nineteenth century, European and American, is brought up to date and vindicated by an original and sensitive vision.

22-34 EDWARD HOPPER, *Eleven A.M.*, 1926. 28″ × 36″. Hirshhorn Museum and Sculpture Garden, Washington, D.C.

SCULPTURE BEFORE WORLD WAR II

Auguste Rodin (FIGS. 2, 21-82, 21-83, 21-84) was the greatest sculptor of the nineteenth century, an artist whose international reputation rivaled that of Michelangelo and Gianlorenzo Bernini; he was also a great teacher. His reputation brought to his studio in Paris, as pupils or as admirers, many members of the younger generation who would develop new kinds of sculpture, either under Rodin's influence or in reaction against him.

The French sculptor ARISTIDE MAILLOL (1861–1944) turned away from Rodin's evanescent effects of light and broken planes toward a simple and weighty style. He began his career as a painter, executing broadly decorative designs in the manner of Gauguin, and was also known as a graphic artist through his book illustrations. About 1900, Maillol turned to sculpture and, until the end of his life, scarcely deviated from his chosen subject—the female figure—which he interpreted in massive planes and volumes devoid of historical stylization or literary anecdote. One of his first and most important works, the seated figure *Mediterranean* (FIG. 22-35), is conceived as an organization of almost abstract volumes simplified from the endless complexities of the human figure. It has weight and solidity, and the largely unbroken surfaces of the smoothly modeled masses take the light evenly and quietly. The pose itself, familiar in several Tahitian figures by Gauguin, whose art Maillol greatly admired, also has in its tranquil closure,

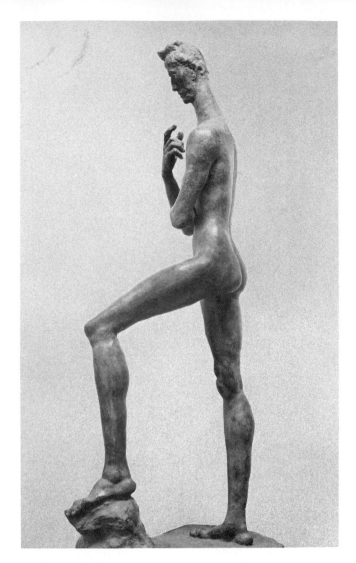

22-36 WILHELM LEHMBRUCK, *Standing Youth*, 1913. Cast stone, approx. 7' 8" high. Museum of Modern Art, New York (gift of Abby Aldrich Rockefeller).

22-35 ARISTIDE MAILLOL, *Mediterranean*, c. 1901. Bronze, approx. 41" high, base 45" × 24¾". Museum of Modern Art, New York (gift of Stephen C. Clark).

monumentality, and dignity more than a little of the Early Classical sculpture of Greece. The figure carries its own meaning (it refers to nothing outside itself; the title "Mediterranean" was added later). The form alone is sufficient to the artist's purpose.

The Expressionistic element in Rodin proved most sympathetic to the young German sculptor WILHELM LEHMBRUCK (1881–1919). Perceiving in Rodin's later work the possibilities of distortion, Lehmbruck developed an impressive style of his own based on the elongation and attenuation of human proportions. His *Standing Youth* (FIG. 22-36)—we have already seen his *Seated Youth* (FIG. 1)—elegantly slender and tall, poses in solemn reverie, making a slow, deliberate, and eloquent gesture, as if participating in some grave ritual. Without specific subject or historical reference, Lehmbruck's figure "tells" by pose and gesture alone; its mood is entirely a function of its form. The extreme proportions recall Medieval (FIG. 9-36) and even Mannerist (FIG. 17-43) attenuation and announce a new freedom to interpret the human figure

22-37 GASTON LACHAISE, *Standing Woman*, 1912–1918. Bronze, 6′ 7″ high, 2′ 5″ wide. Albright-Knox Gallery, Buffalo (James A. Forsyth Fund, 1938).

quite without regard for the measure of it established in antiquity and in the Renaissance.

GASTON LACHAISE (1882–1935), of French descent but active most of his life in the United States, specialized, like Maillol, in sculpture of the female figure and, like Lehmbruck, dealt freely with the proportions of the human body. His life-size *Standing Woman* (FIG. 22-37) is as broadly modeled as Maillol's, but with a more sensuous treatment of the anatomy. The strongly felt movement swells rapidly upward from the lightly poised, delicate feet to the large rounding hips; after a sharp accent in the angle of the waist, it again swells into the broad shoulders and bent arms. There is an elastic, abstract rhythm of both volume and contour and a union of weight and grace. Bronze is an ideal medium for this beautifully contrived equilibrium of opulent mass with delicate supporting strength. If we compare Lehmbruck's *Standing Youth* with Lachaise's figure, we can appreciate the wide variation in the formal and expressive results when the sculptor experiments with noncanonical proportions.

Symbolism and Art Nouveau opened the stylistic troves of other ages and cultures to the modern artist. Thus, the Expressionist sculptor could find in Medieval art both unsophisticated and intense spirituality and abstract forms as yet uncomplicated by Realism. Although the sculptors discovered Romanesque and Gothic art much later than the architects did, they made of their borrowing from it something far more genuine. The works of ERNST BARLACH (1870–1938), a German sculptor much influenced by Medieval carving, combine sharp, smoothly planed forms with intense action and keen expression. His *War Monument* for Güstrow Cathedral (FIGS. 22-38 and 22-39) is one

22-38 ERNST BARLACH, *War Monument*, Güstrow Cathedral, 1927. Bronze. Schildergasse Antoniterkirche, Cologne.

22-39 ERNST BARLACH, *Head*, detail of FIG. 22-38, separately cast. Approx. 13½″ high. Museum of Modern Art, New York (gift of Edward M.M. Warburg).

919

of the most poignant memorials of World War I. The sculptor depicts a dying soul at the moment when it is about to awaken to everlasting life—the theme of death and transfiguration; the rigid economy of surfaces concentrates attention on the superb head. The spiritual anguish evoked by the disaster of war and the release from that anguish through the hope of salvation are rarely expressed as movingly as they are in this work.

Cubism to Constructivism

Although sculpture does not register the major stylistic groupings—Expressionism, Cubism, and Surrealism—as clearly as painting does, we still may discern them. On the other hand, sculpture, the three-dimensional art, is perhaps more at home in the age of metals and industrially produced artifacts; later in the century, it is sculpture in particular that achieves the inevitable linkage of art and technology. The Expressionism of Lehmbruck and Lachaise overlaps the new experience of Cubism, which, in its concern for the creation of the effects of three-dimensional space on a flat surface, was not easily adapted to the sculptural mode. Nevertheless, we can see a development from the Rodinesque mode to total Cubist abstraction in two figures (FIGS. 22-40 and 22-41) by Henri Matisse, who was a sculptor as well as a painter (FIG. 22-3). Although these figures—the first and last of a series of four made between 1909 and 1929—are not in the more characteristic linear mode (or "arabesque," as Matisse called it) preferred by the artist, they reveal with great force a profound change in sculptural vision. *Back I* (FIG. 22-40), the first of these representations of back views of the female nude, is a believable anatomy not far removed from the roughly modeled surfaces of Rodin's sculptures. *Back II* and *Back III* (not illustrated here), made in quick succession in 1913 and 1914, show a rapid breaking up—an abstraction—of the main bodily shapes. *Back IV* (FIG. 22-41), the final version, made in 1929, is the last stage of the disintegration and embodies the emergence of a totally different concept and procedure—the geometrizing, radical simplifications of Cubism.

Matisse's "exercise in the progressive reduction and concentration of form" took place as an exclusively sculptural enterprise, independent of painting. On the other hand, the earlier works of JACQUES LIPCHITZ (1891–1973), born in Poland but long resident in France and the United States, are among the most successful solutions to the problem of developing the spatial feeling of Cubist painting in three dimensions. In *Man with Mandolin* (FIG. 22-42), the continuous form is broken down into planes that, no matter the direction of the light, can be read as flat, shaded surfaces. As with Cubist painting, there is now no single point of view, no continuity or simul-

22-40 HENRI MATISSE, *Back I*, 1909. Bronze, 6' 2¾" high, 3' 10" wide, 7¼" deep. Tate Gallery, London.

22-41 HENRI MATISSE, *Back IV*, 1929. Bronze, 6' 2½" high, 3' 8½" wide, 6¼" deep. Tate Gallery, London.

taneity of image contour. But an even more decisive break with the long tradition of Western sculpture than this analysis of mass into planes is the piercing of the mass. An early example of this new turn can be seen in *Woman Combing Her Hair* (FIG. 22–43) by Russian sculptor ALEXANDER ARCHIPENKO (1887–1964). This statuette, recalling in its graceful contrapposto something of Renaissance Mannerism, introduces in place of the head a void with a shape of its own that figures importantly in the whole design. Enclosed spaces have always existed in figure sculpture—for example, the space between the arm and the body when the hand rests on the hip, as in Verrocchio's *David* (FIG. 16-52). But here there is penetration of the continuous mass of the figure, and shaped space (often referred to as "negative space") occurs with shaped mass in the same design. Archipenko's figure shows the same slipping of the planes that we have seen in pictorial Cubism, and the relation of the planes to each other is similarly complex. Thus, in painting and sculpture, the traditional limits are broken through and the media transformed.

Archipenko's figure is still quasi-representational, but sculpture (like painting) executed within the Cub-

ist orbit tends to cast off the last vestiges of representation. By 1913, UMBERTO BOCCIONI (1882–1916), already mentioned as a Futurist and both painter and sculptor, pushes his forms so far toward abstraction that the title of his *Unique Forms of Continuity in Space* (FIG. 22-44) calls attention to the formal and spatial effects rather than to the fact that the source for these is the striding human figure. The "figure" is so expanded, interrupted, or broken in plane and contour that it disappears, as it were, behind the blur of its movement; only the blur remains. Boccioni's search for plastic means with which to express dynamic movement reaches a monumental expression here. In its power and sense of vital activity, this sculpture surpasses similar efforts in painting (by Boccioni and his Futurist companions) to create images symbolic of the dynamic quality of modern life. To be convinced by it, we need only reflect on how details of an adjacent landscape appear in our peripheral vision when we are traveling at great speed on a highway or in a low-flying airplane. Although Boccioni's figure bears a curious resemblance to the ancient *Nike of Samothrace* (FIG. 5-76), a cursory comparison reveals how the modern work departs from the ancient one.

22-42 *Left:* JACQUES LIPCHITZ, *Man with Mandolin*, 1917. Stone, approx. 29¾" high. Yale University Art Gallery, New Haven, Connecticut (Collection, Société Anonyme).

22-43 *Right:* ALEXANDER ARCHIPENKO, *Woman Combing Her Hair*, 1915. Bronze, approx. 13¾" high. Museum of Modern Art, New York (bequest of Lillie P. Bliss).

22-44 UMBERTO BOCCIONI, *Unique Forms of Continuity in Space*, 1913. Bronze, approx. 43½" high. Museum of Modern Art, New York (bequest of Lillie P. Bliss).

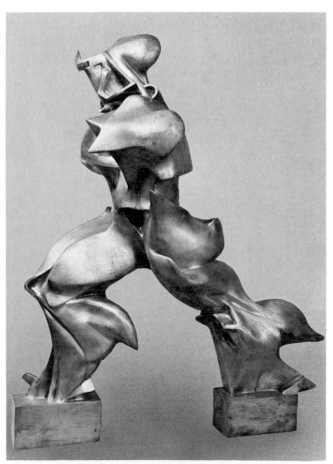

The Romanian sculptor CONSTANTIN BRANCUȘI (1876–1957) carries abstraction to the limit beyond which the representational element is lost entirely. At the same time, he extracts from the material—whether marble, metal, or wood—its maximum effect. It may be that it is with Brancuși's scrupulous attention to the nature of his materials that the pervading doctrine and mystique of modern art—"truth to the material"—arises. This doctrine demands that the artist respect the material, that formal intentions never abuse its peculiar nature. What is appropriate for bronze is not so for marble; what is appropriate for marble is not so for wood; and so on. Respect for the function of the material is a necessity in industrial production. This truth to material goes along with the modern quest for purity or "reality" of form. As the painter Mondrian finds rectilinear form to be most "real," so Brancuși visualizes an extended ovoid shape as the most "natural" shape, and simplifies the most complex natural forms and even natural movements to variations on this fundamental shape. In his famous *Bird in Space* (FIG. 22-45) everything accidental is eliminated or compressed into the most direct and economical expression, yet the form as a whole suggests the essence of a bird's sudden upward movement through air. Even more, there is a remarkable suggestion of airflow, as delineated by modern aerodynamics, and Brancuși's means of conveying flight are not unrelated to those the modern engineer generally uses in designing "streamlined" industrial forms. There is the same study of the nature of the material—the same meticulous attention to proportions, contour, and surface finish. Thus, even at this early stage, the coming together of art and technology is predictable. At the same time, there appears what might be considered a contradiction of the technological connection—namely, *biomorphic abstraction*, in which the artist derives forms from living and growing things.

A friend of Brancuși and Picasso, JULIO GONZALEZ (1876–1942), shared their interest in the artistic possibilities of new materials and new methods borrowed from both industrial technology and traditional metalworking. Constructed or "direct" shapes (using ready-made bars, sheets, rods, or the like) of welded or wrought iron and bronze can produce, in effect, simple or incredibly complex sculptured *spaces* in a kind of fluent openwork, in which the solids function only as contours, boundaries, or dividing planes. In *Woman Combing Her Hair* (FIG. 22-46) by Gonzalez (compare with Archipenko's version of the same subject; FIG. 22-43), fantasy is restrained by no traditional convention of representation, and the actual constructive process is unimpeded by the more demanding methods of carving and casting. Sculptors in the 1960s and 1970s would fully exploit the advantages of this method: linear effects impossible for other

22-45 CONSTANTIN BRANCUȘI, *Bird in Space*, c. 1927. Bronze, unique cast, approx. 54" high. Museum of Modern Art, New York.

22-46 JULIO GONZALEZ, *Woman Combing Her Hair*, c. 1930–1933. Iron, 57" high. Moderna Museet, Stockholm.

modes, flexibility in construction, speed of execution, and easy correction of errors or changes in intention. The direct-metal method in the hands of contemporary sculptors parallels the methods used by the so-called "abstract expressionist" painters. It should be noted that although Gonzalez innovates in material and method, he still thinks (as the title of this piece indicates) of the human figure as a point of departure for abstraction, even though the forms could, like Brancuşi's, stand without external reference to the natural world. After years as an unsuccessful painter, Gonzalez was asked by Picasso for technical help in constructing metal sculpture. From that time, his influence has been continuous, with a special impact on today's sculptors.

Unlike Gonzalez or Brancuşi, De Stijl and Constructivist artists prefer to work with forms that refer not to the natural world but to the worlds of mathematics and mechanism. The search for pure form led naturally to mathematics; its abstract and impersonal beauty could be projected into three dimensions. But it also reflected the sculptor's impulse toward the "engineering" and machining of forms "to specification"—as with the use of a blueprint or plan. Early in the development of Synthetic Cubism, a group of Russian artists working in Moscow became interested in applying industrial engineering techniques to sculpture. Their point of departure was provided by some of the more three-dimensional collages of Picasso, which contained miscellaneous, recognizable objects taken from the environment, such as bottles, pipes, guitars. VLADIMIR TATLIN (1885–1953) saw some of these collages when he visited Picasso in Paris in 1913. On his return to Moscow, he made similar collage reliefs that significantly excluded all representational motifs and recognizable objects. Tatlin's compositions were completely abstract—the first of their kind. He called them "constructions," giving a name to the very influential movement, Constructivism. Tatlin was the moving spirit among a group of progressive Constructivists whose experiments were eventually banned by the new Soviet regime in 1922; some left Russia and spread their ideas and practices through the West.

Shortly before Constructivism was banned in Russia, Tatlin designed a prodigious monument; it was never built, but the model survives (FIG. 22-47). A tower called *Monument to the Third International, 1919–1920,* and intended to be about 1,300 feet high, it was to be a spiraling, leaning, openwork structure composed of steel, wood, and glass and was to contain three vast, moving, geometric elements. A cube, a pyramid, and a cylinder, designed to house facilities for cultural, political, administrative, and scientific activities, would have revolved on their axes at different speeds, ranging from one revolution per year to one per day.

22-47 VLADIMIR TATLIN, *Monument to the Third International,* 1919–1920. Model in wood, iron, and glass. Re-created in 1968 for exhibition at the Moderna Museet, Stockholm.

In 1920, the Constructivists divided and Tatlin allied himself with the so-called Productivists, who renounced art altogether in favor of productive, collective engineering. The Productivist position was rejected by the brothers ANTOINE PEVSNER (1886–1962) and NAUM GABO (1890–1977), who championed the individual freedom of the artist and the right to free experimentation. In 1920, they issued their *Realist Manifesto,* in which they called for the representation of a "new reality":

In order to interpret the reality of life, art must be based upon two fundamental elements: space and time. Volume is not the only concept of space. Kinetic and dynamic elements must be used to express the true nature of time. The static rhythms are no longer sufficient. Art must not be more imitative, but seek new forms.

We have seen something of this last statement already explicit in Brancuşi and Gonzalez, and the rotating elements of Tatlin's *Monument* anticipate the expression of time in space. In their placing of mass to make, enframe, and divide spaces, as we have seen in Gonzalez especially, we have the essential procedure laid down by Pevsner and Gabo in their *Manifesto:*

> Mass and space are two concrete and measurable things. We consider and use space as a new and absolutely sculptural element, a material substance which really enters into construction.

Architecture had always implicitly admitted the reality of space. For sculpture to admit space was a triumph, already announced in Archipenko's "pierced" figure (FIG. 22-43). It now appeared that space could be "sculptured" as well as mass. In their concern with the properties of space, Pevsner and Gabo created objects in which voids acted as forcefully as the elements of solid mass, conceding that, for sculpture, mass and void could be made esthetically equivalent—a radical position indeed in view of the fact that the essence of sculpture had been commonly thought of as pure mass. Gabo turned to the new synthetic plastic materials, as many younger sculptors have since. He used celluloid first and later nylon and lucite for constructions in which space seems to flow through as well as around the transparent materials. His prewar experiments culminated in some of his most subtle postwar compositions. In his *Linear Construction* (FIG. 22-48) space is caught and held in suspension, as it were, by the most delicate combination of hovering planes. In the "fields of force" of physics, conventional "solids" and "voids" alike are only mathematical expressions; in the subatomic universe, solids and voids are always in am-

biguous relation and never definitely one or the other. Like the mathematician, the artist may express his conception of this undecidable relation of space and mass. Like Mondrian, Gabo believed that indeed "such artfully constructed images are the very essence of the reality of the world which we are searching for." In our time, science and art alike make their models of the reality of the physical world.

From the "transparency" of mass and the consequent creation of interior spaces, it seems but a step to the attempt to create actual movement in space. Yet movement must come as a reality in which the positions of the work or of the spectator, or both, are constantly changing. Anticipating today's kinetic sculptors, the American sculptor ALEXANDER CALDER (1898–1976) was the first to set his works in continuous and "natural" (unmotorized) motion. His "mobiles," as they are appropriately called, are made of rods, wires, and sheet-metal forms so balanced that the slightest current of air moves the parts within a carefully planned pattern, creating a constantly shifting "definition" of space. Traditionally, sculpture has had very few standards of space and these have demanded its fixity and sometimes the fixity of the spectator. A remark of Salvador Dali's expresses our traditional view of the sculptural mode: ". . . the least one can expect of sculpture is that it stand still." Calder's work, most often nonrepresentational, is sprightly and witty and contains many unexpected felicities of line and shape. In this respect, it often reminds us of the paintings of Miró (FIG. 22-27). In *Horizontal Spines* (FIG. 22-49), the delicate grace and precision of pure line in the fine steel wires contrast and combine in constantly changing relationships with the sharp accents of the flat shapes.

22-48 NAUM GABO, *Linear Construction*, 1950. Plastic and nylon thread. Private collection.

22-49 ALEXANDER CALDER, *Horizontal Spines*, 1942. Approx. 54″ high. Addison Gallery of American Art, Phillips Academy, Andover, Massachusetts.

Dada and the Fantastic

The biting Dadaist critique of modern life cuts across the whole development of formalizing, abstract sculpture, bringing with it a new permissiveness. Objects out of the ordinary environment of modern life were selected and exhibited in the Dada shows as works of art. Duchamp, with serene impudence, mocked serious artistic intention with chance selections of objects like a bicycle wheel (FIG. 22-50), bottle washer, urinal, corkscrew, and other "ready-made," commonplace things. These André Breton called "manufactured objects promoted to the dignity of objects of art through the choice of the artist." According to Duchamp—and for a generation of artists after him who were profoundly influenced by his art and especially by his attitude—life and art are a matter of chance and arbitrary choice; the essence of the artistic act is willful selection, and each act is individual and unique: "Your chance is not the same as mine, just as your throw of the dice will rarely be the same as mine." This philosophy of utter freedom for the artist is fundamental to the history of art in the twentieth century, and Duchamp can stand as perhaps the shrewdest and most perceptive theorist of

the modern movement. The freedom he granted himself to set up a bicycle wheel (with its fork) on a kitchen stool, he granted to the visitor in allowing him to spin the wheel as he chose.

The "ready-mades" of Duchamp led to "found objects" like the random junk that Schwitters used in his *Merz Pictures* (FIG. 22-23); the collages of Cubism had pointed the way. Interest in "found objects" spread to the public, which began to collect such oddments as rocks, driftwood, and fragments of manufactured objects. A happy conjunction of two ordinary objects, never appearing together in this way, makes up Picasso's *Bull's Head* (FIG. 22-51). The never-failing ingenuity of this modern master turns the handle bars and seat of a bicycle into an image of a bull, beautifully stylized. The work, which might seem only a clever trick, illustrates an important method in modern art—the unexpected unity that two objects can make when taken out of their usual context and brought into a radically new relationship. We have seen this phenomenon of new meanings arising out of uncommon juxtapositions in the case of the seemingly opposed caption and image in painting. Much of the pungency and surprise—the impact—of modern painting and sculpture is the result of such strenuous feats of conjunctive imagination.

Ordinary manufactured objects and utensils can be modified just enough to create a startling paradox. MAN RAY (1890–1976), Duchamp's collaborator in his brief reintroduction of Dada to the United States in 1921, equips a laundry iron with a row of wicked-looking spikes, contravening its proper function of smoothing and pressing (FIG. 22-52). The malicious

22-50 MARCEL DUCHAMP, *Bicycle Wheel*, 1951 (third version after lost original of 1913). Metal wheel mounted on painted wooden stool, 50½" high, 25½" wide, 16⅝" deep. Museum of Modern Art, New York (gift of the Sidney and Harriet Janis Collection).

22-51 PABLO PICASSO, *Bull's Head*, 1943. Handlebars and seat of a bicycle. Galerie Louise Leiris, Paris.

22-52 MAN RAY, *Gift*, c. 1958 (replica after destroyed original of 1921). Painted flatiron with metal tacks, 6⅛" high, 3⅝" wide, 4½" deep. Museum of Modern Art, New York (James Thrall Soby Fund).

humor of *Gift*—seen throughout Dada and, indeed, in much of contemporary art—gives it a characteristic edge that can cut the unwary. Contradiction, paradox, irony, even blasphemy are the bequest of Dada. They are, in the view of Dada and its successors, the free and defiant artist's weapons in what has been called the "hundred years' war with the public."

In these later years of that "war," sculptors, like painters, have explored numerous avenues of possibility. Where human reference would seem to have been once and for all expelled from the sculptor's interest by exclusively formal concerns, it insistently reappears. The English sculptor HENRY MOORE (1898–1986) has created many variations on the human figure; some are more abstract than others, but all reflect

an instinctive feeling for the dignity of the human form. Moore also often disregards the human form in favor of pure biomorphic abstraction and, like his colleague BARBARA HEPWORTH (1903–1975), shows a profound love for and knowledge of natural forms and materials. In such a work as *Reclining Figure* (FIG. 22-53), the massive, interlocking shapes reflect the discipline of abstract art, particularly the architectonic counterpoint of mass and void; but their total visual reality relates the human being to the enduring world of natural experience, even as the smooth, polished wooden surfaces suggest the action of wind and water on natural materials. Quite another treatment of the human figure is found in the works of ALBERTO GIACOMETTI (1901–1966)—a Swiss sculptor, long a resident of Paris, who participated in both the Cubist and Surrealist movements and contributed significant works in each mode. In 1947, however, he turned to representational sculpture to produce unexpectedly poignant figures that seem to be immediate projections of the modern experiences of bewilderment, loss, alienation. At the beginning of this chapter, we referred to Giacometti's *City Square* (FIG. 22-54) as a peculiar projection of the image of the modern, isolated individual in the "lonely crowd." It is noteworthy that Giacometti disapproved of any such classification of his work and believed that he was simply trying to render the effect of great space as it presses around a figure—and nothing more. But this is precisely the point: The lone, modern man is only too aware of the vastness of the space that separates him from his neighbor by only a few feet. The artist's ver-

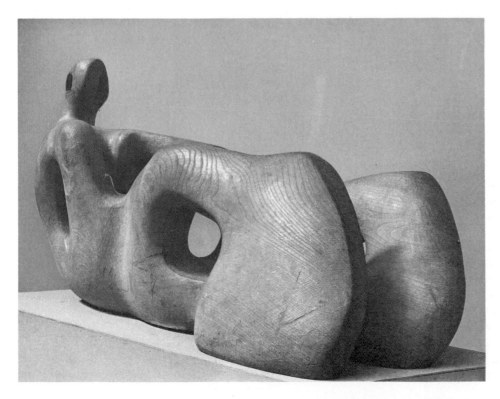

22-53 HENRY MOORE, *Reclining Figure*, 1939. Elmwood, 6' 9" long. Detroit Institute of the Arts (gift of the Dexter M. Ferry, Jr., Trustee Corporation).

22-54 ALBERTO GIACOMETTI, *City Square* (*La Place*), 1948. Bronze, approx. $6\frac{3}{4}''$ high, $23\frac{1}{2}''$ wide, 16'' deep. Museum of Modern Art, New York (purchase).

bally expressed intention and our own verbally expressed interpretation may seem to differ, as is the case so often in modern art; yet we recognize when he is speaking for his age through his art. Giacometti's pencil-thin, elongated figures stride abstractedly through endless space; they never meet and never can. At certain angles, the forms are so attenuated that they almost disappear, as, often in the human condition, people fade noiselessly out of sight. If we compare Giacometti's figures with those in Rodin's *Burghers of Calais* (FIG. 21-82), we can readily appreciate the changes wrought by half a century of revolution in the interpretation of the human being in art.

ARCHITECTURE BEFORE WORLD WAR II

The structural promise of steel and concrete, only partly recognized in the later nineteenth century, finds its fulfillment in the twentieth. Like painting and sculpture, architecture has been revolutionized by industrial materials and by the example of the pure functionalism of machines. Radical contradictions and reversals of tradition, analogous to what we have seen in the figurative arts, have produced architectural styles with no precedent in the past. Architecture, with all the other arts, has been brought within the domain of modern technology. In the words of the critic Siegfried Giedion, "Mechanization takes command!" This does not mean that individual talent became submerged in collective production; rather, architects of genius welcomed the machine and its potential for inspiring new form. Indeed, architecture and engineering were drawn closer and were embodied in one person.

Technology, if not altogether taking the initiative in inspiring modern architecture, is always implicit in it.

It is intriguing that the old Renaissance ideal of the union of theory and practice seems to find its full realization in a style fundamentally different from that of the Renaissance. In any event, we find in the history of modern architecture —more conspicuously than in the past—a kind of tension between the individual architect's impulse toward personal expression and the demand for vast, public, impersonal projects that impose their uniformity on whole cities. Within the titanic scale of modern, collective, public design, the old individualism of a Michelangelo or a Bernini would be likely to lose some of its distinctiveness. The modern architect is more like the Medieval master of works than the isolated Renaissance genius imposing his will on the whole form. To a degree, although modern architecture has its heroes, architects of our time tend, like modern sculptors and painters, to take their characters from the broad, collective movements of style, rather than to create them. Architects like Frank Lloyd Wright seem to be the rule-proving exceptions.

We have seen in "exhibition" architecture (FIGS. 21-86 and 21-87) and in the mercantile buildings of Henry Hobson Richardson (FIG. 21-88) and Louis Sullivan (FIGS. 21-89 and 21-90) the move toward a utilitarian architecture of a large enough scale to accommodate the traffic of thousands of people. The metal frames of the Americans' buildings, like that of Henri Labrouste's Bibliothèque Ste.-Geneviève (FIG. 21-85), are clothed in a fabric reminiscent of traditional styles, although Sullivan was deeply interested in devising an architectural ornament independent of tradition. In this respect, he was the leading American representative of Art Nouveau, which exhibits the typical architectural motif of an undulant, sweeping, serpentine line that wraps about or rises from structural members, its weaving spirals ending in tense scrolls. Easily adaptable to light metal construction, the Art Nouveau style is seen primarily in private houses, although many of the Paris Metro entrances are also decorated with Art Nouveau motifs. A good example of the style is the staircase in the Hotel van Eetvelde (FIG. 22-55), built in Brussels in 1895 by VICTOR HORTA (1861–1947), whose name is particularly associated with the Art Nouveau style in architecture. This decorative experiment was hailed enthusiastically as a truly modern style, although in fact it is the last appearance of the old "craftsman" style of the nineteenth century. A number of influences can be identified in Art Nouveau; they range from the rich, foliated, two-dimensional ornament and craftsman's respect for materials of William Morris' Arts and Crafts movement in nineteenth-century England to the free, sinuous, whiplash curve of Japanese designs. The boldness of Horta's use of metal may also be seen in the light supports, the ductile, curvilinear ornamentation, and the candor with which design and structure are integrated.

In Horta's hands, Art Nouveau was most effective as interior design, although all the arts were under its sway—from architecture to book illustration. On a monumental architectural scale, the style may be

22-55 VICTOR HORTA, staircase in the Hotel van Eetvelde, Brussels, Belgium, 1895.

seen in the Casa Milá apartment house (FIG. 22-56), erected in Barcelona in 1907 by ANTONIO GAUDÍ (1852–1926), an inventive architect who strove mightily to create forms utterly divorced from tradition and as close as possible to the randomness of nature. Here, Gaudí superposes bulky layers of cut stone in restless undulation, banishing the straight line altogether. The surfaces of the stone are left in the rough, suggesting naturally worn rock; entrance portals look like eroded sea caves. Passionate naturalism, seeking to escape from all regularity of artifice into the formless dynamism of nature, has never had more striking expression. Gaudí's work is the spiritual kin of Expressionist painting and sculpture.

The work of Horta and Gaudí provided components for a new and deeply searching art: a declaration of independence from all tradition, a profound respect for nature and the nature of materials, and the expectation of an entirely new architecture. As with painting and sculpture, an age of experiment opened for architecture at the turn of the century. The most striking and original personality in the development of a "modern" architecture is unquestionably FRANK LLOYD WRIGHT (1867–1959), whose experimental projects still startle the world. Always a believer in architecture as "natural" and "organic", Wright sees it in the service of free individuals who have the right to move within a "free" space—that is, as an asymmetrical design in natural surroundings. He seeks to develop an organic unity of planning, structure, materials, and site. He identifies the principle of *continuity* as fundamental to the understanding of his view of organic unity:

> Classic architecture was all fixation. . . . Now why not let walls, ceilings, floors become seen as component parts of each other, their surfaces flowing into each other? . . . You may see the appearance in the surface of your hand contrasted with the articulation of the bony structure itself. This ideal, profound in its architectural implications . . . I called . . . continuity.*

The concept of flux, of constant change, of evolution and progress is inherent in this principle, as it is in the views of Walt Whitman, also a prophet of continuity. It appears, too, in the work of the then greatly influential philosopher Henri Bergson, a contemporary of Wright, who stresses the reality of vitalism, of living process, above any other.

A pupil of Sullivan, Wright could well understand the former's long-debated slogan "form follows function" as the difference between the surface of the hand and its bony structure—the relation being dynamic and necessary, determined yet flexible. His

*Frank Lloyd Wright, *American Architecture*, ed. Edgar Kaufmann (New York: Horizon, 1955), pp. 205, 208.

22-56 ANTONIO GAUDÍ, Casa Milá, Barcelona, Spain, 1907.

vigorous originality was manifested early and, by 1900, he had arrived at a style entirely his own; in his work during the first decade of this century, his cross-axial plan and his fabric of continuous roof planes and screens (derived from Richardson's "shingle-plan" resort houses) defined a new domestic architecture. Although the skeleton frame makes its significant appearance in the works of Sullivan and others, Wright attacks the concept in his studies of other systems. His demand: "no posts, no columns. . . . In my work, the idea of plasticity may now be seen as the element of continuity." He acclaims "the new reality that is space *instead* of matter." As for architectural interiors, he declares: "I came to realize that the reality of a building was not the container but the space within."

These elements and concepts are fully expressed in Wright's Robie House in Chicago (FIG. 22-57), built between 1907 and 1909. This building, like others of his houses at the time, was called a "prairie house." The long, sweeping, ground-hugging lines, unconfined by abrupt limits of wall, seem to reach out toward and to express the great flatlands of the Middle West. This is a good example of Wright's "naturalism" in the adjustment of building to site, although, in this particular case, the confines of the city lot provide less opportunity than do the sites of some of Wright's more expansive suburban villas. In the "wandering" plan of the Robie House (FIG. 22-58), intricately articulated spaces (some, large and open; others, closed) are grouped freely around a great central fireplace. (Wright felt strongly the age-old domestic significance of the hearth.) Wright's new and fundamental spatial arrangement of the interior is matched in his treatment of the exterior. Symmetry is disposed of, the façade disappears, the roofs extend

22-57 FRANK LLOYD WRIGHT, Robie House, Chicago, Illinois, 1907–1909.

929

1. Porch
2. Living room
3. Dining room
4. Balcony
5. Guest room
6. Kitchen
7. Servants
8. Billiard room
9. Children's playroom
10. Entrance hall
11. Boiler room
12. Laundry
13. Garage
14. Court
15. Garden
16. Lavatory or bath
17. Fireplace
18. Bedrooms

Roof

Outdoor walls (garden, terrace, balcony, etc.)

Structures above or below plan level

THIRD LEVEL

SECOND LEVEL

FIRST LEVEL

22-58 FRANK LLOYD WRIGHT, plan of the Robie House, Chicago.

far beyond the walls, the windows are in continuous strips, and the entrance is all but concealed. Masses and voids have come into equilibrium; the flow of space determines the placement of the walls. The "Cubist" aspect of the exterior, with its sharp, angular planes meeting at apparently odd angles, matches the complex play of interior solids, where the solids function not as inert, containing surfaces but as equivalent in role to the spaces in the design.

The implied message of this new architecture is *space*, not *mass*—a space that fits the life of the patron and that is simply enclosed and divided as required. Wright took special pains to meet the requirements of his clients, often designing the accessories of the house himself (including, in at least one case, the gowns of his client's wife!). Discerning clients commissioned his works, but his reputation grew more rapidly in Europe, especially in Holland and Germany, than in America. The publication in Berlin in 1910 of a portfolio of Wright's work hastened the death of Art Nouveau and stimulated younger archi-

tects to turn in the new direction. Had Wright died at that time, his work would still have a revolutionary significance. In 1940, Ludwig Mies van der Rohe, himself a great modern architect, wrote:

At this moment [1911], so critical for us, the exhibition of the work of Frank Lloyd Wright came to Berlin. . . . The encounter was destined to prove of great significance to the European development. . . . The dynamic impulse from his work invigorated a whole generation. His influence was strongly felt even when it was not actually visible.[*]

The International Style

World War I was the dividing line for European architecture, eliminating the blind alley of Art Nouveau and bringing Wright's ideas into broad acceptance and eager expansion. Even until after World War II, American and European architects would practice

[*]In Philip Johnson, *Mies van der Rohe,* rev. ed. (New York: Museum of Modern Art, 1954), pp. 200–201.

what could be called an International style, so closely did they agree on fundamental principles including the new principle of *structure*. In the modern building, the great tensile strength of steel and the great crushing (or compression) strength of concrete are employed together to support enormous loads. The steel framework obviates the historical necessity of bracing thrust pressures with resisting mass and makes heavy bearing walls unnecessary, so that the walls become mere screens or "curtains." The long cantilever, another product of the use of steel, can reach out into space with support at only one end; and with the development of prestressed concrete, load and support become one.* Thus, the demands of stability and support can be subordinated to the concerns of utility and esthetics as never before in the history of architecture.

Another principle basic to the International style deals with a radically different approach to the *plan.* The enormous strength of the new building materials now at the architect's disposal permits an unprecedented flexibility in the planning of the interiors of buildings. With steel and concrete, spans without interior supports can be constructed on a scale that goes far beyond the wildest dreams of earlier builders. The resultant interior space can be arranged and rearranged with movable, nonbearing partitions or thrown open completely for an "open plan." Glass "walls" often make interior and exterior ambiguous. "Out" and "in" become relative terms, like "forward" and "back" in Cubist art. New demands are

*In *reinforced concrete,* steel bars are embedded in concrete and the resulting member combines the respective *tensile* and *compressive* strengths of the two materials. In *prestressed concrete,* the embedded bars are fastened at the ends of the member in such a way that they are kept under tension, thus increasing tensile strength.

placed on the viewer, who now must move through the interior to comprehend its "wandering" space-flow.

The third principle animating the International School, the architectural philosophy of *functionalism,* is naturally related to the new approaches to structure and design. In this view, the function of the building is considered first and determines the building's form. Thus, there is no given form into which a function can be made to fit; a building cannot be made that will function just as well as an art school, a hospital, or a warehouse. The functions to be enclosed must be particularized; a building is then designed to enclose and esthetically express those functions. Just as the plan is determined first by the space, so the function of the building—the activities that are to take place in it—must dictate its form. The parts of the building should visually distinguish its functions; for example, its servant (utility) spaces should be distinct from its primary spaces.

The structural essentials of the International style are graphically shown in the 1914 drawing (FIG. 22-59) by Swiss architect Charles Édouard Jeanneret-Gris (1887–1965), called LE CORBUSIER. A Cubist painter as well as an influential writer on modern architecture, Le Corbusier applied himself principally to the design of the "functional" house, which he describes, in a phrase that has acquired wide currency, as a "machine for living." The drawing shows the skeleton of a dwelling in which the properties of reinforced concrete have been utilized with maximum efficiency. Reinforced concrete slabs, serving the double function of ceiling (for the lower story) and floor (for the upper), are supported by steel posts that rise freely through the interior space of the structure. Exterior walls can be suspended from the projecting edges of

22-59 LE CORBUSIER, perspective drawing for Domino House Project, Marseilles, France, 1914.

the concrete slabs like free-hanging curtains. Because the skeleton is self-supporting, the architect has complete freedom to subdivide the interior as desired with nonbearing walls. Furthermore, the unit shown can be repeated almost indefinitely (as a kind of module), both horizontally and vertically, as indeed it is in most modern office buildings and skyscrapers (see FIGS. 22-66 and 22-67). Although Le Corbusier did not invent the system shown (it had been anticipated about half a decade earlier by PETER BEHRENS, with whom Le Corbusier worked in his early career, and by Walter Gropius), the drawing clearly states the basic structural principles on which much of twentieth-century architecture is based.

Early examples of the International style show its very close relationship to Cubist and Formalist developments in painting. The Schroeder House at Utrecht in Holland (FIG. 22-60), built in 1924 by GERRIT RIETVELDT (1888–1964), shows the influence of the De Stijl purists and—in its sweeping planes and overhanging roofs—of Frank Lloyd Wright. A severe and doctrinaire insistence on the rectilinearity of the planes, which seem to slide across each other like movable panels, makes Rietveldt's house a kind of three-dimensional projection of the rigid but carefully proportioned flat planes in Mondrian's paintings (FIG. 22-20). Ornament is, of course, entirely banished; ADOLPH LOOS, a forerunner of this kind of purist trend, equates ornament with "crime." A triumph of International purism is the Villa Savoye (FIG. 22-61) at Poissy-sur-Seine, near Paris, designed by Le Corbusier. The building is a cube of lightly enclosed and deeply penetrated space, supported, at least visually,

on thin columns (*pilotis*)—a seemingly deliberate analogy with the isolated, "machined" space of an ocean liner; the flat roof-terrace may appropriately be called a "deck," as the modern flat roof commonly is now. There is no façade; the approach does not define an entrance, and one must walk around and through the building to comprehend its layout. Spaces and masses interpenetrate so fluently that there is the familiar Internationalist ambiguity of "inside" and "outside." The machine-planed smoothness of the surfaces, entirely without adornment, the slender "ribbons" of continuous windows, the buoyant lightness of the whole fabric—all present a total effect that is the very reverse of the traditional country house (compare Andrea Palladio's Villa Rotunda and John Vanbrugh's Blenheim; FIGS. 17-52 and 20-4). There are no basement walls of masonry; the "load" hovers lightly on its slender supports, the inverse of the traditional design, which places the light elements above and the heavy ones below. Le Corbusier's use of color—dark-green base, cream walls, and rose and blue superstructure (a windscreen)—is a deliberate analogy with contemporary painting, in which he was actively engaged.

The Villa Savoye is set conspicuously within its site, tending to dominate it, and has a broad view of the landscape. In this way, it *does* resemble the Palladian villa and contrasts sharply with Frank Lloyd Wright's dwellings, which hug and adjust to the landscape, almost as if they were intended to be part of it and concealed by it. Wright's Kaufmann House (FIG. 22-62), built at Bear Run, Pennsylvania, in 1939, crouches within its isolated woodland site, reaching

22-60 GERRIT RIETVELDT, Schroeder House, Utrecht, Netherlands, 1924.

22-61 LE CORBUSIER,
Villa Savoye,
Poissy-sur-Seine, France, 1929.

22-62 FRANK LLOYD WRIGHT,
Kaufmann House ("Falling Water"),
Bear Run, Pennsylvania,
1936–1939.

out almost protectively over a little waterfall. The machine-planed decks of the International style function like the broad overhanging roofs of the Robie House (FIG. 22-57), meeting and intersecting dramatically. Although he disliked the cubic regularity of the International style, here Wright makes a virtue of the contrast between the sharp, clean lines and planes of the International deck and the rockwork and freely falling water of the natural site. Thus, Wright's customary naturalism—his love of free and irregular forms, the "organic" in its unspoiled setting—is beautifully adjusted to the severe regularity of the European designs, as if he were editorializing on the International style.

Wright accepted the machine as a challenge to be met, but he warned against being overcome by it. In Europe, architecture was long dominated by what might be called the "romanticism of the machine." Le Corbusier's vision of the house as a "machine for living" expresses this, and we have seen the broad influence of machine design and dynamics on painting

and sculpture. German architecture, particularly the factories and industrial buildings designed by Gropius (FIG. 22-63), reveals a deep respect for the machine, with its parts precisely tooled, seemingly unrelated, and functioning only as parts of a whole. This may be seen in the Bauhaus in Dessau, West Germany, originally founded in 1906 as the Weimar School of Arts and Crafts by the Dutch architect–designer HENRY VAN DE VELDE (1863–1957). He was an outstanding representative of Art Nouveau, and his educational program emphasized craftsmanship along with free creativity and experimentation. When Van de Velde left Weimar at the outbreak of World War I, he recommended a young German architect, WALTER GROPIUS (1883–1969), as his successor. Gropius assumed the directorship of the school in 1919; he reorganized the various departments of the original school under the new name of Das Staatliche Bauhaus, Weimar, and moved it to the newly built quarters in Dessau in 1925. The redesigned curriculum stressed the search for solutions to contemporary

22-63 WALTER GROPIUS, shop block, the Bauhaus, Dessau, West Germany, 1925–1926.

problems in such areas as housing, urban planning, and high-quality, utilitarian mass production—all vital needs in impoverished post-World War I Germany. Under the guidance of Lyonel Feininger, Kandinsky, and Klee, The Bauhaus, which takes its name from the German word for building *(bau)*, offered courses not only in architecture, but also in music, drama, and, in particular, painting. In design, handicraft was considered the natural training device for mass production and the natural basis for experimental models leading to industrial products. In these respects, and in the minimizing of philosophy and other "verbal" disciplines, the Bauhaus was the earliest working example of much that is still sought in design education. Its training was rooted in the Arts and Crafts movement of earlier generations and in the work of Friedrich Froebel, a German educator, and others' work with children's art, but its vision was firmly fixed on the requirements and potentialities of its day.

Gropius' design for the Bauhaus buildings, which included a workshop, a studio, a school, and an administrative office, firmly established the principles of the International style—an expression of the "machine age" as the Europeans of the 1920s wished to see it. Planned as a series of cells, each with its own specific function, it is the direct expression, in glass, steel, and thin concrete veneer, of the technical program (that is, the function) of the building. The forms are clear, cubic units—the epitome of classicizing purity. The workshop block (FIG. 22-63) is a cage of glass that extends beyond and encloses its steel supports in a realization of Le Corbusier's early schematic sketch (FIG. 22-59). Here, the new concept of flexible structure triumphs. The transparent block makes an equilibrium of inner and outer space.

In the work of LUDWIG MIES VAN DER ROHE (1886–1969), the International style found its most imaginative solutions and perhaps a new order. His German Pavilion (FIG. 22-64), built for the International Exposition at Barcelona in 1929, has a program—an information center and rest house—so simple that the architect was able to concentrate almost exclusively (as is the case for many exposition buildings) on the dramatic principles of the new style. Fine stone and marble, chromium and glass, water and sculpture mold the space and subtly lead the visitor through a succession of areas that vary in degree of enclosure—now open on several sides, now enclosed by two, three, or four walls. Grace and elegance, refined and subtle harmonies, are realized to a degree comparable to that in such eighteenth-century masterpieces as the Hôtel de Soubise (FIG. 20-6) and Robert Adam's Osterley Park House (FIG. 20-24), but in this instance in a language and spirit wholly of the twentieth century.

Although American architecture did not keep up with the progressive International style during the 1920s, the example of its mighty skyscrapers stimulated the imagination of European architects. For a time, the typical American skyscraper was clothed in traditional stylistic features, but something of the new International manner began to appear just at the end of the skyscraper age in the early 1930s. In the Philadelphia Savings Fund Society Building (FIG. 22-65), designed by GEORGE HOWE (1886–1955) and WILLIAM E. LESCAZE (1896–1969), the horizontal banding, ribbon windows, and clean geometric planes of the International style appear on the soaring scale of the American urban office building. Mies van der Rohe had been inspired by the skyscraper as early as 1920, when he made a startlingly beautiful

22-64   LUDWIG MIES VAN DER ROHE, German Pavilion, Barcelona International Exhibition, Spain, 1929.

22-65   GEORGE HOWE and WILLIAM E. LESCAZE, Philadelphia Savings Fund Society Building, Philadelphia, Pennsylvania, 1931–1932.

22-66   LUDWIG MIES VAN DER ROHE, model for a glass skyscraper, 1920–1921. Present location of model unknown.

model for a glass building (FIG. 22-66)—a work that was never carried out but showed a profound understanding of the technical and esthetic possibilities of steel, glass, and concrete in symphonic relationship. The structure's transparency, which may have influenced Gropius' Bauhaus design (FIG. 22-63), the weblike delicacy of its lines, its radiance, and the illusion of movement created by reflection and by light changes seen through it prefigure the contemporary

glass skyscraper slabs of our major cities. Indeed, the model anticipates by 30 years Mies van der Rohe's design—carried out in collaboration with PHILIP JOHNSON (b. 1906)—of the Seagram Building (FIG. 22-67), built in New York City from 1956 to 1958. This towering, prismatic block, raised on piers, is measured out in modular units, each detail of surface and silhouette dictated by Mies van der Rohe's sense for the purity of straight line and uncomplicated, rectilinear shape. Here, the evolution of function–form is completed. The myriad operations performed by thousands of human beings are revealed in a luminous cage of glass that, at the same time, serves as a vast, almost pictorial, reflective surface that mirrors the titanic city. Enclosure and disclosure are simultaneous; the building is the perfect expression of an anonymous public world articulated by innumerable impersonal functions. Yet Mies van der Rohe—no matter his belief that architectural beauty may be as impersonal as its function—spared no pains in his attention to detail, for "God," he said, "dwells in the details."

To the three principles of structure, plan, and functionalism that guide the architect working in the International style should be added a fourth—one deci-

22-67 Ludwig Mies van der Rohe and Philip Johnson,
Seagram Building, New York, 1956–1958.

sive for the characteristic look of the style: *mechanical
control of the interior environment*. If the elevator made
the development of the high-rise building possible,
so air conditioning has made design according to the
new principles possible without respect to geographical location or climatic conditions. Thus, true to their
name, International style buildings resemble one
another, whether they rise in Canada or Brazil, in
Tokyo, New York, Capetown, or Calcutta.

PAINTING AND SCULPTURE
AFTER WORLD WAR II

Since World War II, brilliant variations have been
made on the great central themes stated in the "classical age" of modern art, when most of our contemporary artists were born. The shock of the war and its
"cold" aftermath, the persisting threat of nuclear
annihilation, the widening recognition of human suffering in a large part of the world, and a haunting fear
among many that life has no meaning or value have
sharpened the protest of highly sensitive artists
against a mechanized culture that often appears to
have no place in it for the nonconforming individual.
Expressionism becomes harsher, more defiant and
rebellious; Dadaistic satire, more bitter; and Formalistic art insists on an ever-more-radical abstraction from
the world of appearance. As European–American
civilization broadens into world civilization, a crisis of
values is taking place—or, rather, continues to take
place. Traditional values and the values of organized
modern life are criticized mercilessly and declared to
be largely false. It is almost as if the only value left is
the belief in the artistic process itself on the grounds
that in creativity alone resides true humanity. The
artist's way of life has become a possible model for all
human life, with its religion of free expression, its
pursuit of identity and self-knowledge through art,
and its overtones of prophetic mysticism. On the
other hand, neither art nor artist has escaped the peculiar dynamics of modern society. Art has become a
big business, and the artist might sometimes be
thought of as a kind of piecework employee of ambitious and commercially minded galleries. The work of
art is a commodity on the art "market," and methods
familiar to modern advertising promote it. The old
divisions between the arts are vanishing. Painting,
sculpture, and architecture interfuse, and all are increasingly bound to developments in technology.
The revolution that began even before the century
itself continues at an ever-more-rapid pace.

It is of course impossible to do historical justice to
contemporary events, especially when the men and
women who create them are still living. The selection
and presentation of certain contemporary monuments suggests that a judgment of their superiority
has already been made by history. This is not the
case; historical judgment moves slowly, and its selection of the touchstone masterpieces of the epoch has
scarcely begun for the twentieth century.

At first glance, developments in painting and
sculpture after World War II seem all confusion, with
bewildering overlaps and intersections of tendencies
and influences. Yet closer study reveals a certain
order susceptible of at least rough classification. This

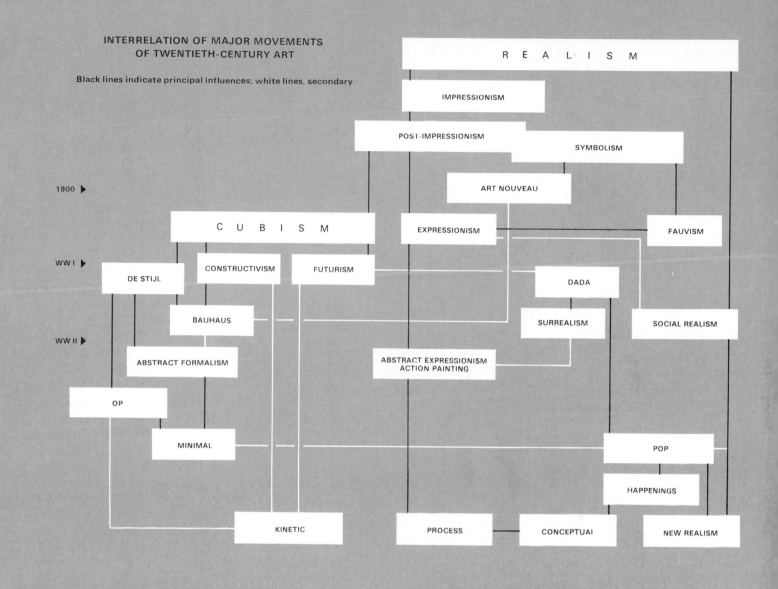

INTERRELATION OF MAJOR MOVEMENTS OF TWENTIETH-CENTURY ART

Black lines indicate principal influences; white lines, secondary

REALISM

IMPRESSIONISM

POST-IMPRESSIONISM

SYMBOLISM

ART NOUVEAU

1900 ▶

CUBISM

EXPRESSIONISM

FAUVISM

WW I ▶

CONSTRUCTIVISM

FUTURISM

DE STIJL

DADA

BAUHAUS

SURREALISM

SOCIAL REALISM

WW II ▶

ABSTRACT FORMALISM

ABSTRACT EXPRESSIONISM ACTION PAINTING

OP

MINIMAL

POP

HAPPENINGS

KINETIC

PROCESS

CONCEPTUAL

NEW REALISM

order appears as a fundamental (though by no means clear-cut) dualism that seems to arise in the work of the fathers of modern art—Cézanne on the one hand, Gauguin and Van Gogh on the other. One can believe it is the old familiar dualism in Western art between "classicizing formalism" directed by intellect and "baroque–romantic expressivism" prompted by sensation and feeling.

As indicated in the chart of twentieth-century art (see above), Cubism and Expressionism and the styles derivative from them dominate the art of the first half of the century (the period before World War II). Some semblance of order can be brought into the seemingly chaotic profusion of postwar trends and styles by grouping them on the basis of artists' approaches to their mediums, which can be either predominantly rational–formalistic or emotional–expressive. Accordingly, most of the postwar trends are grouped as

descendants of either Cubism or Expressionism (although we are aware of the crosscurrents and interchanges of influence) under the generic headings Abstract Formalism and Abstract Expressionism. Admittedly, the organization is rough, oversimplified, and undoubtedly subject to future modifications as increasing distance from contemporaneous events allows us to view them with greater detachment.

Expressionism: Figural and Abstract

Against the Constructivist depersonalization of the work of art and against the prevailing Social Realism, Expressionists after World War II strenuously assert the artist's personality, individuality, identity, even pathology. In this, they can follow the example and the precepts of the distinguished tradition of Expressionism that reaches back to Gauguin, Van Gogh,

Kandinsky, and their contemporaries and successors. But among the later artists, the Expressionist conviction and method seem stronger. Basically, what sets them apart from the earlier Expressionists is the question of whether to retain the human figure and related images or to banish them altogether from painting. The Expressionists accept the first alternative and can be conveniently designated "figural"; the others are "abstract."

The distortion of the human figure in painting for the purpose of the expression of strong emotion is, as we have seen, a very old practice in Western art and by no means solely a modern invention. That distortion works strongly in many works of the British painter FRANCIS BACON (b. 1910), which express an excruciating crisis of nerves that goes well beyond Munch (FIG. 21-76), for example, in its emphasis. A subject that Bacon often returns to is the human being locked in a box-like space by a malignant, glittering mesh of spectral light rays. His 1953 *Number VII from Eight Studies for a Portrait* (FIG. 22-68), painted in 1953, shows us Pope Innocent X (from a Velázquez portrait) as if restrained by a straitjacket and capable of no action but a continuing, dreadful scream. The picture is an almost unbearable image of insane terror. Our age—the "age of psychology"—is obsessed as perhaps no other age before it with the fear and the fact of mental illness.

22-68 FRANCIS BACON, *Number VII from Eight Studies for a Portrait*, 1953. Approx. 60" × 46". Museum of Modern Art, New York (gift of Mr. and Mrs. William A.M. Burden).

The construction of the new art seems almost to require the destruction of the ideals of the old; thus destructiveness, as Gertrude Stein recognized, plays a large role in the new art's vitality: "everything destroys itself in the twentieth century, and nothing continues. . . ." (Compare Jean Tinguely's *Homage to New York,* FIG. 22-86.) This wide destruction involves not only the Cubist shattering of perspective and the denial that there is only one perspective; it also dismisses the traditional notion (both Greek and Renaissance) of beauty in art as being a reflection of human beauty, for, as Gauguin thought, beauty in this sense is nothing but a lie. The Expressionist artist is only too aware of pain and suffering in his age.

Although his intuitive manner of painting seems related to the methods of the Abstract Expressionist painters, Bacon is largely independent of international Abstract Expressionism and provides a kind of figural reaction against the movement's more abstract tendencies. Abstract Expressionism carries all before it after World War II, especially in America, to which the artistic center of gravity appears to shift from Europe. The style—or, rather, method—has its roots in Kandinsky's automatic and spontaneous nonobjectivity and his mystical interpretations of color and line (FIG. 22-10). (The label "abstract expressionism" was attached to Kandinsky's art as early as 1919.) It also owes much to Surrealists like Ernst (FIG. 22-26), who experimented with chance effects of manipulating paint and surface in ways other than by the brush. Most immigrant European artists in the 1930s and 1940s were Constructivists like Mondrian (FIG. 22-20). On the other hand, HANS HOFMANN (1880–1966) developed an expressionistic method of painting in his later years in America that directly preceded the native American school of Abstract Expressionism and had a deep influence on it. Hofmann's double career as artist and art teacher spanned two generations and two continents. As a young man, he was the associate and friend of the founders of abstract art—Matisse, Braque, Picasso. Later, in America, he became an influential teacher and expressed his new ideas in a vigorous, almost violent method of painterly attack. Hofmann charges his surfaces with primary colors of unparalleled richness in jolting contrasts and conflicts—painting impastos densely and with dashing spontaneity, leaving each stroke or splash unmodified. The painted surface becomes only that: a record of the artist's intense experience of paint and of color, of the process of painting—arbitrary, accidental, unthinking, automatic, direct. In *Effervescence, 1944* (FIG. 22-69), Hofmann mixes media (oil, India ink, casein, enamel), a method common in Abstract Expressionist painting. Colors explode in a chaos controlled only by the picture frame—a chaos that seems to have sucked the artist into its swirl and to have painted itself.

22-69 Hans Hofmann,
Effervescence, 1944.
Oil, India ink, casein, and
enamel on plywood,
$54\frac{1}{2}'' \times 36''$.
University Art Museum,
Berkeley, California.

Hofmann's method in effect produces painting that is a record of the producing action, that is almost a *picture* of that action. This is the rationale behind the designation "action painting" attached to many Abstract Expressionist works. Painting is thus a largely uncontrolled, prerational action or event; the process of painting becomes more real than the painted surface.

An artist who certainly must have subscribed to this "action" view and who was the central figure of the New York School in the 1940s and 1950s was JACKSON POLLOCK (1912–1956). Pollock once practiced Social Realism; his abrupt turnabout to Abstract Expressionism typifies the postwar situation in the arts. At the height of his powers, in the years just before his untimely death in 1956, Pollock shared with his brilliant colleagues in New York a collective achievement that has been called the most original and distinctive in the history of American art. The principal method in American Abstract Expressionism (for there were other methods) was the painting-action revealed through the brush gesture and the signature left by the fall and touch of the paint. Pollock would roll out a large canvas on the floor and drip and splatter paint on it while he himself was in energetic motion along its edge or sometimes within it. For him, the expression of the artist's whole content, which is inward, is directed by mysterious psychic forces; hence, in his view, to label the look of such painting "accidental" would be misleading. Yet there is something of the mystique of the materials that we saw in Brancuşi motivating the action painter; the random fall and scatter of the paint emphasizes the liquid nature of the medium itself, which enters into the sum of the painting's qualities. The jarring dynamism of Pollock's large-scale paintings, in turn, echoes the restless, perhaps rootless life style of the postwar years. It manifests too, in its extremely personal nature, the interest of many Expressionist artists in Existentialism, the widely adopted philosophy of the postwar years that stresses absolute freedom of choice in life and art as a human commitment.

In an early (1947) example of Pollock's art, his *Lucifer* (FIG. 22-70), the materials—oil, aluminum paint, and enamel—are dragged, dripped, and splattered from well above the surface in a process of excited movement that has in its tracing and retracing a remarkable coherence of direction and pattern. The painter strives for unplanned immediacy and directness and for an effect of unstudied, spontaneous freshness of statement. As Pollock says ". . . it doesn't make much difference how the paint is put on as long as something has been said. Technique is just a means of arriving at a statement." The state-

ment arrived at is at the same time the record—the signature, as it were—of the creating process itself, which *arrives* at something rather that aims at it intentionally. Modern philosophy, when it is influenced by the views of modern biology, often stresses the reality of process over structure, and if Pollock's painting is an image of anything, it is of process itself in its never-ending, never-wearying creation of nature. Action painting completes, moreover, that introduction of time and motion into the static arts of form that began in Futurism. Now the artist himself is truly in motion; his viewpoint is constantly changing. It is significant that the easel picture is inappropriate for his creative "dance"; as he moves, he looks not out (as from a viewpoint) but *down*, seeing his "landscape" unfold somewhat as we see the earth from an airplane moving through the air some 10,000 feet up. Thus, although action painting may seem strange and formless at first, we need only reflect on the vast new vocabulary of forms that the surface of the earth itself yields to modern eyes and imaginations. To these, add the marvelous, formal complexities of the microcosm and the macrocosm revealed by microphotography and our probing of outer space. The macroscopic and microscopic worlds—where endless and intricate processes weave endless and intricate relationships of living forms—are given a visual presence in the dense, entangled skeins of lines and colors in Pollock's art.

Abstract Expressionism had many possible methods of approach. In the work of FRANZ KLINE (1910–1962), it is a vehicle of very personal psychic revelation, possibly as mysterious to the artist as to the observer. Kline himself admitted that there was no

22-70 JACKSON POLLOCK, *Lucifer*, 1947. Oil, aluminum paint, and enamel on canvas, approx. 3′ 5″ × 8′ 9″. Collection of Mr. and Mrs. Harry W. Anderson.

22-71 FRANZ KLINE, *Painting 1952*, 1955–1956. Approx.
6′ 5″ × 8′ 4″. Present location unknown.

way to find a verbal equivalent or sometimes even a
caption, to express his meaning. He painted, in black
and white on large canvases, ragged bars and stripes
of black enclosing (or overlapped by) rectilinear white
areas as sharp-edged as broken planes of glass (FIG.
22-71). These configurations suggest Chinese characters boldly brushed and greatly magnified, a kind of
ideogram of the artist's psychic states. As hieratic and
quasi-magical shapes, they can be interpreted as the
observer pleases; as purely nonobjective forms in a
wide variety of arrangements, they appeal through
their blunt esthetic force and bold, free execution.

Of the New York action painters, WILLEM DE
KOONING (b. 1904), a native of Holland who began as
a figure and portrait painter, practices a quick alternation between abstract and figural painting. The tension between the two approaches is itself expressive
of De Kooning's attitude; he has been called an "artist
who makes ambiguity a hypothesis on which to
build."* Ambiguity prevails in an art and in an age
where nothing, as De Kooning himself says, is certain
but self-consciousness. Shapes and colors play
through, over, and across one another with no definable order, with no completeness of decision. De
Kooning's best-known works, his series of paintings
of female nudes on large canvases, comprise a gallery
of sometimes harsh and biting, sometimes sinister
and menacing, sometimes jovial and sensuous caricatures. In *Woman I* (FIG. 22-72), the attack is carried out
with manic excitement, the figure slashed out with
brush at arm's length and at full speed. There is a
curious effect, typically ambiguous, of simultaneous
delineation and defacement, of construction and can-
cellation—a conflict between sketch and finished pic-

*Thomas B. Hess, *Willem de Kooning* (New York: Museum of Modern Art, 1968), p. 25.

22-72 WILLEM DE KOONING, *Woman 1*, 1950–1952. Approx.
6′ 4″ × 4′ 10″. Museum of Modern Art, New York (purchase).

ture. The brazen and baleful mask mixes the tooth-
paste smile with the grimace of the death's head. The
enormous sketch is carried through by the compulsive drive that marks the action painter.

That Abstract Expressionism is a good deal less
homogeneous in style than once seemed to be the
case is particularly apparent in the work of MARK
ROTHKO (1903–1973). Although he was a friend and
contemporary of Pollock, Kline, and De Kooning,
Rothko's paintings exhibit none of their aggressive
attack or slashing brushwork. *Four Darks on Red* (FIG.
22-73) dismisses the usual *brio* of "action painting" for
a calm and contemplative mood. Subtle tonal variations transcend the essentially monochromatic theme
and create a mysterious effect of forms or images
hovering in an ambiguously defined space. Where
the dynamics of the other Abstract Expressionists
might be taken as visual metaphors of the hostility
and alienation implicit in contemporary Existential
philosophy, Rothko's work seems more in tune with
a Zen viewpoint—the one, a call to action; the other,
an invitation to meditate. Yet, despite the profound
differences, all these painters share a primary interest
in the painterly problem of painting—that is, a concern with the actual process of applying paint to canvas rather than with questions of narrative content.

22-73 MARK ROTHKO, *Four Darks on Red*, 1958. 8′ 6″ × 9′ 8″. Collection of the Whitney Museum of American Art (gift of the Friends of the Whitney Museum of American Art, Mr. and Mrs. Eugene Schwartz, Mrs. Samuel A. Seaver, Charles Simon, and purchase).

Realism

It is indicative of the diversity of modern trends that, at the height of its vogue, Abstract Expressionism was by no means universally adopted. It was possible in the general debate about styles and the purposes of art for voices old and new to be heard—and in many stylistic accents. The painting of ANDREW WYETH (b. 1917) is still the subject of considerable disagreement among critics. Contemporaneous with the vivid action painting of the New York School, Wyeth treats the American scene with a meticulous Realism in a muted poetic way that has something of the dreaming detachment of Surrealism without Surrealism's fantasy. At first glance, Wyeth's spirit seems utterly untouched by the storms of twentieth-century artistic revolution; but the odd angles of his compositions and his carefully selected perspectives and vignettes show that he is no stranger to experimentation in

modern design. His quiet appeal to the long-established taste of America for realism speaks in pictures like *Christina's World* (FIG. 22-74), a work almost exactly contemporary with Pollock's *Lucifer* (FIG. 22-70). Here, his skilled representation of the optical world does not intrude on the genuinely felt human situation and its gentle pathos. The title, in the modern fashion, seems askew from the theme, and the subject is not given literally but only alluded to, in familiar modern ambiguity. In its own way, the picture is as personal and introspective as the works of the Abstract Expressionists.

Realism in both painting and sculpture has been the prevailing mode of artistic representation in the countries altered or affected by the great revolutions of the twentieth century. In the Soviet Union, as well as in the People's Republic of China (FIG. 12-29), it has become the official style of the state; and in Marxist Socialist movements and regimes throughout the

22-74 ANDREW WYETH, *Christina's World*, 1948. Tempera on gesso panel, approx. $32\frac{1}{4}" \times 47\frac{3}{4}"$. Museum of Modern Art, New York (purchase).

world, Social Realism advertises the merits of revolutionary socialism. Ironically, similar elements are manifest in the official art of Germany and Italy in the 1930s and early 1940s, although their Fascist political philosophy is generally held to be diametrically opposed to that of Soviet Marxism. It would appear that the highly centralized twentieth-century dictatorship not only favors conservative Realism in art but also uses art to achieve propagandistic ends, denying the "art for art's sake" orientation of much modern art. Much the same could be said of many government-subsidized WPA (Works Projects Administration) art projects in the United States during the Great Depression of the 1930s.

Abstract Formalism

An early phase of the Formalist approach is epitomized by the work of the productive and influential American painter STUART DAVIS (1894–1964), the first artist to assimilate French Cubism and naturalize it in the American setting. His long career extends from his exhibit in New York at the Armory show of 1913 (which introduced modern art to the general public in this country) to the 1960s. Beginning with the collage, Davis gradually eliminated all representational and associative forms from his compositions. (There are some exceptions; for example, Davis occasionally introduced advertising signs into his work, anticipating Pop Art.) This process of elimination and the achievement of a total abstraction can be followed in his famous series of "egg-beater" paintings, wherein, beginning with an image of that ordinary kitchen utensil, Davis gradually evolves an organization of line, shape, and color that shows no trace of the origi-

nal image. But Davis was not merely a foreign member of the French school of abstract art. He was an original master who developed his own style, expressive of the vivid syncopation of the American scene; and he was at least partly responsible for raising the level of competence of American painting to that of the European schools. Throughout his career, Davis yielded little to the pressures of new vogues, maintaining with astonishing consistency the principles of Cubist art as he had reinterpreted them to suit his purpose. At the same time, he retained the respect of modern innovators, who acknowledged him as the dean of American abstract painters. In *Colonial Cubism* (FIG. 22-75), Davis shows, in a densely organized composition, the play of angular and rectilinear shapes and flat, hard colors in the characteristic Cubist ambiguity of figure and ground, where "forward" and "backward" alternate rapidly. Here, the "subject" of the painting is nothing but the carefully adjusted elements of a purely formal, two-dimensional order. The whole visual field is a lively vibration of colors and shapes in combination and contrast.

The Formalistic interest represented by Davis withstood the powerful competition of America's original postwar style—Abstract Expressionism or "action painting," with its subjectivity and painterly extravagance. We must keep in mind the context of these movements and countermovements. Restless experimentation, the rapid successions of inventions and obsolescences of stylistic conventions, and the fluctuations of a highly sensitive art market kept producing almost violent reversals of interest and tendency in contemporary art. In the Formalistic reaction to Abstract Expressionism—generally called Post-Painterly Abstraction (a phrase of the critic Clement Greenberg), a movement with such allied manifestations as

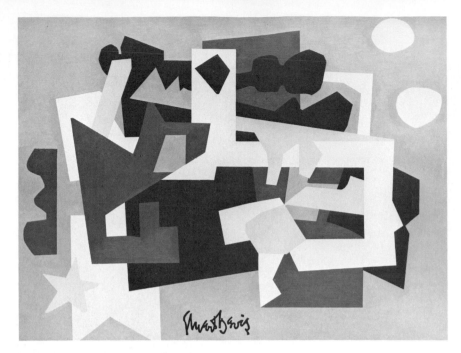

22-75 STUART DAVIS, *Colonial Cubism*, 1954. 45″ × 60″. Collection, Walker Art Center, Minneapolis.

Op Art and Hard-Edge and Color-Field painting—the disciplined line favored by the tradition of Cubism, Constructivism, and De Stijl comes to be appreciated once again, and the painter aims at radical simplicity and purity of shape and color. While Abstract Expressionism was fulminating, BARNETT NEWMAN (1905—1970) was experimenting with the condensation rather than the explosion of forms, searching, as it were, for the still center of shape and color function—rigid linearity and primary color at full intensity. Returning to these elements of painting, Newman seeks their elemental drama in the division, contrast, opposition, advance, and retreat of planes ambiguously spaced but marked off with the authority of lines on a spectrum. His attachment of a

caption to his huge painting *Vir Heroicus Sublimis* (FIG. 22-76) provides a cue for reading the colossal scale, the blood red, and the spare verticals as metaphors of heroism as well as essays in pure color, proportion, and nonperspectival space. Thus, unlike more puristic Formalists, Newman does not exclude meaning; he simply finds a new way to embody it. His influence carried beyond the days of Abstract Expressionism into the later 1960s, when its ostensible purism and radical abstraction guided both painters and sculptors.

An extension of the field of Newman's interest can be found in the work of ELLSWORTH KELLY (b. 1923). His *Red, Blue, Green* (FIG. 22-77)—an example of Color-Field painting, in which subject is excluded

22-76 BARNETT NEWMAN, *Vir Heroicus Sublimis*, 1950–1951. 8′ × 17′ 10″. Museum of Modern Art, New York (gift of Mr. and Mrs. Ben Heller).

22-77 ELLSWORTH KELLY, *Red, Blue, Green*, 1963. Approx. 7′ × 11′ 4″. Courtesy of the Sidney Janis Gallery, New York.

absolutely—shows a scrupulous management of pure color for its own sake and a knife-edge clarity in the contours that contain it. The title declares clearly enough what the artist considers to be the painting's exclusive meaning. The fundamental modern Formalist and Constructivist claim that the "subject" of the painting should be its form and nothing else is here powerfully stressed.

It is but a slight step from an interest in the elementary properties of line, shape, and color to an interest in our mode of perceiving them. Here is the reverse of the whole traditional process of seeing a picture. Originally, we "looked through" the picture "window" of a constructed perspective space; then, with modern art, the canvas itself became the perceptual object, with its arrangement of lines, shapes, and colors. Now, in Perceptual Abstraction, or Op Art, the optical "illusion," which has its seat in the brain, is the object. Thus, the picture is meant to reach out and stimulate, even disturb, our actual seeing. *Current* (FIG. 22-78), painted in 1964 by BRIDGET RILEY (b. 1931), seems to swim in contrary motions. If we stare at it long enough, its vibrations seem to penetrate the eye and cause some discomfort.

It is noteworthy that the elements of the patterns in

22-78 BRIDGET RILEY, *Current*, 1964. Synthetic-resin paint on composition board, approx. 58⅜″ × 58⅞″. Museum of Modern Art, New York (Philip Johnson Fund).

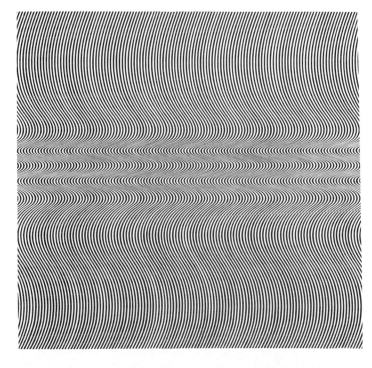

Current stand in a definable, mathematical relation to one another, and patterns like this can be generated by computer. Technologically created forms such as this can produce an esthetic response; for example, the pattern of a sinusoidal wave, with a linearly increasing period, gives an overwhelming impression of motion. Technology has had a most powerful influence on the arts throughout the era since the French Revolution—that era that has no name as yet but "modern." A whole new world of materials and instruments, beginning with the camera (in 1840) and the example of the machine in general, have stimulated—even forced—the arts into radical innovation.

At the same time, much of modern art, as we have seen, is made of reaction *against* the mechanization and standardization of human life imposed by technology. Yet any kind of making—and the artist is engaged in *making* art—inevitably has to acknowledge, adapt to, even yield to the irresistible presence, example, and power of technology. This is especially true of the art of sculpture, which, since World War II, has changed profoundly as it adopted new technological materials and procedures and has come to command as wide a field of action and interest as contemporary painting.

We have already observed in sculpture before World War I and between the world wars the rapid advance of Formalism in the guise of Cubism and Constructivism; the availability of industrial materials and technical procedures accelerated that advance. Gonzalez taught Picasso the method of "direct-metal sculpture," the quasi-industrial procedure of welding together pieces of basic metal "stock" (rod, tube, sheet)—an early instance of the application of modern metalworking techniques to art. This involved the shaping and assembling of metal elements by the artist more or less from the start. EDUARDO PAOLOZZI (b. 1924) went a step farther, welding together (and rendering immobile) elements already machined to perform mechanical functions. This separation of machined elements from their functions is all-important here, both as a kind of reaction against the growing presence in human life of the functioning machine and as an opportunity for the creation of an utterly new medium and Constructivist style. For one thing, the Formalist–Structuralist artist has, in the found object or engine component, a starting point—a "pure" form, already produced, that has no meaning other than its own form. However, Paolozzi can and does arrange these components in unconventional, bizarre ways—as biomorphic constructions, for example. His *Medea* (FIG. 22-79), with its welded aluminum slab and writhing, pipe-like tubules, imposes organic shape on the inorganic material and, at the same time, sets the shapes of the slab and tubules in inorganic–organic opposition. The title is a kind of

22-79 EDUARDO PAOLOZZI, *Medea*, 1964. Welded aluminum, 6' 9" high, 6' wide, 3' 9" deep. National Museum Kröller-Müller, Otterlo, Netherlands.

Dadaist reinforcement of the ambiguity of the piece—a literary reference without images to illustrate it.

Paolozzi's enthusiasm for machine elements not only foreshadows Pop Art, but is itself partly responsible—along with the efforts of his older contemporary DAVID SMITH (1906–1965)—for recent sculptors' fascination with metal sculpture and the simplicity of machined surface. A master of this material and mode, a master of what one might call the "personality" of steel, Smith worked earlier in a delicate, linear, open style. His late *Cubi* compositions (FIG. 22-80), done in the 1960s, are monumental constructions in stainless steel, in which he arranged solid, geometric masses in remarkable equilibriums of strength and buoyancy. Smith, like his Structuralist contemporaries, was at ease in the age of the machine; he declared that machinery was in his nature. "His ambition," writes Barbara Rose

> was to turn his studio into a factory, where he could produce sculpture whose forms were as impressive, monumental, and contemporary as the locomotive. He preferred to work in iron and steel because it "possesses little art history. What associations it possesses are those of this century: power, structure, movement, progress, suspension, destruction, brutality."*

Thus, we find in the art of Smith, and in his charac-

*Barbara Rose, *American Art Since 1900* (New York: Praeger, 1967), pp. 253–54.

22-80 DAVID SMITH, *Cubi XVIII*, 1964.
Stainless steel, 9' 7¾" high. Courtesy of the Museum of
Fine Arts, Boston (gift of Stephen D. Paine) and of the
Estate of David Smith and the Marlborough-Gerson
Gallery, New York.

terization of it, the aim of the Formalist–Structuralist
to eliminate the human element from art altogether—
almost as a source of impurity?—and to present
blunt metal in its unmitigated "power . . . brutality."

It is instructive to turn for the moment from Smith
to the art of LOUISE NEVELSON (b. 1900) to get a sense
of the stylistic diversity and disagreement within contemporary art. (Of course we have witnessed it since
the nineteenth century!) Working in wood—though,
recently, also in metal—Nevelson's style is so markedly different from Smith's that it is hard to believe
they are contemporaries. She uses the easily worked
medium of wood, a favorite of the later Middle Ages
(FIG. 18-29), to create a multiplicity of detail, almost to
confusion, and clusters of reference and association
to things both familiar and mysterious in human experience. Her work appears to be a skillful joinery
that assembles shelves, cupboards, closets, chests,
cabinets, boxes crammed with oddments and fragments of furnishings, and accessories of all periods,
picked up at random. Painted black, white, and gold
(FIG. 22-81), these assemblages of objects and nonob-
jects evoke the apprehensive curiosity we experience
when confronted by unfamiliar, cased collections of
things not inventoried and liable to be puzzling.
Nevelson *intends* her compositions to signify, even if
ambiguously; Smith would banish meaning from
form altogether. The influence of Smith, Paolozzi,
and the great tradition of Constructivism to which
they belong is widely accepted by modern metal
sculptors—even, perhaps, by Nevelson in her later,
monumental work.

In the interest of a sculpture that banishes all refer-

22-81 LOUISE NEVELSON, *An American
Tribute to the British People*, 1960–1965.
Painted wood, 10' 2" × 14' 3". Tate Gallery,
London.

22-82 DONALD JUDD, *Untitled*, 1968. Stainless steel, each box is 4′ square. Collection of Miles Fiterman, Minneapolis, Minnesota.

ence beyond itself, DONALD JUDD (b. 1928)—widely influential as artist and critic, especially in the 1960s—asserts a doctrine of ultimate purity of three-dimensional form, manifest in figures of solid geometry like the cube (FIG. 22-82). Against all two-dimensional space that invites illusionistic figuration, including even Mondrian's paintings (FIG. 22-20), Judd insists that such treatment is a distortion of space, and that only the spatial wholeness of the third dimension in the ultimate reduction of geometry bears the truth of art. Here, he aligns eight brightly machined, identical cubes so that they multiply the reflections of their neighbors and the environment, exhibiting, in their superhuman precision and exactitude, the depersonalized technological order that produces them.

The forms preferred by Judd and many of his contemporaries have been called "minimal" or "primary"; hence, the work of this school is labeled Minimal Art or Primary Art. Typically, RONALD BLADEN (b. 1918), like Judd, reacts against romantic subjectivism (particularly that of Abstract Expressionism and welded metal), personal signature or touch, allusive association—anything extraneous to the form itself. He seeks a purism of simplicity so austere as to remove any trace of the artist's self from his work. The elimination of every vestige of personality amounts to the elimination of the artist himself; the artist seeks to achieve the impersonal, anonymous aspect of the machine. (Few people even wonder who built a particular machine.) Works like Bladen's are often constructed on a great scale, asserting their severity of outline, economy of means, and domination of the environment; above all, they emphasize their isolation from human personality and affects. They are a new kind of object that silently commands the environment, natural or artificial. Bladen's *X* (FIG. 22-83) manifests the Structuralist's credo; a stark, tremendous form, painted black, it confronts the observer with an overpowering weight and awesome blankness. It should be noted that *X* is made of wood, a

full-scale model of the metal object it is designed to become. But metal on this scale is extremely expensive, and the artist must await a patron. Here, the ambition of the metal Structuralist may take him beyond the possibility of realizing his design in his chosen medium, the properties of which inspired the design in the first place.

The great scale of much Minimal Art naturally brought to the fore the problems of the relation of the piece to its site or environment. Concerned that sculpture too emphatically separates its reality from the reality of its site, a number of sculptors trained in Minimal Art, ROBERT SMITHSON (1938–1973) among them, sought a solution to the problem of sculptural site in an entirely new context for their art, the unbounded spread of the earth itself. Their method and results, although widely differing in look, have been

22-83 RONALD BLADEN, *X*, 1967. Painted wood, 22′ high, 26′ wide, 14′ deep. Fischbach Gallery, New York.

called Earth Art, which consists of manipulating vast quantities of earth and rock (usually in desolate terrains in the American West) with earth-moving equipment to produce a new unity of sculpture, site, and context. One Smithson work, *Spiral Jetty* (FIG. 22-84) in Great Salt Lake, Utah, the making of which he filmed, is a vast spiral of earth and stone built out from a shore of the lake that expresses monumentally, although in open form (unlike the closed shapes of Minimal Art), the reality of time, which is missing from sculpture—Minimal or traditional. Smithson's movie carefully describes the forms and life of the whole site, even the difficult approach to it, as he builds within it; he shows both the work and the context in reciprocal relation, sharing the same reality. Against the boundedness and closure of sculpture and its architectural sites, as well as the limits of "differentiated" thinking, Smithson tries for an indissoluble unity of art and nature, much like the suspension of the boundaries between "self" and "nonself" that he asks of the critic. (Smithson was killed when the airplane in which he was surveying a site for a new earth sculpture crashed.) The Earth Artist's work thus is neither imitation of nor flight from physical nature; rather, it asserts the unity of the physical reality of the world. The prodigious energy that goes into this reshaping of physical nature, embodied in the great earth-movers and the masses of earth they lift and place, represents in itself the shaping forces of the physical world in which the artist shares.

Earth Art differs only in method and matter from the Structuralist search for formal truth and purity that leads to the Minimal or Primary constructions inspired by the hard, clean, precisely machined surfaces of industrial metal. But ingredient in the model of machinery (and, indeed, in all nature) is also the fact of motion. Early Constructivists like Tatlin and Gabo perceived this, and the Futurists made it central to their philosophy. Pevsner and Gabo, in their *Realist Manifesto* of 1920, included time with space as a prime reality for the modern experience; and the combination of time and space makes for motion. Motion then must be a reality for modern art, as for modern life, and the construction of forms in motion, powered by some form of motor energy, has come to be called Kinetic Art.

Paolozzi, Smith, Judd, and Bladen all express the power of static form. Artists like POL BURY (b. 1922) say in effect that, for art, motion is as real and as interesting as stasis and is the very model of industrial process. The motion that Bury and his associates in the international movement of Kinetic Art experiment with is not at all like the freely disposed, "air-sketching" of Calder (FIG. 22-49), in which delicately cut and poised filaments and fins move buoyantly on natural currents of air. Rather, it is motion produced

22-84 ROBERT SMITHSON, *Spiral Jetty*, April 1970. Black rocks, salt crystal, earth, red water, algae, 1,500' long, 15' wide. Great Salt Lake, Utah.

22-85 POL BURY, *Broad Flatheads*, 1964. Wood and nails, approx. $39\frac{1}{2}'' \times 29\frac{1}{2}''$. Collection of Mr. and Mrs. Frank M. Titelman, Altoona, Pennsylvania.

by a mechanical drive—the difference between it and Calder's art being somewhat like the difference between a glider and an airplane. Although it is, of course, impossible to represent the kinetic object in a still picture, some sense of it may be had in Bury's *Broad Flatheads* (FIG. 22-85) from the blur caused by the movement of the nails. The movements are very slow and subtle and must be observed carefully over a considerable period of time, much of the work's appeal being derived from the changing relationships of the moving parts. Of course, all sorts and degrees of movement can be made by varying speed, rate of variation, and interval; and these are often augmented by accompanying sound and light effects. Kinetic Art enjoys great currency in the area of pop entertainment, bringing together plastic art, sound, and light into sometimes overpowering orchestration.

Constructivism, in its search for ultimate form and a consistent logic of procedure, can lead to contradictions. It may lead to forms, motions, spaces, and times that are already complete in themselves and do not need the artist's hand (for example, the machined parts and fixed motions of an existing machine). Or, as artists strive to eliminate themselves from the form they have produced, so the form might be made to eliminate itself—that is, to "self-destruct." Or, again, artists might have to concede their own replacement by, say, the machine. Still further, they might intrude meaning on their nonobjective forms by bestowing titles on them. JEAN TINGUELY (b. 1925) seems to have pondered all of these possibilities. At ease with paradox—one of his own being "the only stable thing is movement"—Tinguely builds Kinetic sculptures somewhat in the satiric, Dadaist spirit of Duchamp (FIG. 22-24), often with the droll import of Klee's *Twittering Machine* (FIG. 22-30). Tinguely's art manifests a kind of dangerous playfulness and a gusto for the absurd. His *Homage to New York* (FIG. 22-86)—a giant, motorized, explosive "junk sculpture" crowned with a weather balloon—was designed to destroy itself, which it resolutely did in the garden of the Museum

of Modern Art in New York in 1960. The gesture may have been of profounder historical significance than was first supposed. Earlier, as a spoof of Abstract Expressionism, which held—almost alone—the international art stage of the late 1940s and 1950s, a painting machine designed by Tinguely, called *Metamatic-Automobile-Odorante et Sonore*, produced 40,000 "Abstract Expressionist" paintings during the first Biennial of Paris in 1959. Here, indeed, might be the ultimate elimination of the painter.

22-86 JEAN TINGUELY, *Homage to New York*, 1960, just prior to its self-destruction in the garden of the Museum of Modern Art, New York.

Pop Art and Other Trends

In the later 1950s, the tendencies to total "inwardness" had hardly been established by the mode of Abstract Expressionism before it received a jarring reversal from the rise of a movement—called, among many things, Neo-Dada, but now Pop (for *popular* art)—that has striking resemblances, in both attitude and method, to Dada (although there are important differences). The English critic Lawrence Alloway, who is generally credited with inventing the label "Pop Art," asserts that it refers not so much to the art as to the new attitudes that led to it—principally an acceptance of the prevalence of mass art media, including advertising, industrial design, photography, and cinema. The Pop artist turns outward to his environment—not the natural environment, but the artificial one of mass popular culture—finding material in the manipulated and programed folkways and the mass-produced commodities of modern urban and suburban life. Pop Art challenges the tradition of the "fine arts," insisting that the common culture in its multitudinous forms is as valid as, and indeed continuous with, the fine arts. The tone of Pop Art is for the most part sympathetic with mass culture, although it can range from sympathetic to neutral to hostile. Against the extremely personal and private symbolic utterances of Abstract Expressionism, Pop seeks a hard, tough, impersonal objectivity in the mood of composer John Cage's remark: "Object is *fact*, not symbol." The Pop fact is as visibly in front of us as the cans of soup on our shelves and the billboards along our highways. Its appearance commands our responses daily. It is one of billions of shapes and images that continually rain on us in the visual explosion of the twentieth century. The Pop fact is an expendable object—due in part to its immediacy in our experience and to its significance for that experience. We are continually confronted with the expendable products of Hollywood, Detroit, and Madison Avenue. Taken together, Pop facts make a vast universe of fascinating images, which can, like any "facts," become the source of new fantasies.

The origins of Pop Art are not precisely traceable. It had an early start in London in the mid-1950s, and was restated in New York and Los Angeles in 1960 and for some time after. In London, the influence of Paolozzi (FIG. 22-79) was strong, especially his conviction of the importance of the interaction of the individual and technology, his sincerely cultivated taste for popular culture, and his sense of the presence of a new universe of images with manifold possibilities of significance. Paolozzi was a member of the pioneering Independent Group, which shared his interest in mass culture. Among the members were architects, critics, designers, painters, and sculptors who were especially aware of the lessons of Duchamp's "an-

22-87 RICHARD HAMILTON, *Just What Is It That Makes Today's Homes So Different, So Appealing?*, 1956. Collage, 10¼" × 9¾". Kunsthalle Tübingen, West Germany.

tiart," the collages of Schwitters, and the work of Picasso, much of which owes something to the hard facts of the street culture of Paris. In a small collage (FIG. 22-87), later turned into a photo-mural, RICHARD HAMILTON (b. 1922), a display artist and member of the Independent Group, shows us an interior laden with the images of mass culture—in effect, the contents of a mass mind: muscle man, magazine female, fetish figure, television ad, canned ham, tape recorder, posters, automobile logo, and so on. This is a collage or montage of images lifted from specific contexts and brought together with almost sardonic effect, whether or not the artist intends to make a pointed comment. The images have a kind of realism, while the composition and context repudiate traditional Realism altogether.

Pop Art developed slightly later in America than in England—and differently. The influence of Duchamp's philosophy of art and life was active, as was, to a degree, the influence of Léger's art with its acceptance of the machine culture. Further, the examples of the so-called "cool" Abstract Expressionists like Rothko (FIG. 22-73) and of the Post-Painterly Abstraction or Color-Field painters like Kelly (FIG. 22-77) provided the formal means. In 1955, ROBERT RAUSCHENBERG (b. 1925), whose work bridges Abstract Expressionism and the American Pop movement, began working with collages, which he called "combine painting," composed of photographs, news clippings, prints, and the like. Unlike the collages of Schwitters (FIG. 22-23) and the Dadaists (FIG. 22-24), Rauschenberg's compositions are topical, with reference to events of the day or to commonly seen objects used in the mass environment; they are,

22-88 ROBERT RAUSCHENBERG, *Monogram*, 1959. Construction, 4' high, 6' wide, 6' deep. Collection, Moderna Museet, Stockholm.

moreover, of far greater scale. The evanescence of the referent events and objects is expressed in the ordinariness and expendability of the items chosen by Rauschenberg, which led him naturally to collages or constructions in three dimensions composed of perishable or throwaway materials. In *Monogram* (FIG. 22-88), a stuffed ram wearing an automobile tire is mounted on a collage base, with dense passages of free-brush painting pulling the whole together in a *tour de force* of mixed-media procedure. Dada, Surrealism, and Abstract Expressionism meet here in ambiguous equilibrium.

It is noteworthy that Rauschenberg originally was part of the Abstract Expressionist movement. It is symbolic of his personal rebellion against it— symbolic, perhaps, of the whole reaction of Pop against action painting—that he obtained a drawing from De Kooning, erased it, and then exhibited it as *Erased de Kooning by Robert Rauschenberg*. The gestures of modern artists have much in common, no matter the diversity of their styles.

An early associate of Rauschenberg and of the influential musician John Cage, JASPER JOHNS (b. 1930), like Duchamp, takes the commonplace out of context and makes us *look* at it—not simply use it and throw it away. In *Painted Bronze* (FIG. 22-89), part of the modern cultural landscape—the beer can—is reconstituted as an object not to be discarded but to exist for our attention. Johns goes beyond Duchamp in solemnly exalting the banal by casting it in bronze, faithfully reproducing its label, and placing it firmly on a base, so that the flimsy and disposable container, intended to be used and forgotten, is monumentalized and made permanent as a profoundly symbolic twentieth-century artifact. As has been the case with so many ancient cultures, it is by our manufactured products—at least, by the less perishable ones—that

we are and will be known. The irony of Johns and Duchamp echoes T. S. Eliot's prediction that nothing will survive us but a thousand lost golf balls.

The ephemeral and the banal in popular art naturally attracted the attention of the Pop artist, although we must remember that the Pop philosophy accepts and approves the art (such as illustration and comic strips) and artifacts of mass culture as entirely valid art in themselves. To reconstruct on a giant scale the thudding clichés and earsplitting rhetoric of certain comic strips devoured daily by millions is to comment wordlessly on the taste and fantasy life of the public. A good example of this punishing presentation of what can be forgotten quite as easily as an empty beer can is *Blam!* (FIG. 22-90), painted in 1962 by ROY LICHTENSTEIN (b. 1923). Familiar as the form and iconography are, they create a powerful effect when

22-89 JASPER JOHNS, *Painted Bronze*, 1960. Approx. 5½" high, 8" wide, 4¾" deep. Wallraf-Richartz-Museum, Cologne (Sammlung Ludwig).

22-90 Roy Lichtenstein, *Blam!*, 1962. Approx. 5′ × 6′ 8″. Collection of Richard Brown Baker, New York.

22-91 Claes Oldenburg, *Soft Toilet*, 1966. Vinyl, plexiglass, and kapok, 55″ high, 28″ wide, 33″ deep. Collection of Mr. and Mrs. Victor W. Ganz, New York.

written large and out of context. The new landscape and still life of Pop replace the Traditional; they offer a view of a world in which we are surrounded by garish artifice that only too clearly reflects ourselves.

The new universe of shapes and colors produced by mass culture and its visual explosion supplied Pop Art with its material—its new fact. But, as Rauschenberg shows us (FIG. 22-88), instant fact can be made fantasy simply by shattering factual contexts and realigning and regrouping the elements that compose conventional aggregates of facts. The effect of this process is to surprise and to defeat expectation—the old Dada aim to shake up (*épater*) the observer. The sympathetic neutrality of the Pop attitude toward mass culture could, under the impact of this mischievous Dada impulse, very quickly yield to mockery of that culture through fantastic exaggeration and paradox. This is the case in the art of CLAES OLDENBURG (b. 1929), in which, once more, the example of the good-humoredly cynical Duchamp seems to be influential. Oldenburg's *Soft Toilet* (FIG. 22-91) gives us a shock by knocking our perceptions (categories) of "hard" and "soft" sharply together and confusing our responses. What is conventionally hard, rigid, and prophylactic is shown as soft, sagging, and positively unsanitary. The artist makes fun of our modern dependence on our prized household appliances, which, for the masses, can be the ultimate expressions of civilized living.

The flat, severe planes and hard edges of much modern design find satirical reversal in Pop forms that are soft or that simulate softness. An early example of this whimsical opposition of soft to hard appears, in spirit, in Salvador Dali's reply to Le Corbusier's query concerning how Dali envisioned the architect's future buildings: "soft and hairy." EDWARD KIENHOLZ (b. 1927) uses soft and unresist-

ant materials of almost every kind, made or found, to produce his realistic–fantastic tableaux—three-dimensional constructs that combine theater (stage sets), sculpture, architecture, furniture, and mannequins and recall the grotesquerie of Surrealism while mirroring the tawdry aspects of modern life. His *Birthday* (FIG. 22-92) depicts a hospital maternity room with draped patient and hospital accessories. The pangs of childbirth are represented as great, transparent, plastic arrows rising and branching out from the patient's body. Hard reality and eerie fantasy mingle in this emphatic restatement of the Pop absorption in the forms and events of the mass scene.

The world of fancy that hovers above Pop Art seems to win a place of its own in what has been called Psychedelic Art, presumably because it approximates the visions produced by "mind-expanding" drugs. Its formal roots are in Art Nouveau, Odilon Redon, Kandinsky, Klee, and others of the extremely subjective Expressionist camp. Although worldwide in extent, Psychedelic Art has belonged mostly to the American Pop scene since the late 1960s. Its primary media are the poster and the underground comic strip—the area of Pop already explored by the young. Seemingly a contradiction of Pop factualism, Psychedelic Art presents simply another kind of fact—induced by the drugs that widely circulate among the youthful consumers of Pop Art and culture.

In the study of the art of the twentieth century, we become used to the shock of stylistic contrast. We

22-92 EDWARD KIENHOLZ, *Birthday*, 1964. Tableau, approx. 7' high, 10' wide, 15' deep. The Frederick and Marcia Weismann Foundation.

find yet another contrast in works of the Pop-born school of New Realism or Photo Realism. In *Nedick's* (FIG. 22-93), RICHARD ESTES (b. 1936) gives us the portrait of a familiar, fast-food restaurant and fountain with all the glassy fidelity of a photograph taken through a pristine, plate-glass window with the latest refinement in cameras. We have already seen (FIG. 22-87) the importance of the camera in supplying Pop Art with unlimited images for collages made of fragments taken out of their visual contexts. But here all the images are back in context, pulled together by the habit of a long tradition of Realism and brought into sharp focus by the camera in a single scene in an infinitesimal interval of time. The last gives a peculiar stillness to the picture, arresting all action and concentrating the viewer's attention on the wide range of "information" given. By projecting a photograph onto a canvas and then painting over it, as if it were a cartoon (in the traditional sense of a full-sized, preparatory drawing), the artist uses the camera as a

22-93 RICHARD ESTES, *Nedick's*, 1969–1970. Oil, 48" × 66". Collection of Mrs. Donald Pritzker.

means to the picture—not the photograph as an end in itself. Yet the photograph from which the artist renders is his new "nature," replacing both the natural and artificial environments that traditional Realism draws on or that Pop exhibits without transformation.

Two terms that have come into currency latterly—Process Art and Conceptual Art—seem to be the product of a search for some unifying agent among the widely diverging trends of Post-Pop Art. In a literal sense, the Process artist claims that the act of making an object is more important than the eventual product. If such is the case, the product will have meaning primarily to the artist and to those participating in the "process." This attitude is similar to that of the "action painters" of the Abstract Expressionist movement. In Conceptual Art, in which this notion is seemingly carried one step further, the artistic concept—the creative thought—is more important than either the process or the product. Although based on different premises, Process Art and Conceptual Art tend to differ little in actual practice.

The aim of both Process and Conceptual artists is to eliminate the isolated art object or product as such and to arrange "environments" composed of both objects and audiences. The process of creation and the concepts directing it thereby become superior to any made form. The audience is introduced into a setting that is automated, sometimes in such a way that the audience itself becomes an element of the circuitry—functioning, via "feedback," like a component of some modern electronic system. Objects and audience are the shifting foci of relationships of interdependent events: process is reality, and reality is process—as some modern physicists understand the way of things.* Light, sound, color, and automata (among numerous devices), and materials adapted from industrial technology all function together to saturate audiences with intensified and continually varying sensory experiences. Or, latterly, environments are constructed to reduce sense stimuli and produce an effect of soundless isolation. This extreme "systemic" art supplies "information" that directs audience response, creating a programed situation much like that experienced by astronauts in their spacecraft or, for that matter, by anyone operating a machine (as the latter, if it is not totally automated, compels responses from the former). As receptors of the informational output, audience members need not deal with the images and appearances that stay to be evaluated; they need only react to them. This means that the artist is a node in such a network of

*Cf. the fundamental work of the philosopher Alfred North Whitehead, *Process and Reality*.

22-94 CHRISTO, *Running Fence*, 1976. Steel posts and nylon sheeting, approx. 20' high, 24 miles long. Petaluma, California (now dismantled).

informational relationships, rather than an isolated system. In the transactions between himself and the environment—which includes the audience—the artist becomes part of an unlimited, ceaselessly varying process.

The idea and the event engaged in the creative act, along with the recording of them, are the preoccupation of Christo Javacheff, called CHRISTO (b. 1935). Like the Earth artists (in some respects, he can be considered one) Christo is attracted to the natural environment as a medium. He has, among other projects, wrapped over 1,000,000 square feet of Australian coast in plastic and curtained a canyon at Rifle Gap, Colorado. In 1976, Christo constructed *Running Fence* (FIG. 22-94) across the California hills north of Petaluma to the Pacific Coast. Made of nylon panels (some 20 feet high) fastened to 2,050 steel poles, the fence was 24 miles long; until it was dismantled (it stood two weeks), it was the largest work created by an artist. Christo's objective was the harmonious relation of art and nature. The architecture of the piece articulated—rather than destroyed—the rhythms of the landscape in precisely effected perspectives; their fluid sequences, with fortuitous foreshortenings, made the interplay of the shapes of the hills readable.

The innovative character of the work lay not so much in its esthetic inventiveness and audacious scale as in the wide employment of a variety of hands, resources, decisions, and media that made the process of realization even more of a social than an artistic enterprise. During two years of preparation, permissions had to be gained, court decisions sought, workers assembled, and over $2 million raised (largely through the sale of preliminary drawings by Christo, an excellent draftsman and graphic artist). Of greater significance than the finished product was the fact that two years of preparation and six months of actual work were required for a project that stood for only 14 days! During its limited existence, however, it became the focus of the public media's power to publicize and promote. Innumerable photographs, two movies, three books, a documentary exhibition, reproductions, and postcards—all guaranteeing the familiarity and the permanency of *Running Fence*—it has become perhaps the widest known monument of contemporary art, and pieces of it have been contracted for and sold widely. Here again, the record of an artistic concept and process preserves and validates it in a mode of existence and identity other than its own.

In retrospect, we can note a process in modern art in which the role of the artist is undergoing permutation, as are the once-understood media of painting and sculpture. The artist may now be painter, printmaker, or sculptor; the artist can also be prophet, seer, entrepreneur, producer, performer, entertainer, photographer, filmmaker, ceramist, glassblower, electrician. In schools, colleges, and exhibitions, the title "artist" includes all of these activities and many others; the forms of modern design they share draw them closely together. It may be that we see here the withering away of the special status given by the Renaissance to the "fine arts" and a return to the craft collectivization and, ultimately, to the anonymity of the Middle Ages, or the anonymity of the industrial designer in the modern world.

The media are similarly permuted. The materials of sculpture range from traditional marble and bronze through plastics and nylon to junk. Forms are carved, cast, welded, wired, sewn, glued, painted, and lighted. They are pierced with space, reduced to filaments, set in motion by air currents or electrical means. The framed picture loses its illusionistic picture-perspective space and becomes a painted, two-dimensional object. The frame itself is discarded, the wall takes its place, and, eventually, the gallery or the spaces of physical nature become the setting for the object. The relation of the artist to the viewer through the object becomes problematic, as does the status of the object within the space it occupies with the viewer. Finally, focus moves from the object to the process of its production and to the idea of the object

as conceived, described, recorded. The making of the object, an incomplete and temporary process, is followed by its elimination and by the elimination of the artist as the determiner of its effect on audience or environment. The physical media are replaced by act, performance, and then, by the record of these. Like vapor trails, the arts leave an ephemeral trace.

The art of the twentieth century (commencing in the 1880s!) can perhaps be understood as simultaneously the brilliant debris of a great tradition and an aggregate of elements for new languages of design, in dependence on or rejection of the machine forms of an industrialized world.

Post-Modernism—The Art of the 1970s and 1980s

At present, in some quarters, the art we have been describing as "Modern" is being renamed "Modernist," and its ideology, the set of ideas by which it explains itself, is now called Modernism. This indicates an important shift of historical and critical points of view. The complex of "Modernist" styles originating at the end of the nineteenth century is beginning to be identified as a distinct period; its art-historical development seems to be reaching a conclusion or, at least, a bewildered pause—perhaps a transition to something new. Modernist art and ideology are being revised and reacted against. The revision and reaction go by the name Post-Modernism.

In the previous sections of this chapter, we have sorted out the Modernist styles and traced their development; in passing, we have touched on some of the ideas behind them. In simple summation, the most important axioms of Modernism will be examined here.

Modern art is the consequence of a successful and continuing revolution led by an *avant-garde* of artists and critics who overthrew the Tradition that began in the Renaissance and exhausted itself in the nineteenth century. Their formal method is *abstraction*, by which images referring to objects in the world of sight are progressively distorted or eliminated, leaving the particular painting or sculpture to refer only to itself as a unique thing. The mission and triumph of the *avant-garde* is the "liberation" of the pictorial and sculptural object from any obligation to mean something other than itself. This liberation of the plastic media from all but self-reference makes for a "purification" of visual art, which had been corrupted by its bondage to subject matter drawn from myth, religion, history, literature. The only "truth" for art is to be found not in something extraneous to it, like the forms of nature, but in its own materials, techniques, and forms. All reference otherwise is a lie; the truth of the object is simply *that*, and *what*, it is. The main avenue, up which the *avant-garde* march forever, is abstraction. The truly modern styles all branch from abstraction; all others run counter to it in anachronistic, retrograde reaction. Abstract art and its relatives constitute the only authentic art for our times; this art is always revolutionary and progressive—in a word, "modern." In the search for truth of statement, the Modern artist strives for the ever-more abstractive reduction of the art object, until nothing is left but its minimal elements and the *process* of composing them.

This Modernist ideology, hardened into inflexible doctrine, has exercised considerable control over both artistic procedure and critical judgment. (We are reminded of the influence of the French Royal Academy in the time of Louis XIV; see Chapter 19.) Against this Modernism, Post-Modernism now seems to be in uncertain revolt.

The value and method of abstraction are still acknowledged, even as its absolute claims are being rejected; indeed, it seems still dominant at the very moment it is being sharply challenged. For the referential, mediating function of art—its age-old purpose—is being appealed to once again. The importance of content and meaning is being reaffirmed, and traditional subject matter is being reintroduced: report of optical fact, the human figure, the human environment, narrative, social commentary, imaginative transformation of the commonplace. Increasingly, the world of the photograph is yielding vast quantities of materials for the expression and representation of human experience. One thing is certain; artists, searching in all directions for fresh inspiration, feel that abstraction has reached its limit of invention, that it is a dead end, and that they wish to escape from a stern and doctrinaire formalism that

has narrowed into academic precept. But thus far, the revisionism is incoherent; it has no central theme, no certain direction.

Meanwhile, the play of the art market, with its urgent demands for novelty, stimulates the feverish exploration for innovation at any cost and the rapid turnover of fads and fashions—adding to the confusion of the scene. Old paths are being sought out once more, and old modes are being restored with superficial changes. We find Neo-Primitivism, Neo-Symbolism, Neo-Abstract Expressionism, Neo-Formalism, Neo-Social Realism, even Neo-Impressionism—and hybrids of all of them. Side-by-side with these persist elements of Pop, Op, Minimalism, Conceptualism, Photo Realism, and the like.

It is difficult for us to find a way through what, at present, seems to be both the recapitulation and the deconstruction of Modernism to locate firm evidence of an emerging style that could replace it. Nevertheless, some description can be made of the present situation by pointing to a small selection of artists whose work is Post-Modern by date, if by no agreed-on definition. Many characteristics of art after 1945 remain in evidence: the pieces are very large; the broad, monochrome areas of Color-Field painting persist; the pictorial and sculptural media are combined; "installations" continue to be popular; experiment with both Formalistic and Expressionistic modes goes on.

Julian Schnabel (b. 1951) who disclaims that he is Post-Modernist, makes a powerful restatement of Expressionism, experimenting widely with materials and supports—from broken plates bonded to wood to paint on velvet. *The Walk Home* (FIG. 22-95) is a vast

22-95 Julian Schnabel, *The Walk Home*, 1984–1985. Oil, plates, copper, bronze, fiberglass, and bondo on wood, 9′ 3″ × 19′ 4″. Collection of Aaron Katz.

22-96 LEON GOLUB, *Mercenaries (IV)*, 1980. Oil on canvas, figures life-size. Susan Caldwell Gallery/Barbara Gladstone Gallery.

mosaic of broken crockery, painted and glued to a wooden support. Its origin in the Abstract Expressionism of the New York School is clear, recalling the stippling of Jackson Pollock (FIG. 22-70) and the black slashes of Franz Kline (FIG. 22-71). But the artist amalgamates these techniques in a new and distinctive medium of his own—glazed, tesselated relief. In effect, Schnabel reclaims the great tradition of Medieval mosaic.

The abstractions of Schnabel contrast with works that reaffirm the referential and mediating importance of the human figure in art. The figures in the paintings of LEON GOLUB (b. 1923), usually well over life-size, fiercely express the brutalities of our time—its street violence, terrorism, torture, death squads. In *Mercenaries (IV)* (FIG. 22-96), one of a series on this theme, Golub presents an unforgettable gathering of soldiers of fortune—tough, merciless men who kill for pay and seem here to have just come back from a

mission. In stark relief from the flat ground of monochromatic red, the figures project from a kind of Color-Field painting charged with meaning; it is the color of fire and blood, crime and cruelty. Gnarled, wrinkled, and sweaty, their miscellaneous field garb clings to their hard bodies. Their weapons, bright and ready, are modeled in full tone and contrast with the harshly scraped, flattened surfaces of the bodies. The viewer, part of the space they occupy, cannot help but feel their menacing presence. Here and in his other works, Golub has reference to the news photograph and greatly augments the shock of its often atrocious report.

Drawing fully on the resources of photography, especially as it is found in newspapers and magazines, MARK TANSEY (b. 1949) makes oil paintings that comment wryly and wittily on the contemporary world. His method is to bring persons, things, times, places, and events that are not usually—if ever—

22-97 MARK TANSEY, *Triumph of the New York School*, 1984. Oil on canvas, 6′ 2″ × 10′. Grace Borgenicht Gallery, New York.

associated into new and surprising conjunctions and to render them in fully pictorial tonalities reminiscent of on-the-spot news photography. He prefers monochromatic sepias and gray–greens, recalling the color of old rotogravure pictures printed decades ago in Sunday newspaper supplements. Disparates, incongruities, and contradictories invite the viewer to search out the artist's meaning, to solve the iconographic problems he deliberately sets up. Tansey makes frequent references and allusions to the history of art, one of which, *Triumph of the New York School* (FIG. 22-97), takes for its subject the historical shift of the artistic fulcrum from Paris to New York after 1945. The event is dramatized as a surrender of the French army, clad in the uniforms of World War I on the left, to the American army, in the garb and with the motorized armor of World War II on the right. This, of course, is an event that never happened and, given the pictured circumstances, that could never have happened in this way. We are confronted with a large group portrait of artists and critics, all identifiable. Among the French are Pablo Picasso, Henri Matisse, Guillaume Apollinaire, and André Breton; among the Americans, Clement Greenberg, Jackson Pollock, Robert Motherwell, Harold Rosenberg, and others associated with the New York School. The trig elegance of the French and the firm ground they stand on are metaphors for Abstract Formalism; the slouchiness of the GIs and the puddles beneath their feet stand for the "drip" and "spatter" techniques of "action painting." The surrender theme—with the central officers, the balancing armies, the smoking landscape and the lancers—alludes to Velázquez's great painting *The Surrender of Breda* ("The Lances"), but the allusion is checked by the anachronistic uniforms and the modern armor. The kneeling news photographer signalizes the paradoxicality of the message: this is a veritable photograph of nothing that in fact happened, but the shift of focus of the art world from Paris to New York *did* happen.

Without the domination and push of *avant-garde* abstractionism, artists in the 1970s and 1980s have felt free to wander through and to take second looks at the art-historical past—borrowing, where they are interested, or working old mines for new ores. *Deep Pool* (FIG. 22-98) by NEIL WELLIVER (b. 1929) recalls certain traits of Impressionism—for example, the early water studies of Monet and the rugged rocks in landscapes by Gustave Courbet—but they have been rethought and reinforced by close attention to the optical facts. Welliver's patient analysis and firm technical command recover in a new synthesis features of later nineteenth-century landscape painting, as it passes from Realism to Impressionism.

22-98 NEIL WELLIVER, *Deep Pool*, 1983. Oil on canvas, 8' × 8'. The Collection of Exxon Corporation.

Young European artists from France, Germany, Italy, and Britain, like their American contemporaries, are producing abundantly in a great variety of styles and substyles—and, like the Americans, they aim at the New York galleries, but not exclusively. In the Soviet Union, painting is dominated by a rather heavy-handed kind of Social Realism, which is only occasionally softened by the influence of Western modes. Under the watchful supervision of the authorities, subject matter continues to be an advertisement of the heroism of the Soviet worker. But despite such strictures, a few artists are able to create works that are impressive by any standard of criticism. In one such work, *Construction Workers* (FIG. 22-99) by BORIS MALUEV (b. 1929), the principal figure is an epic hero of labor, fashioned in steel, his towering frame interlocked with the girders he commands. Man and girders almost fuse in a heavy framework of dark, vertical shapes, which, with abstraction of detail, could reduce to a Formalist—even Constructivist—expression of the attributes of brute power.

Ambiguities, conundrums, stretched metaphors, paradoxes, puns, and puzzlements are all part of the ideational equipment of artists working in three dimensions, as well as in two. Viewers of three-dimensional art are also put off-balance and forced to find their own equilibrium. More and more, they are required to complete the meaning of the pieces that

22-99 BORIS MALUEV, *Construction Workers*, 1975. Oil on canvas, approx. 5' 2" × 6' 6". Union of Artists of the USSR.

confront them and to come to terms with the viewing predicament. The esthetic experience—once thought restfully contemplative—now entails surprise and perplexity, requiring the viewer to figure out riddles and to get the point of jokes (when there is a point). There are no rules of interpretation; the viewer is meant to feel uneasy and to be left dangling, or at sea.

Claes Oldenburg, whom we have seen as a leader in the Pop movement (FIG. 22-91), lifts his utilitarian motifs to the giant scale characteristic of much Minimal sculpture. His colossal *Clothespin* (FIG. 22-100) dominates a city square in Philadelphia, as if it were a pedestaled obelisk in a Roman piazza (FIG. 19-4) or in the Place de la Concorde in Paris. The insignificant, domestic utensil takes on the proportions of a civic monument, mocking the pretentious, official architecture that is now merely a foil for it. It is as if Bach were to write an oratorio in honor of a square nail. The incongruity of scale and significance of Oldenburg's *Clothespin* is matched by incongruity of another sort in *Brick Knot* (FIG. 22-101) by WENDY TAYLOR (b. 1945) a British sculptor. The mixed-media construction appears to be a heavy brick pier tied in a knot. The factually impossible is made visibly "real"— we should almost say "sur-real." The impact of the piece derives from our visual association of the contraries "hard" and "soft," "brick" and "rope." The simplicity of form and the large scale are of the Minimal sort, but the imitation of the texture of brick and the referential joke give a quite independent twist to that approach.

A popular and prevalent type of construction, the gallery "installation," brings into a single composition gallery walls, gallery spaces, light, color, form, and illusion, in an endless variety of materials and

shapes; or—at the other extreme—creates neutral blankness of unencumbered space. The installation is impermanent and meant to be dismantled; like

22-100 CLAES OLDENBURG, *Clothespin*, 1976. Steel, 45' high, 18 tons. Centre Square, Philadelphia, Pennsylvania.

22-101 WENDY TAYLOR, *Brick Knot*, 1978. Mixed media, 7' high, 11' 9" wide, 7' 7" deep.

booths after a carnival, it is taken down, but is not likely to be set up again in another place. In this respect, the installation is like Christo's *Running Fence* (FIG. 22-94)—an evanescent phenomenon deliberately created for the moment and sacrificed to time, the only record of it being the photographs made of it. The exuberant clutter of the installation *Rock/Paper/Scissors* (FIG. 22-102) by JUDY PFAFF (b. 1946) suggests the sights and sounds of a New Year's Eve or of a giant kaleidoscope wired for sound. The "subject," of course, is the variety and impact of the materials, shapes, and colors.

22-102 JUDY PFAFF, *Rock/Paper/Scissors*, September 24, 1982–January 9, 1983. Installation. Albright-Knox Art Gallery, Buffalo.

Most of the art we have studied in this book was produced, we may believe, with the intention that it would last. The installation is not expected to last and is not intended to last. In this respect, an installation is analagous to the commodities of industrial manufacture; in the end, all are disposable. Judd—in calling for the permanent installation of his own works, which are not "installations" (FIG. 22-82), and those of masters like Rothko, Kline, De Kooning, Pollock, and Newman—seems to sense that the *avant-garde* period (1945–1975) has ended and to believe that the public should be given the opportunity to view the art of that period in appropriate and lasting settings. The implication can be drawn that the *impermanent* installation, of the kind we have described, marks the end of an era—and is, in any case, perishable and inconsequent.

As the traditional boundaries of the media of painting and sculpture are being erased and as artists work more and more in "multi-media," objects are being produced out of whatever materials suit the artist's esthetic and expressive purposes. At the same time, science and technology are providing new materials and techniques that may or may not be thought of as "art" (unless we wish to define "art" as "what artists do") and that may or may not be the media of the future. We have video art, reporting on magnetic tape a continuum of images that can be instantly combined, recombined, and replayed in an infinite variety of ways; computer-generated art, programing abstract or figural shapes and colors to appear on a display terminal, as on a television screen; light "sculpture" and projection and reflection, having a purity and intensity comparable to laser beams; and holograms, producing perfect illusions of objects in three dimensions, so that they can be "walked around." We can only speculate whether these essentially impermanent media, and others like them, will displace once and for all the more permanent media of painting and sculpture, which, with architecture, have been the subjects of this book.

Much of contemporary art may seem ephemeral and made for the day, but the scientific *conservation* of historical art is being swiftly advanced and is contributing greatly to art-historical knowledge. Since the 1960s, highly refined techniques adapted from industrial, nuclear, space, and medical science, luminescent dating, infrared spectroscopy, infrared reflectography, to name some—represent vast improvements over the older X-ray methods formerly used to get at the physical facts of a work of art. They probe beneath picture surfaces, make cross sections of pigments, detect underpainting and underdrawing, and recover signatures and inscriptions. At the same time, computer science is revolutionizing our methods of the storage and retrieval of art-historical information, making it accessible to research scholarship as never before. Computers organize collections of museums, libraries, slide and photographic archives, and catalogs of shows, sales, and auctions; they index iconographic themes and provenances, as well as compose lexicons and thesauri of artists, artworks, and art terminology. In a new collaboration of scientist and scholar, the full resources of "high-technology" are being placed at the service of conservation and of the history of art. If developments and trends of artistic activity presently seem to be in disarray, our historical knowledge of art is permitting us to discover more secure methods of procedure and ever-more-reliable tests of the data they yield.

ARCHITECTURE AFTER WORLD WAR II

The first 25 years after World War II saw the rapid spread of the International style over the Western world. While Mies van der Rohe was still refining his style, the building type pioneered by him and other members of the CIAM (Congrès Internationale d' Architecture Moderne, founded in 1928) began to dominate the skylines of most major Western cities. Appealing in its structural logic and clarity, the style, although often vulgarized, was easily emulated and quickly became the norm for postwar, commercial, high-rise buildings. We have seen a 1958 example of the type in the Seagram Building of New York (FIG. 22-67).

As early as 1949, Mies van der Rohe demonstrated the flexibility of his style by applying it to domestic architecture. The Lakeshore Drive Apartments (FIG. 22-103) are two of several high-rise apartments which he built along the Chicago waterfront. Some 250 apartments are suspended within the steel frames of the two towers, which are placed and oriented so that a majority of tenants have a view of Lake Michigan. In their appearance—quite similar to the Seagram Building and based on the same structural principles—these apartment blocks seem to bring to full realization Le Corbusier's concept of dwellings as "machines for living." They also prove that the design principles of the International style can be applied equally to commercial and domestic building.

While Mies van der Rohe was bringing his translucent style to ultimate refinement, Le Corbusier was moving in another direction—toward more sculptural, architectural forms. In answer to one of the most insistent contemporary needs—a functional design for urban living—he designed the Unité d' Habitation in Marseilles (FIG. 22-104). Mighty piers (so different from the slender stilts of the Villa Savoye, shown in FIG. 22-61) support the framework

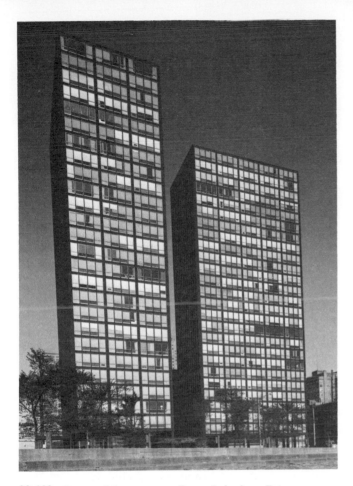

22-103 LUDWIG MIES VAN DER ROHE, Lakeshore Drive Apartments, Chicago, Illinois, 1949–1951.

22-104 LE CORBUSIER, Unité d'Habitation, Marseilles, France, 1946–1952.

that contains 337 apartments of 23 different types. Most of them are two-storied and extend through the entire width of the building, permitting cross ventilation and admitting light from two sides. The apartments are designed as integral, self-contained units that offer maximum privacy, or, as Le Corbusier describes it, "give freedom to the individual within a collective organization," as demanded by our civilization. Recessed porches, each with a sunbreak, are hollowed out of the massive block, so that the building exists neither as a skeletal frame enclosed by a membrane nor as a solid mass. Solids and voids are carefully balanced, as in Greek temples, which, to Le Corbusier, sounded "clear and tragic, like brazen trumpets." Every effort has been made to provide residents with all of the conveniences and some of the luxuries of modern life: the seventh and ninth floors of the 17-story structure contain shopping malls, hotel rooms, restaurants, drug stores, and a post office; the roof has been converted into a park, complete with swimming pool and gymnasium. In short, all of the demands of an entire subdivision of small townhouses are met within a single building block. All of this seems somewhat removed from the rather spartan concept of the "machine for living" advocated by Le Corbusier in the 1920s.

The startling forms of Le Corbusier's Notre Dame du Haut (FIG. 22-105) built at Ronchamp, France, in 1955, challenge us in their fusion of architecture and sculpture in a single expression. Here, in Le Corbusier's own terms, is a "vessel" on a "high place," intended to respond to a "psychology–physiology of the senses" and to "a reverberating landscape, holding the four horizons as witness." (Could the architect have been thinking of the first temple after man's first cataclysm—the ark of Noah stranded on Mount Ararat by the receding waters of the Flood? It is noteworthy that we speculate, as with a work of figurative art, on the architect's possible meaning.) In these powerful, surging masses, these sculptural solids and voids, is a new environment in which man may find new values—new interpretations of his sacred beliefs and of his natural environment. The interior of Notre Dame du Haut (FIG. 22-106) is illuminated fitfully and mysteriously by deeply recessed windows, placed almost randomly. The absence of ornament reminds us not so much of Internationalist purism as of the chaste severity of the Cistercian architecture of the twelfth century. Ronchamp is a unique work that could not possibly find membership in a movement. The extremely personal touch is that of a sculptor who has made a unique masterwork.

22-105   *Left:* LE CORBUSIER, Notre Dame du Haut, Ronchamp, France, 1950–1955.

22-106   *Above:* LE CORBUSIER, interior of Notre Dame du Haut.

The long, incredibly productive career of Frank Lloyd Wright, meanwhile, ends with a testament to art itself—the Guggenheim Museum (FIGS. 22-107 and 22-108), built in New York between 1943 and 1959. The principle of dynamic continuity that guided Wright through his life is triumphantly stated here. The immense structure is boldly composed essentially as a cylinder expanding with height, its floors expressed on the exterior as a spiraling strip of skylight, in levels marked by shadow by day and by light at night. The cantilevered decks of Wright's Kaufmann House (FIG. 22-62) are here drawn around an immense circle, determined by the function of circulation. Visitors are brought by elevator to the top of the building and walk down the gently inclined spiral ramp, viewing the pictures displayed on its outer wall. The bold, monumental design, the assertion of a powerful personality, merges space and void without remainder and, despite its overwhelming strength, subtly sets off the pictures on exhibition. Wright's humanism directs him here, as ever, to serve human needs. In this case, one of the highest experiences given to modern urbanites—delighting in the works of their gifted fellows—is facilitated and honored in a building that itself must be regarded as an enduring contribution. Yet here, Wright—the great Jeffersonian, agrarian democrat—seems to turn his back on the city. The rounded, closed form, like a visitor from outer space, is entirely at odds with the rectilinear urban pattern and fabric. The building

22-107   FRANK LLOYD WRIGHT, Solomon R. Guggenheim Museum, New York, 1943–1959 (exterior view from the north).

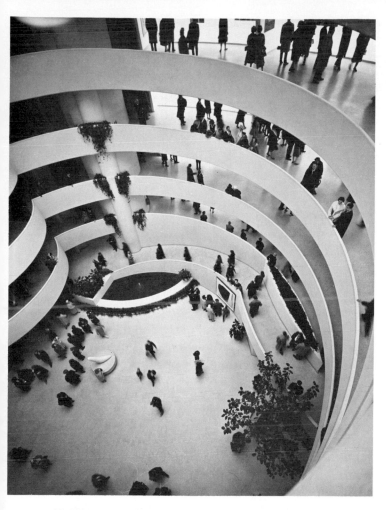

22-108 FRANK LLOYD WRIGHT, interior of the Solomon R. Guggenheim Museum (view from the dome).

turns in on itself, the long gallery area opening onto a 90-foot well of space that seems to provide an environment secure from the hostile city.

The later works of Le Corbusier and Wright illustrate the postwar movement away from the Formalistic rigidity of the International style, with its insistence on a purely rectilinear frame of reference. At the same time, new developments in building technology

increasingly became a part of the expressive vocabulary of the Modern movement. The engineer PIER LUIGI NERVI (1891–1978), using the remarkable tensile strength of prestressed concrete, covers huge spaces with designs that offer dazzling geometric beauty as well as great economy of materials. His method and material make it possible to omit the steel columns of the International style—as in the Palazzetto dello Sport in Rome (FIG. 22-109), built in 1958—and his vast roofs seem to soar daringly with a grace and crispness of detail that leave severe rectilinearity behind and bring a new vision of architectural form, an organic rather than a mechanical one. Yet, despite his more personal statement, Nervi shows keen interest and insight concerning one of the ongoing themes of modern architectural theory: the rational expression of structural elements. With the grace and surety of a Gothic flying buttress (FIGS. 10-10 and 10-19), Nervi's structural members make the force lines of the building visible and carry, with a technical elegance, the lateral thrust of the vault to the ground.

Only four years later, EERO SAARINEN (1910–1961) exploits the malleable nature of concrete to its very limits. We are reminded of the ancient Roman architects who built Nero's Domus Aurea (FIG. 6-50) and the Pantheon (FIG. 6-51) some 1900 years ago and who, without structural steel and with concrete of greatly inferior quality, had similar aspirations. In his design for the Trans World Airlines Terminal at John F. Kennedy International Airport in New York (FIGS. 22-110 and 22-111), Saarinen covers the functional nucleus of the huge layout with four doubly curved concrete shells that rest on massive Y-shaped piers. Two concrete tubes, each 328 feet long, channel the passengers from the check-in counters to the waiting rooms and the finger-docks, through which they board the planes. Even if the layout does not present the final solution, it provides a satisfactory answer to

22-109 PIER LUIGI NERVI, Palazzetto dello Sport, Rome, 1958.

22-110 EERO SAARINEN, Trans World Airlines Terminal, John F. Kennedy International Airport, New York, 1956–1962.

22-111 EERO SAARINEN, interior of the Trans World Airlines Terminal, John F. Kennedy International Airport.

the complex problems of sheltering large crowds of people and of moving them in time-coordinated flows to and from multiple flight departures and arrivals. But Saarinen goes beyond the purely logistical problems, which might well have been solved with the by-now-traditional rectilinear and cubical forms of the International style. Like a sculptor working with steel and concrete on a monumental scale, the architect creates a huge, three-dimensional symbol that stands for "Flight." From a distance, the rooflines of the structure resemble the outstretched wings of a soaring bird. Like arteries, arched bridges transect the building's interior space and echo the forms of plan and ceiling. In sum, Saarinen's forms combine to create the impression of a living organism and they realize to perfection his stated aim—to express the excitement of air travel.

Our summary of trends in modern architecture, of necessity, stresses the contributions of those architects who, in our foreshortened historical perspective, appear to be pioneers in the creation of an archi-

tecture free of reference to earlier architectural styles. It seems certain that Wright, Mies van der Rohe, and Le Corbusier will be recognized by future generations; their work continues to inspire younger architects even as they experiment to expand the horizons of both building form and building technology. The rapid development and exploitation of new engineering possibilities can be seen in a comparison of Nervi's Olympic Palazzetto (FIG. 22-109) with the buildings constructed in Munich by FREI OTTO (b. 1925) for the 1972 Olympic Games (FIG. 22-112). Nervi's structure, light and graceful as it is, seems massive and dense next to Otto's airy, transparent, tent-like enclosures. Part of the difference is due to Otto's revolutionary approach to structure; Nervi, for all his experiments with prestressed concrete, still conceives of structure in traditional terms of *compression*—the principle that underlies all architecture studied in this history, from the Egyptians onward. Otto, on the other hand, exploits the tensile strength of steel to create a structural system based on *tension*, the same engineering principle that permits the construction of the light-appearing but remarkably strong free spans of suspension bridges. No less up-to-date is Otto's selection of a kind of gossamer plastic membrane to sheathe the building—a sheathing that provides shelter without confinement, just as his radical struc-

22-112 FREI OTTO, model for the roof of the Olympic Stadium, Munich, West Germany, 1971–1972.

tural system provides vast enclosures without the interruption of interior supports.

The soaring, graceful forms of Otto's giant tent may appear limited in their application to the solution of more common architectural problems; but just as the Crystal Palace (FIG. 21-86), believed to be a building of limited potential about a century and a half ago, proved to be the prototype of a dominant structural form of our time, so perhaps tension structures will revolutionize architectural concepts of the future. In any case, the same principles can be seen at work in an office building designed by GUNNAR BIRKERTS (b. 1925) in Minneapolis. His Federal Reserve Bank Building (FIG. 22-113) combines the tension of great cables strung in a catenary curve between massive end towers with more traditional compression members that support the stack of floors above the cables. The floors below the catenary are also carried by the cables, but this time in suspension. The result of this extremely complex system is a free-span structure of 330 feet between the supporting towers, which contain service facilities, elevators, fire stairs, and so forth. Le Corbusier's original idea of raising a building on slender columns (*pilotis*) to free the site for other uses is here carried a step further; Birkert's structure leaves an open, virtually unobstructed urban space of over 100,000 square feet, framed and articulated by the office block. The principal functional elements of the bank—the vaults and other high-security facilities—are tucked away beneath the huge ''piazza'' that becomes a gift to the city and a fine urban amenity.

The increasing urbanization of the world population, a byproduct of the Industrial Revolution, has brought into focus one of the critical building problems of our time—the provision of adequate housing for an ever-expanding urban population. With land

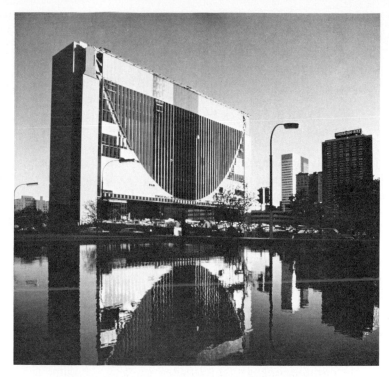

22-113   GUNNAR BIRKERTS, Federal Reserve Bank Building, Minneapolis, Minnesota, 1972–1973.

becoming more and more precious in cities, the single-family house is increasingly being considered an inefficient use of a dwindling resource, and architects have responded with a variety of proposals for mass housing. We have already examined Le Corbusier's contribution in his Marseilles apartment block (FIG. 22-104), with its clear attempt to return a sense of dignity to the urban dwelling by running each apartment the width of the building to approximate the characteristics of a free-standing house. This idea is carried a step further by the young Israeli architect MOSHE SAFDIE (b. 1938) in his Habitat (FIG. 22-114), a demonstration building constructed for Montreal's Expo '67. An experiment in the application of mass

22-114   MOSHE SAFDIE, Habitat, Montreal, Canada, 1967–1968.

production and complete prefabrication to the building industry, Habitat carries Le Corbusier's handling of each apartment as a hypothetically independent unit to its logical realization; here, each apartment is reduced to a single, box-like, precast concrete module made at a plant and trucked to the site. Like outsized children's building blocks, the units were then lifted into their appropriate slots in the matrix of the building by a huge crane. The heroic scale of the undertaking, with its implication of a kind of fully industrialized architecture, seems to fulfill the Crystal Palace's promise of prefabrication (FIG. 21-86). Visually, the building has a boldly sculptured look that appeals both to contemporary sensibilities and to the rational insistence on structural clarity while providing an appropriate setting for modern urban living.

In the later half of the century an ever-broadening public interest in art has fundamentally changed the concept of the museum. No longer the exclusive repository of artistic treasure—administered by curatorial experts and visited only by scholars, connoisseurs, and an educated minority of art lovers—the museum, whether the Guggenheim in New York (FIG. 22-107) or the "Beaubourg" in Paris (FIG. 22-117), invites and receives a general public numbering in the millions. Curatorial and exhibition functions have been expanded and widely diversified to include popular as well as scholarly study of the arts. The traditional halls and galleries are supplemented by libraries, lecture halls, study rooms, motion-picture theaters, and shops that sell audio-visual materials, slides, prints, postcards, reproductions, and imitations. Facilities aimed at enhancing the circulation, comfort, convenience, and even the amusement of

large crowds of visitors place art increasingly in a context of entertainment.

The museums of the nineteenth and earlier twentieth centuries are vast, converted palaces like the Louvre—buildings of palatial scale that overwhelm the artworks or obscure them in ill-lighted, crowded galleries or darkened halls laid out in monotonous, rectilinear plans. In the later twentieth century, the expansionary function that has transformed the museum into a great community center has presented contemporary architecture with one of its major challenges. In a variety of ways, modern architects are addressing the problem of combining the marginal services that encourage large public attendance with the still-primary function of exhibiting works of art effectively.

IEOH MING PEI (b. 1917), an American architect born in China, solves the problem with conspicuous success in his East Building of the National Gallery in Washington, D.C. (FIG. 22-115), for which he won the Gold Medal of the American Institute of Architects in 1978. In Pei's hands, the awkward building site becomes a virtue made from necessity, somewhat as the Campidoglio (FIG. 17-29) did in the hands of Michelangelo. The irregular, trapezoidal site had been set aside in 1937 for expansion of the main building—a handsome, domed, Neoclassical structure of the Jeffersonian type, built in 1941. Bisecting the trapezoid into a larger isosceles triangle and a smaller right triangle, Pei ingeniously maximized his use of the difficult site, producing an esthetically and functionally impressive aggregation of angular masses unified by a vast, faceted skylight 80 feet above a spacious courtyard six levels high. The larger triangle, with its dia-

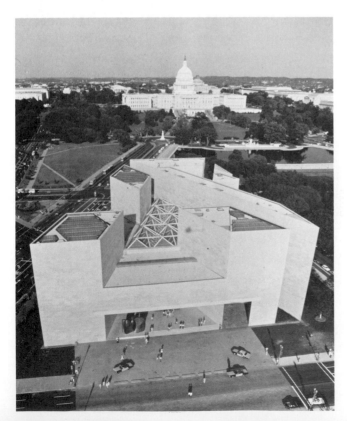

22-115 IEOH MING PEI, National Gallery Addition (East Building), Washington D.C., 1978. *Below:* IEOH MING PEI, site plan of the National Gallery Addition.

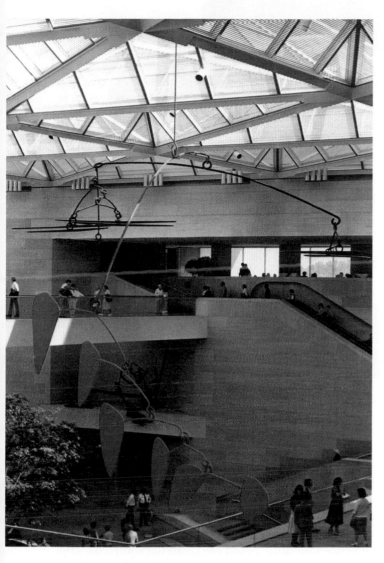

22-116 IOEH MING PEI, interior of the National Gallery Addition. (The mobile shown in the foreground is by ALEXANDER CALDER.)

mond-shaped towers, provides exhibition space; the smaller, with its dramatic wedge shape (the walls meet in a sharp 19° angle) provides space for art-historical research.

The East Building artfully compliments the West Building by aligning with its axis (it is connected with it by an underground, moving walkway) and by wearing a facing of the same pink Tennessee marble that adorns the older building. The centerpiece of a skillful urban composition, the East Building makes the most of the angularity of the site (especially the lines of convergence of the avenues and the great Mall), reflecting in its many contradictory planes and lesser axes the directional sweep and pattern of the adjacent traffic.

The interior (FIG. 22-116) is illuminated by a great skylight made up of glass tetrahedra, set in a complex tracery, that seem to change, multiply, and create

shapes as one moves. The experience of fluid space and transformation of form is intensified by the mobile by Alexander Calder that majestically commands the scene. Bridges, escalators, and stairways casually connect the central space with numerous irregularly shaped and randomly placed galleries of varying dimensions—"houses" diminutive and intimate enough to show very small pictures or ample enough to accommodate the largest canvases of the New York School.

Despite the rich variety of its forms, the whole structure is a marvel of coherence and order and a triumph of craftsmanship down to the least detail; the last is creditable to the donor, who stipulated that no expense be spared in bringing the building to perfection. This collaboration of patron and architect is reminiscent of that of the Medici or the artistic geniuses of the Renaissance. It is significant, moreover, that the building, itself a masterpiece, has been designed to house masterpieces and that it occupies a site continuous with monuments visited and revered by the public as national shrines. The National Gallery— completing the original, Classical design of Pierre Charles L' Enfant, the city planner of Washington, D.C.—has become an unforgettable part of this great ensemble.

In Paris, another new museum—the Georges Pompidou National Center of Art and Culture, known as the "Beaubourg" (FIG. 22-117), opened in 1977— recalls in many ways the spirit, intention, and structure of the Crystal Palace (FIG. 21-86) and of the Galerie des Machines of the Paris International Exhibition of 1889 (FIG. 21-87). This spirit of making the fruits of the arts and sciences accessible to as wide a public as possible is evident throughout the "Beaubourg." The anatomy of this six-level building designed by RICHARD ROGERS (b. 1933) and RENZO PIANO (b. 1937) is fully exposed. So is its "metabolism"—the actual movements and processes it produces, directs, and surrounds. Pipes, ducts, tubes, and corridors are coded in color according to function (red, for the movement of people; green, for water; blue, for air conditioning; yellow, for electricity)—much as in a sophisticated industrial plant. This total "archigraphic" revelation of the structural body is, at the same time, a self-revelation for the public, for the great crowds that flow through the building (some 4,000 visitors a day) can readily perceive its functions, including those that serve their own needs and interests. In addition to art galleries, the building houses a center for industrial design, a library (described as "the first truly open library in France"), science and music centers, conference rooms, research and archival facilities, projection rooms, rest areas, and a restaurant that looks down and through the building to sculptured terraces outside. The meaning and

22-117 RICHARD ROGERS and RENZO PIANO, Georges Pompidou National Center of Art and Culture (the "Beaubourg"), Paris, 1977.

function of the "Beaubourg" is stated simply in the words of a director of the museum, Pontus Hulten:

> If the hallowed, cult-like calm of the traditional museum has been lost, so much the better. . . . We are moving toward a society where art will play a great role, which is why this museum is open to disciplines that were once excluded by museums and which is why it is open to the largest possible public.*

Of course, the building is not without its critics. Detractors have called it a "cultural supermarket" and have pointed out that its exposed entrails require excessive maintenance to protect them from the elements.

Architecture of the last 25 years has shown a growing departure from the doctrines, forms, and practices of the International style; this phase has been called Post-Modern. A new freedom of conception has set in, expressing itself in an almost Baroque inventiveness and elaboration of design. For inspiration, architects range through all the resources provided by the history of architecture; or they may indulge in fanciful, even quixotic experiments in search of novel forms and significance, making use of an ever-richer technology of materials and methods of construction. Not least among their opportunities for inventiveness are those offered by new problems related to environment, energy, and the changing patterns of public and private life. It is little wonder

*Architectural Record (February 1978), p. 103.

that the bewildering diversity of design that has resulted makes identification of a dominant contemporary trend close to impossible. This diversity extends to architectural types. Buildings designed for similar functions can differ so widely in appearance that they seem to have little in common or to be suited for any number of not necessarily consistent uses. The museums we have considered are cases in point. The Guggenheim, the National Gallery Addition, and the "Beaubourg" are all markedly individualistic, unique, and anything but representative of a type.

A familiar architectural type that characterizes the International style in the cities of the world is the concrete, steel, and glass tower—the skyscraper reduced to a sheer, vertical grid. We have seen the perfection of the skyscraper type—a respected formula for more than 20 years—in the Seagram Building in New York (FIG. 22-67). Philip Johnson, who collaborated with Mies van der Rohe on that structure and who, for most of his career, has been close to the International style, has departed from the strictness of the "Miesian" scheme into geometric adventures similar to Pei's in the National Gallery Addition. Like many of his younger contemporaries, Johnson has moved away from the severity of the elementary, solid, geometric figures to much more complex ones. In the Pennzoil Place, in Houston, Texas, Johnson modifies and complicates the skyscraper type, greatly reducing its height and articulating its plan and elevation for dramatic effect (FIG. 22-118). In collaboration with

22 118 PHILIP JOHNSON, JOHN BURGEE, and Associates, Pennzoil Place, Houston, Texas, 1977.

John Burgee and associates, he has erected twin, trapezoidal, dark towers of steel and anodized aluminum, 36 stories high. Angled toward one another, and separated by a 10-foot slot of space, they appear as mirror images. Within the slot, repeating its angle, a glazed atrium rises eight stories from the street.

Johnson's departures belong to a general shifting of Post-Modern design and taste. Criticism of the International style reaches back into the 1940s, when the philosopher and architectural critic Ernst Bloch denounced "modernity" in architecture as "polished death offered as morning-glow," or as "chrome-covered misery." A somewhat less severe critic, architect ROBERT VENTURI (b. 1925), remarks "on the richness and ambiguity of modern experience." In *Complexity and Contradiction in Architecture*, published by the Museum of Modern Art in 1966, Venturi declares:

. . . architects can no longer afford to be intimidated by the puritanically moral language of orthodox

Modern architecture. . . . A valid architecture evokes many levels of meaning and combinations of focus; its space and its elements become readable and workable in several ways at once.

True to form, Venturi, a leader in the Post-Modern movement, has produced work that reflects his words. At Vail, Colorado, Venturi and associates built a four-story vacation lodge (FIG. 22-119), set into a steep slope that, in its elevation reverses the traditional distribution of functions. Here, the private rooms are on the two lower stories; the public rooms, on the two upper. The exterior of the building suggests the rustic mountain cabin, with the flavor of the chalet; Venturi declares it "romantic," in its evocation of a tower among trees. The massive, peaked roof—pulled tightly down—contrasts with the large, lunette-shaped dormers; the abrupt contrast of exterior with interior and the free proportions, asymmetries, and almost random placement of the features certainly avoid all formulas. In frank eclecticism, both outside and inside, borrowings are evident from sources widely separated in time and tone: Palladio, Art Nouveau, the "romantic" Internationalist Alvar Aalto, Le Corbusier. The material throughout is wood (cedar siding and shingles, oak stairs, maple counters), scrupulously handcrafted. The fourth floor dramatically caps the design, in all its "complexity and contradiction," with a vaulted parlor, luminous with outdoor light from the lunette dormers and the sheen of cedar (FIG. 22-120). The building is an expression of a self-conscious manner that deliberately looks away from the conventional wisdoms of the International style.

The multiple aspects of Post-Modern architecture, in all their diversity, share a common rejection of the machined and frigid monotony of the International style. In reaction to the straight-edged, antiseptic forms of the "Miesian" style, a fascination with curvilinear forms, both in plan and elevation, can be observed. The dome, the arch, and the vault are being resurrected—sometimes with whimsical and, occasionally, even humorous results, reminiscent of the Manneristic style of Giulio Romano's Palazzo del Tè (FIGS. 17-48 and 17-49). In Europe, a shift of focus can be discerned—away from a building's efficiency and toward a greater concern for the well-being of its occupants. Although only an undercurrent in architectural thought, the slogan "humanization of the workplace" is gaining currency. Here and there, the science-fiction settings of glass-encased, high-rise office silos are being replaced with three- and four-story buildings, grouped around landscaped courts, to provide workers with a home-like atmosphere in which they can feel like inhabitants rather than robots. The self-glorification of financial and industrial

22-119 ROBERT VENTURI and Associates, Brant–Johnson house, Vail, Colorado, 1977.

22-120 ROBERT VENTURI and Associates, interior of the Brant–Johnson house.

giants, with their ever-higher and more daring skyscrapers, may one day come to an end. At present, however, elephantine high-rises are still sprouting from urban centers, and the revolution of office planning lies in the future.

The great shift in architectural style is accompanied by considerable confusion about the architect's role and purpose, as well as about the nature and goal of the Post-Modern movement itself. In reporting a conference on architectural design, Robert Gutman observes that the members of the conference "expressed dramatically opposite points of view" and that all were applauded to the same degree:

> Architecture, as it shakes off Modernism and the International style, is slouching toward a new architectural order through a chaos of styles that many find alarming and others delight in. . . . Design in architecture, as that pluralism unfolds, is swinging toward humanism; or it is growing more and more victimized by a technocratic society; or it is managing to reconcile the two.*

However historians may interpret these stylistic events, they agree that, as we have already suggested, the function of the architect is often blurred or shared among other persons or agencies. A design is no longer the product of the individual architect, or even of the architectural firm, but reflects the additional influences of a group that includes regulatory agencies, zoning boards, financiers, ecologists, and—not least—the energy-conscious.

A new and pressing demand is that architecture be energy-efficient. A premise of the International style—that the interior environment of a building can be totally controlled by elaborate heating, cooling, and ventilation systems, installed with little effect on the design—presupposes an inexhaustible supply of relatively inexpensive energy to fuel these systems. The rise in cost of energy in the 1970s and the recognition of the finite character of fossil fuels has increasingly elicited the demand that energy consumption be considered at the very beginning of the design process—a fact that could make the principles as well as the look of the International style largely obsolete. Concerning the energy-wasteful building, Richard Stein observes:

> . . . the hope for the future lies in the fundamental reversal in our present commitment to the sealed building, with its massive plant for manufacturing the air and delivering it at predetermined temperatures and velocities and its large lighting apparatus that substitutes a universal switch for selectivity. If these helped cause our problem, their reversal can help solve it.*

With new sources of energy being sought, solar energy has become an attractive field for recent experiment—as the many new residential and commer-

*Journal of the American Institute of Architects, Vol. 67, No. 1 (January 1978), p. 49.

*Architecture and Energy (New York: Doubleday, Anchor Press, 1977), p. 292.

cial buildings using solar techniques testify. In 1978, a design competition for a state office building in Sacramento, California, was won by BUFORD DUKE for an energy-efficient design that combines "maximum exposure for solar generation with minimum exposure for energy conservation." Most of the building's office space is underground, arranged around a great, sunken courtyard, with lightwells providing natural light. Overhead, an urban park provides insulation. At one end of the complex, a six-story tower contains additional office space, but its main purpose is to serve as support for some 12,000 square feet of solar collectors that generate the energy for heating and cooling the building.

Related to the need for energy conservation is the problem of urban sprawl. In keeping with the progressing trend toward specialization, urbanism—once part of the architect's sphere of activity—has become the problem child of a new specialist, the city planner. For a little more than a century (since about 1850), the modern city has been attracting a rural population that has lost its livelihood in the country. Ironically, the explosive growth of cities largely has been a consequence of the enormous rise in agricultural producivity. (If only 5 percent of a population can feed the rest, then the other 95 percent must move to cities and industrial centers to find work.) But yesterday's panacea has lost its charm today, and Aristotle's vision of the "good life" in the city has evaporated in smog, noise, and pollution. Since World War II, metropolitan centers have become increasingly deserted, as people move, if not all the way back, at least closer to the rural surroundings from which their parents and grandparents emigrated. Today, we find the once-bustling, metropolitan cores surrounded by satellite residential towns, complete with shopping and recreational centers, to which disenchanted city workers rush back each evening, fleeing their dehumanized workday surroundings. As a result of this flight back to the country, many urban centers stand dark and deserted for some 14 hours a day five days a week and 24 hours a day on weekends. All this has placed an enormous strain on transportation systems (primarily on highways in the United States), which must move millions of people to and from their jobs, at the cost of commensurate amounts of fuel. And the specter of yet another "doomsday" arises to threaten us not with the Last Judgement or a nuclear holocaust, but with the inevitable depletion of the earth's energy resources.

Thus, one of the most urgent issues confronting the contemporary city planner is how to revitalize urban centers and make them attractive again, so that people will no longer feel the need to vacate them at 5 P.M. each evening. Under the general heading of "urban renewal," numerous solutions have been attempted, but none yet have proved to be entirely successful. Partial answers have been provided: shopping malls, high-rise (!) hotels, convention centers, museums, and occasional designs for public squares.

An interesting example of a public square is the Piazza d' Italia in New Orleans (FIGS. 22-121 and 22-122), which incidentally, also is a fascinating specimen of Post-Modern design. Created by CHARLES MOORE (b. 1925), it illustrates still another of the many facets of Post-Modern architecture—unabashed eclecticism—which here, however, serves a specific purpose. The piazza is dedicated to the Italian colony of New Orleans, and Moore's use of Classical models for its design is meaningful in its direct reference to the Mediterranean origin of Italians and to a region, strewn with Greek and Roman ruins, that evokes ancient cultural reminiscences.

Backed up against a contemporary high-rise and set off from urban traffic patterns, the Piazza d' Italia can be reached on foot from three sides, through gateways of varied design. The approaches lead to an open, circular area partially framed by short segments of colonnades arranged in staggered, concentric arcs, which direct the eye to the composition's focal point: an exedra (a semicircular, walled space, like an apse) on a raised platform that serves as rostrum during the annual festivities of St. Joseph's Day. The piazza's pavement is inlaid with the map of Italy, in which Sicily, the place of origin of the Italian colony's majority, is centrally placed. From there, the Italian boot moves in the direction of the steps that ascend the rostrum and that, geographically, correspond to the Alps. The piazza's most immediate historical reference is to the Greek agora or the Roman forum; on the other hand, its circular form refers to the ideal geometric figure of the Renaissance. The irregular placement of the concentrically arranged colonnade fragments inserts a note of instability into the design that is reminiscent of Mannerism; and illusionistic devices, like the continuation of the piazza's pavement design (apparently through a building and out into the street), are Baroque in character. All of the Classical orders are represented—some with whimsical modifications: fluting defined by rising jets of water; water falling from metopes (Moore calls these "wetopes") and spouting from the mouths of the architect's relief portraits that have been set into spandrels. Twentieth-century touches are provided in the form of stainless-steel columns and capitals, neon collars around the necks of columns, and the framing of various features of the exedra with neon lights.

In sum, the design of the Piazza d' Italia is a complex conglomerate of symbolic, historical, and geographical allusions—some overt, others hidden—

22-121 CHARLES MOORE, model of the Piazza d'Italia, New Orleans, Louisiana, 1976–1980.

22-122 CHARLES MOORE, Piazza d'Italia, view of the exedra (detail of FIG. 22-121).

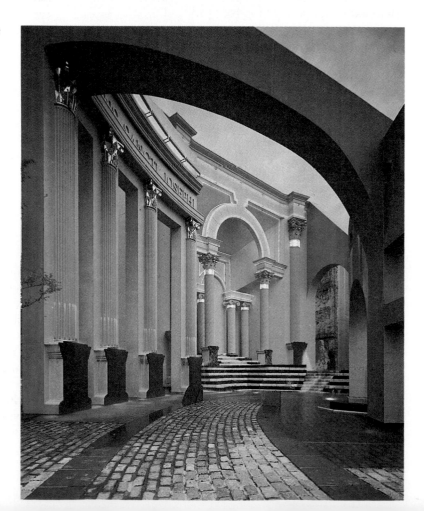

assembled for visual effect and not without humor. The piazza's specific purpose is to give identity (or, to use a favorite Post-Modern expression, a ''heart'') to the Italian community of New Orleans. Its more general purpose is to revitalize an urban area by becoming a focal point and an architectural setting for the social activities of the neighborhood residents. It remains to be seen if it can fulfill this expectation, or if it will become just another curiosity and tourist attraction.

Great works, as we have seen, transcend the stature of any one architect. What philosopher–historian Stephen Toulmin writes of scientific work in this century could well apply to architecture now: ''Ours is not so much a century of *genius* as a century of *scale* and *organization*.'' The International style, developed in the early years of the twentieth century, provided the elements of an architectural language that is recognized and understood throughout the world. It remains the dominant trend in today's building. Its further sophistication and consolidation—however edited, revised, and transformed—will be the work of great collaborations rather than of isolated genius, resembling, as Mies van der Rohe predicted, the corporate architectural creativity of the Gothic world.

EPILOGUE

The transformation of the world by science and technology is the signal fact that separates the modern epoch from all of the past. The influence on architecture is obvious enough; in painting and sculpture, it is perhaps less obvious but certainly just as decisive. The image-making function of the figurative arts, insofar as they simulate appearance, has been largely displaced by the making of objects with or without reference to the public world as we see it. These are the products of the artist's private vision and vocabulary. The ironic, mythic, and social functions of representation have been monopolized by mechanical media—photography, motion pictures, television, and computers. By these means, images can be produced and reproduced in countless millions. The art object itself, through sophisticated means of reproduction, loses its uniqueness and its ''space,'' like the original sound of an orchestral performance reproduced in high-fidelity recording. Reproductions of art and artifacts in special collections are offered for sale as exact duplications. This is analogous to biological cloning or to the standardization and mass production of industrial commodities; the processes employed are quite different from the ones that made the original object. At the same time, there is a multiplication of hands involved—a collectivization of the agents and the agencies of creation. The independent role of the artist as hand craftsman could not help but be fundamentally affected by the fact and the method of mechanized production. And the esthetic values of nonobjective sculpture and painting cannot help but be shared and exchanged with, or even transferred to, the esthetic values we appreciate in the best industrial design.

Meanwhile the Tradition has been dismantled. Has a new one appeared? The triumph of modern art is at the same time its crisis. At the heart of the crisis is a paradox. Modernism, created by the break with tradition, has itself become a ''tradition''; we have seen that Post-Modernism is precisely a reaction against the ''tradition'' of Modernism. Everything now becomes problematical: the purpose of art, the function of the artist, the nature of the media with which the artist works or should work, the artist's relationship to patron and public. Questions abound: What is wanted? What is needed? What is to be done? How is it to be done? This pervasive disagreement is explicit in the very plurality of works and styles, programs and processes, interpretations and assessments.

In the marketplace, where artists compete fiercely, there is unrelenting pressure for novelty, uniqueness, and variety of expression. For economics, as well as science and technology, has touched the art of today and influenced it definitively. The old, direct relationship of artist and patron has been replaced by ''the system''—an unregulated art market managed (sometimes manipulated in concert) by critics, dealers, collectors, gallery owners, museum directors, art schools, and other agencies and institutions. The estimate of the intrinsic value of a work of art is often directly related to its value on the market, and conflicts of interest can render critical and art-historical judgments suspect. As the critic Robert Hughes observes:

> The flight of speculative capital to the art market has done more to alter and distort the way we experience painting and sculpture in the last twenty years than any style, movement, or polemic. . . . The subversion of esthetic experience by monetary value is by now as pervasive and visible as the alteration of unique objects by mass reproduction. Colossal sums of money are exchanged every day on the art market.

Thus, the industrial and the economic worlds have had their way with art and artist—with their integrity and with their independence. But there is no reason to believe that creative power has been sapped, even if it has often been confused and frustrated. As the West has lost its tradition, the non-Western sectors of humanity have lost or modified theirs. To judge by style, an international—a world—art is emerging. As traditional differences disappear and as art gains a wholeness never before known, it may promise spiritual and esthetic experiences of incalculable worth for all the human race.

GLOSSARY

Italicized terms are also defined in the Glossary.

abacus (ab'a·kus) The uppermost portion of the *capital* of a *column*, usually a thin slab.

abstract In painting and sculpture, emphasizing a derived, essential character having little visual reference to objects in nature.

academy A place of study, derived from the name of the grove where Plato held his philosophical seminars. Giorgio Vasari founded the first academy of fine arts, properly speaking, with his Accademia di Disegno in Florence in 1563.

Achaea (a·ka'ya) An ancient section of the northern Peloponnesos; loosely, Greece in general.

Achaean (a·kee'an) Of or pertaining to *Achaea*.

acroterium or **acroterion** (ak·roh·tee' ri·um) In Classical buildings, a figure or ornament usually at the apex of the *pediment*.

addorsed Set back-to-back, especially as in heraldic design.

adobe (a·do'bee) The clay used to make a kind of sun-dried brick of the same name; a building made of such brick.

aerial perspective See *perspective*.

agora (ag'o·ra) An open square or space used for public meetings or business in ancient Greek cities.

aisle The portion of a church flanking the *nave* and separated from it by a row of *columns* or *piers*.

alabaster A variety of gypsum or calcite of dense, fine texture, usually white, but also red, yellow, gray, and sometimes banded.

alla prima (a'la pree'ma) A painting technique in which pigments are laid on in one application, with little or no drawing or underpainting.

altarpiece A panel, painted or sculptured, situated above and behind an altar. See also *retable*.

ambulatory A covered walkway, outdoors (as in a *cloister*) or indoors, especially the passageway around the *apse* and the *choir* of a church.

amphora (am'fo·ra) A two-handled, egg-shaped jar used for general storage purposes.

anamorphic image An image that must be viewed by some special means (such as a mirror) to be recognized.

apadana (ap·a·dan'a) The great audience hall in ancient Persian palaces.

apse A recess, usually singular and semi-circular, in the wall of a Roman *basilica* or at the east end of a Christian church.

arabesque Literally, "Arabian-like." A flowing, intricate pattern derived from stylized organic motifs, usually floral, often arranged in symmetrical *palmette* designs; generally, an Islamic decorative motif.

arcade A series of *arches* supported by *piers* or *columns*.

arcading An uninterrupted series of *arches*.

arch A curved structural member that spans an opening and is generally composed of wedge-shaped blocks (*voussoirs*) that transmit the downward pressure laterally. A **diaphragm arch** is a transverse, wall-bearing arch that divides a *vault* or a ceiling into compartments, providing a kind of firebreak. See also *thrust*.

architectonic Having structural or architectural qualities, usually as elements of a nonarchitectural object.

architrave (ark'i·trayv) The *lintel* or lowest division of the *entablature*; sometimes called the *epistyle*.

archivolt (ark'i·volt) One of a series of concentric *moldings* on a Romanesque or a Gothic arch.

arcuated (ar'kew·ate·id) Of *arch–column* construction.

armature In sculpture, a skeleton-like framework to support material being modeled.

aspara In India, a nymph of the sky or air; in Chinese Buddhism, a heavenly maiden.

atlantes (at·lan'teez; *sing.* **atlas**) Male figures that function as supporting columns. See also *caryatid*.

atmospheric perspective See *perspective*.

atrium (ay'tree·um) The court of a Roman house that is near the entrance and partly open to the sky. Also, the open, colonnaded court in front of and attached to a Christian *basilica*.

avant-garde (a·vahn·gard') Artists whose work is in (or work that reflects) the latest stylistic direction.

avatar (ah'vah·tar) In Hinduism, an incarnation of a god.

axial plan See *plan*.

axis An imaginary line or lines about which a work, a group of works, or a part of a work is visually or structurally organized, often symmetrically.

baldacchino (bal·da·kee'no) A canopy on columns, frequently built over an altar.

barrel vault See *vault*.

bas (bah) **relief** See *relief*.

basilica (ba·sil'i·ka) In Roman architecture, a public building for assemblies (especially tribunals), that is rectangular in plan with an entrance on a long side. In Christian architecture, an early church somewhat resembling the Roman basilica, usually entered from one end and with an *apse* at the other, creating an *axial plan*.

batter To slope inward, often almost imperceptibly, or such an inward slope of a wall.

bay A subdivision of the interior space of a building. In Romanesque and Gothic churches, the transverse *arches* and *piers* of the *arcade* divide the building into bays.

beehive tomb A beehive-shaped type of subterranean tomb constructed as a *corbeled vault* and found on pre-Archaic Greek sites.

belvedere (bell·vuh·dare'eh) An open, roofed story built to provide a scenic view.

ben-ben A pyramidal stone; a *fetish* of the Egyptian god Re.

benizuri-e (ben'i·zur'i-ee) A two-color method of Japanese printing in pink and green that produces strong color vibration.

bevel See *chamfer*.

bhakti (buh·hock'tee) In Hinduism, the devote, selfless direction of all tasks and activities of life to the service of one god; the adoration of a personalized deity.

black-figure technique In early Greek pottery, the silhouetting of dark figures against a light background of natural, reddish clay.

blind arcade (wall arcade) An *arcade* having no actual openings, applied as decoration to a wall surface.

Bodhisattva (bo·dee·sot'va) In Buddhism, a being who is a potential *Buddha*.

bottega (but·tay'ga) A shop; the studio-shop of an Italian artist.

bouleuterion (boo·loo·tee'ri·on) In ancient Greece, an assembly hall or council chamber.

broken color A painting technique using short, thick strokes laid over a ground color to create rich textures and vibrant effects of light.

broken pediment A *pediment* in which the *cornice* is discontinuous at the apex or the base.

Buddha The supreme enlightened being of Buddhism, an embodiment of divine wisdom and virtue. **Buddhist** (*adj.*)

burin (byoor'in) A pointed steel tool for *engraving* or *incising*.

buttress An exterior masonry structure that opposes the lateral thrust of an *arch* or a *vault*. A **pier buttress** is a solid mass of masonry; a **flying buttress** consists typically of an inclined member carried on an arch or a series of arches and a solid buttress to which it transmits lateral *thrust*.

calidarium The hot-bath section of a Roman bathing establishment.

calligraphy Handwriting or penmanship, especially elegant or "beautiful" writing as a decorative art.

camera obscura An ancestor of the modern camera in which a tiny pinhole, acting as a lens, projects an image on a screen, the wall of a room, or the ground-glass wall of a box; used by seventeenth- and eighteenth-century artists as an aid in compositional arrangement.

campanile (kam·pa·neel'eh) A bell tower, usually freestanding.

capital The upper member of a *column,* serving as a transition from the *shaft* to the *lintel.*

Caravaggisti (kara·va·gee'stee) Artists influenced by Caravaggio's dramatically contrasting dark–light effects; painters of "night" pictures in the "dark manner" (*tenebroso*).

cardo The north–south road in Etruscan and Roman towns, intersecting the *decumanus* at right angles.

carrier The material support for a painting (wood, canvas, wall, etc.).

cartoon In painting, a full-size drawing from which a painting is made. Cartoons were usually worked out in complete detail; the design was then transferred to the working surface by coating the back with chalk and going over the lines with a *stylus,* or by pricking the lines and "pouncing" charcoal dust through the resulting holes.

cartouche (kar·toosh') A scroll-like design or medallion, purely decorative or containing an inscription or heraldic device. In ancient Egypt, an oval device containing such elements as *hieroglyphic* names of Egyptian kings.

caryatid (kar'ee·at'id) A female figure that functions as a supporting *column.* See also *atlantes.*

casting In sculpture, duplication of a clay original in plaster or metal by use of a mold.

cella (sel'a) An enclosed chamber (Greek, *naos*), the essential feature of a Classical temple, in which the cult statue usually stood.

centering A wooden framework to support an *arch* or a *vault* during its construction.

central plan See *plan.*

ceramics The art of making objects such as pottery out of clay; also, the objects themselves.

chaitya (chight'yuh) An Indian shrine, especially a Buddhist assembly hall having a votive *stupa* at one end.

chalice A cup or goblet, especially that used in the sacraments of the Christian Church.

chamfer The surface formed by cutting off a corner of a board or post; a *bevel.*

champlevé (shahn·le·vay') A process of enameling in which a design is cut into a metal plate in such a way as to leave thin, raised lines that create compartments to hold the enamel.

chandi A Javanese temple.

chatra See *parasol.*

chevet (sheh·vay') The eastern end of a Gothic church, including *choir, ambulatory,* and radiating chapels.

chevron A zigzag or V-shaped motif of decoration.

chiaroscuro (kee·ar'o·skoor'o) In painting or drawing, the treatment and use of light and dark, especially the gradations of light that produce the effect of *modeling.*

chinoiserie (shee·nwaz·eh·ree') Chinese motifs used as decorations for furniture, in wallpaper, etc., applied largely to eighteenth-century Rococo style.

chiton (kite'on) A Greek tunic, the essential (and often only) garment of both men and women, the other being the *himation* or *mantle.*

choir The space reserved for the clergy in the church, usually east of the *transept* but, in some instances, extending into the *nave.*

ciborium (sih·bor'ee·um) A canopy, often freestanding and supported by four columns, erected over an altar; also, a covered cup used in the sacraments of the Christian Church. See *baldacchino.*

cinquecento (cheenk·way·chain'toh) The sixteenth century in Italian art.

cire perdue (seer pair·dew') The **lost-wax process.** A bronze-casting method in which a figure is modeled in wax and covered with clay; the whole is fired, melting away the wax and hardening the clay, which then becomes a mold for molten metal.

clerestory (kleer'sto·ry) The *fenestrated* part of a building that rises above the roofs of the other parts.

cloison (klwa·zohn') Literally, a partition. A cell made of metal wire or a narrow metal strip (usually gold) that is soldered edge-down to a metal base to hold enamel or other decorative materials.

cloisonné (klwa·zoh·nay') A process of enameling employing *cloisons.*

cloister A court, usually with covered walks or *ambulatories* along its sides.

closed form A *form,* especially in painting, with a *contour* that is not broken or blurred.

cluster pier See *compound pier.*

codex Separate pages of *vellum* or *parchment* bound together at one side and having a cover; the predecessor of the modern book.

coffer A sunken panel in a *soffit,* a *vault,* or a ceiling, often ornamental.

collage (kul·lahzh') A composition made by pasting together on a flat surface various materials such as newspaper, wallpaper, printed text and illustrations, photographs, and cloth. See also *montage.*

colonnade A series or row of *columns,* usually spanned by *lintels.*

colonnette A small *column.*

color See *hue, saturation,* and *value.*

color-field painting A style of painting characterized by radical simplicity (disciplined line) and purity of shape and color.

column A vertical, weight-carrying architectural member, circular in cross section and consisting of a base (sometimes omitted), a *shaft,* and a *capital.*

complementary afterimage The image (in a *complementary color*) that is retained briefly by the eye after the stimulus is removed.

complementary colors Those pairs of colors, such as red and green, that together embrace the entire spectrum. The complement of one of the three *primary colors* is a mixture of the other two. In pigments, they produce a neutral gray when mixed in the right proportions.

compluvium An opening in the center of the roof of a Roman *atrium* to admit light.

compound or **cluster pier** A *pier* composed of a group or cluster of members, especially characteristic of Gothic architecture.

connoisseur (kon·nuh·ser') An expert on works of art and the individual styles of artists.

contour A visible border of a *mass* in space; a *line* that creates the illusion of *mass* and *volume* in space.

contrapposto (kon·tra·poh'stoh) The disposition of the human figure in which one part is turned in opposition to another part (usually hips and legs one way, shoulders and chest another), creating a counter-positioning of the body about its central *axis.* Sometimes called **weight shift** because the weight of the body tends to be thrown to one foot, creating tension on one side and relaxation on the other.

cool color Blue, green, or violet. Psychologically, cool colors are calming, unemphatic, depressive; optically, they generally appear to recede. See also *warm color.*

corbel (kor'bel) A projecting wall member used as a support for some element in the superstructure. Also, courses of stone or brick in which each course projects beyond the one beneath it. Two such structures, meeting at the topmost course, create an arch.

cornice The projecting, crowning member of the *entablature;* also, any crowning projection.

cosmati (koz·ma'tee) Cut-stone *mosaic* inlay decoration in geometric patterns.

cramp or **clamp** A device, usually metal, to hold together blocks of stone of the same course. See also *dowel.*

crenelated (kren'el·ate·id) Notched or indented, usually with respect to tops of walls, as in battlements.

crockct A projecting, foliate ornament of a *capital, pinnacle, gable, buttress,* or spire.

Cro-Magnon (kro-mag'non) Of or pertaining to the *homo sapiens* whose remains, dating from the Aurignacian period, were found in the Cro-Magnon caves in Dordogne, France.

cromlech (krom'lek) A circle of *monoliths.*

crossing The space in a cruciform church formed by the intersection of the *nave* and the *transept.*

crossing square The area in a church that is formed by the intersection (crossing) of a *nave* and a *transept* of equal width.

crown The topmost part of an *arch,* including the *keystone;* also, an open *finial* of a tower.

cruciform (kroo'suh·form) Cross-shaped

crypt A *vaulted* space under part of a building, wholly or partly underground; in Medieval churches, normally the portion under an *apse* or a *chevet.*

cubiculum A small room constructed in the wall of an Early Christian catacomb to serve as a mortuary chapel.

cuneiform (kyoo·nee'ih·form) Literally, "wedge-shaped." A system of writing used in ancient Mesopotamia, the characters of which were wedge-shaped.

Cyclopean (sike·lo·pee'an) Gigantic; vast

and rough; massive. **Cyclopean architecture** is a method of stone construction using large, irregular blocks without mortar.

dado (day'doh) A horizontal band, often decorated, at the base or lower part of a wall or a pedestal.

daguerreotype (dah·gair'oh·type) A photograph made by an early method on a plate of chemically treated metal or glass; developed by Louis J.M. Daguerre.

decumanus (dek·yoo·man'us) The east–west road in an Etruscan or Roman town, intersecting the *cardo* at right angles.

diptych (dip'tik) A two-paneled *altarpiece*; also, an ancient Roman and Early Christian two-hinged writing tablet, or two ivory memorial panels.

dolmen (dohl'men) Several large stones (*megaliths*) capped with a covering slab, erected in prehistoric times.

dome A hemispheric *vault*; theoretically, an *arch* rotated on its vertical *axis*.

dowel In ancient architecture, a wooden or metal pin placed between stones of different courses to prevent shifting. See also *cramp*.

dromos The passage to a *beehive tomb*.

drum The circular wall that supports a *dome*; also, one of the cylindrical stones of which a non-monolithic *shaft* of a *column* is made.

dry point An engraving in which the design, instead of being cut into the plate with a *burin*, is scratched into the surface with a hard steel "pencil." The process is quicker and more spontaneous than standard engraving and lends itself to the creation of painterly effects. Its disadvantage is the fact that the plate wears out very quickly. See also *engraving, etching, intaglio*.

duecento (doo·ay·chain'toh) The thirteenth century in Italian art.

earth colors Pigments, such as yellow ochre and umber, that are obtained by mining; usually compounds of metals.

echinus (eh·ky'nus) In architecture, the convex element of a *capital* directly below the *abacus*.

eclecticism (eh·klek'ti·sism) The practice of selecting from various sources, sometimes to form a new system or style.

écorché (ay·kor·shay') A figure painted or sculptured to show the muscles of the body without skin.

elevation In drawing and architecture, a geometric projection of a building on a plane perpendicular to the horizon; a vertical projection.

embrasure A *splayed* opening in a wall that enframes a doorway or a window.

enamel A vitreous, colored paste that solidifies when fired. See also *champlevé, cloisonné*.

encaustic An ancient method of painting with colored, molten wax in which the wax is fused with the surface by the application of hot irons.

engaged column A column-like, nonfunctional form projecting from a wall and articulating it visually. See also *pilaster*.

engobe (en·gohb') A slip of finely sifted clay used by Greek potters; applied to a pot, it would form a black *glaze* in firing.

engraving The process of *incising* a design in hard material, often a metal plate (usually copper); also, the print or impression made from such a plate. See also *dry point, etching, intaglio*.

entablature The part of a building above the *capitals* of *columns* and below the roof or the upper story.

entasis (en'·tah·sis) An almost imperceptible convex tapering (an apparent swelling) in the *shaft* of a *column*.

epigone An artist of a succeeding and less distinguished generation.

epistyle See *architrave*.

esthetic The distinctive vocabulary and theory of a given *style*.

etching A kind of *engraving* in which the design is *incised* in a layer of wax or varnish on a copper plate. The parts of the plate left exposed are then **etched** (slightly eaten away) by the acid in which the plate is immersed after incising. Etching is one of the most facile of the graphic arts and the one most capable of subtleties of line and tone. See also *dry point, engraving, intaglio*.

extrados (eks·trah'dohs) The upper or outer surface of an *arch*.

façade Usually, the front of a building; also, the other sides when they are emphasized architecturally.

faïence (feye·ahnce') Pottery (except *porcelain*) glazed with compounds of tin; also, any *glazed* earthenware.

fan vault See *vault*.

fenestration The arrangement of the windows of a building.

ferroconcrete See *reinforced concrete*.

fête galante (fet ga·lahnt') An elegant and graceful celebration; often represented in the works of Antoine Watteau and other Rococo painters.

fetish An object believed to possess magical powers, especially one capable of bringing to fruition its owner's plans; sometimes regarded as the abode of a supernatural power or spirit.

fibula A decorative pin, usually used to fasten garments.

figure-ground The visual unity, yet separability, of a form and its background.

filigree A delicate, lace-like, intertwined, ornamental work or design.

fin de siècle (fan·duh·see'akl) Characteristic of the progressive ideas and customs of the last years of the nineteenth century.

finial A knob-like ornament (usually with a foliate design) in which a vertical member, such as a *pinnacle*, terminates.

flamboyant Flame-like, flaming; applied to aspects of Late Gothic style, especially architectural tracery.

flute or **fluting** Vertical channeling, roughly semicircular in cross section and used principally on *columns* and *pilasters*.

flying buttress See *buttress*.

foreshortening The apparent visual contraction of an object viewed as extended in a plane that is not perpendicular to the line of sight; also, the representation of this phenomenon.

form In its widest sense, total structure; a synthesis of all the elements of that structure and of the manner in which they are united to create its distinctive character. The *form* of a work is what enables us to apprehend it. See also *closed form* and *open form*.

formalism Strict adherence to, or dependence on, prescribed forms of execution.

forum The public square or marketplace of an ancient Roman city.

fresco Painting on plaster, either dry **(dry fresco** or **fresco secco)** or wet **(wet** or **true fresco).** In the latter method, the pigments are mixed with water and become chemically bound to the plaster. Also, a painting executed in either method.

fret or **meander** An ornament, usually in bands but also covering broad surfaces, consisting of interlocking geometric motifs.

frieze (freez) The part of the *entablature* between the *architrave* and the *cornice*; also, any sculptured or ornamented band in a building, on furniture, etc.

full round Sculpture in full and completely rounded form (not in *relief*).

gable See *pediment*.

gallery The second story of an *ambulatory* or *aisle*.

garbha griha The *cella* or inner sanctum of the Hindu temple.

gargoyle In architecture, a waterspout (usually carved), often in the form of a *grotesque*.

genre (zhahn'reh) A style or category of art; also, a kind of painting realistically depicting scenes from everyday life.

gesso (jess'oh) Plaster mixed with a binding material and used for *reliefs* and as a *ground* for painting.

glaze A vitreous coating applied to pottery to seal the surface and as decoration; it may be colored, transparent, or opaque, and glossy or *matte*. In oil painting, a thin, transparent, or semitransparent layer put over a color to alter it slightly.

glory See *nimbus*.

golden mean or **golden section** A proportional relation obtained by dividing a line so that the shorter part is to the longer part as the longer part is to the whole. The *esthetic* appeal of these proportions has led artists of varying periods and cultures to employ them in determining basic dimensions.

gopuram (go'poor·am) The massive, ornamented entrance structure of South Indian temples.

gouache (goo·ahsh') *Watercolor* rendered opaque by the addition of a filler, such as gum. It has more body and dries more slowly than the transparent watercolor and lends itself to bright color effects and meticulous detail. Also, a picture painted in this medium.

granulation In jewelry, a method of ornamenting in which small grains of metal (usually gold) are soldered to a flat surface.

graphic arts   Visual arts that are linear in character, such as drawing and *engraving*; also, generally, visual arts that involve impression (printing and printmaking).

graver   A cutting tool used by engravers and sculptors.

Greek cross   A cross in which all the arms are the same length.

grisaille (greez·eye′)   A monochrome painting done mainly in neutral grays to simulate sculpture.

groin   The edge formed by the intersection of two *vaults*.

groin vault   See *vault*.

grotesque   In art, a kind of ornament used in antiquity—and sometimes called (imprecisely) *arabesque*—consisting of representations of medallions, sphinxes, foliage, and imaginary creatures.

ground   A coating applied to a canvas or some other surface to prepare that surface for painting; also, background.

guilloche (gee·ūsh)   An ornament consisting of interlaced, curving bands.

hallenkirche (holl′en·keer·sheh)   A hall church. In this variety of Gothic church, especially popular in Germany, the *aisles* are as high as the *nave*.

haniwa   Sculptured pottery tubes placed around early (archaic) Japanese burial mounds.

harmika   A square enclosure atop the *dome* of a *stupa* from which the *yasti* arises.

hatching   A technique used in drawing, engraving, etc., in which fine lines are cut or drawn close together to achieve an effect of shading.

haunch   The part of an *arch* (roughly midway between the *springing* and the *crown*) at which the lateral *thrust* is strongest.

herringbone perspective   See *perspective*.

hieratic (higher·at′tic)   The priestly supernaturalism disparaging matter and material values that prevailed throughout the Christian Middle Ages, especially in Orthodox Byzantium.

hieroglyphic (high·roh·glif′ic)   A system of writing using symbols or pictures; also, one of the symbols.

himation (him·mat′ee·on)   A Greek *mantle* worn by men and women over the tunic and draped in various ways.

historiated   Ornamented with representations, such as plants, animals, or human figures, that have a narrative—as distinct from a purely decorative—function. Historiated initial letters were a popular form of manuscript decoration in the Middle Ages.

horror vacui (vack′ui)   Literally, "fear of empty space"; crowded design.

hue   The name of a color. The *primary colors* (blue, red, and yellow) together with the *secondary colors* (green, orange, and violet) form the chief colors of the spectrum. See also *complementary colors, cool color, saturation, value, warm color.*

hydria (high′dree·a)   An ancient Greek three-handled water jar.

hypostyle hall   A hall with a roof supported by columns; applied to the colonnaded hall of the Egyptian *pylon* temple.

icon (eye′con)   A portrait or image; especially in the Greek church, a panel with a painting of sacred personages that are objects of veneration. In the visual arts, a painting, a piece of sculpture, or even a building regarded as an object of veneration.

iconography (eye·con·og′ra·fee)   The study dealing with the symbolic, often religious, meaning of objects, persons, or events depicted in works of art.

iconostasis (eye·con·os′ta·sis)   In eastern Christian churches, a screen or a partition, with doors and many *tiers* of *icons*, that separates the sanctuary from the main body of the church.

idealization   The representation of things according to a preconception of ideal *form* or type; a kind of *esthetic* distortion to produce idealized forms. See also *realism*.

illumination   Decoration with drawings (usually in gold, silver, and bright colors), especially the initial letters of a manuscript.

imagines (i·maj′i·nees; *sing.* **imago**)   In ancient Rome, wax portraits of ancestors.

imam (eye·mahm′)   One who leads worshipers in prayer in Moslem services.

impasto (im·pah′stoh)   A style of painting in which the pigment is applied thickly or in heavy lumps, as in many of Rembrandt's paintings.

impluvium   A depression in the floor of a Roman *atrium* to collect rainwater.

impost block   A stone with the shape of a truncated, inverted pyramid, placed between a *capital* and the *arch* that springs from it.

incising   Cutting into a surface with a sharp instrument; also, a method of decoration, especially on metal and pottery.

in situ (si′too)   In place; in original position.

insula   A multi-storied Roman apartment block.

intaglio (in·tal′yoh)   A category of graphic technique in which the design is *incised*, so that the impression made is in *relief*. Used especially on gems, seals, and dies for coins, but also in the kinds of printing or printmaking in which the ink-bearing surface is depressed. Also, an object so decorated. See also *dry point, engraving, etching*.

intarsia (in·tahr′sya)   Inlay work, primarily in wood and sometimes in mother-of-pearl, marble, etc.

intercolumniation   The space or the system of spacing between *columns* in a *colonnade*.

intrados (in·trah′dohs)   The underside of an *arch* or a *vault*.

isocephaly (eye·soh·sef′ah·lee)   The arrangement of figures so that the heads are at the same height.

jataka (jah′tah·kah)   Tales of the lives of the *Buddha*.

ka (kah)   In ancient Egypt, immortal human substance; the concept approximates the Western idea of soul.

kagle   A rough, highly abstracted African (Don) mask.

kakemono (kah′keh·moh·noh)   A Japanese hanging or scroll.

karma (kar′muh)   In Buddhist and Hindu belief, the ethical consequences of a person's life, which determine his or her fate.

keystone   The central, uppermost *voussoir* in an *arch*.

khutbah (koot′bah)   In Moslem worship, a sermon and a declaration of allegiance to a community leader.

kiln   A large stove or oven in which pottery is fired.

kore (kor′ay)   Greek for "girl."

kouros (coor′aus)   Greek for "young man."

krater/crater (kray′ter)   An ancient Greek wide-mouthed bowl for mixing wine and water.

kuang (gwahng)   A Chinese covered libation vessel.

kylix/cylix (kye′liks)   An ancient Greek drinking cup, shallow and having two handles and a stem.

lacquer   A resinous spirit varnish, such as shellac, often colored.

lantern   In architecture, a small, often decorative structure with openings for lighting that crowns a *dome, turret,* or roof.

lapis lazuli (la′pis la′zyoo·lye)   A rich, ultramarine, semiprecious stone used for carving and as a source of *pigment*.

Latin cross   A cross in which the vertical member is longer than the horizontal member.

lectionary   A list, often illustrated, of **lections,** selections from the Scriptures that are read in church services.

lierne (lee·ern)   A short *rib* that runs from one main rib of a *vault* to another.

line   The mark made by a moving point and having psychological impact according to its direction and weight. In art, a line defines space and may create a silhouette or define a *contour*, creating the illusion of *mass* and *volume*.

linear perspective   See *perspective*.

lintel   A beam of any material used to span an opening.

lithography   In graphic arts, a printmaking process in which the printing surface is a polished stone on which the design is drawn with a greasy material. Greasy ink, applied to the moistened stone, is repelled by all surfaces except the lines of the drawing. The process permits linear and tonal *values* of great range and subtlety.

local color   In painting, the actual *color* of an object.

loggia (luh′jee·uh)   A gallery that has an open *arcade* or a *colonnade* on one or both sides.

lost-wax process   See *cire perdue*.

lotiform   In the form of a lotus petal.

lunette   A semicircular opening (with the flat side down) in a wall over a door, a niche, or a window.

luster   A thin *glaze* (usually metallic) sometimes used on pottery to produce a rich, often iridescent color. Used particularly in Persian pottery and in *majolica*.

machicolation (mah·chik′oh·lay·shun)   An opening (in the floor of an overhanging gallery) through which the defenders of a castle dropped stones and boiling liquids on attackers.

madrasah (muh·drah'suh) A combined Moslem school and *mosque*.

magazine A room or building designed for storage.

majolica (ma·jo'lik·ah) A kind of Italian Renaissance pottery coated with a whitish tin-compound enamel, brilliantly painted and often *lustered*.

makimono (mah'kee·moh'noh) A Japanese horizontal scroll.

malanggan (mah·lohng'gahn) Intricately carved Melanesian ceremonial masks.

mandala (man'duh·luh) In Hinduism and Buddhism, a magical, geometric symbol of the cosmos.

mandapa (man·dop'ah) A Hindu assembly hall, part of a temple.

mandorla An almond-shaped *nimbus*, or *glory*, surrounding the figure of Christ.

maniera greca (man·yera'greka) A formal Byzantine style that dominated Italian painting in the twelfth and thirteenth centuries; characterized by shallow space and linear flatness.

mantle See *himation*.

mass The effect and degree of bulk, density, and weight of matter in space. As opposed to plane and area (**volume**), mass is three-dimensional.

mastaba (mah'sta·bah) A bench-shaped ancient Egyptian tomb.

matte (mat) In painting, pottery, and photography, a dull finish.

mbari Ceremonial houses filled with clay sculptures, honoring community deities of the Ibo tribe in Africa.

meander See *fret*.

medium The substance or agency in which an artist works; also, in painting, the vehicle (usually liquid) that carries the *pigment*.

megalith Literally, "great stone"; a large, roughly hewn stone used in the construction of monumental, prehistoric structures. **megalithic** (*adj.*). See also, *cromlech, dolmen, menhir*.

megaron (meh'ga·ron) A rectangular hall, fronted by an open, two-columned porch, traditional in Greece since Mycenaean times.

menhir (men'heer) A prehistoric *monolith*, uncut or roughly cut, standing singly or with others in rows or circles.

merlon The solid part of a battlement.

metope (met'a·pee) The space between *triglyphs* in a Doric *frieze*.

mihrab (mee'rahb) In the wall of a *mosque*, the niche that indicates the direction of Mecca.

minbar (meen'bar) The pulpit in a *mosque*.

miniature A small picture illustrating a manuscript; also, any small portrait, often on ivory or *porcelain*.

modeling The shaping of three-dimensional forms in a soft material, such as clay; also, the gradations of light and shade reflected from the surfaces of matter in space, or the illusion of such gradations produced by alterations of *value* in a drawing or a painting.

module (mod'yool) A basic unit of which the dimensions of the major parts of a work are multiples. The principle is used in sculpture and other art forms, but it is most often employed in architecture, where the module may be the dimensions of an important part of a building, such as a *column*, or simply some commonly accepted unit of measurement (the centimeter or the inch, or, as with Le Corbusier, the average dimensions of the human figure).

molding In architecture, a continuous, narrow surface (projecting or recessed, plain or ornamented) designed to break up a surface, to accent, or to decorate.

monochrome A painting in one color; also, the technique of making such a painting.

monolith A column that is all in one piece (not built up); a large, single block or piece of stone used in *megalithic* structures.

montage (mohn'tahzh) A composition made by fitting together pictures or parts of pictures; also, motion-picture effects produced by superimposing images or showing them in rapid sequence. See also *collage*.

monumental In art criticism, any work of art of unpretentious grandeur and simplicity, regardless of its size.

mortice See *tenon*.

mosaic Patterns or pictures made by embedding small pieces of stone or glass (*tesserae*) in cement on surfaces such as walls and floors; also, the technique of making such works.

mosque A Moslem place of worship.

mudra (muh·drah') A stylized gesture of mystical significance, usually in representations of Hindu deities.

mullion A vertical member that divides a window or that separates one window from another.

mural A wall painting; a *fresco* is a type of mural medium and technique.

naos See *cella*.

narthex A porch or vestibule of a church, generally colonnaded or arcaded and preceding the *nave*.

Naturalism The doctrine that art should adhere as closely as possible to the appearance of the natural world. Naturalism, with varying degrees of fidelity to appearance, recurs in the history of Western art.

nave The part of a church between the chief entrance and the *choir*, demarcated from *aisles* by *piers* or *columns*.

necking A groove at the bottom of the Greek Doric *capital* between the *echinus* and the *flutes* that masks the junction of *capital* and *shaft*.

necropolis (neh·krop'o·lis) A large burial area; literally, a city of the dead.

niello (nee·el'o) Inlay in a metal of an alloy of sulfur and such metals as gold or silver. Also, a work made by this process, or the alloy itself.

nimbus A halo, aureole, or **glory** appearing around the head of a holy figure to signify divinity.

nirvana (neer·vah'nah) In Buddhism and Hinduism, a blissful state brought about by absorption of the individual soul or consciousness into the supreme spirit.

objet d'art (objay·dar') A relatively small object (figurine, vase, etc.) of artistic value.

obverse On coins or medals, the side that bears the principal type or inscription. See also *reverse*.

oculus A round, central opening or "eye" in a *dome*.

odalisque (oh'dah·lisk) An Oriental slave girl or concubine, a favorite subject of such artists as Ingres and Matisse.

oenochoe (eh·nuk'oh·ee) An ancient Greek wine pitcher.

oeuvre (uh'vreh) The whole of an artist's output; literally, the artist's "work."

ogee (oh'jee) A *molding* having in profile a double or S-shaped curve. Also, an *arch*, each side of which has this *form*.

ogive The diagonal *rib* of a Gothic *vault*; a pointed, or Gothic, *arch*. **ogival** (*adj.*)

oil color *Pigment* ground with oil.

open form A *mass* penetrated or treated in such a way that space acts as its environment rather than as its limit. See also *closed form*.

order In Classical architecture, a style represented by a characteristic design of the *column* and its *entablature*. See also *superimposed order*.

orthogonal A line imagined to be behind and perpendicular to the *picture plane*; the *orthogonals* in a painting appear to recede toward a *vanishing point* on the horizon.

pagoda A Buddhist tower with a multiplicity of winged eaves; derived from the Indian *stupa*.

palestra A Roman exercise room.

palette (pal'it) A thin board with a thumb hole at one end on which an artist lays and mixes colors; any surface so used. Also, the colors or kinds of colors characteristically used by an artist.

palmette (pal·met') A conventional, decorative ornament of ancient origin composed of radiating petals springing from a cup-like base.

Panathenaea (pan'a·then·ee'a) The most ancient and important festival of Athens, held in honor of the goddess Athena.

Pantheon (Pan'thee·on) All the gods of a people, or a temple dedicated to all such gods; especially, the Pantheon in Rome (although it is not certain that this was its function).

papyrus (pah·pye'rus) A plant native to Egypt and adjacent lands used to make a paper-like writing material; also, the material or any writing on it.

parasol An umbrella atop a Chinese *pagoda*; a vestige of the **chatra** on an Indian *stupa*.

parchment Lambskin prepared as a surface for writing or painting.

passage grave A burial chamber entered through a long, tunnel-like passage.

pastel Finely ground *pigments* compressed into chalk-like sticks. Also, work done in this *medium*, or its characteristic paleness.

pastiche (pas·teesh') An artistic hodge-podge that imitates or ridicules another artist's style.

patina (pa·teen'a) The green, oxidized layer that forms on bronze and copper.

pediment (ped'i·ment) In Classical architecture, the triangular space (**gable**) at the end of a building, formed by the ends of the sloping roof and the *cornice;* also, an ornamental feature having this shape.

pendentive (pen·den'tiv) A concave, triangular piece of masonry (a triangular section of a hemisphere), four of which provide the transition from a square area to the circular base of a covering *dome.* Although they appear to be hanging (**pendent**) from the dome, they in fact support it.

peripteral (per·ip'ter·al) A style of building in which the main structure is surrounded by a *colonnade.*

peristyle (pair'i·stile) A *colonnade* surrounding a building or a court.

perspective A formula for projecting an illusion of the three-dimensional world onto a two-dimensional surface. In **linear perspective,** the most common type, all parallel lines or lines of projection seem to converge on a single point on the horizon, known as the *vanishing point,* and associated objects are rendered smaller the further from the viewer they are intended to seem. **Atmospheric** or **aerial perspective** creates the illusion of distance by the greater diminution of *color* intensity, the shift in color toward an almost neutral blue, and the blurring of *contours* as the intended distance between eye and object increases. In **herringbone perspective,** the lines of projection converge not on a vanishing point, but on a vertical *axis* at the center of the picture as in Roman paintings.

pi (bee) The Chinese symbol of Heaven, a jade disk.

piano nobile (peea'no no'bee·lay) The principal story, usually the second, in Renaissance buildings.

pictograph A picture, usually stylized, that represents an idea; also, writing using such means. See also *hieroglyphic.*

picture plane The surface of a picture.

pier A vertical, unattached masonry support.

Pietà (peeay·ta') A work of art depicting the Virgin mourning over the body of Christ.

pigment Finely powdered coloring matter mixed or ground with various vehicles to form paint, crayon, etc.

pilaster (pi·las'ter) A flat, rectangular, vertical member projecting from a wall of which it forms a part. It usually has a base and a *capital* and is often *fluted.*

pillar Usually a weight-carrying member, such as a *pier* or a *column;* sometimes an isolated, freestanding structure used for commemorative purposes.

pinnacle A tower, primarily ornamental, that also functions in Gothic architecture to give additional weight to a *buttress* or a *pier.* See also *finial.*

pithos (pith'oss; *pl.* **pithoi**) A large, clay storage vessel frequently set into the earth and therefore possessing no flat base.

plan The horizontal arrangement of the parts of a building, or a drawing or a diagram showing such an arrangement as a horizontal *section.* In **axial plan,** the parts of a building are organized longitudinally, or along a given *axis;* in a **central plan,** the parts radiate from a central point.

plasticity In art, the three-dimensionality of an object. **plastic** (*adj.*)

plein-air painting (plen·air) The representation of the observed effects of outdoor light and atmosphere practiced by some late nineteenth-century Impressionists.

plinth The lowest member of a base; also, a block serving as a base for a statue.

pointillism The method of painting of some French Impressionists in which a white ground is covered with tiny dots of color, which, when viewed at a distance, blend together to produce a luminous effect.

polychrome Done in several colors.

polyptych (pol'ip·tik) An *altarpiece* made up of more than three sections.

porcelain Translucent, impervious, resonant *pottery* made in a base of **kaolin,** a fine white clay; sometimes any pottery that is translucent, whether or not it is made of kaolin.

porphyry (pour'feary) An Egyptian rock containing large crystals in a purplish groundmass.

portico A porch with a roof supported by *columns;* an entrance porch.

post-and-lintel system A *trabeated* system of construction in which two posts support a *lintel.*

potsherds Broken pottery, discarded by earlier civilizations, that settles into firmly stratified mounds over time and provides archeological chronologies.

pottery Objects (usually vessels) made of clay and hardened by firing.

predella The narrow ledge on which an *altarpiece* rests at the back of an altar.

primary colors The *hues* red, yellow, and blue. From these three colors, with the addition of white, it is theoretically possible to mix the full color spectrum. The primary colors cannot be produced by mixing other colors together.

program The architect's formulation of a design problem with respect to considerations of site, function, materials, and aims of the client; also, in painting and sculpture, the conceptual basis of a work.

pronaos (pro·nay'os) The space in front of the *cella* or *naos* of a Greek temple.

propylaeum (prah·pi·lay'um; *pl.* **propylaea**) A gateway building leading to an open court preceding a Greek or Roman temple.

proscenium (pro·seen'i·um) The stage of an ancient Greek or Roman theater.

prostyle A style of Greek temple in which the *columns* stand in front of the *naos* and extend to its width.

provenance Origin; source.

psalter A book containing the Psalms of the Bible.

putto (*pl.* **putti**) A young child, a favorite subject in Italian painting and sculpture.

pylon (pie'lon) The *monumental* entrance of an Egyptian temple.

qiblah (keeb'lah) The direction (toward Mecca) in which Moslems face in prayer. (Often *kibla.*)

quadro-riportato (kwahd·roh·ree·por·tah'toh) The simulation of a wall painting for a ceiling design in which painted scenes are arranged in panels resembling frames on the surface of a shallow, curved *vault.*

quatrefoil (kat're·foyl) An architectural ornament having four lobes or **foils.** See also *trefoil.*

quattrocento (kwat'tro·chain'toh) The fifteenth century in Italian art.

quoin (koin) Large, sometimes *rusticated,* usually slightly projecting stone (or stones) that often form the corners of the exterior walls of masonry buildings.

raking cornice The *cornice* on the sloping sides of a *pediment.*

Ramayana A Sanskrit epic telling of Rama, an incarnation of the Hindu god Vishnu.

rathas Small, freestanding Hindu temples, perhaps sculptured as architectural models.

rayonnant The "radiant" style in thirteenth-century architecture that is associated with the royal Paris court of Louis IX.

realism The representation of things according to nature (without *idealization*).

red-figure technique In later Greek pottery, the silhouetting of red figures against a black background; the reverse of the *black-figure technique.*

reinforced concrete (ferroconcrete) Concrete with increased tensile strength produced by iron or steel mesh or bars embedded in it.

relief In sculpture, figures projecting from a background of which they are part. The degree of relief is designated high, low (**bas**), or sunken (hollow). In the last, the backgrounds are not cut back and the points in highest relief are level with the original surface of the material being carved. A kind of low relief that is hardly more than a scratching of the surface, originated by Donatello, is termed **stiacciata** or **sciacciata.** See also *repoussé.*

reliquary A small receptacle for a sacred relic, usually of a richly decorated, precious material.

repoussé (ruh·poo·say') Formed in *relief* by beating a metal plate from the back, leaving the impression on the face. The metal is hammered into a hollow mold of wood or some other pliable material and finished with a *graver.* See also *relief.*

reserve column In Egyptian rock-cut tombs, a *column* that is hewn from the living rock and serves no supporting function.

respond An engaged *column, pilaster,* or similar structure that either projects from a *compound pier* or some other supporting device or is bonded to a wall and carries one end of an *arch,* often at the end of an *arcade.* A **nave arcade,** for example, may have nine *pillars* and two responds.

retable (ruh·tay′bl) An architectural screen or wall above and behind an altar, usually containing painting, sculpture, carving, or other decorations. See also *altarpiece.*

reverse On coins or medals, the side opposite the *obverse.*

rhyton (right′on) An ancient Greek ceremonial drinking vessel with a base usually in the form of the head of an animal, a woman, or a mythological creature.

rib A relatively slender, molded masonry *arch* that projects from a surface. In Gothic architecture, the *ribs* form the framework of the *vaulting.*

ribbed vault See *vault.*

ridgepole The horizontal beam at the ridge of a roof, to which the upper ends of the rafters attach.

rinceau (ran·so′) An ornamental design composed of undulating foliate vine motifs.

Romanitas (Roh·man·ee·tahs) The religion of the Holy Roman Empire; its ritual and practice was based on imperial dominion.

rose or **wheel window** The large, circular window with *tracery* and stained glass frequently used in the *façades* of Gothic churches.

rotulus A long manuscript scroll used by the Egyptians, Greeks, and Romans; predecessor of the *codex.*

rusticate To give a rustic appearance by *beveling* the edges of stone blocks to emphasize the joints between them. A technique popular during the Renaissance, especially for stone courses at the ground-floor level.

sacra conversazione (sah′krah·cone·ver·sotz·ee·ohn′ee) In Italian, literally ''holy conversation''; a grouping of the Madonna, Child, and Saints in the same spatial setting, so that they appear to be conversing with one another.

sacral-idyllic scene A landscape depicting country life and idealized nature.

Salon The government-sponsored exhibition of works by living artists held in Paris, first biennially and (since the mid-eighteenth century) annually.

samsara (som·sah′rah) In Hindu belief, the rebirth of the soul into a succession of lives.

sarcophagus (sar·kof′a·gus) A stone coffin.

saturation The purity of a *hue;* the higher the *saturation,* the purer the hue. *Value* and saturation are not constantly related. For example, high-saturation yellow tends to have a high value, but high-saturation violet tends to have a low value.

satyr (sat′er) In Greek mythology, a kind of demi-god or deity, a follower of Dionysos, wanton and lascivious and often represented with goat-like ears and legs and a short tail.

scale The dimensions of the parts or the totality of a building or an object in relation to its use or function. In architectural

plans, the relation of the actual size of a structure to its representative size.

scriptorium A Medieval writing room in which scrolls were also housed.

sculpture in the round Freestanding figures, carved or modeled in three dimensions.

secondary colors The colors (green, orange, and purple) that result from mixture of pairs of *primary colors.*

section In architecture, a diagram or representation of a part of a structure or building along an imaginary plane that passes through it vertically.

seicento (say·chain′toh) The seventeenth century in Italian art.

serdab A small, concealed chamber in an Egyptian tomb for the statue of the deceased.

severe style An early, pre-Classical, transitional style of mid-fifth-century Greek statuary that is formal but not rigid in pose and emphasizes the principle of weight distribution; a liberation from the Archaic limitations of frontal rigidity found in Egyptian portrait statues.

sfumato (sfoo·ma′toh) A smoke-like haziness that subtly softens outlines in painting, particularly applied to the painting of Leonardo and Correggio.

sgraffito (zgra·fee′toh) Decoration produced by scratching through a surface layer of plaster, *glazing,* etc., to reveal a different colored *ground;* also, pottery or other ware so decorated.

shaft The part of a *column* between the *capital* and the base.

shaft grave A grave in the form of a deep pit, the actual burial spot being at the base of the shaft or in a niche at the base.

shaman (shah′mon) A priest or medicine man who can influence good and evil spirits; the religion of some American Indians and Eskimos. **shamanism** (*adj.*)

shoji (show′jee) A rice-paper-covered sliding screen that serves as a room divider in traditional Japanese houses.

sikhara (shih′ka·rah) In Hindu temples of Vishnu, the tower above the shrine.

silver point A drawing technique involving the use of a silver-tipped ''pencil'' on a paper with a white *matte* coating; also, the delicate drawings so made.

sinopia or **sinopie** Reddish-brown earth color; also, the *cartoon* or underpainting for a *fresco.*

sistrum An instrument of metal rods loosely held in a metal frame, which jingle when shaken. Peculiarly Egyptian, it was used especially in the worship of Isis and is still used in Nubia.

Siva or **Shiva** (shee′vuh) Hindu god of destruction and creation.

slip Potter's clay dispersed in a liquid and used for *casting,* decoration, and to attach parts of clay vessels, such as handles.

smalto The colored glass or enamel used in *mosaics.*

socle (soh′kel) A molded projection at the bottom of a wall or a *pier,* or beneath a pedestal or a *column* base.

soffit The underside of an architectural member such as an *arch, lintel, cornice,* or stairway. See also *intrados.*

spandrel The roughly triangular space enclosed by the curves of adjacent *arches* and a horizontal member connecting their vertexes; also, the space enclosed by the curve of an *arch* and an enclosing right angle.

splay A large *bevel* or *chamfer.*

splayed opening An opening (as in a wall) that is cut away diagonally so that the outer edges are farther apart then the inner edges. See also *embrasure.*

springing The lowest stone of an *arch,* resting on the *impost block.*

square schematism A church *plan* in which the *crossing square* is used as the *module* for all parts of the design.

squinch An architectural device used to make a transition from a square to a polygonal or circular base for a *dome.* It may be composed of *lintels, corbels,* or *arches.*

stave A wedge-shaped timber; vertically placed staves embellish the architectural features of a building.

stele (stee′lee) A carved stone slab or *pillar* used especially by the ancient Greeks as grave or site markers and for similar purposes.

still life A painting representing inanimate objects, such as flowers, fruit, or household articles.

stoa (stoh′a) In ancient Greek architecture, an open building with a roof supported by a row of *columns* parallel to the back wall.

stringcourse A horizontal *molding* or band in masonry, ornamental but usually reflecting interior structure.

stucco Fine plaster or cement used as a coating for walls or for decoration.

stupa (stoo′puh) A large, mound-shaped Buddhist shrine.

style A manner of treatment or execution of works of art that is characteristic of a civilization, a people, or an individual; also, a special and superior quality in a work of art.

stylobate (sty′loh·bate) The upper step of the base of a Greek temple, which forms a platform for the *columns.*

stylus A needle-like tool used in *engraving* and *incising.*

superimposed orders *Orders* of architecture that are placed one above another in an *arcaded* or *colonnaded* building, usually in the following sequence: **Doric** (the first story), **Ionic,** and **Corinthian.** Superimposed orders are found in Greek *stoas* and were used widely by Roman and Renaissance builders.

sutra (soo′truh) In Buddhism, an account of a sermon by or a dialogue involving the *Buddha.*

swag A kind of decoration for walls, furniture, etc., done in *relief* and resembling garlands and gathered drapery, that was particularly popular in the eighteenth century.

symmetry *Esthetic* balance that is usually achieved by disposing *forms* about a real or an imaginary *axis* so that those on one side more-or-less correspond with those on the other. The correspondence may be in terms of shape, *color,* texture, etc.

tablinum A room behind the *atrium* in a Roman house in which family archives and statues were kept.

tectiforms Shapes resembling man-made structures found painted on the walls of Paleolithic caves.

tell In Near Eastern archeology, a hill or a mound, usually an ancient site of habitation.

tempera A technique of painting using *pigment* mixed with egg yolk, glue, or casein; also, the *medium* itself.

Tenebrists (Ten'i·brists) A group of seventeenth-century European painters who used violent contrasts of light and dark.

tenebroso Painting in the "dark manner"; a technique of the *Caravagisti*.

tenon A projection on the end of a piece of wood that is inserted into a corresponding hole (**mortice**) in another piece of wood to form a joint.

terra cotta Hard-baked clay, used for sculpture and as a building material, that may be *glazed* or painted.

tesserae (tess'er·ee) Small, shaped pieces of glass or stone used in making *mosaics*.

tholos (thoh'los) A circular structure, generally in Classical Greek style; also, an ancient, circular tomb.

thrust The outward force exerted by an *arch* or a *vault* that must be counterbalanced by *buttresses*.

tier A series of architectural rows, layers, or ranks arranged above or behind one another.

tondo A circular painting or *relief* sculpture.

torano (tor'uh·nuh) Gateways in the stone fence around a *stupa*, located at the cardinal points of the compass.

torus A convex *molding* or part of a molding, usually the lowest in the base of a *column*.

totem An animal or object and its representation or image, considered to be a symbol of a given family or clan.

trabeated (tray'bee·ate·id) Of *post-and-lintel* construction.

tracery Branching, ornamental stonework, generally in a window, where it supports the glass; particularly characteristic of Gothic architecture.

transept The part of a *cruciform* church with an *axis* that crosses the main axis at right angles.

trecento (tray·chain'toh) The fourteenth century in Italian art.

trefoil An architectural ornament having three lobes or *foils*. See also *quatrefoil*.

triforium In a Gothic cathedral, the blind, *arcaded* gallery below the *clerestory*.

triglyph A projecting, grooved member of a *Doric frieze* that alternates with *metopes*.

trilithon A pair of *monoliths* topped with a *lintel*; found in *megalithic* structures.

triptych (trip'tik) A three-paneled *altarpiece*.

trompe l'oeil (trohmp loy') A form of illusionistic painting that attempts to represent an object as if it exists in three dimensions at the surface of the painting; literally, "eye-fooling."

trumeau (troo·moh') A *pillar* in the center of a Romanesque or Gothic portal.

turret A small, often ornamental tower projecting from a building, usually at a corner.

tympanum The space enclosed by a *lintel* and an *arch* over a doorway; also, the recessed face of a *pediment*.

ukiyo-e (oo'kee·oh·ee) A style of Japanese *genre* painting ("pictures of the floating world") that influenced nineteenth-century Western art.

Upanishads (oo·pan'i·shads) A series of late Vedic metaphysical treatises dealing with man in relation to the universe.

urna The whorl of hair, represented as a dot, between the brows of a Hindu diety.

ushnisha (ush·nish'uh) Stylized protuberance of the *Buddha's* forehead, emblematic of his superhuman consciousness.

value The amount of light reflected by a *hue*; the greater the amount of light, the higher the value. See also *saturation*.

vanishing point In *linear perspective*, that point on the horizon toward which parallel lines appear to converge and at which they seem to vanish.

vault A masonry roof or ceiling constructed on the *arch* principle. A **barrel** or **tunnel vault**, semicylindrical in cross section, is in effect a deep arch or an uninterrupted series of arches, one behind the other, over an oblong space. In a **cross-barrel vault,** the main barrel (tunnel) vault is intersected at right angles with other barrel (tunnel) vaults at regular intervals. A **quadrant vault** is a half-barrel (tunnel) vault. A **sexpartite vault** is a rib vault with six panels. A **fan vault** is a development of *lierne* vaulting characteristic of English Perpendicular Gothic, in which radiating *ribs* form a fan-like pattern. A **groin** or **cross vault** is formed at the point at which two *barrel (tunnel) vaults* intersect at right angles. In a **ribbed vault,** there is a framework of ribs or arches under the intersections of the vaulting sections.

vellum Calfskin prepared as a surface for writing or painting.

vignette Originally, a decorative element of vine leaves and tendrils; any decorative design in a book or manuscript that is rather small and that has no definite boundaries or frame.

vihara (vee·hah'rah) A Buddhist monastery, often cut into a hill.

vimana (vih·mah'nuh) In Hindu and Buddhist temples, the pyramidal tower above the shrine (composed of the *garbha griha* and the *sikhara*).

Vishnu Hindu god, called "The Preserver," one of whose incarnations is Krishna.

volume See *mass*.

volute A spiral, scroll-like form characteristic of the Greek Ionic *capital*.

voussoir (voo·swahr') A wedge-shaped block used in the construction of a true *arch*. The central voussoir, which sets the arch, is the *keystone*.

warm color Red, orange, or yellow. Psychologically, warm colors tend to be exciting, emphatic, and affirmative; optically, they generally seem to advance or to project. See also *cool color*.

wash In *watercolor* painting especially, a thin, transparent film of color.

watercolor A painting technique using *pigment* (usually prepared with gum) mixed with water and applied to an absorbent surface; also, the *medium* itself. The painting is transparent, with the white of the paper furnishing the lights. See also *gouache*.

weight shift See *contrapposto*.

westwork A multi-storied *mass*, including the *façade* and usually surmounted by towers, at the western end of a Medieval church.

woodcut A wooden block on the surface of which those parts not intended to print are cut away to a slight depth, leaving the design raised; also, the printed impression made with such a block.

yaksha (yak'shah) A divinity in the Hindu and Buddhist pantheon. (*f.* **yakshi**)

yamato-e (yah·mah'toh·ee) A purely Japanese style of sophisticated and depersonalized painting created for the Fujiwara nobility.

yasti (yahs'tee) The mast surmounting the *dome* of a *stupa*.

yu A covered Chinese libation vessel.

Zen A Buddhist sect and its doctrine, emphasizing enlightenment through intuition and introspection rather than the study of scripture. In Chinese, *Ch'an*.

ziggurat (zig'oor·at) A roughly pyramidal structure, built in ancient Mesopotamia, consisting of stages; each succeeding stage is stepped back from the one beneath.

zoomorphism The representation of gods in the form or with the attributes of animals; the use of animal forms in art or symbolism.

BIBLIOGRAPHY

This bibliography lists the basic general books in the field and contains a few entries for monographs and museum exhibition catalogs. There are no entries for periodical articles; for reference to these, consult your library.

Reference Books

Arntzen, Etta, and Rainwater, Robert. *Guide to the Literature of Art History.* Chicago: American Library Association/Art Book Company, 1980.

Bator, Paul M. *The International Trade in Art.* Chicago: University of Chicago Press, 1983.

Broude, Norma, and Garrard, May D., eds. *Feminism and Art History.* New York: Harper & Row, 1982.

Encyclopedia of World Art. 15 vols. New York: McGraw-Hill, 1959–1968, revised 1972.

Feilden, Bernard B. *Conservation of Historic Buildings.* London: Butterworth Scientific Books, 1982.

Fielding, Mantle. *Dictionary of American Painters, Sculptors and Engravers.* New York: James F. Carr, 1965.

Fleming, John; Honour, Hugh; and Pevsner, Nikolaus. *Penguin Dictionary of Architecture.* Baltimore: Penguin, 1980.

Fletcher, Sir Banister. *A History of Architecture.* 18th rev. ed. New York: Scribner, 1975.

Giedion, Siegfried. *The Beginnings of Architecture.* Princeton: Princeton University Press, 1981.

——*Space, Time and Architecture.* 5th ed., rev. and enl. Cambridge: Harvard University Press, 1982.

Gombrich, Ernst Hans Josef. *Art and Illusion.* 5th ed. London: Phaidon, 1977.

Hall, James. *Dictionary of Subjects and Symbols in Art.* Rev. ed. London: J. Murray, 1977.

Hauser, Arnold. *The Sociology of Art.* Chicago: University of Chicago Press, 1982.

Hind, Arthur M. *A History of Engraving and Etching from the Fifteenth Century to the Year 1914.* 3rd rev. ed. New York: Dover, 1963.

Holt, Elizabeth B. *A Documentary History of Art.* 2nd ed. 2 vols. Garden City, N.Y.: Doubleday, 1981.

Huyghe, René, ed. *Larousse Encyclopedia of Byzantine and Medieval Art.* New York: Prometheus Press, 1963; New York: Hamlyn/American (paperbound), 1976.

——*Larousse Encyclopedia of Renaissance and Baroque Art.* New York: Prometheus Press, 1964; Hamlyn/American (paperbound), 1976.

Kostof, Spiro. *A History of Architecture.* Oxford: Oxford University Press, 1985.

Kronenberger, Louis. *Atlantic Brief Lives: A Biographical Companion to the Arts.* Boston: Little, Brown, 1971.

Murray, Peter, and Murray, Linda. *A Dictionary of Art and Artists.* New York: Penguin, 1976.

Myers, Bernard Samuel, ed. *Encyclopedia of Painting: Painters and Painting of the World from Prehistoric Times to the Present Day.* 4th rev. ed. New York: Crown, 1979.

——*Encyclopedia of World Art,* Suppl. vol. 16. Palatine, Ill.: McGraw-Hill/The Publishers Guild, 1983.

Myers, Bernard S., and Myers, Shirley D., eds. *Dictionary of 20th Century Art.* New York: McGraw-Hill, 1974.

Pevsner, Nikolaus. *An Outline of European Architecture.* 8th rev. ed. Baltimore: Penguin, 1974.

Pierson, William H., and Davidson, Martha. *Arts of the United States, A Pictorial Survey.*

1960. Reprint. Athens: University of Georgia Press, 1975.

Placzik, A. K., ed. *Macmillan Encyclopedia of Architects.* 4 vols. New York: Macmillan/Free Press, 1982.

Podro, Michael. *The Critical Historians of Art.* New Haven: Yale University Press, 1982.

Quick, John. *Artists' and Illustrators' Encyclopedia.* New York: McGraw-Hill, 1977.

Rubenstein, Charlotte Streifer. *American Women Artists from Early Indian Times to the Present.* Boston: G.K. Hall/Avon Books, 1982.

Smith, G. E. Kidder. *The Architecture of the United States: An Illustrated Guide to Buildings Open to the Public.* 3 vols. Garden City, N.Y.: Doubleday/Anchor, 1981.

Stierlin, Henri. *Encyclopedia of World Architecture 1978.* 1978. Reprint. New York: Van Nostrand, Reinhold, 1983.

Tufts, Eleanor. *American Women Artists, Past and Present, A Selected Bibliographic Guide.* New York: Garland Publishers, 1984.

——*Our Hidden Heritage, Five Centuries of Women Artists.* London: Paddington Press, 1974.

Waterhouse, Ellis. *The Dictionary of British 18th Century Painters in Oils and Crayons.* Woodbridge, England: Antique Collectors' Club, 1981.

Wittkower, Rudolf. *Sculpture Processes and Principles.* New York: Harper & Row, 1977.

Wölfflin, Heinrich. *The Sense of Form in Art.* New York: Chelsea, 1958.

Young, William, ed. *A Dictionary of American Artists, Sculptors, and Engravers.* Cambridge, Mass.: W. Young, 1968.

chapter 1   The Birth of Art

Bandi, Hans; Breuil, Henri; et al. *The Art of the Stone Age: Forty Thousand Years of Rock Art.* 2nd ed. London: Methuen, 1970.

Bataille, Georges. *Lascaux: Prehistoric Painting or the Birth of Art.* Lausanne: Skira, 1980.

Breuil, Henri. *Four Hundred Centuries of Cave Art.* New York: Hacker, 1979.

Graziosi, Paolo. *Paleolithic Art.* New York: McGraw-Hill, 1960.

Leroi-Gourhan, Andre. *The Dawn of European Art, and Introduction to Paleolithic Cave Painting.* Cambridge: Cambridge University Press, 1982.

——*Treasurers of Prehistoric Art.* New York: Abrams, 1967.

Megaw, J. V. S. *The Art of the European Iron Age.* New York: Harper & Row, 1970.

Renfrew, Colin, ed. *British Prehistory.* London: Duckworth, 1974.

Sandars, Nancy K. *Prehistoric Art in Europe.* Harmondsworth, England: Penguin, 1969.

Trump, David H. *The Prehistory of the Mediterranean.* New Haven: Yale University Press, 1980.

Windels, Fernand. *The Lascaux Cave Paintings.* New York: Viking, 1950.

chapter 2   The Ancient Near East

Culican, William. *The Medes and Persians.* London: Thames & Hudson, 1965; New York: Praeger, 1965.

Frankfort, Henri. *The Art and Architecture of the Ancient Orient.* Baltimore: Penguin, 1971.

Garbini, Giovanni. *The Ancient World.* London: Hamlyn, 1976.

Ghirshman, Roman. *Iran from Earliest Times to the Islamic Conquest.* New York: Penguin, 1978.

Hinz, Walther. *The Lost World of Elam.* New York: New York University Press, 1973.

Kenyon, Kathleen M. *Digging Up Jericho.* New York: Praeger, 1974.

Kramer, Samuel N. *The Sumerians: Their History, Culture, and Character.* Chicago: University of Chicago Press, 1963.

Lloyd, Seton. *The Archaeology of Mesopotamia from the Old Stone Age to the Persian Conquest.* London: Thames & Hudson, 1978.

——*The Art of the Ancient Near East.* New York: Praeger, 1969.

Lloyd, S. H.; Muller, H. W.; and Martin, R. *Ancient Architecture: Mesopotamia, Egypt, Crete, Greece.* New York: Abrams, 1974.

Mellaart, James. *Çatal Hüyük: a Neolithic Town in Anatolia.* New York: McGraw-Hill, 1967.

——*The Earliest Civilizations of the Near East.* New York: McGraw-Hill, 1965.

——*The Neolithic of the Near East.* New York: Scribner, 1975.

Oppenheim, A. Leo. *Ancient Mesopotamia.* Rev. ed. Chicago: University of Chicago Press, 1977.

Parrot, André. *The Arts of Assyria.* New York: Golden Press, 1961.

——*Sumer: The Dawn of Art.* New York: Golden Press, 1961.

Perkins, Ann Louise. *The Art of Dura-Europos.* Oxford: Clarendon Press, 1973.

Porada, Edith, and Dyson, R. H. *The Art of Ancient Iran: Islamic Cultures.* Rev. ed. New York: Greystone Press, 1969.

Woolley, Charles L. *The Art of the Middle East, Including Persia, Mesopotamia and Palestine.* New York: Crown, 1961.

——*The Development of Sumerian Art.* Westport, Conn.: Greenwood Press, 1981.

chapter 3   The Art of Egypt

Aldred, Cyril. *The Development of Ancient Egyptian Art from 3200 to 1315 B.C.* 3 vols. London: Academy Edition, 1973.

Badawy, Alexander. *A History of Egyptian Architecture.* 3 vols. Berkeley: University of California Press, 1973.

Breasted, James. *History of Egypt.* 1909. Reprint. New York: Scribner's, 1964.

Emery, Walter B. *Archaic Egypt.* Baltimore: Penguin, 1972.

Gardiner, Sir Alan Henderson. *Egypt of the Pharaohs.* London: Oxford University Press, 1978.

Lange, Kurt, with Hirmer, Max. *Egypt: Architecture, Sculpture and Painting in Three Thousand Years.* 4th ed. London: Phaidon, 1968.

Lurker, Manfred. *The Gods and Symbols of Ancient Egypt: an Illustrated Dictionary.* New York: Thames & Hudson, 1980.

Mekhitarian, Arpag. *Egyptian Painting.* New York: Skira, 1978.

Smith, E. Baldwin. *Egyptian Architecture as*

Cultural Expression. Watkins Glen, N.Y.: American Life Foundation, 1968.

Smith, William Stevenson, and Simpson, W. *The Art and Architecture of Ancient Egypt.* Rev. ed. New York: Viking, 1981.

Woldering, Irmgard. *Gods, Men and Pharaohs: The Glory of Egyptian Art.* New York: Abrams, 1967.

chapter 4   The Art of the Aegean

Demargne, Pierre. *Aegean Art: The Origins of Greek Art.* London: Thames & Hudson, 1964.

Evans, Arthur. *The Palace of Minos.* 4 vols. 1921–1935. Reprint. New York: Biblo & Tannen, 1964.

Graham, James W. *The Palaces of Crete.* Princeton: Princeton University Press, 1969.

Marinatos, Spyridon, with Hirmer, Max. *Crete and Mycenae.* London: Thames & Hudson, 1960.

Matz, Friedrich. *The Art of Crete and Early Greece.* New York: Crown, 1965.

Pendlebury, John. *The Archeology of Crete.* London: Methuen, 1967.

Schliemann, Heinrich. *Ilios.* 1881. Reprint. New York: B. Blom, 1968. (Other reprints available.)

——*Mycenae.* 1880. Reprint. New York: Arno Press, 1976.

——*Tiryns.* 1885. Reprint. New York: Arno Press, 1976.

Vermeule Emily. *Greece in the Bronze Age.* Chicago: University of Chicago Press, 1972.

Wace, Alan. *Mycenae, an Archeological History and Guide.* New York: Biblo & Tannen, 1964.

Warren, Peter M. *The Aegean Civilizations.* London: Elsevier/Phaidon, 1970.

Willetts, R. F. *The Civilization of Ancient Crete.* Berkeley: University of California Press, 1978.

chapter 5   The Art of Greece

Arias, Paolo. *A History of One Thousand Years of Greek Vase Painting.* New York: Abrams, 1962.

Ashmole, Bernard. *Architect and Sculptor in Classical Greece.* New York: New York University Press, 1972.

Beazley, John D. *Attic Red-Figure Vase-Painters.* 3 vols. 1963. Reprint. New York: Hacker, 1984.

——*The Development of Attic Black-Figure.* Berkeley: University of California Press, 1964.

Beazley, John D., and Ashmole, Bernard. *Greek Sculpture and Painting to the End of the Hellenistic Period.* Cambridge: Cambridge University Press, 1932, 1966.

Berve, Helmut. *Greek Temples, Theatres, and Shrines.* New York: Abrams, 1963.

Blumel, Carl. *Greek Sculptors at Work.* London: Phaidon, 1969.

Brilliant, Richard. *Arts of the Ancient Greeks.* New York: McGraw-Hill, 1973.

Buschor, Ernst. *Greek Vase Painting.* New York: Hacker, 1978.

Carpenter, Rhys. *Greek Sculpture: A Critical Review.* Chicago: University of Chicago Press, 1960.

Charbonneaux, Jean. *Archaic Greek Art.* New York: Braziller, 1971.

Charbonneaux, Jean; Martin, Roland; and Villard, François. *Hellenistic Art.* New York: Braziller, 1973.

Cook, Robert M. *Greek Art: Its Development, Character and Influence.* Harmondsworth, England: Penguin, 1976.

Coulton, J. J. *Ancient Greek Architects at Work.* Ithaca, N.Y.: Cornell University Press, 1977.

Dinsmoor, W. B. *The Architecture of Ancient Greece.* 3rd ed. New York: Norton, 1975.

Havelock, Christine Mitchell. *Hellenistic Art:*

The Art of the Classical World. 2nd ed., rev. New York: W. W. Norton, 1981.

Lawrence, Arnold W. *Greek Architecture.* 2nd ed. Baltimore: Penguin, 1967.

Lullies, Reinhard, and Hirmer, Max. *Greek Sculpture.* Rev. ed. New York: Abrams, 1960.

Pfuhl, Ernst. *Masterpieces of Greek Drawing and Painting.* 2nd ed. Chicago: Argonaut, 1967.

Pollitt, Jerome J. *The Ancient View of Greek Art.* New Haven: Yale University Press, 1974.

——*Art and Experience in Classical Greece.* Cambridge: Cambridge University Press, 1972.

——*The Art of Greece 1400–31 B.C.* Englewood Cliffs, N.J.: Prentice-Hall, 1965.

Richter, Gisela M. *Attic Red-Figure Vases: A Survey.* New Haven: Yale University Press, 1958.

——*A Handbook of Greek Art.* 6th ed. New York: Phaidon, 1969.

——*The Sculpture and Sculptors of the Greeks.* 4th ed. New Haven: Yale University Press, 1970.

Ridgway, Brunilde Sismondo. *Fifth Century Styles in Greek Sculpture.* Princeton: Princeton University Press, 1981.

Robertson, Donald S. *Greek and Roman Architecture.* 2nd ed. Cambridge: Cambridge University Press, 1969.

Robertson, Martin. *Greek Painting.* New York: Rizzoli, 1979.

——*A History of Greek Art.* 2 vols. Cambridge: Cambridge University Press, 1976.

——*A Shorter History of Greek Art.* Cambridge: Cambridge University Press, 1981.

Scranton, Robert L. *Greek Architecture.* New York: Braziller, 1962.

Scully, Vincent J. *The Earth, the Temple and the Gods: Greek Sacred Architecture.* Rev. ed. New York: Praeger, 1969.

Swindler, Mary H. *Ancient Painting.* New Haven: Yale University Press, 1929.

Vermeule, Cornelius C. *Greek and Roman Sculpture in America: Masterpieces in Public Collections.* Berkeley: University of California Press, 1981.

chapter 6   Etruscan and Roman Art

Andreae, Bernard. *The Art of Rome.* New York: Abrams, 1977.

Bianchi Bandinelli, Ranuccio. *Rome, the Late Empire.* New York: Braziller, 1971.

Boethius, Axel. *The Golden House of Nero.* Ann Arbor: University of Michigan Press, 1960.

Brilliant, Richard. *Roman Art, from the Republic to Constantine.* New York: Praeger, 1974.

Brown, Frank Edward. *Roman Architecture.* New York: Braziller, 1961.

Buchthal, Hugo. *Art of the Mediterranean World, A.D. 100 to 1400.* Art History Series 5. Washington, D.C.: Decatur House Press, 1983.

Goldscheider, Ludwig. *Roman Portraits.* London: Phaidon, 1940.

Hanfmann, George. *Roman Art.* Greenwich, Conn.: New York Graphic Society, 1964.

Kraus, Theodor. *Pompeii and Herculaneum: The Living Cities of the Dead.* New York: Abrams, 1975.

MacDonald, William L. *The Architecture of the Roman Empire.* Rev. ed. New Haven: Yale University Press, 1982.

McKay, Alexander G. *Houses, Villas, and Palaces in the Roman World.* Ithaca, N.Y.: Cornell University Press, 1975.

Maiuri, Amedeo. *Pompeii.* 14th ed. Rome: Istituto poligrafico dello Stato, 1970.

——*Roman Painting.* Geneva: Skira, 1953.

Mansuelli, Guido. *The Art of Etruria and Early Rome.* New York: Crown, 1965.

Nash, Ernest. *Pictorial Dictionary of Ancient Rome.* 2nd ed. 2 vols. New York: Praeger, 1968.

Pollitt, Jerome J. *The Art of Rome, 753 B.C.– A.D. 337.* Englewood Cliffs, N.J.: Prentice-Hall, 1966.

Richardson, Emeline. *The Etruscans: Their Art and Civilization.* Chicago: University of Chicago Press, 1976.

Rivoira, Giovanni. *Roman Architecture and Its Principles of Construction Under the Empire.* New York: Hacker, 1972.

Robertson, Donald S. *Greek and Roman Architecture.* 2nd ed. Cambridge: Cambridge University Press, 1969.

Strong, Donald. *Roman Art.* Harmondsworth, England: Penguin, 1980.

Strong, Eugenie. *Art in Ancient Rome.* Ann Arbor, Michigan: University Microfilms, 1979.

Ward-Perkins, John. *Roman Architecture.* New York: Abrams, 1977.

Ward-Perkins, John, and Boethius, Axel. *Etruscan and Roman Architecture.* Harmondsworth, England: Penguin, 1970.

chapter 7   Early Christian, Byzantine, and Islamic Art

Anthony, Edgar W. *A History of Mosaics.* New York: Hacker, 1968.

Arnold, Thomas W. *Painting in Islam.* New York: Dover, 1965.

Aslanapa, Oktay. *Turkish Art and Architecture.* London: Faber & Faber, 1971.

Atil, Esin. *Renaissance of Islam: Art of the Mamluks.* Washington, D.C.: Smithsonian Institution Press, 1981.

Baynes, Norman, and Moss, Henry, eds. *Byzantium.* Oxford: Clarendon Press, 1948.

Beckwith, John. *The Art of Constantinople: An Introduction to Byzantine Art (330–1453).* New York: Phaidon, 1968.

——*Early Christian and Byzantine Art.* New York: Penguin, 1979.

Chatzidakis, Manolis. *Byzantine and Early Medieval Painting.* New York: Viking, 1965.

Creswell, K. A. C., and van Berchem, Marguerite. *Early Muslim Architecture.* 2nd ed. Oxford: Clarendon Press, 1969.

Dalton, Ormonde M. *Byzantine Art and Archaeology.* New York: Dover, 1961.

Demus, Otto. *Byzantine Art in the West.* New York: New York University Press, 1970.

Ettinghausen, Richard. *Arab Painting.* Geneva: Skira, 1977.

——*From Byzantium to Sasanian Iran and the Islamic World.* Leiden: Brill, 1972.

Goodwin, Godfrey. *A History of Ottoman Architecture.* Baltimore: Johns Hopkins University Press, 1971.

Gough, Michael. *The Origins of Christian Art.* New York: Praeger, 1973.

Grabar, André. *The Beginnings of Christian Art, 200–395.* London: Thames & Hudson, 1967.

——*Byzantine Painting.* Geneva: Skira, 1953.

——*The Golden Age of Justinian: From the Death of Theodosius to the Rise of Islam.* New York: Odyssey Press, 1967.

Grabar, André, and Chatzidakis, Manolis. *Greek Mosaics of the Byzantine Period.* New York: New American Library, 1964.

Grabar, Oleg. *The Formation of Islamic Art.* New Haven: Yale University Press, 1973.

Grunebaum, Gustave von. *Classical Islam: A History, 600–1258.* Chicago: Aldine, 1970.

Hamilton, George H. *The Art and Architecture of Russia.* 2nd ed. New York: Viking, 1975.

Hamilton, John A. *Byzantine Architecture and Decoration.* 1933. Freeport, N.Y.: Books for Libraries/Arno, 1972.

Hawley, Walter A. *Oriental Rugs, Antique and Modern.* 1936. Reprint. New York: Dover, 1970.

Hoag, John D. *Islamic Architecture.* New York: Abrams, 1977.

Huyghe, René, ed. *Larousse Encyclopedia of Byzantine and Medieval Art*. See **Reference Books**.

Kitzinger, Ernst. *The Art of Byzantium and the Medieval Ages*. Bloomington: Indiana University Press, 1976.

——*Early Medieval Art in the British Museum*. London: British Museum, 1983.

Krautheimer, Richard. *Early Christian and Byzantine Architecture*. Harmondsworth, England: Penguin, 1975.

Kühnel, Ernst. *Islamic Art and Architecture*. London: Bell, 1966.

Lane, Arthur. *Early Islamic Pottery, Mesopotamia, Egypt and Persia*. New York: Faber & Faber, 1965.

Levey, Michael. *The World of Ottoman Art*. New York: Scribner, 1975.

Lowrie, Walter S. *Art in the Early Church*. New York: Norton, 1969.

MacDonald, William L. *Early Christian and Byzantine Architecture*. New York: Braziller, 1962.

Maguire, Henry. *Art and Eloquence in Byzantium*. Princeton: Princeton University Press, 1981.

Mango, Cyril A. *Byzantine Architecture*. New York: Abrams, 1975.

Meyer, Peter. *Byzantine Mosaics: Torcello, Venice, Monreale, Palermo*. London: Batsford, 1952.

Morey, Charles R. *Early Christian Art*. Princeton: Princeton University Press, 1953.

Pope, Arthur, and Ackerman, Phyllis. *A Survey of Persian Art from Prehistoric Times to the Present*. London: Oxford University Press, 1977.

Rice, David T. *The Appreciation of Byzantine Art*. London: Oxford University Press, 1972.

——*The Art of Byzantium*. New York: Abrams, 1959.

——*Byzantine Art*. London: Variorum Reprints, 1973.

——*Islamic Art*. London: Thames & Hudson, 1975.

Simson, Otto von. *Sacred Fortress: Byzantine Art and Stagecraft in Ravenna*. Chicago: University of Chicago Press, 1976.

Smith, Earl Baldwin. *Architectural Symbolism of Imperial Rome and the Middle Ages*. Princeton: Princeton University Press, 1956.

——*The Dome, a Study in the History of Ideas*. Princeton: Princeton University Press, 1971.

Swift, Emerson H. *Hagia Sophia*. New York: Columbia University Press, 1980.

Volbach, Wolfgang. *Early Christian Mosaics, from the Fourth to the Seventh Centuries*. New York: Oxford University Press, 1946.

Volbach, Wolfgang, and Hirmer, Max. *Early Christian Art*. New York: Abrams, 1962.

Weitzmann, Kurt. *Ancient Book Illumination*. Cambridge: Harvard University Press, 1959.

——*Illustrations in Roll and Codex*. Princeton: Princeton University Press, 1970.

Weitzmann, Kurt, et al. *The Icon*. New York: Knopf, 1982.

chapter 8   Early Medieval Art

Arnold, Bruce. *A Concise History of Irish Art*. Rev. ed. London: Thames & Hudson, 1977.

Beckwith, John. *Early Medieval Art: Carolingian, Ottonian, Romanesque*. New York: Oxford University Press, 1974.

Calkins, Robert G. *Illuminated Books of the Middle Ages*. Ithaca, N.Y.: Cornell University Press, 1983.

Conant, Kenneth. *Carolingian and Romanesque Architecture 800–1200*. 2nd integrated rev. ed. Harmondsworth, England: Penguin, 1978.

Dodwell, C. R. *Anglo-Saxon Art: A New Perspective*. Ithaca, N.Y.: Cornell University Press, 1982.

Finlay, Ian. *Celtic Art, an Introduction*. London: Faber & Faber, 1973.

Goldschmidt, Adolf. *German Illumination*. New York: Hacker, 1970.

Grabar, André, and Nordenfalk, Carl. *Early Medieval Painting from the Fourth to the Eleventh Century*. New York: Skira, 1967.

Harbison, Peter, et al. *Irish Art and Architecture from Prehistory to the Present*. London: Thames & Hudson, 1978.

Henderson, George. *Early Medieval*. Pelican Style and Civilization Series. New York: Penguin, 1972.

Henry, Françoise. *Irish Art During the Viking Invasions, 900–1200 A.D.* Ithaca, N.Y.: Cornell University Press, 1970.

——*Irish Art in the Early Christian Period, to 800 A.D.* Rev. ed. London: Methuen, 1965.

Hinks, Roger P. *Carolingian Art*. Ann Arbor: University of Michigan Press, 1974.

Laszlo, Gyula. *The Art of the Migration Period*. London: Allen Lane, 1974.

Leeds, Edward T. *Early Anglo-Saxon Art and Archaeology*. Westport, Conn.: Greenwood Press, 1970.

Mütherich, Florentine, and Gaehde, J. E. *Carolingian Painting*. New York: Braziller, 1976.

Nordenfalk, Carl. *Celtic and Anglo-Saxon Painting: Book Illumination in the British Isles 600–800*. New York: Braziller, 1977.

Simons, Gerald. *Barbarian Europe*. New York: Time-Life Books, 1979.

Taylor, Harold M., and Taylor, Joan. *Anglo-Saxon Architecture*. 2 vols. Cambridge: Cambridge University Press, 1980.

Wilson, David M., and Klindt-Jensen, Ole. *Viking Art*. London: Allen & Unwin, 1980.

Zarnecki, George. *Art of the Medieval World*. New York: Abrams, 1975.

chapter 9   Romanesque Art

Anthony, Edgar W. *Romanesque Frescoes*. Princeton: Princeton University Press, Westport, Conn.: Greenwood Press, 1971.

Baum, Julius. *Romanesque Architecture in France*. 2nd ed. London: Country Life, 1928.

Bevan, Bernard. *History of Spanish Architecture*. London: Batsford, 1938.

Brooke, Christopher. *The Monastic World, 1000–1300*. London: Elek, 1974.

Clapham, Alfred W. *English Romanesque Architecture After the Conquest*. Oxford: Clarendon Press, 1964.

——*Romanesque Architecture in Western Europe*. Oxford: Clarendon Press, 1959.

Conant, Kenneth. *Carolingian and Romanesque Architecture 800–1200*. Baltimore: Penguin, 1979.

Crichton, George H. *Romanesque Sculpture in Italy*. London: Routledge & Paul, 1954.

Decker, Heinrich. *Romanesque Art in Italy*. New York: Abrams, 1959.

Demus, Otto. *Romanesque Mural Painting*. New York: Abrams, 1970.

Deschamps, Paul. *French Sculpture of the Romanesque Period—Eleventh and Twelfth Centuries*. 1930. Reprint. New York: Hacker, 1972.

Dodwell, C. R. *Painting in Europe 800–1200*. Harmondsworth, England: Penguin, 1971.

Evans, Joan. *Art in Medieval France 987–1498*. Oxford: Clarendon Press, 1969.

Focillon, Henri. *The Art of the West in the Middle Ages*. 2nd ed. London: Phaidon, 1969.

Gantner, Joseph; Pobé, Marcel; and Roubier, Jean. *Romanesque Art in France*. London: Thames & Hudson, 1956.

Gibbs-Smith, Charles H. *The Bayeux Tapestry*. London: Phaidon, 1973.

Grabar, André, and Nordenfalk, Carl. *Romanesque Painting*. New York: Skira, 1958.

Hearn, Millard F. *Romanesque Sculpture in the Eleventh and Twelfth Centuries*. Ithaca, N.Y.: Cornell University Press/Phaidon, 1981.

Holt, Elizabeth Filmore, ed. *A Documentary History of Art, I: The Middle Ages*. Princeton: Princeton University Press, 1981.

Kuback, Hans E. *Romanesque Architecture*. New York: Abrams, 1975.

Kuenstler, Gustav, ed. *Romanesque Art in Europe*. New York: Norton, 1973.

Leisinger, Hermann. *Romanesque Bronzes: Church Portals in Mediaeval Europe*. New York: Praeger, 1957.

Michel, Paul H. *Romanesque Wall Paintings in France*. Paris: Éditions Chêne, 1949.

Morey, Charles R. *Medieval Art*. New York: Norton, 1970.

Pickering, Frederick P. *Literature and Art in the Middle Ages*. Coral Gables: University of Miami Press, 1970.

Porter, Arthur K. *Medieval Architecture*. 2 vols. 1909. Reprint. New York: Hacker, 1969.

——*Romanesque Sculpture of the Pilgrimage Roads*. 1923. Reprint. New York: Hacker, 1969.

Ricci, Corrado. *Romanesque Architecture in Italy*. London: W. Heinemann, 1925.

Rickert, Margaret. *Painting in Britain: The Middle Ages*. 2nd ed. Harmondsworth, England: Penguin, 1965.

Rivoira, Giovanni. *Lombardic Architecture: Its Origin, Development, and Derivatives*. 1933. Reprint. New York: Hacker, 1975.

Saalman, Howard. *Medieval Architecture: European Architecture 600–1200*. New York: Braziller, 1962.

Schapiro, Meyer. *Romanesque Art: Selected Papers*. London: Chatto & Windus, 1977; New York: Braziller, 1976.

Stoddard, Whitney. *Art and Architecture in Medieval France*. New York: Harper & Row, 1972.

——*Monastery and Cathedral in France*. New York: Harper & Row, 1972.

Stone, Lawrence. *Sculpture in Britain in the Middle Ages*. Baltimore: Penguin, 1972.

Swarzenski, Hanns. *Monuments of Romanesque Art*. Chicago: University of Chicago Press, 1974.

Webb, Geoffrey F. *Architecture in Britain: The Middle Ages*. Harmondsworth, England: Penguin, 1965.

Zarnecki, George. *Romanesque Art*. New York: Universe Books, 1971.

——*Studies in Romanesque Sculpture*. London: Darian Press, 1979.

chapter 10   Gothic Art

Adams, Henry. *Mont-Saint-Michel and Chartres*. New York: Doubleday/Anchor, 1959.

Arnold, Hugh. *Stained Glass of the Middle Ages in England and France*. London: A. & C. Black, 1956.

Arslan, Edoardo. *Gothic Architecture in Venice*. London: Phaidon, 1971.

Aubert, Marcel. *The Art of the High Gothic Era*. New York: Crown, 1965.

——*Gothic Cathedrals of France and Their Treasures*. London: N. Kay, 1959.

Bony, Jean. *French Gothic Architecture of the XII and XIII Centuries*. Berkeley: University of California Press, 1983.

Branner, Robert. *Chartres Cathedral*. New York: Norton, 1969.

——*Gothic Architecture*. New York: Braziller, 1961.

Duby, George. *The Age of the Cathedrals*. Chicago: University of Chicago Press, 1981.

Dupont, Jacques, and Gnudi, Cesare. *Gothic Painting*. New York: Rizzoli, 1979.

Evans, Joan. *Art in Medieval France 987–1498*. Oxford: Clarendon Press, 1969.

——*The Flowering of the Middle Ages*. London: Thames & Hudson, 1985.

Fitchen, John. *The Construction of Gothic Cathedrals*. Chicago: University of Chicago Press, 1977.

Focillon, Henri. *The Art of the West in the Middle*

Ages. Vol. 2. Ithaca, N.Y.: Cornell University Press, 1980.

Foster, Richard. *Discovering English Churches*. New York: Oxford University Press, 1982.

Frankl, Paul. *Gothic Architecture*. Baltimore: Penguin, 1963.

———*The Gothic Literary Sources and Interpretations*. Princeton: Princeton University Press, 1960.

Grodecki, Louis, et al. *Gothic Architecture*. New York: Abrams, 1977.

Harvey, John H. *The Gothic World*. New York: Harper & Row, 1969.

Huizinga, Johan. *The Waning of the Middle Ages*. London: E. Arnold, 1970.

Jantzen, Hans. *The High Gothic: The Classic Cathedrals of Chartres, Reims, and Amiens*. New York: Pantheon, 1962.

Johnson, James. *The Radiance of Chartres*. New York: Random House, 1965.

Johnson, Paul. *British Cathedrals*. New York: William Morrow, 1980.

Katzenellenbogen, Adolf. *The Sculptural Programs of Chartres Cathedral*. Baltimore: Johns Hopkins Press, 1959.

Male, Émile. *The Gothic Image: Religious Art in France of the Thirteenth Century*. New York: Harper & Row, 1958.

———*The Gothic Image: Religious Art in the Twelfth Century*. Rev. ed. Princeton: Princeton University Press, 1978.

Mark, Robert. *Experiments in Gothic Structure*. Cambridge: MIT Press, 1982.

Martindale, Andrew. *Gothic Art*. London: Thames & Hudson, 1967.

———*The Rise of the Artist in the Middle Ages and Early Renaissance*. New York: McGraw-Hill, 1972.

Panofsky, Erwin. *Abbot Suger on the Abbey Church of St. Denis and Its Art Treasures*. 2nd ed. Princeton: Princeton University Press, 1979.

———*Gothic Architecture and Scholasticism*. New York: Meridian Books, 1963.

Pevsner, Nikolaus. *The Buildings of England*. 46 vols. Harmondsworth, England: Penguin, 1951–1974.

Robb, David M. *The Art of the Illuminated Manuscript*. Cranbury, N.J.: A. S. Barnes, 1973.

Sauerlander, Willibald, and Hirmer, Max. *Gothic Sculpture in France 1140–1270*. New York: Abrams, 1973.

Sheridan, Ronald, and Ross, Anne. *Gargoyles and Grotesques: Paganism in the Medieval Church*. Boston: New York Graphic Society, 1975.

Simson, Otto von. *The Gothic Cathedral*. 2nd rev. ed. Princeton: Princeton University Press, 1974.

Stoddard, Whitney. *Monastery and Cathedral in France*. Middletown, Conn.: Wesleyan University Press, 1966.

Swaan, Wim. *The Late Middle Ages: Art and Architecture from 1350 to the Advent of the Renaissance*. Ithaca, N.Y.: Cornell University Press, 1977.

Thompson, Daniel. *The Materials and Techniques of Medieval Painting*. New York: Dover, 1956.

Ward, Clarence. *Medieval Church Vaulting*. 1915. Reprint. New York: AMS Press, 1973.

Zarnecki, George. *Art of the Medieval World*. New York: Abrams, 1975.

chapter 11   The Art of India

Archer, William G. *Indian Miniatures*. Greenwich, Conn.: New York Graphic Society, 1960.

———*Indian Paintings from the Punjab Hills*. 2 vols. London: Sotheby Parke Bernet, 1973.

Bachhofer, Ludwig. *Early Indian Sculpture*. 1929. Reprint. New York: Hacker, 1972.

Balasubrahmanyan, S. R. *Early Chola Art—*

Part I. New York: Asia Publishing House, 1966.

———*Early Chola Temples: Parantakat to Rajaraja I, A.D. 907–985*. Bombay: Orient Longman, 1971.

Barrett, Douglas E. *Early Cola Bronzes*. Bombay: Bhulabhai Memorial Institute, 1965.

Barrett, Douglas E., and Gray, Basil. *Painting of India*. Geneva: Skira, 1963.

Basham, Arthur L. *The Wonder That Was India*. 3rd rev. ed. Paris: Arthaud, 1976.

Bhattacharji, Sukumari. *The Indian Theogony, a Comparative Study of Indian Mythology*. London: Cambridge University Press, 1970.

Coomaraswamy, Ananda K. *History of Indian and Indonesian Art*. New Delhi: Munshiram Manaharlal, 1972.

———*Yaksas*. New Delhi: Munshiram Manaharlal, 1971.

Dehijia, Vidya. *Early Buddhist Rock Temples*. Ithaca, N.Y.: Cornell University Press, 1972.

Ghosh, Amalananda. *Ajanta Murals*. New Delhi: Archaeological Survey of India, 1967.

Gopinatha Rao, T. A. *Elements of Hindu Iconography*. 2nd ed. 4 vols. New York: Paragon, 1968.

Gray, Basil, ed. *The Arts of India*. Ithaca, N.Y.: Cornell University Press/Phaidon, 1981.

Groslier, Philippe, and Arthaud, Jacques. *The Arts and Civilization of Angkor*. New York: Praeger, 1957.

Harle, James C. *Gupta Sculpture: Indian Sculpture of the Fourth to the Sixth Centuries A.D.* Oxford: Clarendon Press, 1974.

Kramrisch, Stella. *The Art of India*. 3rd ed. London: Phaidon, 1965.

———*The Hindu Temple*. 2 vols. Delhi: Motilal Banarsidass, 1976.

———*Indian Sculpture*. The Heritage of India Series. London: Oxford University Press, 1933.

Krishna Deva. *Temples of North India*. New Delhi: National Book Trust, 1969.

Lee, Sherman E. *Ancient Cambodian Sculpture*. New York: Intercultural Arts Press, 1970.

Rawson, Philip. *The Art of Southeast Asia*. New York: Praeger, 1967.

Rosenfield, John. *Dynastic Arts of the Kushan*. Berkeley: University of California Press, 1967.

Rowland, Benjamin. *The Art and Architecture of India: Buddhist, Hindu, Jain*. Harmondsworth, England: Penguin, 1977.

Sivaramamurti, C. *South Indian Bronzes*. New Delhi: Lalit Kala Akademi, 1963.

———*South Indian Paintings*. New Delhi: National Museum, 1968.

Srinivasan, K. R. *Temples of South India*. New Delhi: National Book Trust, 1972.

Williams, Joanna Gottfried. *The Art of Gupta India: Empire and Province*. Princeton: Princeton University Press, 1982.

Zimmer, Heinrich, and Campbell, Joseph, eds. *The Art of Indian Asia; Its Mythology*. Bollingen Series 39. 2 vols. Princeton: Princeton University Press, 1983.

chapter 12   The Art of China

Cahill, James. *Chinese Painting*. New ed. Geneva: Skira, 1977; New York: Rizzoli, 1977.

Davidson, J. Leroy. *The Lotus Sutra in Chinese Art: A Study in Buddhist Art to the Year 1880*. New Haven: Yale University Press, 1954.

Gray, Basil, and Vincent, John B. *Buddhist Cave Paintings at Tun-Huang*. Chicago: University of Chicago Press, 1959.

Honey, William B. *The Ceramic Art of China and Other Countries of the Far East*. New York: Beechhurst Press, 1954.

Lee, Sherman E. *Chinese Landscape Painting*. 2nd ed. Cleveland: Cleveland Museum of Art, 1962.

———*Past, Present, East and West*. New York: Braziller, 1983.

Loehr, Max. *The Great Painters of China*. New York: Harper & Row, 1980.

———*Ritual Vessels of Bronze Age China*. New York: Asia Society, 1968.

Mizuno, Seiichi. *Bronzes and Jades of Ancient China*. Tokyo: Nihon Keizai, 1959.

Mizuno, Seiichi, and Nagahiro, Toshio. *A Study of the Buddhist Cave Temples at Lung-Men, Honan*. Tokyo: Zanho Press, 1941.

Munsterberg, Hugo. *Dictionary of Chinese and Japanese Art*. New York: Hacker, 1981.

Rudolph, Richard. *Han Tomb Art of West China*. Berkeley: University of California Press, 1951.

Sickman, Lawrence C., and Soper, Alexander. *The Art and Architecture of China*. Baltimore: Penguin, 1956.

Siren, Oswald. *Chinese Painting: Leading Masters and Principles*. New York: Hacker, 1973.

———*Chinese Sculpture from the Fifth to the Fourteenth Centuries*. 4 vols. 1925. Reprint. New York: Hacker, 1970.

———*A History of Later Chinese Painting*. 1938. Reprint. London: Medici Society, 1970.

Sullivan, Michael. *The Birth of Landscape Painting in China*. Berkeley: University of California Press, 1962.

———*A Short History of Chinese Art*. Berkeley: University of California Press, 1970.

Sullivan, Michael, and Darbois, Dominique. *The Cave Temples of Maichishun*. London: Faber & Faber, 1969.

Weber, Charles D. *Chinese Pictorial Bronze Vessels of the Late Chou Period*. Ascona: Artibus Asiae, 1968.

Willetts, William. *Foundations of Chinese Art*. New York: McGraw-Hill, 1965.

chapter 13   The Art of Japan

Akiyama, Terukazu. *Japanese Painting*. Geneva: Skira; New York: Rizzoli, 1977.

Cahill, James F. *Scholar Painters of Japan: The Nanga School*. New York: Arno Press, 1976.

Drexler, Arthur. *The Architecture of Japan*. New York: Arno Press, 1966.

Fontein, Jan, and Hickman, M. C., eds. *Zen Painting and Calligraphy*. Greenwich, Conn.: New York Graphic Society, 1970.

Hirano, Chie. *Kiyonaga: A Study of His Life and Works*. Cambridge: Harvard University Press, 1939.

Kidder, J. Edward. *Early Japanese Art*. London: Thames & Hudson, 1969.

———*Japanese Temples: Sculpture, Painting, and Architecture*. Tokyo: Bijutsu Shuppansha, 1964.

Lee, Sherman E. *A History of Far Eastern Art*. London: Thames & Hudson, 1975.

———*Japanese Decorative Style*. New York: Harper & Row, 1972.

Paine, Robert, and Soper, Alexander. *The Art and Architecture of Japan*. Baltimore: Penguin, 1955.

Rosenfield, John M. *Japanese Art of the Heian Period, 749–1185*. New York: Asia Society, 1967.

Rosenfield, John M., and Shimada, Shujiro. *Traditions of Japanese Art*. Cambridge: Fogg Art Museum, Harvard University, 1970.

Soper, Alexander. *The Evolution of Buddhist Architecture in Japan*. 1942. Reprint. New York: Hacker, 1978.

Stern, Harold P. *Master Prints of Japan: Ukiyo-e Hanga*. New York: Abrams, 1969.

chapter 14   The Native Arts of the Americas, Africa, and the South Pacific

PRE-COLUMBIAN ART

Bennett, Wendell C. *Ancient Arts of the Andes*. New York: Museum of Modern Art/Arno Press, 1966.

Bernal, Ignacio. *The Olmec World*. Berkeley: University of California Press, 1977.

Bushnell, G. H. S. *Peru*. Rev. ed. New York: Praeger, 1963.

Coe, Michael D. *The Maya*. London: Thames & Hudson, 1980.

Coe, Michael D., and Diehl, R. A. *In the Land of the Olmec*. 2 vols. Austin: University of Texas Press, 1980.

Coe, William R. *Tikal: A Handbook of the Ancient Maya Ruins*. 3rd ed. Philadelphia: University Museum, University of Pennsylvania, 1970.

Emmerich, André. *Sweat of the Sun and Tears of the Moon: Gold and Silver in Pre-Columbian Art*. New York: Hacker, 1977.

Grider, Terence. *Origins of Pre-Columbian Art*. Austin: University of Texas Press, 1982.

Heyden, Doris, and Gendrop, Paul. *Pre-Columbian Architecture of Mesoamerica*. New York: Abrams, 1975.

Kubler, George. *The Art and Architecture of Ancient America: The Mexican, Maya, and Andean Peoples*. 2nd ed. Harmondsworth, England: Penguin, 1975.

Lapiner, Alan C. *Pre-Columbian Art of South America*. New York: Abrams, 1976.

Lehmann, Walter, with Heinrich Doering. *The Art of Old Peru*. New York: Hacker, 1975.

Los Angeles County Museum of Art. *Sculpture of Ancient West Mexico: Nayarit*. Los Angeles: Los Angeles County Museum of Art, 1970.

Mason, John Alden. *The Ancient Civilizations of Peru*. Rev. ed. Harmondsworth, England: Penguin, 1975.

Morley, Sylvanus G. *The Ancient Maya*. 3rd rev. ed. Stanford: Stanford University Press, 1973.

Paddock, John, ed. *Ancient Oaxaca: Discoveries in Mexican Archeology and History*. Stanford: Stanford University Press, 1970.

Pasztory, Esther. *Aztec Art*. New York: Abrams, 1983.

Peterson, Frederick. *Ancient Mexico*. New York: Capricorn Books, 1962.

Pettersen, Carmen L. *The Maya of Guatemala: Their Life and Dress*. Guatemala City: University of Washington Press, 1976.

Proskouriakoff, Tatiana Avenirovna. *A Study of Classic Maya Sculpture*. Washington, D.C.: Carnegie Institute of Washington, 1950.

Robertson, Donald. *Pre-Columbian Architecture*. New York: Braziller, 1963.

Robertson, Merle G.; Rands, Robert L.; and Graham, John A. *Maya Sculpture from the Southern Lowlands*. Berkeley: Lederer, Street & Zeus, 1972.

Rowe, John H. *Chavín Art: An Inquiry into Its Form and Meaning*. New York: Museum of Primitive Art, 1962.

Steward, Julian H. *Handbook of the South American Indians*. 7 vols. New York: Cooper Square Publishers, 1963.

Stierlin, Henri. *Art of the Aztecs, and Its Origins*. New York: Rizzoli, 1982.

Thompson, John E. S. *Maya History and Religion*. Norman: University of Oklahoma Press, 1972.

Wauchope, Robert, ed. *Handbook of Middle American Indians*. 16 vols. Austin: University of Texas Press, 1964–1976.

Weaver, Muriel Porter. *The Aztecs, Maya, and their Predecessors: The Archaeology of Mesoamerica*. 2nd ed. New York: Academic Press, 1981.

NORTH AMERICAN INDIAN AND ESKIMO ART

Boas, Franz. *Primitive Art*. 1927. Reprint. Magnolia, Mass.: Peter Smith, 1962.

Collins, Henry, et al. *The Far North: Two Thousand Years of American Eskimo and Indian Art*. Bloomington, Ind.: Indiana University Press in association with the National Gallery of Art, Washington, D.C., 1977.

Curtis, Edward S. *The North American Indian*. 30 vols. Cambridge: Cambridge University Press, 1907–1930.

Dockstader, Frederick. *Indian Art in America: The Arts and Crafts of the North American Indian*. Greenwich, Conn.: New York Graphic Society.

———*Indian Art of the Americas*. New York: Museum of the American Indian, Heye Foundation, 1973.

Ewers, John C. *Plains Indian Painting*. Stanford: Stanford University Press, 1939.

Feder, Norman. *Two Hundred Years of North American Art*. New York: Praeger, 1972.

Fraser, Douglas. *The Many Faces of Primitive Art*. Englewood Cliffs, N.J.: Prentice-Hall, 1966.

Grant, Campbell. *Rock Art of the American Indian*. 1967. Reprint. New York: Promontory Press, 1974.

Gunther, Erna. *Art in the Life of the Northwest Coast Indians*. Portland, Ore.: Portland Art Museum, 1966.

Harding, Anne D., and Boling, Patricia. *Bibliography of Articles and Papers on North American Indian Arts*. 1938. Reprint. New York: Kraus, 1969.

Murdock, George P., and O'Leary, Timothy. *Ethnographic Bibliography of North America*. 4th ed. New Haven: Human Relations Area Files Press, 1941.

Ray, Dorothy J. *Artists of the Tundra and the Sea*. Seattle: University of Washington Press, 1961.

Ritchie, Carson I. A. *The Eskimo and His Art*. New York: St. Martin's Press, 1976.

Snow, Dean. *The Archaeology of North America/American Indians*. New York: Thames & Hudson, 1980.

Whiteford, Andrew H. *North American Indian Arts*. New York: Golden Press, 1973.

AFRICAN ART

Allison, Philip. *African Stone Sculpture*. New York: Praeger, 1968.

Bascom, William R. *African Art in Cultural Perspective: An Introduction*. New York: Norton, 1973.

Ben-Amos, Paula. *The Art of Benin*. New York: Thames & Hudson, 1980.

Brentjes, Burchard. *African Rock Art*. London: Dent, 1967.

Cornet, Joseph. *Art of Africa: Treasures from the Congo*. London: Phaidon, 1971.

D'Azevedo, Warren L., ed. *The Traditional Artist in African Societies*. Bloomington: Indiana University Press, 1973.

Delange, Jacqueline. *Art and Peoples of Black Africa*. New York: Dutton, 1974.

Elisofon, Eliot, and Fagg, William. *The Sculpture of Africa*. New York: Hacker, 1978.

Eyo, Ekpo, and Willett, Frank. *Treasures of Ancient Nigeria*. New York: Knopf, 1980.

Fagg, William B. *Nigerian Images: The Splendor of African Sculpture*. New York: Praeger, 1963.

Forman, Werner. *Benin Art*. London: Hamlyn, 1960.

Fraser, Douglas F., and Cole, H. M., eds. *African Art and Leadership*. Madison: University of Wisconsin Press, 1972.

Gaskin, L. J. P. *A Bibliography of African Art*. London: International African Institute, 1965.

Laude, Jean. *The Arts of Black Africa*. Berkeley: University of California Press, 1973.

Lieris, Michel, and Delange, Jacqueline. *African Art*. New York: Golden Press, 1968.

Thompson, Robert F. *Black Gods and Kings: Yoruba Art at U.C.L.A.* Bloomington: Indiana University Press, 1976.

———*Flash of the Spirit: African and Afro-American Art and Philosophy*. New York: Random House, 1983

Trowell, Kathleen M. *Classical African Sculpture*. London: Faber & Faber, 1970.

Walker Art Center. *Art of the Congo*. Minneapolis: Walker Art Center, 1967.

Wassing, René S. *African Art: Its Background and Traditions*. New York: Abrams, 1968.

Willett, Frank. *African Art: An Introduction*. London: Thames & Hudson, 1971.

———*Ife in the History of West African Sculpture*. New York: McGraw-Hill, 1967.

OCEANIC ART

Barrow, Tui T. *Art and Life in Polynesia*. Rutland, Vt.: Charles E. Tuttle, 1973.

———*Maori Wood Sculpture of New Zealand*. Rutland, Vt.: Charles E. Tuttle, 1970.

Batterberry, Michael, and Ruskin, Ariane. *Primitive Art*. New York: McGraw-Hill, 1973.

Bernot, Ronald M. *Australian Aboriginal Art*. New York: Macmillan, 1964.

Buck, Peter H. *Arts and Crafts of Hawaii*. Honolulu: Bishop Museum Press, 1964.

Dodd, Edward H. *Polynesian Art*. New York: Dodd, Mead, 1967.

Firth, Raymond. *Art and Life in New Guinea*. 1936. Reprint. New York: AMS Press, 1977.

Fraser, Douglas. *Primitive Art*. London: Thames & Hudson, 1962.

Guiart, Jean. *Arts of the South Pacific*. New York: Golden Press, 1963.

Kooijman, S. *The Art of Lake Sentani*. New York: Museum of Primitive Art, 1959.

Linton, Ralph, and Wingert, Paul. *Arts of the South Seas*. 1946. Reprint. New York: Arno Press, 1972.

Newton, Douglas. *Art Styles of the Papuan Gulf*. New York: Museum of Primitive Art, 1961.

Rockefeller, Michael C. *The Asmat of New Guinea: The Journal of Michael Clark Rockefeller*. Greenwich, Conn.: New York Graphic Society, 1967.

Schmitz, Carl A. *Oceanic Art; Myth, Man and Image in the South Seas*. New York: Abrams, 1971.

Stubbs, Dacre. *Prehistoric Art of Australia*. New York: Scribner, 1975.

Taylor, Clyde R. H. *A Pacific Bibliography: Printed Matter Relating to the Native People of Polynesia, Melanesia, and Micronesia*. 2nd ed. Oxford: Clarendon Press, 1965.

Wingert, Paul. *Primitive Art: Its Traditions and Styles*. Cleveland: World Publishing, 1970.

chapter 15 The "Proto-Renaissance" in Italy

Antal, Frederick, *Florentine Painting and Its Social Background*. London: Kegan Paul, 1948.

Cole, Bruce. *Sienese Painting: From Its Origin to the Fifteenth Century*. Bloomington: Indiana University Press, 1985.

De Wald, Ernest T. *Italian Painting: 1200–1600*. New York: Holt, Rinehart & Winston, 1961.

Fremantle, Richard. *Florentine Gothic Painters from Giotto to Masaccio: A Guide to Painting in and near Florence*. London: Secker & Warburg, 1975.

Marle, Raimond van. *The Development of the Italian Schools of Painting*. 19 vols. 1923–1938. Reprint. New York: Hacker, 1970.

Meiss, Millard. *Painting in Florence and Siena After the Black Death*. New York: Harper & Row, 1973.

Panofsky, Erwin. *Renaissance and Renascences in Western Art*. New York: Harper & Row, 1969.

Pope-Hennessy, John. *Introduction to Italian Sculpture*. 2nd ed. 3 vols. New York: Phaidon, 1970–1972.

Schevill, Ferdinand. *The Medici*. New York: Harper & Row, 1960.

Smart, Alastair. *The Dawn of Italian Painting*. Ithaca, N.Y.: Cornell University Press, 1978.

Stubblebine, James, ed. *Giotto: The Arena Chapel Frescoes*. New York: Norton, 1969.

Venturi, Lionello, and Skira-Venturi, Rosabianca. *Italian Painting: The Creators of the Renaissance*. 3 vols. Geneva; Skira, 1950–1952.

White, John. *Art and Architecture in Italy, 1250 to 1400*. Baltimore: Penguin, 1966.

chapter 16 Fifteenth-Century Italian Art

Baxandall, Michael. *Painting and Experience in Fifteenth Century Italy.* New York: Oxford University Press, 1983.

Berenson, Bernard. *The Italian Painters of the Renaissance.* Ithaca, N.Y.: Phaidon/Cornell University Press, 1980.

————*Italian Pictures of the Renaissance.* Ithaca, N.Y.: Phaidon/Cornell University Press, 1980.

Borsook, Eve. *The Mural Painters of Tuscany.* New York: Oxford University Press, 1981.

Burckhardt, Jacob. *The Civilization of the Renaissance in Italy.* 4th ed. 1867. Reprint. London: Phaidon, 1960.

Chastel, André. *The Age of Humanism.* New York: McGraw-Hill, 1964.

————*Studios and Styles of the Italian Renaissance.* New York: Braziller, 1971.

Cole, Bruce. *Masaccio and the Art of Early Renaissance Florence.* Bloomington: Indiana University Press, 1980.

Decker, Heinrich. *The Renaissance in Italy: Architecture, Sculpture, Frescoes.* New York: Viking, 1969.

De Wald, Ernest T. *Italian Painting, 1200–1600.* New York: Holt, Rinehart & Winston, 1961.

Edgerton, Samuel Y., Jr. *The Renaissance Rediscovery of Linear Perspective.* New York: Harper & Row, 1976.

Ferguson, Wallace K., et al. *The Renaissance.* New York: Henry Holt, 1940.

Gadol, Joan. *Leon Battista Alberti: Universal Man of the Early Renaissance.* Chicago: University of Chicago Press, 1969.

Gilbert, Creighton. *History of Renaissance Art throughout Europe.* New York: Abrams, 1973.

————*Italian Art 1400–1500: Sources and Documents.* Englewood Cliffs, N.J.: Prentice-Hall, 1970.

Godfrey, F. M. *Early Venetian Painters, 1415–1495.* London: Tiranti, 1954.

Hale, John R. *Italian Renaissance Painting from Masaccio to Titian.* New York: Dutton, 1977.

Hartt, Frederick. *History of Italian Renaissance Art.* New York: Abrams, 1979.

Helton, Tinsley, ed. *The Renaissance: A Reconsideration of the Theories and Interpretations of the Age.* Madison: University of Wisconsin Press, 1964.

Heydenreich, Ludwig H., and Lotz, Wolfgang. *Architecture in Italy 1400–1600.* Harmondsworth, England: Penguin, 1974.

Holt, Elizabeth B. *A Documentary History of Art.* 2nd ed. Vol. 1. Garden City, N.Y.: Doubleday, 1957.

Huyghe, René. *Larousse Encyclopedia of Renaissance and Baroque Art.* See **Reference Books.**

Janson, Horst W. *The Sculpture of Donatello.* 2 vols. Princeton, N.J.: Princeton University Press, 1957.

Krautheimer, Richard, and Krautheimer-Hess, Trude. *Lorenzo Ghiberti.* Princeton, N.J.: Princeton University Press, 1956.

Lieberman, Ralph. *Renaissance Architecture in Venice.* New York: Abbeville, 1982.

Lowry, Bates. *Renaissance Architecture.* New York: Braziller, 1962.

McAndrew, John. *Venetian Architecture of the Early Renaissance.* Cambridge: MIT Press, 1980.

Marle, Raimond van. *The Development of the Italian Schools of Painting.* 19 vols. 1923–1938. Reprint. New York: Hacker, 1970.

Meiss, Millard. *The Painter's Choice, Problems in the Interpretation of Renaissance Art.* New York: Harper & Row, 1976.

Murray, Peter. *The Architecture of the Italian Renaissance.* London: Secker & Warburg, 1985.

Murray, Peter, and Murray, Linda. *The Art of the Renaissance.* London: Thames & Hudson, 1981.

Panofsky, Erwin. *Renaissance and Renascences in Western Art.* New York: Harper & Row, 1969.

Pater, Walter. *The Renaissance: Studies in Art and Poetry.* Edited by D. L. Hill. Berkeley: University of California Press, 1980.

Pope-Hennessy, John. *An Introduction to Italian Sculpture.* 2nd ed. 3 vols. New York: Phaidon, 1970–1971.

————*Sienese Quattrocento Painting.* New York: Oxford University Press, 1947.

Schevill, Ferdinand. *The Medici.* New York: Harper & Row, 1960.

Seymour, Charles. *Sculpture in Italy, 1400–1500.* Baltimore: Penguin, 1966.

Symonds, John Addington. *The Renaissance in Italy.* 7 vols. 1875–1886. Reprint. New York: Modern Library, 1935. (Other reprints available.)

Vasari, Giorgio. *The Lives of the Most Eminent Painters, Sculptors, and Architects, 1550–1568.* 3 vols. New York: Abrams, 1979.

Werkmeister, William H., ed. Ferguson, Wallace, et al. *Facets of the Renaissance.* New York: Harper & Row, 1963.

Wittkower, Rudolf. *Architectural Principles in the Age of Humanism.* 4th ed. London: Academy, 1973

chapter 17 Sixteenth-Century Italian Art

Ackerman, James S. *The Architecture of Michelangelo.* London: Zwemmer, 1966.

————*Palladio.* New York: Penguin, 1978.

Bialostocki, Jan. *The Art of the Renaissance in Eastern Europe.* Ithaca, N.Y.: Cornell University Press, 1976.

Blunt, Anthony. *Artistic Theory in Italy, 1450–1600.* London: Oxford University Press, 1975.

Briganti, Giuliano. *Italian Mannerism.* London: Thames & Hudson, 1962.

Castiglione, Baldassare. *The Courtier.* 1528. Reprint. New York: National Alumni, 1907. (Other reprints available.)

Cellini, Benvenuto. *Autobiography.* Reprint. New York: Grolier, 1969. (Other reprints available.)

Einem, Herbert von. *Michelangelo.* London: Methuen, 1976.

Freedberg, Sydney F. *Painting in Italy: 1500–1600.* Harmondsworth, England: Penguin, 1983.

————*Painting of the High Renaissance in Rome and Florence.* 1st rev. New York: Harper & Row, 1975.

Friedlaender, Walter. *Mannerism and Anti-Mannerism in Italian Painting.* New York: Schocken Books, 1965.

Holt, Elizabeth Gilmore, ed. *A Documentary History of Art.* Vol. 2, *Michelangelo and the Mannerists.* Rev. ed. Princeton: Princeton University Press, 1982.

Levey, Michael. *High Renaissance.* Harmondsworth, England: Penguin, 1975.

Murray, Linda. *The High Renaissance and Mannerism.* New York: Oxford University Press, 1977.

Partner, Peter. *Renaissance Rome, 1500–1559: A Portrait of a Society.* Berkeley: University of California Press, 1977.

Pope-Hennessy, John. *Italian High Renaissance and Baroque Sculpture.* 3 vols. Greenwich, Conn.: Phaidon, 1963.

Shearman, John K. G. *Mannerism.* Baltimore: Penguin, 1978.

Venturi, Lionello. *The Sixteenth Century: From Leonardo to El Greco.* New York: Skira, 1956.

Wölfflin, Heinrich. *The Art of the Italian Renaissance.* New York: Schocken Books, 1963.

————*Classic Art.* London: Phaidon, 1968.

Würtenberger, Franzsepp. *Mannerism: The European Style of the Sixteenth Century.* New York: Holt, Rinehart & Winston, 1963.

chapter 18 The Renaissance Outside of Italy

Alpers, Svetlana. *The Art of Describing: Dutch Art in the Seventeenth Century.* Chicago: University of Chicago Press, 1983.

Benesch, Otto. *Art of the Renaissance in Northern Europe.* Rev. ed. London: Phaidon, 1965.

————*German Painting from Dürer to Holbein.* Geneva: Skira, 1966.

Blunt, Anthony. *Art and Architecture in France 1500–1700.* 4th ed. Baltimore: Penguin, 1982.

Chatelet, Albert. *Early Dutch Painting.* New York: Rizzoli, 1981.

Conway, William M. *The Van Eycks and Their Followers.* 1921. Reprint. New York: AMS Press, 1979.

Cuttler, Charles P. *Northern Painting from Pucelle to Bruegel.* New York: Holt, Rinehart & Winston, 1968.

Evans, Joan. *Monastic Architecture in France from the Renaissance to the Revolution.* New York: Hacker, 1980.

Friedlander, Max J. *Early Netherlandish Painting.* New York: Praeger/Phaidon, 1967–1976.

————*From Van Eyck to Bruegel.* 3rd ed. Ithaca, N.Y.: Cornell University Press, 1981.

Fuchs, Rudolph H. *Dutch Painting.* London: Thames & Hudson, 1978.

Hind, Arthur M. *History of Engraving and Etching from the Fifteenth Century to the Year 1914.* 3rd rev. ed. New York: Dover, 1963.

————*An Introduction to a History of Woodcut.* New York: Dover, 1963.

Hitchcock, Henry-Russell. *German Renaissance Architecture.* Princeton: Princeton University Press. 1981.

Huizinga, Johan. *The Waning of the Middle Ages.* 1924. Reprint. New York: Doubleday/Anchor, 1970.

Lassaigne, Jacques, and Delevoy, Robert. *Flemish Painting.* New York: Skira, 1957.

Mather, Frank J. *Western European Painting of the Renaissance.* New York: Cooper Square Publishers, 1966.

Meiss, Millard. *French Painting in the Time of Jean de Berry.* New York: Braziller, 1974.

Panofsky, Erwin. *Early Netherlandish Painting.* Cambridge: Harvard University Press, 1953.

————*The Life and Art of Albrecht Dürer.* 4th ed. Princeton. Princeton University Press, 1971

Puyvelde, Leo van. *The Flemish Primitives.* London: Collins, 1948.

Réau, Louis. *French Painting in the Fourteenth, Fifteenth, and Sixteenth Centuries.* New York: Hyperion Press, 1939.

Snyder, James. *Northern Renaissance Art.* New York: Abrams, 1985.

Stechow, Wolfgang, ed. *Northern Renaissance Art, 1400–1600.* Englewood Cliffs, N.J.: Prentice-Hall, 1966.

Waetzold, Wilhelm. *Dürer and His Time.* Enl. ed. London: Phaidon, 1955.

Whinney, Margaret. *Early Flemish Painting.* London: Faber & Faber, 1968.

Wilenski, Reginald H. *Flemish Painters, 1430–1830.* 2 vols. London: Faber & Faber, 1960.

chapter 19 Baroque Art

Bazin, Germain. *Baroque and Rococo Art.* New York: Praeger, 1974.

Blunt, Anthony, ed. *Baroque and Rococo: Architecture and Decoration.* Cambridge: Harper & Row, 1982.

Chatelet, Albert, and Thuillier, Jacques. *French Painting from Fouquet to Poussin.* Geneva: Skira, 1963.

Fokker, Timon H. *Roman Baroque Art: The History of a Style.* London: Oxford University Press, 1938.

Freedberg, Sydney J. *Circa 1600: A Revolution of Style in Italian Painting.* Cambridge: Harvard University Press, 1983.

Gerson, Horst, and ter Kuile, E. H. *Art and*

Architecture in Belgium 1600–1800. Baltimore: Penguin, 1960.

Haak, Bob. The Golden Age: Dutch Painters of the Seventeenth Century. London: Thames & Hudson, 1984.

Held, Julius, and Posner, Donald. 17th and 18th Century Art. New York: Abrams, 1974.

Hempel, Eberhard. Baroque Art and Architecture in Central Europe. Baltimore: Penguin, 1965.

Hibbard, Howard. Bernini. Harmondsworth, England: Penguin, 1976.

——— Caravaggio. New York: Thames & Hudson, 1983.

——— Carlo Maderno and Roman Architecture, 1580–1630. London: Zwemmer, 1971.

Hinks, Roger P. Michelangelo Merisi da Caravaggio. London: Faber & Faber, 1953.

Howard, Deborah. The Architectural History of Venice. London: B. T. Batsford, 1981.

Kahr, Madlyn Millner. Dutch Painting in the Seventeenth Century. New York: Harper & Row, 1978.

——— Velázquez: The Art of Painting. New York: Harper & Row, 1976.

Kitson, Michael. The Age of Baroque. London: Hamlyn, 1976.

Lees-Milne, James. Baroque in Italy. New York: Macmillan, 1960.

Martin, John R. Baroque. New York: Harper & Row, 1977.

Millon, Henry A. Baroque and Rococo Architecture. New York: Braziller, 1965.

Norberg-Schulz, Christian. Baroque Architecture. New York: Rizzoli, 1985.

Pope-Hennessy, Sir John. The Study and Criticism of Italian Sculpture. New York: Metropolitan Museum, 1981.

Portoghesi, Paolo. The Rome of Borromini. London: Phaidon, 1972.

Powell, Nicolas. From Baroque to Rococo: An Introduction to Austrian and German Architecture from 1580 to 1790. London: Faber & Faber, 1959.

Rosenberg, Jakob; Slive, Seymour; and ter Kuile, E. H. Dutch Art and Architecture, 1600–1800. Baltimore: Penguin, 1979.

Spear, Richard E. Caravaggio and His Followers. New York: Harper & Row, 1975.

Stechow, Wolfgang. Dutch Landscape Painting of the 17th Century. Oxford: Phaidon, 1981.

Summerson, Sir John. Architecture in Britain: 1530–1830. 7th rev. and enl. ed. Baltimore: Penguin, 1983.

Tapie, Victor-Lucien. The Age of Grandeur: Baroque Art and Architecture. New York: Praeger, 1966.

Waterhouse, Ellis Kirkham. Baroque Painting in Rome. London: Phaidon, 1976.

——— Italian Baroque Painting. 2nd ed. London: Phaidon, 1969.

——— Painting in Britain, 1530–1790. 4th ed. New York: Penguin, 1978.

Wittkower, Rudolf. Gian Lorenzo Bernini: The Sculptor of the Roman Baroque. 3rd ed. rev. Oxford: Phaidon, 1981.

Wölfflin, Heinrich. Principles of Art History. 7th ed. New York: Dover, 1950.

chapter 20   The Eighteenth Century: Rococo and the Rise of Romanticism

Bacou, Roseline. Piranesi: Etchings and Drawings. Boston: New York Graphic Society, 1975.

Blunt, Anthony. Art and Architecture in France, 1500–1700. 2nd ed. Harmondsworth, England: Penguin, 1970.

Braham, Allan. The Architecture of the French Enlightenment. Berkeley: University of California Press, 1980.

Chatelet, Albert, and Thuillier, Jacques. French Painting from Le Nain to Fragonard. Geneva: Skira, 1964.

Conisbee, Philip. Painting in Eighteenth-Cen-
tury France. Ithaca, N.Y.: Phaidon/Cornell University Press, 1981.

Hayes, John T. Gainsborough: Paintings and Drawings. London: Phaidon, 1975.

Herrmann, Luke. British Landscape Painting of the Eighteenth Century. New York: Oxford University Press, 1974.

Hitchcock, Henry Russell. Rococo Architecture in Southern Germany. London: Phaidon, 1968.

Irwin, David. English Neoclassical Art. London: Faber & Faber, 1966.

Kalnein, Wend Graf, and Levey, Michael. Art and Architecture of the Eighteenth Century in France. New York: Viking/Pelican, 1973.

Kimball, Sidney F. The Creation of the Rococo. New York: Norton, 1964.

Levey, Michael. Painting in Eighteenth-Century Venice. Ithaca, N.Y.: Phaidon/Cornell University Press, 1980.

Millon, Henry A. Baroque and Rococo Architecture. New York: Braziller, 1961.

Norberg-Schulz, Christian. Late Baroque and Rococo Architecture. New York: Abrams, 1974.

Pierson, William. American Buildings and Their Architects: The Colonial and Neo-Classical Style. Vol. 1. Garden City, N.Y.: Doubleday, 1970.

Pignatti, Terisio. The Age of Rococo. New York: Hamlyn, 1969.

Rosenblum, Robert. Transformations in Late Eighteenth Century Art. Princeton: Princeton University Press, 1970.

Waterhouse, Ellis K. Painting in Britain, 1530–1790. 4th ed. New York: Penguin, 1978.

Whinney, Margaret Dickens. English Art, 1625–1714. Oxford: Clarendon Press, 1957.

——— Sculpture in Britain, 1530–1830. Baltimore: Penguin, 1964.

Whinney, Margaret D., and Millar, Oliver. English Art, 1720–1830. London: H. M. Stationery Office, 1971.

Wittkower, Rudolf. Art and Architecture in Italy, 1600–1750. New York: Penguin, 1980.

chapter 21   The Nineteenth Century: Pluralism of Style

Arnason, H. The Sculptures of Houdon. New York: Oxford University Press, 1975.

Aslin, Elizabeth. The Aesthetic Movement: Prelude to Art Nouveau. New York: Praeger, 1969.

Baudelaire, Charles. The Mirror of Art, Critical Studies. Garden City, N.Y.: Doubleday, 1956.

Boime, A. The Academy and French Painting in the 19th Century. London: Phaidon, 1971.

Brion, Marcel. Art of the Romantic Era: Romanticism, Classicism, Realism. New York: Praeger, 1966.

Brown, Milton. American Art to 1900. New York: Abrams, 1977.

Brunhammer, Yvonne, et al. Art Nouveau— Belgium, France: Catalogue of an Exhibition. Houston: Institute for the Arts, Rice University, 1976.

Canaday, John. Mainstreams of Modern Art. New York: Holt, 1959.

Clark, Kenneth. The Gothic Revival: An Essay in the History of Taste. New York: Humanities Press, 1970.

Clay, Jean. Romanticism. New York: Phaidon, 1981.

Courthion, Pierre. Romanticism. Geneva: Skira, 1961.

Delacroix, Eugène. The Journals of Eugène Delacroix. New York: Phaidon, 1951.

Dixon, Roger, and Muthesius, Stefan. Victorian Architecture. London: Thames & Hudson, 1978.

Eitner, Lorenz. Neo-Classicism and Romanticism, 1750–1850: Sources and Documents on the History of Art. 2 vols. Englewood Cliffs, N.J.: Prentice-Hall, 1970.

Flexner, James Thomas. America's Old Masters. New York: McGraw-Hill, 1982.

Friedlaender, Walter. From David to Delacroix. New York: Schocken Books, 1968.

Gernsheim, Helmut, and Gernsheim, Alison. The History of Photography from the Camera Obscura to the Beginning of the Modern Era. London: Thames & Hudson, 1969.

Hamilton, George H. Nineteenth and Twentieth Century Art. Englewood Cliffs, N.J.: Prentice-Hall, 1972.

Hanson, Anne Coffin. Manet and the Modern Tradition. New Haven: Yale University Press, 1977.

Hawley, Henry. Neo-Classicism, Style and Motif. Cleveland: Cleveland Museum of Art, 1964.

Hilton, Timothy. The Pre-Raphaelites. New York: Praeger, 1974.

Hitchcock, Henry-Russell. Architecture: Nineteenth and Twentieth Centuries. 4th ed. Baltimore: Penguin, 1977.

Holt, Elizabeth B. From the Classicists to the Impressionists: Art and Architecture in the Nineteenth Century. Garden City, N.Y.: Doubleday/Anchor, 1966.

Honour, Hugh. Neo-Classicism. New York: Harper & Row, 1979.

——— Romanticism. New York: Harper & Row, 1979.

Janson, Horst W. 19th Century Sculpture. New York: Abrams, 1985.

Leymarie, Jean. French Painting in the Nineteenth Century. Geneva: Skira, 1962.

Licht, Fred. Sculpture—Nineteenth and Twentieth Centuries. Greenwich, Conn.: New York Graphic Society, 1967.

Loyer, Francois. Architecture of the Industrial Age. New York: Rizzoli, 1983.

Macaulay, James. The Gothic Revival, 1745–1845. Glasgow: Blackie, 1975.

Martinell, César. Gaudi: His Life, His Theories, His Work. Cambridge: MIT Press, 1975.

Middleton, Robin, ed. The Beaux-Arts and Nineteenth Century French Architecture. Cambridge: MIT Press, 1982.

Newton, Eric. The Romantic Rebellion. New York: Schocken Books, 1964.

Nochlin, Linda. Gustave Courbet: A Study of Style and Society. New York: Garland, 1976.

——— Impressionism and Post-Impressionism 1874–1904: Sources and Documents. Englewood Cliffs, N.J.: Prentice-Hall, 1966.

——— Realism and Tradition in Art. New York: Penguin, 1976.

Novak, Barbara. American Painting of the Nineteenth Century. New York: Praeger, 1969.

Novotny, Fritz. Painting and Sculpture in Europe 1780–1880. 2nd ed. Harmondsworth, England: Penguin, 1978.

Pelles, Geraldine. Art, Artists and Society: Origins of a Modern Dilemma, Painting in England and France 1750–1850. Englewood Cliffs, N.J.: Prentice-Hall, 1963.

Pevsner, Nikolaus. Pioneers of Modern Design. Harmondsworth, England: Penguin, 1964.

Rewald, John. The History of Impressionism. New York: Museum of Modern Art, 1973.

Roberts, Keith. The Impressionists and Post-Impressionists. New York: Dutton, 1977.

Rosenblum, Robert. Modern Painting and the Northern Romantic Tradition. New York: Harper & Row, 1975.

Rosenblum, Robert, and Janson, Horst W. 19th Century Art. New York: Abrams, 1984.

Sambrook, James, ed. Pre-Raphaelitism: A Collection of Critical Essays. Chicago: University of Chicago Press, 1974.

Schapiro, Meyer. Modern Art: 19th and 20th Centuries. New York: Braziller, 1980.

Sloane, Joseph C. French Painting Between the Past and the Present: Artists, Critics, and Traditions from 1848 to 1870. Princeton: Princeton University Press, 1973.

Sypher, Wylie. Rococo to Cubism in Art and Literature. New York: Random House, 1960.

Vaughan, William. German Romantic Painting. New Haven: Yale University Press, 1980.

Weisberg, Gabriel P. *The Realist Tradition: French Painting and Drawing, 1830–1900.* Cleveland: Cleveland Museum/Indiana University Press, 1980.

Whiffen, Marcus, and Koeper, Frederick. *American Architecture, 1607–1976.* Cambridge: MIT Press, 1983.

Wood, Christopher. *The Pre-Raphaelites.* New York: Viking Press, 1981.

chapter 22 The Twentieth Century

Amaya, Mario. *Pop Art and After.* New York: Viking, 1972.

Andersen, Wayne. *American Sculpture in Process 1930/1970.* Boston: New York Graphic Society, 1975.

Apollinaire, Guillaume. *The Cubist Painters: Aesthetic Meditations, 1913.* New York: Wittenborn, 1970.

Arnason, H. Harvard. *History of Modern Art: Painting, Sculpture, Architecture.* 2nd rev. and enl. ed. Englewood Cliffs, N.J.: Prentice-Hall, 1977.

Ashton, Dore. *American Art Since 1945.* New York: Oxford University Press, 1982.

Banham, Reyner. *Guide to Modern Architecture.* Princeton: D. Van Nostrand, 1962.

Battcock, Gregory. *Minimal Art: A Critical Anthology.* New York: Studio Vista, 1969.

Battcock, Gregory, ed. *The New Art: A Critical Anthology.* New York: Dutton, 1973.

Benevolo, Leonardo. *History of Modern Architecture.* 2 vols. Cambridge: MIT Press, 1977.

Blake, Peter. *The Master Builder.* New York: Norton, 1976.

Breton, André. *Surrealism and Painting.* New York: Harper & Row, 1972.

Brown, Milton; Hunter, Sam; and Jacobus, John. *American Art: Painting, Sculpture, Architecture, Decorative Arts, Photography.* New York: Abrams, 1979.

Canaday, John. *Mainstreams of Modern Art.* New York: Holt, 1959.

Carter, Peter. *Mies van der Rohe at Work.* London: Pall Mall Press, 1974.

Cassou, Jean, and Pevsner, Nikolaus. *Gateway to the Twentieth Century.* New York: McGraw-Hill, 1962.

Collins, Peter. *Changing Ideals in Modern Architecture, 1750–1950.* London: Faber & Faber, 1971.

Condit, Carl W. *The Rise of the Skyscraper: Portrait of the Times and Career of Influential Architects.* Chicago: University of Chicago Press, 1952.

Cummings, Paul. *Dictionary of Contemporary American Artists.* 3rd ed. New York: St. Martin's Press, 1977.

Curtis, William J. R. *Modern Architecture Since 1900.* Englewood Cliffs, N.J.: Prentice-Hall, 1982.

Diehl, Gaston. *The Moderns: A Treasury of Painting Throughout the World.* Milan: Uffizi, 1961.

Duthuit, Georges. *The Fauvist Painters.* New York: Wittenborn, Schultz, 1950.

Elderfield, John. *The "Wild Beasts": Fauvism and Its Affinities.* New York: The Museum of Modern Art/Oxford University Press, 1976.

Elsen, Albert. *Origins of Modern Sculpture.* New York: Braziller, 1974.

Frampton, Kenneth. *Modern Architecture: A Critical History.* New York: Oxford University Press, 1980.

Giedion-Welcker, Carola. *Contemporary Sculpture: An Evaluation in Volume and Space.* New York: Wittenborn, 1961.

Golding, John. *Cubism: A History and an Analysis, 1907–1914.* Rev. ed. Boston: Boston Book & Art Shop, 1968.

Goodyear, Frank H., Jr. *Contemporary American Realism Since 1960.* Boston: New York Graphic Society, 1981.

Gray, Christopher. *Cubist Aesthetic Theories.* Baltimore: Johns Hopkins University Press, 1953.

Haftmann, Werner. *Painting in the Twentieth Century: A Pictorial Survey.* London: Lund Humphries, 1965.

Hamilton, George Heard. *Painting and Sculpture in Europe.* New York: Penguin, 1983.

Hamlin, Talbot F., ed. *Forms and Functions of Twentieth-Century Architecture.* 4 vols. New York: Columbia University Press, 1952.

Hitchcock, Henry-Russell. *Architecture—Nineteenth and Twentieth Centuries.* New York: Penguin, 1977.

Hunter, Sam. *American Art of the Twentieth Century.* New York: Abrams, 1973.

———*Modern French Painting, 1855–1956.* New York: Dell, 1966.

Hunter, Sam, and Jacobus, John. *Modern Art: Painting, Sculpture, and Architecture.* New York: Abrams, 1985.

Jacobus, John. *Twentieth-Century Architecture: The Middle Years, 1940–1961.* New York: Praeger, 1966.

Janis, Sidney. *Abstract and Surrealist Art in America.* 1944. Reprint. New York: Arno Press, 1969.

Kahnweiler, Daniel H. *The Rise of Cubism.* New York: Wittenborn, Schultz, 1949.

Kaprow, Allan. *Assemblage, Environments, and Happenings.* New York: Abrams, 1966.

Kepes, Gyorgy. *The Visual Arts Today.* Middletown, Conn.: Wesleyan University Press, 1960.

Kraus, Rosalind, E. *Passages in Modern Sculpture.* Cambridge: MIT Press, 1981.

Lake, Carlton, and Maillard, Roger, eds. *Dictionary of Modern Painting.* 3rd rev. enl. ed. New York: Tudor, 1964.

Licht, Fred. *Sculpture of the Nineteenth and Twentieth Centuries.* Greenwich, Conn.: New York Graphic Society, 1967.

Lippard, Lucy R. *Pop Art.* New York: Praeger, 1966.

Lucie-Smith, Edward. *Art in the Seventies.* Ithaca, N.Y.: Cornell University Press, 1980.

———*Art Now: From Abstract Expressionism to Superrealism.* New York: Morrow, 1981.

———*Symbolist Art.* New York: Oxford University Press, 1972.

Lynton, Norbert. *The Modern World.* New York: McGraw-Hill, 1965.

McShine, Kynaston. *An International Survey of Recent Painting and Sculpture.* New York: Museum of Modern Art, 1984.

Martin, Marianne W. *Futurist Art and Theory.* Oxford: Clarendon Press, 1968.

Meyer, Ursula. *Conceptual Art.* New York: Dutton, 1972.

Mondrian, Pieter Cornelius. *Plastic Art and Pure Plastic Art.* 3rd ed. New York: Wittenborn, Schultz, 1952.

Motherwell, Robert, ed. *The Dada Painters and Poets.* New York: Wittenborn, Schultz, 1951.

Nochlin, Linda. *Realism.* Baltimore: Penguin, 1976.

Pehnt, Wolfgang. *Encyclopedia of Modern Architecture.* New York: Abrams, 1964.

Pierson, William. *American Buildings and Their Architects: Technology and the Picturesque.* Vol. 2. Garden City, N.Y.: Doubleday, 1978.

Raymond, Marcel. *From Baudelaire to Surrealism.* London: Methuen, 1970.

Raynal, Maurice. *History of Modern Painting.* 3 vols. Geneva: Skira, 1949–1950.

Read, Herbert. *A Concise History of Modern Painting.* 3rd ed. New York: Praeger, 1975.

———*A Concise History of Modern Sculpture.* Rev. and enl. ed. New York: Praeger, 1964.

Read, Herbert, ed. *Surrealism.* New York: Praeger, 1971.

Riseboro, Bill. *Modern Architecture and Design: An Alternative History.* Cambridge: MIT Press, 1983.

Ritchie, Andrew C. *Abstract Painting and Sculpture in America.* New York: Arno Press, 1969.

———*Sculpture of the Twentieth Century.* New York: Arno Press, 1972.

Rose, Barbara. *American Art Since 1900.* Rev. ed. New York: Praeger, 1975.

Rosenblum, Robert. *Cubism and Twentieth-Century Art.* New York: Abrams, 1976.

Rubin, William S. *Dada, Surrealism and Their Heritage.* New York: Museum of Modern Art, 1977.

Russell, John. *The Meanings of Modern Art.* New York: Museum of Modern Art/Thames & Hudson, 1981.

Schiee, Gert, ed. *Picasso in Perspective.* Englewood Cliffs, N.J.: Prentice-Hall, 1976.

Schlenoff, Norman. *Art in the Modern World.* New York: Bantam, 1965.

Schneede, Uwe M. *Surrealism.* New York: Abrams, 1974.

Schwarz, Arturo. *Marcel Duchamp.* New York: Abrams, 1974.

Scully, Vincent. *American Architecture and Urbanism.* New York: Praeger, 1969.

———*Modern Architecture.* Rev. ed. New York: Braziller, 1974.

Selz, Peter. *German Expressionist Painting.* 1957. Reprint. Berkeley: University of California Press, 1974.

Sotriffer, Kristian. *Expressionism and Fauvism.* New York: McGraw-Hill, 1972.

Tuchman, Maurice. *American Sculpture of the Sixties.* Los Angeles: Los Angeles County Museum of Art, 1967.

Vogt, Paul. *Expressionism: German Painting 1905–1920.* New York: Abrams, 1980.

Whittick, Arnold. *European Architecture in the Twentieth Century.* Aylesbury, England: Leonard Hill Books, 1974.

Wilmerding, John. *American Art.* Harmondsworth, England: Penguin, 1976.

———*The Genius of American Painting.* London: Weidenfeld & Nicolson, 1973.

PICTURE CREDITS

The authors and publisher are grateful to the proprietors and custodians of various works of art for photographs of these works and permission to reproduce them in this book. Sources not included in the captions are listed below.

KEY TO ABBREVIATIONS

ACL   Copyright A.C.L., Brussels
AMNH   American Museum of Natural History, New York
AR   Art Resource, New York
Al   Fratelli Alinari
Bulloz   J.E. Bulloz, Paris
Caisse   Caisse Nationale, Paris
Fototeca   Fototeca Unione, Rome
Gab   Gabinetto Fotografico Nazionale, Rome
Gir   Giraudon
Harding   Robert Harding Picture Library, London
Hir   Hirmer Fotoarchiv, Munich
Mansell   The Mansell Collection, London
Mar   Bildarchiv Foto Marburg
MAS   Ampliaciones y Reproducciones MAS, Barcelona
MN   Cliché des Musées Nationaux, Paris
NYPL   New York Public Library
OI   Courtesy of The Oriental Institute of the University of Chicago
PRI   Photo Researchers, Inc., New York
Scala   Scala Fine Art Publishers
Note: All references in the following credits are to figure numbers.

Paperbound covers Volume I: Scala-AR; Volume II: Museum of Modern Art, New York

Introduction Opening illustration: The British Museum, London; Drawing by Alain, © 1955, 1983 The New Yorker Magazine, Inc.: 11; Al-AR: 9a, 10; Josef Albers: 6, 7; Dr. Thomas Brachert, Courtesy of *Art Bulletin*, Dec. 1971, LIII, 4: 4; Giacomo Brogi-AR: 9b; Hir: 12; Walter Steinkopf: 14.

Part I Opening illustration: Shostal Associates, Inc.
Chapter 1 Aerofilms, Ltd., London: 15; AMNH: 9, 10, 13; Caisse: 7, 8; Colorphoto Hans Hinz, Basel: 1, 4, 6; MAS: 14; © 1982 Scientific American, Inc.: 2, 3; Edwin Smith: 16; Studio Laboric, Bergerac: 5, 12.
Chapter 2 Al-AR: 40; British School of Archeology in Jerusalem: 1, 2; Hir: 10, 12, 19, 24, 27, 31; Arlette Mellaart: 5, 6, 7, 8; James Mellaart: 3, 4; Mansell: 28, 29; MN: 21, 23, 34, 37; OI: 13, 14, 18, 35, 38, 39.
Chapter 3 The Bettmann Archive/BBC Hulton: 11; © Lee Boltin: 39; Reproduced by courtesy of the Trustees of the British Museum: 35, 43; Egyptian Antiquities Organization: 22, 44; Egyptian Expedition, Metropolitan Museum of Art: 18, 20, 34; George Gerster/PRI: 7; Harding: 6, 29, 40, 41; HBJ Collection: 1; Hir: 2, 3, 12, 13, 14, 15, 16, 17, 23, 31, 36; Holle Bildarchiv, Baden-Baden: 27; Mar-AR: 25; MN: 42; OI: 21; © John G. Ross/Harding: 10; © Jim Walston/Taurus Photos, Inc.: 24.
Chapter 4 AR: 14, 15, 16; © Alison Frantz: 25; Courtauld Institute Galleries, London University: 27; Harding: 4, 5, 7, 8, 9, 11, 13, 19, 20, 21, 24, 28, 29, 30, 31; TAP Service: 10; From Christian Zervos, *L'Art des Cyclades*, Éditions Cahiers d'Art, Paris: 1, 2, 3.
Chapter 5 Al-AR: 14, 25, 61, 67, 68, 70, 77, 87; Frederick Ayer III/PRI: 89; Deutsches Archäologisches Institut, Rome: 12; © Robert Ellis/Harding: 57; © Alison Frantz: 39, 40, 41, 53, 54; Gir-AR: 2; Walter Hege: 46; HBJ Collection: 64; Hir: 4, 8, 17, 18, 19, 22, 28, 31, 32, 37, 38, 45, 48, 49, 50, 51, 52, 55, 58, 59, 65, 66, 69, 76, 83, 88; Colorphoto Hans Hinz, Basel: 10; © C.H. Krüger-Moessner: 7, 60; Photo by Herschel Levit: 23; Mar-AR: 73, 74; Ministero Beni Culturali e Ambientali, Rome. Photo: Barbara Malter: 85; MN: 9, 63; Photophile: 42; Josephine Powell, Rome: 62; Courtesy of the Royal Ontario Museum, Toronto, Canada: 44; Scala-AR: 6, 33, 34, 35, 36, 72, 80; Photo: R. Schoder, SJ: 98; Dr. Franz Stoedtner: 27; TAP Service: 16.
Chapter 6 AR: 6, 10, 11, 17, 25, 35, 38, 39, 42, 59, 62, 63, 66, 69, 75, 90, 91; Anderson-AR: 60; Photograph by Bruno Balestrini by courtesy of Electa Editrice, Milan: 50; Frank Brown/Fototeca: 8; Deutsches Archäologisches Institut, Rome: 8, 14, 68, 70, 87, 89; Walter Drayer: 2, 9, 12; Fototeca: 7, 16, 18, 19, 20, 21, 47, 52, 55, 58; Gab: 3, 71; M. Grimoldi: 40, 92; Photo Andre Held: 30; John Johnston: 88; G.E. Kidder-Smith: 85; Foto KLM: 46; Photo by Herschel Levit: 61; From Amedeo Maiuri, *Roman Painting*, Éditions d'Art, Albert Skira: 26; Rhenisches Landesmuseum, Trier: 80, 81; H. Roger-Viollet: 43; Charles Rotkin/PRI: 45; Oscar Savio: 33; Scala-AK: 5, 23, 28, 32, 34, 36, 51, 83, 84; Photo: R. Schoder, SJ: 44; Leonard von Matt/PRI: 64, 65, 72; Courtesy of the Yugoslav National Tourist Office, New York: 77; Zefa: 79.
Chapter 7 © Aerofilms, Ltd.: 67; AR: 43; Al-AR: 11, 35, 36, 37, 51, 65; Anderson-AR: 17, 22, 25, 68; From K.A.C. Creswell, *Early Muslim Architecture*, Clarendon Press: 74; Courtesy of © 1985 Dumbar-

ton Oaks, Trustees for Harvard University, Washington, D.C.: 42; Enrico Ferorelli/DOT: 57; © Alison Frantz: 45, 48; HBJ Collection: 5, 52, 53, 54; Photo Andre Held: 10, 19, 60; Hir: 7, 9, 16, 18, 20, 21, 24, 29, 32, 34, 41; Werner Kalber (from a color proof by Kurt Weitzmann, Princeton): 40; A.F. Kersting, London: 86; G.E. Kidder-Smith: 80; Irving Trust, New York: 72; Linares, Yale University Photo Collection: 78; MAS: 70, 71; Novosti Press Agency: 62; OI: 23; Pontifica Commissione Centrale per l'Arte Sacra in Italia: 3; Josephine Powell, Rome: 55, 56, 77; Ekkehard Ritter: 58, 59; Salmer: 79; Scala-AR: 12, 26, 27, 28, 30, 31, 38, 39; Sergio Sostegni/Fotocielo: 49; Sovfoto: 63; State of Israel, Department of Antiquities and Museums, Jerusalem: 76; Tiers/Holmeyer: 82; Turkish Culture and Information Office: 83; By courtesy of the Board of Trustees of the Victoria and Albert Museum, London: 64; Leonard von Matt/PRI: 84.

Part II Opening illustration: Scala-AR.
Chapter 8 Dr. Harald Busch: 17; De Antonis: 5; HBJ Collection: 19, 20; Hir: 13, 18, 28; Mar-AR: 26; © University Museum of National Antiquities, Oslo, Norway: 3, 4; Wagner Göttingen, Germany: 22; Hermann Wehmeyer: 24, 25.
Chapter 9 Al-AR: 11, 13, 20, 26; © Arch. Phot. Paris/S.P.A.D.E.M.: 33; Bulloz: 27, 31; The Master and Fellows of Corpus Christi College, Cambridge: 39, 41; Caisse: 28; Jean Dieuziade: 4, 24; Gir-AR: 34, 37, 38; J. Guidol/Archive Photographiques, Paris: 29; Hir: 9; HBJ Collection: 10; Evelyn Hofer: 21; A.F. Kersting, London: 17; © Erich Lessing Culture and Fine Art Archives: 35; Jean Roubier, Paris: 1, 6, 14, 23, 25, 30; Scala-AR: 22, 32, 36; Sergio Sostegni/Fotocielo: 19; W.S. Stoddard: 15.
Chapter 10 © Aerofilms, Ltd.: 28; Aero-Photo, Paris: 15; Al-AR: 38, 61, 62, 63; Anderson-AR: 60; Pierre Berger/PRI: 8; Dr. Harald Busch: 52; Electa Editrice: 17; Theo Felton: 57; Gir-AR: 26, 31, 33; HBJ Collection: 1, 3; George Holton/PRI: 58, 64; Mar-AR: 30, 32, 49, 51, 55; Monuments Record, London: 40, 46; Rapho Agence/PRI: 35, 39; Revue Française de l'Électricité: 34; Rheinisches Bildarchiv, Cologne: 56; H. Roger-Viollet: 13, 27; Jean Roubier, Paris: 9, 12, 14; Royal Commission on the Historical Monuments of England: 44, 45; Scala-AR: 28; Helga Schmidt-Glassner: 54; Edwin Smith: 42, 47; W.S. Stoddard: 10, 19; Clarence Ward: 24, 25; Clarence Ward Collection, Photographic Archives, National Gallery of Art, Washington, D.C.: 7, 21, 22, 24, 25, 48.

Part III Opening illustration: Shostal Associates, Inc.
Chapter 11 © Black Star: 32; © J. LeRoy Davidson: 13, 16, 18, 19, 22, 24, 27; © Eliot Elisofon/Time Inc.: 38; Government of India, Archeological Survey of India: 1, 2, 3, 4, 5, 6, 7, 8, 9, 14, 15, 17, 20; HBJ Collection: 26; The Indian Government Tourist Office, New York: 21; Elizabeth Lyons: 33; I. Job Thomas: 23.
Chapter 12 Harry N. Abrams, Inc.: 4; Chavannes: 6; © Joan Lebold Cohen: 30; Courtesy of The Cultural Relics Bureau, Beijing and the Metropolitan Museum of Art, New York: 5; Gir-AR: 27; Harding: 24; HBJ Collection: 15; Magnum: 7, 8; MN: 11; Scala-AR: 10; Audrey R. Topping: 29; Charles Uht: 13; C.C. Wang Family Collection: 26; Langdon Warner's Family: 14.
Chapter 13 Japan National Tourist Organization: 31; National Commission for Protection of Cultural Properties, Tokyo, Japan: 3, 4, 9, 11, 13; From *A History of Far Eastern Art* by Sherman E. Lee, Harry N. Abrams, Inc., Publisher: 6, 10, 27, 28; International Society for Educational Information: 20; Sakamoto Photo Research Laboratory: 5, 8, 12; Shashinka Photo: 16, 17, 18, 23, 24, 25; Spaulding Collection, Museum of Fine Arts, Boston: 30; Yoshi Watanabe: 7; Zauho Press: 26.
Chapter 14 Archaeological Institute of America, reproduced from *Art and Archaeology*, IV, 6, © 1916: 6, 22; Photograph © copyright 1986 by The Barnes Foundation: 55; Chicago Natural History Museum: 15a; Herbert M. Cole: 49; Field photo by Dr. George A. Corbin, Oct. 1972: 62; From H.S. and C.B. Cosgrove, *The Swarts Ruin: A Typical Mimbres Site in Southwestern New Mexico*. Peabody Museum Papers, Vol. 15, No. 1. Reprinted with the permission of the Peabody Museum, Harvard University, Cambridge, Massachusetts: 25; David Gebhard, The Art Galleries, University of California, Santa Barbara: 24; From Campbell Grant, *Rock Art of the American Indian*: 23; Abraham Guillen M.: 17; HBJ Collection: 9; Dr. George Kennedy, University of California, Los Angeles: 46; From J.D. Lajoux, *The*

Rock Painting of Tassili: 40; Archive of Hispanic Culture, Library of Congress: 15b; Courtesy of Museum of the American Indian, Heye Foundation, New York: 21, 30; © National Geographic: 1; National Museum, Lagos, Nigeria: 43; National Park Service, U.S. Department of the Interior: 26, 27; New Mexico State Monuments: 28; Frances Pratt: 2; Photo: Jerry Thompson: 56; From Karl von den Steinen, *Die Marquesaner und ihre Kunst I*: 60; The Wheelwright Museum of the American Indian, Santa Fe: 7; Frank Willett: 41, 42, 46.

Part IV Opening illustration: Scala-AR.
Chapter 15 Al-AR: 2, 4, 5, 9, 12, 13, 15, 16, 17, 18; Anderson-AR: 7, 10, 22, 25; Giacomo Brogi-AR: 3, 20; Gab: 11; Scala-AR: 1, 6, 8, 14, 19, 21, 23, 24.
Chapter 16 Al-AR: 4, 5, 6, 8, 9, 11, 12, 13, 14, 15, 16, 19, 21, 26, 27, 28, 36, 38, 42, 45, 47, 48, 49, 54, 57, 62, 63, 66; Anderson-AR: 17, 24, 30, 31, 39, 41, 53; Marcello Bertoni: 1, 2; Giacomo Brogi-AR: 3, 23, 51; Farbenfotografie: 67; HBJ Collection: 7; La Photothèque: 59; Rollie McKenna/PRI: 40, 44; Scala-AR: 10, 25, 32, 33, 34, 35, 37, 52, 60, 61, 64, 65.
Chapter 17 Harry N. Abrams: 10, 51; Al-AR: 1, 3, 15, 16, 18, 20, 23, 24, 27, 28, 36, 42, 43, 46, 47, 61, 62, 64, 66; Anderson-AR: 4, 31, 38, 39, 48; AR: 50, 56; Harvey J. Barad/PRI: 21; British Architectural Library, London: 11; Caisse: 19; Fototeca: 30, 33; Gir-AR: 22; Scala-AR: 9, 19; Sovfoto: 28; Walter Steinkopf: 24, 39.
Chapter 18 ACL: 7, 8, 9, 20, 21; Al-AR: 18, 55; Artothek, Munich: 41; Giacomo Brogi-AR: 33; Bulloz: 54; Caisse: 1, 51; Gir-AR: 4, 5, 35, 50, 53; L. Gundermann/Photo-Verlag: 29; HBJ Collection: 49; Colorphoto Hans Hinz, Basel: 23; MAS: 22, 56, 57, 58, 59, 60; MN: 25; Rapho Agence/PRI: 61; Studio Remy: 2; Rheinisches Bildarchiv, Cologne: 26; Charles Rotkin/PRI: 52; Scala-AR: 19; Sovfoto: 28; Stedelijke Musea, Louvain: 17; Walter Steinkopf: 24, 39.
Chapter 19 Harry N. Abrams, Inc.: 21; Aero-Photo, Paris: 66; Al-AR: 8, 10, 12, 13, 15, 18, 24, 25, 28, 42, 43, 73; Anderson-AR: 5, 33, 35; © Arch. Phot., Paris/S.P.A.D.E.M.: 72; Avery Library, Columbia University, New York: 1; British Crown Copyright, Reproduced with permission of the Controller of Her Brittanic Majesty's Stationery Office: 75; Giacomo Brogi-AR: 38; © 1966, Henri Dauman. All rights reserved: 69; Gab: 20; Gir-AR: 62, 66; Gene Heil/PRI: 24; A.F. Kersting, London: 4, 65, 76; G.E. Kidder-Smith: 17, 19; Frank Lerner, Munich: 55; Mansell: 61; MAS: 37; MN: 27, 48, 59; Courtesy of NYPL (Astor, Lenox and Tilden Foundations): 67; Photo Henrot: 70; H. Roger-Viollet: 71; Charles Rotkin/PRI: 3; Scala-AR: 7, 9, 23, 26, 30, 32, 34; Helga Schmidt-Glassner: 64; Walter Steinkopf: 58.
Chapter 20 ACL: 39; Al-AR: 1, 2, 7, 12; Bulloz: 36; J. Allan Cash/PRI: 42; British Crown Copyright, Reproduced with permission of the Controller of Her Britannic Majesty's Stationery Office: 5; Caisse: 19; By kind permission of Country Life Magazine: 22, 23; H.B. Fleming & Co.: 21; Gir-AR· 18, 29, 38; Hir: 13; A.F. Kersting, London: 10, 21, 25; Library of Congress: 26; Merisio, Pepi, Bergano, courtesy Art and Architecture Div., NYPL (Astor, Lenox and Tilden Foundations): 3; Erich Muller: 9; Courtesy of the NYPL (Astor, Lenox and Tilden Foundations): 40; Scala: 14, 17; Virginia Chamber of Commerce: 27; Virginia Museum of Fine Arts, Richmond: 33.

Part V Opening illustration: Collection of The Museum of Modern Art, New York.
Chapter 21 Al-AR: 5, 8, 21, 24, 27, 83; AR: 39, 40; Bridgeman-AR: 41; John R. Brownlie/PRI: 2; Bulloz: 7, 20, 23, 35; Caisse: 1; Gir-AR: 15, 16, 57, 81; HBJ Collection: 61, 85, 86, 88, 89, 90; Hedrich-Blessing: 87; A.F. Kersting, London: 3; Photo Kleinhempel: 43; Library of Congress: 79; Mar-AR: 82; MN: 13, 14, 17, 19, 22, 26, 38; Neue Pinakothek, Munich: 50; Novosti: 45; Collection Phoenix Art Museum: 28; H. Roger-Viollet: 4; Scala-AR: 9, 12, 18; Photo courtesy of National-Galerie, Staatliche Museen, Berlin: 33.
Chapter 22 Albright-Knox Art Gallery, Buffalo: 102; Photo by Rudolph Burckhardt, New York: 82; Photo Courtesy of Leo Castelli Gallery, New York: 88, 90; Geoffrey Clements: 91; John Donat: 101; David Gahr: 86; Barbara Gladstone Gallery, New York: 96; © Gianfranco Gorgoni/Contact Press Images: 84; Photo by Carmelo Guadagno: 9; Solomon R. Guggenheim Museum, New York. Photo by Robert E. Mates: 107, 108; HBJ Collection: 55, 57, 58, 71; Photo by David Heald: 13; Lucien Hervé: 59, 61, 104, 105, 106; Colorphoto Hans Hinz, Basel: 5, 20; Institut für Leichte Flachentragwerke, Stuttgart:

112; Photo Kleinhempel: 6; William Lescaze Associates: 65; Courtesy of Marlborough Gallery Inc., New York: 98; MAS: 56; © Norman McGrath: 122; Museum of Modern Art, New York: 63, 66; Office du Film du Québec: 114; Courtesy of The Pace Gallery and Julian Schnabel. Photographed by Phillips/Schwab: 95; Courtesy of the Philadelphia Convention and Visitors Bureau: 100; Robert Phillips for Fortune Magazine: 113; Musée Picasso, Paris: 14; © Margaret K. Porter: 116; Photo: Michel Proulx, *Architectural Record*: 117; Oscar Savio: 109; © foto Stedelijk Museum, Amsterdam: 60; Dr. Franz Stoedtner: 64; © 1956 Ezra Stoller, ESTO: 103; Ezra Stoller, © ESTO: 67; Photo by Don Sudnik, *AIA Journal*: 118; Photo by James A. Sugar © National Geographic Society: 115; Tiofoto: 47; Trans World Airlines: 110, 111; Courtesy of the Union of Artists of the USSR: 99; Malcolm Varon, New York: 21; Venturi and Rauch: 119, 120; Wolfgang Volz, Essen: 94; Galerie Welz: 4; Collection of the Whitney Museum, Gift of Robert and Nancy Kaye: 97.

© S.P.A.D.E.M., Paris/V.A.G.A., New York, 1985: 19-72; 20-25; Part V Opening illustration: 21-1, 75; 22-3, 4, 5, 8, 10, 11, 12, 14, 15, 17, 18, 20, 23, 25, 26, 30, 31, 33, 35, 40, 41, 51, 59, 60, 61, 80, 88, 90, 104, 105, 106.

© A.D.A.G.P., Paris/V.A.G.A., New York, 1985: 22-8, 14, 17, 29, 46, 49, 52, 58.

Illustration Credits
FIG. 3-4 Adapted from the "Later Canon" of Egyptian Art, figure 1 in Erwin Panofsky, *Meaning in the Visual Arts*. Copyright © 1955 by Erwin Panofsky. Used by permission of Doubleday and Company, Inc.
FIGS. 3-19, 28; 5-26; 6-24, 48, 52a, 56; 7-50; 10-59 From Sir Banister Fletcher, *A History of Architecture on the Comparative Method*, 17th ed., rev. by R.A. Cordingly, 1961. Used by permission of the Athlone Press of the University of London.
FIGS. 4-6; 7-1, 8, 33 Hirmer Fotoarchiv, Munich.
FIGS. 5-92, 93, 95 From Richard Brilliant, *Arts of the Ancient Greeks*, 1973. Adapted by permission of McGraw-Hill Book Co.
FIG. 5-96 From J. Charbonneaux, et al., *Hellenistic Art 330–50 B.C.*, 1973. Adapted by permission of George Braziller, Inc.
FIG. 6-49 From J.B. Ward-Perkins, *Roman Architecture*, 1977. Adapted by permission of Electa Editrice.
FIG. 6-54 From Robert Furneaux Jordan, *A Concise History of Western Architecture*, © 1969 by Harcourt Brace Jovanovich, Inc. Reproduced by permission of the publisher.
FIG. 6-76 Deutsches Archäologisches Institut, Rome.
FIG. 6-78 From Fiske Kimball, M. Arch, and G.H. Edgell, *A History of Architecture*, 1918. Used by permission of Harper & Row, Inc., publishers.
FIG. 6-82 From George M.A. Hanfmann, *Roman Art: A Survey of the Art of Imperial Rome*, A New York Graphic Society Book. By permission of Little, Brown and Company.
FIG. 7-66 From Kenneth J. Conant, *Early Medieval Church Architecture*. Used by permission of The Johns Hopkins Press.
FIGS. 7-66, 73 From K.A.C. Creswell, *Early Muslim Architecture*. Adapted by permission of Clarendon Press.
FIG. 7-69 From G. Marçais, *L'Architecture Musulmane d'Occident*. By permission of Arts et Métiers Graphiques, Paris.
FIG. 7-75 Staatliche Museen, Berlin.
FIG. 7-85 From "Sinan" by D. Kuban from *Macmillan Encyclopedia of Architects*, Adolf K. Placzek, Editor-in-Chief, Vol. 4, p. 68. © 1982 by the Free Press, a Division of Macmillan, Inc.
FIG. 9-3 From H. Stierlin, *Die Architektur der Welt*, Vol. 1, p. 147. © 1977 by Hirmer Verlag, Munich.
FIGS. 10-4, 5, 6 From Ernst Gall, *Gotische Kathedralen*, 1925. Used by permission of Klinkhardt & Biermann, publishers.
FIG. 10-18 Used by permission of Umschau Verlag, Frankfort.
FIG. 11-8 From Benjamin Rowland, *The Art and Architectural India*, 1953, Penguin Books.
FIG. 11-29 From Madeleine Giteau, *The Civilization of Angkor*. Adapted by permission of Rizzoli International Publications.
FIG. 14-4 Field Museum of Natural History, Chicago.
FIG. 14-22 From "The Serpent Mound of Adams County, Ohio" by Charles C. Willoughby from *American Anthropologist* 21 (2): 156, 1919. Reproduced by permission of The American Anthropological Association.
FIG. 16-43 From Nikolaus Pevsner, *An Outline of European Architecture*, 6th ed., 1960, Penguin Books, Ltd., © Nikolaus Pevsner, 1943, 1960, 1963.

INDEX

Page numbers in italics indicate illustrations.

Art Nouveau, 874, 879, 884, 885, 891, 919, 927–28, 930, 953

Artemis, Temple of, Corfu, 144, *145*

Asam, Egid Quirin: *Assumption of the Virgin*, 778, *779*

Ascension of Christ and the Mission of the Apostles, The, La Madeleine, Vézelay, 362–63, *362*

Ashikaga period, 472–74

Ashurbanipal Hunting Lions, Nineveh, 60–61, *61*

Ashurnasirpal II at War, Nimrud, 59–60, *60*

Ashurnasirpal II Drinking, Nimrud, 60, *60*

Asie usu figures, 511–12, *512*

Asmat ancestral poles, 516, *517*

Asoka, 420, *421*; palace of, 420

Assumption of the Virgin (Asam), 778, *779*

Assumption of the Virgin, The (Correggio), 630, *630*

Assumption of the Virgin, The, from *The Creglingen Altarpiece* (Riemenschneider), 680–81, *680*

Assyrian art, 17, 56–61

Aswan High Dam, 72n, 88

At the Moulin Rouge (Toulouse-Lautrec), 870–71, *870*

Athena Nike, Temple of, Acropolis, Athens, *139*, 151, 157, *157*

Athena Taking Young Alcyoneus by the Hair, Altar of Zeus and Athena, Pergamon, 171, *171*

Athenodorus (with Agesander and Polydorus): *Head of Odysseus*, 173, *173*; *Laocoön* group, 172, *172*, 173; *Odysseus' Helmsman Falling*, 173, *173*

Athlete (Lysippos), 166, *167*

Augusta Trevirorum, 237–39, *238*

Augustine. *See* St. Augustine

Augustus, 214, 219, 225

Augustus of Primaporta, 225, *225*, 231, *231*

Aula Palatina, Augusta Trevirorum, 238–39, *238*

Aurangabad, India, relief sculpture from, 426, *426*

Aurelian 235

Aurier, Albert, 871

Aurora (Il Guercino), 725–26, *725*, 731

Aurora (Reni), 725, *725*

Australian art, 518

Autumn Mountains (Tung Ch'i-ch'ang), 458, *458*

Avebury, cromlechs at, 37

Avignon Pietà, The (Quarton), 678, *678*

Axis line, 8–9

Aztec art, 486, 491

B

Babylon: art, 55–56; ziggurats, 48

Back I (Matisse), 920, *920*

Back IV (Matisse), 920, *920*

Bacon, Francis, 938; *Number VII from Eight Studies for a Portrait*, 938, *938*

Bacon, Roger, 531, 556

Baining art, 515

Baldassare Castiglione (Raphael), 613, *614*

Ballet Rehearsal (Adagio) (Degas), 859–60, *860*

Balthasar Coymans (Hals), 742–43, *743*

Balzac (Rodin), 880–81, *881*

Bamberg Rider, from Bamberg Cathedral, 406–407, *406*

Bamboo (Wu Chen), 456–57, *457*

Bangwa art, 508

Banqueting House at Whitehall (Jones), 765–66, *766*

Bar at the Folies-Bergère (Manet), 843–44, *843*

Barbarian art. *See* Migration period

Barbaro, Daniele, 640

Barbizon School, 837, 839

Bare Willows and Distant Mountain (Ma Yuan), 455, *455*

Barlach, Ernst, 919–20; *War Monument*, 919–20, *919*

Baroque art, 710–67; architecture, 712–17, 719–23, 758–67, 771–74; English, 765–67; Dutch, 741–53; Italian, 712–32; painting, 723–53, 754–58; Rococo style, 770–85; sculpture, 717–19, 764; Spanish, 732–36

Barrel vaults, 57; Roman, 223–24, *223*; Romanesque, 347

Barry, Charles, 811–12; Houses of Parliament, London (with Pugin), 811–12, *811*

Bartolommeo Colleoni (Verrocchio), 583–84, *583*

Barye, Antoine-Louis: *Jaguar Devouring a Hare*, 17, 814, *814*

"Basilica," Paestum, 141–42, *141, 142*

Basilica of Constantine, Rome, 223, 241, *241*, 242

Basilica Ulpia, Rome, 218–19, *219*

Bastien-Lepage, Jules, 855; *Joan of Arc*, *854*, 855

Bath, The (Cassatt), 862, *862*

Bathers (Picasso), 8, *8*

Baths of Caracalla, Rome, 223, 224–25, *224*

Baths of Neptune, Ostia, *212*, 213

Battle Between Romans and Barbarians, from the Ludovisi Battle Sarcophagus, 260–61, *260*

Battle of Gods and Giants, Pergamon, 170–71, *171*

Battle of Issus, The (Altdorfer), 682, *683*

Battle of Issus, The, Pompeii, 202, 210, 211, *211*

Battle of San Romano, The (Uccello), 567, *568*

Battle of the Gods and Giants, Delphi, 144, *144*

Battle of the Ten Nudes (Pollaiuolo), 585, *585*

Baudelaire, Charles, 675, 821, 827, 839, 841

Bauhaus, the, Dessau (Gropius), 933–34, *934*

Baule figures, 511–12, *512*

Bayeux Tapestry, 364, *364*

Bayon at Angkor Thom, Kampuchea, 436–37, *436, 437*

Beardsley, Aubrey, 873–74; *The Peacock Skirt*, 874, *874*

"Beauborg," the. *See* Georges Pompidou National Center of Art and Culture

Beautiful Bodhisattva Padmapani, Ajanta, 430, *430*

Beauvais Cathedral, France, 390–91, *390*

Beckmann, Max, 897; *Departure*, 896, *897*

Behrens, Peter, 932

Belleville Breviary (Pucelle), 658–60, *659*

Bellini, Giovanni, 596, 642–45, 646, 647, 687; *The Feast of the Gods*, 643–44, *644*; *Madonna of the Trees*, 642, *642*; *San Giobbe Altarpiece*, 642–43, *643*; *San Zaccaria Altarpiece*, 642, 643, *643*

Beni Hasan, rock-cut tombs at, 84–86, *84, 85*

Benin art, 506–507

Benizuri-e, 481

Bergson, Henri, 928

Berlinghieri, Bonaventura, 535; *St. Francis Altarpiece*, 534, *535*; *St. Francis Preaching to the Birds*, 534–35, *535*

Bernard of Clairvaux, 355, 374

Bernardo Rossellino. *See* Rossellino, Bernardo

Bernini, Gianlorenzo, 7, 711, 715–19; baldacchino for St. Peter's, Rome, 716, *716*; Cathedra Petri, Rome, 716–17, *717*; Cornaro Chapel, Santa Maria della Vittoria, Rome, 718, *718*; *David*, 710, 717–18, *717*; *The Ecstasy of St. Theresa*, 520, 718, *718*; St. Peter's, Rome, 7, 713, 715, *715*, *716*; Scala Regia, the Vatican, Rome, 715–16, *716*; Triton Fountain, Rome, 718, *719*

Bertoldo di Giovanni, 615

Betrayal of Jesus, The, from the *Maestà Altarpiece* (Duccio), 535–36, *536*

Bhagavad-Gita, 424

Bibliotheque Ste. Geneviève, Paris (Labrouste), 881–82, *881*

Bicycle Wheel (Duchamp), 925, *925*

Bihzad, 307

Biomorphic abstraction, 922

Bird in Space (Brancuşi), 922, *922*

Birkerts, Gunnar, 967; Federal Reserve Bank Building, Minneapolis, 967, *967*

Birthday (Kienholz), 953, *954*

Birth of the Virgin, The (Ghirlandaio), 586–87, *586*

Birth of the Virgin, The (Pietro Lorenzetti), 545–46, *545*

Birth of Venus, The (Botticelli), 589–90, *590*

Bison with Superposed Arrows, Niaux, 31, *31*

Bison with Turned Head, La Madeleine, *33*

Black-figure technique, 131

Bladen, Ronald, 948; *X*, 948, *948*

Blake, William, 799–800, 801; *Pity*, 800, *800*

Blam! (Lichtenstein), 952–53, *953*

Blenheim Palace, Oxfordshire (Vanbrugh), 772, *773*

Blinding of Polyphemus, The, and *Gorgons*, Eleusis, 129–30, *129*

Bloch, Ernest, 971

Blue Rider movement (Der Blaue Reiter), 895, 898

Boar Avatar of Vishnu, Udayagiri, 425, *425*

Boccioni, Umberto, 904–905, 921; *Unique Forms of Continuity in Space*, 921, *921*

Bodhidharma, 455

Bodhisattva, Early T'ang dynasty, 449, *450*

Bodmer, Karl: *Mandan Chief Mato-Tape*, 502–504, *503*

Boffrand, Germain: Salon de la Princesse, Hôtel de Soubise, Paris, 774–75, *774*

Bonampak, temple at, 489–90; mural from, *490*

Bonheur, Rosa, 853–54; *The Horse Fair*, 854–55, *854*

Book of Lindisfarne, 321–23, *321, 323*, 325, 399

Borgia, Cesare, 604

Borobudur stupa, Java, 432–33, *433*

Borrachos, Los (Velázquez), 733, *733*

Borromini, Francesco, 719–20; San Carlo alle Quattro Fontane, 719–20, *719*; St. Ivo, 720, *720*, *721*

Bosch, Hieronymus, 674–77, 696, 697; *The Carrying of the Cross*, 674–75, *674*; *The Garden of Earthly Delights*, 675–77, *676*; *Hell*, 675–77, *676*; *The Third Day of Creation*, 676, *677*

Botticelli, Sandro, 588–91, 592, 604; *The Birth of Venus*, 589–90, *590*; *Portrait of a Young Man*, 588–89, *588*

Boucher, François, 781; *Cupid a Captive*, 781, *781*

Bouguereau, Adolphe William, 842, 853; *Nymphs and Satyr*, 853, *853*

Bouleuterion, 178

Bound Slave, The (Michelangelo), 617–18, *617*

Bourges Cathedral, France, 384–85, *384, 385*

Bouts, Dirk, 671; *The Last Supper*, 671–72, *671*

Boy in a Red Vest (Cézanne), 866, *866*

Boyle, Richard: Chiswick House, England (with Kent), 772–74, *773*

Bramante, 604, 605–608, 611, 625; Palazzo Caprini, Rome, 608, *608*; St. Peter's, Rome, 606–607, *606*, 625; Sant' Eligio degli Orifici, Rome (with Raphael), 722, *722*; the Tempietto, 605–606, *606*

Brancuşi, Constantin, 922, 923; *Bird in Space*, 922, *922*

Brant–Johnson house, Vail (Venturi and Associates), 971, *972*

Braque, Georges, 900, 903–904; *The Table*, 903–904, *904*

Breakfast Scene, from *Marriage à la Mode* (Hogarth), 784–85, *784*

Breasted, James, 94

Breton, André, 911, 925

Breuil, Abbé, 28, 32

Brick Knot (Taylor), 960, *961*

Bride of the Wind, The (Kokoschka), 895, *895*

Bridge movement (Die Brücke), 895

Brihadesvara Temple, Thanjavur, 429, 430

Broad Flatheads (Bury), 950, *950*

Broederlam, Melchior: *The Flight into Egypt*, 658, *658*; *Presentation, The*, 658, *658*

Bronze-casting technique, 147

Bronze warrior, Athens, 133–34, *134*

Bronzino, 633–34, 635; *Portrait of a Young Man*, 634–35, *634*; *Venus, Cupid, Folly, and Time (The Exposure of Luxury)*, 633–34, *633*

Bruegel, Pieter, the Elder, 696–98; *Hunters in the Snow*, 696–97, *697*; *Peasant Dance, The*, 697–98, *698*

Bruges, Flanders, 657

Brunelleschi, Filippo, 524, 551, 556, 559–63, 564, 575, 577; Florence Cathedral, dome of, 407, *408*, 559–69, *559*; Ospedale degli Innocenti, Florence, 560, *560*; Pazzi Chapel, Florence, 561–63, *562*; *The Sacrifice of Isaac*, 550, 551; Santa Maria degli Angeli, Florence, 562–63, *562*; Santo Spirito, Florence, 560–61

Bruni, Leonardo, 580; tomb of, Santa Croce, Florence (Bernardo Rossellino), 580, *581*

Brygos Painter, 133; *Revelers*, 133, *133*

Buddha, Gal Vihara, 432, *432*

Buddha images, 423–24, 445–48, 465, 470–71

Buddhism, 419–20, 445, 446, 449, 455, 465, 472

Buffalmacco, Buonamico: *The Triumph of Death* (or Traini ?), 546–47, *547*

Hippodameia and the Centaur, Olympia, 149–50, *149*
Hippodamian plan, 177–178, *178*, *179*
Hippodamus, 177
Hippopotamus Hunt, Saqqara, 83, *83*
Hiroshige, Ando, 482
Hispano–America (Orozco), 916, *916*
Hoffman, Hans, 938; *Effervescence, 1944*, 938–39, *939*
Hogarth, William, 8, 784–85; *Breakfast Scene*, from *Marriage à la Mode*, 784–85, *784*
Hokke-kyo (Lotus Sutra), Fujiwara period, 469, *469*
Hokusai, Katsushika, 482; *The Great Wave*, from *Thirty-Six Views of Mt. Fuji*, *482*
Holbein, Hans, the Younger, 682, 690–92; *Christina of Denmark*, 692, *692*; *The French Ambassador*, 691–92, *692*
Holland, art of, 741–53, 867–68. *See also* Flemish art
Holy Apostles, Church of, 283
Holy Sepulchre, Church of the, Jerusalem, 255
Holy Trinity, The (Masaccio), 566–67, *567*
Homage to New York (Tinguely), 950, *950*
Homer, 104, 117, 118, 191
Homer, Winslow, 844, 849; *The Fox Hunt*, 849–50, *849*
Honorius, 265
Honourable Mrs. Graham, The (Gainsborough), 792, *792*
Honthorst, Gerard van. *See* Van Honthorst, Gerard
Hopi art, 499, 500
Hopper, Edward, 917; *Eleven A.M.*, 917, *917*
Horace, 194, 210
Horizontal Spines (Calder), 924, *924*
Horse (Han Kan), 452, *452*
Horse Fair, The (Bonheur), 854–55, *854*
Horsemen, Parthenon, Athens, 155, *155*
Horta, Victor, 928; staircase, Hotel van Eetvelde, Brussels, 928, *928*
Horus, Temple of, at Edfu, 89, *89*
Horyu-ji temple complex, 466
Hotel van Eetvelde, Brussels, staircase in (Horta), 928, *928*
Houdon, Jean Antoine, *Count Cagliostro*, 791, *791*; *Diana*, 791, *791*
Houses: African, 509, *509*; Japanese, 483, *483*; Medieval, 328–29, *329*; Oceanic, 516, *516*; Roman, 201–202, *201*, 214; twentieth-century, 929–33, *929–33*
Houses of Parliament, London (Barry and Pugin), 811–12, *811*
Howe, George: Philadelphia Savings Fund Society Building (with Lescaze), 934, *934*
Hsia Kuei, 455
Hsu Pei-hung, 459
Huang Kung-wang: *Dwelling in the Fu-ch'un Mountains*, 456, *456*
Hue, 12
Hugh of St. Victor, 393
Hughes, Robert, 975
Hugo van der Goes, 672–73; *Adoration of the Shepherds*, 672, *673*; *The Portinari Altarpiece*, 672–73, *672*
Hui Tsung, 454
Huizinga, Johan, 662
Humanism, 522–27, 531, 575, 580, 627, 682, 692
Hunter and Kangaroo, Oenpelli, 518, *519*
Hunters in the Snow (Bruegel), 696–97, *697*
Hydria, *130*
Hyksos period, Egypt, 86
Hypostyle halls, Egyptian, 89–92

I

Ibo mbari house, 509, *509*
Iconoclastic Controversy, 285, 292
Iconography, 6
Iconostasis, 291–92
Icons: Byzantine, 285, 289–92; Russian, 291–92. *See also* Buddha images
Idyllic Landscape, Pompeii, 210, *210*
Ife–Benin style, 505–507
Ife king figure, Yoruba, 505–506, *505*
Igbo Ukwu, 505
Ijo Iphri sculpture, 507, *507*

Iktinos: Parthenon, Athens (with Kallikrates), 151–56
Il Gesù, Rome (Giacomo della Porta and Giacomo da Vignola), 712–13, *712*, *713*
Illumination: Early Christian, 258–60; Early Medieval, 320–23, 324–25; Flemish, 658–61; Gothic, 396–98; Islamic, 307–309; Romanesque, 366–69
Imhotep, 77
Important Personage Seated in a Stylized Niche, Olmec, 487, *487*
Impressionism, 836, 855–62, 881; Post-, 862–71; in Roman wall painting, 209
Improvisation 28 (Kandinsky), 897, 898, *898*
Inca art, 495
Incrustation wall painting, *202*, *203*
India, art of, 418–37; architecture, 420–23, 432–33, 434–37; Buddha images, 423–24; painting, 429–31; sculpture, 420, 422–27, 429, 432–34, 436, 437
Indonesian art, 432–33
Ingres, Jean Auguste Dominique, 18, 824–27, 830, 861; *François Marius Granet*, 826–27, *826*; *Grande Odalisque*, 825–26, *825*; *Oedipus and the Sphinx*, 825, *825*; *Paganini*, 826–27, *826*
Insane Woman (Envy) (Géricault), 820, *820*
Installations, 960–62
Insulae, 213, *214*
Intensity, 12
Intérieur (Le Viol) (Degas), 858, 859, *859*
Interior of the Pantheon (Pannini), 222, *223*
International style: in "proto-Renaissance" painting, 543, 552, 564, 593, 656, 658, 660–61, 678; in twentieth-century architecture, 930–36, 965, 970, 971, 972
Intricate wall painting, 206–208, *207*
Ionic order, 140, *140*, 143, 153, 156–58, 168, 169
Iroquois art, 504, *504*
Isaac and His Sons (Ghiberti), 557, *557*
Ise Shrine, 467–68, *467*
Isenheim Altarpiece, The (Grünewald), 684–87, *685*, *686*
Ishtar Gate, Babylon, 62–63, *62*, *63*; *Lion from the Processional Way* from, 17, 62, *62*
Isidorus of Miletus, 279
Islam, 249, 293–94
Islamic art, 293–309; architecture, 294–305; illumination, 307–309; object art, 307; Ottoman, 303–305; textiles, 307
Italian art: architecture, 5, 559–64, 576–80, 605–10, 620–26, 712–17, 719–23; Baroque, 712–32; fifteenth-century, 550–97; Gothic, 5, 107–11; Mannerism, 631–38; painting, 534–47, 550–59, 580–84, 615–18, 635–36, 719–23, 777, 852, 904–905, 910–11; "proto-Renaissance," 530–47; Renaissance, 550–653; sculpture, 532–34, 550–59, 580–84, 615–18, 635–36, 719–23; sixteenth-century, 600–653; twentieth-century, 904–905
Ixion Room, House of the Vetii, Pompeii, 206, *207*

J

Jack-in-the-Pulpit IV (O'Keeffe), 907–908, *908*
Jacopo da Pontormo: *The Descent from the Cross*, 632, *632*
Jacopo della Quercia, 552, 615, 628; *The Expulsion from the Garden of Eden*, 552, *552*
Jade carvings, Chinese, 440, 442, 445, 460
Jaeger, Werner, 126
Jaggayyapeta, 427
Jaguar Devouring a Hare (Barye), 17, 814, *814*
Jainism, 419
Jamdat Nasr, 45–46
Japanese art, 464–83; architecture, 465, 473–74, 483; Ashikaga period, 472–74; calligraphy, 479; fan painting, 469; Fujiwara period, 468–70; Heian period, 468–71; Kamakura realism, 471–72; Momoyama period, 475–82; native traditions, 464–65; painting, 466, 468–70, 471–73, 474, 475, 479–80; pottery, 464; prints, 480–82, 859–60, 891; screen painting, 475; scroll painting, 468–70, 471–72; tea ceremony, 473–74
Java, art of, 432–33
Jeckyl, Thomas: Peacock Room (with Whistler), 885, *885*

Jefferson, Thomas, 789–90; Monticello, 789–90, *789*; State Capital, Richmond, 790, *790*
Jericho, 40–41
Jesus, 255–56, 294
Joan of Arc (Bastien-Lepage), 854, 855
Jocho: *Amida*, 470–71, *470*
John of Garland, 393
John of Salisbury, 382
Johns, Jasper, 952; *Painted Bronze*, 952, *952*
Johnson, Philip, 970–71; Pennzoil Place, Houston (with Burgee and Associates), 970–71, *971*; Seagram Building, New York (with Mies van der Rohe), 935, *936*
Jones, Inigo, 608, 765–66; Banqueting House at Whitehall, London, 765–66, *766*
Joseph in Egypt, St. Mark's, Venice, 288–89, *288*
Juan de Pareja (Velázquez), 734, *734*
Judd, Donald, 948; *Untitled*, 948, *948*
Judgment of Paris, The (Cranach), 683–84, *684*
Judith and Maidservant with the Head of Holofernes (Gentileschi), 729, *729*
Julii, mausoleum of the, Rome, 256, *256*
Julius II (pope), 606, 611, 620, 638; tomb of, 616–18
Jung, Carl, 915
Jupiter and Semele (Moreau), 872–83, *872*
Just What Is It That Makes Today's Homes So Different, So Appealing (Hamilton), 951, *951*
Justin Martyr, 261
Justinian, 265
Justinian and Attendants, San Vitale, Ravenna, 273, *274*, 275–76, *276*, 542
Justinian and Maximianus, San Vitale, Ravenna, *276*
Juvara, Filippo, *772*; the Superga, Turin, 771–72, *771*
Juvenal, 214

K

Ka-Aper (Sheikh el Beled), Saqqara, 82–83, *83*
Kabuki theater, 480
Kachina spirit mask, 500, *500*
Kagle (mask), Dan, 510–11, *510*
Kaigetsudo family, 480–81
Kailasa Temple, Ellora, 428
Kalf, Willem: *Still Life*, 13, 751, *752*
Kallikrates: Parthenon, Athens (with Iktinos), 151–56; Temple of Athena Nike, Acropolis, Athens, *139*, 157, *157*
Kamakura realism, 471–72
Kamares pitcher, Phaistos, 106–107, *107*, *115*
Kandinsky, Vasily, 897, 898–99, 906, 931, 930, *Improvisation 28*, 897, 898, *898*
Kano School, 474
Kao, 472
Karnak, Temple of Amen-Re at, 89–91, *90*, *91*, 95
Katholikon, Church of the, Hosios Loukas, 13, 282–83, *282*, *283*
Kato Zakro, palace at, 107
Katsura Place, Japan, 476–78, *476*, *477*; gardens of, 477–78; Shokintei from, 473–74, *473*, *474*
Kauffmann, Angelica, 796; *Cornelia, Mother of the Gracchi*, 796, *796*
Kaufmann House ("Falling Water"), Bear Run, Pennsylvania (Wright), 932–33, *933*
Keats, John, 84
Kelly, Ellsworth, 944–45; *Red, Blue, Green*, 944–45, *945*
Kent, William: Chiswick House, England (with Boyle), 772–74, *773*
Kenzan, Ogata, 479
Kepler, Johannes, 710
Khafre: pyramid of, 77, 78, *78*, 79–80, *79*; statue of, 81–82, *81*; valley temple of, 80–81, *82*
Khirbat al-Mafjar, palace at, 299–300
Khufu, pyramid of, Gizeh, 77, 78, *78*, 79
Kienholz, Edward, 953; *Birthday*, 953, *954*
Kinetic Art, 924, 949–50
King Cophetua and the Beggar Maid (Burne-Jones), 851–52, *851*
King Smenkhkare and Meritaten, Tel el-Amarna, 96, *96*
Kiss, The (Rodin), 879–80, *880*
Kiyomasu I, 480

Mshatta, palace at, 299, *299*
Mu-ch'i, 473
Muktesvar Temple, Bhuvanesvar, 428, *428*
Mummy Portrait of a Man, Faiyum, 213, *213*
Munch, Edvard, 875, 894; *The Scream,* 875, *875*
Mungarawai: *The Djanggawul Sisters,* 518, *519*
Mural painting: Byzantine, 264–65; Greek, 161, 162; Indian, 429–30; pre-Columbian, 489–90; Romanesque, 364. *See also* Frescoes; Wall painting
Museo Capitolino, Rome (Michelangelo), 623, *624*
Musicians and Dancers, Thebes, *2,* 93, *93*
Muybridge, Eadweard, 845
Mycenaean art, 117–23; architecture, 117–20; craft art, 121–22; pottery, 122–23
Mykerinus. *See* Menkure
Myron: *Discobolos,* 148–49, *148*
Mythological Scenes, Wu family shrine, Shantung, 443–44, *444*

N

Nagarjunakonda, 427
Nagoya Castle, Japan, 475
Nakht, Tomb of, at Thebes, 93, *93*
Nanga painting, 479–80
Nanni di Banco, 552, 553; *Quattro Santi Coronati,* 552, *553*
Napoleon Bonaparte, 72, 818
Nara period, 465, 471
Nasca art, 493
Nash, John: Royal Pavilion, Brighton, 812–13, *812*
National Gallery Addition, Washington, D.C. (Pei), 968–69, *968, 969*
Naturalism: Baroque, 711; in cave art, 28; Flemish, 665; Japanese, 480; "proto-Renaissance," 531, 534; Renaissance, 534. *See also* Realism
Nature Studies (Okyo), 480, *480*
Navajo art, 499–500
Near East, Ancient, 40–69, 114; Akkad, 53–55; Assyria, 56–61; Babylon, 55–56, 62–63; Çatal Hüyük, 41–44; Elam, 64; Jericho, 40–41; Persia, 64–69; Sumer, 45–52
Nebamun, tomb of, at Thebes, 93–94; wall paintings from, *2, 92,* 93, *93*
Nebuchadnezzar, 62, 64
Necropolis at Caere, 186, *186*
Nedick's (Estes), 954, *954*
Neo-Babylonian art, 62–63
Neoclassicism, 787–90, 795–800
Neolithic art, 36–37, 40–44
Neptune and Amphitrite, House of, Herculaneum, *212,* 213
Neptune and Amphitrite (Gossaert), 694, *694*
Nero, 195, 219–20
Nervi, Pier Luigi, 965; Palazzetto dello Sport, Rome, 965, *965*
Netherlands. *See* Flemish art
Neumann, Balthasar; pilgrimage church of Vierzehnheiligen, 776–77, *776, 777*
Nevelson, Louise, 947; *An American Tribute to the British People,* 947, *947*
New Guinea art, 516–17
New Kingdom, Egypt, 86–94
New Realism, 954–55
New Sacristy, Florence (Michelangelo), 620–21
New York School, 939–41
New Zealand art, 514
Newman, Barnett, 944; *Vir Heroicus Sublimis,* 944, *944*
Newton, Sir Isaac, 710, 731
Ni Tsan, 456
Niaux cave art, 28; *Bison with Superposed Arrows,* 31, *31*
Nicholas of Cusa, 531, 667
Nicola Pisano. *See* Pisano, Nicola
Nietzsche, Friedrich, 850
Night Café, The (Van Gogh), 867–68, *867*
Nightmare, The (Fuseli), 799, *800*
Nike Fastening Her Sandal, Acropolis, Athens, 159–60, *159*
Nike of Samothrace, 169–70, *170*
Niobid Painter: *Argonaut Krater,* 162–63, *162*
Nishiki-e, 481

No plays, 480
Nok head, 505, *505*
Nolde, Emil, 895–97; *St. Mary of Egypt Among Sinners,* 895–97, *896*
Norman architecture, 350–51
Norman Cavalry Charging in the Battle of Hastings, from the *Bayeaux Tapestry,* 364, *364*
North American Indian art, 495–504; Eastern Woodlands, 504; Eskimo, 495–96; Great Plains, 502–504; historic era, 499–504; Northwest Coast, 500–502; prehistoric era, 495–99; Southwest, 499–500
Northern and Southern dynasties, 445–48
Northern Sung dynasty, 453–54
Northwest Coast Indian art, 500–502
Notre Dame Cathedral, Paris, *378,* 379–80, *379;* rose windows, *310,* 378, 388–89, *388; The Virgin of Paris,* from, 398–99, *399*
Notre Dame du Haut, Ronchamp (Le Corbusier), 13, *963, 964*
Novius Plautius: *The Ficoroni Cist,* 192, *192*
Nude Descending a Staircase #2 (Duchamp), 905, *906*
Number VII from Eight Studies for a Portrait (Bacon), 938, *938*
Nymph and Satyr (Clodion), 790–91, *790*
Nymphs, from the Fountain of the Innocents, Paris (Goujon), 701, *701*
Nymphs and Satyr (Bouguereau), 853, *853*

O

Oath of the Horatii (David), 797–98, *797*
Oceanic art, 512–18; Australia, 518; Melanesia, 514–16; Polynesia, 512–14
Octagonal Hall, Domus Aurea, Rome, 220–21, *220*
Octavian, 194, 214
Octopus Jar, The, Gournia, 115, *115*
Odysseus' Helmsman Falling (Agesander, Athenodorus, and Polydorus), 173, *173*
Odyssey Landscapes, Rome, *204,* 205
Oedipus and the Sphinx (Ingres), 825, *825*
Oenochoe, *130*
Oenpelli painting, 518, *518*
Oil paints, introduction of, 646, 656, 665
O'Keeffe, Georgia, 906–908; *Jack-in-the-Pulpit IV,* 907–908, *908*
Okyo, Maruyama, 480; *Nature Studies,* 480
Old King, The (Roualt), 894, *894*
Old Kingdom, Egypt, 81–84, 101
Old Market Woman, 174, *174*
Old Testament Trinity Prefiguring the Incarnation, The (Rublëv), 291–92, *291*
Oldenburg, Claes, 953; *Clothespin,* 960, *960; Soft Toilet,* 953, *953*
Olmec art, 486–87
Olympic Stadium, Munich (Otto), 966–67, *966*
Olynthus, Greece, city plan, 178–79, *179*
Op Art, 944, 945–46
Opéra, the, Paris (Garnier), *812,* 813
Ophelia (Millais), 850–51, *850*
Ophelia (Préault), 878–79, *879*
Orders, Greek, 140–43, 218; Corinthian, 140, 153, 168–69; Doric, 140–43, *140, 142,* 152–53, 156, 161, 168, 169; Ionic, 140, *140,* 143, 153, 156–58, 168, 169
Orientalizing period, Greece, 129–30, 134
Ornate wall painting, 206, *206*
Orozco, José Clemente, 916–17; *Hispano-America,* 916, *916*
Orvieto Cathedral, Italy, 409–10, *409*
Oseberg ship burial, 318, *318*
Osman I, 303
Ospedale degli Innocenti, Florence (Brunelleschi), 560, *560*
Otto, Frei, 966–67; model for roof of Olympic stadium, Munich, 966–67, *966*
Otto III Enthroned Receiving the Homage of Four Parts of the Empire, from the *Gospel Book of Otto III, 338,* 339
Ottonian period (Early Medieval), 303, 305, 333–39
Ovid, 644, 723

P

Pacher, Michael, 681; *St. Wolfgang Forces the Devil to Hold His Prayerbook,* 681, *681*
Paganini (Delacroix), 826–27, *827*
Paganini (Ingres), 826–27, *826*
Pagodas, 461, *461*
Painted Bronze (Johns), 952, *952*
Painting: Abstract Expressionism, 937–42; Abstract Formalism, 943–50; Action painting, 939–41; African, 504–505; American, 793–94, 832–34, 844–45, 848–50, 861–62, 876–77, 906–908, 917, 938–41; Baroque, 723–53, 754–58; Byzantine, 264–65, 285–92; Chinese, 450–59; Constructivism, 909, 910, 945, 959; Cubism, 899–906; Dada, 909–10, 911; Dutch, 741–53, 867–68, 906; Early Christian, 250–52; Egyptian, 83–86, 93–94; English, 784, 792–93, 799–801, 831, 846–47, 850–52, 873–74, 938; Etruscan, 187; Expressionism, 891–99; Fauves, 891–95, 898; Flemish, 596, 658–77, 692–98, 736–40, 779–81; French, 698–99, 754–64, 783–84, 792, 794–96, 817–30, 836–44, 852–67, 870–76, 891–94, 903–904, 909–10, 918; German, 777–79, 834–35, 845–46, 852, 875, 894–98, 909, 911–12, 914–16; Greek, 128–33, 161–63; Impressionism, 855–62; Indian, 429–39; Italian, 534–47, 550–59, 580–84, 615–18, 719–32, 777, 835–36, 852, 904–905, 910–11; Japanese, 466, 468–70, 471–73, 474, 475, 479–80; Mannerism, 632–35, 705, 707; Mexican, 916–17; Minoan, 109–14; Neoclassicism, 795–99; North American Indian, 497, 499–500, 504; Oceanic, 516, 518; Post-Impressionism, 862–71; pre-Columbian, 489; "proto-Renaissance," 534–47; Realism, 836–55, 916–17, 942–43; Renaissance, 564–75, 584–97, 601–604, 610–13, 627–35, 642–52, 658–99; rock-shelter, 34–36; Rococo, 777–85; Roman, 202–11, 213; Romanesque, 364–69; Romanticism, 792–801, 815–35, 850–55, 871–77; Russian, 847–48, 898, 908–909, 942; Social Realism, 916–17; Spanish, 732–36, 815–17, 899–903, 911–14; Stone Age, 27, 34–36; Surrealism, 875–76, 911–14; Symbolism, 871–77, 890–91; twentieth-century, 890–917, 936–46; Venetian, 642–52, 781–82, 890–91; Zen, 455–56, 472–73. *See also* Frescoes; Illumination; Mural painting; Vase painting; Wall painting
Painting (Miró), 912, *912*
Palace Ladies, tomb of Princess Yung-t'ai Shensi, 450–51, *451*
Palace of Versailles, 9, 760–63, *760, 761;* Galerie des Glaces (Hardouin-Mansart and Le Brun), 760–62, *762;* garden façade (Le Vau and Hardouin-Mansart), 760, *761;* park (Le Nôtre), *761,* 762–63; Royal Chapel (Hardouin-Mansart), *762,* 763
Palaces: Aegean, 107–12; Islamic, 296–300; Japanese, 475, 476–78; Minoan, 107–12; Renaissance Palazzos, 608–10; Roman, 235–36
Palatine Chapel of Charlemagne, Aachen, 329, *329*
Palazzetto dello Sport, Rome (Nervi), 965, *965*
Palazzo dei Conservatori, Capitoline Hill, Rome, 623, *624*
Palazzo dei Senatori, Capitoline Hill, Rome, 623, *624, 625*
Palazzo del Tè, Mantua (Giulio Romano), 623, 636–37, *637; The Fall of the Giants* from, 637–38, *638*
Palazzo Caprini, Rome (Bramante), 608, *608*
Palazzo Carignano, Turin (Guarini), 721, *721*
Palazzo Medici–Riccardi, Florence (Michelozzo di Bartolommeo), 563–64, *563*
Palazzo Pubblico, Siena, 410–11, *411,* 543, 546
Palazzo Rucellai, Florence (Alberti), 576–77, *576*
Palladio, Andrea, 606, 608, 640–41, 722, 723; San Giorgio Maggiore, Venice, 641, *641;* Villa Rotonda, Vicenza, *640,* 641
Palmieri, Matteo, 581; bust of (Antonio Rossellino), 581, *581*
Pamphilus, catacomb of, *251*